# Imagery in Psychology

# Imagery in Psychology
## *A Reference Guide*

Jon E. Roeckelein

PRAEGER

Westport, Connecticut
London

#53987030

**Library of Congress Cataloging-in-Publication Data**

Roeckelein, Jon E.
    Imagery in psychology : a reference guide / Jon E. Roeckelein.
       p. cm.
    Includes bibliographical references and indexes.
    ISBN 0–313–32197–3 (alk. paper)
      1. Imagery (Psychology)  I. Title.
    BF367.R64   2004
      153.3'2—dc22      2003070686

British Library Cataloguing in Publication Data is available.

Library of Congress Catalog Card Number: 2003070686
ISBN: 0–313–32197–3

First published in 2004

Praeger Publishers, 88 Post Road West, Westport, CT 06881
An imprint of Greenwood Publishing Group, Inc.
www.praeger.com

Printed in the United States of America

The paper used in this book complies with the
Permanent Paper Standard issued by the National
Information Standards Organization (Z39.48–1984).

10 9 8 7 6 5 4 3 2 1

*In memory of B. Richard Bugelski who was my teacher at SUNY at Buffalo (and my academic-geneologic link to Wilhelm Wundt and the beginnings of scientific psychology) and who attempted— often via rugged and ingenious tactics and pursuits—to understand the phenomenon of imagery; and to all my excellent teachers at Wagner College (New York), especially the psychologists: Gertrude Aull, Eugene Sersen, John Dalland, and Eli Kapostins.*

*To Brad Ettore—a fledgling developer* par excellence*—whose creative imagination and vision transform the mundane and commonplace into works that are exceptional and beautiful.*

# Contents

*Preface* ix

*Introduction* xi

1 Definitions and Domains of Imagery 1
  Images versus Mental Imagery 2
  Afterimagery 23
  Dream Imagery and Levels of Consciousness 29
  Eidetic Imagery 39
  Hallucinations, Illusions, and Delusions 43
  Imagination Imagery 52
  Memory Imagery 60
  Redintegration and Déjà Vu 63
  Sensory Imagery 68
  Synesthesia 69
  Thought Imagery 73

2 Origins and Evolution of Imagery 121
  Images and Imagery in Antiquity and in the Bible 122
  The Image and the Imagery Debate in Philosophy 145
    and Early Psychology
  Early Measurement and Individual Differences 157
    in Imagery
  Selected Early Psychological Imagery Studies 176
    (1890–1959)

3   Modern Theoretical Aspects, Applications,                           293
       and Functions of Imagery
    The Imagery Debate and Imagery Theories in                          294
       Modern Psychology
    Applications and Functions of Imagery                               329

4   Methodological Aspects of Imagery                                   425
    General Scientific Methodology Considerations                       426
    General Measurement Considerations                                  432
    Modern Measurement and Methodology in                               438
       Imagery Research
    Selected Modern Psychological Imagery                               515
       Studies (1960–2003)
    Future Directions in Imagery Research                               537

5   Annotated Bibliography of Imagery Studies                           581
       in Psychology (1960–2003)
    Afterimagery and Synesthesia                                        582
    Applications and Functions of Imagery                               587
    Bibliographies and Reviews of Imagery                               605
    Cognition and Imagery                                               625
    Creativity and Imagery                                              634
    Dreams/Daydreams and Imagery                                        639
    Eidetic Imagery                                                     646
    Imagery Theory                                                      654
    Imagination Imagery                                                 666
    Learning and Imagery                                                674
    Measurement and Tests of Imagery                                    685
    Memory/Working Memory and Imagery                                   693
    Perception/Sensation and Imagery                                    700
    Personality/Individual and Gender Differences                       709
       and Imagery
    Physiology/Neuropsychology and Imagery                              720
    Sports and Imagery                                                  724
    Therapy and Imagery                                                 727
    Thought Imagery                                                     733

*Index*                                                                 735

# *Preface*

Recently, in September 2003, I ran a computer search of the keywords *imagery* and *image* using the WorldCat database, and discovered a total of over 21,430 studies for the search term imagery and a total of over 111,790 studies for the term image; this database cuts across many languages and many different academic disciplines ranging from anthropology to the health sciences to zoology. At the same time, when I searched the more discipline-specific database PsycINFO, I found a total of over 12,990 studies on the topic of imagery and over 32,430 studies focusing on the term image in the psychological literature that have been published from 1887 through 2003. The large number of studies on imagery (and the image) published in the field of psychology (as compared proportionately with the other discipline areas) indicates that the topics of imagery and the image are represented substantially in psychology. According to the figures here—when contrasting WorldCat with PsycINFO—psychology captures over 60 percent of the total number of studies published on imagery (with almost 30 percent of the total number of studies published on the topic of the image) across all disciplines.

The finding that the field of psychology contains such an enormous number of studies on imagery (and the image) requires that a review, reference, and resource book—such as the present work—set up boundaries and criteria concerning the selection of material to be covered. Accordingly, the following parameters serve as the basis for selection of material in this book:

1. The topic of imagery as compared and contrasted with the topic of the image.

2. The topics of imagery and the image in a historical context, including the origins and evolution of the terms in philosophy and early scientific psychology.
3. The topics of imagery and the image from theoretical perspectives, as well as from "applications" and "functional" viewpoints.
4. The topics of imagery and the image as used in experimental/empirical studies involving various methodologies and measurements of imagery.
5. The topics of imagery and the image as projected into future research settings and contexts.
6. The topics of imagery and the image as reported in the modern psychological literature from 1960 through 2003, including—among others— the rubrics of *afterimagery, eidetic imagery, imagination imagery, memory imagery*, and *thought imagery* that comprise a current annotated bibliography of imagery/image studies in psychology.

The aim of this book is to provide a one-volume reference/resource book for the topic of imagery in psychology that covers the definitions/domains of imagery; the origin and evolution of imagery; the past, present, and projected future methodological and theoretical concerns of psychologists regarding the study of imagery and the image; and a scientific, experimental, and empirical account of the topics of imagery and the image as reflected in the recent psychological literature.

In more specific terms, the plan and outline of this book is to provide the following material: the various definitions and domains of imagery, as well as distinguishing the term imagery from the term image (chapter 1); imagery as considered in the Bible and by early philosophers and early scientific psychologists, along with selected early psychological imagery studies (chapter 2); the modern theoretical aspects, functions, and applications of imagery both in psychological and nonpsychological contexts (chapter 3); the various methodological aspects of imagery, including the measurement of imagery, selected modern psychological studies of imagery, and future directions in imagery research (chapter 4); and imagery as indicated in a current (1960–2003) annotated bibliography of imagery studies in psychology (chapter 5). Additionally, this book includes both name and subject indexes for ease in locating particular persons and topics of interest relative to imagery and the image.

# Introduction

The notion of imagery and images as "little pictures in the mind or head" has been a persistent and debatable issue in philosophy and psychology for a relatively long time, appearing in ideas and writings as early as those of the ancient Greek philosophers Plato (c. 427–347 B.C.) and Aristotle (c. 384–322 B.C.). Plato asserted that mental images are like patterns etched in wax where individual differences may be understood in terms of properties of the wax, such as its purity, temperature, and so on (cf. Kosslyn, 1994, p. 1). Aristotle maintained that mental images are copies of sensory input and are the primary symbols of thinking ("The soul never thinks without a mental picture"; see Sommer, 1978, p. 42), along with various other secondary and derivative symbols. Aristotle's powerful influence on the imagery issue remained intact until the seventeenth century when the British philosophers Thomas Hobbes, John Locke, George Berkeley, and David Hume developed and expanded Aristotle's ideas. Included among the innovative approaches and perspectives during this time was the origination and enunciation of the "laws of association" (see Roeckelein, 1998, pp. 44–48) that attempted to explain how simple images may be combined into more complex images and how one image may serve in the recall of other mental images.

Following the formal establishment of psychology as a scientific discipline—most notably via Wilhelm Wundt in 1879 at the University of Leipzig—the discourse on mental imagery passed from the rational/empiricist philosophers to the experimental psychologists who attempted to study images and imagery *scientifically* as part of the larger goal or program of studying the contents of the mind and of human experience.

Also, at about this time, during the late nineteenth century, the so-called "imageless thought" debate arose (i.e., the debate concerning the notion that thought processes are *not* based upon images and that images are *not* necessary for thought to occur) in psychology and highlighted the different theoretical and empirical positions taken by experimental psychologists concerning mental imagery.

With the arrival and popularity of the Behaviorist school of thought in psychology during the early 1900s, the focus on mental imagery shifted from the study of subjective and internal mental states to the study of objective and external behaviors. As a result of this orientation and influence, the study of mental imagery largely waned and lapsed into disfavor among the experimental psychologists, and became a "pariah" that was not much studied in "respectable" departments of psychology. However, by the last half of the twentiethth century, and with the arrival and development of the Cognitive school of thought in psychology, the phenomenon of mental imagery—as a topic for serious scientific study—was revitalized and became, once again, a proper subject matter for psychological investigation.

Interest in the study of imagery in the discipline of psychology in the last 117 years from 1887 through 2003 may be gauged quantitatively, decade by decade, by consulting the computer database PsycINFO. This source shows the following numbers of published studies in the psychological literature relating to the topic of imagery: six studies from 1887 through 1900; thirty-four studies from 1901 through 1910; seventy-nine studies from 1911 through 1920; 168 studies from 1921 through 1930; 247 studies from 1931 through 1940; 101 studies from 1941 through 1950; 165 studies from 1951 through 1960; 513 studies from 1961 through 1970; 2,354 studies from 1971 through 1980; 4,108 studies from 1981 through 1990; and 4,125 plus studies from 1991 through 2003. Thus, it may be seen that interest in the topic of imagery—as reflected by the number of published studies in psychology—steadily increases up to about 1940, takes a downward trend and decreases somewhat in the twenty-year period 1941 through 1960, and then finally makes a dramatic recovery with enormous increases from 1961 to the present. The revival of interest in imagery after about 1960 may be attributable to the modern development and revitalization in psychology of the cognitive emphasis on studying mental phenomena, as well as to the behaviorist's innovative methodologies and contributions and to the neuropsychologist's and physiologist's improved instrumentation for studying internal states (cf. Holt, 1964; Kazdin, 2000, pp. 188–90).

While a number of important books on the topics of *imagery* and the *image* have appeared in the last thirty years—both in psychology (e.g., Block, 1981; Finke, 1989; Forrester, 2000; Hampson, Marks, & Richardson, 1990; Klinger, 1981; Kosslyn, 1980, 1983, 1994; Kunzendorf, 1991; Kunzendorf & Sheikh, 1990; Lusebrink, 1990; Morris & Hampson, 1983; Paivio, 1971/1979; A. Richardson, 1969; J.T.E. Richardson, 1980, 1999; Segal, 1971; Sheehan, 1972; Sheikh, 1983; Shepard & Cooper, 1982; Sommer, 1978) and in nonpsychological disciplines (e.g., Allender, 1991; Rollins, 1989; Samuels & Samuels, 1975; Smart, 1995; Tye, 1991)—there is as yet a great need for a current and comprehensive reference/resource book (and annotated bibliography on recent research) in the area of imagery in psychology. Such a book—as exemplified by the present work—does not attempt to duplicate the style or material in previous books on imagery and the image in psychology, but attempts to provide a synthesis of material, an organization of disparate issues, and a comprehensive review/survey of the existing material on imagery and to supplement previous works in this area. Thus, in consideration of the perceived need for a complementary reference book on the topics of imagery and the image in psychology, the present book is written for those laypersons, teachers, students, and researchers who are interested in gaining a twenty-first-century state-of-the-art appreciation of imagery in psychology.

## REFERENCES

Allender, J. (1991). *Imagery in teaching and learning.* New York: Praeger.

Block, N. (Ed.) (1981). *Imagery.* Cambridge, MA: MIT Press.

Finke, R. A. (1989). *Principles of mental imagery.* Cambridge, MA: MIT Press.

Forrester, M. (2000). *Psychology of the image.* London: Routledge.

Hampson, P. J., Marks, D. F., & Richardson, J.T.E. (Eds.) (1990). *Imagery: Current developments.* London: Routledge.

Holt, R. R. (1964). Imagery: The return of the ostracized. *American Psychologist, 19,* 254–64.

Kazdin, A. E. (Ed.) (2000). *Encyclopedia of psychology.* Vol. 5. New York: Oxford University Press; Washington, DC: American Psychological Association.

Klinger, E. (Ed.) (1981). *Imagery.* New York: Plenum.

Kosslyn, S. M. (1980). *Image and mind.* Cambridge, MA: Harvard University Press.

Kosslyn, S. M. (1983). *Ghosts in the mind's machine.* New York: Norton.

Kosslyn, S. M. (1994). *Image and brain: The resolution of the imagery debate*. Cambridge, MA: MIT Press.

Kunzendorf, R. G. (Ed.) (1991). *Mental imagery*. New York: Plenum.

Kunzendorf, R. G., & Sheikh, A. A. (1990). *The psychophysiology of mental imagery*. Amityville, NY: Baywood.

Lusebrink, V. (1990). *Imagery and visual expression in therapy*. New York: Plenum.

Morris, P. E., & Hampson, P. J. (1983). *Imagery and consciousness*. New York: Academic Press.

Paivio, A. (1971/1979). *Imagery and verbal processes*. New York: Holt, Rinehart & Winston/Hillsdale, NJ: Erlbaum.

Richardson, A. (1969). *Mental imagery*. New York: Springer.

Richardson, J.T.E. (1980). *Mental imagery and human memory*. London: Macmillan.

Richardson, J.T.E. (1999). *Imagery*. Hove, UK: Psychology Press.

Roeckelein, J. E. (1998). *Dictionary of theories, laws, and concepts in psychology*. Westport, CT: Greenwood Press.

Rollins, M. (1989). *Mental imagery: On the limits of cognitive science*. New Haven, CT: Yale University Press.

Samuels, M., & Samuels, N. (1975). *Seeing with the mind's eye: The history, techniques, and uses of visualization*. New York: Random House.

Segal, S. J. (Ed.) (1971). *Imagery: Current cognitive approaches*. New York: Academic Press.

Sheehan, P. W. (Ed.) (1972). *The function and nature of imagery*. New York: Academic Press.

Sheikh, A. A. (Ed.) (1983). *Imagery: Current theory, research, and application*. New York: Wiley.

Shepard, R. N., & Cooper, L. A. (1982). *Mental images and their transformations*. Cambridge, MA: MIT Press.

Smart, C. (1995). *The imagery of Soviet foreign policy and the collapse of the Russian empire*. Westport, CT: Praeger.

Sommer, R. (1978). *The mind's eye*. New York: Delacorte Press.

Tye, M. (1991). *The imagery debate*. Cambridge, MA: MIT Press.

# Chapter 1

# *Definitions and Domains of Imagery*

To what do we refer when we employ terms such as "imagery," "images," or "imaging"? Do we refer to events, processes, or both? Is imagery an explanatory construct or is it a phenomenon to be explained? . . . Answers to these and related questions vary greatly, and it is often unclear whether this variation is due to any genuine differences in the facts and their interpretation or whether some more fundamental conceptual confusions exist.

—A. Richardson, 1983

The word "image" is conventionally applied to configurations presented *to* the eye—photos, paintings, engravings, TV displays, shadows, reflections, and projections—and although there are good reasons for applying the same term to patterns of nervous activity in the visual system, the logical connotations are recognisably different. When it comes to so-called *mental* images, the relevance of the word image is distinctly controversial and although it would be perverse to deny the existence of visual "imaginings" there are those who insist that it is misleading to describe what is "seen" as a visual image.

—J. Miller, 1990

Researchers have conceptualised mental imagery in different ways: as a phenomenal experience, as an internal representation, as a stimulus attribute, and as a cognitive strategy.

—J.T.E. Richardson, 1999

## IMAGES VERSUS MENTAL IMAGERY

*Webster's Third New International Dictionary* (1993) defines the term *image* as a noun (Middle English from Old French, short for *imagene*, from Latin *imagin-*, *imago*; akin to Latin *imitari* to imitate) as "a reproduction of a person or thing . . . a thing actually or seemingly reproducing another . . . exact likeness . . . a tangible or visible representation . . . a mental picture"; and as a verb as "to describe or portray in language especially in an effective or vivid manner . . . to call up a mental picture of . . . reflect, mirror . . . to create a representation of."

*Webster's* (1993) also defines the noun *imagery* (Middle English *imagerie*, from Middle French, from *image* + -*erie* -ery) as "the product of image makers (as a statue, emblem, or idol) . . . ornate or heightened description or figures of speech . . . mental images, especially the products of imagination."

The phenomenon of *mental imagery* (not explicitly defined in *Webster's*, 1993) was first investigated and described in detail by Francis Galton (1879–1880, 1880a, b, 1883; cf. Gregory, 1987, p. 475). The ninth edition of the *Encyclopaedia Britannica* (1875) does not provide a separate entry for the term *image*, but it does contain a substantial entry for the term *image worship*; within this context, the word image is used "to denote any artificial representation, whether pictorial or sculptural, of any person or thing, real or imaginary, which is used as a direct adjunct of religious services." By the time of the publication of the eleventh edition of the *Encyclopaedia Britannica* (1922), the term image has its own separate entry and is defined there as "a copy, representation, exact counterpart of something else." Entomologically, the term image is applied in its Latin form *imago* to an insect which, having passed through its larval stages, has achieved its full typical development. Accordingly, the term is susceptible of two opposite connotations: it implies that the thing to which it is applied is only a copy, and on the other hand, it implies that as a copy it is faithful and accurate.

The *Encyclopaedia Britannica* (1922) describes two uses of the term image as used in the discipline of psychology: the simplest use refers to the physiological impression made by an observed object on the retina of the eye and is connected to the term *afterimage* (or *aftersensation*) that refers to an image that remains when an external stimulus (such as a bright light) is removed. The other use of the term in psychology refers to a purely mental idea that is taken as being observed by the "eye of the mind." Such *mental images* are created or produced *not* by an external stimulus—such as is necessary for a visual image—but by a *mental act* of reproduction. The simplest "ideational" or mental image—often denoted as the "primary memory-image"—is a vivid and distinctive ideal representation of an object that one may maintain or recall by an appropriate effort of attention that occurs immediately after sensing or perceiving the object (cf. "image rotation" in Gregory, 1987, p. 347).

Other general, and more current, sources for the definition and description of the terms image, imagery, and mental imagery are the following references: the *Academic American Encyclopedia* (1998), the *Encyclopedia Americana* (1998), and the *World Book Encyclopedia* (1999). The *Academic American Encyclopedia* (1998) contains entries for the terms image (optical), image and imagery, and image processing. (Obviously, depending on the discipline one has in mind, there are distinctive differences between the ways one may approach and view the terms image and imagery; for example, there are vast differences in orientation, emphasis, terminology, and theory between physicists, philosophers, physiologists, photographers, politicians/political scientists, paleontologists, perceptual/experimental psychologists, and clinical psychologists regarding these terms.) Optical images may be real or virtual, reduced or enlarged in size, and inverted or erect (cf. "stabilization of retinal images" in Gregory, 1987, pp. 682–84). In optical images, mirrors or lenses are devised to form an image of an object by modification of the path of light rays. In this context, a "real" image is formed by rays of light actually passing through the image point and *converging* to a focal point; such a real image may be projected onto a screen that is placed at the image location. On the other hand, a "virtual" image is created via *diverging* rays of light that appear to come from a point that is behind, or within, the lens or mirror; inasmuch as virtual images are formed by diverging rays of light, they cannot be focused at any point and, thus, cannot be projected on a screen as is the case with real images. Moreover, images formed by an ordinary plane mirror are virtual images, those formed by a concave mirror—such as contained in a reflecting telescope are real images—and those formed by a convex lens—such as a magnifying glass—may be either a virtual or a real image, depending on the location of the object (if it lies between the focal point and the lens, the image will be virtual, erect, and magnified, but if it lies beyond the focal point, the image will be real, inverted, and either magnified or reduced, depending on the variable of distance from the lens).

In another entry, the *Academic American Encyclopedia* (1998, p. 51) defines an image as "a representation of what is perceived— the registration on the mind of an object or scene." In the area of literary criticism, the term image is used both for the representations produced in the mind by verbal descriptions, as well as for the descriptions themselves because the mental pictures ("images") may be thought of either as separate from words or as integral features of the verbal descriptions. Also, in the field of literary analysis, the term imagery refers to all language that gives a vivid or concrete picture of something. In this context, imagery resembles that of "figurative" language—such as that involved in so-called "figures of speech," including similes and metaphors. In a substantial entry for the term image processing, the *Academic American Encyclopedia* (1998) describes how image processing modifies pictures to improve their quality via enhancement and restoration, how it extracts information via analysis and pattern recognition, and how it changes image structure via compression and image editing. In this context, images may be processed by optical, photographic, electronic (cf. the terms "image orthicon" in the *World Book Encyclopedia*, 1999, p. 79, and "image tube" in the *Encyclopedia Americana*, 1998, p. 796), and digital-computer methods. See the particular area of study called "diagnostic imaging" or "images of the brain in action" in Gregory (1987, pp. 347–53); this technological field includes concepts and devices such as X-ray computer tomography (CT), positron emission tomography (PET), and nuclear magnetic resonance (NMR) or magnetic resonance imaging (MRI). This technical-laboratory approach to the topic of images permits researchers to study the production of refined anatomical images in vivo, and to consider images as measured in terms of local chemistry, metabolism (i.e., the use of oxygen and glucose), and blood flow within the brain. In a related technical context, in the field of optics, the concept/phenomenon of *holograms* is related, also, to image production. *Webster's* (1989) defines hologram as "a negative produced by exposing a high-resolution photographic plate, without camera or lens, near a subject illuminated by monochromatic, coherent radiation, as from a laser: when placed in a beam of coherent light a true three-dimensional image of the subject is formed."

Overall, the entries in the *Academic American Encyclopedia* (1998) concerning images and imagery are anchored in the nonpsychological fields of literature, optics, and digital computers. However, in the case of the entry for imagery in the *Encyclopedia Americana* (1998, pp. 796–97), where an image is "a concrete representation of something not present to the senses," the field of psychology is indicated as well as the literary arts. In the *Encyclopedia Americana* (1998), an image may be "tied" or "free"—when the image has developed a definite meaning for almost everyone (e.g., the word *sky* suggests "infinity"), it is said to be tied, while if its meaning or value varies widely for different people (e.g., the words *your mother*), it is called a free image. Also, imagery may be figurative or literal: a figurative image involves a change, or "turn," in the basic meaning of words, while a literal image involves no necessary change, or turn, in the meaning of words and gives a direct sensory representation. Moreover, when imagery combines a literal and sensuous quality with an abstract or suggestive aspect, it takes on the characteristics of a "symbol"; when the abstract or suggestive aspect is *directly* expressed, the resulting figure of speech is called a simile, and when the analogy is implied or *indirectly* expressed, the resulting figure of speech is called a metaphor. Thus, the terms image, symbol, metaphor, and simile may all contribute to the meaning of the term *imagery* (cf. DeVries, 2001).

In more explicit psychological terms, the entry for imagery in the *Encyclopedia Americana* (1998) refers to the psychology of Carl Jung that deals with ways in which images strike resonant points in the "collective unconscious" of the human race and, thus, produces "primordial images" or "archetypes" (cf. Jung, 1912, 1964; Roeckelein, 1998, pp. 276–78). The field of psychology is acknowledged, also, in the substantial entry for the image-related term imagination in the *Encyclopedia Americana* (1998, pp. 796–98). Imagination is described as the general term that "applies to the production of mental pictures, or images, when there is no stimulation of the sense receptors." Within this context, images are usually of a visual nature, but they may occur with other forms of perception and may involve more than one of the senses. Furthermore, imagination may be used in two slightly different ways—"imitative" versus "creative"—where imitative imagination is close in meaning to memory and refers to the *reconstruction* in the mind of past events (highly accurate reconstructions are called "eidetic images/imagery"), and creative imagination is related to thought or reasoning that involves the *restructuring* of previous sensory impressions. Various psychological terms are indicated in the discussions in this source on both *imitative* imagination (terms such as "afterimage," "synesthetic image," "hypnogogic image," "illusion," "hallucination," "redintegration," and "déjà vu"), and on *creative* imagination (terms such as "daydreaming," "intelligence," "fantasy," "projection," "creativity tests and stages," "productive creativity," "association of ideas," "dreams," and "intro-spection").

Although there are no separate entries for the terms image and imagery in the *World Book Encyclopedia* (1999), there is reference to these concepts under the entry for *imagination* (p. 79); imagination is defined as "the capacity for considering objects or events in their absence or as they might be"; imagination may refer to many activities such as fantasy, daydreaming, make-believe, and ingenuity. Most often, imagination involves the use of *mental imagery*—the ability to call to mind the sensations of sights, sounds, smells, tastes, and touches that the individual has experienced. It is through mental imagery whereby the person may create mental sensations of conditions or situations that he/she have not have actually experienced ("vicarious" experience), and mental images may substitute for the real thing, thus permitting a person to plan how to paint a picture, how to sculpt a statue, how to arrange a musical composition, or how to draft an architectural work or structure. It is noted, also, that mental imagery is produced by the same parts of the brain as are used in actual perception; this fact may sometimes lead people to mistake objects in their mental images for the real objects (i.e., they may experience "illusions" or "hallucinations").

In the database PsycINFO for the period 1887 through 2003, I discovered that there are over three times as many studies retrievable via the search terms image/images as compared with studies via the search terms imagery/mental imagery. The terms image/images cut across many areas of investigation—including psychology—with a substantial number of studies focusing on "imagery interpretation," "imagery coding," and "image processing" that involve (among other issues) the location, recognition, identification, and description of objects, activities, and terrain that appear in imagery from sources such as photographic, infrared, and ultraviolet techniques and methods (cf. the rubric imagery in the *New Encyclopaedia Britannica* [1997, vol. 29, p. 687]). In this context, for instance, imagery data collected by satellites and high-altitude aircraft reflect one of the most important sources of military/government intelligence, provide information for a huge number of intelligence-collection categories including order of battle and military operations, as well as technical/scientific developments involving computers, television, display systems, environmental design, economics, and arms-limitations treaties. The major emphasis in the present book, however, is *not* on these specialized/

technical areas of image study. The following sample of two dozen studies concerns the topic of the *image(s)* but is considered here to be "extra-psychological" and technical in nature—as regards "mental imagery"—and exemplifies the type of image "processing," "interpretation," and "coding" studies that are *excluded* from further detailed consideration in the present book: see Baumel (1999a); Birnbaum (1962); Brainard and Ornstein (1965); Fraser (1992); Garcia-Perez (1988); Gooley and Barrett (1992); Jacquin (1992); Laymon (1966); Lohmann and Sinzinger (1995); Lu, Williams, and You (2001); Martinek and Zarin (1979); Mouravier (1997); Narita (1994); Roger and Arnold (1994); Rosen (1999); Sancar and Macari (1988); Self and Rhodes (1965); Shapiro (1993); Stark (2000); Taejeong (1992); Tallman (1970); Thomas and Sadacca (1967); Willmorth and Birnbaum (1967); and Wu (1992).

The approach in this book focuses more exclusively on the term mental imagery and considers in detail those imagery studies that are firmly grounded in the discipline of psychology and the psychological literature. Thus, in my initial section heading, "Images versus Mental Imagery," the implicit suggestion is that the term mental imagery (equivalent here to the term imagery) is more closely, and exclusively, allied with the discipline of psychology while the broader, and more diverse, term image(s) (associated with "processing," "coding," and "interpreting" images) involves many other "extra-psychological" and technical disciplines and fields of study. Accordingly, we turn now to those sources containing definitions of the terms image/imagery/mental imagery and other image-related terms within the field of psychology, and survey various psychological dictionaries, encyclopedias, and other works—chronologically arranged, based on publication date—for a more discipline-specific (psychological) understanding of imagery.

Baldwin (1901–1905) describes and discusses the terms image/imagery, image-worship, and imaging. The term image (from the Latin *imago*, a copy or a likeness) is translated into German as *Bild*, into French as *image*, and into Italian as *immagine*. According to Baldwin (p. 516), an image is the "mental scheme in which sensations or the sensory elements of a perception (or earlier image) are revived; the images of the mind taken collectively are known as imagery." Baldwin also refers to images of fancy, images of memory, visual images, auditory images, tactual images, afterimages, and double images. He notes that the image played a large part in the older associationistic psychology where memory and recognition depend on the comparison made between a given presentation and its memory image; however, according to Baldwin, recent experimental evidence has shown cases in which the image plays no apparent role. He states that the theory of the "mental disposition" is a general way of accounting for cases where the "associationistic-image" theory is artificial, especially for those theorists who make dispositions out to be motor tendencies, attention, or attitudes. The term *image-worship* (also called *iconolatry*) refers to giving divine honors to an object that is alleged to be a likeness or imitation of the divinity for which it stands; image-worship may be regarded as a type of idol-worship where the idol need not be a direct likeness or imitation of the divinity, but may merely represent it by simple association. Baldwin notes that it is the characteristic of an idol that it gradually displaces the divinity it represents and tends to become itself the object of worship; this is true, also, of image-worship although the supposed resemblance in this case maintains the thought of the object uppermost in the worshipper's mind and tends to keep in check the process of identification. Baldwin suggests that the evil of image-worship arises out of the temptation to materialize the spiritual. Historically, the controversy over the use of images in worship played a large role in the development of the Christian Church and led, at one time, to a conflict that virtually disrupted the church. That is, the Roman Church has been more tolerant of the use of images and pictures in its liturgy than the Reformed Church, which generally has been most uncompromising in its opposition to image-worship.

Baldwin (1901–1905) essentially defines the term imaging within the context of the disciplines of logic and mathematics; in logic, in one case, imaging refers to any relative condition where the relation must belong to one or the other of two classes, the one embracing the notion that every object has an image, and the other indicating that no object has more than one image (i.e., an imaging must be defined as a generic relation between an object-class and an image-class); in mathematics, any mathematical function of one variable may be regarded as an image ("representation") of its variable according to some mode of imaging. In the final analysis, Baldwin suggests that the term imaging is used as a synonym for the term *substitution*. Note that Baldwin (p. 519) also describes the image-related term imitation as "the performance in movement, thought, or both movement and thought, of what comes through the senses, or by suggestion, as belonging to another individual"; presumably, similar mental dynamics (i.e., reproduction, copy-reinstatement, and representational processes) exist in the phenomenon of imitation as in the case of mental imagery.

Warren (1934) defines the terms image and imagery, as well as a number of image-related words. (For another early account of imagery—in terms of *individual differences*—see Griffitts, 1927.) According to Warren (1934), an image is "an element of experience which is centrally aroused and which possesses all the attributes of sensation; an experience which reproduces or copies in part and with some degree of sensory realism a previous perceptual experience in the absence of the original sensory stimulation." (Cf. Warren's [1934] use of the term image in the field of optics: "the picture or reproduction of an object produced by a lens, reflector, or optical system, as a result to the focusing of the light emanating from each point in the object"; his definition of the term imaging as "forming an image, i.e., picturing, reproducing [applied especially to an image-forming optical system, including that of the eye]"; and his definition of the term *retinal image* [synonymous with the terms "retinal picture" and "retinal impression"] as "the optical image of external objects formed upon the retina by the refracting surfaces of the eye; the consequent pattern of physiological activity excited in the retina and corresponding to the distribution of energy in the optical image" [pp. 131–32].) In Warren's terminology, the term imagery refers to "images taken collectively, or the imaging operation in general"; and mental imagery refers to "the preponderance of a certain mode of sensory content (visual, auditory, etc.) in the imagery experiences of a given individual (used, also, to distinguish one kind of sensory material from another in imagery)" (1934, pp. 132, 164; cf. also Fernald, 1912; Schaub, 1911).

Various other image-related terms defined by Warren include the following: *image/anticipation*—an image that is accompanied by reference to a future time when a corresponding sensory experience is expected; *image/composite*—an image that is derived from a plurality of previous sensory experiences and does not copy any single such experience; *image/general*—an image regarded by the subject as referring to any one of a class of objects; *image/habitual*—an image that regularly or frequently recurs as a representation of a certain meaning; *image/tied*—imaginal content attached to a present perception; and *imago*—the final state of an insect after it has undergone metamorphosis and become sexually mature (as used in the field of biology), and a memory, fantasy, or idealization of a beloved person, formed in childhood and remaining uncorrected in adult life (as used in the field of psychoanalysis).

Drever (1952/1973) defines image as "a revived sense experience, in the absence of the sensory stimulation, e.g., seeing with the mind's eye," and cites several technical word combinations involving the term image: *composite image* (an image based on a number of sensory experiences of the same or similar objects); *generic image* (an image, usually somewhat schematic, capable of representing any one of a class of objects); *hallucinatory image* (an image that has momentarily perceptual character); and *retinal image* (an optical image focused on the retina by the lens system of the eye). (For an early discussion on the "intensity of images," see Schaub [1911].)

English and English (1958) define image, imagery, and mental imagery, as well as a number of image-related terms. An image is a "likeness or copy"; in an *optical image*, it is "a picture of an object produced by focusing with a mirror or lens"; and in a *retinal image*, it is "a picture of an object on the retina when refracted through the optical system of the eye." Additionally, the image—subject to imperfections in the optical system—is a "point-for-point duplication of the plane view of the object." According to English and English (p. 251), the retinal image should be distinguished clearly from all of the following meanings: "a mental copy of something not present to the senses" (this meaning is the most traditional and popular meaning of the term mental imagery); "a composite of a person's concepts, judgments, preferences, and attitudes toward some comprehensive object such as a nation or toward a cause such as pacifism" (this meaning emphasizes the cognitive content of a sentiment—which sometimes may be only loosely organized); "a mature stage of certain insects . . . a representation of a person, etc." (this meaning focuses on the respective biological, and psychoanalytical, meanings of the term *imago*; also see Warren, 1934, p. 132; and, according to English and English, 1958, p. 253, the psychoanalytical interpretation of *imago* includes the notion that an *imago* may influence personal relations at the conscious level, especially by providing a pattern for the kind of person with whom to fall in love; cf. the concept of "father figure"); "a more or less complete representation of the attributes of an object or event once experienced but not now present to the senses, together with recognition of its 'pastness'; a revival that resembles but need not exactly copy a past experience; the image may be sensory or verbal or both" (this meaning emphasizes the "memory" aspects of imagery).

In English and English's (1958) terminology, a mental image is "associated with the activity of *imagining* where the mind contemplates a sort of 'mental stuff'—a copy or *image* of a not-present but objective reality." According to English and English (p. 252), the view of a mental image as both a "nonpresent" and "objective" reality is rather metaphysical and, they state, "those who contend that this metaphysics has no place in psychology find it difficult, on the one hand, to say what the image is or, on the other, to dispense with the term altogether. No sharp line, moreover, can be drawn between the meaning of *image* and of *idea*." Also, English and English (p. 252) note that "while one cannot well say what an image is, we have many terms by which we distinguish different kinds"; among the different kinds of images they describe are the following: *concrete images*— images that have the direct sensory qualities of the original objects (concrete images are further differentiated according to their sensory modality such as visual, auditory, olfactory, gustatory, tactual, and kinesthetic; they may also be referred to as "composite" when they combine more than one sensory modality); *verbal images*—images that represent either an object or a past verbal experience/speech (these images may be distinguished further as visual-visual, auditory-visual, kinesthetic-verbal [writing words], or vocomotor [speaking]); and *general images*—images that are regarded by the individual as standing for any one of a class of objects, and carry a general/global meaning (e.g., "an image of a car," refers to *any* car).

In comparing the verbs imagine and image, English and English (1958, p. 252) state that the term image is "more specific for the meaning *to have* or *to form a mental image*." Other image-related terms defined and discussed by English and English include the following:

- *body image*—the mental representation or picture one has of one's own body at rest or in motion at any moment that is derived from internal sensations, postural changes, contact with outside objects and people, emotional experiences, and fantasies;
- *self-image*—the self one *thinks* oneself to be; this is not a directly observed self-object but a complex concept consisting of one's personality character, status, body and bodily appearance, and so on; it may differ greatly from objective fact;
- *collective image*—an image in the unconscious deriving from racial experience (a "primordial image" or "archetype" (cf. Jung, 1912, 1964);
- *composite image*—an image made up of parts of different "memory images";
- *idealized image*—in psychoanalysis, a false conception of one's virtues and assets developed as a defense against the demands of the "ego ideal"; the

irrationally imagined unconscious image of oneself as he or she should be according to the dictates of "neurotic pride"; it is characterized by the glorified, aggrandized, and perfected qualities derived from a person's previous fantasies, experiences, needs, and capacities (cf. "idealized self");

• *personal image*—a representation in the unconscious of a personal experience (cf. Jung, 1912, 1964);
• *primordial image*—a representation in the unconscious of an experience of the human race; an inherited and unconscious idea or idea-feeling (cf. Jung, 1912, 1964);
• *recurrent image*—a visual, auditory, or other image that returns persistently; and
• *tied images*—mental images attached to a perceptual object, for example, the imagined feel of the rough texture of sandpaper when merely seeing it.

The single term imagery is defined by English and English as "the imagining processes taken collectively; or the process of imagining, in general; the kind of mental images characteristically used in a particular kind of task, or by an individual."

In defining mental imagery, A. Richardson (1969, p. 2) states that "mental imagery refers to (1) all those quasi-sensory or quasi-perceptual experiences of which (2) we are self-consciously aware, and which (3) exist for us in the absence of those stimulus conditions that are known to produce their genuine sensory or perceptual counterparts, and which (4) may be expected to have different consequences from their sensory or perceptual counterparts" (cf. Owens, 1963; A. Richardson, 1983). Bugelski (1971, p. 52) observes that having read A. Richardson's definition of mental imagery here, "we are no closer to understanding the concept because Richardson asks us to accept some kind of conscious experience as the criterion for imagery without having the latter clarified for us." Bugelski also suggests that the attempt by Leuba (1940)—which was endorsed wholly by Mowrer (1960) and partially by Paivio (1969)—to define images as "conditioned sensations" is not much more helpful without a definition of "sensations."

Hinsie and Campbell (1970) define image-related concepts mainly within a psychiatric/psychoanalytical context; typically, their definitions are sprinkled and supplemented with the names of the individuals/references that have employed prominently the various terms in their works. Accordingly, Hinsie and Campbell define the following terms: an *imago image* is "the image or likeness of someone, usually not of the subject himself [*sic*], constructed in the unconscious and remaining therein (the commonest imagos are those of the parents and of those who stand for the parents)" (references cited are E. Jones, C. Jung, and W. Stekel); *image agglutinations* refer to "dreams and twilight states" where "mental activity appears in the form of sensory images"; such images sometimes comprise a scenic arrangement but, with the clouding of consciousness, they disintegrate into fragments of pictures that seem to go on without rules or regulations and, under the influence of affects, again conglomerate into peculiar image groups, the *image agglutinations*; the faces of several persons or several objects of similar emotional value are seen in the dreams as one, and are conglomerated into unity (Freud called this phenomenon "condensation"; reference is E. Kretschmer); *body image* (also called "conceptual image") is "the concept which each person has of his [*sic*] own body as an object in space, independently and apart from all other objects . . . the body image or *body identity* is the conceptualization of the body's structure and functions that grows out of the awareness of the self and one's body in intended action; schizophrenic children are often deficient in the ability to localize, discriminate, or give pattern and meaning to body perceptions" (references are W. Goldfarb and L. C. Kolb); *idealized image* is "the defense of having a false picture of one's virtues and assets; the more unrealistic (idealized) this image is, the more vulnerable is the person amid the vicissitudes of life" (reference is K. Horney).

Other image-related terms provided by Hinsie and Campbell (1970) are *memory image* (via T. Reik and I. Pavlov), that is, anticipation of the recurrence of a past experience and *percept-images* (via A. Storch and E. R. Jaensch), that is, images having hallucinatory aspects, which are common among schizophrenic patients, appear as fantasy or memory images, and represent a primitive level of intellectual life. *Personal images* (via C. Jung) represent the contents of one's personal unconscious domain; *primordial image* (via C. Jung) that is, an imprint, deposit, or engram that arises through a condensation of numerous similar processes; it is also known as *archetype* wherein the most immediate and primordial image is the mother. *Social image* (via T. Burrow) is an affective impression derived from beliefs, prejudices, and opinions deeply ingrained in the individual and in society but having no objective or demonstrable correspondence in actuality. *Unconscious image* (via S. Freud and C. Thompson) is synonymous with "unconscious memory"; it is the retention of mental impressions of an event even though they are not subject to recall into conscious awareness, and invokes the process of "repression." *Hypnagogic imagery* (via

A. Jellinek) are images that occur during the sleep stage between wakefulness and sleep just *before* sleep has set in; *hypnopompic imagery* (via A. Jellinek) are images that occur just *after* the sleeping state and before full wakefulness. *Spontaneous imagery* (via A. Jellinek) are visual images commonly produced in children voluntarily when the eyes are closed; this is not a pathological condition, but may sometimes be misinterpreted as visual hallucinations. Finally *imaginarii* (via D. Beres) is one of three subdivisions of mental disorders characterized by sensory-faculty disturbances, and *imagination* (via D. Beres) is the process of synthesizing mental images into new ideas and the forming of a mental representation of an absent object, an affect, a body function, or an instinctual drive leading to novel images, symbols, phantasies, dreams, ideas, thoughts, or concepts.

Eysenck, Arnold, and Meili (1972) define image as "a mental representation, i.e., one of the senses of 'idea'; any representation, copy, likeness, imitation, or similitude; a mental copy of a sensory quality or experience in the absence of any sensory stimulus; an attitude toward, e.g., a national type"; and mental imagery as "the subjective combination of fragments of earlier perceptions. . . . In contradistinction to impressions derived directly from sense perceptions, the contents of mental images are usually imprecise, less detailed, and without clear localization in space. They do not possess the persistence and continuity of experiential perceptions." Eysenck et al. note that depending on the sense modality involved, there are visual (optical), acoustic (auditory), kinesthetic (motor), tactile, olfactory, and gustatory ideas or images (*concrete images*) (cf. the "three types of imagery" in McKellar, 1972, pp. 36–40); when several sensory systems combine to produce the image, it is known as a *composite image* (or *idea*). Eysenck et al. (1972, p. 262) caution that this type of mental imagery must not be confused with the pseudoperceptual, realistic character of "compulsive hallucinations."

Eysenck et al. (1972) define, also, the following image-related concepts: *image types*—synonymous with "ideational types" and "idea types"; this refers to persons whose mental imagery/ideation is oriented toward a specific sensory modality (cf. "fantasy"). *Imagination* is defined as the ability to call to mind various situations, objects, processes, or individuals that are not present; and *imago* derives historically from the notion of a wax portrait mask placed on a corpse displayed in the Forum in ancient Rome. (Sigmund Freud used the term *imago* to denote the idealizing distortion of personality common during the course of transference in psychoanalysis, and Carl Jung used the term to denote the subsequently effective image of a "reference person"; the term *imago*, in the title *American Imago*, was also adopted as the name of a psychological journal whose contents deal with literary, historical, and mythological topics from a psychoanalytical perspective.) Additionally, Eysenck et al. define *ideomotor image* (synonymous with ideomotor idea where the term ideomotor is equivalent to "ideal of movement," and refers to an idea- or image-controlled emotionally that leads involuntarily to certain motor reactions) and *ideomotor law* (synonymous with "Carpenter effect" and "ideo-real law," and refers to a phenomenon described by the English physiologist W. B. Carpenter in 1879 whereby perceptual and imaginative contents, in particular those relating to perceived and/or imagined movements, may be accompanied by partial or complete involuntary drive impulses that correspond to the motor features of those contents; that is, ideas may produce motor responses by innervation of muscle groups corresponding to those ideas).

Wolman (1973) defines *image* simply as "a mental copy arising from memory of a sense experience in the absence of sensory stimulation," and he describes the following image-related concepts (in equally brief terms):

- *Image agglutinations*—dream image-groups that are representative of the day's thoughts, formed from the conglomeration of discrete images under the influence of affects
- *Body image*—mental representation of one's body emanating from internal sensations, fantasies, emotions, posture, and experiences with outside people and objects
- *Generic image*—a schematic image representing any one of a class of objects
- *Idealized image*—a false and exaggerated estimation of oneself developed from what one would like to be rather than from what one actually is
- *Memory image*—the revival in memory of a past experience in the absence of present sensory stimulation
- *Percept-image*—a memory image or concrete fantasy image containing hallucinatory clarity, commonly seen in schizophrenic patients
- *Primordial image*—same as "archetype," refers to the structural component of the "collective unconscious" that is inherited racially; the "anima," "animus," and "shadow" are the major archetypes
- *Composite imagery*—a single image consisting of the parts of several sensory experiences of similar objects
- *Hypnagogic imagery*—vivid imagery demonstrated during the pre-sleep stage and during the time of falling asleep; cf. Ardis and McKellar, 1956; Leaning, 1925

- *Hypnopompic imagery*—visions experienced during the state after sleep and before wakefulness
- *Imagination*—the constructive reorganization of past perceptual experiences into ideational-level images in a present experience
- *Imago*—idealized and unconscious representations of an important figure from childhood, usually a parental figure, that often influences one's later life

As their entry for the term imagery, Harre and Lamb (1983) state, "See mental imagery"; and the term mental imagery is defined and described as "the supposed 'inner representations' to which people refer in imagining, remembering, and introspection. Imagery, once regarded as too mentalistic for empirical study, is now an important area of research in cognitive psychology, as well as in medicine" (cf. Bower, 1984). Harre and Lamb also note that study and research on imagery revolves around the person's ability to "scan" and manipulate his/her own mental images; moreover, once in existence, images may be "observed" and manipulated as if they, themselves, were objects. For a further discussion of the main types of *imagery*, see Morris and Hampson (1983, pp. 65–90).

Reber (1985) observes that the prefix *ideo-* (e.g., the term ideomotor act is defined as an overt/motor act initiated by an idea) is derived from the Greek language, is distinguished from the prefix *idio-*, and means "idea" or "mental image." Reber's entry (pp. 343–44) for the term *image* states that "the term derives from the Latin for *imitation* and most usages in psychology, both obsolete and contemporary, revolve around this notion; common synonyms are *likeness, copy, reproduction, duplicate*, etc." Among the variations on this central notion, Reber identifies the following concepts (cf. Sutherland, 1996):

- *Optical image*—the reflection of an object by a lens, mirror, or other optical device
- *Retinal image*—the approximate point-by-point depiction of an object cast on the retina when light is refracted by the eye's optical system
- *Auditory image*—an image produced via the auditory system
- *Body image/concept*—one's subjective image of one's own body, specifically in regard to evaluative judgments about how one is perceived by others and how well one is adjusted to such social perceptions; inappropriate or disturbed body image is a feature of many neurotic disorders, for example, in "anorexia nervosa" it is a hallmark symptom (cf. *self-image*—the "self" one supposes oneself to be; many models of neurosis,

in particular, are built on the commonly observed situations in which a person's "real self" is incongruent dramatically with his/her self-image)
- *Collective, archetypal, or primordial image*—the unconscious and inherited ideas and images that are the components of the "collective unconscious" of a group/race of people
- *Fixed, stabilized, or stopped image*—an image that has been fixed or stabilized so that it falls on the same spot on the retina regardless of the eye's movements; under such conditions, the perception fades rapidly, presumably from fatigue of the retinal receptors
- *Hypnagogic* or *hypnogogic images*—images having a hallucinatory-like nature that are experienced when first falling asleep
- *Hypnopompic images*—fleeting hallucination-like images that frequently accompany the first few semiconscious moments during the waking process
- *Idealized image*—a nonveridical sense of one's positive aspects, assumed to develop as a defense against the demands of one's "ego ideal" (cf. *idealized self*—a lofty and perfected portrayal of self concerning what one would like to become)
- *Imagination*—the recombination of memories of past experiences and previously formed images into novel constructions
- *Imago*—unconscious representations of other individuals, typically a parent with whom one may identify closely; this is commonly an idealized portrayal and not necessarily reflective of the true aspects of the person

Reber (1985) defines imagery as "the whole imaging process" that refers, often, only to the actual images themselves, and equates the term mental image with the following historical and definitional variations of the term *image*: within Structuralism, one of the three subclasses of consciousness, the others being "sensations" and "affections." In this context, the image was treated as a mental representation or copy of an earlier sensory experience where the copy was considered to be less vivid than the actual sensory experience; within contemporary cognitive psychology, the image is considered as a "picture in the head" where the picture—also in this context—is not a literal one, but rather a kind of "as if" picture; that is, imagery is viewed as a cognitive process that operates as if one had a mental picture that is an analog of a real-world scene, and the image is not necessarily a reproduction of an earlier event but rather a construction or a synthesis of it. In such a definitional context, the image is no longer viewed merely as a copy, but the picture in the head seems to have the property of being mentally "transformable" or "adjustable"; also, the picture is not necessarily restricted to visual representation only: it may be manifested as an auditory image or a tactile image.

Reber (1985) further describes *emotive imagery* as "imagery that evokes emotion; it is most often used in behavior therapy and cognitive-behavioral therapy for a procedure in which the client images emotion-arousing scenes while relaxed and in a comfortable, protective setting"; he cites, also, various other uses and meanings of the term image: as a general attitude toward some institution; as the elements of dreams; and (as a verb—*to image*) as to "create an image." Reber notes that to image is often used as a synonym of *to imagine*, but the latter may connote "flights of fancy" whereas to image does not carry such a meaning. Moreover, despite the subtle overlap between the concepts of image and imagination, according to Reber, to image something does not exactly involve the same mental processes or acts as to imagine something.

In discussing "principles of mental imagery," Finke (1989, p. 2) defines mental imagery as "the mental invention or recreation of an experience that in at least some respects resembles the experience of actually perceiving an object or an event, either in conjunction with, or in the absence of, direct sensory stimulation." Finke notes in his account of mental imagery that the usage of the term image is different from both its use in the visual sciences to refer to the projection of visual scenes on the back of the retina (e.g., Marr, 1982), and in its use in the memory area ("iconic image") of short-term retention of visual information in sensory mechanisms (e.g., Neisser, 1967; Sperling, 1960). His treatment of mental imagery is distinctive from both retinal imagery and iconic imagery. Finke discusses research that has led to the recent identification of five major "principles of imagery": the principles of implicit encoding, perceptual equivalence, spatial equivalence, transformational equivalence, and structural equivalence. According to Finke, these five principles—taken together—provide a general description of the fundamental characteristics of mental images (cf. Rollins [1989] who discusses two competing views of imagery— pictorialism and descriptionalism—neither of which denies the existence of mental images or of the meaningfulness of the term image; both approaches attempt to account for research that strongly suggests that imaging occurs in *conjunction* with certain tasks involving memory and perceptual-recognition processes).

Kunzendorf (1990, p. 9) discusses mental imagery within the context of psychophysiological theory and research; he proposes that the sensory qualities of images are subjective qualities of objectively distinguishable "structures" in the *peripheral* nervous system, whereas the sensationless qualities of images are subjective qualities of objectively observable "functions" in the *central* nervous system. Thus, Kunzendorf's approach to mental imagery is to apply the "mind-brain identity theory" (cf. Roeckelein, 1998, pp. 324–26) to the psycho-physiology of imagery.

Bugelski (1996) describes the concept of imagery (cf. Bugelski, 1984, 2001; Griffitts, 1927; Hicks, 1924; Holt, 1964; Horne, 1993; Janssen, 1976; Kessel, 1972; Kolers, 1987; Kolers and Smythe, 1979; Lawrie, 1970; McMahon, 1973; Mowrer, 1977; Neisser, 1972; Newton, 1982; Popplestone and McPherson, 1988; Rey, 1981; A. Richardson, 1969; J.T.E. Richardson, 1980, 1999; Roeckelein, 1998; Rollins, 1989; Segal, 1971; Sheehan, 1978; Sheikh, 1984; Shepard, 1978; Sterelny, 1986; Tye, 1991; Von Eckhardt, 1988; Washburn, 1916; Wekker, 1966; Wright, 1983) in an encyclopedic-type entry and indicates that in everyday conversation an image is supposed to be some kind of mental experience, or a picture in the "mind's eye." Such a description is referred to as the "picture metaphor," but imagery also refers to experiences in other perceptual areas such as hearing, tasting, and kinesthesis. Bugelski (1996) notes that Wilhelm Wundt—in the early history of psychology—considered "images" to be one of the three fundamental elements of consciousness (along with feelings and sensations); images were commonly accepted in the early days of psychology (around 1879) as basic psychological phenomena whose reality was not questioned. However, as Bugelski (1996, p. 449) observes, "all imagery is difficult to describe in crisp, neat communication, just as are all internal reactions"; on the other hand, says Bugelski, "the fact that we have trouble describing our images does not make them any less real than toothaches or other pains."

Thomas (1997b) provides a philosophical perspective and approach to the issue of mental imagery; he notes (p. 1) that mental imagery—sometimes called "visualization" or "seeing in the mind's eye"—is an "experience that resembles perceptual experience but which occurs in the absence of the appropriate stimuli for the relevant perception." Such quasi-perceptual events are interpreted by individuals, at some times, as personal reconstructions of actual perceptual experiences from their past, and at other times involve their anticipation of possible—often desired or feared—future experiences and events. (Cf. Heil [1982], Rabb [1975], and Tye [1984] who present an "adverbial" account/theory of imagery, which is the philosophical counterpart to the "perceptual activity" theory in cognitive science [Neisser, 1976]; in the former case, imagery is regarded *not* as "seeing" a mental object—an image—in the mind, but rather it is a type of activity or way of thinking about some actual, or possible, real-world object. In yet other approaches, Kosslyn [1980, 1981, 1987, 1994] presents a "computational quasi-pictorial" theory of imagery, which has become the dominant view in cognitive science; and Paivio [1971, 1977, 1986, 1991, 1995] and Sadoski and Paivio [2001] present a "dual-coding" theory of memory and mental representation that contains much empirical data on the mnemonic effects of imagery. For further discussions on theories of mental imagery, see chapter 3.) In this way, according to Thomas (1997b), imagery plays an important role in both memory and motivation processes, as well as in visuo-spatial reasoning and inventive and creative thought. In his encyclopedic-type entry, Thomas (1997b) touches on the following issues concerning mental imagery: problems of definition and terminology; ancient, medieval, and modern imagery; the rise, demise, and resurrection of imagery in scientific psychology (including references to the works of Wundt, James, Titchener, Jaensch, and Freud); the "imageless thought" controversy; the "Perky experiment"; behaviorist and motor theories of imagery; and imagery in cognitive science. Thomas's (1997b) generous bibliography contains over three hundred citations relating either directly or indirectly to the topic of mental imagery.

Corsini (2002) defines an image as "a likeness or copy of an earlier sensory or perceptual experience recalled without external stimulation," imagery as "mental images considered collectively . . . the particular type of imagery characteristic of an individual person, such as visual, auditory, or kinesthetic imagery," and a number of different kinds of images, including *archetypal-, image agglutinations, imago, body concept–, concrete-, double-, general-, hypnagogic-, idealized-, memory-, percept-, personal-, primordial-, retinal-, self-, social-, stabilized retinal-,* and *tied-images.* (For definitions of these terms, also see English and English [1958], Hinsie and Campbell [1970], Reber [1985], and Warren [1934].) Further, Corsini's (2002, pp. 585, 472–73) dictionary definitions are as follows:

- *Mental imagery* as "phenomenological productions such as pictures, fantasies, hallucinations, or representations of objects, people, or events"
- *Mental image (types)* as "four types of images in terms of clarity and completeness of detail: afterimages, eidetic images, memory images, and imagination images"
- *Image envy* as "an unpleasant feeling of jealousy experienced when appraising another's potential or actual image as more desirable than the person's own"

- *Imagery code* as "the encoding of an object, idea, or impression in terms of its visual appearance"
- *Imagery reactor* as "a person who responds to the environment predominantly in terms of images, usually auditory or visual"
- *Imagery therapy* as "the use of mental images as a therapeutic technique" (cf. "guided affective imagery" and "psycho-imagination therapy")
- *Imagery types* as "based on a questionnaire, Francis Galton concluded that people fell into one of these six types of perception of mental images: auditory, gustatory, motor, olfactory, tactual, visual"
- *Imaginal flooding* as "a type of semi-hypnotic trance in which a person is treated for some obsessive, hypochondrial, or phobic condition by imagining, via vivid speech of the therapist, matters of crucial importance to the specific disorder"
- *Imaginary audience* as "the strong belief among early adolescents that everyone is thinking about them and observing their behavior"
- *Imaginary chromaticity* as "relating to the hue of a color that does not exist naturally in the spectrum"
- *Imaginary companion* as "a fictitious person, animal, or object created by a child; the imaginary companion is given a name, and the child talks to it, shares feelings, and plays with it; it may be used as a scapegoat for the child's misdeeds . . . also known as 'invisible playmate'"
- *Imagination* as "the creation of ideas and images in the absence of direct sensory data, frequently combining fragments of previous sensory experiences into new syntheses; types of imagination include: active, creative, reproductive"
- *Imaging* as "the use of suggested mental images to control bodily processes, including the easing of pain"

Corsini also observes that the term imagery when used in a technical/ laboratory context—such as that of "radioisotopic encephalography"— refers to the process of scanning the brain after injection of a radio-isotope and recording the patterns in graphic form; the imaging in this context may be either static or dynamic (cf. "nuclear imaging").

Katz (2000, p. 187) discusses mental imagery in an encyclopedic-style entry, and defines imagery as "the mental construction of an experience that at least in some respects resembles the experience of perceiving an object or an event, either with or without direct sensory stimulation." (Cf. Singer [2000, p. 227] who—in his discussion of "imagination"—defines mental imagery as "the person's ability to look at some object, or to hear a sound pattern, and then to reproduce that material in thought once it is no longer physically present.") Moreover, Katz briefly discusses the following issues: the philosophical and early psychological inquiries into mental imagery (cf. Candlish,

2001), the study of mental imagery since 1960, imagery and psycho-therapy, and imagery play. Katz also provides a brief bibliography on mental imagery in his article.

Colman (2001, p. 356) defines image in the following ways: "a depiction or likeness of an object; an optically formed representation of an object, such as a retinal image projected by the crystalline lens of the eye on to the retina; a mental representation of a stimulus in the absence of the physical stimulus, formed by imagination or memory; also called a *mental image*; the appearance or character that a person or an organization presents in public; another name for a figure of speech in which a word or phrase is applied to something other than its usual or literal meaning." The term imagery is defined by Colman (p. 356) as "the act or process of forming mental images without stimulation of sense organs, or the mental images formed by memory and imagination, including not only visual images but also images from the other senses, such as hearing, taste, smell, and touch." Other image-related terms defined by Colman (p. 356) include the following:

- *imagen*: a representation of a visual image in long-term memory;
- *image-retinal system*: a subsystem of the visual system, based on direction-sensitive neurons, that computes object-movements from the movement of images across the retina, but is unable on its own to differentiate between retinal movements caused by movements in the environment and those caused by the observer's eye- and head-movements;
- *imaginary companion*: a child's invented or fanciful playmate, friend, or associate, often accompanied with great delusional belief;
- *imaginary contour*: synonymous with the phenomenon of "illusory contour" which is a visual contour in the absence of a lightness or color gradient in the stimulus and which generates form perception without a corresponding retinal image;
- *imago*: an idealized image of an individual, usually a parent, that is acquired and developed in infancy but is maintained in one's unconscious in later life; and
- *imagination*: the process or act of imagery in which mental images are generated in a resultant fashion that have never been experienced previously in perception; involves the notions of resourcefulness and creative ability.

In summary, regarding this first section, the broad concept of image was seen to carry a number of different meanings and connotations that cut across a number of different disciplines, including psychology (general, experimental, abnormal, social, cultural), anthropology, optics, anatomy and physiology, and literature. On the other hand, the concept of mental imagery was considered to be more discipline-specific and exclusive to the field of psychology where various subtypes of mental imagery—such as afterimages, eidetic images, memory images, and imagination images—have been investigated historically by psychologists (cf. Kosslyn, Pinker, Smith, and Shwartz, 1979). Accordingly, the remaining sections of this chapter involve the definition, description, and analysis of the various classes or subtypes of psychological mental imagery.

## AFTERIMAGERY

Warren (1934) provides a serviceable definition of the concept of afterimage, as well as several other related terms such as after-discharge, aftereffect, afterimage/memory, afterimage/negative, afterimage/positive, after-nystagmus, and after-sensation (cf. Brown, 1965; English and English, 1958; McKellar, 1972, pp. 54–55; Morsch and Abbott, 1945; Reber, 1985; Wolman, 1973). According to Warren, an afterimage is "a prolongation or renewal of a sensory experience after the external stimulus has ceased to operate"; Warren notes that the term afterimage implies a central nervous system origin; however, where a peripheral nervous system origin is indicated, the appropriate term to use would be *after-sensation*. The term after-sensation—which is synonymous with the term aftereffect—is defined as "a prolongation or renewal of a sensory experience after the external stimulus has ceased to operate, but while the receptor is presumably still active" (p. 8). The term aftereffect—which is synonymous with the term *after-experience*—is defined by Warren (p. 7) in two ways as "the experience which under certain conditions follows the removal of a stimulus—it may be continuous with the primary experience or may follow after an interval of time" and "an after-image or after-sensation . . . used to avoid the implication of central or peripheral origin." In Warren's terminology, a *negative afterimage* is "an experience which follows another and is dependent upon the prior stimulation, but which is of a quality antagonistic or complementary to the preceding experience; for example, a visual after-image in which black and white relations are reversed and the colors are usually approximately complementary to those of the original sensation" and a *positive afterimage* is "an experience which follows another in the absence of direct stimulation, and reproduces the qualities of the preceding experience" (p. 7). As Warren suggests, this term is synonymous with *positive after-sensation*, and is contrasted with *negative after-sensation/*

*image* in which the qualities are reversed, or complementary; however, the aftereffect following a light stimulus is sometimes termed a positive afterimage if it appears brighter than the surrounding field, and a negative afterimage if it appears less bright (cf. Favreau and Corballis, 1976). In this context, the terms *positive* and *negative* refer to "brightness" only, and not to the "hue" of the image.

Warren (1934) also refers to the *Purkinje afterimage*, which is positive in brightness and complementary in hue to the primary image. (At another place in his dictionary [p. 219], Warren defines the Purkinje afterimage as "the second positive visual after-sensation which appears most plainly in the hue complementary to that of the primary sensation"; a synonymous term for the Purkinje afterimage is called "Bidwell's ghost," named after the English physicist Shelford Bidwell [1848–1909]; cf. Roeckelein, 1998, p. 392.) Moreover, *Purkinje images*—synonymous with the term *Purkinje-Sanson images*—are defined by Warren (p. 219) as "the images of reflection on the anterior and posterior surfaces of the eye-lens" (cf. *Purkinje phenomenon*— "a phenomenon concerning the relative brilliance of different colors, namely, that as the spectrum is darkened, the long-wave end darkens more rapidly than the short-wave end; for example, red appears brighter in an intense general illumination, blue in faint illumination . . . the effect rests upon the transition from cone to rod vision" and *Purkinje figures* are the "shadows cast on the retina by the blood vessels which lie just within the retinal layer of nerve fibers, seen projected outward into the visual field; they are observed when the interior of the eyeball is illuminated by a strong light concentrated on the sclera or white of the eye; they appear branched and tortuous; synonym is *snake figure*"; p. 219).

Finally, Warren (1934) defines *memory afterimage* (a perceptual or sensory experience following another in the absence of direct stimulation, and is like a sort of instantaneous photograph of the preceding perception or sensation); *after-nystagmus* (the continuation of alternate quick and slow phases after stopping, or slowing down, of rotation of the head); and *after-discharge* (the release of neural impulses from an intensely excited nerve center, continuing on after the original exciting stimulus has stopped). (For another subtype of afterimage—called "recurrent imagery"—see Hanawalt [1954] and McKellar [1979] who suggests that "perseverative imagery" is the same as "recurrent imagery.")

In his celebrated work, *The Principles of Psychology*, William James (1890) discusses afterimages in his chapters on imagination, memory, and hypnotism. Within the context of memory, James (vol. 1, p. 645) states,

> As a rule sensations outlast for some little time the objective stimulus which occasioned them. This phenomenon is the ground of those "after-images" which are familiar in the physiology of the sense-organs. If we open our eyes instantaneously upon a scene, and then shroud them in complete darkness, it will be as if we saw the scene in ghostly light throught [*sic*] the dark screen. We can read off details in it which were unnoticed whilst the eyes were open . . . this is the primary positive after-image.

James (1890, vol. 1, p. 645) cites evidence from Helmholtz (1856–1866) concerning afterimages: "According to Helmholtz, one third of a second is the most favorable length of exposure to the light for producing it" (i.e., the "primary positive after-image") ". . . longer exposure, complicated by subsequent admission of light to the eye, results in the ordinary negative and complementary after-images . . . which may (if the original impression was brilliant and the fixation long) last for many minutes." Helmholtz—via James—notes that Gustav Fechner gave the name "memory-after-images" to the instantaneous positive effects found under such conditions, and distinguishes them from ordinary afterimages.

Within the context of his discussion on imagination, James (1890, vol. 2, p. 50) also cites observations made by Gustav Fechner (1860) concerning the differences between afterimages and *images of imagination* (see my later section in this chapter, "Imagination Imagery"). Fechner suggests that afterimages "feel coercive," whereas imagination *images* "feel subject to our spontaneity" and afterimages "seem unsubstantial and vaporous," whereas *imagination-images* "have more body." Moreover, in respective comparisons, afterimages are "sharp in outline," "bright," "almost colorless," "continuously enduring," "cannot be voluntarily changed," "are exact copies of originals," "are more easily got with shut than with open eyes," "seem to move when the head or eyes move," and "in observing after-images, attention seems directed forwards towards the sense-organ." On the other hand, Fechner—via James (1890)—found that imagination-images are "blurred," "are darker than even the darkest black of the after-images," "have lively coloration," "incessantly disappear and have to be renewed by an effort of will," "can be exchanged at will for others," "cannot violate the necessary laws of appearance of their originals (e.g., a man cannot be imagined from in front and behind at the same time)," "are more easily had with open than with shut eyes," "need not follow movements of head or eyes," and "in imagining, the attention feels as if drawn backwards towards the brain." Fechner also suggested that it is impossible to attend to both afterimages and imagination-images at the same time—even when they are of the same object and might be expected to combine.

James (1890, vol. 2, p. 51) asserts in a "universal proposition" that afterimages seem larger if one projects them on a distant screen, and smaller if they are projected on a near one—while no such change takes place in mental pictures. Thus, James adds his own observations to the propositions already cited by Fechner concerning the nature of afterimages. James's universal proposition also invites a consideration of afterimages within the context of "Emmert's law" or the "size-distance invariance hypothesis" (see Roeckelein, 1998, pp. 160–62). Emmert (1881) noted the tendency of a projected image (usually an afterimage) to increase in size in proportion to the distance to which it is projected onto a background surface (this became known as Emmert's law). Boring, Langfeld, and Weld (1939) refer to Emmert's principle as an "after-image law" and, earlier, Ebbecke (1929) proposed a "theory of positive and negative after-images" that assumes that there is only one aftereffect process (which he regards as "after-excitation") in the retina and *not* two opposed aftereffects (cf. Woodworth [1938, p. 560] who offers a modification of Ebbecke's theory by assuming the single retinal aftereffect to be one of adaptation instead of excitation, and proposes a transposing to the cortex the necessary after-excitation to account for the "positive after-image"). Thus, Emmert's law is based on the use of size as a cue in estimating distance and involves the geometry of visual size and depth; this relationship suggests the following equation (known as "Euclid's law." Cf. Woodworth and Schlosberg [1965]: $a = A/D$, where $a$ is the retinal image of an object, A is the actual size of the object, and D is the distance from the object on the retina. This equation states that the farther away an object is, the smaller it should look ["retinal size"]). However, Emmert's law presents an apparent exception to Euclid's law by suggesting that an afterimage actually looks bigger if it is projected on a more distant surface; that is, the judged size of the image is proportional to the distance. In this way, Emmert's law may be said to be a special case of Euclid's law.

The relationship of the variable of *size* to the variable of *distance* was studied, also, by Helmholtz (1856–1866) who maintained that observers learn through experience that an object's physical size remains the same (invariant), although its retinal image size varies with distance. Thus, one's perceptual system records the size of the retinal image and then changes or corrects this information based upon available cues about distance to arrive at judgments of object size. Helmholtz suggested, moreover, that in perceiving object size, people implicitly solve the equation: object size = retinal size × distance (cf. Euclid's law). More recently, this view of size constancy constitutes the "size-distance invariance hypothesis," which implies that accurate perception of an object's distance leads to accurate perception to its size (cf. Epstein, Park, and Casey, 1961). Thus, the relationship between the size-distance invariance hypothesis and Emmert's law is the use in the latter of an afterimage of an object that is projected onto a background surface. In either case, the basic principles concerning the link between perceived *size* and perceived *distance* remain the same.

Emmert's law and the size-distance invariance hypothesis have been invoked as a possible explanation (among others) for one of psychology's classical perceptual illusions—the "moon illusion" (i.e., the experience one has where the perceived size of a full moon observed on the horizon seems much larger than the same moon when viewed overhead at its zenith a few hours later; additionally, this illusion has been called the "celestial illusion" because the effect may occur, also, with regard to the sun).

Another afterimage phenomenon is called the "McCollough effect" (cf. Brown, 1965; McCollough, 1965) or the "color-contingent aftereffect," which is a persistent afterimage produced by saturating the eye with red and green patterns of different angularity: In a typical experiment, a pattern of bright red and black horizontal lines is alternated with a pattern of bright green and black vertical lines every five seconds for several minutes. Following these exposures, a pattern of black-and-white lines at various angles is presented to the viewer and, when the afterimage appears, the horizontal white lines are seen as tinged with green and the vertical lines with red (if one tilts one's head 90 degrees under these conditions, the colors change, taking on the appropriate coloration). For a study on the use of the afterimage method, see Baldwin (1939); for a "demonstration of positive and negative visual after-images," see Stevens (1935); and for other early studies on the afterimage, see the following: "the positive after-image in audition" (Bishop, 1921); "the visual negative after-image" (Braddock, 1924); "the auditory memory after-image" (Dimmick, 1923); "the perception of depth in the after-image" (Ferree and Rand,

1934); "the after-image threshold" (Franz, 1895); "the after-effect of visually observed movement" (Gates, 1934); "the Purkinje after-image" (Judd, 1927); "after-images observed in complete darkness" (Robertson and Fry, 1937); and "visual, cutaneous, and kinaesthetic ghosts" (Swindle, 1917).

Boring (1957, p. 103) notes that the persistence of sensation after the cessation of the stimulus (i.e., aftereffects or afterimages) was known to Sir Isaac Newton who described the circle of light seen on whirling a luminous body (Newton, 1704). Boring (1957) also indicates that there are several references to the phenomenon of aftereffects before Newton in the seventeenth century, most notably those by Robert Boyle in 1663; moreover, several early investigators after Newton in the middle and late eighteenth century refer to aftereffects and afterimages. In 1743, Georges Louis Leclerc, comte de Buffon, coined the phrase "accidental colors" to describe all instances of positive and negative afterimages, the flight of colors, and similar chromatic effects that occur in the absence of a stimulus; in 1765, Benjamin Franklin demonstrated—via what came to be called the "Franklin experiment"—how the afterimage may be positive on the dark field of the closed eyes and negative on a field of white paper when the eyes are open; and in 1786, the physician R. W. Darwin (the father of the evolutionist Charles Darwin) gave a full account of "ocular spectra" and was the first to use the term "spectrum" for an afterimage (a spectrum, or specter, is an "appearance" or "apparition"). Newton also used the word for the ghostly band of colors one sees in the dark when a beam of white light is dispersed by a prism.

Thus, according to Boring (1957), the chief facts concerning afterimages were already available at the start of the nineteenth century. See Franz (1895) who indicates that Aristotle—in his *De Somniis*—described the appearance of an afterimage. According to Franz, this observation seems *not* to be generally known by German writers (Hermann Aubert and Hermann von Helmholtz both credit Peiresc as being the first to mention afterimages). Franz also notes that the fourth to fifth-century philosopher St. Augustine mentions afterimages, as well as various other prominent writers such as Buffon, Goethe, and Newton who all described the appearance of afterimages.

In his chapter on "The Perception of Space," James (1890, vol. 2, pp. 225–30) discusses the phenomenon of *double-images*. (Also see Boring's [1957, p. 105] account of the "horopter"—discovered and defined by Aguilonius in 1613—that supported the view that the two retinas are composed of corresponding points. The horopter is the locus of all points seen as single in binocular vision, that is, the locus of all points whose images fall on corresponding points of the two retinas; in the horizontal plane, it is a circle which passes through the fixation point and the two centers of the eyes.) With the premise that physiologists for a long time have looked for a simple law by which to connect the seen direction and the distance of objects with the retinal impressions they produce, James provides the relative merits and shortcomings of the two main theories that account for this connection: the "theory of identical points" and the "theory of projection." Proceeding from the theory of identical points (i.e., any pair of retinal points in the two eyes which, when the eyes are in the primary position, receive stimuli from the same objective point at infinite distance), James (vol. 2, pp. 224–25) states that "[i]t is an immediate consequence . . . that images which fall upon geometrically disparate points of the two retinae should be projected in disparate directions, and that their objects should consequently appear in two places, or look double." On the other hand, in another part of his inquiry into "the perception of space," James (vol. 2, p. 252) observes that "[a] thoroughgoing anti-sensationalist ought to deny all native tendency to see double images when disparate retinal points are stimulated, because, he should say, most people never get them, but see all things single which experience has led them to believe to be single."

The topic of afterimages/afterimagery is discussed further in chapter 2 ("Origins and Evolution of Imagery") and chapter 5 ("Annotated Bibliography of Imagery Studies in Psychology").

## DREAM IMAGERY AND LEVELS OF CONSCIOUSNESS

*Dream imagery* may be defined as "the sequence of presentations, usually visual, which make up a dream story, or a cross-section (i.e., a momentary scene) from this," and *consciousness* may be defined as "the distinguishing feature of mental life, variously characterized as awareness, the central effect of neural reception, the capacity of having experiences, the subjective aspect of brain activity, or the relation of self to environment" (Warren, 1934, pp. 85, 57). (The useful bibliography compiled by Benjamin Rand in Baldwin [1901–1905, vol. 3, part 2] provides over 340 references on the topics "Dreams and Sleep," over 360 references on "Consciousness," and over 415 references on "Hypnotism and Suggestion"; all citations are dated before the early twentieth century (pre-1901) and include works in the German, French, English, and Italian literature.)

Subcategories of dream imagery include the following: *hypnagogic/hypnogogic imagery* (i.e., images, often hallucination-like, that occur immediately prior to a period of sleep; cf. McKellar and Simpson, 1954; Schacter, 1976); *hypnopompic imagery* (i.e., mental images that may occur immediately after a period of sleep and before full wakefulness; cf. McKellar, 1972, p. 45); and *dream-illusion* (i.e., a dream involving images may be precipitated by an objective sensory stimulus; for example, a ringing alarm clock may stimulate one to dream of a locomotive rapidly passing by the dreamer; cf. Hinsie and Campbell, 1970; Reber, 1985; Tart, 1965a,b, 1966; Wolman, 1973). Subcategories of the term consciousness include the following (cf. Reber, 1995): *preconscious/foreconscious/descriptive unconscious* (i.e., the images, emotions, and knowledge that are not immediately present in consciousness but that are accessible easily); *unconscious/dynamic unconscious* (i.e., a level of mind, and imagery, that is lacking in awareness); and *subconscious* (i.e., a level of mind through which images and other mental elements pass on their way to full consciousness; images that are on the margins of attention and of which one is only vaguely aware); according to Reber (1995), the term *subconscious* should not be used as a synonym for *unconscious*; the term *preconscious* is most often preferred by lexicographic purists over the term subconscious. Early studies on the topic of consciousness include the following: Allin (1896), Angell and Thompson (1899), Armstrong (1898), Arnold (1905), Bain (1894), Baldwin (1895), Bascom (1869, 1875), Bastian (1870), Benedict (1885), Binet (1890), Bogardus (1899), Bradley (1893), Carus (1894, 1895), Child (1893), Cleland (1883–1884), Dana (1894), Davidson (1881), Davies (1877), Delabarre (1892, 1895), Dendy (1893), Dwinell (1880), Gorton (1896), Hall (1901), Herrick (1894, 1896), R. Hodgson (1885), S. Hodgson (1894), James (1887, 1898, 1904), Ladd (1896a,b), Lewes (1877), Marshall (1896, 1901, 1902, 1904), Maudsley (1887), Minot (1902), Montague (1905), Morgan (1896–1897), Myers (1892), Perry (1904), Rehmke (1897), Schofield (1898), Shand (1888, 1891), Smith (1898–1899), Speir (1887–1888), Stanley (1899), Talbot (1895), Woodbridge (1905), and Wundt (1876); and early studies on the topic of *dreams* include the following: Andrews (1900), Bisland (1896), Bradley (1894), Calkins (1893), Clymer (1885), Conover (1791), Crichton-Brown (1895), Cunningham (1864), Dearborn (1899), Drummond (1900), Ellis (1895, 1899), Ermacora (1895),

Fere (1887), Gould (1889), Granville (1882), Greenwood (1894), Gulliver (1880), Hutchinson (1901), Leadbeater (1899), Monroe (1900–1901), Murray (1894), Nelson (1888), Oswald (1889), Popham (1854), Robinson (1893), Scholz and Jowett (1894), Seafield (1865), Shaler (1879), Stanley (1899), Sully (1876, 1889, 1893), Symonds (1851), Titchener (1895), Tryon (1697), Vaschide and Pieron (1901), Vold (1896), Waller (1816), Weed, Hallam, and Phinney (1896), Wilks (1894), Wilson (1884), and Woodworth (1897).

Reber (1995) defines consciousness as "a state of awareness; a state of being conscious . . . a domain of mind that contains the sensations, perceptions, and memories of which one is momentarily aware . . . those aspects of present mental life that one is attending to [*sic*]"; he also indicates that the term consciousness has a distinctly checkered history: it sometimes has represented the central focus of psychology—as viewed within the Structuralist school of psychology, while at other times it has been banned from usage or consideration—as viewed within the Behaviorist school of psychology. Reber (1995) also notes that the ongoing fascination with the concept of consciousness derives from a compelling sense that it serves as one of the fundamental defining features of the human species: to be human is not only to possess self-awareness but also to demonstrate the remarkable ability to scan and review mentally (including imagery and images) the contents of one's awareness. In Reber's usage, the term *conscious* refers to the mental state of an individual who is capable of having sensations and perceptions, of reacting to stimuli, of having feelings and emotions, of having thoughts, ideas, plans, and images, and of being aware of such mental contents. In another dictionary of psychological terms, see Sutherland's (1996, p. 95) interesting dictum—upon ending his definition of consciousness—that "[n]othing worth reading has been written on it." For other approaches to the definition of consciousness, see Reese (2001, pp. 228–29) who observes that the words consciousness, *mind*, and *psyche* have been used synonymously from ancient Greek philosophy to the present, but the underlying concept was never adequately defined. Reese also provides the following historical perspectives and sources regarding consciousness: "Its meaning we know so long as no one asks us to define it, but to give an accurate account of it is the most difficult of philosophical tasks" (see James, 1890, vol. 1, p. 225); "Consciousness can never be defined" (see Ladd, 1896a, p. 300); "Consciousness is that which is present when we are either awake or dreaming, and which is absent when we

are dreamlessly asleep" (see Washburn, 1916, p. 17); "Consciousness
can neither be defined nor described. . . . It cannot be defined by discriminating it from the unconscious, for this either is not known at
all, or else is known only as it exists for consciousness" (see Dewey,
1891, p. 2); "There is probably no word which has been more discussed, or whose meaning remains more obscure, than the word *consciousness*" (see Rignano, 1923, p. 359); also, as noted by Reese, see
Dunlap's (1926) circular-reasoning viewpoint (containing, potentially,
the "stimulus error" fallacy that lies in describing the external object
rather than the internal state it arouses) that consciousness means both
introspective observing of something and the thing so observed by
introspection; and Prince's (1926) assertion that consciousness and
awareness are used often as synonyms. Reese (2001, p. 229) states that
"[v]ery little if any progress has been made in a century of research
on consciousness. We are not even closer to having a satisfactory definition of the term."

In his welcomed account of consciousness, Hilgard (1977, p. 1)
states that "[t]he unity of consciousness is illusory." That is, an individual may perform more than one thing at a time, all the time, where
the conscious representation of such activity is never complete; one's
awareness may shift from one aspect of action outside of one's body
to events inside the body—including events consisting of images and
memories. Moreover, according to Hilgard, because consciousness is
recognized as only partial, it is customary to speak of "paying attention" with the implication that some things going on in the present
may not be attended to; also one's attention may be divided among
two or more streams of thought or courses of action. Within this context, Hilgard invokes the concepts of *hypnosis* and *dissociation,* which
refer to the concealed part(s) of one's total ongoing conscious thought
and action; he maintains that hypnosis is a useful and instructive
mechanism for understanding consciousness in that it may interfere
with, and divide, the normal attentive processes and, also, may alter
the balance between voluntary and involuntary control (cf. James,
1890, vol. 2, pp. 604–7, for a discussion of hallucinations, delusions,
and illusions within the context of hypnosis). Hilgard (pp. 4–16) provides an historical account of the phenomenon of *dissociation* that is
grounded in the more general domain of consciousness. Early accounts
in the psychology of consciousness and the "dual controls" operating in human mental functioning include the notions of a "subconscious mind" versus a "conscious mind"; a "double consciousness";
and an "upper consciousness" versus a "lower consciousness" (cf.

Binet, 1889–1890; Dessoir, 1890; Hartmann, 1869; Janet, 1889; Mishlove, 1975). Thus, such divisions of consciousness had been made, and were being made, when Sigmund Freud began to write in the early 1900s about the role of the unconscious in mental illness.

In his discussion of dissociation theory, Hilgard (1977) traces the development, and decline, of the concept of dissociation. The beginnings of dissociation are attributed typically to Pierre Janet in 1889 who asserted that systems of ideas are "split off" from the major personality and exist as a subordinate personality that is unconscious but capable of becoming represented in consciousness, especially via hypnosis (cf. Sidis, 1898). Janet initially introduced the term subconscious into psychology to refer to a level of cognitive functioning outside of one's awareness that could, on occasion, become conscious. Moreover, according to Whyte (1960), the term unconscious was well-known in philosophy and psychology, and frequently used before Freud's writings further popularized the term (cf. von Hartmann's [1869] famous work entitled "Philosophie des Unbewussten" [Philosophy of the Unconscious]); thus, Freud did not "discover" the unconscious but elaborated significantly on it, based upon his clinical experience. Janet attempted to avoid the semantic and interpretive excesses that had become associated with the term unconscious via his introduction of the term subconscious into the clinical field. Prince (1906, 1909, 1914) introduced another term, *coconscious*, into psychology to refer to the splitting up of normal consciousness into disparate parts. According to Hilgard (1977, p. 15), Prince had his own terminology: he preferred to use the term subconscious as a generic term to include both the concepts of unconscious and coconscious, and he limited the unconscious to neural processes and dispositions whereas the coconscious referred to ideas that do not enter into the content of conscious awareness. The term coconscious made it clear that the ideas of which the person may be unaware are still active and that subconscious activity may still be available concurrently—for instance, as revealed in the behavior of "automatic writing," that is, writing while one's attention is given totally to some other task, or writing that is produced while attending to some content and not to the actual process of writing itself (cf. James, 1889; Muhl, 1930, 1952; Myers, 1887; Skinner, 1934; Taylor, 1932).

Hilgard (1977) notes that Janet's use of the term dissociation was borrowed from the "doctrine of association" that was prevalent in Janet's day (see Roeckelein, 1998, pp. 44–47); if thoughts and memories may be brought to the level of consciousness via the association of ideas, then it follows that those thoughts and memories that are *not* accessible to association must simply be "dissociated" (cf. Sidis [1902) and Prince [1906] who—for a time—both advanced and revitalized Janet's concept of dissociation). Demonstrations and experiments, usually involving hypnosis, designed to test the notion of dissociation have given mixed results (see Hilgard, 1977, pp. 7–10). Barry, Mackinnon, and Murray (1931), Burnett (1925), Janet (1889, 1907), and Prince (1909) report positive results, whereas Hull (1933) and Messerschmidt (1927–1928) apply various qualifications to the experimental findings. For example, Hull (p. 191)—while accepting the positive findings that simultaneous tasks may be carried out with one of them *not* recalled—was not able to accept a "noninterference" interpretation of the results from dissociation experiments (cf. Burnett, 1925), and concluded that the whole concept of dissociation as containing "functional independence" is an erroneous notion. Hilgard suggests that the most important criticisms of dissociation theory depend on the importance assigned to the noninterference between simultaneously occurring tasks in the experiments (cf. Rosenberg, 1959; Stevenson, 1972, 1976).

In discussing the decline of the concept of dissociation, Hilgard (1977) notes that the fading of dissociation theory was very rapid after the first few decades of the twentieth century (a count of the references to dissociation in the first ten volumes of *Psychological Abstracts* from 1927 through 1936 shows twenty abstracts indexed; the next ten volumes index only eight studies; the next ten only two studies, and the next ten only three studies). Contributing to the decline of the notion of dissociation were factors such as the upsurge of interest in psychoanalysis during these early years (e.g., psychoanalysis presented an alternative view of unconscious processes where the term *repression* was substituted for the term dissociation [cf. McDougall, 1938]) and the growth of Behaviorism in America [e.g., behaviorists rejected the mentalistic concepts of consciousness and subconsciousness]. See White and Shevach (1942) who concluded that whatever the nature of the hypnotic state, it is not adequately characterized by dissociation; they recommend that the concept of *suggestion* is more useful than dissociation in explaining the phenomenon of hypnosis (cf. Bernheim [1888/1963]).

By way of defense of the concept of dissociation (cf. Spiegel, 1994), and in advancing his own *neodissociation* interpretation of the concept, Hilgard (1977, pp. 12–14) maintains that the experimental "refutations" of dissociation have rested mainly on an "all-or-nothing" interpretation of the separateness or noninterference between dissociated activities. The originators of dissociation, according to Hilgard, held no such extreme position. Rather, it is reasonable today to reexamine dissociation carefully and to adopt the strategy that the amount of interference between partially dissociated activities is an empirical problem or issue where the old dissociation theory may be reformulated in contemporary terms, taking into account what psychologists have learned recently about brain function, divided attention, and information processing.

Hilgard (1977) suggests that it is useful to assign two modes to consciousness: a receptive mode and an active mode (cf. Deikman, 1971) where the former is reflected in the relatively passive registration of events as they impinge on one's sense organs and the latter is reflected in the active, planning, and voluntary aspects of behavior. Both these modes are demonstrated in the special problems of a "divided consciousness" or "divided control"; memories may be separated so that reflection on experiences registered in the first mode may be disrupted, and, on the other hand, the voluntary and involuntary control systems may be reversed through dissociation so that an activity that is normally involuntary may be brought under voluntary control, for instance, with some compulsive behaviors. (Many issues have appeared, disappeared, and reappeared in the behavioral sciences during the twentieth century. For a discussion of the concepts of consciousness and cognition, including the interpretation of mental imagery, as two such recurrent issues, see Reese [2001].)

Other sources that indicate psychology's (and science's) revived interest—both directly and indirectly—in the concept of consciousness, and levels of consciousness, are the following works: Angell (1913), Burt (1964), Chalmers (1999), Deikman (1971), Ellenberger (1970), Globus, Maxwell, and Savodnik (1976), Hameroff, Kaszniak, and Scott (1998), Hilgard (1980), Jaynes (1977), Kanfer and Marston (1963), Keehn (1964), Lambie and Marcel (2002), Neisser (1967), Ornstein (1972, 1973), Pascual-Leone (1990), Penfield (1975), Piaget (1974), Schwartz and Shapiro (1976), Shallice (1972), Sperry (1969), Tart (1969, 1975), Tononi and Edelman (1998), Woodruff-Pak (1999), and Zeman (2001).

Studies that invoke the relationship between imagery and dreams, memory, and/or levels of consciousness—including hypnosis—may be found in the following sources: Azam (1887), Barber (1969), Barber and Hahn (1962), Beck (1936), Blum (1967), Bowers (1976),

Brenman and Gill (1947), Breuer and Freud (1895), Cass (1942), Cheek (1959), Cheek and Le Cron (1968), Danto (1958), Dement (1972), Dement and Kleitman (1957), Dement and Wolpert (1958), Diamond (1974), Diamond and Taft (1975), Dixon (1971), Erickson (1937), Erikson (1954), French and Fromm (1964), Freud (1900), Fromm and Shor (1972), Gazzaniga (1970), Giddan (1967), Gill and Brenman (1959), Guilleminault, Billiard, Montplaisir, and Dement (1975), Gur and Reyher (1976), Hall (1953), Hall and Van de Castle (1966), Hartmann (1970), Hilgard (1965, 1973a,b), Hilgard and Tart (1966), Hiscock and Cohen (1973), Homme (1965), Kety, Evarts, and Williams (1967), Kroger and Fezler (1976), Kunzendorf (1980), Ladd (1892), Le Cron (1952), Levinson (1967), London (1967), Marks (1983, 1999), Martin (1917), Mayman (1973), McKenley and Gur (1975), Miller (1939), Mitchell (1925), Moss (1967), Mostert (1975), Norman (1976), Orne (1959), Perry (1964, 1973), Prince (1968), Sacerdote (1967), Sarbin and Coe (1972), Schreiber (1973), Sheehan and Perry (1976), Shor (1960), Singer (1966), Spanos and McPeake (1975), Spanos, McPeake, and Churchill (1976), Sutcliffe, Perry, and Sheehan (1970), Tart (1972), Thigpen and Cleckley (1957), Ullman, Krippner, and Vaughan (1973), Weitzenhoffer (1953), Wells (1940), Wickramesekera (1976), Wolberg (1945), and Zikmund (1972).

A very useful Web site (http://www.calstatela.edu/faculty/ nthomas/home.htm) on the scientific, philosophical, and historical approaches concerning the relationships between the topics of consciousness, imagination, mental imagery, and cognition was created and is maintained by Nigel J. T. Thomas, who is a philosopher, cognitive scientist, and historian of science and psychology. N.J.T. Thomas (1998) provides a philosophical perspective on consciousness in his account of the "pre-history of consciousness"; he notes that the experts in the field seem generally to agree that there was no word for consciousness (in anything similar to its modern sense) much before the seventeenth century. Moreover, the word consciousness does not seem to have had any equivalents in other non-English European languages as well, including Ancient Greek and Latin (cf. Wilkes, 1988, 1995). Mayne's (1728/1976) essay was probably the first work devoted to the topic, even though European philosophers had, most likely, discussed the issue ever since the time of the French philosopher/mathematician René Descartes (1596–1650). Wilkes (1988,

1995) reviews the non-European usage of the term consciousness and asserts that there is no word (even in modern usage) in the Chinese, Korean, or other non-Western languages that translates the term consciousness in any satisfactory manner. N.J.T. Thomas (1998) invokes Aristotle's philosophy and suggests that to a very large degree the question of whether there was a conception of consciousness before the seventeenth century becomes the more particular question of whether there was an Aristotelian conception of consciousness. Compare Hardie (1976), Modrak (1981), Rorty (1980), and Wilkes (1988, 1995) who claim that Aristotle did *not* have a conception of consciousness; moreover, modern psychologists such as the Behaviorists J. B. Watson (1930) and B. F. Skinner (1976) saw no need to develop or elaborate on such "mentalistic," "internal-unobservable," and "medieval" terms and constructs such as consciousness or self.

On the issue of the viability of the concept of consciousness, N.J.T. Thomas (1998, p. 2) maintains that he "cannot attain the degree of intellectual sophistication required to disbelieve in consciousness. Consciousness is not a technical notion, but an everyday one . . . present to *me* almost every waking moment." In the final analysis, N.J.T. Thomas (pp. 9–10) suggests that:

> We should be doing all we can to construct a scientific account of the function that Aristotle designated as the imagination and the common sense. Aristotle himself could not . . . give any such account, but in recent decades we have learned things far beyond the dreams of either Aristotle or Descartes about the characteristics and mechanisms of both perception and mental imagery. . . . Bringing our scientific knowledge of imagery to bear on the problem of consciousness, and attempting to theorize imagery as a fundamentally conscious phenomenon, may transform our understanding of both topics.

The following references are among those that are indicated in N.J.T. Thomas's Web site concerning the topic of consciousness: Ando (1965), Audi (1978), Baars (1996, 1997), Beare (1906), Bisiach, Luzzatti, and Perani (1979), Carr (1979), Cazenave, Hall, and Callander (1984), Churchland (1979, 1983, 1985), Clement and Falmange (1986), Cotterill (1995, 1997), Davies and Humphreys (1993), Dennett (1969, 1982, 1991), Ellis (1995), Fodor (1975), Freyd (1987), Gray (1995), Hameroff, Kaszniak, and Scott (1998), Hannay (1973), Hardie (1976), Hayes (1973), Heil (1982), Hinton (1979), Hochberg (1968), Kaufmann (1980), Marcel (1983), Marcel and Bisiach (1988), Marks (1983, 1999), Matthews (1969), Mayne (1728/1976), McMahon (1973), Metzinger (1995), Miller (1984), Modrak (1981), Morris and Hampson (1983), Natsoulas (1978, 1983a,b, 1986–1987), Ramachandran and Hirstein (1997), Ryle (1949), Searle (1992), Slezak (1993), Thomas (2000), Tye (1984, 1988), and Wright (1983).

The Web site created by N.J.T. Thomas has numerous useful links, also regarding the topics of imagination, consciousness, mental imagery, and cognition. Among these links are the following rubrics:

1. Philosophical Issues about Mental Imagery. This provides a brief, but comprehensive, guide to imagery theories in cognitive science and philosophy; it also provides a definition of imagery and covers the history of ideas about the topic in philosophy, experimental psychology, and cognitive science, and outlines the latest theories. The relevance of imagery theory to philosophical issues such as consciousness, intentionality, and mental representation are considered. According to N.J.T. Thomas, the information in this link will appear in a forthcoming edition of the Macmillan/Nature *Encyclopedia of Cognitive Science.*

2. Mental Imagery. Mental imagery is defined. Terminological problems in the field are cited, the history of imagery research in scientific psychology before the birth of cognitive science is discussed, and a large bibliography on mental imagery studies is included. The information in this link appears in the "Stanford Encyclopedia of Philosophy," www online serial, accessible via the following URL: http://www.plato.stanford.edu/entries/mental-imagery/.

3. Imagination. This consists of a concise definition, an extended discussion section, and a brief bibliography on imagination; this information is given in the online "Dictionary of Philosophy of Mind.")

4. A Non-Symbolic Theory of Conscious Content: Imagery and Activity. This introduces the "perceptual activity" theory of imagery.

5. Imagery and the Coherence of Imagination: A Critique of White. Indicates a unified understanding of imagination and imagery.

6. A Stimulus to the Imagination: Essay Review of "Questioning Consciousness." Written by R. D. Ellis, this indicates why imagery-based theories of cognition died and why they might be resurrected.

7. Review of M. Tye's "The Imagery Debate." The "analog" versus the "propositional" debate in mental imagery is discussed.

8. Review of J. Taylor's "The Race for Consciousness." This critiques the identification of "qualia" with "brain states."

9. Imagination, Eliminativism and the Pre-History of Consciousness. The understanding of imagination may be the key to understanding consciousness.

10. A Dialogue between N.J.T. Thomas and P. Hayes Concerning the Concept and Nature of Imagery. This dialogue indicates imagery's functional significance in thought.

Other links in N.J.T. Thomas's Web site include The Study of Imagination as an Approach to Consciousness; Imagery and Knowledge: A Historical Analysis; and Gestalt Psychology as a Theory of Imagination.

Finally, among N.J.T. Thomas's "Link Collections" on his Web site are the following: Imagination Links (Web sites that discuss the nature of imagination and related concepts); Mental Imagery (an extensive listing of Web sites related to the psychology, cognitive science, and philosophy of mental imagery); Applied Mental Imagery (covers imagery-based techniques that are used in clinical psychology, psychotherapy, psychological and spiritual "self-help," pain control, and sports training); Journals (provides Web sites of peer-review journals that cover the topics of consciousness, imagination, and imagery); Links on Dreaming (indicates the relationship between dreams and imagination/imagery); and Links on Consciousness, Cognition, and the Philosophy of Mind (Web sites for *general* information on consciousness, the philosophy of mind, and cognition rather than *specific* information on imagination or mental imagery).

## EIDETIC IMAGERY

Ever since the 1930s, various dictionaries of psychology have defined the phenomenon of *eidetic imagery*. For instance, Warren (1934, p. 90) defines eidetic image as "a clear image (usually visual) which possesses an external or perceptual character, though generally recognized as subjective . . . commonly found among children: rarely after adolescence. Distinguished from imagination by its strong sensory character, and from hallucinations by its nonillusory character (from the German *Anschauungsbild*)." Warren (p. 90) also defines the word *eidetic* as "characterizing such psychic phenomena as depend upon (or are otherwise related to) the capacity for clear projected images (*Anschauungsbilder*); term devised by E. R. Jaensch; translates in German as *eidetische*"; the term *eidetic disposition* is defined (p. 90) as "the ability of certain individuals (especially children) to project images of an unusually lively pseudoperceptual character (the German term is *eidetische Anlage*)"; and the term *Eidetiker, eidetic individual* is defined by Warren (p. 90) as "an individual who possesses the ability to project unusually lifelike (eidetic) images."

A longitudinal sampling of more current psychological dictionary accounts of the term eidetic imagery include those by English and English (1958), Hinsie and Campbell (1970), Popplestone and McPherson (1988), and Reber (1995). English and English (1958, p. 173) define it as "a peculiarly vivid type of imagery: it is practically as if the subject [*sic*] were actually perceiving, although in general he [*sic*] realizes that the imagined object is not literally present to the senses. It is very common in childhood (perhaps universal) and is gradually lost by most persons."

A popular experimental psychology textbook of the 1950s (Osgood, 1953, p. 641) gives a flavor of the procedure involved in, and status of, the phenomenon of eidetic imagery as follows:

> If the child is shown a picture for a few moments and then looks at a gray surface, a memory image is projected so clearly that he can literally count the number of spokes on a wheel or even read forward or backward the letters in an unfamiliar word. These eidetic images are not ordinary visual after-images: the child freely moves his eyes about exploring the object during the original impression rather than rigidly fixing a given point. One especially interesting characteristic of the eidetic image is that the individual appears able at will to focus upon any detail and make it gradually become clearer, the rest of the picture remaining obscure (Kluver, 1930). Another point worth noting, which relates this form of imagery to ego-involvement and other personality factors, is that the probability of the child's producing an eidetic image seems to depend upon the degree of interest in the picture (Allport, 1924). Despite the amount of work that has been done on the problem, however, . . . the basic nature of eidetic imagery is unknown.

Hinsie and Campbell (1970, p. 258) define eidetic as "pertaining to or characterized by clear visualization (even by a voluntary act) of objects previously seen. Eidetic images (also known as primary memory images) are clearer and richer in detail than the usual memory images and are also more intense and of better quality . . . the phenomenon is analogous to a hallucination. Visual eidetic imagery is more common than auditory. Such imagery is rare in adults." Hinsie and Campbell (p. 380) also provide an extensive definition under the term imagery, eidetic that includes the following aspects: it is a term that is intermediate between the ordinary visual memory-image and the afterimage, and it gets its significance for constitutional medicine via the work of E. R. Jaensch—where, although it occurs in 60 percent of children under the age of twelve years, it persists after adolescence only in two types, the *Basedow* type (type B) and the *tetany* type (type T).

Hinsie and Campbell (1970) indicate that the eidetic image differs from the ordinary *memory-image* in six ways: it possesses a pseudo-perceptual quality, it is more accurate in its reproduction of detail, it is superior in clearness and richness of detail, it is more brilliant in coloration, it shows a greater degree of coherence with the projection ground, and it requires more rigid fixation for its arousal. Furthermore, according to Hinsie and Campbell, the eidetic image differs from the afterimage in five ways: it is arousable by a more detailed and complicated object, it is superior in clarity and continues longer in the visual field, it is more dependent on factors of interest, it requires a shorter length of exposure and less rigid fixation for its arousal, and it is subject to voluntary recall even after the passage of considerable time as well as to voluntary control. Note that Sheikh (1984) characterizes eidetic images as forms of perceptlike images containing two types: those resembling prolonged afterimages occasioned by percepts, and those originating in memory or the general process of imagination; these two types are termed "typographic" and "structural" eidetics, respectively. The former type may be hue-positive or hue-negative, but may not consist of wholly accurate representations (even though both types are characterized by detail and clarity). Sheikh notes that eidetics are relatively fixed, and one may scan them for details much like examining a photograph; however, the factor of suggestion may occasion a degree of movement of parts of the image. According to Sheikh, the identification of an image as eidetic is not very reliable because researchers apply different criteria, as well as different methods, to the phenomenon (cf. Ahsen, 1977, 1979; Allport, 1924).

Hinsie and Campbell (1970) make an interesting connection between imagery and personal/medical qualities: the type B is identified more with memory-imagery and has been found in individuals with Basedow's disease (i.e., hyperthyroidism) or the tendency toward it, whereas the type T is associated more with afterimagery and has been observed in persons whose blood calcium and potassium show either evidence of tetany or changes in its direction. Moreover, such differences in imagery—referable to the different biochemical conditions in Basedow's disease and tetany—are thought to be symptomatic of two contrasting types of mind: the integrated, and the disintegrated, respectively. Additionally, according to the studies of E. R. Jaensch (1925/1930), another point of difference between these two distinctive psychosomatic types are the characteristic capillary loops of the individual's nail-beds. (Basedow's disease is characterized by enlargement of the thyroid gland, protrusion of the eyeballs, rapid heartbeat, fine muscular tremors, and general nervousness; also, it is frequently called "Grave's disease," and less commonly called "Begbie's," "Marsh's," "Parry's," "Parsons'," or "Flajani's" disease.)

Popplestone and McPherson (1988) note that the term eidetic derives from the Greek word *eidelon* meaning "idol" or "image," and was brought into wide usage by the German psychologist E. R. Jaensch (1925/1930) who emphasized the phenomenon and its ability to convey the unusual clarity of a likeness. Eidetic imagery may occur in the various sense modalities, but because it has been studied more in the visual sense than in the other modalities it commonly connotes visual images and, in common parlance, people who experience eidetic imagery are described often as possessing a "photographic memory." Kluver (1928, p. 70) states that "eidetic images may be almost photographic in fidelity," but Haber (1979, p. 590) states that "eidetic imagery is not photographic" (also see Haber [1980]). While the phenomenon of eidetic imagery is much more common in children than in adults (cf. Allport, 1928, p. 419; 1924, p. 101), Popplestone and McPherson (1988) note an apparent exception in one individual, E. B. Titchener, the early Structuralist psychologist, whose subjective representations were apparently unusually clear and available for his classroom presentations. Titchener (1909/1973, p. 8) states, "I am able . . . to lecture from any one of the three main cues. I can read off what I have to say from a memory transcript, I can follow the lead of my voice, or I can trust to the guidance of kinaesthesis, the anticipatory feel of the movements of articulation. . . . I draw up in mind's eye a table of contents, written or printed, and refer to it as the hour proceeds."

Reber (1995) observes that the term eidetic imagery derives from the Greek word *eidos* meaning *form* (usually taken to mean "form in the mind"), and is mental imagery that is "vivid and persistent." Reber identifies the critical features of individuals (called "eidetikers") who experience such imagery: a persistence in "seeing" a representation of a visual stimulus some time after its removal, and an insistence that such seeing is a true visual image and not merely a memory for the stimulus. Compare Eysenck, Arnold, and Meili (1972, p. 262) who state that "it is questionable whether, as some argue, 'eidetic' phenomena are qualitatively different from intensive visual images"; and, also, the entry for eidetic image in the *New Encyclopaedia Britannica* (1997, vol. 4, p. 397, *Macropaedia, Ready Reference*), which states that an eidetic image is "an unusually vivid subjective visual phenomenon . . . eidetic images and the objects they represent differ in colour, form, apparent size, position in space, richness of detail, and many other characteristics. . . . Investigations have revealed little about the nature, causes, and significance of eidetic images."

Reber (1995, p. 242) also indicates that "true" eidetic images last for some time and, thereby, are different from *icons* (i.e., brief visual experiences that last for less than two seconds after the termination of a bright stimulus; often called "iconic memory," they are considered by many to be one of a class of phenomena within the "sensory information store," "sensory memory," or "sensory register"; cf. Haber, 1983) and afterimages. Reber notes, also, that eidetic imagery is more common in children (estimates put it at about five in every 100 children) than in adults (estimated at less than one in every 1,000, or even less than one in a million, adults) (cf. Haber, 1979, pp. 591–92; Haber and Haber, 1964; Kluver, 1926).

A number of early (pre-1960) references on eidetic imagery are listed in a section in chapter 2 ("Early Measurement and Individual Differences in Imagery"), and selected early (pre-1960) studies on eidetic imagery are also discussed in another chapter 2 section ("Selected Early Psychological Imagery Studies"); more modern (post-1960) studies on eidetic imagery are discussed in chapter 5 ("Annotated Bibliography of Imagery Studies in Psychology"). Haber (1979, pp. 624–29) provides over 280 references on eidetic imagery for the period 1900 through 1978 under the following rubrics: Empirical Studies of Eidetic Imagery (pre-1964); Empirical Studies of Eidetic Imagery (post-1964); Case Studies of Eidetic Abilities (pre-1964); Case Studies of Eidetic Abilities (post-1964); Theoretical and Review Articles on Eidetic Imagery (pre-1964); Theoretical and Review Articles on Eidetic Imagery (post-1964); Cross-Cultural Studies of Eidetic Imagery; Eidetic Imagery and Neurological Pathology; and General References. Also see Ahsen (1977, 1979) and the more recent bibliography by Hochman (2001) who provides over 700 citations/references on eidetic imagery.

## HALLUCINATIONS, ILLUSIONS, AND DELUSIONS

The image-related phenomenon of *hallucination* is defined by Warren (1934) as an "abnormal misinterpretation of ideational experiences as perceptions," and is synonymous with the term pseudo-perception; he also notes that hallucination is frequently, but not always, indicative of "mental derangement." Additionally, Warren distinguishes hallucinations from both *illusions* and *delusions*. In illusion, there is an erroneous perception of some sense data that presently exists (whereas, in hallucination the error of perception extends to one's supposition that sense data are present but, in actual fact, there is no relevant stimulation being received by the individual's sensory organs [cf. Parish, 1897]). In the case of delusion, there is cognitive misinterpretation of the current situation but not of the facts that are immediately present to the sensory systems (thus, in delusion there is an error of psychological judgment rather than of physiology or sense perception). Warren (p. 131) suggests that illusions are broadly divided into two types: *illusions of memory* (in which the memory is mislocated in time or includes elements not in the original perception) and *illusions of perception* (which include illusions of *motion*—apparent motion of an immobile object or field; *movement*—apparent movement of a rigid member of one's body, or of one's entire body; *orientation*—misinterpretation of the position of one's body in space; *reversible perspective*—illusions occur in flat or solid figures when certain parts appear sometimes nearer, sometimes farther from, the eye, such as in the "staircase illusion" or in the "Necker cube illusion"; and *visual size*—misinterpretation of the spatial relations of objects or figures seen. The most striking of the *spatial illusions* have been named after their discoverers and given eponymous identification, for example, the Hering illusion, the Muller-Lyer illusion, the Poggendorff illusion, the Ponzo illusion, and the Zollner illusion (cf. Perry and Chisholm, 1973; Walk, 1984).

Warren (1934) defines *hallucinatory image* as "an image which seems at the moment to be a perceptual experience," and *hallucinosis* as "a disorder in which the patient is subject to hallucinations without any disorder of consciousness or other setting" (e.g., in *alcoholic hallucinosis* there are hallucinations—usually auditory imagery—of threat and reproach directed toward the patient which arise while he/she is clear but frightened; it is a delirium involving "preserved orientation," is apt to last a number of weeks, and is sometimes difficult to distinguish from schizophrenia). In another place, Warren (pp. 17, 115) defines the term *apparition* (a popular rather than a scientific term that often is used technically in descriptions of visual hallucinations and images) as "a sudden and unexpected appearance of some being or object, usually implying a supernatural manifestation; e.g., a ghost, a 'sign' in the heavens"; the term *ghost* is defined as "a visual appearance attributed to the presence of a disembodied personality; a shadowy semblance of some person or thing"; and *ghost theory* is defined as "a non-technical designation for the theory that religion originated in primitive man's belief in ghosts, or disembodied spirits."

English and English (1958, p. 236) define hallucination as "a false perception which has a compulsive sense of the reality of objects although relevant and adequate stimuli for such perceiving are lacking; the acceptance of sense imagination as real. It is an abnormal phenomenon, though occasionally experienced by normal persons." Also, they define *hallucination/peripheral* as "one clearly suggested by a stimulus; it seems likely that stimulation of a receptor is part of all hallucinations, but the stimulus is often not ascertainable"; and hallucinosis is defined as "the condition of having hallucinations; acute hallucinations (lasting not more than a few weeks) is often marked also by great anxiety; it is usually of toxic origin, particularly alcoholic." In another place, English and English (p. 143) define delusion as "a belief held in the face of evidence normally sufficient to destroy the belief; a delusion must be considered a definitely abnormal phenomenon, even though a normal individual may hold it." Many varieties of delusion are distinguished by indicating the particular belief; for example, *delusion of grandeur* (or *megalomania*) is an "exaggerated belief that one is of exalted station or accomplishment," *delusion of persecution* is "a delusion that other persons are deliberately and unfairly causing the person's efforts to fail or are in some way inflicting hardships on him," and *delusion of reference* is "a false belief that behaviors actually having other significance have malign or derogatory reference to oneself" (p. 143). The term illusion is defined by English and English (p. 251) as a "mistaken perception" where—in some cases—the laws of physics explain the erroneous perception; for example, in a *physical* illusion such as the "bent-pencil-in-water illusion," the laws of optics account for the apparent bending of a pencil that is thrust into a glass of water; in a *psychological* illusion—such as the "waterfall illusion" (see James, 1890, vol. 2, pp. 89, 245–46; Warren, 1934, p. 294)—the explanation lies with the perceiver himself or herself. The following illusion-related terms are also discussed by English and English (p. 251): *illusion/associative, illusion/contrast, illusion/assimilative, illusion/memory, illusion/motion,* and *illusion of movement*. English and English note that in illusion there is always an object, though it is incorrectly perceived, whereas in hallucination the object is either lacking or has only a fantastic similarity to the object for which it is mistaken. Moreover, illusions are normal and subject to "regular rule," whereas hallucinations—though not infrequently experienced by normal persons—are essentially abnormal phenomena. According to English and English, both illusion and hallucination have a compulsive sense of their reality, usually even when one is assured of their unreality (cf. Parish, 1897); also, the term illusion tends to be used loosely by the layperson for the term delusion, but this usage should be avoided (even though the expression "illusion of memory" may be well established for a false memory in which the person firmly believes). In the final analysis, English and English suggest that in actual cases, however, it may be difficult to decide whether one is dealing with illusion, hallucination, or delusion.

The most complete cataloging (at least as sampled here) of the term hallucination ("an apparent perception of an external object when no such object is present") is provided by Hinsie and Campbell (1970, pp. 333–37). In this source, over two dozen varieties of hallucination—some invoking more references to imagery than others—are mentioned. Kappenberg (1984, p. 88) counts thirty-one separate definitions of hallucination in Hinsie and Campbell (1970), but given the "see" and the "same" (synonymous) designations for some of the entries, there are actually less than thirty-one varieties. Using a vivid clinical case study across types of hallucinations, Hinsie and Campbell (p. 333) describe a paranoid patient (sitting alone in a quiet room) who complains that his persecutors (who are miles away) speak directly to him in derogatory terms; moreover, the patient believes implicitly that he feels electrical stimuli over his entire body (the alleged stimuli come from a machine operated by his persecutors). In actual fact, the auditory and tactile stimuli have no source in the environment—rather, they are sensations arising within the patient himself. Thus, according to Hinsie and Campbell, a hallucination is a "sense perception" to which there is no external stimulus; in the patient's experience, then, his "sensations" are "hallucinations" and his "false beliefs" concerning his persecutors are "delusions." In another instance, with the same paranoid patient (who is again sitting alone in an otherwise quiet room), when he hears the crackling of the floorboards he is strongly convinced that the sounds are those of a "telegraph-ticker" sending messages to him from his persecutors (i.e., the patient misinterprets actual stimuli from the environment). In this latter case, it may be said that an "illusion" is a false impression from a real stimulus, but the text that the patient reads into the "crackling sounds-messages" may be called a delusion. Among the types of hallucinations described by

Hinsie and Campbell (1970) are the following: haptic, olfactory, gustatory-taste, auditory, and visual hallucinations. A *haptic hallucination* is one associated with the sensation of touch; in the case of the paranoid patient, again, he may complain that his persecutors are operating an electrical apparatus hidden in the walls of the building and are inducing very disagreeable sensations all over his body via the machine. Moreover, the alleged persecutors may surround the patient with "bad sexual odors," thereby indicating an *olfactory hallucination;* they may put "scum" or "seminal fluid" in his food and trigger a *gustatory/taste hallucination;* they call him a "sexual pervert," thereby indicating an *auditory hallucination;* or they allegedly may grimace and wink at him, thereby precipitating a *visual hallucination* (cf. Barnes and David, 2001; Bliss and Clark, 1962; Manford and Andermann, 1998; Santhouse, Howard, and Ffytche, 2000). Other image-related hallucinations (Hinsie and Campbell, 1970, pp. 334–36) are

- *Auditory peripheric hallucination* (an auditory illusion—mostly involving the hearing of voices—that is experienced as a result of actual auditory sensory stimulation, such as the pouring of water, a person's walking, or the rumpling of paper).
- *Blank hallucination* (a generic term that refers to certain uncanny experiences of sensations of equilibrium and space, such as unclear rotating objects, sensations of crescendo and decrescendo, and rhythmically approaching and receding objects that are localized typically in one's mouth, skin, and hands while—at the same time—positioned in the space immediately surrounding one's body. Commonly, such experiences occur in stress situations, when falling asleep, or in dreams. According to Hinsie and Campbell, the appearance of such hallucinations in a therapeutic context indicates that "primal scene" material will be forthcoming).
- *Diminutive visual, Lilliputian,* or *microptic hallucination* (these terms derive from the six-inch-tall inhabitants of the imaginary island of Lilliput in Jonathan Swift's [1667–1745] novel, *Gulliver's Travels.* The hallucination occurs when objects—generally in the guise of persons—appear to the individual as greatly reduced in size under conditions where there is no object in the environment that stimulates such a perception. Hinsie and Campbell [p. 335] note that, as a rule, Lilliputian hallucinations occur in psychiatric states associated with febrile or intoxicating conditions).
- *Elementary hallucination* (in the visual modality, "unformed visions" such as certain types of lighting, sparks, or a cloudlike partial darkening of the visual field; or, in the auditory modality, simple noises such as knocks, murmurs, or gunshots).

- *Extracampine hallucination* (a visual or haptic hallucination localized outside of the sensory field where, for example, a patient may "see" behind his head a vision of the devil with distinct clarity, or "feel" streams of water issuing from a definite point on his hand).
- *Induced hallucination* (a hallucination aroused in one person by another person; for example, in extreme form, similar to a type of psychosis—"psychosis of association"—in which certain of the mental symptoms of one patient, called the "principal," appear in identical form in one or more other people, called the "associates," who are related closely to the "principal." Such an association is commonly intrafamilial, such as two siblings, a parent and a child, or a wife and husband, but it may also occur among pairs of patients on a psychiatric ward, or in pairs of friends who have been in intimate social contact over a period of time. Hinsie and Campbell note that when the number of people involved in the situation is two, the condition may be called *folie à deux,* when three are involved it may be called *folie à trois,* with four it may be called *folie à quatre,* and with many individuals involved it may be called *folie à beaucoup.* Historically, the psychotic form of the condition is known, also, by other names such as "infectious insanity," "psychic infection," "familial mental infection," "reciprocal insanity," "collective insanity," "double insanity," "influenced psychosis," and "mystic paranoia").

Yet other types of hallucination cited by Hinsie and Campbell (1970, p. 335) are *memory/retroactive hallucination* (according to Freudian theory, material that has been repressed into the unconscious may return to consciousness in the form of a visual image; in a "paranoiac memory-hallucination," the image undergoes a distortion similar to that of the "obsessional neurosis" where an analogous current image replaces one that has been repressed); *motor/psychomotor hallucination* (body sensations where certain parts of one's body are felt to be transferred to somatic regions that are distant from their original, natural, or proper location); *negative hallucination* (the failure to see an object while apparently looking at it; the condition may be induced via hypnosis; cf. McKellar and Tonn, 1967); *negative memory hallucination* (one's denial of something that, in actual fact, has been experienced by the individual); *hallucination of conception/psychic/perception* (in a "conception hallucination," or "psychic hallucination," the hearing of inner voices; and in "perception hallucination," an auditory hallucination where one hears a false noise or sound as emanating from outside oneself); and *psycho-sensorial hallucination* (the combined action of the imagination and the sense organs; when the hallucination is the result of the imagination only—without the addition of a sensory stimulus—it is called a "psychic hallucination"). Finally, Hinsie and Campbell (pp. 335–37) define and describe various other hallucination-related terms such as reflex hallucination, slow-motion hallucination, space-motor hallucination, teleologic hallucination, unilateral hallucination, vestibular hallucination, hallucinogen, hallucinosis, acute hallucinosis, alcoholic hallucinosis, diabetic hallucinosis, and uremic hallucinosis.

In a book containing forty-two contributors from various disciplines, West (1962) provides a good summary—of work up to the 1960s—of the knowledge concerning the phenomena of hallucinations; also, Siegel and West (1975) edited a symposium on hallucinatory behavior and experiences. Hilgard (1977, p. 112) notes that up to the 1960s the topic of hallucinations produced by the experience of being in *sensory-deprived* environments and conditions was a popular issue among psychologists, but since then "the excitement has gone out of the field as the extremes of reported hallucinatory effects have been softened by such findings as those of Orne and Scheibe (1964) that *expectations* [italics added] could greatly influence the phenomena of sensory deprivation without the actual deprivation." Also, Hilgard observes that the interest in drug-induced hallucinations has led to the publication of many new books in the field, including the republication of the classical study of the drug mescaline (originally published in 1928) by Heinrich Kluver (1966).

Other pre-1977 works on hallucinations (cf. Crookes, 1874; Frankel, 1976) were published by Barber and Calverley (1964), Barnett (1965), Beringer (1927), Bowers (1967), Bresowsky (1926), Brierre de Boismont (1853), Campbell (1930), Castaneda (1970), Forster (1930), Giel, Gezahegn, and Van Luijk (1968), Goldstein (1908), Graham (1969), Hartmann (1924), Hibbert-Ware (1825), Hilgard (1972), Johnson (1972), Johnson, Maher, and Barber (1972), Kandinsky (1881), Keup (1970), Kirshner (1973), Kluver (1942), Ludwig (1966), McDonald and Smith (1975), McKellar and Tonn (1967), Medlicott (1958), Orne (1959, 1962), Pick (1922), Salisbury (1968), Sarbin and Juhasz (1967), Scheibel and Scheibel (1962), Schilder (1920), Schultes (1966), Seashore (1895), Seitz and Molholm (1947), Shor (1970), Sidgwick (1894), Silberer (1909/1951), Specht (1914), Sutcliffe (1961), Taylor and Martin (1944), Thale, Westcott, and Salomon (1950), Trustman, Dubovsky, and Titley (1977), Underwood (1960), West (1962), Whitty and Zangwill (1966), Zaretsky and Leone (1974), Zucker (1930), and Zucker and Zador (1930).

Kappenberg (1984) observes that the most common type of hal-lucination—both in its familiarity to the public and its occurrence in clinical evaluations—is the auditory hallucination as experienced by individuals diagnosed as having one of the schizophrenic disorders (cf. Freedman, Kaplan, and Sadock, 1975). Further, hallucinations are associated with any of the several senses, including the vestibular sen-sory system and the emotions. According to Kappenberg, perhaps the closest that the average person comes to experiencing an hallucina-tion occurs in a dream-state during sleep; however, hallucinations may be elicited, also, in an otherwise normal person by electrical stimula-tion to his/her brain (cf. Luria, 1973; Penfield, 1958, 1975). More-over, hallucinations that occur in the absence of electrical brain stimulation may signify the presence of aberrant conditions of the brain; for example, hallucinations that may occur as part of the aura that an epileptic patient experiences prior to a seizure may provide a clue as to the location of cerebral dysfunction—if the sense modality and the type of experienced hallucination are analyzed. In the case of induced hallucinations via ingestion of hallucinogenic drugs, Kappenberg notes that the type of hallucination experienced varies from user to user, and even for the same user over different trials; however, visual hallucinations are the most common experienced by LSD users, while marijuana seems to affect reliably the experience of the passage of time, typically "slowing down" time or experiencing/ perceiving "slow-motion movements" across a period of time. Other drugs may produce hallucinogenic effects mainly as an undesirable or unwanted side effect; for instance, visual hallucinations (e.g., "pink elephants") and emotional "terrors" are experienced frequently by individuals undergoing alcohol withdrawal. Also, extended and con-tinued use of amphetamines has been shown to produce both para-noid ideation and associated hallucinations; the tactile hallucinations experienced by those withdrawing from cocaine are characterized as "the cocaine bug" and felt as "crawling sensations" beneath the person's skin. Under more normal circumstances (e.g., in uninter-rupted long-distance driving), fatigued drivers have reported visual hallucinations after driving for long periods of time on highways that have little or no variation in visual features.

Concerning terminology in the area of hallucinogenic drugs, Kappenberg (1984) notes that some writers argue for a more descriptive name for the hallucinogenic substances—such as the term "psychotomimetic," meaning "mimicking psychosis"—because of their behavioral and emotional effect. However, most hallucinogens produce some, but not all, of the cognitive, emotional, personality, and perceptual changes associated with psychotic experiences. As a consequence, other writers argue that the term "psychedelic" or "mind-expanding/altering" drugs be used for the hallucinogens; such experts assert that most people take such drugs neither for their hallucinatory effect, nor for their ability to induce a psychotic state, but to induce an expanded perceptual state in which one may perceive objects from a different perspective or to experience unknown nuances of perception. Additionally, the chemical and pharmacological classifications of the hallucinogens—as well as the advantages and disadvantages of their usage—are open to argument among the experts in the field (cf. Baudelaire, 1971; DeRopp, 1968; Durr, 1970; Huxley, 1954; Julien, 1975; Leary, 1968).

Finally, while much concern has arisen about the most appropriate term or classificatory system to use for the hallucinogens, experts in the field generally agree that the effects of the hallucinogenic drugs vary considerably depending on the type and amount of drug used, on the attitude or "feeling state" of the user, on the user's knowledge and familiarity with the particular drug, and on factors in the user's immediate environment. (Such considerations—regarding drug variability and unpredictability—are expressed while at the same time acknowledging some very general, common, and predictable expectations vis-à-vis certain of the hallucinogens. For example, the effects of *smoking* marijuana/hashish/cannabis will be felt within five minutes of smoking, whereas the oral *ingestion* of cannabis, or the other psychedelics, typically takes about thirty minutes before an effect is experienced; also, while *duration* of drug effect varies for dosage and drug type, the effects of cannabis last approximately three hours whereas drugs such as LSD typically last for twelve or more hours.) Thus, on the whole, with the possibility of so many variations of these factors, it is difficult to predict with any certainty what response any particular individual will have at a particular time to a particular hallucinogenic drug. Kappenberg (1984) observes that it is in large part due to the various adverse reactions to the hallucinogenic drugs that have led to their demise as psychotherapeutic agents or supplemental aids to psychotherapy; initially, about four decades ago, the hallucinogens were viewed as potentially effective psychopharmacological tools, but today they are perceived generally as too risky for widespread clinical use and are of questionable value for most psychotherapeutic applications.

## IMAGINATION IMAGERY

As early as the 1770s, the topic of imagination touched the history of American psychology in a rather interesting way: via Benjamin Franklin (cf. Zusne, 1975, p. 43). During his stay in France (late 1770s) as the American ambassador, Franklin was appointed by the French government to serve on one of several commissions to investigate the work of Franz Anton Mesmer (1733–1815)—the German physician, hypnotist ("mesmerist"), and proponent of "animal magnetism" who claimed to cure neurotic individuals with various unorthodox methods (cf. Ingmar Bergman's 1958 film, *The Magician*; Bergman, 1958/1988)—who was active in Paris at that time. The findings of the commission were that imagination was the thing that actually was responsible for Mesmer's alleged cures. When one of Mesmer's disciples claimed to achieve cures by having afflicted persons stand under trees that he had "magnetized," Franklin—a preeminent empiricist—performed the experiment of telling some peasants that particular trees had been "magnetized," with the result that those who stood under those particular trees were cured as completely as the patients of Mesmer's disciple, and all of which confirmed to Franklin the commission's previous conclusion that imagination or suggestion was the actual effective means or method of cure and *not* "animal magnetism." Thus, Franklin's experiments were the first instances of the empirical study of the factors involved in *hypnosis* (Zusne, 1984, pp. 137–38).

William James (1890, vol. 2, pp. 44–75) devotes an entire chapter (18) in his book *The Principles of Psychology* to the topic of imagination. He states (p. 44) that "sensations, once experienced, modify the nervous organism, so that copies of them arise again in the mind after the original outward stimulus is gone. No mental copy, however, can arise in the mind, of any kind of sensation which has never been directly excited from without." James asserts that a blind person may dream of sights, and a deaf person may dream of sounds, for years long after he/she has lost his/her sense of vision or hearing. James qualifies this assertion somewhat, at least for vision, with evidence—from Joseph Jastrow in an article, "Dreams of the Blind," in the *New Princeton Review* for January 1888 (cf. Jastrow, 1900)—that if one's blindness occurred *before* the age of five to seven years, the visual centers seem to "decay" and visual dreams and images are gradually "outgrown," but if sight was lost *after* seven years of age, visual imagination seems to survive throughout the blind person's life. For a modern account of the issue of "visual imagery" in *congenitally* totally blind people, see Aleman, VanLee, Mantione, Verkoijen, and De Haan (2001). However, according to James, the person born deaf can never be made to imagine what sound is like, neither can the person born blind ever have mental imagery. Along these lines, James refers to the philosopher John Locke (1690) who observed that "the mind can frame unto itself no one new simple idea." Thus, according to James (p. 44, vol. 2), the original "ideas" of sights and sounds must have been given "from without," and the terms fantasy and imagination are the names given to the faculty of reproducing copies of originals "once felt." Furthermore, the imagination may be called "reproductive" when the copies are literal and "productive" when elements from various different originals are recombined in order to make new wholes. In this sense, afterimages may be classified as sensations rather than as imaginings/imagination, and the most immediate elements of imagination are the "tardy images" of actual experience. James maintains that the phenomena ordinarily ascribed to imagination are those mental pictures of possible sensible experiences that are facilitated by the ordinary processes of associative thought. Further, when the mental pictures are represented with concrete surroundings of dates, they may be called "recollections," but when the mental pictures are freely combined—reproducing no past combination exactly and representing no exact date—the result may properly be called an act of "imagination."

Among the rubrics employed in his chapter on imagination, James (1890) includes the following: "Our Images Are Usually Vague," "Are Vague Images 'Abstract Ideas'?" "Individuals Differ in Imagination," and "The Neural Process Which Underlies Imagination." Among his findings and conclusions concerning imagination, James (vol. 2, pp. 49–74) cites the following: a blurred picture is just as much a single mental fact as is a sharp picture, and the use of either is a new mental function; there are different "imaginations" that must be studied in detail, and not merely a general faculty of mind called "The Imagination." Some individuals have no visual images at all. There are great differences among individuals concerning imagination; our verbal imagination seems to be dependent on actual feelings in lips, tongue, throat, and larynx. Touch-images are very strong in some people; the subjective difference between imagined and felt objects is less absolute than has been claimed previously. The cortical processes that underlie imagination and sensation are not quite as discrete as they may seem to be upon initial examination, and it is almost certain that the imagination-process differs from the sensation-process by its intensity rather than by its locality.

Baldwin (1901–1905, p. 517) defines the term imagination as "the general power or process of having mental images . . . it seems better to use the terms imaging and imagery than imagination." Baldwin describes two "variations" of imagination (similar to those of James, 1890, vol. 2, p. 44): reproductive (old memories) and productive (new creations), but suggests that one restrict the term imagination to the meaning that involves the formation of "new combinations which are made possible by the absence of objective limitations confining the flow of ideas" (p. 517). Furthermore, Baldwin refers to two "kinds" of imagination: fancy (which is relatively passive) and constructive (which is relatively active). He notes, also, that the mind is relatively unrestricted when it passes from sense-perception to its selective involvement with mental imagery: one can imagine combinations of ideas that have never actually been perceived. Such relative freedom in one's mental activities forms the connecting link between imagination in the sense of imagery and in the sense of free selective combination. Moreover, Baldwin asserts that the phenomena of belief and imagination are mutually exclusive inasmuch as imagination is conditioned by *absence* of the objective control from which belief necessarily involves; for instance, "belief-attitudes" and "reality-feelings" are partly excluded in situations of "semblance" or "aesthetic illusions" (e.g., audience members at a theatrical performance are involved in an acknowledged imaginary activity and do not act as they would if the same scenes or events occurred in real life). B. Rand in Baldwin (1901–1905, vol. 3, part 2, pp. 1067–69) provides a very extensive and useful bibliography (nineteenth- and early twentieth-century references) on the topic of imagination (including imagery) consisting of 125 references in the English, German, French, and Italian scientific literature. For example, derived from this bibliography, Coues (1877, pp. 455, 457)—in a florid, literary, and poetic style—refers to imagination as "one of the intellectual faculties that in its highest development is the rarest, most precious, and most splendid of human endowments . . . one excellent and most useful purpose which the imagination subserves at the hands of the gifted few whom the higher development of this faculty makes leaders of thought and watchful guardians of human progress, is, to put men of science on their proper level, and to teach them to know their place." In a more philosophical/psychological style, J. R. Angell (1897) discusses his theoretical differences with G. F. Stout's (1896) account in the area of imagination of the relationship between thought and imagery, that is, "imageless thought," and in a psychological style—based upon empirical data from 100 college-student participants, as well as reference to extended experiments conducted on five other participants—Stetson (1896) describes various types of imagination such as visual, auditory, motor, and tactile imagination. At one point (p. 400), Stetson states, "[W]hatever the predominant type of imagination . . . the individual gains most of his ideas through sight and hearing . . . but the relative ease with which he uses hearing or sight may be as well the result of an original idiosyncrasy as of his type of imagination." Other early (pre-1911) studies on imagination include the following: Armstrong (1894), Bain (1855), Binet (1903), Burnham (1885), Cameron (1897), Chalmers (1900), Chase (1899), Davies (1869), Dearborn (1898), Demangeon (1829), Dugas (1895, 1903), DuPasquier (1821), French (1902), Galton (1880a,b, 1883), Goschen (1893), Greenwood (1892), Hunt (1845), Jastrow (1898), Joly (1877), Kirkpatrick (1893), Lay (1898, 1903), Lovell (1899), Lowell (1894), MacDougal (1898), Michaut (1876), Peillaube (1902), Perky (1910), Philippe (1897, 1903), Ribot (1900), Royce (1898), Souriau (1901), Wiltse (1890), and Witt (1900).

Warren (1934, pp. 131–32) defines imagination as "the reorganization of data derived from past experiences, with new relations, into a present ideational experience" and *imagination image* as "an image, usually built up from several previous sensory experiences and accompanied by reference to an object that has never been perceived by the subject."

English and English (1958, p. 253) define imagination as "a recombination into a new pattern of mental images from past experiences." They identify various processes, functions, and uses (cf. Wolman, 1989, for a similar analysis) of imagining: *anticipatory imagination*—the representation of future events, involving "goal" and "movement" images (respectively, the goal sought, and the movements needed to achieve the goal); *constructive* or *creative imagination*—an intentional recombining either for its own sake or as a plan for action; *fanciful imagination*—also called "images of fancy" in which the individual remains relatively passive and the recombining of portions from past experiences seems to proceed without one's will (e.g., dreams, daydreams, and the imaginings in delusions and hallucinations); and *reproductive* or *memory imagination*—also called "memory images," which are the more or less complete representations of formerly experienced events or objects that are linked with the recognition that it does represent a past actually experienced.

Hinsie and Campbell (1970, p. 381) note that imagination is "not the obverse of reality, but affords . . . a means of adaptation to reality"; they suggest that only with the development of the imaginative process in the child does he/she progress from the capacity to create a mental representation of the absent object (involving a syncretic, sensori-motor-affective, immediate response) to the delayed abstract conceptualized response that is one of the defining characteristics of the human species. Further, according to Hinsie and Campbell, creative imagination and *creative work* designate the process whereby dormant and unrelated contents of the unconscious become associated with the more organized aspect of consciousness to produce something novel.

In Eysenck, Arnold, and Meili (1972), imagination is the ability to call forth pictures of absent individuals, objects, processes, or situations; also, they refer to Carl Jung's work and suggest that imagination includes images of elementary situations (objects, processes, or persons) that appear as "collective human experience"—supposedly without any reference to *specific* human experience. The notion of creative imagination refers to the artistic or scientific combination of such elements into new entities such as philosophic systems, works of art, and scientific hypotheses and planned experimentation.

According to Harre and Lamb (1983), the word imagine and its cognates (e.g., imagination) are used commonly to express a number of different, but closely interrelated, concepts (cf. Warnock, 1976; and Hilgard's [1977, pp. 100–111, 112–14] discussion of "imagination"). They note that philosophers often have found it convenient to discuss the general topic of imagination under the three principal headings of "the imaginative," "the imaginary," and "mental imagery." Moreover, the term imagination has been used by some philosophers (e.g., Hume, 1738; Kant, 1781) to refer to a faculty supposed to be necessarily involved in the process of sense-perception. Harre and Lamb also note that the notion of *imaginativeness* is akin closely to those of creativeness and inventiveness (e.g., a person is said to be imaginative insofar as he/she is able to think of things not thought of by other people); however, it is a wider notion than either creativeness or inventiveness, and involves the ability to understand and appreciate the imaginative creations of other people as well as the feelings of others. Thus, according to Harre and Lamb, imagination shows itself as sensitivity and perceptiveness rather than merely as creativity or inventiveness (cf. Croce, 1902, who suggests that to appreciate a work of art, for instance, one must be able to re-create something of the experience of the original artist without resorting to mere fancifulness). Perhaps the fullest discussions of imaginativeness have occurred in the context of the arts and literature (cf. Engell, 1981; Tyndall, 1872; Van't Hoff, 1878/1967). Harre and Lamb indicate that the discussion of mental imagery has centered mainly on the nature of the similarity between imaging and perceiving, as well as on the relationship between imaging and thinking. Thus, there has been a tendency by some investigators to write as if an image were a sort of picture that may be heard, seen, examined, or felt by—and only by—its owner (e.g., Galton, 1883). However, such a model in which an image is analogous to something perceived has been debated and/ or refuted by various writers (e.g., Ryle, 1949; Sartre, 1940; cf. Hannay, 1971; Shorter, 1952; Strawson, 1970).

Gall (1996, p. 191) refers to imagination as "a complex cognitive process of forming a mental scene that includes elements which are not, at the moment, being perceived by the senses." Moreover, according to Gall, imagination involves the synthetic combining of aspects of experiences or memories into a mental construction that differs from past or present perceived reality, and may anticipate some future reality (cf. Bronowski, 1978). Imagination is not thought to be present in lower animals, but is generally regarded as one of the "higher mental functions." It may be fanciful, fantastic, wishful, or problem solving, and may differ slightly, or even greatly, from "reality," and it is generally considered to be a basis of artistic expression that is indicative—within certain limits—of a healthy, creative, and higher mental-functioning individual. Gall notes that observers as diverse as Plato and S. T. Coleridge have cited two contrasting types of imagination: *imitative* (concerned with mentally reconstructing past events or images, e.g., eidetic imagery, afterimages, synesthetic imagery, hypnagogic imagery, hallucinations, dreams) and *creative* (concerned with thought and involves the restructuring—not merely the retention—of sensory impressions, e.g., daydreaming, right-brain hemisphere activity, intuitive leaps of insight, ability to synthesize existing elements into new wholes).

Thomas (1999a, p. 207) attempts to "illuminate the obscure topic of imagination" (cf. Thomas, 1987, 1989, 1997a,b), asserts that the issues of imagery and imagination are related intimately, and maintains that imagination is used often to identify the faculty of "image production" (i.e., the mental arena in which images appear). Thomas (1999a) argues that neither of the better-known theories of imagery (i.e., the "quasi-pictorial" theory—see Kosslyn, 1980, 1994; and the "description" theory—see Pylyshyn, 1973, 1981) are able to serve as the basis for a general theory of imagination and its role in creative thought. Thomas (1999a) proposes a third theory, called the "perceptual activity" theory, that views imagery as nondiscursive and that relates imagery closely to the concept of "seeing as." This theory rejects the traditional symbolic computational view of imagery as merely mental contents and is compatible with more current approaches in imagery such as the "situated cognition" approach (e.g., Clancey, 1997) of "active vision" as demonstrated in the field of robotics. Thus, according to Thomas (1999a), the issue of imagination may be approached, and accommodated, optimally via the "perceptual activity" theory.

In another instance, Thomas (1999b, p. 1) provides a philosopher's perspective on the topic of imagination, which he defines as "the mental capacity for experiencing, constructing, or manipulating 'mental imagery' (quasi-perceptual experience)." Thomas (1999b) also regards imagination as responsible for fantasy, inventiveness, idiosyncrasy, and creative, original, and insightful thought in general, and sometimes for a much broader range of mental activities dealing with the nonactual, such as supposing, pretending, "seeing as," and thinking of possibilities. Thomas (1999b) notes that imagination—despite being a familiar word of everyday language—is a very complex, highly contested, and evaluatively loaded concept; it often has radically different meanings when used in different contexts. In discussing the concept of imagination, Thomas (1999b) reviews the history of the word; the notion of imagination seems to have been first introduced into philosophy by Aristotle (384–322 B.C.) who suggested that imagination (or "phantasia") is the process by which an image (or "phantasma") is presented to a person, and indicated further that the soul never thinks without a mental image. Thomas (1999b) asserts that such images, or "phantasmas," played a role in the early philosophy of Aristotle much like the role that is played in contemporary cognitive theory by the notion of "mental representations"; compare Anderson (1978), Bickhard and Richie (1983), Blachowicz (1997), Cornoldi, Logie, Brandimonte, Kaufmann, and Reisberg (1996), Cummins (1989, 1996), Farah, Hammond, Levine, and Calvanio (1985), Freyd (1987), Hayes-Roth (1979), Julstrom and Baron

(1985), Kosslyn and Pomerantz (1977), Logie and Denis (1991), Paivio (1986), Palmer (1977, 1978), Shepard (1975), Shepard and Cooper (1982), Slezak, Caelli, and Clark (1995), Sober (1976), Squires (1968), Thomas (1987, 1989), Tweedale (1990), Wiles and Dartnall (1999). In such a tradition, according to Thomas (1999b), imagery—and, thus, imagination also—has an essential role to play in *all* forms of thinking and is not confined to, or has no *special* connection with, the phenomena and processes of creativity and inventiveness. (Further discussion of *theories* of imagery, as well as the work of N.J.T. Thomas, may be found in chapter 3.)

Singer (2000) notes that although scientific psychologists agree that the broader function of imagination ultimately rests on the retention and reshaping of stimulus-derived mental images through human memory, evidence from phenomena such as daydreams and sleeping dreams makes it clear that one may generate complex and elaborate thoughts that surpass very recently-presented objects or events. Singer also suggests that the imaginative dimension of human experience is linked, generally, to four kinds of processes: consciousness/stream of thought, daydreaming, night dreaming, and creativity. Moreover, the processes that provide the novel mixtures of mental images and form them into apparently new storylike scenes are largely outside one's awareness or "cognitive unconscious" (cf. Kihlstrom, 1987). In his discussion of imagination, Singer observes that human beings engage in two broad classes of thought that may provide a foundation for studying and understanding imagination. For example, Bruner (1986) proposed that all human thought takes place along the two dimensions of "paradigmatic" (logical, quasi-mathematical, and orderly processes) and "narrative" (engaging in subjective or conditional kinds of imagery thinking or language) modes of thinking (cf. Epstein, 1998). Singer asserts that it is clear from humans' dreams, spontaneous fantasies, waking dreams, and guided-imagery techniques that the complex associative cognitive structures (such as schemas, scripts, prototypes, episodic memories, and sensory-linked images) that form our brain's storage material (often called "declarative memory") may combine to create new, often bizarre, mental experiences (cf. Csikszentmihalyi, 1990; Klinger, 1990; Singer, 1975; Singer and Bonanno, 1990; Singer and Singer, 1990). Singer (2000) holds that imagination—although derived from memories of actual experiences—is *more* than memory: it is an ongoing and dynamic effort to reshape one's past and to create a whole new range of possibilities that is, in itself, a stimulus to further creativity.

Other published studies and sources on imagination that invoke mental imagery include the following works: Atwood (1971), Barron (1958), Baylor (1972), Berbaum and Chung (1981), Bickhard and Richie (1983), Brandimonte and Gerbino (1993), Brann (1991), Brown (1991), Candlish (1975), Casey (1976), Chambers and Reisberg (1985), Cocking (1991), Corbin (1958), Council, Chambers, Jundt, and Good (1991), Daston (1998), Dilman (1967), Dix (1985), Egan and Nadaner (1988), Finke, Ward, and Smith (1992), Flew (1953), Furlong (1961), Hamlyn (1994), Hilgard (1981), Holton (1996), Ishiguro (1967), Johnson (1993), Kearney (1988), Mayne (1728/1976), McFarland (1985), McKellar (1957), Neisser (1978), Newton (1982, 1989), Nussbaum (1978), Pico della Mirandola (1500/1930), Pressey and Wilson (1974), Robson (1986), Russow (1978, 1980), Ryle (1949), Sarbin (1972), Sarbin and Juhasz (1970), Sartre (1936, 1948), Schofield (1978), Scruton (1974), Sepper (1996), Shorter (1952), Singer (1999), Sparshott (1990), Strawson (1970), Sutherland (1971), Taylor (1981), Thomas (1987, 1997a, 1998, 1999a), Tweney, Doherty, and Mynatt (1981), Van Biervliet (1927), Warnock (1976), Watson (1988), Wedin (1988), and White (1989, 1990).

## MEMORY IMAGERY

In an early usage of the concept of *memory imagery* (cf. Hinsie and Campbell, 1970, p. 380, who equate "primary memory image" with "eidetic image"), William James (1890, vol. 1, p. 646) cites the term *primary memory-image* as employed by Sigmund Exner in Hermann's (1879) *Handbook of Physiology*:

> Impressions to which we are inattentive leave so brief an image in the memory that it is usually overlooked. When deeply absorbed, we do not hear the clock strike. But our attention may awake after the striking has ceased, and we may then count off the strokes. Such examples are often found in daily life. We can also prove the existence of this *primary memory-image*, as it may be called, in another person, even when his attention is completely absorbed elsewhere. . . . This primary memory-image is . . . subjectively quite distinct from every sort of after-image or hallucination. . . . It vanishes, if not caught by attention, in the course of a few seconds. Even when the original impression is attended to, the liveliness of its image in memory fades fast.

Also, in an early discussion of imagery, Gustav Fechner (1860, p. 492) refers to the term *memory-afterimages* and distinguishes them from ordinary afterimages on the following bases (cf. James, 1890, vol. 1, p. 645, footnote): the originals of the memory-afterimages must have been attended to (this is not the case in common visual afterimages); the strain of attention towards the memory-afterimages is inward, as in ordinary remembering, not outward, as in observing a common afterimage; a short fixation of the original is better for the memory-afterimage, a long one for the ordinary afterimage; and the colors of the memory-afterimage are never complementary of those of the original. In another early study, Angell (1900) describes in detail the memory-image theory of discrimination, which he maintained had an exceedingly harmful influence on psychological research in general (cf. Roeckelein, 2000, p. 72).

Bentley (1899) attempted to examine critically the place given the image in the memory literature, to discuss the nature and function of the memory-image and its genetic significance, and to isolate the memory-image for experimental investigation. Bentley (p. 14) notes that the term image has a wide significance in psychology, and has a close connection with vision via the "retinal picture/image" notion. He asserts that the use of image as *retinal picture* is not wholly technical: the image is the copy of the *real* in ordinary speech, and the eye—like a mirror—reflects and reduplicates the world. According to Bentley, the language of psychology has extended the term memory-image from its link to vision to various mental contents that represent a definite past event, without regard to the sense affiliations that the contents may reveal. Moreover, psychology has added to the nomenclature of imagery the terms "positive afterimage," "negative afterimage," "memory afterimage," "phantoms of sensory memory," "hallucinations," and "illusions." Bentley notes that the memory-afterimage seems to be a special case under memory-images proper, and whose limited literature demands new investigations.

In another section, in his discussion of the genetic significance of the image, Bentley (1899, pp. 18, 24) states that

If we take the biological point of view, it seems altogether probable that the memory image was a comparatively late acquirement for the organism . . . our view concerning the lineage of the memory-image is as follows. The earliest conscious reaction upon the environment was provided by intimate connection of pleasurably-toned sensations with reactions appropriate for nutrition. Such reactions developed into complex instinctive actions in presence of both pleasurable and unpleasurable perceptions. Next, the distinction between the familiar and the strange (nascent recognition) appeared. As adaptation became too complicated and too delicate to be entrusted either to instinctive control or to response in face of critical stimulation, a discrimination between the present and the non-present arose with the appearance of general images. These images were excited in a variety of ways, and helped to govern action as peripheral stimulation—special and organic sensations—had done before. Special images set in a definite place in the "future" and the "past" came later, and mediated adjustment for special occasions. Simply as a part of the past the image has had little value, but as an index of the future its function has been important.

Other early studies on memory-imagery (cf. Woodworth, 1938, pp. 39–47) include works by the following investigators: Anderson (1939), Baldwin (1939), Berliner (1918), Bowers (1931), Brown (1935), Burtt (1916), Kuhlmann (1905, 1906, 1907, 1909), Murray (1906), Talbot (1896), and Whipple (1901, 1902).

In more current accounts of the term memory-image, Warren (1934), English and English (1958), Hinsie and Campbell (1970), and Popplestone and McPherson (1988) provide the following definitions:

- "The revival of a former experience in the absence of the appropriate stimuli, the content of the revival being similar to the original experience, but not a copy of it" (Warren, 1934).
- "A more or less complete representation of the attributes of an object or event once experienced but not now present to the senses, together with recognition of its 'pastness'; a revival that resembles but need not exactly copy a past experience. The image may be sensory or verbal or both" (English and English, 1958).
- "Anticipation of the recurrence of a past experience, immediately before its recurrence . . . the memory image may be said to be a part of the conditioned reflex in Pavlov's sense, that is, the memory image is an ingredient of the inner preparedness for the stimulus, and is part and parcel of the individual's total reaction" (Hinsie and Campbell, 1970).
- "The simulation of a previous experience is recognized as personal, and introspective data indicate that the fidelity between the original and the recalled varies from person to person, from time to time, and from topic to topic . . . the imagination image: these representations are on occasion unusual and even startling. They are probably basically memory images inasmuch as there is evidence that the imaginative component is in the

combinations rather than in the ingredients" (Popplestone and McPherson, 1988).

(Also, see immediate memory imagery in McKellar, 1972, pp. 53–54.) Standing, Bond, Hall, and Weller (1972) provide a bibliography of "picture-memory" studies (including memory imagery) that contains 685 items covering articles dating from the nineteenth century up to 1972, but in particular is especially exhaustive for the years 1960 to 1970. In a later section of this book (chapter 2, "Selected Early Psychological Imagery Studies" and in chapter 5, "Annotated Bibliography of Imagery Studies in Psychology"), I provide further material, also, dealing with the topic of memory imagery.

## REDINTEGRATION AND DÉJÀ VU

It is a common experience that sensing a part of a previous situation or event leads to an image of the entire situation/event (e.g., hearing the first few notes of Beethoven's Fifth Symphony brings to mind several of the subsequent notes). Such a process is called *redintegration* and psychologists often use it to explain the phenomenon of déjà vu in which a person feels as if he or she has been in a particular situation or place in some previous time. For example (*Encyclopedia Americana*, 1998, p. 797), one may glance around a room without realizing it, then stare at a window and call up a mental image of the entire room—leading to the feeling that one had been in the room previously (this may also be the underlying aspect in those cases where individuals believe that they have been on earth before in some different form or in some other bodies). Thus, apparently, the phenomenon of mental imagery—in one form or another—seems to be related occasionally to the processes of redintegration and déjà vu.

The Scottish philosopher Sir William Hamilton (1859/1860) first proposed the principle of redintegration, which refers to an impression one has that tends to bring back into consciousness the whole situation of which it was a part at one time. In critiquing the *associationistic doctrine* in psychology (cf. Roeckelein, 1998, pp. 44–48), that a sequence of mental events is a "remembering mind" that contains only one single idea at a time, Hamilton taught—on the other hand—that the process of perception is such that any one of the elements simultaneously experienced is capable—when presented later—

of bringing back the total experience. Thus, according to Hamilton, a person redintegrates in memory the original situation when one recalls not only a series of elements but also a pattern of elements as well. Moreover, Hamilton's *principle of redintegration* suggests that any given mental event is only a part of a much larger whole.

Later, H. Hollingworth (1926) used the term redintegration to describe the "functional" rather than the "recall" process in redintegration when the part acts for the whole context; he also described the *law of redintegration* (1928) as the capability of one aspect of a situation to bring it back in its entirety or the reestablishment of a whole situation or experience by bringing together its several parts (*reintegration*). While the terms redintegration and reintegration are synonymous, essentially—and even though the shorter form (reintegration) is more euphonic—historical usage from William Hamilton (1859/1860) on down favors the spelling "redintegration" (cf. Warren, 1934). The law/principle of redintegration was adopted and used by the Scottish psychologist Alexander Bain (1818–1903), as well as by the American philosopher/psychologist William James (1842–1910). The concept of redintegration has undergone various contextual, logical, and terminological changes over the years, and has served as the starting point for much modern discussion of learning processes.

Various dictionaries of psychology define the concept of redintegration:

1. "The reinstatement of a total presentation, in the form of a memory or idea, upon the appearance of a partial constituent of such (former) presentation; the arousal of a response by a fraction of the stimuli whose combination originally aroused it" (Warren, 1934, p. 226).
2. "The reestablishing of a whole; putting together again (synonymous with 'reintegration'); the principle that the presence in consciousness of one element of a whole tends to the *imaginal* (i.e., pertaining to an *image*, or to the process of *imagining*) revival of others, or of the whole; the principle that presence of a single element of a former event tends to bring about the psychological consequence of the event as a whole; the simple case is that wherein part of the former stimulus situation elicits the response, the 'element of the former event' may be a response, may be a feeling tone, or may be the imaginal or ideational content . . . the principle that any sensory process occurring simultaneously with a response elicited by some other stimulus tends to become capable of independently eliciting the response. This is essentially the principle of classical conditioning or the law of contiguity" (English and English, 1958, p. 446).

3. "Hollingworth's term for the process in which part of a complex antecedent provokes the complete consequent that was previously made to the antecedent as a whole. The conditioned response is an example of redintegration. Redintegration is the basis of the value of souvenirs and keepsakes, which tend to arouse the same attributes as were originally connected with the experiences to which they pertain" (Hinsie and Campbell, 1970, p. 652).
4. "The re-establishment or re-forming of a whole . . . the principle which is characterized by the recall of other elements in the whole or the whole itself when a few of the elements are present in consciousness . . . the principle which holds that a stimulus which is contiguous with a response elicited by another stimulus will in the future tend to elicit that response, i.e., the principle operative in classical conditioning" (Wolman, 1973, p. 316).
5. "Generally, the re-establishing of a whole by the bringing together of its several parts, a 're-integration'; more specifically, the capability of one aspect of a complex stimulus to evoke a response originally associated with the whole stimulus. The recalling of many (or all) of the details of a complex memory upon presentation of one detail ('redintegrative memory')" (Reber, 1995, p. 645).

The experience of déjà vu (French for "already seen") is a common phenomenon and occurs in pathological as well as nonpathological conditions, and may be considered to be any subjectively inappropriate impression of familiarity of a present experience with an undefined past (Brown, 2003; Sno and Linszey, 1990; cf. Kafka, 1991). While déjà vu experiences are not uncommon in normal individuals, it has been established that they are symptoms of temporal lobe seizures. For example, Spatt (2002) argues that déjà vu is the result of faulty and isolated activity of a "recognition memory system" that consists of the parahippocampal gyrus and its neocortical connections; this memory system is responsible for judgments of familiarity and the effect is that a momentary perceived scene is given the features of familiarity that usually accompany a conscious recollection. Spatt maintains that the normal functioning of other brain structures that are involved in retrieval of memories (e.g., the prefrontal cortex and the hippocampus) leads to the strange phenomenological qualities of déjà vu. His hypothesis is able to account for many aspects of déjà vu in healthy individuals, as well as explaining such experiences found in epileptic patients (cf. Adachi, Koutroumanidis, Elwes, Polkey, Binnie, Reynolds, Barrington, Maisey, and Panayiotopoulos, 1999; Bancaud, Brunet-Bourgin, Chauvel, and Halgren, 1994).

Among the dictionaries of psychology that define the phenomenon of déjà vu are the following:

Warren (1934)—"an illusion of recognition in which a new situation is incorrectly regarded as a repetition of a previous experience."

English and English (1958)—"(the term *déjà*) in combination with various adjectives, it refers to an illusion of familiarity; *déjà pensee*, of a new idea that seems familiar; *déjà entendu*, of a new voice that sounds familiar; *déjà vu*, of a new scene that looks familiar."

Hinsie and Campbell (1970, pp. 184–85)—(in addition to defining *déjà entendu, déjà eprouve, déjà fait, déjà pense, déjà raconte*, and *déjà voulu*) define déjà vu as "a feeling of familiarity. When a person upon perceiving something that he has never seen before, has the distinct feeling that he had had the experience some time in the past, the expression *déjà vu* is used. It is not uncommon among psychiatric patients, particularly those with hysteria and epilepsy. . . . Freud suggested that *déjà vu* feelings correspond to the memory of an unconscious phantasy; the experience probably represents a combination of ego defenses in a situation that both symbolizes and stimulates the revival of an anxiety-provoking memory or phantasy. The ego defenses include wish-fulfillment . . . and regressive reanimation of omnipotent feelings (in the form of predicting the future)."

Reber (1995)—"a rather compelling illusion of familiarity with a scene that is actually new. It is thought by some to be due to a response to cues in the new situation that are common to old, roughly similar, experiences; others believe it to be due to a kind of momentary 'short circuit' so that the impression of the scene arrives at the memory store (metaphorically speaking) before it registers in the sensorium. There is some evidence for the latter view since [*sic*] frequent *déjà vu* experiences are symptomatic of certain kinds of brain damage. There are several *déjà* experiences, e.g., *déjà pense* or already thought, *déjà entendu* or already heard."

Various other recent studies in the psychological literature have also examined the déjà vu experience: "a summary of works carried out on 'déjà vu'" (Baumel, 1999b); "memory disorders in psychiatric practice" (Berrios and Hodges, 2000); "recent discoveries about common mental diversities" (Bragdon and Gamon, 2000); "an early Dutch study of déjà vu experiences" (Sno and Draaisma, 1993); "déjà vu experiences and reduplicative paramnesia" (Sno, Linszey, and De Jonghe, 1992); and the "Inventory of Déjà Vu Experiences Assessment" (Sno, Schalken, De Jonghe, and Koeter, 1994).

In summarizing this section on the phenomena of redintegration and déjà vu, an indication of the longitudinal "popularity" (i.e., frequency of usage) of the term redintegration as a formal "lawful" concept in psychology may be found in the results of a survey conducted on over 136 introductory psychology textbooks published between 1885 and 1996 (see Roeckelein, 1998, p. 499). This survey (cf. Roeckelein, 1996) shows that the term law of redintegration was referenced by *none* of the textbook authors writing in the periods 1885 through 1919 (cf. Brockbank, 1919) and 1940 through 1996. Moreover, in the period 1920 through 1939 (cf. Seward, 1928), only 7 percent of the surveyed textbooks mention the law of redintegration. Apparently, at least as indicated in a sampling of introductory psychology textbooks across 112 years of psychology, the concept of redintegration (the law of redintegration) has *not* found widespread usage in mainstream psychology. However, a few current studies in the specialized area of experimental psychology (e.g., Brainerd, 1990; Brown and Hulme, 1995; Gathercole, Pickering, and Hall, 2001; Halldorson, 1999; Hulme, Newton, Cowan, Stuart, and Brown, 1999; Hulme, Roodenrys, Schweickert, Brown, Martin, and Stuart, 1997; Lewandowsky, 1999; Lewandowsky and Farrell, 2000; Murdock, 1993; Schweickert, 1993; Schweickert, Chen, and Poirier, 1999; Turner, Henry, and Smith, 2000) do employ and/or invoke the concept of redintegration. No such empirical data—concerning frequency of usage—apparently exist for the term déjà vu as a formal concept (i.e., as a "theory," "law," "principle," etc.). However, casual observation indicates that the concept déjà vu does seem to have found a place in our common parlance and everyday language usage (e.g., Alvis, 1987; Brainerd, 1979; Carro, 1988; Crismon, 1984; Edwards, 1996; Hudson and Sheffield, 1998; Janet, 1905; Neppe, 1981, 1983; Osborne, 1991; Saint-Alban, 1978; Sno, 1993; Thibault, 1899) and, currently, the term déjà vu probably does have a higher frequency of usage—or is more "popular"—than the term redintegration. For instance, more specifically, I recently (May 2002) conducted keyword searches for the two terms and found corroborating evidence concerning the relative "popularity" of the two terms via the following databases: WorldCat (redintegration = 13 studies and déjà vu = 663 studies); ArticleFirst (redintegration = 8 studies and déjà vu = 372 studies); ECO (redintegration = 7 studies and déjà vu = 27 studies); and CDL/MELVYL (redintegration = 0 studies and déjà vu = 5 studies).

Finally, inasmuch as the concepts of redintegration and déjà vu appear only to be tangentially related to the topic area of imagery/mental imagery, and seem only to be vaguely connected to imagery in the formal definitions (cf. English and English, 1958, p. 446), I do not attempt to provide further detailed discussion of these phenomena now or in later sections/chapters of this book.

## SENSORY IMAGERY

In his discussion of *memory-images*, Woodworth (1938, p. 39) states that

> Many individuals possess the power of calling up "before their mind's eye" pictures of scenes, objects or faces which they have seen; they are said to have strong powers of visual imagery. Some, again, have the power of vividly reproducing sounds "before their mind's ear" and are said to be strong in auditory imagery; and similar powers exist in smell, touch, and perhaps other senses. A memory image is typically a lifelike or vivid reproduction of sensory experience.

Thus, according to Woodworth (1938) and others (cf. Lindauer, 1972, pp. 131–47), while images are commonly referred to as "pictures in the mind's eye," and invoke visual imagery, they could just as well refer to auditory, gustatory, olfactory, and tactile mental representations of the various sensory systems.

Woodworth (1938, pp. 39–40) notes also that there are great individual differences in imagery (cf. Fechner, 1860; Galton, 1879–1880, 1883; Griffitts, 1927). Some persons are strong in visual imagery, others are strong in auditory or in motor imagery. Thus there has developed in psychology a "theory of imagery types" (e.g., the "visualist," the "audile," the "motile," etc.; cf. Raju, 1946). Moreover, Woodworth indicates that in addition to the "pure types" of imagers, there is a "mixed type" to accommodate individuals who report imagery of several senses without any marked preponderance of any one modality. Compare Drever (1952/1973, p. 129) who defines *composite image* as "an image based on a number of *sensory* experiences of the same or similar objects." Further discussions of individual differences in imagery, and measurement of imagery, are given in chapter 4, "Methodological Aspects of Imagery."

In defining images and imagery, in general (it is interesting to observe that *none* of the dictionaries surveyed here explicitly or directly define *sensory imagery* per se) various dictionaries of psychology simply indicate the *sensory aspect* of the mental representations called images. For example, Warren (1934, p. 131) refers to them as "elements of experience which possess all the attributes of *sensation*" and "experiences that reproduce with some degree of sensory realism a previous perceptual experience in the absence of the original *sensory* stimulation" (italics added). English and English (1958, p. 252) define both memory image and mental image with reference to sensory attributes: "a more or less complete representation of the attributes of an object or event once experienced but not now present to the *senses* . . . the image may be *sensory* or verbal or both" and "an image that is said to have the direct *sensory* quality of the original object is 'concrete.' Concrete images are usually further distinguished according to their *sensory* quality as visual, auditory, olfactory, gustatory, tactual, or kinesthetic. They may also be called 'composite' when they combine more than one *sensory* modality" (italics added). Reber (1995, p. 358), at one point, invokes the school of Structuralism (in the history of psychology), which treated the image as "a mental representation of an earlier *sensory* experience, a copy of it. The copy was considered to be less vivid than the *sensory* experience but still consciously recognizable as a memory of it." He also notes, "[T]he picture (in the head) is not necessarily restricted to *visual* representation . . . one can elaborate an *auditory* image . . . a *tactile* image . . . some people claim to even have *gustatory* and *olfactory* images" (italics added). Thus, based on such definitions of imagery and the image that invoke sensory aspects, the notions of sensory systems, sensory imagery, sensations, and sensory modality seem to contribute to the very essence of the phenomenon of imagery itself. However, as Lindauer (1972) observes, sensory imagery per se has been neglected in much of contemporary research—including the study of learning. He argues that sensory imagery as a phenomenological attribute of imagery has been insufficiently explored and little understood (cf. Lindauer, 1969). Accordingly, Lindauer (1972) discusses the sensory aspects of imagery in a general context (including its role in aesthetics and language), provides a review of imagery research involving the sensory dimension, examines the study of individual differences in types of imagery and their relationship to performance variables, gives an account of imagery's role in the learning process, and summarizes some recent (up to 1972) unpublished research on the sensory aspects of imagery.

## SYNESTHESIA

The phenomenon of *synesthesia* (from the Greek *syn* meaning "union" or "together" and *aisthesis* meaning "sensation" or "feeling") is closely related to that of sensory imagery (cf. McKellar, 1957, 1972) in which a stimulus elicits an image in a sensory mode *other than* the one in which the initiating stimulus is presented (e.g., the olfactory stimulus of manure evokes a visual memory image of a farm, or the auditory stimulus of a musical note elicits the visual image of a color). McKellar (1972, pp. 46–47) notes that Sir Francis Galton (1822–1911) traditionally has been linked to the discovery of synesthesia (or synaesthesia)—even though Galton himself refers to other earlier studies on the issue. For example, Galton (1883) describes the association of visual imagery for color with sound (*chromaesthesia*) in a case study that was published earlier in 1873.

In cataloging the various types of synesthesia, Simpson and McKellar (1955) suggest the use of two hyphenated words when describing the many possibilities of synesthesia. Thus, the label "visual-auditory synesthesia" refers to visual imagery of color and shape that accompanies auditory perception; the most common variety of synesthesia is called chromesthesia, *synopsia*, or *chromatic-lexical synesthesia*; that is, words may elicit colors (cf. Domino, 1999; Karwoski and Odbert, 1938; McKellar, 1968). According to this naming convention, the *first* of the two words is taken to specify the imagery, and the *second* word specifies the sensation; thus, in a rare form of synesthesia—called *auditory-visual synesthesia*—auditory imagery accompanies a visual sensation (cf. the more frequently occurring type, *visual-auditory synesthesia*, where the reverse is the case—visual imagery accompanies an auditory sensation). McKellar (1972; cf. p. 48, Figure 1) refers, also, to *visual-algesic synesthesia* (pains that differ in color, or color imagery for pains), *visual-gustatory synesthesia* (color imagery for tastes), *gustatory-visual synesthesia* (taste imagery for colors), and *gustatory-auditory synesthesia* (taste imagery for sounds).

A sample of various dictionaries of psychological terms indicates the following definitions of synesthesia:

"A phenomenon characterizing the experiences of certain individuals, in which certain sensations belonging to one sense or mode attach to certain sensations of another group and appear regularly whenever a stimulus of the latter type occurs; there are various types, of which *colored hearing* (*synopsia*) is the most common; e.g., the vocal sound *o* may appear red" (Warren, 1934, p. 270).

"A condition, found in some individuals, in which perception of a certain type of object is regularly linked with particular *images* from another sensory mode. Thus, in colored hearing (*chromesthesia*) certain sounds regularly evoke imagery of certain colors, often spread out in space in a precise way. *Number form* is imagery of numbers in definite geometrical positions according to their serial order" (English and English, 1958, p. 540).

"Synesthesia (secondary sensation; cf. Stoddart, 1926) . . . are those sensations which accompany sensations of another modality; for example, some people experience with every auditory sensation an accompanying visual sensation: the tone G is perhaps associated with the color red or the tone D with blue. Similar sensations of color may accompany perceptions of taste, touch, pain, heat or cold: they are called 'photisms.' With some people certain words are accompanied by a sense of color, varying with different words (verbochromia). Again, there are secondary auditory sensations called 'phonisms,' secondary taste sensations called 'gustatisms,' secondary smell sensations called 'olfactisms,' and so on" (Hinsie and Campbell, 1970, p. 694).

"The condition in which a sensory experience normally associated with one modality occurs when another modality is stimulated. To a certain extent such cross-modality experiences are perfectly normal; e.g., low-pitched tones give a sensation of softness or fullness while high-pitched tones feel brittle and sharp, the color blue feels cold while red feels warm. However, the term is usually restricted to the unusual cases in which regular and vivid cross-modality experiences occur, such as when particular sounds reliably produce particular color sensations (e.g., *chromesthesia*)" (Reber, 1995).

The *early* literature in psychology (from about 1890 through 1959) on synesthesia is fairly extensive (cf. the *current* work of Cytowic [1989/2002, 1993/1998, 1995]). For example, for *early* reviews, critiques, descriptions, and bibliographies in this area, see Anschutz (1929), Bachem (1949), Banerji (1930), Beltran (1931), Feigenberg (1958), Karwoski and Odbert (1938), Kleint (1940), Krohn (1893), Langfeld (1915, 1919, 1926, 1929), Mayer-Gross (1927), Naito (1936, 1938), Nikiforovski (1937), Oldham (1940), Pierce (1913), Riggs and Karwoski (1934), Ryan (1940), Schliebe (1932), Schiller (1935), Schneider (1932), Seashore (1938), Simpson and McKellar (1955), Simpson, Quinn, and Ausubel (1956), Suarez de Mendoza (1890), Uhlich (1957), Wehofer (1913), Wellek (1930, 1931a,b), Werner (1930, 1934), Wheeler (1920), and Zietz (1935).

For *early* psychological research studies within various subtopics of synesthesia, see the following:

- *Anthropological study* (Peabody, 1918)
- *Blindness* (Anschutz, 1925; Voss, 1929; Wheeler, 1920; Wheeler and Cutsforth, 1922b)
- *Body imagery* (Ananjev and Tornova, 1941; Schilder, 1935)

- *Case studies* (Alford, 1918; Anschutz, 1926; Collins, 1929; Coriat, 1913; Daub, 1937; Dudycha and Dudycha, 1935; Ginsberg, 1923; Lay, 1896; Myers, 1911; Raines, 1909–1910; Whipple, 1900)
- *Colored hearing* (Argelander, 1927; Binet, 1892; Bos, 1931; Calkins, 1895; Claviere, 1899; Daubresse, 1900; Dauffenbach, 1924–1925; English, 1923; Hasebroek, 1935; Hein, 1926; Howells, 1937, 1944; Jachesky and Foradori, 1933, 1935; Karwoski and Odbert, 1938; Kelly, 1934; Kerr and Pear, 1931, 1932; Langfeld, 1914; Lemaitre, 1901; Mahlung, 1926; Ortmann, 1933; Padovani, 1935; Revesz, 1923; Vernon, 1930; Wellek, 1935; Zietz, 1931; Zigler, 1930)
- *Colored letters/alphabet* (Hollingworth and Weischer, 1939; Tordon, 1917)
- *Cultural, social psychological aspects* (Osgood, 1960; Raines, 1909–1910)
- *Emotional, mood, drug aspects* (Cutsforth, 1925; Delay, Gerard, and Racamier, 1951; Gutman, 1936; Odbert, Karwoski, and Eckerson, 1942; Ross, 1938)
- *Gustation* (Downey, 1911; Myers, 1911; Pierce, 1907)
- *Kinaesthesis* (Mainwaring, 1933)
- *Meaning* (Karwoski and Odbert, 1938; Wheeler and Cutsforth, 1922a)
- *Pain* (Coriat, 1913)
- *Pressure, cold* (Dallenbach, 1926)
- *Theoretical aspects* (Deutsch, 1954; Lenzberg, 1923)
- *Thinking, reasoning* (Cutsforth, 1924; Karwoski, Odbert, and Osgood, 1942; Wheeler and Cutsforth, 1925, 1928)

Much of the current research on synesthesia focuses attention on the functioning of the brain's limbic ("emotional") region that is considered to be the coordination center for all of one's senses—which is a contradiction of traditional brain theory. Neurologist R. E. Cytowic (1989/2002, 1995) asserts that the limbic system also is the control center for information-processing activities. Other research suggests that a sex/gender difference—along with a handedness difference—is present in *synesthetes* (i.e., those who experience synesthesia) where a majority of them statistically are left-handed women who possess unusual crossovers in their neural pathways (cf. Motluk, 1994). Moreover, synesthetic experiences seem to be both vivid and involuntary (cf. Pound, 2001). Scientists now estimate that about one in 2,000 people are synesthetic, and that there are nearly as many types of synesthesia as there are permutations of the senses. Current research has also shown that the responses of synesthetes tend to be very precise and reliable when they are asked to link letters and words to their corresponding hues. The results of brain imaging studies shows that such consistency has a physical basis: words activate the vision- and color-processing centers—as well as the language centers—of the synesthete's brain. The question that remains unanswered, however, is how closely the synesthetic response is connected to consciousness (cf. Kher, 2001).

Finally, the following references concerning synesthesia are taken from selected early and current nonpsychological sources: Ackerman (1990/1995), Fleischer (1929), Goode (1999), Gregersen (1998), Guterman (2001), Harrison and Baron-Cohen (1995), Kingman (1928), Marinesco (1931), Marinesco and Sava (1929), Masson (1952), Mattingley, Rich, Yelland, and Bradshaw (2001), Nelson and Hitchon (1995), Reichard, Jakobson, and Werth (1949), Shore (1991), and Silz (1942).

## THOUGHT IMAGERY

The term *thought imagery* is a rather "loaded" concept in light of its historical meaning and context. That is, the notion of thought imagery is an aspect of the "imageless thought" controversy in the history of psychology that peaked in popularity at the turn of the twentieth century between the Structuralist school (e.g., proponents were Wilhelm Wundt and E. B. Titchener) on the one hand and the Wurzburg school (e.g., proponents were Oswald Kulpe, M. M. Meyer, J. Orth, H. J. Watt, and N. Ach) on the other hand (cf. Woodworth, 1906). Briefly, in this controversy concerning the nature of thought and thinking, Wundt (1896) and the Structuralists postulated that consciousness was made up of only three elements: sensations, feelings, and images where images were considered to be the necessary "vehicles of thought." Contrary to this position Kulpe (1893) and the Wurzburg psychologists (i.e., those individuals in the "imageless thought" camp) argued that there was no experimental evidence that imagery is present or essential in various tasks where thinking or judgment is required. Further discussion of this important historical issue concerning imagery in psychology is provided in a section of chapter 2, "The Image and the Imagery Debate in Philosophy and Early Psychology."

Warren (1934)—while *not* explicitly defining the term thought imagery—does define *imageless thought* as "an idea, thought, or train of thinking which is wholly lacking in sensory contents," and *thought* as "a type of ideational experience which is symbolic; subvocal movements; a succession or train of symbolic processes; cognitive experience in general, as distinguished from 'feeling' and 'action'; a single one of several ideas in a course of thinking." Other dictionaries of psychological terms, likewise, do *not* explicitly define thought imagery, but do have entries for imageless thought and thought. For example, English and English (1958, p. 252) define imageless thought as "an idea or thought which, upon careful introspective analysis, reveals no sensations or images. . . . Apparently imageless thinking (e.g., the awareness of relationship) is explained by some as consisting of fleeting kinesthetic and vocomotor sensations and images. . . . Responding to the properties of an object other than those directly revealed by sensory process. This is better called 'non-sensory thinking.' In this meaning, the fact that sensory process may influence the thinking is not denied but the response nonetheless is primarily to nonsensory properties, such as relations," and thought is defined as "a single complex idea that results from thinking; a covert activity involving symbols; the operations of using symbols." (English and English [1958] provide a very extensive set of definitions for the term *symbol*, among which is "a mental process that represents external reality; an *image* or an *idea*; anything that is apprehended as standing for something else [synonym is *sign*].") Hinsie and Campbell (1970) define imageless thought as "a thought completely devoid of optic pictures or representations," and Reber (1995, p. 359) states that imageless thought refers to "a theoretical and empirical debate between the Wurzburg school ('act psychology') and orthodox Structuralism over whether or not all thought processes were based upon images. Although the issue was never fully resolved, the fact that under the same stimulus conditions the Wurzburgers found no evidence for images and the Structuralists found traces of sensory images did not augur well for the method of introspection."

In his celebrated textbook on experimental psychology, Osgood (1953, pp. 640–42) discusses the "role of imagery in thought" in a chapter on "thinking" (cf. Barratt, 1953; Fox, 1914). Osgood notes that the Greek philosophers used the two terms images and ideas interchangeably (e.g., Plato argued that because an image looks just like the original object—but is smaller as it resides within the head—it must be a tiny replica of the original that enters the head through the eyes). Osgood also identifies an issue here: If an image actually is a pattern of activity in nerve fibers, then how can it (the image) look "just like" an object? As a way out of this dilemma, Osgood suggests that images are seldom exact duplicates of original impressions—what appears to be a precisely recalled image proves, upon careful scrutiny, to be lacking in detail. Osgood equates the problem of an image of an object (via a pattern of activity in nerve fibers) to that of a *percep-*

*tion* of an object (also via a pattern of activity in nerve fibers); he identifies the dimension of *intensity* as the major variable along which both perceptions and various types of images may range. (See Holt's [1972, p. 10] suggested usage for the term image where his definition of image does not make the usual distinction between *percept* and mental image. Holt argues that the image that is usually called a percept is as much a construct of the nervous system as is a memory image or hallucination.) According to Osgood (1953), under certain conditions (e.g., taking drugs such as mescal and alcohol), images may become so intense as to rival perceptions; however, Osgood argues, little is known in regard to how toxic conditions and certain drugs can intensify the neural processes that subserve imagery. Other areas that Osgood touches on in his coverage of "imagery and thought" are eidetic imagery, individual differences in imagery, imagery types, synesthetic thinking, the imageless thought controversy, and a critique of the introspective technique. Areas covered by Osgood (1953) regarding *thinking*, in general, include motor activity during thought in humans and animals, concept formation, and abstracting ability. Compare Humphrey's (1951) treatment of thinking in experimental psychology; Woodworth and Schlosberg's (1965, pp. 814–48) treatment of thinking and problem solving in experimental psychology; and McKellar's (1972, pp. 56–58) distinction between "A-Thinking" (autistic thinking) and "R-Thinking" (realistic thinking) vis-à-vis imagery.

Holt (1972, p. 13) uses the term image to refer to a "subjective phenomenon that may have any combination of external and internal influences. When the weight is clearly on the side of sensory input, the common terms *percept* or *perceptual image* will serve interchangeably; and when the weight is on the side of inner, central inputs, I shall speak of *mental images* or of their commonly recognized subtypes like hypnagogic images, drug images, etc." Within his chapter on "the nature and generality of mental imagery," Holt (1972, pp. 16, 18–20, 24, 25, 29, 30) makes repeated reference to the term thought imagery, especially in his discussion of the "interrelatedness of various types of imagery" (see, especially, Tables 2, 3, 5). Presumably, the notion of thought imagery is implicit and operationally defined in Holt's discourse via some empirical data on the interrelationship between certain types of imagery (e.g., hypnagogic-, hypnopompic-, LSD-, isolation-, eidetic-, afterimage-, and dream-imagery). In his section on thought imagery (p. 16), Holt describes his pretest/posttest technique of interviewing participants who were given the drug LSD;

he attempted to measure the "vividness" and "controllability" of thought imagery in a procedure that was similar to Gordon's (1949) technique. Subsequently, judges independently scored the verbal protocols (thought imagery) of the LSD participants on the dimensions of movement, color, sound, and other sensory qualities.

In a section on thought imagery, A. Richardson (1983, p. 27) defines thought imagery, initially, via a negative example: "it is not the type of imagery that can be experienced after fixating a black square or scanning a high contrast picture for 30 seconds." In an earlier publication, A. Richardson (1969, pp. 2–3) defined mental imagery as containing four characteristics, but in a later publication (A. Richardson, 1983, p. 15), he questions the adequacy of the fourth characteristic (i.e., "quasi-perceptual or sensory experiences having different consequences from their sensory or perceptual counterparts") because of the recent increasing evidence that "self-initiated *thought imagery* of a concrete sensory-like kind (i.e., *not* verbal imagery embodied in inner speech) can have results that appear to be indistinguishable from their genuine sensory counterparts." In a more affirmative approach to thought imagery, A. Richardson (1969) distinguishes among four classes or types of imagery: afterimagery, eidetic imagery, imagination imagery, and memory imagery (now called thought imagery). Thus, according to A. Richardson (1969, 1983), the term thought imagery may be equated by some with the notion of memory imagery (cf. J.T.E. Richardson, 1980). The self-appointed task for A. Richardson is to distinguish the various types of imagery— eidetic-, after-, and imagination-imagery—from thought imagery. Essentially, A. Richardson (1969, p. 43; 1983, p. 27) defines thought imagery as "the common and relatively familiar imagery of everyday life. It may accompany the recall of events from the past, the ongoing thought processes of the present or the anticipatory actions and events of the future. Though it may occur as a spontaneous accompaniment to much everyday thought of this kind it is far more amenable to voluntary control than other forms of imagery." However, A. Richardson (1983, p. 27) adds, "Because this description embraces more than images of remembered events, the term 'thought imagery' (Holt, 1972) is now considered a more apt name than 'memory imagery.' . . . Thought images are more often like hazy etchings, often incomplete and easily dissolved if attention is fixed on them for very long." A. Richardson (1983) includes discussions of the topics of "spontaneous thought imagery" and "voluntary thought imagery" in his coverage of thought imagery. See Bugelski (1983, pp. 72–95) who covers the following issues in his discussion of "Imagery and the Thought Processes": imagery and thought; imagery, language, and cognition; thinking as a routine bodily process; the definition of thinking; the thinking process; the nature of imagery; characteristics of imagery; the subjective quality of imagery; the role of language in thinking; the problem of concepts; abstractions; creative thinking; imagery and action: ideomotor action; and imagery and emotion. In one place, Bugelski (1983, p. 92) pays homage to O. H. Mowrer (1960) for making a theoretical and empirical connection between imagery and thought: "To Mowrer's credit, he did not hesitate to introduce imagery to account for denotative meaning, and, as an extension of meaning, to account for the operation of 'symbolic processes' or thinking."

Denis (1991) maintains that one of the "thorniest" issues in the field of imagery is giving a cogent account of its relationship to thinking and thought (cf. Denis, 1989; Denis, Engelkamp, and Richardson, 1988; Kaufmann, 1980, 1984; Kosslyn, 1983; Paivio, 1986; J.T.E. Richardson, 1983). At the heart of the issue, according to Denis (1991), is that the concepts of imagery and thinking both have been defined in a number of diverse ways. For purposes of his discussion, Denis (1991, p. 103) offers the following definition of thinking (cf. Mandler and Mandler, 1964; Newell and Simon, 1972): "that set of mental activities involved in the manipulation of representations with, as outputs, the construction of new pieces of information which can enter into an individual's knowledge base" and asserts that the concept of imagery "covers a set of representational processes dedicated to the evocation of structural, modality-specific properties of objects. The notion of 'mental analogs' reflects the idea that the mental representations constructed through imagery attain a high degree of structural isomorphism with the objects they stand for." Based upon these definitions and assumptions, Denis focuses his attention on the subset of problems called "visual thinking tasks" by way of examining the relationships between imagery and thinking. Denis (1991) notes that there are various ways in which researchers historically have conceptualized the relationships between imagery and thinking; for example, in terms of *equivalence*—where imagery is considered to be the essence of thinking (or, alternatively, thinking is generation and manipulation of images)—or in terms of *nonequivalence*—where imagery is viewed as totally unrelated to thinking (i.e., thinking involves the manipulation of *abstract* representational entities that have *no* counterpart in the *concrete* representations provided by mental imagery). Denis's own perspective is that imagery involves a set of processes that have their *own* properties and that can be energized at various levels of cognitive activity. In this way, according to Denis (1991), imagery is not the *core* of thought processes, but rather a potential *medium* for them; thinking employs representations—some of which are produced by imagery processes and some by more abstract representational systems. Thus, images may be considered to be "models for thinking." Within this framework of defining the concepts of imagery and thought, and their relationships, Denis (1991) discusses the following topics concerning thought imagery: imagery and theories of thinking; the properties of images (e.g., they are economical; they have structural similarity to perceptual representations; they enable online inspection of current hypotheses via their ability to be manipulated in a way that realistically simulates transformations on physical objects); conditions for efficient use of imagery in thinking (cf. Duncker, 1945; Luchins, 1942); and current issues in the area of imagery and thinking, for example, analog representations in reasoning and comparative judgments (cf. Johnson-Laird, 1983; Kahneman and Tversky, 1973); imagery and the processing of spatial descriptions (cf. Huttenlocher, 1968; Mani and Johnson-Laird, 1982); and coherence and validity of images used in visual thinking.

## REFERENCES

*Academic American Encyclopedia.* (1998). Danbury, CT: Grolier.

Ackerman, D. (1990/1995). *A natural history of the senses.* New York: Random House.

Adachi, N., Koutroumanidis, M., Elwes, R., Polkey, C., Binnie, C., Reynolds, E., Barrington, S., Maisey, M., & Panayiotopoulos, C. (1999). Interictal 18-FDG PET findings in temporal lobe epilepsy with *déjà vu. Journal of Neuropsychiatry and Clinical Neurosciences, 11,* 380–86.

Ahsen, A. (1977). Eidetics: An overview. *Journal of Mental Imagery, 1,* 5–38.

Ahsen, A. (1979). Eidetics: Redefinition of the ghost and its clinical application. *Behavioral and Brain Sciences, 2,* 594–96.

Aleman, A., VanLee, L., Mantione, M., VerKoijen, I., & DeHaan, E. (2001). Visual imagery without visual experience: Evidence from congenitally totally blind people. *Neuroreport, 12,* 2601–4.

Alford, L. B. (1918). A report of two cases of synaesthesia. *Journal of Abnormal Psychology, 13,* 1–16.

Allin, A. (1896). The "recognition theory" of perception. *American Journal of Psychology, 7,* 237–48.

Allport, G. (1924). Eidetic imagery. *British Journal of Psychology, 15*, 99–120.

Allport, G. (1928). The eidetic image and the after-image. *American Journal of Psychology, 40*, 418–25.

Alvis, G. (1987). Individual differences in experience of déjà vu, attention, and nervous system strength. Unpublished Master's thesis, Memphis State University.

Ananjev, B., & Tornova, A. (1941). Synesthesia and the body scheme. *Sovetskaia Psikhiatriia, 6*, 555–62.

Anderson, J. R. (1978). Arguments concerning representations for mental imagery. *Psychological Review, 85*, 249–77.

Anderson, V. A. (1939). Auditory memory span as tested by speech sounds. *American Journal of Psychology, 52*, 95–99.

Ando, T. (1965). *Aristotle's theory of practical cognition.* The Hague: M. Nijhoff.

Andrews, G. (1900). Studies of the dream consciousness. *American Journal of Psychology, 12*, 131–35.

Angell, F. (1900). Discrimination of clangs for different intervals of time. *American Journal of Psychology, 12*, 58–79.

Angell, J. R. (1897). Thought and imagery. *Philosophical Review, 6*, 646–51.

Angell, J. R. (1913). Behavior as a category of psychology. *Psychological Review, 20*, 255–70.

Angell, J. R., & Thompson, H. (1899). The relations between certain organic processes and consciousness. *Psychological Review, 6*, 32–69.

Anschutz, G. (1925). Untersuchungen zur analyze musikalischer photismen. *Archiv fur die Gesamte Psychologie, 51*, 155–218.

Anschutz, G. (1926). Untersuchungen uber komplexe musikalische synopsie. *Archiv fur die Gesamte Psychologie, 54*, 129–273.

Anschutz, G. (1929). *The color-tone problem in the general psychical field. Special phenomena of complex optical synesthesia "sight pictures."* Halle, East Germany: Marhold.

Ardis, J., & McKellar, P. (1956). Hypnagogic imagery and mescaline. *Journal of Mental Science, 102*, 22–29.

Argelander, A. (1927). *Das farbenhoren und der synasthetische factor der wahrnehmung.* Jena, East Germany: Fischer.

Armstrong, A. (1898). Consciousness and the unconscious. *Psychological Review, 5*, 650–52.

Armstrong, W. (1894). Imagery of American students. *Psychological Review, 1*, 495–505.

Arnold, F. (1905). Consciousness and its object. *Psychological Review, 12*, 220–49.

Atwood, G. (1971). An experimental study of visual imagination and imagery. *Cognitive Psychology, 2*, 290–99.

Audi, R. (1978). The ontological status of mental images. *Inquiry, 21,* 348–61.

Azam, E. (1887). *Hypnotisme, double conscience et alteration de la personnalite.* Paris: Bailliere.

Baars, B. (1996). When are images conscious? The curious disconnection between imagery and consciousness in the scientific literature. *Consciousness and Cognition, 5,* 261–64.

Baars, B. (1997). *In the theater of consciousness.* New York: Oxford University Press.

Bachem, A. (1949). A new auditory-visual synesthesia. *Acta Psychologica, 6,* 363–64.

Bain, A. (1855). *Senses and intellect.* London: Longmans, Green.

Bain, A. (1880). Statistics of mental imagery. *Mind, 5,* 564–73.

Bain, A. (1894). Definition and problem of consciousness. *Mind, 3,* 348–61.

Baldwin, A. L. (1939). The visual perception of filled and unfilled space by the after-image method. *American Journal of Psychology, 52,* 376–79.

Baldwin, J. M. (1895). Consciousness and evolution. *Science, 2,* 219–22.

Baldwin, J. M. (Ed.) (1901–1905). *Dictionary of philosophy and psychology.* New York: Macmillan. (Also, Gloucester, MA: Peter Smith, 1960.)

Bancaud, J., Brunet-Bourgin, F., Chauvel, P., & Halgren, E. (1994). Anatomical origin of déjà vu and vivid "memories" in human temporal lobe epilepsy. *Brain: A Journal of Neurology, 117,* 71–90.

Banerji, M. (1930). Synaesthesia. *Indian Journal of Psychology, 5,* 147–59.

Barber, T. X. (1969). *Hypnosis: A scientific approach.* New York: Van Nostrand Reinhold.

Barber, T. X., & Calverley, D. (1964). An experimental study of "hypnotic" (auditory and visual) hallucinations. *Journal of Abnormal and Social Psychology, 68,* 13–30.

Barber, T. X., & Hahn, K. (1962). Physiological and subjective responses to pain-producing stimulation under hypnotically suggested and waking-imagined "analgesia." *Journal of Abnormal and Social Psychology, 65,* 222–28.

Barnes, J., & David, A. S. (2001). Visual hallucinations in Parkinson's disease: A review and phenomenological survey. *Journal of Neurology, Neurosurgery, and Psychiatry, 70,* 727–33.

Barnett, B. (1965). Witchcraft, psychopathology, and hallucinations. *British Journal of Psychology, 111,* 474.

Barratt, P. E. (1953). Imagery and thinking. *Australian Journal of Psychology, 5,* 154–64.

Barron, F. (1958). The psychology of imagination. *Scientific American, 199,* 150–66.

Barry, H., MacKinnon, D., & Murray, H. (1931). Studies in personality:

Hypnotizability as a personality trait and its typological relations. *Human Biology, 3,* 1–36.

Bascom, J. (1869). What is consciousness? *American Presbyterian Review, 18,* 478–91.

Bascom, J. (1875). Consciousness. *Bibliotheca Sacra, 32,* 676–702.

Bastian, H. (1870). Consciousness. *Journal of Mental Science, 15,* 501–23.

Baudelaire, C. P. (1971). *Artificial paradise: On hashish and wine as a means of expanding individuality.* New York: Herder and Herder.

Baumel, N. (1999a). Color constancy: The role of image surfaces in illuminant adjustment. *Journal of the Optical Society of America, 16,* 1521–30.

Baumel, N. (1999b). Summary of works carried out on "déjà vu." *Information Psychiatrique, 75,* 235–39.

Baylor, G. W. (1972). A treatise on the mind's eye. Unpublished doctoral dissertation, Carnegie-Mellon University, Pittsburgh.

Beare, J. (1906). *Greek theories of elementary cognition: From Alcmaeon to Aristotle.* Oxford, UK: Oxford University Press.

Beck, L. (1936). Hypnotic identification of an amnesia victim. *British Journal of Medical Psychology, 16,* 36–42.

Beltran, J. R. (1931). Synesthesia. *Revista de Criminologia Psiquiatria y Medicina Legal, 18,* 409–23.

Benedict, W. (1885). Consciousness and the nervous system. *Popular Science Monthly, 26,* 731–50; *27,* 66–77, 150–65.

Bentley, I. M. (1899). The memory image and its qualitative fidelity. *American Journal of Psychology, 11,* 1–48.

Berbaum, K., & Chung, C. (1981). Muller-Lyer illusion induced by imagination. *Journal of Mental Imagery, 5,* 125–28.

Bergman, I. (1958/1988). *The magician.* Motion picture/videotape. Beverly Hills, CA: Nelson Entertainment (The International Collection, #6162, NTSC VHS).

Beringer, K. (1927). *Der meskalin rausch.* Berlin: Springer.

Berliner, A. (1918). The influence of mental work on the visual memory image. *American Journal of Psychology, 29,* 355–70.

Bernheim, H. (1888/1963). *Hypnosis and suggestion in psychotherapy.* New Hyde Park, NY: University Books.

Berrios, G., & Hodges, J. (2000). *Memory disorders in psychiatric practice.* New York: Cambridge University Press.

Bickhard, M., & Richie, D. (1983). *On the nature of representation: A case study of James Gibson's theory of perception.* New York: Praeger.

Binet, A. (1889–1890). *On double consciousness.* Chicago: Open Court.

Binet, A. (1890). Double consciousness in health. *Mind, 15,* 46–57.

Binet, A. (1892). Le probleme de l'audition coloree. *Revue des Deux Mondes, 113,* 586.

Binet, A. (1903). La pensee sans images. *Revue Philosophique, 55,* 138–52.

Birnbaum, A. (1962). Human factors research in image systems: Status report. *U.S. Army Personnel Research Office Technical Research Report, 122*, 1–22.

Bishop, H. G. (1921). An experimental investigation of the positive afterimage in audition. *American Journal of Psychology, 32*, 305–25.

Bisiach, E., Luzzatti, C., & Perani, D. (1979). Unilateral neglect, representational schema, and consciousness. *Brain, 102*, 609–18.

Bisland, E. (1896). Dreams and their mysteries. *North American Review, 162*, 716–26.

Blachowicz, J. (1997). Analog representation beyond mental imagery. *Journal of Philosophy, 94*, 55–84.

Bliss, E., & Clark, L. (1962). Visual hallucinations. In L. J. West (Ed.), *Hallucinations*. New York: Grune and Stratton.

Blum, G. (1967). Experimental observations on the contextual nature of hypnosis. *International Journal of Clinical and Experimental Hypnosis, 15*, 160–71.

Bockar, J. (1981). *Primer for the non-medical psychotherapist*. New York: Spectrum.

Bogardus, H. (1899). The evolution of consciousness. *Metaphysics Magazine* (May), 10–14.

Boring, E. G. (1957). *A history of experimental psychology*. New York: Appleton-Century-Crofts.

Boring, E. G., Langfeld, H., & Weld, H. (1939). *Introduction to psychology*. New York: Wiley.

Bos, M. (1931). Concerning genuine and spurious colored hearing. *Zeitschrift fur Psychologie, 119*, 396–406.

Bower, K. J. (1984). Imagery: From Hume to cognitive science. *Canadian Journal of Philosophy, 14*, 217–34.

Bowers, H. (1931). Memory and mental imagery: An experimental study. *British Journal of Psychology, 21*, 271–82.

Bowers, K. (1967). The effect of demands for honesty upon reports of visual and auditory hallucinations. *International Journal of Clinical and Experimental Hypnosis, 15*, 31–36.

Bowers, K. (1976). *Hypnosis for the seriously curious*. Monterey, CA: Brooks/Cole.

Braddock, C. C. (1924). An experimental study of the visual negative afterimage. *American Journal of Psychology, 35*, 157–66.

Bradley, F. (1893). Consciousness and experience. *Mind, 18*, 211–16.

Bradley, F. (1894). On the failure of movement in dreams. *Mind, 14*, 373–77.

Bragdon, A., & Gamon, D. (2000). *Brains that work a little bit differently: Recent discoveries about common mental diversities*. South Yarmouth, MA: Brainwaves Books.

Brainard, R., & Ornstein, G. (1965). Image quality enhancement. *USAF Aerospace Medical Research Laboratories Technical Report, 65–28*, 1–56.

Brainerd, C. J. (1979). *Déjà vu*. London, Ontario: Psychology Department, University of Western Ontario.

Brainerd, C. J. (1990). *The development of forgetting and reminiscence*. Chicago: University of Chicago Press.

Brandimonte, M., & Gerbino, W. (1993). Mental image reversal and verbal recoding: When ducks become rabbits. *Memory and Cognition, 21*, 23–33.

Brann, E. (1991). *The world of the imagination: Sum and substance*. Savage, MD: Rowman & Littlefield.

Brenman, M., & Gill, M. (1947). *Hypnotherapy: A survey of the literature*. New York: International Universities Press.

Bresowsky, M. (1926). Uber psychogene halluzinationen. *Monatsschrift fur Psychiatrie und Neurologie, 62*, 31–50.

Breuer, J., & Freud, S. (1895). Studies in hysteria. In *Standard Edition*, Vol. 2. London: Hogarth Press.

Brierre de Boismont, A. (1853). *Hallucinations*. Philadelphia: Lindsay & Blakiston.

Brockbank, T. W. (1919). Redintegration in the albino rat. Doctoral dissertation, Catholic University of America. (Also, published in 1919 by Henry Holt, Cambridge, MA.)

Bronowski, J. (1978). *The origins of knowledge and imagination*. New Haven, CT: Yale University Press.

Brown, A. S. (2003). A review of the déjà vu experience. *Psychological Bulletin, 129*, 394–413.

Brown, G.D.A., & Hulme, C. (1995). Modeling item length effects in memory span: No rehearsal needed? *Journal of Memory and Language, 34*, 594–621.

Brown, J. L. (1965). Afterimages. In C. Graham (Ed.), *Vision and visual perception*. New York: Wiley.

Brown, J. R. (1991). *The laboratory of the mind: Thought experiments in the natural sciences*. London: Routledge.

Brown, W. (1935). Growth of "memory images." *American Journal of Psychology, 47*, 90–102.

Bruner, J. (1986). *Actual minds, possible worlds*. Cambridge, MA: Harvard University Press.

Bugelski, B. R. (1971). The definition of the image. In S. J. Segal (Ed.), *Imagery: Current cognitive approaches*. New York: Academic Press.

Bugelski, B. R. (1983). Imagery and the thought processes. In A. A. Sheikh (Ed.), *Imagery: Current theory, research, and application*. New York: Wiley.

Bugelski, B. R. (1984). Imagery. In R. J. Corsini (Ed.), *Encyclopedia of psychology*. Vol. 2. New York: Wiley.

Bugelski, B. R. (1996). Imagery. In R. J. Corsini & A. J. Auerbach (Eds.), *Concise encyclopedia of psychology.* New York: Wiley.

Bugelski, B. R. (2001). Imagery. In W. E. Craighead & C. B. Nemeroff (Eds.), *The Corsini encyclopedia of psychology and behavioral science.* Vol. 2. New York: Wiley.

Burnett, C. T. (1925). Splitting the mind. *Psychological Monographs, 34,* No. 2.

Burnham, W. (1885). Individual differences in imagination in children. *Pedagogical Seminary, 2,* 204.

Burt, C. (1964). Consciousness and behaviorism: A reply. *British Journal of Psychology, 55,* 93–96.

Burtt, H. E. (1916). Factors which influence the arousal of the primary visual memory image. *American Journal of Psychology, 27,* 87–118.

Calkins, M. (1893). Statistics of dreams. *American Journal of Psychology, 5,* 311–43.

Calkins, M. (1895). Pseudochromesthesia. *American Journal of Psychology, 7,* 90.

Cameron, A. (1897). The imagery of one early made blind. *Psychological Review, 4,* 391–92.

Campbell, C. M. (1930). Hallucinations: Their nature and significance. *American Journal of Psychiatry, 9,* 607–23.

Candlish, S. (1975). Mental images and pictorial properties. *Mind, 84,* 260–62.

Candlish, S. (2001). Mental imagery. In S. Schroeder (Ed.), *Wittgenstein and contemporary philosophy of mind.* London: Palgrave.

Carr, T. (1979). Consciousness in models of human information processing. In G. Underwood & R. Stevens (Eds.), *Aspects of consciousness, Vol. 1, Psychological issues.* London: Academic Press.

Carro, P. (1988). *Déjà vu.* New York: Silhouette Books.

Carus, P. (1894). The seat of consciousness. *Journal of Comparative Neurology, 4,* 176–92.

Carus, P. (1895). The physiological conditions of consciousness. *Journal of Comparative Neurology, 5,* 129–38.

Casey, E. (1976). *Imagining: A phenomenological study.* Bloomington: Indiana University Press.

Cass, W. A. (1942). An experimental investigation of the dissociation hypothesis, utilizing a post-hypnotic technique. Unpublished Master's thesis, University of Oregon.

Castaneda, C. (1970). *The teachings of Don Juan: A Yaqui way of knowledge.* Harmondsworth, UK: Penguin.

Cazenave, M., Hall, A., & Callander, E. (Eds.) (1984). *Science and consciousness: Two views of the universe.* Oxford, UK: Pergamon.

Chalmers, D. (1999). First-person methods in the science of consciousness. *Consciousness Bulletin* (Fall), pp. 8, 10–11.

Chalmers, L. (1900). Studies in imagination. *Pedagogical Seminary, 7*, 111–23.

Chambers, D., & Reisberg, D. (1985). Can mental images be ambiguous? *Journal of Experimental Psychology: Human Perception and Performance, 11*, 317–28.

Chase, R. (1899). The imagination in relation to mental disease. *American Journal of Insanity, 56*, 285–94.

Cheek, D. (1959). Unconscious perception of meaningful sounds during surgical anesthesia as revealed in hypnosis. *American Journal of Clinical Hypnosis, 1*, 101–13.

Cheek, D., & LeCron, L. (1968). *Clinical hypnotherapy.* New York: Grune and Stratton.

Child, C. (1893). Statistics of unconscious cerebration. *American Journal of Psychology, 5*, 242–59.

Churchland, P. (1979). *Scientific realism and the plasticity of mind.* Cambridge, UK: Cambridge University Press.

Churchland, P. (1983). Consciousness: The transmutation of a concept. *Pacific Philosophical Quarterly, 64*, 80–95.

Churchland, P. (1985). Reduction, qualia, and the direct introspection of brain states. *Journal of Philosophy, 82*, 8–28.

Clancey, W. (1997). *Situated cognition: On human knowledge and computer representations.* Cambridge, UK: Cambridge University Press.

Claviere, J. (1899). L'audition coloree. *L'Annee Psychologie, 5*, 161.

Cleland, J. (1883–1884). On the seat of consciousness. *Journal of Mental Science, 29*, 147–57, 498–507.

Clement, C., & Falmange, R. (1986). Logical reasoning, world knowledge, and mental imagery: Interconnections in cognitive processes. *Memory and Cognition, 14*, 299–307.

Clymer, M. (1885). The stuff that dreams are made of. *Forum, 5*, 532–44. (Cf. Ellis, 1899; Robinson, 1893; Wilson, 1884.)

Cocking, J. (1991). *Imagination: A study in the history of ideas.* London: Routledge.

Collins, M. (1929). A case of synaesthesia. *Journal of General Psychology, 2*, 12–27.

Colman, A. M. (2001). *Dictionary of psychology.* New York: Oxford University Press.

Conover, F. (1791). *On sleep and dreams.* Philadelphia: Bowen.

Corbin, H. (1958). *Creative imagination in the Sufism of Ibn 'Arabi.* Princeton, NJ: Princeton University Press.

Coriat, I. (1913). A case of synesthesia. *Journal of Abnormal Psychology, 8*, 38–43, 109–12.

Cornoldi, C., Logie, R., Brandimonte, M., Kaufmann, G., & Reisberg, D. (1996). *Stretching the imagination: Representation and transformation in mental imagery.* New York: Oxford University Press.

Corsini, R. J. (2002). *Dictionary of psychology*. Philadelphia: Brunner/Mazel.

Cotterill, R. (1995). On the unity of conscious experience. *Journal of Consciousness Studies, 2*, 290–312.

Cotterill, R. (1997). On the mechanism of consciousness. *Journal of Consciousness Studies, 4*, 231–47.

Coues, E. (1887). Imagination. *Popular Science Monthly, 11*, 455–61.

Council, J., Chambers, D., Jundt, T., & Good, M. (1991). Are the mental images of fantasy-prone persons really more "real"? *Imagination, Cognition, and Personality, 10*, 319–27.

Crichton-Brown, J. (1895). Dreamy mental states. *Lancet*, No. 3749.

Crismon, O. L. (1984). *Eternity and déjà vu*. Oklahoma City, OK: Kwik-Kopy.

Croce, B. (1902). *Aesthetics*. London: Macmillan.

Crookes, W. (1874). *Researches in the phenomena of spiritualism*. London: Burn and Oates.

Csikszentmihalyi, M. (1990). *Flow: The psychology of optimal experience*. New York: Harper & Row.

Cummins, R. (1989). *Meaning and mental representation*. Cambridge, MA: M.I.T. Press.

Cummins, R. (1996). *Representations, targets, and attitudes*. Cambridge, MA: M.I.T. Press.

Cunningham, J. (1864). On sleep and dreams. *Macmillan's Magazine, 9*, 473–81.

Cutsforth, T. (1924). Synaesthesia in the process of reasoning. *American Journal of Psychology, 35*, 88–97.

Cutsforth, T. (1925). The role of emotion in a synaesthetic subject. *American Journal of Psychology, 36*, 527–43.

Cytowic, R. E. (1989/2002). *Synesthesia: A union of the senses*. New York: Springer-Verlag/Cambridge, MA: M.I.T. Press. (Also see *Science News*, June 14, 1986, *129*, 376; *U.S. News and World Report*, November 13, 1989, *107*, 70–72; *Nature*, January 4, 1990, *343*, 30.)

Cytowic, R. E. (1993/1998). *The man who tasted shapes*. New York: Putnam.

Cytowic, R. E. (1995). *Synesthesia: Phenomenology and neuropsychology*. Washington, DC: R. E. Cytowic (Internet Resource). (Also see *Psyche*, July, 1995, *2*, 10.)

Dallenbach, K. (1926). Synaesthesia: "Pressury" cold. *American Journal of Psychology, 37*, 571–77.

Dana, C. (1894). Amnesia or "double consciousness." *Psychological Review, 1*, 570–80.

Danto, A. (1958). Concerning mental pictures. *Journal of Philosophy, 55*, 12–20.

Daston, L. (1998). Fear and loathing of the imagination in science. *Daedalus, 127*, 73–95.

Daub, F. (1937). A case of "synoptic absolute hearing." *Zeitschrift fur Angewandte Psychologie, 52*, 243–50.

Daubresse, M. (1900). L'audition coloree. *Review of Philosophy, 49*, 300.

Dauffenbach, W. (1924–1925). Musik und farbe. *Die Musik, 17*, 344–49.

Davidson, W. (1881). Definition of consciousness. *Mind, 6*, 406–12.

Davies, E. (1869). Training of the imagination. *Contemporary Review, 12*, 25–37.

Davies, M., & Humphreys, G. (Eds.) (1993). *Consciousness: Psychological and philosophical essays*. London: Blackwell.

Davies, W. (1877). Veracity of consciousness. *Mind, 2*, 64–74.

Dearborn, G. (1898). A study of imaginations. *American Journal of Psychology, 9*, 183–90.

Dearborn, G. (1899). The origin of nightmares. *Science, 9*, 455–56.

Deikman, A. J. (1971). Bimodal consciousness. *Archives of General Psychiatry, 25*, 481–89.

Delabarre, E. (1892). The influence of muscular states on consciousness. *Mind, 17*, 379–96.

Delabarre, E. (1895). *Interpretation of the phenomena of double consciousness*. New York: Neale.

Delay, J., Gerard, H.-P., & Racamier, P.-C. (1951). Synesthesias in mescalin intoxication. *Encephale, 40*, 1–18.

Demangeon, J. (1829). *De l'imagination*. Paris: Fortin, Masson.

Dement, W. (1972). *Some must watch while some must sleep*. Stanford, CA: Stanford Alumni Association.

Dement, W., & Kleitman, N. (1957). The relation of eye movements during sleep to dream activity: An objective method for the study of dreaming. *Journal of Experimental Psychology, 53*, 339–46.

Dement, W., & Wolpert, E. (1958). The relation of eye movements, bodily motility, and external stimuli to dream content. *Journal of Experimental Psychology, 53*, 543–53.

Dendy, H. (1893). Recent developments of the doctrine of the sub-conscious process. *Mind, 18*, 370–71.

Denis, M. (1989). *Image et cognition*. Paris: Presses Universitaires de France.

Denis, M. (1991). Imagery and thinking. In C. Cornoldi and M. A. McDaniel (Eds *Imagery and cognition*. New York: Springer-Verlag.

Denis, M., Engelkamp, J., & Richardson, J.T.E. (Eds.) (1988). *Cognitive and neuropsychological approaches to mental imagery*. Dordrecht, The Netherlands: M. Nijhoff.

Dennett, D. (1969). *Content and consciousness*. London: Routledge & Kegan Paul.

Dennett, D. (1982). How to study human consciousness empirically: Or, nothing comes to mind. *Synthese, 53*, 159–80.

Dennett, D. (1991). *Consciousness explained*. Boston, MA: Little, Brown.

DeRopp, R. (1968). *The master game.* New York: Delacorte Press.

Dessoir, M. (1890). *Das Doppel-Ich.* Leipzig: Gunthers Verlag.

Deutsch, F. (1954). Analytic synesthesiology: Analytic interpretation of intersensory perception. *International Journal of Psycho-Analysis, 35,* 293–302.

DeVries, A. (2001). *Dictionary of symbols and imagery.* London: Elsevier Science.

Dewey, J. (1891). *Psychology.* 3rd ed. New York: American Book Company.

Diamond, M. (1974). The modification of hypnotizability: A review. *Psychological Bulletin, 81,* 180–98.

Diamond, M., & Taft, R. (1975). The role played by ego permissiveness and imagery in hypnotic responsivity. *International Journal of Clinical and Experimental Hypnosis, 23,* 130–38.

Dilman, I. (1967). Imagination. *Proceedings of the Aristotelian Society, Supplementary Volume, 41,* 19–36.

Dimmick, C. C. (1923). The auditory memory after-image. *American Journal of Psychology, 34,* 1–12.

Dix, M. R. (1985). An inquiry into the nature of imagination and its roles in cognition. Unpublished doctoral dissertation, La Trobe University.

Dixon, N. (1971). *Subliminal perception: The nature of a controversy.* London: McGraw-Hill.

Domino, G. (1999). Synesthesia. In M. A. Runco & S. R. Pritzer (Eds.), *Encyclopedia of creativity.* Vol. 2. San Diego, CA: Academic Press.

Downey, J. (1911). A case of colored gustation. *American Journal of Psychology, 22,* 528–39.

Drever, J. (1952/1973). *A dictionary of psychology.* Baltimore, MD: Penguin Books.

Drummond, H. (1900). Cause of dreams. *New Church Review, 7,* 548.

Dudycha, G., & Dudycha, M. (1935). A case of synesthesia: Visual pain and visual audition. *Journal of Abnormal and Social Psychology, 30,* 57–69.

Dugas, L. (1895). Recherches experimentales sur les differents types d'images. *Revue Philosophique, 39,* 285–92.

Dugas, L. (1903). *L'imagination.* Paris: Alcan.

Duncker, K. (1945). On problem solving. *Psychological Monographs, 58,* No. 270.

Dunlap, K. (1926). The theoretical aspect of psychology. In M. Bentley (Ed.), *Psychologies of 1925: Powell lectures in psychological theory,* pp. 309–29. Worcester, MA: Clark University.

DuPasquier, S. (1821). *De l'imagination.* Paris: Corti.

Durr, R. (1970). *Poetic vision and the psychedelic experience.* Syracuse, NY: Syracuse University Press.

Dwinell, I. (1880). The mind back of consciousness. *Bibliotheca Sacra, 37,* 369–89.

Ebbecke, U. (1929). (No article title available). *Archiv fur die gesamte Physiologie, 221,* 160–212.

Edwards, P. (1996). *Reincarnation: A critical examination.* Amherst, NY: Prometheus Books.

Egan, K., & Nadaner, D. (Eds.) (1988). *Imagination and education.* London: Open University Press.

Ellenberger, H. F. (1970). *The discovery of the unconscious.* New York: Basic Books.

Ellis, H. (1895). On dreaming of the dead. *Psychological Review, 2,* 458–61.

Ellis, H. (1899). The stuff that dreams are made of. *Popular Science Monthly, 44,* 721–35. (Cf. Clymer, 1885; Robinson, 1893; Wilson, 1884.)

Ellis, R. (1995). *Questioning consciousness: The interplay of imagery, cognition, and emotion in the human brain.* Amsterdam: J. Benjamins.

Emmert, E. (1881). Grossenverhaltnisse der Nachbilder. *Klinical Monatsblatter der Augenheilkunde, 4,* 443–50.

*Encyclopaedia Britannica.* (1875). 9th ed. Edinburgh: Adam and Charles Black.

*Encyclopaedia Britannica.* (1922). 11th ed. New York: Encyclopaedia Britannica.

*Encyclopedia Americana.* (1998). Danbury, CT: Grolier.

Engell, J. (1981). *The creative imagination: Enlightenment to romanticism.* Cambridge, MA: Harvard University Press.

English, H. B. (1923). Colored hearing. *Science, 57,* 444.

English, H. B., & English, A. C. (1958). *A comprehensive dictionary of psychological and psychoanalytical terms.* New York: David McKay.

Epstein, S. (1998). Cognitive-experiential self-theory. In R. Bornstein & J. Masling (Eds.), *Empirical perspectives on the psychoanalytic unconscious.* Washington, DC: APA.

Epstein, W., Park, J., & Casey, A. (1961). The current status of the size-distance hypothesis. *Psychological Bulletin, 58,* 491–514.

Erickson, M. (1937). Development of apparent unconsciousness during hypnotic reliving of a traumatic experience. *Archives of Neurology and Psychiatry, 38,* 1282–88.

Erikson, E. (1954). The dream specimen of psychoanalysis. *Journal of the American Psychoanalytic Association, 2,* 5–56.

Ermacora, G. (1895). Telepathic dreams experimentally induced. *Proceedings of the Society for Psychical Research, 11,* 235–308.

Eysenck, H. J., Arnold, W., & Meili, R. (Eds.) (1972). *Encyclopedia of psychology.* New York: Herder and Herder.

Farah, M., Hammond, K., Levine, D., & Calvanio, R. (1985). Visual and spatial mental imagery: Dissociable systems of representation. *Cognitive Psychology, 20,* 439–62.

Favreau, O., & Corballis, M. (1976). Negative aftereffects in visual perception. *Scientific American, 235,* 42–48.

Fechner, G. (1860). *Elemente der psychophysik.* Leipzig: Breitkopf, Hartel.

Feigenberg, I. M. (1958). On some peculiar abnormalities of perception. *Voprosy Psychologii, 4,* 38–46.

Fere, C. (1887). A contribution to the pathology of dreams and of hysterical paralysis. *Brain, 9,* 488–93.

Fernald, M. R. (1912). The diagnosis of mental imagery. *Psychological Review Monograph Supplement, 14,* No. 58.

Ferree, C., & Rand, G. (1934). Perception of depth in the after-image. *American Journal of Psychology, 46,* 329–32.

Finke, R. A. (1989). *Principles of mental imagery.* Cambridge, MA: M.I.T. Press.

Finke, R. A., Ward, T., & Smith, S. M. (1992). *Creative cognition: Theory, research, and applications.* Cambridge, MA: M.I.T. Press.

Fleischer, E. (1929). *The appearance of colored tones: An epistemological treatise.* Basel: Schwabe.

Flew, A. (1953). Images, supposing, and imagining. *Philosophy, 28,* 246–54.

Fodor, J. (1975). *The language of thought.* New York: T. Crowell.

Forster, E. (1930). Selbstversuch mit meskalin. *Zeitschrift fur die Gesamte Neurologie und Psychiatrie, 127,* 1–14.

Fox, C. (1914). The conditions which arouse mental images in thought. *British Journal of Psychology, 6,* 420–31.

Frankel, F. (1976). *Hypnosis: Trance as a coping mechanism.* New York: Plenum Medical Book Company.

Franz, S. I. (1895). The after-image threshold. *Psychological Review, 2,* 130–36.

Fraser, B. (1992). The evolution of image-editing tools. *MacWEEK, 6,* 54–56.

Freedman, A., Kaplan, H., & Sadock, B. (Eds.) (1975). *Comprehensive textbook of psychiatry.* 2 vols. Baltimore, MD: Williams and Wilkins.

French, F. (1902). The mental imagery of students. *Psychological Review, 9,* 40–104.

French, T., & Fromm, E. (1964). *Dream interpretation: A new approach.* New York: Basic Books.

Freud, S. (1900). The interpretation of dreams. In *Standard edition.* Vols. 4 and 5. London: Hogarth Press.

Freyd, J. (1987). Dynamic mental representations. *Psychological Review, 94,* 427–38.

Fromm, E., & Shor, R. (Eds.) (1972). *Hypnosis: Research developments and perspectives.* Chicago: Aldine-Atherton.

Furlong, E. (1961). *Imagination.* London: Allen & Unwin.

Gall, S. (Ed.) (1996). *The Gale encyclopedia of psychology.* Detroit, MI: Gale.

Galton, F. (1879–1880). Psychometric experiments. *Brain, 2,* 149–62.

Galton, F. (1880a). Mental imagery. *Fortnightly Review, 34,* 312–24.

Galton, F. (1880b). Statistics of mental imagery. *Mind, 5,* 301–18.

Galton, F. (1883). *Inquiries into human faculty and its development.* London: Dent.

Garcia-Perez, M. (1988). HDC: A subroutine library for image processing using Burt's hierarchical discrete correlation. *Behavior Research Methods, Instruments, and Computers, 20,* 317–29.

Gates, L. W. (1934). The after-effect of visually observed movement. *American Journal of Psychology, 46,* 34–46.

Gathercole, S., Pickering, S., & Hall, M. (2001). Dissociable lexical and phonological influences on serial recognition and serial recall. *Quarterly Journal of Experimental Psychology, 54,* 1–30.

Gazzaniga, M. (1970). *The bisected brain.* New York: Appleton-Century-Crofts.

Giddan, N. (1967). Recovery through images of briefly flashed stimuli. *Journal of Personality, 35,* 1–19.

Giel, R., Gezahegn, Y., & Van Luijk, J. (1968). Faith-healing and spirit-possession in Ghion, Ethiopia. *Social Science and Medicine, 2,* 63–79.

Gill, M., & Brenman, M. (1959). *Hypnosis and related states: Psychoanalytic studies in regression.* New York: International Universities Press.

Ginsberg, L. (1923). A case of synaesthesia. *American Journal of Psychology, 34,* 582–89.

Globus, G., Maxwell, G., & Savodnik, I. (Eds.) (1976). *Consciousness and the brain.* New York: Plenum Press.

Goldstein, K. (1908). Zur theorie der halluzinationen. Studien uber normale und pathologische wahrnehmung. *Archiv fur Psychiatrie und Nervenheilkunde, 44,* 584, 1036.

Goode, E. (1999). When people see a sound and hear a color. *New York Times,* February 23, D3 (N), F3 (L).

Gooley, T., & Barrett, H. (1992). Evaluation of statistical methods of image reconstruction through ROC analysis. *IEEE Transactions on Medical Imaging, 11,* 276–84.

Gordon, R. (1949). An investigation into some of the factors that favour the formation of stereotyped images. *British Journal of Psychology, 39,* 156–67.

Gorton, D. (1896). Psychology of the unconscious. *New York Medical Times, 24,* 33, 97.

Goschen, G. (1893). *The cultivation and use of the imagination.* London: Wilson.

Gould, G. (1889). Dreams, sleep, and consciousness. *Open Court, 2,* 1433–36, 1444–46.

Graham, K. (1969). Brightness contrast by hypnotic hallucination. *International Journal of Clinical and Experimental Hypnosis, 17,* 62–73.

Granville, J. (1882). Dreams and their making. *Popular Science Monthly, 20,* 461–68.

Gray, J. (1995). The contents of consciousness: A neuropsychological conjecture. *Behavioral and Brain Sciences, 18,* 659–76.

Greenwood, F. (1892). Imagination in dreams. *Contemporary Review, 62,* 165–82.

Greenwood, F. (1894). *Imagination in dreams and their study.* London: Lane.

Gregersen, P. (1998). Instant recognition: The genetics of pitch perception. *American Journal of Human Genetics, 62,* 221–23.

Gregory, R. (Ed.) (1987). *The Oxford companion to the mind.* Oxford, UK: Oxford University Press.

Griffitts, C. H. (1927). Individual differences in imagery. *Psychological Monographs, 37,* No. 172.

Guilleminault, C., Billiard, M., Montplaisir, J., & Dement, W. (1975). Altered states of consciousness in disorders of daytime sleepiness. *Journal of the Neurological Sciences, 26,* 377–93.

Gulliver, J. (1880). The psychology of dreams. *Journal of Speculative Philosophy, 14,* 204–18.

Gur, R., & Reyher, J. (1976). Enhancement of imagery via free-imagery and hypnosis. *American Journal of Clinical Hypnosis, 18,* 237–49.

Guterman, L. (2001). Synesthetes show their colors. *Chronicle of Higher Education, 48,* A17.

Gutman, E. (1936). Artificial psychoses produced by mescaline. *Journal of Mental Science, 82,* 203–21.

Haber, R. N. (1979). Twenty years of haunting eidetic imagery: Where's the ghost? *Behavioral and Brain Sciences, 2,* 583–629.

Haber, R. N. (1980). Eidetic images are not just imaginary. *Psychology Today,* November, 72–82.

Haber, R. N. (1983). The impending demise of the icon: A critique of the concept of iconic storage in visual information processing. *Behavioral and Brain Sciences, 6,* 1–54.

Haber, R. N., and Haber, R. G. (1964). Eidetic imagery: I. Frequency. *Perceptual and Motor Skills, 19,* 131–38.

Hall, C. S. (1953). *The meaning of dreams.* New York: Harper.

Hall, C. S., & Van de Castle, R. (1966). *The content analysis of dreams.* New York: Appleton-Century-Crofts.

Hall, L. (1901). *The evolution of consciousness.* London: Oxford University Press.

Halldorson, M. (1999). *Redintegration and item recognition: Effects of storage unit size and context.* Ottawa: National Library of Canada. (Also see Halldorson, M. [1998]. Unpublished doctoral dissertation, University of Manitoba.)

Hameroff, S., Kaszniak, A., & Scott, A. (Eds.) (1998). *Toward a science of consciousness II: The second Tucson discussions and debates.* Cambridge, MA: M.I.T. Press.

Hamilton, W. (1859/1860). *Lectures on metaphysics and logic.* London: Blackwood; Boston: Gould and Lincoln.

Hamlyn, D. (1994). Imagination. In S. Guttenplan (Ed.), *A companion to the philosophy of mind.* Oxford, UK: Blackwell.

Hanawalt, N. G. (1954). Recurrent images: New instances and a summary of the older ones. *American Journal of Psychology, 67,* 170–74.

Hannay, A. (1971). *Mental images—a defence.* London: Allen & Unwin.

Hannay, A. (1973). To see a mental image. *Mind, 82,* 161–262.

Hardie, W. (1976). Concepts of consciousness in Aristotle. *Mind, 85,* 388–411.

Harre, R., & Lamb, R. (Eds.) (1983). *Encyclopedic dictionary of psychology.* Cambridge, MA: M.I.T. Press.

Harrison, J., & Baron-Cohen, S. (1995). Synaesthesia: Reconciling the subjective with the objective. *Endeavour, 19,* 157–61.

Hartmann, E. (Ed.) (1970). *Sleep and dreaming.* Boston: Little, Brown.

Hartmann, E. von (1869). *Philosophie des unbewussten.* Berlin: Duncker.

Hartmann, H. (1924). Halluzinierte flachenfarben und bewegungen. *Monatsschrift fur Psychiatrie und Neurologie, 56,* 1–29.

Hasebroek, K. (1935). Concerning color hearing. *Zeitschrift fur Psychologie, 136,* 292–98.

Hayes, J. (1973). On the function of visual imagery in elementary mathematics. In W. Chase (Ed.), *Visual information processing.* New York: Academic Press.

Hayes-Roth, F. (1979). Distinguishing theories of mental representation: A critique of Anderson's "Arguments concerning mental imagery." *Psychological Review, 86,* 376–82.

Heil, J. (1982). What does the mind's eye look at? *The Journal of Mind and Behavior, 3,* 143-149.

Hein, H. (1926). Untersuchungen uber die gesetzmassigkeiten der zuordnung von farben zu tonen. *Archiv fur die Gesamte Psychologie, 56,* 95–176.

Helmholtz, H. (1856–1866). *Handbuch der physiologischen optik.* Leipzig: Voss.

Hermann, L. (1879). *Handbuch der physiologie.* Vol. 2. London: Taylor & Walton.

Herrick, C. (1894). The seat of consciousness. *Journal of Comparative Neurology, 4,* 221–24.

Herrick, C. (1896). Focal and marginal consciousness. *Psychological Review, 3,* 193–95.

Hibbert-Ware, S. (1825). *Sketches of the philosophy of apparitions.* Edinburgh: Oliver and Boyd.

Hicks, G. D. (1924). On the nature of images. *British Journal of Psychology, 15,* 121–48.

Hilgard, E. R. (1965). *Hypnotic suggestibility.* New York: Harcourt Brace Jovanovich.

Hilgard, E. R. (1972). A critique of Johnson, Maher, and Barber's "Artifact in the 'essence of hypnosis': An evaluation of trance logic," with a recomputation of their findings. *Journal of Abnormal Psychology, 79,* 221–33.

Hilgard, E. R. (1973a). A neodissociation interpretation of pain reduction in hypnosis. *Psychological Review, 80,* 396–411.

Hilgard, E. R. (1973b). The domain of hypnosis, with some comments on alternative paradigms. *American Psychologist, 28,* 972–82.

Hilgard, E. R. (1977). *Divided consciousness: Multiple controls in human thought and action.* New York: Wiley.

Hilgard, E. R. (1980). Consciousness in contemporary psychology. *Annual Review of Psychology, 31,* 1–26.

Hilgard, E. R. (1981). Imagery and imagination in American psychology. *Journal of Mental Imagery, 5,* 5–66.

Hilgard, E. R., & Tart, C. (1966). Responsiveness to suggestions following waking and imagination instructions and following induction of hypnosis. *Journal of Abnormal Psychology, 71,* 196–208.

Hinsie, L., & Campbell, R. (1970). *Psychiatric dictionary.* New York: Oxford University Press.

Hinton, G. (1979). Some demonstrations of the effects of structural descriptions in mental imagery. *Cognitive Science, 3,* 231–50.

Hiscock, M., & Cohen, D. B. (1973). Visual imagery and dream recall. *Journal of Research in Personality, 7,* 179–88.

Hochberg, J. (1968). In the mind's eye. In R. Haber (Ed.), *Contemporary theory and research in visual perception.* New York: Holt, Rinehart & Winston.

Hochman, J. (2001). A basic outline search on the eidetic with PsycINFO, MEDLINE, and ERIC. *Journal of Mental Imagery, 25,* 99–215.

Hodgson, R. (1885). The consciousness of eternal reality. *Mind, 10,* 321–40.

Hodgson, S. (1894). Reflective consciousness. *Mind, 19,* 208–21.

Hollingworth, H. (1926). *The psychology of thought.* New York: Appleton.

Hollingworth, H. (1928). *Psychology: Its facts and principles.* New York: Appleton.

Hollingworth, H., & Weischer, V. (1939). Persistent alphabetic synesthesis. *American Journal of Psychology, 52,* 361–66.

Holt, R. R. (1964). Imagery: The return of the ostracized. *American Psychologist, 19,* 254–64.

Holt, R. R. (1972). On the nature and generality of mental imagery. In P. W. Sheehan (Ed.), *The function and nature of imagery.* New York: Academic Press.

Holton, G. (1996). Imagination in science. In G. Holton (Ed.), *Einstein, history, and other passions: The rebellion against science at the end of the twentieth century.* Reading, MA: Addison-Wesley.

Homme, L. (1965). Control of coverants: The operants of the mind. *Psychological Record, 15*, 501–11.

Horne, P. (1993). The nature of imagery. *Consciousness and Cognition, 2*, 58–82.

Howells, T. H. (1937). Experimental development of color-tone synesthesia. *Psychological Bulletin, 34*, 714.

Howells, T. H. (1944). The experimental development of color-tone synesthesia. *Journal of Experimental Psychology, 34*, 87–103.

Hudson, J., & Sheffield, E. (1998). Déjà vu all over again: Effects of reenactment on toddlers' event memory. *Child Development, 69*, 51–68.

Hull, C. L. (1933). *Hypnosis and suggestibility.* New York: Appleton-Century-Crofts.

Hulme, C., Newton, P., Cowan, N., Stuart, G., & Brown, G. (1999). Think before you speak: Pauses, memory search, and trace redintegration processes in verbal memory span. *Journal of Experimental Psychology: Learning, Memory, and Cognition, 25*, 447–64.

Hulme, C., Roodenrys, S., Schweickert, R., Brown, G., Martin, S., & Stuart, G. (1997). Word-frequency effects on short-term memory tasks: Evidence for a redintegration process in immediate serial recall. *Journal of Experimental Psychology: Learning, Memory, and Cognition, 23*, 1217–33.

Hume, D. (1738). *A treatise of human nature.* Oxford, UK: Clarendon Press.

Humphrey, G. (1951). *Thinking: An introduction to its experimental psychology.* London: Methuen.

Hunt, J. (1845). *Imagination and fancy.* London: Smith, Elder.

Hutchinson, H. (1901). *Dreams and their meanings.* London: Longmans, Green.

Huttenlocher, J. (1968). Constructing spatial images: A strategy in reasoning. *Psychological Review, 75*, 550–60.

Huxley, A. (1954). *The doors of perception and heaven and hell.* Middlesex, UK: Penguin Books.

Ishiguro, H. (1967). Imagination. *Proceedings of the Aristotelian Society, Supplementary Volume, 41*, 37–56.

Jachesky, L., & Foradori, I. A. (1933). Colored audition. *Revista de Criminologia, Buenos Aires, 20*, 696–702.

Jachesky, L., & Foradori, I. A. (1935). Contribution to the study of colored hearing. *Anales del Instituto de Psicologia, Universidad de Buenos Aires, 1*, 273–97.

Jacquin, A. E. (1992). Image coding based on a fractal theory of iterated contractive image transformations. *IEEE Transactions on Image Processing, 1*, 18–31.

Jaensch, E. R. (1925/1930). *Eidetic imagery and typological methods of investigation.* 2d ed. (O. Oeser, Trans.). New York: Harcourt Brace.

James, W. (1887). Consciousness of lost limbs. *Proceedings of the American Society for Psychical Research, 1,* 3.

James, W. (1889). Automatic writing. *Proceedings of the American Society for Psychical Research, 1,* 548–64.

James, W. (1890). *The principles of psychology.* 2 vols. New York: Dover.

James, W. (1898). Consciousness under nitrous oxide. *Psychological Review, 5,* 194–96.

James, W. (1904). Does consciousness exist? *Journal of Philosophy, Psychology, and Scientific Method, 1,* 477–91.

Janet, P. (1889). *L'Automatisme psychologique.* Paris: Alcan.

Janet, P. (1905). *A propos du "déjà vu."* Paris: Alcan.

Janet, P. (1907). *The major symptoms of hysteria.* New York: Macmillan.

Janssen, W. (1976). *On the nature of mental imagery.* Soesterburg, Netherlands: Institute for Perception TNO.

Jastrow, J. (1898). The psychology of invention. *Psychological Review, 5,* 307–9.

Jastrow, J. (1900). *Fact and fable in psychology.* Boston: Houghton, Mifflin.

Jaynes, J. (1977). *The origin of consciousness in the breakdown of the bicameral mind.* Boston: Houghton Mifflin.

Johnson, M. (1993). *Moral imagination: Implications of cognitive science for ethics.* Chicago: University of Chicago Press.

Johnson, R.F.Q. (1972). Trance logic revisited: A reply to Hilgard's critique. *Journal of Abnormal Psychology, 79,* 234–38.

Johnson, R.F.Q., Maher, B., & Barber, T. X. (1972). Artifact in the "essence of hypnosis," an evaluation of trance logic. *Journal of Abnormal Psychology, 79,* 212–20.

Johnson-Laird, P. N. (1983). *Mental models: Towards a cognitive science of language, inference, and consciousness.* Cambridge, UK: Cambridge University Press.

Joly, H. (1877). De l'imagination. *Revue Philosophique, 5,* 334–39.

Judd, D. B. (1927). A quantitative investigation of the Purkinje after-image. *American Journal of Psychology, 38,* 507–33.

Julien, R. (1975). *A primer of drug action.* San Francisco: Freeman.

Julstrom, B., & Baron, R. (1985). A model of mental imagery. *International Journal of Man-Machine Studies, 23,* 313–34.

Jung, C. (1912). *The psychology of the unconscious.* Leipzig: Deuticke.

Jung, C. (Ed.) (1964). *Man and his symbols.* New York: Dell.

Kafka, J. S. (1991). Déjà vu and synesthesia. Reply by H. N. Sno and D. H. Linszen. *American Journal of Psychology, 148,* 951–52.

Kahneman, D., & Tversky, A. (1973). On the psychology of prediction. *Psychological Review, 80,* 237–51.

Kandinsky, V. (1881). Zur lehre von den halluzinationen. *Archiv fur Psychiatrie, 11,* 453–58.

Kanfer, I., & Marston, A. (1963). Conditioning of self-reinforcing responses.

An analogue to self-confidence training. *Psychological Reports, 13*, 63–70.

Kant, I. (1781). *Critique of pure reason*. London: Macmillan.

Kappenberg, R. P. (1984). Hallucinations; Hallucinogenic drugs. In R. J. Corsini (Ed.), *Encyclopedia of psychology*. Vol. 2. New York: Wiley.

Karwoski, T. F., & Odbert, H. S. (1938). Color-music. *Psychological Monographs, 50*, No. 2.

Karwoski, T. F., Odbert, H. S., & Osgood, C. E. (1942). Studies in synesthetic thinking. II. The role of form in visual responses to music. *Journal of General Psychology, 26*, 199–222.

Katz, A. (2000). Mental imagery. In A. E. Kazdin (Ed.), *Encyclopedia of psychology*. Vol. 5. New York: Oxford University Press.

Kaufmann, G. (1980). *Imagery, language, and cognition: Toward a theory of symbolic activity in human problem-solving*. Bergen: Universitetsforlaget.

Kaufmann, G. (1984). Mental imagery in problem solving. *International Review of Mental Imagery, 1*, 23–55.

Kearney, R. (1988). *The wake of imagination: Ideas of creativity in Western culture*. London: Hutchinson.

Keehn, J. D. (1964). Consciousness and behaviorism. *British Journal of Psychology, 55*, 89–91.

Kelly, E. L. (1934). An experimental attempt to produce artificial chromaesthesia by the technique of the conditioned response. *Journal of Experimental Psychology, 17*, 315–41.

Kerr, M., & Pear, T. (1931). Unseen drama and imagery: Some experimental observations. *British Journal of Psychology, 22*, 43–54.

Kerr, M., & Pear, T. H. (1932). Synaesthetic factors in judging the voice. *British Journal of Psychology, 23*, 167–69.

Kessel, F. (1972). Imagery: A dimension of mind rediscovered. *British Journal of Psychology, 63*, 149–62.

Kety, S., Evarts, E., & Williams, H. (1967). *Sleep and altered states of consciousness*. Baltimore, MD: Williams and Wilkins.

Keup, W. (Ed.) (1970). *Origin and mechanisms of hallucinations*. New York: Plenum.

Kher, U. (2001). Ah, the blue smell of it! Synesthetes who mix up their senses and the scholars who study them cross paths to compare notes. *Time*, May 21, *157*, 64.

Kihlstrom, J. (1987). The cognitive unconscious. *Science, 237*, 1445–52.

Kingman, R. (1928). Color psychology: A study of the combined esthesias. *Welfare Magazine, 19*, 900–906.

Kirkpatrick, E. (1893). Mental images. *Science, 22*, 227–30.

Kirshner, L. (1973). Dissociative reaction: An historical review and clinical study. *Acta Psychiatrica Scandinavia, 49*, 698–711.

Kleint, B. (1940). *Experiments on perception*. Leipzig: Barth.

Klinger, E. (1990). *Daydreaming*. Los Angeles: Tarcher.

Kluver, H. (1926). An experimental study of the eidetic type. *Genetic Psychology Monographs, 1,* 70–230.

Kluver, H. (1928). Studies on the eidetic type and on eidetic imagery. *Psychological Bulletin, 25,* 69–104.

Kluver, H. (1930). Fragmentary eidetic imagery. *Psychological Review, 37,* 441–58.

Kluver, H. (1942). Mechanisms of hallucinations. In Q. McNemar & M. A. Merrill (Eds.), *Studies in personality in honour of Lewis M. Terman.* New York: McGraw-Hill.

Kluver, H. (1966). *Mescal, and mechanisms of hallucinations.* Chicago: University of Chicago Press.

Kolers, P. (1987). Imaging. In R. Gregory & O. Zangwill (Eds.), *The Oxford companion to the mind.* Oxford, UK: Oxford University Press.

Kolers, P., & Smythe, W. (1979). Images, symbols, and skills. *Canadian Journal of Psychology, 33,* 158–84.

Kosslyn, S. M. (1980). *Image and mind.* Cambridge, MA: Harvard University Press.

Kosslyn, S. M. (1981). The medium and the message in mental imagery: A theory. *Psychological Review, 88,* 46–66.

Kosslyn, S. M. (1983). *Ghosts in the mind's machine: Creating and using images in the brain.* New York: Norton.

Kosslyn, S. M. (1987). Seeing and imagining in the cerebral hemispheres: A computational approach. *Psychological Review, 94,* 148–75.

Kosslyn, S. M. (1994). *Image and brain: The resolution of the imagery debate.* Cambridge, MA: M.I.T. Press.

Kosslyn, S. M., Pinker, S., Smith, G., & Shwartz, S. (1979). On the demystification of mental imagery. *Behavioral and Brain Sciences, 2,* 535–81.

Kosslyn, S. M., & Pomerantz, J. (1977). Imagery, propositions, and the form of internal representations. *Cognitive Psychology, 9,* 52–76.

Kroger, W., & Fezler, W. (1976). *Hypnosis and behavior modification: Imagery conditioning.* Philadelphia: Lippincott.

Krohn, W. (1893). Pseudo-chromaesthesia, or the association of color with words, letters, and sounds. *American Journal of Psychology, 5,* 20–41.

Kuhlmann, F. (1905). The place of mental imagery and memory among mental functions. *American Journal of Psychology, 16,* 337–56.

Kuhlmann, F. (1906). On the analysis of the memory consciousness: A study in the mental imagery and memory of meaningless visual forms. *Psychological Review, 13,* 316–48.

Kuhlmann, F. (1907). On the analysis of the memory consciousness for pictures of familiar objects. *American Journal of Psychology, 18,* 389–420.

Kuhlmann, F. (1909). On the analysis of auditory memory consciousness. *American Journal of Psychology, 20,* 194–218.

Kulpe, O. (1893). *Grundriss der psychologie.* Leipzig: Engelmann.

Kunzendorf, R. G. (1980). Imagery and consciousness: A scientific analysis of the mind-body problem. *Dissertation Abstracts International, 40,* 3448B–49B.

Kunzendorf, R. G. (1990). Mind-brain identity theory: A materialistic foundation for the psychophysiology of mental imagery. In R. G. Kunzendorf & A. A. Sheikh (Eds.), *The psychophysiology of mental imagery: Theory, research, and application.* Amityville, NY: Baywood.

Ladd, G. T. (1892). Contributions to the psychology of visual dreams. *Mind, 1,* 299–300.

Ladd, G. T. (1896a). Evolution and consciousness. *Psychological Review, 3,* 296–300.

Ladd, G. T. (1896b). *Outlines of physiological psychology: A textbook of mental science for academies and colleges.* 5th ed. New York: Scribner's.

Lambie, J. A., & Marcel, A. J. (2002). Consciousness and the varieties of emotion experience: A theoretical framework. *Psychological Review, 109,* 219–59.

Langfeld, H. S. (1914). Note on a case of chromaesthesia. *Psychological Bulletin, 11,* 113–14.

Langfeld, H. S. (1915, 1919, 1926, 1929). Synesthesia. *Psychological Bulletin, 12,* 121–22; *16,* 148–50; *23,* 599–606; *26,* 582–85.

Lawrie, R. (1970). The existence of mental images. *Philosophical Quarterly, 20,* 253–57.

Lay, W. (1896). Three cases of synaesthesia. *Psychological Review, 3,* 92–95.

Lay, W. (1898). Mental imagery. *Psychological Review, Monograph Supplement No. 7,* 1–54.

Lay, W. (1903). Mental imagery. *Psychological Review, 10,* 300–306, 422–25.

Laymon, R. (1966). An experimental study of two methods of indexing tactical imagery. *U.S. Army Technical Research Note, 176,* 1–40.

Leadbeater, C. (1899). *Dreams: What they are.* London: Jarrolds.

Leaning, F. E. (1925). An introductory study of hypnagogic phenomena. *Proceedings of the Society for Psychical Research, 35,* 289–403.

Leary, T. (1968). *The politics of ecstasy.* New York: Putnam.

LeCron, L. (Ed.) (1952). *Experimental hypnosis.* New York: Macmillan.

Lemaitre, A. (1901). *Audition coloree et phenomenes connexes.* Paris: Alcan.

Lenzberg, K. (1923). Zur theorie der sekundarempfindungen und bleulerschen theorie im besondern. *Zeitschrift fur Angewandte Psychologie, 21,* 283.

Leuba, C. (1940). Images as conditioned sensations. *Journal of Experimental Psychology, 26,* 345–51.

Levinson, B. (1967). States of awareness during general anesthesia. In J. Lassner (Ed.), *Hypnosis and psychosomatic medicine.* New York: Springer Verlag.

Lewandowsky, S. (1999). Redintegration and response suppression in serial recall: A dynamic network model. *International Journal of Psychology, 34,* 434–46.

Lewandowsky, S., & Farrell, S. (2000). A redintegration account of the effects of speech rate, lexicality, and word frequency in immediate serial recall. *Psychological Research, 63,* 163–74.

Lewes, G. (1877). Consciousness and unconsciousness. *Mind, 2,* 156–67.

Lindauer, M. S. (1969). Imagery and sensory modality. *Perceptual and Motor Skills, 29,* 203–15.

Lindauer, M. S. (1972). The sensory attributes and functions of imagery and imagery evoking stimuli. In P. W. Sheehan (Ed.), *The function and nature of imagery.* New York: Academic Press.

Locke, J. (1690). *An essay concerning human understanding.* London: Dent.

Logie, R., & Denis, M. (Eds.) (1991). *Mental images in human cognition.* Amsterdam: Elsevier.

Lohmann, A., & Sinzinger, S. (1995). Graphic codes for computer holography. *Applied Optics, 34,* 3172–79.

London, P. (1967). The induction of hypnosis. In J. E. Gordon (Ed.), *Handbook of clinical and experimental hypnosis.* New York: Macmillan.

Lovell, A. (1899). *Imagination and its wonders.* London: Nichols.

Lowell, J. (1894). The imagination. *Century, 47,* 716–21.

Lu, G., Williams, B., & You, C. (2001). An effective World Wide Web image search engine. *Journal of Information Science, 27,* 27–28.

Luchins, A. S. (1942). Mechanization in problem solving. *Psychological Monographs, 54,* No. 248.

Ludwig, A. M. (1966). Altered states of consciousness. *Archives of General Psychiatry, 26,* 225–34.

Luria, A. R. (1973). *The working brain.* New York: Basic Books.

MacDougal, R. (1898). Music imagery: A confession of experience. *Psychological Review, 5,* 463–76.

Mahlung, F. (1926). Das problem der "audition coloree." *Archiv fur die Gesamte Psychologie, 57,* 165–301.

Mainwaring, J. (1933). Kinaesthetic factors in the recall of musical experience. *British Journal of Psychology, 23,* 284–307.

Mandler, J. M., & Mandler, G. (1964). *Thinking: From association to Gestalt.* New York: Wiley.

Manford, M., & Andermann, F. (1998). Complex visual hallucinations: Clinical and neurobiological insights. *Brain, 121,* 1819–40.

Mani, K., & Johnson-Laird, P. N. (1982). The mental representation of spatial descriptions. *Memory and Cognition, 10,* 181–87.

Marcel, A. (1983). Conscious and unconscious perception: An approach to the relations between phenomenal experience and perceptual processes. *Cognitive Psychology, 15,* 238–300.

Marcel, A., & Bisiach, E. (Eds.) (1988). *Consciousness in contemporary science.* New York: Oxford University Press.

Marinesco, G. (1931). On colored hearing. *Presse Medicale, 39,* 743–44.

Marinesco, G., & Sava, V. (1929). Colored hearing. *Bulletin: Section Scientifique, Academie Roumaine, 12,* 4–5.

Marks, D. F. (1983). Mental imagery and consciousness: A theoretical review. In A. A. Sheikh (Ed.), *Imagery: Current theory, research, and application.* New York: Wiley.

Marks, D. F. (1999). Consciousness, mental imagery, and action. *British Journal of Psychology, 90,* 567–85.

Marr, D. (1982). *Vision.* Cambridge, MA: M.I.T. Press.

Marshall, H. (1896). Consciousness and biological evolution. *Mind, 21,* 367–87, 523–38.

Marshall, H. (1901). Consciousness, self-consciousness, and the self. *Mind, 26,* 98–113.

Marshall, H. (1902). The unity process in consciousness. *Mind, 27,* 470–502.

Marshall, H. (1904). Of simpler and more complex consciousness. *Journal of Philosophy, Psychology, and Scientific Method, 1,* 365–75.

Martin, L. (1917). An experimental study of the subconscious. In J. E. Coover (Ed.), *Experiments in psychical research.* Stanford, CA: Stanford University Press.

Martinek, H., & Zarin, A. (1979). The effects of bandwidth compression on image interpreter performance. *U.S. Army Research Institute for the Behavioral and Social Sciences, 396,* 1–70.

Masson, D. (1952). Synesthesia and sound sprectra. *Word, 8,* 39–41.

Matthews, G. (1969). Mental copies. *Philosophical Review, 78,* 53–73.

Mattingley, J., Rich, A., Yelland, G., & Bradshaw, J. (2001). Unconscious priming eliminates automatic binding of colour and alphanumeric form in synaesthesia. *Nature, 410,* 580–82.

Maudsley, H. (1887). The physical conditions of consciousness. *Mind, 12,* 489–575.

Mayer-Gross, W. (1927). On the problem of synaesthesias. *Psychiatrisch-Neurologische Wochenschrift, 29,* 233–35.

Mayman, M. (Ed.) (1973). Psychoanalytic research: Three approaches to the experimental study of subliminal processes. *Psychological Issues, 8,* Monograph 30.

Mayne, Z. (1728/1976). *Two dissertations concerning sense, and the imagination, with an essay on consciousness.* London: J. Tonson/New York: Garland.

McCollough, C. (1965). Color adaptation of edge-detectors in the human visual system. *Science, 149,* 1115–16.

McDonald, R., & Smith, J. R. (1975). Trance logic in tranceable and simulating subjects. *International Journal of Clinical and Experimental Hypnosis, 23,* 80–89.

McDougall, W. (1938). The relation between dissociation and repression. *British Journal of Medical Psychology, 17,* 141–57.

McFarland, T. (1985). *Originality and imagination.* Baltimore, MD: Johns Hopkins University Press.

McKellar, P. (1957). *Imagination and thinking: A psychological analysis.* New York: Basic Books.

McKellar, P. (1968). *Experience and behaviour.* Harmondsworth, UK: Penguin.

McKellar, P. (1972). Imagery from the standpoint of introspection. In P. W. Sheehan (Ed.), *The function and nature of imagery.* New York: Academic Press.

McKellar, P. (1979). Between wakefulness and sleep: Hypnagogic fantasy. In A. A. Sheikh & J. T. Shaffer (Eds.), *The potential of fantasy and imagination.* New York: Brandon House.

McKellar, P., & Simpson, L. (1954). Between wakefulness and sleep: Hypnagogic imagery. *British Journal of Psychology, 45,* 266–76.

McKellar, P., & Tonn, H. (1967). Negative hallucinations, dissociation, and the five stamps experiment. *British Journal of Social Psychology, 1,* 260–70.

McKenley, P., & Gur, R. (1975). Imagery, absorption, meditation, and drug use as correlates of hypnotic susceptibility. Paper presented at the annual meeting of the Society for Clinical and Experimental Hypnosis, Chicago, October 10.

McMahon, C. E. (1973). Images as motives and motivators: A historical perspective. *American Journal of Psychology, 86,* 465–90.

Medlicott, R. W. (1958). An inquiry into the significance of hallucinations with special reference to their occurrence in the sane. *International Journal of Medicine, 171,* 664–77.

Messerschmidt, R. (1927–1928). A quantitative investigation of the alleged independent operation of conscious and subconscious processes. *Journal of Abnormal and Social Psychology, 22,* 325–40.

Metzinger, T. (Ed.) (1995). *Conscious experience.* Hamburg: Schoningh/Academic.

Michaut, N. (1876). *De l'imagination.* Paris: Thorin.

Miller, A. I. (1984). *Imagery in scientific thought.* Boston, MA: Birkhauser.

Miller, J. (1990). The essence of images. In H. Barlow, C. Blakemore, & M. Weston-Smith (Eds.), *Images and understanding.* Cambridge, UK: Cambridge University Press.

Miller, J. G. (1939). Discrimination without awareness. *American Journal of Psychology, 52,* 562–78.

Minot, C. (1902). The problem of consciousness in its biological aspects. *Proceedings of the American Association for the Advancement of Science, 2,* 265–85.

Mishlove, J. (1975). *The roots of consciousness: Psychic liberation through history, science, and experience.* New York: Random House.

Mitchell, T. W. (1925). Divisions of the self and co-consciousness. In C. M. Campbell (Ed.), *Problems of personality: Studies presented to Dr. Morton Prince.* New York: Harcourt, Brace.

Modrak, D. (1981). An Aristotelian theory of consciousness? *Ancient Philosophy, 1*, 160–70.

Monroe, W. (1900–1901). Imagery in dreams. *Fourth International Congress of Psychology*, 175–77.

Montague, W. (1905). The relational theory of consciousness. *Journal of Philosophy, 2*, 309–16.

Morgan, C. L. (1896–1897). Animal automatism and consciousness. *Monist, 7*, 1–18.

Morris, P. E., & Hampson, P. J. (1983). *Imagery and consciousness.* London: Academic Press.

Morsch, J., & Abbott, H. (1945). An investigation of after-images. *Journal of Comparative Psychology, 38*, 47–63.

Moss, C. S. (1967). *The hypnotic investigation of dreams.* New York: Wiley.

Mostert, J. (1975). States of awareness during general anesthesia. *Perspectives in Biology and Medicine* (Autumn), 68–76.

Motluk, A. (1994). The sweet smell of purple. *New Scientist, 143*, 32–37.

Mouravier, S. (1997). Image formation mechanism on the shroud of Turin: A solar reflex radiation model. *Applied Optics, 36*, 8976–82.

Mowrer, O. H. (1960). *Learning theory and the symbolic processes.* New York: Wiley.

Mowrer, O. H. (1977). Mental imagery: An indispensable psychological concept. *Journal of Mental Imagery, 2*, 303–21.

Muhl, A. (1930). *Automatic writing.* Leipzig: Theodor Steinkopff.

Muhl, A. (1952). Automatic writing and hypnosis. In L. M. Le Cron (Ed.), *Experimental hypnosis.* New York: Macmillan.

Murdock, B. (1993). Derivations for the chunking model. *Journal of Mathematical Psychology, 37*, 421–45.

Murray, E. (1906). Peripheral and central factors in memory images of visual form and color. *American Journal of Psychology, 17*, 227–47.

Murray, J. (1894). Do we ever dream of tasting? *Proceedings of the American Psychological Association, New York, 2*, 20–21. (Cf. Titchener, 1895.)

Myers, C. S. (1911). A case of synaesthesia. *British Journal of Psychology, 4*, 228–38.

Myers, F.W.H. (1887). Automatic writing III. *Proceedings of the Society for Psychical Research, 4*, 209–61.

Myers, F.W.H. (1892). The subliminal consciousness. *Proceedings of the Society for Psychical Research, 7*, 298–353; *8*, 333–411.

Naito, K. (1936). A sketch of synesthesia in my experience. *Japanese Journal of Experimental Psychology, 3,* 263–75.

Naito, K. (1938). Some varieties and problems of synaesthesia. *Report of the Congress of the Japanese Psychological Association, 2,* 145–49.

Narita, N. (1994). Subjective-evaluation method for quality coded images. *IEEE Transactions on Broadcasting, 40,* 7–14.

Natsoulas, T. (1978). Consciousness. *American Psychologist, 33,* 906–14.

Natsoulas, T. (1983a). A selective review of conceptions of consciousness with special reference to behavioristic contributions. *Cognition and Brain Theory, 6,* 417–47.

Natsoulas, T. (1983b). Addendum to "consciousness." *American Psychologist, 38,* 121–22.

Natsoulas, T. (1986–1987). The six basic concepts of consciousness and William James's stream of thought. *Imagination, Cognition, and Personality, 6,* 289–319.

Neisser, U. (1967). *Cognitive psychology.* New York: Appleton-Century-Crofts.

Neisser, U. (1972). Changing conceptions of imagery. In P. Sheehan (Ed.), *The function and nature of imagery.* London: Academic Press.

Neisser, U. (1976). *Cognition and reality.* San Francisco, CA: W. H. Freeman.

Neisser, U. (1978). Anticipations, images, and introspection. *Cognition, 6,* 167–74.

Nelson, J. (1888). A study of dreams. *American Journal of Psychology, 1,* 367–401.

Nelson, M., & Hitchon, J. (1995). Theory of synaesthesia applied to persuasion in print advertising headlines. *Journalism and Mass Communication Quarterly, 72,* 346–60.

Neppe, V. (1981). A study of déjà vu experience. Unpublished doctoral dissertation, University of the Witwatersrand, South Africa.

Neppe, V. (1983). *The psychology of déjà vu: Have I been here before?* Johannesburg, South Africa: Witwatersrand University Press.

*New Encyclopaedia Britannica.* (1997). 15th ed. Chicago: Encyclopaedia Britannica.

Newell, A., & Simon, H. A. (1972). *Human problem solving.* Englewood Cliffs, NJ: Prentice-Hall.

Newton, I. (1704). *Opticks.* London: Innys.

Newton, N. (1982). Experience and imagery. *The Southern Journal of Philosophy, 21,* 475–87.

Newton, N. (1989). Visualizing is imagining seeing: A reply to White. *Analysis, 49,* 77–81.

Nikiforovski, V. M. (1937). To the doctrine of synesthesias. *Nevropatologiya i Psikhiatriya, 12,* 18–19.

Norman, D. (1976). *Memory and attention: An introduction to information processing*. New York: Wiley.

Nussbaum, M. (1978). The role of *phantasia* in Aristotle's explanation of action. In M. Nussbaum (Ed.), *Aristotle's De motu animalium*. Princeton, NJ: Princeton University Press.

Odbert, H. S., Karwoski, T. F., & Eckerson, A. B. (1942). Studies in synesthetic thinking. I. Musical and verbal association of color and mood. *Journal of General Psychology, 26*, 153–73.

Oldham, H. (1940). *Child expression in colour and form*. London: John Lane.

Orne, M. (1959). The nature of hypnosis: Artifact and essence. *Journal of Abnormal and Social Psychology, 58*, 277–99.

Orne, M. (1962). Hypnotically induced hallucinations. In L. West (Ed.), *Hallucinations*. New York: Grune and Stratton.

Orne, M., & Scheibe, K. (1964). The contribution of nondeprivation deprivation effects: The psychology of the "panic button," *Journal of Abnormal and Social Psychology, 68*, 3–12.

Ornstein, R. (1972). *The psychology of consciousness*. San Francisco: Freeman.

Ornstein, R. (Ed.) (1973). *The nature of human consciousness*. New York: Viking.

Ortmann, O. (1933). Theories of synesthesia in the light of a case of color hearing. *Human Biology, 5*, 155–211.

Osborne, J. (1991). *Déjà vu*. London: Faber.

Osgood, C. E. (1953). *Method and theory in experimental psychology*. New York: Oxford University Press.

Osgood, C. E. (1960). The cross-cultural generality of visual-verbal synesthetic tendencies. *Behavioral Science, 5*, 146–69.

Oswald, F. (1889). Dreams. *Open Court, 3*, 1597–1600, 1647–50.

Owens, C. A. (1963). A study of mental imagery. Unpublished doctoral dissertation, University of Liverpool, UK.

Padovani, E. (1935). Contribution to the study of colored hearing and its psychological, psychotherapeutic, and pedagogical value. *Societe Italiana di Psichiatria, 20*, 874–77.

Paivio, A. (1969). Mental imagery in associative learning and memory. *Psychological Review, 76*, 241–63.

Paivio, A. (1971). *Imagery and verbal processes*. New York: Holt, Rinehart & Winston.

Paivio, A. (1977). Images, propositions, and knowledge. In J. Nicholas (Ed.), *Images, perception, and knowledge*. Boston, MA: Reidel.

Paivio, A. (1986). *Mental representations: A dual coding approach*. New York: Oxford University Press.

Paivio, A. (1991). Dual coding theory: Retrospect and current status. *Canadian Journal of Psychology, 45*, 255–87.

Paivio, A. (1995). Imagery and memory. In M. Gazzaniga (Ed.), *The cognitive neurosciences*. Cambridge, MA: M.I.T. Press.

Palmer, S. (1977). Hierarchical structure in perceptual representation. *Cognitive Psychology, 9*, 441–74.

Palmer, S. (1978). Fundamental aspects of cognitive representation. In E. Rosch & B. Lloyd (Eds.), *Cognition and categorization*. Hillsdale, NJ: Erlbaum.

Parish, E. (1897). *Hallucinations and illusions: A study of the fallacies of perception*. London: Scott.

Pascual-Leone, J. (1990). Reflections on life-span intelligence, consciousness, and ego development. In C. Alexander & E. Langer (Eds.), *Higher stages of human development: Perspectives on adult growth*, pp. 258–85. New York: Oxford University Press.

Peabody, C. (1918). Certain further experiments in synaesthesia. *American Anthropology, 17*, 143–55.

Peillaube, E. (1902). L'imagination. *Revue Philosophique, 2*, 701–18.

Penfield, W. (1958). *The excitable cortex in conscious man*. Springfield, IL: Thomas.

Penfield, W. (1975). *The mystery of the mind: A critical study of consciousness and the human brain*. Princeton, NJ: Princeton University Press.

Perky, C. (1910). An experimental study of imagination. *American Journal of Psychology, 21*, 422–52.

Perry, C. (1964). Content analysis of dream reports. In J. P. Sutcliffe (Ed.), *The relation of imagery and fantasy to hypnosis*. Sydney, Australia: University of Sydney.

Perry, C. (1973). Imagery, fantasy, and hypnotic susceptibility: A multidimensional approach. *Journal of Personality and Social Psychology, 26*, 208–16.

Perry, C., & Chisholm, W. (1973). Hypnotic age regression and the Ponzo and Poggendorff illusions. *International Journal of Clinical and Experimental Hypnosis, 21*, 192–204.

Perry, R. (1904). Conceptions and misconceptions of consciousness. *Psychological Review, 11*, 282–96.

Philippe, J. (1897). Sur les transformations de nos images mentales. *Revue Philosophique, 43*, 481–93.

Philippe, J. (1903). *L'image mentale*. Paris: Depollier.

Piaget, J. (1974). *The child and reality: Problems in genetic psychology*. (A. Rosin, Trans.). New York: Viking Press.

Pick, A. (1922). Bemerkungen zur lehre von den halluzinationen. *Monatsschrift fur Psychiatrie und Neurologie, 52*, 65–76.

Pico della Mirandola, G. (1500/1930). *On the imagination*. New Haven, CT: Yale University Press.

Pierce, A. H. (1907). Gustatory audition: A hitherto undescribed variety of synaesthesia. *American Journal of Psychology, 18*, 341–52.

Pierce, A. H. (1913). Synaesthesia. *Psychological Bulletin, 10*, 118.

Popham, J. (1854). *Sleep and dreaming*. Dublin: Wolfhound.

Popplestone, J., & McPherson, M. (1988). *Dictionary of concepts in general psychology*. Westport, CT: Greenwood Press.

Pound, A. (2001). Synaesthetic experiences are vivid and involuntary, say scientists. *The Lancet*, March 31, *357*, 1021.

Pressey, A., & Wilson, A. (1974). The Poggendorff illusion in imagination. *Bulletin of the Psychonomic Society, 3*, 447–57.

Prince, M. (1906). *The dissociation of a personality*. London: Longmans Green.

Prince, M. (1909). Experiments to determine co-conscious (subconscious) ideation. *Journal of Abnormal Psychology, 3*, 33–42.

Prince, M. (1914). *The unconscious*. New York: Macmillan.

Prince, M. (1926). Awareness, consciousness, co-consciousness, and animal intelligence from the point of view of the data of abnormal psychology: A biological theory of consciousness. In M. Bentley (Ed.), *Psychologies of 1925: Powell lectures in psychological theory*, pp. 221–43. Worcester, MA: Clark University.

Prince, R. (Ed.) (1968). *Trance and possession states*. Montreal: R. M. Bucke Memorial Society.

Pylyshyn, Z. (1973). What the mind's eye tells the mind's brain: A critique of mental imagery. *Psychological Bulletin, 80*, 1–25.

Pylyshyn, Z. (1981). The imagery debate: Analogue media versus tacit knowledge. *Psychological Review, 88*, 16–45.

Rabb, J. (1975). Imaging: An adverbial analysis. *Dialogue, 14*, 312–18.

Raines, T. H. (1909–1910). Report of a case of psychochromasthesia. *Journal of Abnormal Psychology, 4*, 249–60.

Raju, P. (1946). A note on imagery types. *Indian Journal of Psychology, 21*, 86–88.

Ramachandran, V., & Hirstein, W. (1997). Three laws of qualia: What neurology tells us about the biological functions of consciousness. *Journal of Consciousness Studies, 4*, 429–57.

Rand, B. (1901–1905). Bibliography of philosophy, psychology, and cognate subjects. In J. M. Baldwin (Ed.), *Dictionary of philosophy and psychology*. New York: Macmillan. (Also, Gloucester, MA: Peter Smith, 1960.)

Reber, A. S. (1985). *Dictionary of psychology*. New York: Penguin Books.

Reber, A. S. (1995). *Dictionary of psychology*. 2d ed. New York: Penguin Books.

Reese, H. W. (2001). Some recurrent issues in the history of behavioral sciences. *The Behavior Analyst, 24*, 227–39.

Rehmke, J. (1897). Fundamental conceptions regarding the nature of consciousness. *Philosophical Review, 6*, 449–70.

Reichard, G., Jakobson, R., & Werth, E. (1949). Language and synesthesia. *Word, 5*, 224–33.

Revesz, G. (1923). Uber audition coloree. *Zeitschrift fur Angewandte Psychologie, 21*, 308, 335.

Rey, G. (1981). Introduction: What are mental images? In N. Block (Ed.), *Readings in the philosophy of psychology*. Vol. 2. London: Methuen.

Ribot, T. (1900). Nature of the creative imagination. *International Monthly, 1*, 648–75. (Also see Ribot, T. [1900]. *L'imagination creative*. Paris: Alcan.)

Richardson, A. (1969). *Mental imagery*. London: Routledge & Kegan Paul.

Richardson, A. (1983). Imagery: Definition and types. In A. A. Sheikh (Ed.), *Imagery: Current theory, research, and application*. New York: Wiley.

Richardson, J.T.E. (1980). *Mental imagery and human memory*. London: Macmillan.

Richardson, J.T.E. (1983). Mental imagery in thinking and problem solving. In J. Evans (Ed.), *Thinking and reasoning: Psychological approaches*. London: Routledge & Kegan Paul.

Richardson, J.T.E. (1999). *Imagery*. Hove, East Sussex, UK: Taylor & Francis.

Riggs, L. A., & Karwoski, T. (1934). Synaesthesia. *British Journal of Psychology, 25*, 29–41.

Rignano, E. (1923). *The psychology of reasoning*. New York: Harcourt, Brace.

Robertson, V., & Fry, G. (1937). After-images observed in complete darkness. *American Journal of Psychology, 49*, 265–76.

Robinson, L. (1893). What dreams are made of. *North American Review, 157*, 687–97. (Cf. Clymer, 1885; Ellis, 1899; Wilson, 1884.)

Robson, J. (1986). Coleridge's images of fantasy and imagination. In D. Russell, D. Marks, & J.T.E. Richardson (Eds.), *Imagery 2*. Dunedin, New Zealand: Human Performance Associates.

Roeckelein, J. E. (1996). Citation of *laws* and *theories* in textbooks across 112 years of psychology. *Psychological Reports, 79*, 979–98.

Roeckelein, J. E. (1998). *Dictionary of theories, laws, and concepts in psychology*. Westport, CT: Greenwood Press.

Roeckelein, J. E. (2000). *The concept of time in psychology: A resource book and annotated bibliography*. Westport, CT: Greenwood Press.

Roger, R., & Arnold, J. (1994). Reversible image compression bounded by noise. *IEEE Transactions on Geoscience and Remote Sensing, 32*, 19–25.

Rollins, M. (1989). *Mental imagery: On the limits of cognitive science*. New Haven, CT: Yale University Press.

Rorty, R. (1980). *Philosophy and the mirror of nature*. Oxford, UK: Blackwell.

Rosen, J. (1999). Computer-generated holograms of images reconstructed on curved surfaces. *Applied Optics, 38*, 136–41.

Rosenberg, M. J. (1959). A disconfirmation of the descriptions of hypnosis as a dissociated state. *International Journal of Clinical and Experimental Hypnosis, 7*, 187–204.

Ross, R. T. (1938). Studies in the psychology of the theater. *Psychological Record, 2,* 127–90.

Royce, J. (1898). The psychology of invention. *Psychological Review, 5,* 113–44.

Russow, L.-M. (1978). Some recent work on imagination. *American Philosophical Quarterly, 15,* 57–66.

Russow, L.-M. (1980). Towards a theory of imagination. *Southern Journal of Philosophy, 28,* 353–69.

Ryan, T. A. (1940). Interrelations of sensory systems in perception. *Psychological Bulletin, 37,* 659–98.

Ryle, G. (1949). *The concept of mind.* London: Hutchinson.

Sacerdote, P. (1967). *Induced dreams.* New York: Vantage Press.

Sadoski, M., & Paivio, A. (2001). *Imagery and text: A dual coding theory of reading and writing.* Mahwah, NJ: Erlbaum.

Saint-Alban, D. (1978). *Déjà vu: A novel.* New York: St. Martin's Press.

Salisbury, R. (1968). Possession in the New Guinea highlands. *International Journal of Social Psychiatry, 14,* 113–18.

Sancar, F., & Macari, H. (1988). A situational research approach for discovering the meaning of city image. *Environmental Design Research Association, 19,* 93–98.

Santhouse, A., Howard, R., & Ffytche, D. (2000). Visual hallucinatory syndromes and the anatomy of the visual brain. *Brain, 123,* 2055–64.

Sarbin, T. (1972). Imagination as muted role taking. In P. Sheehan (Ed.), *The function and nature of imagery.* New York: Academic Press.

Sarbin, T., & Coe, W. (1972). *Hypnosis: A social psychological analysis of influence communication.* New York: Holt, Rinehart, & Winston.

Sarbin, T., & Juhasz, J. (1967). The historical background of the concept of hallucination. *Journal of the History of the Behavioural Sciences, 3,* 339–58.

Sarbin, T., & Juhasz, J. (1970). Toward a theory of imagination. *Journal of Personality, 38,* 52–76.

Sartre, J.-P. (1936). *Imagination: A psychological critique.* Ann Arbor, MI: University of Michigan Press.

Sartre, J.-P. (1940). *L'imaginaire.* Paris: Gallimard.

Sartre, J.-P. (1948). *The psychology of imagination.* New York: Philosophical Library.

Schacter, D. (1976). The hypnagogic state: A critical review of the literature. *Psychological Bulletin, 83,* 452–81.

Schaub, A. de Vries (1911). On the intensity of images. *American Journal of Psychology, 22,* 346–68.

Scheibel, M., & Scheibel, A. (1962). Hallucinations and the brain stem reticular core. In L. J. West (Ed.), *Hallucinations.* New York: Grune & Stratton.

Schilder, P. (1920). Uber halluzinationen. *Zeitschrift fur die Gesamte Neurologie und Psychiatrie, 53,* 169–73.

Schilder, P. (1935). *The image and appearance of the human body.* London: Kegan Paul.

Schiller, P. (1935). Interplay of different senses in perception. *British Journal of Psychology, 25,* 465–69.

Schliebe, G. (1932). On motor synesthesias. *Archiv fur die Gesamte Psychologie, 85,* 289–330.

Schneider, K. (1932). General psychopathology in 1931. *Fortschritte der Neurologie, Psychiatrie, und ihrer Grenzgebiete, 4,* 147–61.

Schofield, A. (1898). *The unconscious mind.* London: Allen & Unwin.

Schofield, M. (1978). Aristotle on the imagination. In G. Lloyd & G. Owen (Eds.), *Aristotle on the mind and the senses.* Cambridge, UK: Cambridge University Press.

Scholz, F., & Jowett, M. (1894). *Sleep and dreams.* New York: Funk & Wagnalls.

Schreiber, F. (1973). *Sybil.* Chicago: Regnery.

Schultes, R. E. (1966). The search for new natural hallucinogens. *Lloydia, 29,* 293–308.

Schwartz, G., & Shapiro, D. (Eds.) (1976). *Consciousness and self-regulation: Advances in research.* Vol. 1. New York: Plenum Press.

Schweikert, R. (1993). A multinomial processing tree model for degradation and redintegration in immediate recall. *Memory and Cognition, 21,* 168–75.

Schweikert, R., Chen, S., & Poirier, M. (1999). Redintegration and the useful lifetime of the verbal memory representation. *International Journal of Psychology, 34,* 447–53.

Scruton, R. (1974). *Art and imagination.* London: Methuen.

Seafield, F. (1865). *The literature and curiosities of dreams.* London: Murray.

Searle, J. (1992). *The rediscovery of the mind.* Cambridge, MA: M.I.T. Press.

Seashore, C. E. (1895). Measurements of illusions and hallucinations in normal life. *Studies from the Yale Psychological Laboratory, 3,* 1–20.

Seashore, C. E. (1938). Color music. *Music Educators Journal, 25,* 26.

Segal, S. (Ed.) (1971). *Imagery: Current cognitive approaches.* New York: Academic Press.

Seitz, P., & Molholm, H. (1947). Relation of mental imagery to hallucinations. *Archives of Neurology and Psychiatry, 57,* 469–80.

Self, H., & Rhodes, F. (1965). The effect of simulated aircraft speed on detecting and identifying targets from side-looking radar imagery. *USAF Aerospace Medical Research Laboratories Technical Documentary Report, 64–40,* 1–18.

Sepper, D. (1996). *Descartes's imagination: Proportion, images, and the activity of thinking.* Berkeley, CA: University of California Press.

Seward, G. H. (1928). Recognition time as a measure of confidence: An experimental study of redintegration. Unpublished doctoral dissertation, Columbia University.

Shaler, N. (1879). Sleep and dreams. *International Review, 6,* 234–47.

Shallice, T. (1972). Dual functions of consciousness. *Psychological Review, 79,* 383–93.

Shand, A. (1888). The unity of consciousness. *Mind, 13,* 231–43.

Shand, A. (1891). The nature of consciousness. *Mind, 16,* 206–22.

Shapiro, J. (1993). Embedded image coding using zerotrees of wavelet coefficients. *IEEE Transactions on Signal Processing, 41,* 3445–63.

Sheehan, P. W. (1978). Mental imagery. In B. Foss (Ed.), *Psychology survey No. 1.* London: Allen & Unwin.

Sheehan, P. W., & Perry, C. (1976). *Methodologies of hypnosis: A critical appraisal of contemporary paradigms of hypnosis.* Hillsdale, NJ: Erlbaum.

Sheikh, A. A. (1984). Mental imagery. In R. J. Corsini (Ed.), *Encyclopedia of psychology.* Vol. 2. New York: Wiley.

Shepard, R. N. (1975). Form, formation, and transformation of internal representations. In R. Solso (Ed.), *Information processing and cognition.* Hillsdale, NJ: Erlbaum.

Shepard, R. N. (1978). The mental image. *American Psychologist, 33,* 125–37.

Shepard, R. N., & Cooper, L. (1982). *Mental images and their transformations.* Cambridge, MA: M.I.T. Press.

Shor, R. E. (1960). The frequency of naturally occurring "hypnotic-like" experiences in the normal college population. *International Journal of Clinical and Experimental Hypnosis, 8,* 151–63.

Shor, R. E. (1970). The three-factor theory of hypnosis as applied to the book-reading fantasy and the concept of suggestion. *International Journal of Clinical and Experimental Hypnosis, 18,* 89–98.

Shore, B. (1991). Twice-born, once conceived: Meaning construction and cultural cognition. *American Anthropologist, 1,* 9–28.

Shorter, J. (1952). Imagination. *Mind, 61,* 528–42.

Sidgwick, H. (1894). Report on the census of hallucinations. *Proceedings of the Society for Psychical Research, 26,* 25–422.

Sidis, B. (1898/1973). *The psychology of suggestion.* New York: Arno Press.

Sidis, B. (Ed.) (1902). *Psychopathological researches: Study in mental dissociation.* New York: Stechert.

Siegel, R., & West, L. (Eds.) (1975). *Hallucinations: Behavior, experience, and theory.* New York: Wiley.

Silberer, H. (1909/1951). Report on a method of eliciting and observing certain symbolic hallucination-phenomena. In D. Rapaport (Ed.), *Organization and pathology of thought: Selected sources.* New York: Columbia University Press.

Silz, W. (1942). Heine's synesthesia. *Publications, Modern Language Association of America, 57,* 469–88.

Simpson, L., & McKellar, P. (1955). Types of synaesthesia. *Journal of Mental Science, 101,* 141–47.

Simpson, R., Quinn, M., & Ausubel, D. (1956). Synesthesia in children: Association of colors with pure tone frequencies. *Journal of Genetic Psychology, 89,* 95–104.

Singer, D., & Singer, J. L. (1990). *The house of make-believe: Children's play and the developing imagination.* Cambridge, MA: Harvard University Press.

Singer, J. L. (1966). *Daydreaming: An introduction to the experimental study of inner experience.* New York: Random House.

Singer, J. L. (1975). *The inner world of daydreaming.* New York: Harper & Row.

Singer, J. L. (1999). Imagination. In M. A. Runco & S. R. Pritzer (Eds.), *Encyclopedia of creativity.* Vol. 2. San Diego, CA: Academic Press.

Singer, J. L. (2000). Imagination. In A. E. Kazdin (Ed.), *Encyclopedia of psychology.* Vol. 4. New York: Oxford University Press.

Singer, J. L., & Bonanno, G. (1990). Personality and private experience: Individual variations in consciousness and in attention to subjective phenomena. In L. Pervin (Ed.), *Handbook of personality.* New York: Guilford Press.

Skinner, B. F. (1934). Has Gertrude Stein a secret? *Atlantic Monthly, 153,* 50–57.

Skinner, B. F. (1976). *About Behaviorism.* New York: Vintage Books.

Slezak, P. (1993). Artificial imagery? *Computational Intelligence, 9,* 349–52.

Slezak, P., Caelli, T., & Clark, R. (Eds.) (1995). *Perspectives on cognitive science: Theories, experiments, and foundations.* Stamford, CT: Ablex.

Smith, O. (1898–1899). Evolution of consciousness. *Monist, 9,* 219–33.

Sno, H. N. (1993). The déjà vu experience: A psychiatric perspective. Unpublished doctoral dissertation, University of Amsterdam.

Sno, H. N., & Draaisma, D. (1993). An early Dutch study of déjà vu experiences. *Psychological Medicine, 23,* 17–26.

Sno, H. N., & Linszey, D. H. (1990). The déjà vu experience: Remembrance of things past? *American Journal of Psychiatry, 147,* 1587–95.

Sno, H. N., Linszey, D. H., & DeJonghe, F. (1992). Déjà vu experiences and reduplicative paramnesia. *British Journal of Psychiatry, 161,* 565–68.

Sno, H. N., Schalken, H., DeJonghe, F., & Koeter, M. (1994). The Inventory of Déjà Vu Experiences Assessment: Development, utility, reliability, and validity. *Journal of Nervous and Mental Disease, 182,* 27–36.

Sober, E. (1976). Mental representations. *Synthese, 33,* 101–48.

Souriau, P. (1901). *L'imagination de l'artiste*. Paris: Hachette.

Spanos, N., & McPeake, J. (1975). Involvement in everyday imaginative activities, attitudes towards hypnosis, and hypnotic suggestibility. *Journal of Personality and Social Psychology, 31*, 594–98.

Spanos, N., McPeake, J., & Churchill, B. (1976). Relationships between imaginative ability variables and the Barber Suggestibility Scale. *American Journal of Clinical Hypnosis, 19*, 39–46.

Sparshott, F. (1990). Imagination—the very idea. *The Journal of Aesthetics and Art Criticism, 48*, 1–8.

Spatt, J. (2002). Déjà vu: Possible parahippocampal mechanisms. *Journal of Neuropsychiatry and Clinical Neurosciences, 14*, 6–10.

Specht, W. (1914). Wahrnehmung und halluzinationen. *Monatschrift fur Psychiatrie und Neurologie, 62*, 31–50.

Speir, F. (1887–1888). The antechamber of consciousness. *Popular Science Monthly, 32*, 657–68.

Sperling, G. (1960). The information available in brief visual presentations. *Psychological Monographs, 74*, 1–29.

Sperry, R. (1969). A modified concept of consciousness. *Psychological Review, 76*, 532–36.

Spiegel, D. (Ed.) (1994). *Dissociation: Culture, mind, and body*. Washington, DC: American Psychiatric Press.

Squires, J. (1968). Visualising. *Mind, 77*, 58–67.

Standing, L., Bond, B., Hall, J., & Weller, J. (1972). A bibliography of picture-memory studies. *Psychonomic Science, 29*, 406–16.

Stanley, H. (1899). Artificial dreams. *Science, 9*, 263–64.

Stark, J. (2000). Adaptive image contrast enhancement using generalizations of histogram equalization. *IEEE Transactions on Image Processing, 9*, 889–96.

Sterelny, K. (1986). The imagery debate. *Philosophy of Science, 53*, 560–83.

Stetson, R. (1896). Types of imagination. *Psychological Review, 3*, 398–411.

Stevens, S. S. (1935). A demonstration of positive and negative visual after-images. *American Journal of Psychology, 47*, 497–98.

Stevenson, J. (1972). The effect of hypnotic and posthypnotic dissociation on the performance of interfering tasks. *Dissertation Abstracts International, 33*, 8-B, 3998.

Stevenson, J. (1976). The effect of posthypnotic dissociation on the performance of interfering tasks. *Journal of Abnormal Psychology, 85*, 398–407.

Stoddart, W.H.B. (1926). *Mind and its disorders*. London: Lewis.

Stout, G. F. (1896). *Analytic psychology*. London: Sonnenschein.

Strawson, P. (1970). Imagination and perception. In L. Foster & J. Swanson (Eds.), *Experience and theory*. London: Duckworth.

Suarez de Mendoza, F. (1890). *L'audition coloree.* (Publisher not known).

Sully, J. (1876). On the laws of dream fancy. *Cornhill Magazine, 34,* 555–76.

Sully, J. (1889). Dreams as related to literature. *Forum, 7,* 67–89.

Sully, J. (1893). The dream as a revelation. *Fortnightly Review, 59,* 354–65.

Sutcliffe, J. (1961). "Credulous" and "skeptical" views of hypnotic phenomena: Experiments on esthesia, hallucination, and delusion. *Journal of Abnormal and Social Psychology, 46,* 678–82.

Sutcliffe, J., Perry, C., & Sheehan, P. (1970). The relation of some aspects of imagery and fantasy to hypnotizability. *Journal of Abnormal Psychology, 76,* 279–87.

Sutherland, M. (1971). *Everyday imagining and education.* London: Routledge & Kegan Paul.

Sutherland, S. (1996). *International dictionary of psychology.* New York: Crossroad.

Swindle, P. F. (1917). Visual, cutaneous, and kinaesthetic ghosts. *American Journal of Psychology, 28,* 349–72.

Symonds, J. (1851). *Sleep and dreams.* London: J. Murray.

Taejeong, K. (1992). Side match and overlap match vector quantizers for images. *IEEE Transactions on Image Processing, 1,* 170–86.

Talbot, E. B. (1895). The doctrine of conscious elements. *Philosophical Review, 4,* 154–66.

Talbot, E. B. (1896). An attempt to train the visual memory. *American Journal of Psychology, 8,* 414–17.

Tallman, O. (1970). Processing of visual imagery by an adaptive model of the visual system: Its performance and its significance. *U.S. AFHRD Technical Report, 70-45,* 1–43.

Tart, C. (1965a). The hypnotic dream: Methodological problems and a review of the literature. *Psychological Bulletin, 63,* 87–99.

Tart, C. (1965b). Toward the experimental control of dreaming: A review of the literature. *Psychological Bulletin, 64,* 81–91.

Tart, C. (1966). Types of hypnotic dreams and their relation to hypnotic depth. *Journal of Abnormal Psychology, 71,* 377–82.

Tart, C. (Ed.) (1969). *Altered states of consciousness.* New York: Wiley.

Tart, C. (1972). Measuring the depth of an altered state of consciousness, with particular reference to self-report scales of hypnotic depth. In E. Fromm & R. Shor (Eds.), *Hypnosis: Research developments and perspectives.* Chicago: Aldine-Atherton.

Tart, C. (1975). *States of consciousness.* New York: Dutton.

Taylor, P. (1981). Imagination and information. *Philosophy and Phenomenological Research, 42,* 205–23.

Taylor, S.E.L. (Ed.) (1932). *Fox-Taylor automatic writing, 1869–1892. Unabridged record.* Minneapolis, MN: Tribune-Great West Printing Company.

Taylor, W., & Martin, M. (1944). Multiple personality. *Journal of Abnormal and Social Psychology, 39*, 281–300.

Thale, T., Westcott, G., & Salomon, K. (1950). Hallucinations and imagery induced by mescaline. *American Journal of Psychiatry, 106*, 686–91.

Thibault, E. (1899). Etude de psychologie morbide: Essai psychologique et clinique sur la sensation du "déjà vu." Unpublished doctoral dissertation, University of Bordeaux.

Thigpen, C., & Cleckley, H. (1957). *The three faces of Eve.* New York: McGraw-Hill.

Thomas, J., & Sadacca, R. (1967). Rapid screening of tactical imagery as a function of display time. *U.S. Army BESRL Technical Research Note, 189*, 1–23.

Thomas, N.J.T. (1987). The psychology of perception, imagination, and mental representation, and twentieth century philosophies of science. Unpublished doctoral dissertation, University of Leeds (UK).

Thomas, N.J.T. (1989). Experience and theory as determinants of attitudes toward mental representation: The case of Knight Dunlap and the vanishing images of J. B. Watson. *American Journal of Psychology, 102*, 395–412.

Thomas, N.J.T. (1997a). Imagery and the coherence of imagination: A critique of White. *Journal of Philosophical Research, 22*, 95–127.

Thomas, N.J.T. (1997b). Mental imagery. In E. Zalta (Ed.), *The Stanford encyclopedia of philosophy.* Palo Alto, CA: Stanford University Press (www document; URL: http://plato.stanford.edu/entries/mental-imagery/).

Thomas, N.J.T. (1998). Imagination, eliminativism, and the pre-history of consciousness. Paper presented at the Toward a Science of Consciousness Conference (Tucson III), Tucson, AZ, April 30, 1998.

Thomas, N.J.T. (1999a). Are theories of imagery theories of imagination? *Cognitive Science, 23*, 207–45.

Thomas, N.J.T. (1999b). Imagination. In C. Eliasmith (Ed.), *Dictionary of philosophy of mind* (www document; URL: http://www.artsci.wustl.edu/~philos/MindDict/imagination.html).

Thomas, N.J.T. (2000). A non-symbolic theory of conscious content: Imagery and activity. Paper presented at the Tucson 2000 Conference (Toward a Science of Consciousness), Tucson, AZ, April 14, 2000.

Titchener, E. B. (1895). Dreams of tasting. *American Journal of Psychology, 6*, 505–9. (Cf. Murray, 1894.)

Titchener, E. B. (1909/1973). *Lectures on the experimental psychology of the thought processes.* New York: Arno Press.

Tononi, G., & Edelman, G. (1998). Consciousness and complexity. *Science, 282*, 1846–51.

Tordon, D. (1917). The colour of letters. *Science, 46*, 311.

Trustman, R., Dubovsky, S., & Titley, R. (1977). Auditory perception during general anesthesia—myth or fact? *International Journal of Clinical and Experimental Hypnosis, 25*, 88–105.

Tryon, T. (1697). *A treatise of dreams and visions.* London: T. Salusbury.

Turner, J., Henry, L., & Smith, P. (2000). The development of the use of long-term knowledge to assist short-term recall. *Quarterly Journal of Experimental Psychology, 53*, 457–78.

Tweedale, M. (1990). Mental representations in later Medieval scholasticism. In J.-C. Smith (Ed.), *Historical foundations of cognitive science.* Dordrecht, Netherlands: Kluwer.

Tweney, R., Doherty, M., & Mynatt, C. (Eds.) (1981). *On scientific thinking.* New York: Columbia University Press.

Tye, M. (1984). The debate about mental imagery. *Journal of Philosophy, 81*, 678–91.

Tye, M. (1988). The picture theory of mental images. *Philosophical Review, 97*, 497–520.

Tye, M. (1991). *The imagery debate.* Cambridge, MA: M.I.T. Press.

Tyndall, J. (1872). On the scientific use of the imagination. In J. Tyndall (Ed.), *Fragments of science.* London: Longmans, Green.

Uhlich, E. (1957). Synesthesia in the two sexes. *Zeitschrift fur Experimentelle und Angewandte Psychologie, 4*, 31–57.

Ullman, M., Krippner, S., & Vaughan, A. (1973). *Dream telepathy.* New York: Macmillan.

Underwood, H. (1960). The validity of hypnotically induced hallucinations. *Journal of Abnormal and Social Psychology, 61*, 39–46.

Van Biervliet, J. J. (1927). *La psychologie d'aujourd'hui.* Paris: Alcan. (Also see review by J. Peterson, *American Journal of Psychology.* [1929]. *41*, 483–86.)

Van't Hoff, J. (1878/1967). *Imagination in science.* Berlin: Springer-Verlag.

Vaschide, N., & Pieron, H. (1901). Prophetic dreams in Greek and Roman antiquity. *Monist, 11*, 161–94.

Vernon, P. E. (1930). Synaesthesia in music. *Psyche, 10*, 22–39.

Vold, J. M. (1896). Visual images in dreams. *Science, 4*, 646.

Von Eckardt, B. (1988). Mental images and their explanations. *Philosophical Studies, 53*, 441–60.

Voss, W. (1929). Colored hearing in persons who have lost their vision. *Archiv fur die Gesamte Psychologie, 73*, 407–524.

Walk, R. D. (1984). Illusions. In R. J. Corsini (Ed.), *Encyclopedia of psychology.* Vol. 2. New York: Wiley.

Waller, J. (1816). *A treatise on the incubus or nightmare, disturbed sleep, terrific dreams, and nocturnal visions.* London: Parker.

Warnock, M. (1976). *Imagination.* London: Faber and Faber.

Warren, H. C. (Ed.) (1934). *Dictionary of psychology.* Cambridge, MA: Houghton-Mifflin.

Washburn, M. F. (1916). *Movement and mental imagery: Outlines of a motor theory of the complexer mental processes*. Boston: Houghton Mifflin.

Watson, G. (1988). *Phantasia in classical thought*. Galway, Ireland: Galway University Press.

Watson, J. B. (1930). *Behaviorism*. Chicago: University of Chicago Press.

*Webster's New Universal Unabridged Dictionary*. (1989). New York: Barnes & Noble.

*Webster's Third New International Dictionary, Unabridged*. (1993). Springfield, MA: Merriam-Webster, Inc.

Wedin, M. (1988). *Mind and imagination in Aristotle*. New Haven, CT: Yale University Press.

Weed, S., Hallam, F., & Phinney, E. (1896). A study of dream-consciousness. *American Journal of Psychology, 7*, 405–11.

Wehofer, F. (1913). Farbenhoren (chromatische phonopsien) bei musik. *Zeitschrift fur Angewandte Psychologie, 7*, 1–54.

Weitzenhoffer, A. (1953). *Hypnotism: An objective study of suggestibility*. New York: Wiley.

Wekker, L. (1966). On the basic properties of the mental image and a general approach to their analogue simulation. In *Psychological research in the U.S.S.R.* Moscow: Progress Publishers.

Wellek, A. (1930). Contributions to the problem of synesthesia: General review. *Archiv fur die Gesamte Psychologie, 76*, 193–201.

Wellek, A. (1931a). History and critique of the research on synesthesia. *Archiv fur die Gesamte Psychologie, 79*, 325–84.

Wellek, A. (1931b). Synesthesia in occidental antiquity and the middle ages. *Archiv fur die Gesamte Psychologie, 80*, 120–66.

Wellek, A. (1935). Color harmony and the color piano. *Archiv fur die Gesamte Psychologie, 94*, 348–75.

Wells, W. (1940). Ability to resist artificially induced dissociation. *Journal of Abnormal and Social Psychology, 35*, 261–72.

Werner, H. (1930). Research in the field of sensation. I. The problem of sensation and the experimental methods used in its study. *Zeitschrift fur Psychologie, 114*, 152–66.

Werner, H. (1934). The unity of the senses. *Journal de Psychologie, 31*, 190–205.

West, L. (Ed.) (1962). *Hallucinations*. New York: Grune and Stratton.

Wheeler, R. H. (1920). The synaesthesia of a blind subject. *University of Oregon Publications, 1*, 1–61.

Wheeler, R. H., & Cutsforth, T. (1922a). Synaesthesia and meaning. *American Journal of Psychology, 33*, 361–84.

Wheeler, R. H., & Cutsforth, T. (1922b). Synaesthesia of a blind subject. *University of Oregon Publications, 3*, 104.

Wheeler, R. H., & Cutsforth, T. (1925). Synaesthesia in the development of the concept. *Journal of Experimental Psychology, 8*, 149–59.

Wheeler, R. H., & Cutsforth, T. (1928). Synaesthesia in judging and choosing. *Journal of General Psychology, 1,* 497–519.

Whipple, G. M. (1900). Two cases of synaesthesia. *American Journal of Psychology, 11,* 377–404.

Whipple, G. M. (1901, 1902). An analytic study of the memory image and the process of judgment in the discrimination of clangs and tones. *American Journal of Psychology, 12,* 409–57; *13,* 219–68.

White, A. (1989). Imaginary imagining. *Analysis, 49,* 81–83.

White, A. (1990). *The language of imagination.* Oxford, UK: Blackwell.

White, R. W., & Shevach, B. J. (1942). Hypnosis and the concept of dissociation. *Journal of Abnormal Psychology, 37,* 309–28.

Whitty, C., & Zangwill, O. (Eds.) (1966). *Amnesia.* New York: Appleton-Century-Crofts.

Whyte, L. (1960). *The unconscious before Freud.* New York: Basic Books.

Wickramesekera, I. (1976). *Biofeedback, behavior therapy, and hypnosis.* Chicago: Nelson-Hall.

Wiles, J., & Dartnall, T. (Eds.) (1999). *Perspectives on cognitive science II: Theories, experiments, and foundations.* Stamford, CT: Ablex.

Wilkes, K. V. (1988). Consciousness. In A. J. Marcel & E. Bisiach (Eds.), *Consciousness in contemporary science,* pp. 16–41. UK: Oxford University Press.

Wilkes, K. V. (1995). Losing consciousness. In T. Metzinger (Ed.), *Conscious experience,* pp. 97–106. Lawrence, KS: Allen Press.

Wilks, S. (1894). On the nature of dreams. *Medical Magazine, London, 2,* 597–606.

Willmorth, N., & Birnbaum, A. (1967). Influence of screening and overlapping image on speed and accuracy of photo interpretation. *U.S. Army BESRL Technical Research Note, 182,* 1–37.

Wilson, A. (1884). What are dreams made of? *Gentleman's Magazine, 33,* 279–98. (Cf. Clymer, 1885; Ellis, 1899; Robinson, 1893.)

Wiltse, S. (1890). Mental imagery of boys. *American Journal of Psychology, 3,* 144–48.

Witt, R. (1900). The imaginative faculty. *Westminster Review, 154,* 217–22.

Wolberg, L. (1945). *Hypnoanalysis.* New York: Grune and Stratton.

Wolman, B. (Ed.) (1973). *Dictionary of behavioral science.* New York: Van Nostrand Reinhold.

Wolman, B. (Ed.) (1989). *Dictionary of behavioral science.* 2d ed. San Diego, CA: Academic Press.

Woodbridge, F. (1905). The nature of consciousness. *Journal of Philosophy, 2,* 119–25.

Woodruff-Pak, D. (1999). Review of "Toward a science of consciousness II. The Second Tucson Discussions and Debates." *Journal of Cognitive Neuroscience, 11,* 132–35.

Woodworth, R. S. (1897). Note on the rapidity of dreams. *Psychological Review, 4*, 524–26.

Woodworth, R. S. (1906). Imageless thought. *Journal of Philosophy, Psychology, and Scientific Methods, 3*, 701–8.

Woodworth, R. S. (1938). *Experimental psychology.* New York: Holt.

Woodworth, R. S., & Schlosberg, H. (1965). *Experimental psychology.* Revised edition. New York: Holt, Rinehart, & Winston.

*World Book Encyclopedia.* (1999). Chicago: World Book.

Wright, E. (1983). Inspecting images. *Philosophy, 58*, 57–72.

Wu, X. (1992). Image coding by adaptive tree-structured segmentation. *IEEE Transactions on Information Theory, 38*, 1755–68.

Wundt, W. (1876). Central innervation and consciousness. *Mind, 1*, 161–78.

Wundt, W. (1896). *Grundriss der psychologie.* Leipzig: Engelmann.

Zaretsky, I., & Leone, M. (Eds.) (1974). *Religious movements in contemporary America.* Princeton, NJ: Princeton University Press.

Zeman, A. (2001). Consciousness. *Brain, 124*, 1263–89.

Zietz, K. (1931). Mutual influences of color and sound experiences: Studies in experimentally induced synesthesia. *Zeitschrift fur Psychologie, 121*, 257–356.

Zietz, K. (1935). The problem of synesthesia and the question of the disintegrated type. *Zeitschrift fur Psychologie, 125*, 348–401.

Zigler, M. J. (1930). Tone shapes: A novel type of synaesthesia. *Journal of General Psychology, 3*, 277–87.

Zikmund, V. (1972). Physiological correlates of visual imagery. In P. W. Sheehan (Ed.), *The function and nature of imagery.* New York: Academic Press.

Zucker, K. (1930). Versuche mit meskalin am halluzinanten. *Zeitschrift fur die Gesamte Neurologie und Psychiatrie, 127*, 108–26.

Zucker, K., & Zador, J. (1930). Zur analyse der meskalin—wirkung am normalen. *Zeitschrift fur die Gesamte Neurologie und Psychiatrie, 127*, 15–29.

Zusne, L. (1975). *Names in the history of psychology: A biographical sourcebook.* Washington, DC: Hemisphere Publishing.

Zusne, L. (1984). *Biographical dictionary of psychology.* Westport, CT: Greenwood Press.

# Chapter 2

# *Origins and Evolution of Imagery*

Rock carvings and paintings are designs inscribed on rock surfaces and huge stone monuments in many parts of the world and attributed to primitive man. They have been found on every continent and are usually from prehistoric times. Petroglyphs (rock carvings) are more widespread than pictographs (rock paintings). . . . It is thought that these designs were created for purposes of religious propitiation and sympathetic magic.

         —W. H. Harris and J. S. Levey, 1975

Genesis 1: 26–27. Then God said, "Let Us make man in Our image, according to Our likeness.". . . So God created man in His own image, in the image of God He created him; male and female He created them.

      —*Holy Bible: The New King James Version*, 1984

Those who reject the worship of images call such images "idols" and their veneration "idolatry," holding that they are honored in the place of the true God, and that such worship is highly offensive to God . . . the question of using images or not has been the stuff of bitter religious conflict and even bloody persecution. . . . Two different views of religion, and of the relation to religion of works of art and of the visual senses, lie behind the conflict. Do we use that which is seen, and is made by human hands usually in human form, to lift us to the sacred, because the sacred can in fact live in humans as gods, buddhas, and saints? Or do we find God best by taking away all that is not God, all that is man-made, worshipping him only as spirit and with the help only of words, not of things seen? These are questions that still divide the religious world.

—R. S. Ellwood, 1998

## IMAGES AND IMAGERY IN ANTIQUITY AND IN THE BIBLE

When one focuses on the definitional domain of image in terms of a "likeness, copy, reproduction, or duplicate," and the domain of mental imagery as "a cognitive process where the image is a visual reproduction of an earlier event involving a construction or synthesis of a previously seen stimulus" (e.g., Reber, 1995), then some of the earliest sources and records of physical evidence for imagery in primitive humans are the crude cave paintings and the Paleolithic ("Old Stone Age") art found in Western Europe, especially in the cave paintings in Northern Spain and the Dordogne Valley of southwestern France (cf. Breuil, 1952). It may be mentioned at this point—in this chapter on the "origins" of imagery—that the emphasis in the present section is on a *phylogenetic* analysis of image/imagery and *not* on an *ontogenetic* one. That is, the present section focuses on how people—collectively, as a group—came to view, employ, or regard image(s) and imagery (as well as their symbolic/pictorial significance), and not on how the person—individually—creates, experiences, or demonstrates imagery. For the latter perspective, I provide discussions in the next section of this chapter, as well as in chapters 3 and 4, and how one "has" an image/imagery (cf. Rosenow's [1918] article, "The Genesis of the Image"; and Kosslyn's [1980] chapter 4, "The Origins of Images"—both of which may be considered as involving ontogenetic analyses).

Harris and Levey (1975) note that most of the classical cave-wall paintings were produced during the two vast and overlapping periods of the Aurignacio-Perigordian period (c. 14,000–c. 13,500 B.C.) and the Solutreo-Magdalenian period (c. 14,000–c. 9,500 B.C.). The former period encompasses the powerful Lascaux cave paintings, the outdoor sculpture at Laussel, and the several small female figurines (known as "Venuses") found at several sites; the latter period includes the murals at Rouffignac and Niaux and the cave-ceiling paintings at Altamira, Spain. Both of the great cave-complex masterpiece paintings were discovered by accident: Altamira in 1879 and Lascaux in 1940. The style of the cave paintings is known as "Franco-Cantabrian" and is attributed to Cro-Magnon Man; a variety of styles (thirteen at

Lascaux alone) and techniques are demonstrated in the cave paintings (involving skill and the use of foreshortening and shadowing) that include painting with fingers, sticks, pads of moss or fur; dotting, daubing, and sketching with charcoal and colored materials; and "spray painting" via mouth or hollow bone. The compositions typically show images of animals crowded close to, and on top of, each other, and often include respect for previously applied paintings. In most of the Paleolithic period cave paintings, elegant and simply drawn animal figures (e.g., bison, cattle, horses) predominate, thus suggesting that primitive humans' art and imagery may have contained ritual, ceremonial, sacred, or religious significance that was related to the fundamental activity of hunting. Moreover, depictions of human figures are extremely rare as are group/hunting scenes. Another style of imagery in paintings dominates in eastern Spain and has a strong resemblance to the rock carvings and paintings found in northern and southern Africa; in this case, the pictures are drawn mainly in silhouette, are located on the walls of small, shallow rock shelters, and depict human (as well as animal) figures in scenes of fighting, hunting, ritual, ceremonial, and domestic activities (cf. "Imagery and Subject Matter" in the "History of Painting" in *New Encyclopaedia Britannica, Macropaedia*, vol. 25 [1997], pp. 331–33). Other images are manifest in small sculptured figures and animals and humans found in regions from France to western Siberia and are largely of Aurignacian origin. In this case, the human figures are chiefly female, are often unusually voluptuous, and are regarded typically as fertility goddesses; the "Venus of Willendorf" (in Austria) is one of the most famous of the fertility figures.

Harris and Levey (1975) note that primitive rock carvings (petroglyphs) and rock paintings (pictographs)—which are preserved mainly in dry regions, inside caves and under overhanging cliffs—were created most likely for propitiation of the gods and for use in sympathetic magic and ritual/religious ceremonies. According to Harris and Levey, whatever the early humans' true motives in their use of images and imagery may have been, the prehistoric "artist" reached great aesthetic heights—such as in the Paleolithic art of western Europe, the rock figures attributed to the San of South Africa, and the Tassili cliff paintings discovered in the central Sahara (which suggests that this was once a fertile, and habitable, region). Similar evidence was found in the Alps of northern Italy; the images typically depict wild animals and hunting scenes, whereas the scenes of daily life were shown alongside representations of deities and religious ceremonies. In Neolithic times

(c. 8,000–9,000 B.C.), cows and herdsmen appear in the artistic productions, but rock art seems to have declined and disappeared with
the development of agriculture. Harris and Levey observe that in
Europe and Africa the artistic style was largely "naturalistic," while in
the Americas and Australia the designs were more frequently geometric
or "symbolic" and often approximated a primitive form of writing.

Thus, briefly, images and imagery—as embodied in the earliest
human prelinguistic or preliterate creations involving cave paintings,
rock carvings and paintings, and small sculptures—dates back to the
Paleolithic, or Old Stone Age, period that began about 2 million years
ago and ended in various places between 40,000 and 10,000 years ago.
Harris and Levey (1975) suggest that the most outstanding feature
of the Paleolithic period was the evolution of humans from apelike
creatures, or near humans, to true *Homo sapiens*. In this context, then,
the prehistoric presence of images and imagery is as old as the initial
appearance of the first humans (engaged predominantly in hunting
activities) on earth.

In this chapter, I attempt to trace the origins, functions, and significance of imagery from the employment of images in some of the
earliest sacred records and writings of humans—primarily those of the
Bible—up through the earliest philosophical accounts of imagery to
the premodern accounts of imagery as seen in various early psychological studies of imagery from 1890 through 1959. (Because my
concern and emphasis in this book is mainly on an account of images
and imagery from a *psychological*—rather than an *artistic/pictorial*—
viewpoint, I refrain from making extended analyses of images and
imagery from an art-historian's perspective—a singular topic or approach that would, in itself, take many volumes to cover. In this regard, it may be useful to consult Samuels and Samuels's [1975,
pp. 20–37] chapter 3, "A Brief History of Imagery in Religion, Healing, and Psychology" that includes the following topics: Egyptian and
Hermetic philosophy; Sumarian fertility gods; Patanjali's *Yoga Sutras*;
Tantric visualizations: mandalas; Old Testament visualizations; basic
Christian visualizations; Shamanistic healing rituals; Egyptian medicine; Paracelsus; Christian Science healing; and twentieth-century research in physiology, the image in psychology, and the image in
psychiatry. I suggest at this point only that it is significant for the
present discussion to recognize that imagery apparently had its origins in our preliterate—but artistic—ancestors, most likely those flour-
ishing in the late Paleolithic period.)

In his account of image/imagery in *The Interpreter's Dictionary of the Bible*, V. H. Kooy (1962/1986) notes that imagery is a graphic description or pictorial representation of reality and truth, as opposed to abstract thought. He observes, further, that Orientals traditionally had a love for the concrete and typically expressed their ideas pictorially, without conducting a metaphysical search for absolute goodness, beauty, or truth. Likewise, the Hebrews typically searched for "practical" truth and goodness in the present experience and in existing circumstances. In biblical terms, greed was portrayed by a picture of a greedy man, love by an example of loving, and fear by an image or experience of terror. With such usage of imagery, the distinction between the historical and the imaginative, or between fact and figure, is not clear-cut, and this makes the problem of understanding the actual historical facts of the Bible extremely difficult (it also accounts for the frequent use of story, parable, and proverb in biblical teachings).

Kooy (1962/1986) maintains that the secular and the sacred were one and the same for the ancient Hebrews: the phenomena of nature, the movements of men and of nations, and the woes and fortunes of life were related to God's direct action and control (cf. Isaiah 45: 5–7 where the Lord says "There is no other," "Besides Me there is no God," and "There is no one besides Me"; also, the Lord "causes well-being" and "creates calamity," and it is "The Lord who does all these." In Amos 3: 6, God's power and control are imaged in the question, "If a calamity occurs in a city has not the Lord done it?"). According to Kooy, such a perspective and belief about the world and the divine led to an abundance of anthropomorphisms in Hebraic writings and teachings. Moreover, the use of imagery in the Bible was expressive of the life of the Hebrews who lived between the desert and the sea, and who were dependent on the land for existence. Thus, the hopes, fears, and faith of the Hebrews—in all periods of their history, including nomadic, agricultural, dynastic, exilic, and colonial—are expressed in the imagery of the Bible.

Kooy (1962/1986) notes that the imagery in the Old Testament—based upon the most common and elemental aspects of life—is rich and expressive in its variety of metaphors. For example, God is described in the following diverse ways: as a *father* (e.g., Isaiah 1: 2; 50: 1); as a *husband* (e.g., Jeremiah 31: 32; Isaiah 54: 5; "Ishi," or "my husband" in Hosea 2: 16); as a *teacher* (e.g., Isaiah 28: 26); as a *healer* (e.g., Jeremiah 30: 17); as a *shepherd* (e.g., Psalm 23: 1; Jeremiah 31:

10); as a *judge* (e.g., Isaiah 2: 4; 33: 22); as a *lawgiver* and *king* (e.g., Isaiah 33: 22); as a *champion/warrior* (e.g., Jeremiah 20: 11); as a *winnower* (e.g., Jeremiah 15: 7); as a *farmer/husbandman/vineyardist/vinedresser* (e.g., Isaiah 5: 2–7); as a *smelter* (e.g., Isaiah 1: 25); as a *builder* (e.g., Jeremiah 31: 4); as a *harvester* (e.g., Jeremiah 8: 13); as a *giver of rain* (e.g, Jeremiah 5: 24); as a *leader of the blind* (e.g., Isaiah 42: 16); and as a *stranger/wayfarer* (e.g., Jeremiah 14: 8).

There is a variety of imagery and metaphor, also, in the Old Testament concerning the "chosen nation" status of Israel; for example, Israel is described and depicted in the following ways: as one who is *diseased* (Isaiah 1: 5–6); as a *faithless wife* (Jeremiah 3: 20); as a *wild vine* (Jeremiah 2: 21); as a *wild donkey* (Jeremiah 2: 24); as *well-fed lusty horses* (Jeremiah 5: 8); as *cows of Bashan* (Amos 4: 1); as *God's servant* (Jeremiah 30: 10), as *beloved* (Jeremiah 11: 15), as a *bride* (Jeremiah 2: 2), as a *vineyard* (Isaiah 5: 1–7), and as an *inheritance/heritage* (Jeremiah 12: 7–9).

Kooy (1962/1986) also observes that the New Testament of the Bible is as rich in imagery and metaphor as is the Old Testament. For instance, Jesus speaks of the kingdom of God/heaven in the imagery of a *man sowing seed* (Matthew 13: 24–30), as a *treasure hid in a field* (Matthew 13: 44), and as a *net cast into the sea* (Matthew 13: 44–50). Further, in the New Testament, Jesus finds spiritual truths in the imagery of a *shepherd seeking a lost sheep* (Luke 15: 4–7); as *children at play* (Luke 7: 31–35); as *men at prayer* (Luke 18: 9–14); and as a *woman preparing dough/leaven* (Matthew 13: 33). In the language and parables of the Bible, common and familiar things such as water, wine, wind, light, bread, salt, lamps, vines, and roads all become expressive of spiritual insights and truths where salvation is depicted in figures positioned in the spheres of the family, the slave market, the law court, the marketplace, the temple service, and the mystery cults (cf. a table listing the "Parables of Jesus" in the *New American Standard Bible: Study Bible*, 1999, p. 1493). Kooy (p. 682) suggests that the early biblical writers—via the use of the literary devices of imagery and metaphor—were able to relate matters such as religious-spiritual faith to the life situations and experiences of the people of an earlier era, but—on the other hand—it may present a problem of "distance" or "antiquity" to the modern, present-day interpreter of such imagery. Thus, the problem of interpretation and reinterpretation, and the issue of presenting the gospel in terms of contemporary imagery, is an ever-current need that, according to Kooy, is one of the most important tasks of the biblical scholar in helping to make spiritual truth and faith relevant for modern society.

In substantial entries under the rubric "Image Worship," both the ninth (1875) and eleventh (1922) editions of the *Encyclopaedia Britannica* provide further information on the relationship between images/imagery and religious/spiritual practices. The *Encyclopaedia Britannica* (1875) indicates that most religions of recorded history contain distinctive primitive periods in which "idols" were unknown; for example, in India, the worship of idols was only a secondary phenomenon that was a later degradation of the more primitive worship of ideal gods. Furthermore, various early Greek historians indicate an absence of religious images in the worship ceremonies of the ancient Greeks and Persians. Initially, in such cultures, the powers of nature were worshipped via natural symbols (e.g., trees, serpents, meteoric stones); however, in some cases, temples were built that contained no visible symbols at all. Moreover, even in the early Greek literature (e.g., Homer's epic poems of the eighth century B.C.), there is a paucity of allusions to images of the gods. The same situation seems to have been extant in the ancient Roman culture (e.g., the Greek biographer Plutarch, and later writers, indicate that—for about 170 years after the foundation of Rome in 753 B.C.—images were unknown). The date of the oldest statue in Rome—Diana on the Aventine—has been traced to a period between 577 and 534 B.C.; also, the ancient Germans (via the testimony of the Roman historian Tacitus in the first century A.D.) had gods that were invisible and, moreover, the Germans apparently had neither temples nor images at least up to the first century A.D.

The *Encyclopaedia Britannica* (1875) indicates that the Decalogue, or the Ten Commandments (see Exodus 20: 2–17), contains a clear directive (Exodus 20: 4, 5) against the making of any "idol," "carved image," or "graven image," at least for religious/worship purposes (cf. Deuteronomy 5: 8, 9; 4: 15–18). (The terminology concerning images here varies, depending on the particular version of the Bible that is consulted; for example, the *New American Standard Bible* [1999] uses the terms "graven image" and "idol" in the passages above, whereas the *Holy Bible: The New King James Version* [1984] uses the term "carved image.") The idols or images mentioned in the early books of the Old Testament refer to images of men, birds, fishes, reptiles, and quadrupeds—all of which had already become objects of religious veneration before the dicta of the Decalogue. However, apparently, little is known regarding imagery and various other objects (idols) of potential veneration mentioned in the Bible. For example, there is little certainty concerning the "foreign/strange gods" (alluded to in Genesis 35: 2, 4) that were buried by Jacob under the oak at Shechem, or the "teraphim/household gods" (see Genesis 31: 19) that Rachel stole (and that were her father's). In the latter case, "teraphims" were "household idols" that were small and portable, and are first mentioned in the Bible as having been worshipped in one of the branches of the family of Terah (cf. Joshua 24: 2; Judges 18: 30–31; and the "ephods"—sometimes a holy garment associated with the priesthood, and at other times a pagan object associated with idols—and household idols that are mentioned in Judges 17: 5). Rachel probably took the idols because she thought they would bring her protection and blessing—or, perhaps, she wanted to have something tangible to worship on her long journey ahead, a practice that was much referred to in the later writings of Josephus, a first-century Jewish historian; in any case, apparently, Rachel was not yet free of her "pagan background" (cf. *New American Standard Bible: Study Bible* [1999, p. 47, footnote 31: 19]).

Other biblical passages that refer to the use of teraphims, idols, and ephods at various stages throughout the history of both the Northern and Southern Kingdom are Isaiah 44: 9–17; Hosea 3: 4; Zechariah 10: 2; and 2 Kings 23: 24. Most often, the teraphims were probably rather small in size, but some biblical passages indicate that they sometimes may have been larger, even of human size and form (cf. 1 Samuel 19: 13, 16). The worship of calf images is also mentioned in the Old Testament (e.g., Exodus 32: 4) and was a prominent practice in the religion of the Northern Kingdom since the days of Jeroboam in the early years of 900 B.C. As observed in the *Encyclopaedia Britannica* (1875, p. 711), it is a disputed question concerning calf-image veneration whether the worshipping cult was of Egyptian (there was goat worship, also, by the Egyptians) or of purely Semitic origin.

The entry for "Image Worship" in the *Encyclopaedia Britannica* (1875) indicates that—on the question of the attitude toward religious images assumed by the primitive Christian Church—there can be no doubt that the early Christians were unanimous in their total condemnation of all heathen image-worship and the various immoral customs with which it was associated. A form of iconolatry especially deprecated in the New Testament was the then-prevalent adoration of the images of the reigning emperors (cf. Revelation 15: 2); a common accusation brought against the early Christians by their detractors and enemies was that they had no altars, no temples, no known images, and that they set up no image or form of any god. The *Encyclopaedia Britannica* (1875, pp. 711–14) further provides a lengthy account of the employment of images, idols, pictures, mosaics, statues, sculptures, and paintings in the history of the development of the Western Church and the Eastern Church.

In a completely rewritten entry for "Image Worship" in the eleventh edition of the *Encyclopaedia Britannica* (1922), it is suggested that the two religious votaries kneeling together before a sacred statue/object may hold widely different conceptions of what the extant image is and what it signifies, although the outward attitude of the two persons may be the same. For example, one person may regard the statue/object as a mere image, picture, or representation of a higher entity or being (much like a photograph of a loved one—cherished as a picture, and no more) that is, in itself, devoid of power or value. On the other hand, another person may regard the object as an animated being (much as a little girl regards her favorite doll) that is infused with "soul" and a quality of divinity. Historically, the Latin Church officially promoted certain attitudes in its members concerning sacred pictures, statues, images, and objects—that is, the images are intended to convey to the eyes of the faithful (especially to the illiterate among them) the history of Jesus, of the Virgin Mary, and of the saints. Moreover, in image-worship, images (or idols) are considered to be different, generically, from other religious and miraculous relics (such as fetishes, charms, talismans, or phylacteries) in that they actually *resemble* the power adored (i.e., they have a prototype that is capable of being brought before the eye of the visualizer—which is not necessarily the case with the worship of "unshaped" or "aniconic" gods). Worshippers who set up a sacred stone (or "bethel") believe that a divine power or influence enters the stone, and dwells in it, and they treat the stone as if it were the god itself, kissing it, anointing it with oils, and perhaps even feeding the god(s) within it by pouring out over it the sacrificial blood of slain victims.

Concerning image worship, the *Encyclopaedia Britannica* (1922) raises the questions, "Does the stage of aniconic gods historically precede, and lead up to, the use of pictures and images in the development of human religions—where one may find a 'law of transition' from sacred stock and stone up to picture and image?" and "Is the transition from sacred stone to picture/image a characteristic of a higher stage of religious development?" Early anthropologists postulated such a "law of development" based on the ease with which a pilar of stone or wood could be turned into an image by painting or sculpturing on it the features of eyes, ears, mouth, sexual organs, and so forth, but the facts do not seem to bear out such a scenario (e.g., the "higher" or more "advanced" and "mature" religions deliberately attach greater sanctity to aniconic gods than they do to iconic gods—and this was *not* a result due to artistic incapacity). Some religious faiths (e.g., Islam) embrace a prohibition of pictures and statues because it is felt that if you have a picture of someone, you have the power of harming him through it—it is as dangerous for your enemy to have a picture of you as for him to know your name. The old Hebrew prohibition of graven images was most likely based on a similar superstition, so far as it was not merely due to the physical impossibility for nomads to carry heavy statues from camp to camp and from pasture to pasture. Also, the Jews—possessing no images of Yahweh—were not exposed to the same risk as were idolaters of having their gods stolen by their foes and used against them. Furthermore, the restriction of aniconic worship saved many individuals from excessive superstition for there is nothing that so much stimulates the growth of a mythology as the manufacture of idols. In essence, according to the *Encyclopaedia Britannica* entry, image-worship is a sort of animism: it is a continuance by adults of their childish games with dolls. The old Greek statues moved by themselves, shook their spears, kneeled down, spoke, walked, wept, laughed, winked, and even bled and sweated. Images of Christ, the Virgin Mary, and the saints also have revealed many similar manifestations and miraculous behaviors to the devout.

In the *Illustrated Bible Dictionary* (1980), the term image is defined as "a material representation, usually of a deity," and—unlike the term *idol*, which has a pejorative aspect—image is "objectively descriptive." Throughout the ancient Near East, many images of various deities were discovered in temples and other holy places; many private households also contained a niche where the image of the protective deity of the house was placed. Images were most commonly anthropomorphic (human) or theriomorphic (animal) in form. The form of the image—especially of the theriomorphic type in Egypt—frequently represented some prominent characteristic of the specific deity; for example, an image of a bull depicted the god's power and fertility. A particular image was not intended, necessarily, as a visual representation of the deity, but·as a "dwelling place" of the deity's spirit that allowed the god to be physically present in many different locations simultaneously; thus, the image was usually a "projection" or "embodiment" of the deity. The early Israelites who denied any reality to the deity as represented by the image believed that the worshippers of foreign deities ("idolaters") were paying homage to mere stone or wood objects. Images were constructed in various ways: a *molten image* was cast in a mold from gold, silver, or copper and a *graven image* was carved from stone or wood (a wooden image was often overlaid with precious metals; see Isaiah 40: 19; cf. Isaiah 44: 15–17).

The *Illustrated Bible Dictionary* (1980) gives the following references to images and imagery in the Old Testament: *Images of foreign gods*—Exodus 20: 4–5; Jeremiah 10: 2–10; Hosea 11: 2; Judges 6: 25; 1 Kings 16: 31–33; 2 Kings 21: 3–7; *Images of Yahweh*—Genesis 28: 18–19, 22; Genesis 35: 14; Deuteronomy 16: 21; Genesis 31: 45; Joshua 4: 4–9; Exodus 32: 1–8; Judges 8: 26–27; 1 Kings 12: 28–30; Hosea 8: 4–6; and *Man as the image of God*—Genesis 1: 26–27; Genesis 5: 1–2; Genesis 9: 6 (cf. Berkouwer, 1962; Cairns, 1953; Smith, 1958). Also cited are references to images and imagery in the New Testament (where the emphasis falls on the person of Jesus Christ who is called the "image of God," and whose identification as the "image" of the Father derives from his unique relationship as "preexistent"; the term image, in this context, does not suggest a mere likeness to God or a paradigm of his person—rather, it connotes a sharing in the divine life and as an "objectivization" of the essence of God, where the One who is by nature invisible comes to visible expression in the figure of his Son): 1 Corinthians 11: 7; James 3: 9; 2 Corinthians 4: 4; Colossians 1: 15; Hebrews 1: 3; Philippians 2: 6–11; 1 Corinthians 15: 49; Romans 8: 29; 2 Corinthians 3: 18; 1 John 3: 2. The *Illustrated Bible Dictionary* (1980, p. 685) suggests that the term *image of God* is connected closely with the term *the new man* (Ephesians 4: 24; Colossians 3: 10; cf. Galatians 3: 28), and is a reminder in the Bible that there are important social aspects as to what the image means as it is reproduced in human lives—both in association with the church and in custodianship of nature. Additionally, there is a theological and eschatological dimension to the concept of image in the New Testament where the fulfillment of God's plan for "humanity-in-Christ" awaits the time when Christians' mortal existence will be transformed to a perfect likeness of their Lord (cf. 1

Corinthians 15: 49; Philippians 3: 20–21) and, in this way, the image of "God-in-man" will be restored completely.

In a substantial encyclopedic-type entry under the heading "Image of God," Porteous (1962/1986) discusses the biblical meaning of the term image of God via the evidence, linguistic considerations, and interpretations in the Old Testament, as well as the Pauline view in the New Testament, the traces of the Old Testament in the New Testament, and the New Testament transformation of the image of God idea. For example, Porteous notes that in Genesis 1: 26–27 the words image and *likeness* are used in an interchangeable, but inconsistent, way—which may complicate interpretation of the image of God notion. That is, either man *is* a concrete image of God—in respect of literal physical resemblance—where he may be made *after* an actual concrete model (*mental image*) of God, or man is not viewed in concrete-meaning terms of image but rather in a purely spiritual fashion that invokes words such as "personality," "self-consciousness," "self-determination," "immortality," "reason," "ability to pass judgment," "moral capacity," and "freedom of the will." Furthermore, in regard to sex/gender, Porteous suggests that it is possible that the clear separation in Genesis 1: 27 (i.e., "So God created man in His own image; in the image of God He created him; male and female He created them") of the statement about the distinction between man and woman from that about man's being made in the image of God may imply a rejection of the view found in a Sumerian liturgy that men and women were made after the image of a god and a goddess, respectively. Porteous maintains that the manner in which the creation of man is introduced in Genesis 1: 26 (and the fact that the passage in Genesis 9: 1–7 suggests that human life has a greater sanctity than animal life; cf. Leviticus 20: 15–16)—and where this creation is linked with the image of God—implies that the phrase image of God expresses in some way man's peculiar and unique dignity.

Other observations, conclusions, and notions examined by Porteous (1962/1986) are the following:

- If one starts with the possibility that Genesis portrays man as the image of God in the sense in which a statue may represent an absent ruler (cf. Daniel 3), it may be concluded that man acquires dignity and authority as God's representative.
- Man and animals are distinct and the difference must not be obscured (cf. Psalm 8: 4–8; Leviticus 20: 15–16).

- In the Old Testament, there is a curious oscillation between the belief that God cannot be seen and that he can be seen.
- In Genesis, the concept of "likeness" implies the concept of "distance."
- When one asserts external resemblance, it does not exclude or preclude spiritual resemblance (the Old Testament does not treat man as a duality of soul and body). Anthropomorphisms are used in the Bible in speaking of God and are not a sign of primitive thought.
- When the concrete term image is used in Genesis, it may well be an attempt to convey an abstract idea.
- One may not go far wrong if it is said that the image of God means "personality" (but *not* personality in the sense of the autonomous, self-legislating "self" of the philosophers)—and man is determined by God as his Creator where "image of God" means "what gives authority" which God has given man to exercise and, thereby, implies responsibility.
- In the New Testament, nothing makes clearer the tremendous impact of the revelation of God in Christ than the fact that it has almost completely obliterated the thought of man as being in the image of God and replaced it with the thought of Christ as being the image of God.

In his analysis of the Old Testament, Bruce (1981) notes that the word image translates a number of Hebrew words with different meanings as follows:

1. *Selem*—a copy or counterpart (e.g., Genesis 1: 26–27; 5: 3; 9: 6; Numbers 33: 52; 1 Samuel 6: 5, 11; 2 Kings 11: 18; Amos 5: 26; in Psalm 39: 6, this word is translated "vain shew," and "shadow" is not a good rendering)
2. *Semel*—a resemblance or likeness (e.g., Ezekiel 8: 3, 5; this word is rendered "figure" in Deuteronomy 4: 16 and "idol" in 2 Chronicles 33: 7, 15)
3. *Temunah*—a similitude (e.g., Job 4: 16; elsewhere as "likeness," Exodus 20: 4; or "similitude," Numbers 12: 8; Deuteronomy 4: 12, 15, 16; cf. "form" versus "likeness," Psalm 17: 15)
4. *Maskith*—a picture or representation (e.g., "image" in Leviticus 26: 1)
5. *Massebah*—a pillar (cf. Leviticus 26: 1; Micah 5: 13)
6. *Hammanim*—Canaanite incense altars (e.g., Leviticus 26: 30; 2 Chronicles 14: 5; 34: 4, 7; cf. Isaiah 17: 8; 27: 9; Ezekiel 6: 4, 6)
7. *Teraphim*—household gods (e.g., Judges 17: 5; 18: 14, 17, 18, 20; Hosea 3: 4; Genesis 31: 19; cf. 1 Samuel 19: 13, 16)
8. *Asabbim*—a contemptuous term translated as idols, images (e.g., 2 Samuel 5: 21; Jeremiah 50: 2)
9. *Gillulim*—a term of disparagement for idol blocks (e.g., Jeremiah 50: 2; Ezekiel 8: 10, 12)

10. *Elil*—worthlessness (a word often applied derisively to foreign gods; e.g., Jeremiah 14: 14; Zechariah 11: 17; Job 13: 4)
11. *Pesel*—graven image, carved image (e.g., Judges 18: 18; 2 Chronicles 33: 7, 22; 34: 3, 4)
12. *Massekhah*—molten/molded calf (e.g., Exodus 32: 4, 8; 34: 17; Deuteronomy 9: 12; Leviticus 19: 4; Isaiah 41: 29: 48: 5; Jeremiah 10: 14; 51: 17)

In an analysis of the use of the word image in the New Testament, Vine (1981) indicates that the Greek word *eikon* denotes an image and involves the two ideas of representation and manifestation. In the New Testament, the word *eikon* is used in a number of different ways: as an image or a coin (not a mere likeness)—Matthew 22: 20; Mark 12: 16; Luke 20: 24; as of a statue or similar representation (more than a resemblance)—Romans 1: 23; Revelation 13: 14, 15; 14: 9, 11; 15: 2; 16: 2; 19: 20; 20: 4; and of the descendants of Adam as bearing his image—1 Corinthians 15: 49. Other meanings of the word *eikon* in the New Testament are as of subjects relative to things spiritual—Hebrews 10:1 (the contrast in this passage has been likened to the difference between a statue and the shadow cast by it) and as of the relations between God the Father, Christ, and man (e.g., as of man as he was created as being a visible representation of God—1 Corinthians 11: 7, a being corresponding to the original); the condition of man as a fallen creature has not entirely effaced the image; he is still suitable to bear responsibility, he still has godlike qualities such as love of goodness and beauty—none of which are found in a mere animal; and as of Christ in relation to God—2 Corinthians 4: 4, the image of God, that is, essentially and absolutely the perfect expression and representation of the Archetype, God the Father; in Colossians 1: 15, the "image of the invisible God," that is, Christ is the visible representation and manifestation of God to created beings.

Vine (1981) cites other Greek words that are synonymous with *eikon* (image): *homoioma*—likeness, stresses the resemblance to an archetype, though the resemblance may not be derived, whereas *eikon* is a derived likeness; *eidos*—a shape, form, or an appearance, not necessarily based on reality; *skia*—a shadowed resemblance; *morphe*—the form, as indicative of the inner being; *charakter*—a tool for graving, a stamp or impress (cf. Hebrews 1: 3); and *charagma*—a mark (involves the narrower meaning of the thing impressed, without denoting the special characteristic of that which produces it (e.g., Revelation 13: 16, 17).

Cross and Livingstone (1983) refer to images as "the use of any representations of men, animals, and plants whether carved or painted that was prohibited in the Mosaic Law (Exodus 20: 4) by reason of the danger of idolatry." The description of various types of images is mentioned in other parts of the Old Testament; for example, "Moses made a bronze serpent, and put it on a pole" (Numbers 21: 9); "And you shall make two cherubim of gold; of hammered work you shall make them at the two ends of the mercy seat" (Exodus 25: 18); "So Solomon overlaid the inside of the temple with pure gold. . . . Then he carved cherubim, palm trees, and open flowers on them, and overlaid them with gold applied evenly on the carved work" (1 Kings 6: 21, 35). Curiously, Cross and Livingstone (p. 691) state that "there is no mention of imagery in the New Testament, as at least from the time of the Maccabees the Palestinian Jews had observed the second commandment rigorously" (cf. Vine [1981], and a literal distinction between the terms image and imagery; while the term image actually is used in the New Testament [e.g., 2 Corinthians 4: 4; Colossians 1: 15; Hebrews 1: 3], the derivative term imagery as referring to idols, statues, and images—as objects of worship or veneration and as employed in the Old Testament—does not appear in the New Testament). However, Cross and Livingstone (p. 691) also state that "[i]t was only when the theological significance of the Incarnation came to be more fully grasped, and what was involved in the fact that God had become visible by making human nature better understood, that, to many, there seemed to be no further obstacle to the use of images and other products of the artistic gifts of mankind in the service of the true religion."

Cross and Livingstone (1983) discuss the rise of the use of sacred images beginning with the paintings of the Catacombs—some of which date from the late second century—that are the earliest Christian images and pictures. Such works received great attention in the so-called "iconoclastic controversy" of the eighth and ninth centuries; the final settlement of the controversy went in favor of the use of *icons*, which remain the only form of representation legitimate in the Greek Church, whereas they are not given as much of an important place in the orthodoxy of the Western Church. In the Western Church, the veneration of images (including statues) made slower progress than in the Eastern Church. St. Thomas Aquinas provided a doctrinal basis for the use of such imagery by applying St. Basil's principle that the honor paid to the image passes on to its prototype—the principle that had already been accepted by the church via the Second Council of Nicaea in A.D. 787. The Nicene Council refers to either of two church councils that met at Nicaea, the first in A.D. 325 to deal with the Arian heresy—that is, the doctrine taught by the early Alexandrian Christian priest Arius, c. A.D. 330, that Christ the Son was not consubstantial (i.e., of one and the same substance, essence, or nature) with God the Father—and the second in A.D. 787 to consider the question of the veneration of images; and the Nicene Creed refers to a formal statement of the chief tenets of Christian belief, adopted by the first Nicene Council. Subsequently, in the sixteenth century, the abuses that had developed around the use of sacred images in the later Middle Ages led to a revolt against such images by most of the Reformers (e.g., Zwingli and Calvin) and the Puritans. (The Lutherans were rather more tolerant of a liturgy involving the use of sacred images, and to this day retain the crucifix in their services.) The Council of Trent—which was the ecumenical council of the Roman Catholic Church—met at Trent, Italy, intermittently from 1545 to 1563 and defined church doctrine, as well as condemning the Reformation and its activists and leaders. Moreover, the Council of Trent decreed that due honor should be paid to images of the Lord and the saints on the basis not of any virtue inherent in the image itself, but because in it the person represented is venerated. Such veneration is allowed to be shown only to images of actual human persons, not to such symbolical representations as that of God the Father as a venerable old man or the Holy Ghost as a dove, and similar devices.

In another entry, for *imago Dei* (Latin for image of God), Cross and Livingstone (1983) discuss various theories that have evolved to explain in what the *imago* consists. (According to Catholic theology, the *imago Dei* was obscured, but not lost, in the Fall of Man—in contrast to the *similitudo Dei* [likeness or resemblance of God] which was destroyed by Original Sin but is restored by baptism.) Several Greek fathers (including St. Gregory of Nyssa and St. John of Damascus) identify the *imago* with human free will, while others seek it in man's superiority to the rest of creation or in a quality of man's soul such as simplicity and immortality, or in his reason. According to St. Augustine, the Image of the Trinity is to be found in the intellectual nature of the soul and its three powers: Memory (the Father), Intellect (the Son), and Will (the Holy Ghost). In the mystical theology of the church, the *imago* has an important role as the point at which man's soul may enter into union with God. In Protestant theology, there has been an emphasis on the weakening of the *imago Dei* by the event of the Fall of Man; for example, according to Cross and Livingstone (1983), E. Brunner asserts that there is a "formal image" (constituting man as human and responsible and that serves as the point of contact for grace—which was destroyed by the Fall), and a "material image" (which has been destroyed by the Fall); on the other hand, K. Barth rejects the "formal image" concept and holds man to be corrupted completely by sin and incapable of discovering any kind of truth about God, or himself, apart from the manifestation of revelation.

Young (1982) provides biblical passages and references for a variety of image-related terms, much like Bruce's (1981) approach. For example, there are biblical passages for the terms pillar/idol ("*matstsebah*"), imagery ("*maskith*"), figure/idol ("*semel*"), grief ("*atsab*"), image ("*tselem*"), similitude/form/likeness ("*temunah*"), image/likeness ("*eikon*"), graven objects ("*pesel*," "*pesilim*"), impressed character ("*charakter*"), standing image ("*matstsebah*"), image/work ("*tsaatsuim*"), images/sun ("*chammanim*"), and household gods ("*teraphim*"). Young (1982) also gives similarly formatted biblical references for the terms *imagination, thought, reasoning, mind,* and to *imagine.*

Ellison (1984) provides biblical passages for the following terms (cf. Cruden, 1986; Strong, 1990): idols, idolatrous, and idolatry (124 different passages); imagination, imagine, imagines, and imagining (8 separate passages), and image and images (120 separate cases). The majority of references to the term idol(s) occurs in the books of Leviticus ($n=3$), 1 Kings ($n=4$), 2 Kings ($n=5$), Psalms ($n=7$), Isaiah ($n=14$), Jeremiah ($n=8$), Ezekiel ($n=38$), Hosea ($n=5$), Acts ($n=4$), 1 Corinthians ($n=7$), Revelation ($n=3$); and the majority of references to image/images occurs in the books of Genesis ($n=5$), Deuteronomy ($n=9$), Judges ($n=10$), 2 Chronicles ($n=10$), Isaiah ($n=13$), Daniel ($n=17$), 1 Corinthians ($n=3$), Revelation ($n=10$), Jeremiah ($n=8$), Ezekiel ($n=6$).

Myers (1987) discusses the terms image of God, imagery, and image/idolatry. The concept image of God (p. 515) is "a designation of the distinguishing nature of humanity as originally created; in the New Testament, Jesus Christ restores to fullness the image of God, both in himself and in the redeemed." Myers notes that the central passage for the term image of God is Genesis 1: 26 where Adam is said to have been created *in* God's image (Hebrew *selem*; cf. Genesis 1: 27; 5: 3; 9: 6) and *after* his likeness (Hebrew *demut*; cf. Genesis 5: 1, 3). The precise theological meaning of the phrase "image of

God," says Myers (p. 515) "has been the subject of much scholarly
explanation and speculation. The uses of 'image' in other biblical contexts carry the meaning of concrete representation, as in statues, pictures, and the like. . . . The history of interpretation, however, has
largely rejected a concrete or physical interpretation—since [*sic*] God
is spirit and has no physical form to be represented—in favor of various spiritualizing interpretations such as personality, self-consciousness,
immortality, rationality, freedom of will, moral agency, or creativity"
(cf. Porteus, 1962/1986, p. 683). Myers observes that a purely spiritual interpretation of the concept image of God tends to ignore the
fundamental unitary aspect of Hebrew anthropology where human
nature is viewed as a "psychosomatic unity"; for example, to regard
the concept image of God as rationality solely is a reflection of a
Greek—rather than a Hebrew—perspective. In the Hebrew approach,
reason, volition, the heart, and moral sensibility are a unitary fact, and
suggests that a proper understanding of the image of God is not to
be sought in particular capacities or faculties alone, but rather in the
one nature that they all contain (i.e., in the "wholeness of human
nature" which is not limited to "embodiment"). Within such an interpretation, various human traits may be subsumed, some of which
are implied in other biblical uses of the terms image and likeness (cf.
Genesis 5: 3 where Seth is *in* the likeness of, and *after* the image of,
his father, Adam—a verse that reverses the construction found in
Genesis 1: 26). In this case, Seth's "humanity" (i.e., his resemblance
to Adam) does not omit the physical resemblance. In another issue—
that of murder—murder is prohibited because it violates the image
of God as embodied in the victim (see Genesis 9: 6); this case, also,
must include the aspect of physical violation, although it too suggests
the more abstract concept of the sanctity of human life and, thus, of
human dignity and "standing before God."

Myers (1987, p. 516) identifies another interpretive problem:
whether the concepts of image and likeness are to be distinguished;
biblical usage of the terms is inconsistent, and theologians have developed theories concerning semantic differences in the concepts that
generally, in the final analysis, focus on the effect of the Fall of Man
and the image of God in mankind. Myers notes that neither the Old
Testament nor the New Testament countenance the notion of the
complete loss of the image of God after the Fall (cf. Genesis 9: 6; 1
Corinthians 11: 7; James 3: 9); he maintains that most interpreters
agree that the image of God has been radically affected and distorted
by sin, yet not wholly lost. In the New Testament, the concepts of

image (Greek: *eikon*) and likeness (Greek: *homoioma, homoiosis*) of God are redefined in terms of the personage of Jesus Christ, who is the "image of the invisible God" (Colossians 1: 15), the "express image" of God's nature (Hebrews 1: 3), and the "likeness of God" (2 Corinthians 4: 4). In each case, the image must refer to deity—an exact image would be identical with the original; thus, in Christ dwells the "fullness of God" (Colossians 1: 19; 2: 9), and Christ preexisted in the "form of God" (Philippians 2: 6). Moreover, the image of the "invisible God" became visible in the Incarnation (cf. John 1: 4, 9, 13–14); thus, the Incarnate Word may be, in fact, the prototype of all humanity, and even the body is a part of the image of God—especially in the light of the New Testament doctrine of the eschatological restoration of the image in Christ. Finally, according to Myers (1987), the image of God as revealed in Jesus Christ relates to his significance and purposes (cf. Cocar, 1999): as prophet (revealing the image of God in knowledge), as priest (in holiness), and as king (in lordship and righteousness).

Myers (1987) relates the term imagery to the wealth of pictorial language and graphic literary forms in the Bible on the basis that the Bible deals with supernatural matters that cannot be expressed adequately in direct terms. Myers suggests that the concrete figures that are employed in much of the imagery in the Bible are most appropriate or suitable for the ancient audience for whom the writings were produced; figurative usage abounds in the Bible in the form of anthropomorphisms and in concrete images associated with *agriculture* (e.g., Jeremiah 8: 13; Matthew 13: 24–30), *commerce* (e.g., Luke 19: 11–27), and *domestic life* (e.g., Jeremiah 18: 1–12; Matthew 13: 33). Other image-related genres in the Bible—which employ various symbols and images to point beyond themselves to some truth that is unseen—include the use of *allegory* (an extended metaphor in the form of a story), *fable* (a didactic story with animals or plants acting as humans), *proverb* (a saying, based upon common human experience or observation and indicating wisdom), and *parable* (a brief narrative similar to the allegory but containing a single idea). Many of the verses in the Old Testament book of Psalms, in particular, use imagery and images (metaphors and similes) to represent God. One of the most popular images of God is contained in what is perhaps the best-known of the Psalms: Psalm 23 ("The Lord is my shepherd; I shall not want. . . . And I will dwell in the house of the Lord Forever").

Other imagery (via metaphor/simile) in Psalms includes the following aspects/objects/persons: *shield* (Psalm 33: 20); *judge* (Psalm 7:

11; 9: 16); *creator* (Psalm 8: 3–8); *rock/fortress* (Psalm 18: 2); *avenger* (Psalm 18: 47); *landlord* (Psalm 24: 1); *teacher* (Psalm 25: 8–9); *warrior/savior* (Psalm 35: 1–3); *refuge* (Psalm 9: 9: 46: 1); *redeemer* (Psalm 49: 15); *father* (Psalm 68: 5–6); *mother bird* (Psalm 91: 3–4); *king/ruler* (Psalm 93: 1–2). The concept of eidetic imagery has been employed by Nussbaum (1974) within the context of the Old Testament in his account of "abnormal mental phenomena in the prophets." Nussbaum examines three borderline states between the "normal" and the "abnormal": inspiration, ecstasy, and eidetic imagery. Inspiration is viewed as a state of excitement indicating well-preserved "reality control"; ecstasy is a state of perception where reality has disappeared and "psychotic paralysis" occurs; and eidetic imagery involves dreams, visions, and tactile/auditory experiences. Nussbaum cites examples from the Old Testament of each type of behavior, and he compares and contrasts hallucinations versus revelations in the Old Testament prophets. He also examines, semantically, the occurrence of mania, paranoia, and depression in some of the "great" or literary prophets.

Myers (1987) defines the term idolatry (Greek: *eidololatria*) as the worship of gods other than Yahweh in the Old Testament—especially through the images that represent them (the New Testament extends the concept of idolatry to include any ultimate confidence in something other than God—such as covetousness or surrender to appetites). Myers suggests that the Sumerians in the ancient Near East may have been the first to develop an extensive pantheon (i.e., a temple dedicated to the gods) and mythology; their gods included An (the god of heaven), Ninhursag (the creator of humans), Ki (the earth-god), Enlil (the god of air), Enki (the lord of the waters or the abyss), and Nanna (the moon-goddess, whose daughter was Inanna the wife of Dumuzi). The Babylonians adapted the Sumerian deities Inanna and Dumuzi into their own god, Ishtar (goddess of love and fertility). The Assyrians, in turn, accepted the Babylonian deities (to the Assyrians, Ishtar was equal in power to Ashur, the chief local deity). Egyptian religions grew out of a variety of local systems that eventually merged; most of these mythologies emphasized the emergence of the gods from chaos (sometimes itself regarded as a deity), and eventually the sun-god Re or Ra was regarded as the chief god—creator of other gods, the world, and mankind. The pharoah was regarded often as identical with, or as, the son of Re. Myers notes that Egypt's chief deities were usually represented in human form; others appeared as human bodies with animal heads or were associated with totem animals (e.g., Sebek was represented by the crocodile, Anubis by the jackal's head, and others by the cow, cat, or vulture). The chief gods of the Canaanites were El (the creator) and his son, Baal (a storm and/or vegetation god, also called Haddu or Hadad); both El and Baal were represented by the bull (virility) or as riding on a bull. The fertility goddess, Asherah (Anath, Astarte, or Ashtaroth) was portrayed as particularly bloodthirsty and savage. The cults of Baal and Asherah engaged in excessive carnality, fornication, and drunkenness and, as such, posed a great threat to the devout Israelites.

Myers (1987) relates the various manifestations and forms of idols (e.g., amulets, teraphim, pillars, statues, monuments, incense altars, graven images, molten images, and inlaid wood carvings) to particular passages in the Bible, and provides an extended discussion—along with biblical passages—on the influence of idols and idolatry on the Israelites (who frequently lapsed into pagan worship—even leading at times to human sacrifice; cf. Deuteronomy 12: 31; 2 Kings 3: 27; 17: 17; 2 Chronicles 28: 3). Of course, as Myers observes, idolatry was contrary to the true character of both Israel and its God, and the rejection of idolatry—replacing it with the worship of Yahweh alone— was enunciated in the Mosaic Law (Exodus 20: 3–5) and was evinced, also, in the Israelites' development of a versatile vocabulary concerning idolatry that was rich in derogatory and contemptuous names for idols.

When consulting Strong's (1990, p. 528) concordance as a database/source for assessing the frequency of usage of the term image and image-related terms (cf. Ellison, 1984), it may be seen that the term image occurs ninety-seven times throughout the Bible; the terms imagery and image's each occur once; the term images occurs sixty-nine times; and the terms imagine, imagination, imaginations, imagined, imagineth collectively occur thirty-six times throughout the Bible. Strong (p. 99) identifies biblical passages for the terms idol-makers/idol-making ($n=5$; e.g., Isaiah 45: 16; 2: 20; 44: 9–18); for idols/idolatry ($n=62$; e.g., 1 Corinthians 5: 11; 10: 14; 10: 19, 20; Exodus 20: 1–5; 32: 1–8; 34: 13–16; Judges 8: 24–27; 10: 6– 16; 17: 1–13; 18: 30, 31; 1 Kings 11: 1–8; 12: 26–33; 14: 22–24; 18: 1–46; 21: 25, 26; 2 Kings 16: 3; 17: 5–23; 21: 1–18; 23: 1–20, 26, 27; 2 Chronicles 11: 15; 28: 1–4; 33: 1–11; 14: 3–5; 29: 15– 19); and for image of God ($n=8$; e.g., Genesis 1: 26, 27; 9: 6; 1 Corinthians 11: 7; Colossians 3: 10; 2 Corinthians 3: 18: John 1: 14, 18; Romans 8: 29). In Strong, the notion of imagination ("creating a mental picture; thoughts") is identified as being the following: evil and willful (Genesis 6: 5; Jeremiah 18: 12), deceitful

(Proverbs 12: 20), and vain (Romans 1: 21); and the "cleansing of imagination" is indicated in 2 Corinthians 10: 5. In surveying and researching the visual imagery-related term *vision* in the Bible, Strong's (p. 1143) concordance may be used, also, for assessing the frequency of occurrence of the terms vision and *visions*. The word vision (as used in the Bible, generally, refers to "visual hallucinations," "apparitions," "extra-perceptual experiences or aspects of seeing," "prophesy," "clarity," "revelation" or "foresight") occurs seventy-nine times throughout the Bible, and the word visions occurs twenty-four times. Among the books of the Bible in which the term vision appears, the book of Daniel clearly contains the largest number of references to both vision ($n=22$) and visions ($n=10$). Next in frequency of occurrence, the book of Ezekiel contains thirteen references to vision and five references to visions, and next is the book of Acts, which contains eleven references to vision and one reference to visions. The remaining references to vision and visions are contained in the books of Genesis, Numbers, 1 and 2 Samuel, 1 and 2 Chronicles, Job, Psalms, Proverbs, Isaiah, Jeremiah, Lamentations, Obadiah, Micah, Nahum, Habakkuk, Zechariah, Matthew, Luke, The Revelation, Hosea, Joel, and 2 Corinthians.

A selection of a few passages—illustrating the use of the visual imagery-related terms vision and visions—in the *Holy Bible: New King James Version* (1984) is as follows: Genesis 15: 1 ("After these things the word of the Lord came to Abram in a vision, saying 'Do not be afraid, Abram, I *am* your shield, Your exceedingly great reward'"); Numbers 12: 6 ("If there is a prophet among you, I, the Lord, make Myself known to him in a vision, And I speak to him in a dream"); Job 20: 8 ("He will fly away like a dream, and not be found; Yes, he will be chased away like a vision of the night"); Psalm 89: 19 ("Then you spoke in a vision to Your holy one"); Ezekiel 7: 26 ("Then they will seek a vision from a prophet"); Ezekiel 11: 24 ("And the vision that I had seen went up from me"); Daniel 2: 19 ("Then the secret was revealed to Daniel in a night vision"); Daniel 8: 26–27 ("And the vision of the evenings and mornings which was told is true; Therefore seal up the vision, for *it refers* to many days *in the future*. . . . I was astonished by the vision, but no one understood it").

Other sources for the terms imagery, visions, and *symbolism*—both in general, and in the Bible and other sacred works, in particular—include the following: Armistead (1903/1991), Bohler and Clinebell

(1996), Bryant (1971), Burghardt (1957), Caird and Wright (1997), Childs (1988), Collins (1990), Curtis (1984), Eichhorst (1973), Farisani (1990), Fichtner (1978), Foston (1930), Fries (1995), Geisler (1997), Gibson (1998), Grassi (1987), Grinfield (1837), Harris (1998), Johanning (1965), Kreutz (1983), Lageer (1992), McFarland (2000), Morrison (1983), Newpher (1958), Nussbaum (1974), Olsen (1988), Ryken, Wilhoit, Longman, and Wilhoit (1998), Sechrist (1973), Shepherd (1959), Soules (1968), Vries (1974), Wakefield (1968), Weemes (1632), and Wynkoop (1952).

In summary, regarding the origins and evolution of imagery in primitive or prehistoric times, and in the sacred writings of the Old and New Testament of the Bible, the use of images by early human-kind probably served two main functions or purposes:

1. For early, "uncivilized" humans—such as cave dwellers—*pictorial* images/imagery contained primal (and prelinguistic) sacred, ceremonial, religious, or ritualistic significance as early humans attempted to master and control their environment that included incessant and innumerable natural dangers—especially in their hunting activities involving dangerous animals—that required various conciliatory/adaptive behaviors necessary for both *physical* survival (e.g., cave paintings/images of animals may have aided in identification of the "optimal animals" in future hunting activities) and *psychological* survival (e.g., cave paintings/images of animals and objects may have aided in "capturing the soul or spirit" of the target animal/object and, thus, gain a measure of ascendancy, fearlessness, or control over it).

2. For later, more "civilized" humans—such as the early Jews and Christians during biblical times—the use of *literary* images/imagery in sacred writings and linguistic expressions may have served primarily as a moral/ethical mechanism for the development, unification, and preservation of social, political, cultural, and religious systems or customs (e.g., the diatribes against idols/idolatry)—and the images, symbols, and objects associated with various foreign deities—in the Old and New Testaments helped to advance a newer, more enlightened approach toward God-worship in the Jews and Christians that served to unite them in a common set of beliefs that was "healthy" for the ultimate survival of their special groups, notwithstanding the incessant and bloody "border/boundary wars" that seem to plague various "civilized" nations and seem to jeopardize their very existence.

In these germinal respects, then, it is suggested that the basic function(s) of images and imagery has been to promote the development and survival of the individual and the group—whether by pictorial/symbolic/nonlinguistic or by literary/descriptive/linguistic modes of expression.

> Whatsoever we imagine, is Finite. Therefore there is no Idea, or conception of any thing we call Infinite. No man can have in his mind an Image of infinite magnitude; nor conceive infinite swiftness, infinite time, or infinite place, or infinite power.
>
> —T. Hobbes, 1651/1958

> A Friend of mine knew one perfectly cured of Madness by a very harsh and offensive Operation . . . but whatever Gratitude and Reason suggested to him, he could never bear the sight of the Operator: That Image brought back with it the Idea of that Agony which he suffer'd from his Hands, which was too mighty and intolerable for him to endure.
>
> —J. Locke, 1690/1965

> Ideas, which are observed to be connected with other Ideas, come to be considered as Signs, by means whereof Things, not actually perceived by Sense, are signified or suggested to the Imagination, whose Objects they are, and which alone perceives them. . . . How comes it to pass, that a Set of Ideas, altogether different from tangible Ideas, should nevertheless suggest them to us, there being no necessary Connexion between them? To which the proper Answer is, That this is done in virtue of an arbitrary Connexion, instituted by the Author of Nature.
>
> —G. Berkeley, 1709/1910

> We may divide all the Perceptions of the Mind into two Classes or Species, which are distinguish'd by their different Degrees of Force and Vivacity. The less forcible and lively are commonly denominated Thoughts or Ideas.
>
> —D. Hume, 1748/1963

> Sensations, once experienced, modify the nervous organism, so that copies of them arise again in the mind after the original outward stimulus is gone.
>
> —W. James, 1890

> There has been a remarkable revival of interest in mental imagery among psychologists after a long period of neglect. . . . Some of the questions philosophers have debated remain largely untouched by the current debate in psychology.
>
> —M. Tye, 1991

## THE IMAGE AND THE IMAGERY DEBATE IN PHILOSOPHY AND EARLY PSYCHOLOGY

Rather than using the singular tense in the title phrase "the imagery debate," perhaps a more accurate description of events would be to refer to "the imagery debate*s*," using the plural tense. That is, separate and characteristic debates took place in the two different disciplines of philosophy *and* psychology. Thus, historically, the imagery debate occurred in *both* philosophy and psychology (cf. Tye, 1991, p. xii; and, also, "the debate" actually developed into a series of discussions where each of them had a different emphasis; cf. Kosslyn, 1994, p. 4).

Overall, the imagery debate(s) in the history of philosophy begins with the Greek philosophers Plato and Aristotle, and continues through to the French philosopher René Descartes, the British Empiricist philosophers—including Thomas Hobbes, John Locke, George Berkeley, and David Hume—and the German philosopher Immanuel Kant. In this philosophical arena, the two most important and popular viewpoints were the notion that images are "picturelike representations" and the notion that "imagining is similar to perceiving—under less than optimal conditions." The method typically employed by philosophers to defend these viewpoints was that of *introspection* (i.e., "looking into one's own experience, or one's own mental life, and reporting on the mental contents of one's consciousness").

The earliest explicit accounts of mental images in philosophy seem to derive from the ideas and writings of Plato (427–347 B.C.) and Aristotle (384–322 B.C.). Plato's "wax tablet model" of memory (in his *Theaetetus* 191c, d; cf. Kosslyn, 1981) and his notion of an "inner artist painting pictures in the soul" (in his *Philebus* 39c; cf. Thomas, 2001) initially invoked the idea of images where images were considered to be copies of perceptions and thoughts, and where such a rudimentary model of memory formed the basis for later "stimulus-trace" theories in psychology (cf. Morris and Hampson, 1983, p. 5; Paivio, 1971/1979). Note that Kosslyn (1981, p. 207) observes that Plato—in his likening of memory representations to impressions on a wax tablet—was probably the first theorist to distinguish between *representations* (i.e., the different possible impressions) and the *medium* in which they occur (i.e., the wax tablet). Such a distinction between representations and a medium, according to Kosslyn, has been important in the history of the study of visual mental imagery. Moreover, consistent with the notion of images in a memory context, the early

Greek poet Semonides (aka Simonides) of Amorgos (c. 650 B.C.)—usually credited with the discovery of the mnemonic device called the *method of loci* (i.e., the technique in which the memorizer uses a well-known geographic area or architectural structure as a set of locations where the objects/items to be remembered are "placed" in a visual picture of the location and where, during recall of the material, the person merely takes a "mental walk" down the street and "picks up" the objects where he/she had been mentally placed previously)—asserted that imagery may have a beneficial mediational influence in the memory of information and materials (cf. Morris and Hampson, 1983, p. 5; Yates, 1966).

Following Plato, Aristotle endorsed the "wax impression model" of memory and asserted, further, that mental images are like "inner pictures." In his work, *On the Soul* (*De Anima* 427b, 19), Aristotle makes reference to "calling up a picture—as in the practice of mnemonics—by the use of mental images" (also, see Aristotle, *De Anima*, III, iii, in McKeon, 1941). In another work, *On Memory and Reminiscence* (451a, 19), Aristotle discusses the nature of memory and its processes, and states that "memory has now been explained as the persistent possession of an image, in the sense of a copy of the thing to which the image refers" (see Aristotle, *De Memoria et Reminiscentia*, 450a,b in McKeon, 1941). Aristotle maintained that the ability to employ images in the service of memory was due, primarily, to one's faculty of sensation; he also spoke of imagination as a "feeble sort of sensation" (*Rhetorica*, 1370a). In this regard, Aristotle may be viewed as a forerunner of the later Empiricist psychologists' conception of imagery. For source material on Aristotle's notions of imagery, see the following: Beare (1906), Hett (1957), Lawson-Tancred (1986), McKeon (1941), Modrak (1987), Nussbaum (1978), and Ross (1931). Aristotle's account of the representational content of memory via imagery is that mental images must copy or resemble what they represent; that is—much like real pictures—there must be a resemblance of what is pictorial and not just a representation of them by use of conventional symbols. Aristotle also asserted that "the soul never thinks without a mental image" (*De Anima*, 431a, 15–20), and advanced the notion that the representational aspect of language derives from imagery where spoken words are the symbols of the inner images (*De Interpretatione*, 16a; *De Anima*, 420b). Thus, according to Aristotle, if mental images are inner pictures (i.e., the "picture theory"), then they must be represented in a like manner—a viewpoint that was easily accessible via introspection and one that was very popular with succeeding generations of philosophers.

The next notable contribution in philosophy toward understanding mental imagery took place almost 2,000 years after Aristotle and was made by the French philosopher René Descartes (1596–1650) who suggested that the act of imagining a thing is quite different from the act of thinking or conceiving of that thing. For example, one can easily imagine a pentagon (a five-sided figure) in a way that is different from imagining a hexagon (a six-sided figure); however, it is virtually impossible to imagine a chiliagon (a 1,000-sided figure) as different from a 999-sided figure—even though one may *conceive* of a chiliagon and *conceive* of the way in which it differs from a figure having one more or less sides (cf. Descartes, 1637/1960; and Descartes, *Meditation Six* in *Meditations on First Philosophy*, in Haldane and Ross, 1967). In accord with Aristotle, Descartes adhered to the view that mental images copy the objects they represent. See Tye (1991, p. 4) who suggests that Descartes—in his *Meditation Three* (see Haldane and Ross, 1967)—holds (like Aristotle) that percepts and mental images copy objects in the external world. Thomas (2001) notes that—with certain qualifications and exceptions (especially, the "clear and distinct ideas" of Descartes's epistemology)—the concept of idea(s) that played such a large role in philosophy and cognitive psychological theory from the seventeenth through the nineteenth century are direct descendants of Aristotle's notion of images. Note that the British Empiricist philosophers John Locke (1690/1965) and David Hume (1739/1978) had either implicitly or explicitly identified ideas as images; and in more modern times, in an experimental psychology context, Kantowitz, Roediger, and Elmes (2001, p. 472) equate the terms images and ideas where each represent experiences not actually present.

A contemporary of Descartes, the English philosopher Thomas Hobbes (1588–1679) provides an account of imagery that is important in several respects (Tye, 1991, pp. 4–5): Hobbes emphasizes the lack of specificity or determinacy in many mental images as well as the parallel with seeing ("after the object is removed or the eye shut, we still retain an image of the thing seen, though more obscure than when we see it" [1651/1958, p. 27]). Hobbes presents a rudimentary account of the generation of mental images involving the combination of separate percepts that are stored in memory and that may form entirely novel objects or scenes ("imagination being only of those

things which have been formerly perceived by sense, either all at once
or by parts at several times, the former . . . is simple imagination.
. . . The other is compounded, as when, from the sight of a man at
one time and of a horse at another, we conceive in our mind a cen-
taur" [p. 28]); and Hobbes locates imagery within the brain (Tye,
1991, p. 155, suggests that this interpretation comes from Hobbes's
observations regarding motions in the "internal parts of a man" when
"he sees, dreams, etc." [Hobbes, 1651/1958, p. 27]).

The British Empiricist philosophers—John Locke (1632–1704),
George Berkeley (1685–1753), and David Hume (1711–1776)—
viewed imagery as a central feature of mind wherein (unlike the views
of Descartes and Hobbes) *all* thought was considered to be formed
from the manipulation of either simple images extracted from sense
experience or complex images constructed from these simple images.
In Locke's approach, memory is defined as the retention of images,
language-learning consists of the association of sounds and images, and
object classification/identification consists of the comparison or check-
ing of objects and images (cf. Locke, 1690/1965, Book 2, chapters
1–13; Book 3, chapters 1–3). According to Locke, images ("ideas")
themselves are mental pictures ("the ideas of the nurse and mother
are well framed in their minds, i.e., the minds of children, and, like
pictures of them, represent only those individuals" [1690/1965, Book
3, chapter 3, section 7]). Tye (1991, p. 6) provides a passage from
Locke that seems to refute the "pictorial approach" to imagery; in any
event, says Tye, the ideas or images in Locke's system that are stored
in memory are abstractions, as are the ideas used in classification and
the ideas that function as word meanings. Locke's assertion that ideas
are sometimes abstract is basically supportive of the notion that ideas
are sometimes sketchy, vague, or lacking in detail; in Locke's view (cf.
Tye, 1991, p. 6), apparently, the senses initially provide us with percepts or ideas that are fully determinate, and then the ideas lose some
of their internal details, as well as the particular circumstances associated with their arrival in the mind.

Tye (1991, p. 7) suggests that Locke and the British Empiricists,
generally, gave imagery too broad a role in the workings and function of the mind; for instance, a person may understand the meanings of a multitude of words even though he or she may not be able
to call up an appropriate image for them (e.g., the words *conduct, sake,
character*). However, George Berkeley seems, at least, to appreciate
the relationships between meaning and language where words may be
meaningful even when they are not associated with ideas/images. Tye

(1991, p. 7) notes that Berkeley disagrees strongly with Locke on the issue of abstract ideas (Berkeley asserts not merely that Locke's doctrine of abstract ideas is inconsistent with the act of introspection, but also that Lockean abstract ideas are logically impossible [cf. Bennett, 1971, p. 37]). Although Berkeley accepts the notion that mental images and percepts are entities of the same type—and mental images often are generated by combining percepts stored in memory—he maintains that every idea must have a definite color and shape where the notions of indeterminacy/vagueness have no place in ideas themselves. Note that Berkeley (1710/1950) denies the possibility of "generalized images" or, as he calls them, "general notions" or "abstract ideas." Berkeley suggested that he could imagine particular things such as persons, hands, or eyes, but they must have some particular shape and color; moreover, he asserted that he cannot "by any effort of thought conceive the *abstract* idea" of such things (cf. Woodworth, 1938, p. 43). Furthermore, Berkeley (unlike Locke) holds a "photographic view" of mental pictures that is grounded in the introspective method of reporting phenomena (cf. Berkeley, 1710/1950, sections 10, 13).

David Hume's philosophy of mind and his conception of ideas were influenced by the earlier British Empiricists John Locke and George Berkeley. In Hume's view, thinking consists in the manipulation of ideas where ideas are the "faint images" of sense impressions (cf. Hume, 1739/1978, Book 1, parts 1, 4). Note that Hume (1748/1963) distinguishes images from sensations where the former possess less vivacity or vividness; he asserts that there is a "considerable difference between the perceptions of the mind when a man feels the pain of excessive heat . . . and when he afterwards recalls to his memory this sensation, or anticipates it by his imagination." Hume maintains that such faculties (images) may mimic/copy the perceptions of the senses, but they never wholly achieve the vivacity or force of the original sensation (cf. Woodworth, 1938, p. 44). In this regard—in his assimilation of the intellectual to the sensory—Hume *explicitly* equates the notion of idea with that of image. Hume sides with Berkeley on the issue of Lockean abstract ideas, probably due to Berkeley's forceful refutation of Locke's theory of abstraction (Tye, 1991, p. 10). Hume also attempted to give a plausible account of "representational content" for ideas where he suggested that "resemblance" is not sufficient for "pictorial representation" and that "interpretation" must play a crucial role in the process (cf. Goodman, 1968, pp. 3–31; Kant, 1781/1929, Book 2, p. 182).

Tye (1991, p. 11) concludes, by and large, that philosophers his-torically have held the position that mental images are picturelike rep-resentations that are similar to those that occur during the process of perception. The philosophers, in particular the British Empiricists, allowed the representations to be sketchy, nondetailed, or vague, and they frequently considered resemblance to be the "picturing relation." Also, they often generally exaggerated the role that imagery plays in mental activity and thinking. The method of introspection—and the evidence gained via the "introspective act"—was used by the philoso-phers as the rationale or basis for general adoption of the "pictorial view" of images (cf. Thomas, 1994, p. 291). Tye (pp. 11–12) pre-sents the introspective argument for the pictorial approach to imag-ery in its simplest form: "Mental images *look* like the objects that they represent. In this respect, mental images are similar to realistic public pictures and dissimilar from other public representations, for example, descriptions. Hence, mental images represent in the manner of, or something very like the manner of, real pictures." Tye observes that this viewpoint historically has been enormously influential in shaping the views of philosophers, and it still has some appeal today—despite containing some basic flaws. (For discussions of the various theories of imagery—such as the "pictorial view"—see chapter 3 herein, "Mod-ern Theoretical Aspects, Applications, and Functions of Imagery"; and for a review of philosopher Tye's book, *The Imagery Debate*, see phi-losopher N.J.T. Thomas [1994] who refers to Tye's book as an excellent source for appreciating the debate between the "mental images-as-pictures" [e.g., Kosslyn, 1980, 1994] versus the "mental images-as-descriptions" [e.g., Pylyshyn, 1973, 1981] viewpoints; how-ever, Thomas suggests that Tye has omitted, or greatly abridged, the work of some of the more important imagery theorists [e.g., Shepard, Paivio, Finke, Anderson, Neisser, Palmer, and Marks]. For an early description and estimation of the emerging "sensationalist" psychol-ogy—in its first presentation by Hobbes, its development by Locke and Berkeley, and its culmination in the skepticism of Hume—see Fraser [1891–1892] who attempted to show that the predominating element, or chief source, in the psychological approaches of these philosophers was the notion of *visualization.*)

Following the British Empiricists' study and analyses of mental imagery, the issue began to be investigated by psychologists early in the history of the field of experimental psychology, which was in-augurated in 1879 by the German philosopher, physiologist, and psy-chologist Wilhelm Wundt (1832–1920) at the University of Leipzig.

At about this time, also, the discipline of psychology in general—and the emerging new field of experimental psychology in particular—began to detach itself from the discipline of philosophy. However, the topic of imagery played a pivotal cognitive role in Wundt's theories and laboratory research that was parallel to that of the formulations of the earlier philosophers. Wundt's systematic study of mental phenomena became known as *structuralism,* and its epistemological foundation was based in the philosophers' concept of *associationism* which asserts that higher-order mental or behavioral processes result from the combination/association of simpler mental or behavioral elements. In other words, knowledge that is derived solely through the senses was considered to be stored in the form of ideas or *mental atoms*—where new ideas were formed from associative groups of old ones and where the *principles of grouping* first enunciated by Aristotle (i.e., similarity, contiguity, and contrast) were the chief determining factors.

Reber (1995, p. 60) notes that associationism really has two historically important lines: a philosophical and a scientific (cf. Roeckelein, 1998, pp. 44–48). The philosophical line is best represented by the British Empiricists (such as Locke, Berkeley, Hume, James Mill, and John S. Mill) who needed powerful *antinativist* principles by which complex mental life could be explained by appeal only to experience. Hobbes was the first philosopher to suggest that Aristotle's notion of *relations* could serve as an *associationistic model* of human cognition and thinking. On the other hand, the scientific line is best represented by Hermann von Ebbinghaus (1850–1909) who conducted the first systematic experiments in 1885 on the issue of memory (e.g., Ebbinghaus, 1885). The emphasis in the scientific approach for evidence and data to validate associationist doctrine continued through Ivan Pavlov's (1849–1936) studies on conditioned reflexes (Pavlov, 1927), and Edward Thorndike's (1874–1949) research on *connectionism* (Thorndike, 1907, 1931), and that became, finally, the foundation on which J. B. Watson (1878–1958) built the movement/school known as *Behaviorism* (Watson, 1919/1929).

The scientific/experimental psychological orientation differed from the earlier philosophical approach in a number of ways (Reber, 1995); for example, the "primitive elements" of the philosophers that became connected were no longer ideas or sensations but became operationally defined by experimental psychologists as *stimuli* and *responses.* The philosophers' focus on the *rationalist* analysis of associations that were already formed (via a kind of "armchair introspection") was shifted by the experimental psychologists to attention on the issue of *how* the associations were formed (and, thus, establishing the topic of "learning" as one of the most intensively researched areas in psychology) and the shift from the philosophers' analyses of mentalistic phenomena (available mainly through introspection) to the experimental psychologists' analyses of objectively measurable behavior. Reber observes that the principle of associationism has proven to be one of the most enduring theoretical mechanisms in philosophy and psychology (cf. Roeckelein, 1996) where the basic tenets of associationism have reemerged in recent years in the cognitive sciences under the related term connectionism (i.e., the doctrine that a system—such as a brain—operates as though it were composed of a network of nodes, each of which has at any given time a certain level of activation; each of the nodes, in turn, is assumed to be interconnected with other nodes at different levels of the system in either an *inhibitory* or an *excitatory* manner so that, in effect, activating one node will have specific effects on the others. Also, the whole network is assumed to be dynamic so that as long as inputs are fed into it, it will keep adjusting the activation levels and the strengths of the various interconnections between the nodes). Reber notes that *connectionist models* have proven to be quite powerful and when expressed as *computer models* have provided great insights into human learning, memory, and neurocognitive processes; theories based on such principles are also known as associationist models, *parallel distributed processing models*, and *neural network models*.

The most popular theory of mind adopted by the early experimental psychologists was some version of the approach known as *parallelism*, that is, physical and mental events are synchronous but do not interact (cf. Morris and Hampson, 1983, p. 5). The rise of the methodology within experimental psychology known as *psychophysics* was an attempt to relate psychological (mental/mind) aspects to physical (body) aspects in as direct a way as possible (cf. Fechner, 1860; Muller, 1878, 1903; Watson, 1978, pp. 239–52). Another methodology—introspection—was adopted by the psychologists from the philosophers and was based on the assumption that all the essential aspects of mental functioning are conscious and available through "reporting on one's mental experiences by looking inward into the contents of one's consciousness" Note that Reber (1995, p. 388) observes that the method of introspection is not a true examination of the contents of consciousness as its proponents claimed, but it is, rather, a retrospective glance back at those things that have already passed through consciousness; Reber states that *introspectionism* as an approach to the study of mind is "defunct." In the late 1800s, the method of introspection initiated the formal investigation of imagery in psychology—but it also led, eventually, to its virtual banishment from psychology for about fifty years (beginning around the second decade of the twentieth century). Just before the turn of the twentieth century, Wilhelm Wundt (1897) maintained that the method of introspection was not applicable to the "higher" mental processes that, for him, included perception as well as thought; Wundt insisted that the proper application of introspection was in the area of *sensation* because this was "uncontaminated by meaning." According to Morris and Hampson (1983, p. 5), Wundt could find no real approach for opening up the study of the higher mental/cognitive processes (such as thought); on the other hand, E. B. Titchener (1896)—a student of Wundt's at Leipzig and his leading Structuralist disciple in America at Cornell University—did open up the topic by asserting that *all* cognitive activity is accompanied by images. Such images (in common with sensations) were said to possess the properties of intensity, quality, duration, and clarity, but differed from sensations in their "transparency" (i.e., images were considered by Titchener to be less objective, less realistic, and were easily destroyed than were sensations). By virtue of this viewpoint, according to Morris and Hampson (p. 6), Titchener "equated thought with conscious content that was reducible, in turn, to a series of mental images; (Titchener) opened up imagery and thinking to introspective analysis, since [*sic*] conscious mental content was observable through the 'mind's eye.'"

In a related issue, an early introspective experiment (Perky, 1910) involving imagery cast doubt on the value of definitions of cognitive processes in terms of conscious experience. One of Titchener's students, C. W. Perky, attempted to determine the differences between images and sensory perceptions; she asked her participants to construct conscious images and to project them on a ground-glass screen in front of them, and then to describe introspectively the nature of the images. Sometimes, however, without telling her participants, Perky caused faint pictures actually to be projected onto the screen from the other side; these stimuli were faint but not subliminal. Results showed that her participants could not distinguish between these sensory experiences and the images that they themselves projected—they could not distinguish introspectively between images and sensory perceptions. Leeper (1951, p. 732) notes that Perky's results have often been taken as evidence that there is no useful distinction between perceptual and imaginal processes. However, this conclusion does not follow; according to Leeper, what Perky's results suggest is that the distinction must be made in terms of *functional* relations—particularly in terms of the different origins of the two types of processes, and that it cannot be made by introspective observations of the two processes as such. (Perky's experiment, reactions to it by various other investigators, and related studies are covered in more detail in a later section, "Selected Early Psychological Imagery Studies," in this chapter; cf. Segal and Gordon [1969]; Segal and Nathan [1964].)

Morris and Hampson (1983, p. 6) note that Titchener's approach to the associative issues of thinking and images was "doomed to failure." Psychological experiments in thought and imagery performed at the University of Wurzburg in Germany by Oswald Kulpe (1893) and others (e.g., M. M. Meyer, J. Orth, H. J. Watt, and N. Ach) demonstrated that thinking can, and does, occur *without* any reportable, conscious content or imagery (cf. Humphrey, 1951; Leeper, 1951; Ogden, 1951; Paivio, 1971/1979; Watson, 1978, pp. 308–15). This difference of opinion concerning the relationship between thinking and imagery initiated the famous imageless thought controversy in the history of psychology. Participants in experiments at Wurzburg were asked to give introspective reports of the contents of their consciousness as they carried out specified cognitive tasks; the participants often claimed *not* to experience imagery, but rather reported they had "imageless thoughts" (i.e., conscious contents without any perceptual or sensory qualities). In some tasks at Wurzburg, participants were able to make a correct judgment of difference or equality of weights in the *absence* of imagery (cf. Marbe, 1901). In other experiments at Wurzburg, word-association tasks were arranged such that a participant would respond as quickly as possible with a word to a stimulus word; the person would be given a task (*Aufgabe*) such as responding with a rhyming word, or a subordinate or superordinate word. Under such instructions, the psychologists at Wurzburg found that the answers/responses came rapidly and directly as the result of "determining tendencies," or "sets," again with *no* imagery involved in the participants' "search" for the answer (cf. Bugelski, 1984, p. 185; Buhler, 1907/1908; Watson, 1978, pp. 310–11; Watt, 1905). In rebuttal, Wundt criticized the introspective methodology of the Wurzburg experiments, while Titchener claimed that in his laboratory at Cornell University, similar introspective experiments *always* elicited imagery—although not necessarily visual imagery. Both Wundt and Titchener dismissed the studies at Wurzburg on the basis that they were not actually studying thinking so much as the effects of previous experience where no thinking was really occurring (cf. Wundt, 1908). Thus, Wundt (at Leipzig) and Titchener (at Cornell) favored the notion that imagery occurred during cognitive/thought processes, but Kulpe and others (at Wurzburg) reported *no* images (i.e., espoused the notion of imageless thought) in their experiments (cf. Angell, 1911; Boring, 1957, pp. 401–10, 415–20; Evans, 1975; Thomas, 1997, 2001; Titchener, 1909; Watson, 1978, pp. 309–13).

Watson (1978, p. 311) suggests that distinctions such as those involved in the debates (e.g., imageless thought, introspection, analytical methods) between the warring views of the Wurzburg (Kulpe) and Leipzig (Wundt) schools is "never as clean-cut as enthusiasts would like to believe. . . . From the perspective of today, it can be seen that the views of the Wurzburgers and Wundt were not not incompatible." Watson also notes that while Wundt synthesized the first modern view of a scientific psychology, the work of Kulpe at the Wurzburg school was prophetic of the development of a *holistic* view as distinct from the *elementalist* view of Wundt; the Gestalt school of psychology that came later owed a debt to Kulpe for attempting to deal with both "content" and "act" in the new experimental psychology. Moreover, Kulpe and the Wurzburgers "broadened the scope of introspection and opened the area of the thought processes to experimental study; the essential change they made was to convert introspection into retrospection—the report of past experience, rather than a description of an immediate experience" (p. 314). During the cognitive process, a person thought, memorized, or judged something and then turned around and examined those contents that were experienced during the process; the lack of sensory experience during many of the tasks being studied—in so-called "imageless thought" tasks—was one of the major contributions, according to Watson, of the Wurzburg psychologists.

In summary, it may be said that the debate on imageless thought (as well as other methodological issues) between Wundt's school/followers and Kulpe's school/followers was salubrious for the development of a scientific and experimental psychology. Watson (1978, pp. 314–15) lists the following "prescriptions," procedural developments, or scientific features that are the by-products for psychologists today of the early Wundt-versus-Kulpe viewpoints/approaches: general agreement was reached on *nomotheticism* (i.e., the search for *general* principles that apply to *many* individuals); general agreement was reached on *naturalism* (i.e., the principles discovered are within the realm of natural science and not of some transcendental realm); the concept of *methodological objectivism* was advanced (i.e., the use of methods of studying psychological phenomena that are open to other competent observers who may validate previous findings by replication of one's study); the notion of *quantitativism* was advanced (i.e., the dependence on objective measurement of phenomena); the criterion of *determinism* was adhered to (i.e., the belief that human events are explicable in terms of cause-effect or antecedent-consequent relationships); and the method of *empiricism* was advanced (i.e., the preferred form of knowing about a phenomenon is the use of keen observation within the experimental setting).

> I found that the great majority of the men of science to whom I first applied protested that mental imagery was unknown to them, and they looked on me as fanciful and fantastic in supposing that the words "mental imagery" really expressed what I believed everybody supposed them to mean. They had no more notion of its true nature than a color-blind man, who has not discerned his defect, has of the nature of color. They had a mental deficiency of which they were unaware. . . . On the other hand, when I spoke to persons whom I met in general society, I found an entirely different disposition to prevail. Many men and a yet larger number of women, and many boys and girls, declared that they habitually saw mental imagery, and that it was perfectly distinct to them and full of color.
>
> —F. Galton, 1880

> Psychology cannot attain the certainty and exactness of the physical sciences, unless it rests on a foundation of experiment and measurement. . . . A step in this direction would be made by applying a series of mental tests and measurements to a large number of individuals. The results would be of considerable scientific value in discovering the constancy of mental processes, their interdependence, and their variation under different circumstances.
>
> —J. M. Cattell, 1890

> Galton's greatest contribution to introspective psychology was . . . his study of imagery and of individual differences in imagery. With Fechner in Germany and Charcot in France he is one of the three originators of the conception of ideational types. His questionnaire for determining types and for measuring the vividness of the imagery for the different senses is known to every psychologist.
>
> —E. G. Boring, 1957

Work on individual variation . . . is plagued by a number of theoretical and methodological difficulties in any area of psychology, and imagery is no exception.

—P. E. Morris and P. J. Hampson, 1983

## EARLY MEASUREMENT AND INDIVIDUAL DIFFERENCES IN IMAGERY

With the English naturalist and psychologist Sir Francis Galton (1822–1911), the criterion of *quantification* for the problem of mental imagery was realized—although in a rudimentary way—in the measurement of imagery via the first extensive use of the psychological questionnaire/survey. Galton (1883/1907) became interested in the particular issue of visual mental imagery because of a larger issue: He maintained that evidence of individual differences in mental imagery would help to establish a basis for stating the *differences* in the mental operations of different people (Watson, 1978, p. 329). Also, as with most of his research, Galton's interest in imagery was rooted in his attempt to demonstrate, ultimately, hereditary *similarities*; for example, he found that similarity in imagery is greater between siblings than between persons who are unrelated (Schultz, 1981, p. 128; cf. Galton, 1889/1973, 1869/1962, 1874, 1961; *Encyclopaedia Britannica*, 1955). Woodworth (1938, pp. 39–44) observes that the existence of great individual differences in imagery was first reported by Fechner (1860) and, later with fuller evidence, by Galton (1880) (cf. Galton, 1879–1880).

Eysenck, Arnold, and Meili (1972, p. 262) note that in regard to the interindividual differences in mental imagery, J. M. Charcot inspired a number of attempts to describe so-called "ideational" or "imaginative" types (the visual type or visualizer, the acoustic or auditory type, the motor type, etc.; cf. Charcot, 1890). Several objective methods were developed to more exactly determine the individual dominant type of ideation (e.g., methods involving association analysis, distractors in selective answer tests, questionnaires, picture description, stylistic analysis, etc.; cf. Woodworth and Schlosberg, 1965). Often, however, the validity of these methods has been questioned (e.g., Betts, 1909, asserts that the distinctions between ideational or imaginative types are not justified because there would need to be high correlations between imaginative capacities in different areas). Eysenck et al. observe, also, that for a long time research topics in psychology were focused on the "laws" of ideation (of image reproduction) and on the significance of mental images in thought (problem-solving) processes and concept formation. By way of explaining mental imagery, association psychologists such as G. E. Muller (1911) referred chiefly to the so-called "laws" of coexistence, similarity, succession, and perseveration; and to explain arbitrary ideation (along with the solving of specific tasks on this basis), appeal was made often to the theory of image complexes involving initial, goal, or objective ideas or images. In another viewpoint, the Wurzburg school allowed mental imagery only a subordinate significance in the thought-processes proper (imageless or abstract thinking). Yet another viewpoint—the so-called "motor theory" of thinking and consciousness (e.g., Jacobson, 1929, 1932; Max, 1934, 1935)—points out that mental images (i.e., motor and visual images) are accompanied by changes in the corresponding muscular area, for example, the arm and eye regions Further discussion on the theories of mental imagery is given herein in chapter 3, "A Review of Imagery Theories." However, without much disagreement among psychologists, it is widely recognized that Francis Galton was the first investigator to carry out anything approaching an *empirical* study of the modes and functions of mental imagery.

James (1890, vol. 2, p. 51) suggests that Galton's (1880) work on mental imagery "made an era in descriptive Psychology." James also provides an extensive account of Galton's use of the questionnaire on mental imagery. For instance, Galton's first group of a long series of questions related to the *illumination* (e.g., "Is the image dim or fairly clear? Is its brightness comparable to that of the actual scene?"), the *definition* (e.g., "Are all the objects pretty well defined at the same time, or is the place of sharpest definition at any one moment more contracted than it is in a real scene?"), and the *coloring* (e.g, "Are the colors of the china, of the toast, bread-crust, mustard, meat, parsley, or whatever may have been on the table, quite distinct and natural?") of the mental images that are conjured up when given the following instructions: "Think of your breakfast table as you sat down to it this morning—and consider carefully the picture that rises before your mind's eye."

Woodworth (1938, p. 39) describes both Fechner's (1860) and Galton's (1880) procedures for collecting data on mental imagery. Fechner asked his participants to call up an image of a certain object, and found that while some were able to accomplish this, others were only able, at best, to get a momentary glimpse of an image, after which the image merely turned into "bare thought" of the object. Galton employed the famous "breakfast table" questionnaire, and asked his participants to report on various dimensions of the images that were recalled when imagining the breakfast table scene (cf. Armstrong, 1894; French, 1902). From his first participants—consisting of scholars and men of science—Galton obtained responses that surprised him, for many of them reported an *absence* of images, and were inclined to regard the "mind's eye" as a pure invention of romantic poets. However, on distributing his questionnaire to a wider range or set of participants from "general society," Galton obtained many rather different reports that included habitual experiences of seeing mental images that were both distinct and colorful.

By way of quantification and arrangement of his data, Galton placed his participants in the order of their "power of imagery" as indicated by their reports and, thus, was able to demonstrate the average/median point of the collective responses (Woodworth, 1938). Galton accounted for the relative absence of mental imagery in his "men of science" by reasoning that their habits of highly abstract modes of thinking overshadowed such imagery and it was lost through disuse. With the collection of much more data from all strata of society, Galton eventually found that some scientists did, indeed, have vivid imagery while, on the other hand, some persons in the general population reported a lack of imagery. Moreover, Galton found distinct imagery *types* and, although he referred to types in his data collection and summarization, he emphasized that there was a *gradation* of clarity of imagery from distinct to faint. In this sense, Galton may be said to have favored, implicitly, a *continuum model* over a *discrete-type model* of mental imagery. Following Galton, other investigators of mental imagery popularized the notion of *imagery types* as if this had been Galton's major finding (cf. Watson, 1978, p. 330). Later, however, careful work in this area demonstrated that Galton was correct concerning his gradation (continuum) notion and others were incorrect in their belief that imagery falls neatly into discrete types. It may be mentioned here that the term types as used in this context (i.e., as referring to one's ability to have, or not to have, visual imagery) may be distinguished from the use of the term to differentiate imagery among the various sensory modalities collectively. That is, early researchers found that some individuals are strong in *visual* imagery, but weak in *auditory* imagery; other individuals are strong in *motor* imagery, but weak in *visual* imagery, and so on. In this respect, then, a continuum model may be applied *within* a given sensory modality (a person has "more" or "less" imagery in that modality), while a discrete-type model may be applied *across* modalities when assessing predominance of kind of imagery (e.g., visual, auditory, tactile, motor, etc.) in an individual. It is suggested that one should always be cautious when applying the term type in psychology to describe persons, behavior, or phenomena. Much of the early psychological literature in this area invokes the notion of types where the terms *pure types* and *mixed types* were used to describe a person's ability to experience imagery (a mixed type referred to individuals who reported imagery of several senses with no marked preponderance of any one modality). The next section—"Selected Early Psychological Imagery Studies"— covers various imagery studies that employ the concept of types in this regard.

Today, it seems correct to maintain the notion that the experience, or ability, of having imagery is more or less normally distributed (i.e., it conforms to the *normal curve model*) in the general population with the great majority of individuals having some, but not much, capacity for mental imagery.

Watson (1978, p. 332) evaluates Galton's contributions to psychology in general, including the latter's systematic study of imagery. Essentially, it was Galton who launched the measurement of *individual differences* in psychology even though others had been working in this area (e.g., Helmholtz measured reaction time but had given it up because the time varied so much from trial to trial). It was Galton's insight that individual differences were *not* a "nuisance" to be eliminated but, indeed, should be studied for their own sake (cf. Galton, 1884). Galton was the originator of mental tests; he developed the first extensive use of the method of questionnaire/survey in psychological research, and he strengthened the ties between the evolutionary and developmental approaches in psychology. According to Watson (p. 333), most important among Galton's contributions to psychology was his advancement of *quantitativism*—the desire to count and measure; Galton made the measurement of variability an interesting and important aspect of psychological research.

Following Galton's initial work on imagery, Betts (1909) expanded Galton's questionnaire to give a greater chance for participants to report images of every modality (cf. Cattell, 1897). In addition to visual imagery, and to refine the measurement procedure, Betts asked his participants to call up visually landscapes and faces, to call up auditorily voices and tunes, and to imagine the tactile feeling of velvet and sand, the taste of sugar and salt, the odor of roses and onions, the kinesthetic impressions of running and kicking, and the organic sensations of a headache and hunger. The task of the participant was to grade each image on a seven-point scale ranging from "perfectly clear" to "no image." Betts's results indicated that participants who ranked their imagery high or low in one sense tended to do about the same in the other senses also, so that there was a positive correlation (cf. Galton, 1888; Pearson, 1896) between the reported vividness of imagery of the different senses, instead of the negative correlation as demanded by a type model or theory. The average rating/grade assigned to the visual and auditory images was only slightly higher than the average assigned to the other modalities; the average fell between "very clear" and "moderately clear," except for olfaction/smell images where it fell a little below "moderately clear."

Woodworth (1938, pp. 41–45; cf. Woodworth and Schlosberg, 1965, pp. 720–22) observes that in view of the unstandardized nature of an individual's ratings of his own imagery—at around the turn of the twentieth century—it was necessary to develop objective tests of imagery. The tests were based on the overall assumption that visual work requires visual imagery, auditory work requires auditory imagery, and so forth. The criterion for validating an objective imagery test, at that time, was the subjective report of a trained observer. Many "objective" tests of imagery were studied by Angell (1910) and Fernald (1912) and found to have low validity, though some of them were useful in combination with a subjective report. The various methods used in the objective test of imagery cited by Woodworth (1938, pp. 41–43; and Woodworth and Schlosberg, 1965, pp. 721–22) include the following approaches (cf. chapter 4 herein, "Individual Differences in Mental Imagery"; and Osgood, 1953): the *questionary* (involves presentation of a series of questions designed to elicit images and the dimensions of imagery, such as definition, brightness, colors, and so on, in participants; see Betts, 1909; Galton, 1879–1880); the *association method* (involves tallying the number of association words that seem to belong to each sense modality—or the participant is given five minutes for saying objects that have characteristic colors, and another five minutes for saying objects that have characteristic sounds; see Woodworth and Schlosberg, 1965, pp. 46–48); the *analysis of style* (when an individual uses many words that describe sounds or sounding objects, he or she is identified as an *audile*; similarly, many words describing scenes would make the person a *visualist* or *visile*, etc.); *learning by eye or ear* (determine if the person learns more easily by reading or by listening; the *memory span* may be used as a test for imagery here, on the assumption that a person

who has strong visual imagery will recall digits presented visually better than those given orally); *method of distraction* (while the participant
is learning a list of materials, she is subjected to experimenter-provided
distractions in various sense modalities; theoretically, here, a noise should
bother people who are using auditory imagery, while holding the tongue
between the teeth should distract those who use motor imagery; see
Woodworth and Schlosberg, 1965, pp. 84–87); *spelling method* (the
person with good visual imagery should have little trouble spelling words
backward; however, as Fernald, 1912, points out, visual images of the
letters do not "stay put" well enough to be useful); the *letter square
method* (the participant is required to learn nine, sixteen, or twenty-five
letters or digits, arranged in a square pattern, reading by *rows*; subsequently, he is asked to recall the material by *columns*; see Binet, 1894;
Fernald, 1912; Muller, 1911; Muller and Schumann, 1894); and the
*picture-description method* (the use of visual imagery should permit the
person to give the most complete descriptions of pictures, but results
typically show that participants can do very well on the test by merely
naming the objects as the picture is being examined and, then, remembering only the names; cf. Fernald, 1912). Woodworth and Schlosberg
(1965, p. 722) note that—since Angell's (1910) and Fernald's (1912)
early work and assessments of most of the objective tests for imagery—
work on this issue continued for some years (e.g., Bowers, 1932a,b,c;
Davis, 1932) but had become inactive because of the lack of adequate
experimental methods.

One area, in particular, in the field of mental imagery—that of
eidetic imagery (cf. Hochman, 2001, pp. 100–103, 124–25, for definitions of the eidetic)—has been investigated extensively in the history of imagery measurement and research (cf. Kluver, 1928b, 1930,
1932). The method commonly used in assessing eidetic imagery in
persons is to have them examine a picture or scene and then ask them
to project their image of it on a gray screen, and to behave as if they
were still actually seeing the picture and describe it in as much detail
as possible. The results are frequently called an eidetic image, which
is regarded as a special kind of image. The German psychologist E. R.
Jaensch (1920, 1930) was responsible mainly for attracting early attention to the phenomenon of eidetic imagery. Woodworth and
Schlosberg (1965, p. 722) observe that eidetic imagery is fairly common in children but rare in adults, and it may be related to personality traits; they assert, also, that psychologists know little about the
actual nature of the eidetic image, despite a large number of studies,
and it is not known how the eidetic child establishes his image or

whether it is qualitatively different from the ordinary strong visual imagery of many people. Allport (1924) and Kluver (1926a,b, 1928b, 1932) provide good summaries of early eidetic imagery research. The remaining portion of this section covers early research on the quantitative/measurement aspects of imagery, in particular research on visual imagery and eidetic imagery.

One of the difficulties in the study of visual imagery and its measurement is that—unlike viewing a real object that is "fixed" in space—the visual memory image is rather mobile and frequently nonlocalized. That is, sometimes visual imagery is not definitely localized, sometimes it is localized inside the participant's head (cf. the methodology employed by Holmes, Roeckelein, and Olmstead, 1968, pp. 666–68), sometimes in the space/distance where the original object was, and sometimes out in front of the participant or on the wall in front of him/her. In a series of tests, Lillien J. Martin (1912, 1915) discovered that many of her participants were able to perform what appears, at first glance, to be an impossible feat: They could look at a *real* object, call up beside it an *image* of the same object, and *compare* the image with the object while both were present. Martin reported that her participants saw an image that was usually less vivid in color and vaguer in outline than the real object, and that it had to be constructed with effort whereas the real object was "there" all at once. Moreover, the real object revealed more and more detail on continued examination, whereas further study of the image revealed nothing more than had been noted previously in the original imaged object.

Martin (1915) discusses the protocols from college students who reported that they had seen apparitions (ghosts), and maintains that whether one will see ghosts at all, and what their appearance will be, depends on whether the individual normally projects his/her visual images into space—or is able to do so under the influence of a strong emotional stimulus. Martin found—for some participants with strong visual imagery—that when an object is *casually* thought of, such images are located in the *back* of the person's head, but when thinking of the object in *detail*, the image of it is out in *front* of him/her—the distance away depending on the circumstances under which the image is seen. Moreover, with such vivid visualizers, when the individual projects visual images of someone previously seen, those persons are *translucent* (the participant does not usually "see through" such images, but can easily do so). In other cases, with accompanying emotional experience, various kinaesthetic components are localized largely in the back of the participant's neck and arms. Martin suggests that such *hallucinatory* experiences, as well as others like it, show that it is not necessary to be able to project one's visual images and to do it usually, or very often, in order to have a hallucination. Martin found, also, that many other persons who have strong visual images and usually project them, have never seen an apparition/ghost. However, this "negative aspect" does not vitiate Martin's (1915, p. 257) opinion that "ghosts arise only where one is able to project his images"; that is, those who can project images may, or may not, see ghosts. Further, the hallucination image—when present—must have a content or be accompanied by an emotion that separates it out from other projected visual images.

Of course, in terms of objective and valid imagery measurement, studies such as those of Martin (1912, 1914–1915, 1915) are comparatively unsophisticated—as judged by today's standards—and offer only nonquantitative data based upon the introspective reports of participants operating within the framework of the case study method. (For other interesting early empirical studies on mental imagery, see the work of O. Kulpe [1902], J. Rieffert [1912], E. W. Scripture [1896], and C. W. Perky [1910]—as described by Woodworth [1938, pp. 44–45].)

Two early investigators (i.e., Gengerelli, 1930; Teasdale, 1934; cf. Martin, 1913b) use the term quantitative in the titles of their articles on eidetic imagery. Note that Woodworth (1938, p. 45) observes that persons possessing eidetic imagery were first described by Urbantschitsch (1907) who distinguished between the ordinary memory images that are imagined, and the perceptlike memory images that are seen. The name eidetic was used by Jaensch (1920, 1930) and his associates to convey the idea of an especially *vivid* image. Also, see Jaensch (1922, 1927), Kiesow (1925, 1927), Kluver (1925, 1929, 1930, 1932), Kroh (1922), Purdy (1936), Urbantschitsch (1903, 1905, 1908, 1918), and Zillig (1922, 1930, 1931). Briefly, Gengerelli (1930) conducted four experiments (involving *independent variables* of stimulus-size, and projection-distances of *criterion* card) in which seven stimulus cards contained a different size circle (in two experiments, circles ranged in diameter from 54 mm to 30 mm in incremental differences of 4 mm between circles) were shown to two participants (with the addition of a third participant in the fourth experiment) who were asked to project an image of the circle onto a *criterion* card (containing a line drawing of a 42 mm square) after viewing the circle for 5 seconds. The seven cards were shuffled and placed face downward, and the participants went through the stimulus cards successively. Experimenter's instructions to participants were as follows: "When I say 'up' I want you to pick up with your right hand one of the cards in the pile and look at it for 5 seconds. At the end of this time I shall say 'down,' and after you hand the card to me, I want you to project the circle you just saw onto the square which is tacked up here in front of you, and tell me whether it is too big, too small, or just fits. All you have to say is too small, too big, or just right." Ten judgments (the *dependent variable*)—involving reports of too small, too big, or just right—were obtained for each circle (Gengerelli also collected participants' *introspective* reports), the deck of cards being reshuffled after each run of the seven stimulus cards. Gengerelli expected that circle number 4 (the "halfway" circle of the series, measuring 42 mm in diameter)—having its diameter equal to the length of the sides of the criterion (the square)—would invariably be indicated as fitting the square: the smaller circles as being too small, and the larger circles as being too large. Results from the tests, however, indicated that such an expectation was fulfilled only for the older of the two female participants (the girls were fifteen and eleven years of age). Gengerelli (p. 400) states that the older girl "seems to possess a much more highly developed eidetic proclivity" than the younger girl—which is contrary to the work of Jaensch (1920, 1930), which indicates that eidetic imagery capacity diminishes with age. Another finding by Gengerelli was that the size of the eidetic image decreases as the distance of projection is increased (a result that is similar to Kluver's [1926a] findings. Kluver used projection distances of 25, 100, and 150 cm; of his eighteen participants, twelve demonstrated a diminution in the size of the eidetic images with increase in distance of projection; Kluver's stimulus exposure times were 10 seconds). Gengerelli suggests that certain methods of attack are amenable to the future fruitful quantitative study of eidetic imagery, and of visual imagery in general; for example, he asserts that there is no a priori reason that would render the method of "constant stimuli" (so widely successful in experiments with lifted-weights) to be of no value in investigations of eidetic imagery. Gengerelli (p. 404) states, "Such a method . . . would place research in this field on a quantitative basis such as has not been attained heretofore."

Teasdale (1934) reviews previous work on eidetic imagery (e.g., Allport, 1924; Jaensch, 1930; Kluver, 1926a,b; Roessler, 1928; Zeman, 1925) and describes his own experiments consisting of six independent tests of eidetic imagery. Teasdale (p. 56) notes that work on eidetic imagery typically has been confined to a study of isolated cases and has resulted in claims being made for the significance of the phenomenon without sufficient statistical evidence to support them; he also notes that previous work in this area makes no mention of tests of reliability and indicates that different researchers use different criteria for determining the strength of the eidetic capability. Moreover, according to Teasdale, among those researchers who use the same criteria there does not seem to be a standard method of marking/grading responses. In addition, different investigators use varying experimental conditions; for example, Jaensch (1930) exposed his stimulus pictures to participants for 15 seconds, Allport (1924) for 35 seconds, and Kluver (1926a) used 30 seconds and 60 seconds for two silhouette pictures and 15 seconds for pictures of animals. Teasdale notes that complex pictures, of course, require longer exposure times than simpler ones, but it surprises him that Allport and Kluver should use the same times of exposure for studying eidetic images as Jaensch uses for afterimages.

Teasdale (1934) maintains that not only are the experimental methods used in imagery studies open to criticism but also the results obtained vary widely with different investigators and, in certain cases, are entirely contradictory. For instance, Jaensch's (1930) theory of perceptual development and the claims he makes for the educational significance of eidetic imagery rest largely on the supposition that eidetic ability is strongest in young children and that it decreases with increasing age—but he has only Roessler's (1928) results to support his contention. Other researchers—such as Allport (1924), Bonte (1925), Fischer and Hirschberg (1924), and Liefmann (1928a,b)—all disagree, most of them maintaining that the peak of eidetic phenomena occurs at the age just before puberty. Teasdale attempts to provide reliable and statistically sound evidence of the way in which eidetic phenomena vary in school children between the ages of ten and fourteen years—the age range involved in the dispute regarding the variation of eidetic imagery with age.

Teasdale's (1934) experimental conditions were designed around those used by Jaensch (1930) and Kluver (1926a), which involved a homogeneous dark gray background against which participants projected images after being shown stimulus pictures, and a stopwatch was used to determine the exposure time and duration of the image. (I include detailed descriptions of procedures and materials here to give the reader a flavor for the type of experiments conducted in these early studies of eidetic imagery.) In the first test, a red square (2-inch sides) was presented for fixation for 10 seconds; the goal of this test was to show to the child what was meant by "seeing" something on the gray background. After an interval of 2 to 3 minutes, the same square was presented again for fixation, this time for 20 seconds. The third test consisted of the participant's fixation on a silhouette picture (cf. Jaensch, 1930); participants were asked to fixate on a central feature of the picture, such as the "lady's hand" in the picture. After the exposure time of 15 seconds, the participant was required to look at the gray background and to describe every detail occurring in the image. All the details occurring in the actual picture were printed on a blank form so as to enable the experimenter to record rapidly those seen in the image by marking/checking the appropriate words. Results obtained from the *fixation* of pictures and squares in these tests were not taken into account in the marking; marks were given only where an image was obtained when the participant had only *looked at* the stimulus picture. Any images obtained without fixation of the stimulus being necessary were called the eidetic images. Nonfixation of the stimulus was employed in the fourth, fifth, and sixth tests; in these conditions, the participant was marked/graded as to his/her eidetic imagery ability. Participants (a total of 173 boys) were reminded frequently that the experimenter wished to know what was "seen," not what was "remembered." Teasdale (p. 60) notes that a "definite tension of the eyes was observed when an image appeared"— an interesting datum that is based in an objective, but unmeasured, behavior of the participants. The duration (i.e., the time between the appearance, then disappearance, of the image) and richness of detail (i.e., absence versus presence of image) of the participants' imagery was marked/recorded by the experimenter. Teasdale asserts that long duration is characteristic of eidetic imagery, and also that there is a high correlation between this factor and that of richness of detail.

Teasdale's (1934) system of "marking/grading" was as follows: In the test, three pictures were shown, one at a time, for nonfixating inspection. The maximum number of marks/checks that could be obtained on one picture was twenty-four; of these, eighteen were given for the amount of *detail* seen, and six for *duration* of the image. The six marks for duration were given as follows: 10 seconds—one mark; 30 seconds—two marks; 1 minute—three marks; 2 minutes—four marks; 5 minutes—five marks; and 10 minutes—six marks. The eighteen marks/checks given for detail were given as follows: for an image portraying the silhouette in full detail—twelve marks; for a full reproduction of the background of the picture—six marks. In all the stimulus pictures, the chief features or objects were in black silhouette with the background in delicate colors; the experimenter "used his judgment in allotting marks." The maximum number of marks that could be scored was seventy-two (i.e., twenty-four for each of three pictures). In order to obtain the full twenty-four marks for each picture, the participant had to have an image that reproduced the picture with photographic accuracy and had to last for at least 10 minutes (results showed that the boy who received the largest number of marks obtained a score of forty-nine on the three pictures). Each participant was placed into one of four groups, based upon his marks/score: Group One—over twenty-four marks; Group Two—thirteen to twenty-four marks; Group Three—one to twelve marks; Group Four— no marks. Many boys, after regarding a stimulus picture with nonfixation, obtained an image that contained almost the whole of the detail for a mere instant; images seen in this manner were not considered to be eidetic images, but merely as afterimages. Accordingly, such images were graded as "no marks/no eidetic image."

Teasdale (1934) reasoned that his tests were *valid* because the tests, and the system of marking used, were based on the generally accepted properties of the eidetic image; the stimulus pictures used were those advocated by Jaensch (1930); the method of estimating the ability of the participants by grading them as shown is an improvement on the methods used previously (the previous systems of marking/grading participants take into account *latent* eidetic imagery ability and make use of criteria such as *Emmert's size-distance invariance hypothesis/law*; neither latent eidetic ability nor Emmert's law are accepted in the present experiments, only *manifest* eidetic ability is considered). Teasdale also claims good *reliability* of his experiments based upon his procedure of repeated measurements of one class of boys taken on two separate days with two different selections of stimulus pictures taken from the same series. Among Teasdale's results are the following: if the criterion of eidetic imagery ability is the obtaining of over twenty-four marks, then only 5.8 percent of boys between the ages of twelve to thirteen years are eidetics (if the standard is lower—such as the criterion of obtaining over twelve marks—then 21 percent of the boys are eidetics); the prevalence of eidetic ability *decreases* with *increases* in age. This finding is in agreement with Jaensch's (1930) results; however, again, other investigators—such as Allport (1924), Bonte (1925), Fischer and Hirschberg (1924), Liefmann (1928a,b), and Zeman (1925)—report that the frequency of eidetic imagery is a maximum at about twelve years of age. Teasdale concludes that the inconsistent results obtained previously by different researchers may be due to the use of different standards. (Teasdale provides three differently shaped curves based upon the use of different standards for defining eidetic imagery; for example, if very poor/faint images are counted as eidetic images, then it is seen that there is an *increase* of eidetic ability with *increasing* age, over the range of ten to fourteen years old—a result that is different from Jaensch's 1930 findings.)

In summary, Teasdale (1934) concludes that there are probably two types of eidetic imagery: one that is very prevalent among young children and decreases with increasing age, and one that is not so rich in detail—which does not show such marked divergencies from normal afterimages and which becomes more frequent with increasing age up to fourteen years. The main result of Teasdale's study is that eidetic images that differ markedly from afterimages are found to be more prevalent among young than among older children, over the tested ages of ten to fourteen years. Finally, consideration of Teasdale's study in detail gives an indication of the specific materials used in assessing and measuring eidetic imagery and shows psychologists' increasing concerns in the area of imagery in the early 1900s with matters relating to the validity, reliability, methodology, scoring, quantification, and measurement of imagery phenomena.

Allport (1924) examines the visual memory imagery (eidetic imagery) studies that were performed from 1919 through 1924 at the Marburg Institute for Psychology in Germany under the direction of E. R. Jaensch. Allport notes that Urbantschitsch (1907) employed the German word *anschauungsbild* for eidetic imagery phenomena, and the term was adopted by subsequent writers. The capacity for imagery of this type is designated by Jaensch and his school as the *eidetische anlage*, and the individuals who possess this capacity as *eidetikers*. Allport suggests that it is best to translate *anschauungsbild* as eidetic image, in order not to complicate unnecessarily the terminology, though the term eidographic image would perhaps better characterize the true nature of the phenomenon. Allport distinguishes, also, between the terms visual image (where a former visual perception is merely imagined) and eidetic image (where the original object is actually seen); a person may be able to remember clearly a visual experience and to describe it in detail without necessarily possessing eidetic imagery. The true eidetic image, in distinction from the visual memory-image, revives the earlier optical impression—when the eyes are closed in a dark room, and sometimes when the eyes are normally open—with *hallucinatory clearness* (cf. Kroh, 1920, 1922). This definition also excludes both pathological hallucinations and dream images, but admits various "spontaneous images of phantasy." Allport notes that this special type of psychical afterimage is probably the same phenomenon that has been named by others as *subjective vision* (Muller, 1826), *memory afterimage* (Fechner, 1860), *primary memory-image* (Ward, 1918), *projected memory-image* (Martin, 1912), and *imaginary perception* (Binet, 1899). The credit for first exploring eidetic imagery systematically—and of referring it to its proper realm, that of child psychology—belongs to the Marburg school under E. R. Jaensch.

Allport (1924) divides his discussion of the "descriptive and functional characteristics of eidetic imagery" (where he provides criteria for distinguishing the eidetic image from the memory-image and the afterimage) into fifteen sections:

1. *Localization* (the content of the eidetic image is truly "seen," and it is always "projected" and never localized "within the head")
2. *Richness/clearness in detail* (the eidetic image far surpasses both the memory-image and the afterimage in richness of detail)
3. *Persistence* (the eidetic image continues in the visual field even through prolonged periods of observation, as well as being "recurrent" voluntarily by *eidetikers* even after hours, days, months, or years)
4. *Intensity/weight* (with the qualification of a possible "time-" or "order-error," there is an increase in the intensity/weight of the eidetic image—in comparison to its ground—where it is less dominant than the afterimage, but more dominant than the memory-image)
5. *Corporeity* (the principle of depth may be used to distinguish among the three types of images where a memory-image is two-dimensional, an afterimage seems to be three-dimensional, and the eidetic image appears in "semirelief")
6. *Size of the visual field* (refers to attempts to determine at what distance from the center of the image a peripheral stimulus is effective)
7. *Coloration* (the colors in the eidetic image are often seen as more "brilliant" than in the original object; in such cases, the color appears to be like "frozen gas"—*Flachenfarbe*—without object character)
8. *Conditions of arousal/disappearance* (it seems that a longer time of presentation is required for the arousal of the eidetic image than for the memory-image, and a longer time for the afterimage than for the eidetic image; also, rigid fixation is necessary to the arousal of an afterimage, but less often required for the eidetic image, and practically never required for the memory-image; and while the memory-image is largely subject to voluntary recall, the eidetic image is recallable voluntarily to a lesser degree, and the afterimage not at all)

9. *Selective tendencies* (eidetic images may be secured on the basis of personal interest or affective tone invoked by the subject material or the stimulus objects)

10. *Flexibility* (the content of the eidetic image may undergo striking alterations in imagery reproductions, indicating a close relationship to purely central/ideational imagery)

11. *Coherence* (it seems that the higher the memory-level, the less is the coherence between the image and the perception such that the memory-image is less coherent than the eidetic image which, in turn, is less than the afterimage)

12. *Plasticity* (this is the degree to which an eidetic image may be influenced by the conditions of a preceding experiment/event)

13. *Invariability* (the eidetic image does not seem to conform, as does the afterimage, to Emmert's law; cf. Roeckelein, 1998, pp. 160–62; however, the eidetic image, according to its nature, approaches either the afterimage or the memory-image in regard to the factor of *invariability*)

14. *Displacement in space* (eidetic images are reversed frequently, turned upside down or displaced from right to left)

15. *Fusion* (*eidetikers* may construct *synthetic* images that are not static, but have the properties of continuous movement, alteration, and composite aspects of form and size; a synthetic image may be reproduced after several different objects are placed in a row before the participant and he is asked to look intently at the first object until an eidetic image is aroused, then to project this image upon the next object, and so on until he comes to the end of the series—at which time a unique synthetic, composite, or generic type of image appears)

For the significance of this phenomenon vis-à-vis the theory of the *origin* of generic images, see Binet (1899, p. 118) and Galton (1883/1907, 2d ed., p. 132).

In attempting to answer the question, "What is the *function* of eidetic imagery in mental life?" Allport (1924) recalls Jaensch's (1920, 1930) "genetic" theory that is based on the conception of a progressive series of memory-levels and in which the transition from one level to another is continuous so that the eidetic image now resembles more closely the memory-image and now the afterimage. The experimental evidence on this approach shows that in respect to those attributes that are shared by all three types of images, the eidetic image tends to assume a *middle* position between the afterimage and the memory-image. Moreover, for Jaensch and the Marburg researchers, the doctrine of memory-levels carries additional features: It is for them a genetic as well as a descriptive fact. Memory is a "purposive" if not a "structural" unity, and the afterimage, the eidetic image, and the memory-image represent progressively higher states in a "teleological continuum"—as the individual advances in years he or she comes to depend more and more upon the higher grades of memory, while the lower grades fall into disuse (some investigators ascribe to the afterimage the most primitive qualities and functions in the "memory scale"; others regard the eidetic phenomenon not only as the original form of memory, but also as the ontogenetic source of perception as well). According to this hypothesis or scenario, as the individual makes contact with the environment, and as the needs of the individual change with his/her development, there gradually evolves from the original eidetic experience (i.e., via a primitive and undifferentiated conscious content called an eidetic image) the appearance of true perceptions and true memories with all of their distinctive attributes.

Allport (1924, p. 116) cautions that "the mere fact of resemblance between the various types of imagery does not prove that memory and imagination have evolved through lower stages. On the contrary, memory . . . seems from the beginning to exist as an independent phenomenon. Not all children have eidetic images, and yet all have memory." Allport asserts that the eidetic phenomenon is an intermediate form of imagery in the sense that it shows at one and the same time characteristics that pertain to both the sensory and the ideational realms, but it cannot be shown to be a transitional stage in the evolution of higher forms of imagery from lower. Allport concludes that the function of the eidetic image seems to be to preserve and to elaborate a concrete stimulus situation for the developing child in such a way as to intensify the sensory aspects of experience and, thereby, to enhance for the individual the meaning of the stimulus situation and to enable him/her to repeat and to perfect adaptive responding to the changing environment.

Allport (1928) provides a useful discussion concerning Jaensch's (1920, 1922, 1927, 1930) hypothesis of a continuum involving afterimages, eidetic images, and memory-images. The weakness of the hypothesis, according to Allport, lies in relating eidetic images to afterimages—in reality these phenomena have "only a superficial and accidental resemblance . . . on the other hand, such a close relation obtains between the eidetic image and the memory-image that the former, in all probability, should be considered as merely a limiting case of the latter" (p. 418). Allport (1928) examines the evidence for the alleged affinity that exists between the eidetic image and the afterimage by discussing five issues: the method of discovery of an eidetic imager; the existence of negatively colored eidetic images; the fact that both the eidetic image and the afterimage are localized in visual space; the occasional resemblances in behavior of the two types of image; and the case of the "unitary type" of imager/observer where no afterimages are produced, but where all imagery experience is eidetic.

For other substantive discussions in the area of eidetic imagery, see Ahsen (1977, 1987); Allport (1924); Gray and Gummerman (1975); Haber (1979); Haber and Haber (1988); Hochman (2001); Kluver (1928b, 1930, 1932); Leask, Haber, and Haber (1969); Marks and McKellar (1982); Siipola and Hayden (1965); Stromeyer (1970); Stromeyer and Psotka (1970); and Woodworth (1938). Kluver (1928b, p. 94) observes that the earliest studies on eidetic imagery were concerned chiefly with problems of visual sensation and perception; later studies, however, were concerned with the psychology of thought and memory, and problems of emotional and volitional life. Also, later investigations touched on problems of social, racial, animal, vocational, educational, and abnormal psychology. The later studies attempted to make contributions not only to the field of psychology, but also to the fields of esthetics, philology, ethnology, and mythology, as well as to shed light on problems in the areas of psychotherapy, physiology, anatomy, histology, neurology, embryology, and genetics.

In a later article, Kluver (1932, p. 181) states that "during the last (few) years the majority of investigators have been more interested in eidetic images as indicators of personality trends than in eidetic imagery itself. As a matter of fact, too great an emphasis has been placed on the relation of eidetic imagery to personality." In his review, Kluver (1932, p. 181) covers the *experimental* studies on eidetic imagery that were conducted from 1928 to 1932; he maintains that "it is to be regretted that in the experimental work recently published more attention has been paid to the Marburg hypotheses on 'types,' 'memory-levels,' etc., than to the problems involved in the methods for determining eidetic imagery." Finally, for yet other early (pre-1960) studies, researches, experiments, procedures, methods, individual differences, and measurements in the area of eidetic imagery, see the following sources: Aderhold (1959), Alexander (1904), Ammann (1930), Antipoff (1926), Barber (1959a,b), Baxt (1871), Bender (1938), Bergemann (1925), Beringer (1923), Bibring-Lehner (1928), Blachowski (1936), Bonte (1933, 1934), Bonte, Liefmann, and Roessler (1926), Bousfield and Barry (1933), Bradfield (1939), Bratbak (1944), Broer (1932), Brueckner (1934), Busse (1920),

Carmichael (1925), Cramaussel (1926), Critchley (1951), Dimitrov (1931, 1933, 1937a,b), Downey (1927b), Drummond (1926), Dwelshauvers (1930), Eissler and Rowe (1946), Enke (1933), Feigenberg (1958), Feiman (1935), Fiedler (1935), Finkenstaedt (1940), Fischer (1927), Fischer and Hentze (1934), Flournoy (1926), Floyd (1956), Freiling (1923), Freiling and Jaensch (1923), Friedlaender (1928), Funke (1928), Garfunkel (1929), Gatti (1929), Gatti and Vacino (1926), Geblewicz (1935), Gosser (1921), Gottheil (1921), Gotz (1929), Gressot (1950), Griffitts (1927), Gross (1930), Gutmann (1935), Hansen (1929), Havermans (1936), Hayashi (1934, 1936), Heller (1930), Helson (1933), Henning (1923, 1924), Hensel (1930), Herbertz (1930), Herwig (1921), Higginson (1926), Hirst (1951), Hodges (1936), Hofe (1926), Hofmarksrichter (1931), Husen (1946, 1952), Jackson (1936), Jaensch (1921, 1922, 1923, 1934, 1935a,b), Jaensch and Jaensch (1921), Jaensch and Kretz (1932), Jaensch and Mehmel (1928), Jaensch and Schweicher (1927), Jankowska (1938, 1939), Jelliffe (1928), Jenkin (1935), Joesten (1929), Johannesson (1939), Kao and Lyman (1944), Karger (1925), Kattsoff (1950), Katz (1956), Khaimovich (1937), Kiefer (1956), Kirek (1926), Kluver (1926a,b, 1927, 1928, 1931, 1934), Koffka (1923), Kononova (1929), Kratina (1930), Krellenberg (1922), Kroh (1924, 1952), Krudewig (1953), Lahti (1951), Lang, Polatin, and Hotchkiss (1937), Langfeld (1929), Lenz (1940), Leuner (1955), Leven (1926, 1927), Levin (1932), Loch (1931), Lotz (1937), Luther (1931), Marzi (1933), Marzi and Rende (1943), Masaki (1929), Mata de Gregorio and Poleo (1958), Meenes (1933, 1934, 1937), Meenes and Morton (1936), Meili-Dworetzki (1943), Metz (1929), Miller (1931a,b), Miskolczy and Schultz (1929), Morsch (1942), Morsch and Abbott (1945), Mota (1950), Muller (1935), Myslivecek (1931), Naumova (1934), Neymeyer (1956), O'Neill (1933/1934), O'Neill and Rauth (1934), Ohwaki (1936), Ohwaki and Kihara (1953), Ohwaki, Kaiwa, and Kaketa (1934, 1936), Olasz (1936), Ostrowski (1934), Oswald (1957), Pankow (1955), Pear (1925a, 1927a,b), Peck and Hodges (1937a,b), Peck and Walling (1935), Pedersen (1954), Petty (1939), Peuckert (1939), Pflugfelder (1948), Pinelli (1939), Popov (1934), Quercy (1925, 1926, 1927, 1937), Rauth and Sinnott (1937), Riekel (1950, 1951), Rieti (1932, 1933), Rutten (1940), Ruttmann (1938), Sacristan and Germain (1933), Saltzman and Machover (1952), Scharnke (1927), Schiel (1934), Schilder (1926), Schmeieng (1935, 1936a,b, 1937), Schmidt (1937), Schmitz (1930),

Schmulling (1927/1928), Schultze-Niemann (1940), Schumacher (1928, 1930, 1931), Schwab (1924), Scola (1925, 1927), Shipley (1958), Siebert (1929), Singleton (1954), Smith (1949), Stratton (1917), Susukita (1937), Thacker (1937), Tripp (1926), Wachtel (1932, 1934, 1935), Walker (1927), Walters (1939, 1942), Warren (1921), Weil (1930), Weiskrantz (1950), Wertham (1930), Whitaker (1942), Wilhelm (1927), Zagorovskii (1929), Zaworski (1947), Zeman (1929), Zimmerman (1931), and Ziolko (1953).

> If one were to generalize from this single set of answers, he would conclude that in most people the mind is capable by efforts of all kinds of sense imagery, although as a usual thing its content is limited to one or two special forms.
>
> —F. C. French, 1902

> Sometimes the psychologist . . . would have us believe that the chief distinction between the mental image and the percept is that the former is unreal and the latter real. . . . The two worlds, the imagined and the real, are not finally two worlds. Eventually, the imagined must be realized, the ideal must be made a part of my concrete achievement.
>
> —S. Colvin, 1908

> The difference between Percepts and Images, which seems so obvious, and for practical guidance is in fact known to everybody, has not yet been determined to the satisfaction of psychologists.
>
> —C. Read, 1908

> Until recent years the experimental investigation of images has been comparatively neglected, and even at the present time the subject does not seem to receive either the extended or the detailed study that is given to sensation. Thus, while there have been studies of the general nature of mental imagery, of the memory image, and of the image of imagination, these have treated the subject mostly from the point of view of recognition and recall, and a specific investigation of the attributes of the image has been neglected. Especially meager in the existing experimental work on imagery is reference to its intensive aspect.
>
> —A. de Vries Schaub, 1911

> I would say that I thoroughly agree with the Behaviorists that our efforts should be directed with all possible energy toward the refinement of the methods for the investigation of expression. The

science owes them the deepest gratitude for their reaction against objectively uncontrolled experimentation.

—H. S. Langfeld, 1916

The problem of the exact nature of so-called "images," of the precise character of that which in and through an act of imagining is immediately presented to the apprehending mind, has rarely been seriously faced either in the standard treatises on psychology or in special monographs dealing with imagination and memory.

—G. D. Hicks, 1924

## SELECTED EARLY PSYCHOLOGICAL IMAGERY STUDIES (1890–1959)

This section on selected early (1890–1959) psychological research on imagery is divided into ten parts using the following rubrics: Afterimages; Consciousness/Dreams/Hallucinations/Illusions/Perception; Imagination Imagery; Literature/Music; Meaning/Thinking/ Imageless Thought; Memory Imagery; Methods/General Imagery-Related Studies; Synesthesia; Tactile/Gustatory/Olfactory/Auditory/ Kinesthetics/Motor Imagery; and Visual Imagery. Studies in each part are arranged chronologically, according to publication date, and are selected to give a cross-sectional analysis and insight into the nature and concerns of early imagery research from 1890 through 1959.

### Afterimages

Franklin (1894) reviews work on the afterimage both as conducted by Carl Hess (cf. Hess, 1893) and as discussed by Hermann von Helmholtz (cf. Helmholtz, 1856–1866). In a series of trials, Hess examined the change of tone produced in a given spectral color in a condition where the eye had already been fatigued by gazing at another color; for example, under such circumstances, after looking at red, violet becomes bluish green and green becomes greenish blue; after looking at violet, red becomes reddish yellow; and after looking at blue, red also becomes reddish yellow. Franklin notes that in each of these cases the effect is the same as if the reacting color were mixed with a very considerable amount of the color complementary to that first gazed at. Such a fact, says Franklin (p. 396) is "nothing new for Helmholtz . . . the question is whether the explanation given by

Helmholtz of the after-image which causes the result is sufficient to account for the amount of change produced." Franklin (p. 398) asserts that while the work of Hess "makes no distinct addition to our knowledge of facts, it is still very important in calling renewed attention to the necessity for admitting that when an after-image is produced, some very pronounced physiological process if taking place in the retina." Franklin concludes that "this does not establish an incompatibility with the Young-Helmholtz theory."

Franz (1895) observes that practically nothing had been accomplished before the nineteenth century in the way of exact *measurement* of the afterimage, and presents the results of an attempt to measure the smallest amount of light (i.e., the *threshold* value) that will produce an afterimage. Franz systematically manipulated three physical units (light intensity, light area, and stimulation time) in his apparatus that was used to study the afterimage in four participants. Based upon nearly 3,000 experiments/trials, and upon the definition of the threshold as "that intensity, time, or area which produces an afterimage 75-percent of the number of stimuli," Franz concluded the following: with an exposure time of 1 second and an intensity of 2/25 candle power, the *area* threshold is 4 square millimeters; with the area 64 square millimeters and the intensity 2/25 candle power, the *time* threshold is 1/100 second; and with the area 64 square millimeters and the time of exposure 1 second, the *intensity* threshold is approximately 1/100 candle power. Franz (p. 136) also makes a further analysis based upon a correlation of the physical units used in terms of the production of afterimages—which is a "purely psychological problem" involving the question: "How much time equals how much intensity or area?" Franz proposed the following relationships: Squaring the time equals doubling the intensity or quadrupling the area (and vice versa), and reducing the area to one-fourth equals halving the intensity and taking the square root of the time. Franz suggested that whether these are chance relations—or are, indeed, general ones throughout the phenomena of afterimages—which may not be stated dogmatically at the present time (1895).

Daniels (1895) conducted experiments to determine the *duration* of memory afterimages under conditions of "distracted attention" (cf. Hyslop, 1903) where he attempted to separate the simple persistence of the image (due, most likely, to the "native retentiveness of the nervous substance") from its continuation in associative memory. As a means of distraction, Daniels had his participants rapidly read aloud passages of interesting stories; the image employed was that aroused by the pronunciation of a group of three digits. When the participant was underway in his reading, the three digits were announced by the experimenter within a total time of about 2 seconds. Following a determined interval, at a signal (a tap on the table) from the experimenter, the participant stopped reading the story and attempted to recall the digits that were given; intervals of 0, 5, 10, 15, and 20 seconds were used. One hundred trials each were run at these intervals on each of two participants where each served alternately as participant and experimenter. Results of this procedure indicated that the memory afterimage does not last 15 seconds in a reproducible condition, unless it is "freshened by a re-entrance into consciousness"; if it returns a single time, it may exceed 20 seconds, but not often. Note that Meyer (1902) discusses the duration of the "auditory after-sensation" and critiques the methodologies used in Mayer's work in 1874 against Abraham's studies in 1898. Meyer favors Abraham's approach and states that the "seemingly beautiful method of Mayer turns out to be no method at all" (p. 143). In another context, Lay (1903b) critiques extensively the methodology used by Slaughter (1902) who studied motor, visual, auditory, dermal, gustatory, and olfactory imagery. Lay states that "Dr. Slaughter's paper seems to me to be an example of not a few that have appeared of late in which the conditions of the experiment are not clearly described" and his results "give the impression that there are more words than ideas behind them" (p. 305).

Daniels (1895) notes that the term memory afterimage (*Erinnerungsnachbild*) was introduced by Fechner (1860) who made observations and recordings on visual memory afterimages, and it was described, also, by Exner (cf. James, 1890, vol. 1, p. 646) under the name of the *primary memory-image*. Daniels (pp. 563–64) relates and compares the results of his afterimage study to previous experiments conducted by Dietze (in Wundt's laboratory at Leipzig), Munsterberg, and Wolfe.

Haines and Williams (1905) note that the relationship of the peripherally aroused and the centrally aroused or revived mental processes is in a "very unsatisfactory state" (p. 20; cf. Murray, 1906) and suggest that the *voluntary control* of afterimages offers a way of studying such a relationship. Further, they observe that there are four distinct lines of work on this issue: vivid visualization of memory images (cf. Galton, 1883/1907, pp. 103, 159), control of the color and form of idio-retinal light (cf. Ladd, 1894), afterimages of memory images of color (or of subjectively induced color; cf. Downey, 1901), and control of the color of visual afterimages (cf. Washburn, 1899). Following a review of work in these four areas, Haines and Williams describe their research concerning the problem as to whether the course of the afterimage can be altered or interfered with by mental imagery. Their three-stage procedure involved the daily presentation to two participants (the two researchers themselves) the following: a series of two to six normal afterimages (with a 20-second exposure); then about two memory-images (subjective controls for a given color) beginning when no afterimage effects were present; and finally two or more subjective controls (for a given color) of the afterimage—this afterimage being aroused in the same way as the normal afterimage. Thus Haines and Williams's procedure allowed them to see, side by side: (1) the simple afterimage effect; (2) the simple memory image (imagination product); and (3) the two types of image combined. Based upon their data and analyses, Haines and Williams (p. 36) conclude that it is very clear that "there is an interference of the after-image and the memory image with each other." Moreover, one of the participants felt that his effort to get an effective subjective control of an afterimage led to bringing that control color up from *behind* the afterimage—it started in a small area and spread out over the area of the afterimage. According to Haines and Williams, the effort to get and keep a given color in the field is a very distinct species of mental work, and is equally true whether one is controlling an afterimage or is trying to hold a given color against "chance comers" (i.e., the memory images). Haines and Williams (p. 36) state that this effort involves as much work "as if one should try to lift himself up out of a chair." Finally, Haines and Williams attempt to explain the nature of the interference between the afterimage and the memory image via a discussion of the physical basis involved in these processes. For example, regarding the mechanism of the "revival process," it may be that the *tendency* to discharge toward the peripheral apparatus—there to set up the revival of the sensory process—is sufficient in itself to elicit in the central or cortical sensory cells a process that stands for the revival of the sensory process; thus, it may be considered to be a *symbol* of a copy.

Freeman (1906) reviews the work of the German researcher A. von Szily (1905) concerning the phenomenon of afterimages of motion. Szily repeated all of the experiments that are usually made in studying motion afterimages (e.g., parallel lines that move, rotating disks, etc.), varied the conditions of these experiments, and carried them into great detail. Szily's general conclusions are that the appearance of motion in the afterimage following the perception of motion is due to a purely physiological afterimage of motion and that the seat of this physiological process is somewhere central to the retina. Freeman notes that Szily's article is prefaced by a full historical account of previous experiments on afterimages of motion, as well as of the theories advanced in the explanation of such phenomena.

Two early female researchers, Helen Thompson and Kate Gordon (1907), describe their work on peripheral afterimages with special reference to the brightness of the backgrounds upon which the images were cast (cf. Baird, 1907; Day, 1912; Fernald, 1905). They used nine stimulus colors that were individually shown upon gray backgrounds of differing brightness, and recorded participants' judgments as to the color of the stimulus presentations. Thompson and Gordon discuss their results under the following nine headings: Extent of the Color Field; Color Tone of Stimuli as Perceived; Color Tone of After-images; Intensity and Distinctness of After-images; Color Discrimination in After-images; Duration of After-images; Alterations in the After-image During the Process of Fading; Minor Observations; and Theoretical. Among their theoretical points, Thompson and Gordon make the following assertions: It is possible with the light-adapted eye to arouse peripheral afterimages (their records show more than 4,500 tests ranging from 0-degrees to 93-degrees on the retina). The presence of white light is necessary to the production of the afterimage in the peripheral part of the retina (this may best be explained via the Ladd-Franklin theory of color vision—as opposed to the Hering and Muller theories—which holds that afterimages are due to the successive phases of breakdown in a color molecule); and separate, or independent, observations concerning afterimages on the peripheral retina (viz, a stimulus component may be emphasized that varies more from the background brightness, and an afterimage component may be emphasized that approaches the background brightness) may be considered to be illustrations of the same phenomenon: the tendency to interpret certain degrees of brightness is made in terms of certain color tones (thus, a stimulus shown on a dark ground is being mixed with white by simultaneous contrast, whereas an afterimage in order to be mixed with white light must be shown on a light background). Essentially, according to Thompson and Gordon, stimuli exposed on dark backgrounds—and afterimages cast on light backgrounds—tend to have their lighter color components brought out, but that stimuli shown on light backgrounds—and afterimages on dark backgrounds—tend to have the dark color element come out.

In two separate articles, Swindle (1916, 1917) examines two related aspects of afterimages. In one case, Swindle (1916) discusses successive color induction (i.e., a perceived color or color change that is determined by, or induced by, stimulation in other parts of the visual field) in an owl, in a cockatoo, and in human beings. In his systematic observations, these species demonstrate visual aftereffects that are more definite than mere after-sensations and, otherwise expressed, the aftereffects may be considered to be strong positive afterimages. Swindle asserts that in *successive* induction positive afterimages—some of long duration—may be brought about as "first aftereffects" and that such effects may come about, also, in *simultaneous* induction. Further, Swindle (1916, p. 332) formulates a general law of color induction as follows: "In successive and simultaneous color induction, any color induces first itself and last of all its antagonistic color." Swindle notes that the "first positive afterimage" has been discovered previously and is used by kinematographists, and the "second positive afterimage" also has been observed earlier and been employed by spiritualists in their activities. In another case, Swindle (1917) discusses "visual ghosts" (cf. Martin, 1915), including, also, "cutaneous ghosts" and "kinaesthetic ghosts." He maintains that experimental results indicate the phenomena sometimes experienced in the traditional "visual ghost story" to be only a "positive after-image of long duration." Borrowing Pavlov's (1927) terminology, Swindle (1917, p. 350) refers to visual ghosts as "conditioned visual responses to previously perceived more or less complex patterns of visual stimuli." Ostensibly, according to Swindle, a similar explanation may be applied both to cutaneous ghosts and kinaesthetic ghosts. He states (p. 368), "It seems as if all forms of self-induction are fundamentally the same."

Bishop (1921) suggests that there is *no* positive afterimage of *audition/tone* that is analogous to the positive afterimage of *vision*, and Martin (1912) earlier asserted that the "memory after-image" is a blending of other images, appearing merely to be a unitary process. Combining the two concepts—memory afterimage and auditory afterimage—C. Dimmick (1923) discusses her studies regarding the "auditory memory after-image." Based on Titchener's (1918, p. 74) methodology (in which "the name of 'memory after-image' has been given to an experience which is most familiar, perhaps, in the taking of dictation"), C. Dimmick dictated various sentences (from John Locke's "Essay Concerning Human Understanding") to her participants who were asked, subsequently, to describe their experiences in taking the dictation. C. Dimmick's (p. 12) results suggested to her that in the auditory memory afterimage one is "dealing with a psychologically unique experience" where "there is no positive after-image in audition which would account for the experiences . . . described." C. Dimmick found that the auditory memory afterimage differs considerably from the memory image. It seems to include the characteristics of both the afterimage (in vision) and the memory-image; like an afterimage (in vision), it apparently is "just there," "persistent," and "localized outside of the head" (p. 12). Moreover, like a memory-image, the auditory memory afterimage is less rich, and sometimes less intense, than that involved in the perceptual process. C. Dimmick (p. 12) concludes that "in any classification of images the memory after-image belongs where its name implies, between the after-image and the memory-image. Whether it should be placed nearer the after-image or nearer the memory-image, depends upon differences between the individual observers." Furthermore, according to C. Dimmick (1923), such a dependence upon individual differences in participants seems to make the memory after-image more like the memory-image, but its many sensory characteristics put it in the afterimage group, so that the name *Erinnerungsnachbild* (via Fechner, 1860, p. 491), or memory afterimage, seems well chosen. For further discussion of the "memory after-image," per se, see the following sources: Allport (1930), Bentley (1899), Brown (1935), Erb (1937), Kuhlmann (1906), and Whipple (1901/1902).

   For other early studies on the following aspects/issues of the afterimage, see the following chronologically arranged studies: retinal rivalry in the afterimage (DeVries and Washburn, 1909); effect of illumination on peripheral vision (Day, 1912); projection of the negative afterimage in the field of the closed lids (Angell, 1913); size and distance of projection of an afterimage on the field of the closed eyes (Angell and Root, 1913; cf. Ferree and Rand, 1931); correlation between accuracy of the visual memory afterimage and control of visual imagery (Adler, Williams, and Washburn, 1914); cutaneous afterimages (F. Dimmick, 1916); the influence of illumination changes upon afterimages and the principle of the *dimming contrast effect* (Troland, 1917); latency period and visual aftereffects (Creed and Granit, 1928; Granit, Hohenthal, and Uoti, 1930; Juhasz, 1920; cf. Ebbecke, 1928); the aftereffect of movement in the sense of touch (Thalman, 1922); the negative visual afterimage as a textureless, dimensionless, shapeless, and nonlocalized "film" (Braddock, 1924; Katz, 1911; cf. Levine and Graham, 1937); recurrent visual and kinaesthetic images (Dallenbach, 1924; cf. Bidwell, 1894); the flight of colors in afterimages (Shuey, 1924, 1926); a quantitative study of the Purkinje after-image (Judd, 1927; cf. Frehafer, 1929); color sequences in the after-image of white light (Berry, 1927; cf. Berry, 1922); eye-movements and visual afterimages (Rexroad, 1928; Walters and Gundlach, 1931); an image of "spectacle rims" (Goodman and Downey, 1929); visual purple in the visual afterimage (Karwoski, 1929); apparatus for induc-ing afterimages (Kellogg, 1929); a delayed visual aftereffect (Warren, 1929); a novel experiment with the negative afterimage (Scheidemann, 1933); stereoscopic binocular fusions in the negative afterimage (Washburn and Smith, 1933); aftereffects of visually observed move-ment (Gates, 1934; cf. Ehrenstein, 1925; Fuchs, 1928; Granit, 1927, 1928; Grindley, 1930; Gurnee, 1933; Hunter, 1914, 1915; Sturm, 1931; Thalman, 1921; Wohlgemuth, 1911); depth perception in the afterimage (Ferree and Rand, 1934; cf. H. Muller, 1928); uniocular negative afterimages and rivalry with the vision of the other eye (Sumner and Watts, 1936; cf. Creed and Harding, 1930; Delabarre, 1889; Ebbinghaus, 1890; McDougall, 1904; Parinaud, 1882); pro-jected afterimage size-constancy (Helson, 1936; cf. Maier, 1929; Noll, 1926); afterimages occurring in complete darkness (Robertson and Fry, 1937); and figural aftereffects (Kohler and Emery, 1947; Kohler and Wallach, 1944; Prentice, 1947; cf. Gibson, 1933; Gibson and Radner, 1937).

## Consciousness/Dreams/Hallucinations/Illusions/Perception

Early studies of *dream consciousness* (cf. Calkins, 1894) were con-ducted at Wellesley College (Massachusetts) by Weed, Hallam, and Phinney (1896), and Andrews (1900). Dream consciousness involves the introspective reports and "dream records" of participants who consistently engage in dreaming activities and who remember and record their dreams immediately upon waking or at a later time. *Nightly dreams* and *waking dreams* involve hypnagogic images whose unity underlies all the distinctions of waking and dreaming life. In some dreamers, the presentation of actual, external stimuli produces the consciousness *within* the dream itself of such stimuli; for example, a participant may place flowers or onions by his/her bedside and, sub-sequently, dreams of smelling and tasting objects, or eating salt just before going to sleep may lead to dreams of a thirsty drive through a wilderness. Also, the *converse* effect of a dream may be experienced by the participant: he wakes up tired and lame after having a dream of running a marathon, or smells and tastes onions after dreaming that he eats them. Typically, in these early studies on dream consciousness, dream-imagery occurs far more often than dream-perception (e.g., Weed, Hallan, and Phinney, 1896, p. 406). Contrary to earlier claims that only visual and auditory images occur in dreams, studies by Weed et al. and Andrews contradict this assertion. Although visual images predominate (with auditory images placing second in frequency), there are reported, also, dermal, pressure, gustatory, and olfactory experiences and images as well during the dreaming state. Weed et al. (p. 411) suggest that the continuity of the dream life (in which not only taste and smell images occur, but also explicit thinking, reasoning, and volition are experienced) with the waking life indicates the "likeness of the dream-consciousness to the hypnotic condition." Andrews (p. 131) demonstrates a certain sensitivity toward a desirable rigorous methodological approach to the typical introspective—and highly subjective—method of studying dream consciousness as she states, "No psychologist has as yet discovered what every one of them desires: an experimental method of varying and repeating stimulations of the dream consciousness, which shall not at the same time vitiate the conditions of natural dreaming."

Other early studies concerning the imagery involved in the dreaming state, including daydreams, the psychology of dreams and drowsiness, the form of dreams, and somnambulism, were conducted (in chronological order) by Cason (1923), Frost (1913), Hollingworth (1911a), Jenness and Jorgensen (1941), Jewell (1905), and Smith (1904). In his discussion of day dreams, Smith (p. 465) defines daydreaming as "all those reproductive and imaginative mental states in which there is a greater or less degree of automatism in the images which come before the mind. Its limits would be, on the one hand, the hypnagogic states which immediately precede sleep and on the other, states of purposive thinking in which the mind becomes so filled with the subject that its workings tend to become automatic." Smith collected and analyzed written reports of day dreaming from 1,475 persons, aged seven to ninety years. He summarizes the results with the following points: daydreaming appears to be a normal and universal phenomenon in children and adolescents and continues throughout life (it is especially characteristic of the years of adolescence); the content of the daydream is determined mainly be environment, though its forms (like those of night dreams) are influenced by age, health, and degree of mental development; in early childhood, daydreams (except in the case of exceptionally imaginative children) are made up mostly of memory-images, with actual experiences or stories being reproduced with little change; with the onset of adolescence, there is a marked increase in the complexity and variety of daydream content and the range is greatly widened ("instinct" emotions are frequently reported and dreams of love are characteristic at this age, both altruistic and egoistic emotions are intensified greatly); the content of the daydreams of adults indicated a somewhat closer connection with adult life than those of childhood and adolescence; and the daydreams of the adults of older age were almost entirely memories of the remote past and much time was spent in daydreaming. Smith suggest that the mostly pleasurable state of daydreaming has a danger attached to it because it—like any other mental activity—may become excessive and pass over into pathological states; he notes, also, that marked sex/gender differences were observed in the daydream reports (e.g., boys dream of acquiring a fortune by means of a short and easy process such as some wonderful invention, or by going West and discovering gold; girls, on the other hand, dream of marrying millionaires, or inheriting large fortunes from newly discovered relatives, or of acquiring wealth by becoming famous actresses, musicians, or authoresses).

Jewell (1905) used the questionnaire method to examine the psychology of night dreams (cf. Frost, 1913; Thompson, 1914); he collected over 2,000 dream reports from some 800 persons, mostly students at Normal Schools (schools giving a two-year course to high-school graduates preparing to become teachers). Based upon his analysis of these reports, Jewell makes the following conclusions, among many others: dreams may be prevented by the "power of suggestion" (cf. Feingold, 1915); neither the season, day of the week, nor month, has any noticeable influence on dream imagery, except for local settings such as winter scenery/imagery being more common during the winter months; the emotions and images experienced during dreaming are determined largely by the organic sensations existing at the time; and there is no mode of functioning of the mind in the waking state that may not take place during sleep. Note that early studies on the influence of *suggestion/suggestibility* vis-à-vis imagery and/or dreaming/hypnosis were conducted by Scott (1910), Morgan (1924), and Cason (1925).

Hollingworth (1911a) examines the psychology of the state called *drowsiness* which is the period that usually precedes the sleep state (cf.

Crichton-Brown's [1895] concept of "dreamy mental state" that includes "double consciousness," "loss of personal identity," "a going
back to childhood," "vivid returns of an old dream," "losing touch
with the world," "deprivation of corporeal substance," and "loss of
sense of proportion"). Based upon the introspective reports of only
two observers—Hollingworth himself and his wife—various analyses
were made concerning drowsiness. Hollingworth employed the notion of *imagery types* in his observations where he was classified—based
on imagery tests—as "highly auditory-motor" both as to imagery and
memory type, and as a "poor visualizer," whereas his wife was classified as "visual" and "visual-verbal" in type with almost no "auditory
or motor tendencies." Hollingworth discusses the phenomenon of
drowsiness under the following "principles of composition": transformation of imagery type, substitution, fluid association on a sensory
basis, isolation of associative trains, grandeur and vastness, amnesia for
processes and events, and absence of symbolism. One of
Hollingworth's conclusions, among others, is that "drowsiness hallucination" seems to be a "flashlight" perceptual fusion or complication that is further differentiated by transformation of imagery type,
by tendencies toward grandeur and vastness, and by rapidly developed
amnesia.

Cason (1923) discusses the incidence of, and equivalence of, imagery in the waking state versus imagery in the drowsy state; that is,
he set out to determine to what extent the *nonverbal* imagery present
in the *waking* state is different from that present in the *drowsy* state,
and was concerned primarily with the *presence* rather than with the
*function* of imagery (cf. Davis, 1932). Cason gave eight participants
(six women and two men) a series of subjective tests to determine the
degree of the person's visual, auditory, kinaesthetic, tactual, organic,
olfactory, gustatory, thermal, and pain imagery (cf. Angell, 1910, pp.
77–80, 95–97; Colvin, 1909; Sullivan, 1921); later, he checked his
results via certain objective tests (Angell, 1910; Fernald, 1912). Specifically, Cason attempted to assess the factors of frequency and
vividness in spontaneous, as well as voluntary, imagery present in the
drowsy state (cf. Jenness and Jorgensen, 1941). Based upon the results of participants' introspective reports of their imagery during the
drowsy, waking, and dreaming states, Cason concluded that (1) the
transformation of imagery type when passing from the waking into
the drowsy state is not a typical experience and no general formula
or rule may be stated that will hold for all cases, mainly because there
are marked individual differences (cf. Griffitts, 1927) on this issue; (2)

there is often a very noticeable increase in the relative prominence of auditory imagery when passing from the waking into the drowsy state; and (3) there is a slightly greater similarity between the imagery present in the waking and dream states than between that present in the waking and drowsy states.

Several early writers (e.g., Bichowsky, 1926; Read, 1908; Rogers, 1923; Sidis, 1908) examine the distinction between perception/ sensory processes (the *percept*) and imagery/imagination processes (the image) (cf. Colvin, 1908, pp. 159–60). Read discusses, reviews, and expands on a paper that a Professor Gotch read before the British Psychological Society in June 1907 that dealt with the physiological basis for the distinction between a sensation and its revised image. Essentially, the ideas suggested by Gotch, and elaborated by Read, are the following: perception—as contrasted with images—is a state of relative restriction of consciousness; the difference between percepts and images is due to the reflex of perception that adjusts the sense organ; various features of perception—such as "aggressiveness," "outness," and "steadiness" may be explained by such a difference; and the principle of *reflex of perception* (that adjusts the sense organ) may be illustrated by the phenomena of dreams, hallucinations, attentive thought, and "criminal perversity." Moreover, in pointing out the distinction between percepts and images, Read (p. 328) suggests that "in perception the object holds the eye, but in phantasy the mind's eye has to hold the image. This difference seems to be due to the definite reflex of perception which adjusts the sense organ and maintains the continuity of the stimulus" (cf. Aveling, 1911). Further, Read notes that a circular activity is set up whereby the stimulus excites an adjustment—which maintains the stimulus, which maintains the adjustment, and so on. Read states that "the image has to be sustained by an arbitrary generalized adjustment" (such as is consciously experienced in the reflective state) and that "involves a reinforcement of the reflex from some source of interest" (pp. 328–29).

Sidis (1908) explains his special theory of perception called *the doctrine of primary and secondary sensory elements* (cf. footnote, p. 58) in which the percept itself is regarded as consisting of two classes of elements of sensations: the primary and the secondary sensory elements. (For a discussion of *esthetics* vis-à-vis imagery and the "higher" versus "lower" senses, see Pitkin [1906].) Sidis emphasizes that the secondary sensory elements are *not* images, ideas, or representations, but the secondary elements of the percept are sensations, essentially; also, sensations are different qualitatively from images, ideas, or representations (e.g., "the image of a light does not shine"). Sidis maintains that the sensation (or *presentation*) is given as immediate experience, while the image (or *representation*) is mediate when it is a mental substitute for the immediate experience of the sensation. Sidis (p. 58) states that "there is not a particle of evidence to substantiate the view that ideas or images are copies of sensations in the sense of being weak sensations or 'centrally excited sensations.' There is nothing of the sensory in the idea. The weakest sensation cannot compare with the most vivid representation." Sidis notes that ideational and perceptual processes are not equivalent; the two are different qualitatively: the sensation has intensity, while the image lacks it. Moreover, according to Sidis, the image is a reproduction/representation or symbol of a sensation, but no sensation represents another sensation. Again, a sensation—unlike an image—is not mediate, but immediate experience; also, a sensation bears the mark of externality, whereas an image lacks it. In other terms, a sensation cannot be called up at will, while an image is independent of peripheral stimulations of external objects and is usually under the control of the will; no sensation differs so much from another as the image differs from its corresponding sensation. In summary, according to Sidis, the percept—whether normal or abnormal—does not consist of images, but of primary and secondary sensations; also, the fundamental difference between percept and image lies in what is and what is not common to all individuals: perceptual experience is common, while ideational experience is not common, to all humans (e.g., "I see the sun and other people can share it with me, while my image of the sun is experienced only by myself"; p. 119).

Rogers (1923) discusses a series of experiments in which she examines the role of the image in auditory and tactual perception; this study is an elaboration of her earlier work (Rogers, 1917), which showed that the simple image plays an important and specific role in visual perceptions. In general, Rogers's procedure was to start with auditory and tactual stimuli as simple and meaningless as possible and then to proceed with more complex ones, recording participants' introspective accounts during the progressions. Her purpose was to determine the fundamental relations existing between imagery and perception on three dimensions: the *kinds* of images present in auditory and tactual perceptions; the *function* of the image (cf. Bartlett, 1921; Hollingworth, 1911b); and the *relation* of clearness to the image. Based upon her results, Rogers (1923) draws the following conclusions: auditory and tactual perceptions involve mostly visual, auditory, and tactual images (in this order of frequency from greatest to least); images furnish about one-half of the indirectly aroused processes (52 percent) and organic sensations the other half (48 percent) in auditory perceptions, while in the tactual perceptions the organic processes furnish 61 percent and the imaginal 39 percent of the indirectly aroused processes. An increase in the stimulus complexity is correlated with an increase in the kind of image corresponding to the directly aroused sensations; the simple images have the specific functions in auditory and tactual perceptions of reproductions, interpretation, orientation, and elaboration; and—regarding clearness—most of the visual and auditory images tend to be clear while the tactual tend to be only moderately clear (also, the kind of image vis-à-vis clearness must, of necessity, consider the function involved). Finally, Rogers (1923) asserts that the kind, complexity, and familiarity of the object arousing a perception may be fairly well predicted from the kinds of images involved (cf. Bartlett, 1916), the frequency of the clear versus the unclear processes, and the function of the image in any given case.

Bichowsky (1926) suggests that—based upon the method of introspection—the phenomenon of images is clearly distinct from that of percepts; thus, even the novice's first attempts at introspection almost invariably distinguish the vivid, external, projected, impersonal, and concrete percept from the subjective and meaningful image. On the other hand, when considered as "pure feels," the image and the percept are rather similar and any differences depend not on intrinsic qualities of the two types but on the consciousness of certain unlike relations in which they commonly stand. Therefore, according to Bichowsky, when those factors that depend on relations between content and reference are ignored—the usual basis or "rule" assumed for laboratory introspection—it becomes very difficult to find substantive differences between the image and the percept. In his study, Bichowsky reports on the introspections of his participants who could distinguish images from percepts on the following dimensions: intensity and vividness, subjectivity, privacy, voluntariness, and universality. When participants were asked to report relations between percepts and images, Bichowsky found that a wide field for introspection was opened, that is, that which was concerned with "meanings"; essentially, a percept often appears to lead to, to suggest, or to stimulate, a particular image involving either *intramodal* (for some percepts, the image is of its own mode) or *transmodal* (for other percepts, the image stimulated is of a different mode) stimulation. Moreover, the most striking feature of image stimulation by a percept is that it is always accompanied by the *consciousness* of meaning and of a particular type of meaning, namely, that the stimulated image means or stands for a given percept. Bichowsky (1926, p. 563) concludes that the direct introspective treatment of the meaning of percepts leads to a simple mechanism for the stimulation of an image-center by a percept-center that is similar in principle to that connecting presensation and percept (cf. Bichowsky, 1925). Also, images may be thought of as the activity of a new conscious level, an activity stimulated by percept activity and partly controlling, in its turn, the activity of that lower level exactly as activity of the *percept-arc* may be stimulated by activity in the next lower level—that of the presensation—and, in its turn, may partly control the activity of that level. For early discussions on related issues of imagery and consciousness as occasioned by ingestion of *drug* substances, such as peyote or mescal buttons, see Fernberger (1923), Mitchell (1896), and Prentiss and Morgan (1895); and for the introspective reports of the effects of chloroform on imagery and consciousness, see Jones (1909).

Several early writers have reported on the relationships between imagery and hallucinations (e.g., Rosett, 1939; Town, 1906), conscious attitudes (e.g., Clarke, 1911), and illusions (e.g., Pierce, 1915). Following a review of the theories and work on *endophasia* (i.e., verbal thinking or internal language; e.g., one theory holds that verbal memory depends on visual, auditory, articulatory, and graphic imaging of words), Town employed the case study method to examine the internal speech of several patients at a Pennsylvania insane asylum. As a result, she was able to classify different types of internal speech (cf. Reed, 1916): internal soliloquy, impersonal external dialogue (in which the second person in the dialogue is hallucinatory in character), and personified internal dialogue (also with a hallucinatory second person, along with strong auditory or motor elements). Note that for other early accounts of hallucinatory behavior vis-à-vis imagery, see Sidis (1908, pp. 106–14), Read (1908, pp. 332–33), Rosett (1939), Pasquasy (1947), Pisk (1935), Stoddard (1904), and Thale, Gabrio, and Salomon (1950); compare Humphrey's (1940) review of Rosett's (1939) work. After a brief survey of other researchers' definitions of the term *conscious attitude*, Clarke (1911, p. 215) offers her own: "a phrase to denote certain large and comprehensive experiences, not evidently imaginal in character." Clarke interpreted over 1,400 introspective reports of her participants after they were presented with stimuli to be perceived tactually and gave the following conclusions: the instances in which thought-elements, imageless thoughts, or attitudes are reported as consciousness are not of psychological description but rather of the translation into words of the meaning of a conscious state (i.e., the German *Kundgabe*); the introspections show different stages of clearness and intensity of imagery that permits the connection—via a graded series of intermediate steps—of a complex of vivid and explicit imagery to a vague and condensed consciousness that represents what is called imageless thought; and conscious attitudes may be analyzed into sensations, images, and feelings, or traced genetically to such analyzable complexes, and do not warrant the proposal of any additional "conscious elements." Pierce (1915) examined his own introspections regarding imagery illusions with special reference to the so-called "proofreader's illusion" (i.e., the failure to notice a "low-level" error in written material because one is concentrating on "higher-level" processing such as understanding, meaning, or comprehension). As a result, Pierce was able to distinguish three classes of illusions on the basis of their "examinability": the peripheral or pure illusions that persist under critical examination (e.g., the stable and persistent *spatial illusions* such as the Muller-Lyer illusion); illusions that dissolve rapidly under examination (*mixed illusions* that become finally transformed into a true perception); and illusions that elude examination (e.g., the *proofreader's illusion* which is an *imagery illusion* and contains the maximum grade of instability where the essence of the illusory experience consists of imagery initiated by, but not compounded with, peripheral elements). According to Pierce, all these classes of illusions are identical in function in that they lead to erroneous motor responses even though they do have structural differences (cf. Binet, 1884).

### Imagination Imagery

Stetson (1896) administered a list of test questions related to imagery to a class of 100 college juniors; the questions touched on dreams (e.g., "observe dreams for some time and report on the relative prevalence of the types of images"), recall of materials (e.g., "attempt to recall the forgotten name of a person; recall a piece of music"), memory of breakfast table objects, presence of images for concepts (e.g., concepts of relation, cause-effect, classification), changes in imagination type, and estimation of the types of imagery that predominate on the responses to the questionnaire. Stetson reports that of 100 cases, eighty-two were judged to be predominantly visual in imagery, six were auditory, four were motor, one was tactual, five were equally visualists and

audiles, and two were equally visualists and motiles. Other findings were
that the auditory imagery type constituted a large element in twenty
students, the motor imagery type in ten students, and the tactual type
in four students. None of the participants lacked visual or auditory imagery, but one student lacked motor imagery and three lacked tactual
imagery; it was generally agreed that among all the types of imagery
tactual images play the least role in imagination or imagining activities.
In one place, Stetson (p. 410) states that

> [t]he image-tendency seems to reach its culmination in the early life of
> the adult, along with the aesthetic and emotional impulses. In middle
> life, the use of symbols, even visual, grows less and less, and often fades
> out altogether . . . perhaps the difference between men and women
> . . . may be due to education. The life and education of the girl empha-
> sizes the visual and auditory in their more delicate forms. The boy, on
> the other hand, has a far greater opportunity for the acquisition of motor
> images and impulses . . . imaging has many disadvantages . . . but there
> are also advantages.

In his "study of imaginations," Dearborn (1898) asked sixteen participants, mostly students, between the ages of eighteen to sixty-two
to look at 120 cards containing "chance blots of ink" (p. 184) and
to examine their consciousness by reporting "the first suggested image" (cf. the inkblot "projective tests" of Rorschach [1921] and
Holtzman [1958]; also, see *Psychological Review* [1897, 4, 390–91]).
Based upon his analysis of participants' responses to the inkblot stimuli,
Dearborn (p. 190) states that "it is clear that, as a general principle,
the experience, and especially the early experience of the subject has
important influence" (e.g., one of the participants—a domestic
woman—saw mostly domestic objects, while another participant—an
artist and student of mythology—saw in the blots many fanciful and
picturesque things). Dearborn suggests that "there is evidence here
that the laws of the reproductive imagination, still for the most part
hid in the neural paths, are substantial laws, which may one day be
found entirely out and reduced to words and to more or less of mathematical certainty of statement" (p. 190).

Perky (1910) describes a series of ten formal experiments on the
images involved in imagination. Perky initially examines three separate meanings for the term imagination: ordinary usage, literary usage, and psychological usage; in the last category, she provides over
two dozen referents as a basis for discussion. See the definition of

imagination offered by Colvin (1908, p. 166) "that activity of consciousness in which an object of sensation is experienced as not immediately present to the senses"; thus, according to Colvin, in order to have a true state of imagination there must be the direct experience of an object that is not actually before the senses ("if this experience is lacking there is no mental image"). Colvin asserts that his definition immediately gives a clear distinction between imagination on the one hand, and perception, illusion, and hallucination on the other ("a distinction which psychology has failed always to emphasize, which failure has led to confusion and contradiction"). In her first few experiments—requiring the aid of three experimenters—Perky presented a visual stimulus (that gradually increased in definiteness) to her participants who were asked to imagine the object whose color and form were thus given in perception (cf. the Perky effect—the subjective impression of imagery with the objective presence of a physical stimulus; Roeckelein, 1998, p. 252). Based upon the results of her intensive experiments, Perky makes the following conclusions:

- A distinctly supraliminal visual perception may be mistaken for and incorporated into an image of imagination without the participant's least suspicion that any external stimulus is present to the eye.
- Images of memory may be distinguished from images of imagination as having particularity and personal reference.
- Memory images of sight, sound, and smell involve gross movements of eyes, larynx, and nostrils, while the corresponding imaginations involve no such movements.
- Visual images of memory involve eye movement and general kinaesthesis while visual images of imagination involve steady fixation and lack of general kinaesthesis.
- Memory images are "scrappy" and "filmy," and give no afterimages, while images of imagination are substantial, complete, and sometimes give afterimages.
- The "mood" of memory is that of familiarity or recognition that is intrinsically pleasant, while the "mood" of imagination is that of unfamiliarity or novelty that is intrinsically unpleasant.
- Memory implies imitative movement and the correlated organic sensations (cf. Tarde, 1903), while imagination implies kinaesthetic and organic empathy.
- Memory images arise more slowly, are more changeable in course, and last less long than images of imagination.
- Memory implies roving attention and a mass of associative material while imagination involves concentrated and quasi-hypnotic attention with inhibition of associations.

In essence, Perky reaches the general conclusion that the materials of imagination are akin closely to those of perception stating that "popular psychology looks upon memory as a photographic record of past experience, and regards imagination as working with kaleidoscopic, instable, undependable materials. Precisely the reverse appears to be true" (p. 451). Note that Titchener (1913) attempts to defend Perky's experiments and findings against the criticisms made by Martin (1912) who could not replicate Perky's results. Titchener covers the following issues in his rebuttal: nature of the observers/participants; the possibility of suggestion in the participants (cf. Feingold, 1915); the nature of the task; the voluntary and spontaneous production of imagery; the data of observation and their employment; the number of observations; and the distinction of memory and imagination. Titchener (p. 131) closes by stating that:

> I spoke above of the thanklessness of repeating someone else's work; yet sheer repetition, repetition without variation, is again and again the demand of the psychologist who seeks to bring results together. . . . I shall welcome any repetition of Perky's experiments, whether the outcome be positive or negative, confirmation or contradiction. . . . Meanwhile, I cannot see that Professor Martin's two experimental series are relevant to the points at issue.

In a series of reviews and summaries written for the journal *The Psychological Bulletin*, Baird (1911/1912/1913/1914/1915/1916/ 1917) covers experimental psychological research conducted in the areas of imagery, imagination, memory, learning, and the higher mental processes. In his section on imagery, Baird (1911, pp. 244–45) reviews the work of the following researchers:

Martin (1910) compares movement images that arise when the moving member is seen versus when it is not seen; her results indicate that the "crucial hypothesis" (i.e., the hypothesis that one's idea of movement is most intensive when one sees the moving member) is not universally valid (cf. Van der Noot, 1910; Weil and Nellen, 1910, who examine the concrete imagery possessed by children).

Perky (1910) uses an ingenious experimental procedure, succeeding in showing that the perceptual consciousness is not different, essentially, from the imaginal consciousness; a detailed examination and comparison is made of memory images with imagination images.

Baird (1911) reports, also, that the papers by Abramowski (1910), Betz (1910), Dugas (1910; cf. Dugas, 1903—*American Journal of Psychology*,

*14*, p. 260), Moore (1910), Peillaube (1910), and Pieron (1910) contain additional discussions of the nature, function, and behavior of imagery.

In another section on imagery, Baird (1912, pp. 322–23) reports on the studies by: Angell (1910)—evaluation of various tests of imagery ("none of the purely objective tests prove to be trustworthy"); Feuchtwanger (1911)—compares the results obtained by introspective and objective methods on imagery tests; Meumann (1911)—studies individual differences in dealing with ideational material (cf. Simpson, 1922); Lipmann (1911)—provides an enumeration of apprehension types within the visual type; Schaub (1911)—reports that the visual, auditory, and tactual images possess the attribute of intensity, and the difference between image and sensation is not one of intensity but rather one of texture and context; Lobsien (1911)—notes that auditory memory is equally well developed in girls and boys, and it increases uniformly and progressively with increases in age.

Baird (1913) summarizes the following imagery studies:

Fernald (1912) studied ideational types and the best means of determining the type to which a given individual belongs.

Downey (1912) studied how imagery is employed in representing the self (specifically in cases where there is personal involvement or personal reference in the appreciation of literary material).

Chapin and Washburn (1912) report on experiments (cf. Fox, 1913–1914) in which 193 students were asked to describe the images they use to represent the idea of "meaning" (the imagery reported was either wholly visual, e.g., a page of the dictionary, wholly kinaesthetic, e.g., imagined movements such as groping, grasping, pointing, gazing, etc., or a combination of both visual and kinaesthetic).

Brahn (1912) gives the results of an experimental diagnosis of the memory of a mathematical prodigy named "Dr. Ruckle" whose ideational type was dominantly visual (cf. Muller, 1913).

Martin (1912) investigated the common phenomenon that normal persons sometimes project their visual images into external space; also, she determined the temporal relations and the characteristics of the projected image, and its relation to attention, emotion, and association; she also attempted to discover the differences between perception, the image, and the afterimage, and between the memory image and the imagination image; her study was extended to include auditory and vocal-motor images as well as the imagery of abnormal patients.

Muller (1912) differentiates among four types of localization of visual imagery in which subjective and objective factors are variously combined in the four cases in studying number-forms and chromaesthesia.

Baird (1914) reviews the following studies on imagery:

Claparede (1913) advances the notion of verbal-motor imagery and its role
   in language behavior.
Fernald (1913) studied the mental imagery of two blind adults to determine
   whether they possessed tactual and visual imagery, as well as their individual differences in translating tactual experiences into visual terms (cf.
   Cameron, 1897).
Sylvester (1913) studied 85 blind children in tests with the "form-board"
   (i.e., performance tasks of fitting a set of blocks of varying shapes into
   slots of varying shapes); he found that those children who had always been
   blind showed the least ability in fitting the blocks into the appropriate slots
   and, thus, it seems that those who have ever had visual experiences retain their visual imagery and are assisted by it in interpreting their tactual impressions. In addition, tactual imagery is less effective than a combination of tactual and visual imagery, even in those individuals who are
   limited to tactual imagery alone (cf. Town, 1914).
Ogden (1913) attempted to distinguish images of memory from images of
   imagination, using six participants with 138 memory images and 74 imagination images. He concludes that it is difficult to differentiate the two
   types of images (see p. 408) and refers the distinction to imageless acts
   and contents.
Martin (1913a) presented simple figures to participants who were asked
   not only to draw his/her visual image but also to draw the figure on
   the card as it was remembered; her results show that more accurate drawings were associated with the latter ("remembered") condition and are
   interpreted as evidence for the existence of a "non-sensory remembrance."
Hunter (1913) conducted experiments with white rats, dogs, raccoons, and
   children in which associations were first established between food acces-
   sibility and the appearance of a light (the temporal interval between the
   stimulus—the light, and the reaction—obtaining food, was increased
   gradually until a limit, "delayed reaction," was reached beyond which no
   associations occurred). The rats and dogs "remembered" the association
   by maintaining gross motor attitudes of the whole or part of the body,
   whereas the behavior of the raccoons and the children indicated the presence of "ideas."

In his 1915 review of imagery studies, Baird provides the following summaries:

Adler, Williams, and Washburn (1914) report an absence of correlation between accuracy and control of visual imagery based upon the results from

53 participants who reproduced visual nonsense-figures and then attempted to control their visual imagery.

Thompson (1914) generally concluded, after examining a number of dreams, that in any given person there is no essential difference between the relative preponderance of the various modalities of imagery in dream life as opposed to waking life.

Spaier (1914) examined the evoking of images in participants (cf. Fox, 1913–1914) and found that the image is not fixed and stable, but develops gradually to a maximum and disappears slowly through a twilight stage; also the image is essential to meaning where it is never present to consciousness without being "saturated with meaning" (cf. Moore, 1915).

Dontchef-Dezeuze (1914) attempted to discover a psychological basis for the conditioned reflex by assuming that mental imagery intervenes between the stimulus and the response.

Exemplarsky (1914) found that a combination of several experimental methods must be employed for the optimal diagnosis of ideational type.

Springer (1914) reports results (based on the performance of 494 children, ages seven to fifteen years, on stimulus presentations of numbers in various fashions, e.g., seen versus heard versus pronounced) showing that in young children the best performance was obtained from visual and visual-motor presentations (cf. Gates, 1916).

Kollarits (1914) examines the nature and origin of one's mental representation of various ideas; for example, persons and places that one has never seen are definitely imaged (cf. English, 1916), and it is possible to discover that one's mental picture is the product of associations of various sorts (e.g., an author's nationality, style, name, or opinions may contribute to one's visual representation of that author's appearance).

Claparede's (1914) study is related to Kollarits's (1914) work and indicates that the appearance or the sound of a person's *name* determines one's mental representation of that person (cf. English, 1916).

Baird (1916) provides the following summaries of imagery studies:

Weber (1913, 1915) proposes that the imaginal content of daydreams is dominantly auditory while sleep-dreams are mainly visual in content; also evidence from mental pathology shows that hallucinations tend to be auditory by day and visual at night.

Gordon (1915) provides evidence that the employment of a global visual image (e.g., of a whole word) is the best strategy to use in a mental imagery task involving a spelling test, as compared with the use of a fragmentary visual image (e.g., only single syllables of a word) strategy.

Martin (1915) proposes that whether one will see ghosts depends on whether the person tends (especially under conditions of emotional stimulation) to project his/her visual images into space; also, when visual images are projected under laboratory conditions they do not possess the reality of apparitions or ghosts (the image must have an emotional component which marks it off from other projected visual images).

Baird (1917) gives the following reviews of studies of imagery:

Burtt (1916) reports that the arousal of visual imagery of a stimulus tends to be facilitated by increase of stimulus contour complexity, by increase in its size, by increased duration of exposure (cf. Foster, 1911), by interest/motivation, and by motor reinforcement; also arousal of visual imagery tends to be inhibited by mental and motor distraction.

Clark (1916) based his experiments with six participants and five variations of experimental procedure. This researcher found that changes in clearness of the visual image are often accompanied by objectively verifiable eye-movements, that the correspondence between amount of eye-movement and kind of image may be due to certain conditions of attention, and that the characteristic eye-movements seem to transfer from visual perception to visual imagery.

Langfeld (1916) conducted experiments in which his participants recited the alphabet as rapidly as possible, omitting certain specified letters. Based upon participants' introspections, it was found that their method of inhibiting the pronouncing of the forbidden letter(s) consisted in associating (in a fore-period) some form of inhibition (e.g., vocal organs) with an image of the letter which was to be omitted; also, imagery tended to drop out as the experiments progressed but it reappeared under conditions of difficulty and doubt. (For Langfeld's account of the German writer Carl Stumpf's viewpoints on imagery, see Langfeld [1937, pp. 43–44]; and for an interesting case-study account of two persons possessing verbal-motor and verbal-auditory imagery—almost exclusively, without other types of imagery—see Dallenbach [1927]; also, see Fernberger [1919].)

### Literature/Music

A number of early studies have discussed imagery in the contexts of *literature* (e.g., Downey [1912; see Baird, 1913], Feasey [1927], Learoyd [1896], Tsanoff [1914], Wheeler [1923], Valentine [1923]), *music* (e.g., MacDougal [1898], Weld [1912]), and *aesthetics* (e.g., Bawden [1909]). Learoyd (1896) examines the nature and prevalence of "continued stories" (i.e., imaginary and usually unwritten narratives, prolonged by their inventors, so that they go on through several weeks, months, or years); she collected responses to the question "Have you a continued story?" from 114 children and from 214 female and 148 male college-level students concerning their exposure to continued stories and any related imagery. Learoyd also found that nearly two-thirds of the children had imagined continued stories, and less than a third as many men as women had continued stories; other findings indicate that the stories sometimes gain a great vividness in imagery and almost the force of an illusion.

Inspired by two manuscript copies (one was a clean copy, the other was a near-illegible first draft) of the Russian poet Lermontov's work, Tsanoff (1914) proposed a method for the experimental study of poetic construction: obtain and analyze a poet's first draft(s) of a work (which is an objective account of a spontaneous process and represents an experimental record) and compare it against the poet's final draft(s) and completed copy. In this way, one may trace, step by step, the poet's progress from mood to mood, from word to word, or from image-combination to image-combination. As Tsanoff (p. 535) states, "even the vicious scratches, the impatient or angry jabs with the pen, the idle lettering or sketching on the margin, the occasional smooth-running stanzas—all indicate the progressive ideational-emotional coloring of the poet's consciousness." Thus, according to Tsanoff, an experimental study of poetic construction demands nothing less than an experimental study of the poet himself/herself; if one could trace and establish the actual order in which pen-stroke followed pen-stroke, then one would be in a position essentially similar to that of the experimenter who reads the zigzaggy record on the kymograph/smoked drum provided by his participants.

O. A. Wheeler (1923) describes the *image-formation method* for analyzing an individual's literary appreciation, especially one's appreciation of poetry. Based upon some observations made by Peers (1913) concerning literary appreciation and the reader's imagery ability, Wheeler employed a general preliminary training period in which her participants initially learned to form various kinds of imagery, chiefly visual, auditory, and kinaesthetic. Following such training, specific poems were analyzed via appropriate questioning of the student by the teacher—where the goal was to lead the student to form vivid images overall rather than merely to the translation of one phrase into another (e.g., in studying Shakespeare's "Song on Winter," one would *not* ask, "What does 'keel the pot' mean?"—for that would lead naturally to verbal explanation that may not be accompanied by an image; rather, the teacher may ask, "What can you see 'greasy Joan' doing?" Following such "appropriate" questioning in the image-formation method, the poem would be read straight through again. Wheeler found—via three experiments using the image-formation method— that the factors of duration/mood and rhythm should be emphasized (in addition to the imagery factor) when presenting poetry to students for their greatest appreciation (the method of exposition is deemed to be too critical and analytic, and disturbs the duration and imagery factors; the methods of silent reading and reading aloud by the students gives too little attention to the rhythm factor; and the method of recitation/repetition sacrifices psychological rhythm to the metrical measure). According to Wheeler, what is needed for the duration/ mood and rhythm factors to develop in harmony with the imagery factor is that the poem be read rhythmically with due regard to its meaning, and be read by someone who has training in the art of reading aloud (i.e., the study of literature must be complemented by a study of elocution technique in teachers' training).

Valentine (1923) examines the function of imagery, especially visual imagery, in the aesthetic appreciation of poetry and its relation to feeling. (For an analysis of children's appreciation of poems, in particular for judgments based on imagery, see Feasey [1927, pp. 61–62]; and for an account of the reader's "self-projection" and "empathic projection" onto poetry and literary material, see Downey [1912].) Valentine covers topics such as the possible injury of psychological analysis on aesthetic enjoyment, imagery aroused by emotion, images of associated experiences, the influence of unconscious memories, imagery and condensation, substitution and displacement of imagery, the effects of deliberate imagery, images of symbols, and imagery and the speed of reading poetry. Valentine conducted a number of studies in which his general method was to present multiple readings of a series of poems to students and then collect their written responses to the poetry—after each reading—concerning their pleasure and appreciation of the poems, including any observed imagery. Among Valentine's conclusions are the following:

- A majority of the students tested experienced imagery (especially in poems containing descriptions of natural objects) where, in some cases, the imagery was the main source of pleasure.
- Large individual differences exist in one's appreciation of imagery in the poetry—even the nature poems were highly appreciated by some without employing any perceptible imagery.
- Imagery that is vague and indefinite may be just as helpful as very clear and definite images—though in a different way (e.g., clear visual imag-

ery approximates the actual enjoyment of beautiful scenery; vague imagery tends to be related to a more reflective attitude).
- A "law of compensation/rivalry" is suggested (i.e., visual imagery displaces, or is displaced by, auditory imagery, or by emphasized attention to rhythm, sound, or meaning; moreover, the addition of imagery to one's experience in reading a poem does not necessarily ensure additional enjoyment).
- The functioning of imagery in poetic appreciation is not fully expressed in the statement that the words of the poem produce images which carry feelings with them—what seems to happen, also, is that words of the poem stimulate feeling, which arouses imagery, which then may arouse further feeling, and so on.
- Deliberate attempts to achieve imagery in a poem—by dividing attention and overemphasizing imagery—may spoil the appreciation of a poem, while "self-coaching" in imagery (i.e., "enriching imagery")—when used sparingly—may increase the individual's enjoyment of a poem.

Reporting on imagery in the appreciation of music, MacDougal (1898) notes in his personal "confession" that the power of music to call up particularized images rests upon a process of indirect association that depends on the listener's individual "genius" and experience. He asserts that music is not an intellectual instrument (such as language, which has each element connected with a distinct object), but offers its aesthetic appeal through a very lack of definiteness in its content. The function of music, according to MacDougal, is to produce a mood in the listener instead of communicating a set of definite concepts; the aesthetic worth of music derives from the "plasticity" of its symbols and the wide subjective variation in their interpretation, which permits the play of one's imagination and moods upon them. In a more formal way, and employing an experimental methodology, Weld (1912) examines musical enjoyment; he presented a variety of musical compositions (p. 249) to his participants and made plethysmographic and pneumographic records of their reactions to the materials, as well as analyzing introspective reports of their "music consciousness" experience. Initially, in his discussion of the "history of the problem," Weld notes that the psychology of music enjoyment is related intimately to the problems of "aesthetics" in general, and that it is impossible to review the literature of the former without taking the literature of the latter into account. For one such philosophical and literary account of *aesthetic imagery*, see Bawden (1909) who maintains that—in any optimal theory of the aesthetic consciousness—

*both* the best aspects of the sensationalist (sense) theories *and* intellectualist (ideational) theories must be taken into consideration. Based upon the results obtained from his experimental methodology, Weld makes the following observations:

- The act of listening to music is almost invariably (92 percent of cases) associated with a decrease in volume of blood supply in the participants' forearms; the participants' heart rates were accelerated during the music-period (however, there was no correlation between the tempo of the music and the heart-rate changes).
- There was acceleration of participants' respiration rate and irregularity of amplitude during the music-period (again, there was no correlation between increased breathing rate and musical tempo).
- Participants' introspections indicate that the "music consciousness" is made up of a mass of kinaesthetic and organic sensations, motor, vocal-motor, auditory, and visual imagery, as well as numerous associations many of which are irrelevant, affective, and emotional processes and various phenomena having to do with intellectual enjoyment.

On the whole, in my estimation, Weld's experimental study of musical enjoyment is well-designed, well-balanced, and well-controlled, and makes excellent reference to, and contact with, the psychological literature on the topic; it is an excellent early example and treatment of the issue of imagery in, and appreciation of, musical materials.

## Meaning/Thinking/Imageless Thought

An early experimental study (that is relatively substantial in length as it includes fifty journal pages) on the relationship between imagery and *meaning* (i.e., the awakening of a succession of various events in one's mind such as an inner reading of words, or "sense of meaning" involving suggested images of objects or other words attended by various feelings and emotions) was conducted by Kakise (1911) who examines, specifically, the relations of the events preceding and succeeding the understanding of materials, and then to investigate the nature of the simultaneous events, that is, the "consciousness of meaning" (cf. Chapin and Washburn, 1912; Mead, 1910). Kakise's method of experimentation involved the total introspection of participants in reaction to words or phrases that were taken down and served as the protocols upon which subsequent conclusions were based. Kakise's participants gave two forms of reaction (an active/short mode involving the pressing of an electric key and a passive/prolonged mode involving giving introspections) to various auditorily and visually presented words and phrases ranging on dimensions from familiar (easy) to unfamiliar (difficult) and from concrete to abstract (proverbs), as well as some meaningless visual stimuli (Chinese characters) in some cases. As an aside, in his section "Remarks on the Method," Kakise (p. 15) acknowledges various objections by certain psychologists leveled against the method he adopts. For example, Wundt (1907) referred to such a methodology as a "pseudo experiment" because it satisfies *none* on the four requirements of a psychological experiment: (1) concentration of attention, (2) repetition of the experiment, (3) methodological change of the conditions, and (4) the observer's own determination of the phenomena to be observed. Ultimately, based upon such a methodology and the results from his participants, Kakise provides the following conclusions (among others):

- Depending on whether the stimulus words were visual or auditory determines whether the imagery is visual or auditory-motor.
- The kinds of imagery (whose frequency was markedly affected by participants' individual differences) were motor speech, visual speech, associated (suggested) word-images, and associated object-images in visual terms.
- The frequency of memory-images is conditioned primarily not by the concreteness or abstractness of the stimulus word or by individual differences but by the slowness or quickness of the participant's reaction.
- The customary method of association experiments seems to be too artificial for the study of natural or real associations. Compare the superior qualities of the *Ausfrage* method as described by Messer (1906); also, see the early studies on *association*, vis-à-vis imagery, by Kelley (1913, p. 500), and Hunter (1917); the "feelings of relations" experiment by Gleason (1919); and the "consciousness of relation" study by Woodworth (1908). Whether one achieves the understanding of a word or phrase the concrete representation depends primarily upon the duration variable (i.e., upon the time one reflects upon it).
- The characteristic constituents of the word's meaning are not selective experiences, but a series of different phases of reproduction.
- The notion of "feeling of concept" may be reduced to either "feeling of familiarity" or "feeling of content." Feeling of content (i.e., the awareness of the more or less fused aggregate of incipient associations) is hardly reducible to any specific images, while "feelings of familiarity" (i.e., the most elementary and fundamental form of the reproductive experience is reducible neither to feelings proper nor to intensity-quality attributes of sensations) may be regarded as a third, or retrospective, quality of sensations or other psychic experiences.

For case studies in which individuals were deficient in ability to understand and give meaning to many stimuli (e.g., persons who lack persistent effort and attention, are distracted both by external stimuli—things in their surroundings—and by their own imagery and motor habits, and mingle facts and imagination, probably as a result of their effortless and inefficient thinking and a tendency to follow their own spontaneous suggestions), see the account by Kuhlmann (1904) concerning his participants diagnosed with "imbecility (Mongolian)," "idiocy," and "feeble-mindedness." Also see Kuhlmann (1905).

A number of other early investigators have also examined the relationship between meaning and imagery (e.g., Moore, 1915, 1917; Tolman, 1917; R. H. Wheeler, 1922; cf. Kantor, 1921). Moore (1915, 1917) studied participants reactions to a series of presentations of word- and picture-stimuli in which both types of stimuli designated familiar objects (e.g., knife, tree, lamp), and participants' reaction times were measured; nonsense words and meaningless drawings were used as controls. Moore reports the following results of his studies: meaning comes prior to the visual image and to the kinaesthetic image; meaning in the case of pictures comes prior to the verbal image; and meaning cannot be identical with such images either considered in themselves or as accruing to the sensations involved. Thus, according to Moore (1915, 1917), meaning must be distinguished from imagery.

Tolman (1917) notes that the controversy between the imageless thought adherents and their opponents was given a new aspect by the work of Moore (1915) in his study of the temporal relations of meaning and imagery (which seems to support the contentions of the imageless thought school). Does Tolman provide us with an intentional pun here in that the title of his article about Moore's study is "More Concerning the Temporal Relations of Meaning and Imagery"? Tolman attempted to replicate Moore's (1915) study with a slight initial methodological modification: instead of presenting a purely chance list of names to participants as Moore had done, Tolman presented only names of black (e.g., coal, raven) or white (e.g., snow, swan) objects and the participant—who was given two keys, one for the right hand and one for the left hand—was instructed to react with the right hand if the object was black and with the left hand if the object was white (cf. Tolman's p. 120 where he replicates Moore's method exactly in subsequent testing). Tolman's results, based upon the performance of forty-nine participants (as compared with Moore's eight participants), led him to conclude that the visual image is unnecessary for meaning to occur. Such a finding suggested three possibilities or solutions to Tolman: an "out-and-out" imageless position, an "out-and-out" image, or some sort of compromise. Of the three possibilities, Tolman reasons that a compromise position—which assumes that meaning depends on image, but is itself distinct from the latter—is the best interpretation or solution suggested by his results. Finally, Tolman (p. 138) emphasizes that the value of his study is not so much in the direction of a positive proof of one or the other theory (image versus imageless), as it is in showing that "if a large enough sample of subjects be taken, Dr. Moore's method in no way lends support to the out-and-out imageless position." For an interesting reaction/rebuttal to Tolman's (1917) study by Moore, see Moore (1917) who states in one place (p. 322) that "[i]t is quite possible . . . that some subjects will be found capable of distinguishing between meaning and imagery, in whom the development of images is so rapid that their mental pictures will usually precede their simple unanalyzed meanings. Such a fact would be significant in the study of types of individuals, but would have little bearing on the more theoretical problem of the existence of imageless thought." For a later "constructive criticism" of the studies on meaning by Moore (1919) and McDonough (1919), see R. H. Wheeler's (1922) "introspections regarding the development of meaning" where he concludes that the development of meaning involves three stages: the original or "given" process, a subsequent process that interprets the first, and a third process that constitutes a final interpretation. Thus, there are shifting or developing sensory and imaginal contents (along with a motor "set" attitude, or verbal imagery) in meaning, and these must shift or develop before their antecedents vanish from consciousness. Essentially, according to Wheeler, kinaesthesis occurs in every stage of the process and is the core or vital aspect of the phenomenon called meaning. For a summary of theories on an issue related to meaning—that of *recognition* (cf. Katzaroff, 1911), see Woods (1915, pp. 381–84). Her bibliography on recognition (pp. 384–87) contains over five dozen references, mainly from the German and French literatures. For a study on *word-consciousness* and meaning, see Downey (1927a).

The early investigations on the topic of thinking/thought vis-à-vis imagery include those (chronologically arranged) by Angell (1911), Aveling (1927), Bartlett (1927), Bartlett and Smith (1920), Comstock (1921), Heidbreder (1926), Otis (1920), Pear (1920, 1921, 1923,

1927b), Robinson (1920), Thomson (1920), and Watson (1920). Angell (1911) discusses the controversial issue of imageless thought by bringing together, initially, the relevant English literature on the topic and then presenting the following six provisions/questions concerning the controversy (see other accounts of imageless thought by Woodworth [1938, pp. 784–89] who also makes reference [p. 784] to several early 1900s, studies on imageless thought [by Binet, Marbe, Kulpe, Ach, Watt, Messer, Buhler, and Woodworth]; additional questions/accounts of imageless thought are given by Titchener [1909] and by Humphrey [1951]):

1. Is there an *aspect* of cognitive experience (immediately given in consciousness) that is distinct from sensation and image?
2. Are there *independent moments* of cognitive consciousness in which neither sensation nor image is to be detected?
3. Are alleged "moments of consciousness" in reality automatized forms of perception or of ratiocination?
4. Are alleged "moments of consciousness" in reality instances of unconscious cerebration which produce consequences that then appear in the conscious stream as the results of reflective thought?
5. Are the alleged "moments of rational thinking" cases in which consciousness is monopolized by the awareness of attitudes that render introspection extremely difficult?
6. Is meaning a conscious element separated out and existing apart from both image and sensation?

In his nonexperimental exposition, Angell's (1911) approach is critical of the experiments and theories of R. S. Woodworth and R. L. Thorndike among American writers and of the Wurzburg school among the Germans. Angell's final assessment is to find the doctrine of imageless thought open to suspicion on the following points (cf. Woodworth, 1915):

Experimental investigation of it (including both the problem of reflective consciousness and of voluntary muscular control) is not wholly satisfactory in meeting the demands of ordinary experimental procedure.

To many observers, imageless thought seems to be a sporadic and only occasional phenomenon.

It seems to be almost impossible to describe (except in negative terms) unless purely functional and logical terms are used (suggesting either that the analysis is not yet complete or that the thing analyzed is not really a content of consciousness)."

If Woodworth's variety of imageless thought is to be accepted as genuine, then two generically different kinds of thought material serve one general function (a notion that is at variance with the psychologists' conceptions of the "parsimony" of nature).

There are many well-recognized conscious states that may be readily confused with imageless thought (e.g., the "consciousness of attitude"— springing out of very primitive physiological attitudes—is an important case in point).

The presence of interpretative factors in perception gives no real comfort to belief in imageless thinking.

Angell (1911, p. 323) states, "My own conclusion is that at present, the only demonstrable imageless thought is subconscious, and so primarily a matter of cerebralistic physiology. Even this would be imaginal, if it got above the limen. But I shall try to keep an open mind."

In another nonexperimental exposition on the issues and problems in the thought processes, Otis (1920) argues against J. B. Watson's (1919/1929, p. 316) hypothesis that "thought is merely the action of language mechanisms." Following his discussions in sections on "Examples of thinking," "The material of thought," "Words may be the material of thought," "Language as the symbolization of meaning," "The genesis of language," "The inadequacy of the behaviorist conception of thought," and "Introspection," Otis (pp. 417–19) states.

> There may be no experimental proof whether or not thinking—conscious adjustment to the environment—is invariably accompanied by the actuation of some language mechanism as the larynx, lips, fingers, etc., in the incipient production of some form of language, spoken or written, but the evidence would seem to favor the belief that no such invariable accompaniment is necessary. . . . But thought . . . is not restricted to the material of language . . . nor is it restricted to the action of language mechanisms any more than it is to the mechanism of hearing or of sight or of locomotion.

In the 1920–1921 issue (vol. 11) of the *British Journal of Psychology*, in a five-part series/symposium, F. C. Bartlett and E. M. Smith, G. H. Thomson, T. H. Pear, A. Robinson, and J. B. Watson present their respective viewpoints on the question "Is thinking merely the action of language mechanisms?" The symposium focused on Watson's (1919/1929, chapter 9) discussion of "Explicit and Implicit Language Habits." Bartlett and Smith (1920) conclude that the psychology of thinking—while it must be treated as a scientific study of the conditions and varieties of the thinking *response*—is only *partially* covered by the examination of the modes in which thought is expressed. Thomson (1920, p. 69) emphasizes the meaning of the two words *merely* and *mechanisms* in the original question; if the question means what it would appear to mean to the "plain" man, then his answer is in the negative. However, according to Thomson, if it means that something is always going on in our body when we are thinking— something chiefly compounded of incipient speech movements and impressions—then his answer to the original question is in the affirmative. Pear (1920, p. 79) asserts that he cannot make up his mind whether the Behaviorist really claims that the awareness of meaning is "carried by" (or "goes on in terms of") the several language processes, or it is *identifiable* with them; Pear claims that he does not yet understand all that is involved in the Behaviorist's supposition that thinking consists merely in the action of language mechanisms (cf. Pear, 1921, 1923). Robinson (1920) essentially agrees with Pear (1920) in his condemnation of the "wholesale rejection of imagery" as espoused by Watson (1919/1929). Watson (1920, p. 87) initially gives a "correction of statement" and allows that "the behaviorist has never really held the view that thinking is largely a verbal process in which, occasionally, expressive movements substitutable for word movements (gestures, attitudes, etc.) enter in as a part of the general stream of implicit activity." Moreover, according to Watson (1920), thinking in the narrow sense where learning is involved is a trial-and-error process that is wholly similar to manual trial and error. For early studies of the imagery involved in learning situations, specifically the influence of voluntary movements under positive and negative attitudes and instructions, see Langfeld (1913); and for the imagery in work tasks involving conditions of with- versus without-knowledge-of results, see Arps (1917). For the role of imagery in the game of *chess*, in particular, see Cleveland (1907, pp. 275–305). Watson (1920, p. 104) states that "situations *plus* training and organization (the individual's biography) are the only 'control' factors we need in psychology—either for regulating overt bodily action or implicit thought action." For a more "generous," "conciliatory," or "social" view of Behaviorism vis-à-vis imagery and thinking, see Weiss (1922, pp. 337–39; 342–43); and for a discussion of thought and consciousness involving the concepts of *motor-image* and *social-image*, see Burrow (1924).

Comstock (1921) provides an experimental basis for investigation of the relevancy of imagery to the thought processes (cf. Heidbreder's

[1926] nonexperimental, rational discussion of thinking as an "instinct"). Comstock conducted a series of four experiments involving problem-solving tasks and subsequent introspections by the participants. The aim of the first experiment was to study the imaginal contents of thought with reference to its uses and relevancy to the thought and, additionally, to replicate Fox's (1913–1914) experiment on imagery in thought; in the second experiment, methodological refinements improved the procedure of the first study; the third experiment included an "irrelevancy" factor in materials that was not present in the first two studies; and the fourth experiment studied feelings in addition to the irrelevancy factor. Comstock (p. 229) states her main finding: "all of the experimental work here indicates that there is no irrelevant imagery" (cf. Simpson, 1922, p. 243). Comstock's analysis of irrelevancies on the perceptual level showed that they are principally characterized by a feeling-component. Not only did all of Comstock's participants use imagery but also they frequently expressed a felt need for it—and this dependence on imagery did not seem to be the result of laboratory conditions.

Finally, in the 1927–1928 issue (vol. 18) of the *British Journal of Psychology*, in a three-part series, T. H. Pear, F. Aveling, and F. C. Bartlett give their respective accounts concerning the issue of the relevance of visual imagery to the process of thinking; Pear (1927b) enumerates the difficulties that prevent him from believing that visual images are necessarily "lowly vehicles of thought" and that they are often irrelevant to, or discrepant from, the thought that proceeds independently of them. For Pear's examination of the function of imagery—of *any* kind—in the appreciation of "unseen (radio) drama," as well as an account of synaesthesia, imagery intensity and vividness, and affective tone, see Kerr and Pear (1931). Among Pear's considerations are the following: the characteristics of visual imagery are extremely numerous and varied; the development of visual imagery as a vehicle for thinking passes through different stages, and these stages should receive different names and ought not to be confused; the "biological importance" of the situation in which visual imagery functions should not be neglected; the distinction between *concrete* and *abstract* imagery is not helpful; and the nature of visual imagery makes it difficult to record, but such a hindrance may be minimized. Aveling's (1927) conclusions as to the presence and relevance of imagery regarding thought processes are as follows: thoughts may or may not be accompanied by sensorial elements/images; they remain unimpaired while the imagery tends to become fragmentary, obscure, and even to drop out of consciousness altogether; images, accordingly, are not relevant to thought in the sense of being necessary to it (though they may be relevant as associated with thoughts or illustrative of them); the concept of *universal* tends to be present to consciousness as imageless substantive content, whereas the *individual,* on the other hand, tends to be present as a concept in connection with sensorial contents (images); and the image that best encompasses individual thought is the direct image or percept. Bartlett (1927) makes the assumption that imaging and thinking both possess the general function of enabling the person to deal with situations at a distance; having both—images and being able to think—are further extensions of that process of developing long-distance receptors which is at the basis of the growth of the brain. Bartlett considers "most certainly" (p. 27) that the image is, in general, relevant to the process of thinking; he asserts that in proportion as the *form* of thinking is to be given genuine material to work with, more and more must images be utilized in one's thinking processes. However, according to Bartlett, to say that images are relevant, in general, to the thinking process is not to say that the thinking process is simply the utilization of images. Moreover, says Bartlett, "thinking is biologically subsequent to the functioning of the image-forming processes" (p. 28). Bartlett maintains that—concerning the *content* of image in relation to the aim of the specific process of thinking—it is in every case the thinking itself that determines whether the images that are utilized are relevant, and never the images that sporadically occur which determine the relevance of the thinking they may stimulate.

## Memory Imagery

Several early writers have described the memorial aspects of imagery (cf. the section in chapter 1 herein, "Memory Imagery") under subheadings such as "visual memory," "visual memory image," "memory image," "memory consciousness," and "auditory memory." For example, see chronologically: Talbot (1896), Bentley (1899), Whipple (1901/1902), Kuhlmann (1905, 1906, 1907, 1909), Murray (1906), Finkenbinder (1914), Burtt (1916), Berliner (1918), Bowers (1931a,b, 1932a,b), Elderton (1933), Brown (1935), and Anderson (1939). Bentley's (1899) experimental account (pp. 25–48) of the memory image focuses on the two principal methods of reproduction and recognition, and on two auxiliary methods: comparison and description. He suggests that the least accurate and least used method is that of description that may involve verbal reports, and the motor modes of gesticulatory and mimetic responses; when one looks for small differences in participants' responses, the method of oral description is extremely deficient or impossible (cf. Talbot's, 1896, description of her visual memory training exercises). In his experiments, Bentley's (1899) method of choice is termed the *method of recall and comparison*; it differs from other methods in its ability to scrutinize the actual contents of memory, and in making possible a direct comparison of image and sensation. Bentley presented his participants—who reported their visual imagery—with a series of color-disc stimuli on a Marbe adjustable color-mixer; this apparatus permits the adjustment of color sectors at will during rotation and, in this way, a continuous change of color is possible or, with a short interval for shifting, two successive stimuli may be given without introducing a "space error" into the procedure that tested for visual imagery memory. It is important to note that another "classical error" to be avoided in experiments containing serial, or comparison, stimuli is called the *time-error, time-order error, time-order effect*, or *negative time-error* (cf. Borak, 1921; Fechner, 1860; Kohler, 1923; Kreezer, 1938; Lauenstein, 1932; Needham, 1934a,b, 1935; Pratt, 1933; Stott, 1935; Woodrow, 1935; Woodrow and Stott, 1936). That is, in general, certain observable constant errors in an experiment may be referable to the *temporal order* of presentation of the stimulus materials (cf. Roeckelein, 2000, pp. 96, 118). As an explanation of the time-error effects, Fechner (1860) and others held the doctrine that the comparison of two successive objects/stimuli is based on the comparison of the second with a memory-image of the first. The occurrence of a negative time-error and its increase with the time-interval was explained by assuming that the intensity of the memory-image gradually fades over time; this persistent theory, however, was gradually dropped as a result of phenomenological observations that showed that successive comparisons usually occur in the absence of a memory-image of the first object. As a substitute for the memory-image doctrine, Kohler (1923) revived the notion of a *physiological trace* involving a persisting aftereffect in the brain of the first object/stimulus. Historically, time-errors have been observed in connection with various properties of perceptual experience, such as the attributes of intensity, quality, duration, and extent.

Of the other subsidiary methods employed by Bentley (1899)—such as "recall and selection" involving a Jastrow drop apparatus, the "burette" method involving the observation of light through an aqueous solution of a pigment contained in a thin glass jar, and "direct production" of a color matched to an exemplar color—it is noted (p. 45) that "none of these secondary methods proved to be entirely satisfactory, though each promised some tempting advantage." Bentley suggests—for future research on visual imagery memory and for improvements over his approach—that the following methodologies be employed: for color stimuli—a spectrum with a movable narrow slit, and for brightness—a constant lamp in a sliding plane with a photometric screen for the projection of rays (cf. Griffitts and Baumgartner, 1919). In general, Bentley found that the examination of the qualitative fidelity of simple contents requires more refined and discriminatory methods than he at first thought necessary; that is, for short times, the amount of change in a constant direction of the memory image is quite small and may be isolated only by great care and under the most favorable conditions. Among his conclusions, Bentley gives the following: participants who are preeminently visual may image the color or brightness dimensions directly; the use of names, or verbal descriptions, are important primarily where the verbal type of memory is strong and the visual deficient; there is marked evidence of the influence of feeling on memory; and strain sensations about the head and trunk, along with general bodily sensations, seem to facilitate retention and recognition in certain cases. Bentley's other specific observations include the following: gray and colored discs that are shown and remembered in daylight tend to become lighter in the visual memory; gray discs shown in a dark chamber have a tendency in the visual image to grow dark during an unilluminated interval (no lightening was observed with an unilluminated interval); the condition of the retina with respect to stimulation (cf. Murray, 1906) during the memory interval is important for the memory image (illuminated and unilluminated intervals—where all other conditions are constant—are followed by different judgments with the same memory stimuli); and in all experiments with brightness and color—where a time interval is involved—care should be taken to control the state of the visual organ.

In a four-part series (involving ninety-nine journal pages), Whipple (1901/1902) makes a lengthy analytic study of *pitch memory* that is the counterpart of Bentley's (1899) study of *visual memory* (cf. Lay, 1903a,b). Following an extensive review of the relevant literature on materials, modes, and methodologies, Whipple describes his experimental procedure whose purpose was to trace introspectively the nature and course of the tonal memory image and to analyze the processes of judgment. In his qualitative analysis of tonal memory, Whipple employs discrete stimuli and the modified method of "right and wrong cases," as well as the use of the continuous change (or reaction) method in examination of the judgment-consciousness in the discrimination of clangs and tones. Based upon the intensive testing of his participants' tonal memory, Whipple draws the following conclusions (among other points):

1. The auditory image is but one part of a complex structure that represents the original experience (i.e., the memory image of a tone is not merely a "tonal memory image"; it is that and much more).
2. A tone is held in memory not only as an auditory quality, but also as a definite quality possessing "marks" (e.g., from modalities of vision, temperature and strain sensations, affective reactions, etc.) that help to identify it.
3. The auditory image per se—usually of the timbre of the stimulus and localized at the instrument—attains its maximal excellence about two seconds after the stimulus and, despite the active use of memorial aids such as visualization, contraction of throat muscles, and so on. It wanes gradually, suffering most in intensity (cf. Binet, 1887; Schaub, 1911), less in clearness, and least in quality (it is very diminished at 40 seconds, and often entirely dissipated at 60 seconds).
4. Continued practice with a stimulus of a particular clang color (tonometer or bottle) increases the "serviceability" of the image: it becomes more intense, clearer, and of longer duration.
5. The task of actively holding the image very soon develops a "habit of imaging" (i.e., the image, of itself, becomes insistent to the degree that when exclusion of the image is desired, very active attention toward naturally powerful distractors—such as odors—is needed to repress it for relatively short intervals of about 10 seconds).

Concerning the process of judgment consciousness, Whipple concludes the following:

1. One must differentiate *qualitatively* between judgments of identity and judgments of differences (no matter how the *quantitative* results are treated).
2. The values yielded by the "reaction" method cannot be compared simply with those obtained by the method of "right and wrong cases" (one may not even be able to say that the determination of subjective equality in the former method is akin to the judgment of equality in the latter).

3. The presence of the auditory image is not necessary to the recognition of either difference or equality.
4. The auditory image may be present in the judgment consciousness, but not itself an object of attention (i.e., not serving as a basis for comparison).
5. The auditory image may be an essential component of the judgment consciousness (becoming a direct object of the attention) *after* the attention has once been given to the variables.
6. Judgments of "higher" and "lower," made without conscious reference to the image, are largely analyzable into complexes of strain sensations (with less prominent visual and organic elements).
7. Judgments of difference in which the direction of the difference is unknown are common for some participants—they rarely appear, however, except when there is an actual objective difference.

Finally, Whipple (1901/1902, vol. 13, p. 268) cites certain problems he observed in the course of his investigations (e.g., the "spatiality" of tones), as well as some issues for further experimental work (e.g., the need to study the recognition and discrimination of auditory qualities whose pitch is not that of a single isolated tone, but that of a cadence, a melody, or a chord; such a content would present conditions more nearly approximating those of actual life).

In a series of studies closely related to those of Bentley (1899) and Whipple (1901/1902), Kuhlmann (1906, 1907, 1909) analyzed the memory consciousness in visual and auditory imagery memory. His general goals were to determine the nature of the imagery in the recall of given visual materials (including both meaningless visual forms and pictures of familiar objects) and to determine the nature of memory errors and the factors that produce them. In one case, Kuhlmann (1906) found in participants' recall results that the direct visual imagery showed distinct *grades* of *spontaneity* and differences in the *order* of its *development*. In a second case, Kuhlmann (1907) discovered that the same general causes produced both *conscious changes* and *memory illusions* in his participants' responses: the tendency of the picture's imagery to change to the imagery of the object represented (due to the following reasons: the spontaneity of correct imagery declined with the lapse of time; spontaneity, or the lack of it, was a criterion for accepting imagery as correct or for rejecting it as wrong; the intensity of direct recognition consciousness decreased; the object rather than its picture was more a matter of everyday experience, and its imagery more habitual; more interest and emotional coloring belongs to objects than to their pictures; and to the extent that the picture represents or suggests the object, the imagery of the object is already given). In a third instance, Kuhlmann (1909) analyzes mainly *auditory* imagery and auditory memory consciousness; he concludes that the character of the auditory imagery produced by his participants varied with reference to its completeness, the degree in which the words were recalled in the quality of the individual voice, and the occasional recall of imagery of the voice in its true character without the recall of any words. As a rule, only fragments of sentences and phrases were recalled directly in terms of auditory imagery, the rest being filled in by other methods of recall (sometimes the stimulus words were recalled in the quality of the individual's voice as heard). Also, visual imagery that at first accompanied simultaneously the auditory imagery of the words or followed it, later preceded it and became the chief means of recall. Kuhlmann (1909, p. 218) notes that auditory imagery "could not as a rule be voluntarily controlled directly, but only through the motor processes, or through visual imagery in some instances. Through these aids, the sound was recalled fragment by fragment, leaving usually large gaps to be filled in by motor representatives alone."

Murray's (1906) general objective of study—in three groups of experiments on the peripheral and central factors in memory images—was to examine the appearance, recurrence, and duration in immediate memory of visual images of simple figures. Her specific purpose was to determine whether figures viewed under uniform conditions of attention differ in reproductivity and, if so, whether such differences may be correlated with certain intrinsic characteristics of the figures, such as size, color, brightness, complexity of contour, and outline. The results of Murray's (p. 247) experiments are summed up as follows: neither the attributes of the stimulus (spatial or qualitative) nor the general ocular movements associated with these attributes comprise the important differential factor in visual reproduction; rather, on the contrary, the "reappearance and persistence, distinctness and general accuracy of reproduction are conditioned primarily upon the relation of the stimulus or image to central conditions, and upon certain special motor phenomena accompanying fixation."

Finkenbinder (1914) attempted to determine what mental imagery and procedures or processes are employed by participants in solving problems of various sorts (e.g., math problems, mechanical puzzles), and in subsequent recalling (after a month or more) the problems and their solutions (cf. Brown; 1935, Elderton, 1933; Hill, 1918; and Rachofsky, 1918 for other early problem-solving studies in this area). Finkenbinder (pp. 79–81) makes the following points, among others, based upon his participants' responses to the problem-solving tasks:

1. The act of voluntary recall is characterized by two stages (an initial stage of an *Aufgabe* to recall, involving the act of "searching," and a second stage involving the occurrence of imagery of various sorts).
2. The concrete objects or words of the initial perception, and the images employed during the act of solving problems, are likely to appear (in the form of images) in recall than are the "short cuts" or processes of reasoning where concrete images usher in meanings, and associations are made which then constitute the awareness of relation (i.e., *content* was readily recalled while *act* was almost never recalled).
3. Very few of the unsuccessful trials in the problem-solving area are definitely recalled (the first unsuccessful trial that is made is usually the only one ever recalled).
4. The cues of an abstract and of a concrete nature lead to approximately the same results.
5. Most participants tend to recall more data in visual imagery than was present in visual imagery during the problem-solving task.
6. The problems dealing with logical fallacies, and sentiments, are more often recalled in verbal imagery than are other types of problems.
7. The visual image is decidedly the most dominant feature of recall (feelings of familiarity, of satisfaction, and pauses of attention are seldom recalled—they are never recalled except in connection with imagery).

Finkenbinder (p. 81) notes that from an actual count of factors present in the recall of ten of his problems, it is estimated that approximately 200,000 images (but only 100 other components, mostly of an affective nature) were experienced; of all of Finkenbinder's introspective data, about 90 percent involved visual imagery. For a comparison of visual memory images experienced in the *morning* versus those at *night* (and a study containing results such as the time a participant can keep a mental image during a certain period is longer in the morning than at night and the duration of a single image is longer in the morning than at night), as well as other factors—such as imagery before and after a short period of intensive mental work—see Berliner (1918, pp. 358–66).

Bowers (1931a,b, 1932a,b) conducted several early studies on visual imagery memory (cf. Anderson's [1939, p. 578] study on auditory memory span in which he concludes, among other things, that participants were able to *discriminate* intensities too low for them to be *aware* of them). In one study, Bowers (1931a) collected data from participants in which correlation coefficients were calculated between their images for visual, auditory, and kinaesthetic words and the numbers of times these words were recalled. Among his conclusions are that there is a small, but significant, positive correlation between word scores and mean imagery for words in the case of visual and kinaesthetic terms (with auditory words, the coefficient was zero); scores for words found in the last third of the recalled list yield no higher coefficients with imagery than those in the first third of the list; the lapse of a period of a month seems to result in a higher relationship between imagery for words and word scores in the cases of auditory and kinaesthetic terms (the evidence is rather unclear when visual words are considered); total imagery ratings for pupil-participants have zero correlation with their memory scores; and both for immediate reproduction, and after a one-month lapse, the *order* for recall of the different kinds of words used was auditory, kinaesthetic, and visual. In a second study, Bowers (1932a) attempted to determine if significant differences exist between single (as well as between groups of) lower-case letters in respect of the mean distinctness of their visual images. Among his conclusions, Bowers (1932a, p. 779) reports that consistent differences exist among single lower-case letters regarding the distinctness of their visual images (the *lowest* four letters in distinctness are g, w, q, and y, and the *highest* four letters are i, c, l, and o); he also found that there were differences in two-letter groups (those with the *least* distinct visual images are xg, qw, gt, and mg; those with the *highest* distinct visual images are io, if, la, and oe). Moreover, Bowers reports that the first and second letters of a three-letter group appear to be of equal importance in influencing the distinctness of the visual image, and the feasibility of assessing verbal material—concerning the distinctness of visual images of it—is established (cf. Bowers, 1929, 1931a,b). In a third study, Bowers (1932b) followed up and improved on his earlier experiments (Bowers, 1931a,b, 1932a), principally by employing a larger number of participants than previously used. He also attempted to determine to what extent visual verbal imagery and retention of his original list of forty-five words varied concomitantly. Among his conclusions, Bowers (1932b) lists the following: confirmation of a previous finding (i.e., there is a small but significant positive correlation between the mean concrete imagery attached to visual words by a group of participants and the number of times these words are recalled by the group—this correlation was found, also, between visual verbal imagery for words or letter-groups and memory for them); there is some evidence that participants claiming "high" concrete imagery recall more words than participants whose claimed imagery is "low"; and it is confirmed that words have an order of *memorial precedence* where the order depends considerably on the method of stimulus presentation.

## Methods/General Imagery-Related Studies

Bell and Muckenhoupt (1906) attempted to test the mutual consistency of the various methods suggested by Titchener (1901, vol. 1, part 2, pp. 394–401) for investigating the type of imagery customarily used by a given individual. Note that the methods cited by Titchener (1901), and studied by Bell and Muckenhoupt here, are those developed by early researchers such as Kraepelin, Secor, Binet, Cohn, and Washburn. Because only two of the methods (the revised Galton questionary, and Secor's word method) aim to discover the presence of images other than auditory, visual, or motor, these three types of images only were compared and assessed. Bell and Muckenhoupt's plan was to test intensively only a few ($n$=4) female participants by as many of the methods as possible to see how harmonious the results were with each other. They draw the following conclusions based upon their participants' responses to the visual, auditory, and motor imagery tests: The methods are consistent, generally, in their results. Secor's method gave the least satisfactory results overall (the root of the difficulty here probably lies in the fact that it requires the exercise of perfectly indefinite and uncontrolled processes of association; all the other methods require the participant to revive certain fixed and specified material, such as letters, numbers, and so on; the variations in a method's results are due wholly to the mode of revival but, where words are used, such as in Secor's method, and allowed to suggest images freely, the process is necessarily complicated by all of the factors that occur in making word-associations, for instance, the recent experience of the participants may be a disturbing or confounding factor), and in comparing the results of the relatively objective methods with participants' introspective testimony as to their mental type (i.e., as given in answers to the questionary in Titchener, 1901, pp. 198–200), the questionary results support those of the other objective methods. Finally, Bell and Muckenhoupt suggest that—in determining mental imagery type—tests of the *vividness* of a certain kind of image should be distinguished from tests showing the mere *frequency* of its occurrence (e.g., a person may have a mediocre power of visual imagery—as measured by the definition and vividness of the pictures called up—but may think frequently or habitually in visual terms). Another variable—suggested by Clark, Quackenbush, and Washburn (1913)—which may influence results in experimental studies of individual differences, especially those involving imagery, is called *affective sensitiveness*, that is, a strong personal predisposition toward affective reactions whether of pleasantness or unpleasantness; cf. Washburn, Hatt, and Holt (1923a). Yet another study involving potential individual differences in the methodology of the experimental setting, also involving imagery materials, was conducted by Coover (1913) who reported on the phenomenon of the *feeling of being stared at.*

Colvin (1909) notes (in his review of the history of the methods for determining ideational types) that although the existence of the mental image was pointed out definitely by Aristotle in the third century B.C. in his *De Anima* (see McKeon, 1941), the first attempt to describe accurately its nature was made by Fechner (1860, pp. 469–91) in the comparison of his own mental imagery with his afterimagery. Fechner introspectively analyzed his own visual imagery and found it to be extremely weak and indefinite in comparison with his afterimagery; weaker still was Fechner's ability to call up mental images of other sensory modalities than those of vision—his auditory mental imagery was practically nil, and his olfactory and gustatory memory imagery were nonexistent. It is reported that Fechner's wife, on the other hand, possessed vivid imagery of hearing, taste, and smell, as well as of vision. About twenty years following Fechner's investigations, Galton (1883/1907) took up the imagery problem and attempted to discover by means of a set of questions the characteristics of mental imagery of a much larger number of participants than employed by Fechner. Galton's inquiry, like that of Fechner, chiefly concerned the visual image; it, however, also touched upon sound, taste, smell, dermal (touch, temperature, pain), and organic (fatigue, hunger, and other bodily conditions) imagery. Colvin notes that Galton's questionary covers somewhat over two pages and is appended to the latter's 1883/1907 work (pp. 378–80). Among the other pioneers in the investigation of mental imagery, Colvin mentions the following:

- Charcot—emphasized the existence of distinct ideational types.
- Ballet—who, with Charcot, distinguished the visual, acoustic, motor, and mixed imagery types.
- Taine, Ribot, Binet, and Stricker—who, along with Egger and Dodge, gave an impetus to the study of motor and other verbal types in distinction from concrete imagery; for example, Dodge's work indicates clearly that a person may be "speech-motor" without being "hand-motor" and that the classification created by Charcot—which held to a *single* motor type—was too inclusive. Dodge also found that a person may possess a vivid type of imagery that, however, may not be employed in ordinary thinking (cf. Bell and Muckenhoupt, 1906).

Other early researchers of mental imagery mentioned by Colvin are Meumann, Baldwin, Lay, Titchener, Secor, and Cohn.

Colvin (1909, p. 225) suggests that "one of the most important discussions in recent years on the various ideational types is that of Segal (1908), who maintains that the conclusions reached by Charcot and others as to the existence of sharply distinguished ideational types is not altogether correct." That is, many persons who possess intense visual imagery do not see all the words that they employ in thinking; also, some persons may—for one purpose—think in concrete visual imagery while—for another purpose—may think equally well in acoustic or motor imagery. Individuals apparently think visually regarding concrete objects and in acoustic-motor terms when they utilize words. Thus, according to Segal, the whole doctrine of distinct types is untenable, and that the qualitative conception of ideational types must be abandoned for a quantitative distinction. Most persons belong to a mixed type and, perhaps, possess greater vividness of imagery in one direction than others, but are not for this reason confined to one type of thinking.

Colvin (1909) maintains that the attempt to determine absolute ideational types is hardly possible and that the best one can do is to determine the predominating type for a certain class of sensory or verbal material. Additionally, the problem of determining ideational types is further complicated by the fact that the methods generally employed are defective in many important respects and often lead to results that are contradictory. While the method of introspective analysis is reliable, and may give valuable insights (e.g., Lay, 1898, pp. 32–47), it is tied closely to the area of individual psychology, and one must take care not to come to sweeping general conclusions concerning imagery. Colvin observes that Fechner's questionary method, as developed by Galton and employed by others, has the value of bringing together mass results of introspective analysis, but it is open to other serious objections unless employed with great caution (cf. Titchener [1901, vol. 1, part 2, pp. 387–90] for a good statement of the value and limitations of this method).

According to Colvin (1909), numerous objective methods for determining ideational types have been devised and employed from time to time with a fair degree of success. The most important of many of these are not the numerical results, but rather the introspective analyses by the participants taking these tests. The main value of such tests is realized when testing small groups with skilled laboratory participants, and as *mass* tests, their value is much less. In one type of test, called the *word-method*, participants are required to write out a list of objects distinguished by their color, and a second list distinguished by their sound. An equal amount of time is given for each list, and the person who succeeds better with the first list than with the second is taken to be a visualizer, while the person who gets better results with the second list is held to be of the auditory type. In this case, it is obvious that the participant may in writing this list have no concrete imagery at all; he/she may merely be relying on verbal imagery (cf. Dugas [1895] who determined the imagery-memory type by dictating words and getting from the participant a report of the associations aroused). The methods employed by Binet and by Cohn—of the "letter squares"—described by Titchener (1901), likewise, have their chief value in the introspections of the participants (the letter-squares, however, involve an important principle for the objective determination of visual imagery in that they present—when given to the participant visually—an opportunity to localize a particular letter in a certain place in the square and to reproduce it in its place on a similar blank square; as the correct placing of the letter is dependent to a large degree on the participant's ability to visualize the square, high success in this direction probably indicates considerable concrete visualizing ability).

Colvin (1909) asserts that, at best, attempts to determine individual ideational types in terms of the method of presentation of the material are valuable only in showing that one participant is superior to another in a certain type of imagery, but *not* in deciding which type predominates in a given person. In referring to Meumann, Colvin describes two other objective methods for determining ideational types: the *method of distraction* and the *method of helps*. The former method consists in giving the participant a definite memory task and measuring the exact time that is required to perform it. Then, various distractions are presented (so chosen as to serve as hindrances for various types of ideation); the effect of the distractions on the results of the learning task indicates the ideational type of the participant (it is assumed that the auditory type is more easily distracted by auditory stimuli, the visual type by visual stimuli, and the motor type by an interference with one's inner-speech). The latter method (helps method) is intended to increase the effectiveness of learning (e.g., the visual type is aided by the spatial arrangement of the material presented, but for the auditory type this arrangement may prove to be a hindrance to the learning; the auditory-motor type is aided by the participant pronouncing the words seen or drawing them with finger or pencil). Colvin (p. 229) points out some potential confounds/fallacies with such methods for determining the ideational type of a person. For example, in the distraction method, the time of learning may be lengthened, or reduce its correctness, simply by taking away the attention of the participant from the learning and not by inhibiting the mental imagery employed in the learning. To illustrate this, Colvin cites the experiments performed by Binet, and later by Meumann, on the mathematical prodigy named "Inaudi." As distractions, Binet had Inaudi sing a tone during his calculations—which resulted in lengthening the time Inaudi used in his calculations—and Meumann had Inaudi hold his tongue between his teeth in order to interfere with his inner-speech—which resulted in lengthening the time of Inaudi's performance, in this case nearly threefold. It is quite obvious that such results might have been due, in part at least, to distracted attention and not simply to the inhibition of speech-motor processes. Moreover, Colvin cautions that when using multiple distractions, the type of distractions used in the method (e.g., an extremely bright light; a moderately intense noise; a metronome ticking, etc.) must be properly equated in order to make valid conclusions as to the ideational type of the person.

Another method, called the *method of style* (e.g., Fraser, 1891–1892), attempts to deduce the type of imagery of an author from his writings. Colvin suggests that such an assumption—that the content of particular, selected words as determined by the experimenter gives an index of the imagery in the mind of the author—be questioned. Such a method may indicate something, but it is far from being an adequate test for the ideational type of the participant (e.g., the line of poetry, "And *shook* his drowsy squire awake," may not necessarily evoke motor imagery; it may merely present a visual picture). Colvin (1909, p. 233) maintains that "one of the most fruitful methods of getting at the ideational processes of an individual is by taking note of characteristic errors made in memorizing various kinds of material" (e.g., the visualizer may confuse like-appearing, but different-sounding, letters, syllables, and words; the auditory-minded participant may confuse like-sounding letters, etc.). He notes, also, that the visualizer makes less mistakes in learning consonants, that the auditory-minded makes less mistakes in learning vowels, and that the visualizer succeeds better when memory for spatial localization is involved than does the acoustic-motor type of person, while the latter succeeds better when the presentation of the material is accompanied by rhythm and accent.

Among his conclusions, Colvin (1909) indicates the following:

It is impossible to determine absolute ideational types in most persons.

The determination of ideational types is complicated by the difficulty of obtaining unequivocal methods for such assessments.

The most "trustworthy" method is that of introspective analysis—in its various forms—employed by well-trained participants (cf. a case study of the imagery of an *untrained* introspectionist—a *child* whose imagery was documented across the ages three to five years; Helson, 1933).

Most of the objective methods are open to more or less serious criticism and not one of them alone can be relied upon as the final word.

The objective methods hardly show more than that one person is superior to another in a certain ideational process.

It is extremely difficult to make the various tests for visual, motor, and auditory imagery comparable (cf. Bell and Muckenhoupt, 1906).

The whole issue of motor imagery is still in a very unsatisfactory state.

In considering motor imagery, it should be remembered that much of the so-called "visual imagery" is not actually such, but is really either the kinaesthetic sensations or imagery due to muscular adjustments of the eyes in accommodation, convergence, and orientation of objects in space (cf. Dunlap, 1910; Goldthwait, 1933; Kohler and Emery, 1947; Kohler and Wallach, 1944; Murray, 1906; Stratton, 1897, 1902, 1907).

It is possible—if the methods are tested out and valid comparisons are made—that superior methods of an objective sort may be devised which will conclusively determine whether a given person (under certain conditions) employs predominantly visual or auditory-motor imagery in his/her thinking and—if the former, whether it is concrete or verbal, while—if the latter, whether it is speech-motor, hand-motor, or motor in the sense of a more comprehensive kinaesthetic ideation.

Several early investigators have described experiments, methods, and phenomena that are indirectly or generally, rather than directly or explicitly, related to various issues of mental imagery (e.g., Hicks, 1924; Jacobson, 1925, 1932; Rosenow, 1918). In his discussion of the "genesis of the image," Rosenow (1918, p. 299) indicates that he shares the view of those who hold that the nature of the ideational response is that of an indirect and "nascent motor response," which leads, typically, to a "delayed overt response" and, whereby, the indirect reaction is the "means," and the delayed reaction is the "end." In the solution to the problem of bringing an indirect reaction to the focus of consciousness, Rosenow proposes that researchers study the indirect reactions of the growing, developing child. Following his analysis of the development of a child's indirect movements (including speech) vis-à-vis imagery, Rosenow sums up his "birth of imagery" argument, including the following points:

• On the *structural* side, the peculiarity of the image is that it may occupy the focus of consciousness as an object which, somehow, belongs to the realm distinct from the perceptual; on the *functional* side, the image is the sensory aspect of a nascent activity which, as purposive activity, is indirect with reference to this perceptual realm (in the formation of habits, such indirect reactions are not attended to after the habit is well formed).
• One's habits of thought are not so automatic that such a process can take place—thus, one might classify all nonhabitual purposive activity as "thought" (even though such a classification neglects the "structural differential"—the "nonperceptual texture" of the idea).
• It is suggested that this structural difference is correlated with the fact that thought is indirect *socially*, and is a development of the direct *social* "gesture."
• The elements of thought come to consciousness at a time when privacy of conscious activity in the *presence of others* is of value to the person.

Another early general discussion of mental imagery is provided by Hicks (1924, p. 121) who observes, initially, that "the exact nature of so-called 'images' . . . has rarely been seriously faced," even though psychologists (ever since Hume in the eighteenth century discussed impressions and ideas) have investigated or enunciated—more or less successfully—some interesting empirical facts concerning the processes of remembering and imagining. In an analysis of the nature of images, Hicks (p. 122) advises against simply using new terminology to describe that which eludes explanation (e.g., "What . . . is gained by speaking of psychical phenomena as being subject to a law of 'mnemic causality,' in contradistinction from the law of physical causality that holds of physical phenomena?"). Such phrases are, in themselves, not explanatory in any sense; they are simply pictorial ways of restating something that calls for explanation. Among the propositions and assumptions that Hicks employs in his account of imagery (which is sprinkled here and there with references to classical literary and philosophical works) are the following:

Imagination is continuous with perception and grows out of it; the *occurrence* of any act of perception—the occasioning condition of its *existence* as a state of the mental life—is traceable to the physiological event of bodily stimulation.

The *character* or *nature* of perception, on the other hand, is explicable only by viewing it from within and as in relation to that upon which it is directed.

The process of imagining is of "one piece" with the process of perceiving, but where imagination contains a relatively larger proportion of revived factors; in imagination—where objective imagery is present—there is (as in perception) a real object upon which the "act of discriminating" is directed.

Memory is not necessarily dependent on concrete objective imagery.

One may speak with confidence that there are images connected with the "lower senses" (e.g., taste, smell, touch, temperature, pressure, kinaesthesis).

Kinaesthetic imagery is perhaps the least accessible of all imagery to exact inspection (in this regard, perception—as it occurs in the concrete life of the mind—is not merely a cognitive process but involves a change in the state of feeling and in a certain form of movement; thus, every mode of sense-perception has a tendency, more or less marked, to give rise to kinaesthetic imagery and, in the revival of such sensory experience, kinaesthetic will be naturally involved).

In the mature mental life, motor images repeatedly take the place of motor sensations. Verbal imagination is dependent on actually perceived movements in lips, tongue, and larynx (cf. Watson, 1919/1929, 1920).

In regard to auditory and visual imagery, it is extremely difficult to draw the line between images that are objective and those that are not objective.

Auditory imagery of the objective type is far less frequent than visual imagery of that type.

Visual imagery is found of a more objective type than is found in imagery connected with the other senses.

In the make-believe activities of children, ample evidence is shown of the way in which realization of imagery takes place in connections with sense-perception.

Much of the visual imagery in dreams—especially in the earlier part of the night—is engendered by entoptic phenomena (i.e., visual experiences produced by factors within the eye itself, such as "ocular spectra" or "floaters" which are fibers or granules that naturally float in the eye's vitreous humor and whose shadows appear in the field of vision as little dark moving spots).

External objects and events may gain the attention of a sleeper and elicit trains of dream-imagery in him or her (very common forms of visual perception giving rise to dreams are those of bright moonlight and the sun's rays in the early morning).

Turning now to the more specific topics of early methodologies and applications of imagery in, and imagery to, various settings (cf. discussions of imagery applications in chapter 3), the studies by Jacobson (1925, 1929, 1932) are especially noteworthy. Jacobson (1925, 1929) investigated, and developed, clinical methods of the "involuntary start," of "bringing quiet to the nervous system," and of the "quieting of psychological activities." He maintains (1925, p. 73) that "the problem of diminishing cerebral activities may prove of interest to every psychological school of thought." For example, clinicians might see the issue in terms of a search for a sedative for overactivity of the cerebrospinal and autonomic nervous systems, or for the reduction of nervous irritability and excitement, while others may focus on a physical or physiological means for diminishing and examining a person's psychic processes (including one's "stream of consciousness," states of attention, mental imagery and kinaesthesis, thought processes, emotions, and subvocal speech). Based upon earlier work by Kulpe (1893), Jacobson (1925, p. 74) asserts that "it is but a step from Kulpe's views . . . that the intensive relaxation of movement brings with it a subsidence of voluntary recollection and reflection." Jacobson reasoned that it is logical—if a means might be discovered to relax the tension in certain parts of one's body—that the concomitant attention to a tension-producing external stimulus might be diminished or extinguished altogether (cf. Washburn, 1916, p. 32; Watson, 1919/1929, p. 15). Jacobson (1925, pp. 76–78) presents a brief summary of his "technique of progressive relaxation" in which the person learns how to relax the principal muscle groups of his body to an extreme degree (this implies the reduction of impulses along motor and associated portions of the nervous system inasmuch as "it is generally agreed among physiologists that there are no specific inhibitory fibers to the striated muscles").

Jacobson's technique of relaxation is "progressive" in three aspects: the individual relaxes a group of muscles (e.g., the flexors of the right forearm) further and further each minute; the individual becomes acquainted—in a certain order—with the principal muscle-groups of his/her entire body (and simultaneously relaxes—with each new group—such parts as have received practice previously); and as the individual practices from day to day, he/she progresses toward a "habit of repose" (i.e., he/she tends toward a state in which quiet is automatically maintained—this is not to be confused with what has been known merely or globally as *relaxation*, a state that yet includes a certain degree of "residual tension"; eliminating residual tension is the essential point of Jacobson's method; residual tension only disappears gradually: it may take fifteen minutes of progressive relaxing to relax a single body part, such as the right arm). Further, progressive relaxation is called *general* when the person lies with closed eyes and relaxes "all over," and it is called *relative* when he/she is active, but is relaxed so far as possible during that activity.

Jacobson (1925, pp. 78–84) describes in great detail the records of two participants who learned to relax well as a result of using his relaxation technique that included the employment of imagery-related tasks (e.g., "imagine a motor-car passing"). Among Jacobson's conclusions are the following:

A method is tested and described that successfully relaxes the striated musculature in a progressive manner.

Participants have been trained to continue the process of relaxation—or the *negative* of contraction—to an extreme degree.

A reliable judgment of relaxation may be made of participants by certain objective signs. Participants judge the relaxation by the absence of the sense of muscular tenseness.

The participants did not know in advance that the investigator was studying whether imagery diminishes or not with advancing relaxation of muscles (it *does* diminish).

With visual imagery, participants have a sense of tenseness in muscles of the ocular region (without such faint tenseness, the image fails to appear; with complete ocular relaxation, the image disappears).

Motor or kinaesthetic imagery, as well as visual imagery, may be "relaxed away" (e.g., "inner speech" ceases with progressive relaxation of the muscles of the lips, tongue, larynx, and throat).

Auditory imagery, also, is attended by a sense of tenseness, sometimes felt in the auditory apparatus but characteristically in the ocular muscles (the person tends to look toward the imaged source of sound; with the

relaxation of such looking responses or other tension, the auditory image is absent).

Progressive relaxation is not, as a rule, perfect or complete except for brief
periods of time (it is during such periods that imagery seems altogether
absent).

It seems that natural sleep ensues after the imageless state is maintained for
a relatively prolonged time.

With progressive muscular relaxation, not only imagery but, also, attention,
recollection, thought-processes, and emotion gradually diminish.

In another similar methodological study involving imagery and
progressive relaxation, Jacobson (1932) describes the "electrophysiology of mental activities." Following an excellent review of the
history and beginnings of experimental psychology and its methodologies, Jacobson states that it is his desire to test the possibility that
the muscle-sense and its recording may be objectively verified for the
whole range of an individual's mental experience (cf. Jacobson, 1927,
1930/1931). He discusses his progressive relaxation technique
(Jacobson, 1925), as well as procedures involving the following:
"imagination of movement," "imagination and recollection of various muscular acts" (along with photographic records of participants'
muscular action-potentials), "evidence that specific muscles contract
during imagination," "the galvanic reflex," "an objective measurement
of introspection," "relaxation of mental activities," "visual imagination and recollection," "variation of specific muscles contracting during imagination," and "the speech musculature" (along with over a
dozen worthwhile references from the early psychological literature
regarding "internal speech").

Among his conclusions, Jacobson (1932) makes the following
points:

1. When the participant—lying relaxed with eyelids closed—engages in mental activity such as imagination or recollection, contraction occurs in specific muscles of the body (thus, it is suggested, that the physiology of
mental activity is *not* confined exclusively to closed circuits within the
brain but that larger muscular regions, also, are engaged).
2. During visual imagination or recollection, the muscles that move the eyes
contract, as if the participant were looking at the imagined object.
3. During "inner speech" activities, muscles in the tongue and lips contract
as if to say the words in a swift and abbreviated manner.
4. During imagination or recollection of muscular acts, or of matters involving such an act on the person's part, contraction occurs in some of the
muscle-fibers that would engage in the actual performance of the act.

5. Electrical records, along with subjective reports, indicate that during general progressive relaxation, processes of thinking and imagery dwindle down and then disappear.
6. The action-potentials measured in the present study are shown to be very different from the galvanic reflex recordings.
7. A method of measuring neuromuscular processes in mental activities is demonstrated successfully, and a branch of study—analogous to "physical chemistry" in the discipline of chemistry—is opened now in psychology and which may be called "physical psychology."

## Synesthesia

A number of selected early studies investigating synesthesia (i.e., the "cross-modality" condition in which a sensory experience that is normally associated with one sensory modality is activated when a different sensory modality is stimulated) cut across other subject areas such as "gustatory audition" (e.g., Pierce, 1907), "meaning" (e.g., Wheeler and Cutsforth, 1922b), "reasoning/thinking" (e.g., Cutsforth, 1924), "emotion" (e.g., Cutsforth, 1925), "judging/choosing" (e.g., Wheeler and Cutsforth, 1928), "unseen drama" (e.g., Kerr and Pear, 1931) and "developments" (e.g., Riggs and Karwoski, 1934) (cf. the section in chapter 1 herein titled, "Synesthesia" for references to other early studies on this phenomenon).

In the late nineteenth century, Calkins (1896, p. 90) noted that the "study of the varying forms of persisting abnormal association, usually known as 'colored-hearing' and 'forms,' but grouped together by Theodore Flournoy, under the convenient name *synaesthesia*, has hardly, as yet, completed the stage of scientific observation." Calkins suggests that the physiologists and others—with their guesses of "intertwined nerve fibres" and "subliminal consciousness theory"—are dealing with unverified hypotheses regarding the phenomenon of synaesthesia. She reports, on the other hand, not on conjectures and untested theories but on the continued statistical study of synaesthesia begun formally in 1894 at Wellesley College (where data were collected on synaesthesia as early as 1892). Concerning the frequency of synaesthesia experiences in her participants ($n = 979$)—via the questionnaire and interview methods—Calkins reports that there were 298 persons with synaesthesia and 681 individuals with no synaesthesia. These data include experiences of photisms, pseudochromesthesia, single-word/figure/object forms, symbols, and dramatization of letters, numerals, and other special features. Thus, Calkins estimates that of every ten persons five, at least, have some peculiar or fixed forms of mental imagery, and that of these five, two are likely to have "photisms," and four to possess some "mental form," whereas three have some other kind of "apparently erratic association." Calkins provides other summary statistical data on synaesthesia concerning "varieties of forms," "varieties of pseudo-chromesthesia," "connection of color with sound and with shape," "utility and pleasurableness of pseudo-chromesthesia," "form and location of color/hallucination," "personification (like/dislike; dramatization)," and "even and odd numbers." Finally, Calkins (pp. 102–7) presents a series of preliminary (e.g., "Do you think of particular colors in connection with letters of the alphabet?") and detailed (e.g., "If you have word-color, give your color for the name 'Sara'") questions on synaesthesia that may—it was presumed—serve as a "first step in a systematic investigation" of the phenomenon.

Pierce (1907) describes a case study of a young college woman who experienced gustatory/taste/oral qualities following the hearing of words spoken by the human voice, or of musical and other nonvocal sounds (cf. Downey, 1911, for a case study of colored gustation); that is, the woman had "mouth-experiences" (including the four taste qualities, the cutaneous qualities of pressure and temperature, and various texture-motor qualities) upon the hearing of certain sounds, and such experiences were *not* accompanied by any olfactory qualities (the woman was classified as *anosmic* as she demonstrated a highly deficient sense of smell) (cf. Downey, 1911, p. 539). Pierce (pp. 343–45) presents a list of 150 words that when spoken individually to the woman are given their gustatory equivalents by her (e.g., when she hears the name "Alice," she experiences the taste of "Spanish cream with a sprinkling of sugar"; the name "Alfred" is tasted as "corn-bread in milk"; the word "boy" is tasted as "gum drops"; the word "fancy" tastes like "cold Boston baked beans"; the word "hope" tastes like "celery"; "intelligence" tastes like "raw sliced tomato"; "loud" tastes like "a boiled new potato"; "men" tastes like "hash"; "story" tastes like "stewed cranberries"; etc.). Pierce cautions that one must be careful in such studies to ascertain that one is dealing with an actual or genuine case of synaesthesia and not simply with a case of artificial associations due to a "lively dramatic fancy." In this regard, Pierce offers the following facts that "are more compatible with the theory of synaesthesia than with that of mere suggested imagery" (p. 349): the participant herself testifies that the gustatory experiences come quite unsolicited (i.e., it is "found" and not "manufactured"); many of the woman's experiences are given quite definite locations in the mouth; when in doubt about a stimulus word, the woman slightly pressed her cheeks inwards with her fingers until the satisfactory gustatory equivalent occurred (this suggests the sensory, rather than the imaginary, character of the phenomenon); the erratic nature of the situation—many words and sounds evoking no "tastes" whatever—is precisely like that of the well-known synaesthesias; and the woman's gustatory equivalents possess a "constancy" that is hardly possible apart from a "true" synaesthesia (i.e., after a period of six months, a number of words from the original list were given at random to the woman who described the identical gustatory equivalents in almost precisely the same language as she used on the original test). As concerns the explanation of his participant's condition, Pierce (p. 352) inclines toward the physiological—as contrasted with the psychological—explanation of synaesthesias in general, and states, "Still, here no less than in all known cases of synaesthesias, we can only regret that our theory is so lame while our facts are so secure."

In a series of studies published between 1922 and 1928, T. D. Cutsforth and R. H. Wheeler investigated various issues and aspects relating to synaesthesia. Wheeler and Cutsforth (1922a,b) studied synaesthesia and meaning in two blind participants, one of whom was synaesthetic (i.e., it was Cutsforth himself who was a graduate student in psychology and lost his sight when he was eleven years old), and the other was asynaesthetic (i.e., this person was an advanced student in psychology who lost his sight at the age of nine). Following the testing of the two participants (from 1916–1921), using methodologies involving recognition, auditory, and tactual materials, Wheeler and Cutsforth conclude the following: the real cognitive function of synaesthetic phenomena is now clearer (the appearance of colors constitutes developing auditory or tactual perceptions on the one hand, and further development of the colors indicates shifts from one meaning to another as, for example, from letter-meanings to word-meanings; the aspects of the colors acts, also, as a surrogate for motor responses in "focal consciousness"—as long as the motor phenomena are present as an unnoticed background); synaesthetic phenomena behave in such a manner that they may mean the fulfillment of a task; meanings fail to develop in the absence of the appropriate behavior of synaesthetic colors; synaesthetic imagery constitutes the context for meaning; synaesthetic images operate as a substitute for feelings of familiarity; and synaesthetic images "label" or "interpret" the "object," making it meaningful. Wheeler and Cutsforth (1922b) note that meaning never developed for the two participants until a motor attitude or visualized motor attitude attended other sensory or imaginal contents; this points to the conclusion not only that kinaesthesis is an essential component of the consciousness of meaning, but also that a motor response is necessary for the development of meaning. Cutsforth (1924) reports—in his article on "Synaesthesia in the Process of Reasoning"—on a continuation of the work on the synaesthesia of a blind person begun by Wheeler in 1920 and carried out jointly since then by Wheeler and Cutsforth (1921, 1922a). The objective of these studies was to make an intensive examination of the mental content of a highly synaesthetic person, and to compare his mental content with an asynaesthetic person as a control/ check measure. Based upon his testing of the participants' reasoning processes via material consisting of analogies, absurdities, and simple and difficult abstract problems, Cutsforth (1924) concluded that there were no imageless or nonsensory contents of consciousness in his two participants, that synaesthetic imagery is an invariable and essential component in the development of meaning, that the difference between implicit and explicit meaning holds in reasoning as well as in the simple development of meaning, and that synaesthesia is not an extraneous form of association. (It is essential to the cognitive activities of the person who possesses it inasmuch as it is the only "structural tool" he has of comprehending meanings—it pervades the synaesthete's entire mental life.) Cutsforth (1925) examines the role of emotion in a synaesthetic person who became aware of her synaesthetic processes at about nine years of age. Based upon the auditory, emotional, and tactual testing, among other measures, of the participant, Cutsforth draws the following conclusions:

The process of synaesthesia is distinctly a process of perceiving or of cognizing, the associated imagery of which plays the same role in synaesthetic persons as in asynaesthetic persons.

The associated colors employed by the individual provide the context necessary in the development of meaning.

Synaesthesis runs not only into the use of visual imagery, but also into visual imagery whose significance is emotional and tactual (i.e., visual perceptions contain color-imagery of a synaesthetic character).

All of the participant's mental processes—other than the highly mechanized—contain an emotional increment present in terms of color-imagery.

The same colors, under different interpretative mental sets, function as emotion, as tactual, or as auditory perceptions.

The role of emotion in the participant's mental life is twofold: it functions in undeveloped perceptions, and it is the end-stage in elaborate recognition processes.

Wheeler and Cutsforth (1928) extend their series of introspective studies of synaesthesia into the subject area of "choice," involving the classical methodology of comparative judgment and tests using lifted weights, time intervals, and sound intensities. Their results are compared with those of previous similar studies and confirm the following points, among others: the process of judging (like all other forms of thinking, such as recognizing, choosing, and reasoning) begins either with a conscious or an implied set or predisposition; one's final judgment issues from a shifting of attention from the intensity of sensations of the comparison stimulus to imagery that persisted from the standard stimulus, and from a change that took place in the motor set; processes of judging pass through various stages of mechanization (passing from associated imagery to visual/auditory factors to kinaesthesis, or motor adjustment, as the dominant content); the consciousness of relation turns out to be an *interpretative consciousness* (i.e., there was no elemental relational consciousness, or no imageless process, of any kind); and no particular mental elements are essential to synaesthetes in judging and choosing other than that of kinaesthesis or its synaesthetic substitute (such as visualized kinaesthesis).

Dallenbach (1926) examines a novel form of synaesthesis, that of "pressury" cold (e.g., in a routine experiment on students' "temperature spots," in their forearms, it was discovered that one student observed that some of the cold spots were felt in her *teeth* and *cheeks*). Based upon his further laboratory testing of the student with pressury cold synaesthesis, Dallenbach summarizes his findings as follows: the person's cold spots were of two kinds (*ordinary* spots giving usual experiences, and *toothy* spots giving secondary experiences localized in and around the teeth and cheeks): the toothy cold spots occur on all parts of the body experimented upon (the right and left forearms, upper arms, and legs), though with varying frequency; the secondary experiences aroused by stimulation of the toothy spots were always localized upon the side of the body stimulated. A second mapping—made twenty-four hours after the first—verified 69 percent of the ordinary colds, and 81 percent of the toothy colds. The secondary experiences were described as light, transient, and pressury in quality; and in view of the fact that the participant has a *synaesthetic inheritance* (i.e., her mother possessed a complicated form of synaesthesia and was a student in the same laboratory over twenty-six years ago! The mother was studied and described in detail by Whipple [1900]), there is evidence of the hereditary nature/theory of synaesthesis.

As part of their study on "unseen drama and imagery," Kerr and Pear (1931) report that no less than 24 percent of their participants experienced some form of synaesthesia, including color and texture synaesthesia. They concluded, among other things, that synaesthesia—provoked by the "dramatic" situations contained in their testing procedure—was more unusual, interesting, and emotional than had been presented before in laboratories, and was much more frequent in their procedure than that produced by the previous methods; and they asserted that synaesthesia seems to play an important part in the perception, memory, and thinking of its possessors. Kerr and Pear (p. 49) provide the following references on synaesthesia: Anschutz (1929), Argelander (1927; contains a bibliography of 446 titles), Vernon (1930), and Weller (1931).

Riggs and Karwoski (1934) examine synaesthesia, in general, and synaesthesia in a seven-year-old girl, in particular; they also provide a summary (including twenty-four references) of the literature of synaesthesia in children, a classification system of synaesthesia, and a theory of synaesthesia. According to Riggs and Karwoski, one of the most interesting phases of the child's synaesthesia was the tendency to see the features of people in different colors; apparently, for the child, mere shape was not sufficient in determining the color of the person—but, rather, it was the expressiveness of form in the personality integration of the target person that determined the color that the child experienced (i.e., she "builds personality colors"). Riggs and Karwoski deduce four types of synaesthetic content, or classification, based upon their observations as well as on their study of the literature: accidental association, affectivity, imagery, and thought. The form of synaesthesia called *accidental association* is rarely described as synaesthesia, and may properly be called *pseudo-synaesthesia*; in reality, such cases are a form of simple learning. In the factor called *affectivity*, the pleasantness or unpleasantness of the stimulus is often an influence in making connections or associations. There is a wide range of individual differences in the amount and strength of *imagery* present in synaesthesia, and the nature of the synaesthesia apparently varies in accordance with the character of the individual's imagery. In the fourth type of synaesthetic content—the *thought* or *conceptual*—resides what has been called the meaning of the stimuli in the synaesthetic experience, and there may not be any real image/photism at all for the person. Riggs and Karwoski present a theory of synaesthesia that is based on two fundamental characteristics of synaesthesia that set it apart as a distinct phenomenon: It has its origin in childhood; and its development occurs according to a pattern (i.e., every case of synaesthesia—whether simple or complex, whether emotional or ideational—consists essentially of a parallel arrangement of "two gradient series." Thus, they may be revealed as a series of pitches, intensities, wavelengths, forms, persons, cities, languages, bird-calls, or anything else in keeping with the synaesthete's interests and capacities). The first characteristic—childhood origin—illustrates that there is primitive, undifferentiated sensory experience before the senses have begun to operate independently (hence, it is natural to suggest that spontaneous synaesthetic experience should occur until the differentiation is complete). The second characteristic—the configurational/pattern aspect of synaesthesia—explains the later development of the phenomenon (it is assumed, according to Riggs and Karwoski, that the strength of the configuration is a function of two things: the strength of content—as determined by clearness of imagery; and the strength of the assimilating process—as determined by the individual's intelligence).

## Tactile/Gustatory/Olfactory/Auditory/Kinesthetics/ Motor Imagery

The *extravisual*, or lower, sensory modalities have been studied by a number of early investigators, and include the tactual/tactile, gustatory, olfactory, and kinaesthetic/motor modalities, as well as the more major system of audition in this grouping. For a basic discussion of the lower senses—the "skin senses" and "smell and taste"—see Woodworth (1938, pp. 450–500); and for another account of the lower senses—the cutaneous and chemical senses—see Woodworth and Schlosberg (1965, pp. 267–322). In this section, a very brief account/summary is given for several of these selected early studies.

Monroe (1898) examined the "taste-dream" experiences of twenty female participants who provided 254 dreams as the data for analysis; seventeen taste and eight smell dreams were reported (also, there was a strong visual element in 123 of the dreams, a marked auditory element in seventeen, and a pronounced motor element in thirty-six of the dreams).

Bolger and Titchener (1907) and Harris (1908) both describe the "associative power of smells/odors"; the former investigators report negative results in their efforts to have participants pair, and associate, odors with picture stimuli (the odors were no more effective in subsequent association tests than were nonsense syllables—auditory

stimuli—and were less effective as associative stimuli than simple geometrical figures; for similar negative results concerning this issue, see
Heywood and Vortriede, 1905); the latter researcher (Harris) also
presented participants with a series of odors under conditions that
required the formation of certain definite new associations (involving
different two-digit numbers for each odor), and noted the changes
that took place in both the old and new associations. In this case,
Harris (1908) reports that the affective qualities of the odors seem
to play a subordinate role in the fixing of the numbers-odors associations. Harris further suggests that odors, as a rule, carry a strong "affective coloration" that is weakened and in some cases nearly disappears
with frequent experience; he concludes that the "feeling coloration"
of the odors, and their tendency to recall early associations, run a
somewhat parallel course, thus suggesting that the *feeling* itself may
be an important link in the recall task.

Early studies reporting on the tactual-cutaneous and temperature
sensory systems vis-à-vis imagery are provided by Braddock (1921),
Burnett and Dallenbach (1927), Cook (1915), and Zigler and
Northup (1926). Cook (1915) reviews the psychological literature on
the topic "tactual and kinaesthetic space" for the year 1914; she cites
the following studies: Gemelli (1914a,b,c,d). These findings include
the result that the increased underestimation of cutaneous distance on
the arm, when the latter is out of its normal position, is due to an
increase in visual imagery. For a detailed view of some of Gemelli's
work, see Fernberger (1915). Fitt (1914) agrees with Gemelli's finding that the over- or underestimation of cutaneous distances varies
directly with the size of the two-point threshold; also, the estimation
of cutaneous distances is made more accurate by the presence of clear
and vivid visual imagery. Toltschinsky (1914a,b) gives a detailed report of the "aesthesiometric field" around a given point in the palm
of the left hand. Findings include the following: the field is more or
less circular in form, the fields of nearby points are not juxtaposed but
overlap, and the conception of *local signs* needs revision. Bourdon
(1914) contributes the only study of the year in the field of "kinaesthetic space perception"; he concludes that cutaneous sensations are
*not* the means by which one perceives the movement of the whole
body in a straight line.

Braddock (1921) reports on an experimental study of cutaneous
(pressure, warmth, cold) imagery. Based upon the results from a
double series of cutaneous experiments where participants compared
their sensory-experiences with their imaginal-experiences, she con-

cluded that in cases where the person's imaginal type tends to be one-sided, the imagery ordinarily employed comes up so readily and dominantly that any possible traces of cutaneous imagery are obliterated. In cases where the imaginal type is generalized, cutaneous imagery of pressure, warmth, and cold rarely occurs in subordination to free imagery of vision or kinaesthesis.

Zigler and Northup (1926) studied the degree of accuracy with which participants can make judgments as to the form, or shape, of geometrical figures (e.g., square, equilateral triangle, right-angled triangle, diamond, and hexagon) applied "passively" to the skin (the volar surface of the left forearm at a point midway between the wrist and elbow) with vision excluded. They concluded that tactual *form* is not as definitely apprehended as is tactual *pressure* when vision is excluded and the participant is kept passive during stimulation; also, the stimuli of common geometrical figures must have a main dimension of 12 to 15 mm to yield tactual impressions of determinate shape when stimulation is made on the middle of the forearm (dimensions smaller than this are described by participants as "blunt points without contour," "shapeless pressure," or "mere sensory-pressure stimulation").

Burnett and Dallenbach (1927) report on an experiment concerning the "experience of heat" (cf. Cutolo, 1918) and its related imagery. Participants received stimulation via "temperature grills" through which water of various temperatures flowed (four temperatures for each system, cold and warm), and they gave introspective reports of their cutaneous experiences. Among their results, Burnett and Dallenbach list the following:

- Stimuli (which, when applied singly, are adequate only to cold and warm, and inadequate to ache, pain, and paradoxical cold) may arouse (when combined) the experience of heat.
- *Physiologically*, heat is a fusion of excitations that are normal to cold and warm. *Psychologically*, heat is a simple quality that lies in the pressure-prick-pain continuum (it is near "prick" and closer to "pressure" than to "pain").
- The concomitant arousal of pain and heat seems to condition the experience of "burn." Individual differences must be taken into account in studies on the temperature-pain threshold.
- The experience of cold usually precedes the experience of heat, doubtless because of the longer latent period of warm.
- Heat is variously localized (sometimes seeming "surfacy" and *on* the skin, and sometimes seeming "voluminous" and *in* the arm).

- Afterimages of cold, warm, heat, burn, and wetness were experienced by participants (one person's termperature experiences were synaesthetic in type).

Early studies on the imagery involved in kinaesthetic and bodily/ motor activities and habits are reported (in chronological order here) by Downey (1909), McMein and Washburn (1909), Colvin (1910), Fletcher (1914), Boring and Luce (1917), Sullivan (1921), Shimberg (1924), and Mainwaring (1933). Downey (1909) initially presents a brief history of "muscle-reading" (also, at first, called *mind-reading*)—an area of investigation involving the existence of, and recognition of, involuntary movements (both in the experimenter and/ or the participant) that may serve as clues on the appropriate way to respond in a given situation (e.g., Oskar Pfungst's classical "clever Hans effect/phenomenon"; see Roeckelein, 1998, pp. 95–96). Based upon her experiments in which participants/operators had to find objects hidden by other participants/guides, and where bodily contact/touch (e.g., on the arm or hand) took place as cues between the two participants, Downey (pp. 294–95) notes the following results: those guides in whom the motor impulse is strong indicate the direction of attention by "motor initiative" (this initiative, however, is retarded although often made more precise by concentration on the direction of movement); those guides in whom the motor impulse is less insistent, often find their attention weakened by the test conditions (if, however, attention is thrown on the pathway, i.e., direction of movement, the motor impulse is increased); and a verbal control condition (mentally given) produces a freer and less accurate initiative than does a mentally given visual control condition (the actual innervation of the vocal musculature may possibly have general motor accompaniments). Downey's experience with the participants in her muscle-reading tests led her to expect that the "fit" participants for the test are those who—in daily life—exhibit few inhibitions either in judgment or action, and who are hopeful and confident in their attitude toward things (the "opposing type," on the other hand, are those individuals who are more hesitant in act and judgment, and are more critical and reserved). Downey emphasizes that the bodily movements she studies are usually involuntary variations in muscular tension, not overt movements (cf. the more *overt* involuntary movement aspects involved in automatic writing; e.g., James, 1890, vol. 1, pp. 393–96; Jastrow, 1892; Myers, 1887; Muhl, 1924, 1930). She states (pp. 299–300) that "[i]t is difficult to comprehend without first-hand experience the wonderful accuracy of the operator's response to the slightest variation in the guide's muscular tension . . . such delicacy in reaction gives the operator a unique acquaintance with the guide's mental processes, his uncertainty, his timidity, and the course of his deliberations." Finally, Downey asserts that muscle-reading affords a new method for investigating certain features of bodily orientation and, also, that results from muscle-reading tests recast various notions about certain peculiarities in imagery type. For other early motor/movement studies vis-à-vis imagery, see McMein and Washburn (1909) who attempted to determine whether two relatively complex motor habits (longer card-sorting tasks) interfere with each other in a less or a greater degree than two relatively simple habits (shorter card-sorting tasks). Among their findings is that a participant whose card-sorting learning is guided by a mental picture of a diagram is much less disturbed when the diagram is turned 90 degrees than is a participant whose learning is done largely in motor terms. In another study (introspective report) on motor movement, motor imagery, or "motor ideation," Colvin (1910) emphasizes the point that the mental image is not always due to centrally aroused processes alone, but that, in part, one's imaginal experiences have mixed with them peripheral factors such that it is impossible to separate such experiences out. This is particularly true of motor imagery where it may be doubted that a motor image is ever experienced in the sense of a purely cortical process, and what is commonly called a *motor image* may, in reality, be a *motor sensation*. Colvin (1910) prefers to use the term *motor/mimetic ideation* instead of *motor imagery* where the former is defined as "those kinaesthetic experiences (whether central or peripheral in their origin) which we employ at times in our thinking and which constitute the mind-stuff of certain of our ideational processes" (p. 260).

Fletcher (1914) describes an "experimental" study (more of a theoretical review and analysis) of a motor anomaly—that of stuttering—which involves individuals who are not distinguished physically from other people, who are of normal intelligence, and who demonstrate logical reasoning in their thought processes. Following his definition and differentiation of the term, Fletcher examines stuttering in its physiological and psychological manifestations. The former account includes material on breathing, vocalization, articulation, and accessory movements; the latter account includes material on psychophysical methodologies, emotions, attitudes, imagery, attention, psychoanalysis, association, and hereditary factors. In his section on imagery, as regards stuttering, Fletcher points out that the well-known phenomenon in psychology—that the kinaesthetic images of certain movements of the body affect the power of voluntary control of those movements—is confirmed by the familiar facts of stuttering that seem to take place more readily in those organs whose functioning is too complex to gain direct representation in consciousness (e.g., the act of breathing can be imagined only partially, and more or less abstractly, because the working of the diaphragm cannot be imagined and can be controlled only through the lower arch of the abdominal wall. The diaphragm is especially concerned in the breathing abnormalities found in stuttering). According to Fletcher, the coordination of vocalization with breathing introduces the function of another complication of muscles that does not allow direct imaginal representation. Moreover, the action of the articulatory organs does allow representation in consciousness, and although stuttering speech seems to the eye and to the ear as being primarily a disturbance of articulation, the real "asynergy" is not merely in the articulatory system, but between this system and others, especially that of vocalization (whispering—which involves only the musculature of articulation and breathing—is usually found to be possible for stutterers). Fletcher also points out that the organs of speech are neither completely under voluntary control, nor are they exclusively nonvoluntary; the abstract act of speech may be called voluntary, but the coordinated action of the muscles that execute the details of speech is nonvoluntary. Among his conclusions concerning the behavior of stuttering, Fletcher makes the following points:

- The motor manifestations of stuttering consist of asynergies in the functioning of the three musculatures of speech—breathing, vocalization, and articulation.
- Stutterers differ widely in type of asynergy and, particularly, in accessory movements (e.g., tics, larynx movements, etc.).
- Besides the motor aspects of stuttering, there are other accompanying conditions such as disturbances in pulse-rate, blood distribution, and psychogalvanic variations (such changes appear before, during, and after the speaking interval).
- A "complex state of mind" involving the feeling states seems to be related to the rise of one's stuttering activity.
- In general, the feelings of fear, anxiety, dread, shame, or embarrassment tend to be the precursors of stuttering (they probably all act as both cause and effect, thus constituting, in effect, a "vicious circle/cycle" for the stutterer).

- In addition to states of feeling, stuttering seems to be affected by the quality of the individual's mental imagery, by attention, and by association (all movements that—like those of speech—are incapable of clear and detailed imaginal representation in consciousness are—in the same way as speech— liable to functional disorders that are analogous to stuttering; when a stutterer's attention can be distracted from his/her speech, the stuttering generally ceases).

In the final analysis, Fletcher (1914, p. 249) maintains that stuttering is "essentially a mental phenomenon in the sense that it is due to and dependent upon certain variations in mental state. Hence, the study of stuttering becomes a specifically psychological problem." Note that Fletcher (1914, pp. 249–55) provides a very substantial bibliography on the phenomenon of stuttering, consisting of 152 references from the multinational literature; especially noteworthy in this regard is the German researcher Hermann Gutzmann who has twenty-four studies on stuttering.

In the area of kinaesthesis and kinaesthetic imagery, selected early studies include those conducted by Mainwaring (1933), Shimberg (1924), and Sullivan (1921). Sullivan (1921) initially compares "kinaesthetic sensation" with "kinaesthetic image" and reports the following: the *qualities* in kinaesthetic *sensation* are dull pressure, light pressure, bright pressure, smooth pressure, strain, and ache, while those in kinaesthetic *image* are all pressury—dull, light, and smooth pressure. The *intensity* of kinaesthetic sensation may be anywhere on the intensive scale from strong to weak, while that of the kinaesthetic image is always comparatively weak. The *duration* of kinaesthetic sensation is relatively long, whereas that of the kinaesthetic image is relatively short. The *vividness* of kinaesthetic sensations ranges from high to low, while that of the kinaesthetic image is always high (unless there is an accompaniment by imagery from other sense modalities). The *patterns* for kinaesthetic sensations are, for the most part, tridimensional, while kinaesthetic images always shows the same pattern—a small spot that sometimes increases temporally to a streak and is most often bidimensional. Kinaesthetic sensations have more "body" than kinaesthetic images (what the sensation lacks in any one intensive attribute it makes up for in some other attribute, while the image may be poor in all the intensive attributes except for vividness). Sullivan (1921) also conducted experiments to compare *projected* (e.g., empathy) and *resident* (e.g., memory) kinaesthetic imagery on the bases of quality, intensity, extent, duration, vividness, locality, pattern, and change (e.g., the duration of projected kinaesthesis is always long, while that of resident kinaesthesis is always short; the pattern of projected kinaesthesis has various types of pattern and may be bi- or tridimensional, while resident kinaesthesis is unvaried in pattern, most often being only bidimensional). Among Sullivan's final conclusions are the following points:

- Kinaesthetic images of memory may be distinguished from kinaesthetic sensations by uniformity, simplicity, and lack of "body."
- Kinaesthetic sensations in a perception of movement are varied, complex, and have "body."
- Kinaesthetic imagery may be classified as resident or projected where the former images are referred ordinarily to oneself, and the latter images are referred ordinarily to someone else or something else.
- The distinction between resident and projected kinaesthesis does not reflect merely the functional difference of "self" and "other"—it is correlated with a specific difference of *attitude* on the part of the individual.

For an analysis of attitude vis-a-via the particular kinaesthetic complex of pressure and pain called *hunger* or *appetite*, see Boring and Luce (1917) who conclude that appetite may be adequately described only as a food-seeking attitude or meaning (i.e., a "reaching-out-after-food"); and a psychological account of appetite attempts to describe the sensory processes correlated with this attitude. In the main, the processes consist in the general kinaesthesis of the orientation of the individual toward food—in the muscular activity and the body's automatic movement kinaesthetically sensed. For a basic historical discussion of "conscious attitudes" and kinaesthesis, see Woodworth (1938, pp. 789–90).

Shimberg (1924) describes the role of kinaesthesis in meaning. Following a solid historical introduction to the issue (cf. Moore, 1915, 1917, 1919; Ogden, 1917; Rogers, 1923), she outlines her experimental procedure, which involved the learning of Esperanto words and progressively more complex nonsense syllables, and the recording of participants' reaction times and introspective reports, especially focusing on kinaesthetic processes (e.g., internal speech). Among her initial conclusions, Shimberg makes the following points: the results of her study, as compared with Ogden's (1917) results, are highly dissimilar (Shimberg reports a high frequency of imagery in her participants, while Ogden reports virtually no imagery—that is, imageless contents—in his participants). Shimberg's findings are similar to those of Rogers (1923) who reports that the results of her experiments on perception agree in general with the results of others who maintain that the background—sensational or imaginal—is of fundamental importance to the meaning of perception. The kinaesthetic and organic sensations and the imaginal processes under Rogers's conditions consistently formed a setting for the central visual complex and supplied more of the derived significance than the directly initiated processes themselves. As to the nature of the images that play so great a part in the search for meaning, Shimberg found that kinaesthetic images are most prominent (they represented 57 percent of all images reported by participants), and while many forms of kinaesthesis were represented, internal speech occurred most frequently (it occurred with 71 percent of all stimulus words). However, Shimberg did not find that kinaesthesis was necessary to meaning. On the contrary, meaning was carried sometimes by way of both visual and auditory imagery (cf. similar results found by Ruckmick, 1913, for the perception of rhythm); but wherever reaction times were long and the search for meaning was difficult, kinaesthesis was an almost invariable concomitant. Shimberg finally concludes that images play an extremely important part in the search for meaning; there are individual differences as to the amount and kind of kinaesthesis present in participants' reports, but in some form, especially as internal speech, it is a significant constituent; and meaning may be carried without any kinaesthesis (although kinaesthesis does accompany long reactions and labored searches for complex meanings).

In the context of the recall of musical experience, Mainwaring (1933) examines the nature and quality of various kinaesthetic factors (e.g., kinaesthetic "habit sequence" in the reproduction of music; kinaesthetic "association" in the recall of musical experience). Mainwaring's analyses of his participants' introspective reports (from both children and adults)—concerning their musical recall—suggested to him that there is no reasonable doubt that some form of associated kinaesthetic recurrence, either vocal or manual (or even pedal), is an essential factor in the adequate recall of auditory musical experience. Any purely perceptual recall (e.g., an unaided auditory image) was vague, fleeting, and fragmentary, and limited to the shortest of melodic passages or to the mere perseveration of the last few notes. Mainwaring's experiments suggest, also, that the participants' general tendency is to translate the fleeting auditory recall immediately into those appropriate kinaesthetic impulses that prior experience connected inseparably with the associated sounds. Thus, not only does the sound tend to stimulate the appropriate motor association, but also the process of thinking—in terms of sound—is fundamentally a process of thinking in recurred kinaesthetic experience (i.e., "thinking in music" tends generally to include the recurrence of associated kinaesthetic experience, and often seems to consist almost entirely in the recurrence of such motor associations).

In a final set of selected early studies in this section, Guernsey (1922) and F. L. Dimmick (1923) describe the auditory modality and several factors in its relationship to imagery. Guernsey initially reviews the different apparatuses that have been used historically for determining sound intensity (e.g., pendulums, falling balls, discs, resonators, tuning forks, electromagnets, direct optical methods for observing the motions of a vibrating diaphragm, and telephone transmitters with subsidiary devices; Guernsey's procedure included a combination of the last two apparatuses to study tone, pitch, and intensity limens/ thresholds and sensibilities in her participants). Among her conclusions, Guernsey gives the following: tones of different pitch correlate with different sensitivity in the human ear as indicated by the difference in energy required to elicit response to their liminal stimuli; tones of the upper-middle range are more easily perceived than tones either above or below it; Weber's law—as applied to audition—seems to hold true with a fraction of about one-third throughout the middle range of intensities (the fraction is larger for low tones and for very high tones); and kinaesthetic and auditory imagery are evidently predominant over visual imagery for all participants in the study and, thus, there appears to be some correlation between auditory imagery and the limen of tonal acuity. Note that Guernsey provides over two dozen references on auditory phenomena in her bibliography section, pp. 568–69. F. L. Dimmick studied another auditory phenomenon—that of *auditory tied-images* (i.e., the effect that, in listening to a speaker whose enunciation is not distinct, one fills in the confused or inaudible parts of the speaker's discourse; Titchener [1914, 1915] gives the name *tied-imagery* to the similar phenomenon in the visual modality; and Zigler [1920] conducted an experimental investigation of the *visual tied-image*). Dimmick's procedure involved the presentation of simple auditory forms (e.g., the opening phrases of familiar tunes) to his participants who then gave their introspective reports of the material. Based upon his findings, Dimmick draws the following conclusions: incomplete auditory perceptions are to a great extent filled in by auditory imagery that may be called tied-imagery; such auditory tied-images are probably common to most people; the auditory tied-images are closely akin to the corresponding sensations and differ from them mainly on the perceptive level; and they are akin, also, to the corresponding phenomena in vision where such phenomena are the basis for the wide use in illustrations and advertisements containing incomplete figures.

## Visual Imagery

Due to the fact that this category or mode of sensory imagery is so pervasive (e.g., it cuts across the previous nine categories, especially memory imagery, and afterimages) and popular in the early psychological literature on mental imagery, it is possible only to select out a few exemplary studies from among the many available investigations in this area. Typical of the early visual imagery studies in chronological order are those by Secor (1900), Alexander (1904), Day (1912), Clark (1916), Pear (1925a,b), Bowers (1931b, 1932b), Bousfield and Barry (1933), and Goldthwait (1933). Secor (1900) studied the questions "Is it possible to read without mentally hearing the words, and without feeling them in the throat, mouth, or on the lips?" and "Can one grasp the meaning of printed or written matter through the eye alone, without the aid of articulatory or auditory images?" In other words, Secor attempted to determine whether it is possible to pass from the visual word directly to the sense, without the mediation of articulation (i.e., active, vocal movements) or audition (i.e., passive hearing). Secor notes that the word—as "sign" of an idea—may exist in the mind in four ways: as auditory image, as visual image, and as motor image, either hand-motor or articulatory type (the four centers in the brain corresponding to these four ways of the "word-as-idea-sign" are well localized). Secor suggests, in an a priori "evolution-based" judgment, that two of these centers—the auditory and articulatory—must be more firmly organized and better correlated than the other two inasmuch as they have been in use ever since humans began to utilize vocal signs for communication (i.e., the word has been a sound and/or articulatory movement for a much longer time than it has been either a visual or hand-motor image). Moreover, what is true of the human race/species is also true of the individual case: the child learns to speak (articulation) and hear (audition) words as "words" before it learns to write (hand-motor) or to recognize (vision) the visual word. Following a series of experiments in which Secor determined the memory- and imagery-type(s) of his participants, he tested them on tasks in which they "read by vision alone" (this strategy in methodology placed Secor's participants under conditions that would tend to decrease, or fade out, the auditory and articulatory elements of reading and, thus, attempt to train them to read by the aid of the eye alone). One specific method in this strategic approach was to have participants read paragraphs in a look as rapidly as possible, with the expectation that "the eye would outrun the ear," thus leaving it behind and allowing the auditory element to drop out. Another method was to have participants say the alphabet aloud, or to whistle a tune, while reading a passage (in a variation of this procedure, the experimenter played on a xylophone at the same time the participant was responding). In these cases, also, the intention was to shut off both articulation and audition in the participants. Based upon the data of his participants' introspective reports, as well as on laryngographic recordings, Secor draws the following conclusions: the auditory element is a much more persistent factor in reading than is articulation; both articulation and audition are to be regarded as aids in reading, rather than as absolutely necessary elements; the prominence of the auditory and articulatory elements in reading depends on the memory- and imagery-type of the individual, and upon the amount and kind of reading done by him/her; and it is possible to read without articulation and audition (i.e., via visualization alone). Thus, Secor gives affirmative answers to his initial questions regarding visual reading and mental imagery.

In his nonexperimental observations on visual imagery, Alexander (1904) begins with a general analysis of types and grades of visual imagery (cf. Pear's 1925b ruminations on the privileges and limitations of visual imagery). In reference to the factor of vividness, three intensities/grades may be distinguished: the fleeting (vague, fragile, ephemeral) images of common thinking; the images (miniature copies) that are fixed in attention and become distinct in outline and filled in with substance; and the images that are rich in detail and appear to be of the same approximate size as the actual things, objects, or persons. In another categorization, Alexander types images as *voluntary/memory* images (capable of easily being "called to mind" or retained by an act of will) and *spontaneous/irrelevant* images (they determine their own occurrence, coming and going "of their own accord"). In his discussion of projection and size of visual images, Alexander notes that a satisfactory criterion of the externalization of images is difficult to obtain (it is common experience, however, that visual images appear to most people in a field of vision and, therefore, in that sense, are external—they never seem to be "in the head" per se). One of the problems concerning the externalization of images is that it is quite possible to compare two types of imagery having different referents: a memory image, say, with an afterimage, although the two types are not present in the same referred, or projection, "space." As regards the factor of image size, Alexander "demurs" to James's (1890, vol. 2, p. 51) assertion that "as a universal proposition that *after-images* seem larger if we project them on a distant screen, and smaller if we project them on a near one, whilst no such change takes place in *mental* pictures" (italics added). This "size-distance invariance hypothesis," or Emmert's law as it is called, has received much attention in the psychological literature; see Roeckelein (1998, pp. 160–62) for a discussion of this principle. However, Alexander observes (p. 325) that the size-distance principle is "not an invariable rule" as "some mental images follow precisely the law of after-images, indicating similar retinal excitation . . . the occurrence of an image on the page of a book is plainly conditioned by the angle at which the book is held and is liable to distortion to suit this angle." Alexander concludes for the size of visual images that there is no universal distinction between mental/projected images and afterimages (the latter are mainly sensory manifestations, but all projected images probably, also, involve retinal excitation; cf. Ferree and Rand, 1931). Among his observations, and his own personal introspective insights, Alexander also discusses the issues of the *imagery of dreams* (in dreams and their attendant memory images "there is a curious interlocking of the dream world and the real world," p. 332); the *influencing of imagery* (the most steadfast distinction among images is "that between voluntary and spontaneous imagery, but even this distinction breaks down occasionally," p. 332); and *imagery and ratiocination* ("It is certain enough that we do reason to some extent in pictures . . . the mass of imagery, then, which so presses in upon our normal intellectual life may be no more than a ghostly reminder of what was once the sum and substance of thought," p. 336. Thus, according to such an analysis, a phenomenon such as dream consciousness may simply be a reversion to the earliest forms of mental life when humans had not yet become literate and "socially disciplined").

In an early experimental study of the relationship between visual imagery and attention, Clark (1916) notes that her approach and methodology is based upon the research conducted by Ogden (1913) and Perky (1910) (cf. Koffka, 1912; Martin, 1912). However, there were three salient differences between Clark's experiments and those of Ogden and Perky. Both Ogden and Perky discovered a number of intermediate or "equivocal" images that did not seem to belong either among their "images of imagination" or their "images of memory" (Clark includes in her classification *all* nonverbal/primary images reported by her participants). Ogden obtained negative results regarding the factor of "ocular movement," and Perky found a correspondence between the *kind* of image and the occurrence of ocular movements (Clark observed movements of the eyes by three different methods, one of which was similar to Perky's method); and Clark proposed to discover the factor(s) most closely connected with ocular movements, not simply the kind of image that was usually involved. Clark's first experiment was an analysis of visual imagery in her six trained participants (introspective reports of the visual images aroused by a series of stimulus words). She identified three main groups of images: F-images (associated with familiar, specific objects), U-images (unfamiliar, but specific images), and G-images (general reference images, but lacking in familiarity). Moreover, images were classified as "usual" (having the same *position* in relation to the participant as the perceptual objects commonly occupied); "unusual" (*position* was not characteristic of the perceptual object, or if the imagined object seemed detached from any setting); "unstable" (images that fluctuated, faded quickly, or were soon replaced by other images); "details of images" (many versus few details); "color of images" (present versus absent); "associative processes" (any relevant processes present); "recency" (having occurred within a year); and "somatic reference" (any relationship between part of the body and the images; cf. Perky's [1910, p. 436] term *personal reference* here). Clark (p. 469) provides statistical data (percentages) from her participants for frequencies of each of these image classes. In a second series of four experiments, Clark studied visual imagery vis-à-vis ocular movement and attention For discussion of a "test of control of visual imagery," see Washburn (1914), and Washburn, Hatt, and Holt (1923b). Based upon all her experiences with her six trained introspectionists, Clark draws the following conclusions: If visual images are divided into three groups on the basis of the presence or absence of specific *reference* and *familiarity* of the object, certain other functional characteristics are found to be closely associated with a particular group, or with groups, of images (pure types, however, are relatively rare, and intermediate forms are relatively numerous). There is a correspondence between kind of image and amount of ocular movement that is referable to certain general conditions of attention. Changes in the clearness of the image correspond, largely, to movements of the eyes. Ocular movement is more likely to occur in secondary attention than in primary or derived primary attention; and characteristic ocular movements—and possibly general motor attitudes—seem to be transferred from visual perception to visual imagery.

Bowers (1931b, 1932b) reports on several of his visual imagery experiments. In one case (Bowers, 1931b), he attempted to determine how persons' positions on rating scales of visual imagery are affected by their tendency to exaggerate the clearness or vagueness of their visual images (via the use of photographs—in a graded series of clarity from very clear to blurred to blank—as experimental materials). In this situation, Bowers found the following results: there is a consistent tendency to exaggerate or minimize an estimate of the clarity of visual imagery when using a rating scale; there is some evidence that scores derived from the ratings of images aroused by *words* are more influenced by individual tendencies to over- or underrate the clarity of imagery than those obtained from the use of *photographic* material. In another case (Bowers, 1932b; cf. Bowers, 1929), he attempted to determine if the mean ratings assigned by participants to images evoked by the various items in a picture would show a (similar) relatively constant order of precedence (for Bowers's own test of visual imagery, see Bowers, 1931b). Based upon the imagery-ratings data from over 100 high school student participants, Bowers (1932b) makes the following conclusions: the constituent elements of a picture indicate that relative constancy of imaginal content exists for other visual, auditory, and kinaesthetic stimuli; a significant correlation was found between mean ratings of images aroused by items in a picture and frequency of mention of these items in reports of the picture; an association exists between clarity of image and mean rank of item; and the relationship between imagery and order is *not* of a causal nature.

In four experiments designed to examine the relation of eye-movements to visual imagery, Goldthwait (1933) employed the "mirror-recorder" and the "cine-recorder" in his methodology to obtain objective measures of his participants' eye-movements (cf. Dodge, 1921) during visual-image-production tasks. Goldthwait's study was inspired by the well-known fact that visual perception of an object is usually accompanied by movements of the eyes that suggested to him the possibility that the centrally excited visual image of such an object might, similarly, possess an efferent component of ocular movement (cf., in chronological order: Stratton, 1902; Judd, McAllister, and Steele, 1905; Perky, 1910; Martin, 1912; Ogden, 1913; and Clark, 1916, for background studies indicating—among other things—various degrees of agreement, and disagreement, with the suggested relation between eye-movements and visual imagery). Based upon the results of his experiments, Goldthwait draws the following conclusions: there is no characteristic relation between *type* of visual image and *amount* of accompanying eye-movement; *unclear* visual images are usually accompanied by a greater amount of eye-movement than are *clear* images; the amount of eye-movement tends to *increase* when conditions demand greater *attention* to stimulus materials; and imagery characteristics such as clearness, stability, detailedness, completeness, and duration *cannot* be assigned with much assurance in greater degree to one type of image than to another.

Finally, for this section on early visual imagery studies, the interesting investigations by Bousfield and Barry (1933) on the "visual imagery of a lightning calculator" serve to show another aspect or dimension in the wide range of interests characterizing the early psychologists' concerns with visual imagery. A certain Polish "calculating genius," named Salo Finkelstein, was studied intensively by researchers in the early 1930s both in Europe and the United States (e.g., Sandor, 1932; cf. Mitchell, 1907; also, see the popular 1988 U.S. movie *Rain Man* depicting an idiot savant). Bousfield and Barry report on their examinations, and informal experiments, of Finkelstein's abilities, in particular on his skill in mentally making "lightning-fast" calculations (cf. Mitchell, 1907, who was concerned with the memory types of mathematical geniuses insofar as they were auditory or visual), and note that Finkelstein may be classified as an eidetiker inasmuch as data collected on him are related to the phenomenon of eidetic imagery. Bousfield and Barry suggest that Finkelstein's amazing performance is essentially twofold: he showed an unusual capacity for *memorization* with respect both to learning and retention (e.g., he was able to memorize a visually perceived square of digits, composed of five rows of five digits each, so that the whole series could be repeated in any sequence desired), and he showed an extraordinary *speed* in the mental manipulation of figures (e.g., he was able to give the sum of fifteen digits at a glance, and his speed of addition of three- and four-place numbers exceeded that of an adding machine). Bousfield and Barry were not primarily interested in Finkelstein's speed of calculation but, rather, in the issue of the *type* of imagery that is the basis for Finkelstein's unique talent. For an account of one type of imagery—vis-à-vis numbers—

called *number form* (in which a person may perceive numbers—often involving days of the week, month, or other time- and magnitude-concepts—as organized in space)—see Domino's (1999, p. 598, Figure 1) description of a synesthete's number form. In general, the most striking feature to Bousfield and Barry of Finkelstein's actual process of calculation and memorization was the "normality" of the operations: except for the products, sums, roots, and powers he already definitely knew, every calculation required Finkelstein's deliberate and fully conscious handling of the figures (he used short-cut methods whenever possible but his procedure was always orderly and systematic). The superiority of Finkelstein's processes lies in the fact that he was capable of dealing with large groups of figures (e.g., in the task of addition, the average person is limited to a succession of two- and sometimes three-digit manipulations; Finkelstein, on the other hand, instantaneously perceived the sum of four, five, and six digits, with the result that the sum of a column of figures was given *before* most people could even read the figures; a "superior" adult has a memory span of about eight digits dictated in succession [cf. Miller, 1956]; however, Finkelstein—with the same rate of dictation—was usually able to repeat twenty digits!).

In the course of their experiments on Finkelstein, Bousfield and Barry (1933) found that the process of his memorization of numbers was aided by associations, in particular, including the following varieties: dates of historical events; mathematical associations such as powers, roots, logarithms, and prime numbers; permutations of significant numbers; ascending and descending series; telephone numbers; and numerical characteristics of literary works—such as number of paragraphs contained therein. Moreover, Finkelstein frequently spoke of some numbers as being "nice," or having "niceness," and this was a function of the number of associations aroused in him. In addition, "nice" numbers had an apparent emotional aspect or appeal for Finkelstein; that is, they were appreciated for their "individuality" and automatically aroused aesthetic feelings in him. Such "nice" numbers were not endowed with sex, but they possessed, for him, uniqueness and personal value. When numbers were written in a yellow color—a color the Finkelstein found unpleasant—he could not avoid a reaction of distinct displeasure. It was also observed that when Finkelstein engaged in the more extensive processes of memorization and calculation, he demonstrated a great amount of motor activity such as pacing back and forth, and making gesticulations and facial contortions—there was a definite kinaesthetic component attached to

Finkelstein's performance where there was a feeling of inhibition when such movements were suppressed.

With respect to the question of the employment of visual imagery, it was evident to Bousfield and Barry (1933) that the imaginal process was virtually integrated into the processes that Finkelstein used in memorization and calculation; the imagery was said to serve a "reference function," and images were held in readiness for subsequent reference. Certain of the more prominent features of Finkelstein's imagery for numbers are as follows: the numbers appear to him as if written with chalk on a freshly washed blackboard; the numbers are in Finkelstein's own handwriting regardless of the form of presentation; ordinarily, the number appear to be from 5 to 7 cm in height; the images normally appear to be at a distance of 35 to 40 cm from his eyes; the span of imagery includes about six figures with a definite preference for their horizontal arrangement (e.g., if a list of 200 numbers has been memorized, at any one moment any group of about six figures may be made to stand out clearly); and when the figures are visualized on a background at a distance of about one to one-and-one-half meters, they are about 30 percent smaller and less distinct (i.e., Emmert's law of the proportionate variation of the afterimage size with the distance of the projection background from the eye seems to be *reversed* in this case). Thus, the general issue of visual imagery here necessarily includes a consideration of the afterimage.

Bousfield and Barry (1933) explore the question as to whether Finkelstein's visual imagery is properly designated as eidetic, due to the high degree of definiteness and stability of the imagery of numbers regularly reported by him (cf. Jaensch [1927, 1930] who asserts that the eidetic phenomenon is intermediate between the afterimage and the memory-image; and Allport [1924, 1928] who contends that the eidetic image is a member of the general class of memory-image, and differs from the ordinary memory-image only in degree). The following eight characteristics, criteria, or dimensions concerning eidetic imagery were applied directly to the data collected from Finkelstein: localization, richness in detail (clearness), persistence, selective tendencies, flexibility, invariability, displacement in space, and conditions of its arousal and disappearance. Bousfield and Barry assert that the application of the eight criteria for eidetic imagery definitely indicates that Finkelstein's images of numbers may be classified with certainty as eidetic and that their analysis lends support to Allport's (1924, 1928) conception of the eidetic image as being a special variety of the memory-image. Moreover, their analysis of Finkelstein would place him as a "pure" B-type of eidetiker, according to Jaensch's (1927, 1930) classification system.

In summary, Bousfield and Barry (1933) conclude that their examination of Finkelstein's images of numbers indicates the following: imagery serves a reference function in his mental manipulation of figures; the images experienced by Finkelstein are eidetic; and the eidetic images are phenomenally, and probably actually, related genetically to the memory-image, but essentially unrelated to the afterimage.

## REFERENCES

Abramowski, E. (1910). La resistance de l'oublie et les sentime generiques. *Journal de Psychologie Normal et Pathologie, 7*, 301–31.

Aderhold, E. (1959). The effect of verbal suggestion upon the incidence and characteristics of eidetic imagery in children. Unpublished master's thesis, University of Georgia.

Adler, H., Williams, M., & Washburn, M. F. (1914). The correlation between accuracy of the visual memory after-image and control of visual imagery. *American Journal of Psychology, 25*, 293–95.

Ahsen, A. (1977). Eidetics: An overview. *Journal of Mental Imagery, 1*, 5–38.

Ahsen, A. (1987). *Image psychology and the empirical method.* New York: Brandon House.

Alexander, H. B. (1904). Some observations on visual imagery. *Psychological Review, 11*, 319–37.

Allport, G. W. (1924). Eidetic imagery. *British Journal of Psychology, 15*, 99–120.

Allport, G. W. (1928). The eidetic image and the after-image. *American Journal of Psychology, 40*, 418–25.

Allport, G. W. (1930). Change and decay in the visual memory image. *British Journal of Psychology, 21*, 133–48.

Ammann, E. (1930). Visual hallucinations in eye disorders. *Schweizerische Medizinische Wochenschrift, 60*, 1031–35.

Anderson, V. A. (1939). Auditory memory span as tested by speech sounds. *American Journal of Psychology, 52*, 95–99.

Andrews, G. A. (1900). Studies of the dream consciousness. *American Journal of Psychology, 12*, 131–34.

Angell, F. (1913). Projection of the negative after-image in the field of the closed lids. *American Journal of Psychology, 24*, 576–78.

Angell, F., & Root, W. T. (1913). Size and distance of projection of an after-image on the field of the closed lids. *American Journal of Psychology, 24*, 262–66.

Angell, J. R. (1910). Report of the committee of the American Psychological Association on the standardizing of procedure in experimental tests. *Psychological Monographs, 13*, No. 53, 61–107.

Angell, J. R. (1911). Imageless thought. *Psychological Review, 18*, 295–323.

Anschutz, G. (1929). *Das farbe-ton-problem in psychischen gesamtbereich.* Halle, East Germany: Marhold.

Antipoff, H. (1926). Un cas d'image eidetique spontanee. *Archiv de Psychologie, 20*, 73–74.

Argelander, A. (1927). *Dar farbenhoren und der synasthetische faktor der wahrnehmung.* Jena, Germany: Fischer.

Aristotle (1941a). De anima (On the soul). In R. McKeon (Ed.), *The basic works of Aristotle.* New York: Random House.

Aristotle (1941b). De memoria et reminiscentia (On memory and reminiscence). In R. McKeon (Ed.), *The basic works of Aristotle.* New York: Random House.

Armistead, W. S. (1903/1991). *The Negro is a man: A reply to professor Charles Carroll's book "The Negro is a beast; or, In the image of God."* Salem, NH: Ayer.

Armstrong, A. C. (1894). The imagery of American students. *Psychological Review, 1*, 496–505.

Arps, G. F. (1917). A preliminary report on "Work with knowledge versus work without knowledge of results." *Psychological Review, 24*, 449–55.

Aveling, F. (1911). The relation of thought-processes and percept in perception. *British Journal of Psychology, 4*, 211–27.

Aveling, F. (1927). The relevance of visual imagery to the process of thinking. II. *British Journal of Psychology, 18*, 15–22.

Baird, J. W. (1907). The color sensitivity of the peripheral retina. *Psychological Review, 14*, 46–65.

Baird, J. W. (1911/1912/1913/1914/1915/1916/1917). General reviews and summaries: Memory, imagination, learning, and the higher mental/intellectual processes (experimental). *Psychological Bulletin, 8*, 243–53; *9*, 321–36; *10*, 333–47; *11*, 305–24; *12*, 333–54; *13*, 333–54; *14*, 303–22.

Barber, T. X. (1959a). The after-images of "hallucinated" and "imagined" colors. *Journal of Abnormal and Social Psychology, 59*, 136–39.

Barber, T. X. (1959b). The "eidetic image" and "hallucinatory" behavior: A suggestion for further research. *Psychological Bulletin, 56*, 236–39.

Bartlett, F. C. (1916). An experimental study of some problems of perceiving and imaging. *British Journal of Psychology, 8*, 222–67.

Bartlett, F. C. (1921). The functions of images. *British Journal of Psychology, 11*, 320–32.

Bartlett, F. C. (1927). The relevance of visual imagery to the process of thinking. III. *British Journal of Psychology, 18*, 23–29.

Bartlett, F. C., & Smith, E. M. (1920). Is thinking merely the action of language mechanisms? (I.). *British Journal of Psychology, 11*, 55–62.

Bawden, H. H. (1909). Aesthetic imagery. *Psychological Review, 16*, 124–41.

Baxt, N. (1871). Uber die zeit welch notig ist, damit ein gesichtseindruck zum bewusstein kommt und uber die grosse (extension) der bewussteins wahrnehmung bei einem gesichtseindrucke von gegebener dauer. *Pfluger's Archive Gesammelte Physiologie, 4*, 325–36.

Beare, J. I. (1906). *Greek theories of elementary cognition: From Alcmaeon to Aristotle.* Oxford, UK: Oxford University Press.

Bell, A., & Muckenhoupt, L. (1906). A comparison of methods for the determination of ideational type. *American Journal of Psychology, 17*, 121–26.

Bender, H. (1938). Experimental hallucinations. *Forschungen und Fortschritte: Nachrichtenblatt der Deutschen Wissenschaft und Technik, 14*, 327–29.

Bennett, J. (1971). *Locke, Berkeley, and Hume: Central themes.* Oxford, UK: Clarendon Press.

Bentley, M. (1899). The memory image and its qualitative fidelity. *American Journal of Psychology, 11*, 1–48.

Bergemann, W. (1925). Versuche uber die entwicklung des visuellen gedachtnisses bei schulern. *Zeistschrift fur Psychologie, 98*, 206–11.

Beringer, K. (1923). Experimentelle psychosen durch mescalin. *Zeitschrift fur die Gesamte Neurologie und Psychiatrie, 84*, 426–32.

Berkeley, G. (1709/1910). Essay toward a new theory of vision. In A. Luce & T. Jessop (Eds.), *The works of George Berkeley, Bishop of Cloyne.* Toronto: Nelson.

Berkeley, G. (1710/1950). *A treatise concerning the principles of human knowledge.* LaSalle, IL: Open Court.

Berkouwer, G. C. (1962). *Man: The image of God.* Grand Rapids, MI: Eerdmans.

Berliner, A. (1918). The influence of mental work on the visual memory image. *American Journal of Psychology, 29*, 355–70.

Berry, W. (1922). The flight of colors in the after-image of a bright light. *Psychological Bulletin, 19*, 307–37.

Berry, W. (1927). Color sequences in the after-image of white light. *American Journal of Psychology, 38*, 584–96.

Betts, G. H. (1909). *The distribution and functions of mental imagery.* New York: Teachers College, Columbia University.

Betz, W. (1910). Vorstellung und einstellung. I. Uber wiedererkennen. *Archiv fur die Gesamte Psychologie, 17*, 266–96.

Bibring-Lehner, G. (1928). The influencing of eidetic phenomena by labyrinth stimulation. *Zeitschrift fur die Gesamte Neurologie und Psychiatrie, 112*, 496–505.

Bichowsky, F. R. (1925). The mechanism of consciousness: Pre-sensation. *American Journal of Psychology, 36*, 588–96.

Bichowsky, F. R. (1926). The mechanism of consciousness: Images. *American Journal of Psychology, 37*, 557–64.

Bidwell, S. (1894). On the recurrent images following visual impressions. *Proceedings of the Royal Society of London, 56*, 132.

Binet, A. (1884). La rectification des illusions par appel aux sens. *Mind, 9*, 206–12.

Binet, A. (1887). L'Intensite des images mentales. *Revue Philosophique, 5*, 10–19. (Also, see *American Journal of Psychology* [1887–1888], *1*, 517, for a review of this article.)

Binet, A. (1894). *Psychologie des grands calculateurs, et joueurs d'echecs*. Paris: Hachette.

Binet, A. (1899). *Psychology of reasoning*. Paris: Hachette.

Bishop, H. G. (1921). An experimental investigation of the positive after-image in audition. *American Journal of Psychology, 32*, 305–25.

Blachowski, S. (1936). From eidetic representations to the structure of the personality. *Chowanna, 7*, 65–76.

Bohler, C., & Clinebell, H. (1996). *Opening to God: Guided imagery meditation on scripture*. Nashville, TN: Upper Room Books.

Bolger, E. M., & Titchener, E. B. (1907). Some experiments on the associative power of smells. *American Journal of Psychology, 18*, 326–27.

Bonte, T. (1925). Die personale bedeutsamkeit der eidetischen anlage unter besonderer berucksightigung ihrer beziehung zum intellektuellen leben. *Zeitschrift fur Angewandte Psychologie, 43*, 1–110.

Bonte, T. (1933). Uber die suggestibilitat von eidetikern und nichteidetikern. *Zeitschrift fur Angewandte Psychologie, 44*, 161–92.

Bonte, T. (1934). *Die eidetische anlage und ihre bedeutung fur erziehung und unterricht*. Leipzig: Barth.

Bonte, T., Liefmann, E., & Roessler, F. (1926). Untersuchungen uber die eidetische veranlagung von kindern und jugendlichen. *Zeitschrift fur Angewandte Psychologie, 43*, 300–371.

Borak, J. (1921). Uber die empfindlichkeit fur gewichtsunterschiede bei abnehmender reizstarke. *Psychologische Forschung, 1*, 374–89.

Boring, E. G. (1957). *A history of experimental psychology*. 2d ed. New York: Appleton-Century-Crofts.

Boring, E. G., & Luce, A. (1917). The psychological basis of appetite. *American Journal of Psychology, 28*, 443–53.

Bourdon, B. (1914). Recherches sur la perception des movements rectilignes de tout le corps. *l'Annee Psychologie, 20*, 1–16. (Also, see *Psychological Bulletin* [1915], *12*, 117.)

Bousfield, W., & Barry, H. (1933). The visual imagery of a lightning calculator. *American Journal of Psychology, 45*, 353–58.

Bowers, H. (1929). Constancy of imaginal content. *Journal of Educational Psychology, 20,* 295–98.

Bowers, H. (1931a). Memory and mental imagey: An experimental study. *British Journal of Psychology, 21,* 271–82.

Bowers, H. (1931b). Studies in visual imagery. *American Journal of Psychology, 43,* 216–29.

Bowers, H. (1932a). Factors influencing visual imagery for letter groups. *American Journal of Psychology, 44,* 775–79.

Bowers, H. (1932b). Visual imagery and "observation." *Journal of Educational Psychology, 23,* 441–45.

Bowers, H. (1932c). Visual imagery and retention. *British Journal of Psychology, 23,* 180–95.

Braddock, C. (1921). An experimental study of cutaneous imagery. *American Journal of Psychology, 32,* 415–20.

Braddock, C. (1924). An experimental study of the visual negative after-image. *American Journal of Psychology, 35,* 157–66.

Bradfield, L. (1939). A preliminary study of the incidence and characteristics of auditory eidetic imagery. Unpublished master's thesis, University of Texas at Austin.

Brahn, M. (1912). Die psychologie eines rechenkunstlers. *Zeitschrift fur Padagogik Psychologie, 13,* 529–33.

Bratbak, J. (1944). Eidetic imagery. *Norsk Pedagogisk Tidsskrift, 28,* 64–68.

Breuil, H. (1952). *Four centuries of cave art.* Montignac, Dordogne, France: Centre d'Etudes et de Documentation Prehistoriques.

Broer, F. (1932). The Purkinje phenomenon in positive images. *Zeitschrift fur Psychologie, 125,* 53–69, 71–89.

Brown, W. (1935). Growth of "memory images." *American Journal of Psychology, 47,* 90–102.

Bruce, F. F. (Ed.) (1981). *Vine's expository dictionary of Old Testament words.* Old Tappan, NJ: Revell.

Brueckner, G. H. (1934). A contribution to the psychology of the clairvoyant. *Zeitschrift fur Angewandte Psychologie, 46,* 210–28.

Bryant, C. M. (1971). The image of God in man fulfilled in the New Testament. Unpublished master's thesis, Dallas Theological Seminary.

Bugelski, B. R. (1984). Imageless thought: The Wurzburg school. In R. J. Corsini (Ed.), *Encyclopedia of psychology.* Vol. 2. New York: Wiley.

Buhler, K. (1907/1908). Tatsachen und probleme zu einer psychologie der denkvorgange. *Archiv fur die Gesamte Psychologie, 11,* 297–305; 12, 1–3, 74–92.

Burghardt, W. (1957). *The image of God in man according to Cyril of Alexandria.* Woodstock, MD: Woodstock College Press.

Burnett, N. C., & Dallenbach, K. M. (1927). The experience of heat. *American Journal of Psychology, 38,* 418–31.

Burrow, T. (1924). Social images versus reality. *Journal of Abnormal and Social Psychology, 19*, 230–35.

Burtt, H. E. (1916). Factors which influence the arousal of the primary visual memory image. *American Journal of Psychology, 27*, 87–118.

Busse, P. (1920). Uber die gedachtnisstufen und ihre beziehung zum aufbau der wahrnehmungswelt. *Zeitschrift fur Psychologie, 84*, 1–66.

Caird, G. B., & Wright, N. (1997). *The language and imagery of the Bible.* Grand Rapids, MI: Eerdmans.

Cairns, D. (1953). *The image of God in man.* New York: Philosophical Library.

Calkins, M. W. (1894). A statistical study of dreams. *American Journal of Psychology, 5*, 312–22.

Calkins, M. W. (1896). Synaesthesia. *American Journal of Psychology, 7*, 90–107.

Cameron, A. (1897). The imagery of one early made blind. *Psychological Review, 4*, 391–92.

Carmichael, L. (1925). Eidetic imagery and the Binet test. *Journal of Educational Psychology, 16*, 251–52.

Cason, H. (1923). Imagery in the waking and drowsy states. *American Journal of Psychology, 34*, 486–95.

Cason, H. (1925). Influence of suggestion on imagery in a group situation. *Journal of Abnormal and Social Psychology, 26*, 294–99.

Cattell, J. McK. (1890). Mental tests and measurements. *Mind, 15*, 373–80.

Cattell, J. McK. (1897). Researches in progress in the psychological laboratory of Columbia University: Imagery. *Psychological Review, 4*, 114–15.

Chapin, M. W., & Washburn, M. F. (1912). A study of the images representing the concept "meaning." *American Journal of Psychology, 23*, 109–14.

Charcot, J. M. (1890). *Complete works.* Paris: Fourneville & Brissand.

Childs, J. (1988). The image dei and eschatology: The ethical implications of a reconsideration of the image of God in man within the framework of an eschatological theology. Unpublished doctoral dissertation, Lutheran School of Theology.

Claparede, E. (1913). Existe-il des images verbo-motrices? *Archiv de Psychologie, 13*, 93–103.

Claparede, E. (1914). De la representation des personnes inconnues, et des lapsus linguae. *Archiv de Psychologie, 14*, 301–4.

Clark, H. (1916). Visual imagery and attention: An analytical study. *American Journal of Psychology, 27*, 461–92.

Clark, H., Quackenbush, N., & Washburn, M. F. (1913). A suggested co-efficient of affective sensitiveness. *American Journal of Psychology, 24*, 583–85.

Clarke, H. M. (1911). Conscious attitudes. *American Journal of Psychology*, 22, 214–49.

Cleveland, A. A. (1907). The psychology of chess and of learning to play it. *American Journal of Psychology*, 18, 269–308.

Cocar, B. (1999). Comparison of the concept of the image of God in man in evangelical theology of the 1980s and the 1990s with a strictly biblical interpretation. Unpublished doctoral dissertation, Grace Theological Seminary.

Collins, S. (1990). *Selfless persons: Imagery and thought in Therarad Buddhism.* New York: Cambridge University Press.

Colvin, S. S. (1908). The nature of the mental image. *Psychological Review*, 15, 158–69.

Colvin, S. S. (1909). Methods of determining ideational types. *Psychological Bulletin*, 6, 223–37.

Colvin, S. S. (1910). A marked case of mimetic ideation. *Psychological Review*, 17, 260–68.

Comstock, C. (1921). On the relevancy of imagery to the processes of thought. *American Journal of Psychology*, 32, 196–230.

Cook, H. D. (1915). Tactual and kinaesthetic space. *Psychological Bulletin*, 12, 214–16.

Coover, J. E. (1913). "The feeling of being stared at"—Experimental. *American Journal of Psychology*, 24, 570–75.

Cramaussel, E. (1926). Images eidetiques. *Journal de Psychologie*, 23, 1003–10.

Creed, R. S., & Granit, R. (1928). On the latency of negative after-images following stimulation of different areas of the retina. *Journal of Physiology*, 66, 281–98.

Creed, R. S., & Harding, R. D. (1930). Latency of after-images and interaction between the two retino-cerebral apparatuses in man. *Journal of Physiology*, 69, 423–41.

Crichton-Brown, W. (1895). Dreamy mental states. *The Lancet*, 13, 3749–50.

Critchley, M. (1951). Types of visual perseveration: "Palinopsia" and "illusory visual spread." *Brain*, 74, 267–99.

Cross, F. L., & Livingstone, E. A. (1983). *The Oxford dictionary of the Christian Church.* 2d ed. New York: Oxford University Press.

Cruden, A. (1986). *Cruden's unabridged concordance.* Grand Rapids, MI: Baker Books.

Curtis, E. M. (1984). Man as the image of God in Genesis in the light of ancient Near Eastern parallels. Unpublished doctoral dissertation, University of Pennsylvania.

Cutolo, F. (1918). A preliminary study of the psychology of heat. *American Journal of Psychology*, 29, 442–48.

Cutsforth, T. D. (1924). Synaesthesia in the process of reasoning. *American Journal of Psychology, 35*, 88–97.

Cutsforth, T. D. (1925). The role of emotion in a synaesthetic subject. *American Journal of Psychology, 36*, 527–43.

Dallenbach, K. M. (1924). Recurrent images. *American Journal of Psychology, 35*, 155.

Dallenbach, K. M. (1926). Synaesthesis: "Pressury" cold. *American Journal of Psychology, 37*, 571–77.

Dallenbach, K. M. (1927). Two pronounced cases of verbal imagery. *American Journal of Psychology, 38*, 667–69.

Daniels, A. H. (1895). The memory after-image and attention. *American Journal of Psychology, 6*, 558–64.

Davis, F. C. (1932). The functional significance of imagery differences. *Journal of Experimental Psychology, 15*, 630–61.

Day, L. M. (1912). The effect of illumination on peripheral vision. *American Journal of Psychology, 23*, 533–78.

Dearborn, G. V. (1898). A study of imaginations. *American Journal of Psychology, 9*, 183–90.

Delabarre, E. B. (1889). On the seat of optical after-images. *American Journal of Psychology, 2*, 326–28.

Descartes, R. (1637/1960). *Discourse on method, and meditations.* Indianapolis, IN: Bobbs-Merrill.

DeVries, A., & Washburn, M. F. (1909). A study of retinal rivalry in the after-image. *American Journal of Psychology, 20*, 131–35.

Dimitrov, M. (1931). Psychologie des images eidetiques spontanees. *Annuaire de l'Universite de Sofia, Faculte Historico-Philologique, 27*, 150–62.

Dimitrov, M. (1933). The movement of colors in the field of spontaneous eidetic images. *Annuaire de l'Universite de Sofia, 30*, 1–10.

Dimitrov, M. (1937a). Eidetism and its psychological and pedagogical importance. *Analele di Psihologie (Bucharest), 4*, 160–76.

Dimitrov, M. (1937b). Oscillations in saturation of eidetic colors. *Journal de Psychologie Normale et Pathologique, 34*, 632–41.

Dimmick, C. C. (1923). The auditory memory after-image. *American Journal of Psychology, 34*, 1–12.

Dimmick, F. L. (1916). On cutaneous after-images. *American Journal of Psychology, 27*, 566–69.

Dimmick, F. L. (1923). An experimental study of auditory tied-images. *American Journal of Psychology, 34*, 85–89.

Dodge, R. (1921). A mirror recorder for photographing the compensatory movements of closed eyes. *Journal of Experimental Psychology, 4*, 165–74.

Domino, G. (1999). Synesthesia. In M. A. Runco & S. R. Pritzer (Eds.), *Encyclopedia of creativity.* Vol. 2. San Diego, CA: Academic Press.

Dontchef-Dezeuze, M. (1914). *L'image et les reflexes conditionnels dans les travaux de Pawlow*. Paris: Alcan.

Downey, J. E. (1901). An experience in getting an after-image from a mental image. *Psychological Review, 8*, 42.

Downey, J. E. (1909). Muscle-reading: A method of investigating involuntary movements and mental types. *Psychological Review, 16*, 257–301.

Downey, J. E. (1911). A case of colored gustation. *American Journal of Psychology, 22*, 528–39.

Downey, J. E. (1912). Literary self projection. *Psychological Review, 19*, 299–311.

Downey, J. E. (1927a). Individual differences in reaction to the word-in-itself. *American Journal of Psychology, 39*, 323–42.

Downey, J. E. (1927b). Observations on a visually preoccupied child. *Journal of Applied Psychology, 11*, 52–57.

Drummond, M. (1926). The nature of images. *British Journal of Psychology, 17*, 10–15.

Dugas, L. (1895). Recherches experimentales sur les differents types d'images. *Revue Philosophique, 39*, 285–92.

Dugas, L. (1903). *L'Imagination*. Paris: Octave Doin.

Dugas, L. (1910). Un noveau cas de paramnesie. *Revue Philosophique, 69*, 623–24.

Dunlap, K. (1910). The complication experiment and related phenomena. *Psychological Review, 17*, 157–91.

Dwelshauvers, G. (1930). New experimental researches concerning eidetic imagery. *Journal de Psychologie, 27*, 794–804.

Ebbecke, U. (1928). Uber positive und negative nachbilder, ihre gegenseitige bezeihung, und den einfluss der lokalen adaptation. *Archiv fur die Gesamte Physiologie, 221*, 160–88.

Ebbinghaus, H. (1885). *Uber das gedachtnis*. Leipzig: Duncker.

Ebbinghaus, H. (1890). Uber nachbilder in binocularen sehen und die binocularen farbenerscheinungen uberhaupt. *Pfluger's Archiv fur die Gesamte Physiologie, 46*, 498–508.

Ehrenstein, W. (1925). Versuche uber die beziehungen zwischen bewegungs- und gestaltwahrenehmungen. *Zeitschrift fur Psychologie, 96*, 305–52.

Eichhorst, W. (1973). Man in the image of God: Created and renewed. Unpublished doctoral dissertation, Grace Theological Seminary.

Eissler, K., & Rowe, C. (1946). A note on eidetic imagery in a case of obsessive neurosis. *Journal of Clinical Psychology, 2*, 286–88.

Elderton, M. (1933). An experiment in map scoring and mental imagery tests. *Journal of Applied Psychology, 17*, 376–406.

Ellison, J. W. (Ed.) (1984). *Nelson's Complete concordance of the Revised Standard Version Bible*. 2d ed. Nashville, TN: Thomas Nelson.

Ellwood, R. S. (Ed.) (1998). *The encyclopedia of world religions.* New York: Facts on File.

*Encyclopaedia Britannica.* (1875). 9th ed. Edinburgh: Adam and Charles Black.

*Encyclopaedia Britannica.* (1922). 11th ed. New York: Encyclopaedia Britannica, Inc.

*Encyclopaedia Britannica.* (1955). Galton, Sir Francis. Vol. 9, p. 989. Chicago: Encyclopaedia Britannica Inc.

English, G. (1916). On the psychological response to unknown proper names. *American Journal of Psychology, 27,* 430–34.

Enke, W. (1933). Reply to E. R. Jaensch's "Discussion of problems in eidetics and typology." *Zeitschrift fur Psychologie, 130,* 96–102.

Erb, M. B. (1937). The memorial forms of apprehension. *American Journal of Psychology, 49,* 343–75.

Evans, R. (1975). The origins of Titchener's doctrine of meaning. *Journal of the History of the Behavioral Sciences, 21,* 334–41.

Exemplarsky, W. (1914). A contribution to the study of ideational types. *Publications of the Psychological Institute, Imperial University of Moscow, 1,* 129–212.

Eysenck, H., J., Arnold, W., & Meili, R. (Eds.) (1972). *Encyclopedia of psychology.* New York: Herder and Herder.

Farisani, T. (1990). *In transit: Between the image of God and the image of man.* Grand Rapids, MI: Eerdmans.

Feasey, L. (1927). Children's appreciation of poems. *British Journal of Psychology, 18,* 51–67.

Fechner, G. (1860). *Elemente der psychophysik.* Leipzig: Breitkopt, Hartel.

Feigenberg, I. M. (1958). On some peculiar abnormalities of perception. *Voprosy Psikhologii, 4,* 38–46.

Feiman, G. (1935). *Eideticism and school age.* Moscow: Biomedgiz.

Feingold, G. A. (1915). The influence of suggestion on imagination. *American Journal of Psychology, 26,* 540–49.

Fernald, G. (1905). The effect of background brightness upon the color tone of stimuli in indirect vision. *Psychological Review, 12,* 386–94.

Fernald, M. R. (1912). The diagnosis of mental imagery. *Psychological Monographs, 14,* No. 58, 1–169.

Fernald, M. R. (1913). The mental imagery of two blind subjects. *Psychological Bulletin, 10,* 62–63.

Fernberger, S. W. (1915). Psychophysical methods and tactual space. *American Journal of Psychology, 26,* 300–302.

Fernberger, S. W. (1919). Possible effects of the imaginal type of the subject on aphasic disturbances. *American Journal of Psychology, 30,* 327–36.

Fernberger, S. W. (1923). Observations on taking peyote (*Anhalonium Lewinii*). *American Journal of Psychology, 34,* 267–73.

Ferree, C. E., & Rand, G. (1931). Distance of projection of the visual image in relation to its apparent intensity. *American Journal of Psychology, 43*, 678–84.

Ferree, C. E., & Rand, G. (1934). Perception of depth in the after-image. *American Journal of Psychology, 46*, 329–32.

Feuchtwanger, A. (1911). Versuche uber vorstellungstypen. *Zeitschrift fur Psychologie, 58*, 161–99.

Fichtner, J. (1978). *Man, the image of God: A Christian anthropology.* New York: Alba House.

Fiedler, M. (1935). Some educational implications of the theory of eidetic imagery. Unpublished master's thesis, Smith College.

Finkenbinder, E. O. (1914). The remembrance of problems and of their solutions: A study in logical memory. *American Journal of Psychology, 25*, 32–81.

Finkenstaedt, E. (1940). Visual size: A study of a theory of perception based on eidetics. *Zeitschrift fur Psychologie, 48*, 205–64.

Fischer, G., & Hentze, R. (1934). Discussions of the problems of eidetic and type theory. *Zeitschrift fur Psychologie, 133*, 222–31, 233–46.

Fischer, S. (1927). Die beziehungen der eidetischen anlage zu korperlichen merkmalen: Einen kritik und erwiderung. *Zeitschrift fur die Gesamte Neurologie und Psychiaatrie, 109*, 680–701.

Fischer, S., & Hirschberg, H. (1924). Die verbrietung der eidetischen anlage im jungendalter und ihre beziehung zu korperischen merkmalen. *Zeitschrift fur die Gesamte Neurologie und Psychiatrie, 88*, 241–352.

Fitt, A. B. (1914). Grossenauffassung durch das auge und den ruhenden tastsinn. *Archiv fur die Gesamte Psychologie, 32*, 420–55.

Fletcher, J. M. (1914). An experimental study of stuttering. *American Journal of Psychology, 25*, 201–55.

Flournoy, H. (1926). Eidetisme chez une debile. *Archives de Psychologie, 20*, 73–74.

Floyd, L. G. (1956). Eidetic imagery in normal and psychotic cases: A study in the incidence and characteristics of eidetic imagery in normal and psychotic cases, and a comparative analysis of the groups. Unpublished doctoral dissertation, New York University.

Foster, W. S. (1911). The effect of practice upon visualizing and upon the reproduction of visual impressions. *Journal of Educational Psychology, 2*, 11–22.

Foston, H. M. (1930). *Man and the image of God.* London: Macmillan.

Fox, C. (1913–1914). The conditions which arouse imagery in thought. *British Journal of Psychology, 6*, 420–31.

Franklin, C. L. (1894). The bearing of the after-image. *Psychological Review, 1*, 396–99.

Franz, S. I. (1895). The after-image threshold. *Psychological Review, 2*, 130–36.

Fraser, A. (1891–1892). Visualization as a chief source of the psychology of Hobbes, Locke, Berkeley, and Hume. *American Journal of Psychology, 4,* 230–47.

Freeman, F. N. (1906). After-images. *Psychological Bulletin, 3,* 105–7.

Frehafer, M. K. (1929). Preliminary note on after-images from stimuli of low saturation and short duration. *American Journal of Psychology, 41,* 277–83.

Freiling, H. (1923). Uber die raumlichen wahrnehmungen der jugendlichen im der eidetischen entwicklungsphase. *Zeitschrift fur Sinnesphysiologie, 55,* 69–132.

Freiling, H., & Jaensch, E. R. (1923). Der aufbau der raumlichen wahrnehmungen. *Zeitschrift fur Psychologie, 91,* 321–42.

French, F. C. (1902). Mental imagery of students: A summary of the replies given to Titchener's questionary by 118 juniors in Vassar College. *Psychological Review, 9,* 40–56.

Friedlaender, A. A. (1928). A case of extraordinary memory: A small contribution to the theory of eidetic imagery. *Psychiatrisch-Neurologische Wochenschrift, 30,* 1–202.

Fries, J. C. (1995). Experiencing God: An analysis of the implications of God imagery. Unpublished master's thesis, University of Virginia.

Frost, E. P. (1913). The characteristic form assumed by dreams. *American Journal of Psychology, 24,* 410–13.

Fuchs, F. (1928). Experimentelle studien uber das bewegungsnachbild. *Zeitschrift fur Psychologie, 106,* 267–315.

Funke, H. (1928). Eidetic arithmetic. *Die Hilfsschule, 21,* 582–88.

Galton, F. (1869/1962). *Hereditary genius: An inquiry into its laws and consequences.* London: Collins.

Galton, F. (1874). *English men of science: Their nature and nurture.* London: Macmillan.

Galton, F. (1879–1880). Psychometric experiments. *Brain, 2,* 149–62.

Galton, F. (1880). Statistics of mental imagery. *Mind, 5,* 301–18.

Galton, F. (1883/1907). *Inquiries into human faculty and its development.* London: Macmillan/New York: Dutton.

Galton, F. (1884). Measurement of character. *Fortnightly Review, 36,* 179–85.

Galton, F. (1888). Co-relations and their measurement, chiefly from anthropometric data. *Proceedings of the Royal Society of London, 15,* 135–45.

Galton, F. (1889/1973). *Natural inheritance.* New York: AMS Press.

Galton, F. (1961). Classification of men according to their natural gifts. In J. Jenkins & D. Paterson (Eds.), *Studies in individual differences.* New York: Appleton-Century-Crofts.

Garfunkel, B. (1929). Eidetik bei hilfsschulern. *Zeitschrift fur Angewandte Psychologie, 33,* 304–28.

Gates, A. I. (1916). The mnemonic span for visual and auditory digits. *Journal of Experimental Psychology, 1*, 393–403.

Gates, L. W. (1934). The after-effect of visually observed movement. *American Journal of Psychology, 46*, 34–46.

Gatti, A., & Vacino, G. (1926). Consecutive imagery in the child. *Pubblicazioni dell'Universita Cattolica del Sacro Cuore, 11*, 215–23.

Gatti, F. (1929). Tri-dimensional negative after-images. *Archivio Italiano di Psicologia, 7*, 138–52.

Geblewicz, E. (1935). The psychology of olfactory experiences. *Kwartalnik Psychologiczny, 7*, 187–242.

Geisler, N. (1997). *Creating God in the image of man?* Minneapolis, MN: Bethany House.

Gemelli, A. (1914a). *Il metado degli equivalenti.* Firenze: L.E.F.

Gemelli, A. (1914b). Influence exercee par la position des parties du corps sur l'appreciation des distances tactiles. *Archiv Italiano de Biologie, 61*, 282–96.

Gemelli, A. (1914c). Intorno alla natura del processo di confronto di distanze tattili. *Rivue di Psicologia, 10*, 415–38.

Gemelli, A. (1914d). Un nouvel esthesiometre. *Archiv Italiano de Biologie, 61*, 271–76.

Gengerelli, J. A. (1930). Some quantitative experiments with eidetic imagery. *American Journal of Psychology, 42*, 399–404.

Gibson, J. (1998). *Language and imagery in the Old Testament.* Peabody, MA: Hendrickson.

Gibson, J. J. (1933). Adaptation, after-effect, and contrast in the perception of curved lines. *Journal of Experimental Psychology, 16*, 1–31.

Gibson, J. J., & Radner, M. (1937). Adaptation, after-effect, and contrast in the perception of tilted lines: I. Quantitative studies; II. Simultaneous contrast and the areal restriction of the after-effect. *Journal of Experimental Psychology, 20*, 453–67; 553–69.

Gleason, J. M. (1919). An experimental study of "feelings of relation." *American Journal of Psychology, 30*, 1–26.

Goldthwait, C. (1933). Relation of eye-movements to visual imagery. *American Journal of Psychology, 45*, 106–10.

Goodman, G., & Downey, J. (1929). An image of spectacle rims. *American Journal of Psychology, 41*, 498–502.

Goodman, N. (1968). *The languages of art.* London: Oxford University Press.

Gordon, K. (1915). A study of an imagery test. *Journal of Philosophy, Psychology, and Scientific Methods, 12*, 574–79.

Gosser, A. (1921). Uber die grunde des verschiedenen verhaltens der einzelnen gedachtnisstufen. *Zeitschrift fur Psychologie, 87*, 97–128.

Gottheil, E. (1921). Uber das latente sinnengedachtnis der jugendlichen und seine aufdeckung. *Zeitschrift fur Psychologie, 87*, 73–90.

Gotz, W. (1929). Untersuchungen uber die eidetische anlage bei jungend-lichen niederer intelligenz. *Archiv fur Psychiatrie, 88,* 251–72.

Granit, R. (1927). Uber eine hemmung der zapfenfunktion durch stabah-enerregung beim bewegungshachbild. *Zeitschrift fur Sinnesphysiologie, 58,* 95–110.

Granit, R. (1928). On inhibition in the after-effect of seen movement. *British Journal of Psychology, 19,* 147–57.

Granit, R., Hohenthal, T., & Uoti, A. (1930). On the latency of negative after-images in relation to brightness of stimulus. *Saertryk Acta Ophthalmologie, 8,* 137–54.

Grassi, J. A. (1987). *Healing the heart: The transformational power of bibli-cal heart imagery.* New York: Paulist Press.

Gray, C. R., & Gummerman, K. (1975). The enigmatic eidetic image: A critical examination of methods, data, and theories. *Psychological Bul-letin, 82,* 383–407.

Gressot, M. (1950). Essai sur l'image eidetique et le probleme de la vision. *Schweizer Archiv fur Neurologie und Psychiatrie, 66,* 86–122.

Griffitts, C. H. (1927). Individual differences in imagery. *Psychological Mono-graphs, 37,* No. 172, 1–91.

Griffitts, C. H., & Baumgartner, W. J. (1919). The correlation between vi-sualization and brightness discrimination. *Psychological Review, 26,* 75–82.

Grindley, G. C. (1930). The relation between the rod and cone mechanisms in the after-effect of seen movement. *Journal of Physiology, 69,* 53–59.

Grinfield, E. W. (1837). *A scriptural inquiry into the nature and import of the image and likeness of God in man.* London: Fellowes.

Gross, J. (1930). Studies in the psychology of testimony in children. *Zeitschrift fur Angewandte Psychologie, 37,* 438–59.

Guernsey, M. (1922). A study of liminal sound intensities and the applica-tion of Weber's law to tones of different pitch. *American Journal of Psychology, 33,* 554–69.

Gurnee, H. (1933). Some observations on after-images of bodily movement. *American Journal of Psychology, 45,* 528–30.

Gutmann, M. (1935). A study of the negative after-image of movement. *Archiv fur die Gesamte Psychologie, 93,* 224–46.

Haber, R. N. (1979). Twenty years of haunting eidetic imagery: Where's the ghost? *Behavioral and Brain Sciences, 2,* 583–629.

Haber, R. N., & Haber, L. R. (1988). The characteristics of eidetic imag-ery. In L. K. Obler & D. Fein (Eds.), *The exceptional brain: Neurop-sychology of talent and special abilities.* New York: Guilford Press.

Haines, T. H., & Williams, J. C. (1905). The relation of perceptive and re-vived mental material as shown by the subjective control of visual after-images. *Psychological Review, 12,* 18–40.

Haldane, E., & Ross, G. (Trans.) (1967). *The philosophical works of Descartes.* Cambridge, UK: Cambridge University Press.

Hansen, W. (1929). Uber den gegenwartigen stand der eidetischen forschung. *Vieteljahrsschrift fur Wissenschaftliche Padogogik, 5*, 347–83.

Harris, J. W. (1908). On the associative power of odors. *American Journal of Psychology, 19*, 557–61.

Harris, W. H. (1998). *The descent of Christ: Ephesians 4: 7–11 and traditional Hebrew imagery.* Grand Rapids, MI: Baker Books.

Harris, W. H., & Levey, J. S. (Eds.) (1975). *The new Columbia encyclopedia.* New York: Columbia University Press.

Havermans, F. M. (1936). Eidetic phenomena in our phylogeny? *Mensch en Maatschappij, 12*, 191–99.

Hayashi, S. (1934). The eidetic imagery and the type of children. *Transactions of the Institute of Child Studies, 16*, 689–722.

Hayashi, S. (1936). On eidetic images in members of a picture-loving society in a middle school. *Japanese Journal of Applied Psychology, 4*, 168–70.

Heidbreder, E. F. (1926). Thinking as an instinct. *Psychological Review, 33*, 279–97.

Heller, T. (1930). Eidetik und psychologie der aussage. *Zeitschrift fur Angewandte Psychologie, 35*, 210–12.

Helmholtz, H. von (1856–1866). *Handbuch der physiologischen optik.* Leipzig: Voss.

Helson, H. (1933). A child's spontaneous reports of imagery. *American Journal of Psychology, 45*, 360–61.

Helson, H. (1936). Size-constancy of the projected after-image. *American Journal of Psychology, 48*, 638–42.

Henning, H. (1923). Starre eidetische klang-und-schmerzbilder und die eidetische konstellation. *Zeitschrift fur Psychologie, 92*, 137–76.

Henning, H. (1924). Die neuentdeckte erlebnisklasse der eidetik, die urbilder und der konstitutions-typus. *Deutsche Zeitschrift fur Nervenheilkunde, 81*, 180–86.

Hensel, G. (1930). The optical in Wordsworth: A contribution to the psychology of poetic creation. *Archiv fur die Gesamte Psychologie, 76*, 83–192.

Herbertz, R. (1930). Was ist "eidetik"? *Psychologische Rundschau, 1*, 355–58.

Herwig, B. (1921). Uber den inneren farbensinn der jugendlichen und seine beziehung zu den allgemeinen fragen des lichtsinns. *Zeitschrift fur Psychologie, 87*, 129–210.

Hess, C. (1893). Uber die unvereinbarkeit gewisser ermudungserscheinungen des sehorgans mit der dreifasertheorie. *Archiv fur Ophthalmologie, 39*, 45–70.

Hett, W. S. (Ed.) (1957). *Aristotle VIII: On the soul, Parva Naturalia, on breath.* Cambridge, MA: Harvard University Press.

Heywood, A., & Vortriede, H. (1905). Some experiments on the associative power of smells. *American Journal of Psychology, 16,* 537–41.

Hicks, G. D. (1924). On the nature of images. *British Journal of Psychology, 15,* 121–48.

Higginson, G. D. (1926). Visual perception in the white rat. *Journal of Experimental Psychology, 9,* 337–47.

Hill, D. S. (1918). An experiment with an automatic mnemonic system. *Psychological Bulletin, 15,* 99–103.

Hirst, R. J. (1951). Perception, science, and common sense. *Mind, 60,* 481–505.

Hobbes, T. (1651/1958). *Leviathan.* Cambridge, UK: Cambridge University Press.

Hochman, J. (2001). A basic online search on the eidetic with PsycINFO, MEDLINE, and ERIC. *Journal of Mental Imagery, 25,* 99–215.

Hodges, A. (1936). Racial differences in the eidetic imagery of preschool children. Unpublished master's thesis, University of Texas at Austin.

Hofe, K. (1926). Beitrage zur frage der eidetischen anlage. *Archiv fur Ophthalmologie, 117,* 40–46.

Hofmarksrichter, K. (1931). Visuelle kompensation und eidetik bei taubstummen. *Archiv fur die Gesamte Psychologie, 82,* 329–402.

Hollingworth, H. L. (1911a). The psychology of drowsiness: An introspective and analytical study. *American Journal of Psychology, 22,* 99–111.

Hollingworth, H. L. (1911b). Vicarious functioning of irrelevant imagery. *Journal of Philosophy, Psychology, and Scientific Methods, 8,* 688–92.

Holmes, D. S., Roeckelein, J. E., & Olmstead, J. A. (1968). Determinants of tactual perception of finger-drawn symbols: Reappraisal. *Perceptual and Motor Skills, 27,* 659–72.

Holtzman, W. H. (1958). *Holtzman inkblot technique: Administration and scoring guide.* New York: Psychological Corporation.

*Holy Bible: The New King James Version.* (1984). Nashville, TN: Thomas Nelson.

Hume, D. (1739/1978). A treatise on human understanding. In L. Selby-Bigge & P. Nidditch (Eds.), *David Hume: A treatise of human nature.* Oxford, UK: Oxford University Press.

Hume, D. (1748/1963). *An enquiry concerning human understanding.* LaSalle, IL: Open Court.

Humphrey, G. (1940). Review of "The mechanism of thought, imagery, and hallucination." *American Journal of Psychology, 53,* 159–60.

Humphrey, G. (1951). *Thinking: An introduction to its experimental psychology.* New York: Wiley/London: Methuen.

Hunter, W. S. (1913). The delayed reaction in animals and children. *Animal Behavior Monographs, 2,* 1–86.

Hunter, W. S. (1914). The after-effect of visual motion. *Psychological Review, 21*, 245–77.

Hunter, W. S. (1915). Retinal factors in visual after-movement. *Psychological Review, 22*, 479–89.

Hunter, W. S. (1917). A reformulation of the law of association. *Psychological Review, 24*, 188–96.

Husen, T. (1946). *Studier roerande de eidetiska fenomenen.* Lund, Sweden: Gleerup.

Husen, T. (1952). Studier roerande de eidetiska bildernas fenomenologi, II. *Lunds Universitets Arsskrift, 48*, 1–85.

Hyslop, J. H. (1903). After-images and allied phenomena. *Psychological Review, 10*, 296–97.

*Illustrated Bible Dictionary.* (1980). Grove, IL: Inter-Varsity Press.

Jackson, F. S. (1936). A study of the imagery of an adult eidetiker. Unpublished master's thesis, University of Texas at Austin.

Jacobson, E. (1925). Progressive relaxation. *American Journal of Psychology, 36*, 73–87. (Also, see 1912, *23*, 345–69.)

Jacobson, E. (1927). Action currents from muscular contractions during conscious processes. *Science, 66*, 403.

Jacobson, E. (1929). *Progressive relaxation.* Chicago: University of Chicago Press.

Jacobson, E. (1930/1931). Electrical measurements of neuromuscular states during mental activities. I., II., III., IV., V., VI., VII. *American Journal of Physiology, 92*, 567–608; *94*, 22–34; *95*, 694–702; *95*, 703–12; *96*, 115–21; *96*, 122–25; *97*, 200–209.

Jacobson, E. (1932). Electrophysiology of mental activities. *American Journal of Psychology, 44*, 677–94.

Jaensch, E. R. (1920). Zur methodik experimenteller untersuchungen an optischen anschauungsbildern. *Zeitschrift fur Psychologie, 85*, 37–82.

Jaensch, E. R. (1921). Uber psychophysische konstitutionstypen. *Monatsschrift fur Kinderheilkunde, 2*, 22–29.

Jaensch, E. R. (1922). Uber die subjektiven anschauungsbilder. *Berichte uber den Kongress fur Experimentelle Psychologie, 7*, 3–49.

Jaensch, E. R. (1923). Die volkerkunde und der eidetische tatsachenkries. *Zeitschrift fur Psychologie, 91*, 88–111.

Jaensch, E. R. (1927). Uber eidetik und typologische forschungsmethode. *Zeitschrift fur Psychologie, 102*, 35–56.

Jaensch, E. R. (1930). *Eidetic imagery and typological methods of investigation.* London: Kegan Paul, Trench Trubner/New York: Harcourt Brace.

Jaensch, E. R. (1934). *Eidetische anlage und kindliches seelenleben: Studien und abhandlungen zur grundlegung der eidetik und jugendanthropologie.* Leipzig: Barth.

Jaensch, E. R. (1935a). Das wesen der kindheit und der eidetische tatsachen-kreis. *Gesundheit und Erziehung, 48,* 194–210.

Jaensch, E. R. (1935b). Wege der jugendanthropologie. *Zeitschrift fur Jegendkunde, 5,* 14–25.

Jaensch, E. R., & Jaensch, W. (1921). Uber die verbreitung der eidetischen anlage im jugendalter. *Zeitschrift fur Psychologie, 87,* 91–96.

Jaensch, E. R., & Kretz, A. (1932). Problems in eidetics and typology. IX. Experimental structure-psychological investigations of the apprehension of time with special reference to personal types. *Zeitschrift fur Psychologie, 126,* 312–75. (Also, see *125,* 113–148; *126,* 51–85.)

Jaensch, E. R., & Mehmel, H. (1928). Gedachtnisleistungen eines schwachsinnigen eidetikers. *Psychiatrisch-Neurologische Wochenschrift, 30,* 101–3.

Jaensch, E. R., & Schweicher, J. (1927). *The question at issue between association and functional psychology tested by the eidetic method.* Berlin: O. Elsner.

James, W. (1890). *The principles of psychology.* 2 vols. New York: Dover.

Jankowska, H. (1938). Eidetic images and hallucinations. *Rocznik Psychjatryczny, 34,* 33–60.

Jankowska, H. (1939). Eidetic images and hallucinations. *Kwartalnik Psychologiczny, 11,* 189–230.

Jastrow, J. (1892). A study of involuntary movements. *American Journal of Psychology, 4,* 398–407; *5,* 223–31.

Jelliffe, S. (1928). On eidetic psychology and psychiatric problems. *Medical Journal and Record, 128,* 80–83.

Jenkin, A. M. (1935). Imagery and learning. *British Journal of Psychology, 26,* 149–64.

Jenness, A., & Jorgensen, A. P. (1941). Ratings of vividness of imagery in the waking state compared with reports of somnambulism. *American Journal of Psychology, 54,* 253–59.

Jewell, J. R. (1905). The psychology of dreams. *American Journal of Psychology, 16,* 1–34.

Joesten, E. (1929). Eidetische anlage und bildnerisches schaffen. *Archiv fur die Gesamte Psychologie, 71,* 493–539.

Johannesson, B. (1939). Eidetische untersuchungen in Island. *Zeitschrift fur Psychologie, 146,* 161–81.

Johanning, M. M. (1965). Some aspects of the image of God in man in the works of Origen and Gregory of Nyssa. Unpublished master's thesis, Marquette University.

Jones, E. E. (1909). The waning of consciousness under chloroform. *Psychological Review, 16,* 48–54.

Judd, C. H., McAllister, C. N., & Steele, W. M. (1905). Introduction to a series of studies of eye-movements by means of kinetoscopic photographs. *Psychological Monographs, 7,* 1–16.

Judd, D. B. (1927). A quantitative investigation of the Purkinje after-image. *American Journal of Psychology, 38,* 507–33.

Juhasz, A. (1920). Uber die komplementar-gefarbten nachbilder. *Zeitschrift fur Sinnesphysiologie, 51,* 233–63.

Kakise, H. (1911). A preliminary experimental study of the conscious concomitants of understanding. *American Journal of Psychology, 22,* 14–64.

Kant, I. (1781/1929). *Critique of pure reason.* New York: St. Martin's Press.

Kantor, J. R. (1921). An objective interpretation of meanings. *American Journal of Psychology, 32,* 231–43.

Kantowitz, B., Roediger, H., & Elmes, D. (2001). *Experimental psychology: Understanding psychological research.* Belmont, CA: Brooks/Cole.

Kao, C., & Lyman, R. (1944). The role of eidetic imagery in a psychosis. *Journal of Nervous and Mental Disease, 100,* 355–65.

Karger, P. (1925). Die eidetische anlage der jugendlichen in ihre bedeutung fur die klinik und die schulleistungen. *Klinische Wochenschrift, 4,* 22–47.

Karwoski, T. (1929). Variations toward purple in the visual after-image. *American Journal of Psychology, 41,* 625–36.

Kattsoff, L. (1950). Is eidetic intuition necessary? *Philosophy and Phenomenological Research 10,* 563–71.

Katz, D. (1911). *Die erscheinungsweisen der farben und ihre beeinflussung durch die individuelle erfahrung.* Leipzig: Barth.

Katz, G. G. (1956). An investigation of eidetic imagery in conditions of hypocalcemia, with and without latent tetany. Unpublished doctoral dissertation, New York University.

Katzaroff, D. (1911). La recognition. *Archiv de Psychologie, 11,* 1–78.

Kelley, T. L. (1913). The association experiment: Individual differences and correlations. *Psychological Review, 20,* 479–504.

Kellogg, W. N. (1929). An improved model of McDougall's after-image apparatus. *American Journal of Psychology, 41,* 119.

Kerr, M., & Pear, T. H. (1931). Unseen drama and imagery: Some experimental observations. *British Journal of Psychology, 22,* 43–54.

Khaimovich, M. (1937). Hypnopompic hallucinations in patients after delirium tremens. *Sovetskaya Psikhonevrologiya, 7,* 98–102.

Kiefer, T. (1956). *Der visuelle mensch: Neue untersuchungen, die vorstellungstypen und deren auswirkung auf das geistesleben.* Munich, Germany: Reinhardt.

Kiesow, F. (1925). Zur kritik der eidetik. *Archiv fur die Gesamte Psychologie, 53,* 447–84.

Kiesow, F. (1927). Critical remarks on eidetic imagery, together with observations made upon eidetic and non-eidetic subjects. *Archiv fur die Gesamte Psychologie, 59,* 339–60.

Kirek, H. (1926). Die bedeutung der sensoriellen veranlagung fur die bildung von objekt vorstellungen insbesondere bei eidetikern. *Zeitschrift fur die Behandlung Schwachsinniger und Epileptischer, 46*, 121–23.

Kluver, H. (1925). Description of eidetic phenomena. *Psychological Bulletin, 22*, 331–40.

Kluver, H. (1926a). An experimental study of the eidetic type. *Genetic Psychology Monographs, 1*, 71–230.

Kluver, H. (1926b). Mescal visions and eidetic vision. *American Journal of Psychology, 37*, 502–15.

Kluver, H. (1927). Visual disturbances after cerebral lesions. *Psychological Bulletin, 24*, 316–24.

Kluver, H. (1928a). *Mescal: The divine plant and its psychological effects.* London: Kegan Paul.

Kluver, H. (1928b). Studies on the eidetic type and on eidetic imagery. *Psychological Bulletin, 25*, 69–104.

Kluver, H. (1929). Eidetic images. *Encyclopaedia Britannica.* 14th ed. Vol. 8, p. 112.

Kluver, H. (1930). Fragmentary eidetic imagery. *Psychological Review, 37*, 441–58.

Kluver, H. (1931). The eidetic child. In C. Murchison (Ed.), *Handbook of child psychology.* Worcester, MA: Clark University Press.

Kluver, H. (1932). Eidetic phenomena. *Psychological Bulletin, 29*, 181–203.

Kluver, H. (1934). The eidetic type. *Proceedings of the Association for Research in Nervous and Mental Diseases, 14*, 150–68.

Koffka, K. (1912). *Zur analyse der vorstellungen und ihrer gesetze.* Leipzig: Quelle & Meyer.

Koffka, K. (1923). Uber die untersuchungen an den sogenannten optischen anschauungsbildern. *Psychologie Forschung, 3*, 124–67.

Kohler, W. (1923). Zur theorie des sukzessivvergleichs und der zeitfehler. *Psychologische Forshung, 4*, 115–75.

Kohler, W., & Emery, D. A. (1947). Figural after-effects in the third dimension of visual space. *American Journal of Psychology, 60*, 159–201.

Kohler, W., & Wallach, H. (1944). Figural after-effects: An investigation of visual processes. *Proceedings of the American Philosophical Society, 88*, 269–357.

Kollarits, J. (1914). Observations de psychologie quotidienne. *Archiv de Psychologie, 14*, 225–47.

Kononova, M. (1929). Eidetic phenomena and their relation to psychopathology. *Zhurnal Nevropatologii i Psikhiatrii imeni S. S. Korsakova, 1*, No. 1.

Kooy, V. H. (1962/1986). Image; Imagery. In G. A. Buttrick (Ed.), *The interpreter's dictionary of the Bible.* Nashville, TN: Abingdon Press.

Kosslyn, S. M. (1980). *Image and mind.* Cambridge, MA: Harvard University Press.

Kosslyn, S. M. (1981). The medium and the message in mental imagery: A theory. In N. Block (Ed.), *Imagery*. Cambridge, MA: M.I.T. Press. (Also, see *Psychological Review* [1981], *88*, 46–66.)

Kosslyn, S. M. (1994). *Image and brain: The resolution of the imagery debate*. Cambridge, MA: M.I.T. Press.

Kratina, F. (1930). *The eidetic characteristics of adolescents: A psychological study*. Prague: Orbis-Verlag.

Kreezer, G. (1938). The neurological level of the factors underlying time-errors. *American Journal of Psychology, 51*, 18–43.

Krellenberg, P. (1922). Uber die herausdifferenzierung der wahrnehmungs und vorstellungswelt aus der originaren eidetischen einheit. *Zeitschrift fur Psychologie, 88*, 56–119.

Kreutz, A. (1983). Man the image of God: Its effect on human sexuality and the church. Unpublished master's thesis, Ashland Theological Seminary.

Kroh, O. (1920). Eidetiker unter deutschen dichtern. *Zeitschrift fur Psychologie, 85*, 118–62.

Kroh, O. (1922). *Subjektive anschauungsbilder bei jugendlichen: Eine psychologisch-padagogische untersuchung*. Gottingen: Vandenhoeck & Ruprecht.

Kroh, O. (1924). Die eidetische anlage bei jugendlichen. *Zeitschrift fur Kinderforschung, 29*, 63–69.

Kroh, O. (1952). Die eidetik in neuer beleuchtung. *Psychologische Rundschau, 1*, 257–65.

Krudewig, M. (1953). *Elements of visual perception and representation*. Meisenheim/Glan: Hain.

Kuhlmann, F. (1904). Experimental studies in mental deficiency: Three cases of imbecility (Mongolian) and six cases of feeblemindedness. *American Journal of Psychology, 15*, 391–446.

Kuhlmann, F. (1905). The place of mental imagery and memory among mental functions. *American Journal of Psychology, 16*, 337–56.

Kuhlmann, F. (1906). On the analysis of the memory consciousness: A study in the mental imagery and memory of meaningless visual forms. *Psychological Review, 13*, 316–48.

Kuhlmann, F. (1907). On the analysis of the memory consciousness for pictures of familiar objects. *American Journal of Psychology, 18*, 389–420.

Kuhlmann, F. (1909). On the analysis of auditory memory consciousness. *American Journal of Psychology, 20*, 194–218.

Kulpe, O. (1893). *Grundriss der psychologie*. Leipzig: Engelmann.

Kulpe, O. (1902). Uber die objektivierung und subjektivierung von sinnese-indrucken. *Philosophische Studien, 19*, 508–36.

Kunzendorf, R. G. (1980). Imagery and consciousness: A scientific analysis of the mind-body problem. *Dissertation Abstracts International, 40*, 3448B–49B.

Ladd, G. T. (1894). Direct control of the retinal field. *Psychological Review, 1*, 51–155.

Lageer, K. (1992). Image of God or image of man? Unpublished master's thesis, Asbury Theological Seminary.

Lahti, A. (1951). On the mental character of phantom limbs in the amputees. *Acta Psychologica Fennica, 1*, 59–74.

Lang, H., Polatin, P., & Hotchkiss, S. (1937). Spontaneous eidetic imagery in a case of chronic epidemic encephalitis. *Journal of Nervous and Mental Disease, 85*, 548–55.

Langfeld, H. S. (1913). Voluntary movement under positve and negative instruction. *Psychological Review, 20*, 459–78.

Langfeld, H. S. (1916). Concerning the image. *Psychological Review, 23*, 180–89.

Langfeld, H. S. (1929). Synesthesia. *Psychological Bulletin, 26*, 582–85.

Langfeld, H. S. (1937). Stumpf's "Introduction to psychology." *American Journal of Psychology, 50*, 33–36.

Lauenstein, O. (1932). Ansatz zu einer physiologischen theorie des vergleichs und der zeitfehler. *Psychologische Forschung, 17*, 130–77.

Lawson-Tancred, H. (Ed.) (1986). *Aristotle: De anima (On the soul)*. Harmondsworth, UK: Penguin Books.

Lay, W. (1898). Mental imagery experimentally and subjectively considered. *Psychological Review Monograph Supplements, 2*, No. 3.

Lay, W. (1903a). Imagery. *Psychological Review, 10*, 422–25.

Lay, W. (1903b). Mental imagery. *Psychological Review, 10*, 300–306.

Learoyd, M. W. (1896). The "continued story." *American Journal of Psychology, 7*, 86–90.

Leask, J., Haber, R. N., & Haber, R. B. (1969). Eidetic imagery in children: II. Longitudinal and experimental results. *Psychonomic Monographs, 3*, 25–48.

Leeper, R. (1951). Cognitive processes. In S. S. Stevens (Ed.), *Handbook of experimental psychology*. New York: Wiley.

Lenz, E. (1940). Heredo-psychological group studies using the method of integrational typology. *Zeitschrift fur Psychologie, 148*, 287–360.

Leuner, H. (1955). Experimental catathymic image experiencing as a clinical method of psychotherapy. *Psychotherapie Psychosomatik Medizinische Psychologie, 5*, 185–203.

Leven, D. (1926). Die eidetische anlage der jugendlichen. *Klinische Wochenschrift, 5*, 271–77.

Leven, E. (1927). The eidetic propensity of the young. *Archiv fur Rassen- und Gesellschaftsbiologie Einschliesslich Rassen- und Gesellschaftshygiene, 18*, 431–34.

Levin, M. (1932). Auditory hallucinations in "nonpsychotic" children. *American Journal of Psychiatry, 11*, 1119–52.

Levine, J., & Graham, C. H. (1937). The latency of negative visual after-effects as a function of the intensity of illumination on an adjacent retinal region. *American Journal of Psychology, 49*, 661–65.

Liefmann, E. (1928a). Die eidetische anlage und ihre bedeutung fur die konstitutionstypologie. *Zeitschrift fur die Gesamte Neurologie und Psychiatrie, 116*, 537–58.

Liefmann, E. (1928b). Untersuchungen uber die eidetische veranlagung von schulerinnen einer hoheren madchenschule. *Zeitschrift fur Angewandte Psychologie, 46*, 111–96.

Lipmann, O. (1911). Visuelle auffassungstypen. *Berlin International Kongress fur Experimentelle Psychologie, 4*, 198–201.

Lobsien, M. (1911). Zur entwickelung des akustischen wortgedachtnisses der schuler. *Zeitschrift fur Padagogik Psychologie, 12*, 238–45.

Loch, M. (1931). *Uber eidetik und kinderzeichnung.* Ochsenfurt am Main, Germany: Fritz & Rappert.

Locke, J. (1690/1965). *An essay concerning human understanding.* London: Dent.

Lotz, F. (1937). Integration typology and hereditary characterology. *Beihefte der Zeitschrift fur Angewandte Psychologie und Charakterkunde, 73*, 149–253.

Luther, F. (1931). Die probleme der eidetik Erich Jaenschs und seiner schule. *Zeitschrift fur Menschenkunde, 6*, 401–19.

MacDougal, R. (1898). Music imagery: A confession of experience. *Psychological Review, 5*, 463–76.

Maier, N.R.F. (1929). The illusion of size in pinhole vision. *American Journal of Psychology, 41*, 291–95.

Mainwaring, J. (1933). Kinaesthetic factors in the recall of musical experience. *British Journal of Psychology, 23*, 284–307.

Marbe, K. (1901). *Experimentell-psychologische untersuchungen uber dar urteil, eine einleitung in die logik.* Leipzig: Engelmann.

Marks, D. F., & McKellar, P. (1982). The nature and function of eidetic imagery. *Journal of Mental Imagery, 6*, 1–125.

Martin, L. J. (1910). Zur lehre von den bewegungsvortellungen. *Zeitschrift fur Psychologie, 56*, 401–47.

Martin, L. J. (1912). *Die projektionsmethode und die lokalization visueller und anderer vorstellungsbilder.* Leipzig: Barth. (Also, see *Zeitschrift fur Psychologie* [1912], *61*, 322–546.)

Martin, L. J. (1913a). Concerning the function of the visual image in memory and imagination. *Psychological Bulletin, 10*, 61–62.

Martin, L. J. (1913b). Quantitative untersuchungen uber das verhaltnis unanschaulicher bewusstseinsinhalte. *Zeitschrift fur Psychologie, 65*, 417–28.

Martin, L. J. (1914–1915). Uber die abhangigkeit visueller vorstellungsbilder vom denken. *Zeitschrift fur Psychologie, 70*, 212–21.

Martin, L. J. (1915). Ghosts and the projection of visual images. *American Journal of Psychology, 26*, 251–57. (Also, see *Psychological Bulletin* [1911], *8*, 36–37.)

Marzi, A. (1933). Concerning visual eidetic aptitudes in normal children. *Scritti Onore Kiesow, 1*, 168–77.

Marzi, A., & Rende, U. (1943). Observations on eidetic phenomena in deaf-mute children. *Rivista di Psicologia Normale e Patologica, 39*, 56–65.

Masaki, M. (1929). On "eidetik." *Japanese Journal of Psychology, 4*, 871–82.

Mata de Gregorio, J., & Poleo, M. (1958). El fenomeno eidetico. *Cuadernos Psicologia, Caracas, 1*, 8–11.

Max, L. W. (1934). An experimental study of the motor theory of consciousness: Critique of earlier studies. *Journal of General Psychology, 11*, 112–25.

Max, L. W. (1935). An experimental study of the motor theory of consciousness. *Journal of Comparative Psychology, 19*, 469–86. (Also, see 1937, *24*, 301–44.)

McDonough, A. R. (1919). The development of meaning. *Psychological Monographs, 27*, 443–515.

McDougall, W. (1904). The sensations excited by a single momentary stimulation of the eye. *British Journal of Psychology, 1*, 98–101.

McFarland, D. (2000). Serpent imagery in Revelation 12: 7–12. Unpublished master's thesis, Dallas Theological Seminary.

McKeon, R. (Ed.) (1941). *The basic works of Aristotle.* New York: Random House.

McMein, M., & Washburn, M. F. (1909). The effect of mental type on the interference of motor habits. *American Journal of Psychology, 20*, 282–84.

Mead, G. H. (1910). Social consciousness and the consciousness of meaning. *Psychological Bulletin, 7*, 397–405.

Meenes, M. (1933). Eidetic phenomena in Negro school children. *Psychological Bulletin, 30*, 688–89.

Meenes, M. (1934). The relationship of the eidetic phenomenon to the after-image and to the memory-image. *Psychological Bulletin, 30*, 739–45.

Meenes, M. (1937). The incidence of eidetic imagery in Negro school children. *Journal of Negro Education, 6*, 592–95.

Meenes, M., & Morton, M. (1936). Characteristics of the eidetic phenomenon. *Journal of General Psychology, 14*, 370–91.

Meili-Dworetzki, G. (1943). Observations on a case of visual agnosia with hallucination. *Archiv de Psychologie, 30*, 65–94.

Messer, A. (1906). Experimentell-psychologische untersuchungen uber das denken. *Archiv fur die Gesamte Psychologie, 8*, 1–30.

Metz, P. (1929). *Die eidetische anlage der jugendlichen in ihrer beziehung zur kunstierischen gestaltung.* Langensalza, Germany: H. Beyer & Sohne.

Meumann, E. (1911). Uber den kombinatorischen faktor der vorstellungs-typen. *Zeitschrift fur Padagogik Psychologie, 12,* 115–20.

Meyer, M. (1902). The duration of the auditory after-sensation. *Psychological Review, 9,* 142–43.

Miller, E. (1931a). Affective nature of illusion and hallucination. Part II: Eidetic imagery. *Journal of Neurology and Psychopathology, 12,* 1–13.

Miller, E. (1931b). The eidetic image—An undertone of psychosis: Introduction to a future inquiry. *Proceedings of the Royal Society of Medicine, 24,* 1223–30.

Miller, G. A. (1956). The magical number seven plus or minus two: Some limits on our capacity for processing information. *Psychological Review, 63,* 81–97.

Miskolczy, D., & Schultz, G. (1929). Eidetik und schizophrenie. *Monatsschrift fur Psychiatrie und Neurologie, 72,* 354–60.

Mitchell, F. D. (1907). Mathematical prodigies. *American Journal of Psychology, 18,* 61–143.

Mitchell, S. W. (1896). The effects of *Anhalonium Lewinii* (the mescal button). *British Medical Journal, 2,* 1625–29.

Modrak, D.W.K. (1987). *Aristotle, power of perception.* Chicago: University of Chicago Press.

Monroe, W. S. (1898). A study of taste dreams. *American Journal of Psychology, 10,* 326–27.

Moore, T. V. (1910). *The process of abstraction.* Berkeley: University of California Press.

Moore, T. V. (1915). The temporal relations of meaning and imagery. *Psychological Review, 22,* 177–225.

Moore, T. V. (1917). Discussion: Meaning and imagery. *Psychological Review, 24,* 318–22. (Also, see *Psychological Bulletin* [1915], *12,* 83–84.)

Moore, T. V. (1919). Image and meaning in memory and perception. *Psychological Monographs, 27,* 69–296.

Morgan, J.J.B. (1924). The nature of suggestibility. *Psychological Review, 31,* 463–77.

Morris, P. E., & Hampson, P. J. (1983). *Imagery and consciousness.* New York: Academic Press.

Morrison, J. D. (1983). The Pauline concept of the restoration of the image of God in man. Unpublished master's thesis, Western Conservative Baptist Seminary.

Morsch, J. E. (1942). Further investigation of "eidetic imagery." *Psychological Bulletin, 39,* 611–12.

Morsch, J. E., & Abbott, H. D. (1945). An investigation of after-images. *Journal of Comparative Psychology, 38,* 47–63.

Mota, A. (1950). Eidetismo e alucinacoes; correlacoes dinamicas. *Anais Portugueses de Psiquiatria, 2,* 359–75.

Muhl, A. M. (1924). Automatic writing combined with crystal gazing as a means of recalling forgotten incidents. *Journal of Abnormal and Social Psychology, 19*, 264–73.

Muhl, A. M. (1930). *Automatic writing*. Leipzig: Theodor Steinkopff.

Muller, G. E. (1878). *Zur grundlegung der psychophysik*. Berlin: Gruben.

Muller, G. E. (1903). *Die gesichtspunkte und die tatsachen der psycho-physischen methodik*. Strassburg: Bergmann.

Muller, G. E. (1911). Zur analyse der gedachtnistatigkeit und des vorstellungsverlaufes. *Zeitschrift fur Psychologie Erganzungsband*, No. 5. (Also, see 1913, No. 8; 1917, No. 9.)

Muller, G. E. (1912). Uber die lokalization der visuellen vorstellungsbilder. *Berlin International Kongress fur Experimentelle Psychologie, 5*, 118–22.

Muller, G. E. (1913). Neue versuche mit Ruckle. *Zeitschrift fur Psychologie, 67*, 193–213.

Muller, G. E. (1935). Contribution to eidetic imagery. *Zeitschrift fur Psychologie, 134*, 1–24.

Muller, G. E., & Schumann, F. (1894). Experimentelle beitrage zur untersuchung des gedachtnisses. *Zeitschrift fur Psychologie, 6*, 81–190, 257–339.

Muller, H. K. (1928). Die beobachtung von tiefen effekten bei die binokularen bewegungnachbildern. *Zeitschrift fur Sinnesphysiologie, 59*, 157–65.

Muller, J. (1826). *Uber die phantastischen gesichtserscheinungen*. Coblenz: Holscher.

Murray, E. (1906). Peripheral and central factors in memory images of visual form and color. *American Journal of Psychology, 17*, 227–47.

Myers, A. C. (Ed.) (1987). *The Eerdmans Bible dictionary*. Grand Rapids, MI: Eerdmans.

Myers, F.W.H. (1887). Automatic writing III. *Proceedings of the Society for Psychical Research, 4*, 209–61.

Myslivecek, Z. (1931). Contribution to verbal-auditory hallucinations. *Revue Neurologii a Psychiatrii, 28*, 317–31.

Naumova, V. V. (1934). Acoustic hallucinations and acoustic eidetism. *Sovetskaya Psikhonevrologiya, 6*, 129–30.

Needham, J. G. (1934a). The time-error as a function of continued experimentation. *American Journal of Psychology, 46*, 558–67.

Needham, J. G. (1934b). The time-error in comparison judgments. *Psychological Bulletin, 31*, 229–43.

Needham, J. G. (1935). The effect of the time interval upon the time-error at different intensive levels. *Journal of Experimental Psychology, 18*, 530–43.

*New American Standard Bible: Study Bible*. (1999). Grand Rapids, MI: Zondervan.

*New Encyclopaedia Britannica, Macropaedia.* (1997). Chicago: Encyclopaedia Britannica, Inc.

Newpher, J. D. (1958). Man and the image of God. Unpublished doctoral dissertation, Temple University.

Neymeyer, H. (1956). Uber pathologische eidetismen. *Psychiatrie, Neurologie und Medizinische Psychologie, 8,* 234–57.

Noll, A. (1926). Versuche uber nachbilder. *Psychologische Forschung, 8,* 25–29.

Nussbaum, K. (1974). Abnormal mental phenomena in the prophets. *Journal of Religion and Health, 3,* 194–200.

Nussbaum, M. C. (1978). *Aristotle's De motu animalium.* Princeton, NJ: Princeton University Press.

Ogden, R. M. (1913). Experimental criteria for differentiating memory and imagination in projected visual images. *Psychological Review, 20,* 378–410.

Ogden, R. M. (1917). Some experiments on the consciousness of meaning. *Titchener Commemorative Volume, 1,* 79–101.

Ogden, R. M. (1951). Oswald Kulpe and the Wurzburg school. *American Journal of Psychology, 64,* 4–19.

Ohwaki, Y. (1936). *Eidetic imagery of school children.* Tokyo: Toen-Syobo.

Ohwaki, Y., Kaiwa, T., & Kaketa, K. (1934). Psycho-medical investigation on the eidetic disposition among Japanese children. I. *Tohoku Psychologica Folia, 2,* 57–128.

Ohwaki, Y., Kaiwa, T., & Kaketa, K. (1936). Psycho-medical investigation on the eidetic disposition among Japanese children. II. *Tohoku Psychologica Folia, 4,* 17–50.

Ohwaki, Y., & Kihara, T. (1953). A new research on the so-called "Bocci image." *Tohoku Psychologica Folia, 13,* 157–80.

Olasz, P. (1936). Eidetics in childhood and puberty. *Vigilia, 2,* 94–98.

Olsen, V. N. (1988). *Man, the image of God: The divine design, the human distortion.* Washington, DC: Review/Herald Publication Association.

O'Neill, H. (1933/1934). *Eidetic ability: A detailed study of twenty-three eidetikers.* Washington, DC: The Catholic Education Press.

O'Neill, H., & Rauth, J. (1934). Eidetic imagery. *Catholic University of America Educational Research Monographs, 8,* No. 2.

Osgood, C. E. (1953). *Method and theory in experimental psychology.* New York: Oxford University Press.

Ostrowski, W. J. (1934). *The eidetic imagery of Stanislaus Wyspianski.* Warsaw: D. K. Polskiej.

Oswald, I. (1957). After-images from retina and brain. *Quarterly Journal of Experimental Psychology, 9,* 88–100.

Otis, A. S. (1920). Do we think in words? Behaviorist versus introspective conceptions. *Psychological Review, 27,* 399–419.

Paivio, A. (1971/1979). *Imagery and verbal processes.* New York: Holt, Rinehart & Winston/Hillsdale, NJ: Erlbaum.

Pankow, G. (1955). A visual "primitive reaction" of a paranoid female patient. *Psychotherapie Psychosomatik Medizinische Psychologie, 5,* 19–29.

Parinaud, H. (1882). Du siege cerebral des images accidentelles ou consecutives. *Gazette des Hopitaux, 55,* 459–63.

Pasquasy, R. (1947). Eidetic imagery in "Le Grand Meaulnes." *Cahiers de Pedagogie de l'Universite de Liege, 7,* 102–9.

Pavlov, I. (1927). *Conditioned reflexes.* New York: Dover.

Pear, T. H. (1920). Is thinking merely the action of language mechanisms? (III.). *British Journal of Psychology, 11,* 71–80.

Pear, T. H. (1921). The intellectual respectability of muscular skill. *British Journal of Psychology, 12,* 163–80.

Pear, T. H. (1923). Imagery and mentality. *British Journal of Psychology, 14,* 291–99.

Pear, T. H. (1925a). Modern investigations of mental imagery. *Nature, 115,* 853–55.

Pear, T. H. (1925b). Privileges and limitations of visual imagery. *British Journal of Psychology, 15,* 363–73.

Pear, T. H. (1927a). Recent investigations on visual imagery, with special reference to hallucinations. *Journal of Mental Science, 73,* 195–99.

Pear, T. H. (1927b). The relevance of visual imagery to the process of thinking. *British Journal of Psychology, 18,* 1–14.

Pearson, K. (1896). Regression, heredity, and panmixia. *Philosophical Transactions, 187A,* 253–318.

Peck, L., & Hodges, A. B. (1937a). A study of racial differences in eidetic imagery of preschool children. *Journal of Genetic Psychology, 51,* 141–61.

Peck, L., & Hodges, A. B. (1937b). A study of the eidetic imagery of young Negro children. *Journal of Negro Education, 6,* 601–10.

Peck, L., & Walling, R. (1935). A preliminary study of the eidetic imagery of preschool children. *Journal of Genetic Psychology, 47,* 168–92.

Pedersen, S. (1954). Eidetics, obsessions, and modern art. *American Imago, 11,* 341–62.

Peers, E. A. (1913). Imagery in imaginative literature. *Journal of Experimental Pedagogy, 2,* 278–84.

Peillaube, E. (1910). *Les images: Essai sur la memoire et l'imagination.* Paris: Riviere et Cie.

Perky, C. W. (1910). An experimental study of imagination. *American Journal of Psychology, 21,* 422–52.

Petty, M. C. (1939). An experimental study of certain factors influencing reading readiness. *Journal of Educational Psychology, 30,* 215–30.

Peuckert, W. (1939). Der zweite leib. *Niederdeutsche Zeitschrift fur Volkskunde, 17,* 174–97.

Pflugfelder, G. (1948). Psychological analysis of a case of inherent deficiency in reading and writing. *Monatsschrift fur Psychiatrie und Neurologie, 115,* 55–79.

Pierce, A. H. (1907). Gustatory audition: A hitherto undescribed variety of synaesthesia. *American Journal of Psychology, 18,* 341–52.

Pierce, A. H. (1915). Imagery illusions. The non-visual character of the proofreader's illusion. *Psychological Bulletin, 12,* 1–9.

Pieron, H. (1910). *L'evolution de la memoire.* Paris: Flanmarion.

Pinelli, M. (1939). Contribution to research on visual eidetic images among the mentally abnormal. *Rivista di Psichologia Normale e Patologica, 35,* 255–59.

Pisk, G. (1935). The question of pseudohallucinations accompanying schizophrenia and their relations to eidetic capacity. *Monatsschrift fur Psychiatrie und Neurologie, 92,* 150–56.

Pitkin, W. B. (1906). Reasons for the slight esthetic value of the "lower senses." *Psychological Review, 13,* 363–77.

Popov, E. A. (1934). Visual hallucinations and visual eidetism in delirium tremens. *Sovetskaya Psikhonevrologiya, 6,* 126–28.

Porteous, N. W. (1962/1986). Image of God. In G. A. Butterick (Ed.), *The interpreter's dictionary of the Bible.* Nashville, TN: Abingdon Press.

Pratt, C. C. (1933). The time-error in psychophysical judgments. *American Journal of Psychology, 45,* 292–97.

Prentice, W.C.H. (1947). The relation of distance to the apparent size of figural after-effects. *American Journal of Psychology, 60,* 617–23.

Prentiss, D. W., & Morgan, F. P. (1895). *Anhalonium Lewinii* (Mescal buttons): A study of the drug with especial reference to its physiological action upon man, with report of experiments. *Therapeutic Gazatte, 9,* 577–85.

Purdy, D. M. (1936). Eidetic imagery and plasticity of perception. *Journal of General Psychology, 15,* 437–54.

Pylyshyn, Z. W. (1973). What the mind's eye tells the mind's brain: A critique of mental imagery. *Psychological Bulletin, 80,* 1–25.

Pylyshyn, Z. W. (1981). The imagery debate: Analogue media versus tacit knowledge. *Psychological Review, 88,* 16–45.

Quercy, P. (1925). Les eidetiques. *Journal de Psychologie, 22,* 801–11.

Quercy, P. (1926). Recherches sur l'eidetisme. *Journal de Psychologie, 23,* 702–22.

Quercy, P. (1927). Auto-observation d'hallucinations visuelles. *Journal de Psychologie, 24,* 520–31.

Quercy, P. (1937). *Hallucinations.* Paris: Alcan.

Rachofsky, L. M. (1918). Speed of presentation and ease of recall in the Knox cube test. *Psychological Bulletin, 15,* 61–64.

Rauth, J. E., & Sinnott, J. J. (1937). A new eidetic phenomenon. *Child Development, 8,* 112–13.

Read, C. (1908). On the difference between percepts and images. *British Journal of Psychology, 2,* 323–37.

Reber, A. S. (1995). *The Penguin dictionary of psychology.* 2d ed. New York: Penguin Books.

Reed, H. B. (1916). The existence and function of inner speech in thought processes. *Journal of Experimental Psychology, 1,* 365–92.

Rexroad, C. N. (1928). Eye–movements and visual after-images. *American Journal of Psychology, 40,* 426–33.

Rieffert, J. (1912). Uber die objektivierung und subjektivierung von sinnes-eindrucken. *Berichte uber den Kongress fur Experimentelle Psychologie, 5,* 245.

Riekel, A. (1950). Eidetics: Sensorial memory and its investigation. *Monograficas Psicologicas, Universidad de Buenos Aires, 54,* No. 2.

Riekel, A. (1951). *Eidetica; La memoria sensorial y su investigacion.* Buenos Aires: Universidad de Buenos Aires Press.

Rieti, E. (1932). New contribution to the study of the eidetic visual disposition in the mentally deranged. *Archivio Italiano di Psicologia, 10,* 112–17.

Rieti, E. (1933). Visual eidetic tendencies in children afflicted with mental diseases. *Scritti Onore Kiesow, 1,* 16–26.

Riggs, L. A., & Karwoski, T. (1934). Synaesthesia. *British Journal of Psychology, 25,* 29–41.

Robertson, V. M., & Fry, G. A. (1937). After-images observed in complete darkness. *American Journal of Psychology, 49,* 265–76.

Robinson, A. (1920). Is thinking merely the action of language mechanisms? (IV.). *British Journal of Psychology, 11,* 81–86.

Roeckelein, J. E. (1996). Citation of *laws* and *theories* in textbooks across 112 years of psychology. *Psychological Reports, 79,* 979–98.

Roeckelein, J. E. (1998). *Dictionary of theories, laws, and concepts in psychology.* Westport, CT: Greenwood Press.

Roeckelein, J. E. (2000). *The concept of time in psychology: A resource book and annotated bibliography.* Westport, CT: Greenwood Press.

Roessler, F. (1928). Verbreitung und erscheinungsweise subjektiver optischer anschauungsbilder bei knaben und madchen im alter von 6–10 jahren. *Zeitschrift fur Angewandte Psychologie, 43,* 197–371.

Rogers, A. S. (1917). An analytic study of visual perceptions. *American Journal of Psychology, 28,* 519–36.

Rogers, A. S. (1923). Auditory and tactual perceptions: The role of the image. *American Journal of Psychology, 34,* 250–66.

Rorschach, H. (1921). *Psychodiagnostics.* New York: Grune & Stratton.

Rosenow, C. (1918). The genesis of the image. *Psychological Review, 25,* 297–304.

Rosett, J. (1939). *The mechanism of thought, imagery, and hallucination.* New York: Columbia University Press.

Ross, W. D. (Ed.) (1931). *The works of Aristotle translated into English.* Oxford, UK: Oxford University Press.

Ruckmick, C. A. (1913). Role of kinaesthesis in the perception of rhythm. *American Journal of Psychology, 24,* 359–75.

Rutten, T. (1940). Report on the activities of the Department of Psychology in the R. C. University, Nijmegen, Holland. *Acta Psychologica (The Hague), 5,* 143–56.

Ruttmann, W. J. (1938). The value of E. R. Jaensch's psychological anthropology for education. *Zeitschrift fur Paedagogische Psychologie und Experimentelle Paedagogik, 39,* 273–80.

Ryken, L., Wilhoit, J., Longman, T., & Wilhoit, J. C. (Eds.) (1998). *Dictionary of biblical imagery.* Grove, IL: Inter-Varsity Press.

Sacristan, J., & Germain, J. (1933). Eidetic constitution and general intelligence. *Medicina del Trabajo e Higiene Industrial, 4,* 307–10.

Saltzman, S., & Machover, S. (1952). An inquiry into eidetic imagery with particular relevance to visual hallucinations. *American Journal of Psychiatry, 108,* 740–48.

Samuels, M., & Samuels, N. (1975). *Seeing with the mind's eye: The history, techniques, and uses of visualization.* New York: Random House.

Sandor, B. (1932). Die gedachtnistatigkeit und arbeitsweise von rechenkunstlern. *Charakter, 1,* 47–50.

Scharnke, A. (1927). *The relations between eidetic phenomena and sensory illusions.* Berlin: O. Elsner.

Schaub, A. de Vries (1911). On the intensity of images. *American Journal of Psychology, 22,* 346–68.

Scheidemann, N. V. (1933). A novel experiment with the negative afterimage. *American Journal of Psychology, 45,* 361–62.

Schiel, W. (1934). The significance of retentive and elaborative memorial behavior for the structure of the child of 11 to 12 years. *Zeitschrift fur Psychologie, 132,* 133–75.

Schilder, P. (1926). Psychoanalyse und eidetik. *Zeitschrift fur Sexualwissenschaft, 13,* 56–63. (Also, see *Zeitschrift fur die Gesamte Neurologie und Psychiatrie* [1930], *128,* 784–91.)

Schmeieng, K. (1935). "Second sight" as an ethnological and psychological (Gestalt and eidetic) problem. *Zeitschrift fur Angewandte Psychologie, 48,* 113–23.

Schmeieng, K. (1936a). Eidetic studies on the problem of "second sight." *Zeitschrift fur Psychologie, 139,* 212–80. (Also, see *Niederdeutsche Zeitschrift fur Volkskunde* [1938], *16,* 22–28.)

Schmeieng, K. (1936b). Emotion and volition in eidetic and "occult" experiences. *Bericht uber den Kongreses der Deutschen Gesellschaft fur Psychologie, 6,* 196–200.

Schmeieng, K. (1937). Justice and eidetics. *Monatsschrift fur Kriminalbiologie und Strafrechtsreform, 28,* 113–20.

Schmidt, O. (1937). *Toward the revision of eidetic theory: A consideration with critical objections.* Kiel: Voss.

Schmitz, K. (1930). Uber das anschauliche denken und die frage einer korrelation zwischen eidetischer anlage und intelligenz. *Zeitschrift fur Psychologie, 114,* 289–97.

Schmulling, W. (1927/1928). Aufdeckung latenter eidetischer phanomene und des integrierten typus mit der intermittenzmethode. *Zeitschrift fur Psychologie, 104,* 233; *105,* 89.

Schultz, D. (1981). *A history of modern psychology.* 3rd ed. New York: Academic Press.

Schultze-Niemann, M. (1940). Sound-eidetic phenomena in a neurotic child and its treatment by autogenous training. *Zentralblatt fur Psychotherapie, 12,* 241–48.

Schumacher, W. (1928). The significance of eidetic capacities in children for education. *Die Hilfsschule, 21,* 99–111.

Schumacher, W. (1930). Eidetische fahigkeiten und aufsatzleistung. *Zeitschrift fur Angewandte Psychologie, 37,* 1–55.

Schumacher, W. (1931). Eidetic imagery in children and adolescents. *Die Hilfsschule, 24,* 324–50.

Schwab, G. (1924). Vorlaufige mitteilung uber untersuchungen zum wesen der subjektiven anschauungsbilder. *Psychologie Forschung, 5,* 321–30.

Scola, F. (1925). Uber das verhaltnis von vorstellungsbild, anschauungsbild, und nachbild. *Archiv fur die Gesamte Psychologie, 52,* 297–312.

Scola, F. (1927). Zur theorie der eidetischen phanomene. *Eighth International Congress of Psychology.* Groningen, Germany: Noordhoff.

Scott, W. D. (1910). Personal differences in suggestibility. *Psychological Review, 17,* 147–54.

Scripture, E. W. (1896). Sensation or image? *Science, 3,* 762–63.

Sechrist, A. (1973). *Dictionary of Bible imagery.* New York: Swedenborg Foundation.

Secor, W. B. (1900). Visual reading: A study in mental imagery. *American Journal of Psychology, 11,* 225–36.

Segal, J. (1908). Uber den reproduktionstypen und das reproduzieren von vorstellungen. *Archiv fur die Gesamte Psychologie, 12,* 124–345.

Segal, S. J., & Gordon, P.-E. (1969). The Perky effect revisited: Blocking of visual signals by imagery. *Perceptual and Motor Skills, 28,* 791–97.

Segal, S. J., & Nathan, S. (1964). The Perky effect: Incorporation of an external stimulus into an imagery experience under placebo and control conditions. *Perceptual and Motor Skills, 18,* 385–95.

Shepherd, N. (1959). Man in the image of God. Unpublished master's thesis, Westminster Theological Seminary.

Shimberg, M. (1924). The role of kinaesthesis in meaning. *American Journal of Psychology, 35,* 167–84.

Shipley, T. (1958). The horopter in eidetic subjects. *Psychological Bulletin,* 55, 171–75.

Shuey, A. M. (1924). The flight of colors. *American Journal of Psychology,* 35, 559–82.

Shuey, A. M. (1926). The effect of varying periods of adaptation on the flight of colors. *American Journal of Psychology, 37,* 528–37.

Sidis, B. (1908). The doctrine of primary and secondary sensory elements. *Psychological Review, 15,* 44–68, 106–21.

Siebert, K. (1929). Plastisch-anschauliche gedachtnisbilder. Ein beitrag zur psychologie der halluzinationen und der eidetischen phanomene. *Archiv fur die Gesamte Psychologie, 72,* 517–44.

Siipola, E. M., & Hayden, S. D. (1965). Exploring eidetic imagery among the retarded. *Perceptual and Motor Skills, 21,* 275–86.

Simpson, R. M. (1922). Creative imagination. *American Journal of Psychology, 33,* 234–43.

Singleton, C. M. (1954). Imagery: Measurement and analysis. Unpublished doctoral dissertation, Boston University.

Slaughter, J. W. (1902). A preliminary study of the behavior of mental images. *American Journal of Psychology, 13,* 526–49.

Smith, G.J.W. (1949). *Psychological studies in twin differences with reference to after-image and eidetic phenomena as well as more general personality characteristics.* Lund: Sweden: Gleerup.

Smith, M. (1958). The image of God. *Bulletin of the John Rylands Library, 40,* 473–512.

Smith, T. (1904). The psychology of daydreams. *American Journal of Psychology, 15,* 465–88.

Soules, F. (1968). A historical survey of the doctrine of the image of God in man. Unpublished master's thesis, Columbia Theological Seminary.

Spaier, A. (1914). L'image mentale d'apres les experiences d'introspection. *Revue Philosophique, 77,* 283–304.

Springer, I. (1914). Ideational types in arithmetic. *Journal of Educational Psychology, 5,* 418–22.

Stetson, R. H. (1896). Types of imagination. *Psychological Review, 3,* 398–411.

Stoddard, W.H.B. (1904). The psychology of hallucinations. *Journal of Mental Science, 6,* 25–32.

Stott, L. H. (1935). Time-order errors in the discrimination of short tonal durations. *Journal of Experimental Psychology, 18,* 741–66.

Stratton, G. M. (1897). Vision without inversion of the retinal image. *Psychological Review, 4,* 341–60.

Stratton, G. M. (1902). Eye-movements and the aesthetics of visual form. *Philosophical Studies, 20,* 336–59.

Stratton, G. M. (1907). Eye-movements and visual direction. *Psychological Bulletin, 4,* 155–56.

Stratton, G. M. (1917). The mnemonic feat of the "Shass Pollak." *Psychological Review, 24,* 244–47.

Stromeyer, C. F. (1970). Eidetic images. *Psychology Today,* November, 76–79.

Stromeyer, C. F., & Psotka, J. (1970). The detailed texture of eidetic images. *Nature, 225,* 346–49.

Strong, J. (1990). *The new Strong's exhaustive concordance of the Bible.* Nashville, TN: Thomas Nelson.

Sturm, M. (1931). A study of the direction in the movement after-image. *Psychologische Forschung, 14,* 269–93.

Sullivan, A. H. (1921). An experimental study of kinaesthetic imagery. *American Journal of Psychology, 32,* 54–80.

Sumner, F. C., & Watts, F. P. (1936). Rivalry between uniocular negative after-images and the vision of the other eye. *American Journal of Psychology, 48,* 109–16.

Susukita, T. (1937). On memory images of a perceptual character. *Tohoku Psychologica Folia, 5,* 1–20.

Swindle, P. F. (1916). Positive after-images of long duration. *American Journal of Psychology, 27,* 324–34.

Swindle, P. F. (1917). Visual, cutaneous, and kinaesthetic ghosts. *American Journal of Psychology, 28,* 349–72.

Sylvester, R. H. (1913). The mental imagery of the blind. *Psychological Bulletin, 10,* 210–11.

Szily, A. von (1905). Bewegungsnachbild und bewegungskontrast. *Zeitschrift fur Psychologie und Physiologie der Sinnesorgange, 38,* 81–154.

Talbot, E. B. (1896). An attempt to train the visual memory. *American Journal of Psychology, 8,* 414–17.

Tarde, G. (1903). *The laws of imitation.* New York: Holt.

Teasdale, H. (1934). A quantitative study of eidetic imagery. *British Journal of Educational Psychology, 4,* 56–74.

Thacker, L. H. (1937). An experimental study of eidetic imagery. Unpublished master's thesis, Tulane University of Lousiana, New Orleans.

Thale, T., Gabrio, B. W., & Salomon, K. (1950). Hallucination and imagery induced by mescaline. *American Journal of Psychiatry, 106,* 686–91.

Thalman, W. (1921). The after-effect of seen movement when the whole visual field is filled by a moving stimulus. *American Journal of Psychology, 32,* 429–41.

Thalman, W. (1922). The after-effect of movement in the sense of touch. *American Journal of Psychology, 33,* 268–76.

Thomas, N.J.T. (1994). Review of: Michael Tye's "The imagery debate." *The Journal of Mind and Behavior, 15,* 291–94.

Thomas, N.J.T. (1997). Mental imagery. In E. N. Zalta (Ed.), *Stanford encyclopedia of philosophy*. Palo Alto, CA: Stanford University Press.

Thomas, N.J.T. (2001). Mental imagery, Philosophical issues about. In L. Nadel (Ed.), *Encyclopedia of cognitive science*. New York: Macmillan/Nature.

Thompson, E. R. (1914). An inquiry into some questions connected with imagery in dreams. *British Journal of Psychology, 7*, 300–318.

Thompson, H. B., & Gordon, K. (1907). A study of after-images on the peripheral retina. *Psychological Review, 14*, 122–35.

Thomson, G. H. (1920). Is thinking merely the action of language mechanisms? (II.). *British Journal of Psychology, 11*, 63–70.

Thorndike, E. L. (1907). *The elements of psychology*. New York: Seiler.

Thorndike, E. L. (1931). *Human learning*. New York: Appleton.

Titchener, E. B. (1896). *An outline of psychology*. New York: Macmillan.

Titchener, E. B. (1901). *Experimental psychology: I. Qualitative experiments; II. Instructor's manual*. New York: Macmillan.

Titchener, E. B. (1909). *Lectures on the experimental psychology of the thought processes*. New York: Macmillan.

Titchener, E. B. (1913). Discussion: Professor Martin on the Perky experiments. *American Journal of Psychology, 24*, 124–31.

Titchener, E. B. (1914). A demonstration of "tied-images." *American Journal of Psychology, 25*, 300.

Titchener, E. B. (1915). *Beginner's psychology*. New York: Macmillan.

Titchener, E. B. (1918). *A beginner's psychology*. 2d ed. New York: Macmillan.

Tolman, E. C. (1917). More concerning the temporal relations of meaning and imagery. *Psychological Review, 24*, 114–38.

Toltschinsky, A. (1914a). Recherches sur la forme des champs de discrimination tactile. *Comptes Rendus Societe de Biologique, 76*, 82–83.

Toltschinsky, A. (1914b). Recherches topographiques sur la discrimination tactile. *L'Annee Psychologie, 20*, 160–81. (Also, see *Psychological Bulletin* [1914], *11*, 238.)

Town, C. H. (1906). The kinaesthetic element in endophasia and auditory hallucination. *American Journal of Psychology, 17*, 127–36.

Town, C. H. (1914). The contribution of visual imagery to verbal thought: A comparative study of seeing and blind subjects. *Illinois Medical Journal, 26*, 354–58.

Tripp, E. (1926). Observations sur l'image eidetique. *Archiv de Psychologie, 20*, 53–72.

Troland, L. T. (1917). Preliminary note: The influence of changes of illumination upon after-images. *American Journal of Psychology, 28*, 497–503.

Tsanoff, R. A. (1914). On the psychology of poetic construction: An experimental method. *American Journal of Psychology, 25*, 528–37.

Tye, M. (1991). *The imagery debate*. Cambridge, MA: M.I.T. Press.

Urbantschitsch, V. (1903). Uber die beeinflussung subjektiver gesichtsemp-findunden. *Archiv fur die Gesamte Physiologie, 94,* 347.

Urbantschitsch, V. (1905). Uber sinnesempfingungen und gedachtnisbilder. *Archiv fur die Gesamte Physiologie, 110,* 437.

Urbantschitsch, V. (1907). *Uber subjektive optische anschauungsbilder.* Leipzig: Deuticke.

Urbantschitsch, V. (1908). *Uber subjektive horerscheinungen und subjektive optische anschauungsbilder.* Wien: Deuticke.

Urbantschitsch, V. (1918). Uber unbewusste gesichtseindrucke und deren auftreten im subjektiven optischen anschauungsbilde. *Zeitschrift fur die Gesamte Neurologie und Psychiatrie, 41,* 170–84.

Valentine, C. W. (1923). The function of images in the appreciation of poetry. *British Journal of Psychology, 14,* 164–91.

Van der Noot, L. (1910). Role des sens dans la memorisation chez les enfants. *Revue Psychologie, 3,* 335–42.

Vernon, P. E. (1930). Synaesthesia in music. *Psyche, 10,* 22–39.

Vine, W. E. (Ed.) (1981). *Vine's expository dictionary of Old and New Testament words.* Old Tappan, NJ: Revell.

Vries, A. de (1974). *Dictionary of symbols and imagery.* Amsterdam: North-Holland.

Wachtel, J. (1932). Eidetic images and after-images in mirrored space. *Kwartnalnik Psychologiczny, 3,* 439–46.

Wachtel, J. (1934). Experiments on eidetic disposition in adults. *Kwartalnik Psychologiczny, 5,* 394–401.

Wachtel, J. (1935). A world of new observations: Eidetism and its problems for pedagogy. *Nasza Ksiegarnia (Warsaw), 5,* 1–157.

Wakefield, J. (1968). Man as the image of God according to Saint Thomas Aquinas. Unpublished master's thesis, Marquette University.

Walker, W. (1927). On processes of adaptation in young people and their relation to the phenomena of transformation. *Zeitschrift fur Psychologie, 103,* 323–83.

Walters, A. (1942). A genetic study of geometrical-optical illusions. *Genetic Psychology Monographs, 25,* 101–55.

Walters, P. O. (1939). An experimental study of certain factors influencing eidetic imagery. Unpublished master's thesis, University of Texas at Austin.

Walters, V. W., & Gundlach, R. H. (1931). Eye-movements and visual after-images. *American Journal of Psychology, 43,* 288–89.

Ward, J. (1918). *Psychological principles.* Cambridge, UK: Cambridge University Press.

Warren, H. C. (1921). Some unusual visual after-effects. *Psychological Review, 28,* 453–60.

Warren, H. C. (1929). A delayed visual after-effect. *American Journal of Psychology, 41,* 684.

Washburn, M. F. (1899). Subjective colors and the after-image. *Mind, 8,* 25–34.

Washburn, M. F. (1914). Test for control of visual imagery. *American Journal of Psychology, 25,* 293–95.

Washburn, M. F. (1916). *Movement and mental imagery.* New York: Macmillan.

Washburn, M. F., Hatt, E., & Holt, E. B. (1923a). Affective sensitiveness in poets and in scientific students. *American Journal of Psychology, 34,* 105–7.

Washburn, M. F., Hatt, E., & Holt, E. B. (1923b). The correlation of a test of control of visual imagery with estimated geometrical ability. *American Journal of Psychology, 34,* 103–5.

Washburn, M. F., & Smith, D. L. (1933). Stereoscopic binocular fusion in the original impression and in the negative after-image. *American Journal of Psychology, 45,* 320–21.

Watson, J. B. (1919/1929). *Psychology from the standpoint of a Behaviorist.* Philadelphia, PA: Lippincott.

Watson, J. B. (1920). Is thinking merely the action of language mechanisms? (V.). *British Journal of Psychology, 11,* 87–104.

Watson, R. I. (1978). *The great psychologists.* 4th ed. Philadelphia: Lippincott.

Watt, H. J. (1905). Experimentelle beitrage zu einer theorie des denkens. *Archiv fur die Gesamte Psychologie, 4,* 289–436.

Weber, R. (1913). Reverie et images. *Archiv de Psychologie, 13,* 179–80.

Weber, R. (1915). Voix et visions. *Archiv de Psychologie, 15,* 314–16.

Weed, S., Hallam, F., & Phinney, E. (1896). A study of the dream-consciousness. *American Journal of Psychology, 7,* 405–11.

Weemes, J. (1632). *The portraiture of the image of God in man.* London: T. Cotes.

Weil, H. (1930). Studies in testimony of integrated personality types. *Zeitschrift fur Angewandte Psychologie, 37,* 74–98.

Weil, M., & Nellen, M. (1910). Contribution a l'etude des images chez l'enfant. *Revue Psychologie, 3,* 343–48.

Weiskrantz, L. (1950). An unusual case of after-imagery following fixation of an "imaginary" visual pattern. *Quarterly Journal of Experimental Psychology, 2,* 170–75.

Weiss, A. P. (1922). Behavior and the central nervous system. *Psychological Review, 29,* 329–43.

Weld, H. P. (1912). An experimental study of musical enjoyment. *American Journal of Psychology, 23,* 245–308.

Weller, A. (1931). Zur geschichte und kritik der synaesthesie-forschung. *Archiv fur die Gesamte Psychologie, 79,* 325–84.

Wertham, F. (1930). Eidetic phenomena and psychopathology. *Archives of Neurology and Psychiatry, 24,* 809–21.

Wheeler, O. A. (1923). An analysis of literary appreciation. *British Journal of Psychology, 13,* 229–42.

Wheeler, R. H. (1920). Visual phenomena in the dreams of a blind subject. *Psychological Review, 27,* 313–22. (Also, see "The synaesthesia of a blind subject." *University of Oregon Publications* [1920], *1,* No. 5, 1–61.)

Wheeler, R. H. (1922). The development of meaning. *American Journal of Psychology, 33,* 223–33.

Wheeler, R. H., & Cutsforth, T. D. (1921). The role of synaesthesia in learning. *Journal of Experimental Psychology, 4,* 448–68.

Wheeler, R. H., & Cutsforth, T. D. (1922a). Synaesthesia, a form of perception. *Psychological Review, 29,* 212–20.

Wheeler, R. H., & Cutsforth, T. D. (1922b). Synaesthesia and meaning. *American Journal of Psychology, 33,* 361–84.

Wheeler, R. H., & Cutsforth, T. D. (1928). Synaesthesia in judging and choosing. *Journal of General Psychology, 1,* 497–519.

Whipple, G. M. (1900). Two cases of synaesthesia. *American Journal of Psychology, 11,* 377–404.

Whipple, G. M. (1901/1902). An analytic study of the memory image and the process of judgment in the discrimination of clangs and tones. I., II., III., IV. *American Journal of Psychology, 12,* 409–57; *13,* 219–68.

Whitaker, E. (1942). Unconscious or rare psychic manifestations and spiritism. *Revista de Neurologia e Psiquiatria de Sao Paulo, 8,* 1–10.

Wilhelm, E. (1927). *Die bedeutung der eidetischen forschung fur erziehung und unterricht.* Leipzig: J. Klinkhardt.

Wohlgemuth, A. (1911). On the after-effect of seen movement. *British Journal of Psychology Monograph Supplement, 1,* 1–117.

Woodrow, H. (1935). The effect of practice upon time-order errors in the comparison of temporal intervals. *Psychological Review, 42,* 127–52.

Woodrow, H., & Stott, L. H. (1936). The effects of practice on positive time-order errors. *Journal of Experimental Psychology, 19,* 694–705.

Woods, E. L. (1915). An experimental analysis of the process of recognizing. *American Journal of Psychology, 26,* 313–87.

Woodworth, R. S. (1908). The consciousness of relation. In R. S. Woodworth (Ed.), *Essays philosophical and psychological in honour of William James.* New York: Columbia University Press.

Woodworth, R. S. (1915). A revision of imageless thought. *Psychological Review, 22,* 1–27.

Woodworth, R. S. (1938). *Experimental psychology.* New York: Henry Holt.

Woodworth, R. S., & Schlosberg, H. (1965). *Experimental psychology.* Revised edition. New York: Holt, Rinehart and Winston.

Wundt, W. (1897). *Outlines of psychology.* New York: Macmillan.

Wundt, W. (1907). Scheinexperimentelle. *Psychologische Studien, 3,* No. 4.

Wundt, W. (1908). Kritiche nachlese zur ausfragemethode. *Archiv fur die Gesamte Psychologie, 11,* 445–59.

Wynkoop, M. (1952). A biblical study of man in his relationship to the image of God. Unpublished bachelor of divinity thesis, Western Evangelical Seminary.

Yates, F. A. (1966). *The art of memory.* London: Routledge and Kegan Paul.

Young, R. (1982). *Young's analytical concordance to the Bible.* Nashville, TN: Thomas Nelson.

Zagorovskii, P. L. (1929). The eidetic school and problems of child psychology. *Zhurnal Psikhologii, Pedologii, i Psikhotekhniki, 2,* 83–92.

Zaworski, T. (1947). Acoustical eidetic representations. *Kwartalnik Psychologiczny, 13,* 156–203.

Zeman, H. (1925). Verbreitung und grade der eidetischen anlage. *Zeitschrift fur Psychologie, 96,* 208–26.

Zeman, H. (1929). The science of eidetic and its practical significance. *Die Quelle, 79,* 6–17, 171–76.

Zigler, M. J. (1920). An experimental study of visual form. *American Journal of Psychology, 31,* 273–80.

Zigler, M. J., & Northup, K. M. (1926). The tactual perception of form. *American Journal of Psychology, 37,* 391–97.

Zillig, M. (1922). Uber eidetische anlage und intelligenz. *Fortschrift der Psychologie, 5,* 293–317.

Zillig, M. (1930). Uber die padagogische bedeutung der eidetischen anlage. *Neue Padagogische Studien, 2,* 85–92.

Zillig, M. (1931). Uber eidetische anlage und jugendliche verwahrlosung. *Zeitschrift fur Psychologie, 122,* 205–30. (Also, see 1929, *112,* 302–24.)

Zimmerman, M. (1931). *Eidetik und schulunterricht.* Langensalza, Germany: H. Beyer & Sohne.

Ziolko, H. (1953). Zur bedeutung spontan-eidetischer erscheinungen in der psychiatrie. *Zeitschrift fur Psychotherapie, Psychosomatik, und Medizinische Psychologie, 3,* 171–78.

# Chapter 3

# Modern Theoretical Aspects, Applications, and Functions of Imagery

After fifty years of neglect during the heyday of Behaviorism, mental imagery is once again a topic of research in psychology. ... I have mentioned a problem arising from experiments on imagery and from introspection—that is, we have reason to think we have internal pictures. But we find none in the brain; so what do we make of our reasons to think there are internal pictures? This problem generates the dispute that this book is about. One side, the *pictorialist* side ... agrees that we don't literally have pictures in our brains, but ... nevertheless that our mental images represent in roughly the way that pictures represent. The other side, the *descriptionalist* side ... thinks of mental images as representing in the manner of some nonimagistic representations—namely, in the manner of language rather than pictures.

—N. Block, 1981

Just as imagery was swept out with the receding tide of the early mentalistic psychology of James, Wundt, and their followers, it was swept back in with the rise of cognitive psychology. ... The systematic results obtained in imagery experiments convinced researchers that there was something to the claim that humans have "mental images." ... [T]he role of imagery in information processing took a leap forward when researchers began to think about how one could program a computer to produce specific types of behavior. To program a computer to mimic imagery, one must specify an image representation with particular properties. ... As this method became increasingly popular, researchers soon realized that there were many ways to program a computer to mimic imagery. And this soon resulted in a series of debates about the nature of mental imagery representations.

—S. M. Kosslyn, 1994

## THE IMAGERY DEBATE AND IMAGERY THEORIES IN MODERN PSYCHOLOGY

In the last chapter, we discussed the premodern, or early, imagery debate(s) in philosophy and psychology that included issues such as consciousness, imagination, introspection, and imageless thought that took us up to the early twentieth century (cf. Horowitz, 1970/1978, pp. 63–76). During this early phase, investigators focused on a series of discussions concerning the best approaches, techniques, and rationales for explaining imagery. In this activity, philosophers and psychologists displayed their own unique ways of dealing with the issue of imagery, ranging from logical-rational bases to empirical-experimental emphases (cf. Kolers, 1987, p. 354). Following their hiatus from investigations of imagery for about fifty years (from the early 1900s up to about the 1960s), psychologists once again began to study and debate mental imagery issues. During the present modern era, Block (1981, p. 1) calls imagery "one of the hottest topics in cognitive science" that is based on a "truly spectacular body of experiments." Tye (1991) provides a philosopher's examination of the modern imagery debate, and discusses the two general groups of mental imagery theories: the *pictorialist* group that likens mental images to pictures, and the *descriptionalist* group that likens mental images to linguistic descriptions (cf. Block, 1981, p. 2; Kosslyn, 1980, pp. 11–28); and Kosslyn (1994, pp. 4–20) describes three phases of the modern imagery debate(s) (cf. Kosslyn, 1990, pp. 87–95): consideration of alternative mental representations, potential problems of methodology, and beyond behavioral results. Note that Kosslyn suggests that researchers have worked through the first two phases of the continuing debate and are now in the third and—he hopes—final phase; the subtitle of his 1994 book is *The Resolution of the Imagery Debate* (cf. Reisberg, Pearson, and Kosslyn [2003]).

It should be mentioned at this point that in any discussion of psychological theories of imagery, a potential problem exists concerning categorization. That is, what is meant by the term *psychological* becomes complicated, even confusing sometimes, in light of the present topic of imagery that, in itself, cuts across many discipline areas, often in subtle ways. For example, it is clear enough that the nonpsychological discipline of philosophy may be viewed as a separate field (assuming that psychology became separated from its "parent" philosophy in the late 1800s and began as a new field of scientific investigation characterized by its experimental approach and methodology, or new empirical "way of knowing"); however, inasmuch as the topic area of imagery is, essentially, a "cognitive" problem, it has been adopted by philosophy and many other extra-psychology disciplines (which frequently overlap with the science of psychology) that happen, also, to study "cognition" with their own special tools and techniques (e.g., linguistics, literature; computer science; physiology; neurology; physics/engineering; etc.). In this sense, then, the "problem (imagery) drives the discipline," rather than vice versa where the discipline may exclusively determine or dictate the problem. (For one philosopher's perspective on the cognitive role of imagery in psychology, its impact on imagery theory, and the issues over which one can be "for" or "against" mental images themselves, see Thomas [1989].) Kosslyn (1983, p. 205) reminds us that "although cognitive science is often regarded as a subfield of psychology, the questions it asks and the tools it uses to answer them come from areas as diverse as linguistics, philosophy, and artificial intelligence, as well as experimental psychology." Therefore, in accepting Kosslyn's approach for the present discussion, we may consider cognitive science—and its special study of the issue of imagery—to be a subfield of psychology, and all of the contributions of the extra-psychology disciplines concerning imagery and imagery-related phenomena to be subsumed further under the rubric *cognitive science*. Thus, the issue of imagery is distinctively a cognitive science issue that cuts across many extra-psychology disciplines, including chiefly contemporary psychology; as a practical consequence of this rationale, then, some extra-psychology theories of imagery may be subsumed under the present psychological imagery theories.

## The Imagery Controversy in Modern Psychology

Block (1981) edited a series of papers on mental imagery that included attempts to answer the general questions

- "Do images exist?"
- "Are images phenomenal?"
- "Are the mental representations involved in imagery similar to those involved in perception?"
- "Is there only a single kind of pictorial representation (the 'photographic fallacy')?"

- "Are there different types of descriptional representations as well as different types of pictorial representations?"
- "Is there a definitive resolution to the 'pictorial/descriptional' controversy or debate?"

Block (1981) observes that the modern debate in mental imagery is based on the dispute between the pictorialists—those researchers who argue that one's mental images represent things in approximately the same way that pictures represent things—and the descriptionalists—those who assert that mental images represent things involving some nonimagistic representations, mainly via language/linguistic components or processes. Block notes, in particular, that Dennett (1981a,b) and Pylyshyn (1981) take the descriptionalist position, whereas Fodor (1980, 1981) and Kosslyn, Pinker, Smith, and Shwartz (1981) hold the pictorialist position. Moreover, among other prominent researchers and writers, neither Brown and Herrnstein (1981) nor Schwartz (1981) take sides in the pictorialist-descriptionalist dispute. According to Block, both the pictorialists and the descriptionalists agree that there are mental representations, but the latter consider all mental representations to be descriptional, while the former consider that at least some mental representations/images are pictorial. Furthermore, all the major pictorialists are willing to allow that there are descriptional representations and, thus, they hold that there are at least two kinds of mental representations. Block (1981, pp 3–4) observes, also, that it is not always easy for one reading material on this issue/debate to grasp what is really at stake between the descriptionalists and the pictorialists. The question whether the representations of imagery are pictorial or descriptional is not wholly or directly an empirical question, but it is one of those issues where "everything is up for grabs," including the precise nature of the problem itself.

Block's (1981) own answer to the question "Do mental images exist?" is that the question actually is a conflation of several issues, none of which involves imagery in any important way (the difficulty is the vagueness/ambiguity that is inherent in the term *mental image*—it may denote experiences, internal/neural representations, or intentional objects). To the question "Are images epiphenomenal?" Block emphasizes the difference between the philosophers' use of the term *epiphenomena*—in the present context, mental images are just effects of brain states and never causes of

anything, and the psychologists' use of the term—that epiphenomena may have extraneous effects, for example, an epiphenomenal
occurrence of brain-writing may affect a neurophysiologist who
looks at it (and what makes an epiphenomenon epiphenomenal is
that it plays no causal role in the brain's information-processing activities—thought and reasoning would go on just as they would if
the epiphenomena were not present). Ultimately, Block argues that
the epiphenomenalism issue is a red herring—on some interpretations, it doesn't come to anything about which the disputants
really disagree; on other interpretations, it reduces to the
pictorialism-descriptionalism controversy (where, again, the difficulty lies in the ambiguity-vagueness of the term mental image).
Block (pp. 7–9) considers the term mental image in three ways (as
subjective experiences, as abstract entities, and as the internal/neu-
ral representations involved in imagery), and suggests, finally, that
one may avoid the inherent terminological confusion(s) in the term
mental image by simply adopting the convention of using it to
denote the internal representations involved in mental imagery (inasmuch as *both* the pictorialists and the descriptionalists accept the
notion of *internal representation*). Thus, one may talk *either* of
whether mental images are pictorial or descriptional, *or* of whether
the internal representations involved in mental imagery are pictorial or descriptional.

To the question "Are mental representations involved in imagery
similar to those involved in perception?" Block (1981, p. 10) notes
that the evidence from the experimental literature—to date—points
to the conclusion that the representations of imaging and perceiving
must be treated together as *either* both pictorial *or* both descriptional
(which, unfortunately, does not settle the issue of pictorialism versus
descriptionalism because one may still ask of *both* the representations
of imagery and perception whether they are pictorial or descriptional).
To the question "Is there only a single kind of pictorial representation?" Block suggest that there is a logical fallacy (the *photographic fallacy*) involved in the presupposition of only a *single* type (where one
may think not only of one, but of a variety of types of pictorial representations, for example, photographs versus stick figures,
that differ from one another in the extent to which they involve
"conventions"). Regarding the question "Is there a resolution to the
descriptional-pictorial controversy?" Block maintains that it is too early

in the debate to discuss a definitive resolution of the matter (cf. Kosslyn, 1994).

Brown and Herrnstein (1981) discuss and define the concepts of icon, contrast, metacontrast, attention, filtering, shadowing, image, mental rotation of images, isomorphism, and second-order isomorphism, as well as examine the relevant experimentation on these concepts as conducted by Atkinson and Shiffrin (1968), Moray (1970), Neisser (1967), Perky (1910), Shepard (1978b), and Sperling (1960), among others. Brown and Herrnstein observe that the most convincing experiments on the properties of imagery have usually been visual—even when stimuli are presented orally, participants may be able to call up a visual icon if the heard stimulus has an obvious visual translation (e.g., hearing a letter of the alphabet). However, according to Brown and Herrnstein, there are icons from all the sensory systems—at some level.

In discussing the nature of images, Dennett (1981a) points out the "trap" that the method of introspection presents to a critical analysis of mental imagery and recommends, at one place (p. 55), the abandonment of mental images altogether. Essentially, Dennett argues for the claim that mental images are descriptional (rather than pictorial) and asks whether mental images represent in virtue of resembling what they represent and, thus, deserve to be called images. Dennett (p. 59) maintains that his previous conclusion in 1969—that nothing deserving to be called an image would be discovered in the subpersonal theory of perception and imagination—was "rash and overstated"; he gives a "corrective agnosticism" of his position in his chapter on "Two Approaches to Mental Images" (Dennett, 1981b). In this latter work (cf. Dennett, 1969), Dennett (1981b) examines the viewpoints of both the *iconophiles* (the proponents of mental images) and the *iconophobes* (those who decry/deny mental images) in their respective approaches to mental representations (i.e., the debate focuses on the issue as to whether one's mental representations are more like "pictures/maps" or more like "sentences"). As to his own position on this issue, Dennett (pp. 104–5) states that "with regard to the legitimate scientific agreement about the nature of mental representation, this paper is so far entirely neutral." The goal of Dennett's essay is to "clear the decks so that debate can proceed unhindered by misconceptions about what we might call the metaphysical status of mental images."

Fodor (1981) discusses "imagistic representation" and, according to Block (1981, p. 5), Fodor argues against Dennett insisting that images do exist—that images are "psychologically real." Fodor asserts that the available data indicate that what goes on in imagery is very *like* picturing and very *unlike* describing. Fodor (p. 81) provides an outline of his argument in the following three steps: (1) some behaviors are facilitated when task-relevant information is displayed as an image; (2) one of our psychological faculties serves to construct images that accord with descriptions (i.e., we have a computational system that takes a description as input and gives an output consisting of an image or something that satisfies the description); and (3) the produced image may be rather schematic because how the image is taken (i.e., what role it plays in cognitive processing) is determined not only by its figural properties but also by the character of the description with which it is paired. Fodor notes that the content of images varies quite a bit from person to person where a given image may function to effect different representations in different computational tasks. Fodor's point is that if mental images are "images under descriptions," then their particularities might have very little effect on the role they play in cognitive processes. Fodor (p. 82) poses the question whether *all* mental images are generated from descriptions or whether some psychological processes are "nondiscursive" from beginning to end—in which case the issue becomes an open empirical question where the discovery of the mechanisms by which descriptions and images are related becomes the major focal point.

Schwartz (1981, p. 109) observes that the "public image of private imagery is showing signs of a comeback" and notes, also, that as the imagery debate goes on it is fueled by the fact that there is no consensus on either side on critical issues such as what "counts" as imagery, what it means for an activity to be explained imagistically, or which evidence is to be taken as either supporting or challenging imagist theories (cf. Anderson, 1978). While much of the recent psychological literature on imagery is concerned with the nature of the neural/mental representations involved in the storage and generation of images (i.e., on how the image *itself* is represented), Schwartz takes a different approach by focusing on the question of how images may serve to represent. That is, Schwartz asserts that a better understanding of the relationship between an image and what it purports to be an image of is a necessary prerequisite for unraveling many of the conceptual complexities and perplexities that plague the imagery debate. Following his discussions (based on examples from auditory imagery, as well as visual imagery) of the symbolic use of images, mode versus median distinctions, symbolization/

interpretation, counting modes, analog versus digital processing, pictures/percepts, and propositions/pictures, Schwartz suggests that debates over the nature of the underlying representations of images often turn on the same points that come up in analyzing representation itself via images.

In the initial portion of a two-part research strategy, Kosslyn, Pinker, Smith, and Shwartz (1981) discuss the "demystification" of mental imagery and note that certain issues or objections permeate the history of mental imagery/mental representation. For example, the objections to mental imagery traditionally have been of two forms:

1. It has been argued that imagery cannot serve the functions that have been attributed to it (e.g., an image cannot represent an object or scene uniquely without some interpretive function that picks out certain qualities of the image as being important and others as being incidental; this class of objections maintains that images cannot be the *sole* form of internal representation that exists in human memory—which does not mean that images cannot be one form of representation in memory).
2. Mental imagery as an explanatory construct in psychology contains incoherencies and inconsistencies in the very concept itself (cf. Pylyshyn, 1973; Kosslyn and Pomerantz, 1977), as well as *not* being demonstrative of a well-formed domain in its own right (i.e., imagery is merely one special aspect of a more general processing system; cf. Pylyshyn, 1973).

Kosslyn et al. (1981) attempt to develop a special theory of imagery that hypothesizes that images are temporary spatial displays in active memory that are generated from more abstract representations in long-term memory (the analog here is the notion that visual images are like displays produced on a cathode ray tube [CRT] by a computer program operating on stored data—this is their "CRT metaphor"); their theory posits interpretative mechanisms (a mind's eye) that work over (look at) the internal displays and subsequently classify them in terms of semantic categories. In their terminology, Kosslyn et al. use the term image to refer to representations in active memory, *not* to an experience. Moreover, the experience of "having an image" means that an image representation is present in active memory, but the question as to whether one can have an image representation without the experience is left open by Kosslyn et al. (1981); see their footnote, p. 133. The CRT metaphor of Kosslyn et al. was thought to be capable of providing accounts for most of the available data on imagery (cf. Paivio, 1971b). According to the CRT metaphor, images not only have some pictorial properties but they are of limited capacity and are actively composed. (This simple "protomodel" was used as a heuristic to help construct a "decision tree," where the nodes represented issues and the branches designated alternative positions on the issues; then, sets of experiments were conducted to eliminate branches, and allowed Kosslyn et al. to descend to the next issue.)

Kosslyn et al. (1981) examine the following issues and questions via their CRT metaphor:

- "Are images epiphenomenal?" (Evidence suggests the view that images are *not* simply epiphenomenal concomitants of more abstract underlying processing; thus, it is posited that there exist functional, quasi-pictorial images.)
- "Are images stored intact in long-term memory and later retrieved in toto?" (Evidence shows that forming images is distinguished from retrieving nonimaginal information, and one view—that images are not necessarily retrieved in toto—was supported. Kosslyn et al. give a counter-interpretation of the results where more detailed pictures require more time to image not because they are constructed, but because there are more things to check after the image is retrieved.)
- "Are images retrieved piecemeal or can they be retrieved in units?" (There is good reason to posit that the imagery system has the capacity to retrieve and integrate "chunks" stored separately in long-term memory.)
- "Are images generated only from 'depictive' information or can 'descriptive' information also be used?" (Evidence indicates that image construction may exploit nonpictorial as well as pictorial information from long-term memory; cf. Kosslyn, 1980.)

In their article, "On the Demystification of Mental Imagery," which appeared originally in the journal *The Behavioral and Brain Sciences* (1979, 2, 535–81), Kosslyn, Ball, and Reiser expand their coverage of the topic—over that which appeared later in Kosslyn et al. (1981)—to include the following issues comprising the second part of their two-part research strategy: an overview of the special theory of imagery (the desired form of a psychological theory: theories and models; the computer simulation technique; the theory and general model; data structures; image processes) and the remystification of mental imagery: objections and replies (e.g., are subjects just doing as they're told?; Anderson's argument for agnosticism; the cognitive penetration of mental imagery; evaluating theories and models). In addition to developing their theory/model of imagery in the 1979 issue of *The Behavioral and Brain Sciences*, Kosslyn et al. have the opportunity to respond to various reactions from a number of imagery researchers in a very substantial and heuristic "Open Peer Commentary" section that is appended to Kosslyn et al.'s "demystifying imagery" article. A sample of those imagery experts and international researchers who responded to Kosslyn et al. in the lengthy (twenty-three journal pages, double columns) "Open Peer Commentary" section includes the following (the title of their commentaries are in parentheses):

R. P. Abelson ("Imagining the purpose of imagery")
J. S. Antrobus ("Matters of definition in the demystification of mental imagery")
L. A. Cooper ("Modeling the mind's eye")
J. A. Feldman ("So many models—so little time")
A. Hannay ("Images, memory, and perception")
F. Hayes-Roth ("Understanding mental imagery: Interpretive metaphors versus explanatory models")
G. Hinton ("Imagery without arrays")
P. N. Johnson-Laird ("The 'thoughtless imagery' controversy")
J. M. Keenan and R. K. Olson ("The imagery debate: A controversy over terms and cognitive styles")
R. Duncan Luce ("A conceptual, an experimental, and a modeling question about imagery research")
T. P. Morgan ("The imprecision of mental imagery")
U. Neisser ("Images, models, and human nature")
A. Paivio ("Computational versus operational approaches to imagery")
Z. Pylyshyn ("Imagery theory: Not mysterious—just wrong").
A. Richardson ("Conscious and nonconscious imagery")
C. L. Richman, D. B. Mitchell, and J. S. Reznick ("The demands of mental travel: Demand characteristics of mental imagery experiments")
E. Sankowski ("On demystifying the mental for psychology")
R. C. Schank ("AI, imagery, and theories")
P. W. Sheehan ("Metaphor versus reality in the understanding of imagery: The path from function to structure")
D. L. Waltz ("On the function of mental imagery")

Following the "Open Peer Commentary" section, Kosslyn et al. (1979) give their "Authors' Response" to the many points raised by the numerous commentators. They organize their responses under the following headings: The how, what, and why of mental imagery; Methodology (demand characteristics, decision tree, introspective data); Particulars (our model and theory, the third dimension, image scanning, miscellaneous topics); and Metatheory (the homunculus, internal representation of the world, images as epiphenomena, perception, images and propositions, demystification; ecological validity, theories and models, the debate). Finally, in their 1979 article, Kosslyn et al. provide a substantial references section that contains over 145 references/citations on the issue of mental imagery. In summary, concerning the Kosslyn et al. article on "demystifying imagery"—*plus* the Open Peer Commentary and Authors' Response sections—I suggest that this material is one of the best singular sources for gaining access to, and essential appreciation of, the imagery debate in modern psychology (cf. the section in chapter 5 titled "Imagery Theory," in this book).

Pylyshyn (1981) comments on some of the recent theoretical work on imagery in light of the modern debate over the nature of mental imagery that has occurred in the psychological literature in the mid- and late 1980s. The various positions in the debate have been represented in a number of places by a number of persons, most notably by Anderson (1978), Kosslyn, Pinker, Smith, and Shwartz (1979), Kosslyn and Pomerantz (1977), Paivio (1977), and Pylyshyn (1973, 1978, 1979a,b, 1981). In his analysis, Pylyshyn (1981) makes extensive reference to the Kosslyn et al. (1979) paper because it seems to provide the most explicit formulation of the imagistic, or pictorial/analogical, position. Pylyshyn notes that there is much in the imagery literature that may be debated; for example, Are images continuous or discrete, concrete or abstract, pictorial or discursive/descriptive? Also, do images constitute a fundamentally different form of cognition or are they merely a species of a single form used in all cognitive processing? Are images epiphenomenal or are they functional in cognition (a question that requires an initial theoretical stand concerning the properties of images)?

In Pylyshyn's (1981) view, the central theoretical issue in the imagery controversy (cf. Rollins, 1989, pp. 18–25) is whether the explanation of certain imagery phenomena requires the postulation of special types of processes or mechanisms such as those implied by the term *analog*, as well as determination of the alleged "spatiality" of images (e.g., via experimental findings from studies of "mental rotation" and "mental scanning" of images). Pylyshyn argues that the only real issue that divides the "images versus propositions" proponents in the debate is the question of whether certain aspects of cognition that are associated with imagery ought to be seen as governed by "tacit knowledge" (i.e., whether they should be explained in terms of processes that operate upon symbolic encodings of rules and other representations—such as beliefs and goals—or whether they should be seen as intrinsic aspects of certain representational media or of certain mechanisms that are not changeable in arbitrary ways by tacit knowledge). (Pylyshyn [1980a,b] referred to such mechanisms as comprising the "functional architecture of the mind.") Thus, Pylyshyn (1981) presents arguments and evidence in support of the position that most of the empirical evidence concerning transformations of images (such as mental scanning and rotation) may be best explained by a "tacit knowledge" theory or approach (cf. Fodor, 1968a,b).

In another place, Pylyshyn (1981, p. 164) states what he takes to be "the fundamental bifurcation between the two camps in the imagery debate, between those who advocate the analogue (or intrinsic property of a medium) view and those who advocate the symbolic or tacit knowledge view." According to Pylyshyn, much confusion arises in this debate due to a considerable amount of equivocation regarding exactly what the *referents* of ambiguous phrases—such as "spatial representation" or "preserves metric spatial information"—are intended to be (cf. Kosslyn, Ball, and Reiser, 1979). Pylyshyn asserts that in the debate one is left with a basic empirical question: Which properties of an organism's functioning are attributable to intrinsic (analog) processes and which are attributable to transactions on a tacit knowledge base? In his final analysis, Pylyshyn (pp. 205–6) maintains that in order for a theory of imagery to be "principled," it is necessary to locate the knowledge-independent functional properties correctly; one must be critical in laying a foundation of "cognitively impenetrable" functions to serve as the basic architecture of a formal imagery model, wherein one's models may be "properly constrained" (cf. Rollins, 1989, pp. 25–39).

Kosslyn (1981) develops the notion that images are a special kind of representation that depicts information and occurs in a spatial medium (cf. Ferguson, 1977). He also considers the relative merits of two kinds of accounts of imagery data: those based on the processing of depictive images and those based on the appeal to the influence of task demands/demand characteristics and the use of tacit knowledge. Following his discussion of background assumptions (i.e., the domain of the theory, the form of a cognitive theory of imagery, and specific and general models), Kosslyn provides an overview of his theory of mental image representation and processing that includes discussion of structure, surface representation, underlying deep representations, literal and propositional encodings, and processes. He also provides a section on criticisms of his theory, most notably those offered by Pylyshyn (1979a, 1980a,b, 1981). Kosslyn lists the five most important criticisms of the Kosslyn and Shwartz imagery theory under the following headings: Ad Hoc Theories, Parameters and Free Parameters, The Source of Predictive Power, Cognitive Penetration, and the New Data. In the imagery debate, Kosslyn notes that Pylyshyn offers alternative accounts—the tacit knowledge approach—of the data from imagery experiments that rest on three major claims: the implicit task demands in the experiments lead participants to re-create as accurately as possible the perceptual events that would occur if they were actually observing the analogous situation; participants draw on their tacit knowledge of physics and the nature of the human perceptual system to decide how to behave in an experiment; and the participants have the psychophysical skills necessary to produce the appropriate responses (e.g., by timing the interval between the onset of the stimulus and their pressing a key). Additionally, according to Kosslyn, Pylyshyn makes another assumption in his overall argument: the means by which tacit knowledge is invoked and used must *not* involve a spatial medium.

At one place, Kosslyn (1981, pp. 240–42) makes an evaluation of the two major imagery theories in the debate (i.e., Pylyshyn's "tacit knowledge/descriptionalist" theory and Kosslyn and Shwartz's "CRT or computer simulation model/pictorialist" theory) regarding the traditional theory-testing criteria of precision, generality, falsifiability, parsimony, and heuristic value. Among his conclusions, Kosslyn asserts that advancements have been made in the imagery debate where there is now an abundance of data that place real constraints on theories, and the theoretical positions are now concerned both with explaining the existing data and with collecting new data that are relevant to the issues—this is a very "healthy sign." To the question "What should one make of the apparent widespread dissatisfaction in the field that the so-called imagery-proposition debate has not yet been resolved?" Kosslyn (pp. 243–44) suggests that "[g]iven the complexity of the issues involved, it seems overly optimistic to expect a speedy solution to such a knotty problem. . . . At the present juncture the best we can do is to continue to work out the empirical implications of the respective positions and to continue to collect new data that support one view while putting strain on others" See Kosslyn's earlier (1980, pp. 27–28) discussion of "conclusions from the debate" when he states, "This, then, is the first issue at hand: should we treat the quasi-pictorial images we experience as a special kind of functional representation in human memory, or as an incidental concomitant or special property of more general abstract processing?"

## A Review of Imagery Theories

In addition to Kosslyn's (1980, 1981, 1983, 1994) pictorial theory and Pylyshyn's (1973, 1978, 1979a,b, 1980a,b, 1981) descriptionalist theory (cf. Tye's [1991, pp. 19–76] discussions of "decline of the picture theory in philosophy," "emergence of alternative views," "the picture theory in cognitive psychology," and "mental images as structural descriptions"), a number of other theories/models of mental imagery have been proposed (cf. Juhasz, 1971; Pinker and Kosslyn, 1983, pp. 43–71; Roeckelein, 1998, pp. 251–52; Sheehan, 1972; Sheikh, 1983). In this section, I provide a review/summary of alternative imagery theories, arranged mostly in chronological order (based upon date of publication), which characterizes modern psychology's interest in, and theoretical accounts of, mental imagery.

In his discussion of the "changing conceptions of imagery," Neisser (1972) notes that previously (Neisser, 1967) he argued that the processes of imagery were closely related to those of perception itself; thus, Neisser's theoretical approach may be called the *percept analogy/analogue* theory (cf. Neisser, 1976, 1978, 1979; Neisser and Kerr, 1973). According to Neisser (1972), both imagery and perception are instances of *active* construction, rather than *passive* registration and recall (cf. Gibson, 1966). Following his analyses of "the storehouse conception of mental life," "the problems of introspection," "learning and remembering as cognitive processes," and "the mnemonic uses of imagery," Neisser (1972, p. 244) suggests that in psychology there is a temptation to adopt an oversimplified notion of imagery (e.g., Paivio, 1969, considers images and verbal processes to be "alternative coding systems" that carries the strong implication that images have one definite set of properties whenever they occur). Other simplistic accounts of imagery, according to Neisser (1972), are those by Bower (1970b), Paivio (1970), Palermo (1970), Reese (1970a,b), and Rohwer (1970). Neisser (1972) asserts that there is good reason to believe that the situation is more complicated than that as indicated by many previous researchers. He maintains that the processes and aspects of processes that are called imagery vary enormously even within one person, and certainly between different persons. Neisser (1981, pp. 245–46) suggests that a definition of imagery as related to perception has several advantages: it can cover the range of phenomena that have traditionally been subsumed under perception, it is consistent with most introspective reports (even though not based on introspection), and it can be given an operational interpretation (cf. Atwood, 1971; Brooks, 1967; Segal and Fusella, 1970; Shepard and Metzler, 1971). Finally, in his theoretical approach to show the relationship between imagery and perception, Neisser (1972) describes an experimental demonstration of nonpictorial imagery; such a demonstration supports the view that the mnemonic effectiveness of an image depends *only* on the spatial layout that it represents and *not* on the pictorial quality of that layout (cf. Neisser and Kerr, 1973). Neisser (1972) asserts that instead of referring to images as mental pictures, it would be better to describe mental life traditionally in terms of an "inner world" that allows the inner world of imagery to be constructed in much the same way as the real world is perceived (cf. Sheehan, 1966, 1967), and may help prevent one from underestimating the dimensionality and complexity of imagery.

Paivio's (1972) theoretical approach to imagery is embedded firmly in the topic areas of verbal learning and memory (cf. Paivio, 1969, 1970, 1971b, 1977); he suggests that imagery variables are among the most powerful memory factors ever discovered (cf. reviews of imagery variables by Bower, 1972; Bugelski, 1970; Reese, 1970a,b; and Rohwer, 1970). Paivio (1972) asserts that it is very important to understand precisely why the independent variables that define imagery are so effective (cf. Sheehan and Neisser, 1969; Wickens and Engle, 1970). Following a review of operational approaches to imagery and its effects, Paivio (1972) presents an outline of theoretical interpretations of imagery effects on memory. In his *coding model*, Paivio (1971b, 1982) indicates that there are two main modes of coding experience: "verbal processes"—which involve a functional symbolic system and are assumed to be auditory/motor—and "imaginal processes"—which constitute the representational mode for nonverbal thinking. Paivio's *dual coding hypothesis* states that higher imagery conditions are so effective in learning and memory because they increase the probability that both imaginal and verbal processes play a mediational role in item retrieval (cf. Bower, 1972). According to this approach, both verbal-sequential and imagery-spatial-parallel processing are needed for optimal human functioning; however, because of its concrete/contextual nature, the imagery system appears to be more akin to perception (cf. the Perky effect—the subjective impression of imagery with the objective presence of a physical stimulus; when a person is asked to form a mental image of an object, and a very faint image of the object is then presented on a screen, the projected image may be taken to be the mental image [Perky, 1910]).

In his discussion, Paivio's (1972) theoretical analysis is divided into two major sections: encoding, and storage/retrieval processes. In the encoding process, the crucial factors affecting image discovery are item concreteness, instructional sets, and presentation rate. In the storage/retrieval processes, the following hypothetical factors are related to imagery effects: properties of the memory trace (such as strength or vividness), code redundancy (dual-coding hypothesis), organizational processes occurring during either or both storage/retrieval stages, interference (or freedom from it) during storage/retrieval, and retrieval mechanisms related in particular to the attributes of effective retrieval cues. Paivio's dual-coding hypothesis (that high imagery conditions increase the probability that *both* imaginal and verbal processes play a mediational role in item retrieval) is supported by several kinds of evidence and offers a parsimonious explanation of the superiority of pictures over concrete words and of the latter over abstract words in various memory tasks.

In his section on "convergent evidence on effective imagery," Paivio (1972, pp. 273–74) indicates that a number of writers (e.g., Mowrer, 1960; Sheffield, 1961; Skinner, 1953; Staats, 1961) have interpreted images as *conditioned sensations* or *perceptual responses* where words may function as one important class of conditioned stimuli, and where Paivio (1969) suggested earlier that such an interpretation might be appropriate in the case of concrete, high-imagery words. Paivio (1972) asserts that whether one accepts such a "classical conditioning model," there seems to be no good alternative to some kind of associative explanation of the acquisition of word imagery. Paivio's theoretical approach that includes the notion that nonverbal images can function as powerful mediators of learning and memory is supported by the results of studies involving a number of different converging operations, among which are scaled attributes of stimulus items, subjective reports, nmemonic instructions, experimentally acquired concreteness, and individual differences in imagery as inferred from sensory deficits and tests of imagery ability. In summary, among his other findings, Paivio conducted a series of experiments that showed that concrete words (i.e., nouns that represent easily visualizable things) are easier to learn than abstract words, and that this difference is not simply a residue of "word frequency" or "associative potency." Paivio's overall findings strongly suggest that participants commonly use images in the act of memorization (cf. Bower's, 1970a, 1972, more "direct" methods involving instructions to participants to deliberately form linking images in paired-associate experiments and where imaging conditions are superior to other methods employed). For further references to Paivio's experimental work on imagery vis-à-vis verbal learning/memory, see Begg and Paivio (1969); Ernest and Paivio (1969, 1971); Paivio (1965, 1966); Paivio and Begg (1971); Paivio and Csapo (1969); Paivio and Foth (1970); Paivio and Madigan (1970); Paivio and Okovita (1971); Paivio and Rowe (1970); Paivio and Smythe (1971); Paivio, Smythe, and Yuille (1968); Paivio and Yuille (1969); Paivio, Yuille, and Madigan (1968); Paivio, Yuille, and Rogers (1969); Simpson and Paivio (1966); and Yuille and Paivio (1967). For further reactions to, and analyses of, Paivio's (and Bower's) dual-coding theory, see Pinker and Kosslyn (1983, pp. 48–49); and Morris and Hampson (1983, pp. 120–23). Also, note Yuille and Marschark's (1983, p. 135) comment that, historically, "the major force behind the renewed interest in the role of imagery in memory was Paivio."

Horowitz (1972) proposes a *cognitive model* of *image formation* (cf. Horowitz, 1970/1978; Marks, 1987) that is grounded in clinical observations and is an attempt to complement data from experimental investigations of the use of images in perception, information processing, and memory that have employed largely normal participants and a variety of ingenious and diverse methods (cf. Ernest, 1977, 1979). Following his discussion of definitions and an approach strategy ("framework for a cognitive model"), Horowitz (1972) reviews two clinical types of subjective loss of control (inability to form images) vis-à-vis the intensity of images: excessive intensity and inadequate intensity. His other sections include clinical "loss of control over image contents" and "unbidden images as a cognitive response to stressful perceptions." Also, Horowitz (p. 295) presents a "list of criteria for a model of image formation" that includes, among other points, the following criteria: the subjectively experienced image may encode information derived from both immediately external and internal sources; attitudes toward the meaning and implication of information influences the sampling and processing of that information; the storage and compulsive-repetition period is longer than that usually considered for short-term or iconic memory in normal/ordinary circumstances; the repetitiousness, intrusive quality, and unusual intensity may be reduced at times by working through the conceptual and emotional implications of the images; nonconscious defensive operations influence the form and content of subjectively experienced images, and there is a complex relationship between image formation, images, and affect (i.e., emotions act as *motives* for the image formation, emotions are *expressed* in the imagery experience, and images evoke emotional *responses*).

In his development of a conceptual model of image formation based upon clinical observations and an information-processing approach, Horowitz (1972) discusses three issues: the use of the image as a mode of representation of information, the construction of an image from immediately external and internal sources of information, and the processing of an image after it is constructed and experienced. According to Horowitz, such a modeling process—where one models the patterns for information processing through image formation—is analogous to formulating the program by which a computer operates in its particular information processing tasks (cf. Miller, Galanter, and Pribram, 1960; Neisser, 1967). For further discussions of Horowitz's clinical approach and theoretical background, see Horowitz (1964, 1969a,b); and Horowitz, Adams, and Rutkin (1968); compare R. S. Lazarus (1966); Segal (1970); Singer (1970). A substantial bibliography consisting of over 535 citations/references is included in Horowitz (1970/1978).

Pinker and Kosslyn's (1983) review of theories of mental imagery is organized into two sections: theories outlined before 1975 (cf. Kosslyn, 1980; Paivio, 1971b), and those outlined after 1975 (cf. Kosslyn, 1981; Kosslyn, Pinker, Smith, and Shwartz, 1979, 1981). Consistent with Dennett's (1980) usage, Pinker and Kosslyn (1983)—in their discussion—invoke the distinction between iconophiles (theorists who attribute special properties to mental imagery representations, especially giving the "spatial" or "pictorial" nature of images a high theoretical status) and the iconophobes (theorists who assert that images are represented mentally in the same way as other forms of thought without giving special status to some intrinsic "pictorial" or "spatial" property of images). Following an analysis and evaluation/criteria of "theories and models" in general (i.e., "it is important to be as clear as possible about what sort of theoretical statement one is dealing with—general theory, specific theory, general model, and specific model," p. 45; and, "cognitive theories describe function roughly on the one level one would use to describe a computer algorithm. . . . Physiological theories, on the other hand, describe the actual operation of brain cells," p. 44), Pinker and Kosslyn describe the older theories, including Paivio's and Bower's "dual-code" theories, Neisser's "percept-analogy" theory, Hebb's "cell assembly" theory, and various "propositional" theories.

Pinker and Kosslyn (1983) assert that no recent theorist has held the strong "first-order isomorphism" claim that images are literally "pictures in the head," but many theorists have treated images metaphorically as if they *were* pictures. The foremost theorist in this category is Paivio (1971b) who emphasizes that one has two kinds of codes in which to store information: verbal and pictorial. According to Pinker and Kosslyn, Paivio's theory is very closely tied to data concerning the role of different materials in enhancing memory for lists of words and word pairs; they suggest that Paivio intends his views to be a "general theory," but they do not seem to cover a well-defined domain (i.e., the views do not address the results of experimental work on the format, generation, inspection, and transformation of images; cf. Kosslyn, 1980). Pinker and Kosslyn do acknowledge that Paivio cannot be faulted for this failure of his approach inasmuch as most of such experimental work on generation, transformation, and so on was conducted after his theory was formulated. In their final assessment of Paivio's (1971b) theory, Pinker and Kosslyn (p. 48) assert that Paivio's approach "cannot attain process adequacy, let alone explanatory adequacy" (i.e., even for the tasks that are addressed by Paivio's theory, "there is no attempt to specify the way they are actually performed").

Pinker and Kosslyn (1983) note that another dual-code theory was proposed by Bower (1972) who emphasized that one may distinguish between *how* something looked and *what* it looked like (in the former, there is a quasi-pictorial representation, and in the latter, there is something akin to a verbal/propositional representation). In Bower's approach, memory images provide a type of direct contact with the appearance of a thing by re-creating the experience of seeing it; moreover, the verbal/propositional representations do not induce a perceptlike experience but, rather, convey information only about the properties of the thing. According to Bower, the two types of information are stored in two different kinds of codes—a viewpoint that is parallel to Paivio's approach. In Pinker and Kosslyn's (p. 49) assessment, Bower's theory invites the same sort of reservations as does Paivio's theory, although "Bower does attempt to build some measure of process adequacy into his theory. He hypothesizes that a 'common generative grammar' may underlie production of images and verbal strings, and he describes how such a grammar might operate."

Next in Pinker and Kosslyn's (1983) review is Neisser's percept-analogy theory, which characterizes the traditional view of mental imagery that has appeared repeatedly over centuries in psychology and philosophy, that is, that images are percepts that emerge from memory rather than from sensory input. (The picture-in-the-head theories are one type, among many other types, of this viewpoint.) Pinker and Kosslyn suggest that a good example of a "non-pictorial percept-analogy" theory is provided by Neisser (1976, 1978, 1979; Neisser and Kerr, 1973) who adopts Gibson's (1966) automatic and direct approach toward perception (in this viewpoint, there is no picturelike representation, but images—like percepts—are of spatial layouts). Pinker and Kosslyn observe that Neisser rejects Gibson's firm position that *no* processing takes place during perception; rather, according to Neisser, the brain *is* a processing device that does not use distinct representations. Thus, Neisser rejects the "structure-process" distinction that is popular in cognitive psychology and artificial intelligence theories. In Pinker and Kosslyn's (1983) assessment of Neisser's theory, the latter *does* seem to have some measure of the criterion of "behavioral adequacy," while *not* possessing the criteria of "process adequacy" and "explanatory adequacy" (cf. Hampson and Morris, 1978; Keenan and Moore, 1979).

Pinker and Kosslyn (1983) discuss Hebb's (1968) early viewpoint on imagery that is based in neurophysiological mechanisms and processes. According to Hebb, an image is formed when some of the brain's same neurological structures that are activated during perception are activated in the absence of the appropriate sensory input. In this process, certain groups of neurons (called *cell assemblies*) for a recurrent synaptic path are organized hierarchically (e.g., the lowest-order assemblies respond to specific visual contours in particular retinal locations, and higher-order assemblies may be triggered by any one of a set of lower-order contours). Consequently, the activation of some of the higher-order assemblies in the hierarchy produces "fuzzy" or "generic" images, while the activation of the lower-order assemblies produces "sharp" and "detailed" images. Additionally, cell assemblies at a given level are connected by the neural assemblies that trigger particular eye movements, which, as a result, are activated in the same sequence as that which occurs when the individual visually examines an object. In evaluating Hebb's theory, Pinker and Kosslyn (p. 51) suggest that Hebb's views are "clearly intended as a general theory, but unfortunately they are too vague to produce specific theories or specific models for most imagery tasks."

In the category of propositional or structural-description theories, Pinker and Kosslyn observe that such theories posit the notion that image representations are no different in kind from the representations underlying conceptual knowledge and abstract thought. In these theories, the quasi-pictorial feature of images that is accessible via introspection is treated as an epiphenomenon where all mental representations consist of logical propositions that contain symbolic variables and constants (cf. Baylor, 1971; Farley, 1974; Kosslyn 1980, chapter 5). In one specific propositional theory, Moran (1973) hypothesizes that all mental representations (including those underlying images) are "symbolic" where there are no special image conditions. According to this approach, memory consists of a collection of "productions" (cf. Newell and Simon, 1972) that contain two parts: the "condition" that states what information must be in active memory or coming from the senses, and the "action" that is produced. The action typically results in a change of the contents of short-term memory, and, in Moran's theory, there is a single short-term store—having limited capacity—for information from all modalities. The short-term memory contents are constantly in flux as new information either arrives from the senses or is activated from long-term memory. Pinker and Kosslyn (p. 51) suggest that "although Moran claims to have a general theory, he in fact has a specific model. . . . The theory is inconsistent with the basic facts of modality-specific interference (Segal, 1971a,b) and with many of the data on image processing reviewed by Kosslyn et al. (1981); thus it lacks behavioral adequacy."

Under the rubric of "Newer Theories," Pinker and Kosslyn (1983) discuss the following imagery theories and perspectives: Kosslyn, Shwartz, and Pinker's "array" theory, Trehub's "neural networks" theory, Finke's "levels of equivalence" approach, Shepard's "psychophysical complementarity" approach, "artifact" theories, and Hinton's "structural descriptions" approach. In general, the array theories posit different kinds of representation in active visual memory and long-term memory (in active memory, there is an arraylike medium—also subserving visual perception—that mimics a coordinate space). In this approach, objects are depicted by selectively activating cells in this array—just as a matrix in a computer memory may be filled with elements whose matrix distributions define the scene or some object's shape. According to this array analysis, active-memory representations underlie one's experience of imagery, and such quasi-pictorial properties that people report during the imagery experience arise from the structural properties of the underlying representation. Moreover, in contrast, long-term memory stores not only quantitative information (that aids in the display of the depictive representation), but also displays the facts in a symbolic/propositional format. Such propositional information affords the imagining of parts of objects (or objects in novel combinations in the array) and, thus, creates detailed images of scenes or objects.

According to Pinker and Kosslyn (1983), array theories hypothesize at least three kinds of processes: a means of pattern interpretation depicted in the array (analogous to a mind's eye process of pattern recognition in visual perception where given patterns are associated with symbolic descriptions); the activation of processes that fill the array with the contents of long-term memory files; and the data require processes that shift points from cell to cell in various ways (to be able to account for one's ability to execute processes such as mental rotations of objects, size scalings, and translations; cf. Kosslyn et al., 1981). Pinker and Kosslyn maintain that the array theories fare reasonably well on the evaluative criteria of "behavioral adequacy" (they can produce specific theories and models that account for the data in specific tasks) and "process adequacy" (via providing explicit accounts of the internal processes employed in accomplishing tasks in the domain) (cf. Cooper and Shepard, 1973a,b; Finke and Kosslyn, 1980; Kosslyn, 1980; Pinker, 1980; Shepard and Metzler, 1971; Shwartz, 1979).

Pinker and Kosslyn (1983) describe Trehub's (1977) neural networks model of pattern recognition and visual imagery that is similar, substantively, to the array theory (cf. Trehub, 1991). Among the features of Trehub's (1977) model are the following:

- "Mosaic cells" (analogous to the "surface array" in the array theory) that act as contour extractors which transform the two-dimensional retinal intensity array into a two-dimensional neural array where every neuron corresponds to a particular retinal locus (and signals "on" and "off" conditions regarding the presence or absence of an edge at that locus).
- "Filter cells" (consisting of a large number of neurons having dendrites, each of which synapses with every mosaic cell) that act to depict certain shapes and subsequently serve as "templates" or "detectors" for those shapes; "neural axons" that act to generate a visual image of a pattern from memory (analogous to a "picture" subroutine in the array theory). "Command cell synapses" linking all the mosaic cells together and whose activation and constant repetition corresponds to a mental rotation or size scaling operation on the array pattern.
- "Concentric subsets" of mosaic cells whose activation corresponds to "focal attention."

Pinker and Kosslyn view Trehub's proposals as constituting a general model that has behavioral and process adequacy in some respects (e.g., it is consistent with experimental data and results concerning "array structure" in the array theory), but is inadequate in other respects (e.g., in terms of process adequacy, Trehub's "normalize-then-template-match" model defines and employs *two*-dimensional representations, but it is highly likely that shape recognition, in particular, is defined over representations of an object's *three*-dimensional shape). Moreover, Pinker and Kosslyn assert that the explanatory adequacy of Trehub's model may be enhanced via a symbiotic relationship with the more computational array theory that it so closely resembles, and, also, Trehub's model confirms that various mechanisms in the neurophysiological substrate implicated by the array theory may, indeed, be identified and actualized.

In describing Finke's (1980) levels of equivalence approach (e.g., where the visual system may be considered as being composed of a hierarchy of processing levels), Pinker and Kosslyn (1983) suggest that Finke presents a framework in which to interpret imagery phenomena in general. However, like Shepard's (1981) complementarity theory, Finke's levels theory is too heuristic and imprecise to allow the generation of behaviorally and process-adequate models of entire imagery tasks (cf. Finke, 1979, 1989; Finke and Schmidt, 1977, 1978). On the other hand, according to Pinker and Kosslyn, by tying mental images to visual processing stages that may be neurally identifiable, Finke approaches, somewhat, the criterion of explanatory adequacy. In their final analysis, Pinker and Kosslyn (p. 58) applaud Finke's (1980) efforts as "an important contribution to the eventual specification of process-adequate and explanatorily-adequate theories of visual imagery."

Pinker and Kosslyn (1983) assert that Shepard's (1981) psychophysical complementarity approach and his "elegant findings" on the process of mental rotation (Cooper and Shepard, 1973a,b; Shepard and Metzler, 1971) serve as an acid test for all recent theories and models of imagery (cf. Anderson, 1978, 1979; Hayes-Roth, 1979; Hinton, 1979a,b; Kosslyn, 1980; Pinker, 1980). Shepard (1981) integrates data from experiments on mental transformations, shape recognition, and apparent motion, using findings to develop very preliminary hypotheses—often invoking evolutionary theory—about the mental structures and processes involved in imagined transformations. Pinker and Kosslyn (pp. 58–64) make an extensive examination and assessment of some of Shepard's (1981) theoretical proposals; for instance, the comparison of the shapes of two three-dimensional objects/bodies where it takes proportionally more time to complete the task when the objects have greater angular disparity may be explained in terms of the imagined/perceived shape as being represented as a set of points, with each point embedded in a multidimensional "space" with its own non-Euclidean geometry, and where different "spaces" are organized into a hierarchy that weights them according to their relative importance in the organism's visual processing. Pinker and Kosslyn note that Shepard's (1981) highly original ideas are difficult to classify according to their scheme, but suggest that his approach comes close to constituting a "general theory." What makes Shepard's theory especially difficult to compare with the other theories is that its "domain" is not imagery in general (i.e., the generation, storage, and inspection of images), but rather the transformational processes that cut across the topic areas of imagery, pattern recognition, and spatial reasoning. In their final analysis of Shepard's approach, Pinker and Kosslyn (p. 64) suggest that the psychophysical complementarity hypotheses have only moderate behavioral and process adequacy; however, by "considering visual transformations in the context of evolution in a three-dimensional world, Shepard has made greater strides toward explanatory adequacy than one usually finds in discussions of imagery."

Pinker and Kosslyn (1983) briefly discuss various artifact theories of imagery that are not properly theories of imagery per se, but rather of how the data collected in imagery experiments were produced and how they indicate *task demands* or *demand characteristics* of the imagery-eliciting tasks. One example of the view that the data reflect task demands may be seen in Pylyshyn's (1981) analysis of the imagery debate where the data on image scanning and related phenomena (cf. Kosslyn, 1980) are to be explained by reference to four ideas:

1. In order to follow the instructions employed in an image-eliciting task (e.g., "rotate an imagined pattern"), the participants must try to anticipate what would occur in the corresponding actual situation.
2. Participants possess the requisite tacit knowledge to know how objects behave in the analogous physical situation (and how their visual systems record these events).
3. Participants process the requisite psychophysical skills to time their button presses (and other responses) appropriately, thereby mimicking the responses they would have made were they actually viewing the "to-be-imaged" stimulus as described.

4. None of the computations involved in understanding the instructions (as well as accessing, and using, stored tacit knowledge, or making responses) involves the actual manipulation of a quasi-pictorial image.

According to such a viewpoint, everything one knows about the world, physics, and one's own perceptual/cognitive abilities could enter into the production of data in imagery tasks. Note that Pinker and Kosslyn observe that the same argument could be made about *any* cognitive task; for example, participants who require more time to verify the presence of probes in larger memorized sets could actually be a consequence of their simulating the act of searching through longer lists of items on a page (cf. Sternberg, 1966). Pinker and Kosslyn note that Pylyshyn (1981) treats his approach as a general theory, and they assess his viewpoint as containing behavioral adequacy inasmuch as the imagery data resemble those from some corresponding or analogous perceptual tasks (cf. Finke, 1980; Kosslyn, 1981; Kosslyn et al., 1979). However, according to Pinker and Kosslyn, Pylyshyn's view fails to attain process adequacy (i.e., it does not specify the cognitive processing that underlies production of the data—except to indicate that quasi-pictorial images are *not* involved). For another analysis of Pylyshyn's (1979a,b, 1980a,b, 1981) descriptionalist approach, see Tye (1991, pp. 64–71).

The demand characteristics view is similar to the task demands view in that the experimental data are explained without hypothesizing about the processing of a mental image. However, according to Pinker and Kosslyn, in this case the data ostensibly are produced not because of implicit task demands built into the instructions, but rather because participants somehow discern the predictions of the experiment and attempt to "help out" the experimenter. Thus, in this view, it is not following instructions per se that elicits the behavior, but attending to other cues (such as participants' active attempts at guessing the experimental hypothesis) (cf. Mitchell and Richman 1980; Richman, Mitchell, and Reznick, 1979).

As their final theoretical assessment, Pinker and Kosslyn (1983) examine Hinton's (1979a,b) structural descriptions approach that is a variant of the propositional theory of visual representation (in which scenes are represented as graph structures whose nodes correspond to objects and their parts and whose edges are labeled with the spatial relationship that is true of pairs of parts). In Pinker and Kosslyn's analysis, Hinton's theory is differentiated from other structural description theories (e.g., Baylor, 1971; Palmer, 1975) by three features: each part has an intrinsic set of "significant directions," or an "originless Cartesian coordinate system," aligned with it; there is a second set of labels relating the significant directions of each part to a single set of directions aligned with the organism's retinal axes; and every piece of quantitative information is specified by an activated point on a continuous analogue scale (where changing the value of a parameter involves shifting the activated point along the scale to a new position). These three features, respectively, account for the following aspects: the effect of descriptions of the intrinsic shape of an object on image processing (Hinton, 1979b); images having an implicit "vantage point" with regard to which perspective properties can be detected (Pinker, 1980; Pinker and Finke, 1980); and the well-known "gradualness" of mental rotation (Shepard and Metzler, 1971). Pinker and Kosslyn (p. 67) suggest that Hinton's theory is computationally powerful and precise enough to generate specific models for many of the recent empirical findings on imagery, and, thus, it gets high grades on the criterion of behavioral adequacy; however, by excluding processes that fill and transform a visual array, Hinton fails to provide support for a large set of empirical phenomena that may be expressed fairly naturally by processes operating on an array during image-production tasks. In the final analysis, Pinker and Kosslyn (p. 68) indicate that Hinton (1979a,b)—by addressing the viewer-centeredness of images, the incremental nature of image transformations, and the relative ease of examining and transforming different image sub-patterns—has "outlined the most psychologically motivated structural description theory we have seen. If a theory in this class turns out to be correct, it will probably resemble Hinton's; if not, it will probably be because of experiments designed with Hinton's theory and data in mind." For another analysis of Hinton's (1979a,b) approach, see Tye (1991, pp. 71–76).

Among their conclusions concerning imagery theories, Pinker and Kosslyn (1983, p. 68) state that "two trends become apparent, both of them salubrious to the scientific study of imagery." As one moves from the older to the newer theories of mental imagery, it may be observed that: (1) there is an increase in precision and generality of theorizing (e.g., the early theories were either extremely vague—such as Hebb's and Paivio's theories, which prompted Pylyshyn's early critique of imagery theories, or were extremely task-specific—such as Moran's theory); and (2) there is a closer connection of imagery with various biological considerations—such as the architecture and evolution of the higher mammals' visual systems (e.g., the work of

Shepard, Trehub, and Finke). Generally, according to Pinker and Kosslyn, the overall trend in imagery theorizing largely has been made possible by the increasing use of the computer as a modeling medium for complex mental phenomena and by the increasing use of computational processes and structures as the theory-relevant components of hypotheses concerning human cognition. In the view of Pinker and Kosslyn (p. 68), both trends are welcomed because "they herald the day when imagery debates will hinge not on semantic quibbles or ideological loyalties, but on which theory fares best in empirical accuracy, parsimony, and elegance."

Marks (1983a) provides a theoretical review of mental imagery within the context of consciousness (cf. Marks, 1977; Hampson and Morris, 1990; Morris and Hampson, 1983; Shallice, 1972; Thomas, 1999, 2000), and draws the following conclusions, among others:

- Imagery is functionally equivalent to, and complementary to, perception (where the two processes share conscious awareness and are represented by the same neuronal networks in the brain).
- Both visual imagery and visual perception employ the encoding of features extracted from the environment using "scan paths" that vary in the level of consistency across individuals.
- Visual imagery encoding occurs on different levels (on a "neural-network-features" level from which conscious images may be formed, and at a higher, nonconscious level as an "executive" system of abstract-conceptual representation that controls the activity of the lower level).
- Verbal reports of imagery provide highly reliable predictors of cognitive functioning (predictions include fixation rate, scan path consistency, and saccadic distance—all of which are out of the individual's awareness or ability to control).
- Demand characteristics of the task are not good explanatory variables.
- Visualization consists of a set of specific skills that influence a wide range of activities in a highly predictable manner (however, the capacity for the individual to experience high-quality imagery is somewhat determined by context/state conditions that indicate the important role of biological and learning factors in imaging ability).
- The prospect of training and improving one's imagery skills is a promising one, especially in their potential for multisetting applications.

(For further imagery studies conducted by Marks, see Marks 1972a,b, 1973a,b, 1977, 1981, 1983b, 1984, 1985, 1986, 1987, 1999.)

Yuille and Marschark (1983) examine various theoretical interpretations of imagery effects on memory that have appeared in the psychological literature since the publication of Paivio's (1972) review of the stimulus- and individual-difference factors that affect the use of imagery. Yuille and Marschark note that Paivio's dual-coding model of imagery persists as the major statement giving a principal role to imagery in memory; however, according to Yuille and Marschark, in the last decade the most striking recent events have been the negative reactions made to imagery theories. That is, the computer has moved from *metaphor* to *testing-ground* of some psychological models (one consequence of this has been the development of computational models of cognition where the models' proponents have been critical of all the imagery-based interpretations and, as a further result, the so-called "analogue-computational debate" has arisen). Following an analysis of the dual-coding model (cf. Kirby and Das, 1976) and the presentation of some "historical notes" (e.g., review of the notions of Aristotle, Plato, Aquinas, Hume, Wundt, and Ebbinghaus concerning the assignment of a central theoretical role to imagery in memory; cf. Holt, 1964), Yuille and Marschark discuss the reappearance of imagery in models of memory.

Since the 1960s, a variety of studies have established the importance of *mediation* as a strong predictor of performance in verbal learning tasks (e.g., Bugelski, 1962; Bugelski, Kidd, and Segman, 1968; Keiss and Montague, 1965; Paivio and Yuille, 1967; Paivio, Yuille, and Smythe, 1966; cf. Bower, 1970b); during this period, the image-evoking aspect of concrete stimulus materials generally was accepted, but the causal link between imagery and recall was less well defined. Specifically, it was not clear whether imagery effects could be more parsimoniously attributed to other variables such as the specificity-generality dimension (e.g., Paivio, 1963), lexical complexity (e.g., Kintsch, 1972), or meaningfulness (e.g., Paivio and O'Neill, 1970). The factor of meaningfulness—until it "passed away quietly"—proved to the most stubborn of such variables insofar as it was empirically related to learning in virtually all tasks where imagery was facilitative (eventually, meaningfulness was unable to compete with the consistently robust effects of imagery).

According to Yuille and Marschark (1983), Paivio's (1969, 1971b) elaboration of a dual-coding model of memory provided a theoretical framework for the interpretation of imagery effects consistent with virtually all relevant empirical findings in the psychological literature on memory; the model combined a conceptual "peg mnemonic" associative system with a two-process theory of meaning. In their discussion of the "negative reactions to imagery models," Yuille and Marschark note that the work of researchers such as Paivio, Kosslyn, and Shepard represent a *proimagery* position in cognitive psychology (cf. Das, Kirby, and Jarman, 1975), even though they differ somewhat concerning the precise nature of the memory processes underlying imagery (cf. Kieras, 1978). On the other hand, those critics of imagery-based theories reflect a general change that has occurred recently in the study of cognitive processes (cf. Neisser, 1967). The renewed interest in mentalistic concepts via the development of cognitive psychology was a reflection, partly, of substantial advances in computer science. Computer metaphors rapidly appeared in descriptions of human memory (e.g., Atkinson and Shiffrin, 1968), and, rather than serving merely as an analog, the computer has provided the means for testing some psychological theories (e.g., see Anderson and Bower's, 1973, computer program called *HAM*—human associative memory—which represents a theory of psychological functions involved in memory and language). The basic assumption in such modeling attempts is that memory involves an abstract/symbolic code where, for instance, all knowledge may be represented as a propositional network consisting of nodes (which represent concepts) that are connected by links (which represent the relationships between concepts). According to this approach, memory is *amodal*, and imagery effects are interpreted in terms of the *amodal codes*; moreover, images, themselves, are assumed either not to exist or to be epiphenomenal in nature.

In their final section, Yuille and Marschark (1983) speculate about the future status of the imagery debate—which has had a volatile history ranging from total rejection in some investigations to complete acceptance in others; they suggest that the high intuitive appeal of the imagery concept has allowed it to persist despite theoretical diversity, debate, and differences. On the other hand, there are serious problems with imagery theories that advocate a central role for imagery in memory; for example, the most prominent of such models—the dual-coding hypothesis (Paivio, 1969, 1971b)—has several shortcomings (such as the lack of specification concerning the nature, structure, or organization of memory). Moreover, according to Yuille and Marschark, Paivio seems to assume implicitly a *trace* theory of memory involving *imagery traces* in the storage and retrieval of images (see Loftus and Loftus, 1980, for a summary of the difficulties with the trace position), but much current research supports a reconstructive view of memory (and, while Paivio, 1976, has implied his model's compatibility with the reconstructive view, he has not specified how this is achieved). Yuille and Marschark suggest that future questions to be answered in this area are

- "What are the relationships between the different types (e.g., specific versus general concepts) of images?"
- "How do retrieval cues access the appropriate images?"
- "What is/are the specification(s) of the nature and structure of memory?"
- "What is the relationship of language and meaning to imagery?"

Finally, Yuille and Marschark (pp. 148–50) assess various other imagery models and approaches; for example,

"Shepard fares less well than Paivio's on critical examination . . . the prognosis for Shepard's approach is not good."
"Kosslyn stands on firmer ground than the other theorists. . . . However, there seems to exist a fundamental flaw (regarding the computer database) in Kosslyn's approach to imagery modeling. . . . Kosslyn has confirmed the suspicions of those who hold a computational approach to cognition: imagery is a redundant concept."
"Anderson (1978, 1979) has suggested that there is no possibility of resolution of the differences between the computational and imagery positions. . . . [H]e has argued that modifications can be made in each position to account for any empirical outcome. . . . [I]t seems that the antagonists have elected to ignore Anderson and continue the debate, apparently believing that their differences are real, and very much worthy of defense (Kosslyn, 1981; Pylyshyn, 1979c, 1981)."
"Pylyshyn (1980b) has implied that a computational perspective is the only viable one for cognitive psychology."
"Fodor (1980) has been more explicit in offering arguments that no other approach (i.e., the computational) is possible if psychology desires to be a science."

In Yuille and Marschark's (1983) own view, the computer is *not* an adequate metaphor for mental processes, and they support the idea that there is a fundamental difference between humans and computers (e.g., human cognition involves *nonlinear* interactions that cannot be easily embedded into the binary/serial structure of computer computations without seriously affecting the metric/topological interrelations of the internal representations; cf. Grossberg, 1980). Moreover, Yuille and Marschark assert that a Piagetian approach (e.g., Piaget and Inhelder, 1971, 1973) holds promise as a model of cognition that includes both an amodal and an imagery code where images are not elements in mental structures but are tools that the system may employ in problem-solving situations (cf. Kaufmann, 1980); thus, a Piagetian perspective ultimately may offer a reasonable resolution to the computational-imagery debate (cf. Yuille and Catchpole, 1977).

King (1983) examines the theoretical utility of the concept of imagery (cf. Bugelski, 1983; Kroger and Fezler, 1976; Staats and Lohr, 1979; Tondo and Cautela, 1974; Upper and Cautela, 1979) in his *image theory of conditioning*—rather than presenting a theory of imagery, per se—based upon the following assumptions: mental imagery resides between the areas of memory and perception; the experience of a stimulus (in its absence) is perceptual in nature (cf. Perky, 1910; Segal, 1972), but the source of this experience is memory; the effects of perceiving and imagining stimuli on behavior are similar (e.g., Segal and Fusella, 1970; cf. Greenwald, 1970; McGuigan, 1978; Sanford, 1937; Shaw, 1940); and stimulus-produced and memorial representations affect the nervous system in a similar manner. King's (1974a,b, 1978, 1979) image theory of conditioning essentially emphasizes the viewpoint that perceptual processes underlie classical and instrumental conditioning (cf. Leuba, 1940).

Morris and Hampson (1983) devote a chapter to theories of imagery, and employ the following rubrics (along with representative samples of theorists for the various positions) in their evaluative discussion:

- *Picture theories* encompass the notion that an image is like a picture in the mind and that processing an image is akin to dealing with, seeing, rotating, or manipulating the imagined object (Paivio's, 1971b, dual-code theory; Shepard's, 1975, first-order isomorphism approach; and Kosslyn's, 1975, 1978, 1980, 1981, Kosslyn and Pomerantz's, 1977, Kosslyn and Shwartz's, 1977, and Kosslyn et al.'s, 1979, computer simulation model).
- *Nonpictorial models* encompass "description/propositional" theories and "role-playing" models that are critical of pictorial theories and emphasize more than one meaning of the concept "representation" in imagery theories (Anderson and Bower, 1973; Kintsch, 1977; Neisser, 1967, 1976; Pylyshyn, 1973, 1980b, 1981; and Ryle, 1949; cf. Sarbin, 1972).

Morris and Hampson (1983) also make comparisons ("commonalities and disagreements") of the theories concerning the following issues or criteria: the relation between imagery and perception, the general problem of representation, and the status of consciousness and introspection in the various models. Among their conclusions on these issues, Morris and Hampson make the following points:

1. There is at least one prediction that may be derived from all three major approaches to imagery (pictorial, role-playing, and descriptive/propositional): imagery and perception may interfere mutually in certain circumstances (e.g., Neisser's, 1976, model predicts that conflict will occur when a "schema" is used to perform an imagery and a perceptual task at the same time; description theories may argue that confusion may occur whenever spatial descriptions of two or more separate tasks are manipulated in a common working memory; and pictorial theories argue that conflict can arise because both imagery and perception sometimes use the same processes and structures; Morris and Hampson suggest that interference occurs at central—rather than peripheral—processing stages where the equivalence between imagery and perception is most likely at that conceptually-driven level).
2. Most models of imagery—whether pro- or antipictorial—share the assumption that some form of stored information is used by the cognitive system to depict objects and events when thinking about, and imaging, those things.
3. Neisser's (1978) theory contains several weaknesses, especially its treatment of introspection and mental rotation (cf. Hampson, 1979).
4. As well as agreeing on the necessity for some form of internal representation, most theories recognize that there is a close relationship between representations and the processes that use them (in general, the more complex a representational system the simpler the procedures which use it, and vice versa; cf. Anderson, 1978).
5. Two substantive issues for imagery theory are *when* and *how* does top-down processing result in the production of images, rather than simply operating in a "cognitively silent" fashion (cf. Johnson-Laird, 1980).
6. Theories of imagery differ greatly in the role they assign to consciousness (e.g., most description theories maintain that the most basic level of representation may well be nonconscious; pictorial models, on the other hand, give an important place to the conscious, or surface, image) and the credence they give to introspection (e.g., propositional models find disfavor with introspection, while it is used with caution in the alternative approaches).

In their final section on theories of imagery, Morris and Hampson (1983) propose their own program for a theory of imagery and consciousness. Their approach contains a number of theoretical criteria, guidelines, or constraints around which various models may be constructed, including the following aspects:

- A theory of imagery is always related to a particular theory of perception.
- If the view that perception depends on concept-driven, as well as data-driven, processes, is accepted, then imagery probably has more in com-

mon with the former than the latter. Imagery and perception may interfere under certain conditions.

- There are good reasons for rejecting nonstorage models of imagery (e.g., Neisser, 1976) and accepting the notion that information about states of affairs is stored in the form of internal representations.
- Internal representations are controlled by various encoding, storage, and retrieval processes, as well as by the derivation of new representations from old.
- Concerning the exact nature/format of representation, it is not yet established either that propositions are viable alternatives to images, or that the two are equivalent.
- It may be more economical theoretically to store propositions in long-term entities and then to construct mental models from these underlying descriptions.
- Models constructed from an indeterminate description will be arbitrary in either the number of, or arrangement of, its elements or both.
- Images that are experienced consciously probably correspond to those features of models that can be perceived in the objects that they represent.
- The use of high-level representations indicates the need for an overall control system that directs and monitors demanding cognitive tasks in a flexible manner.

See the several constraints on theories of imagery that Kosslyn (1980, pp. 112–73) presents in the discussion of his core theory, as well as his review of the various competing imagery theories.

In the light of such constraints or criteria, Morris and Hampson (1983, pp. 57–62, 144–48) present a general model of cognition labeled the *boss-consciousness* theory (cf. Hampson and Morris, 1990). The basis of this approach is that some central control system is required to explain the many-faceted phenomena of consciousness, introspection, automaticity, and the interrelationships of cognitive processes. In this model, a basic distinction is made between the central ("boss") control function or process and the subordinate ("employee") systems. Moreover, among the characteristics of boss processing are its intentionality and its suitability for performing novel tasks, and where the concept of consciousness is equivalent to the reception of information made available to boss and where introspection is involved in the reporting on this information. Furthermore, the role of boss-consciousness in imaging depends on its specific links with top-down perceptual processing; also, for most of the time, the perceptual employee systems may run without boss involvement even when they are involved in top-down operations. Occasionally, however, when the incoming stimulus information is poor or inadequate, or when perceptual decisions are difficult, boss-consciousness may have to take more direct control of top-down processing. Consequently, according to this model, imagery is the limiting case of perception without any stimulus information (i.e., imagery is equivalent to the perceptual system working in a purely top-down mode, normally under the direct control of a boss program; thus, some organisms have learned the trick of "perceiving without stimulus data"). The whole process of "interrogating the database" and constructing a mental image is what is meant to engage in top-down processing, or to use a mental model, in an imagery mode.

The imagery model proposed by Morris and Hampson (1983) incorporates a distinction between mental models and propositions where the perceivable aspects of models are representations that are expressed in the high-level language that boss deals in and that allow it to plan subsequent processing. Additionally, various other processes characterize boss's functioning where, ultimately, images are the perceivable aspects of models and are organized in a format suitable for boss programs. Finally, whenever a visual or verbal subsidiary task is performed at the same time as an imagery task—and uses boss programs—more general and resource-limited interference effects may occur where the result will be that either the imagery or the subsidiary task, or both, will be affected negatively. Thus, according to Morris and Hampson's boss model, intermodal, as well as intramodal, conflict is a distinct possible outcome in such situations.

In the second half of his book on the imagery debate, philosopher Michael Tye (1991, pp. 77–149) discusses the following issues as he presents his own proposal concerning a theory of imagistic representation: "an alternative to quasi-pictures and structural descriptions (mental images as interpreted symbol-filled arrays)," "image indeterminacy," "the phenomenal aspects of mental images," and "the physical basis of imagery and the causal role of image content." For a review of philosopher Tye's (1991) book by another philosopher who is interested, also, in imagery, see N.J.T. Thomas (1994). Thomas suggests that if one wishes to understand the strengths of the arguments concerning imagery by investigators such as Kosslyn, Pylyshyn, and Hinton, this book is "recommended very warmly" (p. 291); however, if one wishes to understand the underlying mechanisms of imagery, then "Tye's conclusions should be treated with great caution" (p. 291).

As a basis for his own theoretical approach, Tye (1991) adopts the essential elements of Marr's (1982) theory of visual perception ("it is widely considered to be the best theory of vision we have," p. 77). Tye discusses Marr's theory for several reasons: it is useful to have a plausible account of how vision works (cf. Wade, 1998) inasmuch as there are shared mechanisms and representations in imagery and vision; both the pictorial and descriptional approaches take mental images to be significantly similar to certain representations that occur during vision vis-à-vis Marr's theory; and the account of imagery Tye favors draws upon central features of Marr's view. Following a review of Marr's vision theory, Tye presents the following material:

- An elaboration of a serious difficulty for the pictorialist approach to images (i.e., the difficulty of representation of the third dimension in the experience of imagery. "[T]here is good reason to reject the hypothesis that images are 3-D arrays . . . the pictorial approach, as it stands, should be rejected," pp. 84–85).
- Some objections to the theory that images are structural descriptions (e.g., "one compelling objection to Pylyshyn's version of descriptionalism is that it cannot satisfactorily explain away Kosslyn's experimental data on imagery by appeal to the doctrines of task demands and tacit knowledge," p. 86).
- The outline of a view of images as "interpreted symbol-filled arrays" that incorporates aspects of the other (rejected) theories, in conjunction with certain features of Marr's account of vision ("I maintain that the proposed view not only sidesteps the objections I make to pictorialism and descriptionalism but also accommodates a wide variety of data on imagery," p. 77).

Commenting on his overall theoretical approach to imagery, Tye (1991) maintains that he draws heavily on the views of *both* the pictorialists and descriptionalists—without falling exclusively into either camp. At one place (p. 102), Tye declares, "The truth about images, I suggest, is that they are a mixed breed."

Finally, in assessing Tye's approach, Thomas (1994, p. 292) states that "I doubt that Tye would seriously want to deny that the theory which he gives us is much more than a tidied-up version of Kosslyn's 'quasi-pictorial' theory (circa 1983). However, Tye does greatly clarify the notion of a quasi-picture, drawing out its homology with the 'two-and-one-half-D sketch' of Marr's influential visual theory." Thomas's own inclination toward the optimal explanation of imag-

ery, in theoretical terms, is to look for answers beyond "computational representationalism" (i.e., the approach in which mental contents—including images—are held to be identifiable with the data
structures being manipulated by the program which the brain, considered to be a computer, is supposed to be operating). According
to Thomas, nonpictorial and noncomputational representationalistic
imagery theories do exist (although in somewhat underdeveloped
states) in what he calls *perceptual activity theories* (e.g., Neisser,
1976), and which he has advocated elsewhere (e.g., Thomas, 1999).
Thomas (1994, p. 294) draws the following conclusion regarding
Tye's work: "Tye betrays no awareness of the possibility of any sort
of imagery theory beyond pictorialism and descriptionalism. His
book is aptly titled. It is about the (or, at least, an) imagery debate.
It may not be about imagery."

> Any child knows that images are close to the core of existence.
> . . . A corollary of our thesis concerning the survival of images
> from an earlier evolutionary stage must be that they serve signifi-
> cant functions, for otherwise—the scientific Weltanshauung of our
> age suggests—they would be gradually or quickly extinguished.
> —L. W. Doob, 1972

> This aid to selection is the most basic and most important func-
> tion of the image: it structures and creates some order that is
> meaningful and relevant to our physical and our psychological
> needs out of the terrifying chaos that is the world of sight, sound,
> smell, taste, touch, and movement.
> —R. Gordon, 1972

> The role of imagery in cognitive function is one of the oldest and
> most difficult problems investigated by psychologists.
> —D. F. Marks, 1972a

> What is its (imagery's) function in terms of human survival and
> happiness? The answer must be given in evolutionary terms, both
> for the species and for the individual. . . . Imagery permits the ex-
> ploration of various possibilities for action without the time con-
> straints and possible dangers of the real event.
> —R. Sommer, 1978

> Images and affects are conscious aspects of our neural models (or
> of integrated response complexes) when they become activated

... imagery is at the center of the organism's capacity for adaptive action in relation to the world.

—E. Klinger, 1981

Although imagery has been an instrument of therapeutic intervention throughout the recorded history of medicine, recently interest in widely varied imagery techniques has greatly expanded and intensified.

—A. A. Sheikh and C. S. Jordan, 1983

Part of the psychophysical equipment for sustaining good physical health is the mental image and its neural underpinnings.

—R. G. Kunzendorf and A. A. Sheikh, 1990

Substantial gaps in our understanding of imagery remain. Indeed, the fundamental question concerning the *function* of imagery remains almost completely unanswered.

—D. F. Marks, 1990

A number of hypnotic imagery techniques have been demonstrated to be effective in dealing with pain.

—N. E. Brink, 1991

It is suggested that specific functions of cells may be influenced by imagery if the subject is aware of those cellular functions.

—J. Schneider, C. W. Smith, C. Minning, S. Whitcher, and J.
Hermanson, 1991

Although many athletes use imagery to some extent, few appear to develop this skill to its potential.

—D. Smith, 1991

## APPLICATIONS AND FUNCTIONS OF IMAGERY

As indicated in the previous sections of this chapter, the issue of the *nature* of imagery has been, and still is, a much-debated problem of theory in psychology where some researchers have endowed mental images, especially spatial images, with the very properties they are alleged to represent in mind, and other researchers have suggested that all mental experience may be captured with the structured propositional representation of the logician (cf. Janssen, 1976). Yet other investigators of imagery have been concerned with how imaging may *function* in mental life, as well as its *application* to practical problems of everyday life (for a discussion of imagery in the field of advertising, see Alesandrini and Sheikh, 1983). A general notion or assumption here is the acceptance of the fact that an image of a particular experience is sometimes not distinguished readily from the perception of an actual physical encounter with particular objects or events (cf. Kolers and Smythe, 1979). In this section, I indicate the *practical* side of imagery (as distinguished from the previous discussion concerning the *theoretical* side) in regard to the application and functioning of imagery in people's quotidian activities (cf. Sommer, 1978). Accordingly, I review a number of selected studies here (chronologically arranged, mostly) that focus on the application and functioning of mental imagery, and employ in each subsection the following eight organizational rubrics in this discussion: Imagery and General Functions and Applications; Imagery and Creativity; Imagery and Development/Personality; Imagery and Learning/Memory; Imagery and Perception; Imagery and Physiology; Imagery and Sports; and Imagery and Therapy/Visualization Techniques.

## Imagery and General Functions and Applications

In a work on current cognitive approaches to imagery edited by Segal (1971a), chapters include contributions by T. X. Barber (1971), B. R. Bugelski (1971), R. N. Haber (1971), A. Paivio (1971a), and S. J. Segal (1971b). Several of these writers, among others, suggest various functions of imagery. Segal (1971a, pp. 1–3) provides a brief history of imagery and identifies several perspectives and functional features of imagery (by writer):

- Habits of abstract thought tend to reduce imagery—imagery is the product of a relatively unsophisticated organism and is not appropriately included among the higher cognitive functions (Galton).
- Vivid imaging is a defining characteristic of autism (Bleuler).
- Imagery and hallucinations are included in the "primary process" function related to drives, wishes, and the more infantile needs (Freud).
- Imagery does not depend on the stimulus and it is a basic cognitive function (Titchener).
- Imagery is a cognitive function dependent on "cell assemblies" and "phase sequences" (Hebb).
- Mnemonic devices employing imagery facilitate learning and memory (Miller, Galanter, and Pribram; Bugelski; Paivio).
- In the conception of two processing systems—the imagistic and the

verbal—imagery is considered to be a more primitive organizer than language even though there is reciprocity between the two (Paivio).

- The human nervous system possesses the capacity to prolong its awareness of a stimulus beyond the time when the stimulus actually disappears (Haber).
- The "icon" is more relevant than the "eidetic" image to the study of imagery as a cognitive function (Haber).
- The importance of prior sensory experiences for imagery may be studied through analysis of visual imagery in the congenitally blind and auditory imagery in the deaf (Bugelski).
- Imagery and perception function in a similar fashion—the image and percept are analogous (Segal).
- Imagery may be studied profitably (i.e., experimentally) via hypnosis and "hallucinogenic" drugs (Barber).
- Normal imagery is a basic cognitive process in which it is not possible to study cognition adequately without elucidating the functions, especially the adaptive functions, of imagery (Segal).

Doob (1972) asserts that images are *ubiquitous*—they appear universally among all cultures (cf. Doob, 1965, 1966, 1970) and at a very early age among normal, healthy children (cf. Jaensch, 1930; Leask, Haber, and Haber, 1969). In this respect, therefore, images must reflect a human ability that has survived from an earlier evolutionary stage (cf. Price-Williams, 1961; Sommer, 1978, p. 42). Following his distinction between *reported* versus *inferred* images (i.e., in an experiment images are reported when they are mentioned/described verbally by the participants experiencing them, and are inferred by the experimenter via the stimulus materials or observable responses of the participants; for instance, in dream analysis, the experimenter learns about dreams in two ways: from what the dreamer says about them upon awakening or from the dreamer's rapid eye movements that occur during sleep), Doob examines the following issues:

1. Evidence for the *primitive* nature of imagery via dreams and related phenomena, via evidence in nonliterate societies (cf. Goodwin, 1953), and via universal processes/devices/variables/evidence such as the electroencephalogram; the decreasing dependence on environmental conditions with increasing age; the manipulability of images and other modes of storage; conditions of sensory deprivation, isolation, and boredom; and children's learning the vocabulary of their native language (cf. Gan'kova, 1960).

2. The *functions* of imagery (including the expressive/emotive, meaning-fulness, mediating, information-storage, and learning functions that involve the four classes of imagery—after-, eidetic-, memory-, and imagination-images—among others; cf. Betts, 1909; Davis, 1932; Fernald, 1912; Paivio, 1970; Richardson, 1969; Shepard, 1978b; Susukita, 1937; Thorndike, 1907; Waltz, 1979).

3. The notion of "substitute satisfaction" where imagination—when it points toward the future—enables the person to anticipate or create novel so-lutions, or when it functions as fantasy, it allows one to secure substitute satisfaction. (Doob [1972, p. 319] asserts that the reason for the partial or almost complete disappearance of imagery as individuals mature in their society is due to the mastery and use of language which is usually more efficient than imagery and, consequently, images come to have less and less survival value.)

4. The *development* of imagery (advancing the notion that images are pri-mordial because ontogenetic development proceeds in a sequence from percept to imagery, and then to verbal storage; cf. Rohwer, 1970; also, imagery itself develops along the continuum from afterimage to imagi-nation; cf. Piaget, 1962; Piaget and Inhelder, 1966).

Among his conclusions, Doob (1972) makes the following points:

1. Each individual child learns and uses the kind of mediating responses best adapted to the problems facing him/her and, thus, the sequence of im-age and language depends on the cultural and environmental conditions present at the age of learning.

2. Inasmuch as the preverbal child can solve, or resolve, some problems only by internalizing experience and anticipating outcomes, it is reasonable to infer that some of the storage is accomplished through preverbal imag-ery.

3. American children use fantasy that is related statistically to various back-ground conditions involving the family (cf. Singer, 1961).

4. In Western cultures, imagery correlates with certain personality traits (cf. Hummeltenberg, 1939) and other behaviors (e.g., it correlates with less stereotyped views regarding nationality groups, with reported dreams and paper-and-pencil tests of traits of dominance, self-confidence, and seek-ing admiration from others).

5. Among male adolescents, the possession of vivid imagery or fantasy cor-relates with persuasibility.

6. Among American high-school students, their visual and eidetic imagery correlates with their ability to spell.

7. In the ontogenetic hypothesis—which proposes a developmental shift from afterimages eventually to imaginal ones—it may be argued that

afterimages must be more primordial than the others because after involuntary or voluntary exposure they are least subject to control.

Finally, Doob (1972) observes that no data, to date, exist concerning the development of various kinds of imagery in the same samples of children from the same culture. Moreover, according to Doob, the best theory of images must be able to account for the storing of images in the first place (cf. Piaget, 1962, p. 70). Doob states that

> [n]o single investigation or experiment by itself proves the thesis that imagery is one of the basic human attributes. The cumulative evidence, nevertheless, makes one conclusion seem inescapable: although our experiences are labeled promiscuously and stored literally and figuratively in unified and fragmented sentences, phrases, and words, our images survive and continue to increase stimulation in the present and also to assist us, for better or worse, in re-experiencing and remembering the past. (pp. 327–28)

In grappling with the complex issue of the relationship between imagery and the thought processes, Bugelski (1983) incidentally suggests various imagery functions. In one case (p. 74), he notes that imagery and language are the "only meaningful operations in thinking" (cf. Kaufmann, 1980); in a second case (p. 82), in defining images, Bugelski suggests that images function as "conditioned sensory responses" and, as such, are "neural activities" involving sense organs that are accompanied by motor reactions to some degree; and in a third case (p. 83), Bugelski (1983) asserts that the "basic operational function of images" lies in their ability as responses to "generate stimuli" where "image-produced stimulation can lead to other imagery or overt responses." In this respect, according to Bugelski, images are similar in function to Guthrie's (1935) "movement-produced stimuli," Osgood's (1953) "r-subscript-m," and Hull's (1943) "r-subscript-g" values; they are probably most easily described as Hebb's (1949) "cell assemblies" (cf. Greenwald, 1970; Mowrer, 1960). Moreover, Bugelski suggests that one's thinking is controlled often by whatever stimulation evokes one's past experience. On the adult human level, such stimulation is largely verbal and some of the verbalization generates imagery. In his analysis, Bugelski maintains that sometimes one's imagery functions as an aid in the sense of being adjustive and eliminating problems (cf. Bower, 1970a,b, 1972); on the other hand, sometimes one's imagery may function to create new problems. On the issue of imagery and its function in creative think-ing, Bugelski (p. 91) asserts that "creative thinking is no different from any other kind. . . . Thinking just occurs, and what the thinking amounts to is what imagery happens to occur to someone. One can-not bid nor forbid certain images to appear. They occur to appropri-ate stimuli if the appropriate background is there to begin with." In discussing the relationship between imagery and emotions, Bugelski (p. 92) endorses Mowrer's (1960) analysis of the role of language, imagery, and emotion in "what passes for thinking and meaning." Thus, another function of imagery is to account for (denotative) mean-ing and, by extension, to account for the operation of "symbolic pro-cesses" or thinking. Among his conclusions, Bugelski laments the fact that the account of imagery—and its role as a mediator in thinking—may not satisfy many psychologists "because it does not lead imme-diately to easily implemented research hypotheses" (p. 92). On the other hand, especially on the heuristic side, imagery may be described satisfactorily as a dynamic, changing, neural event where there is a prior requirement that imagery be conscious or describable (however, it may be considered by some to be a hypothetical construct like any other conditioned response and with the additional feature of functioning as a mediator over long periods of time) (cf. Bugelski, 1968, 1970, 1971, 1974, 1977, 1979; King, 1978, 1979; Leuba, 1940).

Following his review of various criteria for evaluating the worth of theories of mental processing, Kosslyn (1983, pp. 213–23) discusses some of the practical applications arising from imagery/cognitive sci-ence theories of the mind. (Kosslyn asserts that one of the measures of a good scientific theory is its ability to provide a useful technol-ogy.) Among the practical applications of imagery theory research cited by Kosslyn are the following areas:

• Education—provides investigations concerning the most successful pre-sentation of information that plays to the learner's strengths; provides useful insights for designers of educational programs (e.g., in early edu-cation, children depend heavily on imagery for learning up to about the age of seven years; in designing curriculum materials for this level of edu-cation it seems reasonable, therefore, to emphasize the graphic/pictorial aspect of the materials for optimal performance).
• Human Engineering—in the area of product design, for example, com-puter systems can be designed to be more "user compatible/friendly"; also, computer graphics systems may be created to help architects visual-ize—via "externalizing imagery"—what their finished projects/buildings will look like under various options, conditions, or plans.

- Therapy—regarding interpersonal interactions, much of one's concepts of "self" and "others" is stored, presumably, in his/her brain as mental images; a large part of the therapist's job is to bring one's covert images to the conscious surface and to change or update them in more healthy and adaptive ways; for instance, in treating phobic behaviors, the technique of "systematic desensitization" makes extensive use of imagery materials, procedures, and progressions.
- Artificial Intelligence—in this area, the two general approaches—performance mode and simulation mode—for programming computers to behave in intelligent ways have helped to solve a wide variety of problems, to aid in the processes of perception and seeing, and to facilitate the understanding of language; also, under the fiat that the mind uses and stores depictive images, it is reasonable to program computers to do the job in much the same way.

In one section in their book (chapter 9, pp. 206–39), Morris and Hampson (1983) discuss the uses and functions of imagery, among which are the following applications:

- Problem-solving—in the area of "micro" problems (i.e., relatively simple problems that are solvable fairly easily and quickly), images may be used to retrieve facts about events and objects (cf. Kaufmann, 1984).
- Reasoning—images and mental models may be used to realize internal consistency and logical implications of the semantic information one possesses.
- Creativity—visual imagery has been associated with creativity by many researchers and theorists, although there is little work on the precise link between these two aspects in any systematic way; in particular, it is likely that imagery control is an important variable in the creative process, but deserves more attention in the literature than it has received.

For a general review linking imagery, creativity, and aesthetics, see Lindauer, 1977; and for a specific application of imagery involving the use of an imagery scale in the objective rating of movies and TV programs, see Roeckelein, 2003.

For other discussions on the general functions and applications of imagery, see the following studies: Bartlett (1921, 1925, 1927); Binford (1981); Finke (1989, pp. 150–55); Finke and Shepard (1986); Klinger (1971, 1981); Kohl and Roenker (1980); Kosslyn, Seger, Pani, and Hillger (1990); Lindsay (1988); McKim (1980); Miller (1984/1986); Richardson and Patterson (1986); Roe (1951); Shorr, Robin, Connella, and Wolpin (1989); Shorr, Sobel, Robin, and Connella (1980); Shorr, Sobel-Whittington, Robin, and Connella (1983);

Snodgrass (1991); Thorndike (1907); Vandenberg (1978); and Wolpin, Shorr, and Krueger (1986).

## Imagery and Creativity

Forisha (1983) examines the relationship between creativity and mental imagery (cf. Forisha, 1978a,b, 1981). She previously found that sex/gender and chronological age affects the creativity-imagery relationship, but maturity was not consistently related to either variable. Moreover, she discovered that academic disciplines—and possibly cognitive styles—showed distinctly different patterns associated with creativity and imagery. Following her brief review of the psychological literature on the topics of hemispheric functioning, creativity, imagery, and cognitive styles, Forisha discusses current research findings on the interconnections between the three constructs of creativity, imagery, and cognitive styles. (See also Samuels and Samuels's [1975, pp. 238–62] account of creativity that includes various theories of creativity—such as Sinnott's and Rugg's theories, the conditions that foster creativity, and neurophysiology vis-à-vis creativity.) Among Forisha's conclusions are the following points: the relationship between creativity and imagery is central for some individuals but not for others, and it may vary in terms of one's total personality; the variability in the creativity-imagery relationship may be defined in terms of the dimensions of extraversion-introversion and objectivity-subjectivity (also, men seem to prefer a more structured universe than do women; the women lean more to the intuitive, nonstructured approach and are more extraverted in their orientation; control of imagery does not appear to be a salient factor in women's style); four quadrants have been identified as a framework for studying cognitive styles (subjective-introverted, subjective-extraverted, objective-extraverted, and objective-introverted); and a number of polarities studied by other researchers may be listed as related to the present dimensions of subjectivity and objectivity (i.e., right versus left hemisphere; global versus analytic orientation; people- versus task-oriented; resistance to versus preference for structure; intuitive versus logical; and deductive versus inductive). Forisha cautions that her model is still tentative and open to further empirical examination; however, she asserts that at higher levels of integration, creativity and imagery may ultimately reflect a balance between originality and relevance, imagination and logic, and an ability to utilize both internal and external referents.

Finke (1990) examines creative imagery in a unique way by combining the topics of experimental methodology and creative exploration (cf. Shepard, 1978a, 1988; Weisberg, 1986). Following his discussion of anecdotes of creative discoveries in imagery, Finke presents a new approach to creative insight and invention based upon the notion that creative discoveries and inventions might best be achieved by taking an *indirect* strategy. That is, instead of the *traditional* strategy of starting out by thinking of what kinds of invention are needed (or what new ideas are feasible), the new approach encourages the conception of a general object/shape, for example, that is intuitively interesting in itself, and then goes on to consider its possible uses as the situation demands. This approach is consistent with those general recommendations for *nondirective* thinking that have been made by previous investigators on creativity and problem solving (e.g., DeBono, 1967; Levine, 1987).

According to Finke (1990), with the employment of the indirect approach to creativity, the realization of a new idea or invention is thus largely unanticipated—it merely flows from the structure of an imaginal form; however, it doesn't necessarily follow from any particular form. In effect, there are many possible discoveries that the same imagined shape or form may inspire—depending on the desired or required goal. Finke's notion is that real creativity comes from using the things we create, *not* creating the things we use. His major proposition is that one should consider turning the inventive process *inward* and generate and explore mental images that are called *preinventive forms.* Such forms are the products of the combinational play of visualization and they need not be structured according to particular problems or tasks. The assumption here is that creative insights follow naturally as one explores the many possible interpretations of the preinventive forms. Finke asserts that, with this approach, typically, one ends up by inventing things that one never considered previously, or by discovering solutions to problems that one was not initially trying to solve.

Finke (1990) describes, also, the components of creativity where creative discoveries may be defined on two separate dimensions: the *practicality* of an invention (or the *sensibility* of a concept), and the *originality* of an invention/discovery (cf. Sternberg, 1988, for other dimensions of creativity). In his interesting—and creative "reader participation"—book, Finke reports on the findings of eighteen preinventive forms experiments, where nine of the studies are devoted specifically to discovering creative inventions in imagery. The experimental studies involved more than 800 participants in over 5,000 experimental trials where hundreds of creative inventions were collected. Based upon these experiments, Finke draws the following conclusions (among others): people are capable of making visual discoveries using mental imagery that are not merely the result of sophisticated guessing, experimenter bias, or skilled anticipation; to make creative discoveries in imagery, it is best to imagine combining basic parts/components in an intuitive, exploratory way, and then to mentally "see" if an interesting shape or form emerges; a good strategy to use is to imagine preinventive forms of general interest and potential usefulness, and then to interpret the forms according to particular object categories (versus using the object categories to motivate the forms); and many creative discoveries are inspired by the emergent properties of the preinventive forms themselves (see Gibson's [1979] earlier concept of *affordances* as a precursor to Finke's concept of preinventive forms). In discussing the ecological significance of his experimental research findings, Finke suggests the following implications: his approach allows individuals the opportunity to make discoveries that may have direct application in the real-world environment; it is feasible to develop a creative invention for every preinventive form that individuals generate—given sufficient time to interpret the form; the absence of practice effects in the experiments suggests that the image discoveries are mostly spontaneous in nature and the successful use of the methods does not require lengthy training procedures; and it may be that what really distinguishes creative from noncreative people is that the latter may simply not pursue the possibilities of their creative images. Finally, Finke recommends three things that one may do to promote creative thinking and discovery: generate preinventive forms freely and intuitively; explore the possibilities of the preinventive forms patiently and without preconceptions; and concentrate on restricting one's interpretations to general classes of objects or concepts rather than particular types of inventions or problems.

Houtz and Patricola (1999) review the knowledge base and theory of imagery and creativity, and indicate the various relationships between these two phenomena. They note that a most common definition of creativity is that it is a process that leads to the production of something that is both new and useful; moreover, the process may be primarily cognitive—involving particular creative skills, attitudes, and styles—or it may result primarily in a product, leading to the solution of a particular or practical problem. As regards the phenomenon of imagery, it is generally *internal* cues or motivations as opposed to *external* sensations and perceptions. Imagery has been characterized as *nonverbal memory*. Images may be of objects, events, or action scenes; they may also be short-lived or long-lasting and spontaneously or deliberately generated and manipulated by conscious effort. Further, Houtz and Patricola distinguish between imagery and both sensation and perception (*sensation* refers to the impact of external stimulation on the body's sensory organs resulting in signals being sent along neural pathways to the brain; *perception* refers to the interpretation or meaning given by the mind/brain to the sensory inputs; images may both be *sensed* or *perceived* and, often, individuals may confuse sensation and perception of real objects that are external to themselves with imagined objects). Among the numerous types of imagery-related topics cited are body image, hallucinations, phosphenes, thought images, hypnagogic images, hypnapompic images, eidetic images, and synaesthesia. Following their discussions of the various theories and characteristics of imagery, as well as the effects of imagery on cognitive and affective functioning, Houtz and Patricola describe three categories of research on the relationship between imagery and creativity: studies of creative individuals and their self-reports of imagery experiences during their work; studies showing the correlation between the ability of individuals to generate images, most often visual, and their scores on measures of creativity/creative potential (e.g., scores on vividness of imagery correlate significantly with scores on acceptance of authority, environmental sensitivity, initiative, self-strength, intellectuality, individuality, and artistry); and studies on how the use of imagery affects creative productivity (e.g., imagination training enhances performance for participants who are high imagers, but the effects of such training is negligible on those without imaging ability; also, the effects of imagery on problem solving depend on the nature of the task/problem as well as on the specific training conditions).

Houtz and Patricola (1999) note that certain research has demonstrated the positive effects of imagery training on responses, in particular, to the *Torrance Tests of Creative Thinking* (Torrance, 1966) in the creative strength areas of movement or action and richness of imagery, and that imagery training also has improved creativity scores on other measures, including risk taking, total affect, and personal involvement (cf. Goff and Torrance, 1991). However, Houtz and Patricola caution that—although some studies have shown positive relationships among imagery ability, imagery use, and creative problem-solving performance—many other studies have shown conditional, neutral, or even negative results, and they observe that imagery is not necessarily a guarantee of creative success. Houtz and Patricola (pp. 8–9) cite the following points as to the reasonable conclusions concerning the creativity-imagery relationship that may be drawn from the imagery literature (cf. Torrance, 1995): states of consciousness (other than logical or wakeful states) must be activated, at least for brief intermittent periods; intellectual, volitional, and emotional functions must be brought into play together; there must be realistic encounters with a problem, intense absorption, involvement, commitment, and heightened awareness; there must be a confrontation simultaneously with opposite, contradictory, or antithetical concepts, images, or ideas; and visual, kinaesthetic, auditory, and other sensory modes of thought must be activated. The work by both Joseph Khatena (e.g., Khatena, 1976, 1978, 1983; Khatena and Torrance, 1973, 1976) and Ronald Finke (e.g., Finke, 1990, 1993; Finke, Ward, and Smith, 1992) on the relationship between imagery and creativity is discussed by Houtz and Patricola who suggest that such current research on the topic indicates that imagery's mechanism for new idea–generation is its inherently spatial quality where the *combinatorial and transformative processes* (e.g., Finke, Ward, and Smith's [1992] *Geneplore Model*, which refers to the functions of *generate* and *explore* in creative cognition; and Khatena's [1978, 1983] proposed *synthesis-destructuring-restructuring process* in creative imagination) are essential to the creativity-imagistic thinking relationship (cf. Daniels-McGhee and Davis, 1994). As one uses objects in his/her imagery activities, new forms or possible arrangements are "seen," and from such preinventive forms (e.g., Finke, 1990), one may discover original and useful applications of these forms to particular problems, tasks, or situations.

For other discussions on the relationship between *creativity* and imagery, see the following studies: Anderson and Helstrup (1993); Arieti (1976); Bloomberg (1971, 1976); Edwards (1986); Ernest (1977); Finke (1993); Finke and Slayton (1988); Galton (1874); Gardner (1982); Gotz and Gotz (1979); Gowan (1979); Gur and Reyher (1976); Intons-Peterson (1993); Kassels (1991); Kaufmann and Helstrup (1993); Khatena (1977, 1978); Koestler (1964); Krueger (1976); Peterson (1993); Reed (1993); Roskos-Ewoldsen (1993); Roskos-Ewoldsen, Intons-Peterson, and Anderson (1993); Schmeidler (1965); Shaw and DeMers (1986, 1986–1987); Shepard

(1990); Singer and Switzer (1980); Sobel and Rothenberg (1980); Spotts and Mackler (1967); Martindale (1990; contains a ninety-two-item bibliography on creativity); for a review of the arts and imagery, see Lindauer (1977, 1983); and a meta-analytic review is in LeBoutillier and Marks (2003).

## Imagery and Development/Personality

Lautrey and Chartier (1991) describe a developmental approach to mental imagery that initially examines the assumptions, methodology, and findings of theories of information processing as well as Piagetian theory (cf. Tower's [1983], treatment of the role of imagery in development). Lautrey and Chartier focus specifically on the development of the capacity for mental images of transformation in the child. In their comparison of the Piagetian and information-processing theories, they found that relating these two modes of representation may serve as a powerful tool in conceptualizing the development of spatial operations in particular. Lautrey and Chartier note that whereas Piaget's studies were motivated by the *empiricism-constructivism* controversy, the recent debate vis-à-vis information processing involves the basic issue of the nature of mental imagery (i.e., the *antimental imagery* argument claims that all forms of representation—including mental images—have a propositional or symbolic base; on the other hand, the *promental imagery* position contends that mental images are analog representations, although they do not outright reject the notion of a propositional mode of representation). Thus, most information processing approaches to mental imagery involve the testing of the theories' explanatory power, in particular as regards *isomorphisms*; and, in contrast, the Piagetian approach focuses more specifically on developmental issues involving children's performance on tasks (the information processing studies typically employ trained adult participants and assess their stimulus-transformation abilities). Lautrey and Chartier (pp. 266–67) propose the following dual-processing hypothesis: the type of test situations—especially the features of the paradigm and stimulus type—appeal to varying degrees of two distinct modes of representation and spatial information processing; one mode covers processes in the field of analog representations, and the other mode of processing is compatible with propositional models of representation and Piaget's operational theory.

Lautrey and Chartier (1991) suggest that postulating two coexisting, but distinct, modes of representation of spatial information leads to the issue of their interrelatedness, and raises questions for future developmental research studies such as "Do preferences for a given mode of representation *evolve* over the course of development?" and "What defines the relationships between *age* and *modes* of representation and/or determines the *interaction* between the two modes?"

In the same book containing contributions to the understanding of imagery, both Forisha (1983, pp. 319–23) and Wilson and Barber (1983, pp. 340–87) provide separate discussions and perspectives on the relationship between imagery and personality. Wilson and Barber discuss their research in which they found that excellent hypnotic participants have a profound fantasy (imagery) life where involvement in fantasy plays an important role in producing superb hypnotic performance. In addition, as a serendipitous finding, Wilson and Barber suggest that there exists a small group of individuals—possibly 4 percent of the population—who fantasize a large part of the time, who typically see, hear, smell, touch and fully experience what they fantasize, and who may be characterized as possessing *fantasy-prone personalities* (cf. Barber, Spanos, and Chaves, 1974; Barber and Wilson, 1978–1979; Hilgard, 1970, 1979; McKellar, 1979; Perry, 1973; Sheehan, 1979; Singer, 1977; Sutcliffe, Perry, and Sheehan, 1970; Wilson and Barber, 1981). Forisha (1983) reviews studies that have reported correlates between imagery and personality; for example, uncontrolled imagery is related to neuroticism (cf. Costello, 1956, 1957; Gordon, 1972); imagery clarity is inversely related to introversion and neuroticism (Euse and Haney, 1975); the existence of imagery per se has little relationship to mental health; however, flexible and controlled imagery does appear to be a contributing factor to healthy personalities (cf. Singer and Antrobus, 1972); in lower levels of maturity, imagery may play a strong role in the thought processes of both women and men—without being clearly differentiated from reality (McClelland, 1975); imagery may be more important in the cognitive processes of men when aggression and conquest are not primary themes/goals in their lives (McClelland, 1975); and imagery and fantasy are basic cognitive capacities that may reflect serious pathology or distress, but may also be employed as valuable aids for planning, self-gratification, creative activity, and adaptation (Singer and Antrobus, 1972). Concerning the relationship between imagery and personality, Forisha (p. 320) suggests that "the various uses of imagery could be described in terms of an individual's orientation to the world, or what psychologists have come to call *cognitive styles*" (cf. Broverman, 1960; Goldstein and Blackman, 1978; Richardson, 1977).

Forisha reviews research on cognitive styles under the assumption that studies on the imagery-personality relationship overlap with those dealing with cognitive style. Typical of the personality variables depicting cognitive style are the polar opposites of: "field dependence-independence" (e.g., Witkin and Goodenough, 1977); "origence-intellectence" (e.g., Welsh, 1975); and the Jungian polarities of "intuiting-sensing," "thinking-feeling," and "perceiving-judging" (e.g., Jung, 1923; Myers, 1962). Other approaches toward, and models of, cognitive style are "reflectivity-impulsivity" (e.g., Kagan, Moss, and Siegel, 1963); "complexity-simplicity" (e.g., Barron, 1953); "formal-operational" thought (e.g., Piaget, 1955; Piaget and Inhelder, 1969); "logical-intuitive/verbal-mathematical" (e.g., Hogan, 1980); and "visualizer-verbalizer" (e.g., Richardson, 1977). Forisha maintains that many research studies have appeared in the psychological literature recently that have either used these categories of cognitive style or created new ones (e.g., Goebel and Harris, 1980; Harren, Kass, Tinsley, and Moreland, 1978). However, according to Forisha, few of these studies define any cognitive styles, in particular, that reflect a *balance* of both cerebral hemispheres.

For other studies on the relationship between imagery and developmental/personality processes, see the following: Anooshian and Carlson (1973); Biblow (1973); Bideaud (1988); Childs and Polich (1979); Connolly (1991); D'Zamko and Schwab (1991); Dansky (1980); Dean (1979); Dean and Harvey (1979); Dean, Scherzer, and Chabaud (1986); Fein (1975); Giambra (1977); Giambra and Grodsky (1991); E. J. Gibson (1969); Gold and Henderson (1984); Golumb and Cornelius (1977); Hartmann (1991); Honeycutt (1991); Huckabee (1974); Hughes and Hutt (1979); Hummeltenberg (1939); Ishii (1986); Johnson (1991); Kail (1985); Kail, Pellegrino, and Carter (1980); Kazdin (1978); Kerr, Corbitt, and Jurkovic (1980); Kosslyn (1976); Kunzendorf, Jesses, Michaels, Caiazzo-Fluellen, and Butler (1991); Lazarus (1984); Levin and Pressley (1978); Lusebrink (1991); Maltz (1960); Marks (1977); Marmor (1975, 1977); Martin and Williams (1990); Morra, Moizo, and Scopesi (1988); Mowbray and Luria (1973); Neiworth and Rilling (1987); Panagiotou and Sheikh (1977); Pascual-Leone (1970); Pascual-Leone and Goodman (1979); Piaget (1962); Piaget and Inhelder (1971); Platt and Cohen (1981); Pulaski (1973); Qualls and Sheehan (1983); Reese (1975); Rohwer (1970); Rosser, Ensing, Glider, and Lane (1984); Singer (1961, 1970, 1973, 1974, 1975, 1977); Singer and Antrobus (1963, 1972); Singer and Singer (1977); Smith and Dodsworth (1978); Spanos (1991);

Tower (1983, 1986); Tower and Singer (1980, 1981); Tversky (1973); Wallace (1991); Young, Palef, and Logan (1980).

## Imagery and Learning/Memory

Marks (1972a), Richardson (1972), Lindauer (1972), Paivio (1972), and Sheehan (1972) all include the processes of learning and memory among the important functions of imagery. Marks (1972a) reviews studies dealing with the role of images in memory (literal and associative functions) and assesses the issue of whether imagery helps or hinders accurate recall (cf. Bartlett, 1932, p. 60), who views imagery as a hindrance to remembering). Among his conclusions, Marks (1972a) notes that good visualizers have significantly more accurate recall than poor visualizers; the use of a mnemonic device—the "mental walk"—improves recall of verbal stimuli; and the ability of the individual to evoke and utilize imagery is not fixed, but is influenced by situational variables and, also, the potential for imagery appears to be universal (cf. Luria, 1968; McKellar and Marks, 1982; Paivio, 1969). (For Paivio's [1972] discussion of the role of imagery in learning and memory, see the subsection "A Review of Imagery Theories" earlier in this chapter.)

Richardson (1972) observes that memory imagery is common and familiar in everyday life and accompanies the recall of past events, the ongoing thought processes of the present, and the anticipatory actions and events of the future. Moreover, according to Richardson, memory imagery is more amenable to voluntary control than all the other forms of imagery. Richardson concludes that the measurement, correlates, and adaptive utility of the *control* dimension of memory imagery constitute a relatively unknown domain within the recently rediscovered area of mental imagery (cf. Costello, 1957; Jenkin, 1935; Morrisett, 1956; Richardson, 1967, 1969; Start and Richardson, 1964).

Following his discussion of the general aspects of sensory imagery (language and aesthetics), and sensory imagery and individual differences, Lindauer (1972) relates sensory imagery to learning under the assumption that acquisition and retention processes are basic to an understanding of the origins and functions of imagery in all its various manifestations (cf. Bowers, 1931, 1932; Chowdhury and Vernon, 1964; Dominowski and Gadlin, 1968; Paivio, 1969, 1972; Raser and Bartz, 1968; Walker, 1970). Lindauer notes that while research studies on the sensory aspect of imagery in the study of individual differences have been numerous, the sensory dimension in the area relating imagery to learning has been relatively ignored (cf. Holt, 1964, p. 261; Lindauer, 1969). In one of his analyses, Lindauer (1972, p. 143) reports that despite different relative degrees of imagery potency, apparent imagery differences "based on a high sensory reference . . . act to facilitate learning." Following his outline of a proposed program of research for the area of sensory imagery vis-à-vis learning (cf. Sheehan's [1972], proposed program of research for the area of visual imagery and memory), Lindauer concludes with the following points (among others): there has been an overreliance on limited modes of imagery and materials in most research on individual differences and learning; high imagery for a particular mode (e.g., taste) does not necessarily lead to better recall; different degrees of imagery for sensory materials may be functionally equivalent (e.g., materials with a high degree of sensory reference—whether relatively high or low in their imagery-arousal capacity—may equally facilitate learning); and, in addition to accounting for the imagery and modularity characteristics of the materials to be learned, other important variables to be considered in future imagery/learning research include the type of learning paradigm used, organizational factors, the concrete-abstract attribute of meaning, and individual differences, including sex/gender differences.

Hyman (1993) reports on his mental imagery experiments that were conducted in response to those by Chambers and Reisberg (1985; cf. Chambers and Reisberg, 1992) who found that participants could *not* discover the alternative interpretation of an ambiguous figure by using mental imagery (cf. Finke, Pinker, and Farah, 1989; Kaufmann and Helstrup, 1993, p. 142). In his research, Hyman tried to discover how manipulation of visual information using imagery was similar to other memory tasks, such as the reconstruction of a story (cf. Hyman and Neisser, 1991). Phrasing the issue of imagery-based discovery in the language of reconstructive memory—rather than the language of perception and perception-imagery equivalences—provided Hyman with an alternative view of the problem. Following the description of his experiments, and based upon their results, Hyman (1993) concluded that mental images of classical ambiguous figures *can* be reversed—especially when participants are given appropriate instructions. Thus, when explicit instructions concerning how to manipulate an ambiguous figure are provided, participants are able to discover an alternative interpretation of such figures. Hyman notes that it is likely that imaging relies on the visual system for its processing much as perceiving does; however, Hyman suggests, looking at an image is not the same as looking at a picture, and not all tasks that can be accomplished when looking at a visual display will be completed with the same facility when one relies on mental images. Hyman maintains that a primary distinction between perception and imagery is the *source* of the information used by the visual system: in perception that source is the world, while in imagery it is memory. As a result of this assumption, Hyman attempts to frame most of his imagery research in terms of similarities between imagery and *memory* rather than between imagery and *perception*.

For other discussions of imagery vis-à-vis learning/memory, see the following studies: Alesandrini (1982); Anderson (1975); Andreani (1988); Annett (1988); Baddeley (1988); Begg (1973, 1978, 1983); Begg and Anderson (1976); Begg and Clark (1975); Begg and Paivio (1969); Bower (1970a,b); Bugelski (1986); Cautela and McCullough (1978); Conway (1988); Conway, Kahney, Bruce, and Duce (1991); Cooper and Shepard (1973b, 1984); Cornoldi and De Beni (1988); Davies (1974); Engelkamp (1991); Ernest (1977, 1987); Ernest and Paivio (1969, 1971); Finke and Pinker (1982); Heuer, Fischman, and Reisberg (1986); Hunt and Marschark (1987); Hyman and Neisser (1991); Intons-Peterson (1981, 1984); Jenkin (1935); Kaufmann (1988, 1990); Kazdin and Smith (1979); King (1973, 1974a,b); Leuba (1940); Leuba and Dunlap (1951); Logie and Baddeley (1990); Logie and Marchetti (1991); Lohr (1976); Lutz and Lutz (1977); MacKay (1981); Mandler and Johnson (1976); Marks (1973a,b); Martel (1991); Matthews (1983); McDaniel and Einstein (1991); McDaniel and Pressley (1987); Paivio (1965, 1969, 1971b, 1972); Peterson, Kihlstrom, Rose, and Glisky (1992); Pressley, Borkowski, and Johnson (1987); Qualls and Sheehan (1983); Quinn (1991); Reed (1974); Reisberg and Logie (1993); Reisberg, Wilson, and Smith (1991); Richardson (1991a); Sackett (1934); Saltz and Donnenwerth-Nolan (1981); Savoyant (1988); Stewart (1966); Tolman (1948); Twining (1949); Vandall, Davis, and Clugston (1943); Weber and Harnish (1974); Yuille and Marschark (1984); Zecker (1982); and Zimler and Keenan (1983). (For a *practical* application of imagery in an original, and omnibus/versatile, learning technique and program for the self-control, self-improvement, or self-modification of personal behavior(s), see Roeckelein, 1984, pp. 88–117.)

## Imagery and Perception

In his chapter on *mental maps*, Sommer (1978, p. 169) characterizes mental maps as the "meeting place of geography and psychology" where—because they include sounds, odors, and sociopolitical information—"they are richer and more varied than cartographers' maps." However, to the extent that such perceptual/imaginal devices as mental maps distort and omit significant items, they are more variable and biased than regular cartographic maps (cf. Tolman, 1948). Sommer notes that people's images of places are highly personal; places that are important to an individual tend to be imagined as more vivid, detailed, and exaggerated in scale (e.g., in drawing maps, students tend to enlarge the size of familiar areas and reduce the size of unfamiliar places; see Saarinen, 1973). Sommer (1978) emphasizes the point that—contrary to a persistent belief among many researchers—mental maps (including "auditory maps," "smell maps," "kinaesthetic maps," "specialized maps," and "perceptual maps") are not only interesting but also are very useful in many practical applications as well (e.g., in designing city parks, new building placements, new transportation systems, etc.).

Sheehan and Bayliss (1984) conducted a study on the relationships among the variables of participant's perception of time, imagination, and hypnosis. Time estimation was examined in seventy-two hypnotic and nonhypnotic participants (undergraduate psychology students, ages ranging from seventeen to fifty-three years) who judged the temporal duration of intervals that varied in their degree of "crowding" with suggested events versus relatively empty intervals (cf. Roeckelein, 2000, pp. 56, 66, 97, 119, 120–35). Sheehan and Bayliss note that research has failed to answer the question whether suggestions that an objectively empty interval that is crowded with events will lead to a shorter (or longer) interval than when suggestions are given that a participant should simply sit and wait for further instructions (cf. Doob, 1971, who reviews equivocal evidence on this issue). Current theorizing, however, about hypnotized participants suggests that the sense of time of hypnotized persons will be different during an interval filled with suggested events—as compared with a temporal interval that is objectively empty—because of their special capacity for imaginative absorption (cf. Barber and Calverley, 1964; Bowers, 1979; Bowers and Brenneman, 1979; Cooper and Erickson, 1954; Cooper and Rodgin, 1952). Sheehan and Bayliss (1984) employed a 3 × 2 × 3 factorial research design to study the problem where three instructional treatments (hypnotic, task-motivated, and unmotivated imagination control), two levels of hypnotic susceptibility (high and low), and three time perception/estimation conditions (mind-blank, actually filled interval, and suggested mental-walk) were studied with repeated measurements from participants on a 120-second time interval estimation task. The main prediction made by Sheehan and Bayliss was that—across participants—time estimates for the interval filled with suggested events should differ from the empty interval and be more like those for the interval filled with actual events. However, it was guessed, hypnotic participants should lose track of time most easily through their imaginative involvement, and the level of their susceptibility to hypnosis should be related to such an effect. Based upon their experimental results, Sheehan and Bayliss found that time perception/estimation conditions generally had a major impact—as predicted—but instructional context did not have an effect. Further, anomalies in the results for high-susceptible, hypnotized participants indicate that imaginative involvement (although relevant to the data) does not explain adequately the variability of the time estimation effects that were found.

In one of his chapters within the larger domain or issue of a proposed "psychology of the image"—ranging from philosophy, sociology, dreams, and psychoanalysis to advertising, photography, film, and fashion—Forrester (2000, chapter 2) discusses the relationship between perception and imagery; he notes that for individuals with normal vision, to see with the mind's eye evokes a picture of perception where there is not a great deal of difference between an internal or external image—what one "sees" inside is an image of what one has already seen outside. Similarly, according to Forrester, to consider perception as "image stimulation/inscription" on a retinal tableau conjures up ideas of nonconscious automatic perceptual processing where brain-mind cognitive transformations allow for the phenomenon of perception. Forrester suggests that there are at least two meanings for the term perception: the reception of information through the senses and "mental insight" that includes processes dependent on expectations and memories. The psychology of visual perception seems to have concentrated on the former meaning, according to Forrester, and has avoided asking the question "Under what conditions may it be claimed that one 'sees' anything at all?"—leaving such issues to phenomenology and philosophy.

One of the aims of Forrester's (2000) discourse is to analyze critically the contemporary views of perception in order to understand why—among other things—perceptual psychology continues to provide the framework within which theories of mental imagery are formulated and explained. Following his examination of the topics of "perception as sensation and as cognition," "constructivist theories of perception," "ecological approaches to perception," "visual imagery in psychology," and "learning how to see—the interdependence of sensation and culture," Forrester draws the following conclusions concerning the relationship between perception and mental imagery:

- Although such a relationship is analytically differentiated from the content of mental images themselves, the constructs, language, and pretheoretical assumptions of the research field rest exclusively on the dominant ideas within contemporary visual theory. Mental imagery research has very little to say regarding mental images that are "nonvisual" (i.e., sound, touch, or kinaesthetically based image sensation)—a seemingly curious omission given the fact that being touched by, or touching, someone may give rise to rich imagery and associations; academic psychological research on images and imagery remains constrained by the theoretical frameworks found in the traditional study of perception (with the possible exception of the perspective found in Barlow, Blakemore, and Weston-Smith, 1990).
- The methodology employed in much mental imagery research—in particular the social practices where individuals are asked to respond to this or that mental image—serves to produce an account of internal processes based on a philosophically debatable account of perception.
- The notion of mental imagery in psychology seems to be largely interdependent with that of "internal representation" (the idea of representation found in cognitive psychology, and cognitive science, has a distinctly "picturelike" quality, and a portraiture or iconic depiction).
- There does not appear to be a potentially fruitful link between contemporary mental imagery research in psychology and a semiotically informed psychology of the image (perhaps the main reason for this is that mental imagery research remains predicated on unexamined assumptions about perception and the relationship between perception and imagery).

Essentially, in Forrester's view, our current ideas about mental imagery continue to be dominated by the metaphors and ideas of visual perception and, apart from ecological psychology, the traditional perspective of imagery is that it is visionlike and supplemented by knowledge or representational processes—always internal and separate somehow from the outside world. Forrester suggests that psychology has yet to consider seriously the proposition that it is through language, in particular, that one differentiates the inside milieu from the outside world (cf. Begg, 1983).

For other discussions of imagery related to perception and perceptual phenomena, see the following studies: Andersen (1987); Antonietti (1991); Bethell-Fox and Shepard (1988); Biederman (1987); Briggs (1973); Byrne (1979); Carpenter and Eisenberg (1978); Chambers and Reisberg (1985); Cooper (1976a,b, 1991); Cooper and Podgorny (1976); Corballis (1988); DeVega (1988); Downs and Stea (1973); Farah (1985); Finke (1980, 1985, 1986, 1989, pp. 29–58); Finke and Kurtzman (1981); Finke, Pinker, and Farah (1989); J. J. Gibson (1966, 1979); Hampson, Marks, and Richardson (1990, pp. 5–10); Helstrup and Anderson (1991); Intons-Peterson (1983); Intons-Peterson and McDaniel (1991); Intons-Peterson and Roskos-Ewoldsen (1989); Kerr (1983); Klopfer (1985); Kolinsky, Morais, Content, and Cary (1987); Kosslyn, Ball, and Reiser (1978); Larkin and Simon (1987); Lee (1962); Loarer and Savoyant (1991); Lynch (1960); Mackay (1958); Marmor and Zabeck (1976); Marr and Nishihara (1978); Milgram (1972); Millar (1990); Osherson, Kosslyn, and Hollerbach (1990); Parsons (1987); Peronnet, Farah, and Gonon (1988); Peruch and Savoyant (1991); Pinker and Finke (1980); Podgorny and Shepard (1978); Potter (1976); Reed and Johnsen (1975); Reisberg and Chambers (1991); Richardson (1991a); Rock, Wheeler, and Tudor (1989); Roskos-Ewoldsen (1989); Samuels and Samuels (1975); Shepard (1984); Slee (1980); Southworth (1969); Tarr and Pinker (1989); Thompson and Klatzky (1978); Tuan (1975); Tversky (1975); and Van der Veur (1975).

## Imagery and Physiology

Zikmund (1972) notes that the traditional difficulty in shaping a satisfactory general and comprehensive definition of mental imagery applies equally well to imagery's physiological bases; he observes, also, that the majority of physiological studies of mental imagery have been based on the experiential similarity between imaging and perceiving (cf. Kulpe, 1893; Leuba, 1940; Oswald, 1957; Sheehan, 1966). Zikmund suggests that the physiological mechanisms of mental imagery phenomena may be discussed at two different levels: the physiological mechanisms *underlying* particular mental imagery phenomena (i.e., mechanisms that—under various physiological or pathological conditions—give perceptual experiences in the person in the absence of appropriate sensory stimulation from the outer world) and the physiological consequents and/or changes *accompanying* various kinds of mental images. Moreover, according to Zikmund, most physiological studies of mental imagery—from both levels—have been concerned with the visual modality (a perspective that he, himself, represents exclusively). Included among Zikmund's observations in his discussions of the physiological changes and bases of visual imagery are the following points (cf. Horowitz, 1970/1978, pp. 245–79): certain physiological changes may reflect certain alterations in the general arousal of the central nervous system, changes in attention, or changes in emotions that vary considerably depending on the individual, one's attitude to the imagined content, and the actual conditions under which an image takes place. (For the role of imagery in sexual behavior, see Przybyla, Byrne, and Kelley, 1983.) Zikmund reviews the physiological changes that accompany visual imagery from the most general dimension (e.g., autonomic changes) to some rather specific dimensions (e.g., changes in the bioelectric activity of the brain, changes in oculomotor activity). He also presents data indicating that following/pursuit eye-movements may be recorded in some participants during vivid visual imagery of moving objects (such a type of eye "gaze" movement, forming the slow phase of the optokinetic nystagmus [OKN], is an inherent component of the mechanisms of visual motion perception and may be used as a physiological indicator that characterizes vivid visual imagery under certain conditions) (cf. Sommer, 1978, pp. 49–52).

Among his conclusions, Zikmund (1972) makes the following points:

- Autonomic changes, such as heart rate, respiration, and plethysmographic changes do not seem, ultimately, to be suitable indicators of visual imagery (due to the fact that such changes predominantly reflect more general reactions or the central nervous system to various kinds of stimuli).
- The amount of "alpha" blocking in EEG (electroencephalogram), and of saccadic eye movements in EOG (electro-oculogram), are not completely satisfactory as indicators in detecting visual imagery at the physiological level (both of these parameters are related to different mental events and to more general changes in the functional state of the central nervous system).
- Evidence suggests that there exists a similarity between the physiological processes underlying visual perception and those occurring while sensory experience of vivid visual imagery takes place (the view is supported that—during vivid visual imagery—complex visual and oculomotor components of visual perception mechanisms are reactivated).

- Two possible mechanisms are responsible for OKN during visual imagery of optokinetic stimuli: vivid visual images/hallucinations involve a component of retinal stimulation which is mediated by hypothesized centrifugal impulses from the brain structures activated when a visual image arises (with excitement of the retinal elements, retino-eye movement feedback mechanisms give rise to OKN in the same way as they do during visual perception).
- The close integration of the visual and oculomotor mechanisms in visual motion perception is reflected in simultaneous reactivation of both these mechanisms during vivid visual imagery (the evocation of a visual image results in reactivation of an appropriate eye-movement pattern; thus, neurophysiological mechanisms engaged in visual imagery seem to be somewhat similar to those underlying visual perception).

Note that Zikmund (1972) provides a substantial references section containing over 130 citations/references related to imagery and physiological correlates; see, for example, Barratt (1956); Deckert (1964); Drever (1958); Golla, Hutton, and Walter (1943); Jacobson (1930, 1932); Noton and Stark (1971); Slatter (1960); Zikmund (1966).

Ley (1983) notes that the assumption that the right cerebral hemisphere mediates cognitive activities involving imagery was enunciated more than 100 years ago by the English neurologist J. Hughlings Jackson in 1874 (cf. Jackson, 1874, 1876/1958, 1880; Wigan, 1844). Ley reviews a number of current experimental studies on cerebral laterality and imagery that indicate the primary role of the *right* hemisphere in various imagery processes. However, according to Ley, sufficient data have not yet been collected to warrant serious consideration of left-hemispheric mediation of such imagery functions as rotation, orientation, or visualization (cf. Bakan, 1980). Among his conclusions, Ley makes the following points:

- Removal of, or damage to, various parts of the right hemisphere often leads to loss/disturbance of visualization, visual memory, visual dreaming, and the vividness of imagery, as well as impairment to imagery-based learning or performance on spatial tasks containing imageable components.
- Compensation for verbal memory deficits due to left-hemisphere injury may be achieved by teaching the patient to use imagery mnemonics that are mediated by the intact right hemisphere.
- Electrical stimulation of the right temporal lobe generally produces patients' reports of rich imagery and other visual hallucinatory impressions similar to those present in epileptic auras and night dreams.

- EEG and GSR studies of normal participants show that increased activation of their right hemisphere accompanies their imagery experiences.
- Left lateral eye movements (via right-hemispheric activation) correlates with the preferred use and clarity of images, as well as with increased performance on imagery tasks.
- Visual-recognition studies of laterally presented abstract and concrete words show a right hemispheric capacity to "read," store, or otherwise mediate the processing of high-imagery words.

Following his speculations on some possible reasons for a right hemisphere superiority for imagery functions (e.g., it is consistent with many dual-processing models of hemispheric function; cf. Bower, 1970a; Dimond, 1972; Paivio, 1978), Ley (1983) suggests some directions that future research in this area may take: new studies are needed to further clarify the role played by imagery in tests of spatial visualization (to understand the relationship between such factors as imagery control/vividness and performance tests of visual-spatial ability); new studies are needed that emphasize *intra-* as well as *inter-* hemispheric activity underlying imagery processes (to understand the correspondence between specific hemispheric tracts and particular imagery tasks); new research is needed that attempts to experimentally extricate hemispheric effects for imagery versus emotional experiences (just as imagery and visual-spatial factors need to be teased apart); and refinement is needed of behavioral measures of cerebral-laterality effects (as compared with, and for control of, cognitive-strategy effects).

Richardson (1991b) discusses the structures and processes within the brain that mediate mental imagery, as well as the results of neuropsychological research into the cerebral mechanisms underlying the phenomenal experience of mental imagery (cf. Richardson, 1980, 1990). Among the several methodological strategies that have been employed in understanding the cerebral mechanisms responsible for mental imagery are the following: the collection of behavioral data from normal, intact individuals (e.g., presenting discrete verbal stimuli solely to one hemisphere); the collection of data from online recordings of brain activity while participants are carrying out specific experimental tasks (e.g., the use of electrophysiological measures such as event-related potentials or electroencephalograms); and the collection of data from patients who have suffered physical damage to the central nervous system (e.g., head injuries/trauma; cerebral tumors; surgical treatment side-effects). Richardson (1991b) notes that recently the functional dissociation of the two cerebral hemispheres vis-à-vis the processing of verbal and nonverbal information appears to provide direct support for the dual-coding theory of verbal and imaginal symbolic functioning (cf. Paivio, 1971b; Sheikh, 1977). Moreover, the assumption that the right cerebral hemisphere is specialized somehow for mental imagery is a popular one today (cf. Ehrlichman and Barrett, 1983). However, alternative hypotheses must be examined and assessed on this issue (e.g., imagery is most likely dependent on several different components or subsystems rather than a single mechanism localized within just one cerebral hemisphere; cf. Kosslyn, 1980).

Following his review of the research on mental imagery from several perspectives (i.e., imagery considered as a phenomenal experience, as an internal representation, as a stimulus attribute, and as a mnemonic strategy), Richardson (1991b) draws the following conclusions:

- Verbal reports of the loss of imagery as a phenomenal experience do *not* seem to be related to damage to the right cerebral hemisphere, nor to surgical separation of the two hemispheres (such reports, though, appear to be linked to damage to the posterior portion of the left cerebral hemisphere).
- The study of patients who have undergone callosal-sectioning indicates that the neural mechanisms for generating mental images are located within the left hemisphere (perhaps the left inferior occipital region), while the right hemisphere probably plays a role in the transformation of mental images.
- The stimulus attributes of imageability and concreteness appear to evoke cortical activation in a relatively symmetrical, bilateral manner (where their effects on learning and memory—with some exceptions—are not lessened by localized damage to either the left or right cerebral hemispheres).
- The efficacy of imagery as a mnemonic strategy does not seem to depend on the integrity of the right hemisphere (also, it is available as an effective means of encoding verbal material even in patients who have undergone callosal-sectioning surgical separation of the two hemispheres).
- Training and instructions in the use of mental imagery may prove to be totally ineffective in patients with damage to the medial temporal lobe or the diencephalon, but this seems to be merely one aspect of a general issue with cognitive mediation rather than any specific problem with imagery itself (also, there is a some evidence that the occipitotemporal region of the left cerebral hemisphere may contain the neural mechanisms responsible for imaginal encoding).

In the final analysis, at least with regard to research up to the 1990s, according to Richardson (1991b), mental imagery is *not* a unitary function but a complex system of interrelating components where many such components are not localized within the right cerebral hemisphere and may well be related closely to the components responsible for perceptual analysis and linguistic comprehension that are located within the left cerebral hemisphere.

Further discussions on these issues regarding the relationship between imagery and physiological/neuropsychological aspects may be found in the following studies: Achterberg (1984); Ahsen (1984); Andersen (1987); Arabian (1982); Arabian and Furedy (1983); Barbut and Gazzaniga (1987); Basso, Bisiach, and Luzzatti (1980); Bauer and Craighead (1979); Begg (1973); Bisiach and Berti (1990); Bisiach, Luzzatti, and Perani (1979); Blizard, Cowings, and Miller (1975); Brown (1984); Bruyer and Racquez (1985); Carroll, Baker, and Preston (1979); Carroll, Mazillier, and Merian (1982); Cermak (1975, 1980); Corballis (1982); Corballis and Sergent (1988, 1989); Crovitz, Harvey, and Horn (1979); Cuthbert, Vrana, and Bradley (1991); Davidson and Schwartz (1977); Dodds (1978); Duke (1968); Eccles (1958); Ehrlichman and Weinberger (1978); Ehrlichman and Weiner (1980); Farah (1984, 1988); Farah, Gazzaniga, Holtzman, and Kosslyn (1985); Farah, Hammond, Levine, and Calvanio (1988); Farah, Levine, and Calvanio (1988); Farah, Peronnet, Gonon, and Giard (1988); Finke (1989, pp. 147–50); Flor-Henry (1990); Friedland and Weinstein (1977); Galin (1974); Gazzaniga and LeDoux (1978); Goldenberg (1989); Goldenberg, Artner, and Podreka (1991); Goldenberg, Podreka, and Steiner (1990); Gottschalk (1974); Hale (1982); Harris and Robinson (1986); Hawkins (1976); Haynes and Moore (1981); Hearne (1978); Herrington and Schneidau (1968); Ikeda and Hirai (1976); Jacobson (1930); Jones and Johnson (1978, 1980); G. Jones (1977, 1988); M. Jones (1974); Jones-Gotman (1979); Jones-Gotman and Milner (1978); Jordan and Lenington (1979); Kosslyn (1991); Kosslyn, Holtzman, Farah, and Gazzaniga (1985); Kosslyn, VanKleeck, and Kirby (1990); Kunzendorf (1981, 1984); Kunzendorf and Sheikh (1990); Lang, Kozak, Miller, Levin, and McLean (1980); Lang, Levin, Miller, and Kozak (1983); Lang, Melamed, and Hart (1970); Langhinrichsen and Tucker (1990); Leber (1979); Lehmann and Koukkou (1990); Levine, Warach, and Farah (1985); Ley (1979, 1984); Marks (1990); Marks, Marset, Boulougouris, and Huson (1971); Martindale (1990); Marzillier, Carroll, and Newland (1979); Meskin and Singer (1974); Morse, Martin, and Furst (1977); Ogden (1985); Ohkuma (1985); Oswald

(1957); Paivio (1973); Paul (1969); Price (1975); Prigatano (1983, 1987); Qualls (1982); Raichle (1990); Ratcliff (1979); Richardson and Barry (1985); Richardson, Cermak, Blackford, and O'Connor (1987); Rider, Floyd, and Kirkpatrick (1985); Robbins and McAdams (1974); Roberts and Weerts (1982); Roland and Friberg (1985); Schwartz (1984); Schwartz, Brown, and Ahern (1980); Segal and Glickman (1967); Sergent (1990); Shaw (1938); Sheikh and Kunzendorf (1984); Shore (1979); Simpson and Climan (1971); Slatter (1960); Spiegel and Barabasz (1990); Sunderland (1990); Van Loon-Vervoorn, Elzinga-Plomp, and Hennink (1991); Walter and Yeager (1956); Wein (1979); Weinberg, Walter, and Crow (1970); and Ziegler, Klinzing, and Williamson (1982).

## Imagery and Sports

Suinn (1983) discusses sports performance theory and indicates a conceptual model that links performance to psychological training goals (cf. Suinn, 1980). For instance, sports performance may be seen as the product of aptitude and skill acquisition where the latter is analyzable into three components: strengthening the correct responses, extinguishing/controlling incorrect responses, and transferring correct responses to game conditions. In turn, the three components are divided into various subgoals involving motor, ideomotor, or ideational/mental rehearsal responses. Following his review of studies on the potential value of imagery rehearsal in athletics, Suinn concludes that, in general, the evidence based on research in this area is not conclusive, and controlled studies with large sample sizes are relatively rare. According to Suinn (1983), there is only tentative support for the apparent value of imagery rehearsal in skill enhancement among proficient athletes. Some of the goals targeted by imagery rehearsal studies include the following: improving the correct skills associated with accuracy (e.g., Kolonay, 1977; Noel, 1980; Nideffer, 1971); reduction of incorrect responses of conditioned emotionality associated with stress (e.g., Bennett and Stothart, 1978); control of the incorrect responses concerning negative-evaluative or negative-cue instructional cognitions (e.g., Gravel, Lemieux, and Ladouceur, 1980; Desiderato and Miller, 1979; Meyers, Cooke, Cullen, and Liles, 1979); using imagery to deal with athletes who "choke" during competition (e.g., Winning Associates, 1978); and using "visual motor behavior rehearsal" (VMBR) for optimal/adaptive behavior (Suinn, 1976b, 1979, 1980, 1984b; Weinberg, Seabourne, & Jackson, 1981).

More recently, Suinn (1994) advances the discussion of mental imagery and visualization in sports, in particular, via use of the VMBR technique (cf. Suinn, 1984a). According to Suinn (1994, p. 27), "VMBR follows specific steps, including relaxation followed by the use of imagery to practice aspects of motor performances; in common with imagery rehearsal, generally, VMBR is a covert activity which involves sensory-motor sensations that reintegrate reality behaviors, and which include neuromuscular, physiological, and emotional involvement." The advantage of using imagery rehearsal over other versions of mental practice is in the principle underlying learning that it is enhanced to the degree that the conditions of practice are similar to those of game and competition conditions—under which the performance is to be exhibited subsequently. For instance, in practicing basketball, imagining making a free throw *as if* the crowd were present would be much more effective than merely thinking "noncrowd," and where using imagery rehearsal would be the closest to actually making the free throw during the real game itself. Among the several advantages of VMBR as a form of imagery rehearsal (Suinn, 1984a, 1994) are the following: VMBR is a standardized training method that is subject to description and, therefore, replication; the use of VMBR apparently does not demand special skills such as those required in the development of imagery using hypnosis; and VMBR has been researched recently to the point that there are now available published reports concerning its efficacy. Following his examination of the procedures involved in VMBR, as well as the goals and research foundations of VMBR training, Suinn (1994) makes the following conclusions:

- VMBR has been subject to sufficient research and application as to be considered a reasonable procedure to use for mental rehearsal or visualization training.
- VMBR is, in itself, no more than a tool whose application is influenced by a number of variables (e.g., goals of the athlete; design of the particular imagery scenes needed to reach specific goals).
- VMBR is a type of practice, specifically mental practice, which is an adjunct to physical practice/training and is adjusted to the needs of the athlete, the particular competitive experience/event, and the amount of time before the next event.
- VMBR is a skill where practice and training are essential for maximum benefits (also, in the VMBR training steps, relaxation is shortened and the visualization content is altered as the athlete shows progress).
- Performance enhancement of athletic skills is the end product of a number of factors (e.g., level of physical skill, the amount of prior experience in

competitive events, the presence of incorrect responses, and the availability and strength of correct psychological responses).

For further discussions concerning VMBR and visualization in *sports*, see the following studies: Andre and Means (1986); Corbin (1972); Epstein (1980); Feltz and Landers (1983); Gough (1989); Gould, Weinberg, and Jackson (1980); Green (1992); Hale (1982); Hall and Erffmeyer (1983); Harris and Robinson (1986); Hatfield, Landers, and Ray (1984); Housner (1984); Jowdy and Harris (1990); Murphy, Jowdy, and Durtschi (1989); Ryan and Simons (1981, 1983); Suinn (1976a, 1980); Weinberg, Seabourne, and Jackson (1982); and Wrisberg and Ragsdale (1979); compare Carpenter (1984); MacKay (1981); Oxendine (1968); Richardson (1967); Suinn (1985, 1989, 1992); Suinn, Morton, and Brammell (1979).

Sheikh and Korn (1994) edited a book containing discussions on imagery in sports and physical performance. The following is a sample of articles, by author(s), along with the author(s)'s main conclusions:

Enhancing Athletic Performance through Imagery: An Overview (J. J. Janssen and A. A. Sheikh)—while it is suggested that imagery may be an effective method for enhancing athletic performance, it is clear, also, that imagery practice—when used inappropriately—has the potential for producing decrements in performance; a complex relationship seems to exist between factors impacting on the effectiveness of imagery practice, including the effects of sex/gender differences and various imaginal styles, cognitive styles, participants' detailed self-reports concerning the disparity between what is actually imagined versus what is given via imagery instructions, longitudinal effects of intensive imagery training in laboratory and field settings, stress management ability in competition, pain and fatigue management, and stamina and arousal-level control. Among the theories concerned with the issue of how imagery functions to enhance performance are the psychoneuromuscular, symbolic learning, bioinformational, attention-arousal set, covert-conditioning, set-efficacy, and triple-code theories (for a similar discussion of theories in this area, see Budney, Murphy, and Woolfolk's chapter 6 in Sheikh and Korn [1994, pp. 98–103]).
Visualization in Sports (R. M. Suinn)—VMBR research initially grew from case study illustrations to more recent sophisticated research designs; VMBR training contributes to the enhancement of sport performance across a wide variety of different sports; the VMBR approach to mental practice seems to require the synergistic involvement of both relaxation and mental imagery.

Developing Self-Talk to Facilitate the Use of Imagery among Athletes (L. B. Green)—elite performers use internal/kinaesthetic imagery rather than the external/visual imagery used by less-skilled athletes; there seems to be a lack of appropriate self-talk and imagery used by less-than-elite performers/ athletes.

The Role of Imagery in Perfecting Already Learned Physical Skills (N. McLean and A. Richardson)—focuses on the use of mental practice by athletes already possessing well-established skills (synonyms in the psychological literature for the term "mental practice" include "symbolic rehearsal," "imaginary practice," "implicit practice," "mental rehearsal," "conceptualizing practice," "cognitive rehearsal," "behavior rehearsal," "psychomotor rehearsal," and "overt rehearsal") in many studies in this area, the level of skill of participants is not defined adequately—broad categories such as "novice" and "experienced" need to be replaced by more precise definitions of base-rate skill; there is a need, also, for more rigorous assessment of the actual use of the mental practice procedure during practice and prior to, and during, actual performance; mental practice generally yields better results than no-practice, but adding mental practice to physical practice does not, in general, add significantly to the effect of physical practice alone; with the "elite" athlete, mental practice may enable the efficient transfer of skills from practice to competition, rather than to directly enhance the level of skill; and for the "elite" athlete, mental practice is most likely to work via the motivational/cognitive systems rather than by affecting the learning process/system.

Imagery and Motor Performance: What Do We Really Know? (A. J. Budney, S. M. Murphy, and R. L. Woolfolk)—concludes that imagery, clearly, is no panacea in this area; relatively superficial and brief applications of positive imagery to the acquisition/rehearsal of skills, and the creation of "mindsets," has not resulted in dramatic, consistent, or substantive effects on athlete's performance as often promised; however, the negative effects of imagery ("failure imagery" or "wrong type of imagery") seem to produce immediate and meaningful decrements in performance; and sport psychologists should become more cautious in their widespread application of imagery techniques.

Other articles/chapters in Sheikh and Korn (1994), by author, include Imagery Perspectives and Learning in Sports Performance (B. D. Hale); Imagery and Motor Skills Acquisition (C. Hall, D. Schmidt, M.-C. Durand, and E. Buckolz); Optimal Arousal, Stress, and Imagery (H. L. Rishe, E. W. Krenz, C. McQueen, and V. D. Krenz); Channeling Addictive Energy into Healthy Training (J. Dahlkoetter); The Use of Imagery in the Rehabilitation of Injured Athletes (L. B. Green); Optimal Sports Performance Imagery (E. Miller); Transformational Imagery for Sports Excellence (J. T. Shaffer; cf. Shaffer, 1986); Mental

Imagery in Enhancing Performance: Theory and Practical Exercises (E. R. Korn); Improving Imaging Abilities (A. A. Sheikh, K. S. Sheikh, and L. M. Moleski).

For further discussions concerning the relationship between *sports/physical/motor performance* and mental imagery, see the following studies: Annett (1985); Barr and Hall (1992); Bilodeau and Bilodeau (1961); Bird (1984); Blair, Hall, and Leyshon (1993); Budney and Woolfolk (1990); Clark (1960); Corbin (1967, 1972); Davis (1990); Deschaumes-Molinaro, Dittmar, and Vernet-Maury (1991); Feltz and Landers (1983); Feltz and Reissinger (1990); Feltz, Landers, and Becker (1988); Fenker and Lambiotte (1987); Freeman (1933); Garfield (1984); Gordon (1990); Goss, Hall, Buckolz, and Fishburne (1986); Gould, Weinberg, and Jackson (1980); Green (1992); Greenspan and Feltz (1989); C. R. Hall (1980); R. G. Hall (1971); Hall and Buckolz (1981); Hall, Buckolz, and Fishburne (1989); Hall, Pongrac, and Buckolz (1985); Hall, Rodgers, and Barr (1990); Harris and Harris (1984); Heckler and Kaczor (1988); Hinshaw (1991–1992); Hird, Landers, Thomas, and Horan (1991); Housner and Hoffman (1978, 1981); Howe (1991); Ievleva and Orlick (1991); Isaac (1992); Jones (1965); Kaczor (1990); Kelsey (1961); Kendall, Hrycaiko, Martin, and Kendall (1990); Kohl and Roenker (1980, 1983); Kohl, Roenker, and Turner (1985); Korn (1986); Lane (1980); Lang (1977); Larsson (1987); Lee (1990); Lippman (1989); Mahoney and Avener (1977); Martens (1984); McBride and Rothstein (1979); McCaffrey and Orlick (1989); McFadden (1982); Meacci and Price (1985); Mendoza and Wichman (1978); Meyers, Cooke, Cullen, and Liles (1979); Meyers, Schleser, and Okwamabua (1982); Minas (1978); Mumford and Hall (1985); Murphy (1990); Murphy, Woolfolk, and Budney (1988); Nideffer (1971, 1985); Noel (1980); Onestak (1991); Phipps and Morehouse (1969); Porter and Foster (1986); Powell (1973); Riley and Start (1960); Rodgers, Hall, and Buckolz (1991); Rushall (1988); Ryan and Simons (1981, 1982, 1983); Samuels (1969); Savoyant (1988); Schomer (1986); Shaffer (1988); Shaw (1938, 1940); Smith (1987, 1991); Smyth (1975); Start (1962); Start and Richardson (1964); Stebbins (1968); Steel (1952); Tower (1982); Twining (1949); Tynes and McFatter (1987); Uhestahl (1982); Ulich (1967); Vandall, Davis, and Clugston (1943); VanGyn, Wenger, and Gaul (1990); Vealey (1986, 1988); Vedelli (1985); Washburn (1916); Wehner, Vogt, and Stadler (1984); Weinberg (1982); Weinberg, Gould, and Jackson (1980); Whelan, Mahoney, and Meyers (1991); White, Ashton, and Lewis (1979); Whiteley (1962);

Wilkes and Summers (1984); Woolfolk, Murphy, Gottesfeld, and Aitken (1985); Woolfolk, Parrish, and Murphy (1985); Woolman (1986); Wrisberg and Anshel (1989); and Ziegler (1987).

## Imagery and Therapy/Visualization Techniques

In her discussion of a "very private world"—and following her sections on the complexity and elusiveness of imagery and image modality and the artist—Gordon (1972) suggests in a section titled "Imagery and Psychotherapy" that not only psychologists but also psychotherapists have thought and proposed much concerning the character of images, their function, their possible roots, and their development (cf. Gordon, 1962). Gordon (1972) maintains that in the context of therapeutic analysis, imagery functions primarily as a means of "clothing" and gives form to conscious and unconscious experiments. According to Gordon, analysts are tempted to consider the person's psyche as consisting essentially of images that picture all of one's vital activities—including unconscious and even archaic fantasies (cf. Jung, 1923, p. 555, who viewed every image as the "concentrated expression of the total psychic situation"). In one place, Gordon (p. 73) asserts that "nearly all psychotherapeutic procedures depend in greater or smaller measure on the presence of imagery." She even suggests (p. 73) that "the different types of therapy can be distinguished from one another in terms of the extension and the comprehensiveness of the patient's imaginal worlds." Gordon concludes that imagery serves several important biological and psychological functions: it helps the organism to arrange the complexity of sensory stimuli into meaningful patterns that allow the release of instinctual reactions in appropriate situations, and it enables humans to classify, to abstract, and to relate present perceptions to past experience (thus aiding the processes of learning and adaptation), and to tolerate present frustrations for future satisfactions. However, imagery functions as the raw material of one's capacity to imagine and to symbolize, and even to serve as the basis for the human need to make art.

Samuels and Samuels (1975, pp. 181–207) describe the practical use of visualization techniques within the discipline of psychology, including the work of Freud, Breuer, Jung, Kubie, Sacerdote, Beck, Wolpe, Jacobson, Stampfl, LeChron, Kretschmer, Happich, Leuner, Assagioli, Gerard, Desoille, Frederking, Perls, and Mauz. Among the practical aspects, therapies, and specific techniques of visualization and imagery discussed by Samuels and Samuels are the following:

automatic function of images, receptive visualizations, intensely emotional fancy-images, primary process thought, Jungian visualization/mandalas, active imagination, archetypal/primordial images, hypnagogia/induced reveries/dream without distortion, induced dreams, spontaneous visualization control, forward time projection, systematic desensitization, imagery to lessen anxiety, progressive relaxation, autosuggestion, aversive training, implosive therapy, hypnosis/hypnotherapy, automatic writing, age regression/progression, time distortion, meditative techniques, symbolic consciousness, guided affective imagery (GAI), psychosynthesis, symbolic visualization, directed day dreams, deep relaxation and symbolism, and positive symbol visualization. (Samuels and Samuels [1975, p. 226] also describe Carl Simonton's use of visualization in the treatment of cancer.)

Sheikh and Jordan (1983) discuss and examine some of the clinical and therapeutic uses of mental imagery (cf. Horowitz, 1974, 1978; Sheikh, 1977, 1978, 1984; Sheikh and Panagiotou, 1975). In presenting the basis and assumptions for the efficacy of imagery in the clinic, Sheikh and Jordan indicate a number of characteristics of the imagery mode that make it a suitable tool for clinical work. Among these aspects are the following (including researchers):

- Imagery represents the central core of perceptual, retrieval, and response mechanisms.
- Imagery and perception are experientially and neurophysiologically comparable processes and cannot be distinguished from each other by any intrinsic qualities (Klinger, 1980; Kosslyn, 1980; Neisser, 1976; Richardson, 1969; Segal and Fusella, 1970; Sheikh and Shaffer, 1979).
- Images act as the sources of activation and guide behavior by representing the goal object (McMahon, 1973; Mowrer, 1977).
- Individuals seem to act more on the basis of imaginal consequences than on actual probabilities (Shepard, 1978b; Tower and Singer, 1981).
- Meaning is dependent largely on images—words arouse images that have accompanying emotional responses which, in turn, are the source of the meaning of words (Bugelski, 1970; Forisha, 1979).
- Images provide a unique opportunity to examine the integration of motivation, perception, subjective meaning, and realistic abstract thought (Shorr, 1980; cf. Escalona, 1973).
- Imagery may be the main access to important preverbal memories or to memories encoded at developmental stages in which language was not yet predominant (Kepecs, 1954; Sheikh and Panagiotou, 1975).
- Imagery has the power to produce a wide variety of physiological changes (Barber, 1961, 1969, 1978; Barber, Chauncey, and Winer, 1964; Craig,

1969; Jacobson, 1929; Jordan and Lenington, 1979; Paivio, 1973; Sheikh, Richardson, and Moleski, 1979; Sheikh, Twente, and Turner, 1979).

- Imagery often opens up new avenues of exploration when therapy appears to come to a halt (Singer, 1974).
- The image mode permits the spanning of the conscious-unconscious continuum more readily than does overt or covert language (Jellinek, 1949; Panagiotou and Sheikh, 1974, 1977; Sheikh and Panagiotou, 1975).
- Guided daydream images may produce therapeutic consequences in the absence of any interpretation by the guide or intellectual insight by the client (Klinger, 1980; Leuner, 1977, 1978).
- Solutions rehearsed at the imaginal level during therapy appear to generalize outside of the therapy milieu (Klinger, 1980; Richardson, 1969).

Sheikh and Jordan (1983, pp. 395–414) discuss a number of imagery-based therapeutic methods (cf. Jordan, 1979; Shapiro, 1974; Sheikh and Panagiotou, 1975; Sheikh and Shaffer, 1979; Singer, 1974; Singer and Pope, 1978), including the following approaches:

- Imagery substitution/dialogue method (Binet, 1922; Crampton, 1974; Janet, 1898)
- Emergent imagery/meditation/predetermined scenes (Happich, 1932; Kretschmer, 1969)
- Ascending-descending in imaginal space (Caslant, 1921; Singer, 1974)
- Autogenic training (Schultz and Luthe, 1959)
- Imagery-level conflict resolution and directed revery (Guillerey, 1945)
- Psychoanalytical use of imagery (Breuer and Freud, 1955; Clark, 1925; Horowitz, 1968, 1970/1978, 1974, 1978; Jung, 1926/1960; Kanzer, 1958; Kosbab, 1974; Reyher, 1963, 1977, 1978; Shorr, 1972, 1978; cf. Jordan, 1979)
- Active imagination (Jung, 1935/1976)
- Use of imagery in the "oneirotherapies," that is, "dream therapy" or "waking-dream therapy" (Desoille, 1961, 1965; Fretigny and Virel, 1968; Leuner, 1977, 1978; Virel, 1968)
- Psychosynthesis (Assagioli, 1965; cf. Crampton, 1969; Gerard, 1964)
- Behavior/cognitive-behavior therapy and systematic desensitization (Brown, 1969; Cautela, 1977; Kretschmer, 1922; Lazarus and Abramovitz, 1962; Rachman, 1968; Salter, 1949; Stampfl and Levis, 1967; Wolpe, 1958, 1969; cf. Anderson, 1980; Dunlap, 1932; Kazdin, 1978; Malleson, 1959; Meichenbaum, 1977, 1978; Sheikh and Panagiotou, 1975; Singer, 1974; Strosahl and Ascough, 1981; Wolpe and Lazarus, 1966)
- Cognitive-affective restructuring (Beck, 1970; Gendlin, 1978; Morrison, 1979, 1980; cf. Tomkins, 1962/1963)

- Eidetic psychotherapy (Ahsen, 1965, 1968, 1977; Dolan and Sheikh, 1976, 1977; Panagiotou and Sheikh, 1974; Sheikh, 1978, 1983; Sheikh and Jordan, 1981)
- Hypnosis and imagery (Barber, 1978; Barber, Spanos, and Chaves, 1974; Barber and Wilson, 1979; Sheehan, 1979)
- Humanistic-transpersonal approaches (Crampton, 1969; Gerard, 1964; Hammer, 1967; Jaffe and Bresler, 1980; Perls, 1970, 1972; Sheikh, 1983; Sheikh, Twente, and Turner, 1979; Shorr, 1978; Singer, 1974, 1979; Watkins, 1976)
- Group settings and applications of imagery (Ahsen, 1977; Jordan, Davis, Kahn, and Sinnott, 1980; Perls, 1970; Saretsky, 1977; Schutz, 1967; Shorr, 1978)

Sheikh and Jordan (1983, p. 413) note that their coverage of the imagery-based therapies "is by no means intended to convey that exclusive dependence on images is the royal road to therapeutic success" (cf. Singer and Pope, 1978). They also caution the reader that—although the literature on the clinical uses of imagery is replete with clinicians' testimonies regarding the diagnostic-efficacy of mental images—not much systematic work has been done in this area. According to Sheikh and Jordan, the existing diagnostic tests concerning the meaningful use of mental images in the clinic need extensive refinement to be of real value to practitioners, and studies of reliability and validity in this area are "sadly lacking" (p. 422). Finally, among the numerous mechanisms that presumably underlie the effective use of imagery in the clinic, Sheikh and Jordan cite several *common* elements—which have been extracted—that are shared by all approaches (cf. Meichenbaum, 1978; Singer, 1974):

- The client's clear discrimination of his/her own ongoing fantasy processes
- The therapist's clues to the client concerning alternative ways to approach various situations
- Awareness in the client of generally avoided situations
- The therapist's encouragement to the client to engage in covert rehearsal of alternatives
- Decrease of fear in the client of making overt approaches to the avoided situations
- General increase in the client's positive affect via novelty inherent in the imagery experience
- The client's feeling of control gained by the monitoring and rehearsing of various images
- The modified meaning, or changed internal dialogue, that precedes, attends, and follows instances of maladaptive behavior
- The client's mental rehearsal of alternative responses that lead to greater coping skills

Based upon their review and analysis of the relationship between imagery and good physical health, Kunzendorf and Sheikh (1990) note that depression and schizophrenic hallucination are two different responses to the disturbing self-awareness that results from individuals' *monitoring* certain images (cf. Kunzendorf, 1985–1986). For instance, some depressed people start feeling melancholy and stop generating imagery—in response to their self-awareness that threatening images come from within; other depressed individuals stop imaging better worlds and start feeling melancholy—in response to their self-awareness that escapist images are "only imaginary" (cf. Schultz, 1978, 1984). In either case, according to Kunzendorf and Sheikh, when depressed people stop imaging vividly, they not only stop innervating the sensory neurons that are subjectively experienced as images, but also stop activating the immune functions that are neurally connected with imaging; as a result, depression is associated with immune deficiency and poor physical health. In contrast to the depressive pattern, schizophrenic hallucination is associated with the resumption of vivid imaging and the restoration of physical health; some hallucinating individuals stop monitoring stressful images and start experiencing paranoid hallucinations, while other hallucinators stop monitoring vivid images of better worlds and start experiencing vivid hallucinations of them. Evidence indicates that schizophrenics who generate such *unmonitored* hallucinations during psychotic episodes do not—during their normal states of self-consciousness—image as vividly or as frequently as do normal people.

Kunzendorf and Sheikh (1990) observe, also, that the vivid hallucinations of schizophrenics (just like the vivid images of normal people) innervate sensory nerves, activate immune functions, and counteract poor physical health. However, unlike normal imagers, schizophrenic hallucinators have cognitive modes that fail to monitor the difference between imaged sensations and perceived sensations, as well as possessing immune systems that fail to differentiate between diseaseful substances and allergenic substances. Thus, schizophrenia is typically associated with immune hypersensitivity. According to this theoretical perspective, the unmonitored hallucinations of such individuals take the place of a healthy imagination and, as a consequence, serve both to counteract depression and to counterbalance immune deficiency. In one place, Kunzendorf and Sheikh (p. 196) suggest that modern psychology may do well to tolerate all short-term hallucinating—not only hypnotic hallucinating but also ritualized and/or spontaneous hallucinating—in stressful situations that would otherwise be depressing psychologically and unhealthy physically. Note that Kunzendorf and Sheikh's article contains a generous bibliography consisting of 109 citations/references pertaining to the relationship between imagery and health.

For further discussions and treatments of imagery vis-à-vis therapy, see the following studies: Achterberg (1985); Achterberg and Lawlis (1984); Achterberg, Kenner, and Lawlis (1988); Achterberg, Lawlis, Simonton, and Simonton (1977); Ader (1981); Ahsen (1978); Armstrong (1953); Bakan (1991); Benson (1975, 1985); Brett and Starker (1977); Brigham and Toal (1991); Cautela (1977); Cohen (1938); Crawford and MacLeod-Morgan (1986); Fiore (1988); Flor-Henry (1990); Gaston, Crombez, and Dupuis (1989); Gold (1991); Gruber, Hall, Hersch, and Dubois (1988); H. R. Hall (1983, 1984, 1989, 1990); Hanley and Chinn (1989); Heil (1982); Holden (1978); Hookham (1991); Horowitz (1970/1978, pp. 328–61); Jaffe and Bresler (1980); Jasnoski and Kugler (1987); Jordan (1979); Klinger (1971, 1980, 1981, pp. 259–386); Korn (1982, 1983); Korn and Johnson (1983); Kroger and Fezler (1976, pp. 97–136); Kruck and Sheikh (1986); Lang (1977, 1979); Langhinrichsen and Tucker (1990); Lazarus (1977, 1982); Ley (1979); Locke and Colligan (1986); Mavromatis and Richardson (1984); McMahon (1976); McMahon and Sheikh (1986); Naruse and Obonai (1953); Richardson (1964, 1967); Rogers, Dubey, and Reich (1979); Rossi (1986); Rossi and Cheek (1988); Scarf (1980); Schaub, Anselmo, and Luck (1991); Schneider, Smith, Minning, Whitcher, and Hermanson (1991); Schwartz (1984); Schwartz, Weinberger, and Singer (1981); Seitz and Molholm (1947); Shacham (1979); Sheikh, Kunzendorf, and Sheikh (1989); Shorr (1972, 1974, 1978, 1983); Simonton, Matthews-Simonton, and Creighton (1978); Singer (1974, 1979); Sommer (1978, pp. 138–67); Spanos and O'Hara (1990); Spanos and Radtke (1981–1982); Starker (1986); Starker and Jolin (1982); Waters and McDonald (1973); Westcott and Horan (1977); White (1978); Worthington and Shumate (1981); and Yarmey (1984).

## REFERENCES

Achterberg, J. (1984). Imagery and medicine: Psychophysiological speculations. *Journal of Mental Imagery, 8*, 1–14.

Achterberg, J. (1985). *Imagery and healing.* Boulder, CO: Shambhala.

Achterberg, J., Kenner, C., & Lawlis, G. F. (1988). Severe burn injury: A comparison of relaxation, imagery, and biofeedback for pain management. *Journal of Mental Imagery, 12*, 71–88.

Achterberg, J., & Lawlis, G. F. (1984). *Imagery and disease: A diagnostic tool for behavioral medicine.* Champaign, IL: Institute for Personality and Ability Testing.

Achterberg, J., Lawlis, G. F., Simonton, O. C., & Simonton, S. (1977). Psychological factors and blood chemistries as disease outcome predictors for cancer patients. *Multivariate Experimental Clinical Research, 3,* 107–22.

Ader, R. (1981). *Psychoneuroimmunology.* New York: Academic Press.

Ahsen, A. (1965). *Eidetic psychotherapy: A short introduction.* Lahore, Pakistan: Nai Matbooat.

Ahsen, A. (1968). *Basic concepts in eidetic psychotherapy.* New York: Brandon House.

Ahsen, A. (1977). *Psycheye: Self-analytic consciousness.* New York: Brandon House.

Ahsen, A. (1978). Neural-experimental growth treatment of accidental traumas, debilitating stress conditions and chronic emotional blocking. *Journal of Mental Imagery, 2,* 1–22.

Ahsen, A. (1984). The triple code model for imagery and psychophysiology. *Journal of Mental Imagery, 8,* 15–42.

Alesandrini, K. L. (1982). Imagery-eliciting strategies and meaningful learning. *Journal of Mental Imagery, 6,* 125–40.

Alesandrini, K. L., & Sheikh, A. A. (1983). Research on imagery: Implications for advertising. In A. A. Sheikh (Ed.), *Imagery: Current theory, research, and application.* New York: Wiley.

Andersen, R. A. (1987). The role of the inferior parietal lobule in spatial perception and visual-motor integration. In F. Plum, V. B. Mountcastle, & S. R. Geiger (Eds.), *Handbook of physiology: The nervous system and higher functions of the brain.* Part 2. Bethesda, MD: American Physiological Society.

Anderson, J. R. (1978). Arguments concerning representations for mental imagery. *Psychological Review, 85,* 249–77; *86,* 379–90.

Anderson, J. R. (1979). Further arguments concerning representations for mental imagery: A response to Hayes-Roth and Pylyshyn. *Psychological Review, 86,* 395–406.

Anderson, J. R., & Bower, G. H. (1973). *Human associative memory.* New York: Holt, Rinehart, and Winston.

Anderson, M. P. (1975). Imaging as a self-control response to enhance voluntary tolerance of an aversive stimulus. *Dissertation Abstracts International, 36,* 899B–900B.

Anderson, M. P. (1980). Imaginal processes: Therapeutic application and theoretical models. In M. J. Mahoney (Ed.), *Psychotherapy process: Current issues and future trends.* New York: Plenum Press.

Anderson, R. E., & Helstrup, T. (1993). Multiple perspectives on discovery and creativity in mind and on paper. In B. Roskos-Ewoldsen, M. J.

Intons-Peterson, & R. E. Anderson (Eds.), *Imagery, creativity, and discovery: A cognitive perspective.* Amsterdam: North-Holland.

Andre, J., & Means, J. (1986). Rate of imagery in mental practice: An experimental investigation. *Journal of Sport Psychology, 7,* 124–28.

Andreani, O. (1988). Imagery and memory. In M. Denis, J. Engelkamp, & J.T.E. Richardson (Eds.), *Cognitive and neuropsychological approaches to mental imagery.* Boston: M. Nijhoff.

Annett, J. (1985). Motor learning: A review. In H. Heuer, U. Kleinbeck, & K. Schmidt (Eds.), *Motor behavior: Programming, control, and acquisition.* New York: Springer-Verlag.

Annett, J. (1988). Imagery and skill acquisition. In M. Denis, J. Engelkamp, & J.T.E. Richardson (Eds.), *Cognitive and neuropsychological approaches to mental imagery.* Boston: M. Nijhoff.

Anooshian, L., & Carlson, J. S. (1973). A study of mental imagery and conservation within the Piagetian framework. *Human Development, 16,* 382–94.

Antonietti, A. (1991). Why does mental visualization facilitate problem-solving? In R. H. Logie & M. Denis (Eds.), *Mental images in human cognition.* Amsterdam: North-Holland.

Arabian, J. M. (1982). Imagery and Pavlovian heart rate decelerative conditioning. *Psychophysiology, 19,* 286–93.

Arabian, J. M., & Furedy, J. J. (1983). Individual differences in imagery ability and Pavlovian heart rate decelerative conditioning. *Psychophysiology, 20,* 325–36.

Arieti, S. (1976). *Creativity: The magic synthesis.* New York: Basic Books.

Armstrong, C. P. (1953). Some notes on imagery in psychophysical therapy. *Journal of General Psychology, 48,* 231–40.

Assagioli, R. (1965). *Psychosynthesis: A collection of basic writings.* New York: Viking.

Atkinson, R. C., & Shiffrin, R. M. (1968). Human memory: A proposed system and its control processes. In K. W. Spence & J. T. Spence (Eds.), *The psychology of learning and motivation.* Vol. 2. New York: Academic Press.

Atwood, G. (1971). An experimental study of visual imagination and memory. *Cognitive Psychology, 2,* 290–99.

Baddeley, A. D. (1988). Imagery and working memory. In M. Denis, J. Engelkamp, & J.T.E. Richardson (Eds.), *Cognitive and neuropsychological approaches to mental imagery.* Boston: M. Nijhoff.

Bakan, P. (1980). Imagery raw and cooked: A hemispheric recipe. In J. Shorr, G. Sobel, P. Robin, & J. Connella (Eds.), *Imagery: Its many dimensions and applications.* New York: Plenum Press.

Bakan, P. (1991). Imagery and the sinistrality of symptoms. In R. G. Kunzendorf (Ed.), *Mental imagery.* New York: Plenum Press.

Barber, T. X. (1961). Physiological aspects of hypnosis. *Psychological Bulletin, 58*, 390–419.

Barber, T. X. (1969). *Hypnosis: A scientific approach.* New York: Van Nostrand.

Barber, T. X. (1971). Imagery and "hallucinations": Effects of LSD contrasted with the effects of "hypnotic" suggestions. In S. J. Segal (Ed.), *Imagery: Current cognitive approaches.* New York: Academic Press.

Barber, T. X. (1978). Hypnosis, suggestions, and psychosomatic phenomena: A new look from the standpoint of recent experimental studies. *American Journal of Clinical Hypnosis, 21*, 13–27.

Barber, T. X., & Calverley, S. (1964). Toward a theory of "hypnotic" behavior: An experimental study of "hypnotic time distortion." *Archives of General Psychiatry, 10*, 209–16.

Barber, T. X., Chauncey, H., & Winer, R. (1964). The effect of hypnotic and nonhypnotic suggestions on parotid gland response to gustatory stimuli. *Psychosomatic Medicine, 26*, 374–80.

Barber, T. X., Spanos, N. P., & Chaves, J. F. (1974). *Hypnosis, imagination, and human potentialities.* Elmsford, NY: Pergamon.

Barber, T. X., & Wilson, S. C. (1978–1979). The Barber Suggestibility Scale and the Creative Imagination Scale: Experimental and clinical applications. *American Journal of Clinical Hypnosis, 21*, 84–108.

Barber, T. X., & Wilson, S. C. (1979). Guided imagining and hypnosis: Theoretical and empirical overlap and convergence in a new Creative Imagination Scale. In A. A. Sheikh & J. T. Shaffer (Eds.), *The potential of fantasy and imagination.* New York: Brandon House.

Barbut, D., & Gazzaniga, M. S. (1987). Disturbances in conceptual space involving language and speech. *Brain, 110*, 1487–96.

Barlow, H., Blakemore, C., & Weston-Smith, M. (Eds.) (1990). *Images and understanding.* Cambridge, UK: Cambridge University Press.

Barr, K., & Hall, C. R. (1992). The use of imagery by rowers. *International Journal of Sport Psychology, 23*, 243–61.

Barratt, P. E. (1956). Use of the EEG in the study of imagery. *British Journal of Psychology, 47*, 101–14.

Barron, F. (1953). Complexity-simplicity as a personality variable. *Journal of Abnormal and Social Psychology, 48*, 163–72.

Bartlett, F. C. (1921). The function of images. *British Journal of Psychology, 11*, 320–27.

Bartlett, F. C. (1925). Feeling, imaging, and thinking. *British Journal of Psychology, 16*, 16–28.

Bartlett, F. C. (1927). The relevance of visual imagery to thinking. *British Journal of Psychology, 18*, 23–29.

Bartlett, F. C. (1932). *Remembering.* London: Cambridge University Press.

Basso, A., Bisiach, E., & Luzzatti, C. (1980). Loss of mental imagery: A case study. *Neuropsychologia, 18*, 435–42.

Bauer, R. M., & Craighead, W. E. (1979). Psychophysiological responses to the imagination of fearful and neutral situations: The effects of imagery instructions. *Behavior Therapy, 10*, 389–403.

Baylor, G. W. (1971). A treatise on mind's eye. Unpublished doctoral dissertation, Carnegie-Mellon University.

Beck, A. T. (1970). Role of fantasies in psychotherapy and psychopathology. *Journal of Nervous and Mental Diseases, 150*, 3–17.

Begg, I. (1973). Imagery and integration in the recall of words. *Canadian Journal of Psychology, 27*, 159–67.

Begg, I. (1978). Imagery and organization in memory: Instructional effects. *Memory and Cognition, 6*, 174–83.

Begg, I. (1983). Imagery and language. In A. A. Sheikh (Ed.), *Imagery: Current theory, research, and application.* New York: Wiley.

Begg, I., & Anderson, M. (1976). Imagery and associative memory in children. *Journal of Experimental Child Psychology, 21*, 480–89.

Begg, I., & Clark, J. (1975). Contextual imagery in meaning and memory. *Memory and Cognition, 3*, 117–22.

Begg, I., & Paivio, A. (1969). Concreteness and imagery in sentence meaning. *Journal of Verbal Learning and Verbal Behavior, 8*, 821–27.

Bennett, B. K., & Stothart, C. M. (1978). The effects of a relaxation-based cognitive technique on sports performance. Paper presented at the Congress of the Canadian Society for Motor Learning and Sport Psychology, Toronto, Canada.

Benson, H. (1975). *The relaxation response.* New York: Morrow.

Benson, H. (1985). *Beyond the relaxation response.* New York: Berkley Books.

Bethell-Fox, C. E., & Shepard, R. N. (1988). Mental rotation: Effects of stimulus complexity and familiarity. *Journal of Experimental Psychology: Human Perception and Performance, 14*, 12–23.

Betts, G. H. (1909). The distribution and functions of mental imagery. *Teachers College, Columbia University Contributions to Education,* No. 26, 1–99.

Biblow, E. (1973). Imaginative play and the control of aggression. In J. L. Singer (Ed.), *The child's world of make-believe.* New York: Academic Press.

Bideaud, J. (1988). Rotation of mental image with respect to children and adults. In C. Cornoldi (Ed.), *Imagery and cognition proceedings of the second workshop on imagery and cognition.* University of Padova, Italy.

Biederman, I. (1987). Recognition-by-components: A theory of human image understanding. *Psychological Review, 94*, 115–47.

Bilodeau, E. A., & Bilodeau, I. M. (1961). Motor skills and learning. *Annual Review of Psychology, 12*, 243–80.

Binet, A. (1922). *L'etude experimentale de l'intelligence.* Paris: Costes.

Binford, T. O. (1981). Inferring surfaces from images. *Artificial Intelligence, 17*, 205–44.

Bird, E. (1984). EMG quantification of mental rehearsal. *Perceptual and Motor Skills, 59,* 899–906.

Bisiach, E., & Berti, A. (1990). Waking images and neural activity. In R. G. Kunzendorf & A. A. Sheikh (Eds.), *The psychophysiology of mental imagery: Theory, research, and application.* Amityville, NY: Baywood.

Bisiach, E., Luzzatti, C., & Perani, D. (1979). Unilateral neglect, representational scheme, and consciousness. *Brain, 102,* 609–18.

Blair, A., Hall, X., & Leyshon, X. (1993). Imagery effects on the performance of skilled and novice soccer players. *Journal of Sport Sciences, 11,* 95–101.

Blizard, D., Cowings, P., & Miller, N. E. (1975). Visceral responses to opposite types of autogenic-training imagery. *Biological Psychology, 3,* 49–55.

Block, N. (Ed.) (1981). *Imagery.* Cambridge, MA: M.I.T. Press.

Bloomberg, M. (1971). Creativity as related to field independence and mobility. *Journal of Genetic Psychology, 118,* 3–12.

Bloomberg, M. (1976). An inquiry into the relationship between field-independence-dependence and creativity. *Journal of Psychology, 67,* 127–40.

Bower, G. H. (1970a). Analysis of a mnemonic device. *American Scientist, 58,* 496–510.

Bower, G. H. (1970b). Imagery as a relational organizer in associative learning. *Journal of Verbal Learning and Verbal Behavior, 9,* 529–37.

Bower, G. H. (1972). Mental imagery and associative learning. In L. Gregg (Ed.), *Cognition in learning and memory.* New York: Wiley.

Bowers, H. (1931). Memory and mental imagery. *British Journal of Psychology, 21,* 271–82.

Bowers, H. (1932). Visual imagery and retention. *British Journal of Psychology, 23,* 180–95.

Bowers, K. S. (1979). Time distortion and hypnotic ability: Underestimating the duration of hypnosis. *Journal of Abnormal Psychology, 88,* 435–39.

Bowers, K. S., & Brenneman, H. A. (1979). Hypnosis and the perception of time. *International Journal of Clinical and Experimental Hypnosis, 27,* 29–41.

Brett, E. A., & Starker, S. (1977). Auditory imagery and hallucinations. *Journal of Nervous and Mental Disease, 164,* 394–400.

Breuer, J., & Freud, S. (1955). Studies in hysteria. In J. Strachey (Ed.), *The standard edition of the complete psychological works of Sigmund Freud.* London: Hogarth Press.

Briggs, R. (1973). Urban cognitive distance. In R. M. Downs & D. Stea (Eds.), *Image and environment.* Chicago: Aldine.

Brigham, D. D., & Toal, P. O. (1991). The use of imagery in a multimodal psychoneuroimmunology program for cancer and other chronic diseases. In R. G. Kunzendorf (Ed.), *Mental imagery.* New York: Plenum Press.

Brink, N. (1991). Dealing with pain: The psychological mechanisms that intensify pain. In R. G. Kunzendorf (Ed.), *Mental imagery.* New York: Plenum Press.

Brooks, L. R. (1967). The suppression of visualization by reading. *Quarterly Journal of Experimental Psychology, 19,* 289–99.

Brooks, L. R. (1968). Spatial and verbal components of the act of recall. *Canadian Journal of Psychology, 22,* 349–68.

Broverman, D. M. (1960). Dimensions of cognitive style. *Journal of Personality, 28,* 167–85.

Brown, B. M. (1969). The use of induced imagery in psychotherapy. *Psychotherapy: Theory, Research, and Practice, 6,* 120–21.

Brown, J. M. (1984). Imagery coping strategies in the treatment of migraine. *Pain, 18,* 157–67.

Brown, R., & Herrnstein, R. J. (1981). Icons and images. In N. Block (Ed.), *Imagery.* Cambridge, MA: M.I.T. Press.

Bruyer, R., & Racquez, F. (1985). Are lateral differences in word processing modulated by concreteness, imageability, both, or neither? *International Journal of Neuroscience, 27,* 181–89.

Budney, A. J., & Woolfolk, R. L. (1990). Using the wrong image: An exploration of the adverse effects of imagery on motor performance. *Journal of Mental Imagery, 14,* 75–86.

Bugelski, B. R. (1962). Presentation time, total time, and mediation in paired-associate learning. *Journal of Experimental Psychology, 63,* 409–12.

Bugelski, B. R. (1968). Images as mediators in one-trial paired-associate learning. II. Self-timing in successive lists. *Journal of Experimental Psychology, 77,* 328–34.

Bugelski, B. R. (1970). Words and things and images. *American Psychologist, 25,* 1002–12.

Bugelski, B. R. (1971). The definition of the image. In S. J. Segal (Ed.), *Imagery: Current cognitive approaches.* New York: Academic Press.

Bugelski, B. R. (1974). Images as mediators in one-trial paired-associate learning. III. Sequential functions in serial lists. *Journal of Experimental Psychology, 103,* 298–303.

Bugelski, B. R. (1977). Imagery and verbal behavior. *Journal of Mental Imagery, 1,* 39–52.

Bugelski, B. R. (1979). *Principles of learning and memory.* New York: Praeger.

Bugelski, B. R. (1983). Imagery and the thought processes. In A. A. Sheikh (Ed.), *Imagery: Current theory, research, and application.* New York: Wiley.

Bugelski, B. R. (1986). Memory and imagery. In A. A. Sheikh (Ed.), *Inter-

*national review of mental imagery.* Vol. 2. New York: Human Sciences Press.

Bugelski, B. R., Kidd, E., & Segman, J. (1968). Image as a mediator in one trial paired-associate learning. *Journal of Experimental Psychology, 76,* 69–73.

Byrne, R. W. (1979). Memory for urban geography. *Quarterly Journal of Experimental Psychology, 31,* 147–54.

Carpenter, P. A., & Eisenberg, P. (1978). Mental rotation and the frame of reference in blind and sighted individuals. *Perception and Psychophysics, 23,* 117–24.

Carpenter, W. (1984). *Principles of mental physiology.* New York: Appleton-Century-Crofts.

Carroll, D., Baker, J., & Preston, M. (1979). Individual differences in visual imaging and the voluntary control of heart rate. *British Journal of Psychology, 70,* 39–49.

Carroll, D., Mazillier, J., & Merian, S. (1982). Psychophysiological changes accompanying different types of arousing and relaxing imagery. *Psychophysiology, 19,* 75–82.

Caslant, E. (1921). *Methodede developpement des facultes supranormales.* Paris: Edition Rhea.

Cautela, J. R. (1977). Covert conditioning: Assumptions and procedures. *Journal of Mental Imagery, 1,* 53–64.

Cautela, J., & McCullough, L. (1978). Covert conditioning: A learning-theory perspective on imagery. In J. L. Singer & K. S. Pope (Eds.), *The power of human imagination.* New York: Plenum.

Cermak, L. S. (1975). Imagery as an aid to retrieval for Korsakoff patients. *Cortex, 11,* 163–69.

Cermak, L. S. (1980). Comments on imagery as a therapeutic mnemonic. In L. W. Poon, J. L. Fozard, D. Arenberg, & L. W. Thompson (Eds.), *New directions in memory and aging.* Hillsdale, NJ: Erlbaum.

Chambers, D., & Reisberg, D. (1985). Can mental images be ambiguous? *Journal of Experimental Psychology: Human Perception and Performance, 11,* 317–28.

Chambers, D., & Reisberg, D. (1992). What an image depicts depends on what an image means. *Cognitive Psychology, 24,* 145–74.

Childs, M. K., & Polich, J. M. (1979). Developmental differences in mental rotation. *Journal of Experimental Child Psychology, 27,* 339–51.

Chowdhury, K. R., & Vernon, P. E. (1964). An experimental study of imagery and its relation to abilities and interests. *British Journal of Psychology, 55,* 355–64.

Clark, L. V. (1960). Effect of mental practice on the development of a certain motor skill. *Research Quarterly, 31,* 560–69.

Clark, P. (1925). The phantasy method of analyzing narcissistic neurosis. *Psychoanalytic Review, 13,* 225–32.

Cohen, L. H. (1938). Imagery and its relations to schizophrenia symptoms. *Journal of Mental Science, 84,* 284–346.

Connolly, J. F. (1991). Adults who had imaginary playmates as children. In R. G. Kunzendorf (Ed.), *Mental imagery.* New York: Plenum Press.

Conway, M. A. (1988). Images in autobiographical memory. In M. Denis, J. Engelkamp, & J.T.E. Richardson (Eds.), *Cognitive and neuropsychological approaches to mental imagery.* Boston: M. Nijhoff.

Conway, M. A., Kahney, H., Bruce, K., & Duce, H. (1991). Imaging objects, routines, and locations. In R. H. Logie & M. Denis (Eds.), *Mental images in human cognition.* Amsterdam: North-Holland.

Cooper, L. A. (1976a). Demonstration of a mental analog of an external rotation. *Perception and Psychophysics, 19,* 296–302.

Cooper, L. A. (1976b). Individual differences in visual comparison processes. *Perception and Psychophysics, 19,* 433–44.

Cooper, L. A. (1991). Dissociable aspects of the mental representation of visual objects. In R. H. Logie & M. Denis (Eds.), *Mental images in human cognition.* Amsterdam: North Holland.

Cooper, L. A., & Podgorny, P. (1976). Mental transformations and visual comparison processes: Effects of complexity and similarity. *Journal of Experimental Psychology: Human Perception and Performance, 2,* 503–14.

Cooper, L. A., & Shepard, R. N. (1973a). Chronometric studies of the rotation of mental images. In W. G. Chase (Ed.), *Visual information processing.* New York: Academic Press.

Cooper, L. A., & Shepard, R. N. (1973b). The time required to prepare for a rotated stimulus. *Memory and Cognition, 1,* 246–50.

Cooper, L. A., & Shepard, R. N. (1984). Turning something over in the mind. *Scientific American, 251,* 106–14.

Cooper, L. F., & Erickson, M. H. (1954). *Time distortion in hypnosis: An experimental and clinical investigation.* Baltimore: Williams and Wilkins.

Cooper, L. F., & Rodgin, D. W. (1952). Time distortion in hypnosis and nonmotor learning. *Science, 115,* 500–502.

Corballis, M. C. (1982). Mental rotation: Anatomy of a paradigm. In M. Potegal (Ed.), *Spatial abilities: Developmental and physiological foundations.* New York: Academic Press.

Corballis, M. C. (1988). Recognition of disoriented shapes. *Psychological Review, 95,* 115–23

Corballis, M. C., & Sergent, J. (1988). Imagery in a commissurotomized patient. *Neuropsychologia, 26,* 13–26.

Corballis, M. C., & Sergent, J. (1989). Mental rotation in a commissurotomized patient. *Neuropsychologia, 27,* 585–98.

Corbin, C. B. (1967). The effects of covert rehearsal on the development of a complex motor skill. *Journal of General Psychology, 76,* 143–50.

Corbin, C. B. (1972). Mental practice. In W. P. Morgan (Ed.), *Ergogenic aids and muscular performance*. New York: Academic Press.

Cornoldi, C., & De Beni, R. (1988). Weaknesses of imagery without visual experience: The case of the total congenital blind using imaginal mnemonics. In M. Denis, J. Engelkamp, & J.T.E. Richardson (Eds.), *Cognitive and neuropsychological approaches to mental imagery*. Boston: M Nijhoff.

Costello, C. G. (1956). The effects of prefrontal leucotomy upon visual imagery and ability to perform complex operations. *Journal of Mental Science, 102,* 507–16.

Costello, C. G. (1957). The control of visual imagery in mental disorder. *Journal of Mental Science, 102,* 840–49.

Craig, K. D. (1969). Physiological arousal as a function of imagined, vicarious, and direct stress experiences. *Journal of Abnormal Psychology, 73,* 513–20.

Crampton, M. (1969). The use of mental imagery in psychosynthesis. *Journal of Humanistic Psychology, 9,* 139–53.

Crampton, M. (1974). *An historical survey of mental imagery techniques in psychotherapy and description of the dialogic imaginal integration method*. Montreal: Quebec Center for Psychosynthesis.

Crawford, H. J., & MacLeod-Morgan, C. (1986). Hypnotic investigations of imagery: A critical review of relationships. In A. A. Sheikh (Ed.), *International review of mental imagery*. Vol. 2. New York: Human Sciences Press.

Crovitz, H., Harvey, M., & Horn, R. (1979). Problems in the acquisition of imagery mnemonics: Three brain-damaged cases. *Cortex, 15,* 225–34.

Cuthbert, B. N., Vrana, S. R., & Bradley, M. M. (1991). Imagery: Function and physiology. *Advances in Psychophysiology, 4,* 1–42.

Daniels-McGhee, S., & Davis, G. A. (1994). The imagery-creativity connection. *Journal of Creative Behavior, 28,* 151–76.

Dansky, J. (1980). Make-believe: A mediator of the relationship between play and associative fluency. *Child Development, 51,* 526–29.

Das, J. P., Kirby, J., & Jarman, R. F. (1975). Simultaneous and successive synthesis: An alternative model for cognitive abilities. *Psychological Bulletin, 82,* 87–103.

Davidson, R. J., & Schwartz, G. E. (1977). Brain mechanisms subserving self-generated imagery: Electrophysiological specificity and patterning. *Psychophysiology, 14,* 598–602.

Davies, P. (1974). Conditioned after-images. *British Journal of Psychology, 65,* 191–204.

Davis, F. C. (1932). The functional significance of imagery experiences. *Journal of Experimental Psychology, 15,* 630–61.

Davis, H. (1990). Cognitive style and nonsport imagery in elite ice hockey performance. *Perceptual and Motor Skills, 71,* 795–801.

Dean, A. L. (1979). Patterns of change in relations between children's anticipatory imagery and operatory thought. *Developmental Psychology, 15,* 153–63.

Dean, A. L., & Harvey, W. O. (1979). An information-processing analysis of a Piagetian imagery task. *Developmental Psychology, 15,* 474–76.

Dean, A. L., Scherzer, E., & Chabaud, S. (1986). Sequential ordering in children's representations of rotation movements. *Journal of Experimental Child Psychology, 42,* 99–114.

De Bono, E. (1967). *New think: The use of lateral thinking in the generation of new ideas.* New York: Basic Books.

Deckert, G. H. (1964). Pursuit eye movements in the absence of a moving visual stimulus, *Science, 143,* 1192–93.

Denis, M. (1985). Visual imagery and the use of mental practice in the development of motor skills. *Canadian Journal of Applied Sport Sciences, 10,* 4–16.

Dennett, D. C. (1969). *Content and consciousness.* New York: Humanities Press.

Dennett, D. C. (1980). *Brainstorms.* Montgomery, VT: Bradford Books.

Dennett, D. C. (1981a). The nature of images and the introspective trap. In N. Block (Ed.), *Imagery.* Cambridge, MA: M.I.T. Press.

Dennett, D. C. (1981b). Two approaches to mental images. In N. Block (Ed.), *Imagery.* Cambridge, MA: M.I.T. Press.

Deschaumes-Molinaro, C., Dittmar, A., & Vernet-Maury, E. (1991). Relationship between mental imagery and sporting performance. *Behavioural Brain Research, 45,* 29–36.

Desiderato, O., & Miller, I. B. (1979). Improving tennis performance by cognitive behavior modification techniques. *The Behavior Therapist, 2,* 19.

Desoille, R. (1961). *Theorie et pratique du reve eveille dirige.* Geneva: Mont Blanc.

Desoille, R. (1965). *The directed daydream.* New York: Psychosynthesis Research Foundation.

De Vega, M. (1988). Mental imagery and perception: Modularity or functional equivalence? In M. Denis, J. Engelkamp, & J.T.E. Richardson (Eds.), *Cognitive and neuropsychological approaches to mental imagery.* Boston: M. Nijhoff.

Dimond, S. J. (1972). *The double brain.* Baltimore: William & Wilkins.

Dodds, A. G. (1978). Hemispheric differences in tactuo-spatial processing. *Neuropsychologia, 16,* 247–54.

Dolan, A. T., & Sheikh, A. A. (1976). Eidetics: A visual approach to psychotherapy. *Psychologia, 19,* 210–19.

Dolan, A. T., & Sheikh, A. A. (1977). Short-term treatment of phobias through eidetic imagery. *American Journal of Psychotherapy, 31*, 595–604.

Dominowski, R. L., & Gadlin, H. (1968). Imagery and paired-associate learning. *Canadian Journal of Psychology, 22*, 336–48.

Doob, L. W. (1965). Exploring eidetic imagery among the Kamba of Central Kenya. *Journal of Social Psychology, 67*, 3–22.

Doob, L. W. (1966). Eidetic imagery: A cross-cultural will-o'-the-wisp? *Journal of Psychology, 63*, 13–34.

Doob, L. W. (1970). Correlates of eidetic imagery in Africa. *Journal of Psychology, 76*, 223–30.

Doob, L. W. (1971). *Patterning of time.* New Haven, CT: Yale University Press.

Doob, L. W. (1972). The ubiquitous appearance of images. In P. W. Sheehan (Ed.), *The function and nature of imagery.* New York: Academic Press.

Downs, R. M., & Stea, D. (Eds.) (1973). *Image and enviroment.* Chicago: Aldine.

Drever, J. (1958). Further observations on the relation between EEG and visual imagery. *American Journal of Psychology, 71*, 270–76.

Duke, J. (1968). Lateral eye movement behavior. *Journal of General Psychology, 78*, 189–95.

Dunlap, K. (1932). *Habits: Their making and unmaking.* New York: Livewright.

D'Zamko, M. E., & Schwab, L. (1991). Children's reactions to imagery experiences. In R. G. Kunzendorf (Ed.), *Mental imagery.* New York: Plenum Press.

Eccles, J. (1958). The physiology of imagination. *Scientific American, 199*, 135.

Edwards, B. (1986). *Drawing on the artist within: A guide to innovation, invention, imagination, and creativity.* New York: Simon & Schuster.

Ehrlichman, H., & Barrett, J. (1983). Right hemispheric specialization for mental imagery: A review of the evidence. *Brain and Cognition, 2*, 55–76.

Ehrlichman, H., & Weinberger, A. (1978). Lateral eye movements and hemispheric asymmetry: A critical review. *Psychological Bulletin, 85*, 1080–101.

Ehrlichman, H., & Weiner, M. S. (1980). EEG asymmetry during covert mental activity. *Psychophysiology, 17*, 228–35.

Engelkamp, J. (1991). Imagery and enactment in paired-associate learning. In R. H. Logie & M. Denis (Eds.), *Mental images in human cognition.* Amsterdam: North-Holland.

Epstein, M. L. (1980). The relationship of mental imagery and mental rehearsal to performance of a motor task. *Journal of Sport Psychology, 2*, 211–20.

Ernest, C. H. (1977). Mental imagery and cognition: A critical review. *Journal of Mental Imagery, 1*, 181–216.

Ernest, C. H. (1979). Visual imagery ability and the recognition of verbal and nonverbal stimuli. *Acta Psychologica, 43*, 253–69.

Ernest, C. H. (1987). Imagery and memory in the blind: A review. In M. A. McDaniel & M. Pressley (Eds.), *Imagery and related mnemonic processes: Theories, individual differences, and applications.* New York: Springer-Verlag.

Ernest, C. H., & Paivio, A. (1969). Imagery ability in paired-associate and incidental learning. *Psychonomic Science, 15*, 181–82.

Ernest, C. H., & Paivio, A. (1971). Imagery and verbal associative latencies as a function of imagery ability. *Canadian Journal of Psychology, 25*, 83–90.

Escalona, S. K. (1973). Book review of "Mental imagery in children" by Jean Piaget and Barbel Inhelder (New York: Basic Books). *Journal of Nervous and Mental Diseases, 156*, 70–77.

Euse, F. J., & Haney, J. N. (1975). Clarity, control ability, and emotional intensity of image: Correlations with introversion, neuroticism, and subjective anxiety. *Perceptual and Motor Skills, 40*, 443–47.

Farah, M. J. (1984). The neurological basis of mental imagery: A componential analysis. *Cognition, 18*, 245–72.

Farah, M. J. (1985). Psychophysical evidence for a shared representational medium for mental images and percepts. *Journal of Experimental Psychology: General, 114*, 91–103.

Farah, M. J. (1988). Is visual imagery really visual? Overlooked evidence from neuropsychology. *Psychological Review, 95*, 307–17.

Farah, M. J., Gazzaniga, M., Holtzman, J., & Kosslyn, S. M. (1985). A left hemisphere basis for visual mental imagery? *Neuropsychologia, 23*, 115–18.

Farah, M. J., Hammond, K., Levine, D., & Calvanio, R. (1988). Visual and spatial mental imagery: Dissociable systems of representation. *Cognitive Psychology, 20*, 439–62.

Farah, M. J., Levine, D., & Calvanio, R. (1988). A case study of mental imagery deficit. *Brain and Cognition, 8*, 147–64.

Farah, M. J., Peronnet, F., Gonon, M., & Giard, M. (1988). Electrophysiological evidence for a shared representational medium for visual images and percepts. *Journal of Experimental Psychology: General, 17*, 248–57.

Farley, A. M. (1974). VIPS: A visual imagery and perception system; the result of protocol analysis. Unpublished doctoral dissertation, Carnegie-Mellon University.

Fein, G. (1975). A transformational analysis of pretending. *Developmental Psychology, 11*, 291–96.

Fenker, R. M., & Lambiotte, J. G. (1987). A performance enhancement program for a college football team: One incredible season. *Sport Psychologist, 1,* 224–36.

Feltz, D. L., & Landers, D. M. (1983). The effects of mental practice on motor skill learning and performance: A meta-analysis. *Journal of Sport Psychology, 5,* 25–57.

Feltz, D. L., Landers, D. M., & Becker, B. (1988). A revised meta-analysis of the mental practice literature on motor skill learning. In D. Druckman & J. Swets (Eds.), *Enhancing human performance: Issues, theories, and techniques.* New York: National Academy Press. (Also, see *Journal of Sport Psychology* [1983], *5,* 25–27.)

Feltz, D. L., & Reissinger, C. A. (1990). Effects of in vivo emotive imagery and performance feedback. *Journal of Sport and Exercise Psychology, 12,* 132–43.

Ferguson, E. (1977). The mind's eye: Nonverbal thought in technology. *Science, 197,* 827–36.

Fernald, M. R. (1912). The diagnosis of mental imagery. *Psychological Monographs, 14,* No. 58, 1–169.

Finke, R. A. (1979). The functional equivalence of mental images and errors of movement. *Cognitive Psychology, 11,* 235–64.

Finke, R. A. (1980). Levels of equivalence in imagery and perception. *Psychological Review, 87,* 113–32.

Finke, R. A. (1985). Theories relating mental imagery to perception. *Psychological Bulletin, 98,* 236–59.

Finke, R. A. (1986). Mental imagery and the visual system. *Scientific American, 254,* 88–95.

Finke, R. A. (1989). *Principles of mental imagery.* Cambridge, MA: M.I.T. Press.

Finke, R. A. (1990). *Creative imagery: Discoveries and inventions in visualization.* Hillsdale, NJ: Erlbaum.

Finke, R. A. (1993). Mental imagery and creative discovery. In B. Roskos-Ewoldsen, M. J. Intons-Peterson, & R. E. Anderson (Eds.), *Imagery, creativity, and discovery: A cognitive perspective.* Amsterdam: North-Holland.

Finke, R. A., & Kosslyn, S. M. (1980). Mental imagery acuity in the peripheral visual field. *Journal of Experimental Psychology: Human Perception and Performance, 6,* 126–39.

Finke, R. A., & Kurtzman, H. S. (1981). Mapping the visual field in mental imagery. *Journal of Experimental Psychology: General, 110,* 501–17.

Finke, R. A., & Pinker, S. (1982). Spontaneous imagery scanning in mental extrapolation. *Journal of Experimental Psychology: Learning, Memory, and Cognition, 8,* 142–47.

Finke, R. A., Pinker, S., & Farah, M. J. (1989). Reinterpreting visual patterns in mental imagery. *Cognitive Science, 13,* 51–78.

Finke, R. A., & Schmidt, M. J. (1977). Orientation-specific color after-effects following imagination. *Journal of Experimental Psychology: Human Perception and Performance, 3,* 599–606.

Finke, R. A., & Schmidt, M. J. (1978). The quantitative measure of pattern representation in images using orientation-specific color after-effects. *Perception and Psychophysics, 23,* 515–20.

Finke, R. A., & Shepard, R. N. (1986). Visual functions of mental imagery. In K. Boff, L. Kaufman, & J. Thomas (Eds.), *Handbook of perception and human performance.* Vol. 2. New York: Wiley.

Finke, R. A., & Slayton, K. (1988). Explorations of creative visual synthesis in mental imagery. *Memory and Cognition, 16,* 252–57.

Finke, R. A., Ward, T. B., & Smith, S. M. (Eds.) (1992). *Creative cognition: Theory, research, and application.* Cambridge, MA: M.I.T. Press.

Fiore, N. A. (1988). The inner healer: Imagery for coping with cancer and its therapy. *Journal of Mental Imagery, 12,* 79–82.

Flor-Henry, P. (1990). Schizophrenic hallucinations in the context of psychophysiological studies of schizophrenia. In R. G. Kunzendorf & A. A. Sheikh (Eds.), *The psychophysiology of mental imagery: Theory, research, and application.* Amityville, NY: Baywood.

Fodor, J. A. (1968a). The appeal to tacit knowledge in psychological explanation. *Journal of Philosophy, 65,* 627–40.

Fodor, J. A. (1968b). *Psychological explanation: An introduction to the philosophy of psychology.* New York: Random House.

Fodor, J. A. (1980). Methodological solipsism considered as a research strategy in cognitive psychology. *Behavioral and Brain Sciences, 3,* 63–109.

Fodor, J. A. (1981). Imagistic representation. In N. Block (Ed.), *Imagery.* Cambridge, MA: M.I.T. Press.

Forisha, B. L. (1978a). Creativity and imagery in men and women. *Perceptual and Motor Skills, 47,* 1255–64.

Forisha, B. L. (1978b). Mental imagery and creativity: Review and speculation. *Journal of Mental Imagery, 2,* 209–38.

Forisha, B. L. (1979). The outside and the inside: Compartmentalization or integration. In A. A. Sheikh & J. T. Shaffer (Eds.), *The potential of fantasy and imagination.* New York: Brandon House.

Forisha, B. L. (1981). Patterns of mental imagery and creativity in men and women. *Journal of Mental Imagery, 5,* 85–96.

Forisha, B. L. (1983). Relationship between creativity and mental imagery: A question of cognitive styles? In A. A. Sheikh (Ed.), *Imagery: Current theory, research, and application.* New York: Wiley.

Forrester, M. (2000). *Psychology of the image.* London: Routledge.

Freeman, G. L. (1933). The facilitation and inhibitory effect of muscular tension upon performance. *American Journal of Psychology, 45,* 17–52.

Fretigny, R., & Virel, A. (1968). *L'imagerie mentale.* Geneva: Mont Blanc.

Friedland, R., & Weinstein, E. (1977). Hemi-inattention and hemispheric specialization: Introduction and historical review. *Advances in Neurology, 18,* 1–31.

Galin, D. (1974). Implications for psychiatry of left and right cerebral specialization. *Archives of General Psychiatry, 31,* 572–83.

Galton, F. (1874). *English men of science, their nature and nurture.* London: Macmillan.

Gan'kova, Z. A. (1960). On the interrelation of action, image, and speech in the thinking of children of preschool age. *Voprosy Psikhologii, 1,* 69–77. (Also, see *Psychological Abstracts* [1962], *36,* 1FC69G.)

Gardner, H. (1982). *Art, mind, and brain: A cognitive approach to creativity.* New York: Basic Books.

Garfield, C. C. (1984). *Peak performance: Mental training techniques of the world's greatest athletes.* Los Angeles, CA: Tarcher.

Gaston, L., Crombez, J., & Dupuis, G. (1989). An imagery and meditation technique in the treatment of psoriasis: A case study using an A-B-A design. *Journal of Mental Imagery, 13,* 31–38.

Gazzaniga, M. D., & LeDoux, J. E. (1978). *The integrated mind.* New York: Plenum Press.

Gendlin, E. T. (1978). *Focusing.* New York: Everest House.

Gerard, R. (1964). *Psychosynthesis: A psychotherapy for the whole man.* New York: Psychosynthesis Research Foundation.

Giambra, L. M. (1977). A factor analytic study of daydreaming, imaginal process, and temperament: A replication of an adult male life-span sample. *Journal of Gerontology, 32,* 675–80.

Giambra, L. M., & Grodsky, A. (1991). Aging, imagery, and imagery vividness in daydreams: Cross-sectional and longitudinal perspectives. In R. G. Kunzendorf (Ed.), *Mental imagery.* New York: Plenum Press.

Gibson, E. J. (1969). *Perceptual learning and development.* New York: Appleton-Century-Crofts.

Gibson, J. J. (1966). *The senses considered as perceptual systems.* Boston: Houghton Mifflin.

Gibson, J. J. (1979). *The ecological approach to visual perception.* Boston: Houghton Mifflin.

Goebel, B. L., & Harris, E. L. (1980). Cognitive strategy and personality across age levels. *Perceptual and Motor Skills, 50,* 803–11.

Goff, K., & Torrance, E. P. (1991). Healing qualities of imagery and creativity. *Journal of Creative Behavior, 25,* 296–303.

Gold, J. R. (1991). Repairing narcissistic deficits through the use of imagery. In R. G. Kunzendorf (Ed.), *Mental imagery.* New York: Plenum Press.

Gold, S. R., & Henderson, B. B. (1984). Adolescent daydreaming. In A. A. Sheikh (Ed.), *International Review of Mental Imagery.* Vol. 1. New York: Human Sciences Press.

Goldenberg, G. (1989). The ability of patients with brain damage to generate mental visual images. *Brain, 112*, 305–25.

Goldenberg, G., Artner, C., & Podreka, I. (1991). Image generation and the territory of the left posterior cerebral artery. In R. H. Logie & M. Denis (Eds.), *Mental images in human cognition*. Amsterdam: North-Holland.

Goldenberg, G., Podreka, I., & Steiner, M. (1990). The cerebral localization of visual imagery: Evidence from emission computerized tomography of cerebral blood flow. In J. J. Hampson, D. F. Marks, & J.T.E. Richardson (Eds.), *Imagery: Current developments*. London: Routledge.

Goldstein, K. M., & Blackman, S. (1978). Assessment of cognitive style. In P. McReynolds (Ed.), *Advances in psychological assessment*. Vol. 4. San Francisco: Jossey-Bass.

Golla, F., Hutton, E., & Walter, W. G. (1943). The objective study of mental imagery. I. Physiological concomitants. *Journal of Mental Science, 89*, 216–23.

Golumb, C., & Cornelius, C. (1977). Symbolic play and its cognitive significance. *Developmental Psychology, 13*, 246–52.

Goodwin, A.J.H. (1953). *Cave artists of South Africa*. Cape Town: Balkema.

Gordon, R. (1962). *Stereotypy of images and belief as an ego defence*. London: Cambridge University Press.

Gordon, R. (1972). A very private world. In P. W. Sheehan (Ed.), *The function and nature of imagery*. New York: Academic Press.

Gordon, S. (1990). A mental skills training program for the Western Australian State Cricket Team. *Sport Psychologist, 4*, 222–30.

Goss, S., Hall, C. R., Buckolz, E., & Fishburne, G. (1986). Imagery ability and the application and retention of movements. *Memory and Cognition, 14*, 469–77.

Gottschalk, L. A. (1974). Self-induced visual imagery, affect arousal, and autonomic correlates. *Psychosomatics, 15*, 166–69.

Gotz, K. O., & Gotz, K. (1979). Personality characteristics of professional artists. *Perceptual and Motor Skills, 49*, 327–34.

Gough, D. (1989). Improving batting skills with small college baseball players through guided visual imagery. *Coaching Clinic, 27*, 1–6.

Gould, D., Weinberg, R., & Jackson, A. (1980). Mental preparation strategies, cognition, and strength performance. *Journal of Sport Psychology, 2*, 329–39.

Gowan, J. C. (1979). The production of creativity through right hemisphere imagery. *Journal of Creative Behavior, 13*, 39–51.

Gravel, R., Lemieux, G., & Ladouceur, R. (1980). Effectiveness of a cognitive behavioral treatment package for cross-country ski racers. *Cognitive Therapy and Research, 4*, 83–90.

Green, L. B. (1992). The use of imagery in the rehabilitation of injured athletes. *Sport Psychologist, 6,* 416–28.

Greenspan, M., & Feltz, D. (1989). Psychological interventions with athletes in competitive situations: A review. *Sport Psychologist, 3,* 219–36.

Greenwald, A. G. (1970). Sensory feedback mechanisms in performance control: With special reference to the ideo-motor mechanism. *Psychological Review, 77,* 73–99.

Grossberg, S. (1980). Human and computer rules and representations are not equivalent. *Behavioral and Brain Sciences, 3,* 136–38.

Gruber, B., Hall, N., Hersch, S., & Dubois, P. (1988). Immune system and psychological changes in metastatic cancer patients using relaxation and guided imagery: A pilot study. *Scandinavian Journal of Behavior Therapy, 17,* 25–46.

Guillerey, M. (1945). Medecine psychologique. In M. Guillerey, *Medecine officielle et medecine heretique.* Paris: Plon.

Gur, R. C., & Reyher, J. (1976). Enhancement of creativity via free-imagery and hypnosis. *American Journal of Clinical Hypnosis, 18,* 237–49.

Guthrie, E. R. (1935). *The psychology of learning.* New York: Harper & Row.

Haber, R. N. (1971). Where are the visions in visual perception? In S. J. Segal (Ed.), *Imagery: Current cognitive approaches.* New York: Academic Press.

Hale, B. D. (1982). The effects of internal and external imagery on muscular and ocular concomitants. *Journal of Sport Psychology, 4,* 379–87.

Hall, C. R. (1980). Imagery for movement. *Journal of Human Movement Studies, 6,* 252–64.

Hall, C. R., & Buckolz, E. (1981). Recognition memory for movement patterns and their corresponding pictures. *Journal of Mental Imagery, 5,* 97–104.

Hall, C. R., Buckolz, E., & Fishburne, G. (1989). Searching for a relationship between imagery ability and memory of movements. *Journal of Human Movement Studies, 17,* 89–100.

Hall, C. R., Pongrac, J., & Buckolz, E. (1985). The measurement of imagery ability. *Human Movement Science, 4,* 107–18.

Hall, C. R., Rodgers, W. M., & Barr, K. A. (1990). The use of imagery by athletes in selected sports. *Sport Psychologist, 4,* 1–10.

Hall, E. G., & Erffmeyer, E. S. (1983). The effects of visuo-motor behavior rehearsal with videotaped modeling on free throw accuracy of intercollegiate female basketball players. *Journal of Sport Psychology, 5,* 343–46.

Hall, H. R. (1983). Hypnosis and the immune system: A review with implications for cancer and the psychology of healing. *American Journal of Clinical Hypnosis, 25,* 92–103.

Hall, H. R. (1984). Imagery and cancer. In A. A. Sheikh (Ed.), *Imagination and healing.* Amityville, NY: Baywood.

Hall, H. R. (1989). Research in the area of voluntary immunomodulation: Complexities, consistencies, and future research considerations. *International Journal of Neuroscience, 47*, 81–89.

Hall, H. R. (1990). Imagery, psychoneuroimmunology, and the psychology of healing. In R. G. Kunzendorf & A. A. Sheikh (Eds.), *The psychophysiology of mental imagery: Theory, research, and application.* Amityville, NY: Baywood.

Hall, R. G. (1971). The imaginal and verbal components in the acquisition of a perceptual-motor skill. Unpublished doctoral dissertation, Washington State University.

Hammer, M. (1967). The directed daydream technique. *Psychotherapy: Theory, Research, and Practice, 4*, 173–81.

Hampson, P. J. (1979). The role of imagery in cognition. Unpublished doctoral dissertation, University of Lancaster (UK).

Hampson, P. J., Marks, D. F., & Richardson, J.T.E. (Eds.) (1990). *Imagery: Current developments.* London: Routledge.

Hampson, P. J., & Morris, P. E. (1978). Unfulfilled expectations: A criticism of Neisser's theory of imagery. *Cognition, 6*, 79–85.

Hampson, P. J., & Morris, P. E. (1990). Imagery, consciousness, and cognitive control: The BOSS model reviewed. In P. J. Hampson, D. F. Marks, & J.T.E. Richardson (Eds.), *Imagery: Current developments.* London: Routledge.

Hanley, G. L., & Chinn, D. (1989). Stress management: An integration of multidimensional arousal and imagery theories with case study. *Journal of Mental Imagery, 13*, 107–18.

Happich, C. (1932). Das bildbewusstsein als ansatzstelle psychischer behandling. *Zeitblatter der Psychotherapie, 5*, 663–67.

Harren, V., Kass, R., Tinsley, H., & Moreland, J. (1978). Influence of sex role attitudes and cognitive styles on career decision making. *Journal of Counseling Psychology, 25*, 390–98.

Harris, D. V., & Harris, B. L. (1984). *The athlete's guide to sports psychology: Mental skills for physical people.* Champaign, IL: Leisure Press.

Harris, D. V., & Robinson, W. (1986). The effects of skill level on EMG activity during internal and external imagery. *Journal of Sport Psychology, 8*, 105–11.

Hartmann, E. (1991). Thin and thick boundaries: Personality, dreams, and imagination. In R. G. Kunzendorf (Ed.), *Mental imagery.* New York: Plenum Press.

Hatfield, B., Landers, D., & Ray, W. (1984). Cognitive processes during self-paced motor performance: An electroencephalographic profile of skilled marksmen. *Journal of Sport Psychology, 6*, 42–59.

Hawkins, W. H. (1976). Alpha rhythm and heart rate correlates of mental imagery. *Dissertation Abstracts International, 37*, 3112B.

Hayes-Roth, F. (1979). Distinguishing theories of representation: A critique of Anderson's "Arguments concerning mental imagery." *Psychological Review, 86,* 376–92.

Haynes, W. O., & Moore, W. H. (1981). Sentence imagery and recall: An electroencephalographic evaluation of hemispheric processing in males and females. *Cortex, 17,* 49–62.

Hearne, K.M.T. (1978). Visual imagery and evoked-responses. *Psychological Research, 40,* 89–92.

Hebb, D. O. (1949). *The organization of behavior.* New York: Wiley.

Hebb, D. O. (1968). Concerning imagery. *Psychological Review, 75,* 466–77.

Heckler, J. E., & Kaczor, L. M. (1988). Application of imagery theory to sport psychology: Some preliminary findings. *Journal of Sport Psychology, 10,* 363–73.

Heil, J. (1982). Visual imagery change during relaxation meditation training. *Dissertation Abstracts International, 43,* 2338B.

Helstrup, T., & Anderson, R. E. (1991). Imagery in mental construction and decomposition tasks. In R. H. Logie & M. Denis (Eds.), *Mental images in human cognition.* Amsterdam: North-Holland.

Herrington, R. N., & Schneidau, P. (1968). The effect of imagery on the waveshape of the visual evoked responses. *Experientia, 24,* 1136–37.

Heuer, F., Fischman, D., & Reisberg, D. (1986). Why does vivid imagery hurt colour memory? *Canadian Journal of Psychology, 40,* 161–75.

Hilgard, J. R. (1970). *Personality and hypnosis: A study of imaginative involvement.* Chicago: University of Chicago Press.

Hilgard, J. R. (1979). Imaginative and sensory-affective involvements in everyday life and in hypnosis. In E. Fromm & R. E. Shor (Eds.), *Hypnosis: Developments in research and new perspectives.* Hawthorne, NY: Aldine.

Hinshaw, K. E. (1991–1992). The effects of mental practice on motor skills performance: Critical evaluation and meta-analysis. *Imagination, Cognition, and Personality, 11,* 3–35.

Hinton, G. E. (1979a). Imagery without arrays. *Behavioral and Brain Sciences, 2,* 555–56.

Hinton, G. E. (1979b). Some demonstrations of the effects of structural descriptions in mental imagery. *Cognitive Science, 3,* 231–50.

Hird, J., Landers, D., Thomas, J., & Horan, J. (1991). Physical practice is superior to mental practice in enhancing cognitive and motor task performance. *Journal of Sport and Exercise Psychology, 8,* 281–93.

Hogan, R. (1980). The gifted adolescent. In J. Adelson (Ed.), *Handbook of adolescent psychology.* New York: Wiley.

Holden, C. (1978). Cancer and the mind: How are they connected? *Science, 200,* 1363–69.

Holt, R. R. (1964). Imagery: The return of the ostracized. *American Psychologist, 19,* 154–64.

Honeycutt, J. M. (1991). Imagined interactions, imagery, and mindfulness/ mindlessness. In R. G. Kunzendorf (Ed.), *Mental imagery*. New York: Plenum Press.

Hookham, V. (1991). Imagery in conjuction with art therapy. In R. G. Kunzendorf (Ed.), *Mental imagery*. New York: Plenum Press.

Horowitz, M. J. (1964). The imagery of visual hallucinations. *Journal of Nervous and Mental Disease, 138*, 513–23.

Horowitz, M. J. (1968). Visual thought images in psychotherapy. *American Journal of Psychotherapy, 22*, 55–75.

Horowitz, M. J. (1969a). Flashbacks: Recurrent intrusive images after use of LSD. *American Journal of Psychiatry, 126*, 4.

Horowitz, M. J. (1969b). Psychic trauma: Return of images after a stress film. *Archives of General Psychiatry, 22*, 565–69.

Horowitz, M. J. (1970/1978). *Image formation and cognition*. New York: Appleton-Century-Crofts.

Horowitz, M. J. (1972). Image formation: Clinical observations and a cognitive model. In P. W. Sheehan (Ed.), *The function and nature of imagery*. New York: Academic Press.

Horowitz, M. J. (1974). *Image techniques in psychotherapy*. New York: Behavioral Science Tape Library.

Horowitz, M. J. (1978). Controls of visual imagery and therapeutic intervention. In J. L. Singer & K. S. Pope (Eds.), *The power of human imagination*. New York: Plenum Press.

Horowitz, M. J., Adams, J., & Rutkin, B. (1968). Visual imagery on brain stimulation. *Archives of General Psychiatry, 19*, 469–86.

Housner, D. (1984). The role of visual imagery in recall of modeled motoric stimuli. *Journal of Sport Psychology, 6*, 148–58.

Housner, L., & Hoffman, S. J. (1978). Imagery and short-term motor memory. In G. C. Roberts & K. M. Newell (Eds.), *Psychology of motor behavior and sport*. Champaign, IL: Human Kinetics.

Housner, L., & Hoffman, S. J. (1981). Imagery ability in recall of distance and location. *Journal of Motor Behavior, 13*, 207–23.

Houtz, J. C., & Patricola, C. (1999). Imagery. In M. A. Runco & S. R. Pritzker (Eds.), *Encyclopedia of creativity*. Vol. 2. San Diego, CA: Academic Press.

Howe, B. L. (1991). Imagery and sport performance. *Sports Medicine, 11*, 1–5.

Huckabee, M. W. (1974). Introversion-extraversion and imagery. *Psychological Reports, 34*, 453–54.

Hughes, M., & Hutt, C. (1979). Heart-rate correlates of childhood activities: Play, exploration, problem-solving, and daydreaming. *Biological Psychology, 5*, 253–63.

Hull, C. L. (1943). *The principles of behavior*. New York: Appleton-Century-Crofts.

Hummeltenberg, M. (1939). Vorstellungstypus, gedachtnis, und gesamt-personlichkeit. *Zeitschrift fur Psychologie, 147*, 10–37.

Hunt, R. R., & Marschark, M. (1987). Yet another picture of imagery: The roles of shared and distinctive information in memory. In M. A. McDaniel & M. Pressley (Eds.), *Imagery and related mnemonic processes: Theories, individual differences, and applications*. New York: Springer-Verlag.

Hyman, I. E. (1993). Imagery, reconstructive memory, and discovery. In B. Roskos-Ewoldsen, M. J. Intons-Peterson, & R. E. Anderson (Eds.), *Imagery, creativity, and discovery: A cognitive perspective*. Amsterdam: North-Holland.

Hyman, I. E., & Neisser, U. (1991). *Reconstructing mental images: Problems of method*. Report No. 19. Atlanta, GA: Emory Cognitive Project, Emory University.

Ievleva, L., & Orlick, T. (1991). Mental links to enhanced healing: An exploratory study. *Sport Psychologist, 5*, 25–40.

Ikeda, Y., & Hirai, H. (1976). Voluntary control of electroderman activity in relation to imagery and internal perception scores. *Psychophysiology, 13*, 330–33.

Intons-Peterson, M. J. (1981). Constructing and using unusual and common images. *Journal of Experimental Psychology: Human Learning and Memory, 7*, 133–44.

Intons-Peterson, M. J. (1983). Imagery paradigms: How vulnerable are they to experimenters' expectations? *Journal of Experimental Psychology: Human Perception and Performance, 9*, 394–412.

Intons-Peterson, M. J. (1984). Faces, rabbits, skunks, and ducks: Imaginal comparisons of similar and dissimilar items. *Journal of Experimental Psychology: Learning, Memory, and Cognition, 10*, 699–715.

Intons-Peterson, M. J. (1993). Imagery's role in creativity and discovery. In B. Roskos-Ewoldsen, M. J. Intons-Peterson, & R. E. Anderson (Eds.), *Imagery, creativity, and discovery: A cognitive perspective*. Amsterdam: North-Holland.

Intons-Peterson, M. J., & McDaniel, M. A. (1991). Symmetries and asymmetries between imagery and perception. In M. A. McDaniel & C. Cornoldi (Eds.), *Imagery and cognition*. New York: Springer-Verlag.

Intons-Peterson, M. J., & Roskos-Ewoldsen, B. (1989). Sensory-perceptual qualities of images. *Journal of Experimental Psychology: Learning, Memory, and Cognition, 15*, 188–99.

Isaac, A. R. (1992). Mental practice: Does it work in the field? *Sport Psychologist, 6*, 192–98.

Ishii, M. M. (1986). Imagery techniques in the works of Maxwell Maltz. In A. A. Sheikh (Ed.), *Anthology of imagery techniques*. Milwaukee, WI: American Imagery Institute.

Jackson, J. H. (1874). On the nature of the duality of the brain. *Medical Press, 1,* 19.

Jackson, J. H. (1876/1958). Case of large cerebral tumor without optic neuritis and with left hemiplegia and imperceptionl. In J. Taylor (Ed.), *Selected writings of John Hughlings Jackson.* New York: Basic Books.

Jackson, J. H. (1880). On right- or left-sided spasm at the onset of epileptic paroxysms, and on crude sensation warnings and elaborate mental states. *Brain, 3,* 192–206.

Jacobson, E. (1929). Electrical measurements of neuromuscular states during mental activities. I. Imagination of movement involving skeletal muscles. *American Journal of Physiology, 91,* 567–608.

Jacobson, E. (1930). Electrical measurements of neuromuscular states during mental activities. II.; III. Imagination and recollection of various muscular acts; Visual imagination and recollection. *American Journal of Physiology, 94,* 22–34; *95,* 694–712. (Also, see *American Journal of Physiology* [1931], *96,* 115–21.)

Jacobson, E. (1932). Electrophysiology of mental activities. *American Journal of Psychology, 44,* 677–94.

Jaensch, E. R. (1930). *Eidetic imagery and typological methods of investigation.* New York: Harcourt, Brace.

Jaffe, D. T., & Bresler, D. E. (1980). Guided imagery: Healing through the mind's eye. In J. E. Shorr, G. E. Sobel, P. Robin, & J. A. Connella (Eds.), *Imagery: Its many dimensions and applications.* New York: Plenum Press.

Janet, P. (1898). *Nervoses et idees fixes.* Paris: Alcan.

Janssen, W. (1976). *On the nature of the mental image.* Soesterberg, Netherlands: Institute for Perception.

Jasnoski, M. L., & Kugler, J. (1987). Relaxation, imagery, and neuro-immodulation. *Annals of the New York Academy of Sciences, 496,* 722–30.

Jellinek, A. (1949). Spontaneous imagery: A new psychotherapeutic approach. *American Journal of Psychotherapy, 3,* 372–91.

Jenkin, A. M. (1935). Imagery and learning. *British Journal of Psychology, 26,* 149–64.

Johnson, M. K. (1991). Reflection, reality monitoring, and the self. In R. G. Kunzendorf (Ed.), *Mental imagery.* New York: Plenum Press.

Johnson-Laird, P. N. (1980). Mental models in cognitive science. *Cognitive Science, 4,* 71–115.

Jones, G. E. (1977). The influence of stimulus context and somatic activity on phasic heart rate response during imagery. *Dissertation Abstracts International, 37.* 4208B–9B.

Jones, G. E. (1988). Images, predicates, and retrieval cues. In M. Denis, J. Engelkamp, & J.T.E. Richardson (Eds.), *Cognitive and neuropsycho-*

*logical approaches to mental imagery.* Dordrecht, The Netherlands: M. Nijhoff.

Jones, G. E., & Johnson, H. J. (1978). Physiological responding during self-generated imagery of contextually complete stimuli. *Psychophysiology, 15,* 439–46.

Jones, G. E., & Johnson, H. J. (1980). Heart rate and somatic concomitants of mental imagery. *Psychophysiology, 17,* 339–47.

Jones, J. G. (1965). Motor learning without demonstration of physical practice, under two conditions of mental practice. *Research Quarterly, 36,* 270–76.

Jones, M. K. (1974). Imagery as a mnemonic aid after left temporal lobectomy: Contrast between material-specific and generalized memory disorders. *Neuropsychologia, 12,* 21–30.

Jones-Gotman, M. (1979). Incidental learning of image-mediated or pronounced words after right temporal lobectomy. *Cortex, 15,* 187–97.

Jones-Gotman, M., & Milner, B. (1978). Right temporal lobe contribution to image mediated verbal learning. *Neuropsychologia, 16,* 61–71.

Jordan, C. S. (1979). Mental imagery and psychotherapy: European approaches. In A. A. Sheikh & J. T. Shaffer (Eds.), *The potential of fantasy and imagination.* New York: Brandon House.

Jordan, C. S., Davis, M., Kahn, P., & Sinnott, R. (1980). Eidetic imagery group methods of assertion training. *Journal of Mental Imagery, 4,* 41–48.

Jordan, C. S., & Lenington, K. T. (1979). Physiological correlates of eidetic imagery and induced anxiety. *Journal of Mental Imagery, 3,* 31–42.

Jowdy, D., & Harris, D. (1990). Muscular responses during mental imagery as a function of motor skill. *Journal of Sport and Exercise Psychology, 12,* 191–201.

Juhasz, J. B. (1971). Greek theories of imagination. *Journal of the History of the Behavioral Sciences, 7,* 39–58.

Jung, C. (1923). *Psychological types.* London: Routledge & Kegan Paul.

Jung, C. G. (1926/1960). The structure and dynamics of the psyche. In C. G. Jung, *Collected works.* Vol. 8. Princeton, NJ: Princeton University Press.

Jung, C. G. (1935/1976). The symbolic life. In C. G. Jung, *Collected works.* Vol. 18. Princeton, NJ: Princeton University Press.

Kaczor, L. M. (1990). Bioinformational theory of emotional imagery and imagery rehearsal: A process and outcome investigation of performance enhancement. Unpublished doctoral dissertation, University of Maine.

Kagan, J., Moss, M., & Siegel, I. (1963). Psychological significance of styles of conceptualization. *Monographs of the Society for Research in Child Development, 28,* 73–112.

Kail, R. (1985). Development of mental rotation: A speed-accuracy study. *Journal of Experimental Child Psychology, 40,* 181–92.

Kail, R., Pellegrino, J., & Carter, P. (1980). Developmental changes in mental rotation. *Journal of Experimental Child Psychology, 29*, 102–16.

Kanzer, M. (1958). Image formation during free association. *Psychoanalytic Quarterly, 27*, 465–84.

Kassels, S. (1991). Transforming imagery into art: A study of the life and work of Georgia O'Keeffe. In R. G. Kundendorf (Ed.), *Mental imagery*. New York: Plenum Press.

Kaufmann, G. (1980). *Imagery, language, and cognition: Toward a theory of symbolic activity in human problem-solving*. Bergen: Universitetsforlaget.

Kaufmann, G. (1984). Mental imagery in problem solving. In A. A. Sheikh (Ed.), *International Review of Mental Imagery*. Vol. 1. New York: Human Sciences Press.

Kaufmann, G. (1988). Mental imagery and problem solving. In M. Denis, J. Engelkamp, & J.T.E. Richardson (Eds.), *Cognitive and neuropsychological approaches to mental imagery*. Boston: M. Nijhoff.

Kaufmann, G. (1990). Imagery effects on problem solving. In P. J. Hampson, D. F. Marks, & J.T.E. Richardson (Eds.), *Imagery: Current developments*. London: Routledge.

Kaufmann, G., & Helstrup, T. (1993). Mental imagery: Fixed or multiple meanings? Nature and function of imagery in creative thinking. In B. Roskos-Ewoldsen, M. J. Intons-Peterson, & R. E. Anderson (Eds.), *Imagery, creativity, and discovery: A cognitive perspective*. Amsterdam: North-Holland.

Kazdin, A. E. (1978). Covert modeling: The therapeutic application of imagined rehearsal. In J. L. Singer & K. S. Pope (Eds.), *The power of human imagination: New methods in psychotherapy*. New York: Plenum Press.

Kazdin, A. E., & Smith, G. (1979). Covert conditioning: A review and evaluation. *Advances in Behavior Research and Therapy, 2*, 57–96.

Keenan, J. M., & Moore, R. E. (1979). Memory for images of concealed objects: A reexamination of Neisser and Kerr. *Journal of Experimental Psychology: Human Learning and Memory, 5*, 374–85.

Keiss, H. O., & Montague, W. E. (1965). Natural language mediataors in paired-associate learning. *Psychonomic Science, 3*, 549–50.

Kelsey, I. B. (1961). Effects of mental practice and physical practice upon muscular endurance. *Research Quarterly, 32*, 47–54.

Kendall, G., Hrycaiko, D., Martin, G., & Kendall, T. (1990). The effects of an imagery rehearsal, relaxation, and self-talk package on basketball game performance. *Journal of Sport and Exercise Psychology, 12*, 157–66.

Kepecs, J. G. (1954). Observations on screens and barriers in the mind. *Psychoanalytic Quarterly, 23*, 62–77.

Kerr, N. H. (1983). The role of vision in "visual imagery" experiments:

Evidence from the congenitally blind. *Journal of Experimental Psychology: General, 112,* 265–77.

Kerr, N. H., Corbitt, R., & Jurkovic, G. (1980). Mental rotation: Is it stage related? *Journal of Mental Imagery, 4,* 49–56.

Khatena, J. (1976). Original verbal imagery and its sense modality correlates. *Gifted Child Quarterly, 20,* 180–92.

Khatena, J. (1977). Advances in research on creative imagination imagery. *Gifted Child Quarterly, 21,* 433–39.

Khatena, J. (1978). Frontiers of creative imaginative imagery. *Journal of Mental Imagery, 2,* 33–46.

Khatena, J. (1983). Analogy imagery and the creative imagination. *Journal of Mental Imagery, 7,* 127–34.

Khatena, J., & Torrance, E. P. (1973). *Thinking creatively with sounds and words: Norms-technical manual (research edition).* Lexington, MA: Personnel Press.

Khatena, J., & Torrance, E. P. (1976). *Manual for Khatena-Torrance Creative Perception Inventory.* Chicago: Stoelting.

Kieras, D. (1978). Beyond pictures and words: Alternative information processing models for imagery effects in verbal memory. *Psychological Bulletin, 85,* 532–54.

King, D. L. (1973). An image theory of classical conditioning. *Psychological Reports, 33,* 403–11.

King, D. L. (1974a). An image theory of instrumental conditioning. *Psychological Reports, 35,* 1115–22.

King, D. L. (1974b). Perception, binocular fusion, and an image theory of classical conditioning. *Perceptual and Motor Skills, 39,* 531–37.

King, D. L. (1978). Image theory of conditioning, memory, forgetting, functional similarity, fusion, and dominance. *Journal of Mental Imagery, 2,* 47–62.

King, D. L. (1979). *Conditioning: An image approach.* New York: Gardner.

King, D. L. (1983). Image theory of conditioning. In A. A. Sheikh (Ed.), *Imagery: Current theory, research, and application.* New York: Wiley.

Kintsch, W. (1972). Abstract nouns: Imagery versus lexical complexity. *Journal of Verbal Learning and Verbal Behavior, 11,* 59–65.

Kintsch, W. (1977). *Memory and cognition.* New York: Holt, Rinehart and Winston.

Kirby, J. R., & Das, J. P. (1976). Comments on Paivio's imagery theory. *Canadian Psychological Review, 17,* 66–68.

Klinger, E. (1971). *The structure and function of fantasy.* New York: Wiley.

Klinger, E. (1980). Therapy and the flow of thought. In J. E. Shorr, G. E. Sobel, P. Robin, & J. A. Connella (Eds.), *Imagery: Its many dimensions and applications.* New York: Plenum Press.

Klinger, E. (1981). The central place of imagery in human functioning. In E. Klinger (Ed.), *Imagery: Concepts, results, and applications.* Vol. 2. New York: Plenum Press.

Klopfer, D. S. (1985). Constructing mental representations of objects from successive views. *Journal of Experimental Psychology: Human Perception and Performance, 11*, 566–82.

Koestler, A. (1964). *The act of creation.* New York: Macmillan.

Kohl, R. M., & Roenker, D. L. (1980). Bilateral transfer as a function of mental imagery. *Journal of Motor Behavior, 12*, 197–206.

Kohl, R. M., & Roenker, D. L. (1983). Mechanism involvement during skill imagery. *Journal of Motor Behavior, 15*, 179–90.

Kohl, R. M., Roenker, D., & Turner, P. (1985). Clarification of competent imagery as a prerequisite for effective skill imagery. *International Journal of Sport Psychology, 16*, 37–45.

Kolers, P. A. (1987). Imaging. In R. L. Gregory (Ed.), *The Oxford companion to the mind.* New York: Oxford University Press.

Kolers, P. A., & Smythe, W. E. (1979). Images, symbols, and skills. *Canadian Journal of Psychology, 33*, 158–84.

Kolinsky, R., Morais, J., Content, A., & Cary, L. (1987). Finding parts within figures: A developmental study. *Perception, 16*, 399–407.

Kolonay, B. J. (1977). The effects of visuo-motor behavior rehearsal on athletic performance. Unpublished master's thesis, City University of New York.

Korn, E. R. (1982). *Pain management with relaxation and mental imagery.* Audiotape. La Jolla, CA: PCA Press.

Korn, E. R. (1983). The use of altered states of consciousness and imagery in physical and pain rehabilitation. *Journal of Mental Imagery, 17*, 25–34.

Korn, E. R. (1986). The uses of relaxation and mental imagery to enhance athletic performance. In M. Wolpin, J. E. Shorr, & L. Krueger (Eds.), *Imagery. Vol. 4. Recent practice and theory.* New York: Plenum Press.

Korn, E. R., & Johnson, K. (1983). *Visualization: The uses of altered states of consciousness and imagery in the health professions.* Homewood, IL: Dow Jones-Irwin.

Kosbab, F. P. (1974). Imagery techniques in psychiatry. *Archives of General Psychiatry, 31*, 283–90.

Kosslyn, S. M. (1975). Information representation in visual images. *Cognitive Psychology, 7*, 341–70.

Kosslyn, S. M. (1976). Using imagery to retrieve semantic information: A developmental study. *Child Development, 47*, 434–44.

Kosslyn, S. M. (1978). Measuring the visual angle of the mind's eye. *Cognitive Psychology, 10*, 356–89.

Kosslyn, S. M. (1980). *Image and mind.* Cambridge, MA: Harvard University Press.

Kosslyn, S. M. (1981). The medium and the message in mental imagery: A theory. In N. Block (Ed.), *Imagery.* Cambridge, MA: M.I.T. Press. (Also, see *Psychological Review* [1981], *88*, 46–66.)

Kosslyn, S. M. (1983). *Ghosts in the mind's machine: Creating and using images in the brain*. New York: W. W. Norton.

Kosslyn, S. M. (1990). Mental imagery. In D. N. Osherson, S. M. Kosslyn, & J. M. Hollerbach (Eds.), *Visual cognition and action: An invitation to cognitive science*. Vol. 2. Cambridge, MA: M.I.T. Press.

Kosslyn, S. M. (1991). A cognitive neuroscience of visual cognition: Further developments. In R. H. Logie & M. Denis (Eds.), *Mental images in human cognition*. Amsterdam: North-Holland.

Kosslyn, S. M. (1994). *Image and brain: The resolution of the imagery debate*. Cambridge, MA: M.I.T. Press.

Kosslyn, S. M., Ball, T. M., & Reiser, B. J. (1978). Visual images preserve metric spatial information: Evidence from studies of image scanning. *Journal of Experimental Psychology: Human Perception and Performance, 4*, 47–60.

Kosslyn, S. M., Ball, T. M., & Reiser, B. J. (1979). Visual images preserve metric spatial information: Evidence from studies of image scanning. *Journal of Experimental Psychology: Human Perception and Performance, 4*, 47–60.

Kosslyn, S. M., Holtzman, J. D., Farah, M. J., & Gazzaniga, M. S. (1985). A computational analysis of mental image generation: Evidence from functional dissociations in split-brain patients. *Journal of Experimental Psychology: General, 114*, 311–41.

Kosslyn, S. M., Pinker, S., Smith, G. E., & Shwartz, S. P. (1979). On the demystification of mental imagery. *Behavioral and Brain Sciences, 2*, 535–81.

Kosslyn, S. M., Pinker, S., Smith, G. E., & Shwartz, S. P. (1981). On the demystification of mental imagery. In N. Block (Ed.), *Imagery*. Cambridge, MA: M.I.T. Press.

Kosslyn, S. M., & Pomerantz, J. R. (1977). Imagery, propositions, and the form of internal representations. *Cognitive Psychology, 9*, 52–76.

Kosslyn, S. M., Seger, C., Pani, J., & Hillger, L. A. (1990). When is imagery used? A diary study. *Journal of Mental Imagery, 14*, 131–52.

Kosslyn, S. M., & Shwartz, S. P. (1977). A simulation of visual imagery. *Cognitive Science, 1*, 265–95.

Kosslyn, S. M., & Shwartz, S. P. (1981). Empirical constraints on mental imagery. In J. Long & A. Baddeley (Eds.), *Attention and performance*. Hillsdale, NJ: Erlbaum.

Kosslyn, S. M., VanKleeck, M., & Kirby, K. (1990). A neurologically plausible model of individual differences in visual mental imagery. In P. J. Hampson, D. F. Marks, & J.T.E. Richardson (Eds.), *Imagery: Current developments*. London: Routledge.

Kretschmer, E. (1922). *Kretschmer's textbook of medical psychology*. London: Oxford University Press.

Kretschmer, W. (1969). Meditative techniques in psychotherapy. In C. Tart (Ed.), *Altered states of consciousness*. New York: Wiley.

Kroger, W. S., & Fezler, W. D. (1976). *Hypnosis and behavior modification: Imagery conditioning.* Philadelphia, PA: Lippincott.

Kruck, J. S., & Sheikh, A. A. (1986). Alexithymia: A critical review. In A. A. Sheikh (Ed.), *International review of mental imagery.* Vol. 2. New York: Human Sciences Press.

Krueger, T. H. (1976). *Visual imagery in problem solving and scientific creativity.* Derby, CT: Seal Press.

Kulpe, O. (1893). *Outlines of psychology.* London: Swan Sonnenschein.

Kunzendorf, R. G. (1981). Individual differences in imagery and autonomic control. *Journal of Mental Imagery, 5,* 47–60.

Kunzendorf, R. G. (1984). Centrifugal effects of eidetic imaging on flash electroretinograms and autonomic responses. *Journal of Mental Imagery, 8,* 67–76.

Kunzendorf, R. G. (1985–1986). Hypnotic hallucinations as "unmonitored" images: An empirical study. *Imagination, Cognition, and Personality, 5,* 255–70.

Kunzendorf, R. G., Jesses, M., Michaels, A., Caiazzo-Fluellen, G., & Butler, W. (1991). Imagination and perceptual development: Effects of auditory imaging on the brainstem evoked potentials of children, adult musicians, and other adults. In R. G. Kunzendorf (Ed.), *Mental imagery.* New York: Plenum Press.

Kunzendorf, R. G., & Sheikh, A. A. (1990). Imaging, image-monitoring, and health. In R. G. Kunzendorf & A. A. Sheikh (Eds.), *The psychophysiology of mental imagery: Theory, research, and application.* Amityville, NY: Baywood.

Lane, J. F. (1980). Improving athletic performance through visuo-motor behavior rehearsal. In R. M. Suinn (Ed.), *Psychology in sports: Methods and applications.* Minneapolis, MN: Burgess.

Lang, P. J. (1977). Imagery in therapy: An information processing analysis of fear. *Behavior Therapy, 8,* 862–86.

Lang, P. J. (1979). A bio-informational theory of emotional imagery. *Psychophysiology, 16,* 495–512.

Lang, P. J., Kozak, M., Miller, G., Levin, D., & McLean, A. (1980). Emotional imagery: Conceptual structure and pattern of somatovisceral response. *Psychophysiology, 17,* 179–92. (Also, see *Psychophysiology* [1981], *18,* 196.)

Lang, P. J., Levin, D., Miller, G., & Kozak, M. (1983). Fear behavior, fear imagery, and the psychophysiology of emotion: The problem of affective response integration. *Journal of Abnormal Psychology, 92,* 276–306.

Lang, P. J., Melamed, B. G., & Hart, J. A. (1970). Psychophysiological analysis of fear modification using an automated desensitization procedure. *Journal of Abnormal Psychology, 76,* 229–34.

Langhinrichsen, J., & Tucker, D. M. (1990). Neuropsychological concepts of mood, imagery, and performance. In R. G. Kunzendorf & A. A. Sheikh (Eds.), *The psychophysiology of mental imagery: Theory, research, and application.* Amityville, NY: Baywood.

Larkin, J. H., & Simon, H. A. (1987). Why a diagram is (sometimes) worth ten thousand words. *Cognitive Science, 11,* 65–99.

Larsson, G. (1987). Routinization of mental training and organization: Effects on performance and well-being. *Journal of Applied Psychology, 72,* 81–91.

Lautrey, J., & Chartier, D. (1991). A developmental approach to mental imagery. In C. Cornoldi & M. A. McDaniel (Eds.), *Imagery and cognition.* New York: Springer-Verlag.

Lazarus, A. A. (1977). *In the mind's eye.* New York: Rawson Associates.

Lazarus, A. A. (1982). *Personal enrichment through imagery.* Three audio-cassettes. New York: Guilford/BMA Audio Cassettes.

Lazarus, A. A. (1984). *The mind's eye: The power of imagery for personal enrichment.* New York: Guilford Press.

Lazarus, A. A., & Abramovitz, A. (1962). The use of "emotive imagery" in the treatment of children's phobias. *Journal of Mental Science, 108,* 191–95.

Lazarus, R. S. (1966). *Psychological stress and the coping process.* New York: McGraw-Hill.

Leask, J., Haber, R. N., & Haber, R. B. (1969). Eidetic imagery in children: II. Longitudinal and experimental results. *Psychonomic Monograph Supplements, 3,* 25–48.

Leber, W. R. (1979). Stimulus familiarity and muscular involvement as determinants of image-produced arousal. *Dissertation Abstracts International, 40,* 1928B–29B.

LeBoutillier, N., & Marks, D. F. (2003). Mental imagery and creativity: A meta-analytic review study. *British Journal of Psychology, 94,* 29–44.

Lee, C. (1990). Psyching up for a muscular endurance task: Effects of image content on performance and mood state. *Journal of Sport and Exercise Psychology, 12,* 66–73.

Lee, T. R. (1962). Brennan's law of shopping behavior. *Psychological Reports, 11,* 662.

Lehmann, D., & Koukkou, M. (1990). Brain states of visual imagery and dream generation. In R. G. Kunzendorf & A. A. Sheikh (Eds.), *The psychophysiology of mental imagery: Theory, research, and application.* Amityville, NY: Baywood.

Leuba, C. (1940). Images as conditioned sensations. *Journal of Experimental Psychology, 26,* 345–51.

Leuba, C., & Dunlap, R. (1951). Conditioning imagery. *Journal of Experimental Psychology, 41,* 352–55.

Leuner, H. (1977). Guided affective imagery: An account of its development. *Journal of Mental Imagery, 1,* 73–92.

Leuner, H. (1978). Basic principles and therapeutic efficacy of guided affective imagery. In J. L. Singer & K. S. Pope (Eds.), *The power of human imagination*. New York: Plenum Press.

Levin, J., & Pressley, M. (1978). A test of the developmental imagery hypothesis in children's associative learning. *Journal of Educational Psychology, 70,* 691–94.

Levine, D., Warach, J., & Farah, M. (1985). Two visual systems in mental imagery: Dissociation of "what" and "where" in imagery disorders due to bilateral posterior cerebral lesions. *Neurology, 35,* 1010–18.

Levine, M. (1987). *Effective problem solving.* Englewood Cliffs, NJ: Prentice-Hall.

Ley, R. G. (1979). Cerebral asymmetries, emotional experience, and imagery: Implications for psychotherapy. In A. A. Sheikh & P. T. Shaffer (Eds.), *The potential of fantasy and imagination.* New York: Brandon House.

Ley, R. G. (1983). Cerebral laterality and imagery. In A. A. Sheikh (Ed.), *Imagery: Current theory, research, and application.* New York: Wiley.

Ley, R. G. (1984). Right hemispheric processing of emotional and imageable words. In A. A. Sheikh (Ed.), *International Review of Mental Imagery.* Vol. 1. New York: Human Sciences Press.

Lindauer, M. S. (1969). Imagery and sensory modality. *Perceptual and Motor Skills, 29,* 203–15.

Lindauer, M. S. (1972). The sensory attributes and functions of imagery and imagery evoking stimuli. In P. W. Sheehan (Ed.), *The function and nature of imagery.* New York: Academic Press.

Lindauer, M. S. (1977). Imagery from the point of view of psychological aesthetics, the arts, and creativity. *Journal of Mental Imagery, 1,* 343–62.

Lindauer, M. S. (1983). Imagery and the arts. In A. A. Sheikh (Ed.), *Imagery: Current theory, research, and application.* New York: Wiley.

Lindsay, R. K. (1988). Images and inference. *Cognition, 29,* 229–50.

Lippman, L. G. (1989). Positive versus negative phrasing in mental practice. *Journal of General Psychology, 117,* 255–65.

Loarer, E., & Savoyant, A. (1991). Visual imagery in locomotor movement without vision. In R. H. Logie & M. Denis (Eds.), *Mental images in human cognition.* Amsterdam: North-Holland.

Locke, S., & Colligan, D. (1986). *The healer within: The new medicine of mind and body.* New York: E. P. Dutton.

Loftus, E. F., & Loftus, G. R. (1980). On the permanence of stored information in the human brain. *American Psychologist, 5,* 409–20.

Logie, R. H., & Baddeley, A. D. (1990). Imagery and working memory. In P. J. Hampson, D. F. Marks, & J.T.E. Richardson (Eds.), *Imagery: Current developments.* London: Routledge.

Logie, R. H., & Marchetti, C. (1991). Visuo-spatial working memory:

Visual, spatial, or central executive? In R. H. Logie & M. Denis (Eds.), *Mental images in human cognition*. Amsterdam: North-Holland.

Lohr, J. M. (1976). Concurrent conditioning of evaluating meaning and imagery. *British Journal of Psychology, 67*, 353–58.

Luria, A. R. (1968). *The mind of a mnemonist*. New York: Basic Books.

Lusebrink, V. B. (1991). Levels of imagery and visual expression. In R. G. Kunzendorf (Ed.), *Mental imagery*. New York: Plenum Press.

Lutz, K., & Lutz, R. (1977). The effects of interactive imagery on learning: Application to advertising. *Journal of Applied Psychology, 62*, 493–98.

Lynch, K. (1960). *Image of the city*. Cambridge, MA: M.I.T. Press.

MacKay, D. (1981). The problem of rehearsal or mental practice. *Journal of Motor Behavior, 13*, 274–85.

Mackay, J. R. (1958). The interactance hypothesis and boundaries in Canada: A preliminary study. *Canadian Geographer, 3*, 1–8.

Mahoney, M., & Avener, M. (1977). Psychology of the elite athlete: An exploratory study. *Cognitive Therapy and Research, 1*, 135–41.

Malleson, N. (1959). Panic and phobias: Possible method of treatment. *Lancet, 1*, 225–27.

Maltz, M. (1960). *Psycho-cybernetics: A new way to get more living out of life*. Englewood Cliffs, NJ: Prentice-Hall.

Mandler, J. M., & Johnson, N. S. (1976). Some of the thousand words a picture is worth. *Journal of Experimental Psychology: Human Learning and Memory, 2*, 529–40.

Marks, D. F. (1972a). Individual differences in the vividness of visual imagery and their effect on function. In P. W. Sheehan (Ed.), *The function and nature of imagery*. New York: Academic Press.

Marks, D. F. (1972b). Relative judgment: A phenomenon and a theory. *Perception and Psychophysics, 11*, 156–60.

Marks, D. F. (1973a). Visual imagery differences and eye movements in the recall of pictures. *Perception and Psychophysics, 14*, 407–12.

Marks, D. F. (1973b). Visual imagery differences in the recall of pictures. *British Journal of Psychology, 64*, 17–24.

Marks, D. F. (1977). Imagery and consciousness: A theoretical review from an individual differences perspective. *Journal of Mental Imagery, 2*, 275–90.

Marks, D. F. (1981). Imagery, knowledge, and the individual. *Journal of Mental Imagery, 5*, 47–50.

Marks, D. F. (1983a). Mental imagery and consciousness: A theoretical review. In A. A. Sheikh (Ed.), *Imagery: Current theory, research, and application*. New York: Wiley.

Marks, D. F. (1983b). Signal detection theory applied to imagery and states of consciousness. *International Imagery Bulletin, 1*, 39–51.

Marks, D. F. (1984). The new structural approach to image formation, psychophysiology, and psychopathology. *Journal of Mental Imagery,* *8,* 95–104.

Marks, D. F. (1985). Imagery paradigms and methodology. *Journal of Mental Imagery, 9,* 93–106.

Marks, D. F. (Ed.) (1986). *Theories of image formation.* New York: Brandon House.

Marks, D. F. (1987). Problems with the triple code model. *Journal of Mental Imagery, 11,* 102–5.

Marks, D. F. (1990). On the relationship between imagery, body, and mind. In P. J. Hampson, D. F. Marks, & J.T.E. Richardson (Eds.), *Imagery: Current developments.* London: Routledge.

Marks, D. F. (1999). Consciousness, mental imagery, and action. *British Journal of Psychology, 90,* 567–85.

Marks, I., Marset, P., Boulougouris, J., & Huson, J. (1971). Physiological accompaniments of neutral and phobic imagery. *Psychological Medicine, 1,* 299–307.

Marmor, G. S. (1975). Development of kinetic images: When does the child first represent movement in mental images? *Cognitive Psychology, 7,* 548–59.

Marmor, G. S. (1977). Mental rotation and number conservation: Are they related? *Developmental Psychology, 13,* 320–25.

Marmor, G. S., & Zabeck, L. A. (1976). Mental rotation by the blind: Does mental rotation depend on visual imagery? *Journal of Experimental Psychology: Human Perception and Performance, 2,* 515–21.

Marr, D. (1982). *Vision.* San Francisco: Freeman.

Marr, D., & Nishihara, H. K. (1978). Representation and recognition of the spatial organization of three-dimensional shapes. *Proceedings of the Royal Society of London, B-207,* 187–217.

Martel, L. D. (1991). The role of guided imagery in educational reform: The integrative learning system. In R. G. Kunzendorf (Ed.), *Mental imagery.* New York: Plenum Press.

Martens, R. (1984). Imagery in sport. *Sports Medicine, 8,* 213–30.

Martin, M., & Williams, R. (1990). Imagery and emotion: Clinical and experimental approaches. In P. J. Hampson, D. F. Marks, & J.T.E. Richardson (Eds.), *Imagery: Current developments.* London: Routledge.

Martindale, C. (1990). Creative imagination and neural activity. In R. G. Kunzendorf & A. A. Sheikh (Eds.), *The psychophysiology of mental imagery: Theory, research, and application.* Amityville, NY: Baywood.

Marzillier, J., Carroll, D., & Newland, J. (1979). Self-report and physiological changes accompanying repeated imaging of a phobic scene. *Behavior Research and Therapy, 17,* 71–77.

Matthews, W. A. (1983). The effects of concurrent secondary tasks on the use of imagery in a free recall task. *Acta Psychologica, 53,* 231–41.

Mavromatis, A., & Richardson, J.T.E. (1984). Hypnagogic imagery. In A. A. Sheikh (Ed.), *International Review of Mental Imagery*. Vol. 1. New York: Human Sciences Press.

May, J., & Johnson, H. (1973). Physiological activity to internally-elicited arousal and inhibitory thoughts. *Journal of Abnormal Psychology, 82,* 239–45.

McBride, E. R., & Rothstein, A. L. (1979). Mental and physical practice and the learning and retention of open and closed skills. *Perceptual and Motor Skills, 49,* 359–65.

McCaffrey, N., & Orlick, T. (1989). Mental factors related to excellence among top professional golfers. *International Journal of Sport Psychology, 20,* 256–78.

McClelland, D. (1975). *Power: The inner experience*. New York: Halstead.

McDaniel, M. A., & Einstein, G. O. (1991). Bizarre imagery: Mnemonic benefits and theoretical implications. In R. H. Logie & M. Denis (Eds.), *Mental images in human cognition*. Amsterdam: North-Holland.

McDaniel, M. A., & Pressley, M. (Eds.) (1987). *Imagery and related mnemonic processes: Theories, individual differences, and applications*. New York: Springer-Verlag.

McFadden, R. S. (1982). An investigation of the relative effectiveness of two types of imagery rehearsal applied to enhance skilled athletic performance. Unpublished doctoral dissertation, University of Toronto.

McGuigan, F. J. (1978). Imagery and thinking: Covert functioning of the motor system. In G. E. Schwartz & D. Shapiro (Eds.), *Consciousness and self-regulation: Advances in research and theory*. Vol. 2. New York: Plenum.

McKellar, P. (1979). Between wakefulness and sleep: Hypnagogic fantasy. In A. A. Sheikh & J. T. Shaffer (Eds.), *The potential of fantasy and imagination*. New York: Brandon House.

McKellar, P., & Marks, D. F. (1982). Imagery in learning theory: The return of the ostracized. *Journal of Mental Imagery, 6,* 47–51.

McKim, R. H. (1980). *Experiences in visual thinking*. Belmont, CA: Wadsworth.

McMahon, C. E. (1973). Images as motives and motivators: A historical perspective. *American Journal of Psychology, 86,* 465–90.

McMahon, C. E. (1976). The role of imagination in the disease process: Pre-Cartesian history. *Psychological Medicine, 6,* 179–84.

McMahon, C. E., & Sheikh, A. A. (1986). Imagination in disease and healing processes: A historical perspective. In A. A. Sheikh (Ed.), *Anthology of imagery techniques*. Milwaukee, WI: American Imagery Institute.

Meacci, W., & Price, E. (1985). Acquisition and retention of golf putting skill through the relaxation, visualization, and body rehearsal intervention. *Research Quarterly for Exericse and Sport, 16,* 176–79.

Meichenbaum, D. (1977). *Cognitive-behavior modification: An integrative approach*. New York: Plenum Press.

Meichenbaum, D. (1978). Why does using imagery in psychotherapy lead to change? In J. L. Singer & K. S. Pope (Eds.), *The power of human imagination*. New York: Plenum Press.

Mendoza, D., & Wichman, H. (1978). "Inner" darts: Effects of mental practice on performance of dart throwing. *Perceptual and Motor Skills, 47*, 1195–99.

Meskin, B., & Singer, J. L. (1974). Daydreaming, reflective thought, and laterality of eye movements. *Journal of Personality and Social Psychology, 30*, 64–71.

Meyers, A., Cooke, C., Cullen, J., & Liles, L. (1979). Psychological aspects of athletic competitors: A replication across sports. *Cognitive Therapy and Research, 3*, 361–66.

Meyers, A., Schleser, R., & Okwamabua, T. (1982). A cognitive-behavioral intervention for improving basketball performance. *Research Quarterly for Exercise and Sport, 13*, 344–47.

Milgram, S. (1972). A psychological map of New York City. *American Scientist, 60*, 194–200.

Millar, S. (1990). Imagery and blindness. In P. J. Hampson, D. F. Marks, & J.T.E. Richardson (Eds.), *Imagery: Current developments*. London: Routledge.

Miller, A. I. (1984/1986). *Imagery in scientific thought: Creating 20th century physics*. Boston: Birkhauser/Cambridge, MA: M.I.T. Press.

Miller, G. A., Galanter, E., & Pribram, K. H. (1960). *Plans and the structure of behavior*. New York: Holt.

Minas, S. C. (1978). Mental practice of a complex perceptual-motor skill. *Journal of Human Movement Studies, 4*, 102–7.

Mitchell, D. B., & Richman, C. L. (1980). Confirmed reservations: Mental travel. *Journal of Experimental Psychology: Human Perception and Performance, 6*, 58–66.

Moran, T. P. (1973). The symbolic imagery hypothesis: A production system model. Unpublished doctoral dissertation, Carnegie-Mellon University.

Moray, N. (1970). *Attention: Selective processes in vision and hearing*. New York: Academic Press.

Morra, S., Moizo, C., & Scopesi, A. (1988). Working memory (or the MOperator) and the planning of children's drawings. *Journal of Experimental Child Psychology, 46*, 41–73.

Morris, P. E., & Hampson, P. J. (1983). *Imagery and consciousness*. New York: Academic Press.

Morrisett, L. H. (1956). The role of implicit practice in learning. Unpublished doctoral dissertation, Yale University.

Morrison, J. K. (1979). Emotive-reconstructive psychotherapy: Changing constructs by means of mental imagery. In A. A. Sheikh & J. T. Shaffer (Eds.), *The potential of fantasy and imagination*. New York: Brandon House.

Morrison, J. K. (1980). Emotive-reconstructive therapy: A short-term psychotherapeutic use of mental imagery. In J. E. Shorr, G. E. Sobel, P. Robin, & J. A. Connella (Eds.), *Imagery: Its many dimensions and applications*. New York: Plenum Press.

Morse, E., Martin, J., & Furst, M. (1977). A physiological and subjective evaluation of meditation, hypnosis, and relaxation. *Psychosomatic Medicine, 5,* 304–24.

Mowbray, C., & Luria, Z. (1973). Effects of labeling on children's visual imagery. *Developmental Psychology, 9,* 1–8.

Mowrer, O. H. (1960). *Learning theory and the symbolic processes*. New York: Wiley.

Mowrer, O. H. (1977). Mental imagery: An indispensable psychological concept. *Journal of Mental Imagery, 1,* 303–26.

Mumford, B., & Hall, C. R. (1985). The effects of internal and external imagery on performing figures in figure skating. *Canadian Journal of Applied Sport Sciences, 10,* 171–77.

Murphy, S., Jowdy, D., & Durtschi, S. (1989). *Report on the United States Olympic Committee Survey on Imagery Use in Sport: 1989.* Colorado Springs, CO: U.S. Olympic Training Center.

Murphy, S., Woolfolk, R., & Budney, A. (1988). The effects of emotive imagery on strength performance. *Journal of Sport and Exercise Psychology, 10,* 334–45.

Murphy, S. M. (1990). Models of imagery in sport psychology: A review. *Journal of Mental Imagery, 14,* 153–72.

Myers, I. B. (1962). *The Myers-Briggs type indicator manual*. Princeton, NJ: Educational Testing Service.

Naruse, G., & Obonai, T. (1953). Decomposition and fusion of mental images in the drowsy and post-hypnotic hallucinatory state. *Journal of Clinical and Experimental Hypnosis, 1,* 23–44. (Also, see 1955, *3,* 2–23.)

Neisser, U. (1967). *Cognitive psychology*. New York: Appleton.

Neisser, U. (1972). Changing conceptions of imagery. In P. W. Sheehan (Ed.), *The function and nature of imagery*. New York: Academic Press.

Neisser, U. (1976). *Cognition and reality*. San Francisco: Freeman.

Neisser, U. (1978). Anticipations, images, and introspections. *Cognition, 6,* 167–74.

Neisser, U. (1979). Images, models, and human nature. *Behavioral and Brain Sciences, 2,* 561.

Neisser, U., & Kerr, N. (1973). Spatial and mnemonic properties of visual images. *Cognitive Psychology, 5,* 138–50.

Neiworth, J. J., & Rilling, M. E. (1987). A method for studying imagery in animals. *Journal of Experimental Psychology: Animal Behavior Processes, 13*, 203–14.

Newell, A., & Simon, H. A. (1972). *Human problem solving.* Englewood Cliffs, NJ: Prentice-Hall.

Nideffer, R. M. (1971). Deep muscle relaxation: An aid to diving. *Coach and Athlete, 24*, 38.

Nideffer, R. M. (1985). *Athlete's guide to mental training.* Champaign, IL: Human Kinetics.

Noel, R. C. (1980). The effect of visuo-motor behavior rehearsal on tennis performance. *Journal of Sport Psychology, 2*, 220–26.

Noton, D., & Stark, L. (1971). Scan path in eye movements during pattern perception. *Science, 171*, 308–11.

Ogden, J. A. (1985). Contralesional neglect of constructed visual images in right and left brain-damaged patients. *Neuropsychologia, 23*, 273–77.

Ohkuma, Y. (1985). Effects of evoking imagery on the control of peripheral skin temperature. *Japanese Journal of Psychology, 54*, 88–94.

Onestak, D. M. (1991). The effects of progressive relaxation, mental practice, and hypnosis on athletic performance: A review. *Journal of Sport Behavior, 14*, 247–82.

Osgood, C. E. (1953). *Method and theory in experimental psychology.* New York: Oxford University Press.

Osherson, D. N., Kosslyn, S. M., & Hollerbach, J. M. (1990). *Visual cognition and action: An invitation to cognitive science.* Vol. 2. Cambridge, MA: M.I.T. Press.

Oswald, I. (1957). The EEG, visual imagery, and attention. *Quarterly Journal of Experimental Psychology, 9*, 113–18.

Oxendine, J. (1968). *Psychology of motor learning.* New York: Meredith.

Paivio, A. (1963). Learning of adjective-noun paired associates as a function of word order and noun abstractness. *Canadian Journal of Psychology, 18*, 146–55.

Paivio, A. (1965). Abstractness, imagery, and meaningfulness in paired-associate learning. *Journal of Verbal Learning and Verbal Behavior, 4*, 32–38.

Paivio, A. (1966). Latency of verbal associations and imagery to noun stimuli as a function of abstractness and generality. *Canadian Journal of Psychology, 20*, 378–87.

Paivio, A. (1969). Mental imagery in associative learning and memory. *Psychological Review, 76*, 241–63.

Paivio, A. (1970). On the functional significance of imagery. *Psychological Bulletin, 73*, 385–92.

Paivio, A. (1971a). Imagery and language. In S. J. Segal (Ed.), *Imagery: Current cognitive approaches.* New York: Academic Press.

Paivio, A. (1971b). *Imagery and verbal processes.* New York: Holt, Rinehart and Winston.

Paivio, A. (1972). A theoretical analysis of the role of imagery in learning and memory. In P. W. Sheehan (Ed.), *The function and nature of imagery*. New York: Academic Press.

Paivio, A. (1973). Psychophysiological correlates of imagery. In E. J. McGuigan & R. A. Schoonover (Eds.), *The psychophysiology of thinking*. New York: Academic Press.

Paivio, A. (1976). Images, propositions, and knowledge. In J. M. Nicholas (Ed.), *Images, perception, and knowledge*. Dordrecht, Holland: Reidel.

Paivio, A. (1977). Images, propositions, and knowledge. In J. M. Nichols (Ed.), *Images, perception, and knowledge*. Dordrecht, Holland: Reidel.

Paivio, A. (1978). Dual coding: Theoretical issues and empirical evidence. In J. M. Scandura & C. J. Brainerd (Eds.), *Structural/process models of complex human behavior*. Leiden, Netherlands: Nordhoff.

Paivio, A. (1982). The empirical case for dual coding. In J. Yuille (Ed.), *Imagery, cognitions, and memory*. Hillsdale, NJ: Erlbaum.

Paivio, A., & Begg, I. (1971). Imagery and associative overlap in short-term memory. *Journal of Experimental Psychology, 89*, 40–45.

Paivio, A., & Csapo, K. (1969). Concrete-image and verbal memory codes. *Journal of Experimental Psychology, 80*, 279–85.

Paivio, A., & Foth, D. (1970). Imaginal and verbal mediators and noun concreteness in paired-associate learning: The elusive interaction. *Journal of Verbal Learning and Verbal Behavior, 9*, 384–90.

Paivio, A., & Madigan, S. (1970). Noun imagery and frequency in paired-associate and free recall learning. *Canadian Journal of Psychology, 24*, 353–61.

Paivio, A., & Okovita, H. W. (1971). Word imagery modalities and associative learning in blind and sighted subjects. *Journal of Verbal Learning and Verbal Behavior, 10*, 506–10.

Paivio, A., & O'Neill, B. J. (1970). Visual recognition thresholds and dimensions of word meaning. *Perception and Psychophysics, 8*, 273–75.

Paivio, A., & Rowe, E. J. (1970). Noun imagery, frequency, and meaningfulness in verbal discrimination. *Journal of Experimental Psychology, 85*, 264–69.

Paivio, A., & Smythe, P. C. (1971). Word imagery, frequency, and meaningfulness in short-term memory. *Psychonomic Science, 22*, 333–35.

Paivio, A., Smythe, P. C., & Yuille, J. C. (1968). Imagery versus meaningfulness of nouns in paired-associate learning. *Canadian Journal of Psychology, 22*, 427–41.

Paivio, A., & Yuille, J. C. (1967). Mediation instructions and word attributes in paired-associate learning. *Psychonomic Science, 8*, 65–66.

Paivio, A., & Yuille, J. C. (1969). Changes in associative strategies and paired-associate learning over trials as a function of word imagery and type of learning set. *Journal of Experimental Psychology, 79*, 458–63.

Paivio, A., Yuille, J. C., & Madigan, S. (1968). Concreteness, imagery, and meaningfulness values for 925 nouns. *Journal of Experimental Psychology, 76* (1, Pt. 2).

Paivio, A., Yuille, J. C., & Rogers, T. B. (1969). Noun imagery and meaningfulness in free and serial recall. *Journal of Experimental Psychology, 79*, 509–14.

Paivio, A., Yuille, J. C., & Smythe, P. C. (1966). Stimulus and response abstractness, imagery, and meaningfulness, and reported mediators in paired-associate learning. *Canadian Journal of Psychology, 20*, 362–77.

Palermo, D. S. (1970). Imagery in children's learning: Discussion. *Psychological Bulletin, 73*, 415–21.

Palmer, S. E. (1975). Visual perception and world knowledge: Notes on a model of sensory-cognitive interaction. In D. A. Norman & D. E. Rumelhart (Eds.), *Explorations in cognition*. San Francisco: Freeman.

Panagiotou, N., & Sheikh, A. A. (1974). Eidetic psychotherapy: Introduction and evaluation. *International Journal of Social Psychiatry, 20*, 231–41.

Panagiotou, N., & Sheikh, A. A. (1977). The image and the unconscious. *International Journal of Social Psychiatry, 23*, 169–86.

Parsons, L. M. (1987). Imagined spatial transformations of one's hands and feet. *Cognitive Psychology, 19*, 178–241.

Pascual-Leone, J. (1970). A mathematical model for the transition rule in Piaget's developmental stages. *Acta Psychologica, 32*, 301–45.

Pascual-Leone, J., & Goodman, D. (1979). Intelligence and experience: A neo-Piagetian approach. *Instructional Science, 8*, 301–67.

Paul, G. L. (1969). Physiological effects of relaxation training and hypnotic suggestion. *Journal of Abnormal Psychology, 74*, 425–37.

Perky, C. W. (1910). An experimental study of imagination. *American Journal of Psychology, 21*, 422–52.

Perls, F. (1970). *Gestalt therapy verbatim*. New York: Bantam.

Perls, F. (1972). *In and out of the garbage pail*. New York: Bantam.

Peronnet, F., Farah, M. J., & Gonon, M.-A. (1988). Evidence for shared structures between imagery and perception. In M. Denis, J. Engelkamp, & J.T.E. Richardson (Eds.), *Cognitive and neuropsychological approaches to mental imagery*. Boston: M. Nijhoff.

Perry, C. (1973). Imagery, fantasy, and hypnotic susceptibility: A multidimensional approach. *Journal of Personality and Social Psychology, 26*, 217–21.

Peruch, P., & Savoyant, A. (1991). Conflicting spatial frames of reference in a locating task. In R. H. Logie & M. Denis (Eds.), *Mental images in human cognition*. Amsterdam: North-Holland.

Peterson, M. A. (1993). The ambiguity of mental images: Insights regarding the structure of shape memory and its function in creativity. In B. Roskos-Ewoldsen, M. J. Intons-Peterson, & R. E. Anderson (Eds.), *Imagery, creativity, and discovery: A cognitive perspective*. Amsterdam: North-Holland.

Peterson, M. A., Kihlstrom, J., Rose, P., & Glisky, A. (1992). Mental images can be ambiguous: Parts, wholes, and strategies. *Memory and Cognition, 20,* 107–23.

Phipps, S. J., & Morehouse, C. A. (1969). Effects of mental practice on the acquisition of motor skills of varied difficulty. *Research Quarterly, 40,* 773–78.

Piaget, J. (1955). *The growth of logical reasoning.* New York: Basic Books.

Piaget, J. (1962). *Plays, dreams, and imitation in childhood.* New York: Norton.

Piaget, J., & Inhelder, B. (1966). *L'image mentale chez l'enfant.* Paris: Presses Universitaires.

Piaget, J., & Inhelder, B. (1969). *The psychology of the child.* New York: Basic Books.

Piaget, J., & Inhelder, B. (1971). *Mental imagery in the child.* New York: Basic Books.

Piaget, J., & Inhelder, B. (1973). *Memory and intelligence.* New York: Basic Books.

Pinker, S. (1980). Mental imagery and the third dimension. *Journal of Experimental Psychology, 109,* 354–71.

Pinker, S., & Finke, R. A. (1980). Emergent two-dimensional patterns in images rotated in depth. *Journal of Experimental Psychology: Human Perception and Performance, 6,* 244–64.

Pinker, S., & Kosslyn, S. M. (1983). Theories of mental imagery. In A. A. Sheikh (Ed.), *Imagery: Current theory, research, and application.* New York: Wiley.

Platt, J., & Cohen, S. (1981). Mental rotation task performance as a function of age and training. *Journal of Psychology, 108,* 173–78.

Podgorny, P., & Shepard, R. N. (1978). Functional representations common to visual perception and imagination. *Journal of Experimental Psychology: Human Perception and Performance, 4,* 21–35.

Porter, K., & Foster, F. (1986). *The mental athlete: Inner training for peak performance.* Dubuque, IA: W. C. Brown.

Potter, R. B. (1976). Directional bias within the usage and perceptual fields of urban consumers. *Psychological Reports, 38,* 988–90.

Powell, G. E. (1973). Negative and positive mental practice in motor skill acquisition. *Perceptual and Motor Skills, 37,* 423–25.

Pressley, M., Borkowski, J. G., & Johnson, C. J. (1987). The development of good strategy use: Imagery and related mnemonic strategies. In M. A. McDaniel & M. Pressley (Eds.), *Imagery and related mnemonic processes: Theories, individual differences, and applications.* New York: Springer-Verlag.

Price, A. D. (1975). Heart rate variability and respiratory concomitants of visual and nonvisual "imagery" and cognitive style. *Journal of Research in Personality, 9,* 341–55.

Price-Williams, D. R. (1961). A study concerning concepts of conservation of quantities among primitive children. *Acta Psychologica, 18,* 297–305.

Prigatano, G. P. (1983). Visual imagery and the corpus callosum: A theoretical note. *Perceptual and Motor Skills, 56,* 296–98.

Prigatano, G. P. (1987). Recovery and cognitive retraining after craniocerebral trauma. *Journal of Learning Disabilities, 20,* 603–13.

Przybyla, D., Byrne, D., & Kelley, K. (1983). The role of imagery in sexual behavior. In A. A. Sheikh (Ed.), *Imagery: Current theory, research, and application.* New York: Wiley.

Pulaski, M. (1973). Toys and imaginative play. In J. L. Singer (Ed.), *The child's world of make-believe.* New York: Academic Press.

Pylyshyn, Z. W. (1973). What the mind's eye tells the mind's brain: A critique of mental imagery. *Psychological Bulletin, 80,* 1–24.

Pylyshyn, Z. W. (1978). Imagery and artificial intelligence. In C. W. Savage (Ed.), *Perception and cognition: Issues in the foundations of psychology.* Minnesota Studies in the Philosophy of Science, Vol. 9, Minneapolis: University of Minnesota Press.

Pylyshyn, Z. W. (1979a). Imagery theory: Not mysterious—just wrong. *Behavioral and Brain Sciences, 2,* 561–63.

Pylyshyn, Z. W. (1979b). The rate of "mental rotation" of images: A test of a holistic analogue hypothesis. *Memory and Cognition, 7,* 19–28.

Pylyshyn, Z. W. (1979c). Validating computational models: A critique of Anderson's indeterminacy of representation claim. *Psychological Review, 86,* 383–94.

Pylyshyn, Z. W. (1980a). Cognitive representation and the process-architecture distinction. *Behavioral and Brain Sciences, 3,* 154–69.

Pylyshyn, Z. W. (1980b). Computation and cognition: Issues in the foundation of cognitive science. *Behavioral and Brain Sciences, 3,* 111–33.

Pylyshyn, Z. W. (1981). The imagery debate: Analog media versus tacit knowledge. In N. Block (Ed.), *Imagery.* Cambridge, MA: M.I.T. Press.

Qualls, P. J. (1982). The physiological measurement of imagery: An overview. *Imagination, Cognition, and Personality, 2,* 89–101.

Qualls, P. J., & Sheehan, P. W. (1983). Imaginative, make-believe, experiences and their role in the development of the child. In M. L. Fleming & D. W. Hutton (Eds.), *Mental imagery and learning.* Englewood Cliffs, NJ: Educational Technology Publication.

Quinn, J. G. (1991). Encoding and maintenance of information in visual working memory. In R. H. Logie & M. Denis (Eds.), *Mental images in human cognition.* Amsterdam: North-Holland.

Rachman, S. (1968). *Phobias: Their nature and control.* Springfield, IL: Thomas.

Raichle, M. (1990). Images of the functioning human brain. In H. Barlow, C. Blakemore, & M. Weston-Smith (Eds.), *Images and understanding.* Cambridge, UK: Cambridge University Press.

Raser, G. A., & Bartz, W. H. (1968). Imagery and paired-associate recognition. *Psychonomic Science, 12,* 385–86.

Ratcliff, G. (1979). Spatial thought, mental rotation, and the right cerebral hemisphere. *Neuropsychologia, 17,* 49–54.

Reed, S. K. (1974). Structural descriptions and the limitations of visual images. *Memory and Cognition, 2,* 329–36.

Reed, S. K. (1993). Imagery and discovery. In B. Roskos-Ewoldsen, M. J. Intons-Peterson, & R. E. Anderson (Eds.), *Imagery, creativity, and discovery: A cognitive perspective.* Amsterdam: North-Holland.

Reed, S. K., & Johnsen, J. A. (1975). Detection of parts in patterns and images. *Memory and Cognition, 3,* 569–75.

Reese, H. W. (1970a). Imagery and contextual meaning. *Psychological Bulletin, 73,* 404–14.

Reese, H. W. (1970b). Imagery in children's learning: A symposium. Introduction. *Psychological Bulletin, 73,* 383–84.

Reese, H. W. (1975). Verbal effects in children's visual recognition memory. *Child Development, 46,* 400–407.

Reisberg, D., & Chambers, D. (1991). Neither pictures nor propositions: What can we learn from a mental image? *Canadian Journal of Psychology, 45,* 336–52.

Reisberg, D., & Logie, R. H. (1993). The ins and outs of working memory: Overcoming the limits on learning from imagery. In B. Roskos-Ewoldsen, M. J. Intons-Peterson, & R. E. Anderson (Eds.), *Imagery, creativity, and discovery: A cognitive perspective.* Amsterdam: North-Holland.

Reisberg, D., Pearson, D., & Kosslyn, S. M. (2003). Intuitions and introspections about imagery: The role of imagery experience in shaping an investigator's theoretical views. *Applied Cognitive psychology, 17,* 147–60.

Reisberg, D., Wilson, M., & Smith, J. D. (1991). Auditory imagery and inner speech. In R. H. Logie & M. Denis (Eds.), *Mental images in human cognition.* Amsterdam: North-Holland.

Reyher, J. (1963). Free imagery, an uncovering procedure. *Journal of Clinical Psychology, 19,* 454–59.

Reyher, J. (1977). Spontaneous visual imagery: Implications for psychoanalysis, psychopathology, and psychotherapy. *Journal of Mental Imagery, 2,* 253–74.

Reyher, J. (1978). Emergent uncovering psychotherapy: The use of imagoic and linguistic vehicles in objectifying psychodynamic processes. In J. L. Singer & K. S. Pope (Eds.), *The power of human imagination.* New York: Plenum Press.

Richardson, A. (1964). Has mental practice any relevance to physiotherapy? *Physiotherapy, 50,* 148–51.

Richardson, A. (1967). Mental practice: A review and discussion. *Research Quarterly, 38,* 95–107, 263–73.

Richardson, A. (1969). *Mental imagery*. London: Routledge & Kegan Paul.

Richardson, A. (1972). Voluntary control of the memory image. In P. W. Sheehan (Ed.), *The function and nature of imagery*. New York: Academic Press.

Richardson, A. (1977). Verbalizer-visualizer: A cognitive style dimension. *Journal of Mental Imagery, 1*, 109–26.

Richardson, A., & Patterson, Y. (1986). An evaluation of three procedures for increasing imagery vividness. In A. A. Sheikh (Ed.), *International review of mental imagery*. Vol. 2. New York: Human Sciences Press.

Richardson, J.T.E. (1980). *Mental imagery and human memory*. London: Macmillan.

Richardson, J.T.E. (1990). Imagery and memory in brain-damaged patients. In P. J. Hampson, D. F. Marks, & J.T.E. Richardson (Eds.), *Imagery: Current developments*. London: Routledge.

Richardson, J.T.E. (1991a). Gender differences in imagery, cognition, and memory. In R. H. Logie & M. Denis (Eds.), *Mental images in human cognition*. Amsterdam: North-Holland.

Richardson, J.T.E. (1991b). Imagery and the brain. In C. Cornoldi & M. A. McDaniel (Eds.), *Imagery and cognition*. New York: Springer-Verlag.

Richardson, J.T.E., & Barry, C. (1985). The effects of minor closed head injury upon human memory: Further evidence on the role of mental imagery. *Cognitive Neuropsychology, 2*, 149–68.

Richardson, J.T.E., Cermak, L. S., Blackford, S. P., & O'Connor, M. (1987). The efficacy of imagery mnemonics following brain damage. In M. A. McDaniel & M. Pressley (Eds.), *Imagery and related mnemonic processes: Theories, individual differences, and applications*. New York: Springer-Verlag.

Richman, C. L., Mitchell, D. B., & Reznick, J. S. (1979). Mental travel: Some reservations. *Journal of Experimental Psychology: Human Perception and Performance, 5*, 13–18.

Rider, M., Floyd, J., & Kirkpatrick, J. (1985). The effect of music, imagery, and relaxation on adrenal corticosteroids and the reentrainment of circadian rhythms. *Journal of Music Therapy, 22*, 46–58.

Riley, E., & Start, K. (1960). The effect of spacing of mental and physical practices on the acquisition of a physical skill. *Australian Journal of Physical Education, 20, 13*–16.

Robbins, K., & McAdams, D. (1974). Interhemispheric alpha asymmetry and imagery mode. *Brain and Language, 1*, 189–93.

Roberts, R. J., & Weerts, T. C. (1982). Cardiovascular responding during anger and fear imagery. *Psychological Reports, 50*, 219–30.

Rock, I., Wheeler, D., & Tudor, L. (1989). Can we imagine how objects look from other viewpoints? *Cognitive Psychology, 21*, 185–210.

Rodgers, W., Hall, C., & Buckolz, E. (1991). The effect of an imagery training program on imagery ability, imagery use, and figure skating performance. *Journal of Applied Sport Psychology, 3*, 109–25.

Roe, A. (1951). A study of imagery in research scientists. *Journal of Personality, 19*, 159–70.

Roeckelein, J. E. (1984). *Self-control program and laboratory experiments.* Lexington, MA: Ginn.

Roeckelein, J. E. (1998). *Dictionary of theories, laws, and concepts in psychology.* Westport, CT: Greenwood Press.

Roeckelein, J. E. (2000). *The concept of time in psychology: A resource book and annotated bibliography.* Westport, CT: Greenwood Press.

Roeckelein, J. E. (2003). A multidimensional-scale model for rating movies and TV programs objectively. Unpublished manuscript, July 2, Mesa Community College, Mesa, AZ.

Rogers, M., Dubey, D., & Reich, P. (1979). The influence of the psyche and the brain on immunity and disease susceptibility: A critical review. *Psychosomatic Medicine, 41*, 243–64.

Rohwer, W. D. (1970). Images and pictures in children's learning: Research results and educational implications. *Psychological Bulletin, 73*, 393–403.

Roland, P. E., & Friberg, L. (1985). Localization of cortical areas activated by thinking. *Journal of Neurophysiology, 53*, 1219–43.

Rollins, M. (1989). *Mental imagery.* New Haven, CT: Yale University Press.

Roskos-Ewoldsen, B. (1989). Detecting emergent structures of imaginal patterns: The influence of imaginal and perceptual organization. Unpublished doctoral dissertation, Indiana University, Bloomington.

Roskos-Ewoldsen, B. (1993). Discovering emergent properties of images. In B. Roskos-Ewoldsen, M. J. Intons-Peterson, & R. E. Anderson (Eds.), *Imagery, creativity, and discovery: A cognitive perspective.* Amsterdam: North-Holland.

Roskos-Ewoldsen, B., Intons-Peterson, M. J., & Anderson, R. E. (1993). Imagery, creativity, and discovery: Conclusions and implications. In B. Roskos-Ewoldsen, M. J. Intons-Peterson, & R. E. Anderson (Eds.), *Imagery, creativity, and discovery: A cognitive perspective.* Amsterdam: North-Holland.

Rosser, R., Ensing, S., Glider, P., & Lane, S. (1984). An information-processing analysis of children's accuracy in predicting the appearance of rotated stimuli. *Child Develolpment, 55*, 2204–11.

Rossi, E. L. (1986). *The psychobiology of mind-body healing: New concepts in therapeutic hypnosis.* New York: W. W. Norton.

Rossi, E. L., & Cheek, D. B. (1988). *Mind-body therapy: Methods of ideodynamic healing in hypnosis.* New York: W. W. Norton.

Rushall, B. S. (1988). Covert modeling as a procedure for altering an athlete's psychological state. *Sport Psychologist, 2*, 131–40.

Ryan, E. D., & Simons, J. (1981). Cognitive demand, imagery, and frequency of mental rehearsal as factors influencing acquisition of motor skills. *Journal of Sport Psychology, 3,* 35–45.

Ryan, E. D., & Simons, J. (1982). Efficacy of mental imagery in enhancing mental rehearsal of motor skills. *Journal of Sport Psychology, 4,* 41–51.

Ryan, E. D., & Simons, J. (1983). What is learned in mental practice of motor skills: A test of the cognitive-motor hypothesis. *Journal of Sport Psychology, 5,* 419–26.

Ryle, G. (1949). *The concept of mind.* London: Hutchinson.

Saarinen, T. F. (1973). Student views of the world. In R. M. Downs & D. Stea (Eds.), *Image and environment.* Chicago: Aldine.

Sackett, R. (1934). The influence of symbolic rehearsal upon the retention of a maze habit. *Journal of General Psychology, 10,* 376–95.

Salter, A. (1949). *Conditioned reflex therapy.* New York: Farrar, Strauss.

Saltz, E., & Donnenwerth-Nolan, S. (1981). Does motoric imagery facilitate memory for sentences? A selective interference test. *Journal of Verbal Learning and Verbal Behavior, 20,* 322–32.

Samuels, M., & Samuels, N. (1975). *Seeing with the mind's eye: The history, techniques, and uses of visualization.* New York: Random House.

Samuels, T. E. (1969). The effects of mental practice on the acquisition of a perceptual-motor skill. Unpublished doctoral dissertation, Washington State University.

Sanford, R. N. (1937). The effects of abstinence from food upon imaginal processes: A further experiment. *Journal of Psychology, 3,* 145–59.

Sarbin, T. R. (1972). Imagining as muted role-taking: A historical-linguistic analysis. In P. W. Sheehan (Ed.), *The function and nature of imagery.* New York: Academic Press.

Saretsky, T. (1977). *Active techniques and group psychotherapy.* New York: Jason Aronson.

Savoyant, A. (1988). Mental practice: Image and mental rehearsal of motor action. In M. Denis, J. Engelkamp, & J.T.E. Ricardson (Eds.), *Cognitive and neuropsychological approaches to mental imagery.* Boston: M. Nijhoff.

Scarf, M. (1980). Images that heal: A doubtful idea whose time has come. *Psychology Today,* September, 32–46.

Schaub, B. G., Anselmo, J., & Luck, S. (1991). Clinical imagery: Holistic nursing perspectives. In R. G. Kunzendorf (Ed.), *Mental imagery.* New York: Plenum Press.

Schmeidler, G. R. (1965). Visual imagery correlated to a measure of creativity. *Journal of Consulting Psychology, 29,* 78–80.

Schneider, J., Smith, C. W., Minning, C., Whitcher, S., & Hermanson, J. (1991). Guided imagery and immune system function in normal subjects: A summary of research findings. In R. G. Kunzendorf (Ed.), *Mental imagery.* New York: Plenum Press.

Schomer, H. H. (1986). Mental strategy training programme for marathon runners. *International Journal of Sport Psychology, 18,* 133–51.

Schultz, J. H., & Luthe, W. (1959). *Autogenic training: A physiological approach to psychotherapy.* New York: Grune & Stratton.

Schultz, K. D. (1978). Imagery and the control of depression. In J. L. Singer & K. S. Pope (Eds.), *The power of human imagination.* New York: Plenum Press.

Schultz, K. D. (1984). The use of imagery in alleviating depression. In A. A. Sheikh (Ed.), *Imagination and healing.* Amityville, NY: Baywood.

Schutz, W. C. (1967). *Joy: Expanding human awareness.* New York: Grove Press.

Schwartz, G. E. (1984). Psychophysiology of imagery and healing: A systems perspective. In A. A. Sheikh (Ed.), *Imagination and healing.* Amityville, NY: Baywood.

Schwartz, G. E., Brown, S., & Ahern, G. (1980). Facial muscle patterning and subjective experience during affective imagery: Sex differences. *Psychophysiology, 17,* 75–82.

Schwartz, G. E., Weinberger, D. A., & Singer, J. A. (1981). Cardiovascular differentiation of happiness, sadness, anger, and fear following imagery and exercise. *Psychosomatic Medicine, 43,* 343–64.

Schwartz, R. (1981). Imagery—There's more to it than meets the eye. In N. Block (Ed.), *Imagery.* Cambridge, MA: M.I.T. Press.

Segal, S. J. (1970). Imagery and reality: Can they be distinguished? In W. Keup (Ed.), *Origin and mechanisms of hallucinations.* New York: Plenum.

Segal, S. J. (Ed.) (1971a). *Imagery: Current cognitive approaches.* New York: Academic Press.

Segal, S. J. (1971b). Processing of the stimulus in imagery and perception. In S. J. Segal (Ed.), *Imagery: Current cognitive approaches.* New York: Academic Press.

Segal, S. J. (1972). Assimilation of a stimulus in the construction of an image: The Perky effect revisited. In P. W. Sheehan (Ed.), *The function and nature of imagery.* New York: Academic Press.

Segal, S. J., & Fusella, V. (1970). Influence of imaged pictures and sounds on detection of visual and auditory signals. *Journal of Experimental Psychology, 83,* 458–64.

Segal, S. J., & Glickman, M. (1967). Relaxation and the Perky effect: The influence of body position and judgments of imagery. *American Journal of Psychology, 60,* 257–62.

Seitz, P., & Molholm, H. (1947). Relation of mental imagery to hallucinations. *Archives of Neurology and Psychiatry, 57,* 469–80.

Sergent, J. (1990). The neuropsychology of visual image generation. *Brain and Cognition, 13,* 98–129.

Shacham, S. (1979). The effects of imagery monitoring, sensation monitoring, and positive suggestion on pain and distress. *Dissertation Abstracts International, 40,* 2906B–7B.

Shaffer, J. T. (1986). Transformational fantasy. In A. A. Sheikh (Ed.), *Anthology of imagery techniques*. Milwaukee, WI: American Imagery Institute.

Shaffer, J. T. (1988). *Be your own coach, therapist, healer*. St. Louis, MO: Well-Being Center.

Shallice, T. (1972). Dual functions of consciousness. *Psychological Review, 79*, 383–93.

Shapiro, D. L. (1974). The significance of the visual image in psychotherapy. *Psychotherapy: Theory, Research, and Practice, 7*, 209–12.

Shaw, G. A., & De Mers, S. T. (1986). The relationship of imagery to originality, flexibility, and fluency in creative thinking. *Journal of Mental Imagery, 10*, 65–74.

Shaw, G. A., & De Mers, S. T. (1986–1987). Relationships between imagery and creativity in high-IQ children. *Imagination, Cognition, and Personality, 6*, 247–62.

Shaw, W. A. (1938). The distribution of muscular action potentials during imaging. *Psychological Record, 2*, 195–216.

Shaw, W. A. (1940). The relation of muscular action potentials to imaginal weight lifting. *Archives of Psychology, 35*, 1–50.

Sheehan, P. W. (1966). Functional similarity of imaging to perceiving: Individual differences in vividness of imagery. *Perceptual and Motor Skills, 23*, 1011–33. (Also, see pp. 391–98.)

Sheehan, P. W. (1967). Visual imagery and the organizational properties of perceived stimuli. *British Journal of Psychology, 58*, 247–52.

Sheehan, P. W. (Ed.) (1972). *The function and nature of imagery*. New York: Academic Press. (Also, see Sheehan's chapter, "A functional analysis of the role of visual imagery in unexpected recall.")

Sheehan, P. W. (1979). Hypnosis and the process of imagination. In E. Fromm & R. E. Shor (Eds.), *Hypnosis: Developments in research and new perspectives*. Hawthorne, NY: Aldine.

Sheehan, P. W., & Bayliss, D. J. (1984). Time estimation, imagination, and hypnosis. In A. A. Sheikh (Ed.), *International Review of Mental Imagery*. Vol. 1. New York: Human Sciences Press.

Sheehan, P. W., & Neisser, U. (1969). Some variables affecting the vividness of imagery in recall. *British Journal of Psychology, 60*, 71–80.

Sheffield, F. D. (1961). Theoretical considerations in the learning of complex sequential tasks from demonstration and practice. In A. A. Lumsdaine (Ed.), *Student response in programmed instruction*. NAS-NRS Publication No. 943. Washington, DC: National Academy of Sciences.

Sheikh, A. A. (1977). Mental images: Ghosts of sensations? *Journal of Mental Imagery, 1*, 1–4.

Sheikh, A. A. (1978). Eidetic psychotherapy. In J. L. Singer & K. S. Pope (Eds.), *The power of human imagination*. New York: Plenum Press.

Sheikh, A. A. (Ed.) (1983). *Imagery: Current theory, research, and application.* New York: Wiley.

Sheikh, A. A. (Ed.) (1984). *Imagination and healing.* New York: Baywood.

Sheikh, A. A., & Jordan, C. S. (1981). Eidetic psychotherapy. In R. J. Corsini (Ed.), *Handbook of innovative psychotherapies.* New York: Wiley.

Sheikh, A. A., & Jordan, C. S. (1983). Clinical uses of mental imagery. In A. A. Sheikh (Ed.), *Imagery: Current theory, research, and application.* New York: Wiley.

Sheikh, A. A., & Korn, E. R. (Eds.) (1994). *Imagery in sports and physical performance.* Amityville, NY: Baywood.

Sheikh, A. A., & Kunzendorf, R. G. (1984). Imagery, physiology, and psychosomatic illness. In A. A. Sheikh (Ed.), *International Review of Mental Imagery.* Vol. 1. New York: Human Sciences Press.

Sheikh, A. A., Kunzendorf, R. G., & Sheikh, K. S. (1989). Healing images: From ancient wisdom to modern science. In A. A. Sheikh & K. S. Sheikh (Eds.), *Eastern and western approaches to healing: Ancient wisdom and modern knowledge.* New York: Wiley.

Sheikh, A. A., & Panagiotou, N. (1975). Use of mental imagery in psychotherapy: A critical review. *Perceptual and Motor Skills, 41,* 555–85.

Sheikh, A. A., Richardson, P., & Moleski, L. (1979). Psychosomatics and mental imagery: A brief review. In A. A. Sheikh & J. T. Shaffer (Eds.), *The potential of fantasy and imagination.* New York: Brandon House.

Sheikh, A. A., & Shaffer, J. T. (Eds.) (1979). *The potential of fantasy and imagination.* New York: Brandon House.

Sheikh, A. A., Twente, G., & Turner, D. (1979). Death imagery: Therapeutic uses. In A. A. Sheikh & J. T. Shaffer (Eds.), *The potential of fantasy and imagination.* New York: Brandon House.

Shepard, R. N. (1975). Form, formation, and transformation of internal representations. In R. L. Solso (Ed.), *Information processing and cognition: The Loyola Symposium.* Hillsdale, NJ: Erlbaum.

Shepard, R. N. (1978a). Externalization of mental images and the act of creation. In B. S. Randhawa & W. E. Coffman (Eds.), *Visual learning, thinking, and communication.* New York: Academic Press.

Shepard, R. N. (1978b). The mental image. *American Psychologist, 33,* 125–37.

Shepard, R. N. (1981). Psychophysical complementarity. In M. Kubovy & J. R. Pomerantz (Eds.), *Perceptual organization.* Hillsdale, NJ: Erlbaum.

Shepard, R. N. (1984). Ecological constraints on internal representations: Resonant kinematics of perceiving, imagining, thinking, and dreaming. *Psychological Review, 91,* 417–47.

Shepard, R. N. (1988). The imagination of the scientist. In K. Egan & D. Nadaner (Eds.), *Imagination and education.* New York: Teachers College Press.

Shepard, R. N. (1990). *Mind sights*. New York: Freeman.

Shepard, R. N., & Metzler, J. (1971). Mental rotation of three-dimensional objects. *Science, 171*, 701–3.

Shore, D. L. (1979). The effectiveness of verbal and visual imagery mnemonics in the remediation of organically based memory deficits. *Dissertation Abstracts International, 40*, 1916B.

Shorr, J. E. (1972). *Psycho-imagination therapy: The integration of phenomenology and imagination*. New York: Intercontinental Medical Book Corp.

Shorr, J. E. (1974). *Psychotherapy through imagery*. New York: Intercontinental Medical Book Corp.

Shorr, J. E. (1978). Clinical uses of categories of therapeutic imagery. In J. L. Singer & K. S. Pope (Eds.), *The power of human imagination*. New York: Plenum Press.

Shorr, J. E. (1980). Discoveries about the mind's ability to organize and find meaning in imagery. In J. E. Shorr, G. E. Sobel, P. Robin, & J. A. Connella (Eds.), *Imagery: Its many dimensions and applications*. New York: Plenum Press.

Shorr, J. E. (1983). *Psychotherapy through imagery*. New York: Thieme-Stratton.

Shorr, J. E., Robin, P., Connella, J. A., & Wolpin, W. (Eds.) (1989). *Imagery: Current perspectives*. Vol. 5. New York: Plenum Press.

Shorr, J. E., Sobel, G. E., Robin, P., & Connella, J. A. (Eds.) (1980). *Imagery: Its many dimensions and applications*. Vol. 1. New York: Plenum Press.

Shorr, J. E., Sobel-Whittington, G., Robin, P., & Connella, J. A. (Eds.) (1983). *Imagery: Theoretical and clinical applications*. Vol. 3. New York: Plenum Press.

Shwartz, S. P. (1979). Studies of mental image rotation: Implications for a computer simulation of visual imagery. Unpublished doctoral dissertation, Johns Hopkins University.

Simonton, O. C., Matthews-Simonton, S., & Creighton, J. L. (1978). *Getting well again*. New York: Bantam Books.

Simpson, H. M., & Climan, M. H. (1971). Pupillary and electromyographic changes during an imagery task. *Psychophysiology, 8*, 483–90.

Simpson, H. M., & Paivio, A. (1966). Changes in pupil size during an imagery task without motor involvement. *Psychonomic Science, 5*, 405–6.

Singer, J. L. (1961). Imagination and waiting ability in young children. *Journal of Personality, 29*, 396–413.

Singer, J. L. (1970). Drives, affects, and daydreams: The adaptive role of spontaneous imagery or stimulus-independent mentation. In J. S. Antrobus (Ed.), *Cognition and affect*. Boston: Little, Brown.

Singer, J. L. (1973). *The child's world of make-believe.* New York: Academic Press.

Singer, J. L. (1974). *Imagery and daydream methods in psychotherapy and behavior modification.* New York: Academic Press.

Singer, J. L. (1975). *The inner world of daydreaming.* New York: Harper.

Singer, J. L. (1977). Imagination and make-believe play in early childhood: Some educational implications. *Journal of Mental Imagery, 1,* 127–44.

Singer, J. L. (1979). Imagery and affect psychotherapy: Elaborating private scripts and generating contexts. In A. A. Sheikh & J. T. Shaffer (Eds.), *The potential of fantasy and imagination.* New York: Brandon House.

Singer, J. L., & Antrobus, J. S. (1963). A factor analytic study of daydreaming and conceptually-related cognitive and personality variables. *Perceptual and Motor Skills, 17,* 187–209.

Singer, J. L., & Antrobus, J. S. (1972). Daydreaming, imaginal processes, and personality: A normative study. In P. W. Sheehan (Ed.), *The function and nature of imagery.* New York: Academic Press.

Singer, J. L., & Pope, K. S. (1978). The use of imagery and fantasy techniques in psychotherapy. In J. L. Singer & K. S. Pope (Eds.), *The power of human imagination.* New York: Plenum Press.

Singer, J. L., & Singer, D. G. (1977). Television viewing and imaginative play in preschoolers. *National Science Foundation Grant Progress Report.* New Haven, CT.

Singer, J. L., & Switzer, E. (1980). *Mind play: The creative uses of imagery.* Englewood Cliffs, NJ: Prentice-Hall.

Skinner, B. F. (1953). *Science and human behavior.* New York: Macmillan.

Slatter, K. H. (1960). Alpha rhythm and mental imagery. *Electroencephalography and Clinical Neurophysiology, 12,* 851–59.

Slee, J. A. (1980). Individual differences in visual imagery ability and the retrieval of visual appearances. *Journal of Mental Imagery, 4,* 93–113.

Smith, D. (1987). Conditions that facilitate the development of sport imagery training. *Sport Psychologist, 1,* 237–47.

Smith, D. (1991). Imagery in sport: An historical and current overview. In R. G. Kunzendorf (Ed.), *Mental imagery.* New York: Plenum Press.

Smith, P., & Dodsworth, C. (1978). Social class differences in the fantasy play of preschool children. *Journal of Genetic Psychology, 133,* 183–90.

Smyth, M. M. (1975). The role of mental practice in skill acquisition. *Journal of Motor Behavior, 7,* 199–206.

Snodgrass, L. L. (1991). The importance of mental imagery in map reading. In R. G. Kunzendorf (Ed.), *Mental imagery.* New York: Plenum Press.

Sobel, R. S., & Rothenberg, A. (1980). Artistic creation as stimulated by superimposed versus separated visual images. *Journal of Personality and Social Psychology, 39,* 953–61.

Sommer, R. (1978). *The mind's eye: Imagery in everyday life.* New York: Delacorte Press.

Southworth, M. (1969). The sonic environment of cities. *Environment and Behavior, 1,* 49–70.

Spanos, N. P. (1991). Imagery, hypnosis, and hypnotizability. In R. G. Kunzendorf (Ed.), *Mental imagery.* New York: Plenum Press.

Spanos, N. P., & O'Hara, P. A. (1990). Imaginal dispositions and situation-specific expectations in strategy-induced pain reductions. *Imagination, Cognition, and Personality, 9,* 147–56.

Spanos, N. P., & Radtke, H. L. (1981–1982). Hypnotic visual hallucinations as imaginings: A cognitive-social psychological perspective. *Imagination, Cognition, and Personality, 1,* 147–70.

Sperling, G. (1960). The information available in brief visual presentations. *Psychological Monographs, 74,* No. 498.

Spiegel, D., & Barabasz, A. F. (1990). Psychophysiology of hypnotic hallucinations. In R. G. Kunzendorf & A. A. Sheikh (Eds.), *The psychophysiology of mental imagery: Theory, research, and application.* Amityville, NY: Baywood.

Spotts, J. V., & Mackler, B. (1967). Relationships of field-dependent and field-independent cognitive styles to creative test performance. *Perceptual and Motor Skills, 24,* 239–68 (*Monograph Supplement 2-24*).

Staats, A. W. (1961). Verbal habit families, concepts, and the operant conditioning of word classes. *Psychological Review, 68,* 190–204.

Staats, A. W., & Lohr, J. M. (1979). Images, language, emotions, and personality: Social behaviorism's theory. *Journal of Mental Imagery, 3,* 85–106.

Stampfl, T., & Levis, D. (1967). Essentials of therapy: A learning theory-based psychodynamic behavioral therapy. *Journal of Abnormal Psychology, 72,* 496–503.

Starker, S. (1986). From image to hallucination: Studies of mental imagery in schizophrenic patients. In A. A. Sheikh (Ed.), *International review of mental imagery.* Vol. 2. New York: Human Sciences Press.

Starker, S., & Jolin, A. (1982). Imagery and hallucination in schizophrenic patients. *Journal of Nervous and Mental Disease, 170,* 448–51.

Start, K. B. (1962). The influence of subjectively assessed games ability on gain in motor performance after mental rehearsal. *Journal of General Psychology, 67,* 169–72.

Start, K. B., & Richardson, A. (1964). Imagery and mental practice. *British Journal of Educational Psychology, 34,* 280–84.

Stebbins, R. J. (1968). A comparison of the effects of physical and mental practice in learning a motor skill. *Research Quarterly, 39,* 714–20.

Steel, W. I. (1952). The effect of mental practice on the acquisition of a motor skill. *Journal of Physical Education, 44,* 101–8.

Sternberg, R. J. (Ed.) (1988). *The nature of creativity.* Cambridge, UK: Cambridge University Press.

Sternberg, S. (1966). High-speed scanning in human memory. *Science, 153*, 652–54.

Stewart, J. C. (1966). An experimental investigation of imagery. *Dissertation Abstracts, 27*, 1285B.

Strosahl, K. D., & Ascough, J. C. (1981). Clinical uses of mental imagery: Experimental foundations, theoretical misconceptions, and research issues. *Psychological Bulletin, 89*, 422–38.

Suinn, R. M. (1976a). Body thinking for Olympic champs. *Psychology Today, 36*, 38–43.

Suinn, R. M. (1976b). Visual motor behavior rehearsal for adaptive behavior. In J. Krumboltz & C. Thoresen (Eds.), *Counseling methods.* New York: Holt.

Suinn, R. M. (1979). Behavioral applications of psychology to U.S. world class competitors. In P. Klavora (Ed.), *Coach, athlete, and the sport psychologist.* Toronto: University of Toronto Press.

Suinn, R. M. (1980). Psychology and sports performance: Principles and applications. In R. M. Suinn (Ed.), *Psychology in sports: Methods and applications.* Minneapolis: Burgess.

Suinn, R. M. (1983). Imagery and sports. In A. A. Sheikh (Ed.), *Imagery: Current theory, research, and application.* New York: Wiley.

Suinn, R. M. (1984a). Visual motor behavior rehearsal: The basic technique. *Scandinavian Journal of Behavior Therapy, 13*, 131–42.

Suinn, R. M. (1984b). *Visuo-motor behavior rehearsal: A demonstration.* Videotape Demonstration, ABC Television, Long Beach, CA.

Suinn, R. M. (1985). *The seven steps to peak performance: Manual for Olympic teams.* Fort Collins, CO: Colorado State University, Department of Psychology. (Also, see *The Behavior Therapist* [1985], *8*, 155–59.)

Suinn, R. M. (1989). Future directions in sport psychology research: Applied aspects. In J. Skinner (Ed.), *Future directions in exercise/sport research.* Chicago: Human Kinetics Books.

Suinn, R. M. (1992). Psychological techniques for individual performance enhancement: Imagery. In R. Singer, M. Murphey, & L. Tennant (Eds.), *Handbook on research in sport psychology.* New York: Macmillan.

Suinn, R. M. (1994). Visualization in sports. In A. A. Sheikh & E. R. Korn (Eds.), *Imagery in sports and physical performance.* Amityville, NY: Baywood.

Suinn, R. M., Morton, M., & Brammell, H. (1979). *Psychological and mental training to increase endurance in athletes.* Washington, DC: Final Report to U.S. Olympic Women's Athletics Developmental Subcommittee.

Sunderland, A. (1990). The bisected image? Visual memory in patients with visual neglect. In P. J. Hampson, D. F. Marks, & J.T.E. Richardson (Eds.), *Imagery: Current developments.* London: Routledge.

Susukita, T. (1937). Uber die wahrnehmungsmassigen vorstellungsbilder von wirklichkeitscharakter. *Tohoku Psychologica, 5*, 1–20.

Sutcliffe, J. P., Perry, C., & Sheehan, P. W. (1970). The relation of some aspects of imagery and fantasy to hypnotizability. *Journal of Abnormal Psychology, 76,* 279–87.

Tarr, M., & Pinker, S. (1989). Mental rotation and orientation-dependence in shape recognition. *Cognitive Psychology, 21,* 233–82.

Thomas, N.J.T. (1989). Experience and theory as determinants of attitudes toward mental representation: The case of Knight Dunlap and the vanishing images of J. B. Watson. *American Journal of Psychology, 102,* 395–412.

Thomas, N.J.T. (1994). Review of Michael Tye's "The imagery debate." *The Journal of Mind and Behavior, 15,* 291–94.

Thomas, N.J.T. (1999). Are theories of imagery theories of imagination? An active perception approach to conscious mental content. *Cognitive Science, 23,* 207–45.

Thomas, N.J.T. (2000). A non-symbolic theory of conscious content: Imagery and activity. Paper presented at the Toward a Science of Consciousness Conference, Tucson, AZ, April 14.

Thompson, A. L., & Klatzky, R. L. (1978). Studies of visual synthesis: Integration of fragments into forms. *Journal of Experimental Psychology: Human Perception and Performance, 4,* 244–63.

Thorndike, E. L. (1907). On the function of visual images. *Journal of Philosophy, Psychology, and the Scientific Methods, 4,* 324–27.

Tolman, E. C. (1948). Cognitive maps in rats and man. *Psychological Review, 55,* 189–208.

Tomkins, S. (1962/1963). *Affect, imagery, and consciousness.* 2 Vols. New York: Springer.

Tondo, R. R., & Cautela, J. R. (1974). Assessment of imagery in covert reinforcement. *Psychological Reports, 34,* 1271–80.

Torrance, E. P. (1966). *Torrance tests of creative thinking. Verbal, forms A and B; Norms-technical manual.* Princeton, NJ: Personnel Press.

Torrance, E. P. (1995). *Why fly: A philosophy of creativity.* Norwood, NJ: Ablex.

Tower, R. B. (1982). Imagery training: A workshop model. *Imagination, Cognition, and Personality, 2,* 153–62.

Tower, R. B. (1983). Imagery: Its role in development. In A. A. Sheikh (Ed.), *Imagery: Current theory, research, and application.* New York: Wiley.

Tower, R. B. (1986). Imagery and families. In A. A. Sheikh (Ed.), *International review of mental imagery.* Vol. 2. New York: Human Sciences Press.

Tower, R. B., & Singer, J. L. (1980). Imagination, interest, and joy in early childhood. In P. E. McGhee & A. J. Chapman (Eds.), *Children's humour.* London: Wiley.

Tower, R. B., & Singer, J. L. (1981). The measurement of imagery: How can it be clinically useful? In P. C. Kendall & S. Holland (Eds.), *Cognitive-behavioral interventions: Assessment methods*. New York: Academic Press.

Trehub, A. (1977). Neuronal modesl for cognitive processes: Networks for learning, perception, and imagination. *Journal of Theoretical Biology, 65*, 141–69.

Trehub, A. (1991). *The cognitive brain*. Cambridge, MA: M.I.T. Press.

Tuan, Y.-F. (1975). Images of mental maps. *Annals of the Association of American Geographers, 65*, 205–13.

Tversky, B. (1973). Pictorial and verbal encoding in preschool children. *Developmental Psychology, 8*, 149–53.

Tversky, B. (1975). Pictorial encoding of sentences in sentence-picture comparison. *Quarterly Journal of Experimental Psychology, 27*, 405–10.

Twining, W. E. (1949). Mental practice and physical practice in learning a motor skill. *Research Quarterly, 20*, 432–35.

Tye, M. (1991). *The imagery debate*. Cambridge, MA: M.I.T. Press.

Tynes, L. L., & McFatter, R. M. (1987). The efficacy of psyching strategies on a weight-lifting task. *Cognitive Therapy and Research, 11*, 327–36.

Uhestahl, L. E. (1982). Inner mental training for sport. In T. Orlick, J. Partington, & J. Sanela (Eds.), *Mental training for coaches and athletes*. Ottawa, Ontario: Coaching Association of Canada.

Ulich, E. (1967). Some experiments on the formation of mental practice training in the acquisition of motor skills. *Ergonomics, 10*, 411–19.

Upper, D., & Cautela, J. R. (1979). *Covert conditioning*. Elmsford, NY: Pergamon Press.

Vandall, R., Davis, R., & Clugston, H. (1943). The function of mental practice in the acquisition of motor skills. *Journal of General Psychology, 29*, 243–50.

Vandenberg, B. (1978). Play and development from an ethological perspective. *American Psychologist, 33*, 724–38.

Van der Veur, B. (1975). Imagery rating of 1,000 frequently used words. *Journal of Educational Psychology, 67*, 44–56.

Van Gyn, G., Wenger, H., & Gaul, C. (1990). Imagery as a method of enhancing transfer from training to performance. *Journal of Sport and Exercise Psychology, 12*, 366–75.

Van Loon-Vervoorn, W. A., Elzinga-Plomp, A., & Hennink, J. H. (1991). Effortful and automatic activation of imagery: Evidence from right brain damage. In R. H. Logie & M. Denis (Eds.), *Mental images in human cognition*. Amsterdam: North-Holland.

Vealey, R. S. (1986). Imagery training for performance enhancement. In J. M. Williams (Ed.), *Applied sport psychology: Personal growth to peak performance*. Palo Alto, CA: Mayfield.

Vealey, R. S. (1988). Future directions in psychological skills training. *Sport Psychologist, 5,* 318–36.

Vedelli, J. (1985). Mental rehearsal in sport. In L. Bunker, R. Rotella, & A. Reilly (Eds.), *Sport psychology: Psychological considerations in maximizing sport performance.* New York: McNaughton & Nunn.

Virel, A. (1968). *Histoire de notre image.* Geneva: Mont Blanc.

Wade, N. J. (1998). *A natural history of vision.* Cambridge, MA: M.I.T. Press.

Walker, H. J. (1970). Imagery ratings for 338 nouns. *Behavior Research Methods and Instrumentation, 2,* 165–67.

Wallace, B. (1991). Hypnotic susceptibility, imaging ability, and information processing: An integrative look. In R. G. Kunzendorf (Ed.), *Mental imagery.* New York: Plenum Press.

Walter, R. D., & Yeager, C. L. (1956). Visual imagery and electroencephalographic changes. *Electroencephalography and Clinical Neurophysiology, 8,* 193–99.

Waltz, D. L. (1979). On the function of mental imagery. *Behavioral and Brain Sciences, 2,* 569.

Washburn, M. F. (1916). *Movement and mental imagery.* Boston: Houghton.

Waters, W. F., & McDonald, D. G. (1973). Autonomic response to auditory, visual, and imagined stimuli in a systematic desensitization context. *Behavior Research and Therapy, 11,* 577–85.

Watkins, M. J. (1976). *Waking dreams.* New York: Harper.

Weber, R. J., & Harnish, R. (1974). Visual imagery for words: The Hebb test. *Journal of Experimental Psychology, 102,* 409–14.

Wehner, T., Vogt, S., & Stadler, M. (1984). Task specific EMG-characteristics during mental training. *Psychological Research, 46,* 389–401.

Wein, K. S. (1979). The effects of direct and imaginal stimulation on physiological and self-report measures: A test of the continuity assumption. *Dissertation Abstracts International, 39,* 6149B–50B.

Weinberg, H., Walter, W. G., & Crow, H. J. (1970). Intracerebral events in humans related to real and imaginary stimuli. *Electroencephalography and Clinical Neurophysiology, 29,* 1–9.

Weinberg, R. (1982). The relationship between mental preparation strategies and motor performance: A review and critique. *Quest, 33,* 190–213.

Weinberg, R., Gould, D., & Jackson, A. (1980). Cognition and motor performance: Effect of psyching-up strategies on three motor tasks. *Cognitive Therapy and Research, 4,* 239–45.

Weinberg, R., Seabourne, T., & Jackson, A. (1981). Effects of visuo-motor behavior rehearsal, relaxation, and imagery on karate performance. *Journal of Sport Psychology, 3,* 228–38.

Weinberg, R., Seabourne, T., & Jackson, A. (1982). Effects of visuo-motor behavior rehearsal on state-trait anxiety and performance: Is practice important? *Journal of Sport Psychology, 5,* 209–19.

Weisberg, R. (1986). *Creativity, genius, and other myths.* New York: Freeman.

Welsh, G. (1975). *Creativity and intelligence: A personality approach.* Chapel Hill, NC: Institute for Research in Social Science.

Westcott, T. B., & Horan, J. J. (1977). The effects of anger and relaxation froms of *in vivo* emotive imagery on pain tolerance. *Canadian Journal of Behavioral Science, 9,* 216–23.

Whelan, J., Mahoney, M., & Meyers, A. (1991). Performance enhancement in sport: A cognitive behavioral domain. *Behavior Therapy, 22,* 307–27.

White, K. D. (1978). Salivation: The significance of imagery in its voluntary control. *Psychophysiology, 15,* 196–203.

White, K. D., Ashton, R., & Lewis, S. (1979). Learning a complex skill: Effects of mental practice, physical practice, and imagery ability. *International Journal of Sports Psychology, 10,* 71–79

Whiteley, G. (1962). The effect of mental rehearsal on the acquisition of motor skill. Unpublished diploma in education dissertation, University of Manchester, UK.

Wickens, D. D., & Engle, R. W. (1970). Imagery and abstractness in short-term memory. *Journal of Experimental Psychology, 84,* 268–72.

Wigan, A. L. (1844). *The duality of the mind.* London: Longman.

Wilkes, R. L., & Summers, J. J. (1984). Cognitions, mediating variables, and strength performance. *Journal of Sport Psychology, 6,* 351–59.

Wilson, S. C., & Barber, T. X. (1981). Vivid fantasy and hallucinatory abilities in the life histories of excellent hypnotic subjects ("somnambules"): Preliminary report with female subjects. In E. Klinger (Ed.), *Imagery: Concepts, results, and applications.* New York: Plenum Press.

Wilson, S. C., & Barber, T. X. (1983). The fantasy-prone personality: Implications for understanding imagery, hypnosis, and parapsychological phenomena. In A. A. Sheikh (Ed.), *Imagery: Current theory, research, and application.* New York: Wiley.

Winning Associates. (1978). *Athletes' homework manual.* Morgantown, WV: W. Associates.

Witkin, H. A., & Goodenough, D. R. (1977). Field dependence and interpersonal behavior. *Psychological Bulletin, 84,* 661–89.

Wolpe, J. (1958). *Psychotherapy by reciprocal inhibition.* Stanford: Stanford University Press.

Wolpe, J. (1969). *The practice of behavior therapy.* New York: Pergamon.

Wolpe, J., & Lazarus, A. A. (1966). *Behavior therapy techniques.* New York: Pergamon.

Wolpin, W., Shorr, J. E., Krueger, L. (Eds.) (1986). *Imagery: Recent practice and theory.* Vol. 4. New York: Plenum Press.

Woolfolk, R., Murphy, S., Gottesfeld, D., & Aitken, D. (1985). Effects of mental rehearsal of motor task activity and mental depiction of task outcome on motor skill. *Journal of Sport Psychology, 7*, 191–97.

Woolfolk, R., Parrish, W., & Murphy, S. (1985). The effects of positive and negative imagery on motor skill performance. *Cognitive Therapy and Research, 9*, 335–41. (Also, see *Journal of Sport Psychology* [1985], *7*, 191–97.)

Woolman, N. (1986). Research on imagery and motor performance: Three methodological suggestions. *Journal of Sport Psychology, 8*, 135–38.

Worthington, E. L., & Shumate, M. (1981). Imagery and verbal counseling methods in stress inoculation training for pain control. *Journal of Counseling Psychology, 28*, 1–6.

Wrisberg, C. A., & Anshel, M. H. (1989). The effect of cognitive strategies on the free throw shooting performance of young athletes. *Sport Psychologist, 3*, 95–104.

Wrisberg, C. A., & Ragsdale, M. (1979). Cognitive demand and practice level: Factors in the mental rehearsal of motor skills. *Journal of Human Movement Studies, 5*, 201–8.

Yarmey, A. D. (1984). Bizarreness effects in mental imagery. In A. A. Sheikh (Ed.), *International Review of Mental Imagery*. Vol. 1. New York: Human Sciences Press.

Young, J., Palef, S., & Logan, G. (1980). The role of mental rotation in letter processing by children and adults. *Canadian Journal of Psychology, 34*, 265–69.

Yuille, J. C., & Catchpole, M. J. (1977). The role of imagery in models of cognition. *Journal of Mental Imagery, 1*, 171–80.

Yuille, J. C., & Marschark, M. (1983). Imagery effects on memory: Theoretical interpretations. In A. A. Sheikh (Ed.), *Imagery: Current theory, research, and application*. New York: Wiley.

Yuille, J. C., & Marschark, M. (1984). Imagery and children's learning: An issue of declining developmental interest? In A. A. Sheikh (Ed.), *International Review of Mental Imagery*. Vol. 1. New York: Human Sciences Press.

Yuille, J. C., & Paivio, A. (1967). Latency of imaginal and verbal mediators as a function of stimulus and response concreteness-imagery. *Journal of Experimental Psychology, 75*, 540–44.

Zecker, S. (1982). Mental practice and knowledge of results in the learning of a perceptual motor skill. *Journal of Sport Psychology, 4*, 52–63.

Ziegler, S. G. (1987). Comparison of imagery styles and past experience in skills performance. *Perceptual and Motor Skills, 64*, 579–86.

Ziegler, S. G., Klinzing, J., & Williamson, K. (1982). The effects of two stress management training programs on cardiorespiratory efficiency. *Journal of Sport Psychology, 4*, 280–89.

Zikmund, V. (1966). Oculomotor activity during visual imagery of a moving stimulus pattern. *Studia Psychologica, 8*, 254–74.

Zikmund, V. (1972). Physiological correlates of visual imagery. In P. W. Sheehan (Ed.), *The function and nature of imagery*. New York: Academic Press.

Zimler, J., & Keenan, J. M. (1983). Imagery in the congenitally blind: How visual are visual images? *Journal of Experimental Psychology: Learning, Memory, and Cognition, 9,* 269–82.

# Chapter 4

# *Methodological Aspects of Imagery*

The overall position adopted and advanced in this book and, most particularly, in this chapter, is that the topic of mental imagery may best (i.e., most validly and scientifically) be approached and examined from the perspective of scientific methodology, principles, or procedures. That is, the phenomenon of imagery may optimally be studied and understood by the application of methodologies that have at their core the basic tenets of the scientific attitude or orientation, including the concepts of determinism, causality, empiricism, and, especially, the experimental method where a premium is placed on the control of variation and different classes of variables (cf. Ahsen, 1985/1987; Ward, 1985; and Yuille, 1985, 1986) who express other viewpoints on this issue). Thus, with my approach, it is recommended that the unique phenomenon of mental imagery (i.e., the *psychology of imagery*) should be treated as any other issue or topic that is examined generally by scientific principles, criteria, and methods.

In this chapter, I review the methodological aspects of mental imagery, including general scientific methodologies, general measurement considerations, modern measurement and methodology in imagery research, selected modern psychological imagery studies and exemplars (1960–2003), and future directions in imagery research.

> Science is both open-minded and skeptical. It is skeptical of any idea that is not supported by objective evidence; it is open-minded about any idea that is supported by objective evidence. . . . There is no psychology without science . . . using the scientific approach in psychology has allowed psychologists to improve common

sense, to disprove certain superstitions, and to make enormous progress in understanding how to help people.
—M. Mitchell and J. Jolley, 2001

In determining if a relationship is causal, we look for three conditions: covariation of cause and effect, time precedence of the cause, and no alternative explanations. Science has four key values: (1) empiricism . . . (2) skepticism . . . (3) keeping conclusions tentative so that they can be changed on the basis of new evidence, and (4) making the processes and results of science public.
—B. E. Whitley Jr., 2002

If we define scientific psychology (as well as science in general) as a repeatable, self-correcting undertaking that seeks to understand phenomena on the basis of empirical observation, then we can see several advantages to science compared to (other) methods . . . empirical observation and self-correction are the hallmarks of the scientific method. . . . All science has data and theory. What distinguishes among the different sciences, and among the subspecialties within a science like psychology, is the different techniques used.
—D. G. Elmes, B. H. Kantowitz, and H. L. Roediger III, 2003

According to modern physics, scientists do not record events. Instead, scientists record their *observation of events.* They record their experience of the world and base their science on these perceptions. This development amounts to a simple acceptance of the fact that in science we can get no closer to the world than our observations of it. . . . A major characteristic of science is a reliance on information that is *verifiable through experience.* That is, it must be possible for different people in different places and at different times using a similar method to produce the same results.
—W. J. Ray, 2003

## GENERAL SCIENTIFIC METHODOLOGY CONSIDERATIONS

Scientific methodology is a valid way in psychological research to acquire knowledge about a particular phenomenon of interest (e.g., mental imagery). Various writers and researchers have considered the characteristics of the scientific approach to make it the most desirable way to gain valid insights into the nature of people and things in the world (e.g., Elmes, Kantowitz, and Roediger, 2003; Kantowitz, Roediger, and Elmes, 2001; Mitchell and Jolley, 2001; Ray, 2003; Rosnow and Rosenthal, 2002; Whitley, 2002). In discussions of the fundamental issues of fixation of belief and sources of knowledge, the methods of science often are contrasted with other extra-scientific modes of knowing regarding the nature of certain phenomena. The classical perspective in such comparisons is provided by the American philosopher C. S. Peirce (1877) who contrasted the scientific way of knowing with three other methods of establishing or "fixing" beliefs: the method of authority, the method of tenacity, and the a priori method. The easiest and simplest way of fixing one's belief concerning some issue or phenomenon is via the method of authority where some legitimately perceived authority's word(s), pronouncement(s), or statement(s) are taken simply on faith. In the method of tenacity, individuals often steadfastly refuse to alter their current or acquired knowledge regarding some phenomenon—regardless of new evidence that may be presented to them that is contrary to their former beliefs. In the third nonscientific method, the a priori method, beliefs about some thing are often fixed without any actual prior study of, experience with, or examination of the phenomenon in question. Such basic methodologies concerning one's knowledge about a phenomenon are popular collectively because they offer to the individual the great advantages of affording substantial or maximum cognitive security, as well as requiring only a minimum amount of effort or cognitive expenditure on the person's part.

In Peirce's (1877) view, a fourth method—the *scientific method*—fixes one's belief about something on the basis of experience that essentially is tentative and always open to alteration depending on the nature of new and relevant discoveries or evidence. At the most fundamental level, science rests on the assumption that events in our world have causes and that such causes are discoverable through controlled observation; such a belief—that observable causes determine events—is known in scientific psychology (as well as in natural science, and philosophy) as *determinism*. Reber (1985/1995) asserts that most contemporary social scientists—if they think about the issue of determinism at all—take a position that may be described as *uncomfortable pragmatism*; that is, in their day-to-day work they treat events, objects, and persons as *probabilistically determined* and chalk up what they cannot predict accurately to as-yet-unknown factors of causation. In his entry for scientific method, Reber notes that many persons—

both lay people and scientists alike—have protested that psychology is not a science because of the lack of precision in its procedures and lack of generalizability of its principles (for comparisons of psychology with other sciences on this issue, see Roeckelein, 1997a,b; and Simonton 2002, pp. 348–55). However, Reber suggests that what makes a given discipline a science has very little to do with the definitiveness of its findings or the precision of its laws. Rather, according to Reber, the issue rests upon whether practitioners adhere to the accepted canons of scientific methodology (cf. Mitchell and Jolley, 2001, p. 9), among which are the following:

- Appropriate definition of a given problem
- Statement of the problem in a manner whereby it may be tied into existing theory and known empirical fact; the formulation of a testable hypothesis (commonly, today, involving the logic of "falsification"—that is, putting hypotheses in a form that maintains the notion that scientific theories cannot be proven to be true but only subjected to attempts at refutation, and where a given scientific theory—via hypothesis testing—is demonstrably "correct," "accepted," or "supported" because it has not yet been shown to be false)
- The determination of the procedures and operations to be employed in the research
- The maintenance of proper experimental control
- Collection and analysis of the data—where, in accordance with the findings, the hypotheses are either rejected or supported
- The modification of the existing body of scientific knowledge to accommodate the new findings

Reber (1985/1995) indicates, also, that the doctrine of *empiricism* is the touchstone of science, that experimental control is essential, and that falsifiable hypotheses are a necessity for the domain of scientific methodology.

Mitchell and Jolley (2001) identify a number of criteria whereby the field of psychology may be assessed concerning its claim to be a true scientific endeavor (cf. Stanovich, 1990); that is, to what extent does psychology achieve the following goals: the discovery of general rules; the collection of objective evidence; the development of testable statements/hypotheses; the exercise or practice of skepticism and open-mindedness; demonstration of the abilities to be creative and productive; and the collection of publicly shared knowledge that may be replicated. Mitchell and Jolley (pp. 18–27) also provide a discussion concerning the validity (truth) of the experimental method where the researcher attempts to develop causal statements about the relationships between her/his manipulated variables.

Whitley (2002) examines several broad and specific research strategies that may be employed in psychological research. In his section on data collection (pp. 411–22), Whitley discusses the use of the Internet (or World Wide Web) to collect data for psychological research—a relatively recent practice occurring after about 1996. Note that Whitley observes that in 2000, the American Psychological Society's Web page contained links to eighty-six sites regarding studies being conducted on the Internet; the location is http://psych.hanover.edu/research/exponnet.html. These studies covered a wide range of topics in psychology, including neuropsychology, cognition, personality, sensation and perception, and social psychology. Internet research may take a variety of forms: experiments, personality measures, attitude and behavior surveys, participant and nonparticipant observation, and focus groups (cf. Birnbaum, 2000; Buchanan and Smith, 1999a,b; Hewson, Laurent, and Vogel, 1996; James, 1999). For a discussion of mental imagery/imaginary manipulation/mental rotation in the context of experimental design and research methods, see Mook (2001, pp. 180–83).

Elmes, Kantowitz, and Roediger (2003) examine the following topics: the basics of scientific psychology, experimentation in psychology, and the practice of scientific psychology (cf. Ray, 2003). Among their observations, suggestions, and distinctions are the following points:

- All approaches to science share certain basic elements, the most important of these being *data* (empirical observations) and *theory* (organization of concepts that permit prediction of data) (see Rosnow and Rosenthal, 2002, pp. 10–11 for a brief discussion of the importance of *mental imagery* to the scientific enterprise; they note that "the history of ideas teaches us that good scientific *theories*, to be influential, must reflect a way of thinking that includes images").
- The *inductive* approach (reasoning proceeds from particular data to a general theory) versus the *deductive* approach (reasoning proceeds from a general theory to particular data).
- *Hypothesis* (a very specific and testable statement that may be evaluated from observable data) versus *generalization* (a broader statement that cannot be tested directly, but may be used to derive other testable hypotheses).
- Classes of *variables* (cf. Kantowitz, Roediger, and Elmes, 2001, pp. 56–72; Ray, 2003, pp. 32–36)—*intervening* variables (constructs that *summarize*

the effects of several variables), *independent* variables (conditions, events, or variables that are *manipulated* by the experimenter), and *dependent* variables (variables that are observed, recorded, or *measured* by the experimenter).

- Three criteria for evaluating a theory are *parsimony* ("economy" of the theory—the fewer the statements in a theory, the better the theory), *precision* (theories that employ mathematical equations or computer programs are generally more precise and better than those that use loose verbal statements—all other things being equal), and *testability* (if a theory is not open to being tested, it can never be disproved—via the doctrine/logic of "falsifiability"). Belief in a particular theory *increases* as it survives tests that could reject it.
- *Validity* (the "truth" of the observations and measures) and *reliability* (the "consistency" of the observations and measures).
- *Measurement* procedures and scales (behavioral data derived from different scales indicate different things and the kinds of conclusions one may draw depend in part on the scale one uses).
- *Psychometric* and *psychophysical* measures (many are self-report methods that yield psychological data from a personal-subjective perspective rather than from objective measurements derived via direct observations).

In summary, the importance of scientific methodology—in particular, for psychological research—lies in the recommended application here of its experimental method(s) to psychological phenomena, including the investigation of mental imagery. The scientific methods, especially the empirical-experimental approaches, are superior over nonscientific approaches in that scientific procedures fix belief about a phenomena on the basis of experience wherein a repeatable and self-correcting process occurs within the framework of empirical (i.e., that which is sensed or experienced) observation that has the great advantage of making scientific data open to public, and repeatable, verification. Another crucial aspect of scientific methodology is the determination of causality; it is suggested here that the use of psychological experiments in studying the topic of mental imagery may lead to the most valid causal inferences that yield strong scientific support for the phenomenon. Although scientific psychologists may recognize that the explanations for behavior (such as how one experiences imagery) gained through experimentation are only tentative, they are willing to conclude that *A* causes *B* to occur if an experiment is conducted in which *A* (the *independent variable*) is systematically varied (where all other extraneous or outside factors are controlled) and it is observed that *B* (the *dependent variable*) occurs with some probability greater than chance and where variations of $B$ are highly predictable from the variations in $A$. In this manner, $A$ and $B$ are said to *covary*, or occur together, and because $A$ occurs first in the sequence, it may confidently be said that $A$ is the *cause* of $B$. Finally, in the scientific methodology domain, one may refer to the *functional relationship*s between two sets of variables where the manipulated independent variables cause the measured dependent variables; thus, within this terminological context, and for psychological study of mental imagery especially, all *experiments* (i.e., causal determination strategy/design involving manipulation of independent variables, control of extraneous or "nuisance" variables, and measurement of dependent variables) are assumed to be *empirical* in nature, but *not* all *empirical* studies (i.e., those involving only the description, observation, and/or collection of data and *not* the causal determination of the relationships between variables) are assumed to be *experimental* in nature. However, it is suggested here that *both* empirical and experimental methodologies—with preference being given to the latter—are the recommended approaches for a truly scientific examination and understanding of a given psychological phenomenon, such as that of mental imagery.

> This is the purpose of measurement: to provide quantitative descriptions of the characteristics of objects or individuals.
> —F. G. Brown, 1984/1994

> Measurement may be defined as the assignment of numerals to represent certain nonnumerical properties of a set of objects.
> —H. O. Gulliksen, 1984/1994

> Anything that exists, be it the intensity of painful feelings or your attitude toward spinach, exists in some amount. Anything that exists in some amount can be measured. Measurement is a systematic way of assigning numbers or names to objects and their attributes.
> —B. H. Kantowitz, H. L. Roediger III, and D. G. Elmes, 2001

> If a measure is to be sensitive to differences between participants, participants must differ on the measure. However, it is not enough that different participants get different scores. Instead, different participants must get different scores because they differ on what you are trying to measure.
> —M. Mitchell and J. Jolley, 2001

The term "modality of measurement" refers to the manner in which one measures a person's traits . . . the three most commonly used modalities (are): self-report, behavioral, and physiological. . . . Measures of the same construct at different levels can differ from one another on three characteristics—information content, appropriate statistical tests, and ecological validity. It is important to bear these considerations in mind when choosing a level of measurement.

—B. E. Whitley Jr., 2002

Two of the first questions we are faced with in doing research are "What can we measure?" and "What do the measurements mean?" A number may be used in a variety of ways . . . numbers may be used in terms of four specific properties: identify, magnitude, equal intervals, and absolute zero. We can use these properties to help us define levels of measurement, or scales of measurement.

—W. J. Ray, 2003

## GENERAL MEASUREMENT CONSIDERATIONS

One of the first, and most important, topics covered in psychological research methods classes and experimental psychology classes, is that of *measurement*. Brown (1984/1994) discusses measurement, definitions of measurement, types of measurement scales, and criteria of good measurement within the context of psychological research. In general, psychological research emphasizes the relationships among observable *variables* (i.e., entities or things that have the capability of undergoing changes in amount, quantity, or quality), and psychological theory focuses on the relationships among *constructs* (i.e., logical or intellectual creations consisting of concepts, categories, or complexes of objects all of which share some common attributes or properties where there is an internal, mental, or psychological representation of the shared attributes). Moreover, according to Brown, in both theory and research the relationships between variables and constructs are expressed most precisely and accurately when they are expressed in quantitative terms. Additionally, if these relationships are to be expressed qualitatively, the variables also must be given quantitative values. Thus, in the most general sense, the purpose of measurement, especially psychological measurement, is to give a rational or quantitative basis for the descriptions of the characteristics and attributes of objects and persons.

Among the various available definitions of the process of measurement, the one most commonly employed (cf. Brown, 1984/1994) by researchers indicates that measurement is the procedure of assigning numerals to objects or events according to a set of rules. In the field of psychology, including the phenomenon of mental imagery (cf. McLemore, 1976), the objects or events often are persons and what is measured are the person's attributes or characteristics (e.g., extent, degree, or frequency of experiencing imagery), and, thus, psychological measurement is defined as the assignment of numerals to the person's characteristics according to rules. As Brown (1984/1994) observes, this definition implies that three sets of factors are involved in measurement: the attributes of persons, the numerical values assigned, and the rules and procedures for relating the numbers assigned to the individual's characteristics. The goal of the measurement process is to produce an isomorphic relationship where the numerical representation (i.e., the scale values that are assigned) corresponds accurately to differences in the levels of the attribute/characteristic among people (also called the *empirical reality*). The advantages of using quantitative descriptions—over the use of qualitative or verbal descriptions—is that the former are finer, more precise, and more accurate. The quantitative descriptions are also more objective—leading to greater agreement among independent observers; they facilitate communication, and they are more economical (parsimonious) than qualitative descriptions. In the quantitative approach, a relationship or a large set of data may be expressed by one, or only a few, quantitative value(s).

In considering the rules and procedures of measurement, Brown (1984/1994) suggests that while certain standards apply to all types of measurement—such as the clear specification, standardization, and replicability of the procedures—the exact procedures used may vary depending on the attribute being measured (e.g., ability and achievement tests attempt to measure attributes that are different from those involved in personality inventories or vividness of imagery experiences). The definition of the characteristic under study often dictates the appropriate measurement procedure(s) to be employed; however, in all cases, the procedures and rules that are used must be consistent with the purpose(s) of the measurement and the definition of the characteristic. The general rules employed in psychological measurement usually indicate *magnitude*—the extent or degree to which a person exhibits the characteristic—and *proximity*—the degree of similarity between two, or more, individuals. Of course, when measuring physical attributes (such as a person's height), the process is fairly direct, while in measuring psychological attributes (such as a person's sense of humor or her/his imagery experiences), the process is likely to be indirect and involve inferences from observable effects. Furthermore, in many psychological contexts, a given attribute (e.g., an individual's imaging ability) may be measured by several different methods; thus, for example, imaging ability may be measured by a self-report inventory, by observers' ratings of the participant, by behavioral-task measures, or by physiological indices. Whether such diverse methods produce similar results and interpretations—and converge to "pin down" a phenomenon—is open to empirical investigation. Along these methodological lines involving diverse procedures (and converging operations) where any set of two or more experimental operations allow the selection or elimination of alternative hypotheses or concepts that could explain an experimental result—see Garner, Hake, and Eriksen (1956, pp. 150–51); compare Holmes, Roeckelein, and Olmstead (1968, p. 663).

Inasmuch as different sets of rules and procedures may be used to make a measurement, different types of *measurement scales* may be derived; such scales are distinguishable on several bases or dimensions. Four types of basic measurement scales (in ascending order) have been distinguished (Stevens, 1951; cf. Stevens, 1946): nominal, ordinal, interval, and ratio scales. The scales are *hierarchical* where the higher-level scales—such as the interval and ratio scales—have all the properties of the lower-level scales—such as the nominal and ordinal scales—plus additional features (cf. Brown, 1984/1994, p. 349; Kantowitz, Roediger, and Elmes, 2001, pp. 179–84; Mitchell and Jolley, 2001, pp. 128–38; Ray, 2003, pp. 83–86; Whitley, 2002, pp. 350–52; Wolins, 1978).

Among the controversial issues and problems associated with measurement, and measurement theory, are the following:

- The numbers generated by a measure usually do not correspond perfectly to a psychological reality.
- It is not always easy to pair the scale of measurement one needs for a particular study with the measures one actually uses, that is, different research questions require different scales of measurement (Mitchell and Jolley, 2001, pp. 132–38).
- The design of a measuring instrument depends on a theoretical understanding—which is not always complete or adequate—of the underlying concept/construct (Ray, 2003, p. 85).

- The relationship between measurement scales and statistics (the method of summarizing and communicating the results gained from scalar data and measurements) is often confused—for instance, traditionally (cf. Mitchell, 1986; Stevens, 1946) it has been taught that there is a "one-to-one" correspondence between the scale of measurement used (i.e., nominal, ordinal, interval, or ratio) and the statistic chosen (e.g., t-test, sign test, binomial test, analysis of variance, etc.).
- However, statisticians—as well as most present-day experimental psychologists—no longer hold this "one-to-one correspondence" view, they point out simply that where a number comes from does *not* determine the appropriate statistical test that must be used (cf. Gaito, 1960, 1980, 1986; Lord, 1953), and "statistics do not know or do not care where your numbers come from—it does not matter to a statistic whether your numbers mean what you claim they do, much less whether your experiment was performed well or poorly" (Ray, 2003, pp. 86–87).
- The type(s) of scale(s) one should consider, and choose, for one's particular research problem may be an issue. Some writers claim that only procedures that involve "magnitude" are true measurements, and nominal scales should not be considered as such (cf. Nunnally, 1978), whereas other writers assert that measurement scales should have fixed units where only interval and ratio scales may properly be called measurement (cf. Jones, 1971).
- Some investigators indicate that while one may assume that certain measurement procedures achieve a given level of measurement there is no empirical or valid evidence that they do (cf. Allen and Yen, 1979; also see Coombs, Dawes, and Tversky, 1981, who assert that no existing measurement model fits the assessment of certain psychological/cognitive abilities such as intelligence; cf. Coombs, 1950).
- Many psychologists maintain that test scores usually represent only ordinal measurement—yet test scores are interpreted generally as if they were on an interval scale (Brown, 1984/1994, p. 349; cf. Gardner, 1975).
- Although the nature of the measurement scale does not dictate what statistical method(s) must be used to analyze the data, it must be considered when interpreting the data (Brown, 1984/1994, p. 350; cf. Anderson, 1961).

Historically, in the measurement area of *scaling* (i.e., the evaluation of subjective psychological experience and the development of a numerical system for its measurement) many researchers have studied the relationship between stimulus intensity and the intensity of the sensation/response produced by that stimulus. For instance, Fechner (1860/1966) proposed that sensation/response magnitude is proportional to the logarithm of the stimulus intensity. More recently,

Thurstone (1927) asserted that one class of psychophysical methods (such as the method of *average error*) assumes that the researcher is able to obtain and control some physical measurement of stimulus intensity, whereas other classes of methods (such as the method of *paired comparisons*) may be employed in cases where precise measurement and controlled variation of the stimulus intensity is not possible. Moreover, Thurstone suggested that the latter type of scaling methods provides the experimenter with tools for the quantitative measurement of subjective qualities for which there are no direct or relevant stimulus measurements, for example, aesthetic appreciation of works of art; nationality preferences; varieties of mental imagery experiences (cf. Thurstone and Jones, 1957).

In his discussion of scaling (cf. Torgerson, 1958), Gulliksen (1984/ 1994, p. 262) defines measurement as the "assignment of numerals to represent certain non-numerical properties of a set of objects" and maintains that—for measurement to exist—there must be two relations present among the attributes in a given set of objects: precedence and coincidence (cf. Gulliksen, 1956). The basic method of experimentation, according to Gulliksen (1984/1994), for psychological scaling is the method of paired comparisons (also used in psychophysics; cf. Roeckelein, 1968a)—to use this method it is not necessary that the investigator obtain some relevant measure of stimulus intensity, but it is only necessary that the researcher be able to present the same stimulus a number of times. In assessing the *law of comparative judgment*, for instance, the participant is presented, in turn, with all the possible pairs of the set of objects being scaled, and where—for each pair—the participant gives a judgment as to the characteristic/attribute being scaled (e.g., "Which of the two objects is brighter, more vivid, higher quality, etc.?"). In situations where a participant is required to perceive or judge a set of objects as differing in more than one dimension, the issue of *multidimensional scaling* becomes relevant. In the last several decades, there have been numerous developments in the area of experimental and analytical methods for studying multidimensional scaling (cf. Bock and Jones, 1968; Carroll and Arabie, 1980; Coombs, 1976; Golledge and Rayner, 1980; Green and Rao, 1972; Kruskal and Wish, 1978; Luce, Bush, and Galanter, 1963; Nishisato, 1978; Shepard, Romney, and Nerlove, 1972; Torgerson, 1958; Tucker, 1960; Tucker and Messick, 1963).

Finally, as regards scaling in psychology, generally, Reber (1985/ 1995) notes that the most common procedures may be summarized under three classes: *interval* scaling, *ratio* scaling (cf. Roeckelein, 1968b,c, 1971), and *nonmetric* scaling. Moreover, in multidimensional scaling, a search is made—via statistical procedures—for a small set of dimensions that will provide the best fit for a large number of data points.

In summary, the importance of accurate, reliable, and valid measurement in science—in particular, in scientific psychological research—lies in the appropriate choice of measurement procedures and scale(s) to "pin down" the phenomenon under study where a maximum of quantifiable data is collected and analyzed according to established statistical and mathematical rules, methods, and tests. It is suggested here that the desideratum for measurement in psychological research, including the study of mental imagery, is the employment of the higher-order scales of measurement (such as interval and ratio scales), the use of multidimensional scaling techniques, and the application of converging-operations measurements (cf. Richardson, 1985a,b) for the purpose of formulating, ultimately, the strongest possible scientific statements concerning deterministic and causal relationships among the variables that define and comprise the phenomenon under investigation.

> The historical roots of imagery and scientific methodology in psychology are discussed. . . . Discussion involves general psychological methodology, modern imagery research and myth; also, cross-disciplinary analysis of imagery concepts is provided to strengthen the argument for a contemporary image psychology in which experimental method, clinical technique, and context related field methodologies altogether present a special viewing of mental phenomena.
>
> —A. Ahsen, 1985/1987

> The renaissance in interest in mental imagery has produced a host of new facts about imagery and new ways of theorizing about it. We truly have learned more about imagery in the past 15 years than in all the preceding centuries combined and the end of progress in not in sight.
>
> —S. M. Kosslyn, 1985

> It is proposed that experiential perspectives provide a meaningful and necessary complement to experimental methods in the investigation of mental imagery and related processes. . . . This discourse is by no means intended to be a disparagement of scientific

methodology, but rather to emphasize that "objective" observational and psychometric techniques represent but one approach to the assessment of mental imagery.

—C. Ward, 1985

An overriding methodological problem is the relative difficulty of providing an unambiguous external criterion for the internal process of imagery. Also unsolved are such specific problems as: vividness versus ease of imagery as determinants (or correlates) of image-mediated performance, interpretation of imagery integration and its effects, the complex nature and predictive uncertainty of individual differences, and neural mechanisms of imagery.

—A. Paivio, 1988

How could one go about doing scientific experiments to discover the actual properties and functions of images? This presents one of the most difficult yet exciting challenges for a research scientist.

—R. A. Finke, 1989

## MODERN MEASUREMENT AND METHODOLOGY IN IMAGERY RESEARCH

At first glance (as Mook [2001, p. 183] notes), it is not clear how images and mental imagery can be studied scientifically or experimentally at all; that is, what can one observe? Images seem to be locked up inside one's head; you may "see" your images, and I may "see" mine, but I can't "see" yours. You may be asked to *describe* your images, but attempts to study images and imagery in this way are prone to getting bogged down in subjective and solipsistic confusions. However, there are strategies and methods available that may be used to study imagery on a more objective and scientific basis; for example, instead of requiring participants to describe their images, a researcher could ask participants to *use* their images in the performance of some task—in this way, the task and its measure (say, reaction time) are "out there" where all "outsiders" may objectively observe them. Moreover, by varying the conditions of the task, one may learn something about the "hidden" events that allow participants to perform the given tasks (cf. Shepard and Metzler's [1971] imagery/mental rotation experiments, which are viewed widely as a landmark in cognitive psychology and methodology and are excellent examples of how the researcher may turn subjective events into objective events; also see Shepard, 1978b, and Shepard and Cooper, 1982).

Finke (1989) also maintains that one reason the scientific study of mental imagery is so challenging and difficult is that imagery is a subjective phenomenon, and, unlike physical objects, mental images are not directly observable and their properties and functions must always be inferred. One simply cannot rely mainly on the information that individuals give about their images because subjective reports are notoriously inaccurate and unreliable. Another reason for the difficulty in the scientific study of mental imagery is that images are extremely elusive: they may suddenly appear at one moment and then quickly fade away the next moment. Finke suggests that *experimental methods* are needed that permit the researcher not only to infer the properties of images in an objective and scientific manner, but also to elicit reliably the images themselves.

In this section on measurement and methodology in imagery research, the material is organized into four content areas: theory, tactics, and strategy in mental imagery measurement; individual differences in mental imagery; questionnaires, scales, and tests of imagery; and other measures and correlates of imagery.

## Theory, Tactics, and Strategy in Mental Imagery Measurement

In an editorial in the inaugural issue of the *Journal of Mental Imagery*, Sheikh (1977) indicates that the influential psychologist J. B. Watson (1913b) regarded mental images to be nothing more than "mere ghosts of sensations" and of no functional significance whatever. Watson's judgment and behavioristic orientation led to the relegation of mental imagery and other mentalistic concepts to the background of the psychological scene. However, in the post-1960s, there has been a marked resurgence of interest in imagery by psychologists of varied specialties and persuasions where, according to Sheikh's overview, the significance of imagery and the importance of its scientific scrutiny and inquiry have been established beyond doubt (cf. Ahsen, 1968; Paivio, 1971; Sheehan, 1972). For instance, Sheikh notes that Paivio and his associates, and other researchers, have employed a methodology in studying imagery that would satisfy even the strictest of Behaviorists and in which numerous studies have demonstrated that imagery plays an important role in language, memory, and thought. Such research has revealed the functional characteristics that distinguish imagery from verbal symbolic processes and includes support from neuropsychological and clinical work. More specifically, in theoretical terms, it seems that there are at least two main encoding systems: a verbal-sequential one and an imagery-spatial-parallel processing one, where both are needed for optimum functioning. Furthermore, Sheikh observes that the imagery system—due to its concrete and contextual nature—appears to be much akin to perception (e.g., it has been demonstrated that an image and a percept cannot be distinguished from each other on the basis of any intrinsic qualities of either phenomenon; cf. Perky, 1910; Segal, 1971). In the clinical and therapeutic fields, evidence exists that the events in one's past may be reproduced—and the associated affect be reexperienced—more effectively through imagery than through verbal labels applied to the event (cf. Jellinek, 1949; Singer, 1974). Consequently, clinical psychologists have found mental imagery to be a valuable aid for use during therapeutic interaction and intervention, especially in dealing with psychosomatic problems (e.g., Ahsen, 1972; Sheikh and Panagiotou, 1975). Other lines of evidence indicate that imagery may provide access to significant memories encoded at developmental stages when language was not yet present or predominant (e.g., Ahsen, 1968; Kapecs, 1957).

In his "testimony" concerning the importance of the issue of mental imagery for psychology, Mowrer (1977) recounts his early academic experience with reaction-time measurement that set the stage for his later interest in the concept of imagery. Essentially, Mowrer's early experiments on preparatory set and expectancy demonstrated that the reaction time required to make a motor response (such as releasing a telegraph key) may serve as a sensitive index to events that occur in the participant's head and elude explanation in purely behavioristic terms (cf. Mowrer, 1938, 1940, 1941; Mowrer, Raymond, and Bliss, 1940). Moreover, Mowrer indicates that even so rudimentary a phenomenon as variations in reaction time under certain conditions powerfully supports recognition of "mental life," including such phenomena as expectation and imagery. Mowrer's early experimental work that implicated the notions of expectancy and imagery in the fields of learning and motivation went unheralded for a number of years. (For a systematic account of Mowrer's approach in this area, see Mowrer, 1960a,b; in these works, he suggests that an image may be regarded as a *conditioned sensation* (or perception) where images may become so strong or vivid that they often may be misinterpreted as the real thing; also, part of the meaning of many words is visual or imaginal, and when one "thinks," with the subvocal equivalents of words, there tends to be a constant byplay of images; cf. King, 1973, 1974a,b, 1976.) Following his description of various experiments demonstrating central (mental) elements in preparatory set, his examination of various subjective methods of measuring preparatory set (expectancy), and his account of systematic learning theory and imagery, Mowrer (1977) indicates his disappointment concerning the reception that his two books (published in 1960) received from the psychological community ("both of them were favorably, but not exactly enthusiastically, reviewed," p. 319), and he "abandoned virtually all further research and writing with respect to the psychology of learning" (p. 320). After about ten years—following the publication of his two books in 1960—Mowrer indicates that the books were considered to be "old books" in the field. But, then, as Mowrer recounts, an article appeared in the psychological literature (McMahon, 1973) that rediscovered, refreshed, and rejuvenated his work and theoretical approach to mental imagery. McMahon (1973, pp. 484–85) states that "O. Hobart Mowrer deserves the credit for having been the first in contemporary psychology to unabashedly use the term 'imagery' in the context of motivation and for giving the image a place of such prominence as to make it indispensable to his system. . . . The image enters Mowrer's theory as a mechanism of self-regulation and of the direction of behavior . . . the image serves as a standard or ideal of some sort—as a 'thermostat.' His analogy of the function of the image with that of a thermostat can be exemplified by Miller, Galanter, and Pribram's (1960) TOTE model, which stands for the sequence: test, operate, test, exit. Mowrer's thermostatic image provides the standard; that is, the information necessary for the organism to know whether or not things are as they should be. Whenever there is a discrepancy between the actual and the ideal, the organism is motivated to take action to correct the discrepancy." Mowrer concludes that McMahon's (1973) article is "right on target" and provides an even better historical context—and a more vivid and clear formulation—than he was able to give to his own strategic conception of the role of imagery in his work, especially his 1960b book, *Learning Theory and the Symbolic Processes.*

In another article in the inaugural issue of the *Journal of Mental Imagery*, Bugelski (1977) reviews the theory, tactics, and strategy involved in imagery research vis-à-vis verbal behavior that appeared in psychology following the early 1960s. Bugelski (p. 39) notes that "the strange and phenomenal case of the revival of interest in imagery in the last two decades may well be highlighted in future histories of science," and "the renewal of interest in imagery after its demise in the earlier quarters of this century under the attack of behaviorists has been noted by many commentators" (e.g., Bower, 1972; Holt, 1964; Paivio, 1971; Richardson, 1969; Segal, 1971; Sheehan, 1972). In particular, Bugelski reviews criticisms of the imagery theoretical construct as developed by Pylyshyn (1973) and Brewer (1974) and serves as a background for the analysis of the role of words in verbal learning and thinking. Pylyshyn and Brewer, respectively, regard imagery as lacking in utility as a "proper" mechanism for accounting for cognitive behavior, and for the higher mental processes, including the explanation of meaning. Bugelski notes that the revival of interest in imagery occurred in the context of a revolution in verbal learning (cf. Bugelski, 1971); the revolution brought about the rejection of the use of nonsense syllables in verbal learning experiments and the substitution of ordinary words, sometimes in sentences or paragraphs, and a new concern for what the learner/participant had to contribute to the learning and retrieval processes (where, now, the learner was viewed as engaged in *subjective organization* using structures, themes, schemata, and other processes—such as imagery—to assist in the learning activity).

Bugelski (1977) notes that in the history of psychology J. B. Watson (1924) and B. F. Skinner (1957) may be cited as two researchers of verbal behavior who maintained a "correct" psychological orientation. According to Bugelski, although both Watson and Skinner did not succeed in accounting for all language behavior, they must be commended for their strategy of staying with the tools, procedures, and assumptions of the psychological laboratory, and what they found were *psychological* data, *not* the data of grammarians, logicians, or poets. However, both Watson and Skinner—in their treatment of verbal behavior in line with a strictly behavioral approach—tended to ignore the unobservable, inner behavior of experimental participants, and some psychologists have attributed a gross strategic error to the work of Watson and Skinner in their refusal to deal with internal, mediational processes.

Bugelski (1977) notes that there are at least two kinds of tactical errors that are common to psychologists in their treatment of verbal behavior: an overemphasis on the role of words in thinking and the converse or paradoxical error of underemphasizing or misinterpreting the role of words in thinking and other behaviors. He also observes that what might be regarded as a misuse of words in psychological research is surprising in view of the fact that in the birth year of psychology—1879—Sir Francis Galton had suggested a potentially useful approach. That is, Galton (1879) selected seventy-five words, looked at them one at a time, and timed himself while he conjured up two "thoughts" to each word; in essence, Galton asked himself, "What do I think of when I look at this word?" He found that when he looked at a word, say *knife*, he did not think of a fork; rather, he thought of a knife, and a particular knife at that. Additionally, in four repetitions of the mental exercise, months apart, Galton tended to have the same thoughts for the same words—about 50 percent of the time. In effect, the results of Galton's mental exercise showed that he described most of his reactions in terms of imagery, involving more or less static and/or histrionic/action images. In Galton's study, images were described as coming from different life periods (e.g., childhood—39 percent; adulthood—46 percent; and maturity—15 percent).

In summary, Bugelski (1977) attempts to indicate the tactical ways in which words have been employed in psychological research and experiments that have not been particularly fruitful. Words in such a traditional context have been valued as things in themselves, instead of being appreciated as either stimuli for internal responses or as responses to such internal activities with presumed stimulus-generating properties; Bugelski asserts that words can become components of verbal habits that run off more or less by themselves unaccompanied by any significant happenings inside the individual—people may learn vocal responses that sound like words but have little or no meaning to either speaker or listener (e.g., consider the pseudowords *takete* and *malumba*). Bugelski's point is that words are not associated with each other, and they do not exist except as sounds in the air or printed marks or symbols on paper. Verbal stimuli generate neural processes that, in some instances, initiate vocal or written responses; moreover, various sensory responses may be conditioned to sound of words and occur as images or conditioned sensory, perceptual responses. According to Bugelski (p. 51), "to lose sight of this caveat is to forfeit the scientific investigation of what goes on when we learn and think."

Shepard (1978b) rejects the assumption made by some writers (e.g., Pylyshyn [1973]) that mental images are only subjective epiphenomena that play little or no functional role in significant processes of human thought. Rather, he asserts that imagery, especially visual imagery, has played a central role in the origin of his (and other scientists', inventors', and writers' most creative ideas. Shepard describes two (of the many) lines of scientific and technological development of great significance in which mental imagery appears to have played a prominent role: the areas of electromagnetic fields and molecular structures (cf. Ferguson, 1977; Shepard, 1978a). Shepard (1978b) also examines the difficult issues of studying and measuring mental images empirically, and presents an experimental tactic, or device, for the externalization of visual and mental images. In his section on "How Can Mental Images Be Studied?" Shepard (pp. 131–35) notes that past studies of mental imagery have used a largely correlational methodology or strategy and have relied heavily on the participants' introspective ratings of their own mental imagery where the results do not convey much information about the nature of a mental image itself or about its relation to a perceptual image. A better way to approach the study of mental images, according to Shepard, is to employ strategically one or more paradigms in which comparisons are made of participants' performance in conditions that are as nearly identical as possible, with the exception that in one condition the relevant stimuli are physically present whereas in another condition they are only remembered or imagined (cf. Shepard and Podgorny, 1978). Shepard (1978b) names his paradigms as follows: *second-order isomorphism* (in which the proposed equivalence between perception and imagination implies a more abstract or second-order isomorphism where the functional relations among objects as imagined mirror the functional relations among those same objects as actually perceived; cf. Shepard and Chipman, 1970); *reaction time* to a corresponding external *test stimulus* (based upon the assumption that perception and imagination use much of the same neural circuitry, it may be said that to imagine a particular object is to place oneself in a unique state of readiness for the actual perception of that particular object); *reaction time* to a spatially *localized probe* (in which evidence is provided that the very same mechanisms are operative in imagery as in perception; cf. Podgorny and Shepard, 1978); and *mental transformation* (in which dynamic kinds of imagery, especially *mental rotation processes*, are studied; cf. Cooper, 1975, 1976; Cooper and Podgorny, 1976; Cooper and Shepard, 1973, 1975, 1978; Metzler and Shepard, 1974; Robins and Shepard, 1977; Shepard, 1975; Shepard and Cooper, 1982; Shepard and Feng, 1972; Shepard and Judd, 1976; Shepard, Kilpatric, and Cunningham, 1975; Shepard and Metzler, 1971).

Sommer (1978, 1980) suggests various strategies for imagery research. In one case (1978), he provides the items that comprise the

Galton Questionnaire for assessing visual imagery. In another case (1980), Sommer examines the disparity between the results obtained from nomothetic versus ideographic studies; nomothetic investigations involving group comparisons tend to give inconsistent and inconclusive results, while ideographic studies—typically using a case study approach or strategy—are strongly supportive of the importance of imagery. Sommer discusses the methods for bridging the gap between these two strategies, and makes suggestions regarding the issue of subject sampling and the form of distribution of imagery ability in the population, the development of performance tests and training procedures, and the intensive investigation of nonimagers. Sommer (1980) notes that, normally, the researcher who has obtained negative results for a long period of time would be likely to drop the particular line of investigation; however, in the case of visual imagery, there is another strategy, or line of research, that produces very different findings, namely, the ideographic studies of eidetic imagers (cf. Luria, 1968; Stratton, 1917; Stromeyer, 1970). Sommer asserts that if there is any single factor that has kept alive his own interest in imagery research over the past decades, it has been the careful, patient, and convincing work of the *ideographic* (single case studies) researchers. Moreover, the tasks, self-report measures, and sampling procedures used in *nomothetic* (group comparisons studies) research have been subject to a number of criticisms (along with the criticisms leveled against the ideographic strategy—such as the lack of generalizability). Among these are the following:

- The range of participants has been extremely limited—while Galton's (1883/1907) early studies used people from the general population, virtually all succeeding researchers have recruited students, mostly college students, as participants.
- The tasks used in testing imagery—such as recalling objects from a series projected on a screen at the front of a room—have tended to be trivial (i.e., there is no connection between performance and anything important in the lives of the participants; various studies whose results show no relationship between visual imagery and IQ scores raise doubts as to the validity of the traditionally implicit assumption that recalling details from a picture, or the order of letters in a letter square, may be done more quickly and efficiently with visual imagery than without it.
- The mnemonic devices commonly used by college students to remember classroom notes tend to be nonvisual (cf. Sommer, 1978).
- The problems with self-report measures used to assess imagery have been acknowledged by virtually all researchers—there are difficulties in defining

imagery and in making distinctions as to degrees of clarity and control.
- The earliest self-report measures were developed largely on the basis of face validity—without checks on internal consistency (more recent instruments which have been item- and factor-analyzed are more acceptable concerning the criterion of reliability, but they still have validity problems in view of the vagueness of the concept of imagery for many participants).

Concerning general research strategies in imagery research, Sommer (1980) suggests that with a mental phenomenon as complex and poorly defined as is imagery, it is fruitless to rely on a single research strategy or approach; while any individual researcher is free to employ a single data-gathering procedure, any attempt at integration/synthesis must rely on a multimethod approach (cf. Webb, Campbell, Schwartz, and Sechrest, 1966). The multimethod strategy assures a complementarity of benefits and limitations between different research techniques, and, according to Sommer (1980), although each method has its particular shortcomings, these tend to be somewhat different limitations than are found in other methods. For example, the questionnaire is excellent in terms of economy and range of topics covered, but weak in control and interpretation of the meaning of responses/answers; brain wave recordings via the EEG are strong in objectivity, but weak in understanding/interpretation and efficiency; and the personal interviewing technique rates highly in understanding and elaboration of responses, but poorly in objectivity, control, and economy. Sommer maintains that putting all these methods together provides something desirable in the way of economy *plus* control *plus* elaboration of responses. Another suggestion offered by Sommer (p. 119) is that cross-cultural/cross-national studies of imagery ability, in particular, must await the development of better tools and tactics for studying imagery, and recommends that "bridges" be constructed between the nomothetic and ideographic strategies for investigating mental imagery where the development of new research models incorporate both lines of inquiry. Note that Sommer (1978) provides a useful bibliography on imagery in his notes section—containing over 220 references/citations; he also provides a useful adaptation of Galton's (1883/1907) original questionnaire containing twenty-one items for assessing visual imagery.

In an interesting tactical approach, Algom and Lewin (1981–1982) studied the following experimental question: "Do two separate, and independently developed, models of mental imagery tap into the same underlying psychological phenomena?" Empirical propositions derived from a general cognitive-information model and a biofeedback model were tested simultaneously within the design of a single experiment where three measures of imagery (quantity, vividness, and controllability) were employed. Algom and Lewin note that researchers traditionally have been aware of the need for a construct-validation of the concept of imagery; however, most of the construct validatory attempts have been of a statistical nature using mainly factor-analytic techniques as the chief method of data reduction gathered by interview and questionnaire methods. Algom and Lewin assert that while such studies have contributed greatly to the organization of the many multifaceted imagery phenomena, and to the development of important measurement devices, they still do not fill the gap between the different empirical approaches to the study of mental imagery. As an alternative strategy, Algom and Lewin combined the *stimulus independent mentation* (SIM) paradigm (cf. Antrobus, 1968; Antrobus, Singer, and Greenberg, 1966) and the *biofeedback* paradigm (cf. Barratt, 1956; Brown, 1966, 1970, 1971; Kamiya, 1969; Stoyva and Kamiya, 1968) into a simultaneous application within the framework of a single experiment. The results of their study support the major hypothesis indicated in their experimental question; that is, the manipulation of imagery either by imposing a heavy load on the cognitive system or by making use of biofeedback techniques produces a predictable set of results. Moreover, the data suggest that differential combinations of the values of the two types of tactical manipulations may be conceptualized as varied states of *fantasy-deprivation*, or at least of *fantasy-disturbance*, where subsequent magnitude of imaginary activity is a direct function of the strength of the disturbance (cf. Algom, 1980; Algom and Lewin, 1976).

Sheehan (1982–1983) suggests that the work on imaginative consciousness currently is in a time-period when the earlier questions of *how* imagery functions have come to be replaced by questions about *why* imagery operates in the way that it does. According to Sheehan, it is paradoxical that current debate in the field has come full circle where those persons researching imagery/imagination claim that it makes little sense to talk about images as such at all. The current era is characterized by a preoccupation with process and structure in which the real complexities of imagery phenomena—and their possible interactions with the test conditions that surround them—are lost. Sheehan notes that in researchers' relentless search for proof of structure, psychology has acquired a rich assortment of ingenious methodologies and paradigms for demonstrating the functional utility of

imagery itself, but also, polarization is seen among the theoretical alternatives where important questions concerning the mediating role
of imagery have come to be overlooked. For instance, contemporary
research in the field has not studied the issues of whether individual
differences in imagery are fundamental or pervasive enough in character as to be critical to task performance, whether imagery works in
a way that there is generalization over different types of imagery tasks,
or whether imagery is selected by participants over other strategies that
may work equally well under various appropriate circumstances.

Sheehan (1982–1983) notes that methods of measuring/testing for
imagery obviously have an impact on the actual emergence of imagery phenomena, and the interweaving of relationships of method,
function, and process represents a major issue for consideration in
imagery research. Sheehan examines some of the evidence related to
various methods and tactics used in studying imagery. Among the
methods he reviews are the following: mental travel, mental rotation,
images in the "back of the head," and eidetic imagery (cf. Sheehan,
1982). Sheehan (1982–1983) maintains that the important advances
in the field of imagery research are the change in status accorded to
the variable of *aptitude for imagery,* and the growing consensus in the
field that participants should be asked what they think about their performance on their imagery tasks. However, according to Sheehan, despite such advances, the person-treatment interactions in imagery
research remain elusive (i.e., there has been a failure to explore the
complex interactions between individual differences in imaginative
capacity and the actual stimulus factors residing in the imaging tasks
or situations). Sheehan concludes that the interplay between function,
process, and method is an intricate one and argues that the interplay
is best considered within a strategic framework that acknowledges the
relevance of particular interactions between the participants' capacities or aptitudes for imagery, the participants' cognitions, and the
constraints of the stimulus situations in which the participants are
placed; furthermore, it may be premature to argue that the evidence
is unequivocal concerning the structural similarity of imagery to perception, although such similarity may eventually prove to be the case.

In another strategic approach, related to his earlier one (Bugelski,
1977), Bugelski (1982) provides a theoretical analysis of mental imagery that makes imagery a function of learning (cf. King, 1978,
1979), as well as suggesting that learning is a corresponding function
of imagery and that imagery may be described in Hullian terms as a
*hypothetical construct.* Following his attempt to show how imagery has

a central role in learning (via discussions on "the status of the learning problem," "autoshaping and incidental learning," "the nature of learning," "conditioning as imagery formation," "voluntary behavior," "instrumental conditioning and imagery," "ideomotor action," "the subjective aspects of imagery," "image as epiphenomenon," and "imagery and psychotherapy"), Bugelski's (1982) article is followed, in turn, by a number of heuristically important peer commentaries concerning his theoretical position. In regard to his article, following all the commentaries and reactions made to his paper, Bugelski provides a rejoinder or "a comment on the comments" section, taking, individually, each contributor's remarks into account. As Bugelski notes, "Each had something of interest to provide and I find that I cannot group them for any general answers and will have to respond to them individually" (p. 67). (An extensive and useful bibliography related to contributors' remarks, and containing over 185 entries, is appended [pp. 85–92] to Bugelski's article, following his rejoinder.)

J.T.E. Richardson (1985a) reports on a tactical approach studying mental imagery that involves *converging operations* (cf. Richardson, 1985b). As Garner, Hake, and Eriksen (1956) point out, it is normally considered necessary to specify more than one procedure because otherwise some particular posited hypothetical construct (such as imagery) would simply come to be identified with the particular research instrument currently being used to measure that construct. Richardson examines the adequacy of the operational indicators that are employed in experimental investigations of mental imagery. Four types of experimental procedures have been used in such research (cf. Paivio, 1975): the comparison of individual participants in terms of their use of mental imagery (cf. Simpson, Molloy, Hale, and Climan, 1968); the manipulation of the imageability or concreteness of the stimulus material; the administration of instructions to use mental imagery in carrying out particular tasks; and the disruption of mental imagery by means of concurrent perceptual or spatial tasks. As Richardson (1985a) notes, there are a great many conceptual and methodological problems in this area, but each of these procedures has been found to produce reliable empirical effects, especially in tests of human learning and memory (cf. Richardson, 1980). Richardson (1985a) also suggests that what is needed to clarify the predictions relating to the possible interactive relationships among the operational indicators defining mental imagery is a device that would permit one to monitor independently the availability and the efficacy of mental imagery in cognitive tasks. One such way of studying the availability of different categories of learning mediators is to ask participants to describe the strategies that they use to deal with different stimulus items; the efficacy of a particular type of mediator may then be evaluated by relating the appropriate subjective reports to an objective measure of performance.

J.T.E. Richardson (1985a) observes that a few experiments have used formal questionnaires to study the types of mediators employed in verbal learning tasks, and their findings may be summarized: imaginal mediators are more likely to be reported after the administration of imagery instructions, and in the case of concrete material than in the case of abstract material; the memorability of a particular item is directly related to the number of participants who report the use of mental imagery to learn that item; in the recall of concrete material, the performance of a particular participant is related directly to the number of imaginal mediators reported by that participant; and in the recall of abstract material, the performance of a particular participant is unrelated to the number of imaginal mediators reported. Richardson conducted an experiment that tested the assumption that imagery instructions enhance the availability of imaginal mediators, but not their efficacy (his design involved a paired-associate learning task using both a between-participants and a within-participants manipulation); in a second experiment, Richardson tested the assumption that mental images are effective mediators only in the case of concrete (but not abstract) material. Thus, regarding the tactical approach employed here, mediator reports in the two conditions provide an additional point of leverage in evaluating the convergence of the various operational procedures for investigating mental imagery (cf. Richardson, 1985b). Based upon his findings, Richardson (1985a) concludes the following: imagery instructions enhance the availability of imaginal mediators rather than their efficacy; stimulus concreteness enhances both the availability and efficacy of such mediators; mental imagery is not an effective mediating device in the case of abstract material; imagery instructions enhance the availability of imaginal mediators in the case of both concrete and abstract material; and such instructions may depress the recall of items that fail to produce imaginal mediators.

In two separate issues of the *Journal of Mental Imagery*, Ahsen (1985/1987) published the same article (also see Ahsen, 1989): "Image Psychology and the Empirical Method." (In the 1987 issue, Ahsen's article is followed by a number of open peer commentaries and, in turn, by his rejoinders ["comment on the comments"].) Ahsen (1985/1987)—a strong influential force, theoretician, organizer, strategist, proponent of eidetic psychotherapy, and synthesizer of mental imagery research in psychology (as well as across other disciplines, including education, sociology, literature, and mythology) since the 1960s—provides an extensive discussion of the historical roots of imagery vis-à-vis scientific methodology and strategy in psychology. Essentially, Ahsen argues for a contemporary image psychology in which experimental/empirical methodologies, clinical techniques, and context-related field methodologies are combined together to provide a special perspective of mental pheonomena. (For a comprehensive review of Ahsen's prodigious and far-reaching image psychology, and his image model [p. 15], see Hochman, 1994.) Along with his examination of the notion of experience and its close association with imagery starting from Descartes and Locke (where both the relevance and irrelevance of Cartesian dualism to imagery studies is outlined with special emphasis placed on Locke's empiricism and his theory of reflection regarding sense data), Ahsen (1985/1987) discusses several issues concerning reflection and its various forms not accounted for in Locke's approach nor in later theories of empiricism in psychology. Additionally, Ahsen's discussion includes the issues of general psychological methodology, modern imagery research and myths, and cross-disciplinary analyses of imagery concepts.

Regarding strategy in research, Ahsen (1985/1987) notes that deficiencies in modern experimental psychology may be traced directly to the twisting of the goals of empiricism and its historical intentions; such a twist created pseudometaphysical, antiexperiential trends in current experimental methodologies, and changes them at times into "form without content." Ahsen suggests that the care and the search for *content* progressively diminishes as the experimental *form* increases its hold; this inverse correspondence between method and truth leads to an ascendance of *form* where the final outcome is often emphasis on the elegance of the experimental design without attention being paid to the *content* of the experience itself (cf. Yuille, 1985, 1986, who asserts that excessive control and precision paradoxically lead to loss of meaning and value in research paradigms).

At another place, in another perspective of strategy, Ahsen (1985/1987, pp. 15–27) makes a bold statement about the empirical method concerning sense data: empiricism cannot postpone an open-ended treatment of imagery operations at both the personal and the social level; one needs to involve ideas of animism and mythology as much as ideas of technology in order to understand the nature of operations in the modern world. According to Ahsen, a mental object—whether social, natural, or manufactured—is a simultaneous *combination* of all these aspects, and is "real" only in that sense. He suggests that the "baffling mix" of mechanics, myth, metaphor, and politics must be described through a scientific strategy or methodology that does not merely distinguish between abstract truth and operation, but describes the operations as they exist and are carried out, or can be carried out in the historical process. In addition, because misinterpretation is currently a part of the whole process concerning discovery of truth, one cannot hope to have a truth-seeking science but only an empirical science. In the final analysis, according to Ahsen, in an empirical view of imagery a picture is no longer a mere copy but a veritable power, a material process, a meaning, a symbol, and a metaphor—where the picture has split off from its origin and makes new associations.

In his section on the mechanics of imagery, Ahsen (1985/1987) advances the notion of a *Triple Code Model* (ISM) related to the fact that most modern theories of metaphor imply a tripartite model (cf. Ricoeur, 1979; Marks, 1987). The three elements—imagination/image (I), feeling/emotion/somatic response (S), and cognition/semantic relevance/meaning (M)—may appear in different theories under different names or different sequential arrangements, but they imply the same tripartite relationship. The psychological theory involving the acronym *ISM* was first discussed by Ahsen in 1965 (cf. Ahsen, 1984b). According to Ahsen (1985/1987), although the ISM is not explicitly formulated in the classical theory of rhetoric or in later literary theories of imagination, it is nevertheless implied in all such theories as well as in all psychological theories. In Ahsen's ISM model, the *structural* aspects define the whole metaphorical process: the image, the feeling, and the meaning (i.e., ISM), which, all together, produce a single, undivided, and unified effect. In the ISM formulation, the feeling and emotion (S) stand between image (I) and the meaning (M); the basic minimal unit of psychological experience that involves imagery is the ISM sequence—the interconnected operations may be found in this three-dimensional unity that is comprised of a vivid image (I), a somatic or body response (S), and a meaning (M) where it is important to note that normal imagery experiences tend to occur mostly in the I-S-M order/sequence. Moreover, the image is accompanied by a somatic/body response (S) that is always a specific type—skeletal, proprioceptive, motor-neural impulse, sensory experience, and so on, and a measure of meaning. Sometimes, however, for various reasons, the ISM does not occur in its proper order. There are six basic operational variations (order/sequences) of the ISM, namely, ISM, IMS, MIS, MSI, SIM, and SMI. Ahsen (pp. 30–33) provides examples for each of the different six basic operational variations of the ISM. For instance, in the IMS sequence, a person may mistake a piece of rope for a snake and immediately become fearful and run away; here the somatic response is initiated via a misunderstanding where in the IMS the image (I) appears first, is followed by the meaning (M), and then the somatic response (S). Such emphasis upon *sequencing*, or order of events in a sequence, is reminiscent of the distinguishing characteristics of several of the competing theories of emotion—such as the classical theory, the James-Lange theory, and the Cannon-Bard theory (see Roeckelein, 1998, pp. 87–88, 162–64, 273–74). Also the *tripartite* ISM model seems to be reflective of the charm and popularity in psychology of "three-ness" or tripartite models—such as Freud's tripartite personality (id, ego, superego) and Berne's "I'm OK" tripartite dynamics (parent, adult, child) in his script theory. Does this attraction for tripartite models in psychology derive from the traditional and theologically powerful Christian notion of the Trinity comprised of Father, Son, and Holy Ghost?

In his examination of Ricoeur's (1979) operational strategy in the literary field, especially as regards the aspect of metaphor, Ahsen (1985/1987) notes that Ricoeur distinguishes between the psychological theory of metaphor and the literary theory of metaphor, which, essentially, contains the seeds of dissension between psychology and literature. Ahsen asserts that such a literary theory of metaphor (as formulated by Ricoeur) has a serious problem associated with it and one that has consistently been the center of controversy in the psychological theory of imagery—namely, the mechanics of vividness in an image. Ahsen suggests that Rocoeur's approach does not adequately take into account the dimension or factor of *subliminal imagery*, and this omission provides a departure point for Ahsen to discuss the controversy around the issue of imagery vividness and the *vividness paradox* (cf. Ahsen, 1985, 1986a, 1987, 1988, 1990) in psychological research. Ahsen (1985/1987) notes that in psychological studies the relationship between imaginal mediators and cognitive performance has been established mostly as correlational, but the search for a direct causal mechanism linking vividness of imagery and recall continues on (cf. Marks, 1972). According to Ahsen, the vividness-unvividness dimension is an inseparable part of the image and in this connection the vividness does not embody pure recall, but rather the embodiment of the attitude toward recall; therefore, the image is not a memory, but a symbol in a sense (cf. Marks, 1987b). Ahsen contends that attempts to employ memory methods to study imagery (e.g., Paivio, 1972) tend to confuse the imagery process as a whole with memory, and memory is the "worst view" one may expect to inject in the study of imagery because it leads to serious problems in understanding the function of imagery mechanics in the flow of mental processes and their relationship to vividness. For further discussion, elaboration, commentaries, and critiques of the *unvividness paradox* notion, see the *Journal of Mental Imagery*, 1985, *9(3)*, 1–18; 1986, *10(1)*, 1–8; 1987, *11(1)*, 13–60; and 1988, *12(3,4)*, 1–184.

In summary, concerning Ahsen's (1985/1987) strategy and tactics in imagery research, he suggests that the type of operational dynamic involved in imagery experience, and not merely memory recall, is the key to the vividness paradox. He notes that Marks's Vividness of Visual Imagery Questionnaire (cf. Marks, 1989) is an excellent test that provides a fair mix of the mechanical and the dynamic to show the efficacy of the vividness in performing mental tasks that resemble life (i.e., the test takes one beyond the self-report issue into the dynamics of what mechanics are involved in the self-reports and shows that vividness and imagery do correlate when the dynamics are taken into account). In strategic terms, the real argument in imagery, according to Ahsen, is consideration of the importance of what may be called *introspective operationalism*, based on introspective monitors that are realized through empirical evidence. Furthermore, regarding strategy in imagery research, Ahsen asserts that the *convergent* approach to imagery (e.g., Richardson, 1985a,b) is useful but, at the same time, a *divergent* approach is needed, also, which involves the other more dynamic side of imagery operations and which comprises more of what the essence of working with imagery encompasses. Ahsen suggests that, once and for all, imagery researchers need to go beyond Pylyshyn's (1973) propositional view of imagery and base imagery research firmly in the introspective area, both in the experimental laboratory and in the field study of imagery effects. Ahsen looks forward to the advent of what he calls the *New Structuralism* in psychology (cf. Ahsen, 1986b; Marks, 1984, 1986). For a discussion by E. R. Hilgard of Ahsen's (1986b) notion of the New Structuralism, see Hilgard (1993); in his commentary, Hilgard expresses certain reservations about the New Structuralism as a general theory of consciousness (he guesses that perhaps it may only be a theory of image formation). Hilgard (1993, p. 434) observes that the theory of New

Structuralism "appears to begin as a theory of image formation and does indeed say very significant things about images, but then, without quite saying so in so many words, it soon appears to become a general theory as a psychology of consciousness, a new paradigm for psychology, and seems to have no defined boundaries at all." For a comprehensive list of works by Ahsen (over eighty citations), see "Imagery Bibliography" in the *Journal of Mental Imagery*, 1994, *18*, 2–5; also see Hochman, 1994, pp. 111–13.

Kearsley (1985) tacitly examines strategic and tactical issues in imagery research, in particular with respect to the field of *human geography* (i.e., humans' use of the earth with which they interact through the medium of images of the environment and of society). (For a discussion of the role of imagery in *architectural* thought, see Downing, 1987.) Currently, according to Kearsley, a preoccupation with marxist and phenomenological perspectives has led to a decline in overt interest in the nature of human imagery, but the image—whether specifically acknowledged or not—remains a cornerstone of geographic inquiry. Kearsley asserts that, in general, too little attention has been given by geographers to what was being measured, and too much was given to the mode of analysis of the derived measurements. Geographers were sure of the logic of their statistical techniques, but chose to ignore the extent to which the images that were measured were truly representative of the mental processes of humans. Thus, asserts Kearsley, it may be that many of the images that geographers have elicited and processed may be no more than artifacts of the recovery process, and it may be inevitable that the tentative links between behavioral geography and environmental psychology may have to be broadened to include the fundamental aspects or cores of both disciplines. Also, across time, the study of images in geography seems to have polarized into two camps (humanists versus positivists), so that differences of method, rather than similarity of aims, are emphasized. Kearsley suggests that the tactic of the recovery and analysis of mental maps is one significant area—but not the only one—where fruitful cooperation between the polar/alternate positions might take place. In terms of practical applications regarding imagery in human geography, Kearsley himself has conducted studies that have measured the public images—held by New Zealanders—of the impact of various energy developments and industrial projects on their communities, as well as measuring the private images that people hold concerning the scenic values, and land utility, in a number of resource-development situations.

In his review of imagery paradigms, Marks (1985, p. 93) observes that "methodology is the handmaiden of theory." He examines the five traditional strategies/paradigms that have been used in the study of imagery: experimental-cognitive (Fechner, Wundt, and Galton); psychoanalytical-dissociationist (Freud, Charcot, and Janet); behaviorist (Watson, Holt, and Skinner); neuropsychological (Flourens, Luria, and Hebb); and developmental (Piaget and Inhelder). A sixth approach—called the New Structuralism (Ahsen)—is a synthesis of several aspects of the other five strategies. Marks notes that while each paradigm has made a contribution to the understanding of imagery, large gaps in knowledge remain due to a general neglect of image structure and of its relationships to the individual's past and future psychological development. Marks asserts that methods in science are a function of theoretical aims, and, in his review, he attempts to clarify this relationship with special reference to imagery. Marks notes that although the New Structuralism strategy involves the experimental methods of the laboratory, it bases its assumptions on the insights originally obtained through clinical research and therapy (e.g., Ahsen, 1965, 1968, 1972, 1977b, 1982). Moreover, recent laboratory studies conducted with nonclinical samples have provided confirmation of some of the basic hypotheses of the New Structuralism approach (e.g., Marks, 1984, 1986; Marks and McKellar, 1982; Molteno, 1984). Essentially, the New Structuralist methodology differs radically from other paradigms because it deliberately and explicitly sets out to obtain as complete a phenomenological report as possible of the participant's imagery that is produced following standard instructions; the results so obtained show that introspection provides a highly reliable and valid indicator of imagery quality, content, and structure (cf. Kaufmann, 1981; Marks, 1983; Yuille, 1985, 1986). Marks (1985) observes that the New Structural paradigm is young and is still developing; however, because it has borrowed its conceptual and methodological tools from other approaches elsewhere, it may not lay claim in any sense—Kuhnian (Kuhn, 1962) or otherwise—to be revolutionary. Note that in this account, it may be suggested, the New Structuralism may more appropriately be called a research *strategy* rather than a *paradigm* (cf. Neisser, 1972a,b; Segal and Lachman, 1972). Marks maintains that the strategy of controlled introspections, supported by objective measures of somatic responses, provide the necessary methodology for investigating mental imagery.

Ward (1985) examines the strategic biases in favor of scientific methodology and experimental design in psychological inquiry, in general, and the investigation of mental imagery, in particular. Ward offers some reflections on the limitations and shortcomings of scientific method with respect to the study of mental imagery, and examines some prejudices and paradoxes in the field. In her review of scientific methods in psychology (cf. Barratt, 1971), Ward identifies the four major methodological approaches (i.e., observational, correlational, experimental, and quasi-experimental methods; cf. Cronbach, 1957) typically employed by scientific psychologists, and indicates that clinical methods and case studies may be used, also, but for the most part psychological inquiry appears to be nomothetic rather than idiographic. Ward notes that the observational approach is common among all the scientific methods, but description and explanation vary due to the fact that while all sciences are *empirical*, not all are *experimental* (cf. Crano and Brewer, 1972). Ward (1985) maintains that the preference in psychology has been overwhelmingly in favor of experimental methods and causal explanations, despite the fact that only a portion of psychological studies meets these criteria (cf. Ward, 1978). She observes, also, that while the nature of mental imagery research poses problems for adherence to conventional experimentation, the preference for experimental data and the prejudice against other scientific approaches is "blatantly apparent" (1985, p. 115) (cf. Ashton, 1982; Haber, 1982; Marks and McKellar, 1982). Furthermore, Ward suggests that a major problem with psychological thinking generally and with the study of consciousness and mental imagery in particular is the failure to recognize the complementarity of the objective and subjective strategies (cf. Blackburn, 1971; Bronowski, 1960; Globus and Franklin, 1980).

Ward (1985) identifies three significant reservations that scientific psychologists seem to hold with respect to experiential approaches to knowledge in the study of mental imagery: the intangible nature of the subject matter, the requirement of an objective observer, and the viewing of experiential methods as subjective and inappropriate for scientific investigation (cf. Govinda, 1973). Among the limitations of scientific methodology, Ward indicates that mental imagery research is confined often to psychological laboratories and artificially induced altered states of consciousness where these topics are rarely examined as naturally occurring phenomena; subjective experiences are isolated in an experimental session rather than in their usual and more meaningful contexts (cf. Ahsen, 1977a; Doob, 1982; Goleman, 1977; Ludwig, 1966; Marks and McKellar, 1982; Pelletier, 1978; Schuman, 1980; Wallace, 1959; Zusne, 1983). According to Ward, the artificiality of laboratory tests and associated research is restricted in their overall potential to contribute to comprehensive theory/theorizing. Moreover, many psychologists wishing to examine mental imagery in relatively unfamiliar societies, for example, many fear invading certain anthropological domains or various cultural practices and culturally instituted dissociative states that rely heavily on mental imagery (such as drug-induced hallucinogenic experiences, meditative practices, mediumistic trance and healing states, ritual and clinical possession, and mourning practices). While Ward does admit that the application of the objective scientific strategy to the area of mental imagery has yielded many worthwhile findings (such as brain research on hemispheric dominance in fantasy patterns, chemical basis of hallucination, psychophysiological correlates of meditative states, and advances in the study of eidetic imagery), she also forcefully advances the notion that *experiential* perspectives and research strategies are required for the proper understanding of mental processes, especially consciousness and mental imagery.

In his perspective concerning strategy for studying imagery, Yuille (1985) suggests that two factors, in particular, render the laboratory an inappropriate setting for the study of mental imagery (cf. Yuille, 1986, 1987): the powerful *context effects* of experimental situations and the *cognitive penetrability* of most imagery experiments. Following his (1985) review of the history of the concept of mental imagery (including the classical period of Athenian culture, the European, Arabic, Hellenic, and Judeo-Christian philosophers, Descartes, the British Empiricists, and the twentieth-century Behaviorists and cognitive scientists), Yuille discusses the methodological choices that researchers in the field made when mental imagery returned to psychology as a "respectable" topic for study (after a short hiatus and an ostracism in North American psychology between the early 1900s up to about the mid-1950s). Yuille assesses the success of the combination of the new cognitive psychology with the rigorous experimental techniques and technologies of the Behaviorists and, in particular, evaluates the issue of whether the evolved experimental methodology is appropriate for the study of mental imagery (Yuille—before his actual discussion—gives his "up-front" answer to this issue in the negative, p. 139). Yuille develops his argument against experimental methodology, initially, with a definition of it (i.e., laboratory-based hypothesis-testing in which control is the primary concern; cf. Stevens, 1939) and a brief discussion of its historical roots (e.g., agriculture, physics, chemistry), followed by a description of the failings of that methodology (e.g., it doesn't account adequately for the context-dependent nature of most human activity; cf. Petrinovich, 1979); the dynamics of the experimental situation compounds the futility of an experimental psychology of cognition—due to the implicit demands of its methodology, an experiment is actually an elegant and sophisticated method of controlling human behavior. Yuille concludes with some comments concerning how imagery research should be divorced from the experimental method along with some notions about nonexperimental strategies for collecting data about mental imagery, for example, problems concerning cognition exist in experiments such as Shepard's (1978) mental rotation paradigm (cf. Steiger and Yuille, 1983; Yuille and Steiger, 1982; also the mental scanning experimental paradigm of Kosslyn, Ball, and Reiser, 1978) ("blatantly exhibits the effect of task demands").

To bolster his argument, Yuille (1985, p. 141) considers the typical pattern of a psychological experimental investigation: the experimenter designs the experiment to test (which generally means support) an hypothesis; materials are selected, instructions are prepared, the experimental context is controlled, and a decision is made concerning which aspects of behavior are to be recorded and how they are to be recorded. Then the experiment is run, but suppose that the results are not what the experimenter expected—at this point the experiment is labeled a *pilot study* and various changes are made in the procedure, materials, and so on. This process is repeated until the right combination of experimental manipulations is discovered (only the "final" experiment appears in print in the psychological literature). According to Yuille, such a refinement, or such an approximation-by-steps procedure, is commonplace in psychology and is assumed to be legitimate science, for example, see Finke and Pinker (1983, p. 403) who state, "We noted that several of our early pilot experiments had failed to show evidence for mental image scanning. . . . We were therefore interested to see whether we could influence the selection of strategies." Thus, as with most effective researchers, Finke and Pinker did succeed in finding the right combination of factors and were, in turn, successful in supporting their particular hypothesis (cf. McGuire, 1973; Rosenthal, 1966).

Yuille (1985) suggests that some defenders of the laboratory methodology strategy have misunderstood the particular problem of *cooperative participants*. For instance, Berkowitz and Donnerstein (1982) observe that participants do not try to confirm the experimenter's hypothesis because they are usually ignorant of it. However, according to Yuille, the issue here is not whether the participants are able to infer the nature of the experimental hypothesis and then, subsequently, try to confirm it; the consciousness of the participants about the experimental hypothesis is irrelevant. Rather, says Yuille, the point is that the dynamics of the experimental situation *control* the participant's behavior; in effect, the context offers little choice for the participant where everything "conspires" to encourage the participant to conform to the situation, with or without his or her awareness. At one place, Yuille (p. 142) advances the idea that the methodology inherent in experimental psychology is not only futile (cf. Yuille, 1986), but it is also "conceptually destructive."

In critiquing experimental methodology, Yuille (1985) examines and assesses both the mental scanning experiments of Kosslyn and his associates (e.g., Kosslyn, Ball, and Reiser, 1978) and the associative learning paradigm of Paivio (e.g., Paivio, 1971, 1983). In the former case, great task demands are exerted on the participants in these experiments. Yuille notes that in some studies (e.g., Mitchell and Richman, 1980; Richman, Mitchell, and Reznick, 1979) it has been shown that the task demands are sufficiently clear in such paradigms or strategies that the volunteer-participants will frequently verbalize them! Thus, for instance, participants in such studies may correctly estimate how they *would* perform the mental scanning task *without actually* doing it (cf. Intons-Peterson, 1983; Intons-Peterson and White, 1981; where the a priori experimenter-knowledge determined the likelihood of participants producing the desired mental scanning effects; specifically, those experimenters who were naïve about the expected latency effect generally did *not* obtain it, while those experimenters who expected it *did* obtain it). As regards Paivio's (1971, 1983) associative learning strategy, Yuille maintains that there are some complications linked with Paivio's dual-coding model, and while Paivio's basic argument is that the *concreteness effect* may be attributed to the value of mental images as mnemonics, some recent research (e.g., Jonides, Kahn, and Rozin, 1975; Kerr, 1983; Zimler and Keenan, 1983) raises problems for this conclusion as some investigators report that congenitally blind participants show no impairment relative to sighted persons in their memory for words with visual referents, and that instructions to use imagery were equally facilitative and effective for blind as well as sighted participants. Yuille asserts that—for the associative learning strategy—it is the selection of participants that proves critical for the provision of evidence for either a pro- or an anti-imagery position.

In summary, Yuille (1985) maintains that various specific experimental strategies or paradigms (i.e., mental rotation, mental comparisons, mental scanning, and associative learning) provide strong illustrations of the more general difficulties associated with the experimental investigation of mental imagery—in the search for precision, experimenters have sacrificed meaningful investigation where the more one tries to exercise control, the more impoverished becomes the phenomenon of interest. Yuille recommends that imagery psychology does not need more or better experiments, but it does need to discard experimental methodology in the study of context-dependent processes and replace it with field-based research, perhaps supplemented with carefully documented case studies and biographical essays (e.g., Runyon, 1982). Such a proposition, says Yuille, is not anti*empirical*, but only anti*experimental*. (Alternative methodologies are available that explore cognition in situ; e.g., Neisser, 1982; also note the therapeutic role of imagery as representing alternative strategies/paradigms for imagery research; e.g., Anderson, 1980; Hammer, 1984; Leuner, 1977; Sheikh and Jordan, 1983; Simonton, Matthews-Simonton, and Creighton, 1978; Singer, 1974; Strosahl and Ascough, 1981.) In the final analysis, Yuille suggests that experimentalists leave their laboratories and join their critical abilities with the practical concerns of clinicians and therapists in a new combined, cooperative, and strategic effort that will produce, ultimately, an effective, rational, and useful methodology for the study of mental imagery.

Other discussions regarding the theory, tactics, and strategies employed both in mental imagery research and measurement may be found in the following studies:

- Finke (1986)—uses a method for measuring the limits of resolution in mental imagery that is based on techniques common to visual psychophysics.
- Ahsen (1986a)—discusses the issues of ability, diagnosis, age, context, and dynamics vis-à-vis imagery measures such as Marks's Vividness of Visual Imagery Questionnaire (VVIQ), Sheehan's Vividness of Imagery Scale (VIS), Betts's Questionnaire Upon Mental Imagery (QMI), and Gordon's Test of Visual Imagery Control (GTVIC).
- McConkey and Nogrady (1986)—studies the psychometric aspects of the individual versus group versions of the Visual Elaboration Scale in two independent experiments.
- Parrott (1986)—studies the effect of imagery training strategies to stimulate adaptive use of imaginal processes compared to a verbal creativity training program.
- Ahsen (1986b)—in a *tour de force*, analyzes the roots, and the theoretical

scope, of historical Structuralism as a strategy/method and practical application in the cross-disciplinary study of imagery; develops a novel reformulation of the old Structuralism in a strategy termed the "New Structuralism" (cf. Hilgard, 1993); advances the notion of the Triple Code Model, ISM, that is proposed as the basic unit of psychological experience involving imagery. Also note that Ahsen's concept of "unvividness" is not just the absence of "vividness" but an orthogonal quality of the image and where unvividness enables the image to act on consciousness in a way that vividness cannot; unvivid images are used extensively in art and literature to create desired effects that could not be achieved otherwise. A large references section containing over 175 references/citations is provided.

- Ahsen (1987)—discusses the complex and strategic role of the "unvividness paradox" concept in imagery formations, especially in the context of imagery tests such as the QMI, VVIQ, and GTVIC; reviews, and responds to, various critiques of the notion of "unvividness" as made by Hilgard, Marks, and Sheehan; makes the argument that unvivid experience is a separate and independent function in general imagery structures.

Among the relevant *sources* on tactics and strategy in imagery methodology and measurement are the following:

- *Journal of Mental Imagery* (1987), *11(3,4)*, 1–295 presents, again, the enormously rewarding and thought-provoking article entitled "Image Psychology and the Empirical Method" by A. Ahsen (cf. Ahsen, 1985/1987), but in this version, an extensive and heuristically valuable "Open Peer Commentary and Response" section is included where numerous ($n=37$) reactions are made to Ahsen's strategic approach; a generous references section, consisting of over 380 citations/references, concludes Ahsen's monumental and creative expository and editorial tasks.
- Ahsen (1988)—critiques, and advances, the notion of "unvividness paradox" (cf. Ahsen, 1987) through an analysis of visual ads selected from newspapers and magazines showing how they are constructed to convey their messages and the special role that "unvividness" plays in the making of such ads.
- Begg (1988)—suggests that imagery is a tool that allows performance of many useful tasks, and that the problem for students of conscious structure is to recognize that the same structure is the percept, the image, the trace, and the meaning, depending on the questions one asks.
- Reisberg and Heuer (1988)—argue that the degree of detail in an image is uneven and, hence, a unidimensional measure (such as vividness) cannot fully characterize visual imagery; examines the methodological issue of how images may be assessed or quantified.

- Richardson (1988)—emphasizes that imagery researchers must be clear concerning their conceptual and operational definitions of mental imagery, as well as being explicit about the theoretical, methodological, and applied issues that follow the conceptual/operational definitions and bases; highlights the differences between the two main strategies in imagery research: the individual difference approach and the New Structuralism approach.
- Wallace (1988)—describes the use of visual search tactics by poor imagers who were trained to be more efficient in a visual search task.
- Paivio (1988)—examines methodological and conceptual obstacles that prevent a deeper scientific understanding of imagery, in particular the problem of the relative difficulty of developing an unambiguous external criterion for the internal process of imagery.
- Pinker (1988)—describes the "computational theory of mind," a central strategy/dogma at the heart of cognitive science (which is analogous to the doctrine of atomism in physics, the germ theory of disease in medicine, and plate tectonics in geology), and which posits that mental processes are formal manipulations of symbols/programs consisting of sequences of elementary processes made accessible by the information-processing capabilities of neural tissue; proposes a theory in which images are considered as patterns of activation in a three-dimensional array of cells accessed by two overlayed coordinate systems (a fixed viewer-centered spherical coordinate system, and a movable object-centered or world-centered coordinate system); such a strategy allows the researcher (within a single framework) to generate, inspect, and transform images, as well as attend to locations, and recognize shapes.
- Slack (1988)—examines a theoretical approach that allows access to visuospatial information held in long-term memory by individuals who report their use of mental imagery.

Yet other concerns regarding theory, tactics, and strategy in imagery research are discussed in the following studies:

- Denis (1988)—presents an overview of the major theoretical and methodological issues related to the study of the association between imagery and prose processing (cf. Desrochers, 1988).
- Baddeley (1988)—suggests that a strategic approach that employs the concept of "working memory" offers a useful framework for understanding imagery; the approach assumes a "central executive" aided by two slave systems, an "articulatory loop," and a "visuo-spatial sketchpad" (cf. Quinn, 1988, who reports on an experiment that uses an "interface paradigm" to study coding processes in the "visuo-spatial sketchpad;" also see Bischof, 1988; Brooks, 1967; Segal, 1908).
- Kaufmann (1988)—presents a theory which assumes that translating a

problem from a propositional to an analog format gives access to a set of simpler cognitive processes of a perceptual kind.

- Helstrup (1988)—examines how imagery may alternatively be conceptualized as a representation system or as a cognitive-operations system.
- Savoyant (1988)—gives an overview of the theoretical accounts of mental practice, and distinguishes two conceptual intervention tactics/modes in motor skill: planning/organizing of the motor sequence, and motor programming and control.
- Whiting (1988)—presents a general framework for the area of motor control and motor learning in which the "image of the act" is distinguished from the "image of achievement."
- McDaniel (1988)—explores the use of several strategies that are used to study the role of imagery in learning, including material and instructional manipulation, presentation of interfering tasks, and individual differences techniques; also, possible pitfalls of each approach are discussed.
- Perrig (1988)—examines the distinctions made for memory codes, in particular image versus motor encoding strategies.
- Marschark (1988)—notes that empirical findings in the cognitive/imagery research area indicate a *functional* role for imagery in human cognition, but neither the older findings nor the newer ones require the conclusion that images serve as analog representations in long-term memory (rather, the results from most studies are consistent with the idea that concreteness and imagery effects derive from differential processing of distinctive and relational information for high- and low-imagery materials/contexts).
- Richardson, Denis, and Engelkamp (1988)—discuss the strategies and paradigms that have been employed in European research on imagery and cognition, including the designs indicating the relationship between imagery and linguistic representations, between imagery and action-motor activity, and between imagery and brain mechanisms; in the area of brain research, two principal strategies are distinguished: the identification of neurophysiological and neuroanatomical manifestations and bases of imagery processes in intact participants, and the evolution of the performance of patients with brain damage.
- Hishitani (1989)—provides some comments concerning tactics employed in imagery research where, in particular, the notion is advanced of using "imagery experts" to promote understanding of mental imagery; "imagery experts" are defined as particular individuals (such as expert abacus operators) who can easily generate and manipulate vivid imagery as a useful tool to solve tasks (cf. Hatano, Miyake, and Binks, 1977; Hatano and Osawa, 1983; Hishitani, 1984a,b).

A very interesting debate in the literature and instructive series of point-counterpoint articles—initiated by A. Ahsen—in the *Journal of*

*Mental Imagery* (1989, *13*, 1–30; 1990, *14*, ix–xi, 1–259) examines some issues surrounding the influential Behaviorist strategy/approach in science in general and various methodological and reporting tactics of mental imagery in particular. Briefly, Ahsen (1989) responds to the comments and reactions made by H. J. Eysenck and B. F. Skinner concerning Ahsen's earlier (1985/1987, pp. 159 ff) disclosures relative to J. Wolpe's and A. Lazarus's misreporting of scientific facts and data (regarding earlier events in 1967 centering on the issue of the testing of the efficacy of behavior therapy); Ahsen (1989) examines the main questions and issues raised by Eysenck and Skinner, and some crucial points are identified concerning the issue of scientific misconduct in psychological Behaviorism. Following Ahsen's discussion regarding the "Wolpe/Lazarus misreporting affair" (for a very *concise* one-page account of this affair, see "Misrepresentations" in the *Journal of Mental Imagery*, 1990, *14*, vi), B. R. Bugelski (see Bugelski, 1990, p. v; Ahsen, 1989, p. 13) issued a statement (titled "Bugelski-Hilgard Statement")—supported and cosigned by E. R. Hilgard—containing the following strategic propositions: A more stringent measure of peer review needs to be applied in the reporting of methods and research in the Behaviorist circles; a reevaluation and a restatement of the Behaviorist research is needed to remove the blemish on the future image of Behaviorism as a science; a fresh restatement of Behaviorism and its principles and applications is required. Then, Bugelski requests feedback/reactions to his statement from readers to inform him—via publication in the *Journal of Mental Imagery*—of their views on this issue, and suggests that readers submit their positive and/or negative evaluations and guidelines for a restatement of Behaviorist research (cf. Bugelski, 1989; Eysenck, 1989).

In turn, following Bugelski's plea as indicated in "Bugelski-Hilgard Statement," the *Journal of Mental Imagery* (1990, 14, pp. ix–259) devoted an entire issue (under the editorship of A. Ahsen) to the topic entitled "Behaviorists' Misconduct in Science: The Untold Story of the Image in Cognitive Psychology." In his preface, Ahsen states the dual purpose of the volume: to provide an expose on scientific misconduct and to give a restatement of imagery history. In another case, an entire issue of the *Journal of Mental Imagery* (1993b *17[1,2]*) provides discussions concerning strategies and paradigms in mental imagery research. A series of articles on this topic by A. Ahsen, under the rubric "Imagery Paradigms," includes the following titles: Introductory Remarks on Imagery Paradigms in Psychology; Imagery Paradigm: Imaginative Consciousness in the Experimental and Clinical Setting; Thunder in the Tissue Box; Zero Ground; The Running Stream; Divided Consciousness Operations: Vivid and Unvivid Imagery Responses and Their Analyses; A Commentary on Imagery Tests; Dynamics of Hemispheric Imagery: Vivid and Unvivid in Mental Functioning; Heartbeat as Stimulus for Vivid Imagery: A Report on Individual Differences in Imagery Function; Hot Image: An Experimental Study of Enhanced Sensory Connection to the Mental Image, With Clinical Implications; Slow Potentials, TOTE, TOTEM, ISM, and Neo-Dissociation (cf. Hochman, 1994, pp. 55–60).

In their chapter in an edited volume on imagery in sports, Budney, Murphy, and Woolfolk (1994) discuss strategic and methodological issues in research, in particular on the relationship between imagery/ mental practice and motor performance (cf. literature reviews of the methodology employed in mental practice by Corbin, 1972; and Richardson, 1967). A primary problem identified in this area is the great variability in procedures (under the label of *mental practice*, participants engage a wide range of diverse strategies, and imagery scripts—usually poorly described—differ greatly across studies). According to Budney et al., although studies may indicate the ratio of mental to physical practice, the amount of time spent in each, and the latency between the two, should be examined more systematically. Furthermore, in the view of Budney et al., across imagery studies the literature is plagued by failure to control for, and to assess, the quality of mental practice or mental preperformance imagery; the limited data available suggest that vividness and control are related to the efficacy of mental practice, but such conclusions are supported only by weak strategies such as quasi-experimental, anecdotal, and correlational studies that link more vivid and controlled imagery with the more successful, elite athletes and performers.

Ahsen (2000) examines current imagery theory and practice, and advances the strategic use of various devices, techniques, and approaches popular in the history of learning experiments (late nineteenth century), in particular, the employment of mazes, problem boxes, and images/discrimination cues (cf. Ahsen, 1993c). Ahsen (2000) draws parallels between the two fields—current imagery theory and early learning experiments—and indicates how imagery research has come to rely heavily on the strategy of mere vividness imagery ability and has abandoned its earlier link to learning dynamics. For instance, Ahsen notes that the earlier discrimination studies in the learning-dynamics strategy had come from the field of psychophysics (Fechner, 1860, 1876), but they also generated the study of imagery vividness via the questionnaire method of Galton (1883/1907). Moreover, imagery tests came directly out of psychophysics, which was concerned with the psychological scaling of objects that may be arranged on a physical continuum, and the area called *psychometrics*, on the other hand, deals with construction of psychological scales having no convenient physical continuum on which to arrange the stimulus objects. According to Ahsen, based upon the psychophysical method, Galton (1883/1907) was the first one to quantify a strictly psychological function, namely, the vividness of mental images; psychophysics made the first attempts to deal with the tactical problems of scaling, and Fechner's (1876) original method of choice—in dealing with aesthetics—gradually developed into the *ranking method* and the *method of paired comparisons* (cf. Cohn, 1894) used today (Ahsen notes that logically and mathematically the method of paired comparisons is reducible to that of *constant stimuli* and the ranking method is reducible to that of *paired comparisons*). Ahsen maintains, via his discussion of scaling methods and imagery scales, that the imagery vividness tests were not originally designed as *dynamic* tests and they tell one nothing about how imagery works in a dynamic operation; however, according to Ahsen, when such tests are used strategically in *conjunction with* some form of paired comparison involving both vividness and unvividness aspects (cf. Ahsen, 1985, 1987, 1988), one gets values that begin to reflect the dynamics dimension of imagery.

In his section on vividness interlocked with dynamics, Ahsen (2000, p. 7) indicates his specific tactical approach to the "vividness vis-à-vis dynamics" issue that involves a three-step procedure: ask the participant to see and rate the vividness of an image (where any item provided in an imagery test will suffice); ask the participant to keep her/his *father* in mind (mental father filter) while seeing the same image and rate the vividness again; and ask the participant to keep his/her *mother* (mental mother filter) in mind while seeing the same original image and rate the vividness a third time. The use of this procedure is based on the assumption that the straightforward measurement of vividness by itself does not yield the sought-after dynamics; however, if fluctuations in vividness are shown to be a measure of some kind of implicit performance—as the three-step procedure provides—then "less" and "more" vividness gives an indication of the underlying dynamics involved. Use of this procedure with respect to all the items of the foremost, popular imagery tests (i.e., Marks's [1973] VVIQ, Sheehan's [1967a] QMI, and Gordon's [1949] TVIC) showed that each participant's vividness responses went into violent dips and peaks as extreme as the opposite ends of the scale, suggesting that such a tactical approach touches some underlying dynamic functions (cf. Ahsen, 1985).

Finally, in another tactical variation, Ahsen (2000, pp. 26–47) initially discusses the parallels among what animals, children, and adults tend to do during typical *learning experiments*, during the *normal routine* behavior of individuals in daily life, and in *educational* and *clinical* situations when someone is being instructed or being guided. Ahsen suggests that there is not any true difference among these four formal situations, and the essence of any *change* that occurs follows much the same principles that are found universally in every situation. Ahsen draws out similarities in the dynamics under four separate headings (learning experiments, normal routine, educational, and clinical contexts) and the four parallels are presented that involve thirty situations (which contain units of behavior that appear, functionally, as necessary segments at various stages when learning any new skill). The thirty situations are selected from notable early experiments (e.g., Kluver, 1932; Lashley, 1942; Morgan, 1894; Munn, 1931; Tolman, 1932; cf. Woodworth and Schlosberg, 1954). A sample of the thirty situations involve the following variables and behaviors: drawing attention, initial hesitancy, initial exploration, shock, punishment versus surprise, left-right tendency, delay in memory, free exploration, discrimination, position habit, solution cues, conflict and uncertainty, place learning, multisensory involvement, and reinforcement. Subsequently, in his discussion of learning genomes, Ahsen (2000, pp. 46–47) supplements his "30 parallel tactics" concerning imagery situations with a "100 learning genomes tactics" (*genonomy* is defined as "the study of laws of relationships with reference to classification of the organism"). Basically, Ahsen's *learning genomes* in each of the thirty parallels are progressive and attempt to elaborate on the dynamic features in each parallel. Thus, Ahsen's (2000) tactic of learning genomes represents a "learning manual that an experimenter, educator, or therapist may keep in mind while pursuing actual living operations" (p. 46), and where the manner in which the genomes combine in a particular task indicate the learning genomes for that task.

For further discussions of the theory, tactics, and strategies in mental imagery measurement and research, see the remaining portions of this chapter, as well as chapter 5 ("Annotated Bibliography of Imagery Studies in Psychology [1960–2003]")—especially studies under the sections "Applications and Functions of Imagery," "Learning and Imagery," "Measurement and Tests of Imagery," "Perception/Sensation and Imagery," "Personality/Individual and Gender Differences and Imagery," and "Physiology/Neuropsychology and Imagery."

## Individual Differences in Mental Imagery

In his popular and successful book on experimental psychology, Osgood (1953, p. 641) notes in his section on the role of imagery in thought that marked individual differences exist in imagery where people differ in both the general vividness of their imagery and the modality in which they are most proficient. Not only famous historical figures (e.g., Beethoven relied on his auditory imagery even after going deaf; Zola's writings are full of references to olfactory imagery), but psychologists, as well, vary among themselves concerning the form of imagery most vividly experienced, and such differences have helped to shape their theories on the issue. For example, Stricker (1880) relied heavily on kinaesthetic imagery himself and assumed that this ability was widespread among most people; he was supposedly unable to imagine words such as *mutter* and *bubble* while he held his mouth open. Osgood observes that—unfortunately for Stricker's theory— most other psychologists could imagine such words under such circumstances. Moreover, Galton (1883/1907)—a psychologist with lucid visual imagery—was surprised to discover that many scientists seemed to have *no* visual imagery at all; in attempting to account for such a finding (that men of science could have ideas *without* any attendant visual images), Galton anticipated the *motor theory of thought* (e.g., Watson, 1914; cf. Osgood, 1953, pp. 648–55; Roeckelein, 1998, pp. 200–201, 477) by asserting that the "missing faculty" was replaced by other serviceable modes of conception, chiefly connected with the individual's "incipient motor sense"—not only of the eyeballs but also of the muscles generally. Osgood (1953) also notes that since Galton's time a number of objective studies of imagery have been conducted with most of them designed to separate people into imagery types (cf. Woodworth, 1938, pp. 41–44). Among the specific procedures and methods employed in the early objective studies of individual differences in imagery are the following (cf. the section in chapter 2 herein entitled "Early Measurement and Individual Differences in Imagery"):

*Association* method—participants are required to name as many objects (having characteristic colors, sounds, etc.) as they can in a limited amount of time.

*Learning* method—participants learn material presented either orally or visually with the assumption being that one's prominent or preferred type of imagery determines the ease with which learning occurs under each type of condition.

*Distraction* method—participants are distracted (by auditory stimuli, by visual stimuli, or by having to hold one's tongue between one's teeth) while attempting to learn a set of materials (the assumption in this method is that if the individual is utilizing a given type of imagery in learning, he or she will suffer more from distractions within the same modality).

Osgood observes that the entire proposition that there are distinct types of people who emphasize one form of imagery over other forms is made suspect by results obtained in early studies such as those by Betts (1909). Betts expanded Galton's (1883/1907) early type of questionnaire approach to include several forms of imagery (instead of just one type) and found that ratings of imagery vividness for the various sensory modalities were intercorrelated highly (e.g., a participant who expresses experiences of vivid *visual* imagery may generally claim the presence of other imagery—such as vivid *olfactory* or *auditory* imagery—as well). Osgood suggests that a type theory of imagery would demand that good visualizers, for instance, be relatively poor in the other sensory modalities; however, in the final analysis, Osgood expresses doubt as to the validity of this particular approach (i.e., the questionnaire method) in discerning individual differences in imagery.

Goldberger (1961) conducted an experiment on imagery and individual differences within a larger context of the study of perceptual isolation; he attempted to discover whether a limited form of sensory deprivation or homogeneous stimulation (via participants' wearing of translucent eye-cups for periods up to forty minutes) could elicit vivid visual imagery in participants that is similar to that found with multisensorial deprivation of much longer periods of time. The original study in this area—linking imagery to homogeneous stimulation occurred in an incidental fashion in an investigation of color adaptation under visual *ganzfeld* conditions (i.e., via gluing eye-cups consisting of halved ping-pong balls over participants' eyes to produce, in effect, a homogeneous, nondifferentiated visual field)—was conducted by Hochberg, Triebel, and Seaman (1951). During

Goldberger's testing procedure, when, and if, the participant reported an image, the experimenter made an inquiry as to the nature of the image (e.g., the person was asked to compare it with a previously ex-perienced afterimage). Goldberger reports the following results:

1. All of the sixteen participants experienced a fairly vivid afterimage (the afterimage was seen "out there," although all participants *knew* that it was a subjective phenomenon).
2. The majority of participants reported what seemed to be "idio-retinal" phenomena (i.e., phosphenes, luminous dust, pulsations of light, shadow, color) during all phases of the ganzfeld experience/exposure; moreover, in one set of individual-differences observations, about one half of the participants reported the phenomena described by Hochberg et al. (1951), viz, that the visual field gradually turned gray and, in some cases, the field quickly resumed its former brightness.
3. Only five participants in the forty-minute condition (as compared with nine out of fourteen participants in an eight-hour isolation condition) reported phenomena classifiable as imagery; in only two of these cases were the image comparable in intensity to those reported in previous studies containing eight-hour isolation conditions (e.g., Holt and Goldberger, 1959).

Further, concerning individual differences, when images were reported by participants, the images were experienced as being less vivid than the afterimages (only one participant felt that they were of equal in-tensity). Goldberger asserts that the only conclusion concerning meth-odology that one may draw from his study is that a brief (up to forty minutes) ganzfeld procedure is not a particularly powerful method for promoting the kind of imagery obtained under longer-period (eight hour) isolation conditions; also, whether a prolonged homogeneous visual field *alone* could account for the emergence of hallucination-like images typically found in longer-term isolation experiments is open to investigation. Goldberger notes that it would be difficult to answer such a question experimentally without confounding the variable of visual homogeneity with such factors as immobility, confinement, and boredom, which are inherent factors in a prolonged ganzfeld proce-dure. Finally, as regards methodology in this area, Goldberger sug-gests that prolonged immobility—combined with the effects of a group of personality-difference variables involving, in particular, pas-sivity, intellectual flexibility, and emotional freedom/independence—be joined with the factor of visual homogeneity in facilitating the experience of imagery in isolation experiments. For a study that examines sex/gender differences (and reports negative findings) in body imagery/orientation under sensory deprivation conditions of brief duration, see Reed and Kenna, 1964.

In a study concerned with individual differences (initially determined via a series of personality tests, including an embedded-figures test; Witkin, 1950; cf. Eagle, Wolitzky, and Klein, 1966) and the relationship between descriptions of visual imagery produced by rhythmic photic stimulation, Freedman and Marks (1965) found that persons who have the ability to suspend their "generalized reality-orientation" report more imagery than those who don't possess the ability; also, individuals' levels and abilities of imagination and suggestibility seem to be other salient individual-difference factors in the experience of visual imagery under photic stimulation conditions (cf. Blum, 1956; Walter and Walter, 1949). Freedman and Marks observe that the published literature in this area of photic stimulation shows that sensory-deprivation imagery is related to the following personality and individual-difference variables: controlled and accepted primary process, emotional responsiveness, vividness of imagery in everyday life, history of hypnagogic experience, autistic and imaginative self-concept, suggestibility, hypnotizability, and field independence. Moreover, the concept of suspension of the generalized reality-orientation brings such variables into a unified frame of reference, and provides a theoretical basis for extending their relevance to photic stimulation imagery. Based upon the results of their study, Freedman and Marks identified a certain personality syndrome—involving imaginativeness, emotional responsiveness, and a tendency to mystical-type experiences—in their photic stimulation procedure, and suggest that it may have relevance for a wide variety of situations that are conducive to "unreal" experiences as well as for all kinds of imagery (cf. Goldberger and Holt, 1961a,b; Holt and Goldberger, 1960; Leiderman, 1962).

Sheehan (1966) examines individual differences in vividness of imagery and the functional similarity between imaging and perceiving (cf. Sheehan, 1965). He notes that it is a common fact that individuals differ in their capacity to image, but little is known about how this cognitive ability functions, as well as its operative mechanisms. Sheehan's studies generally attempt to control past experience and objectively measure individual differences in reported vividness of waking memory imagery. His suggested method of study requires participants first to image, and then the experimenter relates individual differences in participants' introspective reports to measurable features of imaging responses where imaging behavior is defined by specification of the correspondence between imagery and past perception. Sheehan (1966) asserts that no imagery can occur that is not composed of elements arising out of actual perceptual experience of some kind: images must depend on previous perception. Based upon the results of three experiments, Sheehan makes the following conclusions:

- Individual differences in imaging are related to individual differences in the relationship between the two sets of behavior—perceptual and imaging.
- The relationship between imagery vividness and the correspondence between the two sets of behavior is a nonlinear one—*good* vivid imagers tend to behave similarly as they do when they perceive, but *poor* imagers behave both similarly and dissimilarly.
- The participants' given instructions concerning imaging and recall indicates there are different memorial accounts of the perceptual stimulus: imaging behavior is more akin to perceptual behavior than to recall behavior.
- Familiarity alone cannot account for individual differences in vividness ratings—practice only increases the variance of individual differences already existing regardless of the participants' experience with the imaged object.
- Imagery vividness bears some relationship to the degree of complexity of the stimulus: more complex stimuli are not imaged as vividly as less complex stimuli, and other stimulus characteristics (such as stimulus "meaning") require further study.

Sheehan notes that his results do not account for the essential correspondence between imaging and perceiving—they indicate only that a behavioral relationship exists and refer only to the *form* of that relationship, and the most plausible explanation of results seems to lie with the variables underlying individual differences in modes of representation (e.g., the use of coding and other symbolic devices), rather than with the study of identity of the mechanism underlying the two process of imaging and perceiving.

Lindauer (1972, pp. 134–36) examines individual differences vis-à-vis sensory imagery, in particular; he briefly reviews the history of imagery research and notes that Galton's (1883/1907) questionnaire was rich in its ability to arouse sensory images and represents the first systematic study of imagery, focusing on the aspect of individual differences and a person's capacity to evoke different kinds of sensory images. Lindauer notes that interest in types of imagery remains today, particularly as indicated in tests of imagery. For instance, Brower's (1947) study employs a brief imagery test of the relative predominance of several sensory modalities in which participants were asked if they could see, hear, taste, smell, and feel a pan of onions frying on a stove. However, Sheehan's (1967a,b) research is more representative of a long line of imagery-test development; for example, in Sheehan's approach, participants rated the vividness of the imagery that was evoked when they were given stimulus phrases (pertaining to seven modalities)—such as "the sun sinking below the horizon" for the visual modality. Sheehan (1967a,b) discovered individual differences among participants concerning a general imaging ability across the whole range of sensory modes—rather than a specialization or concentration of imagery in one particular sense. (Cf. McKellar, 1957, 1965, who found that mental imagery seems to vary in the domain of one or other of the sense modes, and that visual and auditory modes are the most predominant. Elsewhere McKellar [1968] rejects any crude typology based on such differences but, on the other hand, he does affirm the *availability* of sensory images that seem to be fairly equally distributed among the senses.) However, as Lindauer points out, availability is not the same as the predominance or frequency-of-use of imagery (cf. Bowers, 1929, who established for visual- and auditory-imagery words that they remain relatively constant over time). In essence, participants who display imagery can use a variety of modalities, but they are likely to use one or another mode more than others. The differentiation between availability and predominance—and their relationship to voluntary and spontaneous imagery—says Lindauer, remains unclear; also, there is inconclusive evidence linking individual differences in sensory imagery to various psychological dimensions and physical skills (cf. Neisser, 1970). Lindauer notes that other lines of imagery research make less of a distinction between sensory modalities than between *visualizers* and *verbalizers* (cf. Roe, 1951, 1953; Short, 1953), or they emphasize the visual mode and its various attributes—such as high versus low imagery and concrete versus abstract reference—and other dimensions such as personality factors (cf. Stewart, 1965), physiological indices such as the pupillary and galvanic skin response (cf. Colman and Paivio, 1969), and comparisons in visual imagery for pictures versus words (cf. Paivio and Yarmey, 1966). Lindauer observes that an exception to the narrow preoccupation in imagery research with only one or two senses is the work of Sarbin and Juhasz (1970) who refer to the different roles played by various modalities activated in imagination episodes. Moreover, according to Lindauer, an even more critical feature of imagery research occurs in the study of individual differences in sensory imagery where there is an overreliance on correlations between factors already existing in participants rather than directly manipulating those variables presumed to be responsible for imagery (cf. Cronbach, 1957); however, Lindauer asserts that research—especially in the area of learning where imagery variables have been manipulated directly—has been relatively indifferent to the role of individual differences in imagery.

Marks (1977) suggests that the most stubborn and uncontroversial observation about the mental image is the enormous variation in the quality of images reported by different individuals. Using an imagery model consisting of consciousness and visual cognition, Marks develops several testable predictions about individual differences in cognitive functioning. Additionally, he asserts that most theories in experimental psychology are tested nomothetically by manipulating an independent variable(s) across experimental conditions and then measuring the effects on some dependent variable(s). In many cases, it is possible—when testing certain classes of theories—to treat people (as well as manipulating other conditions or treatments) as independent variables in experiments by varying the people rather than the conditions (cf. Underwood, 1975). Based upon his definition of imagery as "a conscious, quasi-perceptual experience," Marks (p. 280) maintains that it is necessary to use self-report measures of individual differences in his experimental approach (cf. Richardson, 1979), and he finds that the tactic of between-participants comparisons is more interesting and powerful than comparisons of performance at different imagery levels within participants. Marks employs two main stages in his approach: first, finding a discriminating and reliable measure of imagery differences; and, second, devising tasks sensitive enough to detect performance differences that may be reasonably predicted to occur as a result of the participant-variation observed in the first stage. See Sheehan (1967a,b) who obtained results with such a tactic that best predicted incidental rather than intentional recall; for reviews of this area, see Marks (1972) and Sheehan (1972); also, for a verbalizer-visualizer questionnaire, see Richardson (1977a,b), for a ways of thinking questionnaire, see Paivio (1971), and for his own Vividness of Visual Imagery Questionnaire (VVIQ), see Marks (1972, 1973). In summary, Marks (1977) suggests that there is significant value in the self-report measures of imagery vividness in the prediction of a wide variety of cognitive performances having great individual differences such as perceptual recognition, mental practice, encoding of visual and verbal stimuli, and ability to recall, recognize, and retrieve material from memory.

Hilgard (1977, p. 101) points out that to the extent that imagination is a matter of revived perception, it is often described according to sensory images, corresponding to the sensory modalities of vision, audition, touch, gustation, olfaction, and kinesthesis; also, with the development of Galton's (1883/1907) and Betts's (1909) questionnaires to assess individual differences in imaging ability, it became possible to get a *score* (from a number of opportunities in each modality) both for one's general imaging ability and for the relative vividness of imagery corresponding to one or another of the sensory systems. According to Hilgard, because of the *reductive* psychology of the early twentieth century (wherein the search was on for the simple elements out of which more complex experiences could be constructed), it was assumed that vividness of imagery was likely to be the basis for creative imagination, and, consequently, the early studies tended to use the imagery scale to the neglect of other aspects of imagery (cf. Gordon, 1949, 1950, who called attention to imagery beyond its vividness dimension/aspect). Along the lines of individual differences in imagery, Hilgard (1977) examines, in particular, the relationship between vividness of imagery and hypnotizability; his hypothesis is that the hallucinatory ability of the highly hypnotizable individual may rest on an underlying capacity to form and recognize images. Hilgard observes that the results of the experimental studies on this issue have been interesting because sometimes a significant correlation is found between imagery and hypnotizability, and sometimes not; sometimes the correlation is significant for women and not for men, but occasionally it is the other way around. According to Hilgard, one problem is that the correlations are commonly so low that—even though positive—they may fluctuate considerably with sample size or other aspects of experimentation; a common finding regarding individual differences in this area is that the relationship between hypnotizability and imagery is curvilinear, with the highly hypnotizable showing high imagery and the low hypnotizable showing little imagery—but imagery, in itself, is not predictive of hypnotizability because many with high imagery are not hypnotizable. Hilgard (1977) suggests that the role of imagination in hypnosis requires some ability on the individual's part to make use of the images that are present in some special way if imagery capacity is to lead to hypnotizability; he indicates, also, that Marks's (1973) imagery questionnaire/scale has shown promise in relating visual imagery to hypnotizability, and it moves beyond merely assessing imagery vividness into the area of creative imagination because the scale involves some manipulation of the obtained images.

In his account of mental imagery vis-à-vis human memory, Richardson (1980, p. 117) provides an entire chapter on the issue of individual differences in mental imagery ("one of the most complex and least conclusive of the areas of experimental investigation concerning mental imagery"). Initially, Richardson examines the oldest method used by psychologists for studying individual differences in imagery: the comparison of individual participants in terms of their reports concerning the vividness and manipulability of their experienced mental imagery. Richardson argues that on both conceptual and empirical grounds that this strategy of introspection does not constitute a useful approach for psychological research. However, according to Richardson, an important respect in which individuals vary in their cognitive capacities and imagery is as the result of neurological disorders, an area in which well-replicated findings show that neurological damage at different locations within the brain affects imagery and language skills in different ways. Also, neuropsychological research of this nature suggests that mental imagery consists of several components, each of which, again, may be differentially affected by neurological damage at different cerebral locations. For example, damage to the posterior regions of the brain—especially to the parietal lobes of the cerebral cortex—tends to produce impaired performance in imagery tasks where short-term working memory operates in the representation, preservation, and manipulation of spatial and pictorial information; also, although deficits in spatial thinking may result from damage to either side of the brain, they are more likely following damage to the right cerebral hemisphere. However, the relative frequency of deficits in right-hemisphere damaged patients seems to vary from task to task, and, thus, physiological mechanisms in both hemispheres may contribute to the use of mental imagery as a short-term, nonverbal, working memory but in which different tasks make different demands of the components in the two parietal lobes. Richardson indicates that the role of the right cerebral hemisphere is more salient when considering the factor of *pictorial* memory; while damage to the left cerebral hemisphere typically leaves performance on certain tasks unimpaired—such as retention of complex visual displays not readily described or labeled—the retention of nonverbal patterned stimuli is particularly affected by damage to the right temporal lobe. In summary, concerning evidence in this area for assessing individual

differences, vis-à-vis brain damage, it is suggested that the parietal
lobes constitute the neuroanatomical basis of nonverbal short-term
memory, whereas the right temporal lobe contains the neuroanatomical basis of nonverbal long-term memory (historically, an analogous
distinction for *verbal* memory has been made with respect to the left
parietal and left temporal lobes). Finally, Richardson recommends that
research on individual differences in mental imagery be conducted,
also, in the following content areas: eidetic imagers—individuals who
experience particularly vivid, detailed, and persistent visual imagery;
blind and/or deaf participants—individuals who may be lacking in
certain sorts of mental imagery; and participants who appear to have
radically superior mnemonic abilities where mental imagery is implicated. (Richardson gives a generous references section, containing over
425 citations/references on mental imagery vis-à-vis memory.)

Slee (1980) conducted four experiments in which individual differences in visual imagery ability were used to test hypotheses based on
a theoretical analysis of the functional significance of imagery in visual
memory (cf. Slee, 1976). In the (1980) analysis, visual imagery has a
special function, but only in relation to specific memory tasks, that
is, those tasks that require the retrieval of appearances or basic features,
of visual structure. Taken together, Slee's findings provide a validation
of the constructs of *conceptual-representation* and *appearance-
representation* where the former construct seems to be a normal and
common component of visual recall in all participants, but the latter
construct is an extra component whose occurrence depends, in large
part, on an individual's visual imagery ability. Slee's experimental results, then, support the hypothesis that visual imagery, as indexed by
individual differences in imagery ability, is advantageous in the retrieval
and representation of appearance information and, also, results indicate that imagery has no special role in relation to the retrieval/rep-
resentation of conceptual information. Finally, Slee suggests that future
differential research on the role of imagery in visual memory may
benefit from employment of an accompanying *theoretical* rationale for
the selection of experimental tasks.

In relating individual differences in imagery to *autonomic control*,
Kunzendorf (1981) notes that the German physiologist (and history's
first psychophysicist) Ernst Weber (1795–1878)—according to Ribot
(1906/1973)—used images to control his heart rate voluntarily.
However, historically, in light of Betts's (1909), Fernald's (1912), and
Thorndike's (1907) demonstrations that individual differences in visual imagery are unrelated to individual differences in visual memory

and visual thinking, the behaviorist J. B. Watson (1913a,b) convinced the psychological community at the time that private experiences—such as mental images—are epiphenomenal having no causal influence on any publicly observable behaviors. It is only recently that studies of individual differences in mental imagery and in functionally related behaviors (including autonomically controlled behaviors) have re-appeared. According to Kunzendorf, the earlier and current findings that subjectively reported vividness of visual imagery are uncorrelated with individual differences in the accuracy of visual memory are consistent with two recent approaches to imaging ability: that imaging ability reflects the participant's mastery of transformational rules used both to generate imaginal sensations from deep structure neural codes and to decode perceptual sensations into deep structure universals and that imaging ability reflects the participant's access to image-specific neurological states with central and peripheral components. Moreover, the latter approach to individual differences in imaging anticipates recent demonstrations that individual differences in mental imagery do correlate with the voluntary control of autonomic processes (e.g., Carroll, Baker, and Preston, 1979; Hirschman and Favaro, 1977; Ikeda and Hirai, 1976; White, 1978). Kunzendorf asserts that before one can understand and explain the apparent relationships between imagery ability and autonomic control, one needs to know whether specific imaging ability or general imaging ability is involved; thus, in testing whether better imagers are better at voluntarily producing differences between, say, hand temperatures, Kunzendorf's experiment initially identifies participants both in terms of their specific ability to image temperature and—in terms of their general ability—to image the sensations of several modalities. Specifically, by way of measuring individual differences in visual, auditory, tactile/muscular, and heat imagery, Kunzendorf administered eight separate imaging ability tests, including Prevalence of Imagery (PI) tests and Vividness of Imagery (VI) questionnaires, to his participants. Subsequently, each participant was asked to image one hand becoming colder and the other hand becoming hotter, and then to image the opposite temperature in each hand. Kunzendorf found that the extent to which imaging-inducing measurable hand-temperature differences in the instructed direction was correlated positively with higher PI imagery scores across all sensory modalities, but uncorrelated with all VI scores. Finally, Kunzendorf discusses possible relationships among imaging ability, hypnosis, and biofeedback training concerning their psychosomatic effects, as well as mechanisms to account for the mind-body relationship between autonomic control and multimodal imaging ability (cf. Barber, 1965, 1978; Danaher and Thoresen, 1972; Kunzendorf, 1980; Maslach, Marshall, and Zimbardo, 1972; Miller, 1978; Rehm, 1973; Roberts, Schuler, Bacon, Zimmerman, and Patterson, 1975; Sheikh, Richardson, and Moleski, 1979; Tuke, 1872; Wagman and Stewart, 1974).

Morris and Hampson (1983) provide a chapter entitled "Individual Differences and Dimensions of the Image" in their work on imagery and consciousness. Two general themes are covered in their chapter: research on individual differences in imagery abilities has concentrated on a limited number of dimensions of the image that may, ultimately, prove to be trivial; and research has paid too little attention to the integration of such work on dimensions into a general model of imagery (the concept of individual variation as a cognitive skill, according to Morris and Hampson, is "theoretically cleaner" if it can be related to some more general aspect of processing, and scores on difference measures may then be seen as parameters that specify the operating characteristics of the particular system under study). In the first two sections of their chapter on individual differences, Morris and Hampson examine the two major dimensions of the image that have been most investigated: vividness and control, as well as discussing some of the main subjective and objective attempts to measure them (including single-subject studies). Among the shortcomings in this research area, Morris and Hampson note that most studies have concentrated largely on the visual modality and, while some imagery tests—such as Sheehan's (1967a,b) Questionnaire Upon Mental Imagery (QMI) test—do assess auditory, gustatory, olfactory, and other types of imagery, there may be an overemphasis on the importance of visual imagery (and, perhaps, one result of this bias has been that only a limited number of image dimensions have been studied). Within this framework the most immediate and compelling dimension of the visual image, that is, vividness, has been assumed to be the primary source of individual variance. Morris and Hampson suggest that the same assumption may be made about imagery in other modalities; also, no attempts, apparently, have been made to study the variable of control in auditory, or other, imagery. According to Morris and Hampson, even within the study of visual imagery there are a number of processes and properties that may vary *between* individuals as well as *within* individuals; for example, before images are experienced, they must be retrieved, constructed, or cued in some way and such variations—regarding individual differences—have not been studied systematically.

Further, in Morris and Hampson's view, after images have been re-trieved, they may be transformed by being rotated, expanded, con-tracted, or otherwise deformed, and to suggest that a single dimension—such as control—can cover all of these situations may be misleading. It is possible that individuals who are superior in rotation of their images may be inferior in their ability to alter image size; moreover, the aspect of control may be a general, rather than a spe-cific, factor and, by examining the performance of participants across a battery of reaction-time experiments, for example, such an issue may be resolved. Morris and Hampson note that images in other "extravisual" sensory modalities may have qualities that are, as yet, undiscovered. For a discussion of such qualities, at least in the area of auditory imagery, see Reisberg (1993), and Handel (1993). One important specific issue in this regard is the relation between verbal imagery and verbal rehearsal (cf. Baddeley and Hitch, 1974). Accord-ing to Morris and Hampson, there is a deeper reason why the inte-gration of individual-differences research and studies of imagery's structure has not been fully achieved: difference testing is a part of the general area of psychometrics—a traditional area noted for its *lack* of theory concerning cognitive processes and structure (cf. Sternberg, 1977, for an extended discussion of the limitations of traditional meth-ods of studying individual differences, the benefits of well-formulated functional models, and the contributions that individual differences and variations may make to an understanding of human cognition).

Sutherland, Harrell, and Isaacs (1987) examine the stability of in-dividual differences (in 120 African-American undergraduate women participants) in image vividness ratings over three time intervals, as well as studying the relationship between individual differences in imag-ery ability and affective responses elicited by image scenes (involving racially noxious materials) depicting realistic life events. Participants were given a battery of psychometric tests, including Sheehan's (1967a) revision of the Betts QMI, and—based on their imagery scores—were categorized either as *vivid* or *nonvivid* imagers, and were given training and experimental sessions. Findings indicate that im-agery vividness ratings exhibited consistency and stability over time, and that vivid imagers—as compared with nonvivid imagers—reported greater affective arousal to the various "racial-discrimination" image scenes that were given. Sutherland et al. suggest that even though a stable characteristic was tapped in their study, the ability to engage in vivid imagery should *not* be viewed as an immutable trait. (See Ahsen [1984a] who indicates that imagery vividness may be increased in nonvivid imagers by training them to voluntarily increase heart rate during imagery; cf. Arabian and Furedy [1983], Broadway [1972], and Morris and Gale [1974].)

Cohen and Saslona (1990) note that while impressive progress has been made in demonstrating the possible roles of visual imagery in a variety of cognitive tasks, the results concerning individual differences in imagery are still disappointing (cf. Griffitts, 1927; Hiscock, 1978); they suggest that part of the problem may lie in the lack of careful distinction between the reported vividness of visual imagery and the frequency of its use. Cohen and Saslona designed a study to demonstrate that the latter dimension of imagery self-report (i.e., frequency of use) is highly predictive of incidental color memory. Their participants completed the "frequency of imagery use" items from a battery of imagery tests, followed by a test for incidental recall of the colors, relative locations, and details of the items. Their findings indicate that the frequency of imagery use was correlated highly with the number of colors correctly recalled, but imagery vividness exhibited near-zero correlations with both imagery frequency and color recall (cf. Christal, 1958) and an inverse correlation with recall of locations (spatial memory). Due to the fact that Cohen and Saslona found that habitual visualizers differ in their recall of visual information (e.g., color memory), they maintain that this result is noteworthy—considering the lack of consistency of results in the literature on self-report measures of imagery differences; moreover, they express confidence that their results are not an artifact of either experimenter-bias or demand characteristics of the situation—to which studies involving self-report imagery measures seem to be especially susceptible (cf. Berger and Gaunitz, 1977; Katz, 1983)—because their study contained a *double-blind technique* (i.e., neither the participants nor the actual administrator of the experimental materials knew the purpose of the study). Finally, Cohen and Saslona attempt to explain their finding of an inverse correlation for spatial memory but not for color memory: one guess is that some tasks require greater discriminations to be made between items (their color recognition test contained fairly easy discriminations, while their spatial memory task contained fairly difficult discriminations; cf. Ernest, 1977; Gur and Hilgard, 1975; Heuer, Fischman, and Reisberg, 1986; Naveh-Benjamin, 1987; Reisberg, Culver, Heuer, and Fischman, 1986; Turner, 1978).

In his book on individual differences in imaging, Richardson (1994) discusses the nature, measurement, origins, consequences, and applications of such differences. (For a review of Richardson's [1994] book, see Kunzendorf [1996–1997] who indicates that Richardson addresses the issues of individual differences in imagery with "scientific integrity and scholarly insight.") Concerning the nature of imagery, Richardson (p. 1) defines a mental image as "a kind of percept-like event usually experienced in the complete absence of any corresponding pattern of sensory stimulation." According to Richardson, the most common manifestation of mental imagery is called *thought imagery* because it may be observed by most people as a spontaneous accompaniment to much of their thinking, that is, recalling past events, planning future actions, and solving problems (cf. Richardson, 1983). Following a review of various definitions of, and approaches to, mental imagery (e.g., Bugelski, 1970; Paivio, 1971; Lang, 1979; Kosslyn, 1987, 1991), Richardson (1994) notes that relatively stable individual differences have been found for three conceptually and methodologically distinct qualities of thought imagery: the typical level of vividness achievable, the typical degree of control that can be exercised, and the average, habitual, or preferred mode for the spontaneous conscious representation of thought content (two other aspects—imager orientation/position, and image location—are identified, also). In this regard, according to Richardson, more studies are needed in the internal/external orientation preferences such as those indicated in the "forehead writing test" in which, when asked to simulate printing one's name on one's forehead, some individuals will print it as if written by someone *outside* oneself (i.e., *external* orientation; cf. Holmes, Roeckelein, and Olmstead, 1968). In his examination of the origins of individual differences in imaging, Richardson reviews the potential influence of intelligence, personality, ethnicity, gender, and family on individual's imaging behavior. Other significant effects include the association of uncontrollable images with neurotic traits and the association of vivid images with familial rewards and the effects of laboratory training on both the subjectively experienced image and its physiological manifestations. In his account of the physiological and cognitive consequences of imaging, Richardson focuses on the degree to which individual differences concerning consequences covary with individual differences in subjectively experienced imagery. For example, concerning the psychophysiological factors, it is observed that vivid imagers' images of emotion, gustation, and heat evoke large increases in heart rate, salivary flow, and local skin temperature, respectively; and, concerning the cognitive factors, it is observed that vivid imagers—when they are not imaging—perceive with greater breadth and speed, and when they are imaging, they experience more perceptual illusions. In addition, vivid imagers seem to show more creative-thinking capacity. Richardson notes that only the activities of learning and remembering are equivocal as to the effects of individual differences in imaging. (He finds that the correlations between imaging and *intentional* learning, for instance, are not reliably greater than zero, and he argues that positive correlations between imaging and *incidental* learning are traceable to vivid imagers' range and speed of perceptual encoding; in other analyses, Richardson asserts that mental imagery is functionally associated with perceptual and motor abilities and *not* with memory ability.) Regarding his chapter on the applied aspects of imagery, Richardson examines three areas or contexts: clinical psychology (especially the issues of anxiety and depression), health psychology (especially health loss, health improvement, and health preservation), and sport psychology (especially the topics of motivation, learning, mental practice, and imaging abilities). Richardson suggests that the possession of vivid imagery and a *belief* in the efficacy of an image-based intervention seem to be important ingredients in achieving a variety of personality and socially desirable changes in the fields of clinical, health, and sport psychology (also, conversely, a strong belief, say, that one has a particular illness—coupled with the vivid imaging of its somatic and behavioral consequences—may increase the likelihood of such consequences actually taking place). Finally, Richardson provides three valuable appendices at the end of his book, containing the following: copies of seven widely used imagery tests/inventories—Absorption Scale (AS); Short Form of Betts's Inventory (QMI); Vividness of Visual Imagery Questionnaire (VVIQ); Abbreviated Imagination Inventory (AII); Verbalizer-Visualizer Questionnaire (VVQ); Visual Elaboration Scale (VES); and Control of Visual Imagery Questionnaire (CVIQ); a listing of intertest correlations among the seven tests; and a cross-cultural study of individual differences by A. Richardson, A. A. Sheikh, R. J. Lueger, and P. N. Tariq ("Developmental Origins of Individual Differences in Ability to Form Voluntary Thought Images: A Cross-Cultural Study"). Note that Richardson (1994) provides a very substantial references section on imagery, containing over 570 references/citations.

Further studies dealing with individual differences vis-à-vis imagery may be found in chapter 5 herein, "Annotated Bibliography of Imagery Studies in Psychology (1960–2003)," especially materials included under the section "Personality/Individual and Gender Differences and Imagery."

## Questionnaires, Scales, and Tests of Imagery

As a result of Galton's (1883/1907) famous "inquiries" involving his breakfast-table questionary, the area in which individual differences were first systematically studied was that of mental imagery. Galton's finding that many scientists and scholars reported complete absence of visual imagery spawned numerous investigations into the functions of imagery in the thinking process. One early study by Bartlett (1927), for example, concluded that imagery tends to appear when blockages occur in trains of thought—but that visual reproductions of experience are more distorted and condensed, generally, than are verbalized memories. Since the early studies, many other researchers assumed that people could be classified into imagery types (e.g., "visiles," "audiles," "motiles," etc.) or, more simply, into "visualizers" and "verbalizers" and, further, that such differences played an important role in the perception and retention of various kinds of information (e.g., visualizers should be taught differently from verbalizers, and would be more superior at different skills). Chowdhury and Vernon (1964) note that apparently there were no reliable methods of establishing an individual's type in this area—where probably mixed types were more common than pure types—and interest in this issue eventually diminished.

Following Galton's (1883/1907) lead, even more systematic investigations of introspective data concerning mental imagery were conducted by other researchers; for example, Betts (1909), Carey (1915), and Burt (1938). Betts (1909) expanded Galton's original questionary, giving a better chance for multimodal images to be reported and asking participants to grade each of their images on a seven-point scale ranging from "perfectly clear" to "no image." Betts's results showed that those individuals who ranked their imagery as high or low in one sensory modality tended to do the same in the other modalities and, also, that there was little or no relation between the use of visual imagery in several intellectual tasks and the person's abilities on those tasks. After studying several of the objective tests of imagery, Carey (1915) concluded that they were of little value, and preferred to employ the reliable, introspective, and subjective reports obtained from schoolchildren; she also noted that there was a tendency for negative correlations to occur between tests of higher mental processes and strength of visual imagery (thus suggesting that imagery may even be *detrimental* to academic studies; cf. Brower, 1947, who found no relation between the reported intensities of images of several modalities and scores on the Otis Intelligence Test). Burt (1938) reports that questionnaire techniques may be made to yield more meaningful results through the application of complex types of analysis such as "between-person correlations" and "factorization."

Chowdhury and Vernon (1964) assert that while a number of objective tests have been proposed for assessing the strength of imagery, there are no cases in which there is convincing evidence for their validity (cf. Carey [1915] and Woodworth [1938] for summaries in this area); they note that as early as 1899, Angell and Thompson observed that respiratory rhythms seem to vary with respect to the type of mental imagery present (also, the rhythm was regular, generally, during voluntary attention, but it became irregular when there was a tendency to verbalize—as when participants were asked to recall nonsense syllables; cf. Golla and Antonovitch, 1929a; Golla, Hutton, and Walter, 1943; Paterson, 1935; Short, 1953; Wittkower, 1934). Chowdhury and Vernon attempted to replicate Short's (1953) study for two reasons: to compare his method of classifying imagery with the traditional questionnaire approach and other alleged objective tests and to explore the potential associations between individual differences in imagery vis-à-vis other abilities/interests (cf. Chowdhury, 1956). Based upon the results of their study, Chowdhury and Vernon were able to identify four distinct imagery categories: visual-passive, auditory-passive, visual-active against verbal, and kinaesthetic. They report that a greater number of relationships have been observed between the introspective imagery categories and measures (self-ratings) of interests than with either the information or ability tests, or with other measures alleged to be diagnostic of imagery; they suggest, also, that more extensive records should be collected in a variety of situations to explore the consistency with which participants employ different modalities and, thus, help resolve the discrepancy between their introspective data and questionnaire data.

Sheehan (1967a) asked 280 undergraduate student volunteer participants to rate images related to 150 selected items from Betts's (1909) original long imagery questionnaire. Results from the ratings were analyzed separately for each sensory modality and five items were selected (from each of the seven tested modalities) that represented relatively pure measures of the imagery component accounting for the major part of the variance of scores in each modality. Sheehan's resultant complete scale then was administered to an independent sample of sixty student participants and ratings among sensory modalities were analyzed again to establish that this shortened form of Betts's questionnaire measured a general ability to image. A cross-validation procedure run on the test showed the predictive value of the new scale to be high (.92); thus, the high correlation between the total imagery scores on Sheehan's new short version and Betts's original, older, long version of the test indicated that the new form predicted participants' overall imagery scores essentially as well as the older, and longer, complete questionnaire. Sheehan's results indicate that his form/scale of the older imagery test is a potentially useful tool for measuring mental imagery in both clinical and experimental situations. In a subsequent study, Sheehan (1967b) attempted to establish the reliability of his short version of Betts's imagery questionnaire (cf. Evans and Kamemoto, 1973), and to assess its suitability for testing with American college students. Based upon the results of his studies, Sheehan (1967a,b) concludes that his data so far show that his short-version imagery test measures a general imaging ability, and is a valid (Sheehan, 1967a) and reliable (Sheehan, 1967b) scale that is suitable for use with individuals in situations other than those in which the test was developed.

Christiansen and Stone (1968) designed a study to compare high and low imagery-evoking nouns as mediators in a mediate-association paradigm of the form "A-B, B-C, A-C," along with the use of an innovative control regarding participants' (240 seventh-grade students) ability to form visual images. In their procedure, Christiansen and Stone gave their participants the Guilford-Zimmerman (1956) Spatial Visualization Test and the Memory-for-Designs Test (Graham and Kendall, 1956). The scores combined to give a total visual imagery score; the 120 participants with the highest visual imagery scores were designated as *visualizers*, and the remaining 120 participants were designated as *nonvisualizers*. Subsequently, participants from these two categories were assigned separately, at random, to one of four conditions (experimental groups one and two, and control groups one and two); thus, because visualizers and nonvisualizers were grouped separately, there were eight final groups. Then, each group received five training trials on two twelve-pair paired-associates training lists (the "A-B, B-C" lists). Concrete nouns (e.g., pig, pencil) were used as "B" terms with one experimental group and one control group, and abstract nouns (e.g., energy, humor) were used as "B" terms with the other experimental and control groups; a recognition task was used to test for mediation. An analysis of variance of the data showed no significant learning-rate differences among experimental participants on either training list. Further, the "A-C" test scores of the experimental and control participants were used as a basis of comparison in determining the roles of visual imagery and level of mediator abstractness in the study. Christiansen and Stone found that learning was more effective in paradigms containing imagery-evoking materials and is similar to other previous results (e.g., Bugelski, 1962a,b; Paivio, 1963; Paivio and Yarmey, 1965). In other results, Christiansen and Stone found that visualizers scored significantly higher on the "A-C" test than nonvisualizers and suggest that an individual's ability to form visual images is a factor in mediated association (cf. Miller, Galanter, and Pribram, 1960, who hypothesized that visual images have the power to mediate the recall of the mediator or associates of the mediator in verbal learning tasks). Christiansen and Stone found that maximum mediation was obtained with visualizers in paradigms in which concrete nouns were used as mediators; conversely, it was found that minimum mediation occurred with abstract mediators in paradigms designed for nonvisualizers.

Based upon the assumption that onomatopoeic words (i.e., the formation of a word—such as *buzz* or *cuckoo*—by imitation of sounds) have the potency to produce original responses both by their meaning and "music," Khatena (1969) developed the Onomatopoeia and Images Test (OIT) as a test of originality for adults using word stimuli that include semantic and sound elements to evoke imaginative responses. (For four measures of visual imagination, see Rimm and Bottrell [1969].) Khatena's item-selection procedure produced twenty words of intermediate difficulty and ten words for each of the final two forms of the OIT. The words on Form 1 are meander, rumble, crackle, buzz, boom, moan, ooze, growl, thud, and jangle; and the words on Form 2 are crank, ouch, murmur, groan, jingle, whisp, flop, zoom, stutter, and fizzy. Following test administration and scoring, Khatena calculated test-retest, and split-half, reliabilities for four different samples of college students. Validity indices were derived from several sources: *concurrent* validity was determined via correlations between scores on the OIT and scores on the Sounds and Images test (Cunnington and Torrance, 1965); *criterion* validity was determined via correlations between originality scores on the OIT and scores on a creative activation/achievement questionnaire, as well as scores from participants' creativity self-ratings. Khatena asserts that his OIT—by containing both intellectual and emotional components—has promise in many diverse situations for the assessment of originality in participants (for a good discussion of the nature and function of the creative imagination and its imagery correlates, including the issue of measurement, see Khatena [1978]).

In a study on the intercorrelations among imagery tasks, Simpson, Vaught, and Ham (1971) obtained intercorrelations for nine measures of performance in an attempt to assess any general ability reflected on those tasks involving visual imagery. The nine measures included the following: paired-associate learning tasks (high versus low imagery words); memory-for-designs (Benton Visual Retention Test); maze performance (accuracy in two haptic-visual form recognition tasks); tracing of irregular shapes/passive; tracing of shapes/active; eidetic imagery task (memory-imagery task); mental map task (relative directions, locations, and distances); picture-completion task (items from the Wechsler Adult Intelligence Scale); and rod-and-frame test. Participants were thirty college students who performed the tasks during two 1-hour sessions; they were told the purpose of the study, encouraged to use visual imagery, and asked to report how the tasks were performed. However, no specific training in using or recognizing images was given to participants. Of the thirty-six correlations possible among pairs of the different tasks, Simpson et al. found twenty-one to be positive; however, only six of the correlations were significant (four were positive and two were negative correlations). Simpson et al. conclude that there is little evidence—based upon the results of their study—of a general visual imagery ability, either in terms of the number of positive correlations or in the number of significant correlations. In one analysis, based on participants' responses to questions asked following each task, Simpson et al. found that the use of visual images was *least* often cited for the paired-associate learning tasks, suggesting to them that much of the contemporary research on imagery may have been conducted on a *less* than optimal task (cf. Paivio, 1969).

Richardson (1977b) describes the development of a research instrument—the Verbalizer-Visualizer Questionnaire (VVQ)—which measures individual differences on a verbalizer-visualizer dimension of cognitive style. Initially, Richardson examines the early research in the area of the verbalizer-visualizer dimension, including experiential data (e.g., Griffitts, 1927; Roe, 1951), physiological data (e.g., Chowdhury and Vernon, 1964; Golla and Antonovitch, 1929; Golla, Hutton, and Walter, 1943; Paterson, 1935; Short, 1953; Wittkower, 1934; cf. Richardson, 1969, for a review of this area), and behavioral data (e.g., Bartlett, 1932), and two lines of contemporary research (cerebral hemispheric specialization [e.g., Nebes, 1974], and lateral eye movements in visual imagery [e.g., Bakan, 1969; Bakan and Strayer, 1973]). Such data converged to give impetus to the construction of a verbalizer-visualizer questionnaire (cf. Richardson, 1977a). Richardson (1977b) extracted fifteen critical items from Paivio's (1971) longer eighty-six-item Ways of Thinking (WOT) questionnaire and this served as the basis for his VVQ instrument; his fifteen-item questionnaire (example items: "I enjoy learning new words"; "I read rather slowly"; "I seldom dream") appears to be unaffected by any social desirability response biases, and it obtained an acceptable level of test-retest reliability. Based upon the results of six validating studies of the VVQ, Richardson asserts that the VVQ provides a stable index of an individual's cognitive style that may be used to predict theoretically relevant events of an experiential, behavioral, and physiological kind, as well as aid in the study of many problems concerned with the sequential and parallel processing of cognitive events. Finally, Richardson suggests that the relation of his VVQ to eye-movement responses has a systematic component, but the conditions that control this component require study in their own domain (cf. Bakan, 1971; Day, 1964; Ehrlichman, Weiner, and Baker, 1974; Etaugh, 1972).

White, Sheehan, and Ashton (1977) provide an excellent survey of self-report measures concerning individual differences in imagery ability; they outline the history of such measures and evaluate the reliability, validity, and other statistical characteristics of existing psychometric studies of self-report measures. Among the measures that White et al. discuss are the following: Galton's (1883/1907) breakfast-table questionary; Betts's (1909) QMI—the "most widely-used and influential measure of imagery vividness"; Marks's (1973) VVIQ; Singer's (Singer and Antrobus, 1970) Imaginal Process Inventory (IPI); Paivio's (1971) Individual Differences Questionnaire (IDQ); Richardson's (1977b) VVQ; Gordon's (1949) GTVIC; Sheehan's (1967a,b) QMI; Lane's (1974) Questionnaire on Imagery Control (QIC); and Cautela's (Cautela and Tondo, 1971) Imagery Survey Schedule (ISS). White et al. note that in spite of many decades of work the range of tests available to assess imagery types, imagery vividness, and imagery control is not extensive, and whether this reflects an assumed faith in the validity of the instruments that have been developed or a lack of commitment to the precise measurement of individual differences is difficult to assess. Moreover, according to White et al., when the aspect of function can be studied successfully with only a passing mention of individual differences in ability, the field of imagery must still be considered as surveyed incompletely; even those researchers who have been actively interested in such differences have devised no radically new tests. For example, Sheehan's (1967a,b) QMI was derived from the original test constructed by Betts (1909) and Marks's VVIQ constitutes a further development by simply using more of the same type of items.

Following their examination of the psychometric properties (i.e., reliability and validity) of imagery measures, White et al. (1977) conclude that factor analytic studies of test structure have yielded diverse factor patterns depending on the method of analysis adopted, item content, and questionnaire format; nevertheless, according to White et al., results have been encouraging in the respect that interpretable patterns have generally been found, and some of these may be related to known physiological patterns of sensory system functioning (however, the possibility of contamination of results by participants' response sets should be considered as posing a potential threat—in particular where experimenters wish to show the presence of a general imaging-ability factor). White et al. note, also, that several studies have been conducted that relate scores from different imagery tests (mainly Betts's QMI and Gordon's GTVIC—in which both significant and nonsignificant correlational-based evidence has been reported; however, factor analytic evidence shows that both of these particular tests load on a common factor). White et al. suggest that one way of viewing such diverse evidence (as on the QMI and GTVIC) is to consider that these tests tap into different aspects of imaginal ability (i.e., control and vividness) and these may represent different facets of the same imaginal process (i.e., image evocation). In an examination of the relationship between self-report imagery measures and the variable of social desirability response-set effects (including social setting, and participant's expectancies), White et al. conclude that participants' expectancies about response do affect test scores, at least to some extent.

In other analyses, White et al. (1977, pp. 159–62) examine sex/gender and age differences ("the reason why women invariably report more vivid imagery than men has never been explained"; and "observed age differences in vividness of evoked images—with increases in imagery associated with age increases—has no extant explanation for such a change"); hypnotizability (cf. Hilgard, 1981, p. 15); physiological correlates; and self-control/biofeedback. Among the conclusions from their survey of self-report measures, White et al. make the following points: Betts's QMI has promoted a substantial body of imagery research (cf. Woodworth's, 1910, review of Betts's 1909 work). The data from most of the imagery scales continue to emphasize the *function* of imagery rather than its *nature* (cf. Neisser, 1972a,b). There is a surprising degree of reliability for self-report tests of imagery both in terms of the internal consistency of the scales and their test-retest stability over time, but the criterion of construct validity has yet to be established. The evidence to date firmly points to the predictive utility of the test scales—each of them appears to be associated meaningfully with specific correlates or selected performance functions. There is no direct way of knowing factually that the inventories reviewed here measure imagery rather than some other process that is related to function, and there are several general properties of self-report tests of imagery functioning that pose considerable problems for establishing their validity as measuring instruments (e.g., "Do the stimulus items on the scales mean the same thing to every participant?" "Do the scales contain 'demand characteristics' that may be artifacts that contaminate the tests' results?") See Slee's 1976 VES inventory), which attempts to check on the intended *meaning* of the tests' items for participants. White et al. provide a valuable references section on imagery, containing over 160 bibliographic items/citations.

Sheehan, McConkey, and Law (1978) discuss imagery facilitation and performance on Wilson and Barber's (1976) Creative Imagination Scale (CIS) (cf. Barber and Wilson, 1979). Sheehan et al. (1978) administered the CIS to 303 participants in tape-recorded format under waking instructions; the instructions were intended to actively elicit participants' ability to think with, and imagine along with, the suggestions that were given. The cognitive variables chosen for correlational analyses were absorption, imagery vividness, and visual imagery/control. An important argument in the imagery literature (e.g., White et al., 1977) is whether scales of imagery measure a general ability to image, or a number of different dimensions/factors. Thus, Sheehan et al. focused on the question of whether the CIS measures a single ability/cognitive dimension. Among the analyses performed on the collected data, Sheehan et al. employed the following procedures: normative analysis, structural analysis, and correlational analyses (across both sexes/genders, the four measures that were used—CIS, TAS, QMI, GTVIC—were interrelated appreciably and seemed to tap into cognitively similar components of test performance). Sheehan et al. conclude that the CIS reliably focuses on participants' thinking and imagining capacities, and the scale's unidimensional structure makes it a useful instrument for accessing participants' internal processing as it relates to the factor of suggestibility. Finally, Sheehan et al. suggest that using a variety of techniques, rather than a single instrument, may promote greater physiological and behavioral control, and a number of them may clearly be used in conjunction with the CIS as a meaningful imagery-measuring device.

In his excellent chapter on individual differences, Richardson (1980) discusses various introspective questionnaires, imagery-control tests, mediators, spatial ability tests, and coding-preference/coding-ability distinctions. Richardson (pp. 118–30) provides critical reviews of the foremost imagery tests, including Betts's QMI, Sheehan's short version QMI, Marks's VVIQ, Gordon's TVIC, Singer's IPI, and Cautela's ISS. He also examines the critical issues inherent in imagery testing such as reliability and predictive construct validity of the tests, participants' expectations (including specific experimental and task conditions, demand characteristics of the tasks, participants' readings, possible rumors, prior attitudes toward imagery in one's particular subculture, and other social desirability factors), experimenter effects, intercorrelations among the tests, and various correlates of imagery tests. In his concluding remarks, Richardson observes that contemporary research on individual differences in mental imagery employs two approaches: the subjective approach (involving participants' introspective reports concerning their mental images and the use which they make of them) and the objective approach (relies on measures of the participants' performance on tasks requiring the use of mental imagery). While Richardson maintains that a dual-coding approach may be appropriate for certain contexts (e.g., pictorial memory), he concludes that to date there is inadequate empirical support for the dual-coding theory (certain findings present "grave difficulties" for that position), and, rather, propositional theories seem to offer a more promising means of developing future studies in the areas of memory processes, organization, and function.

In asking his question "What is wrong with imagery questionnaires?" Kaufmann (1981) notes that with imagery questionnaires, the participants are asked, typically, to evoke an image of a specified object and then to rate the vividness of their image on a graded scale; subsequently, scores are compared with performance on other tasks supposed to involve imagery. Following his review of early studies showing that imagery as measured by the questionnaire approach and related to other factors (e.g., scholastic aptitude) appears to be devoid of any functional significance, Kaufmann suggests that an alternative interpretation is that the questionnaire technique simply "does not hit its aim" and that low or zero correlations with other variables may be the consequence of methodological difficulties inherent in the rating scale approach. Among the flaws in the imagery questionnaire technique, according to Kaufmann, is that imagery constitutes a very private world and most people probably have little training in comparing their imagery experiences as to vividness, coloring, and so on; also, it is likely that the same language is used by different individuals to refer to highly varying imagery experiences and, as well, it is reasonable to argue that the task of rating imagery experiences on a seven-point scale must be a very difficult one (i.e., an objective frame of reference is lacking in a task that is highly ambiguous). Kaufmann maintains that it is necessary to put the issue to a critical test by comparing the effect of a between- and within-subjects analysis of the *same* ratings (cf. Kaufmann, 1976); he asserts, also, that the rating scale approach to the study of imagery seems to be infected by a serious methodological flaw that may explain the fact that ambiguous and, most often, negative results are found when the individual differences approach is used to study imagery and its relation to other variables. On the positive side, Kaufmann (1981) suggests that it is reasonable to employ objective performance tests as a way of assessing individual differences in imaging ability (cf. Berger and Gaunitz, 1977; Comstock, 1921; Di Vesta and Sunshine, 1974; Fox, 1914; Hargreaves and Bolton, 1972; Juhasz, 1972, 1977; Kaufmann, 1980; Kessel, 1972; Kieras, 1978; Marks, 1972; McKelvie and Demers, 1979; McKelvie and Rohrberg, 1978; McKelvie and Gingras, 1974; Neisser, 1970; Shaver, Pierson, and Lang, 1975; Sheehan and Neisser, 1969; Switras, 1978). For more information on Kaufmann's article, see the section in chapter 5 herein entitled, "Measurement and Tests of Imagery."

Edwards and Wilkins (1981) report on two studies concerning the correlative properties of Richardson's (1977b) VVQ. In one study, they asked 142 participants to complete the VVQ, the Marlowe-Crowne Social Desirability Scale (M-CSDS; Crowne and Marlowe, 1960), two forms of Gordon's (1949) GTVIC, Sheehan (1967a) QMI, the Space Test (ST) of the Chicago Tests of Primary Mental Abilities (Thurstone and Thurstone, 1941), and the Space Relations Test (SRT) of the Differential Aptitude Tests (Bennett, Seashore, and Wesman, 1974). The scores on the tests were entered in a regressive equation to evaluate their contribution to the VVQ score (the regression component of the total variance was found here to be significant; most of the variance was due to the subjective imagery scales). In the second study, Edwards and Wilkins had 127 participants complete the VVQ, the M-CSDS, the GTVIC, the QMI, and the SRT and Verbal Reasoning Test (VRT) of the Differential Aptitude Tests (Bennett et al., 1977); these scores were analyzed in a 2 × 3 analysis of variance using participant's sex/gender and Verbalizer-Visualizer-Mixed cognitive style as grouping variables (no main effects or interactions involving cognitive style were found). Edwards and Wilkins (1981) express some doubts about the construct validity of the VVQ and its failure to discriminate between performances on the other scales in terms of Paivio's (1971) conceptualization of imagery and verbal processes as independent and parallel in function (cf. Forisha, 1975). In their second study, they found that verbalizers and visualizers—as defined by the VVQ—did not differ significantly from the mixed group nor from each other on self-reports of imagery or on the aptitude tests. Edwards and Wilkins suggest that a dichotomous scale may be inappropriate for measuring the two processing modes (imagery and verbal), and conclude that the construct validity of the VVQ remains to be shown (cf. Antonietti and Giorgetti, 1996–1997; McGrath, O'Malley, Dura, and Beaulieu, 1989).

In their chapter on individual differences, Morris and Hampson (1983, pp. 92–99) discuss the dimensions of the image and their measurement. They note the following three implicit assumptions in the construct of imagery: images vary on the dimension of vividness/brightness, individuals can assess (even though in a subjective manner) the vividness dimension, and persons possessing more vivid imagery have better imagery. Following their review of earlier work on imagery measurement, Morris and Hampson offer criticisms of subjective measures of imagery, examine objective and performance measures, discuss intercorrelations between tests, and indicate possible imagery-processing preferences. Among their observations are the following points (cf. Ernest, 1977; Paivio, 1971):

- Absolute standards are lacking for different participants to use in relating to specific test items (e.g., how does a particular individual—as compared with the experimenter's frame of reference—know at what level of vividness to rate his/her image?).
- Without having some theoretical rationale for assuming that imagery abilities remain relatively constant over time, it is hard to establish test-retest reliability.

- Subjective measures may be criticized most severely on the grounds of a lack of validity (predictive and construct validity are more difficult to achieve than simple "face" validity).
- It is not at all clear, typically, as to what *imagery* abilities are being assessed.
- The general finding seems to be that whereas self-ratings and spatial/objective measures both correlate well among themselves (cf. Morris and Gale, 1974), self-ratings and spatial measures are often poorly intercorrelated.
- There are two ways to interpret correlations on two measures of imagery—the two tests may be different ways of measuring the *same* imagery ability, or the two tests happen to measure *different* imagery abilities but that participants who have a certain level of one ability tend, on the average, to have a similar level of the other ability.
- The self-reports of vividness—if reliable—tap aspects of the image as "representation," whereas measures such as spatial tests are mainly tapping into "control" processes.
- The current so-called "visualizer-verbalizer" distinction weakly resembles the older, much discredited, version of the "typological" approach (cf. the IDQ of Paivio, 1971; Sullivan and Macklin, 1986).

Additionally, Morris and Hampson (pp. 99–113) examine the issues of correlates of vividness and control scores (including participant variables, cognitive correlates, arousal and behavior, and manipulation of images), and single-subject/participant studies (cf. Luria, 1968).

In an instructive debate in the literature on visual imagery, P. J. Chara Jr., and D. F. Marks provide differing viewpoints, specifically, on the issue of the construct validity of Marks's (1973) VVIQ. Initially, Marks (1988) attacked Chara's critique of the construct validity of the VVIQ (in two recent studies by the latter [Chara and Verplanck, 1986; Chara and Hamm, 1988]), contending that the validity of the VVIQ has been established substantially over a fifteen-year period in dozens of studies (inferring that Chara's research is an isolated aberration) and that Chara's research is theoretically and methodologically flawed. Chara (1989) addresses these objections and examines, further, the issue of the construct validity of the VVIQ; he asserts—contrary to Marks's statement—that the validity of the VVIQ has not been established in the literature. For studies in which the VVIQ's validity has been questioned (on both theoretical and methodological grounds), see Berger and Gaunitz (1977, 1979); Kaufmann (1981, 1983); Kerr and Neisser (1983); McKelvie and Rohrberg (1978); J.T.E. Richardson (1978, 1979, 1980, p. 141). Furthermore, according to Chara (1989), not all of the ten studies presented by Marks provide support for VVIQ's validity (cf. Gur and Hilgard, 1975). Chara (1989, p. 160) reviews his notion of construct validity (i.e., it "requires a logical and empirical analysis of the theoretical foundation of the questionnaire; hypotheses are drawn from this foundation, research conducted, and then a determination is made as to whether the theoretical foundation can account for the data"), and then asserts that Marks misses the point when he questions the validity and reliability of the recall measures used by Chara and Verplanck (1986). Chara claims that the measures Marks refers to were performance tasks developed on the basis of the hypothetico-deductive reasoning needed to assess the questionnaire's construct validity. Chara (1989) asserts that Marks confuses approaches used in assessing *construct* validity with those needed to assess *criterion-related* validity. Chara concludes, again, that the construct validity of Marks's (1973) VVIQ has not been empirically established. Note that Chara and Hamm (1989) also studied the VVIQ via a series of visual memory tasks where participants were shown a picture after completing the VVIQ—their ability to recall that picture was then probed through a free-recall procedure, a drawing task, two spatial-recall tasks, and a multiple-choice questionnaire. Chara and Hamm (1989) found that scores on the VVIQ were unrelated statistically to performance on any of the memory tasks, thereby demonstrating, also, a lack of support for VVIQ's construct validity as a measure of visual memory imagery.

In a rejoinder to Chara (1989), Marks (1989b) refers to his extensive bibliography of approximately 150 items related to the VVIQ (Marks, 1989a). The bibliography includes some fifty reports in which VVIQ scores have been employed as a means for manipulating vividness of visual imagery as an independent experimental variable and fifty, or so, other research reports in which VVIQ score has been used as a dependent variable or correlated with other variables of performance, psychophysiology, or self-reported experience. Marks (1989b) claims that it is hazardous to attempt an assessment of the construct validity of an instrument by examining only a small sample of the total literature as Chara (1989), Chara and Hamm (1989), and Kaufmann (1981) attempted to do. Marks asserts that only by looking at the research findings in totality (cf. Marks, 1989a) may a balanced assessment of VVIQ's construct validity be obtained. Further, Marks (1989) suggests that Chara (1989) erroneously construed *construct* validity as independent of *criterion-related* validity (cf. Anastasi, 1988, pp. 153, 163). According to Marks, this error is compounded by Chara and Verplanck's (1986) assumption that the VVIQ assesses purely memory imagery (further problems arise in Chara's selective reporting of the relevant literature—he used only six of approximately one hundred other available studies that have used VVIQ scores as an independent or dependent variable). Marks notes—in disagreement with Chara's interpretation—that Kerr and Neisser's (1983) discussion of the perceptual characteristics of imagery actually does have relevance to the imagery construct embodied in the VVIQ. For another, different and interesting point-counterpoint exchange in the imagery literature concerning, in particular, the fundamental relationship between imagery and perceptual experience—a relationship that tends to be overlooked when imagery is equated purely with memory functioning (as Marks attributes to Chara's position), see the following materials (chronologically arranged): Neisser and Kerr (1973); Keenan and Moore (1979); Keenan (1983); Kerr and Neisser (1983).

Essentially, Marks (1989b) maintains that there is much more to his VVIQ than simply memory; examination of the VVIQ items, and experience with its use, indicates that the VVIQ taps into areas of experience for which extramemory factors—such as imagination, creativity, and absorption—play an influential role. Moreover, detailed exploratory work suggests the importance of content, context, dynamics, sequence, and structure in providing image experience in varying degrees of vividness and unvividness (cf. Ahsen, 1985, 1986; Hilgard, Marks, and Sheehan, 1987; Yarmey, 1975). Marks suggests that variations occur (as one would expect) in vividness ratings when the VVIQ scale is administered in different contexts, but this does not imply problems with validity (as claimed by Chara, 1989), but merely participants' sensitivity to surrounding conditions—surely a positive feature. Finally, Marks (1989b) asserts that all of the relevant imagery research on the issue must be considered together to enable one to make a detailed examination of the consistencies and interrelationships in behavioral measures, psychophysical parameters, and VVIQ scores. The totality of research utilizing the VVIQ—together with Chara and Verplanck's (1986) and Chara and Hamm's (1988) studies—provide evidence concerning VVIQ's construct validity. Marks (pp. 462–63) states that Chara's (1989) contribution has "helped to clarify some of the more fundamental problems that have so often been compounded and confused in the history of imagery research—in spite of the present controversy on the issue, there are undoubtedly many re-search problems which the VVIQ, and related instruments, may be expected to help solve."

Finally, regarding the Marks-Chara debate on the construct valid-ity of the VVIQ, McKelvie (1990) attempts to clarify the opposing positions and argues that—although some of Chara's (1989) logical criticisms merit attention—Chara's empirical work is methodologically unsound. On the other hand, McKelvie suggests, also, that Marks (1988, 1989b) needs to specify more clearly his concept of imagery vividness in order that critical experimental predictions may be made. McKelvie reviews the notions of *construct* validity (i.e., it refers to the extent that a test measures a postulated attribute and is particularly relevant when there is no ready criterion available for the test to pre-dict) and *criterion-related* validity (i.e., it requires evidence that the test in question correlates adequately with an accepted criterion, whereas construct validity is based on evidence from a variety of sources, including those pertinent to other kinds of validity; cf. Anastasia, 1988), and observes that judgments about construct validity emerge out of the hypothetico-deductive method of theorizing in which one, essentially, makes a *decision* and not a *conclusion* about construct validity (cf. Cronbach and Meehl, 1955; Tukey, 1970). McKelvie suggests that because there is no obvious single criterion ready for the VVIQ to predict, *both* Chara and Marks are correct to focus on the notion of the construct validity of the test (for Chara, the VVIQ is designed to measure the vividness of *memory* imagery, whereas Marks conceives of imagery as a quasi-perceptual experience that may or may not involve memory; cf. McKelvie, 1986). Follow-ing his summary of, and commentary on, both Chara's and Marks's arguments in detail, McKelvie (1990) concludes that the exchange in the literature between Chara and Marks has been "spirited," with merit on both sides. However, on the whole—given the methodological doubts about much of Chara's work—McKelvie agrees with Marks that Chara's data should *not* seriously affect one's overall assessment of the construct validity of the VVIQ on the basis of current evidence.

Ahsen (1993a) provides a commentary on imagery tests, in gen-eral, and discusses, in particular, the VVIQ, QMI, GTVIC, AA-VVIQ, AA-QMI, AA-TVIC (the AA prefixes in these latter three tests indi-cate Ahsen's revisions of these previously developed tests), AQUIP, and EPT tests of imagery in the light of his notion of *parental filters* (i.e., evoking a parental figure, mother and/or father, in the activity of imagining or creating internal images of mother/father within the context of imaging, including dream analysis; cf. Ahsen, 1972, 1992). Ahsen (1993a) examines, also, imagery testing against the background of critiques offered by the originators of these imagery tests and highlights the complexities of the issues involved in this topic area.

The *Journal of Mental Imagery* (1993, *17 [1,2]*) published a series of articles on the topic imagery paradigms (see the earlier subsection in this chapter titled "Theory, Tactics, and Strategy in Mental Imagery Measurement" for more information on this issue), which includes material on imagery tests and testing. Among these articles are the following: Sussman (1993), Marks (1993), McKelvie (1993), and Molteno (1993). This issue of the journal also provides appendixes containing copies of the following imagery tests: VVIQ, QMI, GTVIC, AA-VVIQ, AA-QMI, AA-TVIC, and AQUIP. Sussman (1993) reports on her administration of Ahsen's Adapted Vividness of Visual Imagery Questionnaire (AA-VVIQ) (cf. Ahsen, 1990, 1991) to two sample student groups containing a total of seventy-seven participants; the results of her study are compared with Ahsen's results—also using the AA-VVIQ—from studies conducted in Pakistan and the United States with special regard to the role of the mother/father filters on imagery vividness. Sussman (1993) found that the use of the father filter generally suppresses—while the mother filter enhances—imagery vividness. This finding confirms Ahsen's (1990, 1991) results that male dominance tends to suppress imagery functions and their associated potentials in consciousness, whereas the female influence tends to encourage access to these potentials. Sussman's results also indicate that there may be other gender, racial, and cultural differences in imagery testing performance and that filters focusing on such gender/radical/cultural factors may be productive for future imagery research.

Marks (1993) reanalyzes data reported by Ahsen (1990) regarding the AA-VVIQ, and using the traditional method of correlational analysis, Marks's findings confirm the high test-retest reliability of the VVIQ (counter to Ahsen's findings, based on an equivalence factor) and suggests that although VVIQ may be used to study either states of consciousness or mental contents, its dominant function is to provide a trait-measure of individual differences in imagery vividness. Marks asserts that Ahsen's conclusions were based on an ad hoc method of analysis that assumed that high test-retest reliability requires a high proportion of identical scores (equivalence) for individual items; however, according to Marks, equivalence cannot be equated with test-retest correlation as Ahsen's analysis assumed. Marks recommends that further research be conducted on the image-dimming effect to determine whether consistent effects may be obtained in this context with the VVIQ approach.

McKelvie (1993) conducted three studies to investigate the hypothesis that Ahsen's filter instruction (i.e., to keep father or mother in mind during imaging) would affect VVIQ's reliability and mean scores. In his first study, McKelvie reanalyzed Ahsen's (1990, 1991) data to test whether imagery ratings were less vivid under the father filter than under the mother filter (at least for women participants); however, correlations between parental filters were in accord with a reliability standard of .75. In his second study, McKelvie collected new data that indicated a replication of the effect of filters on mean scores, but gave a higher estimate of filter reliability (and values of delayed test-retest for each filter) that were similar to previous estimates for the VVIQ. In his third study, McKelvie found that although the correlations with the GTVIC for both the original and alternate forms of the VVIQ were similar, they were not significant and were lower than previous estimates. Based upon the results of his three studies, McKelvie concluded that the use of various statistical techniques to develop distinctions within the imagery dynamics and the effect of filters on mean scores should be investigated further, but that imaging a parent (mother/father filter) on the VVIQ does not jeopardize its use as a research instrument, that is, "the effects of parental filter demonstrated here do not constitute a serious practical problem for the researcher" (p. 359).

Molteno (1993) describes an attempt to replicate some of Ahsen's (1972) observations and to evaluate some alternate explanations for the findings. Participants were first-year psychology students who completed a variety of group-administered questionnaires, including an item from Ahsen's (1972) Eidetic Parents Test (EPT) and the Beating Heart experiment. On the basis of their responses to the group test, forty-five participants were selected for the second study—which consisted of an individually administered modified form of the EPT. In the second study, dependent variables included a measure of psychopathology; a measure of attitudes to mother, father, and self before and after the EPT; and measures of heart rate taken over the course of test administration. Moreover, participants were grouped according to gender, imagery ability as measured by the VVIQ, perceived position of father, and ease with which the parental images could be reversed. Molteno found that Ahsen's (1993a) observation of a bias toward the father-on-the-left position imagery was confirmed in the individual-, but not in the group-testing situation; also, Ahsen's view—that certain parental configurations in the participant's response to EPT may be associated with increased psychopathology—was supported by her findings. Molteno concludes that her studies indicate a tendency for the father-right position to be associated with an increased incidence of psychopathology, with more negative evaluations of the parents (especially the father), and ratings of the father as much more or less dominant (potent) than the mother. These findings are all consistent with (and, thus, support) Ahsen's view that rejection of the father as being too strong or too weak (as a result of interparental conflict) may be of fundamental importance in the development of psychopathology; on the other hand, it is emphasized that the observed effects were often small and their significance was based only on correlational analyses, and their utility in the individual case has yet to be demonstrated under carefully controlled conditions. In the final analysis, according to Molteno, Ahsen's eidetic therapy approach (involving imagery with parental-figure filters), in particular, is a procedure worthy of serious consideration and deserves more detailed and comprehensive assessment.

In his book on individual differences in imaging, Richardson (1994) includes an entire chapter on the measurement of imaging differences (pp. 13–43); in that chapter, he notes that ever since modern measures of imagery first began to appear in the 1960s, a number of criticisms have been leveled at them regarding their validity (cf. Berger and Gaunitz, 1977; Chara and Verplanck, 1986; Kaufmann, 1981, 1983; J.T.E. Richardson, 1980, 1988); the strongest criticisms have been made in relation to vividness measures that employ rating scales. Richardson (1994) maintains that many of the criticisms are based on misunderstandings regarding the nature of imagery vividness and its influence on the performance of different tasks (i.e., if inappropriate tasks are chosen, any observed individual differences in imaging abilities will be irrelevant to the outcome, and prediction failures cannot be used as a basis for criticism). Initially, Richardson examines some general problems of measurement (e.g., all measurement is subject to error, and such error may be reduced by holding other extraneous variables constant; in psychological testing, in general, variables—such as innate general ability, effects of the immediate environment, culture, training, fatigue, will/interest/motivation, experimental error, and specific abilities—are all potential sources of variation that require attention and control). In the context of imagery measurement, in particular, control of variables—such as rapport between participant and experimenter, compliance with instructions, elimination of "faking good or bad behaviors," understanding the distinction between *vividness of knowing* versus *vividness of imaging*, periodic checks to ensure that ratings of imagery vividness are modality-specific if that is a task requirement, and checks to control overreliance on, and persistent use of, a single rating category by participants—is necessary for optimum and valid results. In other cases involving imagery measurement, imagery ratings should be taken when participants are relatively relaxed because individual differences in mood, or other affective states, may produce unwanted variations in imagery vividness ratings (cf. Ahsen, 1990, who found that holding one's mother in mind while completing an imagery questionnaire resulted in more vivid ratings than when holding one's father in mind). Richardson notes that it may be possible to control some of these problems by using imaging measures that do not require vividness ratings; for instance, the VVQ (a measure of preferences) contains sets of statements followed by appropriate response categories in which the participant chooses a response that is dependent on long-term self-knowledge built up over a lifetime—much like information tapped by the traditional personality inventories.

In his discussion of voluntary imaging abilities, Richardson (1994, pp. 16–32) examines the properties of various types of imagery measures and their research underpinnings, including the following: *general* measures of *vividness* (i.e., the QMI, the Abbreviated Imagination Inventory, and the Absorption Scale); *general* measures of *controllability* (i.e., the Controllability of Imagery Questionnaire, the Questionnaire on Mental Imagery Control, and the Survey of Mental Imagery); a *specific* measure of *vividness* (i.e., the VVIQ); and a *specific* measure of *controllability* (i.e., the Controllability of Visual Imagery Questionnaire). In his section on spontaneous imaging preferences, Richardson (pp. 32–41) examines the properties of, and research with, the following tests: Individual Difference Questionnaire (IDQ), Verbal-Imagery Code Test (VICT), Verbal-Imagery Learning Style Test (VILST), Verbalizer-Visualizer Questionnaire (VVQ), Prevalence of Visual Imagery Test (PVIT), Associative Experience Test (AET), and the Visual Elaboration Scale (VES). Following his review and examination of these imagery tests, Richardson draws the following conclusions (among others): it is desirable to intercorrelate scores from the available imagery tests and then to factor-analyze the resulting matrix (in order to answer the issue of the postulation of conceptually distinct imaging characteristics); it is assumed that after extracting the significant factors and rotating them to an appropriate criterion, conceptually similar tests should load with the same factor (i.e., convergent validity is assessed); and conceptually different tests should load on other factors (i.e., discriminant validity is assessed).

Ideally, according to Richardson (1994), at least three tests should be available for the measurement of each imaging characteristic, and the correlation of each with each may be known (presently, such information is available on four tests of vividness, on only one test of controllability, and on two tests of preference/style). Richardson asserts that confirmation of a resultant factor structure may be made when information becomes available on at least two more tests for the measurement of both preference and controllability (involving both theoretically relevant objective measures and self-report measures). Furthermore, Richardson notes that the QMI measure of general vividness and the VVIQ measure of specific vividness in the visual modality provide the most impressive data across tests regarding the criterion of reliability; these two tests, also, are among the most frequently used for the measurement of vividness and, moreover, they have impressive data regarding the criterion of construct validity. Finally, Richardson suggests that future research be conducted to overcome the deficiencies in, and insufficient evidence on, the reliability of the majority of the preference and controllability imagery tests.

The *Journal of Mental Imagery* (1995, *19 [3,4]*) contains a target article by S. J. McKelvie (1995) giving a critical quantitative review of the VVIQ as a psychometric test of individual differences in visual imagery vividness, followed by a number of "open peer commentaries," and finishing with McKelvie's responses to the commentaries. Initially, McKelvie assesses the construct validity of Marks's (1973) VVIQ on the basis of a quantitative review of content validity, reliability, and criterion-related validity; Marks's examination revealed a number of flaws in the areas of test instructions, items, rating scale, and distribution of scores that challenges the content validity of the VVIQ. On the other hand, McKelvie found that there was acceptable evidence concerning participants' reported vividness ratings and social desirability factors where the latter often pose contamination problems for data results, analysis, and interpretation. Moreover, reliability was acceptable for the test's internal consistency, barely acceptable for its test-retest condition, and unacceptable for both immediate and delayed alternate-form conditions. McKelvie discovered that the effects of social desirability and context indicate, also, that the factor of vividness resembles a typical performance trait; in another analysis, for 263 individual estimates across seventy-one criterion tasks, the validity of the VVIQ was deemed to be acceptable (however, the correlations varied from high through low, respectively, for self-report, cognitive/perceptual, and memory tasks—with the last of these only marginally acceptable). Based upon the results of his extensive examinations, review, and analysis of the VVIQ, McKelvie concludes that the evidence, overall, is favorable to the construct validity of the VVIQ, but that it might be improved further if certain features of the test are altered and that will make the VVIQ a more valuable testing tool as both an independent and dependent variable in future imagery research. McKelvie provides a generous references section at the end of his article, consisting of over 250 references/citations from the imagery research literature.

In response to McKelvie's (1995) target article (100-plus pages) on the VVIQ, the following individuals (with their commentary titles in parentheses) contributed material: A. Ahsen ("Self-Report Questionnaires: New Directions for Imagery Research"); F. S. Bellezza ("Factors That Affect Vividness Ratings"); A. Campos ("Twenty-Two Years of the VVIQ"); C. Cornoldi ("Imagery and Meta-Imagery in the VVIQ"); M. Denis ("Vividness of Visual Imagery and the Evaluation of Its Effects on Cognitive Performance"); E. R. Hilgard ("Commentary on McKelvie's 'The VVIQ as a Psychometric Test of Individual Differences in Visual Imagery Vividness'" [note that Hilgard here, p. 139, states that "[w]hile this review is thorough . . . its approach places a heavy burden on the reader, and I am afraid that not many readers will be able to follow the exposition in detail"]); S. Hishitani ("Toward a Deeper Understanding of Vividness: Some Points Inspired from McKelvie's Article"); A. N. Katz ("What We Need Is a Good Theory of Imagery Vividness"); G. Kaufmann ("Stalking the Elusive Image"); R. G. Kunzendorf ("VVIQ Construct Validity: Centrally Excited Sensations Versus Analog Representations and Memory Images"); D. F. Marks ("New Directions for Mental Imagery Research"); D. G. Pearson ("The VVIQ and Cognitive Models of Imagery: Future Directions for Research"); A. Richardson ("Guidelines for Research with the VVIQ"); J.T.E. Richardson ("Gender Differences in the Vividness of Visual Imagery Questionnaire: A Meta-Analysis"); P. W. Sheehan ("The VVIQ—Directions Emerging"); J. A. Slee ("Vividness is in the Mind—But Not Necessarily the Mind's Eye—of the Cognizer"); and B. Wallace ("The VVIQ—A Good But Dynamic Measure of Imaging Ability"). Finally, in a fifty-page follow-up response to the "open peer commentaries," McKelvie (1995) makes the following points ("The VVIQ and Beyond: Vividness and Its Measurement"), among others: identification is made of the elements of vividness—where the visual experience is similar to perceptual experience—in terms of *clarity* (brightness and sharpness) and *liveliness*, as well as indicating the importance of the factor of *dynamics*; while the VVIQ has the advantages and merits of speed of administration and ease of scoring, the major issue still remains: To what extent is the VVIQ a valid measure of vividness of visual imagery? Stronger effects concerning the validity of the VVIQ might emerge for VVIQ-task relationships if studies are edited for the quality of their controls—this would be particularly useful with memory-focused studies where the validity coefficients are weakest and where there has been some controversy; the newly revised VVIQ—containing new items, new instructions, and a new (McKelvie, 1995, pp. 251–52) rating scale—offers a more promising test for future validity studies; and an appeal is made for more studies to be conducted on the effects of vividness as a manipulated experimental variable (in conjunction with, and supplemented by, the VVIQ) and for new self-report tests of specific theory-based imagery processes that have functional value.

For further discussion of questionnaires, scales, and tests of imagery, see the section "Measurement and Tests of Imagery" in chapter 5 herein.

### Other Measures and Correlates of Imagery

In this section, I briefly discuss and examine several ancillary measures and correlates of mental imagery, including such approaches as electroencephalographic (EEG), eye-movement, and pupillary-response changes, and various other physiological measurements used in conjunction with imagery research.

Marjerrison and Keogh (1967) employed a perceptual deprivation method via a modified ganzfeld technique to study alpha frequencies measured from occipital EEGs (cf. Zubek and Welch, 1963; Zubek, Welch, and Saunders, 1963) in schizophrenic patients (cf. Reitman and

Cleveland, 1964, who demonstrated an increased body-image organization in schizophrenics and a contrasting disintegration of body-
image functions in a comparison group of nonpsychotic patients, also,
via a perceptual deprivation technique). Marjerrison and Keogh found
no significant correlations between changes in EEG alpha frequency
and the scaled reports of visual imagery amount and quality—even
though within-session beta frequency time percentage decreases previously had been found to relate to increased amounts of visual imagery (cf. Marjerrison, 1966).

Simpson, Molloy, Hale, and Climan (1968) continuously photographed participants' pupillary reactions while they attempted to generate images suggested by stimulus words (cf. Hess, 1965; Hess and
Polt, 1964). Participants were required to press a key when an image
occurred as well as to describe, subsequently, the image. Simpson et
al. found a significant increase in participants' pupil *size* during the
imagery task, but differential amounts of dilation were not related
precisely to the levels of task difficulty (the eighteen stimulus-word
nouns contained three levels of task difficulty in terms of the previously rated ease with which the words evoke sensory images). Regarding the *magnitude* of pupil dilation, present results are consistent with
previous reports (e.g., Paivio and Simpson, 1966) that pupil size increases while participants attempt to generate mental images; additionally, in previous studies, the amount of pupil dilation during the image
period differed among the word types employed (cf. Simpson and
Paivio, 1966, 1968); however, across studies overall, the magnitude
of pupil dilation during the imagery task only generally reflects task
difficulty. On the other hand, the *latency* of pupil dilation for the different types of words was consistent with the levels of task difficulty,
suggesting that the *latency* measure is a more sensitive index of difficulty than is the *magnitude* measure of pupil dilation in the imagery
task (cf. Paivio and Simpson, 1968).

Reyher and Morishige (1969) monitored participants' vertical elec-
trooculograms (EOGs), EEGs, electromyograms (EMGs), rapid eye
movements (REMs), and heart rates (HRs) under a visual imagery
condition (free imagery) and under a dream-recall condition; their
results showed that only the dream-recall condition was associated with
EEG alpha desynchronization. Moreover, the imagery involved in the
dream-recall condition was characterized by the following: more primary process, more kinetic imagery, more frequent episodes of imagery, longer durations of images, and greater heart rate than during

the free imagery condition. However, both conditions (free imagery and dream-recall) were related to an equal increase in REMs; Reyher and Morishige discuss the differences between the imagery conditions in terms of the type of tasks involved in the two situations. (For other relevant studies in this area, see the following: Antrobus and Singer, 1965; Barratt, 1956; Burns, 1967; Costello and McGregor, 1957; Dement and Kleitman, 1957; Golla, Hutton, and Walter, 1943; Jasper and Cruikshank, 1937; Reyher, 1963; Reyher and Smeltzer, 1968; Roffwarg, Dement, Muzio, and Fisher, 1962; Stoyva and Kamiya, 1968.)

Colman and Paivio (1970) continuously photographed participants' pupillary activity (magnitude and latency of pupillary dilation) during mediator-formation and paried-associate (PA) learning tasks containing noun items (abstractness and concreteness of the nouns and mediation instructions—imagery, verbal, or none—were manipulated variables). Colman and Paivio found that the PA data confirmed previous findings regarding the strong positive effects of concreteness, especially as a stimulus variable; moreover, learning was best under the *imagery* mediation set where its superiority over the *verbal* mediation condition was greatest in the case of pairs with abstract nouns. They noted, also, that pupil size during learning was largest when *no* mediation instructions were given and when stimulus members were abstract, thus supporting an interpretation in which pupillary dilation is viewed as an index of cognitive task difficulty (cf. Kahneman and Beatty, 1966).

Hale and Simpson (1970) conducted two studies (a between-groups design and a within-subjects design) to determine the effects of eye movements on the latency and vividness of visual images; eye movements were manipulated under three instruction-conditions (to *actually* make eye movements while generating images to noun-pairs; *not* to make *actual* eye movements but only to *think* about making eye movements while generating images to noun-pairs; and *not* to make *actual* eye movements and *not* to think about making eye movements while generating images to noun-pairs). The noun-pairs were manipulated under two conditions: five noun-pairs consisted of *high* imagery-evoking words, and five consisted of *low* imagery-evoking words. Hale and Simpson found that the results of both the between-groups design and the within-subjects design showed significant effects of noun-pair type on both the latency (rate of discovery) and the vividness of images where the fastest and most vivid images occurred under the high-imagery noun-pairs condition.

However, the effects of the eye movement conditions on latency and image-vividness were not significant in either of the two experimental designs. Thus, Hale and Simpson conclude that their results do *not* support the hypothesis that eye movements are necessary for visual imagery or even that eye movements enhance visual imagery (cf. Amadeo and Shagass, 1963; Asher and Ort, 1951; Gaarder, 1967; Hebb, 1968; Lorens and Darrow, 1962); however, they also conclude that ocular activity, in some cases, may be related, ultimately, to imagery, especially in situations involving images of a moving stimulus (cf. Deckert, 1964; Zigmund, 1966).

A. Richardson (1978) notes that in the past few years interest has grown greatly in the experimental investigation of initial lateral eye movements (LEMs)—study of a behavior that typically occurs when a person responds to questions requiring reflective thought (cf. Bakan, 1969, 1971; Bakan and Strayer, 1973), perhaps even involving imagery (cf. Cheney, Miller, and Rees, 1982). Richardson observes, also, that previous research on initial LEMs do not always show such responses/activity to be valid indicators of either the assumed cognitive (cerebral hemispheric) style preferences of the participant or of the psychological functions (cerebral hemisphere) assumed to be operative when a participant is engaged in different mental tasks. Richardson reviews and identifies various participant, task, and tester variables that have been employed in the initial eye movement studies. Based upon the results of his study, Richardson draws the following tentative conclusions: the direction of LEM is influenced by the cognitive style of the tester and the sex/gender and cognitive style of the participant, while the direction of vertical eye movements (VEMs) is influenced primarily by the sex/gender of the tester; however, to the extent that type of question affects the direction of LEMs, the present results are inconsistent with Bakan's (1969) hypothesis regarding a possible link between hemispheric activation and contralateral conjugate LEMs (cf. Ashton and Dwyer, 1975; Barnat, 1974; Crouch, 1976; Day, 1964, 1967; Duke, 1968; Ehrlichman and Weinberger, 1978; Ehrlichman, Weiner, and Baker, 1974; Etaugh, 1972; Galin and Ornstein, 1974; Gur, Gur, and Harris, 1975; Hiscock, 1977; Hines and Martindale, 1974; Kinsbourne, 1972; Kocel, Galin, Ornstein, and Merrin, 1972; Weiner and Ehrlichman, 1976; Weiten and Etaugh, 1974). In another study involving eye movements, but more closely related to imagery production, Cheney, Miller, and Rees (1982) tested a working model (cf. Bandler and Grinder, 1979) that suggested that eye movement direction is indicative of sensory modality of imagery. Cheney et al. asked participants questions designed to evoke imagery in six sensory modalities (visual, auditory, kinaesthetic, tactile, gustatory, and olfactory). Data were obtained concerning the variables of sensory modality, sequence, and vividness of images. Cheney et al. found that participants did report images in the modes as intended by the questions, but they did *not* obtain evidence to support the proposed relationship between eye movements and the participants' reported imagery. In other analyses, Cheney et al. found that—except for the visual modality—imagery does not generally occur in single modalities alone but involves multimodal experience, which is a finding that may be important in attempts to study variables of imagery within separate sense modalities (e.g., the measurement of imagery vividness in a particular modality may be influenced by vividness of images in other modalities occurring simultaneously or in close sequence). In the final analysis, Cheney et al. conclude that if further studies continue to find complex patterns of results (similar to their results), then perhaps one should look beyond simple one-to-one correspondence models relating over behavior (such as LEMs and VEMs) to covert phenomena (such as imaging).

Jordan and Lenington (1979) review various correlates of imagery and note the following conditions/results:

- Studies demonstrating the physiological correlates of mental imagery (cf. Paivio, 1973; Zikmund, 1972) have been equivocal due to the variety of mental images studied and the difficulty of separating the inextricably interwoven processes of imaging and perceiving.
- The three major categories in which studies of the physiological correlates of mental imagery have been conducted include changes in bioelectrical activity of the brain, changes in autonomic functions, and changes in eye movement activity.
- Several EEG studies studies (e.g., Barratt, 1956; Slatter, 1960) report suppression of the EEG alpha rhythm during reports of visual imagery (cf. studies of EEG recordings of participants categorized as "nonvisualizers" as containing little alpha rhythm, e.g., Simpson, Paivio, and Rodgers, 1967).
- Studies investigating autonomic functions as correlates of imagery have produced the most consistent results, e.g., May and Johnson, 1973, found that images elicited by associations to affect-loaded words produced increases in heart rate and respiration but not in electrodermal responses; Chowdhury and Vernon, 1964, indicate a correlation between a regular-irregular dimension of breathing and visual imagery scores; Yaremko and

Butler, 1975, note that imagining a tone or shock, and actual presentation of these stimuli, produce comparable habituation in the GSR. Barber, 1978, observes that a whole host of autonomic responses may be increased or inhibited via images produced by hypnotic suggestion.

- In the area of the physiological effects of imagery (cf. Mathews, 1971), most studies (and controversy) deal with the supposed relationship between eye movement activity and mental imagery (cf. Hebb, 1968).
- In regard to dream- and waking-images, various studies attest to the predictability of eye movements attending these images (cf. Antrobus, Antrobus, and Singer, 1964; Deckert, 1964; Lorens and Darrow, 1962; Roffwarg, Dement, Muzio, and Fisher, 1962).
- Some researchers indicate an absence of eye movements with images of imagination (e.g., Perky, 1910) and daydream thought (e.g., Singer, 1966).

In their own experimental study, Jordan and Lenington (1979) employed a two-factor design—with repeated measures on phases of treatment—to compare the effectiveness of eidetic imagery (cf. Ahsen, 1965, 1968) versus induced-anxiety instructions (cf. Sipprelle, 1967) in producing quantitative and qualitative physiological changes in fifteen female and male medical student participants. During the treatment phases (involving different balanced conditions of anxiety, eidetics, and relaxation instructions), continuous physiological recordings were made of HR, galvanic skin response (GSR), respiration, and eye movements (EMs). Based upon their experimental conditions, Jordan and Lenington found—as predicted—that eidetic imagery produced significant EM changes, but the induced-anxiety condition did not; moreover, the hypothesis that eidetic imagery produces *discrete* arousal—while induced-anxiety produces *diffuse* arousal—was confirmed for the GSR and HR data. Among their conclusions, Jordan and Lenington assert that the dramatic presence of EM during eidetic focusing, and the absence of EM during induced-anxiety, support the hypothesis that eidetic imagery involves obvious oculomotor activity (cf. Ahsen, 1977a). On the other hand, Jordan and Lenington (1979) acknowledge, again, that most previous studies of the relationship between EM and a variety of types of images have yielded equivocal results (e.g., Antrobus, Antrobus, and Singer, 1964; Lorens and Darrow, 1962; Paivio and Simpson, 1967; Simpson and Paivio, 1968; Singer, 1966).

In a theory-based review/survey of studies that show a link between imagery and physiological responses, Richardson (1984) suggests how better theory and better experimental design may optimize the imagery-physiological response connection (cf. Arnold, 1984a,b). Richardson notes that a number of different writers have provided discussions regarding the links that might exist between experienced mental imagery and physiological measures (e.g., Mangan, 1982; Morris and Hampson, 1983; Richardson, 1969; Zikmund, 1972; cf. Arnold, 1984a, who views *imagination* as an integral part of the sequence of psychological activities from perception to action, and who invokes specific physiological/cerebral structures by asserting that *sensory imagination* is mediated by a circuit from limbic areas via amygdala and sensory thalamic nuclei to sensory cortical association areas, and *motor imagination* is mediated by a circuit from limbic areas via amygdala and dorsomedial thalamic nuclei to prefrontal association areas). According to Richardson (1984), the links are basically of three types (but almost always have reference to visual thought, or memory, imagery). One link is between changes in the attributes of a visual image (i.e., its accuracy, vividness, duration, etc.) and the corresponding changes in some neurological substrate (so far, it has proved impossible to establish any such isomorphic relationships). A second type of link is between currently experienced imagery and any physiological activity that may accompany it (e.g., one's breathing span may covary with some aspect of experienced imagery and, thus, be an indicator that imagery is present without having any reference to the actual material substrate of that imagery; again, according to Richardson, it has not proved possible to establish links between the two factors that are uncontaminated by other processes, e.g., attention, that lead independently to physiological changes in emotional or cognitive arousal). A third type of link is of a functional nature and involves study of the content of experienced imagery as a stimulus and the physiological consequences that may follow (according to McMahon, 1976, anecdotal accounts of such links may be found as far back as Aristotle's writings; cf. Tuke, 1872).

Further, Richardson (1984) discusses physiological responses to imaged stimuli under two content headings: physiological responses resulting from *instructions* to participants to image (including empirical studies involving the measures of HR, GSR, and systolic blood pressure, as well as indicating a theoretical position related to the empirical findings) and physiological responses resulting from differences in participants' *ability to construct* vivid thought images (including empirical studies involving the measures of respiration rate, GSR, salivation response, HR, and a theoretical position related to these empirical findings). Based upon his review, Richardson draws the following conclusions: it is important to take the common-sense definition of an image seriously (cf. Lang, 1979) because it seems impossible to avoid discussing these perceptlike experiences whose properties make the most theoretical sense in understanding how physiological responses are mediated; researchers need to spend more time on the identification and measurement of relevant individual difference variables (with added attention given to imagery dimensions such as modality, prevalence, vividness, controllability, and absorption); and researchers need to ensure that their experimental designs always include relevant individual difference/person variables along with the relevant stimulus variables (cf. Ashton and White, 1980; Eysenck, 1983; Kunzendorf, 1981; Owens, 1968).

Initially, in his section on the assessment of mental imagery, Sheikh (2001) notes that self-reports/questionnaires traditionally have been the most frequently used method for measuring individual differences in imaging ability; such measures have examined three aspects of imagery ability: vividness/clarity of the images, imagery types (e.g., modality differences regarding the clearest images experienced), and imagery control (e.g., participants' ability to manipulate their images voluntarily) (cf. Sheehan, Ashton, and White, 1983; Tower and Singer, 1981; White, Sheehan, and Ashton, 1977). Sheikh observes, also, in his discussion of ancillary measures of imagery, that another group of methods measures the aspects of consciousness that reflect experience more directly than do the traditional self-report measures. Among such supplemental measures cited by Sheikh are the thought-sampling method (e.g., Klinger, 1978) and the experiential analysis technique (e.g., Sheehan, McConkey, and Cross, 1978); the major difference between these types of assessment and the self-report inventories is that the latter draw on retrospective reports of experience while the former draw upon the ongoing stream of consciousness. Furthermore, attempts to infer imaging ability have been derived from behavioral performances, the most compelling of such performance tests are those developed in conjunction with the investigation and assessment of eidetic imagery, for instance, the random-dot stereogram test (Sheehan, Ashton, and White, 1983). Also, related to these types of performance/ability tests are those that are spatial in nature—tests whose aim is to arouse imagery and that focus, in particular, on the mental manipulation of spatial relationships, for instance, the spatial-relations subtest of Thurstone's Test of Primary Mental Abilities, the Flag Test, the Space Relations Test, and the Minnesota Paper Form Board (cf. Ernest, 1977; Sheehan, Ashton, and White, 1983; Thurstone, 1938; Thurstone and Thurstone, 1962).

Further discussions of other measures and correlates—including behavioral and physiological approaches—of mental imagery may be found in chapter 5 herein, especially studies under the sections "Measurement and Tests of Imagery" and "Physiology/Neuropsychology and Imagery."

> What happened? . . . [W]hy were images once something every psychologist knew a good deal about and took quite seriously, only to become a minor matter worthy of only brief mention in textbooks and less concern in the laboratory or clinic, until their very recent renaissance?
>
> —R. R. Holt, 1964

> I propose to see what sort of analytical treatment can be made of the image and, equally, of its relation to sensation, perception, and thought.
>
> —D. O. Hebb, 1968

> One of the difficulties facing any investigator interested in examining the nature and function of imagery ability is to determine what techniques of measurement to use in classifying individuals as high or low, or vivid or weak, in imagery ability.
>
> —C. H. Ernest, 1977

> Imagery, we believe, is a fundamental process in the individual's adaptation, physical and psychological, to life. The idea that behavior occurs within the environment is one of the most deceptive half-truths that psychology has yet produced. Behavior takes place within the *cognized environment*, a very different thing.
>
> —D. F. Marks and P. McKellar, 1982

> Use of mental imagery has spread recently in the general framework of learning and psychotherapy procedures. It is predictable that the proliferation of imagery techniques will continue on and contribute toward the further development of an imagery paradigm.
>
> —A. Ahsen, 1982

Men and women probably have been alleged to differ from each other in all areas of psychological functioning at some time or another, and mental imagery is no exception to this.

J.T.E. Richardson, 1991

The relative neglect of motor imagery as a research tool is in some ways surprising since both waking imagery and dreaming commonly involve imaginary activities such as rearranging the furniture. . . . Evidence of the participation of motor responses in imagery comes from a variety of experimental paradigms in pure and applied psychology.

—J. Annett, 1995

## SELECTED MODERN PSYCHOLOGICAL IMAGERY STUDIES (1960–2003)

In his much-heralded article, which served to formally reintroduce the issue of mental imagery back into the psychological community and mainstream, after a long hiatus, Holt (1964, p. 255) lists (and defines) thirteen principal types of imagery (the list derives from E. G. Boring [Holt, 1964, p. 255 footnote] who got it from Titchener [1915, pp. 73–79] who, in turn, most likely got it from Fechner [1860, sections 40–44]): image, thought image, phosphene, synesthesia, body image, phantom limb, hypnagogic image/hallucination, eidetic image, hallucination, paranormal hallucination, pseudo-hallucination, dream image, and sensory conditioning. Among the imagery-related concepts that Holt (1964) does *not* include as types of imagery in his examination of the issue are afterimages, spiral aftereffect, autokinetic phenomenon, figural aftereffects, standard visual illusions, and imagination. Holt notes that there was a great deal of attention given to images of all kinds during the initial development of scientific psychology before, and around, the turn of the twentieth century. However, despite the emergence of eidetic imagery, in particular, as a topic of extensive study between World Wars I and II, psychologists generally lost interest in the phenomenon of imagery; then, in the 1960s, this negative trend was reversed and signs began to appear that the thirteen major types of imagery attracted psychologists' attention once again.

Following his review of the history of the banishment of imagery from psychology (including discussions of the "new psychology" of the 1890s—essentially a science of mind, its contents, and their laws, as revealed by observation and experiments, Galton's contributions, the Wurzburg School of imageless thought, Titchener's influence, Ach's notion of *set* or *determining tendency*, and the impact of J. B. Watson and S. Freud on imagery study), Holt (1964) observes that the challenging manifestoes of Behaviorism in the early 1900s seemed to be the beginning of a new era of "objective scientific progress" for psychology (cf. Hebb, 1960, who characterized this era as the "American revolution of psychology" that—much like a political revolution—carried things to extremes; for example, imagery, attention, states of consciousness, and other such central concepts of the earlier era were banished from psychology as being too "mentalistic"). Holt—as Hebb (1960) proposed a few years earlier—asserts that the "American revolution of psychology" in the early 1900s demonstrated two stages of development: the first phase was characterized by the banishment or "defeat" of the notions of thought, imagery, volition, attention, and other seditious concepts from psychological investigation; and the second phase was characterized by the "victory" of securing an enduring place in psychology for the "objective operational method." Furthermore, according to Holt, the comeback of imagery in psychology seems to have been achieved largely by developments outside the areas of theoretical, experimental, or clinical psychology (where such developments needed new conceptual and operational definitions of the whole spectrum of types of imagery).

Among the several factors that Holt (1964) identifies as being important in the reemergence of imagery in psychology are

- The presence of various practical problems that pushed for solution in engineering psychology (e.g., imagery "hallucinations" of radar operators working for long periods at a time, of truck drivers going long distances, of jet pilots attempting to fly straight and level at high altitudes, of snowcat operators in polar exploration activities, and of astronauts and cosmonauts piloting complex new aircraft for long periods of time).
- Firsthand reports and accounts of individuals who have been isolated or imprisoned in concentration camps, and interrogated by police or guards, for long periods of time (involving conditions of prolonged isolation, sleep deprivation, and multiple regressive or deleterious aspects of forcible indoctrination/thought reform).
- Informal, self-experiments and self-exploration by nonresearch persons involving "mind-expanding" or "hallucinogenic" drugs (e.g., LSD, peyote, mescaline).
- Formal research in psychology laboratories on the effects of sensory and perceptual deprivation (e.g., Goldberger and Holt, 1961c).

- Emergence of popular interest in parapsychological phenomena (e.g., flying saucers, space aliens, telepathically transmitted messages, and imagery).
- Advances in brain research (e.g., occurrence of hallucinations, imagery, and dreamlike states during epileptic seizures, or following brain surgery; developments in photic stimulation, EEG, and brain-imaging techniques; effects of direct stimulation of the brain; functioning of particular parts of the brain, for instance, the brain-stem reticular activating system, the hippocampus, the amygdala/limbic area, and major lobes of the brain).
- Developments in dream research (e.g., objective study of dreaming states involving REMs).
- The recent burgeoning of a "new psychology of thinking" (e.g., the "cognitive revolution" in psychology which suggests new methodologies and metaphors for studying old problems such as thinking, problem-solving, perception, attention, learning, and memory).
- The advances in model-building (cf. Freud, 1885/1966) concerning cognitive activity that involves neuropsychological, anatomical, and physiological factors.
- The emergence of information theory, the high-speed computer, and interest in artificial intelligence.

Holt (1964) maintains that the important point about the "new psychology of thinking" is that it is no longer necessary to assume that thought/cognitive processes are identical with what may be reported by the thinker in terms of *conscious contents*—whether imageless or not (cf. Freud's, 1915/1957, early notion of the unconscious and modern psychology's concession—via the new psychology of thinking— that consciousness is neither a necessary nor a defining property of cognitive processes). According to Holt, two other related bodies of work have helped, also, to bring imagery back into psychologists' consideration: studies of creativity (cf. Roe, 1951) and experiments on the effects of marginal and subliminal stimuli (cf. Eagle, 1962; Fisher, 1954; Klein, 1959). Moreover, developmental cognitive research (e.g., Piaget, 1945/1952) focusing on imagery, in particular, has been influential in the reemergence of imagery in psychology. In Holt's (p. 261) view, there's been a "striking dearth" of phenomenological and taxonomic investigations in the psychological literature on imagery; and, finally, Holt's finding that all kinds of imagery do not fall on a single continuum (but may involve separate mechanisms) seems to him to call for a reconsideration of the issue of hallucination (cf. Ziskind and Augsberg, 1962; Zuckerman and Cohen, 1964) in perceptual isolation studies/conditions ("it is being rediscovered that normal, prosaic folk, and not just psychotics, can hallucinate, given the right circumstances," p. 263).

Hebb (1968) discusses the content and mechanisms of imagery based upon his interest in thought processes in general; he suggests that the renewed increase in psychologists' attention to imagery is due to several factors, including the place that imagery holds in studies of paired-associate learning, the convincing demonstrations of eidetic imagery, and the hallucinatory activity reported in conditions of monotony, perceptual isolation, and sleep deprivation. Hebb argues that the reporting of, or description of, imagery need not always involve the traditional introspective method, and cites the phenomenon of the *phantom limb* (i.e., somesthetic imagery) as a case in point. In this condition, the individual who has had an arm or leg amputated experiences a hallucinatory awareness of the part that had been cut off (in some instances, the person also reports pain in which the fingers or toes are curled up with cramp). Hebb maintains that persons reporting such experiences as the phantom limb are not strictly cases of introspection because one is still dealing with a mechanism of response to the environment—though the mechanism (due to the missing body part) is now functioning abnormally. In Hebb's view, a report by a person of sensation from a phantom limb is not an introspective report (no excitation can originate in the missing limb, but the same excitation, in principle, may arise at higher central regions in the pathway by spontaneous firing of neurons).

Hebb (1968, p. 468) asserts that "the mechanism of imagery is an aberrant mechanism of exteroception, not a form of looking inward to observe the operations of the mind," and, understood as such, the description of an imagined object has a proper place in the realm of objective psychology. Following his distinction between the concepts of *sensation* (i.e., the activity of receptors and the resulting activity of the afferent pathway up to, and including, the cortical sensory area) and *perception* (i.e., the central/cortico-diencephalic activity that is directly excited by sensation), Hebb notes that *different* sensations or sensory patterns may give rise to the *same* perception (e.g., as in the perceptual constancies), and the *same* sensory pattern may give rise to *different* perceptions (e.g., as in ambiguous figures). Regarding the pattern of activity involved in imagery, Hebb suggests that the ordinary memory image and the eidetic image arise from perception, but this doesn't mean that the memory image is identical with perception—even though eidetic imagery may be so identified.

Essentially, Hebb (1968) attempts to analyze imagery in physiological terms and proposes the following notions: eye-movement activity has an organizing function in the process; first-order cell assemblies are the foundation of vivid specific imagery; and higher-order cell assemblies are the foundation of less specific imagery and the nonrepresentational or abstract conceptual processes. Hebb (p. 471) acknowledges that the status of his theory of cell assemblies is incomplete, even paradoxical, because "it has a way of leading to experiments that both support and disprove it." In accounting for eidetic imagery, in particular, Hebb proposes that the eidetic image includes the activity of first-order cell assemblies that are characteristic of perception but absent in the case of the memory image; and in his account of hallucination and hypnagogic imagery, Hebb relates them, as well as the memory image, to various forms of thought. In summary, Hebb's (1968) theoretical analysis of imagery in terms of lower- and higher-order cell assemblies implies a continuum from the very vivid imagery of hallucination through the less vivid memory image to the completely abstract conceptual activity that is nonrepresentational in nature; this analysis includes auditory and verbal imagery as well as somesthetic imagery, and Hebb asserts that it must be a mistake to make a dichotomy between visual imagery and thought, or to identify abstract ideas with verbal processes. Finally, Hebb suggests that the difference between those who have little imagery and those who have an abundance of imagery may not be a difference of thought mechanisms, but more of a difference in image retrievability.

Lindauer (1969) conducted two studies concerning imagery and sensory modality; in the first study, he established the sensory values of auditory, gustatory, olfactory, tactual, and visual words (this was done because he alleges that much research on imagery typically uses material lacking in sensory content—which is an essential attribute of imagery). In his second study, Lindauer measured participants' imagery for the sensory material in terms of both vividness and ease-of-evocation. Thus, the purpose of Lindauer's investigation was to correct certain shortcomings in previous imagery research by providing a set of materials in which *both* the imaginal and sensory content of words in five modalities are standardized and, thereby, provide suitable materials for researchers to use in future systematic study in this area. Following the collection of data in his two studies, Lindauer constructed an imagery index for the words in the five sensory categories by combining the vividness and ease-of-evocation data. Based upon the results of his imagery index, Lindauer found high-imagery values for tactual and gustatory words, intermediate-imagery values for visual and olfactory words, and low-imagery values for auditory words. Lindauer reasons that because most studies of imagery have incorporated—at best—only two sensory modalities (audition and vision), previous investigations must have assessed imagery in relatively low, limited, or divergent ways (cf. Sheehan's, 1967a, imagery test that uses thirty-five phrases pertaining to seven modalities). He suggests that contradictions and inconsistencies in the literature on the extent and effectiveness of imagery may be due in large part to the employment of materials that did not maximize fully or effectively the occurrence of imagery in participants. In one place, Lindauer (pp. 210–12) provides a valuable table for imagery researchers to use in future studies; the table contains an alphabetized listing of 228 words relating to the variances of sensory modality and the frequency, vividness, and ease-of-evocation of imagery.

Sheehan and Neisser (1969) studied the role that imagery plays in the recall of materials and note that at least three different functions of images are possible in the recall process: the participant uses his or her image directly as the *sole* source of information; the image is *only one* source of the information (other sources include stored verbal descriptions); and the image is present but the participant bases her or his response entirely on *other kinds* of information. Furthermore, among the factors that may be relevant in recall conditions, Sheehan and Neisser cite the following: the actual stimulus materials used; the wording of the instructions; the implicit demand characteristics of the experimental setting; and the individual differences of the participants themselves. Sheehan and Neisser explore several variables that have been studied only rarely in imagery recall conditions, including imagery and recall; incidental learning; individual differences; and experimenter effects.

Participants in Sheehan and Neisser's (1969) study were preselected for high and low imagery, and were required, subsequently, to complete imagery tasks involving stimulus materials consisting of two types of colored block designs. With one type of design, participants were asked repeatedly either to produce visual images and copy them, or to recall the designs with the aid of imagery and other resources of memory; and with the other type of design, participants were exposed to materials presented under incidental learning conditions. Overall, results indicate no differences in accuracy between the high- versus low-imagery participants, but the superior-recalled designs were described, generally, as being accompanied by more vivid imagery; additionally, a slight experimenter effect was observed in the study; and the reported vividness, but not accuracy, of imagery increased following an introspective probe of the participants. Further, in the second type of block design condition, the images reported by participants in the subsequent, unexpected recall situation were much more vivid than those in the rest of the experiment. Sheehan and Neisser (1969) conclude that it's probably best to think of the image as just one source of information—among others—that may be used in a recall task; the reported vividness of imagery during recall seems to be a function of several experimental and procedural variables, and the relation between imagery vividness and accuracy is stronger under some conditions than others. Sheehan and Neisser found that instructions proved to be a rather ineffective technique for manipulating recall strategies, but the introduction of an incidental learning task produced a marked increase in the amount of reported imagery; thus, according to Sheehan and Neisser (1969), it is suggested—conversely, and by extension—that imagery may play a special role in the recall of incidentally presented stimulus materials.

Paivio (1969) explores the functional significance of nonverbal imagery and verbal processes in associative meaning, mediation, and memory. The two hypothesized process of nonverbal imagery and verbal symbolic processes are operationally defined by Paivio in terms of stimulus attributes and experiential procedures that are designed to render them available differentially as memory codes or associative mediators. Paivio assumes that imagery availability varies directly with the factor of item-concreteness or image-evoking value, whereas verbal processes are viewed as independent of concreteness but linked functionally to codability and meaningfulness. Moreover, Paivio hypothesizes that the characteristics of stimuli interact with the factors of mediation instructions, presentation rates, and type of memory task. Based upon subjective reports and performance data from experimental tests of his two-process model, Paivio indicates that imagery-concreteness is the most salient stimulus aspect yet to be identified among meaningful items, while meaningfulness, itself, and various other attributes, are relatively ineffective. Paivio indicates, also, that both nonverbal imagery and verbal symbolic processes may be manipulated by mediation instructions but that imagery is a preferred mediator when at least one member of the stimulus-response pair is relatively concrete;

moreover, the two processes are effective in differing ways depending on whether the memory task is sequential or nonsequential. Paivio's argument, essentially, is that imagery is a viable and useful explanatory concept in accounting for associative learning and memory, and that the variables and theoretical views he discusses in relation to paired-associate learning of nouns have been extended to include picture-word comparisons and learning situations other than paired-associates situations (such as recognition-memory, free-recall, memory-span, and serial-learning studies). Paivio's references section contains over 130 citations/references relevant to his exposition on the role of mental imagery in associative learning and memory.

Reese (1970b) reports on a symposium—which he chaired—concerning imagery in children's learning; among the participants in the symposium were A. Paivio (1970), W. D. Rohwer (1970), H. W. Reese (1970a), and D. S. Palermo (1970). Reese (1970b, p. 383) observes—judging from the attendance by psychologists at meetings where papers on imagery were delivered, from the number of imagery research reports, the number of imagery-report reprint requests, and other inquiries—that "the study of imagery, that is, the study of the effects of inferred imagery, has again become not only respectable in psychology, but also relatively popular." Reese (1970b) notes that the main thrust of the symposium was theoretical, especially with respect to the role of imagery in children's learning; however, the theoretical analyses are applicable beyond the period of childhood, and extend into adulthood. Moreover, there is a developmental trend in the field that indicates that imagery is more effective with increasing age; each contributor to the symposium suggested an interpretation of this trend and discussed supporting evidence for it. Following his review of the historical background of the concept of imagery, Paivio (1970) outlines his own "conceptual-peg" hypothesis, which states that the image serves as a peg for storage and retrieval of the response item; in Paivio's approach, the young child's problem is not in the use of the image for storage (encoding), but in the retrieval (decoding) process. Rohwer (1970) concludes that imagery is most effective when a verbal tag is stored with the image, and where the developmental trend (i.e., more effective use of imagery with increasing age) results from the young child's failure to store such verbalizations. Reese (1970a) explores six alternative explanations of the developmental trend: deficiency in the covert verbalization of the imagery materials, defective visual memory, deficiency of production, mediation deficits, excessive leveling of figurative conceptions, and failure to read the imagery materials. Reese's argument focuses on the last interpretation. Palermo (1970) points out the difficulties in all three of the positions endorsed by the participants in the symposium, and he discusses their approaches in the context of the apparent revolutionary changes that are taking place within the field of psychology. Palermo suggests, also, that due to the evident difficulty of constructing a behavioristic account of the issue, it may be best to move outside the behavioristic paradigm (cf. Reese's, 1970a, "leveling of figurative conceptions" hypothesis that may, according to Palermo, hold promise in accounting for the available data on imagery in children's learning).

Ernest (1977) provides a critical review of the literature on the issue of imagery ability and cognition from 1967 to 1977, especially as it relates to individual differences in imagery ability in the areas of memory, learning, and perceptual and conceptual processes. Ernest attempts to position the literature on imagery ability within the context of other operational approaches to imagery; she contrasts the relative merits of self-ratings and objective measures of imagery as predictors of cognitive functioning. Ernest's review demonstrates, in particular, the inappropriateness of making any global statements concerning the construct validity of the self-ratings method as compared with more objective measures of imagery ability. Ernest maintains that although both inter-test correlational data and some evidence from behavioral studies suggest that the factors of vividness, habitual use, and control of imagery share common variance, the nature of their differences is apparent, also. Among Ernest's general findings and conclusions are the following points:

- Imagery vividness is related reliably to the incidental recall of both verbal and nonverbal stimuli.
- The ability to experience vivid imagery appears to facilitate the retrieval of detail or content information from memory (however, it does not seem to be facilitative when the task requires the implementation of strategies for recall).
- The Individual Differences Questionnaire provides imagery scores that are predictive of speed of image generation made to abstract words, and characterizing participants as "verbalizers" or "visualizers" on the basis of such scores is predictive of some aspects of verbal recall (also, there is evidence—via eye-movement studies—that the visualizer-verbalizer dichotomy may reflect participants' strategy differences in processing information).

- Evidence from behavioral studies, as well as correlations with spatial tests of imagery, establish the construct validity of the Gordon Test of Visual Imagery Control as a measure of the ability to manipulate or control visual imagery mentally (also, the test has predicted paired-associate learning under conditions of imagery priming, incidental recall, and divergent thinking).
- Spatial tests, and performance measures, of imagery are related significantly to all aspects of the cognitive functions that were reviewed, although the relationship is not always a positive one.
- Several common patterns seem to emerge from review of studies in the various areas covered, the most prominent being that imagery is likely to be used as a processing strategy by high spatial imagers if the experimental environment encourages cues, or primes its use (when such conditions are present, imagery as an ability facilitates performance in ways similar to those when imagery is defined as an attribute of stimuli or a mediational strategy).
- Effective priming conditions include the use of pictorial stimuli, instructions to use imagery as a processing strategy, presentation of pictures (and words) in homogeneous rather than heterogeneous word lists, and the presentation of words in a meaningful context such as prose.

Finally, Ernest suggests that there is a need for closer study of the relationships among the factors of imagery ability, verbal processing, and sex/gender differences. She asserts that such study is equally as important when imagery is defined by self-ratings as by spatial tests in light of the occasional imagery vividness differences in women (but not men), and in view of the almost total neglect of individual differences in verbal habits/skills in the research literature on the self-ratings approach. Ernest's review is accompanied by a references section that contains over 145 citations/references related to imagery ability and cognition.

Marks and McKellar (1982) provide a "target article" on the topic of the nature and function of eidetic imagery that is followed by an "open peer commentary" section containing reactions from over thirty respondents. Marks and McKellar note that the phenomenon of eidetic imagery has puzzled and perplexed many researchers who have studied it; moreover, different terms have been used by those involved in its study. For example, Urbantschitsch (1907) originally gave the German term *Anschauungsbild* to the phenomenon; Muller (1826) named it *subjective vision*, Fechner (1860/1966) called it *memory afterimage*, Ward (1883) termed it *primary memory-image*, Martin (1912) called it *projected memory-image*, Binet (1889) refers to it as *imaginary perception*, and Galton (1883/1907, p. 99) refers to the phenomenon but without giving it any special name. In their initial discussion, Marks and McKellar (p. 4) define eidetic imagery as "any mental imagery projected into the sensory environment which cannot be attributed to a material change in sensory input and which is known to the imager to be subjective"; subsequently, they explore a wide range of eidetic experiences with special emphasis on structural methods of induction. In more specific terms, Marks and McKellar's empirical findings in this area indicate a distinction between *typographic* and *structural* eidetikers. A useful differentiation between these two kinds of eidetic imagery is that the former is induced primarily by an immediately preceding external stimulus, while the latter is evoked purely by exercising the imagination (cf. Ahsen, 1977a). Marks and McKellar's examination of various subtypes of eidetic imagery (e.g., "scrying," "crystal-vision," or "crystallomancy"—the ability to project visual images in crystal, mirrors, liquids, shiny metals, and other transparent or reflecting materials—ghosts—spirits; apparitions; imaginary playmates; auras; phantom limbs; and out-of-body experiences) suggests that more awareness of the phenomena—especially its autonomy—may dispel many supernatural interpretations of normal experiences. Marks and McKellar note, also, that as eidetic imagery of the more overt and dramatic kind goes into disuse during adolescence, an age-related increase in the incidence of psychosis involving hallucinations occurs; moreover, there seems to be an age-related increase in hallucinations among mentally healthy individuals; Marks and McKellar suggest that these trends possibly may be related in some way in which the issue of the aetiology of hallucinosis is tied in with a person's failing attempts to suppress or control her/his socially embarrassing, but highly autonomous, eidetic capabilities.

Among the conclusions in Marks and McKellar's (1982) "comment on the comments" rejoinder section are the following points (among others): all human beings can project and experience imagery that is known to be subjective and that is not dependent on a change in sensory input; eidetic imagery is a continuum along which only individuals at the extreme end have been identified and labeled, previously, as eidetikers (the distinction between typographic and structural eidetic imagery helps in understanding this continuum); structural methods for inducing eidetic imagery are more sensitive and useful than typographic methods for many experimental and clinical purposes; and psychological constructs—which serve, typically, to draw attention to similarities and differences along a continuum regarding a particular phenomenon—should not be reified, and eidetic imagery is no exception. Finally, the references section appended to Marks and McKellar's article, the "open peer commentary," and the rejoinder sections contains over 240 citations/references relevant to the issue of eidetic imagery. For further material on Marks and McKellar's (1982) article, see the section "Eidetic Imagery" in chapter 5 herein.

Finke (1985) reviews contemporary theories that indicate relationships between mental imagery and visual perception; he examines three general types of such theories: structural (i.e., mental images exhibit the same spatial and pictorial properties as real/actual physical objects), functional (i.e., the formation and transformation of mental images contribute to the capacity for object recognition and comparison-making), and interactive theories (i.e., imagery contributes directly to ongoing perceptual processes). Finke critically evaluates the evidence for each type of theory from the following four alternative-hypotheses/ explanations aspects: experimenter bias, task-induced demand characteristics, tacit knowledge, and eye movements. The major conclusion that Finke (1985) draws from his review is that none of the three types of imagery theories is perfectly free from challenges from at least some of the alternative accounts. Briefly, the structural theories seem to be most susceptible to the factor of experimenter bias and strongest with the eye-movement aspect; the functional theories seem weakest vis-à-vis the factor of tacit knowledge and strongest regarding experimenter bias; and the interactive theories are susceptible to both experimenter bias and eye-movement alternatives, but are stronger concerning the aspect of tacit knowledge. In comparing the three types of theories, Finke found that the functional theories have received the most extensive support, followed—in turn—by the structural, and then the interactive, theories. In Finke's view, the interactive theories are in greatest need of further testing and confirmation. Finally, Finke suggests that when the three types of theories are considered collectively, there are implications that go beyond the evaluation of specific types of imagery theories by showing that—although each theory may be susceptible to one or more of the alternative explanations—no single alternative can explain adequately the total evidence for all three types of theories; according to Finke, this conclusion lends strong support to the general claim—shared by most imagery researchers—that imagery does actually resemble perception in some very fundamental ways. Finke's lengthy references section contains over 160 citations/references relevant to the issue of the relationship between mental imagery and perception.

In a "target article" concerning verbal hallucinations (VHs or "voices") and language production in schizophrenia—and followed by an "open peer commentary" section (with over a dozen contributors), as well as a rejoinder section—Hoffman (1986) proposes that the crucial feature identifying hallucinations is the experience of unintendedness; such an experience is nonpathological during the individual's passive conscious states but may be pathological when occurring during the person's goal-directed cognitive processing. Hoffman presents a model of schizophrenic speech disorganization that hypothesizes a disturbance of discourse planning specifying communicative intentions; such conditions may generate, also, unintended verbal imagery. Thus, essentially, Hoffman attempts to develop a cognitive-processing model by linking conceptually VHs and speech disorganization (or loose associations). The major progressive features of Hoffman's argument are the sensory properties of VHs are not distinct from ordinary verbal imagery; VHs are verbal images that are accompanied by a feeling of unintendedness; disruptions in language-planning processes associated with schizophrenia may cause verbal images to be experienced as unintended; and when such images are dissonant with concurrent cognitive goals, then the experience of unintendedness provides the basis for the sustained conviction of a "nonself" origin. Following the description of his model, Hoffman reviews the merits and limitations of various other theories of schizophrenic hallucinations (e.g., theories of: poor-auditory attention; response-set difficulties; information-overload; relationship of hallucinations to dreaming during sleep; subliminal cognitive processes; language-output processes; associative-memory disturbances) in comparison with his own approach. In his rejoinder to the commentators, Hoffman organizes his material under several headings (e.g., "Other Theories of Hallucinations"; "Inner Speech and Verbal Imagery") and responds to the comments within such a framework. Finally, in his summary section, Hoffman (p. 543) states that the most substantive criticisms offered by the commentators were those pertaining to hallucinatory phenomena in normal individuals, and in cross-cultural variables in psychopathology; another sensitive issue emphasized by the commentators concerns whether disordered speech in schizophrenia is a top-down or a bottom-up disturbance. The lengthy references section of Hoffman's (1986) article contains over 260 citations on the issue of VHs and language-production processes in schizophrenia (cf. Aleman, deHaan, Boecker, Hijman, and Kahn, 2002; Holmes, 1998).

Kosslyn (1987) hypothesizes that the capacities for imagery, visual recognition, navigation, and tracking share certain high-level processing subsystems; he presents an alternative way to understand visual hemispheric specialization, in particular. Kosslyn's approach—which focuses on high-level visual prosesses (as opposed to low-level sensory visual processing)—is based on the notion of *natural computation* (e.g., Marr, 1982) in which the brain may be understood in terms of processing subsystems that interpret and transform data in various ways. His theory is developed, also, in light of an analysis of problems that must be solved by the visual system, along with the computational, neurological, and behavioral constraints on the solutions to such problems. Following the description and formulation of his theory, Kosslyn uses various inferences about perceptual subsystems to develop his notions of how mental images are generated; he provides evidence from studies of split-brain patients, and other neuropsychological findings, in support of computational theory—which involves, also, a "computational mechanism" to account for how visual function becomes lateralized in the brain. Kosslyn's exposition is organized around six main headings (cf. Kosslyn, 1991): Visual Perception and Visual Imagery, Components of Image Generation, Mechanisms of Hemispheric Differentiation, Neuropsychological Evidence for Specialized Representations of Spatial Relations, Image Transformations (cf. Mast and Kosslyn, 2002), and Variability in Lateralization and Task Performance.

Among his conclusions, Kosslyn (1987) makes the following points:

1. By using a computational approach in conjunction with neurological and behavioral data, it has been possible to hypothesize a total of twelve subsystems (each system having an input, a purpose, and an output) that may be used in both visual imagery and visual perception (the twelve subsystems are identified as shape encoding, spatiotopic map construction, categorical relations encoding, coordinate location encoding, visual memory activation, categorical relations access and interpretation, coordinate location access, attention shift, position alteration, part realignment, speech output controller, and search controller).
2. By using several ideas about the macroproperties of the brain, it is possible to generate predictions of how these subsystems become lateralized.

3. The natural computation/mechanistic approach appears to have advantages over the traditional approach that employs simple dichotomous dimensions regarding hemispheric differences.
4. By building a computer simulation model, one may develop new hypotheses about other possible subsystems.
5. Variability of the magnitude and frequency one finds in the neuropsychological literature is probably not simply a result of measurement error, and the present approach may give insights into such variability.
6. The present theory has a "modular" aspect to it which allows one to account, ultimately, for all of the major findings on visual hemisphericity (cf. Bradshaw and Nettleton, 1981; Hardyck, 1983; White, 1969).
7. An acknowledged weakness of the present theory is that it specifies only a few of the subsystems, and there are clearly many more (cf. Pinker, 1985).
8. Also, the present approach has almost nothing to contribute concerning the details of the mechanisms that control and direct attention.
9. One may test the present theory by constructing a simulation model and examine differences in how it lateralizes depending on the precise parameter values that are fed into the model (e.g., one may "lesion" the model and note the effects of disrupting the system/model in selected ways; using the findings from this strategy, one may make precise predictions of behavioral deficits following brain damage).

The references section following Kosslyn's article contains over 180 references/citations that relate to the issue of seeing/imaging in the cerebral hemispheres.

Based upon the supportive results of experiments on the perception of briefly presented pictures by human participants, Biederman (1987) conceptualizes the perceptual recognition of objects to be a process in which the image of the input is segmented at regions of deep concavity into an arrangement of simple geometric components (such as cylinders, blocks, cones, and wedges). His approach, called *recognition-by-components* (RBC), assumes that a modest set (approximately thirty-six) of generalized-cone components called "geons" may be derived from contrasts of five detectable properties (curvature, collinearity, symmetry, parallelism, and cotermination) of edges in a two-dimensional image. According to Biederman, RBC provides a principled account of the previously undecided relation between the classic principles of human pattern recognition and perceptual organization (i.e., the constraints toward regularization or "good figure" characterize not the complete object but the object's components). Also, a "principle of componential recovery" may account for the major phenomena of object recognition (i.e., if an arrangement of two or three geons are recovered from the input, objects may be recognized quickly even when they are occluded, rotated in depth, novel, or degraded extensively). Biederman concludes that the characterization of object perception provided by RBC closely resembles some current views as to how speech is perceived. In both cases, the ease with which one is able to code tens of thousands of words or objects is solved by mapping that input onto a modest number of "primitives": fifty-five phonemes for speech and thirty-six components for object recognition—and then using a representational system that codes and accesses various combinations of these primitives. He suggests, also, that in object perception, the primitive components may have their origins in the fundamental principles by which individuals make inferences about a three-dimensional world based simply on the perception of edges of a two-dimensional image.

In discussing gender differences in imagery, cognition, and memory, J.T.E. Richardson (1991) conceptualizes mental imagery in four different ways: as a phenomenal experience, as an internal representation, as a stimulus attribute, and as a mnemonic strategy. Initially, Richardson distinguishes between the term *sex* (the biological differences between women and men based on their anatomical, physiological, and chromosomal features) and *gender* (the sociocultural differences between men and women on the basis of the traits and behaviors that are conventionally associated with the two groups of people). Thus, Richardson's article may most properly be viewed as referring to *gender*, rather than *sex*, differences because in the majority of mental imagery studies that are reviewed, the participants are categorized on the bases of their outward appearance and behavior rather than in terms of their biological attributes. Subsequently, Richardson examines various theories of gender differences and emphasizes, further, the distinction between theories of sex- versus gender-differences, or between biologically based versus socioculturally based theories (cf. Anderson, 1987; Buffery and Gray, 1972; Fairweather, 1976; Feingold, 1988; Forisha, 1981; Harris, 1978; Harshman, Hampson and Berenbaum, 1983; Harshman and Paivio, 1987; Hyde, 1981; Hyde, Geiringer, and Yen, 1975; Hyde and Linn, 1988; Jacklin, 1981; Linn and Petersen, 1986; Maccoby and Jacklin, 1974; McGee, 1979; McGlone, 1980; Nyborg, 1983; Rosenthal and Rubin, 1982; Sherman, 1978; Tapley and Bryden, 1977; Unger, 1979; Yen, 1975). Subsequent to his review of the literature, Richardson draws the following summarizations and conclusions:

1. Women produce higher ratings than men on imagery vividness and controllability, though the effect is small and often nonsignificant (cf. J.T.E. Richardson, 1995).
2. Beyond early adolescence, male participants achieve higher scores than female participants on tests of spatial ability (where tests of mental rotation, in particular, often produce substantial effects).
3. There are no reliable differences between men and women in the effects of stimulus imageability, or imagery instructions, in tests of learning and memory.
4. Women are less likely than men to use mental imagery as a mnemonic device, but they are more likely to recall those items where mental imagery has been so used (as a result, any gender differences in recall ability seem to be in favor of women rather than of men).

Richardson (1991) provides a generous references section containing 150 citations/references relevant to the issue of gender differences in imagery, cognition, and memory.

In the 1992 (*16 [1,2]*) issue of the *Journal of Mental Imagery*, Ahsen (1992) provides a "target article" on the topic of prolucid dreaming (cf. Ahsen, 1988), which is followed by over a dozen respondents' commentaries, as well as a final section by Ahsen on metaprolucids. Ahsen (1992) notes that the term *lucid* (as in lucid dreams) seems to have a special connection to the term *vividness* that has been used extensively in discussions and research on mental imagery; he emphasizes that the experience associated with the lucid dream may be found, also, in many imagery experiences during waking life. Further, Ahsen (p. xi) "designs" and defines the term *prolucid* as "that special quality in consciousness experience which accounts for most of the imagery transformations. The term *prolucid* refers to a struggle between wakefulness and sleep, between vivid and unvivid, involving the consciousness principle at many levels." Ahsen suggests that when one admits that there is more than just vividness or conscious meaning in the image—that the bodily/somatic response is involved, also, in the generation of meaning—then one may be able to account for the role that the term *lucidity* occupies in the formation of images. Moreover, Ahsen maintains that prolucid dreaming may be involved in the many interactions that take place among the activities, events, and factors of dreams; lucid dreams; sleep awareness; emergence of symbols, metaphors; rational thought; social structures; emerging and decaying civilizations; and the "more cosmic play of the universe which surrounds us" (p. xi). Following his general description of the method of prolucid dreaming (i.e., a new approach to dream research which combines elements of lucid dreaming, ordinary dream-work, and imagery filters in consciousness), Ahsen outlines the specific, basic induction procedures used in prolucid dream analysis; the instructions to participants include the following steps: recall a dream, any dream; consciously interpret the dream; think of your *mother* and keep her in mind and, as you do this, see the dream and go through its experience again; then, think of your *father* and keep him in mind and, as you do this, see the dream and go through its experience again. Ahsen notes that these steps are pursued in an experiential manner, which means that the participant must enter the act of *actually seeing* the dream image in the mind again; he finds that keeping one's mother or father in mind—with or without their images—while seeing the dream images somehow reactivates the dream mechanism so that the dream is now actually experienced in the waking state (the mother and father figures appear to be "activating filters" that interact with the images of the dream in a way similar to a camera's filter, which either shuts out or admits certain aspects of light depending on the filter's design and its intended special dramatic pictorial effect). Ahsen refers to three types of dreams: the original sleep dream; the prolucid M-dream (the dream that is seen while the *mother* is kept in mind); and the prolucid F-dream (the dream that is seen while the *father* is kept in mind); all three types of dreams are experienced in the mind as similar, except that the original dream is recalled while the M-dream and the F-dream are waking experiences that are fresher and of longer duration. Typically, participants characterize the prolucid dreams as better than sleep dreams because prolucid dreams carry more experiential "thrust," containing more detail and substance than possessed by the original recalled dream. According to Ahsen, the primary attraction or benefit of the open-ended prolucid dreaming technique lies in its ability for meaningful and relevant expansion of dream content where it allows the participant to have a larger availability of consciousness material for such dream-content processing. Finally, in his meta-prolucids rejoinder section, following the commentaries on his article, Ahsen integrates his responses to the commentators within a new discussion concerning further perspectives on the prolucid dreaming technique of interlocking waking consciousness with dream consciousness, along with other prolucid perspectives—that invoke alternate physiologies (via symptoms and parental genetics), the examination of myths and archetypes (e.g., prayer) as potentially useful filters (in addition to the already posited parental filters), and the consideration of the special class of images traditionally called *eidos* or *essences,* which disclose and define the foundations of mental phenomena.

The 1995 (*86 [2]*) special issue of the *British Journal of Psychology* explores the relatively lesser-studied fields and problems of motor imagery, the nature of imaginary actions, and the processes shared by overt and imagined actions. Taking part in this discussion are the following investigators: Annett (1995), White and Hardy (1995), Hall, Bernoties, and Schmidt (1995), Vogt (1995), Engelkamp (1995), Salway and Logie (1995), Marks and Isaac (1995), and Williams, Rippon, Stone, and Annett (1995). Annett (1995) notes that there is increasing evidence that motor processes are involved in the generation and manipulation of images, particularly if those images are in any way representative of overt motor acts; he suggests that motor imagery is clearly an area where studies in cognitive psychology converge with new techniques in brain physiology and seem likely to shed new light on some very old problems in psychology. White and Hardy (1995) report on two experiments that examine the relative efficacy of different imagery perspectives on slalom-type and gymnastic-type tasks, involving either an internal visual imagery condition or an external visual imagery condition; they found that on the slalom-task, in a retention test, the *external* visual imagery participants focused on the *speed* of performance, while the *internal* visual imagery participants focused on the *accuracy* of performance. White and Hardy interpreted their findings as suggesting that internal visual imagery is more effective than the external condition for the planning of action in response to changes in a visual field; however, in the gymnastics-task, external visual imagery was found to be more effective than the internal condition for both initial learning and subsequent retention tests.

Hall, Bernoties, and Schmidt (1995) conducted studies that support the hypothesis that imaginary practice may create interference effects (via an experimental-conditions retroactive interference paradigm) that are similar in nature to actual physical practice outcomes. Vogt (1995) conducted three experiments to study the effects of observational, mental, and physical practice on the performance of cyclical movement sequences; his findings suggest that performance, observation, and imagery of sequential patterns involve a common process—characterized as *event generation*—that is either related to an articulatory system (as in the case of physical practice), synchronized with an external event (as in the case of observational practice), or may "run free" without articulatory of perceptual coupling (as in the case of imagery). Vogt's (1995) article includes a references section with over sixty references/citations to studies relating to imagery and motor processes. Engelkamp (1995) found—in paired-associate learning experiments in which unrelated action-verb pairs served as stimuli— that under conditions of enactment-instructions better free recall occurred than under standard learning (and two imagery) conditions, which indicates that enactment conditions provide excellent item-specific information. Also, in a cued-recall condition, it was found that motor encoding hinders stimulus-pair integration and efficient context encoding. Essentially, Engelkamp found that there are participant differences between the following two situations: the encoding processes if one imagines actions that other people perform versus the encoding processes if one imagines oneself performing them and imagining oneself performing an action versus actually performing the action.

In other studies on the relationship between imagery and motor processes, Salway and Logie (1995) report on their use of a dual task methodology that demonstrates that the matrix versus verbal versions of a task rely on separate, specialized cognitive resources, one of which is involved, also, in action-generation; however, under a condition in which a secondary task (i.e., the random generation of numbers) was very demanding on the participants' cognitive resources, both the matrix and verbal tasks were performed poorly, suggesting that each task relies heavily on a common, general purpose resource as well as on their respective specialist resources. Thus, Salway and Logie show that whether performance of a visuospatial or of a verbal task is disrupted by a secondary task (such as random number generation) depends on the nature of the task with which it is combined; they found, also, that the participants' mental imagery system plays a role in the generation of movement. Marks and Isaac (1995) used brain-mapping techniques to study the topographical distribution of EEG activity accompanying visual and motor imagery in four different tasks (e.g., finger touching, fist clenching). Their results showed that participants' EEG alpha waves were attenuated in vivid images during visual imagery (especially in the left posterior quadrant of the cortex), but enhanced during motor imagery. Moreover, after eliminating possible alternative explanations—such as demand characteristics and instrument artifacts—Marks and Isaacs viewed their data as providing strong evidence of the construct validity of the two imagery tests (VVIQ and VMIQ) that were used. Finally, Williams, Rippon, Stone, and Annett (1995) recorded brain-electrical-activity maps from participants as the latter performed a mental rotation test, and completed a vividness-of-movement imagery questionnaire. Overall, the results found by Williams et al. confirm the hypothesis of the involvement of motor, as well as spatial, processes in dynamic imagery; also, their study suggests that some specific EEG measures/sites/regions may provide a useful index of variation in imagery ability. The references section in Williams et al.'s article contains over fifty citations/references relevant to the relationship between imagery and motor processes. For further studies on the motor aspects of imagery, and the imaginary or imagined aspects and features of motor actions, see the following recent studies: Conway, Pleydell-Pearce, Whitecross, and Sharpe (2003); Lutz (2003); Maruff, Wilson, and Currie (2003); Petit, Pegna, Mayer, and Hauert (2003); Reed (2002); Schwoebel, Boronat, and Coslett (2002); Wilson (2003); Wolbers, Weiller, and Buechel (2003).

A "target article" on guided imagery and education by S. M. Drake (1996)—along with an "open peer commentary" section, a response to commentaries section, and a section authored by A. Ahsen (1996)—appears in the 1996 (*20 [1,2]*) issue of the *Journal of Mental Imagery*. Drake chose to use a phenomenological approach and methodology in her study (cf. Giorgi, 1985, 1987). Following her review of the guided imagery/visualization literature in the field of education (cf. Allender, 1991), Drake describes the experience of visualization as reported by six teachers who used the guided imagery technique in their lives and classrooms (cf. Cunningham [1992] and Simonton, Matthews-Simonton, and Creighton [1978] for accounts of the effects of guided imagery in the field of health/well-being). Drake notes that the problem with attempting to relate various theoretical orientations to the issue is that the definition of the term *guided imagery*, itself, is not clear and encompasses the topics of images, imagination, dreams, and daydreams. Thus, it is difficult to distinguish the scientific research aspects of guided imagery. In her methodology with the teachers, the term *visualization* was very serviceable, was widely adopted, and appeared to mean that the produced images—usually following a storyline—were guided by oneself, while the term *guided imagery* was used when the imagery was produced and guided by a tape recording or another person. Based upon data/protocol analyses of the teachers' experiences, Drake found that eight characteristics of three different levels of visualization (i.e., behavioral-cognitive, insight, and transpersonal) were common to all the teachers. Drake's article is accompanied by a references section containing over

230 references/citations relevant to the issue of the theory, practice, and experience of guided imagery.

In Drake's (1996) response to commentaries rejoinder section, she notes that contributors' responses widely affirm the power of imagery as an educational tool. (In a seeming reaction to such acceptance, she gave the following title to her rejoinder section: "Toward a Theory of Guided Imagery in Education.") Finally, in the concluding section, Ahsen (1996) provides an overall critique of guided imagery that argues for more scientific rigor in the area, a closer interaction among the academic classroom, the business office, and the psychological laboratory, and a greater sensitivity to some of guided imagery's roots in literary theory. Ahsen's material is organized into three parts: *imagery origins* (including the issues of guided imagery and psychological research; guidance and the resolution of conflict; consciousness, poetics, and the scientific method); *the dream house* (including descriptions of the "house image" and "mother/father figure" imagery); and *learning ability and disability* (including description of the "nature photograph" conceptualization). For other, more recent studies in the area of guided imagery, see the following sources: J. Ayres and T. A. Ayres, (2003); A. Bakke, M. Purtzer, and P. Newton (2002); L. Hernandez-Guzman, S. Gonzalez, and F. Lopez (2002); and K.-S. Yip (2003).

> Research, of course, will continue to examine the pattern of dependence between the various measures that exist and will persist in its attempt to answer the basic question of whether one underlying process accounts for subjects' performance when artifacts associated with subjects' test behavior are removed.
> —P. W. Sheehan, R. Ashton, and K. White, 1983

> It is recommended that the first step for future directions of study should consist of a codification of extant literatures. Such an effort within imagery psychology would render a valuable service not only to psychology, but also to scholars from sister disciplines who may increasingly recognize the critical role that imagery may play within their provinces, as a factor contributing to the explanation of human action.
> —G. Count-van Manen, 1991

> The fact that positive imagery has not been conclusively shown to enhance athletic activities by the research conducted to date is not equivalent to demonstrating that it can have no beneficial

effects on performance. The effects may be there, but we have simply not investigated the responses under conditions that would clearly reveal them.

—A. J. Budney, S. M. Murphy, and R. L. Woolfolk, 1994

It is true that error lies about us everywhere, and that the price of good science is eternal paranoia. . . . The overall results reported here should engender a well-founded optimism concerning the future of experiential imagery studies.

—A. Richardson, 1994

Every elementary theory about imagery hangs in mid-air, because it is not sufficiently real in the dramatic sense. In an astounding way, imagery, being incipiently dramatic, is more real than the so-called real world. That is where the imagery research should begin.

—A. Ahsen, 1995

The computer and the Internet offer so many fascinating possibilities for imagery research and applications that now, at the threshold of the twenty-first century, we are beginning to envision this adventure into the future.

—A. Ahsen, 2001

Writing dictionary word-entry definitions and digests may be likened to the art of placing a face on a coin. Drastically restricted in area, the result must come up with a reasonable encapsulation of the profile's distinctive features. . . . The secret is this: capture the essence, the bare minimum. . . . With particular reference to the *Stanford Encyclopedia of Philosophy's* entry on *Imagery* . . . it settles for less than the bare minimum. Consequently, the resemblance between its idea of imagery and that in the field of reality is fatally poor.

—J. Weinbaum, 2001

## FUTURE DIRECTIONS IN IMAGERY RESEARCH

In their chapter on assessment of mental imagery, Sheehan, Ashton, and White (1983, pp. 212–14) provide a section on directions for future research that includes the following ideas:

- Concerning individual differences in cognitive abilities, the significance of aptitude needs to be examined at a particular point of time for particular groups of people (it seems likely that analysis of the combinations between ability and test conditions will index the relevance of other processes that may also be important—processes that have been relatively neglected in imagery research).

- Processes that relate to the display of emotion and motivation need to be examined where experience-based modes of assessment are better equipped to indicate their importance than are the more constrained measures of imagery function, such as the traditional objective tests and self-report scales.

- Future imagery research needs to apply different assessment procedures in order to examine more closely the convergent—as opposed to the discriminative—validity of the various tests that may be used; the use of "in vivo thought-sampling" of participants in imagery studies—in conjunction with laboratory assessment methods—would allow researchers to obtain more detailed information about the participants' thoughts that occur during the experimental procedures (such sampling of cognitive data in a variety of ways would help both to discount alternative explanations of obtained results, e.g., the view that participants respond in the experimental setting in terms of the judged propriety of their behavior; and to assist in the reinforcement of most researchers' belief that the various modes of assessment, and tests of imagery, sample processes in common).

- Increasingly, new studies will be conducted to relate imagery to physiological functioning (e.g., study of how images affect a wide variety of physiological responses, such as different changes in EEG patterns between the two cerebral hemispheres as a result of participants' employing different cognitive modes, or in solving different tasks—such as spatial or verbal-arithmetic problems; study of the effect of individual differences in imagery ability on the extent of lateralization of cerebral function— where it may be predicted that good imagers will have faster reaction-times, and will process imaginal stimuli faster and more accurately than will poor imagers; also, it may be predicted that the interaction of concrete/high-imagery-related words with motor or other cognitive performance will be greater in those participants possessing more vivid or intense imagery).

- Psychophysical methodologies and studies of imagery will continue to be a fruitful source of data on imagery ability and its function (e.g., images may not only affect, even cause, bodily reactions, but they may influence, also, the magnitude of such effects).

A lengthy references section is appended to the chapter by Sheehan et al. and contains over 130 citations/references that are relevant to the issue of assessment of mental imagery, including directions for future research.

As part of a special issue of the *Journal of Mental Imagery* (1991, *15 [1,2]*) examining the topic of the relationship between imagery and the discipline of sociology, G. Count-van Manen (1991, pp. 35–59) provides a section on future directions for mental imagery. The "target article" in this issue is also provided by Count-van Manen, and her title is "George Herbert Mead on Mental Imagery: A Neglected Nexus for Interdisciplinary Collaboration with Implications for Social Control"; for critical reactions and commentaries to her article, see Johnson (1991) and Schwalbe (1991), among others. Count-van Manen identifies reciprocal interests in the fields of psychology, social psychology, sociology, and criminology vis-à-vis the issue of mental imagery (cf. Ahsen, 1984c), and suggests the development of new subspecializations—in both sociology and social psychology—of mental imagery (cf. Meltzer, 1991). As an illustration of future research for mental imagery in these areas, Count-van Manen cites the mental imagery impact of terrorist tactics on social units/populations by dissident groups as a means of social control. Moreover, in future research, it may be studied whether the impact of various terrorist tactics (such as lynchings, bombings, brutality, cruelty) over extended time periods tend to depress one's learning and memory abilities, as well as influencing one's social-symbolic imagery (cf. Mead, 1934; Blumer, 1969) in ways that serve to perpetuate intergenerational violence. Count-van Manen examines the implications of symbolic-imagery interaction learning (as a major learning alternative model to behaviorism; cf. Gross, 1978) where the impact of the two approaches are expected—as determined via future study—to contrast in the development of interpersonal learning processes, and as reflected in variables and constructs such as the self, empathy, autonomy, judgment, creativity, and morality. Further, she asserts that the most underdeveloped and/or neglected aspects of the field of mental imagery are those that focus on macrostructural environments hypothesized to affect the contents and processing of mental images—whether emanating from catastrophic historical events (such as terrorist-suicide bombings, war, genocide, and famine), or from the numerous and diverse forms assumed by human cultural, economic, political, and social groupings.

Another recommentation by Count-van Manen for future research in mental imagery consists of the codification of extant literatures where a standard scientific format may be followed and include subtopics on the following: the varying definitions of the concept of mental imagery (cf. Richardson, 1969, 1983); the current state of theoretical directions (cf. Marks, 1986; Sheikh, 1983); the extant major hypotheses, organized by the perspective of the researcher as to whether imagery is viewed arbitrarily as an independent, intervening, or dependent variable; and the weight/substance of empirical evidence of the current theoretical and hypothesized formulations. Finally, Count-van Manen (1991, pp. 54–56) suggests that there are practical—and researchable—human engineering implications of the social-symbolic imagery-interaction processes for massive educational efforts. In effect, her suggestion for the future in this area is a greater macro- and microtheoretical integration—along with relevant class-room-projects and changes in national educational policy—that is more amenable to innovative approaches (involving learning and morality processes) for solving human problems. For other studies on the social/cultural aspects of imagery, including advertising, see the following: Blair, Ma, and Lenton (2001); Bolls (2002); Rychlak (2003); Scott and Batra (2003); Stern (2003); Stewart (2002).

Regarding auditory imagery and inner speech, Reisberg, Wilson, and Smith (1991) suggest future research on the theory of the inner ear, the inner voice, and the lexical ear (cf. Baddeley, 1981, 1986, 1988; Baddeley and Lewis, 1981; Besner, 1987). Based upon their observation that there is a certain diversity within the set of tasks requiring judgments about sound, Reisberg et al. suggest that the inner-voice/inner-ear partnership is one means through which a stimulus-support may be provided—but there are others, also. For instance, in some situations, the participant creates a kinesthetic stimulus, and then perceives it through the channels of proprioception. According to Reisberg et al., the general principle of stimulus-support, and the importance of self-produced stimulus-support, applies equally to imagery in other modalities, and this issue is clearly in need of further exploration in imagery research. They indicate, also, that other research on the lexical ear involving imagery is needed (e.g., perhaps musicians can activate the sound of single chords—just as efficient readers activate whole-word logogens—and then make judgments about such mental representations; it is suggested that the inner ear would be required, say, if the particular judgment demanded analysis of the chords into their component notes). Based upon their survey of a wide range of phenomena (including data from memory, schizo-phrenia, speech perception, music, and reading processes), Reisberg et al. maintain that the mental resource area of auditory imagery is a particularly rich domain that is open to much new research (cf. Reisberg, 1993).

In their chapter on imagery and motor performance—and following their discussion of methodological issues in imagery research—Budney, Murphy, and Woolfolk (1994) indicate some future research issues concerning the relationship between imagery and performance, especially athletic activities. They recommend the future study of the following factors/variables:

- Idiographic versus nomothetic approaches. (Virtually all investigations of imagery in the imagery-motor performance area have employed aggregated/nomothetic data and averaged-effects. What is needed are more idiographic studies to determine if there are individuals for whom imagery may make a positive difference. The single-participant and matched designs are effective future strategies to use to detect imagery effects in the individual.)
- Low external validity (to correct this, future studies should be more longitudinal in nature where athletes, for instance, are given intensive imagery training under field conditions for several months or years).
- Complex interactive effects (future research may test whether imagery might "work" most effectively when combined with other elements or factors; e.g., combining relaxation training with imagery training, combining imaginal rehearsal with positive self-verbalization, or combining and interspersing mental with physical practice may help in understanding the complicated interactive effects of imagery operating in many individuals, including athletes).

Moreover, Budney et al. observe—based upon the current popularity of imagery interventions and use by athletes, coaches, and sport psychologists—that a new generation of research issues has been established, including needed study of the following topics: skill acquisition, skill maintenance, event-planning of performance, stress management, self-efficacy enhancement, and arousal regulation. Budney et al. provide a lengthy references section containing seventy-five citations/references that relate to the issue of imagery, sports, and motor performance. For further studies on imagery vis-à-vis sports and motor performance, see the following: Cumming (2002); Weinberg, Butt, Knight, Burke, and Jackson (2003).

In one of his chapters on individual differences in thought imagery, A. Richardson (1994) recommends methodological improvements and suggests directions and topics for future imagery research. Among his selected areas of interest are the following: ambiguity in the mean-

ing given to the concept of vividness; possible replacements on imagery tests of visual items referring to people by items having a more
neutral content; the three relatively independent imaging abilities of
vividness, control, and preference should serve as "provisional markers" when producing new imagery tests or modifying old ones; the
participant-selection process should be carried out by someone other
than the experimenter; when employing correlational analyses on data,
make corrections for skewedness of data; and, in future studies, the
researcher should take participant-motivational variables into account
as well as imagery-ability variables.

In a "target article," McKelvie (1995) discusses the VVIQ as a useful psychometric tool of individual differences in visual imagery vividness, and suggests future research, in particular, with the VVIQ. (For
further discussion of McKelvie's important article, see the earlier subsection titled "Questionnaires, Scales, and Tests of Imagery" in this
chapter.) Among his recommendations, McKelvie makes the following points:

1. Future studies should focus attention on the construct validity of the
   VVIQ.
2. Future studies should reduce ambiguity in the operational definition of
   the factor of vividness.
3. In instructions to participants, the often-used implicit demand that a visual image be experienced should be removed, and replaced by a more
   neutral directive containing the words "whether" or "if."
4. Broaden the range of scores obtained on imagery rating scales by increasing the number of scale-points to six or seven.
5. To improve the reliability of the VVIQ, increase the number of test items.
6. Drop the practice of rating items on the VVIQ twice, with eyes open or
   closed.
7. Future experimental designs should be double-blind to reduce the likelihood that participants (and experimenters) make a connection between
   the VVIQ and the criterion task(s).
8. Researchers in future studies should include better experimental control
   conditions in order to exclude alternative explanations for obtained results.

In a special issue of the *Journal of Mental Imagery* (2001, *25
[1,2]*) dealing with the topic of imagery and the Internet, a number
of contributors provide insights, perspectives, and directions for new
investigations in imagery research. In his editorial in that issue, Ahsen
(2001) sets the tone for the modern relationships between the

computer/Internet and imagery research (Ahsen's "new initiative" may be viewed online at the following addresses: www.journalof mentalimagery.com and www.imagery_iia). Among the observations, recommendations, and statements offered by contributors to the journal issue are the following (with contributor's name in parentheses):

1. The Internet has provided a new term/concept for psychology, "psychotherapy online" which may ultimately replace face-to-face contact with a long-distance connection via the novel modality of Internet communication where coaching, support, and counseling are available to individuals in a manner similar to "tele-medicine" which treats patients from distant locations.

2. In the context of a visual culture theory and its applications, a theory of the "virtual mind" (cf. "virtual reality") would become a central focal point and lift human imagination from its traditional status or place into a context involving greater personal freedom.

3. Moreover, when mental images via the computer medium are activated and employed, one may achieve what might be called "self-therapy in a virtual time-space" (A. Ahsen).

4. The computer, e-mails, faxes, teleconferences, and the Internet stand in service of the image.

5. The birth of the Internet invites imagery (P. McKellar).

6. It is suggested that the International Imagery Association (IIA) set up a Web page with the following content: a searchable index of titles, and preferably abstracts, of all previous issues of the *Journal of Mental Imagery* (cf. Hochman, 2001); a set of bibliographies for the major subfields within mental imagery research, so that anyone interested in imagery, at whatever level, may find out more information (cf. "Imagery Bibliography, 1977–1991," *Journal of Mental Imagery*, 1994, *18*, 1–277).

7. Readily accessed full-text copies of the major instruments for measurement of imaging capacity.

8. Readily accessed full-text copies of key articles about the applications of mental imagery research.

9. The e-mail and postal directions of all members of the IIA as a means of facilitating communication (A. Campos).

10. It is obvious, as psychologists become more and more computer and Internet dependent, that all psychological journals—those dealing with imagery, as well as other topics—will eventually appear on the Internet for downloading and reading.

11. Paper-versions of journals are becoming increasingly more expensive and space-consuming; an electronic version of a journal would be inexpensive,

would save valuable library storage space, and would be more convenient and easy for the general reader and researcher to access (B.
Wallace).

12. It is difficult to disregard Ahsen's enormous contribution of several
decades of study and research in the field of mental imagery (J.
Weinbaum).

13. Why we are being exposed to such poor scholarship on the Internet,
in certain instances, in the management of scientific notions concerning imagery is beyond comprehension (T. D. Nixon).

14. In locating various sites under the search term "psychotherapy online,"
it may be discovered in the category of "psychotherapy delivery over
the Internet" that there are four modalities: real time, video telecon-
ferencing, e-mail, and Web telephony.

15. There are a number of Web sites provided here concerning mental
health, therapy, and names and credentials of psychotherapists and
psychological practitioners, in addition to "mental imagery" sources and
Web sites online.

16. The several advantages, as well as the limitations of, online psychotherapy are identified (B. M. Landau).

17. A review of mental imagery in the French language is available on the
World Wide Web (O. Hamel).

18. A basic online search concerning the concept of the "eidetic" using the
multiple sources of PsycINFO, MEDLINE, and ERIC is provided
(Hochman, 2001).

## REFERENCES

Ahsen, A. (1965). *Eidetic psychotherapy: A short introduction.* New York:
Brandon House.

Ahsen, A. (1968). *Basic concepts in eidetic psychotherapy.* New York: Brandon
House.

Ahsen, A. (1972). *Eidetic Parents Test and analysis.* New York: Brandon
House.

Ahsen, A. (1977a). Eidetics: An overview. *Journal of Mental Imagery, 1,* 5–
38.

Ahsen, A. (1977b). *Psycheye: Self-analytic consciousness.* New York: Brandon
House.

Ahsen, A. (1982). Imagery in perceptual learning and clinical application.
*Journal of Mental Imagery, 6,* 157–86.

Ahsen, A. (1984a). Heartbeat as a stimulus for vivid imagery: A report on
individual differences in imagery function. *Journal of Mental Imagery, 8,* 105–10. (Also, see *Journal of Mental Imagery* [1993], *17,* 261–
66.)

Ahsen, A. (1984b). ISM: The triple code model for imagery and psychophysiology. *Journal of Mental Imagery, 8*, 15–42.

Ahsen, A. (1984c). *Trojan horse: Imagery in psychology, art, literature, and politics.* New York: Brandon House. (Also, see Hilgard, E. R. [1984]. Review of the books *Trojan horse* and *Rhea complex* by Akhter Ahsen. *Journal of Mental Imagery, 11*, 161–62.)

Ahsen, A. (1985). Unvividness paradox. *Journal of Mental Imagery, 9*, 1–18.

Ahsen, A. (1985/1987). Image psychology and the empirical method. *Journal of Mental Imagery, 9*, 1–40; *11*, 1–295.

Ahsen, A. (1986a). Prologue to unvividness paradox. *Journal of Mental Imagery, 10*, 1–8.

Ahsen, A. (1986b). The New Structuralism: Images in dramatic interlock. *Journal of Mental Imagery, 10*, 1–92.

Ahsen, A. (1987). Epilogue to unvividness paradox. *Journal of Mental Imagery, 11*, 13–59.

Ahsen, A. (1988). Imagery, unvividness paradox, and the paradigm of control. *Journal of Mental Imagery, 12*, 1–44.

Ahsen, A. (1989). Scientific misconduct in behaviorist circles: A response to Eysenck's and Skinner's response. *Journal of Mental Imagery, 13*, 1–20.

Ahsen, A. (1990). AA-VVIQ and imagery paradigm: Vividness and unvividness issue in VVIQ research programs. *Journal of Mental Imagery, 14*, 1–58.

Ahsen, A. (1991). A second report on AA-VVIQ: Role of vivid and unvivid images in consciousness research. *Journal of Mental Imagery, 15*, 1–32.

Ahsen, A. (1992). *Prolucid dreaming.* New York: Brandon House. (Also, see *Journal of Mental Imagery* [1992], *16*, 3–84; *Journal of Mental Imagery* [1988], *12*, 1–70.)

Ahsen, A. (1993a). A commentary on imagery tests. *Journal of Mental Imagery, 17*, 153–96.

Ahsen, A. (1993b). Introductory remarks on "Imagery paradigms in psychology;" Imagery paradigm: Imaginative consciousness into the experimental and clinical setting. *Journal of Mental Imagery, 17*, 3–49.

Ahsen, A. (1993c). *Learning ability and disability: An image approach.* New York: Brandon House.

Ahsen, A. (1995). Self-report questionnaires: New directions for imagery research. *Journal of Mental Imagery, 19*, 107–23.

Ahsen, A. (1996). Guided imagery: The quest for a science. *Journal of Mental Imagery, 20*, 165–204.

Ahsen, A. (2000). Image and maze: Learning through imagery functions. *Journal of Mental Imagery, 24*, 1–60.

Ahsen, A. (2001). Imagery online: Editorial. *Journal of Mental Imagery, 25*, 1–2.

Aleman, A., deHaan, E., Boecker, K., Hijman, R., & Kahn, R. (2002). Hallucinations in schizophrenia: Imbalance between imagery and perception? *Schizophrenia Research, 57,* 315–16.

Algom, D. (1980). Mental imagery: A case study in the logical development of a scientific concept. In D. Algom, *Studies in education.* Haifa: Haifa University Press.

Algom, D., & Lewin, I. (1976). Four theoretico-historical approaches to the study of imagination. *Megamot, 22,* 298–314.

Algom, D., & Lewin, I. (1981–1982). An experimental cross-validation of mental imagery. *Imagination, Cognition, and Personality, 1,* 49–65.

Allen, M., & Yen, W. (1979). *Introduction to measurement theory.* Monterey, CA: Brooks/Cole.

Allender, J. (1991). *Imagery in teaching and learning.* New York: Praeger.

Amadeo, M., & Shagass, C. (1963). Eye movements, attention, and hypnosis. *Journal of Nervous and Mental Disease, 136,* 139–45.

Anastasi, A. (1988). *Psychological testing.* New York: Macmillan.

Anderson, M. (1980). Imaginal processes, therapeutic applications, and theoretical models. In M. J. Mahoney (Ed.), *Psychotherapy process: Current issues and future directions.* New York: Plenum Press.

Anderson, N. H. (1961). Scales and statistics: Parametric and nonparametric. *Psychological Bulletin, 58,* 305–16.

Anderson, N. S. (1987). Cognition, learning, and memory. In M. A. Baker (Ed.), *Sex differences in human performance.* Chichester, UK: Wiley.

Angell, J. R., & Thompson, H. B. (1899). The relations between certain organic processes and consciousness. *Psychological Review, 6,* 32–69.

Annett, J. (1995). Imagery and motor processes: Editorial overview. *British Journal of Psychology, 86,* 161–68.

Antonietti, A., & Giorgetti, M. (1996–1997). A study of some psychometric properties of the Verbalizer-Visualizer Questionnaire. *Journal of Mental Imagery, 20,* 59–68.

Antrobus, J. S. (1968). Information theory and stimulus-independent thought. *British Journal of Psychology, 59,* 423–30.

Antrobus, J. S., Antrobus, J. S., & Singer, J. L. (1964). Eye movements accompanying daydreaming, visual imagery, and thought impression. *Journal of Abnormal and Social Psychology, 69,* 244–52.

Antrobus, J. S., & Singer, J. L. (1965). Eye movements during fantasies: Imagining and suppressing fantasies. *Archives of General Psychiatry, 12,* 71–76.

Antrobus, J. S., Singer, J. L., & Greenberg, S. (1966). Studies in the stream of consciousness: Experimental enhancement and suppression of spontaneous cognitive processes. *Perceptual and Motor Skills, 23,* 399–417.

Arabian, J. M., & Furedy, J. J. (1983). Individual differences in imagery ability and Pavlovian heart rate decelerative conditioning. *Psychophysiology, 20,* 325–31.

Arnold, M. B. (1984a). Imagery and psychophysiological response. *Journal of Mental Imagery, 8,* 43–50.

Arnold, M. B. (1984b). *Memory and the brain.* Hillsdale, NJ: Erlbaum.

Asher, E., & Ort, R. (1951). Eye movements as a complex indicator. *Journal of General Psychology, 45,* 209–17.

Ashton, R. (1982). Mist: Comments on Marks and McKellar. *Journal of Mental Imagery, 6,* 31–32.

Ashton, R., & White, K. D. (1980). Sex differences in imagery vividness: An artefact of the test. *British Journal of Psychology, 71,* 35–38.

Ashton, V., & Dwyer, J. (1975). The left: Lateral eye movments and ideology. *Perceptual and Motor Skills, 41,* 248–50.

Ayres, J., & Ayres, T. A. (2003). Using images to enhance the impact of visualization. *Communication Reports, 16,* 47–56.

Baddeley, A. (1981). The concept of working memory: A view of its current state of probable future development. *Cognition, 10,* 17–23.

Baddeley, A. (1986). *Working memory.* Oxford, UK: Clarendon Press.

Baddeley, A. (1988). Imagery and working memory. In M. Denis, J. Engelkamp, & J.T.E. Richardson (Eds.), *Cognitive and neuropsychological approaches to mental imagery.* Dordrecht, The Netherlands: M. Nijhoff.

Baddeley, A., & Hitch, G. (1974). Working memory. In G. H. Bower (Ed.), *The psychology of learning and motivation.* Vol. 8. New York: Academic Press.

Baddeley, A., & Lewis, V. (1981). Inner active processes in reading: The inner voice, the inner ear, and the inner eye. In A. M. Lesgold & C. A. Perfetti (Eds.), *Interactive processes in reading.* Hillsdale, NJ: Erlbaum.

Bain, A. (1880). Mr. Galton's statistics of mental imagery. *Mind, 5,* 564–73.

Bakan, P. (1969). Hypnotizability, laterality of eye movements, and functional brain asymmetry. *Perceptual and Motor Skills, 28,* 927–32.

Bakan, P. (1971). The eyes have it. *Psychology Today, 4,* 64–67, 96.

Bakan, P., & Strayer, F. F. (1973). On reliability of conjugate lateral eye movements. *Perceptual and Motor Skills, 36,* 429–30.

Bakke, A. C., Purtzer, M., & Newton, P. (2002). The effect of hypnotic-guided imagery on psychological well-being and immune function in patients with prior breast cancer. *Journal of Psychosomatic Research, 53,* 1131–37.

Bandler, R., & Grinder, J. (1979). *Frogs into princes: Neuro-linguistic programming.* Moab, UT: Real People Press.

Barber, T. X. (1965). Physiological effects of "hypnotic suggestions": A critical review of recent research (1960–1964). *Psychological Bulletin, 63,* 201–22.

Barber, T. X. (1978). Hypnosis, suggestions, and psychosomatic phenomena: A new look from the standpoint of recent experimental studies. *American Journal of Clinical Hypnosis, 21,* 13–27.

Barber, T. X., & Wilson, S. C. (1979). Guided imagining and hypnosis: Theoretical and empirical overlap and convergence in a new creative imagination scale. *Journal of Mental Imagery, 2,* 67–88.

Barnat, M. R. (1974). Some personality correlates of the conjugate lateral eye movement phenomenon. *Journal of Personality Assessment, 38,* 223–25.

Barratt, P. E. (1956). Use of the EEG in the study of imagery. *British Journal of Psychology, 47,* 101–14.

Barratt, P. E. (1971). *Bases of psychological methods.* New York: Wiley.

Bartlett, F. C. (1927). The relevance of visual imagery to the process of thinking. *British Journal of Psychology, 18,* 23–29.

Bartlett, F. C. (1932). *Remembering.* Cambridge, UK: Cambridge University Press.

Begg, I. (1988). What does the vividness of an image tell us about the value of imagery? *Journal of Mental Imagery, 12,* 45–56.

Bellezza, F. S. (1995). Factors that affect vividness ratings. *Journal of Mental Imagery, 19,* 123–29.

Bennett, G., Seashore, H., & Wesman, A. (1974). *Fifth edition manual for the differential aptitude tests.* New York: The Psychological Corporation.

Berger, G. H., & Gaunitz, C. B. (1977). Self-rated imagery and vividness of task pictures in relation to visual memory. *British Journal of Psychology, 68,* 283–88.

Berger, G. H., & Gaunitz, C. B. (1979). Self-rated imagery and encoding strategies in visual memory. *British Journal of Psychology, 70,* 21–24.

Berkowitz, L., & Donnerstein, E. (1982). External validity is more than skin deep. *American Psychologist, 37,* 245–57.

Besner, D. (1987). Phonology, lexical access in reading, and articulatory suppression: A critical review. *Quarterly Journal of Experimental Psychology, 39A,* 467–78.

Betts, G. H. (1909). The distribution and functions of mental imagery. *Teachers College, Columbia University, Contributions to Education, 26,* 1–99. (Also, see same titled book [1972], New York: AMS Press.)

Biederman, I. (1987). Recognition-by-components: A theory of human image understanding. *Psychological Review, 94,* 115–47.

Binet, A. (1889). *Psychology of reasoning.* Paris: Alcan.

Birnbaum, M. (Ed.) (2000). *Psychological experiments on the Internet.* San Diego, CA: Academic Press.

Bischof, K. (1988). The effects of central versus peripheral distraction on visual and verbal learning. In M. Denis, J. Engelkamp, & J.T.E. Richardson (Eds.), *Cognitive and neuropsychological approaches to mental imagery.* Dordrecht, The Netherlands: M. Nijhoff.

Blackburn, T. (1971). Sensuous-intellectual complementarity in science. *Science, 172,* 1003–7.

Blair, I., Ma, J., & Lenton, A. (2001). Imagining stereotypes away: The moderation of implicit stereotypes through mental imagery. *Journal of Personality and Social Psychology, 81,* 828–41.

Blum, R. H. (1956). Photic stimulation, imagery, and alpha rhythm. *Journal of Mental Science, 102,* 160–67.

Blumer, H. (1969). *Symbolic interactionism.* Englewood Cliffs, NJ: Prentice-Hall.

Bock, R. D., & Jones, L. V. (1968). *The measurement and prediction of judgment and choice.* San Francisco: Holden-Day.

Bolls, P. D. (2002). I can hear you, but can I see you? The use of visual cognition during exposure to high-imagery radio advertisements. *Communication Research, 29,* 537–63.

Bower, G. H. (1972). Mental imagery and associative learning. In L. Gregg (Ed.), *Cognition in learning and memory.* New York: Wiley.

Bowers, H. (1929). Constancy of imaginal content. *Journal of Educational Psychology, 20,* 295–98.

Bradshaw, J. L., & Nettleton, N. C. (1981). The nature of hemispheric specialization in man. *The Behavioral and Brain Sciences, 4,* 51–91.

Brewer, W. F. (1974). The problem of meaning and the interrelations of the higher mental processes. In W. B. Weiner & D. S. Palermo (Eds.), *Cognition and the symbolic processes.* New York: Wiley.

Broadway, C. M. (1972). Personality correlates of imagery ability. *Dissertation Abstracts International, 32,* 5433-B.

Bronowski, J. (1960). *The common sense of science.* Middlesex, UK: Penguin.

Brooks, L. R. (1967). The suppression of visualization by reading. *Quarterly Journal of Experimental Psychology, 19,* 289–99.

Brower, D. (1947). The experimental study of imagery. I. The relation of imagery to intelligence; II. The relative predominance of various imagery modalities. *Journal of General Psychology, 37,* 199–200; 229–31.

Brown, B. B. (1966). Specificity of EEG photic flicker responses to color as related to visual imagery ability. *Psychophysiology, 2,* 197–207.

Brown, B. B. (1970). Recognition of aspects of consciousness through association with EEG alpha activity represented by a light sign. *Psychophysiology, 6,* 442–52.

Brown, B. B. (1971). Awareness of EEG subjective activity relationship detected within a closed feedback system. *Psychophysiology, 7,* 451–64.

Brown, F. G. (1984/1994). Measurement. In R. J. Corsini (Ed.), *Encyclopedia of psychology.* Vol. 2. New York: Wiley.

Buchanan, T., & Smith, J. L. (1999a). Research on the Internet: Validation of a World Wide Web mediated personality scale. *British Journal of Psychology, 90,* 125–44.

Buchanan, T., & Smith, J. L. (1999b). Using the Internet for psychological research: Personality testing on the World Wide Web. *Behavior Research Methods, Instruments, and Computers, 31,* 565–71.

Budney, A., Murphy, S., & Woolfolk, R. (1994). Imagery and motor performance: What do we really know? In A. A. Sheikh & E. R. Korn (Eds.), *Imagery in sports and physical performance*. Amityville, NY: Baywood.

Buffery, A.W.H., & Gray, J. A. (1972). Sex differences in the development of spatial and linguistic skills. In C. Ounsted & D. C. Taylor (Eds.), *Gender differences: Their ontogency and significance*. Edinburgh: Churchill Livingstone.

Bugelski, B. R. (1962a). Learning and imagery. *Journal of Mental Imagery, 6*, 1–92.

Bugelski, B. R. (1962b). Presentation time, total time, and mediation. *Journal of Experimental Psychology, 63*, 409–12.

Bugelski, B. R. (1970). Words and things and images. *American Psychologist, 25*, 1001–12.

Bugelski, B. R. (1971). The definition of the image. In S. Segal (Ed.), *Imagery: Current cognitive approaches*. New York: Academic Press.

Bugelski, B. R. (1977). Imagery and verbal behavior. *Journal of Mental Imagery, 1*, 39–52.

Bugelski, B. R. (1982). Learning and imagery. *Journal of Mental Imagery, 6*, 1–92.

Bugelski, B. R. (1989). Commentary on scientific misconduct: Sins of omission. *Journal of Mental Imagery, 13*, 27–30.

Bugelski, B. R. (1990). Bugelski-Hilgard statement. *Journal of Mental Imagery, 14*, vii. (Also, see A. Ahsen [1989], 13.)

Burns, B. (1967). The effect of repression on visual imagery. Unpublished master's thesis, Michigan State University.

Burt, C. (1938). Factor analysis by sub-matrices. *Journal of Psychology, 6*, 339–75.

Carey, N. (1915). Factors in the mental processes of schoolchildren. I. Visual and auditory imagery. *British Journal of Psychology, 7*, 453–90.

Carroll, D., Baker, J., & Preston, M. (1979). Individual differences in visual imaging and the voluntary control of heart rate. *British Journal of Psychology, 70*, 39–49.

Carroll, J. D., & Arabie, P. (1980). Multidimensional scaling. *Annual Review of Psychology, 31*, 607–49.

Cautela, J. R., & Tondo, T. R. (1971). Imagery survey schedule. Unpublished imagery questionnaire, Boston College.

Chara, P. J., Jr. (1989). A questionable questionnaire: A rejoinder to Marks. *Perceptual and Motor Skills, 68*, 159–62.

Chara P. J., Jr., & Hamm, D. A. (1988). A semantic analysis of the imagery questionnaire. *Perceptual and Motor Skills, 66*, 113–14.

Chara P. J., Jr., & Hamm, D. A. (1989). An inquiry into the construct validity of the Vividness of Visual Imagery Questionnaire. *Perceptual and Motor Skills, 69*, 127–36.

Chara P. J., Jr., & Verplanck, W. S. (1986). The imagery questionnaire: An investigation of its validity. *Perceptual and Motor Skills, 63*, 915–20.

Cheney, S., Miller, L., & Rees, R. (1982). Imagery and eye movements. *Journal of Mental Imagery, 6*, 113–24.

Chowdhury, K. R. (1956). An experimental study of imagery and its relations to abilities and interests. Unpublished doctoral dissertation, University of London.

Chowdhury, K. R., & Vernon, P. E. (1964). An experimental study of imagery and its relation to abilities and interests. *British Journal of Psychology, 55*, 355–64.

Christal, R. E. (1958). Factor analytic study of visual memory. *Psychological Monographs, 73*, No. 466.

Christiansen, T., & Stone, D. R. (1968). Visual imagery and level of mediator abstractness in induced mediation paradigms. *Perceptual and Motor Skills, 26*, 775–79.

Cohen, B., & Saslona, M. (1990). The advantage of being an habitual visualizer. *Journal of Mental Imagery, 14*, 101–12.

Cohn, J. (1894). Experimentelle untersuchungen uber die gefuhlsbetonung der farben, helligkeiten, und ihrer combination. *Philosophische Studien, 10*, 562–603.

Colman, F. D., & Paivio, A. (1969). Pupillary response and galvanic skin response during an imagery task. *Psychonomic Science, 16*, 296–97.

Colman, F. D., & Paivio, A. (1970). Pupillary dilation and mediation processes during paired-associate learning. *Canadian Journal of Psychology, 24*, 261–70.

Comstock, C. (1921). On the relevance of imagery to the process of thought. *American Journal of Psychology, 32*, 196–230.

Conway, M., Pleydell-Pearce, C., Whitecross, S., & Sharpe, H. (2003). Neurophysiological correlates of memory for experienced and imagined events. *Neuropsychologia, 41*, 334–40.

Coombs, C. H. (1950). Psychological scaling without a unit of measurement. *Psychological Review, 57*, 148–58.

Coombs, C. H. (1976). *A theory of data.* New York: Wiley.

Coombs, C. H., Dawes, R. M., & Tversky, A. (1981). *Mathematical psychology: An elementary introduction.* Englewood Cliffs, NJ: Prentice-Hall.

Cooper, L. A. (1975). Mental transformation of random two-dimensional shapes. *Cognitive Psychology, 7*, 20–43.

Cooper, L. A. (1976). Demonstration of a mental analog of an external rotation. *Perception & Psychophysics, 19*, 296–302.

Cooper, L. A., & Podgorny, P. (1976). Mental transformations and visual comparison processes: Effects of complexity and similarity. *Journal of Experimental Psychology: Human Perception and Performance, 2*, 503–14.

Cooper, L. A., & Shepard, R. N. (1973). Chronometric studies of the rotation of mental images. In W. G. Chase (Ed.), *Visual information processing*. New York: Academic Press.

Cooper, L. A., & Shepard, R. N. (1975). Mental transformation in the identification of left and right hands. *Journal of Experimental Psychology: Human Perception and Performance, 1,* 48–56.

Cooper, L. A., & Shepard, R. N. (1978). Transformations on representations of objects in space. In E. C. Carterette & M. Friedman (Eds.), *Handbook of perception: Space and object perception*. Vol. 8. New York: Academic Press.

Corbin, C. B. (1972). Mental practice. In W. P. Morgan (Ed.), *Ergogenic aids and muscular performance*. New York: Academic Press.

Costello, C., & McGregor, P. (1957). The relationships between some aspects of visual imagery and the alpha rhythm. *Journal of Mental Science, 103,* 786–95.

Count-van Manen, G. (1991). Future directions for mental imagery. *Journal of Mental Imagery, 15,* 35–59.

Crano, W., & Brewer, M. (1972). *Principles of research in social psychology*. New York: McGraw-Hill.

Cronbach, L. J. (1957). The two disciplines of scientific psychology. *American Psychologist, 12,* 671–84.

Cronbach, L. J., & Meehl, P. E. (1955). Construct validity in psychological tests. *Psychological Bulletin, 52,* 281–302.

Crouch, W. W. (1976). Dominant direction of conjugate lateral eye movements and responsiveness to facial and verbal cues. *Perceptual and Motor Skills, 42,* 167–74.

Crowne, D. P., & Marlowe, D. (1960). A new scale of social desirability independent of psychopathology. *Journal of Consulting Psychology, 24,* 349–54.

Cumming, J. L. (2002). Competitive athletes' use of imagery and the deliberate practice framework. *Dissertation Abstracts International, 63(5-B),* 2565.

Cunningham, A. (1992). *A healing journal: Overcoming the crisis of cancer*. Toronto: Key Porte.

Cunnington, B. F., & Torrance, E. P. (1965). *Sounds and images: Teachers guide and recorded text (adult version)*. New York: Ginn.

Danaher, B. G., & Thoresen, C. E. (1972). Imagery assessment by self-report and behavioral measures. *Behaviour Research and Therapy, 10,* 131–38.

Day, M. E. (1964). An eye movement phenomenon relating to attention, thought, and anxiety. *Perceptual and Motor Skills, 19,* 443–46.

Day, M. E. (1967). An eye movement indicator of type and level of anxiety: Some clinical observations. *Journal of Clinical Psychology, 66,* 438–41.

Deckert, G. H. (1964). Pursuit eye movements in the absence of a moving stimulus. *Science, 143,* 1192–93.

Dement, W., & Kleitman, N. (1957). The relation of eye movements during sleep to dream activity: An objective method of the study of dreaming. *Journal of Experimental Psychology, 53,* 339–46.

Denis, M. (1988). Imagery and prose processing. In M. Denis, J. Engelkamp, & J.T.E. Richardson (Eds.), *Cognitive and neuropsychological approaches to mental imagery.* Dordrecht, Netherlands: M. Nijhoff.

Desrochers, A. (1988). Imagery, memory, and prose processing. In M. Denis, J. Engelkamp, & J.T.E. Richardson (Eds.), *Cognitive and neuropsychological approaches to mental imagery.* Dordrecht, Netherlands: M. Nijhoff.

Di Vesta, F. J., & Sunshine, P. M. (1974). The retrieval of abstract and concrete materials as functions of imagery, mediation, and mnemonic aids. *Memory and Cognition, 2,* 340–44.

Doob, L. W. (1982). Structural eidetic images in African societies. *Journal of Mental Imagery, 6,* 44–46.

Downing, F. (1987). Imagery and the structure of design inquiry. *Journal of Mental Imagery, 11,* 61–86.

Drake, S. M. (1996). Guided imagery and education: Theory, practice, and experience. *Journal of Mental Imagery, 20,* 1–58.

Duke, J. D. (1968). Lateral eye movement behavior. *Journal of General Psychology, 78,* 189–95.

Eagle, M. (1962). Personality correlates of sensitivity to subliminal stimulation. *Journal of Nervous and Mental Disorders, 134,* 1–17.

Eagle, M., Wolitzky, D., & Klein, G. (1966). Imagery: Effect of a concealed figure in a stimulus. *Science, 151,* 837–39.

Edwards, J. E., & Wilkins, W. (1981). Verbalizer-Visualizer Questionnaire: Relationship with imagery and verbal-visual ability. *Journal of Mental Imagery, 5,* 137–42.

Ehrlichman, H., & Weinberger, A. (1978). Lateral eye movements and hemispheric asymmetry: A critical review. *Psychological Bulletin, 85,* 1080–101.

Ehrlichman, H., Weiner, S., & Baker, A. (1974). Effects of verbal and spatial questions on initial gaze shifts. *Neuropsychologia, 12,* 265–77.

Elmes, D. G., Kantowitz, B. H., & Roediger, H. L., III. (2003). *Research methods in psychology.* 7th edition. Belmont, CA: Wadsworth/Thomson.

Engelkamp, J. (1995). Visual imagery and enactment of actions in memory. *British Journal of Psychology, 86,* 227–40.

Ernest, C. H. (1977). Imagery ability and cognition: A critical review. *Journal of Mental Imagery, 2,* 181–216.

Etaugh, C. F. (1972). Personality correlates of lateral eye movements. *Perceptual and Motor Skills, 34,* 751–54.

Evans, I. M., & Kamemoto, W. S. (1973). Reliability of the short form of Betts' questionnaire upon mental imagery: A replication. *Psychological Reports, 33,* 281–82.

Eysenck, H. J. (1983). Personality as a fundamental concept in scientific psychology. *Australian Journal of Psychology, 35,* 289–304.

Eysenck, H. J. (1989). Behavior therapy, cognition, and the use of imagery. *Journal of Mental Imagery, 13,* 21–26.

Fairweather, H. (1976). Sex differences in cognition. *Cognition, 4,* 231–80.

Fechner, G. T. (1860). *Elemente der psychophysik.* Leipzig: Breitkopf & Hartel.

Fechner, G. T. (1860/1966). *Elements of psychophysics.* English edition. D. H. Howes & E. G. Boring (Eds.). New York: Holt, Rinehart and Winston.

Fechner, G. T. (1876). *Vorshule der asthetik.* Leipzig: Breitkopf & Hartel.

Feingold, A. (1988). Cognitive gender differences are disappearing. *American Psychologist, 43,* 95–103.

Ferguson, E. S. (1977). The mind's eye: Nonverbal thought in technology. *Science, 197,* 827–36.

Fernald, M. R. (1912). The diagnosis of mental imagery. *Psychological Monographs, 14,* 1–169.

Finke, R. A. (1985). Theories relating mental imagery to perception. *Psychological Bulletin, 98,* 236–59.

Finke, R. A. (1989). *Principles of mental imagery.* Cambridge, MA: M.I.T. Press.

Finke, R. A., & Pinker, S. (1983). Directional scanning of remembered visual patterns. *Journal of Experimental Psychology: Learning, Memory, and Cognition, 9,* 398–410.

Fisher, C. (1954). Dreams and perception. *Journal of the American Psychoanalytical Association, 3,* 380–445.

Forisha, B. (1975). Mental imagery and verbal processes: A developmental study. *Developmental Psychology, 11,* 259–67.

Forisha, B. (1981). Patterns of creativity and mental imagery in men and women. *Journal of Mental Imagery, 5,* 85–96.

Fox, C. (1914). The conditions which arouse mental images in thought. *British Journal of Psychology, 6,* 420–31.

Freedman, S. J., & Marks, P. A. (1965). Visual imagery produced by rhythmic photic stimulation: Personality correlates and phenomenology. *British Journal of Psychology, 56,* 95–112.

Freud, S. (1885/1966). Project for a scientific psychology. In J. S. Strachey (Ed.), *The standard edition of the complete psychological works of Sigmund Freud.* Vol. 1. London: Hogarth Press.

Freud, S. (1915/1957). The unconscious. In J. S. Strachey (Ed.), *The standard edition of the complete psychological works of Sigmund Freud.* Vol. 1. London: Hogarth Press.

Gaarder, K. (1967). Some patterns of fixation saccadic eye movements. *Psychonomic Science, 7,* 145–46.

Gaito, J. (1960). Scale, classification, and statistics. *Psychological Review, 67*, 277–78.

Gaito, J. (1980). Measurement scales and statistics: Resurgence of an old misconception. *Psychological Bulletin, 87*, 564–67.

Gaito, J. (1986). Some issues in the measurement-statistics controversy. *Canadian Psychology, 27*, 63–68.

Galin, D., & Ornstein, R. (1974). Individual differences in cognitive style. I. Reflective eye movements. *Neuropsychologia, 12*, 367–76.

Galton, F. (1879). Psychometric experiments. *Brain, 2*, 149–62.

Galton, F. (1880). Statistics of mental imagery. *Mind, 5*, 301–18.

Galton, F. (1883/1907). *Inquiries into human faculty and its development.* London: Macmillan/London: Dent.

Gardner, P. (1975). Scales and statistics. *Review of Educational Research, 45*, 43–57.

Garner, W. R., Hake, H. W., & Eriksen, C. W. (1956). Operationism and the concept of perception. *Psychological Review, 63*, 149–59.

Giorgi, A. (1985). Sketch of a psychological phenomenological method. In A. Giorgi (Ed.), *Phenomenology and psychological research.* Pittsburgh, PA: Duquesne University Press.

Giorgi, A. (1987). Phenomenology and the research tradition in the psychology of the imagination. In E. Murray (Ed.), *The imagination and phenomenological psychology.* Pittsburgh, PA: Duquesne University Press.

Globus, G., & Franklin, S. (1980). Prospects for the scientific observer of perceptual consciousness. In J. Davidson & R. Davidson (Eds.), *The psychobiology of consciousness.* New York: Plenum Press.

Goldberger, L. (1961). Homogeneous visual stimulation (ganzfeld) and imagery. *Perceptual and Motor Skills, 12*, 91–93.

Goldberger, L., & Holt, R. R. (1961a). A comparison of isolation effects and their personality correlates in two divergent samples. *Final Report WADD Contract No. AF 33(616)-6103.* New York University Research Center for Mental Health.

Goldberger, L., & Holt, R. R. (1961b). Experimental interference with reality contact: Individual differences. In P. Solomon & P. Kubanzky (Eds.), *Sensory deprivation.* Cambridge, MA: Harvard University Press.

Goldberger, L., & Holt, R. R. (1961c). Studies on the effect of perceptual alteration. *USAF ASD Technical Report, No. 61-416.* Wright-Patterson Air Force Base, Ohio.

Goleman, D. (1977). *The varieties of the meditation experiences.* New York: Dutton.

Golla, F. L., & Antonovitch, S. (1929a). The relation of muscular tonus and the patellar reflex to mental work. *Journal of Mental Science, 75*, 234–41.

Golla, F. L., & Antonovitch, S. (1929b). The respiratory rhythm in its relation to the mechanism of thought. *Brain, 52*, 491–509.

Golla, F. L., Hutton, E. L., & Walter, W. G. (1943). The objective study of mental imagery. I. Physiological concomitants. *Journal of Mental Science, 89*, 216–22.

Golledge, R. G., & Rayner, J. N. (Eds.) (1980). *Multidimensional analysis of large data sets.* Minneapolis, MN: University of Minnesota Press.

Gordon, R. (1949). An investigation into some of the factors that favour the formation of stereotyped images. *British Journal of Psychology, 39*, 156–67.

Gordon, R. (1950). An experiment correlating the nature of imagery with performance on a test of reversal of perspective. *British Journal of Psychology, 41*, 63–67.

Govinda, L. (1973). The two types of psychology. In R. Ornstein (Ed.), *The nature of human consciousness.* San Francisco: Freeman.

Graham, F. K., & Kendall, B. S. (1956). *Memory-for-Designs Test.* Missoula, MT: Psychological Test Specialists.

Green, P. E., & Rao, V. R. (1972). *Applied multidimensional scaling.* New York: Holt, Rinehart and Winston.

Griffitts, C. H. (1927). Individual differences in imagery. *Psychological Monographs, 39*, No. 172.

Gross, E. (1978). Toward a symbolic interactionist theory of learning: A rapproachement with Behaviorism. *Studies in Symbolic Interaction, 1*, 129–45.

Guilford, J. P., & Zimmerman, W. S. (1956). *A manual of instructions and interpretations for the Guilford-Zimmerman Aptitude Survey.* Beverly Hills, CA: Sheridan Supply Co.

Gulliksen, H. O. (1956). Measurement of subjective values. *Psychometrika, 21*, 229–44.

Gulliksen, H. O. (1984/1994). Scaling. In R. J. Corsini (Ed.), *Encyclopedia of psychology.* Vol. 3. New York: Wiley.

Gur, R. C., & Hilgard, E. R. (1975). Visual imagery and the discrimination of differences between altered pictures simultaneously and successively presented. *British Journal of Psychology, 66*, 341–45.

Gur, R. E., Gur, R. C., & Harris, L. J. (1975). Hemispheric activation, as measured by the subjects' conjugate lateral eye movements, is influenced by experimenter location. *Neuropsychologia, 13*, 35–44.

Haber, R. N. (1982). Must all imagery be eidetic? *Journal of Mental Imagery, 6*, 52–54.

Hale, S. M., & Simpson, H. M. (1970). Effects of eye movements on the rate of discovery and the vividness of visual images. *Perception & Psychophysics, 9*, 242–45.

Hall, C., Bernoties, L., & Schmidt, D. (1995). Interference effects of mental imagery on a motor task. *British Journal of Psychology, 86*, 181–90.

Hammer, S. (1984). The mind as healer. *Science Digest, 100*, 47–49.

Handel, S. (1993). Review of D. Reisberg's book, "Auditory imagery." *American Journal of Psychology, 106,* 470–75.

Hardyck, C. (1983). Seeing each other's points of view: Visual perceptual lateralization. In J. B. Hellige (Ed.), *Cerebral hemispheric asymmetry: Method, theory, and application.* New York: Praeger.

Hargreaves, D., & Bolton, N. (1972). Selecting creativity tests for use in research. *British Journal of Psychology, 63,* 451–62.

Harris, L. J. (1978). Sex differences in spatial ability: Possible environmental, genetic, and neurological factors. In M. Kinsbourne (Ed.), *Asymmetrical function of the brain.* Cambridge, UK: Cambridge University Press.

Harshman, R. A., Hampson, E., & Berenbaum, S. A. (1983). Individual differences in cognitive abilities and brain organization. I. Sex and handedness differences in ability. *Canadian Journal of Psychology, 37,* 144–92.

Harshman, R. A., & Paivio, A. (1987). "Paradoxical" sex differences in self-reported imagery. *Canadian Journal of Psychology, 41,* 287–302.

Hatano, G., Miyake, Y., & Binks, M. (1977). Performance of expert abacus operators. *Cognition, 5,* 47–55.

Hatano, G., & Osawa, K. (1983). Digit memory of grand experts in abacus-derived mental calculation. *Cognition, 15,* 95–110.

Hebb, D. O. (1960). The American revolution. *American Psychologist, 15,* 735–45.

Hebb, D. O. (1968). Concerning imagery. *Psychological Review, 75,* 466–77.

Helstrup, T. (1988). Imagery as a cognitive strategy. In M. Denis, J. Engelkamp, & J.T.E. Richardson (Eds.), *Cognitive and neuropsychological approaches to mental imagery.* Dordrecht, Netherlands: M. Nijhoff.

Hernandez-Guzman, L., Gonzalez, S., & Lopez, F. (2002). Effect of guided imagery on children's social performance. *Behavioural and Cognitive Psychotherapy, 30,* 471–83.

Hess, E. (1965). Attitude and pupil size. *Scientific American, 212,* 46–54.

Hess, E., & Polt, J. (1964). Pupil size in relation to mental activity during simple problem-solving. *Science, 143,* 1190–92.

Heuer, F., Fischman, D., & Reisberg, D. (1986). Why does vivid imagery hurt colour memory? *Canadian Journal of Psychology, 40,* 161–75.

Hewson, C. M., Laurent, D., & Vogel, C. M. (1996). Proper methodologies for psychological and sociological studies conducted via the Internet. *Behavior Research Methods, Instruments, and Computers, 28,* 186–91.

Hilgard, E. R. (1977). *Divided consciousness: Multiple controls in human thought and action.* New York: Wiley.

Hilgard, E. R. (1981). Imagery and imagination in American psychology. *Journal of Mental Imagery, 5,* 5–65.

Hilgard, E. R. (1993). The New Structuralism: A discussion. *Journal of Mental Imagery, 17*, 433–37.

Hilgard, E. R., Marks, D. F., & Sheehan, P. W. (1987). Unvividness paradox: A discussion. *Journal of Mental Imagery, 11*, 1–12.

Hines, D., & Martindale, C. (1974). Induced lateral eye movements and creative and intellectual performance. *Perceptual and Motor Skills, 39*, 153–54.

Hirschman, R., & Favaro, L. (1977). Relationship between imagery and voluntary heart rate control. *Psychophysiology, 14*, 120.

Hiscock, M. (1977). Eye movement asymmetry and hemispheric function: An examination of individual differences. *Journal of Psychology, 97*, 49–52.

Hiscock, M. (1978). Imagery assessment through self-report: What do imagery questionnaires measure? *Journal of Consulting and Clinical Psychology, 46*, 223–30.

Hishitani, S. (1984a). Imagery experts. *Seishin Preview, 4*, 4–9. (In Japanese.)

Hishitani, S. (1984b). The study of imagery differences: Its significance and the issue of methodology. *Japanese Psychological Review, 27*, 410–27. (In Japanese with English summary.)

Hishitani, S. (1989). The usefulness of studies of imagery experts in imagery research. *Journal of Mental Imagery, 13*, 119–34.

Hochberg, J., Triebel, W., & Seaman, G. (1951). Color adaptation under conditions of homogeneous visual stimulation (ganzfeld). *Journal of Experimental Psychology, 41*, 153–59.

Hochman, J. (1994). Ahsen's image psychology. *Journal of Mental Imagery, 18*, 1–118.

Hochman, J. (2001). A basic online search on the eidetic with PsycINFO, MEDLINE, and ERIC. *Journal of Mental Imagery, 25*, 99–215.

Hoffman, R. E. (1986). Verbal hallucinations and language production processes in schizophrenia. *The Behavioral and Brain Sciences, 9*, 503–48.

Holmes, D. S. (1998). *Hearing voices*. Rileyville, VA: Shenandoah Psychology Press.

Holmes, D. S., Roeckelein, J. E., & Olmstead, J. A. (1968). Determinants of tactual perception of finger–drawn symbols: Reappraisal. *Perceptual and Motor Skills, 27*, 659–72.

Holt, R. R. (1964). Imagery: The return of the ostracized. *American Psychologist, 19*, 254–64.

Holt, R. R., & Goldberger, L. (1959). Personological correlates of reactions to perceptual isolation. *USAF WADC Technical Report, No. 59-735*. Wright-Patterson Air Force Base, Ohio.

Holt, R. R., & Goldberger, L. (1960). Research on the effects of isolation on cognitive functioning. *WADD Technical Report 60-260*. Wright-Patterson Air Force Base, Ohio.

Hyde, J. S. (1981). How large are cognitive gender differences? A meta-analysis using omega-squared and *d*. *American Psychologist, 36,* 892–901.

Hyde, J. S., Geiringer, E. R., & Yen, W. M. (1975). On the empirical relation between spatial ability and sex differences in other aspects of cognitive performance. *Multivariate Behavioral Research, 10,* 289–309.

Hyde, J. S., & Linn, M. C. (1988). Gender differences in verbal ability: A meta-analysis. *Psychological Bulletin, 104,* 53–69.

Ikeda, Y., & Hirai, H. (1976). Voluntary control of electrodermal activity in relation to imagery and internal perception scores. *Psychophysiology, 13,* 330–33.

Intons-Peterson, M. J. (1983). Imagery paradigms: How vulnerable are they to experimenters' expectations? *Journal of Experimental Psychology: Human Perception and Performance, 9,* 394–412.

Intons-Peterson, M. J., & White, A. R. (1981). Experimenter naivete and imaginal judgments. *Journal of Experimental Psychology: Human Perception and Performance, 7,* 833–43.

Jacklin, C. N. (1981). Methodological issues in the study of sex-related differences. *Developmental Review, 1,* 266–73.

James, S. (Ed.) (1999). *Doing Internet research.* Thousand Oaks, CA: Sage.

Jasper, H., & Cruikshank, R. (1937). Electro-encephalography. II. Visual stimulation and the after-image as affecting the occipital alpha rhythm. *Journal of General Psychology, 17,* 29–48.

Jellinek, A. (1949). Spontaneous imagery: A new psychotherapeutic approach. *American Journal of Psychotherapy, 3,* 372–91.

Johnson, J. M. (1991). A Meading of the minds. *Journal of Mental Imagery, 15,* 138–40.

Jones, L. V. (1971). The nature of measurement. In R. L. Thorndike (Ed.), *Educational measurement.* Washington, DC: American Council on Education.

Jonides, J., Kahn, R., & Rozin, P. (1975). Imagery instructions improve memory in blind subjects. *Bulletin of the Psychonomic Society, 5,* 424–26.

Jordan, C. S. (1984). Psychophysiology of structural imagery in post-traumatic stress disorder. *Journal of Mental Imagery, 8,* 57–66.

Jordan, C. S., & Lenington, K. T. (1979). Physiological correlates of eidetic imagery and induced anxiety. *Journal of Mental Imagery, 3,* 31–42.

Juhasz, J. B. (1972). On the reliability of two measures of imagery. *Perceptual and Motor Skills, 35,* 874.

Juhasz, J. B. (1977). Some conceptual limits on reliability estimates of imaging. *Perceptual and Motor Skills, 44,* 1023–31.

Kahneman, D., & Beatty, J. (1966). Pupil diameter and load on memory. *Science, 154,* 1583–85.

Kamiya, J. (1969). Operant control of the EEG, alpha rhythm, and some of its reported effects on consciousness. In C. Tart (Ed.), *Altered states of consciousness*. New York: Wiley.

Kantowitz, B. H., Roediger, H. L., III, & Elmes, D. G. (2001). *Experimental psychology: Understanding psychological research*. 7th edition. Belmont, CA: Brooks/Cole.

Kapecs, J. G. (1957). Observations on screens and barriers in the mind. *Psychoanalytic Quarterly, 28*, 62–77.

Katz, A. N. (1983). What does it mean to be a high imager? In J. Yuille (Ed.), *Imagery, memory, and cognition*. Hillsdale, NJ: Erlbaum.

Katz, A. N. (1995). What we need is a good theory of imagery vividness. *Journal of Mental Imagery, 19*, 143–46.

Kaufmann, G. (1976). Is imagery a cognitive appendix? *Reports from the Institute of Psychology, 1*, University of Bergen, Norway.

Kaufmann, G. (1980). *Visual imagery and its relation to problem solving: A theoretical and experimental inquiry*. Oslo, Norway: Universitetsforlaget.

Kaufmann, G. (1981). What is wrong with imagery questionnaires? *Scandinavian Journal of Psychology, 22*, 59–64.

Kaufmann, G. (1983). How good are imagery questionnaires? A rejoinder to David Marks. *Scandinavian Journal of Psychology, 24*, 247–49.

Kaufmann, G. (1988). Mental imagery and problem solving. In M. Denis, J. Engelkamp, & J.T.E. Richardson (Eds.), *Cognitive and neuropsychological approaches to mental imagery*. Dordrecht, The Netherlands: M. Nijhoff.

Kaufmann, G. (1995). Stalking the elusive image. *Journal of Mental Imagery, 19*, 146–50.

Kearsley, G. W. (1985). Methodological change and the elicitation of images in human geography. *Journal of Mental Imagery, 9*, 71–82.

Keenan, J. M. (1983). Qualifications and clarifications of images of concealed objects: A reply to Kerr and Neisser. *Journal of Experimental Psychology: Learning, Memory, and Cognition, 9*, 222–30.

Keenan, J. M., & Moore, R. E. (1979). Memory for images of concealed objects: A reexamination of Neisser and Kerr. *Journal of Experimental Psychology: Human Learning and Memory, 5*, 374–85.

Kerr, N. H. (1983). The role of vision in "visual imagery" experiments: Evidence from the congenitally blind. *Journal of Experimental Psychology: General, 112*, 265–77.

Kerr, N. H., & Neisser, U. (1983). Mental images of concealed objects: New evidence. *Journal of Experimental Psychology: Learning, Memory, and Cognition, 9*, 212–21.

Kessel, F. S. (1972). Imagery: A dimension of mind rediscovered. *British Journal of Psychology, 63*, 149–62.

Khatena, J. (1969). "Onomatopoeia and images": Preliminary validity study of a test of originality. *Perceptual and Motor Skills, 28*, 335–38.

Khatena, J. (1978). Frontiers of creative imagination imagery. *Journal of Mental Imagery, 2,* 33–46.

Kieras, D. (1978). Beyond pictures and words: Alternating information processing models for imagery effects in verbal memory. *Psychological Bulletin, 85,* 532–54.

King, D. L. (1973). An image theory of classical conditioning. *Psychological Reports, 33,* 403–11.

King, D. L. (1974a). An image theory of instrumental conditioning. *Psychological Reports, 35,* 1115–22.

King, D. L. (1974b). Perception, binocular fusion, and an image theory of classical conditioning. *Perceptual and Motor Skills, 39,* 531–37.

King, D. L. (1976). Learned and perceived reinforcer response strengths and image theory. *Bulletin of the Psychonomic Society, 7,* 438–41.

King, D. L. (1978). Image theory of conditioning, memory, forgetting, functional similarity, fusion, and dominance. *Journal of Mental Imagery, 2,* 47–62.

King, D. L. (1979). *Conditioning: An image approach.* New York: Gardner Press.

Kinsbourne, M. (1972). Eye and head turning indicates cerebral lateralization. *Science, 176,* 539–41.

Klein, G. S. (1959). On subliminal activation. *Journal of Nervous and Mental Disorders, 128,* 293–301.

Klinger, E. (1978). Models of normal conscious flow. In K. S. Pope & J. L. Singer (Eds.), *The stream of consciousness: Scientific investigations into the flow of human experience.* New York: Plenum Press.

Kluver, H. (1932). Eidetic phenomena. *Psychological Bulletin, 29,* 181–203.

Kocel, K., Galin, D., Ornstein, R., & Merrin, E. (1972). Lateral eye movements and cognitive mode. *Psychonomic Science, 27,* 223–24.

Kosslyn, S. M. (1985). Stalking the mental image? *Psychology Today,* May, 23–28.

Kosslyn, S. M. (1987). Seeing and imagining in the cerebral hemispheres: A computational approach. *Psychological Review, 94,* 148–75.

Kosslyn, S. M. (1991). A cognitive neuroscience of visual cognition: Further developments. In R. H. Logie & M. Denis (Eds.), *Mental images in human cognition.* Amsterdam: North-Holland.

Kosslyn, S. M., Ball, T., & Reiser, B. (1978). Visual images preserve metric spatial information: Evidence from studies of image scanning. *Journal of Experimental Psychology: Human Perception and Performance, 4,* 47–60.

Kruskal, J. B., & Wish, M. (1978). *Multidimensional scaling.* Beverly Hills, CA: Sage.

Kuhn, T. S. (1962). *The structure of scientific revolutions.* Chicago: University of Chicago Press.

Kunzendorf, R. G. (1980). Imagery and consciousness: A scientific analysis of the mind-body problem. *Dissertations Abstracts International, 40,* 3448B–49B.

Kunzendorf, R. G. (1981). Individual differences in imagery and autonomic control. *Journal of Mental Imagery, 5,* 47–60.

Kunzendorf, R. G. (1996–1997). Review of "Individual differences in imaging" by Alan Richardson. *Imagination, Cognition, and Personality, 16,* 214–17.

Lane, J. B. (1974). Imagination and personality: The multi-trait investigation of a new measure of imagery control. *Dissertation Abstracts International, 35,* 6099-B.

Lang, P. J. (1979). A bio-information theory of emotional imagery. *Psychophysiology, 16,* 495–512.

Lashley, K. S. (1942). An examination of the "continuity theory" as applied to discriminative learning. *Journal of General Psychology, 26,* 241–65.

Leiderman, P. H. (1962). Imagery and sensory deprivation: An experimental study. *Technical Report MRL-TDR-62-28.* Wright-Patterson Air Force Base, Ohio.

Leuner, H. (1977). Guided affective imagery: An account of its development. *Journal of Mental Imagery, 1,* 73–92.

Lindauer, M. S. (1969). Imagery and sensory modality. *Perceptual and Motor Skills, 29,* 203–15.

Lindauer, M. S. (1972). The sensory attributes and functions of imagery and imagery evoking stimuli. In P. W. Sheehan (Ed.), *The function and nature of imagery.* New York: Academic Press.

Linn, M. C., & Petersen, A. C. (1985). Emergence and characterization of sex differences in spatial ability: A meta-analysis. *Child Development, 56,* 1479–98.

Lord, F. M. (1953). On the statistical treatment of football numbers. *American Psychologist, 8,* 750–51.

Lorens, S., & Darrow, C. (1962). Eye movements, EEG, ESR, and EKG during mental multiplications. *Electroencephalography and Clinical Neurophysiology, 14,* 739–46.

Luce, R. D., Bush, R. R., & Galanter, E. (1963). *Handbook of mathematical psychology.* New York: Wiley.

Ludwig, A. M. (1966). Altered states of consciousness. *Archives of General Psychiatry, 15,* 225–34.

Luria, A. R. (1968). *The mind of a mnemonist.* New York: Basic Books.

Lutz, R. S. (2003). Covert muscle excitation is outflow from the central generation of motor imagery. *Behavioural Brain Research, 140,* 149–63.

Maccoby, E. E., & Jacklin, C. N. (1974). *The psychology of sex differences.* Palo Alto, CA: Stanford University Press.

Mangan, G. L. (1982). *The biology of human conduct: East-West models of temperament and personality.* Oxford, UK: Pergamon.

Marjerrison, G. (1966). The effects of pheniprazine on visual imagery in perceptual deprivation. *Journal of Nervous and Mental Disorders, 142,* 254–64.

Marjerrison, G., & Keogh, R. P. (1967). Electroencephalographic changes during brief periods of perceptual deprivation. *Perceptual and Motor Skills, 24,* 611–15.

Marks, D. F. (1972). Individual differences in the vividness of visual imagery and their effect on function. In P. W. Sheehan (Ed.), *The function and nature of imagery.* New York: Academic Press.

Marks, D. F. (1973). Visual imagery differences in the recall of pictures. *British Journal of Psychology, 64,* 17–24.

Marks, D. F. (1977). Imagery and consciousness: A theoretical review from an individual differences perspective. *Journal of Mental Imagery, 2,* 275–90.

Marks, D. F. (1983). In defense of imagery questionnaires. *Scandinavian Journal of Psychology, 24,* 243–46.

Marks, D. F. (1984). The new structural approach to image formation, psychophysiology, and psychopathology. *Journal of Mental Imagery, 8,* 95–104.

Marks, D. F. (1985). Imagery paradigms and methodology. *Journal of Mental Imagery, 9,* 93–106.

Marks, D. F. (Ed.) (1986). *Theories of image formation.* New York: Brandon House.

Marks, D. F. (1987a). Problems with the triple code model. *Journal of Mental Imagery, 11,* 102–5.

Marks, D. F. (1987b). Resolving the unvividness paradox. *Journal of Mental Imagery, 11,* 3–9.

Marks, D. F. (1988). The misuse of imagery questionnaires. *Perceptual and Motor Skills, 66,* 932–34.

Marks, D. F. (1989a). Bibliography of research utilizing the Vividness of Visual Imagery Questionnaire. *Perceptual and Motor Skills, 69,* 707–18.

Marks, D. F. (1989b). Construct validity of the Vividness of Visual Imagery Questionnaire. *Perceptual and Motor Skills, 69,* 459–65.

Marks, D. F. (1993). The VVIQ: A measure of mental contents, state, or trait? *Journal of Mental Imagery, 17,* 337–45.

Marks, D. F. (1995). New directions for mental imagery research. *Journal of Mental Imagery, 19,* 153–67.

Marks, D. F., & Isaac, A. R. (1995). Topographical distribution of EEG activity accompanying visual and motor imagery in vivid and non-vivid imagers. *British Journal of Psychology, 86,* 271–82.

Marks, D. F., & McKellar, P. (1982). The nature and function of eidetic imagery. *Journal of Mental Imagery, 6,* 1–124.

Marr, D. (1982). *Vision.* San Francisco: Freeman.

Marschark, M. (1988). The functional role of imagery in cognition? In M. Denis, J. Engelkamp, & J.T.E. Richardson (Eds.), *Cognitive and neuropsychological approaches to mental imagery*. Dordrecht, The Netherlands: M. Nijhoff.

Martin, L. J. (1912). Die projektionmethode und die lokalization visueller und anderer vorstellungsbilder. *Zeitschrift fur Psychologie, 61*, 321–542.

Maruff, P., Wilson, P., & Currie, J. (2003). Abnormalities of motor imagery associated with somatic passivity phenomena in schizophrenia. *Schizophrenia Research, 60*, 229–38.

Maslach, C., Marshall, C., & Zimbardo, P. (1972). Hypnotic control of peripheral skin temperature: A case report. *Psychophysiolgy, 9*, 600–605.

Mast, F. W., & Kosslyn, S. M. (2002). Visual mental images can be ambiguous: Insights from individual differences in spatial transformation abilities. *Cognition, 86*, 57–70.

Mathews, A. W. (1971). Psychophysiological approaches to the investigation of desensitization and related procedures. *Psychological Bulletin, 76*, 73–91.

May, J., & Johnson, H. (1973). Physiological activity to internally-elicited arousal and inhibitory thoughts. *Journal of Abnormal Psychology, 82*, 239–45.

McConkey, K. M., & Nogrady, H. (1986). Visual Elaboration Scale: Analysis of individual and group versions. *Journal of Mental Imagery, 10*, 37–46.

McDaniel, M. A. (1988). Empirical approaches to a functional analysis of imagery and cognition. In M. Denis, J. Engelkamp, & J.T.E. Richardson (Eds.), *Cognitive and neuropsychological approaches to mental imagery*. Dordrecht, The Netherlands: M. Nijhoff.

McGee, M. G. (1979). Human spatial abilities: Psychometric studies and environmental, genetic, hormonal, and neurological influences. *Psychological Bulletin, 86*, 889–918.

McGlone, J. (1980). Sex differences in human brain asymmetry: A critical survey. *The Behavioral and Brain Sciences, 3*, 215–63.

McGrath, R., O'Malley, W. B., Dura, J., & Beaulieu, C. (1989). Factors analysis of the Verbalizer-Visualizer Questionnaire. *Journal of Mental Imagery, 13*, 75–78.

McGuire, W. J. (1973). The yin and yang of progress in social psychology: Seven koan. *Journal of Personality and Social Psychology, 26*, 309–20.

McKellar, P. (1957). *Imagination and thinking*. New York: Basic Books.

McKellar, P. (1965). The variety of human experience. In R. S. Daniel (Ed.), *Contemporary readings in general psychology*. Boston: Houghton.

McKellar, P. (1968). *Experience and behavior*. Baltimore, MD: Penguin.

McKelvie, S. J. (1986). Effects of format of the Vividness of Visual Imagery Questionnaire on content validity, split-half reliability, and the role of memory in test-retest reliability. *British Journal of Psychology, 77*, 229–36.

McKelvie, S. J. (1990). The Vividness of Visual Imagery Questionnaire: Commentary on the Marks-Chara debate. *Perceptual and Motor Skills, 70*, 551–60.

McKelvie, S. J. (1993). Reliability of the Vividness of Visual Imagery Questionnaire across "parental filter" and alternate form. *Journal of Mental Imagery, 17*, 347–61.

McKelvie, S. J. (1995). The VVIQ as a psychometric test of individual differences in visual imagery vividness: A critical quantitative review and plea for direction. *Journal of Mental Imagery, 19*, 1–106.

McKelvie, S. J., & Demers, E. G. (1979). Individual differences in reported visual imagery and memory performance. *British Journal of Psychology, 70*, 51–57.

McKelvie, S. J., & Gingras, P. P. (1974). Reliability of two measures of visual imagery. *Perceptual and Motor Skills, 39*, 417–18.

McKelvie, S. J., & Rohrberg, M. N. (1978). Individual differences in reported visual imagery and cognitive performance. *Perceptual and Motor Skills, 46*, 451–58.

McLemore, C. W. (1976). Factorial validity of imagery measures. *Behaviour Research and Therapy, 14*, 399–408.

McMahon, C. E. (1973). Images as motives and motivators: A historical perspective. *American Journal of Psychology, 86*, 465–90.

McMahon, C. E. (1976). The role of imagination in the disease process: Pre-Cartesian history. *Psychological Medicine, 6*, 179–84.

Mead, G. H. (1934). *Mind, self, and society.* Chicago: University of Chicago Press.

Meltzer, B. N. (1991). Mead on mental imagery: A complement to Count-van Manen's views. *Journal of Mental Imagery, 15*, 17–34, 169–78.

Metzler, J., & Shepard, R. N. (1974). Transformational studies of the internal representation of three-dimensional objects. In R. Solso (Ed.), *Theories in cognitive psychology: The Loyola Symposium.* Potomac, MD: Erlbaum.

Miller, G., Galanter, E., & Pribram, K. (1960). *Plans and the structure of behavior.* New York: Holt, Rinehart, and Winston.

Miller, N. E. (1978). Biofeedback and visceral learning. *Annual Review of Psychology, 29*, 373–404.

Mitchell, D. B., & Richman, C. L. (1980). Confirmed reservations: Mental travel. *Journal of Experimental Psychology: Human Perception and Performance, 6*, 58–66.

Mitchell, J. (1986). Measurement scales and statistics: A clash of paradigms. *Psychological Bulletin, 100*, 398–407.

Mitchell, M., & Jolley, J. (2001). *Research design explained.* 4th ed. New York: Harcourt.

Molteno, T. (1984). Imagery in the Eidetic Parents Test. Unpublished master's thesis, University of Otago, Dunedin, New Zealand. (Also, see Molteno, T. [1981]. Imagery: Heart rate responses to pleasant and unpleasant scenes. Unpublished postgraduate diploma dissertation, University of Otago.)

Molteno, T. (1993). Imagery in the Eidetic Parents Test. *Journal of Mental Imagery, 17*, 363–432.

Mook, D. G. (2001). *Psychological research: The ideas behind the methods.* New York: W. W. Norton.

Morgan, C. L. (1894). *An introduction to comparative psychology.* London: Scott.

Morris, P. E., & Gale, A. A. (1974). A correlation study of variables related to imagery. *Perceptual and Motor Skills, 38*, 659–65.

Morris, P. E., & Hampson, P. J. (1983). *Imagery and consciousness.* New York: Academic Press.

Mowrer, O. H. (1938). Preparatory set (expectancy)—A determinant in motivation and learning. *Psychological Review, 45*, 61–91.

Mowrer, O. H. (1940). Preparatory set (expectancy)—Some methods of measurement. *Psychological Monographs, 52*, No. 2.

Mowrer, O. H. (1941). Preparatory set (expectancy)—Further evidence of its "central" locus. *Journal of Experimental Psychology, 28*, 116–33.

Mowrer, O. H. (1960a). *Learning theory and behavior.* New York: Wiley.

Mowrer, O. H. (1960b). *Learning theory and the symbolic processes.* New York: Wiley.

Mowrer, O. H. (1977). Mental imagery: An indispensable psychological concept. *Journal of Mental Imagery, 2*, 303–26.

Mowrer, O. H., Raymond, N., & Bliss, E. (1940). Preparatory set (expectancy)—An experimental demonstration of its "central" locus. *Journal of Experimental Psychology, 26*, 357–72.

Muller, J. (1826). *Uber die phantastischen gesichtserscheinungen.* Coblenz: Holscher.

Munn, N. L. (1931). An apparatus for testing visual discrimination in animals. *Journal of Genetic Psychology, 15*, 342–53.

Naveh–Benjamin, M. (1987). Coding of spatial location information: An automatic process? *Journal of Experimental Psychology: Learning, Memory, and Cognition, 13*, 595–605.

Nebes, R. D. (1974). Hemispheric specialization in commissurotomized man. *Psychological Bulletin, 81*, 1–14.

Neisser, U. (1970). Visual imagery as process and as experience. In J. S. Antrobus (Ed.), *Cognition and affect.* Boston: Little, Brown.

Neisser, U. (1972a). A paradigm shift in psychology. *Science, 176*, 620–30.

Neisser, U. (1972b). Changing conceptions of imagery. In P. W. Sheehan (Ed.), *The function and nature of imagery.* New York: Academic Press.

Neisser, U. (1982). *Memory observed.* San Francisco: Freeman.

Neisser, U., & Kerr, N. H. (1973). Spatial and mnemonic properties of visual images. *Cognitive Psychology, 5*, 138–50.

Nishisato, S. (1978). *Multidimensional scaling: A historical sketch and bibliography.* Toronto: Ontario Institute for Studies in Education.

Nunnally, J. (1978). *Psychometric theory*. New York: McGraw-Hill.

Nyborg, H. (1983). Spatial ability in men and women: Review and new theory. *Advances in Behaviour Research and Therapy, 5*, 89–140.

Osgood, C. E. (1953). *Method and theory in experimental psychology*. New York: Oxford University Press.

Owens, W. A. (1968). Toward one discipline of scientific psychology. *American Psychologist, 23*, 782–85.

Paivio, A. (1963). Learning of adjective-noun paired associates as a function of adjective-noun word order and noun abstractness. *Canadian Journal of Psychology, 17*, 370–79.

Paivio, A. (1969). Mental imagery in associative learning and memory. *Psychological Review, 76*, 241–63.

Paivio, A. (1970). On the functional significance of imagery. *Psychological Bulletin, 72*, 385–92.

Paivio, A. (1971). *Imagery and verbal processes*. New York: Holt, Rinehart and Winston.

Paivio, A. (1972). A theoretical analysis of the role of imagery in learning and memory. In P. W. Sheehan (Ed.), *The function and nature of imagery*. New York: Academic Press.

Paivio, A. (1973). Psychophysiological correlates of imagery. In F. J. McGuigan & R. A. Schoonover (Eds.), *The psychophysiology of thinking*. New York: Academic Press.

Paivio, A. (1975). Neomentalism. *Canadian Journal of Psychology, 29*, 263–91.

Paivio, A. (1983). The empirical case for dual coding. In J. C. Yuille (Ed.), *Imagery, memory, and cognition*. Hillsdale, NJ: Erlbaum.

Paivio, A. (1988). Basic puzzles in imagery research. In M. Denis, J. Engelkamp, & J.T.E. Richardson (Eds.), *Cognitive and neuropsychological approaches to mental imagery*. Dordrecht, The Netherlands: M. Nijhoff.

Paivio, A., & Simpson, H. M. (1966). The effect of word abstractness and pleasantness on pupil size during an imagery task. *Psychonomic Science, 5*, 55–56.

Paivio, A., & Simpson, H. M. (1967). Pupillary responses during imagery tasks as a function of stimulus characteristics and imagery ability. *Research Bulletin No. 45*, Department of Psychology, University of Western Ontario, Canada.

Paivio, A., & Simpson, H. M. (1968). Magnitude and latency of the pupillary response during an imagery task as a function of stimulus abstractness and imagery ability. *Psychonomic Science, 12*, 45–46.

Paivio, A., & Yarmey, A. D. (1965). Abstractions of the common element in mediated learning. *Psychonomic Science, 2*, 231–32.

Paivio, A., & Yarmey, A. D. (1966). Pictures versus words as stimuli and responses in paired-associate learning. *Psychonomic Science, 5*, 235–36.

Palermo, D. S. (1970). Imagery in children's learning: Discussion. *Psychological Bulletin, 73*, 415–21.

Parrott, C. A. (1986). Visual imagery training: Stimulating utilization of imaginal processes. *Journal of Mental Imagery, 10*, 47–64.

Paterson, A. S. (1935). The respiratory rhythms in normal and psychotic subjects. *Journal of Neurology and Psychopathology, 16*, 36–53.

Pearson, D. G. (1995). The VVIQ and cognitive models of imagery: Future directions for research. *Journal of Mental Imagery, 19*, 167–70.

Peirce, C. S. (1877). The fixation of belief. *Popular Science Monthly, 12*, 1–15. (Also, see *Charles Sanders Peirce: The essential writings.* [1972]. E. C. Moore [Ed.]. New York: Harper and Row.)

Pelletier, K. (1978). *Toward a science of consciousness.* New York: Delta Books.

Perky, C. W. (1910). An experimental study of imagination. *American Journal of Psychology, 21*, 422–52.

Perrig, W. J. (1988). On the distinction of memory codes: Image versus motor encoding. In M. Denis, J. Engelkamp, & J.T.E. Richardson (Eds.), *Cognitive and neuropsychological approaches to mental imagery.* Dordrecht, The Netherlands: M. Nijhoff.

Petit, L., Pegna, A., Mayer, E., & Hauert, C. (2003). Representation of anatomical constraints in motor imagery: Mental rotation of a body segment. *Brain and Cognition, 51*, 95–101.

Petrinovich, L. (1979). Probabilistic functionalism: A conception of research method. *American Psychologist, 34*, 373–90.

Piaget, J. (1945/1952). *Play, dreams, and imitation.* New York: Norton.

Pinker, S. (1985). Visual cognition: An introduction. In S. Pinker (Ed.), *Visual cognition.* Cambridge, MA: M.I.T. Press.

Pinker, S. (1988). A computational theory of the mental imagery medium. In M. Denis, J. Engelkamp, & J.T.E. Richardson (Eds.), *Cognitive and neuropsychological approaches to mental imagery.* Dordrecht, The Netherlands: M. Nijhoff.

Podgorny, P., & Shepard, R. N. (1978). Functional representations common to visual perception and imagination. *Journal of Experimental Psychology: Human Perception and Performance, 4*, 21–35.

Pylyshyn, Z. (1973). What the mind's eye tells the mind's brain. *Psychological Bulletin, 80*, 1–24.

Quinn, G. (1988). Interference effects in the visuo-spatial sketchpad. In M. Denis, J. Engelkamp, & J.T.E. Richardson (Eds.), *Cognitive and neuropsychological approaches to mental imagery.* Dordrecht, The Netherlands: M. Nijhoff.

Ray, W. J. (2003). *Methods toward a science of behavior and experience.* 7th edition. Belmont, CA: Wadsworth/Thomson.

Reber, A. S. (1985/1995). *The Penguin dictionary of psychology.* New York: Penguin.

Reed, C. L. (2002). Chronometric comparisons of imagery to action: Visualizing versus physically performing springboard dives. *Memory and Cognition, 30,* 1169–78.

Reed, G. F., & Kenna, J. C. (1964). Sex differences in body imagery and orientation under sensory deprivation of brief duration. *Perceptual and Motor Skills, 18,* 117–18.

Reese, H. W. (1970a). Imagery and contextual meaning. *Psychological Bulletin, 73,* 404–14.

Reese, H. W. (1970b). Imagery in children's learning: A symposium. *Psychological Bulletin, 73,* 383–84.

Rehm, L. P. (1973). Relationships among measures of visual imagery. *Behaviour Research and Therapy, 11,* 265–70.

Reisberg, D. (Ed.) (1993). *Auditory imagery.* Chicago: University of Illinois Press.

Reisberg, D., Culver, C., Heuer, F., & Fischman, D. (1986). Visual memory: When imagery vividness makes a difference. *Journal of Mental Imagery, 10,* 51–74.

Reisberg, D., & Heuer, F. (1988). Vividness, vagueness, and the quantification of visualizing. *Journal of Mental Imagery, 12,* 89–102.

Reisberg, D., Wilson, M., & Smith, J. D. (1991). Auditory imagery and inner speech. In R. H. Logie & M. Denis (Eds.), *Mental images in human cognition.* Amsterdam: North-Holland.

Reitman, E., & Cleveland, S. (1964). Changes in body image following sensory deprivation in schizophrenic and control groups. *Journal of Abnormal and Social Psychology, 68,* 168–76.

Reyher, J. (1963). Free imagery: An uncovering procedure. *Journal of Clinical Psychology, 19,* 454–59.

Reyher, J., & Morishige, H. (1969). Electroencephalogram and rapid eye movements during free imagery and dream recall. *Journal of Abnormal Psychology, 74,* 576–82.

Reyher, J., & Smeltzer, W. (1968). The uncovering properties of visual imagery and verbal association: A comparative study. *Journal of Abnormal Psychology, 73,* 218–22.

Ribot, T. (1906/1973). *Essay on the creative imagination.* Chicago: Open Court/New York: Arno Press.

Richardson, A. (1967). Mental practice: A review and discussion, Parts I & II. *Research Quarterly, 38,* 95–107, 263–73.

Richardson, A. (1969). *Mental imagery.* New York: Springer/London: Routledge & Kegan Paul.

Richardson, A. (1977a). The meaning and measurement of memory imagery. *British Journal of Psychology, 68,* 29–43.

Richardson, A. (1977b). Verbalizer-visualizer: A cognitive style dimension. *Journal of Mental Imagery, 1,* 109–26.

Richardson, A. (1978). Subject, task, and tester variables associated with initial eye movement responses. *Journal of Mental Imagery, 2,* 85–100.

Richardson, A. (1979). Dream recall frequency and vividness of visual imagery. *Journal of Mental Imagery, 3*, 65–72.

Richardson, A. (1983). Imagery: Definition and types. In A. A. Sheikh (Ed.), *Imagery: Current theory, research, and application.* New York: Wiley.

Richardson, A. (1984). Strengthening the theoretical links between imaged stimuli and physiological responses. *Journal of Mental Imagery, 8*, 113–26.

Richardson, A. (1988). What is the question? *Journal of Mental Imagery, 12*, 103–14.

Richardson, A. (1994). *Individual differences in imaging: Their measurement, origins, and consequences.* Amityville, NY: Baywood.

Richardson, A. (1995). Guidelines for research with the VVIQ. *Journal of Mental Imagery, 19*, 171–77.

Richardson, J.T.E. (1978). Mental imagery and memory: Coding ability or coding performance? *Journal of Mental Imagery, 2*, 101–16.

Richardson, J.T.E. (1979). Correlations between imagery and memory across stimuli and across subjects. *Bulletin of the Psychonomic Society, 14*, 368–70.

Richardson, J.T.E. (1980). *Mental imagery and human memory.* London: Macmillan.

Richardson, J.T.E. (1985a). Converging operations and reported mediators in the investigation of mental imagery. *British Journal of Psychology, 76*, 205–14.

Richardson, J.T.E. (1985b). Subjects' reports and converging operations in the investigation of mental imagery. *Journal of Mental Imagery, 9*, 107–12.

Richardson, J.T.E. (1988). Vividness and unvividness: Reliability, consistency, and validity of subjective imagery ratings. *Journal of Mental Imagery, 12*, 115–22.

Richardson, J.T.E. (1991). Gender differences in imagery, cognition, and memory. In R. H. Logie & M. Denis (Eds.), *Mental images in human cognition.* Amsterdam: North-Holland.

Richardson, J.T.E. (1995). Gender differences in the Vividness of Visual Imagery Questionnaire: A meta-analysis. *Journal of Mental Imagery, 19*, 177–87.

Richardson, J.T.E., Denis, M., & Engelkamp, J. (1988). European contributions to research on imagery and cognition. In M. Denis, J. Engelkamp, & J.T.E. Richardson (Eds.), *Cognitive and neuropsychological approaches to mental imagery.* Dordrecht, The Netherlands: M. Nijhoff.

Richman, C. L., Mitchell, D. B., & Reznick, J. S. (1979). Mental travel: Some reservations. *Journal of Experimental Psychology: Human Perception and Performance, 5*, 13–18.

Ricoeur, P. (1979). The metaphysical process as cognition, imagination, and feeling. In S. Sacks (Ed.), *On metaphor*. Chicago: University of Chicago Press.

Rimm, D. C., & Bottrell, J. (1969). Error measures of visual imagination. *Behaviour Research and Therapy, 7*, 63–69.

Roberts, A., Schuler, J., Bacon, J., Zimmermann, R., & Patterson, R. (1975). Individual differences and autonomic control: Absorption, hypnotic susceptibility, and the unilateral control of skin temperatures. *Journal of Abnormal Psychology, 84*, 272–79.

Robins, C., & Shepard, R. N. (1977). Spatio-temporal probing of apparent rotational movement. *Perception & Psychophysics, 22*, 12–18.

Roe, A. (1951). A study of imagery in research scientists. *Journal of Personality, 19*, 459–70.

Roe, A. (1953). *The making of a scientist*. New York: Dodd, Mead.

Roeckelein, J. E. (1968a). Simplicity as a principle in tactual form perception. *Psychonomic Science, 13*, 195–96.

Roeckelein, J. E. (1968b). Tactual size perception with the method of magnitude estimation. *Psychonomic Science, 13*, 295–96.

Roeckelein, J. E. (1968c). The effect of set upon length estimation in active touch perception. *Psychonomic Science, 13*, 193–94.

Roeckelein, J. E. (1971). Magnitude estimations of filled time as a function of the statistical properties of tone sequences. *Dissertation Abstracts International, 32(5-B)*, 3042.

Roeckelein, J. E. (1997a). Hierarchy of the sciences and terminological sharing of laws among the sciences. *Psychological Reports, 81*, 739–46.

Roeckelein, J. E. (1997b). Psychology among the sciences: Comparisons of numbers of theories and laws cited in textbooks. *Psychological Reports, 80*, 131–41.

Roeckelein, J. E. (1998). *Dictionary of theories, laws, and concepts in psychology*. Westport, CT: Greenwood Press.

Roffwarg, H., Dement, W., Muzio, J., & Fisher, C. (1962). Dream imagery: Relationship to rapid eye movements of sleep. *Archives of General Psychiatry, 7*, 235–58.

Rohwer, W. D. (1970). Images and pictures in children's learning: Research results and educational implications. *Psychological Bulletin, 73*, 393–403.

Rosenthal, R. (1966). *Experimenter effects in behavioral research*. New York: Appleton.

Rosenthal, R., & Rubin, D. B. (1982). Further meta-analytic procedures for assessing cognitive gender differences. *Journal of Educational Psychology, 74*, 708–12.

Rosnow, R. L., & Rosenthal, R. (2002). *Beginning behavioral research: A conceptual primer*. Upper Saddle River, NJ: Prentice-Hall.

Runyon, W. M. (1982). *Life histories and psychobiography: Explorations in theory and method*. New York: Oxford University Press.

Rychlak, J. F. (2003). *The human image in postmodern America*. Washington, DC: American Psychological Association.

Salway, A.F.S., & Logie, R. H. (1995). Visuospatial working memory, movement control, and executive demands. *British Journal of Psychology, 86*, 253–69.

Sarbin, T. R., & Juhasz, J. B. (1970). Toward a theory of imagination. *Journal of Personality, 38*, 52–76.

Savoyant, A. (1988). Mental practice: Image and mental rehearsal of motor action. In M. Denis, J. Engelkamp, & J.T.E. Richardson (Eds.), *Cognitive and neuropsychological approaches to mental imagery*. Dordrecht, The Netherlands: M. Nijhoff.

Schuman, M. (1980). The psychophysiological model of meditation and altered states of consciousness: A critical review. In J. Davidson & R. Davidson (Eds.), *The psychobiology of consciousness*. New York: Plenum Press.

Schwalbe, M. L. (1991). Directions for a sociology of mind: Comment on Count-van Manen and Meltzer. *Journal of Mental Imagery, 15*, 154–56.

Schwoebel, J., Boronat, C., & Coslett, H. (2002). The man who executed "imagined" movements: Evidence for dissociable components of the body schema. *Brain and Cognition, 50*, 1–16.

Scott, L. M., & Batra, R. (Eds.) (2003). *Persuasive imagery: A consumer response perspective*. Mahwah, NJ: Erlbaum.

Segal, E. M., & Lachman, R. (1972). Complex behavior as higher mental processes: Is there a paradigm shift? *American Psychologist, 27*, 46–55.

Segal, S. (1908). Uber den reproducktionstypus und das reproduzieren von vorstellungen. *Archiv fur die Gesamte Psychologie, 12*, 124–30.

Segal, S. J. (1971). Processing of the stimulus in imagery and perception. In S. J. Segal (Ed.), *Imagery: Current cognitive approaches*. New York: Academic Press.

Shaver, P., Pierson, L., & Lang, S. (1975). Converging evidence for the functional significance of imagery in problem solving. *Cognition, 3*, 359–75.

Sheehan, P. W. (1965). The investigation of visual imagery and some of its correlates. Unpublished doctoral dissertation, University of Sydney, Australia.

Sheehan, P. W. (1966). Functional similarity of imaging to perceiving: Individual differences in vividness of imagery. *Perceptual and Motor Skills, 23*, 1011–33.

Sheehan, P. W. (1967a). A shortened form of Betts' questionnaire upon mental imagery. *Journal of Clinical Psychology, 23*, 386–89.

Sheehan, P. W. (1967b). Reliability of a short test of imagery. *Perceptual and Motor Skills, 25*, 744.

Sheehan, P. W. (Ed.) (1972). *The function and nature of imagery*. New York: Academic Press.

Sheehan, P. W. (1982). Eidetic imagery and the influence of method. *Journal of Mental Imagery, 6,* 86–88.

Sheehan, P. W. (1982–1983). Imaginative consciousness: Function, process, and method. *Imagination, Cognition, and Personality, 2,* 177–94.

Sheehan, P. W. (1995). The VVIQ—Directions emerging. *Journal of Mental Imagery, 19,* 187–89.

Sheehan, P. W., Ashton, R., & White, K. D. (1983). Assessment of mental imagery. In A. A. Sheikh (Ed.), *Imagery: Current theory, research, and application.* New York: Wiley.

Sheehan, P. W., McConkey, K. M., & Cross, D. G. (1978). The experiential analysis technique: Some new observations on hypnotic phenomena. *Journal of Abnormal Psychology, 87,* 570–73.

Sheehan, P. W., McConkey, K. M., & Law, H. (1978). Imagery facilitation and performance on the Creative Imagination Scale. *Journal of Mental Imagery, 2,* 265–74.

Sheehan, P. W., & Neisser, U. (1969). Some variables affecting the vividness of imagery in recall. *British Journal of Psychology, 60,* 71–80.

Sheikh, A. A. (1977). Mental images: Ghosts of sensations? *Journal of Mental Imagery, 1,* 1–3.

Sheikh, A. A. (Ed.) (1983). *Imagery: Current theory, research, and application.* New York: Wiley.

Sheikh, A. A. (2001). Mental imagery. In W. E. Craighead & C. B. Nemeroff (Eds.), *The Corsini encyclopedia of psychology and behavioral science.* New York: Wiley.

Sheikh, A. A., & Jordan, C. S. (1983). Clinical uses of mental imagery. In A. A. Sheikh (Ed.), *Imagery: Current theory, research, and application.* New York: Wiley.

Sheikh, A. A., & Panagiotou, N. C. (1975). Use of mental imagery in psychotherapy: A critical review. *Perceptual and Motor Skills, 41,* 555–85.

Sheikh, A. A., Richardson, P., & Moleski, L. M. (1979). Psychosomatics and mental imagery: A brief review. In A. A. Sheikh, & J. T. Shaffer (Eds.), *The potential for fantasy and imagination.* New York: Brandon House.

Shepard, R. N. (1975). Form, formation, and transformation of internal representations. In R. Solso (Ed.), *Information processing and cognition: The Loyola Symposium.* Hillsdale, NJ: Erlbaum.

Shepard, R. N. (1978a). Externalization of the image and the act of creation. In B. S. Randhawa & W. E. Coffman (Eds.), *Visual learning, thinking, and communication.* New York: Academic Press.

Shepard, R. N. (1978b). The mental image. *American Psychologist, 33,* 125–37.

Shepard, R. N., & Chipman, S. (1970). Second-order isomorphism of internal representations: Shapes of states. *Cognitive Psychology, 1,* 1–17.

Shepard, R. N., & Cooper, L. A. (1982). *Mental images and their transformations.* Cambridge, MA: M.I.T. Press.

Shepard, R. N., & Feng, C. (1972). A chronometric study of mental paper folding. *Cognitive Psychology, 3,* 228–43.

Shepard, R. N., & Judd, S. A. (1976). Perceptual illusion of rotation of three-dimensional objects. *Science, 191,* 952–54.

Shepard, R. N., Kilpatric, D., & Cunningham, J. (1975). The internal representation of numbers. *Cognitive Psychology, 7,* 82–138.

Shepard, R. N., & Metzler, J. (1971). Mental rotation of three-dimensional objects. *Science, 171,* 701–3.

Shepard, R. N., & Podgorny, P. (1978). Cognitive processes that resemble perceptual processes. In W. K. Estes (Ed.), *Handbook of learning and cognitive processes.* Hillsdale, NJ: Erlbaum.

Shepard, R. N., Romney, A. K., & Nerlove, S. B. (Eds.) (1972). *Multidimensional scaling: Theory and applications in the behavioral sciences.* New York: Seminar Press.

Sherman, J. A. (1978). *Sex-related cognitive differences: An essay on theory and evidence.* Springfield, IL: Thomas.

Short, P. L. (1953). The objective study of mental imagery. *British Journal of Psychology, 44,* 38–51.

Simonton, D. K. (2002). *Great psychologists and their times: Scientific insights into psychology's history.* Washington, DC: American Psychological Association.

Simonton, O. C., Matthews-Simonton, S., & Creighton, J. L. (1978). *Getting well again: A step-by-step, self-help guide to overcoming cancer for patients and their families.* Toronto: Bantam Books/Los Angeles: Tarcher.

Simpson, H. M., Molloy, F., Hale, S., & Climan, M. (1968). Latency and magnitude of the pupillary response during an imagery task. *Psychonomic Science, 13,* 293–94.

Simpson, H. M., & Paivio, A. (1966). Changes in pupil size during an imagery task without motor response involvement. *Psychonomic Science, 5,* 405–6.

Simpson, H. M., & Paivio, A. (1968). Effects on pupil size of manual and verbal indicators of cognitive task fulfillment. *Perception & Psychophysics, 3,* 185–90.

Simpson, H. M., Paivio, A., & Rodgers, T. B. (1967). Occipital alpha activity of high and low imagers during problem solving. *Psychonomic Science, 8,* 49–50.

Simpson, W., Vaught, G., & Ham, M. (1971). Intercorrelations among imagery tasks. *Perceptual and Motor Skills, 32,* 249–50.

Singer, J. L. (1966). *Daydreaming: An introduction to the experimental study of inner experience.* New York: Random House.

Singer, J. L. (1974). *Imagery and daydream methods in psychotherapy and behavior modification.* New York: Academic Press.

Singer, J. L., & Antrobus, J. S. (1970). *Imaginal processes inventory.* New York: Authors.

Sipprelle, C. N. (1967). Induced-anxiety. *Psychotherapy: Theory, Research, and Practice, 4,* 36–40.

Skinner, B. F. (1957). *Verbal behavior.* New York: Appleton-Century-Crofts.

Slack, J. M. (1988). Reading mental images. In M. Denis, J. Engelkamp, & J.T.E. Richardson (Eds.), *Cognitive and neuropsychological approaches to mental imagery.* Dordrecht, The Netherlands: M. Nijhoff.

Slatter, K. H. (1960). Alpha rhythms and mental imagery. *Electroencephalography and Clinical Neurophysiology, 12,* 851–59.

Slee, J. A. (1976). The perceptual nature of visual imagery. Unpublished doctoral dissertation, Australian National University, Canberra.

Slee, J. A. (1980). Individual differences in visual imagery ability and the retrieval of visual appearances. *Journal of Mental Imagery, 4,* 93–113.

Smith, R. C. (1986). Studying the meaning of dreams: Accurate definition of the independent variable. *Biological Psychiatry, 21,* 989–96.

Smith, R. C. (1989). The meaning of dreams: A current warning theory. In J. Gackenbach & A. A. Sheikh (Eds.), *Dream images: A call to mental arms.* Farmingdale, NY: Baywood.

Sommer, R. (1978). *The mind's eye: Imagery in everyday life.* New York: Delacorte Press.

Sommer, R. (1980). Strategies for imagery research. *Journal of Mental Imagery, 4,* 115–21.

Stanovich, K. E. (1990). *How to think straight about psychology.* Glenview, IL: Scott, Foresman.

Steiger, J. H., & Yuille, J. C. (1983). Long term memory and mental rotation. *Canadian Journal of Psychology, 37,* 367–89.

Stern, B. B. (2003). Masculinism(s) and the male image: What does it mean to be a man? In T. Reichert & J. Lambiase (Eds.), *Sex in advertising: Perspectives on the erotic appeal.* Mahwah, NJ: Erlbaum.

Sternberg, R. J. (1977). *Intelligence, information processing, and analogical reasoning: The componential analysis of human abilities.* Hillsdale, NJ: Erlbaum.

Stevens, S. S. (1939). Psychology and the science of science. *Psychological Bulletin, 36,* 221–63.

Stevens, S. S. (1946). On the theory of scales of measurement. *Science, 103,* 677–80.

Stevens, S. S. (1951). Mathematics, measurement, and psychophysics. In S. S. Stevens (Ed.), *Handbook of experimental psychology.* New York: Wiley.

Stewart, H. (1965). Sensory deprivation, personality, and visual imagery. *Journal of General Psychology, 72,* 145–50.

Stewart, R. K. (2002). Increasing perceived susceptibility to tobacco-related illness through imagery and social comparison. *Dissertation Abstracts International, 63(4-B),* 2076.

Stoyva, J., & Kamiya, J. (1968). Electrophysiological studies of dreaming as the prototype of a new strategy in the study of consciousness. *Psychological Review, 75,* 192–205.

Stratton, G. M. (1917). The mnemonic feat of the Shass Pollak. *Psychological Review, 24,* 244–47.

Stricker, S. (1880). *Studien uber die sprachvorstellungen.* Vienna: Holder.

Stromeyer, C. (1970). Eidetikers. *Psychology Today,* November, 77–80.

Strosahl, K. D., & Ascough, J. C. (1981). Clinical uses of mental imagery: Experimental foundations, theoretical misconceptions, and research issues. *Psychological Bulletin, 89,* 422–38.

Sullivan, G. L., & Macklin, M. C. (1986). Some psychometric properties of two scales for the measurement of verbalizer-visualizer differences in cognitive style. *Journal of Mental Imagery, 10,* 75–86.

Sussman, J. L. (1993). Imagery: A feminist perspective. *Journal of Mental Imagery, 17,* 319–35.

Sutherland, M., Harrell, J., & Isaacs, C. (1987). The stability of individual differences in imagery ability. *Journal of Mental Imagery, 11,* 97–104.

Switras, J. E. (1978). An alternate form instrument to assess vividness and controllability of mental imagery in seven modalities. *Perceptual and Motor Skills, 46,* 379–84.

Tapley, S. M., & Bryden, M. P. (1977). An investigation of sex differences in spatial ability: Mental rotation of three-dimensional objects. *Canadian Journal of Psychology, 31,* 122–30.

Thorndike, E. L. (1907). On the function of visual images. *Journal of Philosophy, Psychology, and Scientific Methods, 4,* 324–27.

Thurstone, L. L. (1927). A law of comparative judgment. *Psychological Review, 38,* 273–86.

Thurstone, L. L. (1928). The absolute zero in intelligence measurement. *Psychological Review, 35,* 175–97.

Thurstone, L. L. (1938). *Primary mental abilities. Psychometric Monographs No. 1.* Chicago: University of Chicago Press.

Thurstone, L. L., & Jones, L. V. (1957). The rational origin for measuring subjective values. *Journal of the American Statistical Association, 52,* 458–71.

Thurstone, L. L., & Thurstone, T. G. (1941). *The Chicago tests of primary mental abilities.* Washington, DC: The American Council on Education.

Thurstone, L. L., & Thurstone, T. G. (1962). *SRA primary mental abilities.* 1962 ed. Chicago: Science Research Associates.

Titchener, E. B. (1915). *A beginner's psychology.* New York: Macmillan.

Tolman, E. C. (1932). *Purposive behavior in animals and men.* New York: Appleton-Century-Crofts.

Torgerson, W. S. (1958). *Theory and methods of scaling.* New York: Wiley.

Tower, R. B., & Singer, J. L. (1981). The measurement of imagery: How can it be clinically useful? In P. C. Kendall & S. Holland (Eds.),

*Cognitive-behavioral interventions: Assessment methods.* New York: Academic Press.

Tucker, L. R. (1960). Intra-individual, and inter-individual multidimensionality. In H. O. Gulliksen & S. J. Messick (Eds.), *Psychological scaling: Theory and applications.* New York: Wiley.

Tucker, L. R., & Messick, S. J. (1963). Individual difference model for multidimensional scaling. *Psychometrika, 28,* 333–67.

Tuke, D. H. (1872). *Illustrations of the influence of the mind upon the body in health and disease, designed to elucidate the action of the imagination.* London: J. & A. Churchill.

Tukey, J. W. (1970). Conclusions versus decisions. In P. Badia, A. Haber, & R. P. Runyon (Eds.), *Research problems in psychology.* Reading, MA: Addison-Wesley.

Turner, R. G. (1978). Individual differences in ability to image nouns. *Perceptual and Motor Skills, 47,* 423–34.

Underwood, B. (1975). Individual differences as a crucible in theory construction. *American Psychologist, 30,* 128–34.

Unger, R. K. (1979). Toward a redefinition of sex and gender. *American Psychologist, 34,* 1085–94.

Urbantschitsch, V. (1907). *Uber subjektive optische anshauungsbilder.* Leipzig: Deuticke.

Vogt, S. (1995). On relations between perceiving, imagining, and performing in the learning of cyclical movement sequences. *British Journal of Psychology, 86,* 191–216.

Wagman, R., & Stewart, C. (1974). Visual imagery and hypnotic susceptibility. *Perceptual and Motor Skills, 38,* 815–22.

Wallace, A.F.C. (1959). Cultural determinants in response to hallucinatory experiences. *Archives of General Psychiatry, 1,* 58–69.

Wallace, B. (1988). Imaging ability, visual search strategies, and the unvividness paradox. *Journal of Mental Imagery, 12,* 173–84.

Walter, V. J., & Walter, W. G. (1949). The central effects of rhythmic sensory stimulation. *EEG and Clinical Neurophysiology, 1,* 57–86.

Ward, C. (1978). Methodological problems in attitude measurement. *Representative Research in Social Psychology, 9,* 64–68.

Ward, C. (1985). Scientific methodology and experiential approaches to the study of mental imagery. *Journal of Mental Imagery, 9,* 113–26.

Ward, J. (1883). Psychology. *Encyclopaedia Britannica.* 9th ed. Vol. 20, 37–85.

Watson, J. B. (1913a). Image and affection in behavior. *Journal of Philosophy, Psychology, and Scientific Methods, 10,* 421–28.

Watson, J. B. (1913b). Psychology as the Behaviorist views it. *Psychological Review, 20,* 158–77.

Watson, J. B. (1914). *Behavior: An introduction to comparative psychology.* New York: Holt.

Watson, J. B. (1924). *Behaviorism.* New York: W. W. Norton.

Webb, E., Campbell, D., Schwartz, R., & Sechrest, L. (1966). *Unobtrusive measures: Nonreactive research in the social sciences.* Chicago: Rand McNally.

Weinbaum, J. (2001). A bad coin: Commentary on imagery and the Internet. *Journal of Mental Imagery, 25,* 45–46.

Weinberg, R., Butt, J., Knight, B., Burke, K., & Jackson, A. (2003). The relationship between the use and effectiveness of imagery: An exploratory investigation. *Journal of Applied Sport Psychology, 15,* 26–40.

Weiner, S. L., & Ehrlichman, H. (1976). Ocular motility and cognitive processes. *Cognition, 4,* 31–43.

Weiten, W., & Etaugh, C. (1974). Lateral eye movements as a function of cognitive mode, question sequence, and sex of subject. *Perceptual and Motor Skills, 38,* 439–44.

White, A., & Hardy, L. (1995). Use of different imagery perspectives on the learning and performance of different motor skills. *British Journal of Psychology, 86,* 169–80.

White, K. D. (1978). Salivation: The significance of imagery in its voluntary control. *Psychophysiology, 15,* 196–203.

White, K. D., Sheehan, P. W., & Ashton, R. (1977). Imagery assessment: A survey of self-report measures. *Journal of Mental Imagery, 1,* 145–70.

White, M. J. (1969). Laterality differences in perception: A review. *Psychological Bulletin, 72,* 387–405.

Whiting, H. (1988). Mediation in learning complex cyclical actions. In M. Denis, J. Engelkamp, & J.T.E. Richardson (Eds.), *Cognitive and neuropsychological approaches to mental imagery.* Dordrecht, The Netherlands: M. Nijhoff.

Whitley, B. E., Jr. (2002). *Principles of research in behavioral science.* 2nd ed. New York: McGraw-Hill.

Williams, J. D., Rippon, G., Stone, B. M., & Annett, J. (1995). Psychophysiological correlates of dynamic imagery. *British Journal of Psychology, 86,* 283–300.

Wilson, M. (2003). Imagined movements that leak out: Comment. *Trends in Cognitive Sciences, 7,* 53–55.

Wilson, S. C., & Barber, T. X. (1976). *The Creative Imagination Scale as a measure of hypnotic responsiveness: Applications to experimental and clinical hypnosis.* Medfield, MA: Medfield Foundation.

Witkin, H. A. (1950). Individual differences in ease of perception of embedded figures. *Journal of Personality, 19,* 1–15.

Wittkower, E. (1934). Further studies in the respiration of psychotic patients. *Journal of Mental Science, 80,* 692–704.

Wolbers, T., Weiller, C., & Buechel, C. (2003). Contralateral coding of imagined body parts in the superior parietal lobe. *Cerebral Cortex, 13,* 392–99.

Wolins, L. (1978). Interval measurement: Physics, psychophysics, and metaphysics. *Educational and Psychological Measurement, 38*, 1–9.

Woodworth, R. S. (1910). Mental imagery. Review of G. H. Betts' (1909) "The distribution and functions of mental imagery." *Psychological Bulletin, 7*, 351–52.

Woodworth, R. S. (1938). *Experimental psychology.* New York: Holt.

Woodworth, R. S., & Schlosberg, H. (1954). *Experimental psychology.* New York: Holt, Rinehart and Winston.

Yaremko, R. M., & Butler, M. C. (1975). Imaginal experience and attenuation of the galvanic skin response to shock. *Bulletin of the Psychonomic Society, 5*, 317–18.

Yarmey, A. D. (1975). Introspection and imagery reports of human faces. *Perceptual and Motor Skills, 41*, 711–19.

Yen, W. M. (1975). Sex-linked major-gene influences on selected types of spatial performance. *Behavior Genetics, 5*, 281–98.

Yip, K.-S. (2003). The relief of a caregiver's burden through guided imagery, role-playing, humor, and paradoxical intervention. *American Journal of Psychotherapy, 57*, 109–21.

Yuille, J. C. (1985). A laboratory-based experimental methodology is inappropriate for the study of mental imagery. *Journal of Mental Imagery, 9*, 137–50.

Yuille, J. C. (1986). The futility of a purely experimental psychology of cognition: Imagery as a case study. In D. F. Marks (Ed.), *Theories of image formation.* New York: Brandon House.

Yuille, J. C. (1987). Image: A vital concept at risk. *Journal of Mental Imagery, 11*, 154–58.

Yuille, J. C., & Steiger, J. H. (1982). Nonholistic processing in mental rotation: Some suggestive evidence. *Perception & Psychophysics, 31*, 201–9.

Zikmund, V. (1966). Oculomotor activity during visual imagery of a moving stimulus pattern. *Studia Psychologica, 4*, 254–74.

Zikmund, V. (1972). Physiological correlates of visual imagery. In P. W. Sheehan (Ed.), *The function and nature of imagery.* New York: Academic Press.

Zimler, J., & Keenan, J. M. (1983). Imagery in the congenitally blind: How visual are visual images? *Journal of Experimental Psychology: Learning, Memory, and Cognition, 9*, 269–82.

Ziskind, E., & Augsberg, T. (1962). Hallucinations in sensory deprivation—method or madness? *Science, 137*, 992–93.

Zubek, J. P., & Welch, G. (1963). Electroencephalographic changes after prolonged sensory and perceptual deprivation. *Science, 139*, 1209–10.

Zubek, J. P., Welch, G., & Saunders, M. (1963). Electroencephalographic changes during and after 14 days of perceptual deprivation. *Science, 139*, 490–92.

Zuckerman, M., & Cohen, N. (1964). Is suggestion the source of reported visual sensations in perceptual isolation? *Journal of Abnormal and Social Psychology, 68,* 655–60.

Zusne, L. (1983). Imagery as magic, magic as natural science. *International Imagery Bulletin, 1,* 28–29.

# Chapter 5

# *Annotated Bibliography of Imagery Studies in Psychology (1960–2003)*

The material for the annotated bibliography in this chapter is organized around the following eighteen rubrics: Afterimagery and Synesthesia; Applications and Functions of Imagery; Bibliographies and Reviews of Imagery; Cognition and Imagery; Creativity and Imagery; Dreams/Daydreams and Imagery; Eidetic Imagery; Imagery Theory; Imagination Imagery; Learning and Imagery; Measurement and Tests of Imagery; Memory/Working Memory and Imagery; Perception/Sensation and Imagery; Personality/Individual and Gender Differences and Imagery; Physiology/Neuropsychology and Imagery; Sports and Imagery; Therapy and Imagery; Thought Imagery. (Note: Definitions and discussions of these headings are given in chapters 1, 3, and 4.)

The studies cited in this bibliography are chosen selectively. When it is necessary to choose between studies (regarding which ones to include here), the criterion of "traditionalist" experimental psychology is employed to select studies. That is, studies containing an explicit experimental/empirical basis or format—with clearly defined independent and dependent variables—are preferred over those studies that do not contain such specifications or elements. Also, theoretical articles are included, and very short articles (one or two pages in length)—when chosen—generally are given only brief annotations. This selection strategy is necessary especially in light of the magnitude and wealth of the extant literature on imagery in psychology: since 1887, there have been over 13,000 studies (as determined via PsycINFO, and using *only* the search term *imagery*) published on the topic of *imagery* in psychology. My writing approach, generally, is to avoid redundancy of reference and citation; however, in a few cases, studies cited in a previous chapter are included in this chapter. This is due to the importance—in my estimation—of such works for a better understanding of *imagery in psychology* and where such repetition is employed deliberately to emphasize particular issues, suggestions, findings, strategies, methodologies, and/or conclusions.

The result of the application of these criteria, strategies, and qualifications is the present annotated bibliography that contains over 400 entries from the psychological literature on imagery research from 1960 through 2003. The general format for most entries in this chapter includes the following information (where appropriate): statements concerning the participants involved, the materials used, and the results of the study. Also, the use of a single asterisk (*) at the end of an annotation indicates that the study mainly employed an *empirical* (data collection) methodology, whereas the use of a double asterisk (**) at the end of an annotation denotes that the study employed an *experimental* (causal determination) methodology. Finally, a Notes section is attached to many of the entries. This is a space-saving measure that allows reference to be made to other important studies that are related to the particular topic of the entry and—rather than providing a full description of those studies that would mean taking up more valuable page space—I merely cite them for the interested reader. No evaluations of the quality or superiority of studies are made or intended when comparing a full-annotated study with a cited-only study contained in the Notes section.

## AFTERIMAGERY AND SYNESTHESIA

1. Atkinson, R. P. (1994–1995). Enhanced afterimage persistence in waking and hypnosis: High hypnotizables report more enduring afterimages. *Imagination, Cognition, and Personality, 14,* 31–41. Examines the moderating influences of hypnotic susceptibility level (high versus low) and visuospatial skill level (high versus low) on afterimage persistence in waking and hypnotic states. Participants were eighty male and female college students who were given two scales of hypnotic susceptibility and a mental rotations test. Results indicate that participants' visuospatial skills—as measured by the mental rotations test—did not significantly influence first afterimage intervals or afterimage durations. It is suggested that future studies examine the multivariate contributions of cognitive strategies, contextual effects of hypnosis, attentional and imagery skills, and other factors on afterimage persistence variability.**

**2.** Cytowic, R. E. (2002). *Synesthesia: A union of the senses.* New York: Springer-Verlag/Cambridge, MA: M.I.T. Press. Provides one of the most exhaustive accounts of synesthesia in the psychological literature. Among the findings are the following: synesthetes are more likely to be women than men; synesthetes are apt to be intelligent, to have a superior memory, and to be left-handed; they are typically sensitive, moody, and artistic. Cytowic's interviews with synesthetes indicate that most of them tried to tell other people of their experiences but were met with disbelief; however, few synesthetes would be willing—social awkwardness notwithstanding—to exchange their "sixth sense" for more "normal" perception (for many synesthetes, the joining of the senses is an intensely pleasurable experience). Cytowic suggests that the synesthetes' cortex is not centrally involved in synesthetic experience as it would have to be if language or imagination were key explanatory factors; rather, according to Cytowic, phylogenetically older subcortical brain structures—known collectively as the limbic system—seem to be at work. Cytowic calls synesthesia a kind of "cognitive fossil," a state in which perceptual adjustments to the world are suspended, and where such perception is closer to the actuality of what it really means to perceive the environment. Also see the following related sources: Rader, C. M., and Tellegen, A. (1987). An investigation of synesthesia. *Journal of Personality and Social Psychology, 52,* 981–87; Lemley, B. (1984). Synesthesia: Seeing is feeling. *Psychology Today, 18,* 65; Humphreys, G. (1990). Synesthesia: A union of the senses. (Book review). *Nature, 343,* 30; Marschall, L. A. (1993). The man who tasted shapes. (Book review). *The Sciences,* Nov.–Dec., *33,* 44; Cytowic, R. E. (1986). The look of music. *Science News,* June 14, *129,* 376; Goode, E. E. (1989). A mingling of the senses. *U.S. News and World Report,* Nov. 13, *107,* 70–72; Cytowic, R. E. (1998). *The man who tasted shapes.* New York: Putnam/Cambridge, MA: M.I.T. Press; Cytowic, R. E., and Wood, F. B. (1982). Synesthesia II: Psychophysical relationships in the synesthesia of geometrically shaped taste and colored hearing. *Brain and Cognition, 1.* 36–49; Marks, L. E. (1975). On colored-hearing synesthesia: Cross-modal translations of sensory dimensions. *Psychological Bulletin, 82,* 303–31; McKellar, P. (1997). Synaesthesia and imagery: "Fantasia" revisited. *Journal of Mental Imagery, 21 (3&4),* 41–53.

**3.** Gardner, G. T., and Weintraub, D. J. (1968). Tracking afterimage shrinkage during fading. *Perception and Psychophysics, 3,* 361–63. Eleven college student and faculty participants adjusted the distance of a comparison stimulus of fixed size in which the size changes of projected afterimages were tracked during the fading phase. Results indicate that foveal afterimages, and extrafoveal afterimages, contracted slightly over time where the foveal afterimages fade more rapidly and contract to a greater extent than do extrafoveal afterimages. It was concluded that—although individual variability is high—afterimages do tend to shrink in size over time.**

**4.** Hubbard, T. L. (1996). Synesthesia-like mappings of lightness, pitch, and melodic interval. *American Journal of Psychology, 109,* 219–38. Synesthesia-like mappings between visual lightness and auditory pitch, and between visual lightness and melodic interval were studied under conditions in which college-student participants rated how visual lightness and auditory pitches, and visual lightness and melodic interval "fit together"; in the former case, lighter stimuli were reported to fit better with higher pitches, and darker stimuli fit better with lower pitches; in the latter case, with melodic interval, lighter stimuli were chosen for ascending melodic intervals, and darker stimuli were chosen for descending melodic intervals. It was concluded that systematic mappings may be found among lightness, pitch, and melodic interval. The author provides a twenty-six-item references section on synesthesia, mapping, and imagery.**

**5.** Hupka, R. B., Zaleski, Z., Otto, J., Reidl, L., and Tarabrina, N. V. (1997). The colors of anger, envy, fear, and jealousy: A cross-cultural study. *Journal of Cross-Cultural Psychology, 28,* 156–71. Participants were 661 college students from Germany, Mexico, Poland, Russia, and the United States who provided word associations or verbal synesthesia between concepts of color and particular emotions. The between-participants variable was emotion-words; students indicated on six-point rating scales the extent to which the emotions of anger, envy, fear, and jealousy reminded them of twelve terms/names of color. Results indicate that—for all nations studied—the colors of anger are black and red, that of fear is black, and jealousy is red. The authors suggest that such cross-modal associations originate both in universal human experiences and in culture-specific conditions and variables—such as literature, language, and mythology.*

**6.** Kemp, S. E., and Gilbert, A. N. (1997). Odor intensity and color lightness are correlated sensory dimensions. *American Journal of Psychology, 110,* 35–46. Examines cross-modal associations between vision and olfaction and attempts to determine whether perceptual dimensions of odor vary systematically with those of vision. Participants were fifty individuals recruited via newspaper advertisements who were asked to match color chips (from among 1,565 color samples) to five odors (aldehyde C-16, caramel lactone, cinnamic aldehyde, galbanum, and methyl anthranilate) presented at three concentrations; participants also rated odor intensity. Findings indicate that for three odors (methyl anthranilate, cinnamic aldehyde, and galbanum) there were significant negative correlations between color value and perceived odor intensity. Overall, for the experience of synesthesia, the results suggest that stronger odors are associated with darker colors; also, the cross-modal relationship between colors and olfaction seems to be dimensional: color lightness varies inversely with perceived odor intensity. Such findings parallel the dimensional relations observed between other modalities, for example, lightness (vision) varies with loudness (audition).**

7. Kunzendorf, R. G. (1989). After-images of eidetic images: A developmental study. *Journal of Mental Imagery, 13*, 55–62. Following his operational definition of *eidetic images* as "imaged sensations that produce measurable after-images similar to the after-images of perceived sensations," Kunzendorf examined the directed imagery of 418 public school and college students (participants' ages ranged from five to twenty-four years old). Findings indicate that the images of the younger participants produced more afterimages with the retinal characteristics of perceptual afterimages than did those of the older individuals. The results suggest that both subjective and objective manifestations of eidetic imagery decrease from age five to age twenty-four. Subjectively, an eidetic image (a visual image that "appears to be in the real world") was experienced by 46 percent of the participants under fifteen years old, and by only 22 percent of the participants over fifteen years of age. Objectively, an after-effect of eidetic imaging (an image-inducing afterimage that—like a common perceptual afterimage—obeys Emmert's Law) was exhibited by 40 percent of the eidetic imagers under fifteen years old, and by only 18 percent of the eidetic imagers over fifteen years old. The finding that afterimages of eidetic images obey Emmert's Law suggests that eidetic imagery innervates the retina as well as the brain. Kunzendorf notes that eidetic images are not hallucinations—even though they produce afterimages and other peripheral characteristics of percepts; thus, Kunzendorf preserves the clinically important distinction between eidetic images and hallucinations despite the psychophysiological similarities between percepts and eidetic images.\*\*

8. Melara, R. D. (1989). Similarity relations among synesthetic stimuli and their attributes. *Journal of Experimental Psychology: Human Perception and Performance, 15*, 212–31. Describes four experiments designed to study the similarity relations extant among bimodal attributes that correspond in synesthetic terms (e.g., high pitch and white color), and among stimuli formed by the combination of these attributes either congruently (e.g., black/low, white/high) or incongruently (e.g., black/high, white/low). Two hypotheses were tested: synesthetic-type stimuli are viewed as wholes on the basis of their overall similarity; and nonidentical congruent stimuli are more dissimilar than nonidentical incongruent stimuli. Measures included rating scales and response latencies where two experiments studied similarity among individual attributes (using an individual differences scaling procedure) and two other experiments investigated bimodal stimuli effects. Results of the synesthetic-type comparisons indicate that the overall similarity hypothesis was supported; however, there was no support for the hypothesis concerning perceived congruity/incongruity among stimulus wholes—even though participants were sensitive apparently to correspondence/noncorrespondence among attributes. The author proposes a two-process theory in which stimulus formation (i.e., intersensory processing) occurs independently of the abstraction quality that characterizes cross-sensory meaning (i.e., figurative processing).\*\*

**9.** Seitz, J. A. (1998). Nonverbal metaphor: A review of theories and evidence. *Genetic, Social, and General Psychology Monographs, 124,* 95–119. Among the traditional views of the concept of *metaphor* is that metaphor is a property of language behavior; other approaches to understanding metaphor are the synesthetic and cognitive views. In his review of metaphor theories, Seitz notes that the three general views that account for metaphoric behavior may be differentiated on the following bases: the received or Aristotelian view states that metaphor is largely a property of language (in perceiving similarity, for instance, language simply "indexes" itself); the cognitve view explains metaphor as a general property of symbol systems; and—according to the synesthetic view—metaphor involves the ability to recognize similarities across different sensory domains and provides the foundation for metaphoric behavior (such an ability seems to have evolved naturally in human primates with the maturation of the cross-modal zones in the parietal cortex). Concerning the synesthetic view, it is suggested that perceptual similarities become available to verbal processes when the child begins to map sensory codes onto the abstract representations of language (e.g., the young child may readily map polar adjectives—such as warm/cold—onto swatches of color, musical tones, line patterns, and objects felt while blindfolded). According to the synesthetic view, it is not until the child's sensory modalities emerge as independent perceptual categories (at about four years of age) that they are able to respond in a truly metaphorical fashion. However, the author argues largely for the cognitive view in which metaphor is thought to be more properly construed as a cognitive process that is brought to bear on diverse symbolic instantiations such as music, language, film, painting, photography, dance, architecture, and sculpture.

**10.** Stevenson, R. J., Boakes, R. A., and Prescott, J. (1998). Changes in odor sweetness resulting from implicit learning of a simultaneous odor-sweetness association: An example of learned synesthesia. *Learning and Motivation, 29,* 113–32. Describes two experiments with college-student participants who reported their sensory experiences when the odors of lychee and water chestnut were paired both with sucrose and with ordinary water. Overall results indicate that the odor of such substances paired with sucrose smelled sweeter to the participants than did the same substances when paired with ordinary water. Based upon such findings, the researchers conclude that the experience of odor sweetness, in particular, is a learned response ("learned synesthesia") because—in fact—the nose has no olfactory sensory receptors that are designed for, or dedicated to, the sensory-perceptual assessment of "sweetness."** Also see Wolpin, M., and Weinstein, C. (1983). Visual imagery and olfactory stimulation. *Journal of Mental Imagery, 7,* 63–74.

**11.** Terwogt, M. M., and Hoeksma, J. B. (1995). Colors and emotions: Preferences and combinations. *Journal of General Psychology, 122,* 5–17. Participants were individuals in three age groups: seven-year-old children, eleven-year-old children, and adults who initially used the paired-comparisons method to determine their preferences for colors and emotions; later, they were asked to connect colors to emotions by selecting an appropriate color under given instructions. Results indicate that within age groups, the participants demonstrated consistent preference colors and emotions, but the preferences differed from one age group to another. The researchers formulated, and tested successfully, the most parsimonious hypothesis that colors and emotions are connected to each other on the basis of the preferences given to each of them in their own domain; thus, they found that it was not necessary to refer to some complex process, other than individual's preferences, to explain the connections between colors and emotions.**

12. Wollen, K. A., and Ruggiero, F. T. (1983). Colored-letter synesthesia. *Journal of Mental Imagery, 7*, 83–86. Describes a case study (small sample size having *n*=1) of a woman participant who demonstrated that spoken or written alphabetic letters (e.g., letters printed in black) produced photisms of color in her; the woman was given Stroop-like tasks to determine whether the photisms were produced automatically and involuntarily, as well as to determine whether they could be ignored by her. The Stroop task required that the woman say the *color* in which letters were printed on stimulus cards; she had great difficulty and response-interference on this task when a stimulus matrix contained letters printed in colors that were different from those of her experienced photisms. In further tasks, the woman was able to name the photisms she experienced to letters printed in black as rapidly as she could name the colors in a matrix of colored circles, which led the researchers to conclude that the woman's photisms were immediately and automatically evoked and were not mediated by some perceptual process that consumed an appreciable amount of time.**

## APPLICATIONS AND FUNCTIONS OF IMAGERY

13. Ahsen, A. (1981). Imagery in hemispheric asymmetries: Research and application. *Journal of Mental Imagery, 5*, 157–94. Examines the current imagery research in the complex area of hemispheric asymmetries and notes many insights and clarities of the issue, as well as many misinterpretations and confusions. Ahsen advances the notion of the *geometric* vertical meridian as an *imaginal* vertical meridian, and provides general discussions, as well as case studies, of the applications of hemispheric research to education and psychotherapy. Also see Wallace, B., and Turosky, D. D. (1994). Hemispheric laterality, imaging ability, and hypnotic susceptibility. *Journal of Mental Imagery, 18 (3&4)*, 183–95; Rotenberg, V. S., and Arshavsky, V. V. (1995). The "entropy" of right hemisphere activity and the restorative capacity of image thinking. *Journal of Mental Imagery, 19 (1&2)*, 154–59.

14. Ahsen, A. (1984). Reading of image in psychology and literary text. *Journal of Mental Imagery, 8*, 1–32. Discusses the issue of the traditional

practice of the commingling and unification of psychological method and literary form where mythic imagery and literary consciousness flourished interdependently and harmoniously. Ahsen notes that following the rise of industrialism and its attendant division of labor, the original notion of the unity of consciousness also suffered a similar divisiveness; following this split, the tripartite model in literature (i.e., the elements of the author, the text, and the reader) became popular. In his essay, Ahsen analyzes the role of the reader, in particular, vis-à-vis the creative complexities, problems, and opportunities that are reflected by the tripartite model, and the implications of this milieu for the understanding of imagery.

**15.** Allender, J. S. (1991). *Imagery in teaching and learning: An autobiography of research in four world views.* New York: Praeger. Examines how elementary school children may use mental imagery to facilitate their learning of arithmetic, spelling, and vocabulary, and how imagery techniques may be useful, also, as effective tools in the adult learning process. Allender's findings are accompanied by supporting data, which are then connected to practical applications and explain how imagery activities tap into one's learning potential.

**16.** Barrett, T. J. (1985). Interactive imagery and recall of advertisements: Interactive imagery, noninteractive imagery, and printed text. *Psychological Reports, 56,* 922. This study attempts to improve on an earlier investigation by Lutz and Lutz (1977) on the effect of interactive imagery on recall of advertisements (an interactive advertisement integrates a brand and product pictured in some mutual action; a noninteractive advertisement pictures either a brand or product, but not both). Results showed that mean recall scores were greater significantly for both interactive and noninteractive imagery than for the control condition. It is suggested that when the content of advertisements is held constant, the use of imagery—whether interactive or noninteractive—facilitates the reader's recall.** Also see Lutz, K., and Lutz, R. (1977). Effects of interactive imagery on learning: Application to advertising. *Journal of Applied Psychology, 62,* 493–98.

**17.** Begg, I. (1988). What does the vividness of an image tell us about the value of imagery? *Journal of Mental Imagery, 12,* 45–56. Proposes that the variable of vividness is a quality or attribute that people connect to a subjective experience. It is suggested that the *value* of the imagery process lies in its ability to provide a great deal of information economically where it is helpful to determine whether particular tasks require the same aspects as those that are inherent features of imaging. Begg concludes that the ultimate goal in assessment of imagery vividness is to relate the functions of imagery to the requirements and needs of specific consequential tasks where the *structure* of images is only of secondary importance.

**18.** Begg, I., Upfold, D., and Wilton, T. D. (1978). Imagery in verbal communication. *Journal of Mental Imagery, 2,* 165–86. Discusses the important role played by mental imagery in the acquisition of communication skills and imagery's contribution to communicative success in fluent speakers. Presents several experiments regarding interpersonal communication and gives theoretical and linguistic analyses of the communication process. These authors suggest that people remember best the perceptual aspects of events (via imagery) in which such perceptual data are integral to the meaning of words learned in the context of external events. It is concluded that certain practical approaches may be taken for communicating effectively; for example, one may replace complex, unfamiliar terms with simpler, more concrete ones (such as replacing the word *sinistrality* with the term *left-handedness*, or *comprehension* with *grasping*).**

**19.** Bohan, M., Pharmer, J., and Stokes, A. (1999). When does imagery practice enhance performance on a motor task? *Perceptual and Motor Skills, 88*, 651–58. Describes a 3 × 2 (physical practice × pretest-posttest) split-plot design that investigates the effects of imagery practice on the acquisition of a discrete target behavior at three different stages of learning. Data indicate that imagery practice is most beneficial in the early stages of learning and show an inverse relationship between experience and efficiency of imagery practice. Results are consistent with other studies (e.g., flight training, basketball) in which imagery practice of motor tasks enhances performance on the target activity.**

**20.** Booth, R. D., and Thomas, M. O. (1999). Visualization in mathematics learning: Arithmetic problem-solving and student difficulties. *Journal of Mathematical Behavior, 2*, 169–90. Participants in this study were thirty-two students, ages eleven through fifteen years, who had been identified previously as having mathematics difficulties; they were assigned to one of two groups on the basis of their visuospatial abilities/scores. Initially, on standard mathematical tests, there was no difference between groups in terms of mathematical performance, but one group demonstrated higher visuospatial skills than the other group. Subsequently, all participants were interviewed in a procedure in which arithmetic word problems were given to them and had to be solved in three different modes: orally, with a picture, and with a diagram. Results indicate that the group with the higher visuospatial skills performed at a significantly higher level on the problems than did the group with the lower visuospatial skills. Discussion is provided concerning the relevance and application of the variable of visuospatial skills to the learning of mathematics.**

**21.** Borduin, B., Borduin, C., and Manley, C. (1994). The use of imagery training to improve reading comprehension of second graders. *Journal of Genetic Psychology, 155*, 115–18. Participants in this study were twenty-eight second-graders from four classrooms in a socioeconomically diverse elementary school in the Midwest. Seven students from each classroom were selected randomly and assigned to one of four experimental groups: an imagery training group (in which students were taught how to make mental images of each text page and how to make visual and verbal representations

of the mental images before going to the next section of text); two corrective training groups (via two teachers, one in each group—to control for
"teacher effects"—in a directed reading group with group discussion); and
a "no instruction" group of students (in which no training or instruction
was given, but the students independently read the text). The researchers
conclude that second graders' inferential reasoning about written text may
be improved through planned instruction in the use of imagery, and present
findings that are consistent with similar studies of older children.**

**22.** Burns, A., Biswas, A., and Babin, L. (1993). The operation of visual
imagery as a mediator of advertising effects. *Journal of Advertising, 22,* 71–
85. Provides a framework for testing the notion of visual imagery as a mediating factor and potential moderator in certain advertising strategies that
elicit attitude and intentions differences in consumers. Describes empirical
research for the independent variables of instructions to imagine versus none;
and abstract versus concrete wording in an advertisement; and for the dependent variables of: attitude toward the ad, attitude toward the brand, and
behavioral intentions. Research hypotheses were tested in a 2 × 2 × 2 factorial design where participants (377 college students—each assigned to one
of the eight treatment groups) responded to a print advertisement for an
automobile. Overall results indicate that the vividness of visual imagery operates as a latent cognitive construct when concrete wording is used in advertising copy. The references section in this study contains over fifty items/
citations related to the issue of imagery in advertising.**

**23.** Cooper, G. C. (1986). Imagery in Toni Morrison's novels: The black
perspective. *Journal of Mental Imagery, 10,* 41–52. This essay describes the
application of, and presence of, imagery in black culture. The author argues
that imagery as manifested in black culture is a reflection of a "socially and
culturally reinforced holistic cognitive style" that may be viewed in that
culture's language; moreover, imagery is not merely a supplement to black
language, but is itself a language rooted in the "black experience."

**24.** Davis, J., and Brown, C. (2000). Mental imagery: In what form and
for what purpose is it utilized by counselor trainees? *Journal of Mental Imagery, 24,* 73–82. Notes that imagery as an intervention technique has been
shown to be effective, even superior in some cases, to other interventions
in such areas as career counseling, diversity training, stress counseling for
treatment of trauma such as rape and childhood sexual abuse, symptom
management for persons with AIDS or cancer, and physical disabilities rehabilitation. In this exploratory study, counselor trainee attitudes, knowledge,
and utilization of mental imagery techniques were investigated; participants
were fifty-seven counselor trainees at three universities who completed the
Imagery Attitude Scale. Among the conclusions was the notion that a counselor trainee's theoretical orientation is unrelated to perceived benefits of
mental imagery; thus, counselor trainees of varied theoretical orientations
agree that mental imagery may be beneficial to clients.*

**25.** Davis, L. L., and Lennon, S. J. (1989). Apparel advertising appeals as a function of apparel classification: Trendy versus classic. *Perceptual and Motor Skills, 68,* 1011–14. Participants were sixty-one female college students who were presented with eight pairs of advertisements (four represented trendy styles, and four represented classic styles) of four apparel products; and they completed a twelve-item questionnaire on which they made evaluative comparisons between the two ads in each pair. Findings confirm the researchers' prediction that apparel styling affects evaluations of advertising appeals. The present findings suggest that not all apparel should be advertised the same way, and personal variables, as well as apparel styling, need to be taken into account when measuring appeal toward apparel advertisements.*

**26.** Doll, M. (1983). Hearing images. *Journal of Mental Imagery, 7,* 135–42. Reviews the proposition that language serves two different functions: ordinary public discourse (whose purpose is to give literal clarity and to achieve logical order) and poetic appreciation (whose purpose—via images and imagery—is to activate the imagination). In this essay, the author suggests a method of "hearing" images as a way of responding imaginatively to the second function—that of poetic discourse; in effect, a reader of poetry—in listening to sounds, fragmented stories, juxtaposed meanings and images—hears an imaginal, rather than a conceptual, logic.

**27.** Downing, F. (1987). Imagery and the structure of design inquiry. *Journal of Mental Imagery, 11,* 61–86. In this application of imagery to the discipline of architecture, Downing proposes that the memory of past place-experience creates an "image bank" of critical source material for an architectural designer; such "place-imagery" acts as a bridge between past-experience and the creation of new places. This essay examines the characteristics of design inquiry by citing examples of architects at work and relates the relevant research to the design process; it is suggested that the notion of place-imagery has inspirational value and is useful for formulating what a future place could be like.

**28.** Esrock, E. J. (1986). The inner space of reading: Interviews with John Hawkes, Carlos Fuentes, and William Gass on visual imaging. *Journal of Mental Imagery, 10,* 61–68. Reports on interviews made by the author with three fiction writers (Hawkes, Fuentes, and Gass) concerning the latters' visual imagery and other sensory reactions when reading literature. Taken as a whole, the responses of Hawkes, Fuentes, and Gass show striking and instructive individual differences: Hawkes describes rich sensory experiences of cinemagraphic character that radiate outward from verbal text; Gass describes primarily sonoral and conceptual experiences that are ruled strictly by texts whose integrity depends on their readers and not on the construction of detailed sensory scenarios; and Fuentes—like Hawkes—describes rich sensory perceptions, but—like Gass—claims that they are not cinemagraphic but require verbal support.*

**29.** Fairweather, M., and Sidaway, B. (1993). Ideokinetic imagery as a postural development technique. *Research Quarterly for Exercise and Sport, 64,* 385–92. Describes two experiments (with a total of fifty-five participants) designed to study the use of ideokinetic imagery to improve posture by spinal realignment for the relief of low back pain. The results of this study supports the value of an adapted form of ideokinetic imagery that incorporates kinesthetic awareness exercises to improve posture and reduce low back pain; moreover, in particular, this postural development technique improved lordosis and kyphosis angles and reduced self-perception of low back pain— although exercise alone produced no lasting improvement. It is suggested that the present approach is a step toward the development of an inexpensive and relatively simple technique that improves posture and reduces low back pain *without* the need for drugs or other medical treatment.*

**30.** Fleckenstein, K. S. (1992). The writer's eye on image: Revising for definition and depth. *Journal of Mental Imagery, 16,* 109–16. Examines the notion of whether writers of literary texts—those mainly designed to elicit an emotion response from the reader—alter or craft images to increase the potential intensity of a reader's response. Using a protocol analysis methodology of the work of W. B. Yeats, it was found that Yeats did, indeed, revise his expository text for the presumed purpose of increasing the definition and metaphoric depth of the image and, thereby crafted a more evocative and engaging image for readers.*

**31.** Galyean, B.-C. (1982–1983). The use of guided imagery in elementary and secondary schools. *Imagination, Cognition, and Personality, 2,* 145– 51. Reports on the use of imagery activities in school classes where such activities are usually integrated into the standard curriculum in two ways: as preparatory to learning and within the lesson itself. When imagery is used in the lesson itself, it falls into one or more of three categories: guided cognitive imagery, guided affective imagery, and guided transpersonal imagery; whenever two or more of these operate within a single lesson, it is called *confluent imagery.* Reports that many teachers in the United States use imagery activities to sharpen students' focusing and attention skills.

**32.** Harris, E. L. (1986). Snow as a literary image for a schizophrenic state. *Journal of Mental Imagery, 10,* 69–78. Describes the application of the image of *snow* (in Conrad Aiken's short story, *Silent Snow, Secret Snow*) to the later stages of the onset of schizophrenia in a twelve-year-old boy. Although the story is a literary work, rather than a scientific/clinical case study, it does indicate how an image—such as snow—may serve as a basic communication device for portraying a child's increasing detachment from the real world; the snow increasingly buries everyday reality from the boy's perception. In this application of imagery to a literary product, the image of snow functions mainly to symbolize the various stages of a schizophrenic boy's decline and various aspects of his impaired functioning.

**33.** Hogg, M., Cox, A., and Keeling, K. (2000). The impact of self-monitoring on image congruence and product/brand evaluation. *European Journal of Marketing, 34*, 641–66. Proposes a conceptual model that connects one function of attitudes (i.e., the maintenance of self-esteem and self-identity) to the public and private contexts of self-concepts, as well as to the subsequent extrinsic and intrinsic congruence between product brand choice and evaluation. Employs the Self-Monitoring Scale to explore the connection between the social and psychological aspects of self-presentation and maintenance of self-identity, and to assess the relationship between self-concept and product symbolism. Presents the quantitative and qualitative findings of a study of the alcoholic soft-drinks market in the United Kingdom (participants were men and women, ages eighteen to twenty-five years old, who frequented nightclubs at least once every two weeks). Results give empirical support for conceiving the self as a "divisible entity"; also, distinct differences were observed between the self-monitoring groups when specific brand names were target variables, and served as the basis of several implications for marketing practice.*

**34.** Homer, P. M., and Gauntt, S. G. (1992). The role of imagery in the processing of visual and verbal package information. *Journal of Mental Imagery, 16*, 123–44. Describes an attempt to replicate directly the stimuli in the marketing context by comparing package designs that include both verbal and visual components; the effects of processing mode (nonimagery versus imagery) on consumer reactions to verbal and visual package information were studied. Participants were 231 college students enrolled in advertising courses who were assigned randomly to one level of each of the experimental conditions (package design and processing style); processing styles were manipulated by providing differing instructions among the sample groups designed to induce either imagery (two levels) or nonimagery processing (one level). To induce visual imagery processing, participants either were told to imagine (mentally visualize) the package information or were shown a series of ten slides of paintings and advertisements judged to be high in visual imagery; the other half of the students, who received no such imagery instructions or picture presentation, comprised the nonimagery group. Following exposure to the experimental manipulations, all participants completed a questionnaire concerning their attitudes toward the package, brand attitudes, and purchase intentions (prior to these evaluative judgments, unaided product and brand name recall were measured in respondents). Results indicate that brand attitudes, attitudes toward the package, and purchase intentions were all affected by the interaction of the package design and processing mode.**

**35.** *Journal of Mental Imagery, 7* (1984), 105–26. Special section: Perspectives, projects, and training facilities. In this issue of the journal, various applications of imagery are described in the following topic areas: drama therapy, that is, the intentional use of creative drama—often involving imagery techniques—toward the psychotherapeutic goals of symptom relief, emotional and physical integration, and personal growth; family life settings; prison/inmate settings; and halfway-house settings. Also see Ahsen, A. (1982). Principles of imagery in art and literature. *Journal of Mental Imagery, 6*, 213–50; Ahsen, A. (1984). Imagery, drama, and transformation. *Journal of Mental Imagery, 8*, 53–78; Drummond, J. (1984). The theatergoer as imager. *Journal of Mental Imagery, 8*, 99–104. Fleshman, B. (1984). Mime and movement training with mental imagery. *Journal of Mental Imagery, 8*, 91–98; Count-van Manen, G. (1984). Drama-imagery processes as socialization: An interdisciplinary perspective. *Journal of Mental Imagery, 8*, 1–52.

**36.** Kaplan, F. F. (1988–1989). Imagery, ego development, and nuclear attitudes. *Imagination, Cognition, and Personality, 8*, 105–19. Examines some variables—in this application of imagery to a social/political/moral issue—concerning the differentiation of individuals who oppose the nuclear arms race. Participants were thirty-eight industrial-research facility employees (women and men, ages twenty-four to seventy years old), who gave responses to the following materials: a demographic data form, an ego-development measure, a questionnaire dealing with nuclear attitudes and information and two imagery questions (one about the consequences of nuclear war, and one about images of anger). As part of the data analysis, participants were assigned to one of three nuclear attitude groups: supporters of the status quo, fence sitters, and antinuclear protesters. Results of the survey indicate that protesters were more likely to be better educated women who had a tendency to be better informed about nuclear issues, and who also had a belief that nuclear war is imminent. In terms of imagery, the protesters showed a trend toward greater production of concrete images of nuclear war than the other two groups. An appendix to this article includes the twenty-item Nuclear Issues Questionnaire that was employed in the study.*

**37.** Katz, A. N. (1992). Beliefs and the activation of mental imagery. *Journal of Mental Imagery, 16*, 145–66. Proposes a working model for exploring the conditions under which individuals use imagery in their everyday lives; at the core of the model are the beliefs one holds about one's own imagery abilities. Three studies were conducted involving 176 college-student participants who completed a series of imagery questionnaires. Among the results of these studies is that persons who believe themselves to be high imagers possess belief and personality structures characteristic of high imagery persons. The explanation favored by Katz for his findings is that the knowledge that is relevant about imagery is represented in two separable systems: one is specialized by generic, impersonal facts (e.g., what one knows to be true about imagery), whereas the second system is specialized for specific, personal, or autobiographical facts (e.g., what one believes about *oneself* relevant to imagery). An appendix attached to this article includes the "Imager-Schematic" (twenty-five items) and "Non-Schematic Control" (twenty-five items) terms used in the study.*

**38.** Kohanim, M., and Johnson, J. (2000). Using images as a foundation for natural language processing. *Computational Intelligence, 4,* 596–605. Advances a new framework for knowledge-representation that is based on modality-dependent (i.e., sight, touch, and sound) images, and affords greater communication using natural languages. The major premise of the model is that natural language processing depends not only on grammatical rules, but also on topics/entities, their attributes or states, and other supported events on a time/space continuum.

**39.** Korol, C., and von Baeyer, C. (1992). Effects of brief instruction in imagery and birth visualization in prenatal education. *Journal of Mental Imagery, 16,* 167–72. Participants were sixty pregnant women (with a median age of twenty-seven years old) who were recruited from fourteen prenatal classes taught at community health clinics. A battery of tests was administered to the participants on three occasions (immediately before the first prenatal class, at the end of classes, and two weeks before term—in six imagery and eight nonimagery classes) and included the following measures: an absorption scale, an anxiety scale, and a questionnaire regarding knowledge of the process of labor and delivery and of the accompanying emotions and physical sensations. Results indicate that the hypothesis that a birth visualization format improves memory for information about labor and delivery given in prenatal classes was *not* supported; also, the hypothesis that the use of imagery would be preferred by women who possess a high degree of absorption (i.e., the ability to focus attention on an image) was *not* supported. It is concluded that brief training in imagery—given to groups by instructors with minimal experience in the technique—seems *not* to produce the dramatic results that have been attributed to more intensive imagery instruction.*

**40.** Kosslyn, S. M., Seger, C., Pani, J. R., and Hillger, L. A. (1990). When is imagery used in everyday life: A diary study. *Journal of Mental Imagery, 14,* 131–52. Claims to be the first modern survey of the everyday uses of imagery; in two studies involving different data-collection strategies, participants either simply kept a diary over the course of a week recording instances of images as they occurred, or recorded instances of imagery hourly, or more frequently, for a single day. In the first study, images were noted in an unstructured way, but in the second study, images were described with the aid of a questionnaire. Results from the use of the different methodologies indicate a high level of similarity among participants; in one analysis, most of the images reported by all participants had no discernible purpose. Other similarities among diary-keepers included the following: most images occurred in isolation (not as part of some sequence); most images (more than 50 percent) reported by the participants were visual; and no gender differences in imagery were observed across participants.*

**41.** Lennings, C. J. (1996). Adolescent aggression and imagery: Contributions from object relations and social cognitive theory. *Adolescence, 31,*

831–40. Presents a case study of a sixteen-year-old boy in a youth detention center who was referred for his high level of aggressiveness involving an alleged vicious assault on another individual. The study indicates how to use imagery manipulation in a quasi-therapeutic setting to modify behavior in a short period of time. Among the interventions used with the boy were guided imagery and visualization techniques (through a progression of images—many involving the boy's past experiences, in particular, with disturbed attachments he had with his abusive but idealized father—the ultimate goal was to achieve behavioral change in the boy). It was concluded that the use of imagery in such a context is most effective if psychodynamic principles (based on an understanding of the manipulation of internal objects) and social-cognitive principles (based on adequately operationalized cognitive-behavioral therapies) are used in combination.*

**42.** Lindberg, C., and Lawlis, G. F. (1988). The effectiveness of imagery as a childbirth preparatory technique. *Journal of Mental Imagery, 12,* 103–14. In this application of imagery to the childbirth process/activity, participants were thirty-six primiparous women in three groups who were studied using anxiety, pain, and overall health of the babies as dependent variables. The independent variables of the labor and delivery training classes included basic education of labor and delivery, respiration behavior, relaxation of muscles via imagery, and participation of a coach; the goal of the classes was to reduce the amount of pain experienced in labor/delivery and to decrease the amount of medication received by the women (e.g., medication given to mothers typically affects the Apgar ratings of their infants). Based upon the results of the training procedures, it was concluded that the type of training a mother uses preparing for labor and delivery may enhance the immediate health of her child; also, this study adds to the increasing evidence that supports the Triple Code Model in which the image is assumed to be a primary independent variable, with consequent change in somatic outcomes expressed in physical functioning of both mother and infant.**

**43.** Lucca, C. A., and Jennings, J. L. (1993). The impoverishment of human experience and eidetic imagination through the manipulation of language: The systematic destruction of language in Orwell's *1984. Journal of Mental Imagery, 17,* 141–58. This essay describes an application/relationship of imagery to literature and indicates—via the storyline in George Orwell's 1948 novel *1984*—how the impoverishment of language acts to extinguish eidetic imagination and independent thinking, while breaking social bonds and cultural identity. The authors cite four fundamental functions of language that are necessary for meaningful human existence: it is the primary means of organizing one's experiences; it acts as a preorganizing agent of one's experiences and perceptions; it is the basis of social exchange; and it provides one the means for transcendence of place, time, and socio-cultural miliueu.

**44.** Mandl, B. (1986). Images of transformation: Joyce's Ulysses in midlife. *Journal of Mental Imagery, 10*, 79–86. In this application/relationship of imagery to literature, the author examines the images in James Joyce's 1914 novel *Ulysses*, in particular those associated with the main character/hero's (Leopold Bloom's) midlife feelings and perceptions; the Mandl traces the images relating to androgyny, marriage, and paternity that indicate that Bloom moves through a concentrated phase of development during the course of an intensively introspective day. Mandl examines Bloom's concerns about midlife in relationship to those typically discussed in the recent literature on male midlife experiences; in terms of the particular storyline/theme, much attention is given to the aspect of symbolic fatherhood—vis-à-vis the character Stephen Dedalus—in which Bloom as a mentor figure to Dedalus is both a transformational instrument and the emblem/image of his (Bloom's) generativity. Also see Wentworth, J. A. (1986). Bloom's self-therapy in *Ulysses*: Images in action. *Journal of Mental Imagery, 10*, 127–36.

**45.** Martin, B. A., and McCracken, C. A. (2001). Music marketing: Music consumption imagery in the UK and New Zealand. *Journal of Consumer Marketing, 18*, 426–36. In this application of imagery to the field of consumer marketing, cross-country differences in marketing imagery in music videos broadcast in the United Kingdom and New Zealand are examined. Results of the survey suggest that music videos in the United Kingdom have more references to brand names, fashion imagery, "darkside" products, and role model behavior outcomes than do music videos in New Zealand. Additionally, overall, pop music marketing references contain predominantly visual imagery, while hard rock marketing references contain more "darkside" products, brand name references, and punishment outcomes.*

**46.** McKellar, P. (1987). Coleridge, the imaged albatross, and others. *Journal of Mental Imagery, 11*, 113–24. In this essay, McKellar focuses on the theme of altered states of consciousness, in particular as it manifests in three literary works: Coleridge's *Ancient Mariner*, Dostoevsky's *Brothers Karamazov*, and du Maurier's *Trilby*. The consciousness states of waking-sleeping, hypnosis, and hallucination are considered in these works and indicate psychology's connection to, and interest in, the imaginary characters and contexts created by fiction writers. McKellar suggests that poetry, literature, and drama—often via the device of imagery—have paved/illuminated the pathway for psychologists to follow in their theoretical and practical attempts to understand human behavior.

**47.** Miller, W. J. (1982). Descent into Heller: Mythic imagery in *Catch-22*. *Journal of Mental Imagery, 6*, 145–56. In this application/relationship of imagery to literature, Miller examines Joseph Heller's 1961 novel *Catch-22* from the perspective of its systematic subliminal appeal. It is suggested that this unorthodox novel helps readers to rediscover their "forgotten language" through hidden mythic images that appeal to them on an unconscious level. Miller argues that the unacknowledged component that made

*Catch-22* eventually such a great literary and financial success was in its powerful subliminal appeal through the application of various imagery mechanisms and devices.

**48.** Milojkovic, J. D. (1982). Chess imagery in novice and master. *Journal of Mental Imagery, 6,* 125–44. Describes two experiments in the application of imagery to the game of chess (cf. Saariluoma, 1995). The first study was designed to examine the image scanning effects for chess novices and a chess master in a task concerning the translation and capture of pieces in memory-generated representations of highly simplified chess positions; the second study involved an analogous task for direct viewing of the same chess positions. Results of both experiments based on reaction-time data indicate that there are systematic differences between chess novices and the chess master. It is concluded that there appears to be some support for a representational-development hypothesis that states that with increasing chess skill either the image changes or the nature of the transformation on the chess image changes. The references section of this article contains over seventy items/citations relevant to the issues relating imagery to the game of chess.* Also see Saariluoma, P. (1995). *Chess players' thinking: A cognitive psychological approach.* London: Routledge.

**49.** Morgan, P. (1986). Poetic pictorial multivalency: Milton's *L'Allegro* and its illustrators. *Journal of Mental Imagery, 10,* 87–102. In this essay, Morgan discusses the visual aspects of John Milton's 1632 pictorial poem *L'Allegro,* as well as its reference back to a visual archetype, Ripa's portrait of "happiness," together with the many illustrations beginning in 1645 (down to the middle of the twentieth century) that the poem inspired (e.g., illustrations/engravings/drawings/paintings by Romney, Reynolds, Blake, Fuseli, and Frost). Morgan argues that such ancillary illustrations, visual representations, and images enlarge one's sense of the visual richness of Milton's poem, its interpretation in terms of the landscape and the human figure, and its underlying spiritual essence.

**50.** Parker, L. J. (1983). Is story image? Reflections of a storyteller. *Journal of Mental Imagery, 7,* 127–38. This essay proposes that some great stories function imagistically because they elicit, repeatedly, different interpretations in the reader or listener. It is as if some stories act like two counterforces that are pulling apart simultaneously, but seem—at the same time—to work together to produce the single story's varied appeal on two dimensions: the narrative aspects of the story itself, and the readers'/listeners' individual styles of cognition. In this context, according to Parker, the person's interpretations and experiences as listener or reader flash imagistically across that space between literature and life, and contribute both to one's understanding of the story as well as to the historical, mythological, and personal levels of consciousness.

**51.** Parrott, C. A. (1986). Visual imagery training: Stimulating utilization of imaginal processes. *Journal of Mental Imagery, 10,* 47–64. Participants were sixty university engineering students who volunteered to be part of an imagery-training group or of a verbal-creativity training group. The goal was to assess the effect of imagery training strategies in stimulating the adaptive use of imaginal processes in students. Dependent variable measures included conjugate lateral eye movement (CLEM) patterns and imagery/spatial ability tests. Among the findings of this study were: the distinct lateralization (via eye movements) of imaginal processes was *not* supported by the data, although right hemisphere functioning as a preferred mode was associated with greater facilitation with imagery training; also, superior performance was observed through training in the nonpreferred mode as indexed by CLEMs. It was noted that utilization of the capabilities of both hemispheres—or alternative processing modes—seems to be superior to rigid reliance on just one cognitive style in problem-solving contexts.**

**52.** Peterson, R. (1986). Sylvia Plath's lunar images: "Metamorphoses of the moon." *Journal of Mental Imagery, 10*, 103–12. In this application/relationship of imagery to literature, Peterson analyzes Sylvia Plath's frequent use of lunar imagery in her poetry that results in the evolution of a private symbol. According to Peterson, Plath's early work presents the moon as a cliché (an orb of green cheese), as supernatural light, or as a symbol of death; however, in her later work, Plath's symbol/image of the moon represents her soul.

**53.** Prince, S. (1992). *Visions of empire: Political imagery in contemporary American film.* New York: Praeger. In this application of imagery to the field of politics—via the artistic device of film—Prince explores the functions of film as a medium of political communication. This includes not just the propaganda film, but the various ways in which conventional narrative films demonstrate, question, or criticize the established social values that underlie American attitudes toward social, historical, and political events. Contents of the book include the following issues: a theoretical framework for viewing some basic features of the political landscape of the Reagan era; the major cycles of political films; the images of the new Cold War films that gave attention to the fears of the Soviet menace; various histories and mythologies on film of the Vietnam War as examples of the symbolic reconstruction of social memory; the images of the politicized science fiction films that offer critical commentaries on the pathologies of contemporary urban society and capitalism; and the place of politics in Hollywood films.

**54.** Roberts, D. S., and MacDonald, B. E. (2001). Relations of imagery, creativity, and socioeconomic status with performance on a stock-market e-trading game. *Psychological Reports, 88*, 734–40. Participants in this study of the application of imagery to the milieu of the stock market were 368 college students enrolled in an administration studies program. The dependent variable measures included imagery, creativity, and socioeconomic status (SES) scores and their relationship to performance in a stock-market trading game. Analyses using multiple regression procedures indicate that imaging scores were a greater predictor of stock-trading performance in the participants than were creativity and SES scores, even though the latter were predictors, also, but to a lesser degree.*

**55.** Rosenberg, H. S., and Epstein, Y. M. (1991). Alone together: Collaborative imagery in visual art-making. *Journal of Mental Imagery, 15,* 157–70. Based upon interviews made with twenty visual artists, it was determined the extent to which artists engage in mental imagery strategies whereby they allow their materials, their mental images, and their paintings-in-progress to participate actively in the art-making process. Transcribed tapes of the interviews were scanned for imagery-related statements and references; results indicate that the artists did mention that their mental images, their paintings, and their artist's materials participate actively in the creative process—from creating the original idea through selling the product/piece. It is indicated that a richer time to question visual artists is while they are in the *process* of painting, instead of after completion of the work—it is at this time that most of the imagery-related phenomena seem to emerge and reach a peak.*

**56.** Singer, D. G. (1978). Television and imaginative play. *Journal of Mental Imagery, 2,* 145–64. Discusses the influence of television on the social and cognitive development, imagination, and aggressive behavior of young children. Among the issues reviewed by Singer are the following: television viewing time, preferences and functions of television viewing, properties of television, television and cognitive-skill acquisition, television commercials and imagination, and television and aggression. The author makes the following suggestions for future research and applications based upon her review of the psychological literature of the effects of television on children's various behaviors: more experiments are needed on the relationship of television and children's imaginative play; more research is needed concerning the effects of television viewing on children's language development and the efficacy of modeling behavior in children; and more data are needed on the use of television in daycare centers to teach children how to play or become more imaginative. Singer argues that television has great potential as a teacher, but only if adults *actively* engage children in their viewing; the passive or unrestricted viewing of television may prevent children from reading, playing, or exploring other creative uses of their time. The references section of this article contains over 100 items/citations related to the issue of television and imaginative play.

**57.** Smart, C. (1995). *The imagery of Soviet foreign policy and the collapse of the Russian empire.* Westport, CT: Praeger. In this application/relationship of imagery to the field of international politics, the author explores how Soviet leaders shaped the image of their nation since the death of Joseph Stalin; it is suggested that this was a cumbersome task of image management because the leadership's legitimacy rested on certain values and aims that were fundamentally incongruous with those of the international system. Each

Soviet leader approached the task with a different strategy, with each strategy having direct consequences for Soviet behavior both abroad and at home. The author analyzes the dynamics of foreign policy and image management from Khrushchev and Brezhnev through Gorbachev and Yeltsin.

**58.** Squyres, E. M., and Craddick, R. A. (1984). Rorschach and archetype: Examining the correspondence. *Journal of Mental Imagery, 8,* 91–104. Suggests that participants/clients responses to the Rorschach inkblot test are in the form of personalized images; however, Rorschach responses traditionally have stimulated a great deal of argument regarding specific meanings attributable to them. It is noted that certain periods of art, for instance, the Paleolithic and Neolithic eras, have been invoked in discussions of the structural similarity between art forms and the Rorschach plates; also, Jung's concept of the archetype has been invoked similarly to describe and articulate the correspondence between the Rorschach plates and the language of images reflected from areas of early human experience. These researchers asked Jungian analysts to submit myths and/or fairy tales in an effort to substantiate and amplify the archetypal nature of individuals' responses to the Rorschach plates, and to assess how such responses reflect one's level of personal integration and various themes common to human experience. An appendix to this article identifies and defines ten archetypal themes (e.g., one theme is "the experience of one's matriarchal source") corresponding to the Rorschach inkblot stimuli.*

**59.** Suler, J. (1990). Images of the self in Zen meditation. *Journal of Mental Imagery, 14,* 197–204. This essay represents an application of imagery to the self-actualizing practice of Zen meditation; Zen training and *zazen* lead to a state of being in which all thought, memory, and emotion dissolve—it is a state of egolessness, of "no-mind" and "no-self"; a sign of progress in the Zen form of meditation is the presence of vivid imagistic sensations called *makyo*. Such images, theoretically, are indicative of previously covert features of self-structure that are brought to the surface of one's consciousness. It is suggested that the activation of the "observing self" facilitates one's imagistic experiences, and it is the images of makyo in Zen meditation that serve as balancing mechanisms in the dynamism between the integration of the self, on one hand, and the dissolution of the self, on the other hand.

**60.** Sullivan, G. L., and Macklin, M. C. (1988). Vividness-unvividness effects in print advertising: An experimental investigation. *Journal of Mental Imagery, 12,* 133–44. Participants in this study were fifty-four college male and female students who were asked to evaluate mock-up advertisements for three products: a brand of red wine, a brand of four-wheel-drive passenger car, and a brand of tennis balls. The covariates employed in the study consisted of a measure of product involvement, a measure of visual imaging ability, gender, and culture. Each participant was assigned randomly to one of two experimental conditions: vivid or unvivid (pallid) imagery in ads.

Based on participants' assessments and perceptions of the effectiveness of the advertisements, the following results were noted: contrary to popular advertising wisdom, the vivid print ads proved no more effective than unvivid/pallid ads on a range of advertising copy-testing criteria. It is suggested that other variables (aside from the vivid-unvivid aspect)—such as product class involvement, beliefs, attitudes, purchase intentions, cultural background, and gender—may offer better explanatory power than ad copy vividness in predicting participants' reactions to advertising materials.**

**61.** Taylor, R. E., and Smith, L. (1986). A transformational journey into inner emptiness in Akhter Ahsen's epic poem "Manhunt in the desert." *Journal of Mental Imagery, 10,* 121–26. In this application/relationship of imagery to literature, the authors examine Ahsen's poem "Manhunt in the Desert" that is characterized as an inner journey whereby the pilgrim protagonist, a desert wanderer, develops reconciliation between ego and soul; in the spirit of Dante's "Inferno" and Bunyan's "Pilgrim's Progress," the main character is on a spiritual search that takes him through dangerous and unknown territory where he encounters a series of archetypal figures who aid the traveler's inner growth process. In Ahsen's account, abundant imagery is presented that resonates with the unconscious and undeveloped aspects of the pilgrim's personality; following a series of "psychic deaths" invoking Christian mythology and creation, and a vision of white swans—the historical symbol of hermaphroditism and the coming together of the masculine and feminine principles as the polarities of the psychic progress toward conscious integration—the traveler's journey ends with a vision of completeness and imagistic wholeness. Also see Cirlot, J. E. (1962). *A dictionary of symbols.* New York: Routledge and Kegan Paul.

**62.** Tess, D., Hutchinson, R., Treloar, J., and Jenkins, C. (1999). Bizarre imagery and distinctiveness: Implications for the classroom. *Journal of Mental Imagery, 23,* 153–70. In this application of imagery to the classroom and the field of education, the researchers examine the efficacy of bizarre imagery in enhancing the recall of information in sixty high-school student participants. An experimental group viewed slides of five English romantic era poets, with only the poet Byron dressed in bizarre garb (the bizarre image was operationally defined as Byron in his unusual attire). A control group saw all poets in ordinary dress/attire. Results of recall tests indicate that the bizarre imagery (i.e., Byron's slide) was more memorable than the average of the other four poets (Blake, Shelley, Coleridge, Keats) for participants in the experimental condition across time. It was concluded that the following results may have implications for the classroom: bizarre imagery appears to enhance recall performance; bizarre imagery enhances recall performance on immediate recall and delayed retention tasks; bizarre imagery, as a stimulus variable, seems to enhance recall performance in a sample of college-bound high school seniors; and a restricted version of the distinctiveness theory is a useful tool in accounting for the effectiveness of bizarreness as a mnemonic aid. The references section of this article contains over fifty citations related to imagery and learning/memory.**

**63.** Thompson, W. B. (2000). Is a bee bigger than a flea? A classroom mental imagery activity. *Teaching of Psychology, 27*, 212–14. Describes the application of imagery to the field of education where a simple classroom activity quickly and reliably replicates the following phenomenon (called the *symbolic distance effect*) involving imagery that is useful for classes in cognitive psychology: when individuals decide which of two imagined objects is bigger, their decision time increases as the size difference between the two objects decreases. Students are asked to read a list of twenty-four animal pairs (two lists are provided in the article, one for large size differences and another for small size differences) and decide which animal in each pair is larger. Typically, students require more decision time for small size differences (e.g., bee versus flea) than for large size differences (e.g., bear versus flea). It is suggested that this activity involves the generation and comparison of mental images and, thus, is a good method to use to introduce students to research on imagery and mental representation.* Also see Foltz, G., Poltrock, S., and Potts, G. (1984). Mental comparison of size and magnitude: Size congruity effects. *Journal of Experimental Psychology: Learning, Memory, and Cognition, 10*, 442–53; Holyoak, K., Dumais, S., and Moyer, R. S. (1979). Semantic association effects in a mental comparison task. *Memory and Cognition, 7*, 303–13; Moyer, R. S. (1973). Comparing objects in memory: Evidence suggesting an internal psychophysics. *Perception and Psychophysics, 13*, 180–84; Paivio, A. (1975). Perceptual comparisons through the mind's eye. *Memory and Cognition, 3*, 635–47; Sharma, U., and Srivastava, A. (1993). Type of material and mental size comparison among children. *Psychologia, 36*, 179–84.

**64.** Unnava, H. R., and Burnkrant, R. E. (1991). An imagery-processing view of the role of pictures in print advertisements. *Journal of Marketing Research, 28*, 226–31. Participants were 107 college students (recruited from introductory marketing classes) who were asked to assess print advertisements in an experimental design containing two independent variables (two levels of imagery, high versus low; and two levels of picture, presence versus absence); the target ad for a consumer product (a camcorder with the fictitious name of Digitron) consisted of four central ideas, and the picture manipulation involved presenting those ideas with, or without, pictures. Based on the results of participants' ratings of the product, the hypothesis of imaginal processing is supported whereby pictures increase recall of verbal information by increasing the likelihood that the verbal information will be represented by dual codes (a verbal code and an imaginal code). When participants are exposed to low imagery information, the addition of pictures exemplifying that information increases the likelihood that dual codes will form and, as a result, participants' ability to recall that information increases.

It is concluded that internally generated visual imagery may substitute for externally provided pictures, and support is given for the power of imaginal processing and its role in moderating the effects of pictures in print advertisements. In terms of practical application, when an advertising copywriter addresses an audience that is likely to process the verbal information semantically (e.g., high involvement audience), it is suggested that recall objectives are met by high imagery copy whether it is or is not accompanied by pictures. Further, when the verbal information is low in imagery, provision of pictures having the verbal claims results in increased audience recall.**

**65.** Vaccaro, K. C. (1997). Teaching strategies: The application of found images in dance and sport. *Journal of Physical Education, Recreation, and Dance, 68*, 45–49. In this essay, it is argued that imagery is a cognitive-behavioral tool in sport psychology that may be used to improve students' performance in physical education contexts by enhancing their concentration and promoting their self-discovery. The author suggests that while her article may be directed to all dance and sport, it focuses particularly on the performance of a dancer/skater who used "found images" (i.e., the use of preexisting schematics, pictures, or drawings in the instruction of physical movements) to improve functional body alignment; improvement of alignment for dancers and athletes is offered as a method for increasing one's movement and energy efficiency and is a possible strategy to use for injury prevention.*

**66.** Weaver, R., L., Cotrell, H. W., and Michel, T. A. (1985). Imaging: A technique for effective lecturing. *Journal of Mental Imagery, 9*, 91–108. In this essay/review on the application of imagery to education, seven methods of imaging are examined where likely benefits for the classroom/lecturing situation include increased interest, learning, involvement, and creativity on the part of students. It is concluded that the seven methods for using imaging (i.e., examples/illustrations; instructional aids; trigger words; exercises/activities, daydreams/fantasies, organization features, and giving instructions)—when related to the lecturing format—stimulates meaning and involvement for students concerning the target information/message in a powerful and effective manner.

**67.** Whissell, C. (2001). The emotionality of William Blake's poems: A quantitative comparison of "Songs of innocence" with "Songs of experience." *Perceptual and Motor Skills, 92*, 459–67. In this application of imagery to literature, the author makes a content analysis of the words contained in William Blake's poems "Songs of Experience" and "Songs of Innocence" by reference to a "dictionary of affect" that lists the imagery, pleasantness, and activation of several thousand words. Results indicate that the Innocence poems were more active and pleasant than the Experience poems; however, both sets of these poems were rich in imagery, pleasant in tone, and more emotional when compared to normative English usage and the work of romantic writers who were contemporaries of Blake.*

**68.** White, D. J. (1988). Taming the critic: The use of imagery with clients who procrastinate. *Journal of Mental Imagery, 12,* 125–34. In this essay on the application of imagery to the university clinic/counseling center, the author examines the common student complaint of not being able to complete work on time—procrastination—for some students, such procrastinating behavior results in lowered grades, poor performance, and incompleted courses. The use of imagery is suggested as a therapeutic technique and a way to attend to the behavioral, cognitive, and emotional counterparts of procrastination. Also see Ahsen, A. (1982). Imagery in perceptual learning and clinical application. *Journal of Mental Imagery, 6,* 157–86; Kosbab, F. (1974). Imagery techniques in psychotherapy. *Archives of General Psychiatry, 31,* 283–90; Morrison, J., and Cometa, M. (1980). A cognitive, reconstructive approach to the psychotherapeutic use of imagery. *Journal of Mental Imagery, 4,* 35–41.

**69.** Yates, L. G. (1986). Effect of visualization training on spatial ability test scores. *Journal of Mental Imagery, 10,* 81–92. Examines the effect of a visualization training program upon the performance of male college student participants on tests of spatial orientation (cube-comparisons) and spatial visualization (paper-folding). It was found that participants who received the training performed significantly better on the visualization retest after training than did participants who did not receive training. However, no evidence was found that the visualization training program had any effect on the spatial-*orientation* (as distinguished from the spatial-*visualization*) test scores. It was suggested that such visualization training—combined with visualization exercises designed for a specific discipline (e.g., mathematics, chemistry, biology)—may improve students' performance in specific subject areas. In terms of improvement in experimental design and methodology, it was recommended that future research in this area should provide an intermediate activity between the pretest and posttest for the control group that would eliminate the alternative explanation for results (showing experimental versus control group differences) as due to the extra attention that the experimental group received.\*\* Also see Sommer, R. (1980). Strategies for imagery research. *Journal of Mental Imagery, 4,* 115–21.

## BIBLIOGRAPHIES AND REVIEWS OF IMAGERY

**70.** Ahsen, A. (Ed.) (1989). Mental imagery abstracts: Journal of mental imagery, 1977–1989. *Journal of Mental Imagery, 13,* 1–295. Presents a useful, handy, and felicitous compilation/collection of abstracts of articles published in the *Journal of Mental Imagery* from 1977 through 1989, Volume 1 through Volume 13. The original Table of Contents for each volume is reproduced and appears before the collection of abstracts for the respective volumes.

**71.** Ahsen, A. (Ed.) (1994). Imagery bibliography: Journal of mental imagery, 1977–1991. *Journal of Mental Imagery, 18*, 1–277. This is a very important, valuable, and useful bibliography on mental imagery. According to the editor, Akhter Ahsen, this special issue of the *Journal of Mental Imagery* was actually conceived many years before 1994. Ahsen initially assisted Alan Richardson in gathering references from the field of mental imagery, which Richardson later independently enriched with citations from *Psychological Abstracts, Psychological Index*, and bibliographies on imagery in *The Behavioral and Brain Sciences*, 1980 (for eidetic imagery) and *Psychonomic Science*, 1972 (for inferred imagery), as well as books and review articles on imagery (the work continued to develop entirely through Richardson's own efforts). In 1993, Richardson presented *A Bibliography of Books, Articles, and Theses on Mental Imagery (1872–1976)*, providing a classified set of references to the theoretical and empirical literature for the period 1872–1976. Ahsen indicates that this (1993) work may be obtained by writing to Alan Richardson, Department of Psychology, The University of Western Australian Nedlands, Western Australia 6009. The Table of Contents in Richardson's work includes the following topics/rubrics: books on mental imagery, mental imagery in psychotherapy and behavior therapy, mental imagery as an inferred construct, physiological correlates of mental imagery, afterimagery and related phenomena, eidetic imagery, thought imagery, and imagination imagery. Ahsen's strategy for the journal's bibliography was to compile references alphabetically—rather than chronologically—from those citations that appeared in the bibliographies of the articles published in the *Journal of Mental Imagery* from its inception in 1977 through 1991. Ahsen's massive bibliography contains well over 6,000 references/citations related to the topic of mental imagery.

**72.** Baddeley, A. (1989). Some reflections on visual imagery. *European Journal of Cognitive Psychology, 1*, 333–35. Presents some introductory remarks on a symposium on visual imagery held in 1988 in the United Kingdom. Baddeley notes that the most striking feature of the papers in the symposium is their diversity, ranging from a general theoretical review of the role of imagery in working memory to the specific question of how blind persons use imagery in memory, and from the relationship between rated vividness and the effectiveness of imagery to the role of expertise in the recall of chess positions.

**73.** Barlow, H., Blakemore, C., and Weston-Smith, M. (Eds.) (1990). *Images and understanding: Thoughts about images and ideas about understanding*. Cambridge, UK: Cambridge University Press. Among the contents in this collection of essays on images are the following topics/titles: The essence of images: What does the brain see? How does it understand? Pictorial instructions; Computer-generated cartoons; The tricks of colour; Three stages in the classification of body movements by visual neurons; Visual processing of moving images; Animal language; Are the signs of language arbitrary? Understanding the digital image; Images and thought: Thinking with a computer; How do we interpret images? Images and meaning: Scientific images—perception and deception. The approaches to understanding vision in these essays are wide-ranging and go from the visual psychologists' and psychophysicists' attempts to explore the limitations of the visual system (e.g., how one responds to color, shape, and movement) to the application by artists and craftsmen of the principles of vision (e.g. in painting pictures, drawing caricatures, making movies, and recording body movements).

**74.** Beaudry, I. D. (1996–1997). Book review. *Body images: Development, deviance, and change,* by T. F. Cash and T. Pruzinsky (1990). New York: Guildford Press. *Imagination, Cognition, and Personality, 16,* 120–21. This reviewer concludes that the target book is informative, interesting, and consistently high in quality, and that readers will find in it a good introduction into the historical, methodological, developmental, and clinical issues involved in body-image research and practice. It is suggested that the book is a useful source of material for courses containing the topics of body-self, body-image development, and dance and movement therapy.

**75.** Block, N. (Ed.) (1981). *Imagery.* Cambridge, MA: M.I.T. Press. Following his introductory chapter ("What Is the Issue?"), Block organizes the chapters in this book with the following titles/topics (with contributors name in parenthesis): Icons and images (R. Brown and R. J. Herrnstein); The nature of images and the introspective trap (D. C. Dennett); Imagistic representation (J. A. Fodor); Two approaches to mental images (D. C. Dennett); Imagery—There's more to it than meets the eye (R. Schwartz); On the demystification of mental imagery (S. M. Kosslyn, S. Pinker, G. E. Smith, and S. P. Shwartz); The imagery debate: Analog media versus tacit knowledge (Z. Pylyshyn); The medium and the message in mental imagery: A theory (S. M. Kosslyn). Block points out that two of the eight chapters are about imagery experiments (rotation of mental images; scanning mental images), but the focus of the book is on the debate about what the experiments *show,* in particular, whether a *descriptionalist* or a *pictorialist* position is supported. The references section at the end of this book contains over 270 citations/references related to the various issues surrounding mental imagery.

**76.** Brink, N. E. (1993–1994). Book review. *Taming the diet dragon: Using language and imagery for weight control and body transformation,* by C. C. Kirk (1992). St. Paul, MN: Llewellyn. *Imagination, Cognition, and Personality, 13,* 271–73. This reviewer notes that the target book takes account of the unconscious dynamics blocking maintenance of a healthy weight; it is suggested that the book provides a well-organized program and integrates cognitive-behavioral techniques, guided-imagery techniques, hypnotic-imagery techniques, and other approaches for uncovering the interfering unconscious dynamics. One of the imagery techniques offered in the book is the imagery of the literal "burning of fat," an idea analogous to Carl Simonton's notion of "imagining cancer cells at war and being destroyed," and expanded in the many new techniques now offered in the field of psychoneuroimmunology where one may be trained, specifically, to change his/her rate of metabolism (i.e., by imagining climbing into one's body and exploring those body mechanisms affecting metabolism, clients have been able to increase dramatically the rate their bodies burn fat).

**77.** Denis, M., Engelkamp, J., and Richardson, J.T.E. (Eds.) (1988). *Cognitive and neuropsychological approaches to mental imagery.* Dordrecht, The Netherlands: Martinus Nijhoff. Reflects the concerns of, and the products from, the European Workshop on Imagery and Cognition, which was designed to be a forum for the exploration of current issues in imagery research. Following the two papers in Part 1 ("Key Issues in Imagery Research") by the workshop's keynote speakers, Allan Paivio ("Basic Puzzles in Imagery Research") and Steven Pinker ("A Computational Theory of the Mental Imagery Medium"), Part 2 ("Imaginal Coding and the Processing of Verbal Information") contains papers dealing with contributions on the nature of imaginal coding, its connections with the representation of visual information in long-term memory, and the ties between this form of coding and the processing of linguistic information. Part 3 ("Imagery Processes in Adaptive Behavior") of the volume focuses more directly on imagery as an adaptive process. Part 4 ("Imagery, Action, and Emotion: Imagery and the Brain") explores the relationships between imaginal and motor representations in memory systems, emotional imagery in the framework of a cognitive approach, neuropsychological approaches to mental imagery including detailed characterizations of the neural substrate and mechanisms of visual imagery, and the incidence of brain damage and sensory handicaps on the elaboration and mnemonic use of visual imagery. In the final section, Part 5 ("Concluding Remarks"), it is suggested that future work on mental imagery address the "externalization" or communication of mental imagery and the exploration of the relationship between human development and mental imagery.

**78.** Evans, F. J. (1967). Suggestibility in the normal waking state. *Psychological Bulletin, 67,* 114–29. This review assesses the concept of *suggestibility* as observed in normal participants under waking, nonhypnotic conditions. Based on data from factor analytic studies, it was found that the traditional classification of *primary* and *secondary* suggestibility as presented by previous researchers is *not* confirmed. It is concluded that three types of suggestibility, some implicating imagery, are identified currently: primary/passive motor suggestibility, challenge suggestibility, and imagery/sensory suggestibility. The references section of this article contains over seventy citations/references related to the topic of suggestibility.

**79.** Finke, R. A. (1989). *Principles of mental imagery.* Cambridge, MA: M.I.T. Press. Among the contents of this book are the following issues: information retrieval using mental images; visual characteristics of mental images (e.g., the principle of perceptual equivalence); spatial characteristics of mental images (e.g., the principle of spatial equivalence); criticisms of the image-scanning experiments; transformations of mental images (e.g., mental rotation); the principle of transformational equivalence; criticisms of the mental rotation experiments; mental constructions and discoveries (e.g., the principle of structural equivalence); criticisms of experiments on imagined constructions; principles, foundations, and applications (e.g., unifying principles versus formal models); and neurological foundations of mental imagery. The excellent references section in this book contains over 400 citations/references relating to the issue of the principles of mental imagery.

**80.** Forisha, B. L. (1978). Mental imagery and creativity: Review and speculations. *Journal of Mental Imagery, 2*, 209–37. This review of the literature on the relationship between imagery and creativity indicates that such a relationship is affected by both personality orientations and sex/gender differences. A developmental model of personality structure is proposed that focuses on the variations in differentiation and integration within which imagery and creativity are examined; within this framework, certain hypotheses are made about the vividness and dimness, the control and autonomy, and the flexibility and rigidity of mental imagery. Forisha suggests that at lower levels of development, imagery may be a hindrance to creative and abstract thinking, but that at higher levels of development, imagery is both necessary and vital to the creative process. The references section of this article contains over 100 citations/references relating to the issue of the relationship between imagery and creativity.

**81.** Forrester, M. (2000). *Psychology of the image.* London: Routledge. This work outlines a theoretical framework bringing together the semiotic concepts developed by C. Peirce, the sociological insights of E. Goffmann, and the psychoanalytic notions of J. Lacan. These theorists have influenced image studies significantly in the disparate fields of fashion, advertising, photography, film studies, and psychology. Forrester concludes that given the importance of images in contemporary life, a significant task for psychology—including a *psychology of the image*—in the new millennium will be to understand the relationship between external images and the internal ideas and feelings individuals hold about themselves. The excellent bibliography at the end of this book contains over 500 references/citations relating to the topic of the psychology of the image.

**82.** Gray, E., Pitta, D., and Tall, D. (2000). Objects, actions, and images: A perspective on early number development. *Journal of Mathematical Behavior, 18*, 401–13. This review of the research evidence covering a period of time of over ten years on the issue of imagery and early development of numeracy in children generally indicates the existence of qualitatively different thinking in elementary number development. Overall findings indicate that in the abstraction of numerical concepts from numerical processes, qualitatively different outcomes may arise because children concentrate on different objects, or different aspects of the objects, that are components of numerical processing. It is the authors' contention that different *perceptions* of these objects—whether mental or physical—are at the heart of different cognitive styles that lead to a child's success or failure in elementary arithmetic.*

**83.** Haggerty, R. (1981). Book review. *The mythic image*, by Joseph Campbell (1975). Princeton, NJ: Princeton University Press. *Journal of Mental Imagery*, 5, 197–99. The reviewer suggests that Campbell's book is not the type of book than one *cannot* put down; its "power and magnetism" require that one repeatedly set it aside and return to it later. Campbell's book consists of two distinct, but complementary aspects: a portfolio of paintings, statuary, and architecture from various ancient civilizations and a profound text that focuses on the power of the image. At the heart of Campbell's work is the conviction that there exists in the depths of the human psyche a universal Jungian-like imagistic reality that is the source of all religion, art, philosophy, science, and politics; in this milieu, the mythologies of the great ancient civilizations are presented and explored. Campbell's chapter on Kundalini Yoga is central to the major thesis of the book; it is also pertinent to the science of psychology: the clear delineation of the levels of human consciousness expands the traditional western knowledge of the mind beyond its fixation with the sexually obsessive, the grotesque, and the demonic features of a mechanistic technology and opens it to more life-affirming, life-sustaining, and visionary aspects. Haggerty asserts that beneath the scholarship and intellectual brilliance of Campbell's *The Mythic Image* there is a subtle feeling of personal testament involving an invitation to, and promise of, a potential transformational process waiting for the reader's discovery.

**84.** Hampson, P. J., Marks, D. F., and Richardson, J.T.E. (Eds.) (1990). *Imagery: Current developments.* London: Routledge. Contents in this review of the state of the art of imagery include the following topics/issues: the relationships between imagery, body, and mind; a neurological model of individual differences in visual mental imagery; imagery, consciousness, and cognitive control: the BOSS model; imagery and working memory; imagery and blindness; imagery and action: encoding of verbs and nouns; imagery effects on problem solving; enhancing one's knowledge about images; the photographic image; imagery and affect; clinical and experimental approaches to imagery and emotion; cerebral localization of visual imagery; the bisected image and visual memory in patients with visual neglect; and imagery and memory in brain-damaged patients. Hampson et al. note that three points may be made concerning the overall nature of the psychological research in their book: many profound theoretical questions are asked that go far beyond the narrow concern with the status of imagery as a mental representation that characterized research during the 1970s; imagery is *par excellence* a topic for multidisciplinary and interdisciplinary research; and imagery is a topic that is advanced equally by multinational research efforts.

**85.** Hannay, A. (1971). *Mental images: A defence*. London: Allen and Unwin. In this philosophical essay on imagery, Hannay defends the validity of, and study of, mental imagery against various negations posed by philosophical positions such as those of Dennett, Ryle, Shorter, and Sartre. One of Hannay's principal aims is to show that there is no good argument for getting rid of mental images. Hannay suggests that in the area of mental imagery some speculative "room to play" remains in philosophy, though "it is a good deal more cramped than it seemed before the analysts went into business, and offers a somewhat hostile environment to speculators not adept with at least some of the tools of the analytical trade."

**86.** Hilgard, E. R. (1987). Book review. *Rhea complex: A detour around Oedipus complex*, by Akhter Ahsen (1984). New York: Brandon House. *Journal of Mental Imagery*, *11*, 161. The reviewer notes that Ahsen provides an imaginative and provocative account on the use of ancient myths to help understand contemporary problems; Ahsen goes back in mythology to supplement and correct Freud's Oedipal Project. Although Freud was preoccupied with the father-mother-son motives and jealousies—to the neglect of the importance of siblings—Ahsen emphasizes and symbolizes the attractions between siblings by starting with the mythical figure of Rhea. More in the spirit of Jung than of Freud, Ahsen finds the mythical anecdotes a basis for understanding subliminal material that emerges in the images of the patients treated by his Eidetic Therapy approach.

**87.** Hilgard, E. R. (1987). Book review. *Trojan horse: Imagery in psychology, art, literature, and politics*, by Akhter Ahsen (1984). New York: Brandon House. *Journal of Mental Imagery*, *11*, 162. Hilgard notes that Ahsen's book is a collection of fascinating essays that covers an enormous amount of ground where the hope is that the vitalized concept of the image might lead to a unification of literature and psychology. Hilgard suggests that there is poetic license in Ahsen's *Trojan Horse* that may both mystify and instruct the reader; nevertheless, the book shows the inherent fascination of imagery, the tricks imagery can play on consciousness, and the practical benefits of its use in the therapeutic context.

**88.** Hinshaw, K. E. (1991–1992). The effects of mental practice on motor skill performance: Critical evaluation and meta-analysis. *Imagination, Cognition, and Personality*, *11*, 3–35. This review of the empirical research on the relationship between mental practice and motor skill performance indicates that the former may enhance the latter appreciably. Furthermore, a host of variables have been shown to mediate the size and direction of such mental practice effects; some of the variables affecting mental practice are the following: sex/gender, age, skill level, task type, use of control group, number and length of trials, duration, sessions, gross mental practice, type of mental practice, instruction, and relaxation prior to visualization. It is concluded that the results of empirical studies and of the meta-analysis point to the complexity of the relationships among variables that influence the effectiveness of mental practice. The combined references and bibliography sections at the end of this article contain over 140 citations/references related to the issue of the relationship between mental practice and motor skills/performance. Also see Epstein, M. L. (1980). The relationship of mental imagery and mental rehearsal to performance of a motor task. *Journal of Sport Psychology, 2*, 211–20; Feltz, D. L., and Landers, D. M. (1983). The effects of mental practice on motor skill learning and performance: A meta-analysis. *Journal of Sport Psychology, 5*, 25–57; Richardson, A. (1967). Mental practice: A review and discussion. Parts 1 and 2. *Research Quarterly, 38*, 95–107, 263–73.

**89.** Hintzman, D. L., and Holyoak, K, J. (1981). Book review. *Image and mind*, by Stephen M. Kosslyn (1980). Cambridge, MA: Harvard University Press. *Journal of Mental Imagery, 5*, 195–204. In back-to-back reviews, both Hintzman and Holyoak give their assessments of Kosslyn's book. In Hintzman's evaluation, there is doubt that Kosslyn's simulation model of imagery can be applied to many of the experimental tasks that Kosslyn discusses without considerable elaboration (the model's weakest feature seems to be the interpretive function, which has the job of responding to information on the visual display). However, while Kosslyn's coverage of imagery in his book is quite narrow, Hintzman suggests that the work is a major statement by a creative and prominent researcher of imagery, and that students of the experimental study of visual imagery would be derelict in failing to read *Image and Mind*. In Holyoak's assessment, Kosslyn's work is one of the two benchmark monographs on the research on mental imagery within the cognitive framework (the other work is Paivio's *Imagery and Verbal Processes*, 1971). Holyoak covers in detail Kosslyn's theoretical approach—whose origin is an explicit analogy, a technologically updated version of the traditional picture metaphor of visual imagery, the cathode-ray tube attached to a computer—and indicates that the theory provides a framework for investigating three-dimensional imagery, the representation of movement in images, the functions of imagery in problem solving, and several other issues. Holyoak suggests that Kosslyn's approach is likely to have a continuing impact on imagery research and will gain the attention of serious students of cognitive psychology.

**90.** Hochman, J. (2001). A basic online search on the eidetic with PsycINFO, MEDLINE, and ERIC, *Journal of Mental Imagery, 25*, 99–215. Provides a valuable online bibliographic search of the mental image phenomenon called the *eidetic* (i.e., eidetic imagery), using the databases PsycINFO, MEDLINE, and ERIC. Following a brief review of the methods used to search these databases, Hochman gives a summary of the searches and provides samples of "bad" and "good" records on eidetic imagery that were retrieved. Included in this article are over seventy pages showing the records retrieved. The number of citations found (containing the terms: eidetic, eidetics, eidetic imagery, eidetic image, eidetic images, eidetic imager, eidetic imagers, eidetiker, eidetikers, and eidetic imaging) in PsycINFO, MEDLINE, and ERIC, respectively, were 1,536, 467, and 134 for a total of 2,137 citations. Also see Hochman, J. (1994). Ahsen's image psychology. *Journal of Mental Imagery, 18,* 1–117; Hochman, J. (1998). Memory and the eidetic: An integration. *Dissertation Abstracts International, 59(5-B),* 2455; Hochman, J. (2000). Image and word in Ahsen's image psychology. *Journal of Mental Imagery, 24,* 1–205.

**91.** Horowitz, M. J. (1978). *Image formation and cognition.* New York: Appleton-Century-Crofts. Among the topics/issues in this work are the following: phenomenology of image formation (types of images; the circumstances that increase image formation); psychodynamics of image formation (early concepts of the role of images in thought; psychodynamics and regulation of image formation; experimental research on the revisualization of traumatic perceptions); neurobiologic influences on image formation (contribution of the eye; influence of the brain on image formation; psychedelic images and flashbacks; hallucinations reconsidered); therapeutic uses of image formation (graphic products and use of image formation in psychotherapy). The bibliography section in this book contains over 530 citations/references related to the issue of image formation and cognition.

**92.** *Imagery.* American Association for the Study of Mental Imagery. In this series of papers from periodical conferences on mental imagery, the following volumes (with editors and titles indicated) have been published: Volume 1: Shorr, J. E., Sobel, G. E., Robin, P., and Connella, J. A. (Eds.) (1980). *Imagery: Its many dimensions and applications.* New York: Plenum Press; Volume 2: Klinger, E. (Ed.) (1981). *Imagery: Concepts, results, and applications.* New York: Plenum Press; Volume 3: Shorr, J. E., Sobel-Whittington, G., Robin, P., and Connella, J. A. (Eds.) (1983). *Imagery: Theoretical and clinical applications.* New York: Plenum Press; Volume 4: Wolpin, M., Shorr, J. E., and Krueger, L. (Eds.) (1986). *Imagery: Recent practice and theory.* New York: Plenum Press; Volume 5: Shorr, J. E., Robin, P., Connella, J. A., and Wolpin, M. (Eds.) (1989). *Imagery: Current perspectives.* New York: Plenum Press. Collectively, in these five volumes, over 120 papers are presented and include the following sample of topics/issues covered: theoretical aspects of imagery, psychoimagination therapy, movement therapy and art therapy, guided imagery and fantasy, clinical perspectives, concepts of imagery, measurement of imagery, hypnosis and imagery, synaesthesia, imagery and cognitive processes, imagery and clinical treatment, mental imagery and creativity, the scientific study of imagination, the physiological measurement of imagery, creative drama and imagery, the uses of self-image imagery in psychotherapy, kinesthetic and kinetic body imagery, spatial memory processing, bizarreness of imagery, imagery and olfactory stimulation, imagery and anxiety reduction, imagery and family therapy, sexual daydreams, humor and imagery, time, the right brain, and imagery, historical perspective of imagery, imagery and group psychotherapy, psychosomatic disorders and imagery, imagery and covert modeling, imagery in the schools, imagery and athletic performance, imagined activity in everyday life, social dimensions of imagery, imagery and grief therapy, imagery and meaning, symbolic aspects of hypnagogic imagery, development and imagery, role-playing and imagery, short-term therapy and imagery.

**93.** Kosslyn, S. M. (1980). *Image and mind.* Cambridge, MA: Harvard University Press. Among the contents of this work are the following topics/ issues: a research program for mental/visual imagery; the debate about imagery; validating the properties of imagery; the origins of images; the core theory (modeling image processing on a computer); generating, inspecting, and transforming visual images; using visual images to answer questions; imagery and cognitive development; imagery in perspective; and reflections/ refutations concerning imagery. Examples of subissues that Kosslyn examines from more general topics are the following: conclusions from the imagery debate; issues/questions concerning the origins of images; and explication of the core theory. The references section at the end of Kosslyn's exposition consists of over 280 citations/references related to the issue of visual imagery and mental representations.

**94.** Kosslyn, S. M. (1983). *Ghosts in the mind's machine: Creating and using images in the brain.* New York: W. W. Norton. Among the contents in this work are the following topics/titles: A ghost in the brain; The exit of the homunculus; Stalking the mental image; The medium and the message; How can we know what we cannot see? Private creations; Computer model of mental imagery; The computer model in action; Appearances remembered; Visual thinking; Differences in people; and The philosophical and the practical—science and the mental image. The bibliography section in Kosslyn's book contains over 130 references/citations that are related to the issue of images and the brain.

**95.** Kosslyn, S. M. (1994). *Image and brain: The resolution of the imagery debate.* Cambridge, MA: M.I.T. Press. This is the third book written by Kosslyn on the topic of visual mental imagery; among the contents of the present work are the following issues: resolving the imagery debates; carving a system at its joints; high-level vision; identifying objects in different locations; identifying objects when different portions are visible; identifying objects in degraded images; identifying contorted objects; identifying objects: normal and damaged brains; generating and maintaining visual images; inspecting and transforming visual images; visual mental images in the brain. Kosslyn concludes that although the mechanisms underlying imagery are not fully understood, there now is enough knowledge to assert that the imagery debates have been resolved. The substantial references section at the end of this book contains over 1,000 citations/references related to the issues of the resolution of the imagery debate and the relationship between the image and the brain.

**96.** Kunzendorf, R. G. (Ed.) (1991). *Mental imagery.* New York: Plenum

Press. Among the contents of this collection of papers on mental imagery are the following topics (with samples of subissues indicated in parenthesis): cognitive studies and applications of mental images (the self and reality monitoring; map reading and imagery; aging and imagery vividness in daydreams; guided imagery and education); private images behind personality traits and interpersonal dynamics (personality, dreams, and imagination; hypnosis and hypnotizability); psychophysiological studies and applications of conscious images (consciousness in general; imagination and perceptual development; imagery and immune system functioning; imagery use for cancer and other chronic diseases; imagery and nursing; imagery in sport); symbolic images in psychopathology and psychotherapy (imagery and narcissistic deficits; art therapy).

**97.** Lewin, B. D. (1968). *The image and the past.* New York: International Universities Press. The contents of this long essay on the concept of the image vis-à-vis the past (which emphasizes the psychoanalytic perspective) includes the following topics: the pictorial past, a detail in the primal scene, the earliest recorded visual memories and Lascaux art, the mind of the embryo, traces and storage, phantoms in the head, psychoanalytic comments on a meditation of Descartes, and Agamemnon's head and the discovery of the mind.

**98.** Loverock, D. S., and Modigliani, V. (1995). Visual imagery and the brain: A review. *Journal of Mental Imagery, 19,* 91–132. Examines the empirical evidence relating to the localization of visual imagery in the brain. This includes the topics of hemispheric specialization, mental rotation, response competition, hemispheric activation, dreaming, regional cerebral blood flow, and electrical brain stimulation. This review finds that there is a trend in the literature away from models of global hemispheric specialization toward componential/computational models that include both sides of the brain viewed as an integrated structure. The reviewers recommend that concurrent and collaborative explorations be carried out from as many different perspectives as possible, including experimental, clinical, and neurophysiological approaches. The references section of this article contains over 170 citations/references related to the issue of visual imagery and the brain.

**99.** Marks, D. F. (1989). Bibliography of research utilizing the vividness of visual imagery questionnaire. *Perceptual and Motor Skills, 69,* 707–18. This bibliography on the Vividness of Visual Imagery Questionnaire (VVIQ) covers the period 1972–1988 and is divided into two sections: the first section contains publications, dissertations, and reports of an *empirical* nature citing studies that have explored the reliability of the questionnaire, or provided evidence concerning the construct validity of the measure; the second section contains *theoretical* and literature reviews, critiques, replies/comments, discussions, and historical precursors. Overall, this bibliography contains 149 references from the literature relating to the VVIQ measure of imagery. Also see Marks, D. F. (1972). Individual differences in the vividness of visual imagery and their effect on function. In P. W. Sheehan (Ed.), *The function and nature of imagery.* New York: Academic Press; Marks, D. F. (1983). Mental imagery and consciousness: A theoretical review. In A. A. Sheikh (Ed.), *Imagery: Current theory, research, and application.* New York: Wiley; Marks, D. F. (1985). Imagery differences: An overview of research on visual image vividness. In D. F. Marks and D. G. Russell (Eds.), *Imagery 1.* Dunedin, New Zealand: Human Performance Assoc.; Marks, D. F. (1986). Imagery, consciousness, and the brain. In D. G. Russel, D. F. Marks, and J.T.E. Richardson (Eds.), *Imagery 2.* Dunedin, New Zealand: Human Performance Assoc.; Sheehan, P. W., Ashton, R., and White, K. (1983). Assessment of mental imagery. In A. A. Sheikh (Ed.), *Imagery: Current theory, research, and application.* New York: Wiley; Strosahl, K. D., and Ascough, J. C. (1981). Clinical uses of mental imagery—experimental foundations, theoretical misconceptions, and research issues. *Psychological Bulletin, 89,* 422–38; White, K., Sheehan, P. W., and Ashton, R. (1977). Imagery assessment: A survey of self-report measures. *Journal of Mental Imagery, 1,* 145–70.

**100.** McKellar, P. (1983). Book review. *Lucid dreams,* by Celia Green (1982). Oxford, UK: Institute of Psychophysical Research. *Journal of Mental Imagery, 7,* 169–70. McKellar reviews this work on lucid dreams (i.e., dreams in which the person is aware that she/he is dreaming; cf. prelucid dreams in which the dreamer is uncertain about whether he/she is, or is not, asleep and dreaming), as well as other related phenomena such as false wakenings, flying dreams, and lucid dreaming in the hypnotic state; also included are discussions of visual and auditory imagery, and imagery for pain, temperature, and taste. McKellar observes that Green is careful to work within the framework of scientific psychology in her discussions of perceptual texture, memory, and hypnotic phenomena.

**101.** McKellar, P. (1987). Book review. *Hypnagogia: The unique state of consciousness between wakefulness and sleep,* by Andreas Mavromatis (1987). London: Routledge and Kegan Paul. *Journal of Mental Imagery, 11,* 159–60. In the first sentence of his review of Mavromatis's book, McKellar states that he chooses his words carefully: "This is an *extremely important* book, and of fundamental relevance to the interests of those concerned with the study of imagery." McKellar notes that the work is intellectually exciting and emotionally satisfying to read in a format that has lively text and is lavishly illustrated with drawings from the realm of pre- and postsleep states, dreams, eidetic visualizations, and other sources (there are twenty-nine pages of references ranging from Aristotle to papers that have been published in the *Journal of Mental Imagery,* as well as twenty-four pages of notes relating to the references and the text). According to McKellar, Mavromatis makes creative use of researches (in up-to-date sources) in content areas that include lucid dreaming, creativity, parapsychology, the schizophrenias, structural eidetic imagery, typographic eidetic imagery, hypnagogic/hypnopompic phenomena, and brain processes and physiological correlates. McKellar recommends highly Mavromatis's book due to its outstanding quality, good readability, and comprehensive coverage of the central issues of imagery psychology.

**102.** Morris, P. E., and Hampson, P. J. (1983). *Imagery and consciousness.* New York: Academic Press. Morris and Hampson argue that while issues of the nature of the processes underlying imagery have attracted a great deal of attention recently, less research has been directed to more fundamental questions such as when do images occur and what are their properties. They assert, also, that there is a danger—without a grounding in such basic facts—that abstract issues of the underlying representation may remain insoluble for lack of appropriate data. Among the contents in their book, Morris and Hampson include the following topics: meta issues—philosophical and methodological problems; the concept of consciousness; qualities and types of imagery; individual differences and dimensions of the image; nature and function of imagery; and theories of imagery. In this well-formatted and well-balanced (between the disciplines of philosophy and psychology) account of imagery, the excellent references section of the book contains over 660 citations/references related to studies on the relationship between consciousness and imagery.

**103.** Murphy, S. M. (1990). Models of imagery in sport psychology: A review. *Journal of Mental Imagery, 14,* 153–72. Examines the research evidence on the efficacy of mental practice, summarizes recent findings on the use of imagery in sport psychology as a "psyching-up" method, and analyzes the history of research on the use of imagery techniques in sport psychology. Some of the problems in this research area identified by Murphy include the following: lack of theory development, lack of attention to individual differences in imaginal processes, inadequate assessment approaches to imaginal experiences, and an overemphasis on the use of imagery techniques to enhance athletic performance. It is suggested that specific elements from theoretical models of imagery—such as Lang's psychophysiological model and Ahsen's Triple Code Model—be incorporated into imagery theory development in sport psychology. The references section in this article contains over sixty citations/references related to the issue of imagery in sport psychology.

**104.** Nucho, A. O. (1991–1992). Book review. *Imagery and visual expression in therapy,* by Vija B. Lusebrink (1990). New York: Plenum Press. *Imagination, Cognition, and Personality, 11,* 103–5. Nucho observes that Lusebrink uses the systems approach and the latter's own original scheme of the Expressive Therapies Continuum in an examination of the functions of imagery in cognition, psychotherapy, and healing. Among the chapter topics are the following: overview of uses of imagery in verbal and art therapies; aspects of creativity; image formation; cognitive developmental aspects of imagery; vividness and control of imagery; ways to enhance imagery; components of, and developmental aspects of, symbols; function and meaning of symbols; neurotic distortion of symbol formation; and depiction and integration of images. Nucho concludes that Lusebrink's book is a scholarly, well-documented presentation of relevant theories and empirical studies, written in a clear, crisp, and parsimonious style. Also see Torrey, S. R. (1993–1994). Book review. *Imagery and visual expression in therapy,* by Vija Lusebrink (1990). New York: Plenum Press. *Imagination, Cognition, and Personality, 13,* 370–72.

**105.** O'Regan, J. K., and Noe, A. (2001). A sensorimotor account of vision and visual consciousness. *Behavioral and Brain Sciences, 24,* 939–73. Examines the difficulties inherent in many current neurophysiological, psychophysical, and psychological approaches to vision that rest on the notion that the brain—in the process of seeing—produces an internal representation of the world. According to the authors, such approaches leave unexplained how the existence of such detailed internal representations produce *visual consciousness.* O'Regan and Noe provide an alternative proposal to this dilemma in which the experience of seeing is conceived to be a way of acting and is a particular way of exploring the environment. In support of their approach, O'Regan and Noe provide several lines of empirical evidence, in particular, evidence from experiments on visual filling-in, sensorimotor adaptation, change blindness, visual stability under eye-movement conditions, color perception, and sensory substitution. The references section of this article contains over 290 citations/references related to the issue of vision and visual consciousness. Also see O'Regan, J. K. (1992). Solving the "real" mysteries of visual perception: The world as an outside memory. *Canadian Journal of Psychology, 46,* 461–88.

**106.** Oyama, T., and Ichikawa, S. (1990). Some experimental studies on imagery in Japan. *Journal of Mental Imagery, 14,* 185–95. This review of imagery research in Japan focuses on twenty experimental studies of mental imagery organized under six topics: short-term visual memory, visual imagery and eye movements, spatial transformation of imagery, kinesthetic/bodily component of imagery, perception and imagery, and individual differences. The authors note that some imagery studies of Japan in the 1970s were conducted for the purpose of testing Paivio's dual-coding hypothesis. Then, in the 1980s, other Japanese studies began to deal with kinesthetic/bodily imagery aspects. In this latter regard, according to the authors, many problems remain unsolved concerning kinesthetic imagery; for example, is cognitive style/information processing in Japanese people affected by using such kinds of imagery from their childhood (if this is so, are there recent changes in this population due to the increased usage of word processors for the Japanese language, including kanjis and calculators)? Such devices do not require long practice using kinesthetic imagery. It is suggested that cross-cultural and cohort studies are needed to investigate such problems; also needed are theoretical models that deal most particularly with kinesthetic/bodily imagery. The authors recommend the use of Ahsen's model, which emphasizes interactions between the components of imagery, somatic response, and meaning, and which is highly amenable to studying the role and mechanisms of kinesthetic and bodily imagery. It is argued that this approach may be fruitful in explaining many of the experimental findings of these Japanese studies on imagery.

**107.** Qualls, P. J. (1982–1983). The physiological measurement of imagery: An overview. *Imagination, Cognition, and Personality, 2,* 89–101. This review of the physiological measurement aspects of imagery indicates that physiological responses made during imagery experiences vary as a function of the nature of the image, and—based on the isolation of a number of parameters that affect the magnitude of physiological changes during imaging—demonstrates that images containing different affective/emotional features are related to different patterns of physiological reactions. Qualls concludes that a substantial body of evidence attests to the fact that physiological measures may give sensitive indices of imaginal processes. It is noted, also, that the affect/emotion involved in the image is an especially important determinant of the accompanying physiological reactions, as well as is the nature of the imagery instructions presented to participants. The references section of this article contains forty-six citations/references related to the issue of the physiological measurement of imagery.

**108.** Reisberg, D. (Ed.) (1992). *Auditory imagery.* Hillsdale, NJ: Erlbaum. This review of the area of auditory imagery contains the following topics/titles: Musical aspects of auditory imagery; Research on memory/imagery for musical timbre; Components of auditory imagery; Speech in the head? Rhyme skill, reading, and immediate memory in the deaf; Subvocalization and auditory imagery: Interactions between the inner ear and inner voice; Constraints on theories of inner speech; The auditory hallucinations of schizophrenia; Auditory imagery and working memory; The representation of pitch in musical images; and The climate of auditory imagery and music. Reisberg observes that this book constitutes a step toward remedying the information imbalance that exists in imagery research studies between the vast amount of published data on visual imagery versus the very little information available on imagery in other modalities, in particular auditory imagery. Also see Sharps, M. J., and Price, J. L. (1992). Auditory imagery and free recall. *Journal of General Psychology, 119,* 81–87; Tracy, R. J., Roesner, L. S., and Kovac, R. N. (1988). The effect of visual versus auditory imagery on vividness and memory. *Journal of Mental Imagery, 12 (3&4),* 145–61; Zatorre, R. J., and Beckett, C. (1989). Multiple coding strategies in the retention of musical tones by possessors of absolute pitch. *Memory and Cognition, 17,* 582–89; Okada, H., and Matsuoka, K. (1992). Effects of auditory imagery on the detection of a pure tone in white noise: Experimental evidence of the auditory Perky effect. *Perceptual and Motor Skills, 74,* 443–48; Summer, L. (1985). Imagery and music. *Journal of Mental Imagery, 9 (4),* 83–90; Zatorre, R. J., Halpern, A. R., Perry, D. W., Meyer, E., and

Evans, A. C. (1996). Hearing in the mind's ear: A PET investigation of musical imagery and perception. *Journal of Cognitive Neuroscience, 8,* 29–46; Yoo, S.-S., Lee, C. U., and Choi, B. G. (2001). Human brain mapping of auditory imagery: Event-related functional MRI study. *Neuroreport: For Rapid Communication of Neuroscience Research, 12,* 3045–49.

**109.** Richardson, A. (1969). *Mental imagery.* New York: Springer. The contents of this early work on imagery include the following basic issues: defining mental imagery, afterimagery, eidetic imagery, memory imagery, and imagination imagery. Richardson examines a wide range of literature to get a useful perspective on the nature of mental imagery and the theoretical, practical, and methodological problems in this area. Richardson states that his task is made difficult by the long time span of more than 100 years and the absence of any systematic reviews of the literature; also, writers who have been primarily philosophical, psychopharmacological, or neurophysiological in their interests have been poorly represented, as are psychologists whose accounts of imagery have been mainly anecdotal, including those writers in the areas of literature and education. Richardson's emphasis in on empirical material of a behavioral and experiential kind as it relates to the nature of imagery qua imagery and as it relates to the part played by imagery in such other cognitive processes as perception, memory, remembering, and thinking. Richardson includes two appendixes at the end of his book: one containing the Betts QMI Vividness of Imagery Scale and the other containing the Gordon Test of Visual Imagery Control. There are over 320 citations in Richardson's references section in support of his discussion of the topic of mental imagery.

**110.** Richardson, J.T.E. (1999). *Imagery.* Hove, East Sussex, UK: Psychology Press/Taylor and Francis. The contents in this recent review (which is one contribution to a series of brief texts for a modular course on cognitive psychology) of issues in mental imagery include the following topics: conceptualizing and investigating imagery; imagery and the brain; is imagery a right-hemisphere function; imagery as a phenomenal experience; Galton's, Betts's, Marks's, and Gordon's questionnaires/tests of mental imagery; the role of imagery in cognition; the loss of mental imagery; brain activity during imagery; imagery as an internal representation; tests of spatial ability; manipulation of mental imagery; mental comparisons; visuo-spatial working memory; images and propositions; imagery in split-brain patients and in unilateral neglect; imagery as a stimulus attribute; imageability; concreteness; hemispheric asymmetries; brain dysfunction; dual coding versus dual processing; imagery as a mnemonic strategy; visualisers and verbalisers; cognitive styles and memory strategies; mental imagery as a mediating device; effects of imagery instructions; interactive and separative instructions; and imagery instructions and brain function. Richardson provides the following summary statements concerning mental imagery: it has been conceptualized in different ways by different researchers; it may be investigated either as a dependent variable or as an independent variable—the two approaches are complementary but involve different kinds of research methodologies and depend on the integrity of structures in the brain—this issue may be studied via the methods of experimental neuropsychology, physiological recording and brain-mapping methods, and examining the effects of brain damage; and it is widely assumed that imagery is based on a *single* mechanism that is localized in the right cerebral hemisphere—however, this specific notion needs to be examined critically, as well as the general idea that imagery is based on a *unitary* mechanism. In this regard, Richardson suggests that structures within the posterior portion of the left hemisphere of the brain seem to be crucial to the generation and the experience of imagery, while structures in the right hemisphere seem to be involved in the transformation and the manipulation of mental images. This excellent work—in which Richardson writes simply and concisely about complex phenomena, as well as successfully combining experiential, behavioral, and neuropsychological perspectives—contains valuable end-of-chapter summaries, and has a useful references section that contains over 290 citations/references related to the study of mental imagery.

**111.** Rollins, M. (1989). *Mental imagery: On the limits of cognitive science*. New Haven, CT: Yale University Press. Contents in this largely philosophical essay on mental imagery include the following topics/titles: The view from Descartes's window; Minding the brain: The theory of internal states; The limits of imagination: Image experiments and methodological constraints; The image controversy; The methodological argument; Cognitive penetrability; The poverty of descriptionalism; Intentional icons; Process and content; and The case for pictorial attitudes. Also see Thomas, N.J.T. (1999). Are theories of imagery theories of imagination? An active perception approach to conscious mental content. *Cognitive Science, 23,* 207–45 (which contains over 200 references cutting across the fields of philosophy, cognition, and psychology); Thomas, N.J.T. (1997). Mental imagery. In E. N. Zalta (Ed.), *The Stanford encyclopedia of philosophy*. Palo Alto, CA: Stanford University Press (this encyclopedia entry contains over 320 useful citations/references to the philosophical, cognitive, and psychological foundations of the phenomenon of mental imagery).

**112.** Sheehan, P. W. (Ed.) (1972). *The function and nature of imagery.* New York: Academic Press. Contents in this excellent and widely well-received review of mental imagery in psychology include the following topics/titles (with contributors indicated in parenthesis): Part 1—Some general viewpoints on imagery: On the nature and generality of mental imagery (R. R. Holt); Imagery from the standpoint of introspection (P. McKellar); A very private world (R. Gordon); Part 2—The Function of Imagery: Individual differences in the vividness of visual imagery and their effect on function (D. F. Marks); Voluntary control of the memory image (A. Richardson); The sensory attributes and functions of imagery and imagery-evoking stimuli

(M. S. Lindauer); A functional analysis of the role of visual imagery in un-expected recall (P. W. Sheehan); Daydreaming, imaginal processes, and personality: A normative study (J. L. Singer and J. S. Antrobus); Assimilation of a stimulus in the construction of an image: The Perky Effect revisited (S. J. Segal); Part 3—The Nature of Imagery: Changing conceptions of imagery (U. Neisser); A theoretical analysis of the role of imagery in learning and memory (A. Paivio); Image formation: Clinical observations and a cognitive model (M. J. Horowitz); The ubiquitous appearance of images (L. W. Doob); Imagining as muted role-taking: A historical-linguistic analysis (T. R. Sarbin); and Physiological correlates of visual imagery (V. Zikmund). Sheehan argues that rigid standardization of procedures in research and theory about mental imagery no longer exist—as demonstrated by the sophistication and variety in the methodology and theory of mental imagery presented by the diverse contributors to the book. Each chapter in this valuable resource book has its own specialized and extensive set of references that relates to the particular topic under discussion.

**113.** Sheikh, A. A. (Ed.) (1983). *Imagery: Current theory, research, and application.* New York: Wiley. This valuable resource/reference and review book on mental imagery contains the following topics in three parts (with contributors indicated in parenthesis): Part 1—Theory; Imagery: Definitions and types (A. Richardson); Theories of mental imagery (S. Pinker and S. M. Kosslyn); Imagery and the thought processes (B. R. Bugelski); Mental imagery and consciousness: A theoretical review (D. F. Marks); Imagery effects on memory: Theoretical interpretations (J. C. Yuille and M. Marschark); Image theory of conditioning (D. L. King); Part 2—Research; Assessment of mental imagery (P. W. Sheehan, R. Ashton, and K. White); Imagery: Its role in development (R. B. Tower); Cerebral laterality and imagery (R. G. Ley); Imagery and language (I. Begg); Relationship between creativity and mental imagery: A question of cognitive styles? (B. L. Forisha); The fantasy-prone personality: Implications for understanding imagery, hypnosis, and parapsychological phenomena (S. C. Wilson and T. X. Barber); Part 3—Applications; Clinical uses of mental imagery (A. A. Sheikh and C. S. Jordan); The role of imagery in sexual behavior (D.P.J. Przybyla, D. Byrne, and K. Kelley); Imagery and the arts (M. S. Lindauer); Imagery and sports (R. M. Suinn); Research on imagery: Implications for advertising (K. L. Alesandrini and A. A. Sheikh). Each of the seventeen chapters in this excellent resource book contains its own specialized and lengthy set of references that are relevant to the mental imagery issues under discussion.

**114.** Sheikh, A. A. (Ed.) (1984). *International review of mental imagery.* Vol. 1. New York: Human Sciences Press. Contents of this volume in the International Review of Mental Imagery Series include the following chapters (with contributors in parenthesis): Imagery and children's learning: An issue of declining developmental interest? (J. C. Yuille and M. Marschark); Mental imagery in problem solving (G. Kaufmann); Bizarreness effects in

mental imagery (A. D. Yarmey); Time estimation, imagination, and hypnosis (P. W. Sheehan and D. J. Bayliss); Imagery, physiology, and psychosomatic
illness (A. A. Sheikh and R. G. Kunzendorf); Adolescent daydreaming (S.
R. Gold and B. B. Henderson); Hypnagogic imagery (A. Mavromatis and
J.T.E. Richardson); Right-hemisphere processing of emotional and imageable
words (R. G. Levy). Each chapter has its own references section, some (e.g.,
Sheikh and Kunzendorf's chapter on imagery and physiology/psychosomatic
illness) containing as many as 280 citations/references related to the chapter topic.

**115.** Sheikh, A. A. (Ed.) (1986). *International review of mental imagery.*
Vol. 2. New York: Human Sciences Press. This volume of the International
Review of Mental Imagery Series contains the following chapters (with con-
tributors in parenthesis): Memory and imagery (B. R. Bugelski); Hypnotic
investigations of imagery: A critical review of relationships (H. J. Crawford
and C. MacLeod-Morgan); An overview of lucid dreaming (J. Gackenbach
and S. LaBerge); Alexithymia: A critical review (J. S. Kruck and A. A. Sheikh);
Lend an ear: Grisly body imagery in common American speech (J. L. Olson);
An evaluation of three procedures for increasing imagery vividness
(A. Richardson and Y. Patterson); From image to hallucination: Studies of
mental imagery in schizophrenic patients (S. Starker); Imagery and families
(R. B. Tower). Among the novel notions in this volume of the series are the
following two examples: Bugelski's observation that for almost a century researchers have depended on secondary/revised—rather than on primary/
actual—memory content (the reports of the participants in memory experiments do not portray what actually occurred to them in learning situations
but represent an edited or censored version of the actual content); and Kruck
and Sheikh's account of a relatively novel phenomenon called *alexithymia*,
which is defined as a cluster of ideoaffective attributes (that are not exclusive to, but often observed in, psychosomatic patients) that involve the following aspects: an inhibition of imagery, fantasy, and symbolic activity; a
difficulty with verbalization of feelings; a concrete operatory style of thought
and behavior; and a stereotypic manner of relating to others. Kruck and
Sheikh discuss this issue, which includes a history of alexithymia, its etiologi-
cal theories, and the clinical and empirical evidence of the phenomenon, as
well as the therapeutic attempts at treating the problem.

**116.** Shepard, R. N., and Cooper, L. A. (Eds.) (1982). *Mental images and
their transformations.* Cambridge, MA: M.I.T. Press. The contents of this
book are organized into three parts (with contributors in parenthesis) as
follows: Part 1—Mental Rotation; On turning something over in one's mind
(R. N. Shepard); Transformational studies of the internal representation of
three-dimensional objects (J. Metzler and R. N. Shepard); Chronometric
studies of the rotation of mental images (L. A. Cooper and R. N. Shepard);
Mental rotation of random two-dimensional shapes (L. A. Cooper); Mental
transformations and visual comparison processes (L. A. Cooper and

P. Podgorny); Demonstration of a mental analog of an external rotation (L. A. Cooper); Part 2—Other Transformations; A chronometric study of mental paper folding (R. N. Shepard and C. Feng); Mental transformations in the identification of left and right hands (L. A. Cooper and R. N. Shepard); Spatial comprehension and comparison processes in verification tasks (R. J. Glushko and L. A. Cooper); Part 3—Apparent Motion; Perceptual illusion of rotation of three-dimensional objects (R. N. Shepard and S. A. Judd); Spatio-temporal probing of apparent rotational movement (C. Robins and R. N. Shepard); Shape, orientation, and apparent rotational motion (J. E. Farrell and R. N. Shepard). In summary, Shepard and Cooper's entire program of research described in this book is predicated on the notion that there are different levels of description of internal processes and that significant theoretical statements about such processes may be framed at a level of abstraction that does not require any commitment to a particular mechanization of these processes within the neurophysiological substrate. All references in this book—upward of 300 citations related to the development and discussion of the topic of mental images and their transformations—are assembled in the back of the book, and do not immediately follow each chapter, owing, perhaps, to the singular nature of the topics under discussion. Also see Pinker, S., and Kosslyn, S. M. (1978). The representation and manipulation of three-dimensional space in mental images. *Journal of Mental Imagery, 2,* 69–83.

**117.** Singer, J. L. (1981—1982). Book review. *Imagery,* edited by Ned Block (1981). Cambridge, MA: M.I.T. Press. *Imagination, Cognition, and Personality, 1,* 193. Singer notes that this slim, but profound, volume deals with the historically tricky question of whether images are simply descriptions of events stored in the brain in some abstract propositional form or whether images have some of the same properties of actual seeing or hearing external stimuli. Block's introductory chapter, according to Singer, is a "gem" in outlining the dimensions and implications of what has become a central controversy in cognitive psychology: the *descriptionist* versus the *pictorial* position. In addition, Block's book leads to a sharpening of issues and a possible solution compromising and extending the two extreme positions. On the short side—inasmuch as the book mainly emphasizes imagery in its role as a reproduction of specific external stimulus configurations—Singer suggests that the philosophers and empirical researchers who have contributed to the book are not yet ready to address the problem of the nature of centrally generated images drawn from long-term memory or of fantasies and planning anticipations that are components of ongoing thought.

**118.** Standing, L., Bond, B., Hall, J., and Weller, J. (1972). A bibliography of picture-memory studies. *Psychonomic Science, 29,* 406–16. Provides a comprehensive and useful bibliography totaling 685 references/citations dating from the nineteenth century to the 1970s (with an especially exhaustive list for the years 1960–1970) of studies on the learning of pictorial material or visual forms. Included are works on eidetic imagery, imagery in verbal learning, pathological visual-memory deficits, facial recognition, object-display learning, and picture memory. The main method employed by the authors was a detailed search of *Psychological Abstracts* from 1927 through 1972, and the examination of the bibliography section in each paper located by that search. For the decade of 1960–1970, another detailed search was made of all journals published by the Psychonomic Society, the Southern Universities Press, the Journal Press, and the American Psychological Association, as well as the *American, British,* and *Canadian Journals of Psychology.*

**119.** Starker, S. (1984–1985). Book review. *Visualization: The uses of imagery in the health professions,* by Errol R. Korn and Karen Johnson. (1983). Homewood, IL: Dow Jones-Irwin. *Imagination, Cognition, and Personality, 4,* 319–20. Korn and Johnson—an internist and a physical therapist, respectively—divide their book into two sections: general concepts (dealing with mind-body interactions, stress, and the basics of imagery) and specific applications (imagery techniques for pain control, holistic health care, and psychotherapy). The authors also provide reviews of brain anatomy and physiology, biofeedback, altered states of consciousness, meditation, autogenic training, relaxation, and hypnosis. Starker suggests that to evaluate this book one must consider the potential readership; psychologists involved in imagery, stress management, or hypnosis research will find little that is new in the book and may perhaps wince at the relatively uncritical acceptance of those studies selected to support the authors' views. However, according to Starker, beginning counselors/therapists, students, nurses, and rehabilitation specialists may find this book to be a good starting place for developing helping skills using fantasy and imagery.

## COGNITION AND IMAGERY

**120.** Ackerman, J. A. (1996). Stares and reflective gaze shifts as an index of cognitive modality. *Journal of Mental Imagery, 20,* 41–58. Discusses an experiment on the relationship between reflective gaze shifts (i.e., spontaneous eye movements that occur in response to a question; eye movements may be lateral, right or left, upward or downward; sometimes there is a fixed look with no movement, called *staring*) and cognitive mode (visual or verbal images). Participants were 109 male physicians who gave answers to forty-one modally ambiguous questions where the first forty questions assessed the participant's eye movement tendencies (via videotape measures) and the last question assessed the relationship between self-reported cognitive mode of imagery (visual versus auditory/verbal) and gaze in response to the same question. Results indicate that there was a significant correlation between self-reported cognitive modality and eye movement response to the last question (question 41). Specifically, participants who stared, or moved their eyes upward, in response to the last question were likely to report a visual image, whereas participants whose gaze shifts were lateral were more likely to report an auditory/verbal image. Additionally, in other analyses, the proportion of participants' upward movements/stares were correlated significantly with their visualizer/verbalizer style, but not with their right-left (lateral eye movement, or LEM) directionality. Ackerman suggests that the focus on the neurological control of eye movements in much LEM research has led to an emphasis on the often overly inclusive right-left LEM categories, rather than on the upward *versus* lateral components of eye movement responses.**

**121.** Adeyemo, S. A. (2001). Mode of presentation and instructions in solutions to practical construction problems. *Perceptual and Motor Skills, 92,* 415–18. Participants were 192 male and female college students who were asked to solve five classical-practical construction problems in which the mode of presentation and the instructions were varied. Results indicate that *visual* presentation was superior to *verbal* presentation of materials in solving practical construction tasks; also, when participants were asked to use either imaginative or memory imagery strategies in solving problems, the imaginative imagery mode yielded a larger number of solutions. Adeyemo concludes that *visual* presentation of materials, and instructions to use *imagination* imagery, facilitated development of solutions to problems, while *verbal* presentation of materials, and instructions to use *memory* imagery, hindered solutions to problems.**

**122.** Algom, D., and Singer, J. L. (1984–1985). Interpersonal influences on task-irrelevant thought and imagery in a signal detection experiment. *Imagination, Cognition, and Personality, 4,* 69–83. Participants were thirty-three paid women and men volunteers from the New Haven/Yale community who were given a signal detection task in four experimental sessions in a complete within-subject counterbalanced design under conditions in which instructions were presented either face-to-face by the experimenter or with minimal contact ("interpersonal-impersonal" condition), and by an experimenter who was the same or opposite sex/gender as the participant ("sex of experimenter" condition). The researchers hypothesized that cognitive processes during a relatively objective auditory signal detection task might reflect the influence of immediately preceding interpersonal contact between the participant and the experimenter, as well as the habitual thinking style or current concerns brought by participants to the experiment. The dependent variables of task-irrelevant thought and imagery in participants were measured via systematic interruptions for frequent reports (via questionnaires) following each of the four experimental sessions. Results of these manipulations indicate a significant influence of an opposite-sex experimenter on participant's reports of task-irrelevant thought with a trend for a similar effect for the interpersonal-impersonal condition. It was concluded that some aspects of interpersonal interaction just prior to a participant's entrance into a traditional psychological experiment may affect considerably the nature of ongoing thought/cognition during what the experimenter might assume to be a fairly comparable condition across participants.** Also see Wollman, N. (1987). Consistency between affect and cognition in interpersonal attraction. *Journal of Mental Imagery, 11,* 119–24.

**123.** Antrobus, J. S., Singer, J. L., and Greenberg, S. (1966). Studies in the stream of consciousness: Experimental enhancement and suppression of spontaneous cognitive processes. *Perceptual and Motor Skills, 23,* 399–417. Describes three experiments (participants were 142 college students)—employing a simple signal detection task under conditions of partial sensory deprivation—that tested a model that related production of spontaneous cognitive events (such as daydreams) to the participant's continuous response to external stimuli. The three experiments demonstrate how some of the basic parameters of fantasy may be defined operationally and how the proposed model may provide a basis for advancing beyond the intuitively apparent personal knowledge that everyone has about his/her own private fantasy life. Results from the three experiments indicate the following: increasing the speed of signal presentation or demands on short-term memory both significantly reduced reports of task-irrelevant cognitive activity and imagery; graded financial reward for accuracy of detection led to progressive decrease in extraneous fantasies; and distressing information prior to the experimental trials increased significantly the reports of spontaneous daydreaming during the signal detection task. It is concluded, among other things, that the specialized signal detection procedure described in this study suggests the possibilities for systematic study of individual differences or abnormalities in the priorities assigned by individuals for attention to inner or external stimulus channels.**

**124.** Aylwin, S. M. (1981). Types of relationship instantiated in verbal, visual, and enactive imagery. *Journal of Mental Imagery, 5,* 67–84. Participants were twenty-four college men and women volunteers who were assigned to one of three encoding conditions (verbal, visual, or enactive instructions) in which their task was to respond (i.e., freely associate) to stimulus sentences (containing animal names) with anything that came to mind—be it a single word, a sentence, or a story. Results indicate that the *verbal* coding condition seems to access a level of typical/conceptual knowledge that is characterized by awareness of differences between the animals, assertions that sentences were meaningless or false, and nonsignificant tendencies to give superordinates and acoustic associations; the *visual* coding and imaging condition resulted in references to body parts, the use of metaphor, and the use of intransitive verbs in present continuous tense; and the *enactive* imagery condition resulted in a temporal and affective perspective with references to reasons and consequences, emotions, personality traits, and the use of transitive verbs indicating direct interaction. It was suggested that structural and experiential approaches to imagery may be united through the notion of instantiation where subjectively different forms of representation instantiate (i.e., represent an abstraction or universal by a concrete instance) different types of propositions from one's semantic memory network.**

**125.** Cornoldi, C., and McDaniel, M. A. (Eds.) (1991). *Imagery and cognition*. New York: Springer-Verlag. This collection of papers on imagery and cognition contains the following (with contributors in parenthesis): Imagery and the brain (J.T.E. Richardson); Symmetries and asymmetries between imagery and perception (M. J. Intons-Peterson and M. A. McDaniel); Visuospatial short-term memory: Visual working memory or visual buffer? (R. H. Logie); Imagery and thinking (M. Denis); Imagery and verbal memory (M. Marschark and C. Cornoldi); Memory of action events: Some implications for memory theory and for imagery (J. Engelkamp); Static versus dynamic imagery (A. Paivio and J. M. Clark); A developmental approach to mental imagery (J. Lautrey and D. Chartier). Each chapter/paper is followed by its own set of references, with some (e.g., Richardson's paper) containing over 100 citations/references related to a particular topic.

**126.** Gibbs, R. W., Strom, L. K., and Spivey-Knowlton, M. J. (1997). Conceptual metaphors in mental imagery for proverbs. *Journal of Mental Imagery, 21*, 83–109. Reports on two studies that explored the mental images associated with American English proverbs. The researchers' hypothesis was that individuals possess highly uniform mental images for many proverbs (e.g., "A rolling stone gathers no moss"), and that such consistency is due to the conceptual metaphors that underlie a proverb's figurative meaning. Examination of participants' mental imagery protocols/reports indicates that the conventional images and knowledge associated with proverbs are constrained by different conceptual metaphors; another set of protocol data indicates that the specific characteristics of mental imagery for proverbs may be predicted from an independent analysis of the metaphors that partly motivate proverbs. When taken together, these analyses of mental imagery vis-à-vis proverbs support the view that the figurative meanings of proverbs are motivated by underlying conceptual metaphors that constitute a large part of humans' ordinary conceptual systems.*

**127.** Horowitz, M. J. (1967). Visual imagery and cognitive organization. *American Journal of Psychiatry, 123*, 938–46. Reports on imagery questionnaire data from 112 participants consisting of naval personnel, art students, and student nurses concerning the spontaneous occurrence of visual imagery (i.e., their ability to form visual images without perception of external objects, and their frequency of experiencing pictorial cognition, a form of thinking in nonverbal representation). Horowitz describes various kinds of visual imagery and the circumstances of their occurrence and enhancement, and also considers the relevant problems of reality testing, purpose, content, and sequential organization. It is suggested that pictorial cognition is a developmentally more primitive system than verbal-conceptual thinking in humans and has adaptive utility as a carrier of affectively charged impulses, ideas, and memories.*

**128.** Hunt, H. T., and Popham, C. (1987). Metaphor and states of consciousness: A preliminary correlational study of presentational thinking. *Journal of Mental Imagery, 11,* 83–99. Forty female college students provided measures of metaphor generation, altered-state experience, and general imaginativeness/creativity in this correlational-design study on the relationship between metaphor and altered states of consciousness. More specifically, the issue explored here was the view that altered states of consciousness are abstract cognitive phenomena that exteriorize the processes normally resident in presentational or metaphoric intelligence. Specific measures included material from the following sources: the ancient Chinese *I-Ching* (Book of Changes), experimental meditation, inventory of past tendency to anomalous subjective states, ratings of capacity for imaginative involvement, physiognomic cues test, and an "imagery" version of the Kelly Role Repertory Grid. Hunt and Popham conclude that their results give some support to the notion that these altered-consciousness variables rest on common symbolic processes where there may be a "developmental trade-off" (within presentational intelligence) between experiencing the immediate impact of "states" and the subordination of such processes to intuitive metaphoric meaning. The references section of this article contains over sixty citations/references related to the issue of the association between metaphor and states of consciousness.*

**129.** Kosslyn, S. M. (1988). Aspects of a cognitive neuroscience of mental imagery. *Science, 240,* 1621–26. Summarizes the findings and results of experimental/empirical studies on mental imagery that illustrate how one may discover structure in mental abilities where none originally was obvious. Kosslyn argues that after initially examining behavior during task performance, various facts about the brain and information-processing analyses can lead to relatively subtle hypotheses about processing; such hypotheses are testable, in part, by assessing selective impairments in neuropathological individuals/populations. Application of this approach indicates that the act of generating a visual mental image involves at least two classes of processes: those that activate stored *shapes* and those that use stored *spatial relations* to arrange shapes into an image. Moreover, according to Kosslyn, the discovery that the *left* hemisphere is better at arranging shapes when *categorical* information is appropriate—whereas the *right* hemisphere is better when *coordinate* information is necessary—suggests that the processes that arrange parts may be decomposed further into two classes that operate on different sorts of information. Kosslyn observes that the findings—under some circumstances—that the left cerebral hemisphere is better at mental imagery may be counterintuitive to many researchers (the left hemisphere has been identified traditionally with language, and the right hemisphere with imagery). However, in Kosslyn's view, neither hemisphere may be said to be the exclusive site of mental imagery; rather, imagery is carried out by multiple processes, not all of which are implemented equally or effectively in the same part of the brain.*

**130.** Posner, M. I., Petersen, S. E., Fox, P. T., and Raichle, M. E. (1988). Localization of cognitive operations in the human brain. *Science, 240,* 1627–31. Examines the results of experimental/empirical studies concerned with the brain-localization of human cognition. Posner et al. note that while the question of the localization of cognition in the human brain is an old and difficult one, current findings/analyses of cognitive operations, and new techniques for the imaging of brain function during cognitive tasks, have combined to give support for a new hypothesis, namely, that elementary *operations* forming the basis of cognitive analyses of human tasks are strictly *localized*; such an idea fits generally well with many network theories today in neuroscience and cognition. Conclusions from this review include the following: the PET data provide strong support for localization of operations performed on visual, phonological, and semantic codes (the ability to localize these operations in studies of average blood flow suggests great homogeneity in the neural systems involved, at least with respect to right-handed participants with good reading skills); visual imagery, word reading, and visual-attention shifting from one location to another are not performed by any single area of the brain; the operations involved in both activation of internal codes and in selective attention obey the general rule of localization of component operations; mechanisms involved in image scanning share components with those in visual spatial attention; an area of the cerebellum seems to perform a critical computation for timing both motor and sensory tasks; and memory studies indicate that the hippocampus performs a computation needed for storage in a way that allows conscious retrieval of the item once it has left current attention. Posner et al. apply the joint anatomical and cognitive approach to the issue of selective attention and the study of deficits in patients with schizophrenia.*

**131.** Pylyshyn, Z. W. (1980). Computation and cognition: Issues in the foundations of cognitive science. *Behavioral and Brain Sciences, 3,* 111–69. In this lengthy philosophical essay on various issues in cognitive science, Pylyshyn examines the computational view of mind, which rests on various intuitions concerning the similarity between computation and cognition, and suggests that they derive from the fact that computers and human organisms are both physical systems whose output is described correctly as being governed by rules acting on symbolic representations. It is proposed that a fundamental hypothesis of this approach, the proprietary vocabulary hypothesis, states that there is a natural domain of human functioning (associated with reasoning, perceiving, and acting) that may be understood in terms of a formal symbolic/algorithmic vocabulary or level of analysis. Pylyshyn discusses the various requisite conditions for a viable and literal view of mental activity as computation; he makes a principled distinction between functions requiring internal representations and those as merely instantiating causal physical/biological laws. Moreover, this distinction is empirically grounded by Pylyshyn in a methodological criterion called the *cognitive impenetrability condition* (e.g., functions are said to be cognitively impenetrable if they cannot be affected by purely cognitive factors such as beliefs, goals, inferences, or tacit knowledge); this criterion allows one to separate the fixed capacities of mind (called its *functional architecture*) from the particular representations/algorithms employed on specific occasions. Pylyshyn argues that the architectural assumptions that are implicit in many contemporary models of cognition neglect the cognitive impenetrability criterion because the required fixed functions are measurably sensitive to goals and tacit knowledge. The references section of this article contains over 130 citations/references related to the various issues in cognitive science, in particular, the computational view of mind.

**132.** Reese, H. W. (1977). Toward a cognitive theory of mnemonic imagery. *Journal of Mental Imagery, 2,* 229–44. This essay/review of mnemonic imagery contains the assumption that visual images are inherently memorable, but due to a spontaneous process of change toward typicality, they lose their particular/individual details, thus making memory in this case impermanent. According to Reese, the process of change (which involves a variable amount of time, sometimes operating immediately, and sometimes remaining incomplete even after several months have passed) results in disintegration of a compound image into separate images of its elements because the compound itself has no typical instance toward which the compound may change. Thus, the process of change leaves nothing to be redintegrated and, thereby, destroys the basis of associative memory. Reese argues that—except for the problem of the time requirement—such an analysis works well for the phenomenon of reconstruction and recall, while its success for the recognition mode is not as certain (working well in some cases, where meaningfulness is involved, but not in other cases). Reese postulates that the process of change does not stop even when an image has come to resemble its typical instance completely; rather, the process continues to change the image to ever more general levels of typicality. The references section of this article contains over seventy citations/references related to cognitive theory vis-à-vis mnemonic imagery.

**133.** Richardson, J.T.E. (1980a). Concreteness, imagery, and semantic categorization. *Journal of Mental Imagery, 4,* 51–58. Participants in this study were sixty-eight college students who engaged in a card-sorting task (as a vehicle for indicated the properties affecting the ease with which a word may be categorized) by employing eighty experimental items (these consisted of eight lists of ten nouns, varying orthogonally as high versus low imageability, high versus low concreteness, and simple versus derived nouns). The participants were assigned randomly to one of three groups: a *categorization* condition, a *story* condition, or a *visual-scene* condition. Results of these manipulations indicate that concreteness and emotionality (but not imageability) are correlated with the number of participants who fail to categorize a given word. Richardson draws the following conclusions: concreteness is a semantic feature that is to be distinguished from the image-arousing potential of stimuli; the effects of arousal on memory may be explained in terms of organizational processes; and a system of abstract propositional descriptions is used in a wide array and variety of sorting tasks.**

**134.** Richardson, J.T.E. (1980b). Mental imagery and stimulus concreteness. *Journal of Mental Imagery*, 4, 87–97. In this essay/review of the relationship between stimulus concreteness and imagery, Richardson suggests—in contrast to findings that are currently in vogue in experimental psychology concerning this relationship—that there now exists strong support for the view that concreteness and imageability have *different* effects upon performance, and that the variable of concreteness should be identified as a feature of lexical organization and *not* as a measure of the image-arousing quality of verbal material. Furthermore, according to Richardson, there is good evidence to suggest that the *imageability* of a stimulus, rather than its *concreteness*, is the effective attribute that determines how easily it can be remembered.*

**135.** Rothenberg, A., and Sobel, R. S. (1980). Creation of literary metaphors as stimulated by superimposed versus separated visual images. *Journal of Mental Imagery*, 4, 77–91. Describes the experimental assessment of the creation of metaphors by means of a special form of cognition involving the active use of mental imagery. The cognitive process, called *homospatial thinking*, consists of the active conception of two or more discrete entities occupying the same space, and is a notion that may lead, ultimately, to the articulation of new identities. Participants were forty-three volunteer writers who each created ten metaphors that were stimulated by pairs of slide photographs under two stimulus conditions: the viewing of the stimulus pairs *superimposed* upon one another and the viewing of the same pairs *separated* on the projection screen. The dependent variable—metaphors produced—was judged independently by two accomplished literary experts. Results of these manipulations indicate that the metaphors that were stimulated by the *superimposed* images were judged to be significantly more creative than those stimulated by the *separated* images. The researchers suggest that their results support the construct/notion of homospatial thinking, and—inasmuch as metaphors generally seem to be paradigms of creative output—there may be a wide applicability of this construct to creative endeavors in other areas (e.g., in science, the relatively recent creation of metaphorical terms such as *black holes in space, strange particles,* and *left- and right-handed molecules* have been useful aids both to descriptive clarity and to further theoretical development).**

**136.** Spanos, N. P., and Radtke, H. L. (1981–1982). Hypnotic visual hallucinations as imaginings: A cognitive-social psychological perspective. *Imagination, Cognition, and Personality, 1,* 147–70. This review of cognitive processes and imagery focuses on research concerning the phenomenology of hypnotic/suggested visual hallucinations as viewed within a cognitive-social psychological framework. The authors argue that suggestions made in the hypnosis-context do not automatically cause participants to respond; they are simply requests communicated within a meaningful social context. Whether or not participants engage in the imaginings requested depends on their interpretation of the situation and their motivations to comply/not comply with its implicit and explicit demands. In short, according to Spanos and Radtke, hypnotic hallucinations—like other hypnotic phenomena—are social behaviors that may best be understood by giving consideration to participants' cognitions of the social context in which they are tested, their motivations to meet certain situational demands, and their ability to carry out the imaginative activities required by those demands. The references section of this article contains over 120 citations/references related to hypnotic visual hallucinations and imagery/imaginings. Also see Kunzendorf, R. G. (1985–1986). Hypnotic hallucinations as "unmonitored" images: An empirical study. *Imagination, Cognition, and Personality, 5,* 255–70; Cross, W., and Spanos, N. P. (1988–1989). The effects of imagery vividness and receptivity on skill training induced enhancement in hypnotic susceptibility. *Imagination, Cognition, and Personality, 8,* 89–103.

**137.** Sullivan, C., Urakawa, K. S., and Cossey, V. L. (1996). Separating the effects of alertness from the effects of encoding in a pitch-imagery task. *Journal of General Psychology, 123,* 105–14. Participants in this study were sixty-five male and female college students who were assigned randomly to one of three groups/conditions—an image group; a specific group; and a nonspecific group—in an experimental setting designed to study perceptual and alerting effects in an auditory signal matching task. Moreover, in this experiment, preparation of participants for a pitch-matching task was the manipulated variable where an effort was made to isolate the degree to which a pitch-image prime activates perceptual codes versus alertness. Results confirm previous findings that imagining the pitch of a tone before its actual presentation improves processing of the actual tone.**

**138.** Unnava, H. R., Agarwal, S., and Haugtvedt, C. P. (1996). Interactive effects of presentation modality and message-generated imagery on recall of advertising information. *Journal of Consumer Research, 23,* 81–88. Participants were 161 female and male college students who completed tasks (the rating of ads in terms of their ability to evoke auditory and visual imagey) in one of two experiments designed to study the proposition that imaging is a cognitive process that employs the same mental resources as perception. Results of the first experiment indicate that when the modality of presentation

matches the modality of imagery provoked by the ad, message recall is reduced compared with the condition containing a mismatch between the
modalities of imagery and message presentation. In the second experiment,
it was found that the facilitating effects of visual imagery on recall are evident only when the modalities of imagery and presentation do not match;
moreover, when the modalities of presentation and imagery match, visual
imaging is suppressed and results in reduced elaboration and reduced recall.
The researchers suggest that their finding that learning declines because of
mutual interference between imaging and perception has important implications for advertising message strategy.**

**139.** Yuille, J. C., and Catchpole, M. J. (1977). The role of imagery in
models of cognition. *Journal of Mental Imagery, 1,* 171–80. This essay/
review discusses the place that the construct of mental imagery occupies in
current cognition models. The authors argue that some models (such as the
verbal-learning, dual-coding, modal storage model) give images too prominent a role in cognition, while other models (such as the recent computer-
based models) neglect the functional importance of imagery. Yuille and
Catchpole offer a compromise position/approach to the issue by adopting
a modification of Piaget's cognitive-developmental theory. Also see Kerr,
N. H., Corbitt, R., and Jurkovic, G. J. (1980). Mental rotation: Is it stage
related? *Journal of Mental Imagery, 4,* 49–56; Duncan, E. M., and Bourg,
T. (1983). An examination of the effects of encoding and decision processes
on the rate of mental rotation. *Journal of Mental Imagery, 7,* 33–55.

## CREATIVITY AND IMAGERY

**140.** Adeyemo, S. A. (1998). Imagery unvividness and social-psychological
implications. *Journal of Mental Imagery, 22,* 79–97. Participants in two studies were 140 female and male college students who completed Ahsen's
Adapted Vividness of Visual Imagery Questionnaire (AA-VVIQ), as well as
completing two creative, practical construction problems in efforts to examine visual imagery vividness and its relationship and implications for creative
thinking. Results from the first study showed that participants had lesser
ability to see images vividly when they kept father in mind (father filter) as
compared with images produced when they kept mother in mind (mother
filter). Additionally, it was found that sex/gender produced a significant effect on creative thinking with women showing superior performance over
men—which is counter to the established findings in the cognitive-creativity
literature. Results from the second study indicate that when the participants'
sister and brother were used as filters, there was greater ability to see images vividly when they kept sister in mind as compared with keeping brother
in mind. Adeyemo concludes that the findings with AA-VVIQ has certain
therapeutic implications where this particular imagery questionnaire may be
employed as a clinical tool for diagnostic purposes (e.g., seeing mother and/

or sister more effectively than father and/or brother in these studies indicates psychological well-being to some clinicians, and differences/problems in one's early interaction with parents and siblings may be reflected in the imagery results when mother versus father, and sister versus brother, filters are employed). The references section of this article contains over seventy citations/references related to imagery unvividness, creativity, and interpersonal experiences/social-psychological factors. Also, an appendix to the article contains the sixteen items from the AA-VVIQ used here with the father/mother and brother/sister filters.*

**141.** Barrios, M. V., and Singer, J. L. (1981–1982). The treatment of creative blocks: A comparison of waking imagery, hypnotic dream, and rational discussion techniques. *Imagination, Cognition, and Personality, 1,* 89–109. Participants were forty-eight men and women who—as a requisite condition were experiencing creative blocks in regard to artistic, literary, scientific, or professional projects—were recruited via ads in local community newspapers in New Haven, CT. Participants were assigned randomly to one of four conditions: (1) waking imagery, (2) hypnotic dream, (3) rational discussion, or (4) control group. One week following the treatment/conditions, participants made "satisfaction" ratings and gave a report of any changes concerning their creative blocks. Results indicate that the waking imagery and hypnotic dream conditions were the most effective in helping to break participants' creative blocks. The researchers conclude that their study opens many possibilities for further study of the role of ongoing imagery and its application to overcome inhibitions or difficulties in resolving specific blocks or impediments to the completion of already initiated artistic or scientific work.**

**142.** Campos, A., and Perez, M. J. (1989). High and low imagers and their scores on creativity. *Perceptual and Motor Skills, 68,* 403–6. Participants were 122 school children, ages ranging from twelve to fifteen years old, who completed the Visual Elaboration Scale and the Torrance Tests of Creative Thinking as part of the effort to study the relation between vividness of imagery and four aspects of creativity: fluency, originality, flexibility, and elaboration, as well as attempting to study the differences in creativity of high versus low imagers. Results via correlational analyses indicate the following: significant correlations between imagery vividness and creativity for girls, but not for boys. Other analyses indicate significant differences between high-versus low-imagers in creativity. The researchers conclude that their findings corroborate those of previous studies concerning the important role that imagery plays in the creative processes; also, their data support other studies showing differences between high- and low-imagery participants in performance on various cognitive tasks.*

**143.** Charlton, S., and Bakan, P. (1988–1989). Cognitive complexity and creativity. *Imagination, Cognition, and Personality, 8,* 315–22. Among the factors that have been associated with creativity are unconventional and nonconforming behavior, openness of experience, broad categorizing, coping well with novelty, acceptance of racial group differences, preference for complexity, tolerance for bipolarity, uncertainty, and ambiguity, and the capacity to conceive and utilize two or more opposite or contradictory ideas, concepts, or images simultaneously. Participants in the study—which hypothesized a positive relationship between high creativity and cognitive complexity—were 112 female and male college students who completed a creative personality test and a test of cognitive complexity. Results indicate that cognitive complexity is related significantly to creativity and, moreover, female participants produce higher scores on the cognitive complex test as compared to male participants' scores.*

**144.** Forisha, B. L. (1981). Patterns of creativity and mental imagery in men and women. *Journal of Mental Imagery, 5*, 85–96. Participants were 320 women and men at two different educational levels (undergraduate and graduate students) in four different academic fields (business, engineering, education, psychology) who completed a creative thinking test, a personality projective test, and two imagery tests. Results indicate that two hypotheses were confirmed (imagery and creativity are related, and this relationship varies by sex/gender, academic discipline, and educational level). One hypothesis was not confirmed (the suggestion that the relationship between imagery and creativity is influenced by levels of socioemotional maturity). It is concluded that the construct of mental imagery may be discriminated along several dimensions (especially a flexibility-rigidity dimension), and also the factor of socioemotional maturity may be differentiated (especially with regard to traits associated with control and autonomy). It is argued that an understanding of such dimensions and discriminations/differentiations may clarify the complex relationship between imagery and creativity.* Also see Campos, A., and Gonzalez, M. A. (1995). Effects of mental imagery on creative perception. *Journal of Mental Imagery, 19 (1&2)*, 67–75.

**145.** Gowan, J. C. (1978). Incubation, imagery, and creativity. *Journal of Mental Imagery, 2*, 23–32. This essay on the relationship between imagery and creativity indicates that the *right*-hemisphere imagery is the mechanism through which the process of incubation produces creative productions. According to the author, incubation is the mental analog of physical gestation in which an ovum is developed into a baby and is the phenomenon that exemplifies the process of metamorphosis involving temporary *left*-hemisphere suppression and *right*-hemisphere imagery activation through which creative results are achieved.

**146.** Harrington, D. M. (1980). Creativity, analogical thinking, and muscular metaphors. *Journal of Mental Imagery, 4*, 13–23. Participants in this study were forty-six male and female college students who completed two scales (analogical- and metaphorical-thinking scale, and the use-of-hands scale) of an individual-styles questionnaire, and a modified adjective check list (involving an imaginative item, and two empirically derived indices via creative-personality scales/scorings). Results indicate that the two empirically derived factors of creative-personality are correlated positively with an index of metaphorical and analogical thinking; also, the scale indexing the use and appreciation of hand movements during speech was correlated positively with both of the creative-personality indices for participants reporting general facility/sensitivity to analogies and metaphors, but not for participants who reported less facility/sensitivity to analogies and metaphors.*

**147.** Jennings, J. L. (1991). Aphorisms and the creative imagination: Lessons in creativity, method, and communication. *Journal of Mental Imagery, 15*, 111–32. In this essay on creative imagination, the author examines the German philosopher Nietzsche's use of aphorisms (i.e., short, concise, and dramatic paragraphs that stand as independent "thought experiments") that were designed by Nietzsche as a systematic method for displaying the poetry and power of the creative imagination for philosophic purposes. Jennings notes that the aphoristic method—due to its inherent disorderly and disjointed character—ultimately caused widespread misunderstanding of Nietzsche's thought. However, on the positive side, Jennings suggests that Nietzsche's mastery of metaphor and eidetic imagery, in particular, is enormously relevant to the modern psychological study of mental imagery.

**148.** Kunzendorf, R. G. (1982). Mental images, appreciation of grammatical patterns, and creativity. *Journal of Mental Imagery, 6*, 183–201. Participants in this study were 113 female and male college students who completed a prevalence of *visual* imagery test, a prevalence of *auditory* imagery test, an after-image task, a vividness of *visual* imagery questionnaire, a vividness of *auditory* imagery questionnaire, and tests of aesthetic preference. Results from these data indicate that better visual imagers are more likely to express aesthetic preferences for grammatically generated figures than do poor imagers, which suggests that visual imaging abilities and aesthetic perceptions are, respectively, productive and comprehensional concomitants to a "visual grammar" whose master varies among individuals. Kunzendorf asserts that creativity involves the grammatically directed imaging of idealized, universal and translated events, and *not* the behaviorally observable production of unusual or divergent responses. The references section of this article contains over eighty citations/references related to imagery and creativity.*

**149.** Lindauer, M. C. (1977). Imagery from the point of view of psychological aesthetics, the arts, and creativity. *Journal of Mental Imagery, 2*, 343–62. Participants in this study were forty-five male and female college students who completed a battery of tests, including a values test, an interview session in which four sets of objective data were collected concerning the participant's aesthetic activities, self-description reports, artistic ability measures, a creativity measure, and two tests of self-rated imagery. Results indicate that imagery among aesthetic individuals is more predictable (i.e., they have a more reliable and predictable capacity to imagize in aesthetic settings) than among nonaesthetic people, and imagery is more likely to be aroused regularly by artistic events for the former persons than for the latter ones. The references section of this article contains over seventy-five citations/references related to the relationships between creativity, imagery, the arts, and psychological aesthetics.*

**150.** McKellar, P. (1995). Creative imagination: Hypnagogia and surrealism. *Journal of Mental Imagery, 19,* 33–42. This essay examines the region between wakefulness and sleep (called *hypnagogia,* or the state of drowsy consciousness adjacent to sleep) where strange dreamlike visions and images occur; in hypnagogia there is an element of surrealism that has captured the imagination and creative productions of various artists/painters, scientists, and writers.

**151.** Parrott, C. A., and Strongman, K. T. (1985). Utilization of visual imagery in creative performance. *Journal of Mental Imagery, 9,* 53–66. This study examines the predictive utility of the aspects of control and vividness of visual imagery in conjunction with verbal and figural divergent thinking tasks of seventy participants, some of whom received "normal" instructions on tasks and others who received instructions to "be creative" on the tasks. Individual differences, as well as intra-individual variability, in using imagery in performance on tasks were found to be a function of imagery ability, task demands, environmental factors, and creative orientation.*

**152.** Rosenberg, H. S., and Pinciotti, P. (1983–1984). Imagery in creative drama. *Imagination, Cognition, and Personality, 3,* 69–76. This essay on the role of imagery in creative drama views mental imagery as the connecting link between such fields as child development, education, psychology, and theater and provides the foundation (called the *iii Framework*) for the area of creative drama. This framework, or conceptual model, contains three iii stages: image, imaging, and imagination that may be applied to creative drama—a field dedicated to dramatic activities with young people aged seven to fifteen years old. The iii conceptualization, according to the authors, is helpful to the arts researcher by providing a systematic framework to illustrate the use of imagery skills within drama, and aids both the scientist and educator in understanding the drama process in children. Also see Rosenberg, H. S. (1987–1988). Visual artists and imagery. *Imagination, Cognition, and Personality, 7,* 77–93; Rosenberg, H. S. (1987). *Creative drama and imagination.* New York: Holt, Rinehart, and Winston; Lindauer, M. S. (1983). Imagery and the arts. In A. A. Sheikh (Ed.), *Imagery: Current theory, research, and application.* New York: Wiley; Rohwer, W. D. (1970). Images and pictures in children's learning: Research results and educational implications. *Psychological Bulletin, 73,* 393–403; Marshall, H., and Hahn, G. (1967). Experimental modification of dramatic play. *Journal of Personality and Social Psychology, 5,* 119–22; Piaget, J., and Inhelder, B. (1971). *Mental imagery and the child.* New York: Basic Books; Singer, J. L.

(1977). Imagination and make-believe play in early childhood: Some educational implications. *Journal of Mental Imagery, 1,* 127–44.

**153.** Roskos-Ewoldsen, B., Intons-Peterson, M. J., and Anderson, R. E. (Eds.) (1993). *Imagery, creativity, and discovery: A cognitive perspective.* Amsterdam: North-Holland. The contents of this volume on the relationship between imagery and creativity (consisting of papers presented at a conference on this issue at Vanderbilt University in May 1991) include the following topics/titles: Imagery's role in creativity and discovery; The ins and outs of working memory; Images are both depictive and descriptive; Imagery, reconstructive memory, and discovery; Mental imagery: Fixed or multiple meanings? The nature and function of imagery in creative thinking; The ambiguity of mental images: The structure of shape memory and its function in creativity; Emergent properties of images; and Mental imagery and creative discovery. According to the editors, one of the major aims of this book is to move the issue of the relationship between imagery and creativity—especially the hypothesized stages of creativity—past the older, yet still unchanged, notions that were suggested seventy-five years ago, and into new cognitive perspectives and new conceptions of creativity.

**154.** Shaw, G. A., and Belmore, S. M. (1982–1983). The relationship between imagery and creativity. *Imagination, Cognition, and Personality, 2,* 115–23. Participants in this study were sixty-seven male and female college students who completed three tests involving three dimensions of creativity, two tests of imagery (the Vividness of Visual Imagery Questionnaire (VVIQ), and the Visual Memory Test), and a test of general verbal abilities. Results using regression analysis statistics indicate that imaging ability via the VVIQ account for significant amounts of variance in all three creativity tests that were administered.*

**155.** Shaw, G. A., and DeMers, S. T. (1986). The relationship of imagery to originality, flexibility, and fluency in creative thinking. *Journal of Mental Imagery, 10,* 65–74. Participants in this study were fifty-four selected, high-IQ (i.e., scores above 115) fifth and sixth grade students who completed the following instruments: the Circles Test, the Just Suppose Test, the Vividness of Visual Imagery Questionnaire (VVIQ), the Visual Memory Test (VM), and the Test of Visual Imagery Control (TVIC). Another eighty-four participants consisted of children in four regular classrooms who were used as a comparison group (i.e., a "normal population" of students). Results of the battery of tests indicate that both verbal and figural tests of creativity are correlated with three imagery measures (vividness, control, and visual memory).*

## DREAMS/DAYDREAMS AND IMAGERY

**156.** Ahsen, A. (1988). Prolucid dreaming: A content analysis approach to dreams. *Journal of Mental Imagery, 12,* 1–70. Examines the current issues in research on consciousness, especially waking and sleep consciousness vis-à-vis the process of dreaming. Ahsen describes a novel experimental procedure, called *prolucid dreaming*, which employs material from a remembered ordinary dream to produce a dynamic state closer to *lucid* dreaming (i.e., during sleep, the lucid dreamer struggles within the context of this special experience and fights the dream mind with his own mind). The procedure of prolucid dreaming—rather than using the techniques of free association or deep concentration—is designed to use parental images (e.g., the dreamer is told to keep his/her mother or father in mind as the dream is recalled) as "activation filters" to restart the dormant dreaming process that may be trapped in a remembered dream. Also, the process may be employed during ordinary cognitive awareness and critical judgment situations. Ahsen suggests that his methodology for dream study is reflective partly of his New Structuralist theory. Also see Ahsen, A. (1986). The New Structuralism. *Journal of Mental Imagery, 10*, 1–92.

**157.** Anthony, S., and Gibbins, S. (1992). Characteristics of the daydreams of deaf women. *Journal of Mental Imagery, 16*, 73–88. Participants in this study of the daydreams of deaf women initially were fifty-two female students at a college for the deaf who completed the Gallaudet Daydreaming Survey, and then the final selected sample consisted of thirty participants who were assigned to one of three groups: low frequency daydreamers (LFD), moderate frequency daydreamers (MFD), and high frequency daydreamers (HFD). Results indicate that participants' self-reported daydreams tend to occur like "mental movies" in sign language or in a combination of signs and lip movements (often expressed in the future tense); the daydreams are positive, happy in context, and more frequently occurring than ten years ago, containing the same characters but with different themes over a period of several months.*

**158.** Antrobus, J. S. (1977). The dream as metaphor: An information-processing and learning model. *Journal of Mental Imagery, 2*, 327–37. In this essay on an information-processing model of dreams, the proposition is advanced that many dream events are constructed partially from the attributes of events that have been perceived and stored during a previous waking period. The author includes suggestions for the experimental test (e.g., use of conditioned, discriminative auditory stimuli, and an avoidance conditioning technique, presented during REM sleep) of the information-processing and learning models of dreams, and draws implications for dream-interpretation and metaphor-based decision making in the mental health professions.*

**159.** Blagrove, M. (1993). The Structuralist analysis of dream series. *Journal of Mental Imagery, 17*, 77–90. Describes a Structuralist approach to dream analysis that emphasizes the progression from scene to scene within, and between, myths (based on the Structuralist's penchant for analyzing myths in terms of their concretization of conflicts in mythmakers' lives); one way of achieving resolution to such conflicts lies in the interpretation of bizarre elements/images in the dreams.*

**160.** Dewitt, T. (1988). Impairment of reality-constructing processes in dream experience. *Journal of Mental Imagery, 12*, 65–78. Describes an impaired consciousness model of dreaming that accounts for the development of dream content (i.e., subjectively real and coherent "stories") in terms of impairment of the dreaming mind's ability to understand its own ongoing experience. Results from analyses of questionnaire data of student participants' reports of their dreams indicate that "slippage" in thought, perception, and memory constitute as aspect of dream experience that is different from the dream's plot-and-character content, and that such an aspect has phenomenal reality for a large proportion of dreamers.* Also see Glicksohn, J. (1989). The structure of subjective experience: Interdependencies along the sleep-wakefulness continuum. *Journal of Mental Imagery, 13 (2),* 99–106.

**161.** Doll, M. (1986). The monster in children's dreams: Night alchemies. *Journal of Mental Imagery, 10*, 53–60. Participants in this study of children's dreams were ninety primary-level students who provided protocols concerning the content of their dreams in an approach that involved the use of the notion of *alchemy* (an ancient art of transformation; as used in the present context, it may be viewed as a Jungian process of "mining the darkness of the soul"). It was found that 43 percent of the children's dreams contained a monster image/element. It is suggested that the child dreamer is allowed in such dream visits to see, touch, and feel things or monsters that they cannot easily put into words. However, by expressing these images creatively via drawings/narrations, the child is able to gain a certain degree of control and power over his or her monsters.*

**162.** Foulkes, D., Bradley, L., Cavallero, C., and Hollifield, M. (1989). Processing of memories and knowledge in REM and NREM dreams. *Perceptual and Motor Skills, 68*, 365–66. Participants in this study of dreaming activities were sixteen young adult males who slept on various nights in a sleep laboratory. Over a period of four nights, the volunteers each reported two REM and two NREM dreams involving imagery. Following this phase, participants attempted to identify possible sources of the dream imagery in their waking memory/knowledge. Results indicate that the participants' average REM dream correspondence (between dream event and identified source) score was significantly higher than the participants' average NREM dream correspondence score. It is suggested that the variable of length probably accounts for a large number of differences found on the dimension of the stages of sleep.* Also see Kerr, N., Foulkes, D., and Jurkovic, G. (1978). Reported absence of visual dream imagery in a normally sighted subject with Turner's syndrome. *Journal of Mental Imagery, 2*, 247–63; Blank, H. R. (1958). Dreams of the blind. *Psychoanalytic Quarterly, 27*, 158–74; Deutsch, E. (1928). The dream imagery of the blind. *Psychoanalytic Review, 15*, 288–93.

**163.** Gackenbach, J., and Schilling, B. (1983). Lucid dreams: The content of conscious awareness of dreaming during the dream. *Journal of Mental Imagery, 7,* 1–13. Participants in this study of lucid dreams were 181 adults who took part in a dream project earlier in 1975 and who were asked to take part in the present follow-up study by providing additional information about their lucid dreams. Results indicate that lucid dreams are structurally distinctive from ordinary or vivid dreams and are predominantly characterized by a sense of balance and control. It was concluded that lucid dreams are more emotional, perceptual, and cognitive than their nonlucid counterparts.* Also see Gackenbach, J. I. (1985–1986). A survey of considerations for inducing conscious awareness of dreaming while dreaming. *Imagination, Cognition, and Personality, 5,* 41–55; Green, C. (1968). *Lucid dreams.* London: Hamish Hamilton; Gackenbach, J. I., and LaBerge, S. (Eds.) (1988). *Conscious mind, sleeping brain: Perspectives on lucid dreaming.* New York: Plenum Press; Jennings, J. L. (1995). Dream-centered dream study: The pursuit of prolucidity. *Journal of Mental Imagery, 19,* 43–66; Wolpin, M., Marston, A., Randolph, C., and Clothier, A. (1992). Individual difference correlates of reported lucid dreaming frequency and control. *Journal of Mental Imagery, 16,* 231–36; Soper, B., Milford, G., and Rosenthal, G. (1994). Dream perspective: A research note. *Journal of Mental Imagery, 18,* 181–82; Gackenbach, J., Heilman, N., Boyt, S., and LaBerge, S. (1985). The relationship between field independence and lucid dreaming ability. *Journal of Mental Imagery, 9,* 9–20.

**164.** Gold, S. R., and Henderson, B. B. (1981). Daydreaming, self-consciousness, and memory monitoring. *Journal of Mental Imagery, 5,* 101–5. Participants in this study were fifty-seven female and male college students who completed a measure of daydreaming frequency and self-consciousness, and also completed a memory-monitoring (paired-associates recall and prediction) task (containing high-imagery and low-imagery items). Results indicate only moderate relationships between frequency of daydreaming and self-consciousness, and neither measure was related to memory-monitoring ability.**

**165.** Gold, R. G., and Gold, S. R. (1982). Sex differences in actual daydream content. *Journal of Mental Imagery, 6,* 109–12. Participants in this study were fifty-two male and female college students who kept a record of their dreams for two weeks, and from this pool the responses of thirty students (fifteen men and fifteen women) who had ten or more scorable/usable daydreams were selected for further analysis. Results indicate that only one significant difference was found between women and men: that of a theme/category of recreation; theme/categories of sexual, aggressive, and heroic daydreams were reported with equal frequency by both sexes/genders.* Also see Kremsdorf, R., Palladino, L., Poleny, D., and Antista, B. (1978). Effects of the sex of both interviewer and subject on reported manifest dream content. *Journal of Consulting and Clinical Psychology, 46,* 1166–

67; Singer, J. L., and Antrobus, J. S. (1972). Daydreaming, imaginal processes, and personality: A normative study. In P. W. Sheehan (Ed.), *The function and nature of imagery*. New York: Academic Press; Gold, S. R., Teague, R. G., and Jarvinen, P. (1981). Counting daydreams. *Journal of Mental Imagery*, 5, 129–32; Gold, S. R., and Gold, R. G. (1982). Actual daydream content and the Imaginal Processes Inventory. *Journal of Mental Imagery*, 6, 169–73; Gold, S. R., and Reilly, J. P. (1985–1986). Daydreaming: Current concerns and personality. *Imagination, Cognition, and Personality*, 5, 117–25; Ramonth, S. M. (1985). Absorption in directed daydreaming. *Journal of Mental Imagery*, 9, 67–86.

**166.** Hearne, K.M.T. (1983). Lucid dream induction. *Journal of Mental Imagery*, 7, 19–23. Participants in this dream study were twelve female college students who spent one night in a sleep laboratory and who—before sleep—were instructed on the lucid dream state; moreover, participants were given four electrical impulses to the wrist during the night when they were asleep and dreaming (this was intended as a cue/signal to the participant that she was dreaming, that is, to make participants become lucid). Results indicate that the technique of causing lucidity in REM sleep was shown to work well in six of the twelve participants, and to be effective briefly in two others. The author notes that a portable battery-powered "dream machine" for home use—based on the present method of external sensory stimulation to produce lucidity—has been developed; first, the device detects REM sleep, and then it automatically administers stimulation.\*\* Also see Hearne, K.M.T. (1981). Control your own dreams. *New Scientist, 91*, 783–85; Hearne, K.M.T. (1987). A new perspective on dream imagery. *Journal of Mental Imagery, 11*, 75–81; Tart, C. T. (1965). Towards the experimental control of dreaming: A review of the literature. *Psychological Bulletin, 64*, 81–91; Tart, C. T. (1987). The world simulation process in waking and dreaming: A systems analysis of structure. *Journal of Mental Imagery, 11*, 145–57; Hearne, K.M.T. (1991). A questionnaire and personality study of nightmare sufferers. *Journal of Mental Imagery, 15*, 55–63; Moss, K. (1989). Performing the light-switch task in lucid dreams: A case study. *Journal of Mental Imagery, 13*, 135–37; Stewart, D. W., and Koulack, D. (1989–1990). A rating system for lucid dream content. *Imagination, Cognition, and Personality, 9*, 67–74; Tholey, P. (1989). Consciousness and abilities of dream characters observed during lucid dreaming. *Perceptual and Motor Skills, 68*, 567–78.

**167.** LeBaron, S., Fanurik, D., and Zeltzer, L. (2001). The hypnotic dreams of healthy children and children with cancer: A quantitative and qualitative analysis. *International Journal of Clinical and Experimental Hypnosis, 49*, 305–19. Participants in this study were fifty-two healthy children and 47 children with cancer, ages six to eighteen years old, who completed the Stanford Hypnotic Clinical Scale for Children (SHCS); responses to the dream item on the SHCS were analyzed for the type and detail of imagery. Results indicate that the hypnotizability scores of both groups of children were similar; however, children with cancer indicated more pleasant than unpleasant fantasy in their hypnotic dreams, and their dream reports contained less fantasy and detail overall than did the group of healthy children.*

**168.** Lequerica, A. (1999). Dream cognition and rapid eye movement sleep in the narcolepsy syndrome. *Journal of Mental Imagery, 23,* 85–98. Participants in this survey were forty women who responded to a newsletter advertisement, and who completed a dreaming/waking consciousness questionnaire designed to examine certain personality traits and cognitive abilities that are correlated with lucid dream frequency and other variations in dreaming style. Results indicate that narcoleptic women exhibit differences when compared with normal women on many of the sleep and dreaming parameters measured, including dream self-reflectiveness, which suggests a tendency toward lucidity.*

**169.** Nielsen, T. A. (1991–1992). A self-observational study of spontaneous hypnagogic imagery using the upright napping procedure. *Imagination, Cognition, and Personality, 11,* 353–66. Describes a procedure called *upright napping* that is used for observing and recording spontaneous hypnagogic imagery, and employs systematic self-observation and recording of imagery that occurs when one falls asleep in an upright, seated position. It is concluded that the upright napping procedure is a useful method for observing spontaneous hypnagogic images in detail, and it facilitates access to hypnagogic imagery during the daytime without elaborate preparations such as sensory deprivation conditions or ganzfeld effects. Thus, the procedure may be helpful for studying dreamlike imagery in circumstances where sleep laboratory methods are unavailable or inappropriate.*

**170.** Rechtschaffen, A., and Foulkes, D. (1965). Effect of visual stimuli on dream content. *Perceptual and Motor Skills, 20,* 1149–60. Participants in this small sample size study of dreams were three young adult men who were "good sleepers" without any unusual sleep behaviors, and who were able to sleep with their eyes taped *open* without the aid of soporifics or other artificial sleep-inducing measures. During sleep, participants' pupils were chemically dilated while their sleep stages were monitored by EEG and eye movement recordings and several objects were illuminated in front of the sleeping participants' open eyes. Results indicate that—although there were a few instances of dream imagery containing light stimulation—there was no evidence of a correspondence between the reported imagery and the specific aspects of the stimulus objects presented to the men. It is concluded that the relative "functional blindness" of sleep found here fails to give support to dream theories that indicate that dream images are determined by retinal excitation patterns.** Also see Oswald, I. (1960). Falling asleep open-eyed during intense rhythmic stimulation. *British Medical Journal, 1,* 1450–55.

**171.** Richardson, A. (1979). Dream recall frequency and vividness of visual imagery. *Journal of Mental Imagery, 3,* 65–72. Participants in this study were eighty-four female and male college students who took part in a replication of, and methodological improvement on, a study of visual imagery and dream recall conducted by Hiscock and Cohen (1973). The present results confirm the findings of the earlier study concerning a significant positive association between dream recall frequency and vividness of voluntarily produced visual imagery.* Also see Hiscock, M., and Cohen, D. B. (1973). Visual imagery and dream recall. *Journal of Research in Personality, 7,* 179–88.

172. Rofe, Y., and Lewin, I. (1980). Daydreaming in a war environment. *Journal of Mental Imagery, 4,* 59–75. Participants in this study on daydreaming were 426 high school students, boys and girls, from central and border towns in Israel who completed three questionnaires: a newly developed daydream questionnaire, an earlier revised daydream questionnaire, and a repression-sensitization scale. Results indicate that repressor participants in both towns experienced fewer daydreams of all types. The authors note that their results are *not* congruent with the catharsis theory of daydreaming (i.e., the Freudian notion that daydreaming has a function of relieving tension), and they conclude that living continuously in a war environment encourages the use of repressive mechanisms both as a method for coping with daily stresses and as a personality type.*

173. Spanos, N., Nightingale, M., Radtke, H., and Stam, H. (1980). The stuff hypnotic "dreams" are made of. *Journal of Mental Imagery, 4,* 99–110. Participants in this study of *hypnotic dreams* (i.e., imaginings elicited from awake persons who have been given a special procedure followed by explicit directions to "have a dream") were ninety female and male college students who were given either a hypnotic-induction procedure, relaxation instructions, or task-motivation instructions and then directed to have a dream. Results indicate that the task-motivated group of participants reported longer, more absorbing, and more diversified dreams than did participants in the hypnotic-induction and relaxation-instructions groups.**

174. Stern, D., Saayman, G., and Touyz, S. (1983). The effect of an experimentally induced demand on nocturnal dream content. *Journal of Mental Imagery, 7,* 15–31. Participants in this dream study were twelve male and female college students who provided laboratory and home dreams, and who were assigned to one of two matched groups as differentiated by sets of simple requests: to attend in their nocturnal dreams to outdoor/nature features or to attend in their nocturnal dreams to urban-setting aspects. Results indicate that the dream contexts/settings/content changed significantly in the predicted direction as given in the respective group requests: in one group, following the administration of the Outdoor/Nature Form, the environmental settings of the dreams became significantly more rural in character, and in the other group, following the administration of the Urban Form, the environmental settings of the dreams became significantly more urban in character.**

**175.** Taylor, P. L., and Fulcomer, M. (1979). Adolescent daydreaming: The IQ effect. *Journal of Mental Imagery, 3*, 107–22. Examines whether some types of self-reported daydreaming increase with higher IQ, while other types have an inverse relationship with IQ. Participants were 166 racially and economically diverse adolescent boys and girls ranging in ages from fourteen to seventeen years old who completed a refined version of the Imaginal Processes Inventory. Results of correlational analyses indicate that both IQ and daydreaming are associated with the demographic variables of age, sex/gender, race, and socioeconomic status.* Also see Singer, J. L., and Antrobus, J. S. (1970). *Imaginal processes inventory.* New York: Center for Research in Cognition and Affect, City University of New York; Singer, J. L. (1966). *Daydreaming: An introduction to the experimental study of inner experience.* New York: Random House; Singer, J. L. (1973). *The child's world of make-believe: Experimental studies of imaginative play.* New York: Academic Press; Singer, J. L. (1974). *Imagery and daydream methods in psychotherapy and behavior modification.* New York: Academic Press; Singer, J. L. (1975). *The inner world of daydreaming.* New York: Harper and Row; Singer, J. L. (1975). Navigating the stream of consciousness: Research in daydreaming and related inner experience. *American Psychologist, 30*, 727–38; Tushup, R. J., and Zuckerman, M. (1977). The effects of stimulus invariance on daydreaming and divergent thinking. *Journal of Mental Imagery, 2*, 291–301; Zhiyan, T., and Singer, J. L. (1996–1997). Daydreaming styles, emotionality, and the big five personality dimensions. *Imagination, Cognition, and Personality, 16*, 399–414.

## EIDETIC IMAGERY

**176.** Ahsen, A. (1977). Eidetics: An overview. *Journal of Mental Imagery, 1*, 5–38. Attempts to provide a comprehensive definition of the phenomenon of eidetic imagery, to examine the criteria for distinguishing eidetics from other forms of images (such as memory image, iconic/short-term memory image, imagination, active imagination/directed daydream, daydream, dream, hypnotic/hypnagogic image, hallucination, free association, thought, Gestalt, and Penfieldian picture), and to review the general characteristics/attributes/variables of eidetics in detail (such as perceptual clarity, outward attention, accommodation tension, localization, subjective feeling, freedom of attention, detail, persistence, recurrence, corporeity, motion, interest, exploration or scanning, time, aura, dynamics, conflict, fusion, corrective thrust, conductive structuration, natural constitution, image versus idea, somatic response, meaning, image-somatic response-meaning, bipolarity, hemispheric behavior, and nuclear progression). Ahsen also describes a new method for the experimental study of eidetics called the *hemispheric structural method* that involves the imaging of one's parents during testing sessions. The references section of this article contains over 115 citations/

references concerning the topic of eidetic imagery and related issues. Also see Ahsen, A. (1972). *Eidetic Parents Test and analysis: A practical guide to systematic and comprehensive analysis.* New York: Brandon House; Ahsen, A. (1973). *Basic concepts in eidetic psychotherapy.* New York: Brandon House; Ahsen, A. (1978). Eidetics: Neural experiential growth potential for the treatment of accident traumas, debilitating stress conditions, and chronic emotional blocking. *Journal of Mental Imagery, 2,* 1–22; Ahsen, A. (1997). Phosphene Imagery Questionnaire: Third eye eidetics, hypnosis, and cosmic fantasy. *Journal of Mental Imagery, 21,* 1–104; Ahsen, A. (1999). Image and reality: Eidetic bridge to art, psychology, and therapy. *Journal of Mental Imagery, 23,* 1–16; Ahsen, A. (2000). Eidetic imagination, science, and spirituality. *Journal of Mental Imagery, 24,* 1–14.

**177.** Dolan, A. T. (1977). Eidetic and general image theory of primary image objects and identification processes. *Journal of Mental Imagery, 2,* 217–27. This essay on eidetic imagery describes the eidetic and general image theories of primary objects and differentiates these image theories from the psychoanalytic and cognitive theories of primary objects. The author suggests that experimental psychology needs to establish techniques for studying the normal image object and, also, to develop experimental techniques to show exactly how the stress is manifested in the image object and how various attempts at relieving the stress generate a variety of behaviors that are reproducible. Also see Dolan, A. T., and Sheikh, A. A. (1976). Eidetics: A visual approach to psychotherapy. *Psychologia: An International Journal of Psychology in the Orient, 19,* 200–209; Dolan, A. T., and Sheikh, A. A. (1977). Short-term treatment of phobia through eidetic imagery. *American Journal of Psychotherapy, 31,* 595–604.

**178.** Doob, L. W. (1966). Eidetic imagery: A cross-cultural will-o'-thewisp? *Journal of Psychology, 63,* 13–34. Participants in this cross-cultural study of imagery were 265 haphazardly selected samples of children and adults in five African societies (Ibo, Kamba, Masai, Somali, Swahili) who were tested for eidetic images in a manner closely resembling that used in two studies of normal and retarded American children. Results indicate that although the incidence of eidetic imagery varied markedly, the phenomenon itself transcended culture: it was reported spontaneously in similar terms everywhere.* Also see Doob, L. W. (1964). Eidetic images among the Ibo. *Ethnology, 3,* 357–63; Doob, L. W. (1965). Exploring eidetic imagery among the Kamba of Central Kenya. *Journal of Social Psychology, 67,* 3–22; Doob, L. W. (1970). Correlates of eidetic imagery in Africa. *Journal of Psychology, 76,* 223–30; Feldman, M. (1968). Eidetic imagery in Ghana: A cross-cultural will-o'-thewisp? *Journal of Psychology, 69,* 259–69.

**179.** Giray, E., Roodin, P., Altkin, W., Flagg, P., and Yoon, G. (1985). A life span approach to the study of eidetic imagery. *Journal of Mental Imagery, 9,* 21–32. Participants in this developmental study of eidetic imagery were 600 adult men and women, ages twenty to ninety-four years old, whose data on frequency of eidetic imaging served as a basis for comparison across the wide range of participant ages. It was hypothesized that the frequency of eidetic imagery is higher in the older/adult-aged participants than among the younger adult groups. Combining the present data with previous data collected by the authors on participants ranging in age from five to eighteen years old, results indicate that a significant higher frequency of eidetic imagery was present in the age groups five to seven, and in the age groups sixty to ninety-four. This pattern of frequency of eidetic imagery yields a U-shaped function when plotted with respect to age.* Also see Giray, E., Altkin, W., Vaught, G., and Roodin, P. (1976). The incidence of eidetic imagery as a function of age. *Child Development, 47,* 1207–14; Giray, E., Altkin, W., and Barclay, A. (1976). Frequency of eidetic imagery among hydrocephalic children. *Perceptual and Motor Skills, 43,* 187–94; Giray, E., and Barclay, A. (1977). Eidetic imagery: Longitudinal results in brain-damaged children. *American Journal of Mental Deficiency, 82,* 311–14; Giray, E., Altkin, W., Roodin, P., and Vaught, G. (1977). The enigmatic eidetic image: A reply to Gray and Gummerman. *Perceptual and Motor Skills, 44,* 191–94; Gummerman, K., and Gray, C. (1971). Recall of visually presented material: An unwonted case and a bibliography for eidetic imagery. *Psychonomic Monograph Supplements, 4,* 189–95 (this article contains 115 citations/references related to eidetic imagery); Gummerman, K., Gray, C., and Wilson, J. (1972). An attempt to assess eidetic imagery objectively. *Psychonomic Science, 28,* 115–18; Gray, C., and Gummerman, K. (1975). The enigmatic eidetic image: A critical examination of methods, data, and theories. *Psychological Bulletin, 82,* 383–407.

**180.** Glicksohn, J., Salinger, O., and Roychman, A. (1992). An exploratory study of syncretic experience: Eidetics, synaesthesia, and absorption. *Perception, 21,* 637–42. Participants were ten female and male adults, ages twenty to fifty-four years old, who were tested on a battery of tasks that included the elicitation of structural and typographic eidetic imagery, and color-mood and color-hearing synaesthesia. Results indicate that both structural and typographic eidetic imagery were correlated with the measures of synaesthesia.* Also see Glicksohn, J., Steinbach, I., and Elimalach-Malmilyan, S. (1999). Cognitive dedifferentiation in eidetics and synaesthesia: Hunting for the ghost once more. *Perception, 28,* 109–20.

**181.** Haber, R. N., and Haber, R. B. (1964). Eidetic imagery: I. Frequency. *Perceptual and Motor Skills, 19,* 131–38. Participants in this study were 151 elementary school boys and girls who were tested with various visual stimuli in an eidetic imagery task (i.e., participant stares at a visual object/figure, such as a colored square, placed on an easel for a short time, and then the experimenter quickly removes the stimulus and asks the participant what he/she now sees in the space previously occupied by the stimulus). Results indicate that eighty-four of the 151 children reported images of at least one of the stimulus pictures. A positive relationship was found, also, between accuracy and duration, although the only participants who had both very high accuracy and duration scores were those who saw images of all four pictures. It is concluded that—contrary to a large amount of literature on the issue—the prevalence of eidetic imagery in elementary school-children is quite low, only about 8 percent; however, those few children who did demonstrate their eidetic imagery ability were so impressive in their reports that it is concluded that eidetic imagery does, indeed, exist as a verifiable, identifiable characteristic in children.** Also see Leask, J., Haber, R. N., and Haber, R. B. (1969). Eidetic imagery in children: II. Longitudinal and experimental results. *Psychonomic Monograph Supplements, 3,* 25–48; Haber, R. N. (1969). Eidetic images. *Scientific American, 220,* 36–44; Paine, P. A. (1980). Eidetic imagery and recall accuracy in preschool children. *Journal of Psychology, 105,* 253–58.

**182.** Haber, R. N. (1979). Twenty years of haunting eidetic imagery: Where's the ghost? *Behavioral and Brain Sciences, 2,* 583–629. This review and theoretical analysis of eidetic imagery is derived from the author's ten-year study of elementary school–aged children in which eidetic imagery is said to exist from the children's reports of persisting visual images of stimuli that are no longer in view. Haber notes that eidetikers comprise only a small percentage of children, six to twelve years of age, and are apparently non-existent in adults; moreover, research on eidetic imagery has *not* shown any consistent relationship between the presence of eidetic imagery and other cognitive, emotional, intellectual, or neurological measures. Following an extensive section on "open peer commentaries," and an "author's response" section, a lengthy references section in this article contains over 285 citations/references relevant to the topic of eidetic imagery.* Also see Freides, D., and Kuipers, B. (1982). On Ralph Norman Haber's "Twenty years of haunting eidetic imagery: Where's the ghost?"; Continuing commentary. *Behavioral and Brain Sciences, 5,* 295–98; Haber, R. N., and Haber, L. R. (1988). The characteristics of eidetic imagery. In L. K. Obler and D. Fein (Eds.), *The exceptional brain: Neuropsychology of talent and special abilities.* New York: Guilford Press.

**183.** Jordan, C. S., Davis, M., Kahn, P., and Sinnott, R. H. (1980). Eidetic-imagery group methods of assertion training. *Journal of Mental Imagery, 4,* 41–48. Participants in this study were twelve adult men and women, ages twenty-four to forty-two years old, who sought assertion training and were chosen for two groups (called the *assertion training group* and the *waiting list control group*) matched for age, sex/gender, and level of assertive capacity as determined by pretraining measures of assertiveness. It is concluded that the eidetic approach to cognitive-affective restructuring—which promotes rehearsal and synthesis of verbal, visual, and somatic experience on a private level—is well suited for persons with different levels of social skills.** Also see Jordan, C. S., and Lenington, K. T. (1979). Physiological correlates of eidetic imagery and induced anxiety. *Journal of Mental Imagery, 3,* 31–42.

**184.** Kaylor, C. W., and Davidon, R. S. (1979). Accuracy of recall as a function of eidetic imagery. *Perceptual and Motor Skills, 48,* 1143–48. Participants in this study were twelve third-, fourth-, and fifth-grade students who were identified (from a pool of ninety students) as possessing eidetic imagery, and who were assigned randomly to two groups of six students each where one group was the experimental group and the other was the control group. In a procedure involving presentation of the same stimuli to all students, eidetic imagery was elicited in all participants, but the experimental group was tested for recall accuracy where these students maintained the images, while the control group was tested for recall accuracy after these students blinked their eyes and turned their heads to erase the images. Results indicate that significantly more correct responses were given by the experimental group members than by the control group members.**

**185.** Kubler, G. (1985). Eidetic imagery and paleolithic art. *Journal of Psychology, 119,* 557–65. This essay and review of the relationship between eidetic imagery and paleolithic art deals with the issue vis-à-vis the remote past (from early Aurignacian in the late Holocene period to the early Nuclear period), and notes that more recently, in the nineteenth century, observations by such scientists as Galton, Fechner, and Wundt (as well as others) paved the way for a reexamination of the relationship between eidetic imagery and paleolithic art by virtue of various independent perceptions and analyses made by more modern investigators of the issue.

**186.** Kunzendorf, R. G. (1984). Centrifugal effects of eidetic imaging on flash electroretinograms and autonomic responses. *Journal of Mental Imagery, 8,* 67–75. Participants in this study were twenty female and male college students who were tested for the effects of imaging on three physiological measures: electroretinograms (in conjunction with viewing and imaging green and red flashes of light), hand temperatures (in conjunction with imaging left and right hands, respectively, in snow and fire contexts), and heart rates (in conjunction with imaging one's body tilting backward). Results indicate that imaginally induced color-specific electroretinograms were correlated positively with vividness of visual imagery, with voluntary control of local skin temperature, and with autonomic control of heart rate.** Also see Kunzendorf, R. G. (1981). Individual differences in imagery and autonomic control. *Journal of Mental Imagery, 5,* 47–60; Kunzendorf, R. G. (1988). Vivid images, eidetic images, and hallucinations: "Unvivid" differences. *Journal of Mental Imagery, 12,* 75–80; Kunzendorf, R. G. (1989). After-images of eidetic images: A developmental study. *Journal of Mental Imagery, 13,* 55–62; Kunzendorf, R. G. (1993). The "three pens" test for autohypnotic hallucinating: Hypnotic virtuosos versus eidetic imagers versus control subjects. *Journal of Mental Imagery, 17,* 133–40.

**187.** Marks, D., and McKellar, P. (1982). The nature and function of eidetic imagery. *Journal of Mental Imagery, 6,* 1–124. Examines the phenomenology of a wide range of eidetic experiences relative to structural methods of induction in which eidetic images were elicited by a suggestion, thought, idea, or memory image. Results indicate that eidetic imagery is characteristically constructive, autonomous, dynamic, and displays natural progressions and movements. The article is followed by a commentary section comprised of thirty researchers' reactions to Marks and McKellar's exposition, as well as a final section giving the authors' rebuttals to the comments.*

**188.** Matsuoka, K., Onizawa, T., Hatakeyama, T., and Yamaguchi, H. (1987). Incidence of young adult eidetikers, and two kinds of eidetic imagery. *Tohoku Psychologica Folia*, 46, 62–74. Participants in this study were fifteen Japanese college students who were selected and identified as *typographic eidetikers* (i.e., picture-induced) from an original pool of 327 students. The selection procedure involved two steps: a questionnaire screening test concerning eidetic experiences and an interview with eidetic tests in the laboratory to identify typographic and spontaneous eidetikers. It is concluded that the two kinds of eidetic imagery found in this study—typographic and voluntary/spontaneous—are related and depend on some common ability or mechanism.* Also see Matsuoka, K. (1989). Imagery vividness, verbalizer-visualizer, and fantasy-proneness in young adult eidetikers. *Tohoku Psychologica Folia*, 48, 25–32.

**189.** Miller, S., and Peacock, R. (1982). Evidence for the uniqueness of eidetic imagery. *Perceptual and Motor Skills*, 55, 1219–33. Participants in this study were 259 boys (twelve to fourteen years old) who were tested for eidetic imagery, the results of which indicated a little over 3 percent of the boys who experienced eidetic imagery; subsequently, four experiments were conducted on this selected sample to test the eidetikers accuracy, superimposition ability, and interference/illumination effects on their memory. Results showed that the eidetikers were superior to control participants on tests of accuracy of report and superimposition of images, but the researchers note that the differences were of a low magnitude.**

**190.** Myers, S. A., and Austrin, H. R. (1985). Distal eidetic technology: Further characteristics of the fantasy-prone personality. *Journal of Mental Imagery*, 9, 57–66. Participants in this study were 200 male and female college students who volunteered to be tested concerning aspects of the so-called "fantasy-prone" personality in an attempt to replicate the findings of an earlier study by Wilson and Barber (1982). The following battery of tests and instruments was administered to the participants: an inventory of childhood memories and imaginings, an extra-sensory perception survey, a locus of control scale, a death-anxiety scale, an absorption scale, and a personality inventory. Results provide support for the earlier study by Wilson and Barber, as well as clarifying some of the major personality features of the fantasy-prone personality in terms of eidetic imagery.* Also see Wilson, S. C., and Barber, T. X. (1982). The fantasy-prone personality: Implications for understanding imagery, hypnosis, and parapsychological phenomena. In A. A.

Sheikh (Ed.), *Imagery: Current theory, research, and application*. New York: Wiley.

**191.** O'Connor, K. P., and Gareau, D. (1991). The role of context in eidetic imagery. *Journal of Mental Imagery, 15,* 151–56. Participants in this study on the persistence of perceptual context in the recall of eidetic imagery were twenty adult men and women volunteers from the normal population who took part in a six-step imagery procedure involving the imaging of their parents. Participants were asked to recall and describe their parents in a variety of supplied and elicited past perceptual contexts. Results indicate that all participants spontaneously produced images of their parents and, after attempts to modify the setting of the spontaneous image by eliciting competing contexts, three-fourths of the participants still associated the same context with their parental image (both at the end of the procedure and one week following testing).*

**192.** Paivio, A., and Cohen, M. (1979). Eidetic imagery and cognitive abilities. *Journal of Mental Imagery, 3,* 53–64. Participants in this study were 242 boys and girls from eight elementary schools (grades two and three) who were given a battery of tests, including eidetic-imagery and figural/spatial, imagery-vividness, and verbal ability tests. The eidetic-imagery test data were factor analyzed and showed two correlated factors: a nonmemory factor representing eidetic imagery as a subjective phenomenon and a memory/recall factor; analysis of the ability tests data indicated three factors defined by the spatial, verbal, and imagery-vividness tests; and analyses of the combined eidetic and cognitive tests data indicated that subjective eidetic imagery is unrelated to the other cognitive factors, but the eidetic-memory test scores were correlated positively with one verbal ability test.*

**193.** Richardson, A., and Cant, R. (1970). Eidetic imagery and brain damage. *Australian Journal of Psychology, 22,* 47–54. This study attempted to verify the incidence of eidetic imagery as reported in previous studies that examined brain damaged children (e.g., one study reported that eight out of sixteen brain damaged children had eidetic imagery as compared with one out of eighteen retarded children, and as compared with twelve out of 151 normal children); participants in the present study were sixty-two female and male children and young adults (ages ranging from six to twenty-six years old) who suffered various forms of brain damage; another group of participants were sixty-one normal, non–brain damaged male and female young adults (ages ranging from nine to thirteen years old). Based upon the results from testing the participants on eidetic imagery tasks, it was found that only one out of sixty-two brain injured individuals possessed eidetic imagery, and only three out of sixty-one normal participants demonstrated eidetic imagery. The authors also discuss the relationship between eidetic imagery and the medical condition called *palinopsia* (i.e., the persistence/recurrence of visual images in certain forms of brain lesions/disturbance after the exciting stimulus object has been removed).* Also see Bender, M., Feldman,

M., and Sobin, A. (1968). Palinopsia. *Brain, 91*, 321–38; Critchley, M. (1951). Types of visual perseveration: Paliopsia and illusory visual spread. *Brain, 74*, 267–99; Richardson, A. (1984). Eidetic imagery and emotionality. *Psychologia: An International Journal of Psychology in the Orient, 27*, 152–56; Richardson, A., and Di Francesco, J. (1985). Stability, accuracy, and eye movements in eidetic imagery, *Australian Journal of Psychology, 37*, 51–64; Harris, L. J., and Richardson, A. (1986). A note on two problems associated with obtaining samples of eidetikers. *Psychologia: An International Journal of Psychology in the Orient, 29*, 112–16; Richardson, A., and Harris, L. J. (1986). Age trends in eidetikers. *Journal of Genetic Psychology, 147*, 303–8; Richardson, A. (1986). A follow-up study of nine typographic eidetikers. *Psychologia: An International Journal of Psychology in the Orient, 29*, 165–75.

**194.** Sheehan, P. W. (1973). The variability of eidetic imagery among Australian aboriginal children. *Journal of Social Psychology, 91*, 29–36. Participants in this study were twenty aboriginal children (ages eight to twelve years old) living in the Northern Territory of Australia who had previously been identified as possessing a high incidence of eidetic imagery. Comparisons of eidetic imagery performance were made between this group of children and another community of nineteen aboriginal children who were more isolated from Western cultural effects. Results indicate that there was great variability of frequency of eidetic imagery across the two aboriginal groups where it was observed to be lower in the more isolated group, and where it was more stable in the first group of children.* Also see Sheehan, P. W., and Stewart, S. J. (1972). A cross-cultural study of eidetic imagery among Australian aboriginal children. *Journal of Social Psychology, 87*, 179–88; Sheehan, P. W. (1968). Color response to the TAT: An instance of eidetic imagery. *Journal of Psychology, 68*, 203–9.

**195.** Siipola, E. M., and Hayden, S. D. (1965). Exploring eidetic imagery among the retarded. *Perceptual and Motor Skills, 21*, 275–86. Participants in this study were thirty-four mentally retarded (equally divided between two categories: brain injured and familial retarded) children and young adults (ages eight to twenty-four years old) who were given a commonly used test for eidetic imagery. Results indicate a percentage of eidetikers among the retarded individuals that is more than three times greater than that observed in normal, nonretarded groups of children and young adults.*

**196.** Twente, G., Turner, D., and Haney, J. (1978). Eidetics in a hospital setting and private practice: A report on eidetic therapy procedures employed with 69 patients. *Journal of Mental Imagery, 2*, 275–90. Describes the incorporation of eidetic imagery therapy and tests into an insight-oriented psychiatric hospital program, as well as into affiliated private practice units, for the treatment of sixty-nine patients whose diagnoses ranged from adolescent adjustment reaction to schizophrenia. The authors draw the following conclusions: eidetic therapy is highly effective and possesses many valuable attributes in a variety of settings (e.g., it identifies areas of conflict quickly, provides direction in psychotherapy, and maintains the quality of insight-oriented treatment); and the method is taught easily to potential therapists, is easily supervised and transferred, and represents a short-term therapeutic approach for resolving long-term negative patterns.

**197.** Zelhart, P. F., Markley, R. P., and Bieker, L. (1985). Eidetic imagery in elderly persons. *Perceptual and Motor Skills, 60,* 445–46. Participants in this survey were fifty-nine healthy volunteers (ages sixty-six to ninety years old) who were recruited from rest homes and apartment complexes for the elderly in the Midwest. Results indicate that *none* of the fifty-nine participants possessed eidetic imagery, which is a finding that is in direct opposition to earlier studies that reported dramatic age-related increases in the incidence of eidetic ability of individuals sixty years old and older.* Also see Wasinger, K., Zelhart, P. F., and Markley, R. P. (1982). Memory for random shapes and eidetic ability. *Perceptual and Motor Skills, 55,* 1076–78; Giray, E., Roodin, P., Altkin, W., Flagg, P., and Yoon, G. (1985). A life span approach to the study of eidetic imagery. *Journal of Mental Imagery, 9,* 21–32.

## IMAGERY THEORY

**198.** Ahsen, A. (1981). Mental imagery: New perspectives. *Journal of Mental Imagery, 5,* 1–4. In this editorial article, Ahsen outlines a new task for the *Journal of Mental Imagery*: to move forward in further elaboration of the central theoretical and practical role of images in the interconnected fields and dimensions that include sensory, perceptual, affective, cognitive, behavioral, motivational, and therapeutic variables; it is suggested that images are unique in that they exist in all sensory modalities and modes of human functioning, and serve to synthesize and transform experience at all levels.

**199.** Ahsen, A. (1985). Image psychology and the empirical method. *Journal of Mental Imagery, 9 (2),* 1–40. Sets the tone for the contents of this edition of the *Journal of Mental Imagery* via examination of the historical and theoretical roots of imagery and scientific methodology in psychology, including various philosophical positions by writers such as Hobbes, Locke, and Descartes. Ahsen concludes that there exists an interdependency among some common-sense perspectives of phenomena, including viewpoints via rudimentary reflection, ritual reflection, myth reflection, scientific reflection, and political reflection. According to Ahsen, emerging from such interactive reflections was an empirical theory of mind that allowed a very expansive view of the complex phenomenon of imagery. In the next part of this same volume (Vol. 9, part 3), Ahsen contests the notion of *vividness* as it is customarily employed in current imagery theory; the basis of his argument rests on experimental evidence and a functional analysis of so-called "weak" (or "unvivid") imagery vis-à-vis "vivid" imagery, with or without control. Ahsen critiques the current imagery paradigm and indicates that the concept of *unvividness*—and its apparently paradoxical role in mental functions—is separate and distinct from the concept of *vividness*. Ahsen asserts that unvividness, or weak imagery, is not a sign of absence of imagery; rather, it is one of imagery's independent functional attributes. Also see Juhasz, J. B. (1987). Final exercise in Belletristic psychology: In choral response to Akhter Ahsen's "Image psychology and the empirical method." *Journal of Mental Imagery, 11 (3&4),* 78–82; Ahsen, A. (1983). Exile: The contemporary image of man. *Journal of Mental Imagery, 7 (2),* 139–68; Ahsen, A. (1983). Odysseus and Oedipus Rex: Image psychology and the literary technique of consciousness. *Journal of Mental Imagery, 7 (1),* 143–68; Ahsen, A. (1986). New surrealist manifesto: Interlocking of sanity and insanity. *Journal of Mental Imagery, 10 (2),* 1–32; Ahsen, A. (1987). Principles of unvivid experience: The girdle of Aphrodite. *Journal of Mental Imagery, 11 (2),* 1–52; Ahsen, A. (1987). Epilogue to unvividness paradox. *Journal of Mental Imagery, 11(1),* 13–60; Ahsen, A. (1988). Imagery, unvividness paradox, and the paradigm of control. *Journal of Mental Imagery, 12 (3&4),* 1–44; Ahsen, A. (1988). Hypnagogic and hypnopompic imagery transformations. *Journal of Mental Imagery, 12 (2),* 1–50; Ahsen, A. (1989). Hyponoia, hypnosis, and the eidetic: The underneath sense of images, impulses, and thoughts. *Journal of Mental Imagery, 13 (2),* 1–82; Ahsen, A. (Ed.) (1990). Behaviorists' misconduct in science: The untold story of the image in cognitive psychology. *Journal of Mental Imagery, 14 (1&2),* 1–255. (Special Issue); Parker, L. J. (1995). Akhter Ahsen's mythic vision: New surrealism and narratology—A meeting between myth and history. *Journal of Mental Imagery, 19 (1&2),* 1–32; Parker, L. J. (1998). Mythopoesis and the crisis of postmodernism: Toward integrating image and story. *Journal of Mental Imagery, 22 (1&2),* 1–219; Hilgard, E. R., Marks, D. F., and Sheehan, P. W. (1987). Unvividness paradox: A discussion. *Journal of Mental Imagery, 11 (1),* 1–12; Kitamura, S. (1988). Unvivid imagery in vivid reproduction. *Journal of Mental Imagery, 12 (3&4),* 57–62; Richardson, A. (1988). What is the question? *Journal of Mental Imagery, 12 (3&4),* 103–13; Richardson, J.T.E. (1988). Vividness and unvividness: Reliability, consistency, and validity of subjective imagery ratings. *Journal of Mental Imagery, 12 (3&4),* 115–22; Reisberg, D., and Heuer, F. (1988). Vividness, vagueness and the quantification of visualizing. *Journal of Mental Imagery, 12 (3&4),* 89–102.

**200.** Blackmore, S. (1987). Where am I? Perspectives in imagery and the out-of-body experience. *Journal of Mental Imagery, 11 (2),* 53–66. Briefly reviews and examines the psychological literature on the out-of-body experience (OBE), and advances the theory that OBE is an illusion of reality that involves the substitution of the normal input-driven model of the external world by an internally generated model in the perspective of observer. Blackmore asserts that—just as in visual illusions—the "error" in OBE may provide an insight into the normal operating processes in our perceptual worlds.* Also see Blackmore, S. J. (1984). A psychological theory of the out-of-body experience. *Journal of Parapsychology, 48*, 201–18; Palmer, J. (1978). The out-of-body experience: A psychological theory. *Parapsychology Review, 9 (5),* 19–22.

**201.** Bone, P. F., and Ellen, P. S. (1992). The generation and consequences of communication-evoked imagery. *Journal of Consumer Research, 19*, 93–104. This article provides both a theoretical rationale (based on extant consumer-research literature)—concerning how imagery may influence consumers' purchase-related variables such as attitudes and behavioral intentions—and the results of two empirical studies (involving 306 male and female college participants who assessed various commercial ads) regarding the issues of how self- versus other-relatedness, and situation plausibility, affect the degree of reported imagery and the subsequent influences on brand and ad evaluations. Based on the results of the present two studies, it was found that the focal character and plausibility of an imagined scene influence the degree of imagery elicited by the ad's message (focal character seems to affect directly participants' attitude toward an ad); also, it was observed that imagery directly influences attitude toward an ad but has no affect on attitude toward the brand or participants' behavioral intentions.**

**202.** Count-van Manen, G. (1984). Drama-imagery processes as socialization: An interdisciplinary perspective. *Journal of Mental Imagery, 8 (1),* 1–51. This essay examines interdisciplinary theoretical viewpoints on the nature and mechanisms of socialization and of theater-drama, and of the relationship between them; an evolving model called the *transformation theater* is described along with its elements of family imagery exercises and role playing within the theater context. The references section of this article contains over ninety-five citations/references related to the topic of drama-play-imagery processes vis-à-vis socialization.

**203.** Gillespie, G. (1989). Lights and lattices and where they are seen. *Perceptual and Motor Skills, 68*, 487–504. This unique, theoretical, introspective, and imaginative essay discusses characteristics of internal visual images and includes the following topics: lucid dreams, dream images, stable intense lights, the "place" where dreams are seen, visual scanning in dreams, stable intense lights as scannable, the dome effect, hypnopompic patterns as "flat," the internal dome as illusion, and the visual representation of direction. Gillespie's observations on light and lattice imageries may be placed in the context of current research and theory on cognitive imagery, ordinary and lucid dreaming, altered states of consciousness, active perception, and representational geometric imagery in scientific thought. Also see Hunt, H. (1989). A cognitive-psychological perspective on Gillespie's "Lights and lattices": Some relations among perceptions, imagery, and thought. *Perceptual and Motor Skills, 68*, 631–41; Gillespie, G. (1990). Use of subjective information in scientific psychology: III. The internal image during visual perception: An introspectionist analysis. *Perceptual and Motor Skills, 70*, 963–83.

**204.** Goossens, C. (1994). Enactive imagery: Information processing, emotional responses, and behavioral intentions. *Journal of Mental Imagery, 18 (3&4),* 119–49. This essay describes a theoretical imagery model called the *mental imagery processing* (MIP) model that provides a conceptual framework to study the effect of enactive imagery on affective and behavioral responses. The model may be applied to a number of situations, including consumer behavior and hedonistic advertising. The references section of this article contains over eighty-five citations/references related to the topic of enactive imagery.

**205.** Green, C., and Leslie, W. (1987). The imagery of totally hallucinatory or "metachoric" experiences. *Journal of Mental Imagery, 11 (2),* 67–74. These authors propose the theoretical term *metachoric experiences* to denote hallucinatory experiences in which the whole of the visual field is replaced by an hallucinatory one. The authors discuss cases of apparitions as examples of metachoric experiences occurring in the waking state and compare the integration of hallucinatory elements with that which occurs in the case of eidetic imagery.

**206.** Haber, R. N. (1981). The power of visual perceiving. *Journal of Mental Imagery, 5 (2),* 1–40. In this essay on various theoretical aspects of perception and imagery, Haber argues that humans' superior comprehension, retention, and retrieval of visually presented/represented information is due to the *automatic* processing of visual scenes and pictures, with the result that they are organized *immediately* in perception without the need for additional cognitive attention or effort. An "open peer commentary" section follows this article and contains instructive reactions to Haber's exposition; also, a "comment on the comments" section is included. The references section of this article contains over sixty citations/references related to visual perception and imagery.*

**207.** Hampson, P. J., and Morris, P. E. (1979). Cyclical processing: A framework for imagery research. *Journal of Mental Imagery, 3,* 11–22. Presents a theoretical model of imagery as an internal analog of the perceptual cycle; the model is an extension of an earlier general theory of perception (Neisser, 1976), and attempts to synthesize previous analog and propositional approaches to imagery. The references section of this article contains fifty citations/references related to the cyclical processing model for imagery research. Also see Hampson, P. J., and Morris, P. E. (1978). Unfulfilled expectations: A criticism of Neisser's theory of imagery. *Cognition, 6,* 79–85; Marks, D. (1977). Imagery and consciousness: A theoretical review from an individual differences perspective. *Journal of Mental Imagery, 1,* 275–90; Neisser, U. (1976). *Cognition and reality.* San Francisco: Freeman; Yuille, J. C., and Catchpole, M. J. (1977). The role of imagery in models of cognition. *Journal of Mental Imagery, 1,* 171–80.

**208.** Honeycutt, J. M. (1998–1999). Differences in imagined interactions as a consequence of marital ideology and attachment. *Imagination,*

*Cognition, and Personality, 18,* 269–83. Examines the relationship between attachment theory and a marital model of typology based on traditional, independent, and separate ideologies with respect to the imagined inter-actions, or covert dialogues, that persons have with relational partners. Participants in this study were seventy-two married couples (ages eighteen to sixty-four years old) who completed a survey of imagined interaction, a marital types/relational dimensions survey, and an attachment styles mea-sure (which tapped "secure," "avoidant," and "anxious/ambivalent" styles). Results indicate that the idea of sharing as a marital ideology is associated with a secure attachment, that an anxious/ambivalent attachment is asso-ciated with having discrepant imagined interactions, and that a secure at-tachment is related to rehearsal of messages that are vivid and nondiscrepant from real/actual encounters.*

**209.** Kaufmann, G. (1985). A theory of symbolic representation in prob-lem solving. *Journal of Mental Imagery, 9 (2),* 51–69. This author points out several potential shortcomings of current cognitive approaches concern-ing the nature and function of mental representations and argues that prob-lem solving may be useful as a general paradigm in the study of cognitive processes where symbolic activity is a major component of the cognitive sys-tem. The references section of this article contains over 100 citations/ref-erences related to the issue of symbolic representation in problem solving.* Also see Kaufmann, G. (1980). *Imagery, language, and cognition: Toward a theory of symbolic activity in human problem-solving.* Oslo: Universitets-forlaget; Kaufmann, G. (1984). Mental imagery in problem solving. *Inter-national Review of Mental Imagery, 1 (1),* 23–55; Kaufmann, G. (1986). The conceptual basis of imagery models: A critique and a theory. In D. Marks (Ed.), *Theories of image formation.* New York: Brandon House.

**210.** Kosslyn, S. M., Pinker, S., Smith, G. E., and Shwartz, S. P. (1979). On the demystification of mental imagery. *Behavioral and Brain Sciences, 2,* 535–81. In this "required reading" article on mental imagery, the authors address the central issues in mental imagery research of *what* a theory of mental imagery might look like, and *how* one might begin to formulate such a theory. A theory of image representation and processing is proposed, in-cluding a discussion of its empirical foundations. This excellent and lengthy article is accompanied both by "open peer commentary" and "authors' re-sponse" sections; the references section of this article contains over 140 ci-tations related to the issues of theory and models of mental imagery. Also see Nishizaka, A. (2003). Imagination in action. *Theory & Psychology, 13,* 177–208.

**211.** Kosslyn, S. M. (1981). The medium and the message in mental imagery: A theory. *Psychological Review, 88,* 46–66. This article advances the notion of a computational theory of imagery that hypothesizes that visual mental images are transitory data structures which occur in an analog spa-tial medium. Such "surface" forms are generated from more abstract or "deep" representations in the individual's long-term memory storage and where, once formed, may be operated on in various ways.

**212.** Lavin, M. W., and Agatstein, F. (1984). Personal identity and the imagery of place: Psychological issues and literary themes. *Journal of Mental Imagery, 8 (3)*, 51–66. This essay presents a theoretical viewpoint concerning the psychological and social significance of *place* in relation to issues of identity. Places are defined as named and bounded physical spaces that have been invested with social and personal meanings. The authors argue that places, both real and imagined, serve to symbolize, organize, and express both personal identity and particular situated identities.

**213.** Lyman, B. (1984). An experiential theory of emotion: A partial outline with implications for research. *Journal of Mental Imagery, 8(4)*, 77–86. In this essay, an outline for an experiential theory of emotion based on imagery is presented with reference to a definition of emotion, the initiation of emotion, and the bases for differences in emotion. The present theory relates largely to Ahsen's (1982, 1984) ISM, or triple code model, of imagery in that the image is viewed as carrying emotion or feeling-meanings with it. Also see Ahsen, A. (1982). Imagery in perceptual learning and clinical application. *Journal of Mental Imagery, 6*, 157–86; Ahsen, A. (1984). ISM: The triple code model of imagery and psychophysiology. *Journal of Mental Imagery, 8*, 15–42; Mandler, G. (1984). Consciousness, imagery, and emotion—with special reference to autonomic imagery. *Journal of Mental Imagery, 8 (4)*, 87–94; Hanley, G. L., and Chinn, D. (1989). Stress management: An integration of multidimensional arousal and imagery theories with case study. *Journal of Mental Imagery, 13 (2)*, 107–18; Thayer, R. E. (1978). Toward a psychological theory of multidimensional activation (arousal). *Motivation and Emotion, 2*, 1–34.

**214.** Marks, D. F. (1984). The New Structural approach to image formation, psychophysiology, and psychopathology. *Journal of Mental Imagery, 8 (4)*, 95–104. Advances the New Structural theory of image formation based in the clinical work of Ahsen (1965, 1977) and promoted by Marks (1985). The traditional theories of image formation have been formulated within five major paradigms: psychoanalytic, behavioristic, neuropsychological, developmental, and cognitive. However, the present author argues that some fundamental issues concerning the relationship among imagery, psychophysiology, and psychopathology have remained unanswered by the traditional paradigms. The New Structural theory employs—as one of its major databases—introspectively obtained reports of imagery experience, and uses a number of standard measures/instruments to obtain image reports for a series of "scenes," some of which may be repeated on a number of different occasions; also, various neuropsychological and psychophysiological methods are employed for recording the somatic components of the image, in conjunction with the participant's verbal reports, and his/her interpretation of the somatic and semantic features of the image. All these data are related to the participant's developmental history and goals for the future. Essentially, the structural theory of image formation assumes that there is a "triple coding" of images that takes the following form(s): a quasi-perceptual experience occurring in consciousness, that is, the image (I); a psychophysiological component, that is, the somatic response (S); and an interpretation, or meaning, component in the verbal-semantic system, that is, the meaning (M). Thus, the triple ISM code is normally present for all imagery, all of the time. Also see Ahsen, A. (1965). *Eidetic psychotherapy: A short introduction.* New York: Brandon House; Ahsen, A. (1977). Eidetics: An overview. *Journal of Mental Imagery, 1(1),* 5–38; Marks, D. F. (1985). Toward a structural theory of image formation. In D. F. Marks (Ed.), *Theories of image formation.* New York: Brandon House.

**215.** Martin, M., and Jones, G. (1999). Motor imagery theory of a contralateral handedness effect in recognition memory: Toward a chiral psychology of cognition. *Journal of Experimental Psychology: General, 128,* 265–82. Describes five experiments with left- and right-handed participants that investigate recognition memory for the orientation of heads (e.g., on coins, stamps, etc.), and question the assumption that cognitive processes are independent of handedness. Data from the experiments—involving over 3,000 male and female college student participants—show consistent evidence of a general contralateral handedness effect where left-facing heads are more likely to be recalled correctly by right-handed persons, whereas right-facing heads are more likely to be recalled correctly by left-handed individuals. Results are discussed via motor-imagery versus hemispheric-differences explanations; however, support is given to the hypothesis that the effect is a consequence of differences between handedness groups in terms of specific patterns of underlying motor activation rather than in differences of cerebral-hemispheric functioning.**

**216.** Monguio-Vecino, I., and Lippman, L. G. (1987). Image formation as related to visual fixation point. *Journal of Mental Imagery, 11 (1),* 87–96. Initially, participants in this study were sixteen right-handed student volunteers who were presented with medium-high or medium-low imagery words as they fixated visually on either of two points that were associated with the visual-construct or auditory-remembered dimensions of the Neuro-linguistic Programming (NLP) theory that were used as aides in the retrieval of images. Participants rated the intensity of elicited visual images, and then the latency of image formation was measured; the entire experiment was replicated using another group of thirty-three student participants in which various modifications concerning possible bias and "demand characteristics of the situation" were employed. Results of these studies indicate the positive effects of word imagery, but no evidence was found concerning the influence of the variable of visual fixation point. It is concluded that—due to the lack of relationship between eye fixation and strength or speed of imagery formation—the validity of an important assumption of NLP theory (but not necessarily of the entire NLP theory itself) is questionable.**

**217.** Naruse, G. (1987). Imagery and altered states of consciousness. *Journal of Mental Imagery, 11 (2)*, 137–44. In this essay, the author provides a schematic representation of the progressive process of the dissociation of normal consciousness to the altered state of consciousness; in this theoretical approach, it is posited that repetitive experiences of the altered state of consciousness integrates both the normal and altered states into a widely well-reorganized mental state/activity whereby the individual is able to choose any state/field of mental activity freely. Also see Naruse, G. (1983). On the training of imaginal mental activity. *International Imagery Bulletin, 1,* 13–14; Naruse, G. (1984). On imaginal mental activity and imaginal mental state. *Archives of Psychology, Faculty of Education, Kyushu University, 28 (2),* 787–806; Mavromatis, A. (1987). On shared states of consciousness and objective imagery. *Journal of Mental Imagery, 11 (2),* 125–30.

**218.** Pipes, R., Bowers, M., Hilton, K., Mathews, L., and Oates, D. (1997). Suspiciousness, mental simulation, and norm theory. *Journal of Social Psychology, 137,* 421–27. This article describes seven studies (involving a total of over 360 male and female college-student participants) that were conducted to test various predictions based on *norm theory* (e.g., Kahneman and Miller, 1986). It is concluded—based upon data from various subpopulations of U.S. college students—that the variable of suspiciousness is *not* influenced by the number of absolute ways an event may occur. Thus, it is suggested that the question of whether norm theory is supported by studies in which the ease of mental simulation is manipulated is still an open one, and the present results underscore the important role for the scientific enterprise of the replication of earlier research and past studies, especially those in which positive results are reported for a phenomenon. Also see Kahneman, D., and Miller, D. T. (1986). Norm theory: Comparing reality to its alternatives. *Psychological Review, 93,* 136–53; Miller, D. T., Turnbull, W., and McFarland, C. (1989). When a coincidence is suspicious: The role of mental simulation. *Journal of Personality and Social Psychology, 57,* 581–89.

**219.** Posey, T. B., and Losch, M. E. (1983–1984). Auditory hallucinations of hearing voices in 375 normal subjects. *Imagination, Cognition, and Personality, 3,* 99–113. This study describes a test of predictions made by Jaynes's (1976) theory of the evolution of human consciousness, which speculates that unconscious language use by the right hemisphere of the brain produced frequent auditory hallucinations in primitive people, and suggests why hearing such voices would be less common today, that is, hearing voices is reduced in frequency among modern people due, in part, to an inhibitory action of the language and self-awareness faculties of the left hemisphere. Participants in this survey were 375 female and male college students who completed a two-part questionnaire involving auditory hallucinatory experiences. Results from the questionnaire indicate that over 70 percent of the sample reported some experience with brief auditory hallucinations of the voice type in wakeful situations (hypnagogic and hypnopompic hallucinations were reported, also). It is concluded, overall, that several of Jaynes's theoretical points on this issue are supported by the present data.* Also see Jaynes, J. (1976). *The origins of consciousness in the breakdown of the bicameral mind.* Boston: Houghton Mifflin; Forrer, G. R. (1960). Benign auditory and visual hallucinations. *Archives of General Psychiatry, 3,* 119–22; Hilgard, E. R. (1980). Consciousness in contemporary psychology. In M. Rosenzweig and L. W. Porter (Eds.), *Annual Review of Psychology, 31.* Palo Alto, CA: Annual Reviews, Inc.

**220.** Pylyshyn, Z. W. (1973). What the mind's eye tells the mind's brain: A critique of mental imagery. *Psychological Bulletin, 80,* 1–24. This essay presents a critique of contemporary research that employs the notion of a mental image as a theoretical construct to describe one form of memory representation. The author argues that to understand "what we know" requires the supposition of abstract mental structures that are not accessible to conscious control and that are propositional and conceptual in nature rather than sensory or pictorial. Pylyshyn describes the relative merits of several alternative modes of representation, such as procedures, propositions, and data structures, and also discusses the probable nature of the representation involved when individuals use visual images. Thus, in Pylyshyn's view, the representation corresponding to the image is more like a *description* than it is to a picture. Also see Beech, J. R. (1980). An alternative model to account for the Clark and Chase picture verification experiments. *Journal of Mental Imagery, 4,* 1–11.

**221.** Pylyshyn, Z. W. (1981). The imagery debate: Analogue media versus tacit knowledge. *Psychological Review, 88,* 16–45. This article on theory in the area of mental imagery focuses on the alleged spatial nature of images, on the disagreements between the *analog* and *propositional* theoretical approaches, and on recent findings regarding the *scanning* and *rotation* of mental images. The author advances a *tacit knowledge* account of image-processing over the analog account because the former approach has more generality, and also because certain empirical results show that both mental rotation and mental scanning transformations, in particular, may be affected critically by varying instructions given to participants, as well as the precise form of the task employed. According to Pylyshyn, unless the goal is set of establishing the correct functional architecture or medium in order to *constrain* properly the proposed models (of imagery), the theorist may find himself or herself in the position of having as many free parameters as there are independent observations.

**222.** Quill, W. G. (1999). Subjective, not cognitive psychology: The revolutionary theory of the twenty-first century. *Journal of Mental Imagery, 23*

*(1&2)*, 117–51. This essay indicates that much of modern psychology's main objective of studying the individual person is misguided and misconceived, and reviews the historical development of psychology from the "frequently maligned" German psychologist Wilhelm Wundt in the late nineteenth century to American psychology in the twentieth century. The author argues that the truly revolutionary view of psychology for the twenty-first century resides not in cognitive psychology, but in *subjective* psychology where such a perspective is expressed and exemplified, in particular, by the author's *own* earlier work (Quill, 1972) in which the long history of Western philosophical and psychological thought is combined with Wundt's theoretical and conceptual approaches, as well as integrating subsequent reactions to Wundt's system, including the Behaviorism, psychoanalysis, and cognitive approaches. Also see Quill, W. G. (1972). *Subjective psychology: A concept of mind for the behavioral sciences and philosophy.* New York: Spartan/Macmillan; Cartwright, D. S. (1980). Exploratory analyses of verbally stimulated imagery of the self. *Journal of Mental Imagery, 4,* 1–21.

**223.** Reese, H. W. (2001). Some recurrent issues in the history of behavioral sciences. *Behavior Analyst, 24,* 227–39. This essay identifies and discusses several issues in the history of behavioral sciences that have appeared, disappeared, and reappeared during the twentieth century, including the construct of consciousness (both in humans and nonhuman animals), the method of introspection, and the topic of cognition (including the interpretation of mental imagery and the role of language in thought processes). Essentially, Reese argues that the *literal* recurrence of issues is rare, and that the typical apparent recurrence involves only the *labels* of the issue(s). Reese offers a possible explanation for the apparent cycles that is based on a suggestion by J. B. Watson (1913, p. 175) who asserted that important issues—once found to be intractable and then discarded—are reborn and revitalized when newer theories and methods emerge and old issues are now viewed "from a new angle and in more concrete settings." Also see Watson, J. B. (1913). Psychology as the Behaviorist views it. *Psychological Review, 20,* 158–77.

**224.** Rosenberg, B. A. (1979). A possible function of lateral eye movements. *Journal of Mental Imagery, 3,* 73–84. This essay examines three current theories of lateral eye movements (personality-type, internal processing, orienting response), and concludes that no single theory yet accounts for lateral eye movement behavior. It is suggested, following analyses of typology theory, gating-out theory, and orientation theory, that a new synthesis—involving hemispheric specialization and gating-out theory—is a reasonable approach toward understanding lateral eye movement behavior. Also see Salas, J., DeGroot, H., and Spanos, N. P. (1989). Neuro-linguistic programming and hypnotic responding: An empirical evaluation. *Journal of Mental Imagery, 13,* 79–90.

**225.** Sarbin, T. R., and Juhasz, J. B. (1978). The social psychology of hallucinations. *Journal of Mental Imagery, 2,* 117–44. This essay on theoretical concerns in the area of hallucinatory behavior approaches the issue from a social psychological perspective, and includes discussions of the definition of hallucination and the issues of the characteristics of imaginings, the occasions for reporting them, and the conditions for placing negative valuations on such reports. The authors suggest that imagining may be treated as an iconic coding system, which tends to be of high personal importance for an individual and tends to occur in situations of high cognitive tension. Also see Juhasz, J. B. (1971). Greek theories of imagination. *Journal of the History of the Behavioral Sciences, 7,* 39–58; Juhasz, J. B. (1972). An experimental study of imagining. *Journal of Personality, 40,* 588–600; Sarbin, T. R. (1967). The concept of hallucination. *Journal of Personality, 35,* 359–80; Sarbin, T. R., and Juhasz, J. B. (1967). The historical background of the concept of hallucination. *Journal of the History of the Behavioral Sciences, 3,* 339–58; Sarbin, T. R., and Juhasz, J. B. (1970). Toward a theory of imagination. *Journal of Personality, 38,* 52–76; Sarbin, T. R., and Juhasz, J. B. (1975). The social context of hallucinations. In R. K. Siegel and L. J. West (Eds.), *Hallucinations: Behavior, experience, and theory.* New York: Wiley; Sarbin, T. R., Juhasz, J. B., and Todd, P. (1971). The social psychology of "hallucinations." *Psychological Record, 21,* 87–93.

**226.** Scott, L. M. (1994). Images in advertising: The need for a theory of visual rhetoric. *Journal of Consumer Research, 21,* 252–73. This essay concerning advertising images analyzes and critiques previous consumer research for its underlying assumption that pictures are reflections of reality, and presents a case against such an assumption. An alternative view—that visuals are a convention-based symbolic system—is provided and indicates that pictures must be possessed cognitively or centrally rather than absorbed automatically or peripherally.

**227.** Staats, A. W., and Lohr, J. M. (1979). Images, language, emotions, and personality: Social Behaviorism's theory. *Journal of Mental Imagery, 3,* 85–106. This essay and review of the literature systematizes and elaborates the image theory of social Behaviorism. This theory of images is based on fundamental conditioning principles where images are the stimuli produced by conditioned sensory responses, and where images may have, or elicit, emotional reactions; thus, according to this approach, images may have reinforcing properties and, also, elicit approach responses in cases of positive emotions and avoidance responses in cases of negative emotions.

**228.** Thomas, N.J.T. (1989). Experience and theory as determinants of attitudes toward mental representation: The case of Knight Dunlap and the vanishing images of J. B. Watson. *American Journal of Psychology, 102,* 395–412. In this philosophical and historical essay on mental imagery, the author discusses three separate issues (i.e., whether individuals ever really do have a mental image; the nature of imagery's underlying mechanism; and determination of the cognitive function, if any, of imagery) over which psychologists and philosophers may be for or against mental images. Thomas asserts that conflation of these issues may lead to theoretical differences being mistaken for experiential differences, and cites the examples of J. B. Watson and K. Dunlap as cases in point (Thomas suggests that Dunlap's approach toward imagery may be characterized as "pictorial iconophobia," while Watson's approach toward imagery may be described as "functional *and* experiential iconophobia"). The references section of this article contains over 110 citations related to the historical and theoretical analysis of mental imagery. Also see Dunlap, K. (1912). The case against introspection. *Psychological Review, 19,* 404–13; Dunlap. K. (1914). Images and ideas. *Johns Hopkins University Circular* (March), *3,* 25–41; Thomas, N.J.T. (1987). *The psychology of perception, imagination, and mental representation, and twentieth century philosophies of science.* Doctoral dissertation, University of Leeds, Leeds, UK; Watson, J. B. (1913). Image and affection in behavior. *Journal of Philosophy, Psychology, and Scientific Methods, 10,* 421–28; Watson, J. B. (1919). *Psychology from the standpoint of a Behaviorist.* Philadelphia, PA: Lippincott.

**229.** Thomas, N.J.T. (1999). Are theories of imagery theories of imagination? An *active perception* approach to conscious mental content. *Cognitive Science, 23,* 207–45. This philosophical essay on imagery theories asks the question "Can theories of mental imagery (conscious mental contents) formulated within the field of cognitive science give insight into the obscure concept of imagination?" Thomas examines three theoretical perspectives as a background for answering that question: descriptive theory, quasi-pictorial theory, and perceptual-activity theory. Thomas suggests that an "active perception" approach to conscious mental content via the perceptual-activity theory is a good candidate to serve as the basis for a *general* theory of imagination and its associative role in the creative thinking processes. The references section of this article contains over 215 citations related to the issue of the relationship between imagery theory and imagination. Also see Pylyshyn, Z. W. (2002). Mental imagery: In search of a theory. *Behavioral and Brain Sciences, 25,* 157–237; Thomas, N.J.T. (2002). The false dichotomy of imagery. *Behavioral and Brain Sciences, 25,* 311.

**230.** Tye, M. (1991). *The imagery debate.* Cambridge, MA: M.I.T. Press. The author's overall aim in this book is to show how the philosophical and psychological theories of imagery relate to one another and to propose a comprehensive view of mental imagery that not only addresses the issue of imagistic representation, but also suggests answers to questions concerning the subjective, phenomenal aspects of imagery, imagery indeterminacy, the physical basis of imagery, and the causal role of image content. Essentially, the imagery debate is between two groups of theories: those that liken mental images to *pictures* and those that liken them to linguistic *descriptions*. Ultimately, after arguing that both pictorialist and descriptionalist theories encounter difficulties of one sort or another, the author presents a "mixed" proposal of his own that is influenced most strongly by the views of Stephen

Kosslyn and David Marr. The Notes section at the end of the book contains over 240 notes and references related to the topic of the imagery debate. Also see Kosslyn, S. M. (1980). *Image and mind.* Cambridge, MA: Harvard University Press; Kosslyn, S. M. (1983). *Ghosts in the mind's machine.* New York: W. W. Norton; Kosslyn, S. M. (1994). *Image and brain: The resolution of the imagery debate.* Cambridge, MA: M.I.T. Press; Marr, D. (1982). *Vision.* San Francisco: Freeman.

## IMAGINATION IMAGERY

**231.** Ahsen, A. (1999). Imagination imagery. *Journal of Mental Imagery, 23 (3&4),* 1–265. In this special theme issue of the *Journal of Mental Imagery,* Ahsen notes that the subject of imagination presents many challenging problems, as it is concerned directly with the phenomenon of images and how images, impressions, and ideas interplay in the processes of thinking, remembering, and behaving. Ahsen suggests that the whole complex network of interaction rests on the phenomenon of images itself, and where the basis of all these processes involves imagination in some form or another. As just one example of Ahsen's creative, imaginative, and far-reaching agenda, he invokes the notion of the *hologram,* which provides a useful model for understanding how imagery functions across neurological, biological, and psychological dimensions. Ahsen asserts that by exploiting holographic potentials in a deeper way, one may produce various healing effects in the mind and body, and demonstrates many "mind over body" encounters and how they are achieved. To indicate the profound possibilities in this notion, the hologram is described in several areas ranging from optical holography to the holograms studied in the areas of neurology, embryology, and perception psychology. Within this context, Ahsen suggests how the novel idea of *image cloning* may progress along lines already demonstrated in the field of genetics and gene technology. Also see Juhasz, J. B. (1972). An experimental study of imagining. *Journal of Personality, 40 (4),* 588–600; Juhasz, J. B. (1969). Imagination, imitation, and role taking. Unpublished doctoral dissertation, University of California, Berkeley; Juhasz, J. B. (1971). Greek theories of imagination. *Journal of the History of the Behavioral Sciences, 7,* 39–58.

**232.** Bryant, R. A., Bibb, B. C., and McConkey, K. M. (1991). Imagining and faking blindness. *Journal of Mental Imagery, 15 (3&4),* 37–43. Participants in this study of imagination were forty-four female and male college students who were selected on the basis of their extreme scores (very high or very low imagery scores) on a mental imagery questionnaire, and who were given, subsequently, a range of imagination tasks to complete. More specifically, the experiment examined the affect of visual information on a decision task, and a condition where low- and high-imagery participants, respectively, were asked either to imagine ("simulate") or to fake ("real") blindness. Results indicate that participants' responses were influenced more by the visual information after, rather than during, the request for imagined (simulated) blindness, while the real and simulating participants were similar on the decision task. Thus, whereas real and simulating participants—who reported complete blindness—responded similarly on behavioral measures, they demonstrated distinctively different patterns on subjective measures.**

**233.** Conklin, C. A., and Tiffany, S. T. (2001). The impact of imagining personalized versus standardized urge scenarios on cigarette craving and autonomic reactivity. *Experimental and Clinical Psychopharmacology, 9*, 399–408. Participants in this study were sixty adult cigarette smokers who described situations/scenarios in a cue-reactivity paradigm designed to study the effects of personalizing imagery materials on their reactivity to smoking cues. Results indicate that the variable of personalization led to greater vividness, positive mood, and relevance ratings as compared to various other script forms.**

**234.** Drake, S. D., Nash, M. R., and Cawood, G. N. (1990–1991). Imaginative involvement and hypnotic susceptibility: A re-examination of the relationship. *Imagination, Cognition, and Personality, 10*, 141–55. Participants in this study were 134 male and female college students who were assigned randomly to one of three groups: hypnotic context/temporally contiguous (Group 1), hypnotic context/temporally noncontiguous (Group 2), and nonhypnotic/temporally noncontiguous (Group 3). Following the administration of three scales of absorption/imaginativeness to the participants, a hypnotizability scale was given to them. Results indicate that participants in Group 1—who were given the three scales immediately before hypnosis—showed the usual positive correlation between each of the three scales and hypnotizability; and participants in Groups 2 and 3—who were given the three scales twenty-four to thirty-six hours before hypnosis—yielded data that showed no significant correlation between hypnotizability and the three scales of imagination/absorption.**

**235.** Glicksohn, J., Mourad, B., and Pavell, E. (1991–1992). Imagination, absorption, and subjective time estimation. *Imagination, Cognition, and Personality, 11*, 167–76. In this study of the interaction of trait and task variables in determining duration judgment, participants were twenty-six female and male college students who constituted two groups: a high absorption and a low absorption group. Participants viewed a series of paired slides and were asked to relate to each pair in one of two task-conditions—a metaphor-production task and a story-production task—that were carried out in an objective interval of fifteen minutes. Following the task, participants were asked, retrospectively, to give their verbal estimations of the duration of this interval period. Results indicate a significant interaction between absorption and task for the variables of average time to respond and average time of (length of) response.**

**236.** Gonzalez-Ordi, H., and Miguel-Tobal, J. J. (2001). Suggestibility as a moderator variable in anxiety-imagined situations. *Sociedad Espanola Para El Estudio De La Ansiedad y El Estres, 7,* 89–110. Participants in this study on the relationships among the variables of suggestibility, imagery, and anxiety were forty female students at a Spanish university who were identified as either highly suggestible or slightly suggestible, and who were given the following experimental conditions: an imagined anxiety-provoking/threatening scenario induced by the experimenter (or selected by the participant), or an imagined anxiety-provoking test situation induced by the experimenter (or selected by the participant). Results indicate that highly suggestible participants scored higher than the slightly suggestible participants on the level of real and imagined emotional involvement for all conditions.\*\*

**237.** Honeycutt, J. M., Zagacki, K. S., and Edwards, R. (1992–1993). Imagined interaction, conversational sensitivity, and communication competence. *Imagination, Cognition, and Personality, 12,* 139–57. Participants in this study on the relationship between imagination and communication were 131 female and male college students who completed the following measures: the Survey of Imagined Interaction, the Conversational Sensitivity Measure, and the Communication Competency Assessment Instrument. The following results were obtained: features of imagined interaction predict both conversational sensitivity and self-reported communication competence; mental experiences of communication (i.e., imagined interaction) activate sensitivity to conversations and provide knowledge structures for competent interaction; and overall conversational sensitivity has a mediating role in communication competence.\*

**238.** Hull, C. R., and Render, G. F. (1984). The effect of relaxation, fantasy journeys, and free imagery on control and vividness of imagery. *Journal of Mental Imagery, 8 (2),* 67–78. Participants in this study were ninety-six male and female college students who comprised eight classes where classes were assigned randomly to one of the three treatment groups or to a control group. Before the treatments were administered, all students were pretested with a survey of mental imagery to assess their vividness of imagery and control of imagery. The following treatments were given: one 10-minute session of relaxation exercises; one 25-minute session of relaxation coupled with fantasy journey exercises; one 25-minute session of relaxation coupled with free imagery exercises; the control group received no treatment. Following the administration of treatments, all participants were posttested with a different form of the same survey of mental imagery. Results indicate only one significant treatment-by-measure interaction out of a possible total of seventeen interactions, and led to the conclusion that treatments consisting of a single session of relaxation, relaxation plus fantasy journey, or relaxation plus free imagery have *no* influence on the vividness and controllability of imagery.\*\* (Editorial note: The present study found negative, no-difference, or nil, results; nevertheless, this particular journal published the study. It is refreshing to have access to studies where the results are not positive, and gratifying to know that some psychological journals suspend the "positive-only-results" policy [as a prerequisite to publication of articles]. Indeed, one may learn not only from positive findings, but negative findings as well! Kudos to the journal.)

**239.** Iachini, S., Giusberti, F., and Cicogna, P. (1995–1996). Imagery and emotions. *Imagination, Cognition, and Personality, 15,* 59–73. Participants in this study were thirty female and male college students who were asked to visualize the images associated with six emotional categories: three positive (i.e., happiness, cheerfulness, and surprise) and three negative (i.e., fear, sadness, and anger); additionally, participants were asked to do the following: evaluate the movement and vividness of the images produced on a scale from zero to ten; answer a questionnaire consisting of pairs of opposites; and provide a verbal report of the images produced. Results indicate that formal regularities are present in the imaginative representation of emotional categories, and that various thematic contents characterize different emotions.*

**240.** Ito, M. (1999). Imagined movement and response programming. *Journal of Mental Imagery, 23 (1&2),* 71–84. Participants in this study were twenty-four male and female graduate and undergraduate college students who generated data in a reaction time (RT) task where it was required that two homogeneous force responses be executed in rapid succession. Based upon data from participants' first response as being *imagined* versus *actual,* the results indicate that the actual-movement and task-relevant imagined-movement conditions produced shorter RTs than the task-irrelevant imagined-movement and control conditions when the interstimulus interval was at one second, but no differences occurred in RTs when the interval was at three seconds. Overall, it was concluded that response programming may occur during participants' *imagined* movements as well as during their *actual* movements.** Also see Corriss, D., and Kose, G. (1998). Action and imagination in the formation of images. *Perceptual and Motor Skills, 87,* 979–83.

**241.** Jackson, S. W. (1990). The imagination and psychological healing. *Journal of the History of the Behavioral Sciences, 26,* 345–58. In this essay, the author traces the history of the concept of imagination and its role as a crucial aspect in various schemes of faculties, powers, and functions of the soul/mind, including its importance in certain modes of psychological healing. According to the author, a notable exception to the recent trend away from the concept of the imagination and its language is Carl Jung's (1961) notion of *active imagination,* along with its associative psychotherapeutic technique that attempts to translate the client's emotions into images, or to find the images that are concealed in the client's emotions. Most recently, there has been an emergence of a whole array of psychotherapeutic uses of the imagination subsumed under the labels "guided imagery techniques" and "guided affective imagery." Also see Jung, C. G. (1961). *Memories, dreams, reflections*. New York: Pantheon; Singer, J. L., and Pope, K. S. (Eds.) (1978). *The power of human imagination: New methods in psychotherapy*. New York: Plenum; Sheikh, A. A. (Ed.) (1984). *Imagination and healing*. Farmingdale, NY: Baywood.

**242.** Lynn, S. J., and Rhue, J. W. (1987). Hypnosis, imagination, and fantasy. *Journal of Mental Imagery, 11 (2),* 101–11. This review focuses on three questions: Are participants' nonhypnotic imaginations related to hypnotic susceptibility? Do some fantasy-prone participants have a common set of personality attributes and experiences, including an ability to respond to hypnotic suggestions? What are the childhood developmental antecedents of individuals who score at the extremes of measures of fantasy, imagination, and hypnotic ability? By examining correlational studies (which used measures of absorption in hypnoticlike experiences and imagination), experimental studies (which used high and low hypnotizable participants' responses to actual stimuli presumed to be conducive to imagination-behaviors), and interview research (which employed hypnotizable and fantasy-prone participants), the authors are able to provide tentative answers to the three questions.

**243.** Picco, F., Brouillet, D., and Syssau, A. (2001). Is the model of a situation constructed based on the reading of a story presented in the form of images? *Bulletin de Psychologie: France, 54,* 417–26. Participants in this study were thirty-three female and male students at a French university. Following the administration of a pretest to determine the students' image comprehensibility, participants were given six stories, each containing four images (where the *essential* versus *peripheral-graphic* elements of each image were made distinctive) as part of a two-stage experiment on image learning and recall. Results indicate that participants recalled the viewed images more easily and rapidly than they did the unviewed images.*

**244.** Rabinowitz, A., and Heinhorn, L. (1984–1985). Empathy and imagination. *Imagination, Cognition, and Personality, 4,* 305–12. Participants in this study were 141 tenth- and eleventh-grade boys and girls in an Israeli high school who completed an imaginal processes inventory and an empathy scale (imagination was assessed via the daydreaming and night-dreaming scales of the former inventory, and empathy was assessed on an Israeli version of the latter scale). Results indicate that the greater an individual's imagination, the more empathy the person will show—a finding that is congruent with other research findings regarding imagination (e.g., Frank, 1978; Singer, 1966, 1975).** Also see Frank, S. (1978). Empathy through training in imagination. In J. L. Singer and K. S. Pope (Eds.), *The power of human imagination*. New York: Plenum Press; Singer, J. L. (1966). *Daydreaming: An introduction to the experimental study of inner experience*. New York: Random House; Singer, J. L. (1975). *The inner world of daydreaming*. New York: Harper & Row.

**245.** Reynolds, K., West, S., Clapper, R., and Suter, D. (1987–1988). Arousal as a mediator of behavioral confirmation. *Imagination, Cognition, and Personality, 7,* 129–35. Participants in this study were 145 male and female college students who completed tasks involving a memory drum outfitted with two levels of the Stroop color-word test (in the difficult list on the drum the words *red, green,* and *blue* were printed in incongruous colors; and in the easy list condition, the words *lot, safe,* and *close* were printed in the colors red, green, and blue). In both list conditions, difficulty and easy, the participant was required to pronounce the color in which the word was printed and to ignore the word itself (each list consisted of ninety items, and were presented at a rate of one item per second). The dependent variable of interest in this study was the number of errors committed by each participant on the Stroop task. Results indicate that an interaction was present between the difficulty of list and type of explanation variables; in the difficult list condition, participants who imagined and explained success or failure made more errors on the Stroop task than participants who explained a neutral event.**

**246.** Rhue, J., Lynn, S., Henry, S., Buhk, K., and Boyd, P. (1990–1991). Child abuse, imagination, and hypnotizability. *Imagination, Cognition, and Personality, 10,* 53–63. Participants in this study were 100 male and female college-student volunteers who were assigned to one of four groups based on previous screening data: sexually abused; physically abused; loss of parent prior to ten years of age; an intact family in which both biological parents were still living. Participants completed pencil and paper questionnaires, two personality inventories, an ideation scale, a perceptual aberration scale, a cognitive-slippage scale, and measures of absorption, imaginative involvement, and hypnotizability. The study was designed to test Hilgard's (1970, 1974) hypothesis that hypnotizability is related to a history of physical punishment and to imaginative involvements. Results indicate that there is no support for the hypothesis that increased hypnotizability is associated with a history of physical or sexual abuse (however, it was found that physically and sexually abused participants were more prone to fantasy than participants in both of the other nonabused control conditions).** Also see Hilgard, J. R. (1970). *Personality and hypnosis: A study of imaginative involvement.* Chicago: University of Chicago Press; Hilgard, J. R. (1974). Imaginative involvement: Some characteristics of the highly hypnotizable and nonhypnotizable. *International Journal of Clinical and Experimental Hypnosis, 22,* 238–56; Hilgard, J. R. (1979). Imaginative and sensory-affective involvement in everyday life and hypnosis. In E. Fromm and R. Shor (Eds.), *Hypnosis: Developments in research and new perspectives.* New York: Aldine.

**247.** Richardson, A., and McAndrew, F. (1990). The effects of photic stimulation and private self-consciousness on the complexity of visual imagination imagery. *British Journal of Psychology, 81,* 381–94. Participants in this study were forty female college students who were selected from a pool of

300 male and female Australian students who completed a screening questionnaire dealing with experiences of hypnagogic imagery, photic stimulation, and private-self consciousness (PSC) and who completed tasks in photic stimulation trials. Measures were taken of the participants' reported images or sensations during the photic flashing/stimulation tasks; the major dependent variable was an imagery-complexity score ranging from one (the simplest kind of visual experience) to four (the most complex kind of visual experience). Results indicate that—as predicted—more complex images were reported under the averaged 6 and 10 hertz photic frequencies than under the 18 hertz condition, under the 6 than the 10 hertz condition, and under the high PSC than the low PSC condition.**

**248.** Shmukler, D. (1982–1983). Early home background features in relation to imaginative and creative expression in third grade. *Imagination, Cognition, and Personality, 2,* 311–16. Participants in this longitudinal study were seventy-three third-grade girls and boys who were observed and tested originally when they were enrolled in preschool. Four criteria of creative and imaginative expression were used to assess the third graders' present level of expression in those areas, and were shown to be related to the earlier measures and evaluations of their imaginative predisposition.*

**249.** Sim, J., and Lyman, B. (1987–1988). The experiential themes of various emotions. *Imagination, Cognition, and Personality, 7,* 265–84. Participants in this study were ninety-three Canadian female and male college students who were asked to provide narrative reports concerning emotional situations where twenty-two emotion terms were selected by the experimenters for their familiarity and representativeness (the terms were amusement, anger, anxiety, boredom, contentment, curiosity, depression, disgust, excitement, fear, friendliness, guilt, happiness, hatred, hope, jealousy, joy, loneliness, love, sadness, shame, and surprise). From the list of twenty-two terms, each participant was assigned randomly four emotions to describe. The data collected consisted of the experiential themes extracted from the participants' descriptions. Results indicate that the frequency of correct theme identifications were significant for all twenty-two of the emotions; most theme statements had references to physiological sensations being present in consciousness.*

**250.** Singer, J. L. (1977). Imagination and make-believe play in early childhood: Some educational implications. *Journal of Mental Imagery, 1,* 127–43. This essay notes that the child's creations of settings, times, and characters not present in the immediate environment (i.e., imaginative play) is one of the major forms of play in preschool and early school-age children. The author suggests that—while such make-believe play is not often verbalized aloud by children after ages seven or eight—there is reason to believe that interest in such play continues on into adolescence and becomes a part of the adolescent's daydreaming.

**251.** Stillman, J., and Kemp, T. (1991). Visual versus auditory imagination: Image qualities, perceptual qualities, and memory. *Journal of Mental*

*Imagery, 17 (3&4)*, 181–93. Participants in this study were thirty-eight male and female students in a New Zealand university who rated fifteen imagined sounds and sights given in a taped account of a trip to the beach (five items were selected to evoke visual imagination, five sounds were selected to evoke auditory imagination, and five items were selected to evoke both visual and auditory imagination). During regular, periodic pauses in the narrative, participants made ratings orally of their images on a seven-point scale; half of the participants rated how *real* their images seemed to them, and half rated how *vivid* their images seemed. Results show that more auditory than visual items were recalled (which is consistent with the coding-redundancy hypothesis of memory), and the use of the term *vividness* to rate image quality seems to disadvantage or underrate the auditory modality.* For a methodology similar to the present one, see an earlier study by Tracy, R. J., Tracy, J. K., and Ramsdell, C. L. (1985). The relationship between imagination and memory. *Journal of Mental Imagery, 9 (3)*, 91–108.

**252.** Stotland, E., and Smith, K. D. (1993–1994). Empathy, imagining, and motivation. *Imagination, Cognition, and Personality, 13,* 193–213. This essay/review presents a conception of empathy as a process in which the individual shares an emotion with another person because he or she perceives the other to be experiencing that particular emotion. It is suggested that the core of the empathizing process is the ability of *imagining* the other person's feelings, the latter of which are influenced and shaped by social, individual, learning, and motivational factors.

**253.** Tower, R. B. (1984–1985). Preschoolers' imaginativeness: Subtypes, correlates, and maladaptive extremes. *Imagination, Cognition, and Personality, 4,* 349–64. Participants in this study were forty-three preschool/nursery school boys and girls whose behaviors were observed and rated by teachers, and who provided data for teachers' evaluations of them on child description scales, imaginativeness scales, differential emotion scales, a child adjective checklist, a child interview, and art scales. Results of the observational, behavioral, and interview measures indicate that the conceptual and empirical value of imaginativeness has two dimensions: expressive and constructive. While optimal levels of constructive imaginativeness correlates with other indexes of healthy child development, the correlations were found to be fewer and tended to be weaker in the case of expressive imaginativeness.*

**254.** Tracy, R. J., and Barker, C. H. (1993–1994). A comparison of visual versus auditory imagery in predicting word recall. *Imagination, Cognition, and Personality, 13,* 147–61. Participants in this study were 132 male and female college students who were asked to imagine a future trip to a beach, and rated subsequently the visual imagery or the auditory imagery of twenty-seven stimulus words, phrases, or objects (e.g., sand, waves, bonfire, volleyball game, etc.); later, the participants were asked to recall the objects. Data from participants' imagery reports, ratings, and recall indicate that visual imagery and word recallability were positively correlated. However, in contrast, auditory imagery and recallability were related curvilinearly: objects rated as easy to hear or difficult to hear were recalled better than objects of intermediate audibility. Two appendixes—containing the rating scale and questionnaire used—are given at the end of the article.*

## LEARNING AND IMAGERY

**255.** Anderson, A. (1997). Learning strategies in physical education: Self-talk, imagery, and goal-setting. *The Journal of Physical Education, Recreation, and Dance, 68*, 30–35. In this essay/review of learning strategies—including the use of imagery in the area of physical education—the author defines learning strategies as cognitive tools that are used to manage systematically the thought processes associated with knowledge and skill acquisition. In one case, a distinction is made between mental imagery and mental practice where the former refers to a mental process that occurs when a person imagines an experience, whereas the latter is a descriptive term for a particular technique used by athletes and other individuals for various goals. With mental imagery, the person sees the image, feels the movements and/or the environment in which it takes place, and hears the sounds related to the movement: the crowd, the water, the starting gun; in the individual's mind, it is the next best thing to actually being there. Unlike daydreaming, imagery is controlled consciously by the person; the individual is aware of the images and may manipulate the images.

**256.** Campbell, R., and DeHaan, E.H.F. (1998). Repetition priming for face speech images: Speech-reading primes face identification. *British Journal of Psychology, 89*, 309–23. This study describes three experiments on imagery and speech-reading (i.e., classifying a facial image in terms of speech-sound) that involved the participation of seventy-two female and male postgraduate students and staff at two European universities. The following results were obtained: identity decisions for personally familiar faces are sensitive to a previous image of that person's face making a speech sound (i.e., identity decisions are primed by speech-reading); speech-sound matching is not faster for known faces seen earlier in a different task (i.e., speech-reading is not primed by identification); knowledge of familiar faces may interfere with classification of face images for speech (i.e., unfamiliar faces are speech-read faster); and repeating a speech-classification task may give rise to form- rather than to face-based priming.*

**257.** Campos, A., Perez, M. J., and Gonzalez, M. A. (1996–1997). The interactiveness of paired images is affected by image bizarreness and image vividness. *Imagination, Cognition, and Personality, 16*, 301–7. Participants in two experiments on image vividness and bizarreness were 1,058 female and male high school students who completed a vividness of imagery questionnaire, were exposed to pairs of words, and were asked to visualize interactive images as an aid to recall of the words; some participants were asked to form normal interactive images and others were asked to form bizarre interactive images. Results indicate that bizarre images are more interactive than normal images and, likewise, vivid images are more interactive than nonvivid images; however, imaging ability had no effect on between-image interaction.**

**258.** Cautela, J. R., and Wisocki, P. A. (1969). The use of imagery in the modification of attitudes toward the elderly: A preliminary report. *Journal of Psychology, 73,* 193–99. Participants in this imagery study were forty-nine male and female college students who received a checklist composed of eighteen positive and twenty-two negative statements about elderly persons, and were asked to rate each item along a scale of varying response tendency according to how they felt about each item. One week later the experimental group of participants was asked to imagine a scene in which their lives were saved by an elderly person; they were told to practice imagining this scene at least twice each day; ten days later, the experimental (imagery) and control (nonimagery) groups of participants were given the same questionnaire to complete. Results indicate that the experimental group had a significant positive increase in attitudes toward the aged; the control group scores showed a slightly negative nonsignificant change in attitudes.**

**259.** Cornoldi, C., Rigoni, F., Tressoldi, P. E., and Vio, C. (1999). Imagery deficits in nonverbal learning disabilities. *Journal of Learning Disabilities, 32,* 48–57. Participants in this study were eleven Italian boys and girls, ages seven to thirteen years old, who were diagnosed previously as having nonverbal learning disabilities and who exhibited, subsequently, deficits in the use of visual imagery and visuospatial working memory. The children completed a battery of four tasks requiring visuospatial working memory and visual imagery: a memory task composed of pictures and their positions (pictures task), a task that required them to memorize the positions filled in a matrix (passive matrix task), a task to imagine a pathway along a matrix (active matrix task), and a task to learn groups made up of three words using a visual interactive imagery strategy (word-imagery or TV-screen task). When compared with a control group of forty-nine "normal" children, the nonverbal learning disabled children scored lower on all the tasks, showing deficits in the use of visuospatial working memory and visual imagery.*

**260.** Davidson, R. E., and Adams, J. F. (1970). Verbal and imagery processes in children's paired-associate learning. *Journal of Experimental Child Psychology, 9,* 429–35. Participants in this study were sixty-four second-grade boys and girls who were assigned randomly to one of four independent groups: JP, JC, NJP, or NJC where the letter combinations referred to the imagery and verbalization variables used; the imposed imagery conditions were represented by joined pictures (J), not joined (NJ), or side-by-side pictures; and the imposed verbalization conditions were represented by a prepositional phrase (P) and a conjunction phrase (C). Thus, combinations of the levels produced the four experimental treatments involving syntactic and imagery mediators. Results of learning trials indicate that both kinds of mediators facilitated the learning of noun pairs in paired-associate learning tasks, but a minimal language cue (i.e., prepositional connective) was more effective on performance than was imagery.**

**261.** DiVesta, F. J., and Ross, S. M. (1978). The effects of imagery ability and contextual saliency on the semantic interpretation of verbal stimuli. *Journal of Mental Imagery, 2,* 187–98. Participants in this study were 120 female and male college students who generated data in a paired-associate learning and transfer task; the experimental design employed was a 3 × 2 × 2 factorial analysis of variance where the independent variables were imagery ability (high and low imagers), learning context (word, picture, or control), and transfer concept (related or unrelated to the context in the original learning task); the major dependent variable in both the learning and transfer phases of the study was the number of correct responses vis-à-vis the word lists. Results indicate that verbal contexts have little, although positive, effect on transfer of information, whereas the pictorially presented context have strong positive effects on transfer to a related concept, and lesser, but negative, transfer effects to an unrelated concept.**

**262.** Doheny, M. O. (1993). Effects of mental practice on performance of a psychomotor skill. *Journal of Mental Imagery, 17 (3&4),* 111–18. Participants in this study were ninety-five female and male college sophomores enrolled in a clinical nursing course who completed a vividness of movement imagery questionnaire and who were assigned randomly to one of four treatment groups: mental practice only; relaxation only; combined mental practice and relaxation; control (no treatment). Results indicate that there were no significant effects of group assignment/treatment on injection performance; however, a significant effect was found concerning imagery level vis-à-vis performance (it was especially true for participants rated as high imagers), and suggests that mental practice does affect learning and performance of motor skills.**

**263.** Dominowski, R. L., and Gadlin, H. (1968). Imagery and paired-associate learning. *Canadian Journal of Psychology, 22,* 336–48. Describes three experiments on the relationship between imagery and paired-associate learning where over 240 male and female college students completed paired-associates learning tasks. In the first experiment, the rate of paired-associate learning varied with the type of stimulus, from fastest to slowest: pictures (P), object names (ON), and category names (CN); the stimulus materials had similar levels of meaningfulness, and the ON stimuli had shorter imaginal latencies than the CN stimuli. In the second experiment, the ON-CN difference was replicated, but presentation of the appropriate P along with an ON or CN on the first study trial did not aid in the acquisition of either list. The third experiment studied the short-term retention of word pairs; on a measure of conditional recall, forgetting occurred over a period of 18 seconds (mostly in the first 3 seconds), but was unaffected by the type of stimulus used. The researchers suggest that the present experiments show that P, ON, and CN conditions produce different learning rates when used as stimuli in paired-associate lists, but the interpretation of such differences—in terms of differential use of imaginal mediation—seems to be open to question.**

**264.** Ernest, C. H., and Paivio, A. (1971). Imagery and verbal associative latencies as a function of imagery ability. *Canadian Journal of Psychology, 25*, 83–90. Participants in this study were seventy-seven female and male college students who completed an imagery test battery consisting of two spatial manipulation tasks, and an individual-differences questionnaire (this measure yields both a verbal and an imagery score). The reaction times (RTs) of participants high or low in imagery ability were recorded under instructions to elicit a *verbal* associate or arouse an *image* to concrete and abstract noun stimuli. Results indicate that the latencies of the RTs were shorter significantly for the high than for the low imagers, for the concrete than for the abstract words, and for the verbal than for the imagery instructions.**

**265.** Gehring, R. E., and Toglia, M. P. (1989). Recall of pictorial enactments and verbal descriptions with verbal and imagery study strategies. *Journal of Mental Imagery, 13 (2)*, 83–97. Describes two experiments designed to assess the relative efficacy of learning and recall of enactments versus descriptions of events under conditions where participants covertly employ either verbal-sentence or pictorial-imagery study strategies. Based upon the results from forty-one male and female college-student participants, the present study confirms previous research showing that pictorial rehearsal is possible with compound picture/word stimuli and that it may enhance cued recognition memory when the cues are picture fragments.** Also see Alesandrini, K. L. (1982). Imagery-eliciting strategies and meaningful learning. *Journal of Mental Imagery, 6*, 125–40; Bellezza, F. S., and Day, J. C. (1986). The effects of visual imagery of priming memory. *Journal of Mental Imagery, 10*, 9–25; Bichsel, J., and Roskos-Ewoldsen, B. (1997). The effects of practice on the recognition of emergent properties in visual imagery. *Journal of Mental Imagery, 21 (1&2)*, 105–26.

**266.** Giesen, C., and Peeck, J. (1984). Effects of imagery instruction on reading and retaining a literary text. *Journal of Mental Imagery, 8 (2)*, 79–89. Participants in this study were forty-seven Dutch female college students who were assigned randomly to either an imagery instruction condition or to a control condition; in the former condition, participants were asked to form mental images while reading a 2,300-word story, while in the control condition participants were instructed merely to read the story carefully. Results indicate that the experimental group showed better performance than the control group on subsequent questions dealing with concrete-explicit, contradictory, and spatial information items.**

**267.** Groninger, L. D. (2000). Face-name mediated learning and long-term retention: The role of images and imagery processes. *American Journal* *of Psychology, 113,* 199–219. Describes three experiments where over 170 male and female college-student participants were presented with videotapes in which twenty-four students introduced themselves while the participants were given image mediators as learning aids. The first experiment tested participants' recall after one week, the second experiment after three weeks, and the third experiment after two weeks with an added condition involving image-clarity. Results indicate that there is a clear relationship between ratings of image clarity of faces and the later recall of names learned with image mediators. It appears that a reconstructed mental image of a face is isomorphic with the face recognition unit that allows one to recognize a face as having been seen before.**

**268.** Hollenberg, C. K. (1970). Functions of visual imagery in the learning and concept formation of children. *Child Development, 41,* 1003–15. Participants in this study were sixty-four elementary school boys and girls who scored in the upper and lower quartiles of their grades on tests of visual imagery, and who were tested subsequently in an experimental setting that simulated the learning of verbal labels. Results point clearly to a contrast between high- versus low-imagery children in their styles of learning; the high-imagery children demonstrated superior skill in learning specific associations of name and object, yet apparently had less tendency to group into categories a number of objects with the same name. The low-imagery children, on the other hand, appeared to have a superior capacity to form nonverbal meaning categories and to deal with new experiences according to these categories, although they had less facility in the initial specific learning of the names of objects that were members of these categories.*

**269.** Holzman, A. D., and Levis, D. J. (1991). Differential aversive conditioning of an external (visual) and internal (imaginal) CS: Effects of transfer between and within CS modalities. *Journal of Mental Imagery, 15 (3&4),* 77–90. Participants in this study were eighty-eight male college-students who provided data in this mixed design (permitting a comparison to be made of transfer effects of both *between* and *within* participants) that tested the assumption that the construct of imagery may function as a conditioned cue eliciting emotional responding; a classical fear conditioning paradigm was employed in which the conditioning effects of an *externally* presented conditioned stimulus (CS)—that is, a visual stimulus—were compared in the extinction phase with an *internally* presented CS—that is, instructions to imagine; the dependent variable measures employed were skin conductance magnitude and response-frequency scores. Results indicate the successful conditioning effects for the internal CS condition which compares favorably to the external CS data. Thus, support is given here for the position that the laws and parameters governing the conditioning of internal cognitive stimuli are similar to those established with exteroceptive stimuli.**

**270.** Iaccino, J. F., and Sowa, S. J. (1989). Bizarre imagery in paired-associate learning: An effective mnemonic aid with mixed context, delayed testing, and self-paced conditions. *Perceptual and Motor Skills, 68,* 307–16. Participants in this study were forty female and male college students who were presented randomly with three paired-associate lists to learn: normal, bizarre, and mixed lists; all participants were presented with the same sets of sentences for each paired-associate list, and the sentences within each list consisted of stimulus-response pairs of high-imagery nouns. An example of a sentence from the normal list is "the *burglar* found a *necklace*"; an example of the bizarre list is "the *minister* ate the *bible* during services"; and an example of the mixed list is "a *butterfly* takes off with the *coin.*" Half of the participants were tested on an immediate cued-recall condition for each list while the other half of the participants were tested after a one-week retention interval; participants were subdivided further on the basis of whether the presentation was self-paced or forced-paced. Results based on the number of correct terms recalled and imaged appropriately for each list indicated a three-way interaction where the bizarre imagery condition aided immediate recall under the "combined mixed context, self-paced condition." However, concerning the delayed-recall group of participants, context was the determining factor in performance and not presentation pace.** Also see Anderson, D. C., and Buyer, L. S. (1994). Is imagery a functional component of the "bizarre imagery" phenomenon? *American Journal of Psychology, 107,* 207–22.

**271.** Jamieson, D. G., and Schimpf, M. G. (1980). Self-generated images are more effective mnemonics. *Journal of Mental Imagery, 4,* 25–33. Describes three experiments in a paired-associate learning task where participants were thirty male and female college students and nursing students who adopted one of two types of image processing, one in which participants formed images in response to a description given, and a second in which participants generated their own images; all experiments involved a paired-associate learning task in which participants read—and then used—imagery to relate to each of several word pairs; upon later testing, participants were shown the first word of each pair and required to recall the second. Results indicate that generating one's own images internally yields better recall performance than does generating images specified externally by the experimenter.**

**272.** Lowrie, T. (1996). The use of visual imagery as a problem-solving tool: Classroom implementation. *Journal of Mental Imagery, 20 (3&4),* 127–39. Participants in this imagery and learning study were eighty-seven sixth-grade boys and girls who provided data in two experiments on the impact of a visual-spatial learning program on the problem-solving strategies of elementary school children. In the first experiment/activity, the influence of the training program on the methods (visual versus nonvisual) was assessed concerning students' attempts to solve mathematical word problems. The second experiment/activity assessed the impact a visual learning setting has on students' ability to solve problems that require either spatial or analytical knowledge/skills. The results of the first experiment suggest that the visual-spatial learning program did not have a significant effect on the methods—visual or nonvisual—that students used to solve mathematical word problems; and the results of the second experiment indicate the effect of training on success at solving particular types of mathematical problems.*

**273.** Marmurek, H., and Hamilton, M. E. (2000). Imagery effects in false recall and false recognition. *Journal of Mental Imagery, 24 (1&2),* 83–95. Participants in this study were ninety-six female and male college students who listened to fifteen word lists comprising associates of a common nonpresented target word while forming images of either the words' referents or the words printed in a specific font/script. Subsequent to immediate recall and delayed recognition tests, the participants completed picture memory tests, the results of which were used to identify participants as poor or good imagers. The experimental design used was a 3 × 2 between-subjects design (three levels of encoding: referent-imaging, font-imaging, control; and two levels of imagery: high versus low); participants were assigned randomly to one of the three encoding conditions. Results of this study—that tested the hypothesis that imagery facilitates accurate memory and exacerbates false memory—indicate that the immediate recall data are consistent generally with the view that accurate and false memory are driven by common processes; correct recall was poorer following font-imaging than following referent-imaging.**

**274.** Mueller, J. H., and Jablonski, E. M. (1970). Instructions, noun imagery, and priority in free recall. *Psychological Reports, 27,* 559–66. Describes two experiments in which sixty female and male college-students were recruited to test the role of instructions about mnemonics in free recall with a mixed-list of high- and low-imagery items. The experimental design in the first experiment was a 2 × 2 × 2 mixed factorial where the between-participants factors were picture instructions (not given versus given), and sentence instructions (not given versus given), with item imagery (high versus low) as the within-participant factor; and the experimental design in the second experiment was a 2 × 2 × 2 × 2 mixed factorial where picture strategy (not given versus given) and list composition (not informed versus informed) varied between participants, and item imagery (high versus low) and item frequency (high versus low) were the within-participants factors. In the first experiment in which instructional sets varied—with participants instructed to combine words into sentences, mental pictures, or both, or left to their own strategy—results indicate that the pictures group was superior on both high- and low-imagery items. In the second experiment—employing an own strategy only along with pictures instructions for lists varying independently on imagery and frequency, with half of the participants in each group informed of the general composition of the list—results indicate that the pictures set was effective only for the high-imagery items.**

**275.** Paivio, A. (1971/1979). *Imagery and verbal processes.* New York: Holt, Rinehart and Winston/Hillsdale, NJ: Erlbaum. In this well-received and widely referenced book, the author presents a systematic theoretical and factual account of the role of higher mental processes in human learning and memory, and certain aspects of the psychology of language and perception. The major theme of the book is its dual emphasis on nonverbal imagery and verbal processes/inner speech as memory codes and mediators of behavior. An example of the author's summary concerning imagery mediation in learning and memory is the following (p. 351): "The results of numerous studies involving imagery instructions, training on imagery-mnemonic systems, and use of pictures as mediators completely validate the basic assumption behind the classical memory techniques: They can be extraordinarily powerful as memory aids." The useful references section at the end of the book contains over 1,000 citations/references (three dozen of these refer to Paivio's own experimental research) in support of his review of imagery and verbal processes and his postulated two-process approach regarding memory codes and mediators of the higher mental processes in human learning.

**276.** Rimm, D. C., Alexander, R. A., and Eiles, R. R. (1969). Effects of different mediational instructions and sex of subject on paired-associate learning of concrete nouns. *Psychological Reports, 25,* 935–40. Participants in this study were eighty male and female college students who were assigned randomly to one of four treatment conditions: minimal instructions; rote rehearsal, verbal mediation, and visual imagery mediation, and who were required to learn the same paired associates with stimulus and response members being concrete nouns, and approximately equated for imagery values, concreteness values, and meaningfulness values. The training and test procedures were continued until participants were able to complete two successive errorless test trials; the dependent variables were number of trials and errors to criterion. Results based on a two-way analysis of variance test (instructional sets, and sex/gender of participant) indicate that acquisition of material was greatly facilitated under the *visual imagery mediation* (i.e., requiring that the participant create an imagined scene depicting both objects which the words of the associate-pair represented) condition; this finding is consistent with previous findings. However, discrepant with previous findings is the present result of participants' performance under the *verbal mediation* condition (i.e., requiring the participant to use a sentence or phrase containing both members of a given associate-pair) in which their scores were significantly lower as compared with performance scores under the visual imagery mediation instructions/condition. Results indicate, also, that the sex/gender of the participant was not related significantly to performance in this study.**

**277.** Reese, H. W. (1970). Imagery in children's paired-associate learning. *Journal of Experimental Child Psychology, 9,* 174–78. Participants in this study were seventy-one nursery school boys and girls who were assigned randomly to one of four treatment groups (imagery/pictorial-context, replicated-control, new-control, and verbal-context), and given a paired-associates learning/training task to complete; training continued until participants made three consecutive errorless trials. Results indicate that the verbal-context and imagery/pictorial effects are again reliable, but a predicted age difference was not observed in that the imagery condition was equally effective in younger and older preschool children.**

**278.** Richardson, J.T.E. (2000). The availability and effectiveness of imaginal mediators in associative learning: Individual differences related to gender, age, and verbal ability. *Journal of Mental Imagery, 24 (1&2)*, 111–35. Participants in this study were 515 male and female college students (between the ages of seventeen to sixty-nine years old) who were required to learn paired-associates (common concrete nouns) under standard instructions and under imagery instructions. The dependent variables were the probability of correct recall, the unconditional probability of reporting imaginal mediators, and the conditional probability of correct recall given the report of imaginal mediators both under standard instructions and under imagery instructions. Results indicate that the effectiveness of imaginal mediators was greater in women than in men, but only under imagery instructions; the effectiveness of imaginal mediators was greater in younger than in older participants, but only for men; and the availability of imaginal mediators was greater in participants of high verbal ability than those of low verbal ability, but only for men. The references section of this article contains over ninety citations related to the relationships among the variables of gender, age, verbal ability, and imagery.**

**279.** Steinberg, G. M., and Glass, B. (2001). Can the five-step strategy enhance the learning of motor skills in older adults? *Journal of Aging and Physical Activity, 9*, 1–10. Participants in this study were thirty adult men and women (mean age of sixty-five years) who volunteered to take part in an investigation of the effectiveness of a five-step strategy (FSS) program as an instructional strategy for older adults and its influence on adults' level of anxiety. Results based on retention scores of the adults indicate that the FSS group learned a golf-putting task better than did the control group of participants who did not use the FSS.**

**280.** Tracy, R. J., Betts, W. R., and Ketsios, P. (1994–1995). The effect of abstract and concrete contexts on the imageability and recallability of words. *Imagination, Cognition, and Personality, 14*, 227–45. Participants in this study were sixty-six female and male college students who were assigned randomly to one of three context conditions (abstract-abstract, concrete-concrete, mixed), and who were required to rate on a seven-point scale a series of sample words according to the ease with which the words aroused imagery. Results indicate that in the mixed context condition (abstract-concrete), participants rated the abstract and concrete words mixed within the same set of words in a manner that was similar to the way words were rated according to a normal standard; concrete words were rated as more imageable than abstract words; and in the unmixed contents (abstract-abstract or concrete-concrete) groups, where participants rated only abstract words or only concrete words, it was found that concrete and abstract words no longer differed in rated imageability.**

**281.** Wallace, B., and Persanyi, M. W. (1993). Imaging ability, hypnotic susceptibility, and responses to imagery-laden words. *Journal of Mental Imagery, 17 (3&4)*, 195–206. Participants in this study were eighty-four male and female college students selected from a pool of 248 students; selection was based on either high or low scores on a hypnotic susceptibility scale, and scores on a vividness of visual imagery questionnaire. The experimental task involved a recall and recognition test of high- and low-imagery value nouns in a series of paired-associate learning trials. Results of the recall and recognition tests indicate that participants who were judged to be vivid imagers, as well as high in hypnotic susceptibility, showed superior performance as compared to other factorial group combinations, but only for high-imagery nouns.**

**282.** Weber, R. J., and Castleman, J. (1970). The time it takes to imagine. *Perception and Psychophysics, 8*, 165–68. Describes three experiments that studied the effects of visual and speech imagery in letter processing; participants were forty-one female and male college students. In the first experiment, participants were selected on the basis of possessing visualizing ability concerning their projection of an imaginary visual image of letters of the alphabet on a blank screen; in the second experiment, an attempt was made to objectively indicate visual imagery processes by having participants identify spatial properties of letters of the alphabet as they are visualized; and in the third experiment, arbitrary or visual properties of alphabetic letters were employed. Results indicate that in the first two experiments speech imagery is more rapid than visual imagery (about six letters per second for speech versus about two letters per second for vision); also, on postexperimental measures of the subjective fatigue of participants, the visual imagery conditions were perceived as more fatiguing than the speech conditions.** Also see Cocude, M., and Denis, M. (1988). Measuring the temporal characteristics of visual images. *Journal of Mental Imagery, 12*, 89–101; D'Angiulli, A. (2001). Phenomenal and temporal aspects of visual mental image generation: Validating retrospective report in vividness through latency analysis. *Dissertation Abstracts International, 61(9-B)*, 5015.

**283.** Weir, D., and Richman, C. L. (1996). Subject-generated bizarreness: imagery or semantic processing. *American Journal of Psychology, 109*, 173–85. Participants in this study were seventy-two male and female college students who generated data in a 3 × 2 × 2 mixed experimental design where the within-participants variable was the type of sentence or image to be generated (bizarre or common), the between-participants factors were three types of generation tasks (imagery, sentence, or imagery plus sentence generation), and two types of material presentation (twenty-four single nouns or twelve pairs of nouns); half of the participants generated common sentences or images from the same words that the other half used to generate bizarre sentences or images; stimuli consisted of twenty-eight high-imagery, high-concrete, and high-meaningful concrete nouns from a standardized/ normative list of nouns. The dependent variables included three measures of recall of the noun materials: number of nouns recalled, number of sentences accessed, and the number of items per sentence recalled. Results indicate that subject-generated materials produced the bizarreness effect when participants were instructed to image, to create sentences, or to perform both tasks.** Also see McDaniel, M. A., and Einstein, G. O. (1986). Bizarre imagery as an effective memory aid: The importance of distinctiveness. *Journal of Experimental Psychology: Learning, Memory, and Cognition, 12*, 54–65; Wollen, K. A., and Margres, M. G. (1987). Bizarreness and the imagery multiprocess model. In M. A. McDaniel and M. Pressley (Eds.), *Imagery and related mnemonic processes: Theories, individual differences, and applications.* New York: Springer-Verlag; Einstein, G. O., McDaniel, M. A., and Lackey, S. (1989). Bizarre imagery, interference, and distinctiveness. *Journal of Experimental Psychology: Learning, Memory, and Cognition, 15*, 137–46; Hirshman, E. (1988). The expectation-violation effect: Paradoxical effects of semantic relations. *Journal of Memory and Language, 27*, 40–58; Hirshman, E., Whelley, M. N., and Palij, M. (1989). An investigation of paradoxical memory effects. *Journal of Memory and Language, 28*, 594–609; Imai, S., and Richman, C. L. (1991). Is the bizarreness effect a special case of sentence reorganization? *Bulletin of the Psychonomic Society, 29*, 429–32; Kroll, N. E., and Tu, S. (1988). The bizarre mnemonic. *Psychological Research, 50*, 28–37; Worthen, J. B. (1997). Resiliency of bizarreness effects under varying conditions of verbal and imaginal elaboration and list composition. *Journal of Mental Imagery, 21 (1&2)*, 167–93; Dopkins, S. (1996). The role of imagery in the mental representation of negative sentences. *American Journal of Psychology, 109*, 551–65; Fritsch, T., and Larsen, J. D. (1990). Image-formation time is not related to recall of bizarre and plausible images. *Perceptual and Motor Skills, 70*, 1259–66.

**284.** Wharton, W. P. (1987–1988). Imagery and the comprehension of college history tests: Free response measure. *Imagination, Cognition, and Personality, 7*, 323–33. Participants in this study were 192 male and female college freshmen who rated the interest value and comprehension of passages from a standard American History college textbook; two treatments were used of each of four different war periods: the original form followed the text exactly; and the revised form injected into the passages the variable of image-forming words (at an average rate of eight per 100 words). Results indicate that significantly higher scores of comprehension by participants in a free-response test situation are obtained for the revised, imagery-injected passages as compared to the original, untreated passages.** Also see Wharton, W. P. (1985). Imagery and readability of textbooks. In A. A. Sheikh and K. S. Sheikh (Eds.), *Imagery in education*. Farmingdale, NY: Baywood; Wharton, W. P. (1980). Higher-imagery words and the readability of college history texts. *Journal of Mental Imagery, 4*, 129–47.

## MEASUREMENT AND TESTS OF IMAGERY

**285.** Ahsen, A. (1990). AA-VVIQ and imagery paradigm: Vividness and unvividness issue in VVIQ research programs. *Journal of Mental Imagery, 14 (3&4)*, 1–58. Participants in this study were sixty male and female college students who completed Ahsen's adapted version of the Vividness of Visual Imagery Questionnaire (AA-VVIQ), and showed performances of over 200 percent *less* ability to see images vividly when they kept "father" in mind as compared to keeping "mother" in mind when making responses on the imagery test. Moreover, no sex/gender differences were observed among the participants' responses on the imagery questionnaire. In addition to presenting the participants' imagery data in its entirety, Ahsen provides the introduction, test rehearsal, test instructions, and imagery items of the AA-VVIQ.*

**286.** Ahsen, A. (1991). A second report on AA-VVIQ: Role of vivid and unvivid images in consciousness research. *Journal of Mental Imagery, 15 (3&4)*, 1–31. Participants in this imagery study were forty-eight female students from a college in Pakistan who completed Ahsen's adapted version of the VVIQ (i.e., the AA-VVIQ); these participants showed 190 percent *less* ability to see images vividly on the imagery questionnaire when they kept "father" in mind as compared to when they kept "mother" in mind. These results have high agreement with a previous study by Ahsen (1990; see previous entry).*

**287.** Ahsen, A. (1992). Imagery of prayer: A pilot experiment on concepts and content. *Journal of Mental Imagery, 16 (3&4)*, 1–72. Describes the development of an imagery test by the author, called *Ahsen's Questionnaire Upon Imagery of Prayer* (AQUIP); the eight aspects of the test are one's personal view of prayer; forgetting the personal view of prayer; imagery of entering a shop/store to buy something; imagery of a lake in the middle of mountains; imagery of the shop while prayer is kept in mind; imagery of the lake while prayer is kept in mind; imagery of the prayer without the shop or the lake; and comments on the images of the shop, the lake, and prayer under various conditions. Data on the AQUIP from forty adult male and female participants are presented and discussed along with the prevailing concepts of prayer in several theologies. Ahsen provides the directions, rating scale, and AQUIP test items along with the data from the participants who were involved in the pilot study of the AQUIP.*

**288.** Ahsen, A. (1997). Phosphene imagery questionnaire: Third eye, eidetics, hypnosis, and cosmic fantasy. *Journal of Mental Imagery, 21 (1&2)*, 1–104. Describes the development of the author's Phosphene Imagery

Questionnaire (PIQ), which is a twenty-section (with five parts in each section) imagery inventory that involves the experiences of seeing hallucinatory forms (such as dots, circles, and colors), spontaneous scenic images, images of the "third eye," developmental images, and mythological images, including modern images of the extraterrrestrial (ET). Ahsen provides directions and test items for the PIQ, as well as indicating some future research directions that the PIQ, and phosphene investigations, might take (e.g., useful for studying sleepiness/drowsiness, spontaneous imagery, alter self-image, childhood self-image, happiness, success, creativity, memory, organ analysis, phobias, learning disabilities, synaesthesia, allergies, expressiveness, ecology, and "prophets, gods, and aliens").*

**289.** Antonietti, A., and Giorgetti, M. (1996). A study of some psychometric properties of the Verbalizer-Visualizer Questionnaire. *Journal of Mental Imagery, 20 (3&4)*, 59–68. Participants in this study of the internal structure, discriminating capacity, and reliability of an imagery test were 300 male and female college students who completed the Verbalizer-Visualizer Questionnaire (VVQ) as developed by Richardson (1977). Results based on participants' responses to the VVQ indicate the following limitations: there were no close correlations between the items; factor analysis of the VVQ was not consistent with its alleged unidimensional nature; the split-half procedure used for reliability assessment indicated significant but not high correlation coefficients; and scores on the VVQ were influenced by gender differences.* Also see Richardson, A. (1977). Verbalizer-Visualizer: A cognitive style dimension. *Journal of Mental Imagery, 1*, 109–26; Boswell, D. L., and Pickett, J. A. (1991). A study of the internal consistency and factor structure of the Verbalizer-Visualizer Questionnaire. *Journal of Mental Imagery, 15 (3&4)*, 33–36; McGrath, R. E., O'Malley, W. B., Dura, J. R., and Beaulieu, C. (1989). Factors analysis of the Verbalizer-Visualizer Questionnaire. *Journal of Mental Imagery, 13*, 75–78; Parrott, C. A. (1986). Validation report on the Verbalizer-Visualizer Questionnaire. *Journal of Mental Imagery, 10 (4)*, 39–42; Sullivan, G. L., and Macklin, M. C. (1986). Some psychometric properties of two scales for the measurement of verbalizer-visualizer differences in cognitive style. *Journal of Mental Imagery, 10 (4)*, 75–85.

**290.** Baker, S. R., Hill, D., and Paterson, J. (1990). A study on the sequencing effect of images. *Journal of Mental Imagery, 14 (3&4)*, 59–63. Participants in this study of imaging sequences were 108 male and female college graduate students who completed the Creative Imagination Scale (CIS) and who comprised an "original criterion" group, and fifty-six other graduate students who completed a reordered CIS using the Guttman Scaling technique and who comprised a "new scale" group of participants. The CIS consists of ten images that participants are asked to experience with their eyes closed; after the images are administered, participants are then asked to compare what they experienced in the imagery exercise with what they think they would have actually experienced if the experiences would have been real. The results of the reordered CIS indicated a scale containing an improved reliability and internal validity as well as an increase in "reality involvement" that was now measurable.*

**291.** Bernstein, D. M., and Belicki, K. (1995–1996). On the psychometric properties of retrospective dream content questionnaires. *Imagination, Cognition, and Personality, 15*, 351–64. Participants in this study were 106 female and male college students who completed a dream content questionnaire, kept a fourteen-day dream diary on two separate occasions, completed two trait personality inventories, and measures of spatial ability and imaginativeness. Results based on test-retest reliability measures and protocol analyses indicate that: the dream content questionnaire shows acceptable reliability, as well as discriminant and construct validity.*

**292.** Bott, J., and Klinger, E. (1985–1986). Assessment of guided affective imagery: Methods for extracting quantitative and categorical variables from imagery sequences. *Imagination, Cognition, and Personality, 5*, 279–93. Participants in this study were twelve female and male college students who completed the MMPI, an interview questionnaire, and a modified form of the Guided Affective Imagery (GAI) inventory (Leuner, 1984) during which the experimenter served as the guide, using the motif of the meadow; the GAI sessions were tape-recorded, transcribed, and rated by the use of the seven-part GAI Rating Instrument. Results indicate that participants' image transformations are spontaneous even with experimenter interventions that disrupt the flow of the individual's imagery, and that increases in reported detail of imagery require experimenter intervention. Also see Leuner, H. (1984). *Guided affective imagery: Mental imagery in short-term psychotherapy.* New York: Thieme-Stratton; Leuner, H. (1977). Guided affective imagery: An account of its development. *Journal of Mental Imagery, 1*, 73–91; Hudetz, J. A., and Hudetz, A. G. (2000). Relationship between relaxation by guided imagery and performance of working memory. *Psychological Reports, 86*, 15–20; Ahsen, A. (1996). Guided imagery: The quest for a science. *Journal of Mental Imagery, 20*, 165–204.

**293.** Campos, A. (1998). A measure of visual imaging capacity: A preliminary study. *Perceptual and Motor Skills, 87*, 1012–14. Describes the development of a new performance-based imagery test, the Vividness of Visual Imagery Test (VVIT), by the author who recruited 351 Spanish male and female college students as participants in assessing the VVIT and its capacity for imaging in adults. The VVIT is a twenty-one-item inventory where each item requires the participant to visualize a given object and select one of two descriptions of that object, one of which is correct (score 1) and one incorrect (score 0); for example, "How many lines are there in a capital 'e': (a) 3, (b) 4." The overall score may range between 0 (low imaging capacity) and 21 (high imaging capacity). Results based on correlational analyses of the VVIT with the other imagery tests indicate various psychometric limitations of the VVIT.*

**294.** Eton, D. T., Gilner, F. H., and Munz, D. C. (1998). The measurement of imagery vividness: A test of the reliability and validity of the Vividness of Visual Imagery Questionnaire and the Vividness of Movement Imagery Questionnaire. *Journal of Mental Imagery, 22 (3&4)*, 125–35. Participants in this assessment study of two measures of imagery vividness, the VVIQ and the VMIQ, were 125 female and male college students—athletes and nonathletes—who completed both the VVIQ and the VMIQ, as well as a demographics questionnaire that measured amount of mental imagery use and degree of athletic participation. Among the results of data analyses are the following: varsity athletes reportedly made use of imagery to the greatest extent followed by recreational athletes, with nonathletes reporting the lowest usage of imagery in sport.* Also see Hall, C. R., and Martin, K. A. (1997). Measuring movement imagery abilities: A revision of the Movement Imagery Questionnaire. *Journal of Mental Imagery, 21 (1&2)*, 143–54; Isaac, A., Marks, D. F., and Russell, D. G. (1986). An instrument for assessing imagery of movement: The Vividness of Movement Imagery Questionnaire (VMIQ). *Journal of Mental Imagery, 10 (4)*, 23–30.

**295.** Gissurarson, L. R. (1992). Reported auditory imagery and its relationship with visual imagery. *Journal of Mental Imagery, 16 (3&4)*, 117–22. Describes the development of a new scale intended to measure auditory imagery where 160 adult men and women (ages sixteen to eighty-two years old) were recruited via advertisements and served as participants in the generation of data for the assessment of the new scale. Participants completed a vividness of visual imagery test, a control of visual imagery test, and the author's new Auditory Imagery Scale (AIS); the AIS requires that the participant engage in the imagery of sounds (e.g., imagine: sounds growing *loud* and *faint* as in "the sound of a car driving in the road in front of a house"). Results indicate that acceptable internal reliability coefficients were obtained, and all of the items of the AIS loaded on a single component in a factor analytic assessment; moreover, the AIS correlates significantly with the vividness of visual imagery and the control of visual imagery tests.*

**296.** Glicksohn, J. (1991). Cutting the "Gordonian Knot" using absorption and dream recall. *Journal of Mental Imagery, 15 (3&4)*, 49–54. Participants in this evaluative study of the twelve-item Gordon Test of Visual Imagery Control (GTVIC) were seventy-two male and female college students who completed the GTVIC, an absorption scale, and a subjective experience questionnaire. Results of data analyses indicate that the GTVIC's factor of movement correlates well with absorption, and the GTVIC's factor of color correlates with that of dream recall.* Also see White, K. D., and Ashton, R. (1977). Visual imagery control: One dimension or four? *Journal of Mental Imagery, 2*, 245–51.

**297.** Gliner, J. A., and Gliner, G. S. (1984). Use of multidimensional scaling of imagery in assessing the organization of environmental stresses in memory. *Journal of Mental Imagery, 8 (2)*, 45–56. Participants in this study were sixteen male and female college students who categorized nine different environmental stresses into similar groupings under three different conditions (each condition was based on a different time period as to when the stress was to be imagined). A multidimensional scaling technique, called *INDSCAL*, was employed to determine how persons organize their memory structure concerning the relationships among different environmental stresses. Results of participants' performance on the categorization task indicated that each specified time period yielded a two-dimensional solution based on the perception of threat and perceived *psychological* threat (e.g., making a speech in front of a large group of people) was used to label the X axis on a graph, whereas perceived *physical* threat (e.g., being subjected to extremely cold temperatures) was used to represent the Y axis.*

**298.** Heckler, S. E., Childers, T. L., and Houston, M. J. (1993). On the construct validity of the SOP Scale. *Journal of Mental Imagery, 17 (3&4),* 119–32. Participants in this study were 111 female and male college students who were informed that they would view a series of ads and would be asked to rate each ad along a number of different criteria. Following the ad-rating activity, participants were given a recall test concerning the ideas/messages contained in each of the six ads, as well as individual-differences scales (one of which was the Style of Processing Scale [SOP] scale) relative to one's unique information-processing abilities and preferences for visual versus verbal information processing. Results of the data analyses support the nomological validity of the SOP scale.* Also see Reing, A. B. (1983). Correlates of visual-perceptual dysfunction, imaginal behavior, and effective pedagogy: Validation of the Multisensory Imagery Scale (MIS). *Journal of Mental Imagery, 7 (2),* 75–82.

**299.** Huba, G. J., and Tanaka, J. S. (1983–1984). Confirmatory evidence for three daydreaming factors in the Short Imaginal Processes Inventory. *Imagination, Cognition, and Personality, 3,* 139–47. Participants in this study of the Short Imaginal Processes Inventory (SIPI) were 121 female and male college students who completed the SIPI as part of a larger study of inner experience, mood, and drug use. The SIPI is a forty-five-item inventory with three scales of fifteen items each; the items are answered with five-point alternatives (cf. Huba, Singer, Aneshensel, and Antrobus, 1982). Results involving a confirmatory factor analysis of the SIPI showed that the three hypothesized general factors of positive-constructive daydreaming, guilt-fear of failure daydreaming, and poor attentional control were found in the predicted manner.* Also see Huba, G. J., Singer, J. L., Aneshensel, C. S., and Antrobus, J. S. (1982). *Manual for the Short Imaginal Processes Inventory.* Port Huron, MI: Research Psychologist Press.

**300.** Kaufmann, G. (1981). What is wrong with imagery questionnaires? *Scandinavian Journal of Psychology, 22,* 59–64. Reviews research evidence that shows that the questionnaire method/approach often employed in imagery research is inadequate and open to criticism. According to Kaufmann, while *experimental* techniques in imagery research typically show strong effects across a wide range of cognitive tasks, the use of imagery *questionnaires* in such research yields negative and ambiguous results. It is hypothesized that the questionnaire method—when used in the study of imagery—is contaminated by a significant methodological flaw based on differences in subjective conceptions involving the particular rating scale(s) used.* Also see Hiscock, M. (1978). Imagery assessment through self-report: What do imagery questionnaires measure? *Journal of Consulting and Clinical Psychology, 46,* 223–30.

**301.** Kihlstrom, J. F., Glisky, M. L., Peterson, M. A., Harvey, E. M., and Rose, P. M. (1991). Vividness and control of mental imagery: A psychometric analysis. *Journal of Mental Imagery, 15 (3&4),* 133–42. Participants in this study were 2,813 female and male college students who comprised three separate samples and who completed imagery tests consisting of either the Betts's QMI or Marks's VVIQ, each coupled with Gordon's TVIC. Results of participants' performances on these tests indicate a distribution of responses on all three scales (QMI, VVIQ, and TVIC) that were highly skewed with most participants reporting at least moderately clear and vivid images.* Also see Morrison, P. R., and White, K. D. (1984). Imagery control: What is really being measured? *Journal of Mental Imagery, 8 (2),* 13–18; Sacco, G., and Reda, M. (1998). The Italian form of the Questionnaire Upon Mental Imagery (QMI). *Journal of Mental Imagery, 22 (3&4),* 213–27; Slee, J. A. (1988). Vividness as a descriptor and index of imagery. *Journal of Mental Imagery, 12 (3&4),* 123–32; Walczyk, J. J., and Taylor, R. W. (2000). Reverse-spelling, the VVIQ, and mental imagery. *Journal of Mental Imagery, 24 (1&2),* 177–88; Walczyk, J. J., and Hall, V. C. (1988). The relationship between imagery vividness ratings and imagery accuracy. *Journal of Mental Imagery, 12 (3&4),* 163–71; Wallace, B., Turosky, D. L., and Kokoszka, A. (1992). Variability in the assessment of imagery vividness. *Journal of Mental Imagery, 16 (3&4),* 221–30.

**302.** Lorenz, C., and Neisser, U. (1985). Factors of imagery and event recall. *Memory and Cognition, 13,* 494–500. Participants in this study were forty-six male and female college students who completed thirteen tasks, including the following instruments: nine mental imagery measures (e.g., the VVIQ, QMI, VVQ), a number of memory measures, and two measures of the observer/field distinction concerning point-of-view. Results based on correlational analyses, correlation matrix, and principal components analysis indicate three distinct imagery factors (vividness/control; spatial manipulation; and spontaneous elaboration), and a fourth ancillary factor (childhood memory). Also see DiVesta, F. J., Ingersoll, G., and Sunshine, P. (1971). A factor analysis of imagery tests. *Journal of Verbal Learning and Verbal Behavior, 10,* 471–79; McConkey, K. M., and Nogrady, H. (1986). Visual elaboration scale: Analysis of individual and group versions. *Journal of Mental Imagery, 10,* 37–46; Slee, J. A. (1980). Individual differences in visual imagery ability and the retrieval of visual appearances. *Journal of Mental Imagery, 4,* 93–114; Myers, S. A. (1983). The Wilson-Barber Inventory of Childhood Memories and Imaginings: Children's form and norms for 1,337 children and adolescents. *Journal of Mental Imagery, 7,* 83–94.

**303.** Monteiro, K. P., Macdonald, H., and Hilgard, E. R. (1980). Imagery, absorption, and hypnosis: A factorial study. *Journal of Mental Imagery, 4,* 63–81. Participants in this study were ninety-two male and female college students who completed a battery of tests, including the following: two hypnotic susceptibility scales, a creative imagination scale, a mental imagery questionnaire, an absorption scale, and various other subscales of ideomotor behavior and cognitive alterations. Results based on an orthogonal varimax rotation procedure identified four factors: an amnesia/cognitive factor representing one of two main components of hypnotic responsiveness; an ideomotor factor; a creative-imagination factor; and an absorption/imagery factor.*

**304.** Quittner, A., and Glueckauf, R. (1983). The facilitative effects of music on visual imagery: A multiple measures approach. *Journal of Mental Imagery, 7,* 105–19. Participants in this imagery study were ninety male and female college students who were placed into four categories of imaging ability on the basis of their scores on a creative imagination scale. Later, each participant received three experimental treatments in counterbalanced order across participants: control, relaxation, and music conditions. The dependent variables were multiple measures used to assess the effects of the treatments on the production of visual imagery, and included EEG recordings, event-recorder measures, and rating scales. Results indicate that the imagery production of the participants was higher significantly under the music treatment (i.e., "imagine sitting in the midst of a forest," followed by the introduction of music during which participants engaged in free imagery) than under either the relaxation or control conditions.** Also see Viser, V. J., and Gordon, T. (1996). Mental imagery and emotional responses to opposing types of music. *Journal of Mental Imagery, 20 (3&4),* 169–90; Stratton, V. N., and Zalanowski, A. H. (1991–1992). The interfering effects of music with imagery. *Imagination, Cognition, and Personality, 11,* 381–88.

**305.** Rinaldo, R., and Okada, R. (1993). A test of the relationship between imagery vividness and social desirability across subject selection procedures. *Journal of Mental Imagery, 17 (3&4),* 171–80. Participants in this study—which tested the hypothesis that the relationship between imagery vividness and social desirability would be stronger when the customary practice of requiring participant-anonymity was eliminated—were eighty-seven male and female college students, as well as volunteers recruited via an advertisement asking for participants in a study on mental imagery and word recognition. All participants completed the Vividness of Visual Imagery Questionnaire (VVIQ) and the Marlowe-Crowne (M-C) measure of social desirability. Participants completed the measures either alone with an experi-menter, or by having participants identify themselves on the questionnaires; also, a third procedure was employed—for comparison with the other two procedures—where participants responded anonymously. Results of the data analyses indicate a weak, but significant, relationship between the VVIQ and M-C.* Also see Crowne, D. P., and Marlowe, D. (1964). *The approval motive.* New York: Wiley; Walczyk, J. J. (1995). Between- versus within-subjects assessments of image vividness. *Journal of Mental Imagery, 19 (1&2),* 161–75.

**306.** Rizziello, J., and Suler, J. (1992). A computer program for the block figure imagery test: A preliminary report. *Journal of Mental Imagery, 16 (3&4),* 205–10. Describes a computer program for a block figure imagery test (cf. Brooks, 1968; Suler and Katkin, 1988) in which participants—while imaging a series of twenty block-shaped letters and numbers that are posi-tioned between parallel lines—categorize each corner of the figure as either touching, or not touching, one of the lines. The computer program gives the instructions for the task, presents the twenty figures, and records three types of error scores, as well as response-duration time.* Also see Brooks, L. R. (1968). Spatial and verbal components of the act of recall. *Canadian Journal of Psychology, 22,* 349–68; Suler, J. R., and Katkin, E. S. (1988). Mental imagery of fear-related stimuli. *Journal of Mental Imagery, 12,* 115–24.

**307.** Specht, J. A., and Martin, J. (1998). Individual differences in imagi-nal and verbal thinking habits of grade 6 students. *Journal of Mental Imag-ery, 22 (3&4),* 229–36. Participants in this study were 214 sixth-grade boys and girls who completed a shortened version (containing thirty items, fif-teen verbal and fifteen imaginal) of the Individual Differences Questionnaire (IDQ), which is an eighty-six-item questionnaire originally designed to mea-sure adult learners' imaginal and verbal thinking habits and skills (cf. Paivio, 1971). Results of participants' performance data treated by factor analyses indicated a two-factor solution that fit the original IDQ structure; the re-sulting IDQ contains twenty-five items with twelve imaginal items and thir-teen verbal items, and demonstrates acceptable reliability for each of the scales.* Also see Paivio, A. (1971). *Imagery and verbal processes.* New York: Holt, Rinehart, and Winston; Paivio, A., and Harshman, R. (1983). Factor analysis of a questionnaire on imagery and verbal habits and skills. *Cana-dian Journal of Psychology, 37,* 461–83; Bertolo, H., Paiva, T., Pessoa, L., Mestre, T., Marques, R., and Santos, R. (2003). Visual dream content, graphical representation and EEG alpha activity in congenitally blind sub-jects. *Cognitive Brain Research, 15,* 277–84; Burton, L., and Fogarty, G. (2003). The factor structure of visual imagery and spatial abilities. *Intelli-gence, 31,* 289–318; Knauff, M., Fangmeier, T., Ruff, C., and Johnson-Laird, P. N. (2003). Reasoning, models and images: Behavioral measures and cor-tical activity. *Journal of Cognitive Neuroscience, 15,* 559–73; Lequerica, A.,

Rapport, L., Axelrod, B., Telmet, K., and Whitman, R. D. (2002). Subjective and objective assessment methods of mental imagery control: Construct validation of self-report measures. *Journal of Clinical and Experimental Neuropsychology, 24*, 1103–16; Peterson, E., Deary, J., and Austin, E. (2003). The reliability of Riding's Cognitive Style Analysis test. *Personality and Individual Differences, 34*, 881–91; Swaab, T., Baynes, K., and Knight, R. (2002). Separable effects of priming and imageability on word processing: An ERP study. *Cognitive Brain Research, 15*, 99–103; Jorgensen, C. (2003). *Image Retrieval.* Lanham, MD: Scarecrow Press.

**308.** Vooijs, M. W., Beentjes, J.W.J., and VanDerVoort, T.H.A. (1992–1993). Dimensional structure of the Imaginal Processes Inventory for Children (IPI-C). *Imagination, Cognition, and Personality, 12*, 45–53. Participants in this two-part study were 743 Dutch boys and girls in grades three to six who completed a Dutch translation of the IPI-C, which is a test that distinguishes between themes and modes of children's fantasies. In the present samples of Dutch children, a principal components analysis performed on the subscales resulted in three factors that parallel the three fantasy styles found for American children. The three reliable fantasy styles are positive-intense, heroic-aggressive, and dysphoric fantasy styles. An appendix to this study contains all the items for the three newly constructed scales.* Also see Rosenfeld, E., Huesmann, L. R., Eron, L. D., and Torney-Purta, J. V. (1982). Measuring patterns of fantasy behavior in children. *Journal of Personality and Social Psychology, 42*, 347–66.

## MEMORY/WORKING MEMORY AND IMAGERY

**309.** Baddeley, A., and Andrade, J. (2002). Working memory and the vividness of imagery. *Journal of Experimental Psychology: General, 129*, 126–45. Describes seven experiments—involving 126 male and female college-student participants from an applied psychology unit participant panel—designed to study the factors that influence and determine the experiential vividness of images within a working memory framework (*working memory* is a functional system for processing, and short-term storage of, information in performing complex cognitive tasks; it has three subsystems: the central executive, the visuospatial sketchpad, and the phonological loop). Participants were required to rate the vividness of auditory and visual images while performing tasks that disrupted differentially the visuospatial and phonological systems of working memory. Overall results indicate that working memory and long-term memory—especially the variables of meaningfulness, activity, stimulus familiarity, and bizarreness—are involved in the experience of vividness.**

**310.** Bichsel, J., and Roskos-Ewoldsen, B. (1999). Imaginal discovery, working memory, and intelligence. *Journal of Mental Imagery, 23 (1&2)*, 17–34. Participants in this study were ninety-four female and male college students who each were tested on four tasks involving the relations among individual differences in working memory capacity, intelligence, and the ability to discover emergent properties of a visual image where the discovery task involved the mental synthesis of imagined parts; during the imaginal discovery task, half of the participants responded under a time pressure, whereas the other half were given unlimited time. Results indicate that visual working memory related more strongly than verbal working memory to discovery.*

**311.** Campos, A., Lopez, A., and Perez, M. J. (1998–1999). Non-compliance with instructions in studies of the use of imagery as a memory aid. *Imagination, Cognition, and Personality, 18*, 241–49. Participants in this study were 500 Spanish male and female high school students who were given lists of thirty-two word pairs and asked to form normal or bizarre images as aids to remembering the words in each pair; participants also completed a questionnaire regarding the type of imagery used in each case, and produced scores that permitted independent judges to classify each participant as a *complier* or *noncomplier*. Results based on participants' performance in these tasks indicate that the proportion of noncompliers was larger significantly among participants instructed to use bizarre images than those participants who were instructed to use normal images.* Also see Campos, A., and Perez, M. J. (1997). Mnemonic images and associated pair recall. *Journal of Mental Imagery, 21 (3&4)*, 73–82.

**312.** Cornoldi, C., DeBeni, R., Cavedon, A., Mazzoni, G., Giusberti, F., and Marucci, F. (1992). How can a vivid image be described? Characteristics influencing vividness judgments and the relationship between vividness and memory. *Journal of Mental Imagery, 16 (3&4)*, 89–107. Participants in this study consisting of four experiments were 103 Italian male and female college students who generated images using one of six characteristics (color, context, detail, genericity, saliency, shape/contour) at a time, and subsequently completed a recall task of their productions. The main results on vividness of participants' performance in the four experiments are the following: when images are generated using only one characteristic for different stimuli, or for the same stimuli, any of the six characteristics of the image influence vividness ratings to an equal extent; when an image generated both immediately, and as the outcome of progressive construction contains all six characteristics, then some of them are more likely to influence vividness (first of all, shape/contour) than are others, and one characteristic (genericity) loads vividness negatively (in this condition, some characteristics are reported more often than others); participants with high scores on imagery tests tend to evaluate their images as more vivid than do participants with low scores.** Also see Raspotnig, M. A. (1997). Subcomponents of imagery and their influence on emotional memories. *Journal of Mental Imagery, 21 (3&4)*, 135–45; Reisberg, D., Culver, L. C., Heuer, F., and Fischman, D. (1986). Visual memory: When imagery vividness makes a difference. *Journal of Mental Imagery, 10 (4)*, 51–74.

**313.** Dickel, M. J., and Slak, S. (1983). Imagery vividness and memory for verbal material. *Journal of Mental Imagery, 7*, 121–25. Participants in this study were thirty female and male college students who were initially evaluated as good or poor vivid imagers based on the VVIQ self-report measure of imagery ability, and who then either generated their own images to pairs of nouns or had the images suggested to them. Results based on participants' performance on recall tests indicate that the number of pairs of nouns recalled was not related to imagery vividness, and that self-generated imagery resulted in superior recall as compared to the suggested imagery condition.** Also see Tracy, R. J., Pabis, M., and Kilburg, D. (1997–1998). The effect of schematic context on mental imagery. *Imagination, Cognition, and Personality, 17*, 191–214.

**314.** Hall, C., and Buckolz, E. (1982–1983). Imagery and the recall of movement patterns. *Imagination, Cognition, and Personality, 2*, 251–60. Participants in this study on the effects of instruction on imagery recall were forty male and female college students who were presented with a list of movement patterns varying in imagery values and subsequently given a recall test; half of the participants were instructed to mentally image each pattern, while the other half were given no mnemonic strategy. Results indicate that free recall was no better for the imagery-instructed participants than for those who were given no such instructions.**

**315.** Hubbard, T. L., Kall, D., and Baird, J. C. (1989). Imagery, memory, and size-distance invariance. *Memory and Cognition, 17*, 87–94. Discusses three experiments that examined the size-distance invariance hypothesis (SDIH) regarding remembered and imaged stimuli. Participants were 121 male and female college students who were provided with various sets of names of familiar objects, imagery tasks, and memory tasks dealing with size- and distance-features. The following experiments were conducted with their respective results. Participants gave remembered and imaged distances of familiar objects and imaged distance of nondescript rods in Experiment 1, with the result that the relationship between stated size and distance is more adequately described by power functions with exponents less than one than by the more restricted SDIH. In Experiment 2, participants gave distance estimates to recalled and imaged familiar objects and described the visual context in which each object was situated, with the result that there were no significant differences between distance estimates based on memory and those based on imagery. Participants in Experiment 3 estimated the distances to objects in an actual outdoor setting, with the result being a linear relationship between estimated and physical distance, and suggests that the lower exponents obtained in the first two experiments were not merely artifacts of the distance-judgment methodology.**

**316.** Hudetz, J., Hudetz, A., and Klayman, J. (2000). Relationship between relaxation by guided imagery and performance of working memory.

*Psychological Reports, 86,* 15–20. Participants were thirty female and male employees in a university's department of anesthesiology who were assigned randomly to one of three treatment groups (a guided imagery relaxation audiotape group, a popular dance audiotape group, and a no-treatment control group). All participants were given a letter-number sequencing test before and after a ten-minute period of their assigned treatment. Results indicate that the groups' mean test scores increased after the condition of relaxation by guided imagery, but not after the music and no-treatment conditions.**

**317.** Higbee, K. L., Markham, S. K., and Crandall, S. (1991). Effects of visual imagery and familiarity on recall of sayings learned with an imagery mnemonic. *Journal of Mental Imagery, 15 (3&4),* 65–76. Participants in this study were thirty-five male and female college students who generated data in a 2 × 2 × 2 × 3 factorial design with repeated measures on the last three factors; the factors were mnemonic (peg; control), imagery (high, low), familiarity (high, low), and recall measure (immediate, delayed, cued). The material that the participants were required to learn consisted of a list of twelve sayings (e.g.,"curiosity killed the cat") that were selected from a longer standard list of sayings that had been scaled previously for visual imagery and familiarity (cf. Higbee and Millard, 1983). Results of the analysis of variance indicated significant main effects for all four factors (mnemonic, imagery, familiarity, and recall measure).** Also see Higbee, K. L., and Millard, R. J. (1983). Visual imagery and familiarity ratings for 203 sayings. *American Journal of Psychology, 96,* 211–22; Hunter, I.M.L. (1977). Imagery, comprehension, and mnemonics. *Journal of Mental Imagery, 1,* 65–72; Hwang, Y., Renandya, W., Levin, J., Levin, M., Glasman, L. D., and Carney, R. (1999). A pictorial mnemonic numeric system for improving students' factual memory. *Journal of Mental Imagery, 23 (1&2),* 45–69; D'Angiulli, A., and Reeves, A. (2002). Generating visual mental images: Latency and vividness are inversely related. *Memory and Cognition, 30,* 1179–88; DeBeni, R., and Moe, A. (2003). Presentation modality effects in studying passages: Are mental images always effective? *Applied Cognitive Psychology, 17,* 309–24; Spivey, M., and Geng, J. (2001). Oculomotor mechanisms activated by imagery and memory: Eye movements to absent objects. *Psychological Research/ Psychologische Forschung, 65,* 235–41; Ayres, J., and Ayres, T. A. (2003). Using images to enhance the impact of visualization. *Communication Reports, 16,* 47–55.

**318.** Ishai, A., and Sagi, D. (1997). Visual imagery: Effects of short- and long-term memory. *Journal of Cognitive Neuroscience, 9,* 734–42. Examines the various functional properties and underlying brain structures that are common, apparently, between visual imagery and perception, and describes an attempt to differentiate the conditions under which visual imagery interferes with, or facilitates, visual perception. Using their newly designed experimental paradigms (employing detection tasks of a Gabor target), the authors found that imagery-induced interference and facilitation are memory-dependent where visual recall of common objects from long-term memory may interfere with perception, while facilitation occurs on short-term memory tasks.* Also see Craver-Lemley, C., and Reeves, A. (1992). How visual imagery interferes with vision. *Psychological Review, 99,* 633–49; Farah, M. (1989). Mechanisms of imagery-perception interaction. *Journal of Experimental Psychology: Human Perception and Performance, 15,* 203–11; Gabor, D. (1946). Theory of communication. *Journal of the Institute of Electrical Engineers* (London), *93,* 429–57; Ishai, A., and Sagi, D. (1995). Common mechanisms of visual imagery and perception. *Science, 268,* 1772–74; Ishai, A., and Sagi, D. (1997). Visual imagery facilitates visual perception: Psychophysical evidence. *Journal of Cognitive Neuroscience, 9,* 476–89.

**319.** Kavanagh, D., Freese, S., Andrade, J., and May, J. (2001). Effects of visuospatial tasks on desensitization to emotive memories. *British Journal of Clinical Psychology, 40,* 267–80. Participants in this study were eighteen male and female college students who were given repeated exposure to emotive memories—under three exposure conditions (eye movement, visual noise, and exposure alone)—in an attempt to study whether relief of distress from competing visuospatial sketchpad (VSSP) of working memory tasks during imaginal exposure is accomplished at the cost of impaired desensitization. Results indicate that vividness and distress during imaging were lower during the eye movement exposure condition than in the exposure-only condition; also, reduction in emotional responses from baseline to postexposure sessions was equal for the three exposure conditions.**

**320.** Markham, R., and Hynes, L. (1993). The effect of vividness of imagery on reality monitoring. *Journal of Mental Imagery, 17 (3&4),* 159–70. Participants in this study were sixty male and female college students who were distinguished by their scores on the VVIQ as high-imagery or low-imagery individuals; participants were presented with simple and complex symmetrical geometric shapes to rate for complexity (half of the stimuli were presented as half-shapes about their axis of symmetry); two of the four groups of participants were asked to imagine the half-shapes as complete forms before rating them. Results indicate that high-imagery participants given such instructions made more errors than the other groups of participants when later recalling the form of the figures.** Also see Kahan, T. L., and Johnson, M. K. (1990). Memory for seen and imagined rotations of alphanumeric characters. *Journal of Mental Imagery, 14 (3&4),* 119–29; Kunzendorf, R. G. (1992–1993). The effect of image vividness on reality monitoring. *Imagination, Cognition, and Personality, 12,* 197–205; Kunzendorf, R. G., and Karpen, J. (1996–1997). Dissociative experiences and reality-testing deficits in college students. *Imagination, Cognition, and Personality, 16,* 227–38.

**321.** McDaniel, M. A., and Pressley, M. (Eds.) (1987). *Imagery and related mnemonic processes: Theories, individual differences, and applications.* New York: Springer-Verlag. Among the contents in this edited volume are the following topics/titles: Dual coding and encoding; Mnemonic devices and schemas; Theory of encoding and retrieval in use of imagery-based mnemonic techniques; Bizarre imagery; Shared and distinctive information in memory; The picture superiority effect; Individual differences and control of imagery processing; Prose processing; Imagery and memory in the blind; Socioeconomic status and imagery; Adolescence and imagery; Strategy development and imagery; Brain damage and imagery; Educational applications of mnemonics; Mnemonic training; and Study effectiveness. Also see Marschark, M. and Surian, L. (1989). Why does imagery improve memory? *European Journal of Cognitive Psychology, 1,* 251–63; Massironi, M., Rocchi, P. and Cornoldi, C. (2001). Does regularity affect the construction and memory of a mental image in the same way it affects a visual trace? *Psicologica (Universidad de Valencia Facultad de Psicologia, Spain), 22,* 115–42; McDougall, S., and Velmans, M. (1993). Encoding strategy dynamics: When relationships between words determine strategy use. *British Journal of Psychology, 84,* 227–48; Murray, S. O., and Baldwin, D. A. (1996). An analysis of drawing performance based on visually versus verbally generated mental representations. *Journal of Mental Imagery, 20 (3&4),* 153–68; McKelvie, S. J., and Eberman, C. (2001). Visual imagery in recognition and source memory for audiotape and text. *Perceptual and Motor Skills, 92,* 771–76; Paddock, J. R., and Terranova, S. (2001). Guided visualization and suggestibility: Effect of perceived authority on recall of autobiographical memories. *Journal of Genetic Psychology, 162,* 347–56; Riske, M. L., Wallace, B., and Allen, P. A. (2000). Imaging ability and eyewitness accuracy. *Journal of Mental Imagery, 24 (1&2),* 137–48; Dobson, M., and Maskham, R. (1993). Imagery ability and source monitoring: Implications for eyewitness memory. *British Journal of Psychology, 84,* 111–18; Rubini, V., and Cornoldi, C. (1985). Verbalizers and visualizers in child thinking and memory. *Journal of Mental Imagery, 9,* 77–90; White, H. (1988–1989). Sex differences in vivid memories. *Imagination, Cognition, and Personality, 8,* 141–53.

**322.** Persensky, J. J., and Senter, R. J. (1970). An investigation of "bizarre" imagery as a mnemonic device. *Psychological Record, 20,* 145–50. Participants in this study were 179 female and male college students who learned two serial verbal lists under various instruction treatments: free learning (FL)—participants were instructed to learn the material by whatever method he/she would normally use, and with no "peg" (stimulus) words available; paired-associate learning (PA)—participants were given standard paired associate learning instructions; and mnemonic techniques (MN)—participants were instructed to form bizarre images involving the peg and response members of the pairs of words. Results of participants' performance on recall tests indicate that the MN condition best facilitated performance as compared with the FL and PA conditions.** Also see Kroll, N., Jaeger, G., and Dornfest, R. (1992). Metamemory for the bizarre. *Journal of Mental Imagery, 16 (3&4),* 173–90; Lang, V. A. (1995). Relative association, interactiveness, and the bizarre imagery effect. *American Journal of Psychology, 108*, 13–35; Ironsmith, M., and Lutz, J. (1996). The effects of bizarreness and self-generation on mnemonic imagery. *Journal of Mental Imagery, 20 (3&4)*, 113–26; Mercer, C. (1996). The bizarre imagery effect on memory. *Journal of Mental Imagery, 20 (3&4)*, 141–52; Richardson, J.T.E., and Rossan, S. (1994). Age limitations on the efficacy of imagery mnemonic instructions. *Journal of Mental Imagery, 18 (3&4)*, 151–63; Sharpe, L., and Markham, R. (1992). The effect of the distinctiveness of bizarre imagery on immediate and delayed recall. *Journal of Mental Imagery, 16 (3&4)*, 211–20; Tomasulo, D. J. (1982–1983). Effects of bizarre imagery on children's memory. *Imagination, Cognition, and Personality, 2*, 137–44; Webber, S. M., and Marshall, P. H. (1978). Bizarreness effects in imagery as a function of processing level and delay. *Journal of Mental Imagery, 2*, 291–99.

**323.** Saariluoma, P., and Kalakoski, V. (1997). Skilled imagery and long-term working memory. *American Journal of Psychology, 110*, 177–201. Participants in this study were twenty-seven highly skilled and moderately skilled chess players who provided data in one or more of four separate experiments on the relationship between skilled imagery and working memory. Participants were presented with a series of chess games and asked to follow the moves in the games, and subsequently asked to reconstruct chess-piece positions in recall tests. Results indicate that "blindfold chess" imagery formation is independent of the modality of presented information, but it depends chiefly on the piece location information; the more skilled experts' static and dynamic chunks of information formation gave them greater superiority in encoding speed and accuracy as compared to the medium-skilled players.** Also see Binet, A. (1966). Mnemonic virtuosity: A study of chess players. *Genetic Psychology Monographs, 74*, 127–64 (original work published in 1893); Fine, R. (1965). The psychology of blindfold chess: An introspective account. *Acta Psychologica, 24*, 352–70; Hishitani, S. (1989). The usefulness of the studies of imagery experts in imagery research. *Journal of Mental Imagery, 13*, 119–34; Hishitani, S. (1990). Imagery experts: How do expert abacus operators process imagery? *Applied Cognitive Psychology, 4*, 33–46; Holding, D. H. (1985). *The psychology of chess skill.* Hillsdale, NJ: Erlbaum; Saariluoma, P. (1991). Aspects of skilled imagery in blindfold chess. *Acta Psychologica, 77*, 65-89; Hatta, T., and Miyazaki, M. (1989–1990). Visual imagery processing in Japanese abacus experts. *Imagination, Cognition, and Personality, 9*, 91–102.

**324.** Smith, R. T., and Weene, K. A. (1991). The effects of hypnosis on recall of high and low imagery paired-associated words. *Journal of Mental Imagery, 15 (3&4)*, 171–76. Participants in this study were twenty female adult volunteers, ages thirty-six to forty-six years old, who were assigned randomly to one of two treatment groups: hypnotized, and nonhypnotized/control conditions. The stimuli material to be learned were fifteen pairs of low-imagery words, fifteen pairs of high-imagery words, and ten mixed "filler" pairs; the recall stimuli were single words from each of the thirty experimental pairs. Results indicate that the high-imagery word pairs were recalled better than the low-imagery word pairs, and that the hypnosis condition was more effective in recall than the nonhypnotized condition.**

**325.** Yuille, J. C. (Ed.) (1983). *Imagery, memory, and cognition: Essays in honor of Allan Paivio.* Hillsdale, NJ: Erlbaum. Contents in this edited book on imagery/memory include the following topics/titles: Spatial-imagery ability, sex differences, and hemispheric functioning; High-imagers; Picture memory; Imagery instructions and memory organization; Pictures and words in semantic decisions; Comprehension in comparative judgments; Mental color codes; Schemas/images in self-recognition; Paivio's dual-coding model of meaning; Representational memory; Expectancy, equilibration, and memory; Crisis in theories of mental imagery; Emotion, imagery, and verbal codes; and The empirical case for dual coding. The chapters in this book are based on presentations made to a conference held at the University of Western Ontario in June 1981, and marked the tenth anniversary of the publication of Allan Paivio's landmark book *Imagery and Verbal Processes.* Also see Boles, D. B. (1989). Word attributes and lateralization revisited: Implications for dual coding and discrete versus continuous processing. *Memory and Cognition, 17,* 106–14.

## PERCEPTION/SENSATION AND IMAGERY

**326.** Ahsen, A. (1997). Visual imagery and performance during multisensory experience, synaesthesia and phosphenes. *Journal of Mental Imagery, 21 (3&4),* 1–40. This study emphasizes the dynamic relationship that visual imagery has with other sensations in the measurement, exploration, training procedures, and performance of visual imagery variables. The issues, problems, and solutions are indicated, along with examples of multisensory experience, synaesthesia, and the phosphenes. Among the topics covered in Ahsen's essay are the following: the riddles of performance, the third eye, vividness and unvividness, visuality among other senses, paired-arrows experiment (a study of multisensory target shooting), ISM model and mind-body unity, and the heart imagery in seven stages. Also see Gilbert, A. N., Crouch, M., and Kemp, S. E. (1998). Olfactory and visual mental imagery. *Journal of Mental Imagery, 22 (3&4),* 137–46; Ahsen, A. (1993). Heartbeat as stimulus for vivid imagery: A report on individual differences and imagery function. *Journal of Mental Imagery, 17,* 261–66 (also see the same article in *Journal of Mental Imagery,* 1984, *8,* 105–10).

**327.** Bagnara, S., Simion, F., Tagliabue, M. E., and Umilta, C. (1988). Comparison processes on visual mental images. *Memory and Cognition, 16,* 138–46. Participants in this study were fifty-four Italian male and female college students who generated data in three experiments designed to test whether visual mental images and visual perceptual representations have equivalent structural properties and undergo equivalent comparison processes. The authors conclude that the present findings support the equivalence hypothesis in the visual modality where images and percepts are deemed to be equivalent in structure and involve equivalent processing mechanisms.**

**328.** Baird, J., and Harder, K. (2000). The psychophysics of imagery. *Perception and Psychophysics, 62,* 113–26. Describes five experiments—involving seventy-six female and male college students as participants—designed to study the extent to which the interrelations among subjective magnitudes activated by images corresponds to those for subjective magnitudes activated by physical stimuli. Tasks required participants to imagine the magnitude of lights, sounds, and smells under various conditions. Results indicate that persons' estimates based on images demonstrates many of the same patterns as those based on actual physical stimuli. Discussion is provided of two models designed to handle psychophysical tasks—the sensory aggregate model and the judgment option model—in accounting for present results.**

**329.** Brosgole, L., and Maranion M. (1998). Visual imagery and the vertical-horizontal velocity illusion: A failure to confirm Cerf-Beare's findings. *Journal of Mental Imagery, 22 (3&4),* 113–23. Participants in this study were twenty-four male and female adults, ages eighteen to thirty-three years old, who volunteered to provide data in tasks involving the vertical-horizontal velocity illusion; one group of participants consisted of visualizers (those individuals who were able to imagine movement through space), and another group consisted of nonvisualizers (persons who used a counting strategy in the tasks). The aim of the study was to reproduce Cerf-Beare's (1993) finding that there is a vertical-horizontal velocity illusion with imaginary stimuli. Participants were presented with stimuli on a computer screen that moved either horizontally or vertically between two anchor points; the stimuli displaced one-third of the way across the screen and then stopped moving; the task of the participants was to imagine that the stimuli were continuing to move and signal when they reached the end anchors. Results based on participants' responses to three different stimulus velocities indicated that there were no significant directional differences in the time required to reach the different end points, thus failing to confirm Cerf-Beare's (1993) findings.** Also see Cerf-Beare, A. (1993). Visual imagery and the horizontal-vertical illusion pattern. *Journal of Mental Imagery, 17,* 95–110; Olivier, G., and DeMendoza, J.L.J. (2001). Generation of oculomotor images during tasks requiring visual recognition of polygons. *Perceptual and Motor Skills, 92,* 1233–47; Wallace, B. (1984). Apparent equivalence between perception and imagery in the production of various visual illusions. *Memory and Cognition, 12,* 156–62; Pressey, A. W., and Wilson, A. E. (1974). The Poggendorff illusion in imagination. *Bulletin of the Psychonomic Society, 3,* 447–49; Reisberg, D., and Morris, A. (1985). Images contain what the imager puts there: A nonreplication of illusions in memory. *Bulletin of the Psychonomic Society, 23,*

493–96; Wallace, B. (1984). Creation of the horizontal-vertical illusion through imagery. *Bulletin of the Psychonomic Society, 22,* 9–11.

**330.** Farley, F. H., and Cohen, A. (1978). Imagery-based perceptual centering and decentering: Experimental effects and individual differences. *Journal of Mental Imagery, 2,* 199–207. Participants in this study were seventy-three female and male college students who provided data in a 2 × 2 design involving cutaneous stimulation and consisting of imagined location of the experimenter (in front or behind the participant), and imagined location of a clock (frontal or dorsal) with two different order of stimulation (left shoulder–right side, or right side–left shoulder). Results indicate that only the variable of stimulus location had a significant effect on locus of perception, and it is suggested that *decentering* is the dominant mode of perception when the *whole* body is the anchor for the participants' perceptual judgments, while *centering* is the dominant mode of perception when the *head* only is the anchor for the perceptual judgment; also, no sex/gender differences were found.** Also see Holmes, D. S., Roeckelein, J. E., and Olmstead, J. A. (1968). Determinants of tactual perception of finger-drawn symbols: Reappraisal. *Perceptual and Motor Skills, 27,* 659–72.

**331.** Fiss, H., Goldberg, F. H., and Klein, G. S. (1963). Effects of subliminal stimulation on imagery and discrimination. *Perceptual and Motor Skills, 17,* 31–44. Participants in this two-part imagery/perception study were thirty-seven college students and unemployed actors, ages twenty-one to forty-five years old, who sketched/drew spontaneously arising images after being exposed to a subliminal visual stimulus. Results based on participants' verbal reports of their perceptual experiences indicate that while the stimuli exerted a distinctive effect on participants' produced images, they failed to affect the participants' discriminatory abilities.** Also see Parker, A. (2000). An experimental study of the influences of magical ideation and sense of meaning on the attribution of telepathic experience. *Journal of Mental Imagery, 24 (1&2),* 97–110.

**332.** Haber, R. N. (1983). The impending demise of the icon: A critique of the concept of iconic storage in visual information processing. *Behavioral and Brain Sciences, 6,* 1–54. In this essay, the author argues that in perception the notion of an icon as a brief storage of information persisting after stimulus termination cannot possibly be useful in any typical visual information-processing task because the visual world that provides the stimuli for perception is continuous and not chopped up by tachistoscopes, and—because persons' eyes and heads are rarely motionless—no realistic circumstances exist in which having a frozen iconic storage of information could be beneficial; rather, the presence of such an icon interferes with the processes of perception. Haber examines cases of normal perception and reviews experimental evidence on the topics of temporal integration, saccadic suppression, masking, and the photoreceptor basis of visual persistence to demonstrate that a storage of excitation cannot be a useful mechanism for storing information. A lengthy, and excellent, "open peer commentary" section follows Haber's article. Following the commentaries, Haber provides an equally excellent "author's response" section. Finally, the references section at the end of the article contains over 225 citations related to the issues surrounding the icon and iconic memory.

**333.** Holmes, D. S., Roeckelein, J. E., and Olmstead, J. A. (1968). Determinants of tactual perception of finger-drawn symbols: Reappraisal. *Perceptual and Motor Skills, 27,* 659–72. Participants in this study were twenty-six U.S. Army enlisted men who generated data as a result of the experimenter's finger-drawn symbols on participants' foreheads (twenty-eight symbols were drawn on each participant's forehead). The researchers manipulated "set to *respond*" (inside/outside) while "set to *perceive*" remained free to vary; the same participants served in the experimental and control conditions (within-subjects design). In the experimental condition, participants were compelled to adopt an inside perspective in order to respond but were free to perceive with either an inside or outside perspective. It was reasoned, logically, that—because response perspective was held constant—actual *responses* should be an accurate reflection of *perception*. In the control conditions, no attempt was made to force adoption of a perceptual *or* response perspective; therefore, actual responses in the control conditions might or might not be an accurate reflection of perception. It is argued that the different measurement techniques used in the control and experimental conditions represent converging operations (cf. Garner, Hake, and Eriksen, 1956). Results indicate that the main hypothesis of this study (i.e., that all participants perceive figures traced on the forehead as if from an *internal* or *inside* perspective) was supported in that reports of internal perception/ perspective occurred more than 97 percent of the time. In a follow-up, replication study with twenty other male volunteers performing under the same experimental and control conditions, it was observed that 100 percent of the responses were in the expected direction (i.e., an internal or inside perspective). It is suggested that introduction of a "mobile perceiver" (as in various other previous studies) that is free of the physical body is unnecessary conceptually to account for the facts of tactual perception of figures; and terms such as *internal/external* and *mirror-image/same-image* may have derived from, and probably lead to, conceptual confusion and seem to contaminate the spatial orientation of the participant with that of the experimenter.** Also see Garner, W. R., Hake, H. W., and Eriksen, C. W. (1956). Operationism and the concept of perception. *Psychological Review, 63,* 149–59; Duke, J. D. (1966). Perception of finger drawings upon the body surface. *Journal of General Psychology, 75,* 305–14; Natsoulas, T. (1967). On the perception of cutaneous figures. *Psychological Record, 17,* 43–48; Natsoulas, T., and Dubanoski, R. A. (1964). Inferring the locus and orientation of the perceiver from responses to stimulation of the skin. *American Journal of Psychology, 77,* 281–85; Yonge, G. D. (1965). A reinterpretation of the Natsoulas and Dubanoski study. *American Journal of Psychology, 78,* 677–83; Corcoran, D. W. (1977). The phenomena of the disembodied eye or is it a matter of personal geography? *Perception, 6,* 247–53; Hass, R. G. (1984). Perspective taking and self-awareness: Drawing an E on your forehead. *Journal of Personality and Social Psychology, 48,* 788–98.

**334.** Kirk, C. C., and Griffey, D. C. (1995–1996). The effects of imagery and language cognitive strategies on dietary intake, weight loss, and perception of food. *Imagination, Cognition, and Personality, 15,* 145–57. Participants in this study were forty-eight adult men and women who were recruited via news releases/ads in a Wisconsin college town, and who were assigned randomly into experimental and control groups in a study dealing with a new program for weight loss. All participants were weighed, completed a personal information form and informed consent form, and a perception of food evaluation pretest; the control group was dismissed and returned six weeks later for posttesting; the experimental group was given the treatment materials (that included a "Personal Power Pack," and two types of suggestion—a cassette tape of imagery instructions and language suggestions with printed instructions). Results of data treatment indicate that the experimental group experienced a significant average weight loss of 4.9 pounds, and decreased total daily caloric intake by approximately 200 calories per day; the control group gained an average of one pound with a slight increase in daily caloric intake.**

**335.** Kitamura, S. (1985). Similarities and differences between perception and mental imagery. *Journal of Mental Imagery, 9 (2),* 83–92. This essay/review of the psychological literature focuses on the differences and similarities between perception and imagery, specifically in regard to Kurt Lewin's (1951) field theory conceptualization and formulation. It is argued that—regarding aspects in the environment, persons, and events—there is no difference between perception and imagery; however, regarding the notions of *life space* or a *total situation* (including the self as a perceiver or doer), there is a distinct difference between perception and imagery. Also see Lewin, K. (1951). *Field theory in social science.* New York: Harper and Brothers; Howe, E. S. (1985). High communality among judgments of imagined and perceived novel visual dot patterns. *Journal of Mental Imagery, 9 (3),* 45–56; Fallik, B., and Eliot, J. (1985). Intuition, cognitive style, and hemispheric processing. *Perceptual and Motor Skills, 60,* 683–97; Fery, Y.-A. (2003). Differentiating visual and kinesthetic imagery in mental practice. *Canadian Journal of Experimental Psychology, 57,* 1–10; Michelon, P., and Biederman, I. (2003). Less impairment in face imagery than face perception in early prosopagnosia. *Neuropsychologia, 41,* 421–41; Shepard, R. N. (2003). A funny thing happened on the way to the formulation: How I came to frame mental laws in abstract spaces. In R. J. Sternberg (Ed.), *Psychologists defying the crowd: Stories of those who battled the establishment and won.* Washington, DC: American Psychological Association; Tuschen-Caffier, B., Voegele, C.,

Bracht, S., and Hilbert, A. (2003). Psychological responses to body shape exposure in patients with bulimia nervosa. *Behaviour Research and Therapy,* *41*, 573–86; Tversky, B. (2003). Structures of mental spaces: How people think about space. *Environment and Behavior, 35,* 66–80.

**336.** Klatzky, R. L., and Martin, G. L. (1983). Categorical and idiosyncratic imagery as preparation for object perception. *Journal of Mental Imagery, 7,* 1–17. Participants in this study were forty male and female college students who provided data in an attempt to examine the preparatory function of a response-prime in picture perception by manipulating participants' a priori familiarity with featural details of the stimulus pictures. Results of the two studies conducted here indicate the following: in the first experiment, the effect of a verbal prime (object name) was independent from object familiarity, and both verbal and picture primes had an equivalent influence on decisions about familiar objects. In the second experiment, the verbal-prime results were replicated when stimuli were degraded as well as intact. Overall results suggest that the effect of pictorial familiarization is functionally independent from preparation.**

**337.** Kunzendorf, R. G., Thompson, D., and Butler, W. (1995–1996). Percepts considered as "bundles of sensations": The confusion of percepts with afterimages. *Imagination, Cognition, and Personality, 15,* 311–20. Participants in this study were eight male and female college students who were presented with pink light and white light stimuli, respectively to the left and right eyes, and required to make white-pink discriminations initially, and subsequently had their discriminations tested: with pink afterimagery superimposed on the white stimulus, with no pink afterimagery present, and with pink afterimagery superimposed on the pink stimulus. Results of this multiphase procedure indicate that when pink afterimagery is superimposed on white flashes in the right eye, white flashes become harder to discriminate from pink flashes in the left eye; however, when pink afterimagery is superimposed on pink flashes in the left eye, pink flashes become neither easier nor harder to discriminate from white flashes in the right eye. The authors conclude that consistent with the historical assertion that the percept is a "bundle of sensations," the present results show that a pink afterimage—which is the epitome of a sensation—is confused with a pink percept and, considered with other aspects of the present findings, presents a problem for the realists, physiologists, and Behaviorists who have attempted theoretically to reduce the afterimage to something less mentalistic than a sensation.**

**338.** McGuinness, D., and Brabyn, L. B. (1984). In pursuit of visuo-spatial ability. Part I: Visual systems. *Journal of Mental Imagery, 8 (2),* 1–12. Participants in this three-experiment study were 108 male and female high-school and college students who were given a battery of perceptual tests including tests of binocular convergence and divergence, local and global stereopsis, veridical depth perception, and visual acuity, and the results of which were compared to participants' performance on a spatial relations test. Results indicate that the only significant relationship was between spatial ability and global stereopsis; the overall pattern of results suggest that global stereopsis and visuospatial ability share some common central neural mechanism, but this is unrelated to more peripheral mechanisms; moreover, sex/ gender differences were found in the spatial relations test in only one of the three experiments, in favor of the male students.**

**339.** Okubo, M., and Takano, Y. (2001). Absence of perceptual segmentation in image generation by normals. *Japanese Psychological Research, 43,* 121–29. Participants in this study—concerned with the question of whether normal individuals conduct perceptual segmentation while generating visual menatal images—were ninety-six male and female native Japanese speakers who completed one of three tasks: seeing *hiragana* characters and generating a mental image of the corresponding *kanji* characters; seeing *kanji* characters; and seeing *hiragana* characters without generating the image of the *kanji* characters. Results of participants' performance on these tasks indicate that generating an image of a *kanji* character does not transfer to the decision as to whether the visually presented *kanji* character is vertically segmented or not, whereas it does transfer to a semantic decision as to whether the *kanji* character had a concrete or abstract meaning; the task of seeing a *kanji* character transferred to both types of decisions; and the task of seeing *hiragana* characters without generating an image of the *kanji* characters transferred to neither decision (perceptual segmentation decision or semantic decision).**

**340.** Roberts, D.S.L., and Macdonald, B. E. (2000). Influence of protagonists' race and salience and participants' imagery skill on recognition, inferences, and perception. *Journal of Mental Imagery, 24 (1&2),* 149–67. Participants in this study—concerned with the influence of individual's imagery skill, as well as salience and racial content, in an ambiguous film on viewer's information processing—were 240 Canadian white male and female college students who were shown one of four versions of a film; versions of the film differed only with respect to the race of the the actors who were all white, all Asian, one white among Asians, or one Asian among whites. Results based on participants' responses to the film indicate that a bimodal distribution was obtained for story comprehension (with half of the participants making inferences consistent with a *thief* schema, and the other half with a *philanthropist* schema); other results show that participants' higher imagery skill and salience of the central protagonist led to better recognition, less polarized story inferences, and more positive impressions. The researchers attribute the effects of imagery skill and salience to vivid mental images or complex visual representations which, in turn, are viewed within Ahsen's (1988) imagery paradigm (e.g., vivid or salient images are the product of counterbalanced vivid and unvivid information).** Also see Ahsen, A.

(1988). Imagery, unvividness paradox, and the paradigm of control. *Journal of Mental Imagery, 12,* 1–44.

**341.** Roder, B., and Rosler, F. (1998). Visual input does not facilitate the scanning of spatial images. *Journal of Mental Imagery, 22 (3&4),* 165–81. Participants in this study—that investigated whether performance in a spatial imagery task depends on the modality that is used to explore a spatial layout (visual versus haptic) or on the visual condition of the participant (sighted versus blind)—were fifty-one sighted male and female students who explored a spatial map either haptically, visually, or haptically visually, and twelve congenitally blind male and female students who explored the layout haptically. Following the stimulation conditions and complete acquisition of the layout, all participants were tested with a mental image scanning task (on command of two auditory signals, participants had to imagine an object flying on the direct route from one landmark to another on the mental map). Results of participants' performance on these tasks indicate that the time of the imagined movement was a linearly increasing function of the distance between the two involved objects in all groups.** Also see Ewart, A. G., and Carp, F. M. (1963). Recognition of tactual form by sighted and blind subjects. *American Journal of Psychology, 76,* 488–92; Lanca, M., and Bryant, D. J. (2001). Euclidean metric representations of haptically explored triangles. *American Journal of Psychology, 114,* 377–409.

**342.** Roskos-Ewoldsen, B. (1998). Recognizing emergent properties of images and percepts: The role of perceptual goodness in imaginal and perceptual discovery. *Journal of Mental Imagery, 22 (3&4),* 183–212. Participants in this study—consisting of three experiments that investigated discovery within imagined and perceived patterns—were 390 female and male college students who were required to construct patterns by imagining (or drawing) one part and then another, and subsequently mentally synthesizing the parts. Participants were tested under various conditions: with one of the original parts; with parts that emerged from the synthesis, or with nonparts. The results from the first experiment indicated that emergent parts are discoverable, but less so than the original parts; in the second experiment, the affect of perceptual organization was studied by varying the goodness of the pattern and the goodness of the parts; and the third experiment examined the goodness of the parsing condition. Overall results indicate that imaginal discovery is facilitated when the pattern is poor and the parts are good, and when the parsing is good.**

**343.** Rossi, A. M., Sturrock, J. B., and Solomon, P. (1963). Suggestion effects on reported imagery in sensory deprivation. *Perceptual and Motor Skills, 16,* 39–45. Participants in this study—which examined the extent to which verbal reports of experienced imagery in sensory deprivation conditions are affected by suggestion—were eighteen male college students who were required to experience the same standard series of eleven images under four conditions: hypnosis, sensory deprivation (involving halved ping-pong balls covering participants' eyes, and earphones covering their ears), drug (placebo), and normal. At the end of each condition, participants completed a questionnaire dealing with the clarity and vividness of their experienced images. Results indicate that there was a significant increase in the reported vividness of imagery experienced under the hypnosis condition; moreover, the findings of *no* reported increases in vividness of imagery under the other two experimental conditions here (i.e., the placebo and sensory deprivation conditions) indicates that the variable of suggestion has little or no influence on the verbal reports of imagery experienced under those conditions.** Also see Heinemann, L. G. (1970). Visual phenomena in long sensory deprivation. *Perceptual and Motor Skills, 30*, 563–70; Stewart, H. (1965). Sensory deprivation, personality, and visual imagery. *Journal of General Psychology, 72*, 145–50.

**344.** Segal, S. J. (1968). Patterns of response to thirst in an imaging task (Perky technique) as a function of cognitive style. *Journal of Personality, 36*, 574–88. Participants in this study—which investigated the effect of perceived needs on fantasy and reality-testing using an adaptation of the Perky (1910) technique—were thirty-eight female student nurses who were asked to imagine various need-relevant and neutral items, and as they described the imagery, a faint stimulus was presented to their view supraliminally. The nature of the reported imagery, and the accuracy with which participants detected the stimulus, were compared both in thirsty and nonthirsty/sated participants. Results indicate that there was a slight but significant tendency for thirsty participants to be less accurate than nonthirsty participants in reporting the stimulus and more likely to assimilate the colors and forms of the stimulus into their imagery descriptions.** Also see Perky, C. W. (1910). An experimental study of imagination. *American Journal of Psychology, 21*, 422–52; Segal, S. J. (1964). The Perky effect: Incorporation of an external stimulus into an imagery experience under placebo and control conditions. *Perceptual and Motor Skills, 18*, 385–95; Segal, S. J., and Glicksman, M. (1967). Relaxation and the Perky effect: The influence of body position on judgments of imagery. *American Journal of Psychology, 80*, 257–62; Segal, S. J., and Gordon, P.-E. (1969). The Perky effect revisited: Blocking of visual signals by imagery. *Perceptual and Motor Skills, 28*, 791–97; Giddan, N. S. (1966). Effect of thirst on stimulus recovery and spontaneous imagery. *Perceptual and Motor Skills, 23*, 631–38.

**345.** Trotto, P. A., and Tracy, R. J. (1993–1994). The effect of implied motion on the recall of interactive pictures. *Imagination, Cognition, and Personality, 13*, 249–58. Participants in this study—which explored the effects that implied motion have on the processing of visual information—were sixty-eight male and female college students in a pilot sudy, and 128 female and male college students in the main study, who generated data in a 2 × 2 × 2 factorial design where the first factor was motion (implied motion or stationary). The second factor was viewing time (short or long); and the third factor was picture order (random-order one or random-order two); participants were assigned randomly to each experimental condition in which sixteen picture pairs were presented and where, subsequently, participants wrote a description of the stimuli observed, as well as rating the imageability of each pair; after all the pictures were given, the participants were asked to free recall the stimulus pairs. Results of the studies indicate that implied motion pictures that are presented at a short viewing time are more nameable and better recalled than stationary pictures presented at a short viewing time; however, when participants are given more time to view visual information, implied motion and stationary pictures are equally nameable and recalled.\*\*

**346.** Wallace, B. (1990). Imagery vividness, hypnotic susceptibility, and the perception of fragmented stimuli. *Journal of Personality and Social Psychology, 58,* 354–59. Participants in this study—which investigated the role of hypnotic susceptibility level (high or low) and imaging ability (vivid or poor) in the performance of Gestalt closure tasks—were eighty-eight female and male college students who provided data in two experiments. In the first study, participants were required to identify fragmented stimuli in closure-speed tests, and in the second study, participants reported on fragmented stimuli that were projected to the right eye and subsequently produced an afterimage; also, participants were asked to identify the composite (if possible) and to report on the duration of the afterimage. Results from both experiments indicate that hypnotic susceptibility level and imaging ability influenced reports of Gestalt closure.\*\*

## PERSONALITY/INDIVIDUAL AND GENDER DIFFERENCES AND IMAGERY

**347.** Anderson, R. E. (1973). Individual differences in the use of imaginal processing. Unpublished doctoral dissertation, University of California, San Diego. Describes three experiments—with male and female college-student participants—conducted to help resolve various discrepancies between the results of previous studies that directly manipulated the use of imaginal processing and those obtained from studies of individual differences in imagery ability. It is concluded that—given a distinction between the possession of imagery ability and the use of imagery—the results obtained from individual differences studies in imagery ability are compatible with the results of studies in which either instructional set or stimulus concreteness are varied; that is, for imagery ability to exert a positive influence on retention, imaginal processing must be elicited by the experimental task, the experimental stimuli, or by suitable instructions; when any of these conditions are met, high-imagers show superior retention of material. The references section at the end of this work contains over 120 citations related to the issue of individual differences in imagery and imaginal processing.\*\* Also see Hall,

V. C., Talukder, A., and Esposito, M. (1989). Individual differences in the ability to learn and recall with or without imagery mnemonics. *Journal of Mental Imagery, 13*, 43–54; Stricklin, A. B., and Penk, M. L. (1980). Vividness and control of imagery in personality types. *Journal of Mental Imagery, 4*, 111–14; Dean, G. M., and Morris, P. B. (2003). The relationship between self-reports of imagery and spatial ability. *British Journal of Psychology, 94*, 245–73; Toyota, H. (2002). The bizarreness effect and individual differences in imaging ability. *Perceptual and Motor Skills, 94*, 533–40.

**348.** Baron, G., and Cautela, J. R. (1983–1984). Imagery assessment with normal and special needs children. *Imagination, Cognition, and Personality, 3*, 17–30. In this essay/review of covert conditioning and other imagery-based techniques used in the treatment of a variety of children's clinical problems, the authors present a behavioral perspective and procedures on the clinical use of imagery with children. The authors provide several case studies in their attempts to set down some objective criteria concerning a child's readiness to use imagery, and clinical guidelines for assessing and monitoring a child's ongoing use of imagery. They provide, also, a Functional Imagery Survey for use by clinicians to assess a child's capabilities in imaging.*

**349.** Brown, D., Forte, M., Rich, P., and Epstein, G. (1982–1983). Phenomenological differences among self hypnosis, mindfulness mediation, and imaging. *Imagination, Cognition, and Personality, 2*, 291–309. Describes a survey of 122 male and female participants—via a questionnaire called the Profile of Trance, Imaging, and Meditation Experience (TIME)—in the examination of the differences in phenomenological quality of three types of awareness experiences: self-hypnosis, waking deaming, and mindfulness meditation (i.e., a retreat format/setting in which the routine involves a continuous alternation between hourly periods of sitting and walking meditation over a span of sixteen hours daily). Analyses of the survey data reveal a number of phenomenological dimensions in the areas of attention, thinking, memory, imagery, body sensations, emotions, time sense, reality sense, and sense of self that distinguish among the experiences of practitioners of the three types of awareness training.*

**350.** Campos, A., and Sueiro, E. (1993). Sex and age differences in visual imagery vividness. *Journal of Mental Imagery, 17 (3&4)*, 91–94. Participants in this study were 289 Spanish male and female volunteers, ages fourteen to sixty years old, who completed the Vividness of Visual Imagery Questionnaire; this instrument contains sixteen items scored on a five-point vividness scale, administered once with the eyes open and once with the eyes closed (the lower the score, the more vivid the imagery). Results of participants' data treated by a two-way analysis of variance (sex-by-age) indicate that visual imagery vividness is influenced significantly by sex/gender, but age by itself, and the cross-term, showed no significant effects.

**351.** Cocude, M., Charlot, V., and Denis, M. (1997). Latency and duration of visual mental images in normal and depressed subjects. *Journal of*

*Mental Imagery, 21 (1&2)*, 127–42. Participants in this study were sixteen adult men and women volunteers without any psychiatric history (control group) and sixteen adult men and women inpatients diagnosed as suffering from severe depression (experimental group); the control and experimental groups were matched for socioeconomic status and education (both groups had similar number of years of secondary education). Participants were presented with nouns and asked to form visual mental images in response to the words; the generation latencies and durations of images—as shown by participants' pressing a key—were recorded. Results for the control group indicate that the higher the noun imagery value, the shorter the generation latencies, but that imagery value did not influence image duration (this pattern remained constant across two sessions conducted three weeks apart). On the other hand, the depressed participants failed to form images, especially in response to low imagery nouns, but this effect was reduced significantly by antidepressant treatment.**

**352.** Cornoldi, C., DeBeni, R., Roncari, S., and Romano, S. (1989). The effects of imagery instructions on total congenital blind recall. *European Journal of Cognitive Psychology, 1*, 321–31. Participants in this two-experiment imagery study were twenty-eight totally and congenitally blind (TCB) Italian adult men and women, and twenty-eight normally sighted (control) Italian adult men and women volunteers who where matched for age, level of education, and sex/gender. All participants were presented (read to them by the experimenter) a series of concrete, high-frequency Italian nouns, and asked to form a common or bizarre image for each, describe it in a short sentence, and keep it in mind until the next noun was read; another group of participants in the verbal group were given a noun asked to form a simple common or bizarre sentence (noun plus verb plus noun), and rehearse it in the time available. Subsequently, participants were asked to predict what type of material (common versus bizarre) they remembered best; and they were also given an incidental free recall test of the materials. Results of two experiments indicate that the TCB participants—in a free recall task of unrelated nouns—may take advantage of imagery instructions independently of the particular requirement to form either common or bizarre images.** Also see Aleman, A., VanLee, L., Mantione, M., Verkoijen I., and DeHaan, E. (2001). Visual imagery without visual experience: Evidence from congenitally totally blind people. *Neuroreport: For Rapid Communication of Neuroscience Research, 12*, 2601–4; Cornoldi, C., and Guglielmo, A. (2001). Children who cannot imagine. *Korean Journal of Thinking and Problem Solving, 11*, 99–112; Barolo, E., Masini, R., and Antonietti, A. (1990). Mental rotation of solid objects and problem-solving in sighted and blind subjects. *Journal of Mental Imagery, 14 (3&4)*, 65–74; Marchant, B., and Malloy, T. E. (1984). Auditory, tactile, and visual imagery in PA learning by congenitally blind, deaf, and normal adults. *Journal of Mental Imagery, 8 (2)*, 19–32; Miller, L. (1985). Mindsight: Mental images of the blind. *Psychology Today, 19*, 14.

**353.** Council, J. R., Chambers, D., Jundt, T. A., and Good, M. D. (1990–1991). Are the mental images of fantasy-prone persons really more "real"? *Imagination, Cognition, and Personality, 10,* 319–27. Participants in this two-part study were sixty-eight female and male college students who initially completed a fantasy-proneness inventory and an imagery-vividness questionnaire. Subsequently, an experimental procedure involving four steps was presented: perceptual training on reversible figures; forming a visual image of an ambiguous figure; perceptual training on the drawing of another ambiguous figure; and recalling the visual image encoded in the second step, and attempting to discover its alternative interpretations. Results indicate that of the sixty-eight participants who completed the imagery task, only seven found the alternative construal of an ambiguous figure ("Jastrow's Duck/Rabbit" figure) by inspecting their mental images of this figure.\*\*

**354.** Ernest, C. H., and Paivio, A. (1971). Imagery and sex differences in incidental recall. *British Journal of Psychology, 62,* 67–72. Participants in this two-experiment study of gender/sex differences in imagery were 138 female and male college students who completed imagery tests that identified them as high, medium, or low imagers, and were given, subsequently, tests for incidental recall in two studies involving pictures and words as stimulus material; the free recall instructions, although informing the participants that the items were printed in different colors, stressed the recall of the words and pictures only. Following trials of presentation of stimuli, a test of incidental learning was given concerning the previously presented stimulus items. In the first experiment, high-imagery men showed superior performance over the low-imagery men in intentional free recall of words, but the reverse relation occurred with women participants; no relation was observed between imagery ability and incidental recall for stimulus color. In the second experiment, results indicate that high-imagery participants were more accurate than low imagers in the recognition task; and, also, high-imagery women—but not men—demonstrated superior incidental recall of the stimuli as compared with the low-imagery women.\*\*

**355.** Gaddes, W. H., McKenzie, A., and Barnsley, R. (1968). Psychometric intelligence and spatial imagery in two Northwest Indian and two white groups of children. *Journal of Social Psychology, 75,* 35–42. Participants in this cross-cultural study of imagery were 124 elementary school boys and girls, ages six to fourteen years old, in four groupings: white, rural children; white, urban children; Indian (Vancouver Island Salish), urban children; and Indian (Kwakiutl), rural/isolated children. The dependent variables were scores on batteries of intelligence tests, including performance on spatial imagery items; the independent variable included two racial groups, Northwest Indian and Canadian white children. Results of participants' performance on the tests demonstrated neither superiority nor inferiority of spatial imagery of the Indian children when compared with white children matched broadly for age, sex/gender, intelligence, and socioeconomic status.\*

**356.** Giambra, L. M. (1988–1989). The influence of subject-experimenter sexual congruence on the frequency of task-unrelated imagery and thought: Further evidence. *Imagination, Cognition, and Personality, 8,* 249–60. Participants in this four-experiment study concerning task-unrelated imagery and thought (TUIT) were 330 male and female volunteers, ages seventeen to ninety-two, who provided TUIT data in a vigilance task where the focal variable was the sex/gender of the experimenter and the participant. Results indicate that in all experiments there were more TUITs when the experimenter and participant were of the *opposite* sex/gender than when they were of the *same* sex/gender (however, only one experiment found a significant relationship).**

**357.** Goldston, D. B., Hinrichs, J. V., and Richman, C. L. (1985). Subjects' expectations, individual variability, and the scanning of mental images. *Memory and Cognition, 13,* 365–70. Participants in this study were seventy-two male college students who provided data in a mental imagery scanning task (concerning the map of a fictional island) that involved four different instructional-set groups: a positive-expectation group, a negative-expectation group, a zero-expectation group, and a no-expectation group. Results from participants' performance on the mental map scanning task indicate that individual participants' scanning-time/distance correlations vary as a function of instructional-set (and, hence, a priori expectations), and reveal a large degree of individual variability in scanning-time/distance correlations.**

**358.** Gralton, M. A., Hayes, Y. A., and Richardson, J.T.E. (1979). Introversion-extraversion and mental imagery. *Journal of Mental Imagery, 3,* 1–10. Participants in this study were forty female and male college students who provided data in a standard learning-recall task involving lists of concrete and abstract nouns; they also completed a personality inventory from which scores on the dimension of introversion-extraversion were obtained. Essentially, this study was designed to test the hypothesis that the participants' extraversion would be negatively correlated with their ability to use mental imagery as a mnemonic code. Results indicate that the prediction was confirmed where findings indicate a negative correlation between extraversion and recall. This correlation was found with both concrete and abstract material, and was eliminated when the participants were tested by an experimenter of the opposite sex/gender.** Also see Strelow, B. R., and Davidson, W. B. (2002). Introversion-extraversion, tempo, and guided imagery. *Psychological Reports, 90,* 619–26; Knapp, R. H., and Lapuc, P. S. (1965). Time imagery, introversion, and fantasied preoccupation in simulated isolation. *Perceptual and Motor Skills, 20,* 327–30.

**359.** Honeycutt, J. M., Edwards, R., and Zagacki, K. S. (1989–1990). Using imagined interaction features to predict measures of self-awareness: Loneliness, locus of control, self-dominance, and emotional intensity. *Imagination, Cognition, and Personality, 9,* 17–31. Participants in this study were 290 female and male college students who completed the Survey of Imagined

Interaction (SII), an imagery multidimensional instrument, and provided data for assessment of the multivariate relationship between general characteristics of imagined interactions and various measures of self-awareness and emotional intensity. Data from measures reflecting the factors of loneliness, locus of control, dominance-in-imagined-interaction, and feeling-satisfaction and pleasant-with-an-imagined-interaction were regressed on the general dimensions of the SII, and results from the regression models are examined in terms of imagined interactions associated with, and possibly creating, more self-awareness. It is concluded that structural relationships exist between the general imagined interaction features and the various dependent variables. For instance, having imagined interactions with different individuals on different topics is related to internal locus of control and, in possessing an imagined interaction, the person may call up procedural records that set up action sequences for expected encounters. Moreover, by possessing a variety of imagined interactions, the individual may develop plans for interactions where contingency plans may be conjured up and mentally tested.*

**360.** Isaac, A. R., and Marks, D. F. (1994). Individual differences in mental imagery experience: Developmental changes and specialization. *British Journal of Psychology, 85,* 479–500. Participants in this five-part study—which had the two purposes of examining the developmental changes and differences in visual and movement imagery in male and female children and adults, and examining whether systematic differences in imagery vividness may be measured in specialist groups—were 1,202 female and male adults and children, ages seven to fifty years old, who completed the Vividness of Visual Imagery Questionnaire and the Vividness of Movement Imagey Questionnaire. Results indicate the following: significant increases in imagery vividness for female participants at eight to nine years old, and for male participants at ten to eleven years of age. In general, women report more vivid imagery than men; participants aged seven to fifteen years old with poor movement control were extemely poor imagers with 42 percent reporting no imagery at all; physical education students reported more vivid imagery than students majoring in physics, English, and surveying; significant differences were found between the imagery of elite athletes and that of matched controls; and air traffic controllers and pilots reported significantly more vivid imagery than matched control groups. The references section of this article contains over ninety citations/references related to the issue of individual differences in mental imagery.*

**361.** James, J. W., and Moore, D. M. (1991). Effects of imposed visuals and instructions to image in students of varying ages and cognitive styles. *Journal of Mental Imagery, 15 (3&4),* 91–110. Participants in this study were 197 female and male students in grade levels from fourth to tenth grade who provided data in a 3 × 3 × 3 posttest-only design where the independent variables were cognitive (field dependent, neutral, field independent) as measured by an embedded-figures test, grade level (fourth, seventh, and tenth grades), and teaching strategy (printed words only/control, imposed visuals, and instructions to image); the dependent variable was a written, immediate recall test of twenty-four concrete paired-associate nouns. Results indicate that all three main effects (grade level, cognitive style, and visual strategy) were significant, with no interaction effects present. Two useful appendixes are attached to this article, one containing the experimental word-pairs used, and the other providing the imagery and concreteness ratings of the experimental words employed.** Also see Greeson, L. E. (1989). Modeling and mental imagery use by preschool children as a function of age, task type, and instructional set. *Journal of Mental Imagery, 13,* 39–42; Lutz, B. L. (1980). A study of the relationship between visual imagery and reading comprehension of third and sixth grade children. Unpublished doctoral dissertation, Oklahoma State University; Kitchenham, A. (1997). Gender differences in mental imagery in grade 10s' reader response to a poem. *Journal of Mental Imagery, 21 (3&4),* 111–34.

362. Kelley, K. (1984-85). Sexual fantasy and attitudes as functions of sex of subject and content of erotica. *Imagination, Cognition, and Personality, 4,* 339–47. Participants in this study were 246 male and female college students who viewed stimulus slides containing explicit sexual material. Following this, participants responded to a number of brief scales assessing affective and sexual arousal behavior. Subsequently, participants were asked to create a sexual fantasy scenario/story. Results indicate that when the erotic content of the slides consisted of mild erotica showing men rather than women, the male participants expressed significantly more negative themes in their briefer fantasy productions than did the female participants.* Also see Campagna, A. F. (1985–1986). Fantasy and sexual arousal in college men: Normative and functional aspects. *Imagination, Cognition, and Personality, 5,* 3–20; Hardin, K. N., and Gold, S. R. (1988–1989). Relationship of sex, sex guilt, and experience to written sexual fantasies. *Imagination, Cognition, and Personality, 8,* 155–63; Lentz, S. L., and Zeiss, A. M. (1983–1984). Fantasy and sexual arousal in college women: An empirical investigation. *Imagination, Cognition, and Personality, 3,* 185–202; Kelley, K., and Byrne, D. (1978). The function of imaginative fantasy in sexual behavior. *Journal of Mental Imagery, 2,* 239–46.

363. Klinger, E. (1967). Modeling effects on achievement imagery. *Journal of Personality and Social Psychology, 7,* 49–62. Participants in this two-experiment study were 333 male college-student volunteers who provided data concerning the effects of televised models' nonverbal behavior on stories told to Thematic Apperception Test (TAT)–like pictures; actor-models portrayed achievement-oriented, neutral, or affiliative characters in several roles. Results indicate that participants exposed only visually to achievement-oriented models in interpersonal activity produced higher levels of overall and hero need-achievement (nAch) than did participants who were exposed

to affiliative or neutral models.** Also see Shrable, K., and Stewart, L. H. (1967). Personality correlates of achievement imagery: Theoretical and methodological implications. *Perceptual and Motor Skills, 24,* 1087–98.

**364.** Kunzendorf, R. G., Moran, C., and Gray, R. (1995–1996). Personality traits and reality-testing abilities, controlling for vividness of imagery. *Imagination, Cognition, and Personality, 15,* 113–31. Participants in this study were 178 female and male college students who completed a battery of tests including personality measures and reality-discrimination measures, as well as a timed-discrimination task. In the present task, participants fixated on a dot on a computer screen, perceived a stimulus to one side, imaged an identical stimulus on the other side and rated its vividness while continuing to image. Subsequently, either the dot became a letter P (and participants pressed a button on the side of the *percept* as quickly as possible), or the dot became a letter I (and participants pressed a button on the side of the *image*). Results based on data from participants' image/percept discrimination times over image-vividness ratings indicate that the self-described hallucinators and the personality-test defined paranoids among the participants discriminated percepts less quickly from vivid images, almost as if the greater "central innervation" behind more vivid images was not registered by the psychosis-prone participants.** Also see Kunzendorf, R. G. (1987–1988). Self-consciousness as the monitoring of cognitive states: A theoretical perspective. *Imagination, Cognition, and Personality, 7,* 3–21 (this article contains over 110 citations/references related to self-conscious monitoring).

**365.** Langham-Johnson, S. (1985–1986). Fundamental differences in imagery workspaces in young adults. *Imagination, Cognition, and Personality, 5,* 249–54. Participants in this study were ninety-six female and male college students who completed a twenty-item questionnaire (e.g., "In my mind I have a workspace where I can write and do math problems with mental images") containing nine characteristics of mental imagery workspaces. Results indicate that a significantly higher frequency of mental imagery workspaces were reported by men than by women. In addition characteristics of imagery reported by participants include presence or absence of mental imagery, color, black and white, movement, images of numerals, ability to control the onset and erasure of the mental imagery workspace, and use of imagery to do mathematics.*

**366.** Lyman, B., and Waters, J. (1989). Patterns of imagery in various emotions. *Journal of Mental Imagery, 13,* 63–74. Participants in this study were sixty-two female and male college students who reported on the imagery they felt was present during twenty-six different emotions; the reports were analyzed for the number of images, the kinds of images, and ten qualities of the imagery. Results indicate that there are distinctive patterns of image referents, qualities, and themes that differently characterize a variety of emotions. For example, in a number of negative emotions (anxiety, boredom, depression, envy, guilt, loneliness, rage, and shame) where one might expect imagery of other people to play a major role, people referents are not notably high (they approach a significant level only for the condition of loneliness). This was true, also, for the positive emotions of contentment, happiness, and joy which show notably frequent references to nature, but not to people or to manmade objects/features.* Also see Kovach, B. E. (1988). Imagery, personality, and emotional response. *Journal of Mental Imagery, 12 (3&4)*, 63–73.

**367.** McGuinness, D., and McLaughlin, L. (1982). An investigation of sex differences in visual recognition and recall. *Journal of Mental Imagery, 6*, 203–12. Participants in this two-experiment imagery study were eighty male and female college and high school students who provided data on visual recognition and visual recall tasks using pictorial stimuli. Results of both studies on recognition memory demonstrate that the sexes/genders do *not* differ in their ability to recognize pictorial information; however, in the high school participants, girls were found to exhibit a bimodal distribution with about one-quarter of them showing very superior recognition memory skills, and about one-third showing inferior recognition memory; the boys in this group showed a more uniform distribution concerning recognition memory.* Also see McGuinness, D., and Morley, C. (1991). Sex differences in the development of visuo-spatial ability in pre-school children. *Journal of Mental Imagery, 15 (3&4)*, 143–50; McGuinness, D., and Sparks, J. (1983). Cognitive style and cognitive maps: Sex differences in representations of a familiar terrain. *Journal of Mental Imagery, 7 (2)*, 91–100 (this study shows that men and women *do* exhibit significantly different imagery for topographical domains).

**368.** McKelvie, S. J. (1998). Effects of gender on reported vividness of visual imagery for parents. *Journal of Mental Imagery, 22 (3&4)*, 99–111. Participants in this three-experiment imagery study (involving various factorial designs) were 516 male and female college students who completed the Vividness of Visual Imagery for Parents Questionnaire (VVIPQ) in which respondents rate the vividness of their imagery for each parent on a five-point scale. The VVIPQ was followed by a question in which participants rated their emotional closeness to each parent on a nine-point scale. Results across the experiments indicate that imagery was rated as *less* vivid for fathers than for mothers, but the effect was greater for women than for men; more vivid parental imagery was associated, also, with perceived emotional closeness to parents.* Also see Narchal, R., and Broota, K. D. (1988). Sex differences in vividness of visual imagery under eyes open and eyes closed conditions. *Journal of Mental Imagery, 12 (3&4)*, 81–87.

**369.** Pekala, R. J., Wenger, C. F., and Levine, R. L. (1985). Individual differences in phenomenological experience: States of consciousness as a function of absorption. *Journal of Personality and Social Psychology, 48*, 125–32. Participants in this two-experiment study were 553 female and male college students who completed absorption and introversion-extraversion scales, several stimulus conditions, and subjective-experience mapping inventories in an effort to determine if the personality trait of absorption (i.e., differential responsivity to hypnosis, meditation, marijuana intoxification, and electromyograph biofeedback) correlates with various dimensions of phenomenological experience, and if persons with differing absorption ability experience different states of consciousness. Results indicate that absorption correlates well with increased and more vivid imagery, inward and absorbed attention, and positive affect.* Also see Glicksohn, J., Mourad, B., and Pavell, E. (1991–1992). Imagination, absorption, and subjective time estimation. *Imagination, Cognition, and Personality, 11,* 167–76.

**370.** Richardson, J.T.E., Mavromatis, A., Mindel, T., and Owens, A. C. (1981). Individual differences in hypnagogic and hypnopompic imagery. *Journal of Mental Imagery, 5,* 91–96. Participants in this study/survey were 600 female and male adult volunteers, ages twenty to eighty years old, from the general population who provided extensive biographical and psychometric material, including performance on intelligence scales, and a pictorial memory task that contained a questionnaire on mental imagery. It was found that both types of experience (i.e., hypnagogic and hypnopompic) were reported by a majority of the participants, but were less common in older individuals. Hypnagogic experiences are those imaginal events that occur when *falling* asleep, and hypnopompic experiences are those imaginal events that occur upon *awakening* from sleep. It was found that hypnagogic imagery is more common in women and in those of lower socioeconomic class; neither type of imagery experience was related to either verbal or nonverbal intelligence.*

**371.** Sajjadi-Bafghi, S. H., and Khatena, J. (1985). Effects of autonomy of imagery and time press on production of verbal originality. *Perceptual and Motor Skills, 61,* 787–91. Participants in this study were 114 girls and boys in junior high school who were identified as imagers and who were classified (via an imagery-control questionnaire) as the following concerning the factor of autonomy: high (low controlled), moderate (moderately controlled), and low (high controlled). Participants were assigned randomly to one of two "time-press" conditions: fixed or variable. A sounds and images test was used to measure participants' verbal originality (this measure presents four auditory stimuli, three times, in the form of sounds that range from the simple to complex with intervals between sounds, and participants' responses were scored for originality; incorporated into this procedure were variable time intervals of fifteen and thirty seconds, and unlimited time for presentations one, two, and three, respectively; for the third presentation, participants were allowed to take as much time as they needed). Results of this procedure indicate that participants who were moderately autonomous imagers produced significantly more verbal originality than imagers high and low in autonomy as measured by the sounds and images test.**

**372.** Schredl, M. (2000). Gender differences in dream recall. *Journal of Mental Imagery, 24 (1&2)*, 169–76. Participants in this study/survey were 722 adult men and women volunteers, mean age of thirty-seven years old, from the general population who completed a sleep questionnaire that measured, retrospectively, the aspects of sleep pattern, sleep quality, presleep mood, and dream recall frequency during the previous two weeks. Results indicate that there were significant gender differences on the following variables/factors: sleep quality, nocturnal awakenings, feeling refreshed, emotional balance, dream recall, and engagement in dreams; the factor of tiredness, however, was not distinctive between the male and female participants.* Also see Goldstein, J., and Baskin, D. (1988). Sex differences in daydreaming behavior. *Journal of Mental Imagery, 12 (2)*, 83–90.

**373.** Spanos, N. P., and Brazil, K. (1984). Imagery monitoring and coping suggestions in the reduction of experimentally induced pain. *Journal of Mental Imagery, 8(2)*, 33–44. Participants in this study were eighty male and female college students who provided data in a 4 × 2 × 3 × 4 split-plot design with two between-subject variables (four treatments × high/low pain sensitivity) and two within-subject variables (three immersions × four pain reports); three cold pressor immersions were presented to four goups of participants: (1) imagery monitoring (IM), passive state, IM; (2) IM, IM, IM; (3) suggestion (S), passive state, S; and (4) control group. This study tested the hypothesis that forming a visual image of one's hand during an initial noxious stimulation (i.e., imagery monitoring) lessens the amount of pain and distress reported during later noxious stimulation. Results indicate that an automatic schema hypothesis (cf. Leventhal, 1980) was not confirmed; that is, the *imagery monitoring* treatments did not interact with pain sensitivity.** Also see Leventhal, H. (1980). Toward a comprehensive theory of emotion. *Advances in Experimental Social Psychology, 13*, 139–207.

**374.** Vecchio, L., and Bonifacio, M. (1997). Different images in different situations: A diary study of the spontaneous use of imagery. *Journal of Mental Imagery, 21 (3&4)*, 147–70. Participants in this study were twenty-nine Italian male and female college students who completed a fifty-one-page booklet over the period of one week. Each page in the booklet was devoted to the recording of a single mental image; for each image, participants were required to report the following information: the date and time when the mental image occurred; the modality of the mental image; the situation they were in when the image occurred; a brief/precise description of the image; and an evaluation of their imagery experience on a seven-point scale along the following dimensions: Spontaneous-Voluntary; Intrusive-Effective; Neutral-Emotional; Vague-Vivid; Devoid of Details–Full of Details; Static-Dynamic; Black and White–Colored; Common-Bizarre; and Realistic-Fantastical. Results indicate (among other findings) that most of the imagery experiences reported by the students concerned images they had had while involved in leisure or routine activities (thus, such situations—in which presumably a person's whole attention is *not* focused on a specific task— appear to increase the occurrence of mental images). The authors suggest that the use of *diaries* has proven to be a valid methodology that allows researchers to draw attention to individual differences in imagers and to some aspects of the imagery phenomenon that cannot usually be perceived by using the experimental approach solely.*

## PHYSIOLOGY/NEUROPSYCHOLOGY AND IMAGERY

**375.** Achterberg, J. (1984). Imagery and medicine: Psychophysiological speculations. *Journal of Mental Imagery, 8 (4),* 1–13. In this essay, the author outlines the psychophysiological events that may account for the ancient and persistent use of imagery as a device/tool for medical diagnosis and therapy. She discusses, also, the neurohumoral relations between cognitive processes and the immune system, along with the image's biological bases, in the context of the newly emergent field in psychology called *psychoneuroimmunology.* The author cites recent research demonstrating a relationship between imagery and disease, together with specific immune functions, to support the role of imagery in personal health. Data from such studies suggest that each image has a biochemical, neuroanatomical component, and that imagery may influence—and be influenced by—events and activities at the *cellular* level. Also see Achterberg, J., and Lawlis, G. F. (1984). *Imagery of disease: A diagnostic tool for behavioral medicine.* Champaign, IL: Institute for Personality and Ability Testing; Achterberg, J., Lawlis, G. F., Simonton, O. C., and Simonton, S. (1977). Psychological factors and blood chemistries as disease outcome predictors for cancer patients. *Multivariate Experimental Clinical Research, 3,* 107–22; Ader, R. (1981). *Psychoneuroimmunology.* New York: Academic Press; Locke, S. E., and Hornig-Rohan, M. (1983). *Mind and immunity: Behavioral immunology, an annotated bibliography, 1976–1982.* New York: Institute for the Advancement of Health; Trestman, R. L. (1981). Imagery, coping, and physiological variables in adult cancer patients. Unpublished doctoral dissertation, University of Tennessee, Knoxville.

**376.** Bird, E. I., and Wilson, V. E. (1988). The effects of physical practice upon psychophysiological response during mental rehearsal of novice conductors. *Journal of Mental Imagery, 12 (2),* 51–63. Participants in this study were eight novice music conductors, and their instructor, who provided data in an investigation to assess the ability to see a mental image and the physiological correlates of mental rehearsal (MR). Following the completion of a creative imagery scale and a movement imagery questionnaire— which identified all participants as internal imagers who could elicit visual imagery—various physiological measures, such as electromyograph (EMG), surface finger temperature, left hemisphere electroencephalograph (EEG), and heartrate (HR)—were monitored during rest, mental rehearsal, and actual conducting periods. The participants physically practiced conducting for eight weeks during which no MR training was given; participants' physiological responses were reassessed again, and a conducting performance score was assigned. Subsequently, comparisons were made between the effects of untrained MR before and after eight weeks of physical practice. Results indicate that the more skilled novices and the instructor demonstrated the more frequent and exact EEG pattern similarities in the pre- and posttreatment trials; and psychoneuromuscular facilitation did not appear to be present for the majority of the novices in either pre- or posttreatment trials, as no significant EMG increases were observed during MR.**

**377.** Foster, P. S., Smith, E.W.L., and Webster, D. G. (1998–1999). The psychophysiological differentiation of actual, imagined, and recollected anger. *Imagination, Cognition, and Personality, 18,* 189–203. Participants in this study were thirty-six male and female college students who were assigned randomly to one of three treatment conditions: an actual emotional situation (Actual Anger), Imagined Anger, and Recollected Anger. Participants were informed that they would be connected to a polygraph and that after a period of relaxation they would be asked to either recollect some events from their past or imagine some event that elicited anger (individuals in the Actual Anger group were not informed that an attempt would be made to cause them to react with anger until their participation concluded). Heart rate and skin resistance responses were measured during the establishment of the baseline for each participant; also, the changes in physiological responses measured during the treatment conditions were recorded. Results indicate significant differences for heart rate measures among the three methods/treatments, but not for the skin resistance measure. However, contrary to the expected outcomes, both the Imagined Anger and Recollected Anger groups generated significantly higher heart rate responses than the Actual Anger group participants.**

**378.** Jeannerod, M. (1994). The representing brain: Neural correlates of motor intention and imagery. *Behavioral and Brain Sciences, 17,* 187–202. In this special-issue essay on the topic of how motor actions are represented and coded neurally, the author suggests that action-planning and motor-preparation may be studied using a specific type of representational activity, namely, *motor imagery*. It is suggested that a close functional equivalence exists between motor imagery and motor-preparation as observed by the positive effects of imagining movements on motor learning, the similarity between the neural structures involved, and the similar physiological correlates found in both imaging and preparing. In response to Jeannerod's target article, and also contained in this same journal issue, over two dozen commentaries/reactions are provided. Also see Sirigu, A., Duhamel, J.-R., Cohen, L., Pillon, B., Dubois, B., and Agid, Y. (1996). The mental representation of hand movements after parietal cortex damage. *Science, 273,* 1564–68; Rosen, G., Hugdahl, K., Ersland, L., Lundervold, A., Smievoll, A., Barndon, R., Sundberg, H., Thomsen, T., Roscher, B., Tjolsen, A., and Engelsen, B. (2001). Different brain areas activated during imagery of painful and non-painful "finger movements" in a subject with an amputated arm. *Neurocase, 7,* 255–60; Hugdahl, K., Rosen, G., Ersland, L., Lundervold, A., Smievoll, A., Barndon, R., and Thomsen, T. (2001). Common pathways in mental imagery and pain perception: An fMRI study of a subject with an amputated arm. *Scandinavian Journal of Psychology, 42,* 269–75.

**379.** Kosslyn, S. M., Thompson, W. L., Kim, I. J., Rauch, S. L., and Alpert, N. M. (1996). Individual differences in cerebral blood flow in area-17 predict the time to evaluate visualized letters. *Journal of Cognitive Neuroscience, 8,* 78–82. Participants in this study were sixteen right-handed men who were either college students or medical school students, and who had the task of closing their eyes and visualizing uppercase letters of the alphabet at two sizes, as small as possible or as large as possible while still remaining visible. Participants evaluated a shape characteristic (e.g., curvature of lines) of each letter, and responded as quickly as possible; the cerebral blood flow was normalized to the same value for each participant, and relative blood flow was computed for a set of cerebral regions (in data treatment, the mean response time for each participant in the task was regressed onto the blood flow values). Results indicate that blood flow in area-17 was correlated *negatively* with response time, as was blood flow in area-19, whereas blood flow in the inferior parietal lobe was correlated *positively* with response time.\*\*

**380.** Kunzendorf, R. G., Francis, L., Ward, J., Cohen, R., Cutler, J., Walsh, J., and Berenson, S. (1996–1997). Effect of negative imaging on heart rate and blood pressure, as a function of image vividness and image "realness." *Imagination, Cognition, and Personality, 16,* 139–59. Participants in this two-experiment study were 128 male and female college students who generated data in an attempt to determine how individual differences in mental imagery influence the imaginal control of autonomic arousal. The testing procedure involved measuring image vividness and image "realness," measuring heart rate during one minute of negative imaging, one minute of positive imaging, one minute of negative self-talk, and one minute of positive self-talk. Results indicate that negative imaging induced increases in the heart beat, whereas self-talk did not. In another case, following the completion of the vividness/"realness" task, imaging ability was measured in participants via a series of imagery tests, then heart rate and blood pressure were measured in another task during negative imaging, and then positive imaging; results indicate that negative imaging induced higher pulse rate (as well as higher blood pressure and more intense emotion) in participants whose imagery was more vivid and more "real" and whose predominant image-induced emotion was anger.\*\*

**381.** Kunzendorf, R. G., and Sheikh, A. A. (Eds.) (1990). *The psychophysiology of mental imagery: Theory, research, and application.* Amityville, NY: Baywood. The purpose of this book—containing a collection of papers on imagery and physiology—is to bridge the growing gap between differing approaches taken by psychologists and other psychologists, between cognitive scientists and mentalists, and between researchers and practitioners. For instance, whereas physiological psychologists may study learning from a *limited* neuro*behavioral* perspective, they must approach imagery from an *expanded psycho*physiological perspective; whereas cognitive scientists may use computer programs/metaphors to model the physiological process of imaging, they must employ more subjective models to capture the mental experience of imaging; and whereas practitioners have no real need for research on such issues as short-term memory, they have much to gain from research on the psychosomatic effects of imaging, and on the psychophysiological differences between imaging and hallucinating. Among the contents in this book are the following titles/topics: Mind-brain identity theory: A materialistic foundation for the psychophysiology of mental imagery; Psi mediated emergent interactionism and the nature of consciousness; Waking images and neural activity; Creative imagination and neural activity; Brain states of visual imagery and dream generation; Psychophysiology of hypnotic hallucinations; Schizophrenic hallucincations in the context of psychophysiological studies of schizophrenia; Neuropsychological concepts of mood, imagery, and performance; Imaging, image-monitoring, and health; and Imagery, psychoneuroimmunology, and the psychology of healing. Also see Vrana, S., and Rollock, D. (2002). The role of ethnicity, gender, emotional content, and contextual differences in physiological, expressive, and self-reported emotional responses to imagery. *Cognition and Emotion, 16,* 165–92; Ueda, Y., Kuroiwa, K., Zenjyu, H., Katano, T., Kame, S., Kashiba, H., Yanagida, T., Kitamura, Y., Oshiro, Y., Tokimoto, Y., and Nomura, T. (2000). The study of meditation and image evocation using functional MRI. *Journal of International Society of Life Information Science, 18,* 407–9; Zhang, T., Sakaida, H., Kawano, K., Yamamoto, M., and Machi, Y. (2000). An experiment on cerebral activity during visual imagery. *Journal of International Society of Life Information Science, 18,* 400–403; Mellet, E., Tzourio, N., Denis, M., and Mazoyer, B. (1995). A positron emission tomography study of visual and mental spatial exploration. *Journal of Cognitive Neuroscience, 7,* 433–45; Miller, J. A. (1995). Vision check on the mind's eye. *BioScience, 45,* 245; Various imagery issues (various authors). (2002). *Behavioral and Brain Sciences, 25,* 157–237; O'Craven, K., and Kanwisher, N. (2000). Mental imagery of faces and places activates corresponding stimulus-specific brain regions. *Journal of Cognitive Neuroscience, 12,* 1013–24.

**382.** Persinger, M. A., and Makarec, K. (1991–1992). Interactions between temporal lobe signs, imaginings, beliefs, and gender: Their effect upon logical inference. *Imagination, Cognition, and Personality, 11,* 149–66. Participants in this study were 200 female and male college students who completed a paralogic test, an inventory of childhood memories and imaginings, and a personal philosophy inventory (a measure for discerning possible temporal lobe signs that is based on clinical reports from patients with verified electrical foci within the temporal lobes). Results indicate that both genders exhibit moderately strong correlations between content-selected and factor-analyzed clusters of possible temporal lobe signs, exotic beliefs, and the numbers of childhood imaginings. Moreover, although there were no gender differences between the accuracy of logical statements that contained paranormal or neutral content, the male participants who showed more temporal lobe signs were more accurate for logical items that contained paranormal content. The female participants who showed more imaginings were more accurate for valid than for invalid items; moreover, accuracy for items with paranormal content increased with exotic beliefs but not with conservative religious beliefs for both genders.*

**383.** Reese, C. J. (1999). Hemispheric specialization for categorical and coordinate image generation: A developmental perspective. Unpublished doctoral dissertation, University of California, San Diego. This researcher notes that the *left* cerebral hemisphere is more effective at encoding and using *categorical* spatial relations, while the *right* hemisphere is more adept at encoding and using *coordinate* spatial relations; *categorical* representations involve judgments about the *relative* positions of the components of a visual stimulus, and *coordinate* representations involve computing *precise* metric distances between the components of a visual stimulus. In a set of three studies, the present research assesses the early developmental course of adult and school-aged children's categorical and coordinate image generation abilities. It is concluded that the present findings are consistent with previous studies that posit two separate, yet complementary, lateralized cerebral components for processing categorical and coordinate spatial relations. The references section of this study contains over ninety citations related to the issue of imagery generation and hemispheric specialization.** Also see Kosslyn, S. M., Maljkovic, V., Hamilton, S., Horwitz, G., and Thompson, W. (1995). Two types of image generation: Evidence for left and right hemisphere processes. *Neuropsychologia, 33,* 1485–510.

## SPORTS AND IMAGERY

**384.** Glisky, M. L., Williams, J. M., and Kihlstrom, J. F. (1996). Internal and external mental imagery perspectives and performance on two tasks. *Journal of Sport Behavior, 19,* 3–18. Participants in this study were forty-two male and female college students who completed an imagery assessment questionnaire (yielding scores permitting participants to be classified as internal-imagers or external-imagers) concerning if, and how, imagery is used by the participant, the imagers' natural and preferred imagery perspective, and clarity of imagery. Following this, both cognitive-visual and motor-kinesthetic tasks were given to participants. Results based a 2 × 2 × 2 (imagery perspective × type of task × imagery modality) indicate a main effect of *imagery perspective*, showing higher overall clarity ratings for the internal-imagery participants compared to the external-imagery participants. A main effect of *task* indicates, also, greater clarity on the imagery ratings for a stabilometer task compared to an angles task. Moreover, a main effect of *type of image* showed a higher rating of clarity on the visual images than on the kinesthetic images; however, a significant interaction between task and type of image overrides the significant main effects for these variables.**

**385.** Gordon, S., Weinberg, R., and Jackson, A. (1994). Effect of internal and external imagery on cricket performance. *Journal of Sport Behavior, 17*, 60–75. Participants in this study were sixty-four eighth-, ninth-, and tenth-grade Australian students who completed six 40-minute training sessions on "outswing bowling" (which is a fast bowling technique that accounts for most wickets/dismissals in the game of cricket) in a three-week period. Participants completed, also, a visual imagery questionnaire and a vividness of movement imagery questionnaire, the scores of which allowed the students to be placed into high- and low-imagery groups. Participants were assigned randomly to one of three experimental groups after being matched on general bowling ability and vividness of imagery by the school's cricket-studies coordinator; the three treatments were: control (participants watched a video concerning the art of outswing bowling); external imagery (participants viewed the same video plus receiving instructions on how to image an elite bowler's performance via angle-analysis); and internal imagery (participants viewed the same video plus listening to an elite bowler explaining the kinesthetic experiences of bowling a perfect outswinger). The dependent variables were measures of the students' posttraining net-practice performance in terms of accuracy, degree of swing, and coaching-experts' subjective ratings. Results indicated *no* significant performance differences between the internal and external imagery experimental groups and the control group of participants.**

**386.** Kohl, R. M., and Fisicaro, S. A. (1995). Imaging goal-directed movement. *Research Quarterly for Exercise and Sport, 66*, 17–31. Participants in this four-experiment study of imagery in sport were 128 male and female college students who performed movement tasks in a 2 × 2 × 2 × 3 (Response × Context × Difficulty-Index × Trial Block) factorial design, and a 2 × 2 × 2 × 3 (Response—actual versus imagery × Context—referential versus nonreferential × Target Width/Amplitude × Trial Block) repeated measures design. The four studies were designed to study the influence of imaged tasks and their referential context on movement time. Instructions indicating relative imaged size of stimuli and distance between stimuli were the task manipulations of main interest. The movement task employed was developed by Fitts (1954) where participants are required to repeatedly tap a stylus as quickly and accurately as possible from one stationary target to another in an alternating fashion (by varying target width and amplitude—distance between targets—the experimenter may increase or decrease task difficulty and observe the effect on movement time). Results indicate that movement time for the actual tapping response varies as a function of index of difficulty (ID), whether ID was manipulated by changing target width or target amplitude; also, movement time for actual tapping does not vary when ID is held constant and biases were created in terms of target width or amplitude; and context failed to influence movement time for actual tapping in any of the four experiments. Additionally, the movement times obtained in the referential-context *imagery* condition were similar to movement times found for *actual* tapping which shows that Fitts's (1954) notion applies to *imaged* movement as well as *actual* movement under these conditions. It is concluded that the present findings correspond to predictions based on Fitts's law (Fitts, 1954).** Also see Fitts, P. M. (1954). The information capacity of the human motor system in controlling the amplitude of movement. *Journal of Experimental Psychology, 47,* 381–91.

**387.** Moran, A. (1993). Conceptual and methodological issues in the measurement of mental imagery skills in athletes. *Journal of Sport Behavior, 16,* 156–70. In this essay/review, the author assesses the effectiveness and psychometric properties of different imagery tests, and indicates that current imagery tests lack sufficient theoretical back-up and empirical validation among athletes. Among the author's conclusions and recommendations are the following: there is a disjunction between theory and measurement in visualization research; greater collaboration is needed between researchers from the cognitive and psychometric branches of sport psychology; and rigorous programs of construct validation should be carried out for imagery questionnaires and inventories used in sport research. Also see Feltz, D., and Landers, D. (1983). The effects of mental practice on motor skill learning and performance: A meta-analysis. *Journal of Sport Psychology, 5,* 25–57; Hall, C. R., Rodgers, W. M., and Barr, K. A. (1990). The use of imagery by athletes in selected sports. *The Sport Psychologist, 4,* 1–10; Landers, D. M. (1983). Whatever happened to theory in sport psychology? *Journal of Sport Psychology, 5,* 135–51; Murphy, S. M. (1990). Models of imagery in sport psychology. *Journal of Mental Imagery, 14,* 153–72; Smith, D. (1987). Conditions that facilitate the development of sport imagery training. *The Sport Psychologist, 1,* 237–47.

**388.** Overby, L. Y., Hall, C., and Haslam, I. (1997–1998). A comparison of imagery used by dance teachers, figure skating coaches, and soccer coaches. *Imagination, Cognition, and Personality, 17,* 323–37. Participants in this study were forty-nine coaches and teachers in the areas of dancing, figure skating, and soccer who completed a modified questionnaire based on the Imagery Use Questionnaire and the Survey of Dance Teachers inventory. Results of the survey indicate that all three groups of participants report using mental imagery in their teaching and coaching activities. In terms of imagery perspective, the dance teachers and soccer coaches report using more internal than external imagery, while the figure skating coaches report using both perspectives equally; dance teachers and figure skating coaches employ metaphorical imagery to a greater extent than do the soccer coaches.* Also see Pozzi, E. (1999). Individual preconditions for mental testing. *International Journal of Sport Psychology, 30,* 41–62.

## THERAPY AND IMAGERY

**389.** Abraham, I. L., Neundorfer, M. M., and Terris, E. A. (1993). Effects of focused visual imagery on cognition and depression among nursing home residents. *Journal of Mental Imagery, 17 (3&4),* 61–75. Participants in this study were forty-six female and male elderly nursing home residents who scored high on a geriatric depression scale and who provided data for assessing the effects of focused visual imagery group therapy on cognition and correlates of geriatric depression. Participants were assigned either to a treatment group of a twenty-four-week protocol of focused visual imagery group therapy or to a comparison condition consisting of a twenty-four-week series of educational discussion group sessions. Results indicate that participants in the visual imagery group exhibited a significant improvement in cognition over the span of the study, while participants in the educational discussion group did not show such improvement; moreover, there was *no* observed effect for either group on the geriatric correlates of life satisfaction, hopelessness, or depressive symptomatology.**

**390.** Achterberg, J., Kenner, C., and Lawlis, G. F. (1988). Severe burn injury: A comparison of relaxation, imagery, and biofeedback for pain management. *Journal of Mental Imagery, 12,* 71–87. Participants in this study were 149 severely burn-injured female and male adults who were assigned to one of three treatment groups: relaxation, relaxation and imagery/mental rehearsal, and relaxation and imagery/mental rehearsal plus thermal biofeedback. Each participant received six sessions of the treatment in conjunction with wound care; and multiple psychological and physiological measures of anxiety and pain were recorded and compared with those from a control/nontreatment group of participants. Results indicate that all three treatment groups generally demonstrated some benefit from the intervention/treatment strategies that could not be accounted for by uncontrolled variables in the situation.** Also see Newshan, G., and Balamuth, R. (1990–1991). Use of imagery in a chronic pain outpatient group. *Imagination, Cognition, and Personality, 10,* 25–38; Alden, A. L., Dale, J. A., and DeGood, D. E. (2001). Interactive effects of the affect quality and directional focus of mental imagery on pain analgesia. *Applied Psychophysiology and Biofeedback, 26,* 117–26; Allen, D. G. (1982). Autonomic self-control of clinical relaxation as a function of imagery. Unpublished doctoral dissertation, Utah State University.

**391.** Ahsen, A. (1993). Imagery treatment of alcoholism and drug abuse: A new methodology for treatment and research. *Journal of Mental Imagery, 17 (3&4)*, 1–60. In this lengthy dual essay/review and pilot study of imagery and alcohol/drug abuse, the author presents the history of approaches regarding alcoholism and drug addiction, and gives assessments of current methods for treatment of these maladies and their theoretical underpinnings. A novel methodology involving eidetic imagery is advocated whereby brief but intensive interventions are designed for the purpose of providing immediate relief for sufferers, as well as more long-term support that is based on the use of internal sources of imagery and made available or accessible to the individual without the need for external mechanisms. Participants in Ahsen's study were fifty-eight male and female adult inpatients and outpatients who were being treated (detoxification) for alcoholism or substance abuse and addiction. Ahsen's Adapted Vividness of Visual Imagery Questionnaire (AA-VVIQ) was completed by all participants and showed the following results: the outpatient participants had a greater *inability* to process imagery under the "mother figure" than under the "father figure" condition/scenario—a finding that correlates with other clinical populations or psychotherapy patients tested; on the other hand, the inpatient participants had a greater *inability* to process imagery under the father figure than under the mother figure condition—a finding that correlates with the normal population tested. Also, outpatients demonstrated hemispheric inversion (mother on the left, father on the right) significantly more often than did inpatients who more frequently reported the hemispheric position of father on the left and mother on the right (this result was observed, also, in the general population); the variables of race and ethnic background did not seem to be an important factor in this analysis. It is concluded that the AA-VVIQ serves several useful functions, including therapeutic-setting applications, by providing a mechanism to elucidate important baseline information and transitional stages in the process of discovery in the individual both in clinical and nonclinical contexts. Included in this article, also, is the two-part alcohol and drug abuse questionnaire that was employed, along with instructions for, and items in, the AA-VVIQ.* Also see *Journal of Mental Imagery*, 1980, *4*, 155–68 (section entitled "Imagery Therapy: History Section"); Ahsen, A. (1979). Case histories section. *Journal of Mental Imagery, 3*, 123–54; Jordan, C. S. (1984). Psychophysiology of structural imagery in post-traumatic stress disorder. *Journal of Mental Imagery, 8 (4)*, 51–66; Ahsen, A. (1985). Medial hemispheric imbalance: Experiments on a clinically related imagery function. *Journal of Mental Imagery, 9*, 1–7; Ahsen, A. (1993). *Unvividness paradox: Dynamics of imagery formation.* New York: Brandon House; Ahsen, A. (1996). Menopause: Imagery interventions and therapeutics. *Journal of Mental Imagery, 20 (3&4)*, 1–40.

**392.** Cohen, R. E., Creticos, P. S., and Norman, P. S. (1993–1994). The effects of guided imagery (GI) on allergic subjects' responses to ragweed-pollen nasal challenge: An exploratory investigation. *Imagination, Cognition, and Personality, 13,* 259–69. Participants in the study originally were thirty-four male and female adult volunteers who tested positive on a skin test for ragweed-pollen allergy, and who were paid for their services (however, complete statistical data was obtained for only fourteen of the participants, ages twenty-one to sixty-two years old). Participants were matched and assigned randomly to an experimental or to a control group, and nasal challenges to ragweed-pollen abstract were performed on them to determine baseline levels of two immunologically generated biochemical mediators obtained from nasal secretions and two subjectively reported measures of symptoms. Participants in the experimental group completed a three-week program of guided imagery, while participants in the control group had a no-contact condition. Results indicate that a three-week program of guided imagery enabled allergic participants to suppress immunologically generated TAME-esterase, as determined through responses to ragweed-pollen challenge. When the control group was provided, subsequently, with the treatment program, a within-group, posttreatment analysis indicated, also, a significant suppression of TAME-esterase release.\*\* Also see Abrams, B. (2001). Defining transpersonal experiences of guided imagery and music (GIM). *Dissertation Abstracts International Section A: Humanities and Social Sciences, 61(10-A),* 3817; Housker, J. E. (2001). Houston's model of guided imagery combined with music: Strengthening couples' relationships. *Dissertation Abstracts International Section A: Humanities and Social Sciences, 61(10-A),* 3907; Ettin, M. F. (1988–1989). Book review. *Guided affective imagery: Mental imagery in short-term psychotherapy* by Hanscarl Leuner, New York: Thieme-Stratton, 1984; Leuner, H. (1977). Guided affective imagery: An account of its development. *Journal of Mental Imagery, 1,* 73–92; Ettin, M. F. (1985). Private eyes in a public setting: The use of imagery in group psychotherapy. *Journal of Mental Imagery, 9 (3),* 19–44; Sapp, M. (1994). The effects of guided imagery on reducing the worry and emotionality components of test anxiety. *Journal of Mental Imagery, 18 (3&4),* 165–79; Tusek, D., Church, J. M., and Fazio, V. W. (1997). Guided imagery as a coping strategy for perioperative patients. *Association of Operating Room Nurses Journal, 66,* 644–49.

**393.** Crits-Christoph, P., and Singer, J. L. (1983–1984). An experimental investigation of the use of positive imagery in the treatment of phobias. *Imagination, Cognition, and Personality, 3,* 305–23. Participants in this study were twenty-five male and female adult volunteers recruited through advertisements in a newspaper asking for people with a specific fear or phobia that they would like to overcome. Participants/clients were assigned randomly to either a positive imagery group, an active-involvement imagery group, or a waiting-list control group. Treatment consisted of a maximum of twelve sessions, each one hour in length, and held twice per week for six weeks; control participants were informed that treatment would be delayed for six weeks (after this period, these clients were treated via random assignment by one of the two methods in the study). Results indicate that both groups (positive imagery and active-involvement imagery) showed a large and equal improvement in the severity of their specific fear as compared to the waiting-list control group.\*\*

**394.** Gaston, L., Crombez, J.-C., and Dupuis, G. (1989). An imagery and meditation technique in the treatment of psoriasis: A case study using an A-B-A design. *Journal of Mental Imagery, 13,* 31–38. This case study—involving a female adult as the only participant—describes the effectiveness of an imagey and meditation technique for reducing the severity of the woman's psoriasis symptoms using an A-B-A design (where A is baseline and followup measures, and B is treatment administered; A was undertaken for four weeks, and B lasted for fifteen weeks). Results indicate that while there was a decrease in the severity of the psoriasis symptoms following the use of imagery and meditation techniques, the authors note cautiously that the overall efficacy of the techniques may only be hypothesized.\*\*

**395.** Hart, D. E., and Means, J. R. (1985). Cognitive versus imaginal treatments for cognitively versus imaginally induced dysphoria. *Journal of Mental Imagery, 9,* 33–51. Participants in this study were fifty-six female and male college students who were assigned randomly to one of four mood-induction/treatment combinations: imaginal induction/imaginal treatment, imaginal induction/cognitive treatment, cognitive induction/imaginal treatment, and cognitive induction/cognitive treatment. Each participant was hypnotized, induced into a dysphoric mood (anxiety, restlessness, sadness, dissatisfaction) either imaginally or cognitively, then given one of the two treatment sets; also, a depression adjective checklist was completed by each participant at preinduction, postinduction, and posttreatment stages. Results indicate that there was partial support for a specificity-of-effect hypothesis in that the cognitive treatment was effective only when the sad mood had been cognitively induced, but not when the sad mood had been induced imaginally.\*\*

**396.** Moses, I., and Reyher, J. (1985). Spontaneous and directed visual imagery: Image failure and image substitution. *Journal of Personality and Social Psychology, 48,* 233–42. Participants in this study were forty female and male college students who were asked to visualize the scenes of three stimulus narratives (two aggressive ones—involving parents or parental derivatives with verbal-gestural or physical anger-aggressive components; and one that was affectively neutral but implausible—involving a imagined space odyssey led by a small bird), and to signal (via key-presses) either their successful visualization, or their type of image disparity (image failure or image substitution). It was found that both types of image disparity varied directly with the blatancy of scenes depicting anger and aggression, and showed that image *failure* was more closely related to implausibility, whereas image *substitution* was more closely related to anger-aggression.\*\* Also see Reyher, J. (1977). Spontaneous visual imagery: Implications for psychoanalysis, psychopathology, and psychotherapy. *Journal of Mental Imagery, 2,* 253–73.

**397.** Segal, D., and Lynn, S. J. (1992–1993). Predicting dissociative experiences: Imagination, hypnotizability, psychopathology, and alcohol use. *Imagination, Cognition, and Personality, 12,* 287–300. Participants in this study were eighty-five female and male college students who completed a battery of tests that examined their levels of imagination, psychopathology, hypnotizability, and alcohol use in order to predict various dissociative experiences. Results based on participants' data/scores indicate consistency with the hypothesis that dissociative experiences and imaginative processes are related; other analyses indicate that dissociative experiences in a college population are linked not only to positively valenced, presumably adaptive imaginal activities, but also failures in adaptive cognitive control.*

**398.** Sheikh, A. A. (Ed.) (2002). *Handbook of therapeutic imagery techniques.* Amityville, NY: Baywood. Describes a multitude of imagery techniques useful for psychotherapeutic applications; the approaches are grouped into four general areas: hypnobehavioral techniques, cognitive-behavioral techniques, psychodynamic-humanistic approaches, and humanistic-transpersonal approaches. Among the contents of this book are the following topics/titles: Imagination in disease and healing processes: A historical perspective; Relaxing images in hypnobehavioral therapy; Visualization techniques and altered states of consciousness; Imagery in autogenic training; Neuro-linguistic programming techniques; Imagery techniques in cognitive behavior treatments of anxiety and trauma; Imagery rescripting therapy; Imagery scripts for changing lifestyle patterns; Imagery exercises for health; Imagery techniques in the work of Maxwell Maltz; The oneirotherapies; Psycho-imagination therapy; Emotive reconstructive therapy; Eidetic psychotherapy techniques; Animal imagery, the Chakra System, and psychotherapy; Tsubo imagery psychotherapy; Conception imagery exercise; Images and death psychology: The legacy of Carl Jung; Imagery techniques in psychosynthesis; Guided meditation; Imagery and the conquest of time; and Techniques to enhance imaging ability. Also see Andrea, M. C. (1983). The use of imagery in short-term psychotherapy. *Journal of Mental Imagery, 7 (2),* 119–26; Brink, N. E. (1988–1989). Using imagery as a planning and treatment guide in therapy. *Imagination, Cognition, and Personality, 8,* 187–200; Brown, B. M. (1969). The use of induced imagery in psychotherapy. *Psychotherapy: Theory, Research, and Practice, 6,* 120–21; Dosamantes-Alperson, E. (1985–1986). A current perspective of imagery in psychoanalysis. *Imagination, Cognition, and Personality, 5,* 199–209; Eysenck, H. J. (1989). Behavior therapy, cognition, and the use of imagery. *Journal of Mental Imagery, 13,* 21–26; Farran, E., Jarrold, C., and Gathercole, S. (2001). Block design performance in the Williams syndrome phenotype: A problem with mental imagery? *Journal of Child Psychology and Psychiatry and Allied Disciplines,*

*42,* 719–28; Fiore, N. A. (1988). The inner healer: Imagery for coping with cancer and its therapy. *Journal of Mental Imagery, 12 (2),* 79–82; Geller, J. D., Cooley, R. S., and Hartley, D. (1981–1982). Images of the psychotherapist: A theoretical and methodological perspective. *Imagination, Cognition, and Personality, 1,* 123–33; Grassi, J. A. (1985). Heart imagery: Some new directions in healing and psychotherapeutic applications. *Journal of Mental Imagaery, 9 (4),* 17–31; Hanley, G. L. (1988). The cognitive demands of imagining and perceiving: Implications for using imagery in therapy. *Journal of Mental Imagery, 12 (2),* 91–102; Horowitz, M. J. (1968). Visual thought images in psychotherapy. *American Journal of Psychotherapy, 22,* 55–60; Johnsen, E. L., and Lutgendorf, S. K. (2001). Contributors of imagery ability to stress and relaxation. *Annals of Behavioral Medicine, 23,* 273–81; Johnson, K., and Korn, E. R. (1980). Hypnosis and imagery in the rehabilitation of a brain-damaged patient. *Journal of Mental Imagery, 4,* 35–39; Morrison, J. K., and Cometa, M. S. (1980). A cognitive, reconstructive approach to the psychotherapeutic use of imagery. *Journal of Mental Imagery, 4,* 35–42; Page, S. J. (2001). Mental practice: A promising restorative technique in stroke rehabilitation. *Topics in Stroke Rehabilitation, 8,* 54–63; Prerost, F. J. (1985). A procedure using imagery and humor in psychotherapy: Case application with longitudinal assessment. *Journal of Mental Imagery, 9 (3),* 67–76; Rubin, J. A. (1985). Imagery in art therapy: The source, the setting, and the significance. *Journal of Mental Imagery, 9 (4),* 71–81; Starker, S., and Jolin, A. (1982–1983). Imagery and fantasy in Vietnam veteran psychiatric inpatients. *Imagination, Cognition, and Personality, 2,* 15–21; Yanovski, A., and Fogel, M. L. (1990). Effects of instructions given to reactors and nonreactors to produce visual imagery sequences following an imagined pleasant scene. *Perceptual and Motor Skills, 70,* 891–97; Barnes, J., Boubert, L., Harris, J., Lee, A., and David, A. (2003). Reality monitoring and visual hallucinations in Parkinson's disease. *Neuropsychologia, 41,* 565–74; Nelson, J., and Harvey, A. (2002). The differential functions of imagery and verbal thought in insomnia. *Journal of Abnormal Psychology, 111,* 665–69; Niemeier, J. P. (2002). Visual imagery training for patients with visual perceptual deficits following right hemisphere cerebrovascular accidents: A case study presenting the Lighthouse Strategy. *Rehabilitation Psychology, 47,* 426–37; Phillips, J. (2003). Working with adolescents' violent imagery. In C. A. Malchiodi (Ed.), *Handbook of art therapy.* New York: Guilford Press; Rentz, T. O. (2002). Active-imaginal exposure: Examination of a new behavioral treatment of specific phobia. *Dissertation Abstracts International: Section B: The Sciences and Engineering, 63(4-B),* 2071; Tippett, L., Blackwood, K., and Farah, M. (2003). Visual object and face processing in mild-to-moderate Alzheimer's disease: From segmentation to imagination. *Neuropsychologia, 41,* 453–68; Arbuthnott, K., Arbuthnott, D., and Rossiter, L. (2001). Guided imagery and memory: Implications for psychotherapists. *Journal of Counseling Psychology, 48,* 123–32.

## THOUGHT IMAGERY

**399.** Adeyemo, S. A. (2001). Imagery in thinking and problem solving. *Perceptual and Motor Skills, 92,* 395–98. Participants in this two-experiment imagey study were sixty male and female college students who provided data in a practical-construction task (the classical "hat-rack" problem) in an effort to determine the role of imagery in thinking and problem solving; posttest questioning indicated that two distinct types of imagery were employed to solve the problem: *memory* imagery and *imagination* imagery. It was found that the solvers tended to employ *imagination* in imagery, while the nonsolvers used *memory* in imagery.**

**400.** Antonietti, A., and Colombo, B. (1996–1997). The spontaneous occurrence of mental visualization in thinking. *Imagination, Cognition, and Personality, 16,* 415–28. Participants in this study were 208 female and male college students who completed a seventy-seven-item questionnaire (included in an appendix to the article) where each item related to a situation in which people may experience mental images. A five-point rating scale was used to indicate how frequently the visualizaton process described in the item occurred to the participants. Results showed that the most frequent occurrences of mental visualization are in undirected thinking: participants rated mental imagery high when their mind is able to wander freely (e.g., in daydreaming) or when external stimuli elicit automatically a visual representation.*

**401.** Giambra, L. M., Grodsky, A., Swartz, D. B., and Bernard, M. E. (1997–1998). Task-unrelated image and thought frequency during chronic auditory sensory deprivation: A laboratory study with the severely hearing-impaired. *Imagination, Cognition, and Personality, 17,* 179–89. Participants in this study were thirty-two hearing-impaired, and normal-hearing male and female adult volunteers whose task-unrelated images and thoughts (TUITs) were recorded while they carried out a simple visual vigilance task that required careful, sustained attention. Results indicate, as hypothesized, that the severely hearing-impaired participants reported significantly more TUITs than the normal-hearing participants; and it is concluded that chronic auditory deprivation leads to suboptimal levels of external stimulation that are compensated for by internally generated stimuli, one form of which is the TUITs.**

**402.** Hogenraad, R., and Orianne, E. (1985–1986). Imagery, regressive thinking, and verbal performance in internal monologue. *Imagination, Cognition, and Personality, 5,* 127–45. Participants in this study were eighteen French-speaking female and male college students who provided data in the form of protocols of internal monologue. The aim of the study was to assess a free-associative discourse (via internal monologues obtained by the method of thinking aloud) in terms of both descriptive and deductive analyses. An imagery dictionary and a regressive imagery dictionary (both in French) were used in the descriptive analysis to evaluate the importance and development of images and regressive thinking in three-hour-long internal monologues from participants. Results indicate that a positive relationship exists between images and regressive thinking ("natural cognizings") on the one hand, and the use of markers of congruence (flagged by *and* conjunctions) and incongruence (flagged by *but* conjunctions) on the other hand.*

**403.** Klinger, E., and Cox, W. M. (1987–1988). Dimensions of thought flow in everyday life. *Imagination, Cognition, and Personality, 7,* 105–28. Participants in this study were twenty-nine female and male college students who completed a paper-and-pencil alcohol test and a demographic questionnaire (concerning living conditions, marital status, ethnic background, educational history, and drinking history). Also, participants filled out a twenty-three-item thought-sampling questionnaire (included in the article), an activity report, a state-trait anxiety inventory, and a depression adjective checklist. Participants were given a beeper device that served as a signal for each thought-sampling occasion. Results based on a total of 1,425 thought-sampling occasions, and on intra-participant analyses of thought variables, identified eight orthogonal factors, including visual modality, auditory modality, operantness (directedness), attentiveness to external stimulation, controllability, strangeness (fancifulness/bizarreness), past-time and future-time orientations.* Also see Reise, S. P., and Hurlburt, R. T. (1987–1988). The relations between dimensions of thought reported in two thought-sampling studies. *Imagination, Cognition, and Personality, 7,* 315–21; Parks, C. W., Klinger, E., and Perlmutter, M. (1988–1989). Dimensions of thought as a function of age, gender, and task difficulty. *Imagination, Cognition, and Personality, 8,* 49–62; Starker, S., and Jolin, A. (1983–1984). Occurrence and vividness of imagery in schizophrenic thought: A thought-sampling approach. *Imagination, Cognition, and Personality, 3,* 49–60; Zachary, R. A. (1982). Imagery, ambiguity, emotional arousal, and ongoing thought. *Journal of Mental Imagery, 6,* 93–108.

# Index

A priori method, 427
Abacus operators, 464
Abbreviated Imagination Inventory, 484, 503
Abnormal mental phenomena in the prophets, 140
Absence of images/imagery, 154, 159, 242
Absence of sensory stimulation, 2, 5, 9, 10, 14, 15, 18–24, 28, 69, 147, 350, 483
Absorption, imaginative, 347, 492, 498, 513
Absorption Scale, 484, 503
Abstract ideas/thinking, 5, 53, 77, 133, 138, 148–49, 158, 305, 313, 362, 519
Abstract versus concrete words, 216, 308, 353, 450, 474, 508
Abstracting ability, 75, 149
Abstraction, theory of, 77, 148, 149
Accidental association, 234
Accidental colors, 28
Ach, Narziss Kaspar, 73, 154, 206, 516
Act psychology, 74, 155
Action/acts, 73, 77, 196, 207–8, 229, 313, 362, 464
Activating filters, 532
Active construction versus passive registration, 306

Active imagination, 21, 363
Active memory, 300, 313
Active mode of consciousness, 35
Active vision, 58
Acts and contents, 216
Acute hallucinosis, 49
Adam, 134, 137, 138
Adaptation/adaptive functions, 26, 62, 329, 331, 361, 514
Adequacy criteria, 311–12
Adolescents/adolescence, 21, 39–40, 184–85, 332, 525, 531
Adverbial account/theory, 19
Advertising and imagery, 330, 348, 540
Aesthesiometric field, 236
Aesthetic consciousness/appreciation, 201, 436, 467
Aesthetic illusions, 54
Aesthetics and imagery, 69, 198, 200–201, 251, 335, 467
Affections/affectivity, 17, 234
Affective coloration/tone, 209, 236
Affective sensitiveness, 219
Affordances, 338
After-discharge, 23–24
After-effect(s), 23, 211
After-effect of observed movement, 28
After-excitation, 26
After-experience, 23
Afterimage, early studies of, 61

Afterimage law(s), 26
Afterimage, memory, 23
Afterimage method, 27
Afterimage, negative, 23
Afterimage, positive, 23
Afterimage threshold, 28
Afterimages in complete darkness, 25,
    28, 183
Afterimages versus imagination images,
    25–26, 332
Afterimages/imagery, 2, 5, 7, 20, 23–
    29, 40–41, 57, 75–76, 170–71,
    176–83, 219, 238, 245, 247, 252,
    332, 471, 515, 582–87
After-sensation(s), 2, 23, 181
Age differences, 39–40, 42–43, 162,
    165–66, 168–69, 195, 336, 342,
    491, 522, 525
Aguilonius, 28
Ahsen, Akhter, 425, 439, 450–56,
    461–62, 464–68, 514, 531–33,
    535–37, 539, 542–44
Ahsen's 30 parallel tactics, 468
Ahsen's 100 learning genomes, 468
Ahsen's Adapted Questionnaire Upon
    Mental Imagery, 499–501
Ahsen's Adapted Test of Visual
    Imagery Control, 499–501
Ahsen's Adapted Vividness of Visual
    Imagery Questionnaire, 499–500
Ahsen's Eidetic Parents Test, 499, 501–
    2
Ahsen's Eidetic Therapy approach, 502
Ahsen's image model, 451
Ahsen's new initiative, internet, 543
Alcohol and imagery, 75
Alcoholic hallucinosis, 44, 49
Allegory, 139
Alpha blocking/frequencies, 351, 506
Alphabet letters and imagery, 198,
    217, 230, 298
Altamira cave/ceiling paintings, 122
Alternate physiologies, 532
Alternative coding systems, 306
Alternative hypotheses/explanations,
    354, 526, 538, 542
Ambiguous figures, 345, 518
*American Imago*, 15

*American Journal of Psychology*, 194
American Psychological Society, 429
American revolution of psychology, 516
Amnesia, 186
Amodal codes, 321–22
Amphetamines, 50
Amygdala, 512, 517
Analog processes/representations, 17,
    78, 300, 303, 341, 464
Analog versus propositional debate, 38,
    303, 464
Analogue-computational debate, 303,
    320
Analysis of style method, 161
Aniconic versus iconic gods, 129–30
Anima/animus/animism, 15, 130, 451
Animal magnetism, 52
Anorexia nervosa, 16
Anosmia/anosmic, 230
Anschauungsbild, 39, 169, 524
Anthropologists/anthropology, 71,
    130, 138, 458
Anthropomorphisms, 125, 130, 133,
    139
Anticipation of future events, 19, 76
Anticipatory imagination, 55, 76
Anti-experimental versus anti-empirical,
    458–61
Anti-mental imagery argument, 341, 460
Anti-nativism, 151
Anti-sensationalist, 29
Anxiety, 66, 362, 484, 511
Apparatuses for sound intensity, 244
Apparent motion, 315
Apparitions/appearances/ghosts, 28,
    44, 142, 163–64, 198, 525
Appearance-representation, 478
Appetite, 242
Applications of imagery, x, 226–29,
    293, 329–66, 543, 587–605
Appreciation of music, 198
Aptitude for imagery, 448
Aquinas, St. Thomas, 135, 329
Archetypes, 5, 11, 13, 15, 17, 20, 134,
    362, 532
Architecture and imagery, 455
Architecture/evolution of visual
    systems, 318

Arian heresy, 136
Aristotle, xi, 28, 37, 58, 145–47, 151, 219, 320, 512
Arius, 136
Arousal/disappearance of imagery, 170, 252
Array structure, 315
Array theories, 302, 313–15, 463
Article First database, 67
Articulatory loop/system, 463, 533
Articulatory versus auditory elements, 240, 245–46
Artifact theories, 313, 316
Artificial intelligence (AI), 295, 302, 312, 335, 517
Artificiality of laboratory studies, 458–59
Artistic incapacity, 130
Arts and imagery, 124, 341, 361
Asherah, cult of, 141
As-if experiences, 17, 357
Assessment of mental imagery, 301, 305, 334, 513
Associated hallucinations, 50
Association areas in brain, 512
Association, doctrine of, 33, 63, 151
Association, laws of, xi
Association method in measuring imagery, 154, 157, 161, 203, 470
Association of ideas, 6, 34, 151, 197
Associationist models, 151–52
Associationistic psychology/ associationism, 7–8, 63, 151–52, 158
Associationistic-image theory, 8
Associations/associative thought, 53, 152, 197, 243
Associative Experience Test, 503
Associative mediators/learning/memory, 251, 521–22
Associative potency, 308
Associative powers of smells/odors, 235
Associative processes, 248, 251
Assyrians, 140
Asynergy and articulatory systems, 240
A-thinking (autistic thinking), 75
Athletes/athletics, 356, 359, 541
Atomism, doctrine of, 463
Attention, 3, 8, 25–26, 30, 32, 60, 193, 198, 201, 203–4, 214, 226, 238, 241, 247–50, 298, 351, 486, 512, 516–17, 527, 529
Attention shift, 233, 528
Attitude(s), 8, 10, 14, 190–91, 205–8, 242, 309, 493
Aubert, Hermann, 28
Audile/auditory type, 68, 161
Auditory hallucinations, 47, 50
Auditory maps, 347
Auditory memory, 210
Auditory memory after-image, 27, 181–82
Auditory memory span, 217
Auditory perception, 70, 188
Auditory peripheric hallucinations, 47
Auditory sensation, 178
Auditory tied-images, 244
Auditory/acoustic images/imagery, 7, 11, 16–17, 21, 40, 68–69, 159, 162, 187, 189, 213, 215, 225, 227–28, 235–45, 409, 481, 540–41
Auditory-visual synesthesia, 70
Aufgabe, 154, 216
Auras, 525
Aurignacio-Perigordian period, 122–23
Ausfrage method, 203
Authority, method of, 427
Autism/autistic, 75, 472
Autogenic training, 363
Autokinetic phenomenon, 515
Automatic and direct approaches, 312
Automatic writing, 33, 238, 362
Autonomic control and imagery, 226–29, 478–80
Autonomic functions, 226, 351, 510–11
Autoshaping, 449
Autosuggestion, 362
Availability of images, 474
Average error, method of, 436
Awareness, momentary, 32, 74

Baal, cult of, 141
Babylonians, 140
Back of the head images, 163, 448
Bain, Alexander, 64
Baird's (1911–1917) imagery reviews, 194–98

Basedow type/type B, 41
Basedow's disease, 41–42
Beating heart experiment, 501
Beethoven, Ludwig van, 63, 469
Begbie's disease, 42
Behavior rehearsal, 359
Behavior therapy, 18, 363, 465
Behavioral adequacy, criterion of, 312–18
*Behavioral and Brain Sciences*, 301
Behaviorism, 34, 151, 208, 439–40, 516, 539
Behaviorist school/psychology, xii, 31, 37, 151, 175, 432, 439, 442, 456, 458, 465, 479, 523
Behaviorist theories of imagery, 20, 208
Behaviorists' misconduct in science, 465
Belief and sources of knowledge, 427
Belief/belief-attitudes, 54, 143, 303, 427, 484
Benton Visual Retention Test, 489
Bent-pencil-in-water illusion, 45
Bergman, Ingmar, 52
Berkeley, George, xi, 145, 148–51
Berne's script theory, 453
Bethel/sacred stone, 129
Betts' Questionnaire Upon Mental Imagery, 461, 476, 481, 490–93, 503–4
Between- versus within-participants/subjects, 450, 475, 480, 494, 508
Between-person correlations, 475, 486
Bible, x, 121–22, 124–42
Bible and imagery, 125–28, 131–42
Biblical image-related terms, 131–42
Bibliographies of visual vividness imagery, 455, 542, 605–25
Bibliography, imagery, x, 20, 38, 43, 63, 71, 455, 543, 581–734
Bidwell's ghost, 24
Binocular vision, 29, 183
Bioelectrical activity in the brain, 351, 353, 446, 510, 534
Biofeedback model/approach, 447, 479, 491
Biological aspects, 209–10, 318–19, 361, 530
Blank hallucinations, 47

Bleuler, Paul Eugen, 330
Blind/deaf persons/participants, 52–53, 71, 196, 231–32, 331, 460, 478
Blood flow/pressure, 4, 202, 240, 512
Body concept, 16, 20
Body identity, 13, 507
Body image/imagery, 11, 13, 15–16, 71, 339, 472, 507, 515
Body perceptions, 472
Border/boundary wars, 143
Boring, Edwin Garrigues, 156, 515
Boss-consciousness theory, 325–26
Bottom-up and top-down processes, 324–26
Boyle, Robert, 28
Brain states, 38
Brain theory/research, 72, 152, 310, 464
Brain-damage effects, 66, 352, 464, 477–78, 529
Brain-mapping/imaging techniques, 517, 534–35
Brain-mind cognitive transformations, 152, 348
Brain-stem reticular activating system, 517
Breakfast table questionary, 158–59, 191, 485, 490
Breathing action/rhythms/aspects, 240, 510, 512
"Brief History of Imagery in Religion, Healing, and Psychology, A," 124
Brightness/hue, 24, 180, 212
*British Journal of Psychology*, 207, 209, 533
B-type of eidetiker, 253
Buffon, George Louis Leclerc de, 28
Bugelski, Bergen Richard, 76–77, 333–34, 441–43, 448–49, 465
Bugelski-Hilgard Statement, 465
Burette method, 212

Calculating genius, 250
Calf worship/images, 128
Callosal-sectioning and imagery, 354
Canaanites' gods, 133, 141
Cancer treatment, 362
Cannon-Bard theory, 453

Canons of scientific methodology, 428

Card-sorting tasks, 239

Carpenter effect, 15

Cartesian dualism, 451

Cartographic maps, 347

Carved/graven images, 127, 134

Case studies of synesthesia, 72, 230–35

Case study approach, 43, 72, 164, 198, 204, 230, 445, 461

Catacombs, 135

Categorical relations encoding, 528

Cathode ray tube (CRT), 300

Causality/causation, 156, 326, 425–26, 429–31, 437, 453, 479, 582

Cautela's Imagery Survey Schedule, 490, 493

Cave paintings, 122–23, 143

CDL/MELVYL database, 67

Celestial illusion, 27

Cell-assembly(s) theory, 310, 312, 330, 333, 519

Cells/cellular functions, 329

Central executive, 463

Central nervous system, 19, 23, 178–79, 351

Cerebral hemispheres/laterality/ specialization, 343, 352–54, 490, 509, 529, 538

Cerebralistic physiology, 207

Changing conceptions of imagery, 306

Characteristics of imagery as a clinical tool, 39, 362

Charcot, Jean Martin, 156–57, 220, 456

Chemical senses, 235

Chemistry and imagery measurement, 41

Chess and imagery, 208

Chicago Tests of Primary Mental Abilities, 494

Childhood synaesthesia, 234–35

Children's appreciation of poems, 200

Children's use of imagery in learning, 225, 331, 522–23

Chiliagon, 147

Choice/method of choice, 233, 467

Christian Church and images, 8, 135–36

Christian Church/Christians, 8, 128–29, 131, 135–36, 143, 453

Christian concept of trinity, 453

Chromaesthesia/chromesthesia, 70–71, 195

Chromatic-lexical synesthesia, 70

Cine-recorder, 249

Circular reasoning, 32

Civilized versus uncivilized humans, 143

Clangs/tones discrimination, 213

Classes of variables, 425, 429

Classical conditioning model, 64–65, 308, 323

Classical errors in experiments, 211

Clearness/clarity of images, 20, 40–42, 153, 188, 198, 200, 235, 249–50, 252, 462, 506, 513

Clever Hans effect/phenomenon, 238

Clinical techniques/research, 226–29, 310, 362, 451, 468, 484

Clinical/therapeutic uses of mental imagery, 39, 362

Cocaine bug, 50

Coconscious, 33

Code redundancy, 308

Coding of images, 7, 307, 311, 473, 493

Coding/dual-coding model, 367, 311

Cognition and imagery, 38, 153, 625–34

Cognition in situ, 461

Cognition, model of, 151, 309, 527

Cognition/cognitive behavior/ processes, 1, 10, 17, 35–36, 38, 77–78, 122, 153–55, 206, 225, 232, 295, 299, 303, 309, 317, 319, 322, 325, 328, 330–31, 338, 442, 452, 459, 464, 475, 483, 517, 524

Cognitive model of image formation, 309, 447

Cognitive penetrability/impenetrability, 301, 304–5, 458

Cognitive rehearsal, 359

Cognitive school/psychology/science, xii, 16–17, 19–20, 38, 147, 152, 293–95, 312, 320, 322, 349, 438, 456, 458, 463, 465, 517

Cognitive style(s), 336, 342–43, 489–90, 495, 509

Cognitive theory(s) of imagery, 38, 58, 78, 304, 310

Cognitive unconscious, 59

Cognitive-affective restructuring, 363

Cognitive-behavior therapy, 18, 363
Cognized environment. 514
Coherence of images, 171
Coleridge, Samuel Taylor, 57
Collective human experience, 56
Collective image, 9, 11, 17
Collective insanity, 48
Collective unconscious, 5, 15, 17
Color adaptation, 470
Color recall, 482
Color spectrum, 21, 24
Coloration of images/color, 41, 70,
    73, 149, 156, 158, 170, 178–81,
    183, 230–32, 248, 251
Color-contingent after-effect, 27
Colored gustation, 230
Colored hearing, 70, 72, 229
Colored letters/alphabet, 72, 230
Color-mixer apparatus, 211
Combinations of ideas/aspects, 452
Combinatorial and transformative
    processes, 340
Command cell synapses, 314
Common generative grammar, 311
Commonalities/disagreements of
    imagery theories, 323
Comparative judgment, law of, 436
Compensation/rivalry, law of, 201
Competition/competitive activities,
    356–57
Complementarity theory, 315, 457
Complementary after-images, 25
Complexity/elusiveness of imagery,
    189, 198, 213, 307, 361, 439
Complexity-simplicity dimension, 343,
    473
Componential recovery, principle of,
    529
Composite image/ideas, 10–11, 14–15,
    68–69
Composition principles, 186
Compulsive hallucinations, 14
Computational array theory, 315
Computational mechanism/theory,
    299, 528
Computational quasi-pictorial theory,
    20, 58
Computational theory of mind, 463

Computational-imagery debate, 299,
    320, 323
Computation/computational, 58, 299,
    302, 319–20, 322, 328, 528
Computer algorithm, 300, 310
Computer simulation model(s), 293,
    301, 305, 321, 323, 529
Computers/modeling medium, 4, 6,
    152, 293, 310, 313, 319–20, 328,
    335, 517, 537, 543
Concave/convex lenses, 3
Concentric subsets, 314
Concepts/concept formation, 14, 75,
    77, 158
Conceptual image, 13
Conceptualizing practice, 359
Conceptual-peg hypothesis, 522
Conceptual-representation, 478
Conclusions about imagery theories,
    318
Conclusions from the imagery debate,
    305
Concrete images/imagery, 4, 11, 14–
    15, 20, 69, 132–33, 138–39, 194,
    225, 308, 521
Concrete versus abstract imagery, 77,
    209, 303
Concrete versus abstract words/
    materials, 4, 203, 308, 450, 488
Concrete/high-imagery words, 308, 538
Concreteness effect, 449, 460, 464, 508
Concurrent validity, 488
Condensation, 13, 200
Conditioned sensations/reflexes, 12,
    62, 65, 151, 197, 308, 440
Conditioned sensory responses, 181,
    333, 443
Conditions of image arousal/disap-
    pearance, 170, 252
Conflict resolution and imagery, 363,
    536
Connectionism, 144, 151–52
Conscious versus unconscious, 32,
    206, 324, 361, 363, 517
Consciousness, difficulty of defining,
    31–32, 36–37
Consciousness, early studies of, 30, 35–
    38

Consciousness of attitude, 190, 207, 242
Consciousness of meaning, 190, 202
Consciousness, subcategories of, 17, 19, 30, 33, 73
Consciousness, theory of, 454
Consciousness, two modes of, 35
Consciousness/conscious, 10, 13, 19, 29, 31–33, 35–39, 73, 152–54, 183, 187, 190–91, 193, 197, 206, 210, 224, 302, 319, 323–25, 340, 362, 454, 457, 462, 466, 475, 480, 500, 513, 516–17, 531, 536
Consciousness/dreams/hallucinations/ illusions/perception, 29–39, 183–91
Constant errors in experiments, 211
Constant stimuli, method of, 165, 467
Constraints on imagery theories, 325
Construct(s), 1, 37, 75, 300, 429, 432, 434, 478, 526, 539
Construct validity, 447, 492–93, 495–99, 504–5, 523–24, 534, 542
Construction/synthesis of events, 14, 17, 21, 122
Constructive imagination, 54–55, 512
Constructivism-empiricism controversy, 341
Constructivist theories of perception, 349
Consubstantialism, 136
Content versus form, 210, 451
Context effects of experiments, 458
Contiguity law/principle of, 64, 151
Continued stories, 198–99
Continuous change/reaction method, 213
Continuous versus discrete-type models, 159, 303
Continuum from after-image to imagination, 172
Contrast, principle of, 151
Control, issue of, 344, 425, 428, 451, 458–61, 480–81, 503, 513, 542
Control of imagery, 196, 344, 353, 513, 523
Control of Visual Imagery Questionnaire, 484, 503
Controllability of Imagery Questionnaire, 503

Controllability of thought imagery, 76, 447, 503–4
Controversial issues in measurement, 434–35
Convergent evidence on effective imagery, 308
Convergent validity, 434, 504, 538
Convergent/divergent approaches, 454
Converging operations, 308, 434, 437, 449, 454
Converging/diverging light rays, 3
Cooperative participants, 459
Coordinate location encoding, 463, 528
Core theory, 325
Cornell University, 153–55
Corporeity of images, 170
Corrective agnosticism, 298
Correlates/extra-measures of imagery, 506–14
Correlational method/correlations, 157, 161, 167, 196, 202, 217, 249, 332, 339, 342, 444, 453, 457, 466, 475–76, 479, 482, 484–85, 487, 489, 492–96, 500, 502, 523–24, 542
Correlations between imagery and personality, 342
Council of Trent, 136
Covariations, 431
Creative cognition, 340
Creative discoveries in imagery, 337
Creative imagination, 5, 18, 21, 55–57, 340, 476–77, 489
Creative work/thought, 20, 22, 56, 59, 77, 138, 334, 338, 428, 484, 539
Creativity and imagery, 59, 77, 335, 337, 340, 498, 517, 634–39
Creativity, definition, 338
Creativity, tests of, 339–40
Creativity tests/stages, 5
Criminology and imagery, 539
Criteria for an image formation model, 309
Criteria for evaluating mental processing theories, 334
Criterion of behavioral adequacy, 312–18

Criterion of explanatory adequacy, 311–
    12, 315–16
Criterion of process adequacy, 311–12,
    314–17
Criterion-related validity, 488, 497–99,
    504
Criticisms of imagery theory/methods,
    166, 318
Cro-Magnon Man, 122
Cross-cultural/cross-national studies,
    43, 446, 484, 527
Cross-disciplinary study of imagery, 437,
    451, 462, 536
Cross-modality experiences, 71, 229
Cross-validation, 487
Crowding in temporal intervals, 347
CRT metaphor, 300–301, 305
Crystallomancy, 525
Crystal-vision imagery, 525
Cultural/social psychological aspects of
    synesthesia, 72
Culture(s) and imagery, 331–32, 349, 458
Curvilinear relationship, 476
Cutaneous ghosts, 28, 181
Cutaneous imagery, 182, 236–37
Cutaneous senses, 235
Cytowic, Richard E., 71–72

Damage to brain and effects on
    imagery, 66, 352, 464, 477
Darwin, Charles Robert, 28
Data collection strategies, 429, 582
Daydreaming/daydreams, 5, 6, 55, 57,
    59, 184–85, 197, 362
*De Anima/On the Soul*, 146, 219
*De Somniis*, 28
Debate in the literature on mental
    imagery, 150, 464, 496–99
Debate on visual imagery, 294–306
Decalogue, 127
Decision tree, 301
Declarative memory, 59
Decoding/retrieval process, 522
Deductive approach, 429
Deep structure neural codes, 479
Definitions and domains of imagery, 1–
    78, 158, 161
Deities/deity, 130–31, 139

Déjà entendu, 66
Déjà eprouve, 66
Déjà fait, 66
Déjà pensee/pense, 66
Déjà raconte, 66
Déjà voulu, 66
Déjà vu, 5, 63–68
Delayed overt response, 196, 224
Delayed reaction tests, 196
Delusion of grandeur, 45
Delusion of persecution, 45
Delusion of reference, 45
Delusion versus illusion, 45
Delusional belief/delusions, 22, 32, 43–
    51, 55
Demand characteristics, 302, 304,
    316–17, 319, 459–60, 482, 492–93,
    520, 526, 534
Demystification of mental imagery,
    300–303
Denis, Michel, 77, 87, 100, 365, 374–
    77, 382, 463–64
Denotative meaning, 77, 334
Dependent variables, 165, 430–31, 475,
    505, 540, 581
Depression and imagery, 140, 365–66,
    484
Deprivation, sensory, 331, 470, 472,
    506–7, 516
Depth perception in the after-image, 27,
    183
Descartes, Rene, 36–37, 145, 147, 451,
    458
Description/propositional theories, 58,
    323–24
Descriptionalism/description theory,
    18, 150, 296, 305, 317, 327
Descriptions of early eidetic experiments,
    162–71, 173–75
Descriptions versus use of images, 211
Descriptions/descriptionalist versus
    pictures/pictorialist theories, 150,
    293–98, 303, 306, 317, 323
Descriptive psychology, 158
Descriptive unconscious, 30
Determining tendencies, 154, 516
Determinism/deterministic, 156, 203,
    425–27, 430, 437, 582

Detrimental influence of imagery, 485
Development of imagery, 224, 332–33, 341, 362, 522
Development of meaning, 205
Development/personality and imagery, 341–44
Developmental order of visual imagery, 172, 214, 224, 332
Developmental strategy/paradigm, 160, 229, 341, 440, 456
Diabetic hallucinosis, 49
Diagnostic imaging, 4
Diana on the Aventine, 127
*Dictionary of Philosophy of Mind*, 38
Differential Aptitude Tests, 494–95
Dimensions of creative discovery, 337
Dimensions of the image, 480, 495
Diminutive visual hallucination, 47
Dimming contrast effect, 182
Direct contact, images, 311–12
Direct stimulation of the brain, 50, 353, 517
Directed revery, 363
Discourse-planning disturbance, 527
Discrete versus diffuse arousal, 511
Discrete-type versus continuum models, 159
Discriminant validity, 504
Discrimination(s), 61–62, 217, 225, 466, 481–82
Discrimination of clangs/tones, 213
Displacement in space and imagery, 171, 200
Dissociation/dissociation theory, 32–35, 456
Distance and image/imagery, 3, 26, 133, 170, 182
Distance and size, 26
Distraction/disruption method, 157, 162, 177, 221–22, 449, 470
Divergent thinking, 524
Divided attention, 35
Divided consciousness/control, 35
Doctrine of distinct imagery/ideational types, 219–23
Doctrine of primary/secondary sensory elements, 187
Dorsomedial thalamic nuclei, 512

Double blind technique, 482, 542
Double consciousness, 32, 186
Double images/imagery, 7, 20, 28–29
Double insanity, 48
Dr. Ruckle, mathematical prodigy, 195
Dream consciousness, 35, 183–84, 247, 532
Dream house, 536
Dream illusion, 30
Dream imagery, subcategories, 30
Dream imagery/images, 15, 29–39, 52, 75, 184, 226, 235, 247, 511, 515, 639–46
Dream records/reports, 183, 507
Dream therapy, 363
Dream-perception, 184
Dreams and sleep, 13–17, 29–30, 184
Dreams, early studies, 30
Dreams, lucid, 531–32
Dreams of the blind, 641
Dreams, three types, 532
Dreams/dreaming, 6, 13–15, 18, 29, 32, 35, 39, 55, 184, 191, 197, 226, 235, 331, 348, 362, 517, 531–32, 639–46
Dreamy mental state, 50, 184, 186
Drowsiness hallucination, 186
Drowsiness/drowsy state, 184–87
Drug substances and imagery, 75, 190
Drug-induced hallucinations, 49
Dual controls of mental functioning, 32
Dual-coding hypothesis/theory/ model, 20, 307–11, 320–21, 323, 354, 460, 493
Dual-processing hypothesis, development, 341
Dual-processing models of brain's hemispheres, 353
Duration of drug effects, 51
Duration of memory after-images, 167
Duration, property of, 153, 167, 177–78, 200, 216, 241, 250, 507, 512
Dynamic imagery, 21
Dynamic tests, 467–68
Dynamics factor, 506
Dynamics in learning experiments, 468

Early empirical study of hypnosis, 52

Early measurement of imagery, 157–76
Early psychological imagery studies (1890–1959), x, 124, 176–253
Early studies on synesthesia, 71–72
Early visual imagery studies, 164, 245–53
Ease-of-evocation of imagery, 519
Eastern Church, 129, 135
Ebbecke's after-image theory, 26
Ebbinghaus, Hermann von, 151, 320
ECO database, 67
Ecological significance of research, 338
Ecological validity/approaches, 302, 349
Ecstasy, 140
Education and imagery, 334, 451, 468
Efficient use of imagery/thinking, 78
Ego defenses, 66
Ego ideal, 11, 17
Ego-involvement, 40
Egyptian deities, 128, 130, 140
Egyptians/Egypt, 124, 128, 130, 140
Eidelon, 42
Eidetic disposition, 39
Eidetic image as unreliable, 41, 166
Eidetic image versus after-image, 40–41, 43, 169–70, 172
Eidetic image versus memory-image, 40–41, 170, 172, 252
Eidetic image versus visual image, 40, 169, 252
Eidetic imagery, children versus adults, 39–40, 42–43, 162, 165–66, 168–69
Eidetic imagery, descriptive/functional aspects, 43, 170–71, 524
Eidetic imagery, experimental studies of, 162–71, 173
Eidetic imagery, pre-1960 studies of, 43, 162–71, 173–75
Eidetic imagery, two types, 41, 169
Eidetic imagery/images, 5, 20, 23, 39–43, 57, 60, 75–76, 140, 162, 164–65, 172, 252–53, 331, 339, 448, 458, 511, 513, 515, 518–19, 524–26, 544, 646–54
Eidetic images versus icons, 43
Eidetic psychotherapy, 364, 451, 502
Eidetics, typographic versus structural, 41, 525

Eidetiker/eidetic individual, 39, 42, 169–71, 250, 253, 445, 478, 525
Eidetische anlage, 39, 169
Eidographic image, 169
Eidos/essences, 42, 532–33
Eikon, 134
Electrical/direct brain stimulation, 50, 352, 517
Electrodermal responses, 510
Electroencephalogram/EEG, 331, 351, 353, 446, 506–7, 510, 517, 534–35, 538
Electromagnetic fields, 444
Electromyograms/EMGs, 507
Electro-oculograms/EOGs, 351, 507
Electrophysiology of mental activities, 228, 353
Elementary hallucinations, 47
Eliminativism, 38
Elite athlete(s), 359, 466
Embedded-figures test, 472
Embodiment, 131, 138
Emmert's law/principle, 26–27, 168, 171, 247, 252
Emotion, theories of, 453
Emotional/mood/drug aspects of synesthesia, 72, 232
Emotions/affects, 15, 18, 31, 50, 72, 77, 163, 197–98, 200, 202, 226, 229, 309–10, 332, 334, 351, 353, 356, 452, 472, 483, 488, 538
Emotive imagery, 18, 310, 332
Empathic projection/empathy, 193, 200, 241, 539
Empirical reality, 433
Empirical-experimental approaches, 294, 430–31, 457, 582
Empiricism/empirical study, 43, 52, 75, 156, 164, 425–26, 428–29, 431, 446, 449, 451–52, 512
Empiricism-constructivism controversy, 341
Empiricist philosophers/psychologists, 145–48, 150–51, 458
Employee versus boss systems/processes, 325
Empty versus filled time intervals, 347–48

Encoding/encode, 21, 304, 308–9, 325, 354, 440, 464, 475, 484, 522, 534
*Encyclopedia of Cognitive Science*, 38
Endophasia, 190
Engineering and environmental psychology, 455, 516
Engram, 13
Enriching imagery, 201
Entopic phenomena, 226
Ephods, 128
Epileptic/epilepsy, 65–66, 352, 517
Epiphenomenal/epiphenomena, 296–97, 301–3, 313, 443, 449, 479
Episodic memories, 59
Equivalence factor/scores, 500
Equivalence, levels of, 77
Equivalence versus non-equivalence, 77
Equivocal images, 247
ERIC database, 544
Erinnerungsnachbild, 178, 182
Errors, classical experimental, 211
Errors, constant, 211
Errors, time and order, 211
Eschatological restoration, 131, 139
Esperanto words, 242
*Essay Concerning Human Understanding*, 181
Esthetics and imagery, 187, 192
Ethnicity, 483
Euclid's law, 26–27
Evaluating theories of mental processing, 334
Evaluation of two imagery theories, 305
Event generation, 533
Event-related potentials, 353
Evolution of imagery/evolution theory, 121, 143, 160, 172, 245, 315, 318, 328, 331
Examinability of illusions, 191
Exner, Sigmund, 60, 178
Expectancy experiments, 440–41, 460
Expectations/expectancies, influence of, 49, 348, 460, 491, 493
Experiential analysis technique, 192, 513
Experiential approaches, 151, 426–27, 437, 458, 537
Experimental design(s), 429, 511, 513, 542

Experimental method(s)/methodology, 184, 199, 201–2, 208–9, 228, 295, 337, 425, 428, 430, 439, 449, 457–58
Experimental psychology/psychologists, xi, xii, 3, 40, 67, 74, 147, 150–52, 155, 228, 295, 432, 451, 456, 469, 475, 581
Experimental-cognitive strategy, 456
Experimental-empirical approaches, 156, 173, 184, 209, 295, 430, 451, 457, 581–82
Experimenter-bias/effects, 482, 493, 520, 526
Experimenter's hypothesis/expectations, 317, 459–60
Experiments versus empirical studies, 431
Experts, imagery, 464
Explanatory adequacy criterion, 311–12, 315–16
Explanatory constructs/models, 300, 302, 319, 341
External object versus internal state, 32, 463
External validity, 541
External versus internal imagery, 246, 310, 438, 533
Externalization of images, 246, 444, 483
Exteroception, 518
Extracampine hallucinations, 48
Extraneous/outside factors, 232, 297, 430, 502
Extra-psychology disciplines, 7, 295
Extraversion-introversion dimension, 336
Eye of the mind, 3
Eye-gaze movement, 351
Eye-lens, 24
Eye-movements/EMs, 183, 198, 248–50, 506, 508–11, 519, 523, 526

Fables, 139
Face validity, 446, 496
Factor analysis/analytic approach, 446–47, 491, 504
Factorial research design, 347
Factorization, 486

Failure imagery, 359
Faint images of sense impressions, 149
Faking behaviors, 503
Fall of Man, 136–38
Fallacy, stimulus error, 32
False beliefs, 46
Falsifiability/falsification criterion, 305, 428, 430
Familial mental infection, 48
Familiarity factor(s), 248, 473
Fanciful imagination, 55, 57
Fancy, 7, 18, 54
Fantasy-deprivation/disturbance, 447
Fantasy/fantasies, 5, 6, 14, 20, 53, 58, 332, 342, 361, 364, 458
Fantasy-prone personalities, 342
Fashion and imagery, 348
Father figure, 10, 500, 536
Father filter, mental, 467, 500–501, 532, 536
Father-on-the-left/right position, 502
Fechner, Gustav Theodor, 25–26, 61, 156–58, 178, 220, 435, 456, 467, 515, 524
Feeblemindedness, 204
Feeling coloration, 236
Feeling of being stared at, 219
Feeling of concept, 203
Feeling of content, 203
Feeling of familiarity, 66, 203
Feeling(s), 19, 51, 73, 191, 202, 209, 240, 452
Feelings of relations experiment, 203
Female researchers, early, 180
Fetishes, 129
Field dependence-independence, 343, 472
Field-based research, 451, 454, 461
Figural after-effects, 183, 515
Figurative language and imagery, 4, 5, 22, 139
Film/movies, 348
Filter cells, 314
Filters, mother and father, 467, 500–501, 532
F-images, 248
Finkelstein, Mr. Salo, 250
First after-effects, 181

First positive after-image, 181
First-order isomorphism, 311, 323
Five principles of imagery, 18
Five traditional strategies in studying imagery, 456
Fixed images/fixation, 17, 167
Fixing/establishing beliefs, 427, 430
Flachenfarbe/frozen gas, 170
Flag Test, 513
Flajani's disease, 42
Flashlight perceptual illusion, 186
Flaws in imagery questionnaires, 493–94
Flexibility of images, 171
Flight of colors, 28, 183
Floaters, 226
Flournoy, Theodore, 229
Flow of ideas, 32, 59, 206, 226, 513
Focal attention/consciousness, 231, 314
Folie a beaucoup, 48
Folie a deux, 48
Folie a quatre, 48
Folie a trois, 48
Foreconscious/unconscious, 30
Forehead writing test, 483
Foreign/strange gods, 128, 131, 134, 143
Form in the mind, 42
Form perception, 22
Form versus content, 210, 451
Formal versus material image, 137
Formal-operational thought, 343
Form-board test, 196
Four distinct imagery categories, 20, 332, 486
Four measures of visual imagination, 488
Fragmentary visual image, 197
Framework for a cognitive model, 309
Franklin, Benjamin, 28, 52
Franklin experiment, 28, 52
Franklin's magnetized tree study, 52
Free and tied images, 5, 12, 20
Freedom of the will/freedom, 132, 136, 138, 543
Free-imagery, 507–8
Frequency of imagery use versus availability, 219, 337, 474
Frequency of usage of the term *image* in the Bible, 141–42

Frequency of usage of the term *vision* in the Bible, 142

Frequency of usage of the terms *redintegration* and *déjà vu*, 66–67

Frequency of use of visual imagery, 219, 474, 482

Freud, Sigmund, 13–14, 33, 66, 330, 361, 363, 456, 516–17

Freudian theory, 48, 453

Function(s) of imagery, x, 39, 62, 64, 171, 186, 195, 200–201, 209, 293, 302, 328–66, 448, 464, 514, 524, 587–605

Function of music, 201

Function versus nature of imagery, 492

Functional architecture of the mind, 304

Functional independence, 34, 354

Functional relationships, 154, 431, 444

Functions versus structures, 19, 224, 302

Functions/purposes of images for early humans, 61–62, 143, 172

Fusion and images, 171, 183, 237

Future status of the imagery debate, 321

Future/new directions in imagery research, x, 353, 425, 478, 500, 504–6, 537–44

Fuzzy/generic images, 312

Galton Questionnaire, 160, 218–19, 445–46, 470, 476, 485, 490

Galton, Sir Francis, 2, 21, 70, 156–61, 219–20, 330, 443, 456, 467, 469–70, 473, 476, 485, 516, 525

Galvanic skin response/GSR, 228–29, 240, 353, 474, 511–12

Ganzfeld, 470–71, 506

Gender/sex differences, 72, 132, 185, 192, 195, 199, 336, 345, 472, 476, 483, 491, 505, 509, 515, 524, 530–31, 709–20

Geneplore Model, 340

General measurement considerations, 425, 432–38, 503

General scientific methodology, 425–32

General versus specific theories/models, 310–13, 316–18

Generality criterion, 305, 318

Generalizability/generalization, 428–29, 445

Generalized images, 149

Generalized reality-orientation, 472

Generic/general images, 10–11, 15, 20, 171, 312

*Genesis of the Image*, 122, 224

Genetic theory, 171

Genetics and the image, 61–62, 173, 191, 224, 253

Genonomy/genomes, 468

Geography and imagery, 347, 455

Geons/generalized-cone components, 529–30

Germ theory of disease, 463

Gestalt school of psychology, 39, 155

Ghost theory, 45, 181

Ghostly band of colors, 28

Ghosts of sensations, 439

Ghosts, visual/cutaneous/kinaesthetic, 44, 163, 181, 197, 525

G-images, 248

Global visual imagery, 197, 336

Goal images, 55

God-in-man, image of, 131–32, 134

Gods of the Sumerians, 140

Gods, unshaped/aniconic, 129–30

Goethe, Johann Wolfgang von, 28

Good figure, 529

Good versus poor imagers, 186, 344, 473, 538

Gordon's Test of Visual Imagery Control, 76, 461, 468, 490–91, 493–94, 524

Gradation of imagery, 159

Grades of spontaneity in visual imagery, 214

Gradualness of mental rotation, 318

Graven/carved images, 127, 131, 134

Graves disease, 42

Greek Fathers, 136

Greek philosophy/philosophers, xi, 31, 145

Greek statues, 127, 130

Greek word synonyms for word *image*, 134

Group comparisons studies/methods, 445

Group methods in imagery therapy, 364

Grouping, principles of, 151

Guided affective imagery (GAI), 21, 59, 362

Guided imagery and education, 535–36

Guilford-Zimmerman Spatial Visualization Test, 487

*Gulliver's Travels*, 47

Gustatisms, 71

Gustatory audition, 70, 229

Gustatory images/ideas, 11, 14, 21, 69, 72, 230–31, 235–45, 483

Gustatory-auditory synesthesia, 70

Gustatory-taste hallucinations, 47, 230

Gustatory-visual synesthesia, 70, 230

Gutzmann, Hermann, 241

Gymnastic tasks, 533

Habit of imaging/habit sequence, 213, 243

Habit of repose, 227

Hallucination(s), 5–6, 13, 15, 20, 30, 32, 39–40, 43–51, 55, 57, 61, 75, 164, 190, 230, 339, 352, 515, 517, 519, 527

Hallucination of conception/psychic/ perception, 48

Hallucination/peripheral, 45

Hallucinations, dozens of varieties, 46

Hallucinatory image(s), 10, 17, 44, 164, 190, 471, 516, 527

Hallucinogenic drugs, 50, 331, 458, 516

Hallucinogens, 49, 51

Hallucinosis, 44–45, 49, 525

Hamilton, Sir William, 63–64

Hand temperatures, 479

*Handbook of Physiology*, 60

Handedness, 72

Haptic hallucinations, 47

Haptic-visual recognition tasks, 489

Health aspects/psychology, 342, 484

Hearing/audition, 19

Heart-rate/HR, 42, 202, 351, 478, 482–83, 501, 507, 510–12

Heat, experience of, 237, 483

Heat imagery, 237, 479

Hebb, Donald Olding, 310, 312, 318, 330, 333, 456, 514, 516, 518–19

Hebrew translations of the word *image*, 133–34

Hebrew versus Greek perspectives, 138

Hebrews, ancient, 125, 130, 138

Helmholtz, Hermann Ludwig Ferdinand von, 25–28, 160

Helps, method of, 221–22

Hemispheres of the brain, 336, 343, 353, 458, 466, 528–29, 538

Hereditary similarities, 157, 233

Hering color-vision theory, 180

Hering illusion, 44

Heuristic-value criterion, 305, 315

High and low imagery, 161, 308, 345, 474, 485, 487, 520

Higher mental functions, 57, 153, 191

Higher- versus first-order cell assemblies, 519

Higher versus lower senses, 187

Higher-order assemblies, 312, 519

High-imagery words/conditions, 218, 308, 353, 489, 508

High-level visual processes, 318, 528

Hilgard, Ernest Ropiequet, 32–35, 454, 462, 465, 476

Hippocampus, 65, 517

Historical roots/review of imagery, 123, 437, 451, 458, 465, 473, 522

History of learning experiments, 466

History/theories of imagery, 437, 458, 465, 473

Hobbes, Thomas, xi, 145, 147–48, 150–51

Holistic versus elementalist views, 155

Holograms, 4

Holt, Robert R., xii, 19, 75–76, 94, 320, 345, 442, 456, 471–72, 514–17

Homer, 127

Homo sapiens, 124

Homogeneous stimulation, 470

Homogeneous versus heterogeneous word lists, 524

Homunculus, 302

Horopter, 28

Hot image, 466

House image, 536
Hue versus brightness, 24, 180, 212
Hull, Clark Leonard, 34, 95, 333, 448
Human associative memory/HAM program, 321
Human engineering and imagery, 334, 540
Human geography, 455
Human sacrifice, 141
Humanistic-transpersonal methods, 364
Humanists versus positivists, 455
Humanity-in-Christ, 131
Hume, David, xi, 56, 145, 147–51, 224, 320
Hunger, 242
Hyperthyroidism, 41
Hypnagogic image/imagery, 13, 15, 17, 20, 30, 57, 75, 183–84, 339, 472, 515, 519
Hypnogogic image/imagery, 5, 17, 30
Hypnopompic image/imagery, 14, 16–17, 30, 75, 339
Hypnotism/hypnosis/hypnotizability, 21, 25, 29, 32–35, 52, 329, 331, 342, 347–48, 362, 364, 472, 476, 479, 491, 511
Hypothesis, testable/testing, 334, 428–29, 458–59
Hypothetical construct(s), 334, 448–49
Hypothetico-deductive reasoning, 497, 499
Hysteria, 66

Iconic image/imagery, 18, 43, 129–30, 135, 331
Iconoclastic controversy, 135, 298
Iconolatry, 8, 128
Iconophiles and iconophobes, 298, 310
Icons/iconic memory, 43, 135, 298, 309, 331, 349
Ideal of movement, 15
Idealized image, 10–11, 13, 15, 17, 20
Idealized self, 12, 17
Ideas and images/imagery, 11, 14, 16, 53, 74, 144, 147–49, 151, 196, 224
Ideation, laws of, 157

Ideational image/processes/types, 3, 14, 16, 73, 156–57, 188, 197, 219–23
Identical points theory, 10, 29
Ideomotor acts/action, 16, 77, 449
Ideomotor image, 15
Ideomotor law, 15
Ideo-real law, 15
Idiocy, 204
Idiographic/ideographic studies, 445–46, 457, 541
Idio-retinal phenomena, 178, 471
Idiot savant, 250
Idols/images, 2, 8, 42, 121, 127–29
Idol-worship/idolatry, 8, 121, 127, 130–31, 135, 137, 140–41, 143
Illumination of image(s), 158, 182
Illusion versus delusion, 44–45
Illusion versus hallucination, 44–45
Illusion/assimilative, 45
Illusion/associative, 45
Illusion/contrast, 45
Illusions, 5–6, 32, 43–51, 61, 66, 190–91
Illusions of memory, 44–46
Illusions of motion/movement, 44–45
Illusions of orientation, 44
Illusions of perception, 44
Illusions of reversible perspective, 44
Illusions of visual size, 44
Illusory contour, 22
Image agglutinations, 13, 15, 20
Image as a copy, xi, 2
Image discovery, 308
Image envy, 20
Image evocation, 491
Image location, 163
Image modality and the artist, 361
Image model, 451
Image of God/Father, 131–34, 137–38, 141
Image of the act versus achievement, 464
Image of the Trinity, 136
Image orthicon, 4
Image processing, 3–4, 6–7
Image production, 4, 58
Image psychology, 451

*Image Psychology and the Empirical Method*, 450, 462

Image rotation, 3, 298, 303–4, 314–16, 324, 429, 438, 444, 448, 459–61, 481, 535

Image, significance of, 124

Image size, 246–47, 481

Image stimulation/inscription, 348

Image structure, 456

Image theory of conditioning, 323

Image tube, 4

Image versus imagery/mental imagery, x, 2, 6–7, 22–23

Image worship, 2, 7–8, 127–30

Imageability, 449, 531

Image/anticipation, 9

Image-center and percept-center, 190

Image/composite, 9, 11, 14

Image-dimming effect, 501

Image-eliciting/production tasks, 316, 318

Image-formation method/theory, 199–200, 309–10, 454–55

Image/general, 9

Image/habitual, 9

Image/imagery topics/types, xiii, 1, 7, 9, 11, 14, 19, 21–22, 69, 73, 75, 131, 135, 156–57, 159, 186, 191, 513

Imageless thought, xii, 20, 55, 73–75, 154–55, 158, 190–91, 204–7, 516

Imagen, 22

Image/optical, 3–4, 9–10

Image-produced stimulation, 333

Image-retinal system, 22

Imager orientation/position, 483

Imagery and creativity, 336–41

Imagery and development/personality, 223, 341–44

Imagery and learning/memory, 344–47, 448–49

Imagery and perception, 347–50

Imagery and physical health, 342, 484

Imagery and physiology, 41, 350–56

Imagery and ratiocination, 206, 247

Imagery and sports, 356–61, 466, 541

Imagery and the internet, 429, 537, 542–43

Imagery and therapy/visualization techniques, 361–66

Imagery as a hindrance to remembering, 344

*Imagery Bibliography*, 455, 543

Imagery coding/code, 6–7, 21, 322

Imagery controversy in modern psychology, 295–306

Imagery Debate, The, xiv, 38, 73, 145, 150, 294, 302–3, 326

Imagery experts, 464

Imagery illusion(s), 191

Imagery in nonpsychological contexts, x

Imagery index, 222, 519–20

Imagery interpretation, 6

*Imagery Paradigms*, 465–66, 500, 514

Imagery processes, 78

Imagery reactor, 21

Imagery rehearsal studies, goals of, 356

Imagery tests/testing, 161, 186, 448, 467–68, 473, 500

Imagery theories, review of, 38, 306–29

Imagery theory, 38, 58, 150, 294–329, 526, 654–66

Imagery theory and learning experiments compared, 466–68

Imagery therapy, 21

Imagery traces, 321

Imagery-based therapeutic methods, 363

Imagery-based therapies, limitations of, 364

Imagery-control tests, 480, 493, 513

*Imagery/History of Painting*, 123

Imagery/imaginative types, 18, 20–21, 23, 75, 157, 159, 186, 191, 469, 485, 513

Imagery-spatial-parallel processing system, 307, 440

Images and uncivilized versus civilized humans, 143

Images of brain action, 4

Images of fancy, 7

Image/tied, 9

Imaginal flooding, 21

Imaginal sensations, 64

Imaginal space method, 363

Imaginal/imaginal processes, 17, 64, 154, 307, 361, 490

Imaginarii, 14

Imaginary audience, 21

Imaginary chromaticity, 21

Imaginary contour, 22

Imaginary perception, 170, 525

Imaginary practice, 359

Imaginary/imagined actions, 533–35

Imaginary/invisible companion/ playmate, 21–22, 525

Imagination, Baldwin's two variations/ kinds, 8, 54

Imagination, history of, 58

Imagination image/imagery, 15, 20, 23, 25, 52–60, 76, 175, 191–98, 248, 452, 511, 666–74

Imagination, James's conclusions, 53

Imagination, types of, 57, 59

Imagination versus perception, 145, 154, 472

Imagination/imagine/imaging/ imagining, 1–2, 5–9, 11–12, 14, 16– 18, 21–22, 36, 38, 53–56, 58, 64, 137, 141, 145–49, 172, 176, 187, 192, 225, 228, 332, 347, 434, 452, 472–74, 476, 498, 512, 515, 525, 533–35, 543

Imaginativeness, 56, 447, 466, 472

Imaging/imagery ability, 434, 478–79, 481, 484, 491, 496, 513, 523–24, 542

Imagist theories, 303

Imagistic and verbal processing systems, 303

Imagistic representation, 298, 303

Imago, 2, 7, 9–10, 12, 14–17, 20, 22, 136

*Imago Dei*, 136

Imbecility, 204

Imitation, 8–9, 16

Imitative imagination, 5, 57

Immediate memory imagery, 63

Immortality, 132, 136, 138

Immune functions/systems, 365

Implicit encoding principle, 18

Implicit practice, 359

In vivo images, 4

In vivo thought-sampling, 538

Inability to form images, 156, 159, 309

Inaudi, mathematical prodigy, 222

Incarnate Word/Incarnation, 135, 139

Incidental and intentional learning/ recall, 449, 475, 484, 520, 523–24

Incidental color memory, 482

Incipient motor sense, 469

Incomplete figures, 245

Independent variable(s), 164, 307, 430–31, 475, 505, 540, 581

Indirect strategies in discoveries/ inventions, 337

Individual differences and imagery, 9, 53, 68–69, 75, 156–76, 182, 186, 195–96, 200, 219, 234, 308, 320, 344–45, 448, 463–64, 466, 469–84, 513, 520, 523–24, 537, 541–42, 709–20

Individual Differences Questionnaire, 490, 496, 503, 523

Induced hallucinations, 48

Inductive approach, 429

Infectious insanity, 48

Inferred versus reported images, 331

Influenced psychosis, 48

Influencing of imagery, 247

Information processing/theory, 35, 72, 293, 297, 309–10, 332, 341, 463, 517, 527

Injuries and mental imagery, 66, 352, 464, 477–78

Inner ear and inner voice, 540

Inner pictures, 146

Inner world of imagery, 307

Inner/internal speech, 190, 222, 227– 28, 242, 527, 540

Insane asylum, 190

Inspiration, 140

Instinct emotions, 185

Instinctual drive/instincts, 62, 208–9, 361

Instructions, effects of, 308, 345, 348, 449–50, 460, 473, 479, 492, 501, 508, 511–12, 520–21, 524, 531, 534, 542

Instrument artifacts, 449, 534

Instrumental conditioning, 323, 449

Intellectualist/ideational theories, 202

Intelligence/IQ/intellectual, 5, 136, 149, 235, 445, 471, 483, 485, 488

Intensity/weight of image, 10, 75, 153, 170, 188, 195, 209, 241, 309
Intentional learning, 484
Interface paradigm, 463
Interference of imagery and perception, 179
Intergenerational violence, 539
Internal consistency criterion, 446, 492, 505
Internal cues versus external sensations/ perceptions, 339
Internal representations, 1, 296–97, 300, 302, 322, 324–25, 349, 354, 442, 530
Internal versus external imagery, 348
Internal/external orientation prefer- ences, 336, 483
International Imagery Association, 543
Internet (World Wide Web), 429, 537, 542–43
Interparental conflict, 502
Interpretative consciousness, 149, 233
*Interpreter's Dictionary of the Bible, The* 125
Interval scaling, 437
Intervening variables, 429, 540
Interviewing techniques, 446
Intra- and inter-hemispheric activity, 353
Intramodal and transmodal stimulation, 189
Introspection/introspective, 6, 16, 32, 62, 74–75, 145, 149–50, 151–56, 164–65, 183–84, 186, 188–91, 195, 198, 201–3, 205–7, 209, 216, 220– 21, 223, 228, 233, 239, 242–44, 246–48, 298, 306, 313, 323–25, 444, 454, 456, 472, 477, 485, 493, 518, 521
Introspective operationalism, 454
Intuiting-sensing dimension, 343
Invariability of images, 171
Inventiveness, 20, 56–58
Inventory of Déjà Vu Experiences Assessment, 66
Invisible God, 134, 139
Involuntary reactions/impulses, 15, 35, 72, 238
Irrelevant imagery/irrelevancy factor, 209, 246

Ishtar, 140
Islam, 130
ISM (image, somatic response, meaning) model, 452, 462, 466
Isolation/boredom and imagery, 75, 331, 470–71, 516–17
Isomorphism/isomorphic, 77, 298, 341, 433, 512
Israel as the chosen nation, 126
Israelites/Israel, 126, 131, 141

Jackson, John Hughlings, 352
Jacob, 128
Jacobson, Edmund, 158
Jaensch, Erich Rudolf, 13, 39–40, 42, 170
Jaensch, Walter, 41
James, William, 24–26, 28–29, 52–53, 60, 64, 158, 293
James-Lange theory, 453
Janet, Pierre, 33–34, 456
Jastrow, Joseph, 52, 211
Jesus/Jesus Christ/Christ, 126, 129– 31, 133–34, 136–37, 139
Jews, 130, 135, 143
Josephus, Flavius, 128
*Journal of Mental Imagery*, 439, 441, 450, 454–55, 462, 464–65, 500, 504, 531, 535, 539, 542–43
Judging/choosing, 78, 132, 165, 200, 213, 229, 233, 436
Judgment consciousness, 65, 73, 154, 213–14, 539
Jung, Carl Gustav, 5, 13–14, 56, 362– 63

Kant, Immanuel, 56, 145, 149
Kinaesthetic ghosts, 28, 181
Kinaesthetic maps, 347
Kinaesthetic sensation versus image, 74, 193, 223, 241–42
Kinaesthetic space perception, 236
Kinesthetic/motor images, 11, 14, 19, 42, 72, 74, 163, 182, 193, 202, 204–5, 223, 225–27, 232–33, 235– 45, 251, 469
Kingdoms, Northern and Southern, 128

Kulpe, Oswald, 73, 154–55, 206, 226
*Kundgabe*, 191

Ladd-Franklin color vision theory, 180
Lane's Questionnaire on Imagery
  Control, 490
Language and imagery, 2, 69, 73, 77,
  296, 333, 350
Language production in schizophrenia,
  527–28
Language/verbal behavior, 148, 190,
  196, 207, 527
Laryngographic recordings, 246
Lascaux cave paintings, 122–23
Latency and magnitude measures, 182,
  507–8
Latency effect, 460
Latent eidetic imagery ability, 168
Lateral eye-movements/LEMs, 353,
  490, 509–10
Lateralization, hemispheric, 352–54,
  528, 538
Latin Church, 129
Law of after-images, 247
Law of coexistence, 158
Law of comparative judgment, 436
Law of compensation/rivalry, 201
Law of contiguity, 64, 151
Law of development, 130
Law of mnemic causality, 225
Law of perseveration, 158
Law of physical causality, 225
Law of redintegration, 63–68
Law of similarity, 158
Law of succession, 158
Law of transition, 129
Laws of association, xi
Laws of ideation, 157
Laws of relationships, 468
Laws of the reproductive imagination,
  192
Learning ability/disability, 536
Learning by eye or ear method, 161
Learning experiments, history of, 466–68
Learning genomes, 468
Learning how to see, 349
Learning method/paradigm, 460, 468,
  470

Learning theory and imagery, 441, 448,
  468
*Learning Theory and the Symbolic
  Processes*, 441
Learning/memory and imagery, 64,
  69, 152, 330, 344–47, 448–49,
  466–67, 475, 517, 531, 674–85
Left and right brain hemispheres, 336,
  352, 477
Leipzig, University of, xi, 150, 153, 155,
  178
Lermontov, Mikhail Yurevich, Russian
  poet, 199
Lesion-simulations, 529
Letter square method, 162, 221, 445
Leveling of figurative-conceptions
  hypothesis, 523
Levels of consciousness, 29–39
Levels of equivalence theories, 313, 315
Lexical complexity, 320
Lexical ear, 540
Lightning calculator, visual imagery of,
  250
Likeness, concept of, 2, 10, 16, 132–34,
  136–39
Lilliputian hallucination, 47
Limbic region of brain, 72, 512, 517
Limitations of imagery questionnaires,
  493–94
Limitations of individual difference
  methods, 481
Limitations of scientific method, 457–61
Limitations of visual imagery, 246
Limits of resolution method, 461
Link collections/website, 38–39
Literal/literary images, 5, 22, 139, 143–
  44, 195
Literary appreciation, 199
Literary criticism/analysis and imagery,
  4, 452
Literary theory versus psychological
  theory, 453
Literature/music and imagery, 198–
  202
Little pictures in the mind/head, xi
Liveliness factor, 506
Lobes of the brain, 517
Local signs, concept of, 236

Localization of images, 163, 170, 173, 182, 195, 223, 252, 483
Localized probe, 444
Loci, method of, 146
Locke, John, xi, 53, 145, 147–51, 181, 451
Logical-intuitive/verbal-mathematical dimension, 343
Logic/mathematics and imaging, 8
Long-distance driving, 50
Longitudinal studies, 40, 66
Long-term memory/chunks, 22, 300–301, 313–14, 463–64, 478
Loss of control over imagery contents, 309, 519
Low and high imagery, 218, 474, 485, 487, 489, 508, 520
Lower senses/modalities, 187, 225, 235
Lower-order assemblies, 312, 519
Low-level sensory visual processing, 172, 528
LSD/lysergic acid diethylamide, 50–51, 75–76, 516
Lucid dreams, 531–32
Lucidity of images, 20, 40–42, 153, 188, 198, 200, 469

Maccabees, 135
Macroproperties of the brain, 528
Macro-structural environments, 539
*Magician, The*, 52
Magnetic resonance imaging/MRI, 4
Magnitude and latency measures, 435, 507–8
Magnitude and proximity rules, 433
Main types of imagery, 16
Man as the image of God, 131
Manipulated variables, 430–31, 475
Manipulation of images, 16, 77, 331
Marburg school, 169–71, 173
Marijuana, 50–51
Marking/grading system for images, 166–68
Marks' Vividness of Visual Imagery Questionnaire, 454, 461, 468, 475–76, 484, 490–91, 493, 496–501, 503–6, 534, 542
Marks-Chara imagery debate, 496–99

Marlowe-Crowne Social Desirability Scale, 494
Marr's theory of visual perception, 327, 528
Marsh's disease, 42
Martin, Lillien, J., 163–64
Mathematical prodigy, 222, 250
Maze performance, 466, 489
McCollough effect, 27
Mead, George Herbert, 539
Meaning and synesthesia, 72, 231, 234
Meaning/meaningfulness, 9, 18, 72, 77, 148, 153, 189–91, 195, 197, 199, 202–8, 229, 231–32, 234, 242–43, 309, 320, 332, 334, 361–62, 364, 442–43, 451–52, 462, 473, 488, 492, 521, 524, 531, 542
Measurement and tests of imagery, 685–93
Measurement, controversial issues, 169, 434–35, 502
Measurement, definitions, 431–33, 436
Measurement error, 502, 529
Measurement, purpose, 431–32
Measurement, rules and procedures, 156, 430, 433
Measurement scales and statistics, 432, 435
Measurement scales/procedures/tests/ types, 160, 430, 432, 434–35, 543
Mechanics/mechanism of imagery, 452, 528–29
Mechanization stages, 233
Mediate-association paradigm, 487–88, 521
Mediate/immediate experience, 188
Mediation/mediators/mediational role, 245, 307–8, 320, 332, 334, 442, 449–50, 453, 493, 508, 524
Meditation/meditative, 147, 362–63, 458
MEDLINE database, 544
Megalomania, 45
Memorization/calculation, 250–53
Memory after-images, 24–25, 61, 170, 178, 181–82, 252, 524
Memory consciousness, 69, 210, 214–15

Memory disorders/errors, 66
Memory illusions, 214
Memory imagery/images, 7, 8, 10–11, 13, 15, 20, 23, 25, 40–41, 56, 60–63, 68–69, 76, 164, 170, 175, 182, 185, 193, 203, 210–18, 248, 253, 344, 472, 477, 499, 518
Memory images versus imagination images, 164, 175, 193, 248
Memory imagination, 5, 56
Memory scale, 172
Memory store, 308, 313
Memory trace, 308
Memory-for-Designs Test, 487
Memory-image theory, 145–46
Memory/learning and imagery, 464
Memory-levels and imagery, 171, 173
Memory/memories, 8, 10, 17–18, 25, 31, 35, 65, 136, 145, 148–49, 151, 172, 176–77, 200, 225, 250, 300, 308–9, 311, 313, 321–23, 346, 348, 440, 454, 498, 512, 521, 527, 693–700
Memory/retroactive hallucination, 48
Memory-span studies, 161, 250–53, 522
Men of science, imagery in, 156, 159, 469
Mental act of reproduction/construction, 15, 21
Mental analogs, 77
Mental atoms, 151
Mental disposition theory, 8
Mental father filter, 467
Mental form, 230
Mental imagery theories/models, 20, 150, 158, 294–329, 446
Mental imagery types, 18, 20–21, 23, 75–76, 157, 159, 164, 219, 239
Mental imagery, various definitions of, 2–3, 18, 20–23, 76, 302, 483, 530, 539–40
Mental imagery/images, xiii, 1–3, 6–12, 14, 16–17, 19–22, 35, 37–39, 42, 54, 56, 58, 60, 63, 67, 75–76, 122, 132, 146, 149–50, 156–58, 162, 175, 224, 230, 241, 245, 247, 252, 293, 296–97, 302, 306, 353, 425–26, 429–31, 433, 436–39, 446,

458, 461, 479, 484, 493, 514–15, 526, 530, 544
Mental images as copies of sensory input, xi, 10–11, 15, 17, 20, 146–47
Mental images as patterns in wax, xi, 145–46
Mental images as primary symbols of thinking, xi
Mental insight, 348
Mental maps, 347, 455, 489
Mental mother filter, 467
Mental pictures, 2, 4, 5, 307
Mental practice, synonyms, 359
Mental rehearsal/practice, 356–57, 359, 364, 464, 466, 475, 484, 533, 541
Mental representations, 15, 20, 38, 58, 68–69, 77, 145, 197, 293–96, 300, 540
Mental rotation/scanning of images, 298, 303–4, 314–16, 324, 429, 438, 444, 448, 459–61, 481, 535
Mental tests, 160
Mental transformations, 315, 444
Mental travel, 448
Mental walk, 146, 344
Mentalism/mentalistic, 34, 37, 152, 293, 321, 439, 516
Mescaline/mescal, 49, 75, 190, 516
Mesmer, Franz Anton, 52
Mesmerist, 52
Meta-analysis of VVIQ, 506
Meta-analytic review of imagery-creativity, 341
Metacontrast, 298
Metaphor(s), 4–5, 126, 139, 300, 302, 322, 349, 452–53, 517, 531
Metaphysical/metaphysics, 11, 298
Meta-prolucids, 531–32
Metatheory, 302
Method of association, 157, 161, 203, 470
Method of authority, 427
Method of average error, 436
Method of choice, 233, 467
Method of comparative judgment, 233
Method of constant stimuli, 165, 467
Method of continuous change/reaction, 213

Method of description, 211
Method of distraction/disruption, 157, 162, 177, 221–22, 449, 470
Method of helps, 221–22
Method of learning, 470
Method of loci, 146
Method of paired comparisons, 436, 467
Method of ranking, 467
Method of recall/comparison, 175, 211
Method of right and wrong cases, 213
Method(s) of science, 456
Method of style, 222
Method of tenacity, 427
Methodological objectivism, 156
Methodology and measurement of imagery, x, 178, 218–229, 294, 302, 425–544
Methods of reproduction and recognition, 210, 231
Meyer, M. M., 73, 154
Microptic hallucination, 47
Military/government intelligence, 6
Mill, James, and John Stuart, 151
Mimicking psychosis, 50
Mind, xi, 31, 41, 137, 148, 152, 515, 518
Mind, philosophy/theory of, 39, 148–49, 152
Mind sets in athletes, 359
Mind, two types, 41
Mind-body relationship, 152, 479
Mind-brain identity theory, 19
Mind-expanding/altering drugs, 51, 516
Mind-reading, 238
Mind's ear, 68
Mind's eye, 10, 19, 42, 68, 153, 159, 187, 300, 302, 314, 348
Minnesota Paper Form Board Test, 514
Mirror-recorder, 249
Misconduct, scientific, 465
Misreporting scientific facts/data, 465
Misuse of imagery practice in sports, 359
Mixed illusions, 191
Mixed types of imagers, 68, 160, 220, 485
Mnemonics, 20, 146, 224, 306–8, 330, 344, 352, 354, 445, 460, 478, 530–31

Modality-specific interference, 313
Model-building, 302, 517
Models for thinking, 78, 517
Modern imagery studies, x, 515–37
Modern measurement/methodology in imagery research, 425–544
Modes of knowing, 427
Molecular structures, 444
Molten images, 131, 134
Moments of consciousness, 206
Moments of rational thinking, 206
Monitoring images, 365
Mood and imagery, 193, 200–201
Moon illusion, 27
Morning versus night imagery, 216
Mosaic cells, 314
Mosaic Law, 135, 141
Mother filter, mental, 500–501, 532, 536
Motile/motor type, 68
Motion, after-images, 179–80
Motivation and imagery, 20, 309, 339, 440, 484, 538, 542
Motor control/learning, 464
Motor images/imagery, 21, 68, 159, 162, 198, 208, 220, 223, 227, 232, 235–45, 515, 533, 541
Motor imagination, 228, 512
Motor initiative, 238
Motor sensation, 239
Motor set, 205, 233
Motor tendencies/reactions/processes/performances, 8, 75, 232, 251, 466, 484, 541
Motor theories of imagery, 20
Motor theory of thinking/consciousness, 158, 469
Motor/mimetic ideation, 239
Motor/psychomotor hallucination, 48
Movement images, 8, 42, 55, 194
Movement stimulus/stimuli, 509
Movement-produced stimuli, 333
Movies/film, 348
Movies/TV, objective rating of, 335
Mowrer, Orval Hobart, 77, 334, 440–41
Muller color vision theory, 180
Muller, Georg Elias, 158
Muller-Lyer illusion, 44, 191

Multidimensional scaling, 436–37
Multidimensional space, 316
Multi-method approach/strategy, 446
Multi-modal experience(s), 510
Muscle-reading, 238–39
Muscle-relaxation, 227–29
Music and bodily reactions, 202
Music appreciation, 201, 540
Music consciousness, 201–2
Musical experience, recall, 201, 243
Mystic paranoia, 48
Mystical experiences, 472
Mystical theology, 136
Mythology/myths, 15, 130, 140, 173, 192, 451–52, 532

Names and imagery, 197
Narrative versus paradigmatic thought, 59
Nascent motor response, 62, 224
National type, 43, 332
Natural computation, 528–29
Naturalism, 124, 155
Naturalistic versus symbolic artistic styles, 124
Nature of imagery, 39, 77, 195, 224, 329, 341, 483, 514, 524
Nature photograph concept, 536
Necker cube illusion, 44
Negative after-image/sensation, 23–25, 61, 182
Negative effects of imagery in sports, 359
Negative hallucination, 48
Negative memory hallucination, 48
Negative reactions to imagery models, 320
Negative time-error, 211
Neo-Dissociation approach, 34, 466
Neolithic period, 123
Nerve fibers/systems, 74–75, 229, 331, 463
Neural arrays, 312
Neural axons, 314
Neural impulses/activities/sensation, 24, 72, 297, 314, 333, 443
Neural network models/theories, 152, 313–14, 319, 328

Neurological damage/disorders, 66, 352, 477
Neuron(s), 314
Neurophysiological processes/mechanisms, 297, 299, 312, 315, 362, 517
Neuropsychological strategy/evidence, 353, 429, 456, 517
Neurotic pride, 12
Neuroticism/neurotic traits, 16, 342
New man, 131
New psychology, 515, 517
New psychology of thinking, 517
New Structuralism in psychology, 454–56, 462–63
*New Testament*, 126, 128, 131–35, 137–40, 143
New Zealanders, 455
Newton, Sir Isaac, 28
Nice numbers, 251
Nicene Council, 136
Night dreams, 183–85, 197
Node networks, 152, 321
Nomotheticism/nomothetic, 155, 445–46, 457, 475, 541
Nondirective thinking, 337
Non-Euclidean geometry, 316
Noninterference interpretation, 34–35
Nonlinear interactions, 322
Nonliterate societies, 331
Non-metric scaling, 437
Non-pictorial imagery, 301, 307, 323
Non-pictorial percept-analogy theory, 312, 323
Nonself state, 527
Nonsense syllables/figures, 197, 204, 235, 242, 442, 486
Non-sensory remembrance, 196
Non-sensory thinking, 74
Non-storage models of imagery, 325
Nonverbal images/imagery, 186, 307, 521
Nonverbal memory, 339, 478
Nonvisual imagery, 349
Normal curve model, 160
Normal imagers, 365
Normalize-then-template-match, 315
Normative analysis, 492

Northern and Southern Kingdoms, 128
Nuclear imaging, 21
Nuclear magnetic resonance/NMR, 4
Number form(s)/imagery, 70–71, 195, 250–53
Numbers-orders association, 236

Object recognition, 530
Objections to mental imagery, 300
Objective operational method, 516
Objective rating of movies/TV, 335
Objective scientific progress in psychology, 152, 175–76, 516
Objective tests of imagery/ideational types, 161–62, 164, 195, 221, 223, 469, 485–86, 523
Objective versus subjective approaches/dimension, xii, 184, 186, 225, 228, 336, 430, 438–39, 450
Objective/external behaviors/measures, xii, 152, 249, 479
Observation of events, 426
Observational practice, 533
Obsessional neurosis, 21, 48
Ocular movement, 248–49, 351, 511
Ocular spectra, 28, 226
Old Testament, 124–28, 131–33, 135, 138–40, 143
Olfactisms, 71
Olfactory hallucinations, 47
Olfactory images/imagery, 11, 14, 21, 69, 230, 235–45, 469
*On Memory and Reminiscence*, 146
*On the Soul (De Anima)*, 146
One hundred learning genomes, 468
Oneirotherapies, 363
Onomatopoeia and Images Test, 488
Onomatopoeic words, 488
Ontogenetic versus phylogenetic analyses, 122, 172, 332
Operational definitions of mental imagery, 151, 307, 463, 542
Operational theory, 302, 307, 341
Operational variations of ISM, 453
Optical images/optics, 3, 4, 9, 10, 16, 22, 74
Optokinetic nystagmus/OKN, 351–52
Origence-intellectence, 343

Original Sin, 136
Original sleep dream, 532
Originality and practicality, inventions, 337
Originless Cartesian coordinate system, 318
Origins of imagery, 121–22, 143, 171, 536
"Origins of Images, The," 122
Orth, Johannes, 73, 154
Osgood, Charles Egerton, 40, 74–75, 333, 469–70
Ostracism of mental imagery study, 458
Otis Intelligence Test, 486
Out-of-body experiences, 525
Overt rehearsal, 359

Pain(s), 21, 39, 70, 72, 149, 186, 242, 329
Paired associates/associative learning, 308, 460–61, 487, 489, 508, 518, 522, 524, 534
Paired comparisons method, 436, 461, 467
Paivio's Individual Differences Questionnaire, 490, 496, 503, 523
Paleolithic/Old Stone Age, 122–24
Pantheon, 140
Parables of Jesus, 126
Parables/proverbs, 125, 139
Paradigm(s), 444, 447, 451, 455–56, 460–61, 464–65, 488, 514–15, 523
Paradigmatic versus narrative thought, 59
Paradoxical cold, 237
Parahippocampal gyrus, 65
Parallel-distributed processing models, 152
Parallelism, 152, 529
Paranoiac memory-hallucination, 46, 48, 365
Paranoid ideation, 50, 140
Paranormal hallucination, 515
Parapsychological phenomena, 517
Parental figures/filters, 12, 16–17, 22, 499–501, 503, 532, 536
Parietal lobes, 477–78
Parry's disease, 42

Parsimony/parsimonious, 207, 305–8, 319–20, 430, 433

Parsons' disease, 42

Part realignment, 528

Passive tactual perception, 237

Pathology/psychopathology, 43, 65, 185, 197, 502, 527

Pattern recognition/interpretation, 4, 314, 316

Pavlov, Ivan Petrovich, 13, 62, 151

Peg mnemonics, 320

Peirce, Charles Santiago Sanders, 427

Peiresc, 28

Perceiving-judging dimension, 343

Percept analogy/analogue theory, 306, 310–11

Percept versus mental image, 75, 147, 175, 187, 189, 323, 483

Percept-arc, 190

Percept-images, 13, 15, 20, 41, 75, 147, 149, 187–88, 312, 462

Perception and images/imagery, 5–7, 9, 14, 16, 18–19, 22, 24, 27, 37, 51, 62–63, 71, 74–75, 145, 149–50, 153, 172, 187, 193, 195, 207, 224–25, 232, 243, 249, 295, 297–98, 302, 306–7, 309, 312, 319, 323–26, 330–31, 339, 345–50, 362, 440, 444, 448, 473, 476, 485, 514, 517, 526, 700–709

Perception and sensation, 31, 339, 518

Perception as sensation and as cognition, 349

Perception of rhythm, 243

Perception of space, 28–29

Perception of time, 347

Perception, two meanings, 348

Percept/perceptual image, 15, 41, 75, 210

Perceptual activity theory, 19, 38, 58, 328

Perceptual constancies, 518

Perceptual deprivation/isolation, 470, 506–7, 516–18

Perceptual development theory, 166

Perceptual equivalence principle, 18

Perceptual illusions, 27, 483–84

Perceptual maps, 347

Perceptual recognition, 475, 529

Perceptual responses/processes, 18–19, 27, 308, 348, 506

Perceptual versus imaginal processes, 225, 444

Performance/athletes and imagery, 356, 359, 541

Peripheral and central factors in memory images, 178–80, 191, 506

Peripheral nervous system, 18, 23, 62

Perky, Cheves West/Perky experiment, 20, 153–54, 192–94, 511

Perky effect, 193, 307, 440

Perseverative imagery, 24

Persistence of image, 42, 146, 170, 177, 182, 252

Persistence of sensation, 28

Personal images, 12–13, 20

Personal names and imagery, 197

Personal reference imagery, 195, 248

Personality and eidetic imagery, 162, 173

Personality variables and imagery, 11, 33, 40, 132–33, 138, 173, 234, 332, 471–72, 474, 483, 709–20

Person-treatment interactions, 448

Petroglyphs, 121, 123

Peyote, 190, 516

Pfungst, Oskar, 238

Phantasia, 58

Phantasma, 58

Phantasy images, 10, 13–14, 46

Phantom limb(s), 515, 518, 525

Phantoms of sensory memory, 61

Pharaoh, 140

Phase sequence, 330

Phenomenological productions/ phenomenology, 1, 20, 65, 295, 348, 354, 517, 535

Philosophers/philosophy, x, xi, 3, 19, 21, 33, 36–38, 56, 58, 74, 124, 133, 144–45, 147, 149–52, 294–95, 326, 348, 455–56, 530

"Philosophy of the Unconscious," 33

Phobias/phobic behaviors, 21, 335

Phonisms, 71

Phosphere(s), 339, 471, 515

Photic stimulation, rhythmic, 472, 517

Photisms, 71, 229–30, 234
Photographic fallacy, 295, 297
Photographic materials, 249
Photographic memory, 41–42, 149, 194
Photography and imagery, 3–4, 6, 348
Phylacteries, 129
Phylogenetic versus ontogenetic analyses, 122
Physical basis of imagery, 41, 72, 326
Physical chemistry, 41, 229
Physical damage and mental imagery, 66, 352
Physical health and imagery, 329, 365–66, 535
Physical illusion(s), 45
Physical psychology, 229
Physical versus mental practice, 466, 533, 541
Physiological changes/bases of visual imagery, 351, 362
Physiological imagery theories, 3, 310, 511
Physiological trace, 211
Physiology of the sense organs, 2, 25
Physiology/neuropsychology and imagery, xii, 29, 41, 124, 173, 187, 228–29, 237, 350–56, 491, 510, 512, 519, 538, 720–24
Piaget, Jean/Piagetian theory, 322–23, 332, 341, 456, 517
Pictographs, 121, 123
Pictorial memory, 146, 300, 477, 493
Pictorial representation versus abstract thought, 2, 125, 143, 145, 149
Pictorialism/pictorialist, 18, 139, 144, 148, 150, 293–95, 303, 305–6, 310, 327
Picture and non-pictorial theories/models, 146, 293, 301, 306, 310, 323–24
Picture in the head/mind, xi, 17, 19, 68–69, 311–12
Picture metaphor, 19, 149–50, 298
Picture-completion task(s), 489
Picture-description method, 157, 162
Picture-memory studies, 63
Pictures versus words, 298, 308, 474, 522

Pilot study, 459
Pink elephants, 50
Pioneers of mental imagery study, 456
Pitch/tonal memory/perception, 212–13, 244
Places, images of, 347, 455
Plasticity of images, 171, 201
Plate tectonics, 463
Plato, xi, 57, 74, 145–46, 320
Play, imagery, 22
Plutarch, 127
Poetic appreciation, 200
Poetic construction, experimental study, 199
Poetic factors, duration/mood/rhythm, 200
Poggendorff illusion, 44
Ponzo illusion, 44
Poor and good imagers, 186, 344, 463, 473
Position alteration, 528
Positive after-image, 23–24, 26, 61, 181–82
Positive after-image in audition, 27
Positive after-sensation, 23
Positive and negative after-images, theory, 26–28
Positron emission tomography/PET, 4
Posterior brain regions, 477
Power of imagery, 159, 201
Power of suggestion, 185
Practical aspects of visualization/imagery, 330, 334, 361
Prayer(s), 532
Precision criterion, 305, 430, 461
Preconscious/unconscious, 30
Predetermined scenes, 363
Predictive validity, 492–93, 496, 523
Preference and controllability tests/measures, 493, 504
Prefrontal cortex, 65, 512
Prehistoric images/imagery, 123–24, 143
Prehistory of consciousness, 36, 38
Preinventive forms, 337–38, 340
Preparatory set, 233, 440–41
Prescriptions/scientific features, imageless thought controversy, 155

Pre-sensation, 190
Presentation rates, 308, 521
Preserved orientation, 44
Pressury/pressure cold, 72, 233
Prevalence of Imagery Test, 479, 503
Preverbal imagery, 332, 362
Primal scene, 47
Primary memory-image, 3, 40, 60, 170, 178, 524
Primary positive after-image, 25
Primary sensation, 24
Primary/secondary sensory elements theory, 187–88
Priming conditions, 524
Primitive elements, 151
Primitive humans, 122–23, 133
Primitive nature of imagery, 123, 172, 331
Primordial images, 5, 11–13, 15, 17, 20, 332–33, 362
Principle of componential recovery, 529
Principle of implicit encoding, 18
Principle of perceptual equivalence, 18
Principle of redintegration, 64
Principle of spatial equivalence, 18
Principle of stimulus-support, 540
Principle of structural equivalence, 18
Principle of transformational equivalence, 18
Principles of composition in drowsiness, 186
Principles of grouping, 151
Principles of mental imagery, 18
*Principles of Psychology, The*, 24, 52
Probabilistic determination, 427
Problem-solving studies, early, 158, 209, 215–16, 466
Problem-solving/reasoning/thinking and imagery, 57, 75, 158, 209, 335, 337, 517
Process adequacy criterion, 311–12, 314–17
Processing of images, 3–4, 7, 315–16, 463
Production tasks, 249
Productions, memory, 313
Productive creativity, 6, 339
Productive imagination/imagery production, 2, 5, 53–54, 339, 509

Professor Gotch, 187
Progressive relaxation technique, 226–29, 362
Pro-imagery position, 321, 460
Projected memory-image, 26, 170, 524
Projected versus resident kinaesthetic imagery, 163–64
Projection theory, 29
Projection/projected images, 1, 3, 5, 18, 26, 39–41, 131, 164–66, 182–83, 195, 197–98, 241–42, 246–47, 252, 307
Projective tests, 192
Prolucid dreaming/dreams, 531–32
Prolucid F-dream, 532
Prolucid M-dream, 532
Pro-mental imagery argument, 341
Proofreader's illusion, 191
Properties of images, 78
Prophets/abnormal mental phenomena, 140
Propositional theories, 38, 300–303, 310, 312–13, 317, 324, 341, 454, 493
Proprioception, 540
Prose-processing and imagery, 463
Prototypes/protomodel, 59, 129, 135, 139, 301
Proverbs/parables, 125, 139, 203
Provisional markers for new imagery tests, 542
Psalms, 139–40
Pseudo-chromesthesia, 229–30
Pseudo-experiment, 203
Pseudo-hallucinations, 515
Pseudo-perception, 14, 39, 41, 43
Pseudo-synaesthesia, 234
Psyche, 31, 361
Psychedelic drugs, 51
Psychic hallucination, 48–49
Psychic infection, 48
Psychoanalysis, 10–12, 14–15, 34, 348, 363, 456
Psycho-imagination therapy, 21
*Psychological Abstracts*, 34
*Psychological Bulletin*, 194
Psychological illusion(s), 45
Psychological versus pictorial/artistic viewpoints, 124

Psychology as a science, xi, 428–29
Psychology of music, 201–2, 243
Psychology of the image/imagery, 7, 348, 425, 582
Psychology of thinking, 78
Psychometric measures/psychometrics, 430, 467, 481, 542
Psychomotor rehearsal, 359
Psychopharmacological tools, 51
Psychophysical complementarity theories, 313, 315–16
Psychophysical measures/psychophysics, 152, 305, 316, 329, 430, 436, 467
Psychophysicist/psychophysiology, 19, 478, 483
Psychophysiological theory, 18
Psycho-sensorial hallucination, 48
Psychosis, 525
Psychosis of association, 48
Psychosomatic types/problems/effects, 41, 440, 479
Psychosomatic unity, 138
Psychosynthesis, 362–63
Psychotherapy, 22, 39, 51, 173, 449, 514
Psychotherapy online, 543–44
Psychotic experiences/psychosis, 140
Psychotomimetic substances, 50
PsycINFO database, ix, xii, 6, 544, 581
Public aspects of science, 426, 428, 430
Pupillary response, 474, 506–8
Pure types of imagers, 68, 160, 248, 253, 485
Purkinje after-image/images/figures/ phenomenon, 24, 28, 183
Purkinje-Sanson images, 24
Purpose of imagery, 302
Purposes/functions of images for early humans, 143
Purposive and structural unity, 171–72
Pursuit eye-movements, 351

Qualia, 38
Quantification, 157, 159, 169
Quantitative assessment of imagery study, 164, 169
Quantitative versus qualitative descriptions, 213, 220, 433

Quantitativism, 156, 160
Quasi-experimental methods, 457, 466
Quasi-perceptual experiences, 12, 19, 58, 76, 475, 499
Quasi-pictorial images/theory of imagery, 58, 301, 305, 311, 313, 317, 326–27
Quasi-sensory experiences, 12
Questionary, 161, 218–20, 485, 490
Questionnaire on Mental Imagery Control, 484, 503
Questionnaire(s)/survey(s), 21, 156–60, 185, 191, 219, 446–47, 450, 467, 470, 473, 476, 479, 485–506

*Race for Consciousness,* 38
Rachel, 128
Racially-noxious materials/discrimination, 481
Radio isotopic encephalography, 21
*Rain Man,* 250
Rand, Benjamin, 29, 54
Random-dot stereogram test, 513
Ranking/rating scales, 467
Rapid eye movements/REMs, 331, 507–8, 517
Ra/Re, the sun-god, 140
Rate of discovery, 508
Ratings of images/rating scales, 249, 494
Ratio scaling, 437
Ratiocination and imagery, 206, 247
Rational/empiricist philosophers, xi
Rationalist analysis, 151, 294
Reaction-time measurement studies, 204, 213, 242, 440, 444, 481, 538
Reading processes, 245–46
Real image/imagery, 3, 163, 537
Real self, 17
Reality feelings/control, 54, 140
Reasoning/thinking, 5, 75, 78, 137, 229, 232, 335
Recall and comparison methods, 211, 214, 231
Recall and imagery, xi, 64, 170, 175, 191, 214, 243, 450, 453, 473, 520–21, 531
Recall, incidental versus intentional, 520–21

Receptive mode of consciousness, 35
Reciprocal insanity, 48
Recognition theories, 205, 476
Recognition-by-components/RBC, 529–30
Recognition-memory system, 8, 65, 522
Recollections, 53, 228
Reconstructions in the mind, 5
Reconstructive view of memory, 321–22, 345
Recurrent image/imagery, 12, 24, 170, 182
Recurrent issues, 35
Redintegration, law of, 64, 67
Redintegration/reintegration, 5, 63–68
Redintegrative memory, 65
Reductive psychology, 476
Reduplicative paramnesia, 66
Reference function of imagery, 253
Reference person, 13–14
Reflective thought, 509
Reflectivity-impulsivity dimension, 343
Reflex hallucination, 49
Reflex of perception, 187
Reformers/Reformation, 8, 136
Rehearsal responses/processes, 356
Rehearsal, visual motor behavior/VMBR, 356, 358
Reinforcement, 187, 198
Relations, concept of, 151, 203
Relaxation/progressive relaxation, 18, 226–29, 357, 362, 511, 541
Reliability and validity, 166, 169, 364, 430, 437, 446, 456, 475, 490–93, 495, 497, 500–501, 504
Religions, development, 45, 127, 130
Religious/ritual ceremonies, 121, 123, 127, 143
Remembering mind, 16, 63, 196, 333
Repeatable/self-correcting process, 203, 426, 430
Reported versus inferred images, 331
Representations/reproductions, 1–5, 8–10, 12, 14–17, 20, 41–42, 53, 55–56, 62, 68–69, 74, 77–78, 122, 130–31, 133–35, 138, 145, 149–50, 157, 171, 184, 187–88, 203, 293, 296, 300, 303–5, 310, 312–15, 317,

319, 323–25, 327–29, 341, 464, 477, 496
Repression, 13, 34
Reproduction and recognition methods, 215
Reproductive imagination, 2, 21, 54, 56
Requirements/criteria of a psychological experiment, 203
Resemblance, 149, 172–73
Resident/memory imagery, 241–42
Residual tension, 227
Resolution of the Imagery Debate, xiv, 294
Respiratory/respiration rhythms and images, 202, 240, 351, 486, 510–12
Response-set difficulties/effects, 491, 527
Restructuring of sensory impressions, 5
Retina(s), 9–10, 17–18, 22, 24, 26, 28, 210, 318
Retinal excitation, 22, 26, 247, 352
Retinal image size, 26–28
Retinal image/picture/impression, 2, 9–10, 16–18, 20, 22, 61, 182, 348
Retrievability of images, 301, 308, 321–22, 475, 478, 519, 522
Retroactive interference paradigm, 533
Retrospection versus introspection, 155
Review of imagery ability and cognition, 523
Review of imagery theories, 158, 306–28, 526
Reviews of imagery, 69, 307, 319, 511, 535, 605–25
Revival of imagery research/interest, xii, 20, 144, 309, 320, 437, 439, 441–42, 516–18
Rhythm, perception of, 200, 223, 243
Richardson, Alan, 12, 19, 76, 332, 342–44, 358–60, 482–84, 502–5, 509, 511–12, 537, 541
Richardson, John T. E., xiii, xiv, 1, 19, 76–77, 87, 108, 346, 350, 353–56, 366, 368, 375, 382–84, 408, 437, 449–50, 454, 477–78, 515, 530
Richardson's Verbalizer-Visualizer Questionnaire, 490, 494–95, 503
Richness/clearness of images, 170

Right and left hemispheres, 336, 352–55, 477

Right and wrong cases method, 213

Right-brain hemisphere activity, 57, 352–55, 477

Robotics, 58

Rock carvings and paintings, 121, 123–24

Rod and cone vision, 24

Rod-and-frame test, 489

Role of imagery in thought, 74, 469

Role-playing models, 323–24

Roman Catholic Church, 8, 136

Roman Forum, 14

Rome, foundation of, 127

Rotation of the head, 24

Rotation/scanning of images, 3, 298, 303–4, 314–16, 324, 429, 438, 444, 448, 459, 461, 481, 535

R-subscript-g, 333

R-subscript-m, 333

R-thinking (realistic thinking), 75

Saccadic eye-movements, 319, 351

Sacred images in the church, 130, 135–36

Sacred stone/bethel, 129

Salivation response, 483, 512

Scales of measurement, four types, 432, 434

Scaling issues/procedures, 161, 434–36, 467, 542

Scan mental images/brain, 16, 21, 31, 302–3, 316, 459–61

Scan paths, 319

Schema(s), 59, 324, 442

Schizophrenic/schizophrenia, 13, 15, 44, 50, 365, 506–7, 527–28, 540

Scientific misconduct, 465

Scientific principles and methods, 425, 427, 457, 536

Scientific psychology and imagery, xi, 20, 38, 151, 155, 294–95, 318, 425, 451, 515

Scientific theories, 334, 426, 428

Sclera/white of the eye, 24

Script(s), 59

Script theory, 453

Scrying imagery, 525

Search controller, 528

Second positive after-image, 181

Second positive visual after-sensation, 24

Secondary sensations, 71

Second-order isomorphism, 298, 444

Secor's word method, 218

Seeing as, 58

Seeing in the mind's eye, 10, 19

Selective tendencies and images, 170

Self, 13, 16, 37, 133, 195, 242, 335, 539

Self-awareness, 12, 31, 365

Self-coaching in imagery, 201

Self-consciousness/determination, 132, 138, 365

Self-control, 346, 491

Self-correcting process, 430

Self-help, 39

Self-image/concept, 11, 16–17, 20, 132, 472

Self-initiated thought imagery, 76

Self-projection, 200

Self-report methods/measures/ratings, 229, 308, 339, 430, 432, 434, 445–46, 454, 475, 482, 490–92, 496, 504–5, 513, 523–24, 538

Self-talk and imagery, 358–59

Self-therapy, 543

Self-verbalization, 541

Semantic categories, 300

Semblance situations, 54

Semonides/Semonides of Amorgos, 146

Sensation(s), 5, 8–9, 12, 17, 19, 25, 53–54, 62, 68–71, 73–74, 144, 146, 148–49, 151, 153, 175, 187–88, 191, 195, 203, 206, 211, 339, 349, 357, 365, 514, 518, 700–709

Sensationalist/sense theories, 150, 202

Sense of time, 347

Sense/sensory-perception, 3, 14, 46, 54, 56, 153, 225, 339

Sensorium, 66

Sensory conditioning, 515

Sensory cortical association areas, 512

Sensory deprivation and imagery, 49, 331, 470, 472, 516

Sensory images/imagery, 9–10, 13, 68–69, 188, 344, 473
Sensory information store, 43
Sensory memory/imagination, 18, 43, 512
Sensory modalities and imagery, 9, 11, 14, 42, 69–71, 159, 186, 197, 219, 229, 340, 470, 474, 476, 479, 485–86, 510, 519
Sensory register, 43
Sensory stimulation, absence of, 2, 5, 9–10, 14–15, 18–24, 28, 69, 147, 350, 483
Sensory thalamic nuclei, 512
Sensory-faculty disturbances/deficits, 14, 308
Sensory-linked images, 59
Sequencing of events, 332, 453, 522, 533
Sequential and parallel processing, 490
Serial learning studies, 445, 522
Sets/predispositions, 154, 205, 219, 233, 308, 516
Sex/gender differences, 72, 132, 185, 192, 195, 336, 345, 472, 476, 483, 491, 505, 509, 515, 524, 530–31, 709–20
Sexual behavior and imagery, 351
Shadow(s), 15, 133–34, 226
Shakespeare, William, 199
Shape encoding/recognition, 315, 528
Shape templates/detectors/recognition, 314
Sharp/detailed images, 312
Sheehan's Questionnaire Upon Mental Imagery Test, 468, 480–81, 490, 493–94
Sheehan's Vividness of Imagery Scale, 461
Short Form of Betts's Inventory, 484
Short-term memory, 18, 309, 313, 477
Similarity principle/law, 151, 158
Similes, 4–5, 139
Similitudo Dei, 136
Simonton, Carl, 362
Simultaneous induction, 181
Singer's Imaginal Process Inventory, 490, 493

Single case studies, 445
Single-subject/participant studies, 445, 480, 496, 541
Situated cognition approach, 58
Six variations of ISM, 453
Size cues/images, 26–27, 246, 481
Size of the visual field/visual images, 27, 170, 247
Size-distance invariance hypothesis, 26–27, 168, 247
Skepticism, 426, 428
Skill acquisition/maintenance, 541
Skin senses, 235
Skinner, Burrhus Frederick, 37, 456
Sleep, 13–17, 29–30, 32, 184–85, 197, 532
Sleep deprivation, 516, 518
Slee's Visual Elaboration Scale, 492
Slow potentials, 466
Slow-motion hallucination, 49–50
Smell maps, 347
Smell sense, 230, 235
Snake figure, 24
Social control, 539
Social desirability, 491, 493, 504–5
Social image, 13, 20, 208, 224
Social structures, 531
Social/cultural aspects of imagery, 16, 224, 247, 332, 530, 540
Social-symbolic imagery, 539–40
Sociology and imagery, 348, 451, 539
Solipsistic confusions, 438
Solutreo-Magdalenian period, 122
Somatic response(s)/reference, 248, 452, 456, 531
Somesthetic imagery, 518–19
Somnambulism, 184
Soul, the, xi, 58, 133, 136, 143, 145–46
Sound intensity apparatuses, 244
Sounds and Images Test, 488
Space error, 211
Space, multidimensional, 316
Space projection, 247
Space Relations Test, 494, 513
Space Test, 494
Space-motor hallucination, 49
Spatial displays/layouts, 300, 307, 312, 317

Spatial equivalence principle, 18
Spatial illusions, 191
Spatial memory/tests, 353, 482, 524
Spatial reasoning/thinking/ability, 78, 223, 307, 316, 341, 353, 477, 493, 496, 513, 531
Spatiality of images, 303–4, 310
Spatiality of tones, 214
Spatiotopic map construction, 528
Special theory of imagery, 300–301, 304
Specialization, hemispheric, 528
Specialized maps, 347
Specific techniques of visualization/ imagery, 503
Specificity-generality dimension, 30, 320–21
Spectrum/spectre, 21, 24, 28
Speech disorganization/loose associations, 527
Speech output controller, 528
Speech perception, 21, 190, 530, 540
Speech primitives/components, 530
Speech production, 240
Speech-motor and hand-motor types, 203, 220, 223, 228
Speed of reaction, 203
Spelling method, 162
Spirits, 525
Spiritualists/spiritual, 39, 181
Split-brain patients, 354, 528
Split-half reliability, 488
Split-off of ideas, 33
Spontaneous imagery, 14, 214, 247, 362, 365, 474
Spontaneous images of phantasy, 170
Spontaneous imaging preferences, 214, 503
Spontaneous thought imagery, 76
Spontaneous/irrelevant images, 246
Sport psychology, 484, 541
Sports and imagery, 356–61, 724–27
Sports competition, 356–57
Sports performance theory, 356
Sports training, 39
St. Augustine, 28, 136
St. Basil's principle, 135
Stabilized retinal images, 3, 17, 20

Staircase illusion, 44
*Stanford Encyclopedia of Philosophy*, 38, 537
Static and dynamic imaging, 21
Statistics and measurement scales, 432
Stimuli and responses, 42, 62, 151, 164–65, 197, 203, 521, 530
Stimulus error, 32
Stimulus independent mentation/SIM paradigm, 447
Stimulus-support principle, 540
Stimulus-trace theories, 145
Stopped image, 17
Storage/retrieval processes, 299, 301, 308, 321, 324–25, 332–33
Story reconstruction, 345
Strategy versus paradigm, 456
Stream of thought/consciousness, 32, 59, 206, 226, 513
Stress management, 541
Structural analysis, 18, 492
Structural and typographic eidetikers, 41, 525
Structural aspects/functions, 4, 8, 172, 191, 224, 302, 313, 442, 447, 452, 481, 525
Structural equivalence principle, 18
Structural, functional, and interactive theories, 526
Structural isomorphism, 77
Structural-description theories, 312–13, 317–18, 326, 526
Structuralism school/psychology, 17, 31, 42, 69, 73–74, 151, 153, 462
Structure versus process, 312
Structures versus functions, 18–19, 224
Studies on the imagery-creativity relationship, 340–41
Studies on the imagery-developmental/ personality relationship, 343–44
Studies on the imagery-learning/ memory relationship, 346
Studies on the imagery-perception relationship, 350
Studies on the imagery-physiology relationship, 355–56
Studies on the imagery-sports relationship, 360–61

Studies on the imagery-therapy/ visualization relationship, 366
Studies on visualization and VMBR in sports, 358
Study of imaginations, 192
Stumpf, Carl, 198
Stuttering, 239–41
Style, method of, 222
Subconscious, 30, 32–34, 207
Subconscious versus unconscious, 32
Subjective versus objective events/ approaches, 18, 161, 308, 439, 480, 485, 493, 495
Subjective vision, 170, 179, 524
Subjective/internal mental states, xii, 18, 42, 439, 449
Subliminal consciousness theory, 153, 229
Subliminal imagery/stimulation, 153, 453, 517, 527
Substitute satisfaction and imagery, 332
Substitution, 8, 186, 188, 200, 363
Subvocal movements/speech, 73, 226
Successive color induction, 181
Suggestion/suggestibility, 8–9, 29, 34, 41, 185, 194, 472, 493, 511
Sumerians, 124, 132, 140
Sun illusion, 27
Surface array, 314
Survey of Mental Imagery, 503
Survival, physical/psychological, 143
Swift, Jonathan, 47
Symbol-filled arrays, 326–27
Symbolic computational view, 58, 299, 303, 313
Symbolic/propositional format, 303–4, 313–14, 321, 341
Symbolic rehearsal, 359
Symbols/signs and imagery, xi, 5, 74, 77, 127, 139, 143, 146, 192, 200, 229, 245, 303, 334, 354, 361–62, 443, 463, 521, 531
Symbol/symbolism, 73–74, 122, 139, 142, 179, 186, 207, 299, 307, 452, 454
Synaesthesia theory, 72, 234
Synaesthetic content, four types, 234
Synaesthetic inheritance, 233

Synesthesia/synesthetic image/imagery, 57, 69–73, 75, 209, 229–35, 339, 515, 582–87
Synesthetes, 72–73, 231–32, 251
Synopsia, 70
Synthesis into new wholes, xiii, 14, 17, 21, 53, 57, 122
Synthesis-destructuring-restructuring process, 340
Synthetic images, 5, 171
Systematic desensitization, 335, 362–63

Tacit knowledge, 303–5, 316–17, 327, 526
Tacit knowledge/descriptionalist versus CRT/pictorialist theories, 303–5, 327
Tacitus, 127
Tactile hallucinations, 50
Tactual perception, 188, 237
Tactual/kinaesthetic space, 236
Tactual/tactile images/imagery, 7, 11, 14, 17, 21, 53, 69, 182, 189, 196, 235–45
Talismans, 129
Tardy images, 53
Task demands, 304, 316–17, 327, 459–60
Taste imagery, 230
Taste-dream experiences, 235
Taste/tasting, 19, 235
Taxonomic/taxonomy, 517
Tele-medicine, 543
Teleologic hallucination, 49
Teleological continuum, 172
Temperature grills, 237
Temperature spots/sensations, 213, 230, 233, 479, 483
Temporal lobe seizures, 65
Temporal lobes, 478
Temporal order of stimulus presentation, 211
Temporal relations of meaning and imagery, 204
Ten Commandments, 127
Tenacity method, 427
Tentative conclusions, 426
Teraphims/household gods, 128, 133, 137

Terrorism/terrorist tactics, 539
Terrors, emotional, 50
Test of control of visual imagery, 248
Test(s) of imagery, 249, 467–68, 473, 485–506, 542
Test stimulus, 444
Testability criterion, 430
Testable hypothesis, 428
Test-retest stability/reliability, 488, 492, 495, 500–501
Tetany type/type T, 41
Theoretical aspects of synesthesia, 72
Theories and models, general, 310
Theories of creativity, 336
Theories of emotion, 453
Theories of hallucinations, 527
Theories of recognition, 205, 476, 529–30
Theories of sex- versus gender-differences, 530–31
Theories, scientific, 429, 432
Theory of consciousness, 38, 454–55
Theory of identical points, 29
Theory of image complexes, 158
Theory of image formation, 454–55
Theory of imagery types, 68, 469
Theory of imagistic representation, 326
Theory(s) of mind, 152, 334
Theory of perceptual development, 166
Theory of projection, 29
Theory of reflection, 451
Theory of rhetoric, 452
Theory of thinking, 78
Theory of visual perception, 187, 327
Theory, tactics, and strategy in imagery measurement, 439–69
Theory-testing criteria, 305, 430
Theory/theories of imagery, 20, 26, 38, 59, 150, 158, 323–24, 511, 526
Therapeutic methods, imagery-based, 329, 335, 461
Therapist, speech, 21
Therapy/visualization techniques, 361–66, 727–32
Theriomorphic types, 130
Thermostat analogy, 441
Thinking and imaging, 5, 20, 73–74, 77–78, 149, 154, 224, 244

Thinking and language mechanisms, 207–8
Thinking in music, 244
Thinking-feeling dimension, 343
Thinking/reasoning and synesthesia, 72
Thirteen principal types of imagery, 515
Thirty parallel tactics, Ahsen's, 468
Thomas, Nigel J. T., 57–58
Thorndike, Edward Lee, 151, 153
Thought, imageless, xii, 73–75, 154–55, 158, 190–91, 204–7, 516
Thought imagery versus other types of imagery, 76
Thought imagery/images, 5, 14, 73–78, 339, 483, 512, 515, 541, 733–34
Thoughtless imagery controversy, 302
Thought-sampling method, 513, 538
Thought/thinking processes, xi, 5, 8, 20, 31, 59, 73, 76–78, 137, 149, 153, 155, 158, 190, 205–10, 224, 226, 244, 333, 440, 443, 514
Three classes of illusions, 191
Three criteria for theory-evaluation, 430
Three intensities/grades of vividness, 246
Three phases of modern imagery debate, 294
Three types of imagery/images, 14, 248
Three-dimensional arrays, 4, 170, 315–16, 327, 463, 530
Threshold, after-image, 177
Thurstone's Test of Primary Mental Abilities, 513
Tied and free images, 5, 12, 20, 244
Time estimation, 347–48
Time experience/perception, 50, 347–48
Time projection/distortion, 362
Time-errors, 170, 211
Time-order error/effect, 170, 211
Titchener, Edward Bradford, 42, 73, 153–55, 330, 515–16
To image/to imagine, 11, 18, 137
Tonal memory/image, 212–13, 244
Top-down and bottom-up disturbances/processes, 324–26, 527
Torrance Tests of Creative Thinking, 339

TOTE model, 441, 466
TOTEM model, 466
Trace theory of memory, 321
Training strategies, imagery, 461
Trance, semi-hypnotic, 458
Transference, 14
Transformable/adjustable property, 17, 304
Transformational equivalence principle, 18
Transformations/transformational processes, 186, 304, 316, 318, 341, 479, 528, 531
Transition, law of, 129
Transparency of images, 153, 163
Tripartite model(s), 452, 462
Triple Code Model/ISM, 452, 462
Triple-code theories of performance enhancement, 462
Truth, search for, 125, 428, 430, 452
Two approaches to mental images, 298
Two meanings for the term *perception*, 348
Two modes of representation, 341–42
Two stages of development in psychology, 516
Two-and-one-half-D sketch, 327
Two-dimensional image(s)/representation(s), 170, 315, 530
Two-gradient series, synaesthesia, 235
Two-point threshold, 236
Two-process model, 311, 330, 521
Two-process theory of meaning, 320
Tye, Michael, 38, 294
Type/types concept/model, 157, 159-61, 173, 186, 191, 197, 219–20, 239, 250, 297, 469–70, 473, 485, 513
Typographic and structural eidetikers, 41, 525
Typology/topological approach, 496

Ubiquity of images, 331
U-images, 248
Unbidden images, 309
Uncomfortable pragmatism, 427
Unconscious associated with consciousness, 33
Unconscious image, 13

Unconscious memory, 13, 200
Unconscious representations, 16–17
Unconscious/dynamic unconscious, 11–12, 17, 22, 30, 66, 206
Uncontrollable/uncontrolled images, 342, 483
Unformed visions, 47
Unilateral hallucination, 49
Unintendedness experience, 527
Unitary type of imager, 173
Universal proposition of after-images, 26, 247
Universality of imagery, 210, 344
Unmonitored hallucinations, 365
Unreal experiences, 472
Unseen/radio drama, 209, 229, 234
Unshaped gods, 129–30
Unvividness paradox, 454, 462
Upper versus lower consciousness, 32
Uremic hallucinosis, 49
Usual and unusual images, 248

Validity and reliability, 157, 161, 168–69, 302, 364, 430, 437, 446, 456, 470, 486, 490–93, 496–97, 502–3, 506, 538, 541
Validity/truth of the experimental method, 428, 430
Variability measurement, 160
Variables, classes of, 425, 429, 432
Variation, sources of, 503
Variations of ISM, six operational, 453
Variation/variable control, 194, 425
Vehicles of thought, 73
Veneration of images, 136
Venus of Willendorf, 123
Verbal and pictorial codes, 311
Verbal hallucinations/VHs/voices, 527-28
Verbal-Imagery Code Test, 503
Verbal images/imagery, 10–11, 76, 204–5, 216, 225, 481, 527
Verbal learning and imagery, 307, 309, 320, 450, 508
Verbal learning revolution, 320, 442
Verbal memory, 307, 309, 478
Verbal processes, 4, 208, 307, 332–33, 442, 519, 521

Verbal Reasoning Test, 495
Verbal rehearsal, 481
Verbal versus imagery mediation, 519
Verbal-auditory imagery, 198
Verbal-Imagery Learning Style Test,
  503
Verbalizer-visualizer dimension, 343,
  474–75, 485, 489–90, 495
Verbalizer-Visualizer Questionnaire,
  475, 484, 489
Verbal-motor imagery, 196, 198
Verbal/propositional representations,
  311
Verbal-sequential system, 307, 440
Verbochromia, 71
Vertical eye movements/VEMs, 507,
  509–10
Vestibular hallucination, 49
Vicious cycle for the stutterer, 240
Virgin Mary, 129–30
Virtual image, 3
Virtual mind/reality theory, 543
Virtual time-space, 543
Vision, use of the term in the Bible,
  142
Visual after-image, 23, 40, 183
Visual cognition/thinking, 352, 475
Visual culture theory, 543
Visual Elaboration Scale, 461, 484,
  503
Visual ghost story, 181
Visual ghosts, 28, 181
Visual hallucinations, 14, 44, 47, 142,
  352, 471
Visual hemispheric specialization, 57,
  352–55, 528–29
Visual homogeneity, 471
Visual illusions, 515
Visual image versus eidetic image, 42
Visual imagery control, 248, 492
Visual imagery in congenitally blind
  people, 52–53, 71
Visual imagery, limitations, 163, 246
Visual imagery test(s), 493
Visual images, projection and size,
  246–47
Visual images/imagery, 1, 3, 5, 7, 11,
  17, 21–22, 40, 42, 68–69, 145, 154,
  159–61, 163, 193, 195–97, 200–
  201, 204–5, 209, 216, 223, 225–27,
  232, 236, 245–53, 314, 335, 349,
  480, 512
Visual imagination, 228
Visual memory, 210, 212, 352, 478
Visual memory activation, 528
Visual memory-image, 40, 70, 163,
  169, 178, 193, 210, 212, 216
Visual motor behavior rehearsal/VMBR,
  356–58
Visual negative after-image, 27
Visual perception and eye-movements,
  198, 248–49
Visual perception theory, 313, 526
Visual psychophysics, 461
Visual search tasks, 463
Visual sensation/perception, 188
Visual theory, contemporary, 327
Visual thinking tasks, 77–78
Visual tied-image, 244
Visual-algesic synesthesia, 70
Visual-auditory synesthesia, 70
Visual-gustatory synesthesia, 70
Visualist, 68, 161, 191–92
Visualization/therapy techniques, 361–
  66
Visualization/visualizer, 19, 40, 124,
  129, 150, 157, 163, 178, 186, 221,
  223, 319, 337, 352, 357, 487–88,
  535
Visualizer-verbalizer dimension, 343,
  474–75, 485, 489–90, 496, 523
Visuospatial reasoning, 20, 463, 534
Visuo-spatial sketch pad, 463
Vivid hallucinations, 365
Vivid imagery/vividness, 4, 15, 40, 42,
  72, 76, 149, 156, 159, 161, 163–64,
  178, 186, 189, 199, 209, 219–20,
  236, 241, 246, 308, 332, 339, 352,
  365, 438, 447, 453, 462, 467–70,
  472–74, 476, 480–84, 492–93, 496,
  502, 504, 508–10, 512–13, 520–21,
  523, 531, 542
Vividness of knowing versus imaging,
  503
Vividness of visual imagery, 475, 492–93
Vividness paradox, 453–54

Vividness tests of imagery, 161, 454, 475, 479, 503

Vividness-unvividness dimension, 453, 462, 466–67, 498, 531

Vocomotor sensations/images, 11, 74, 195

Voluntary control of after-images, 41, 170, 178

Voluntary control of autonomic processes, 206, 449, 478–79, 482

Voluntary imaging abilities, 14, 40, 170, 186, 216, 333, 344, 503

Voluntary thought imagery, 76, 208

Voluntary versus involuntary systems, 32, 35, 41, 240

Voluntary versus spontaneous imagery, 14, 215, 247, 474

Voluntary/memory images, 170, 246

Wakefulness/waking state, 14, 16–17, 30, 186–87, 472, 531

Waking dreams/imagery, 183, 186, 511, 515, 532

Waking-dream therapy, 263

Waterfall illusion, 45

Watson, John Broadus, 37, 151, 439, 442, 456, 479, 516

Watt, Henry Jackson, 73, 154, 206

Wax portrait mask, 14

Wax-tablet/impression model of memory, xi, 145–46

Ways of Thinking Questionnaire, 475, 490

Web sites, imagery, 36, 429, 543–44

Web sites on consciousness/mental imagery, 36–37

Weber, Ernst Heinrich, 478

Weber's law, 244

Wechsler Adult Intelligence Scale, 489

Wellesley College, 183, 229

Weltanschauung, 328

Western Church, 129, 135

Wilson/Barber's Creative Imagination Scale, 492–93

Within-individuals and between-individuals, 450, 475, 480, 494, 508

Wolpe/Lazarus misreporting affair, 465

Word consciousness, 190, 205, 217

Word frequency, 308

Word imagery, 190, 217, 231, 245, 362

Word-as-idea-sign, 245

Word-method test of imagery, 154, 218, 221

Words, role in verbal learning/thinking, 217, 362, 442–43

Words versus pictures, 4, 204, 249, 308, 474

Working memory, 324, 463, 477, 693–700

WorldCat database, ix, 67

Worship, image/idol, 2, 7–8

Wrong type of imagery, 359

Wundt, Wilhelm Maximilian, xi, 19, 73, 150, 153–55, 178, 293, 320, 456

Wurzburg school, 73–74, 154–55, 158, 206, 516

X-ray computer tomography/CT, 4

Yahweh, 130–31, 140–41

Young-Helmholtz theory, 177

Zola, Emile, 469

Zollner illusion, 44

## About the Author

JON E. ROECKELEIN is a professor of psychology at Meas Community College in Arizona. He has taught and conducted psychological research for more than thirty years, including research on intelligence systems for the U.S. Army/Department of Defense at the Resources Research Office and Army Research Institute. His earlier books include *The Psychology of Humor* (Greenwood Press, 2002), *The Concept of Time in Psychology* (Greenwood Press, 2000) and *Dictionary of Theories, Laws and Concepts in Psychology* (Greenwood Press, 1988).